International Law

Ethics in Business

THE LEGAL ENVIRONMENT OF BUSINESS AND ONLINE COMMERCE

Business Ethics, E-Commerce, Regulatory, and International Issues

Fifth Edition

HENRY R. CHEESEMAN

Clinical Professor of Business Law
Director of the Legal Studies Program
Marshall School of Business
University of Southern California

PEARSON
Prentice Hall

Upper Saddle River, New Jersey 07458

Library of Congress Cataloging-in-Publication Data
Cheeseman, Henry R.
The legal environment of business and online commerce : business ethics, e–commerce, regulatory, and international issues / Henry R. Cheeseman.—5th ed.
p. cm.
Includes index.
ISBN 0-13-199109-4
1. Business law—United States. I. Title....

KF889.C464 2007
346.7307—dc22 2006041574

AVP/ Executive Editor: Wendy Craven
VP/Editorial Director: Jeff Shelstad
Manager, Product Development: Pamela Hersperger
Project Manager: Kerri Tomasso
Product Development Manager, Media: Nancy Welcher
Marketing Manager: John Wannamaker
Senior Managing Editor, Production: Cynthia Regan
Production Editor: Melissa Feimer
Permissions Coordinator: Charles Morris
Manufacturing Buyer: Diane Peirano
Design/Composition Manager: Christy Mahon
Interior Design: Jill Little
Art Director: Pat Smythe
Cover Design: Anthony Gemmellaro
Cover Photo: Getty Images
Composition: GGS Book Services
Full-Service Project Management: GGS Book Services
Printer/Binder: Quebecor World Dubuque
Typeface: 10.75/13 ACaslon Regular

Pearson Education LTD.
Pearson Education Singapore, Pte. Ltd
Pearson Education, Canada, Ltd
Pearson Education–Japan
Pearson Education Australia PTY, Limited
Pearson Education North Asia Ltd
Pearson Educación de Mexico, S.A. de C.V.
Pearson Education Malaysia, Pte. Ltd.

PEARSON
Prentice Hall

10 9 8 7 6 5 4 3 2
ISBN: 0-13-199109-4

To all of the men and women who have served or now serve in the air force, army, marines, navy, coast guard, reserves, and national guard. Our politicians make this country's decisions, but it is these women and men who serve with dedication, honor, and bravery. To Mark Dixon, my fellow soldier and friend, who died in the Vietnam conflict.

About the Author

Henry R. Cheeseman is Clinical Professor of Business Law and Director of the Legal Studies Program at the Marshall School of Business of the University of Southern California (USC), Los Angeles, California.

Professor Cheeseman earned a Bachelor's degree in Finance from Marquette University, a Master's degree in both Business Administration and in Tax from the University of Southern California, a Juris Doctor (J.D.) degree from the University of California at Los Angeles (UCLA) School of Law, a Masters of Business Administration with emphasis on Law and Economics from the University of Chicago, and a Master's in Law (L.L.M.) degree from Boston University.

Professor Cheeseman earned the "Golden Apple" Teaching Award on many occasions by having been voted the best professor at the Marshall School of Business of the University of Southern California. He has been named a Faculty Fellow at the Center for Excellence in Teaching at USC by the Dean of the Marshall School of Business, and USC's Torch and Tassel Chapter of the Mortar Board has named Professor Cheeseman Faculty of the Month of USC.

Professor Cheeseman writes leading business law and legal environment textbooks that are published by Prentice Hall Publishing Company. These include: *Business Law; Legal, E-Commerce, Ethical, and International Environments; Contemporary Business and Online Commerce; The Legal Environment of Business and Online Commerce; Essentials of Contemporary Business Law,* and *Introduction to Law: Its Dynamic Nature.*

Professor Cheeseman is an avid traveller and amateur photographer. All interior photos for this book have been taken by Professor Cheeseman.

Contents in Brief

Contents

Preface

To the Students

Each semester, as I stand up in front of a new group of business majors in my legal environment class I am stuck by the thought that cases and statutes aside, I know two very important things that they have yet to learn. The first is that I draw as much from them as they do from me. Their youth, enthusiasm, questions, and even the doubts a few of them hold about the relevance of law to their futures fuel my teaching. They don't know that every time they open their minds to look at a point from a new perspective or critically question something they have taken for granted, I get a wonderful reward for the work that I do.

The other thing I know is that both teaching and learning the legal and ethical environments are all about stories. The stories I tell provide the framework on which students will hang everything they learn about the law in my class. It is my hope that long after the specific language of cases or statutes have faded, they will retain that framework. Several years from now, "unintentional torts" may draw only a glimmer of recognition with business managers who learn about them as students in my class this year. However, they will likely recall the story of the woman who sued McDonald's for serving her coffee that was too hot and caused her injuries. The story sticks and gives students the hook on which to hang the concepts.

I remind myself of these two facts every time I sit down to work on writing and revising *The Legal Environment of Business and Online Commerce* as well. My goal is to present the legal environment and ethics in a way that will spur students to ask questions, to go beyond rote memorization. Business law is an evolving outgrowth of its environment, and the legal environment keeps changing. In addition to the social, ethical, and international contexts I have incorporated in previous editions of *The legal Environment of Business and Online Commerce,* this fifth edition emphasizes coverage of Internet law and online commerce as two vital catalysts to the law and a key part of its environment.

It is my wish that my commitment to these goals shines through in this labor of love, and I hope you have as much pleasure in using it as I have had in creating it for you.

Henry Cheeseman

An Integrated Supplements Package

To ensure consistency of style, approach, and coverage among the key *print* and *online supplements*, these critical pieces were created by an author team working in conjunction with Henry Cheeseman. The supplements include:

Companion Website Access at **www.prenhall.com/cheeseman.** This Website will contain an Online Study Guide, including true/false and multiple choice questions, as well as PowerPoint presentations for each chapter. **New!** Free downloadable Student Study Guide with extra true/false, multiple choice, fill-in-the blank and essay questions for extra practice!

Instructors' Manual A comprehensive outline of each text chapter. Also included are terms with definitions, chapter objectives, a key questions checklist, and sample syllabi.

Test Item File A bank of questions specially designed to aid in the preparation of tests. Each question includes a corresponding difficulty level, enabling the easy creation of tailor-made testing material.

TestGen Test management software containing all the material from the Test Item File. This software is completely user friendly and allows instructors to view, edit, and add test questions with a few clicks of the mouse.

PowerPoints A ready-to-use PowerPoint slideshow, designed for classroom presentation. Use "as-is," or edit content to fit your individual class needs.

Instructor's Resource Center on CD A compilation of instructor's tools, including the Instructor's Manual, PowerPoints, Test Item File, and TestGen.

Acknowledgments

When I first began writing this book, I was a solitary figure researching cases in the law library and writing text at my desk. As time passed, others entered upon the scene—editors, research assistants, reviewers, production personnel—and touched the project and made it better. Although my name appears on the cover of this book, it is no longer mine alone. I humbly thank the following persons for their contributions to this project:

The Exceptional Supplements Team and Prentice Hall Professionals

Many thanks to Kerri Tomasso, the Prentice Hall Project Manager who produced the extensive supplements that support this edition of *The Legal Environment of Business and Online Commerce.* The supplements package has been authored by a remarkable team, with exceptional contributions from Ramona Atkins and Linda Fried. I'd also like to recognize Melissa Feimer, my production editor, who skillfully and cheerfully navigated a complex project on a tight deadline. Last, I appreciate the support of Jeff Shelstad, Editorial Director, and Wendy Craven, Executive Editor.

Reviews

I would like to personally thank the following reviewers, who have spent considerable time and effort reviewing the manuscripts for previous and current editions of *The Legal Environment of Business and Online Commerce* and whose comments, suggestions, and criticisms are seen in the final project.

David Austill	Union University
Eli C. Bortman	Babson College
Thomas D. Cavenagh	North Central College
Gregory P. Cermignano	Widener University
Ed Gac	University of Colorado
Gamewell Gantt	Idaho State University
Duane R. Lambett	California State University, Hayward
William Maakestad	Western Illinois University
Gregory McCann	Stetson University
Neal A. Phillips	University of Delaware
James Rittenbaum	St. Louis University
Scott Sandstrom	College of the Holy Cross
Allen Simonson	Montclair State University
S. Jay Sklar	Temple University
Joanic Sompayrac	University of Tennessee-Chattanooga
John A. Wrieden	Florida International University

Personal Acknowledgments

My family: My wife Shou-Yi Kang; my parents—Henry B. and Florence, deceased; my twin brother Gregory and his wife Lana; my sister Marcia; my nephew Gregory and niece Nikki, and the two new additions to the family, my great nieces Lauren and Addison.

The students at the Marshall School of Business at the University of Southern California (USC). Their spirit, energy, and joy is contagious, and I love teaching them (and as important, they teaching me).

Ashley Anderson, an undergraduate and pre-law student at the Marshall School of Business at USC, who has done an absolutely excellent job as my research assistant for the fifth edition of *The Legal Environment of Business and Online Commerce.*

While writing this Preface and Acknowledgment, I have thought about the thousands of hours I have spent researching, writing, and preparing this manuscript. I loved every minute, and the knowledge gained has been sufficient reward for the endeavor.

I hope this book and its supplementary materials will serve you as well as they have served me.

With joy and sadness,
emptiness and fullness,
honor and humility,
I surrender the fruits of this labor

Henry R. Cheeseman

1

Legal Foundations and Global Environment

"Where there is no law, there is no freedom."

—John Locke
Second Treatise of Government, Sec. 57

Chapter Objectives

After studying this chapter, you should be able to:

1. Define law and describe the functions of law.
2. Explain the development of the U.S. legal system.
3. List and describe the sources of law in the United States.
4. Describe the international civil law legal system used in some other countries.
5. Apply critical legal thinking in analyzing judicial decisions.

Chapter Contents

- What Is Law?
- Schools of Jurisprudential Thought
- History of American Law
- Sources of Law in the United States

Every society makes and enforces laws that govern the conduct of the individuals, businesses, and other organizations that function within it. In the words of Judge Learned Hand, "Without law we cannot live; only with it can we insure the future which by right is ours. The best of men's hopes are enmeshed in its success."[1]

Although the law of the United States is primarily based on English common law, other legal systems, such as Spanish and French civil law, also influenced it. The sources of law in this country are the U.S. Constitution, state constitutions, federal and state statutes, ordinances, administrative agency rules and regulations, executive orders, and judicial decisions by federal and state courts.

Businesses that are organized in the United States are subject to its laws. They are also subject to the laws of other countries in which they operate. Businesses organized in other countries must obey the laws of the United States when doing business here. In addition, businesspeople owe a duty to act ethically in the conduct of their affairs, and businesses owe a responsibility not to harm society.

This chapter discusses the nature and definition of law, the history and sources of law, and critical legal thinking, as applied by the U.S. Supreme Court in deciding actual cases.

Statue of Liberty, New York Harbor. The United States of America is a country of laws. For centuries, it has attracted people from around the world because of its democratic principles and constitutional protections.

What Is Law?

A lawyer without history or literature is a mechanic, a mere working mason: if he possesses some knowledge of these, he may venture to call himself an architect.

Sir Walter Scott
Guy Mannering, Chapter 37 (1815)

The law consists of rules that regulate the conduct of individuals, businesses, and other organizations within society. It is intended to protect persons and their property against unwanted interference from others. In other words, the law forbids persons from engaging in certain undesirable activities. Consider the following passage:

> Hardly anyone living in a civilized society has not at some time been told to do something or to refrain from doing something, because there is a law requiring it, or because it is against the law. What do we mean when we say such things? Most generally, how are we to understand statements of the form "x is law"? This is an ancient question. In his *Memorabilia* (I, ii), Xenophon reports a statement of the young Alcibiades, companion of Socrates, who in conversation with the great

Pericles remarked that "no one can really deserve praise unless he knows what a law is."

At the end of the 18th century, Immanuel Kant wrote of the question "What is law?" that it "may be said to be about as embarrassing to the jurist as the well-known question 'What is truth?' is to the logician."[2]

Internet Law & Online Commerce

Students Plug In to the Internet

Every year, millions of students arrive on college campuses and unpack an array of items—clothes, books, furniture, decorations, and their computers. College students used to be judged by the size of their stereo speakers; today it is their computers and their Internet savvy. Ninety percent of college students now own personal computers.

The Internet has revolutionized campus life. Computer kiosks abound around college campuses, occupying more space in libraries, dorm rooms, and hallways of athletic departments. Traditional libraries have become obsolete for many students, as they conduct almost all of their research online. More than 80 percent of college students check out the Web daily, while others communicate through e-mail, pick up course assignments, download course notes, and socialize online. Current university and college students use modern technology and are leading their parents, employers, and sometimes even their professors into the new world of high technology. Today's college students are the leaders of the technology generation.

Universities and colleges are now rated on not only how well they are connected with alumni but also on how well they are connected to computer technology. Some universities have installed software that allows their students to sit anywhere on campus with their laptops and "plug" in to the school's computers. The computer is no longer just a study tool; it has become totally integrated into the lives of college students. Students of the new generation study online, shop online, and even date online.

To help the student understand his or her legal rights and duties, this business law book fully integrates online commerce and Internet law. Through this total integration of online commerce and Internet law, a student will learn traditional business law topics and will also be well versed in his or her legal rights while using the Internet. ■

Definition of Law

The concept of **law** is broad. Although it is difficult to state a precise definition, *Black's Law Dictionary* gives one that is sufficient for this text:

> Law, in its generic sense, is a body of rules of action or conduct prescribed by controlling authority, and having binding legal force. That which must be obeyed and followed by citizens subject to sanctions or legal consequences is a law.[3]

law
That which must be obeyed and followed by citizens subject to sanctions or legal consequences; a body of rules of action or conduct prescribed by controlling authority and having binding legal force.

Functions of the Law

The law is often described by the function it serves within a society. The primary *functions* served by the law in this country are:

1. Keeping the peace, which includes making certain activities crimes.
2. Shaping moral standards (e.g., enacting laws that discourage drug and alcohol abuse).
3. Promoting social justice (e.g., enacting statutes that prohibit discrimination in employment).
4. Maintaining the status quo (e.g., passing laws preventing the forceful overthrow of the government).
5. Facilitating orderly change (e.g., passing statutes only after considerable study, debate, and public input).

> Commercial law lies within a narrow compass, and is far purer and freer from defects than any other part of the system.
>
> Henry Peter Brougham
> *House of Commons, February 7, 1828*

6. **Facilitating planning** (e.g., well-designed commercial laws allow businesses to plan their activities, allocate their productive resources, and assess the risks they take).
7. **Providing a basis for compromise** (approximately 90 percent of all lawsuits are settled prior to trial).
8. **Maximizing individual freedom** (e.g., the rights of freedom of speech, religion, and association granted by the First Amendment to the U.S. Constitution).

Concept Summary *Functions of the Law*

1. Keep the peace
2. Shape moral standards
3. Promote social justice
4. Maintain the status quo
5. Facilitate orderly change
6. Facilitate planning
7. Provide a basis for compromise
8. Maximize individual freedom

Fairness of the Law

The law, in its majestic equality, forbids the rich as well as the poor to sleep under bridges.

Anatole France

On the whole, the American legal system is one of the most comprehensive, fair, and democratic systems of law ever developed and enforced. Nevertheless, some misuses and oversights of our legal system—including abuses of discretion and mistakes by judges and juries, unequal applications of the law, and procedural mishaps—allow some guilty parties to go unpunished.

In *Standefer v. United States*,[4] the Supreme Court *affirmed* (e.g., let stand) the criminal conviction of a Gulf Oil Corporation executive for aiding and abetting the bribery of an Internal Revenue Service agent. The agent had been acquitted in a separate trial. In writing the opinion of the Court, Chief Justice Warren Burger stated, "This case does no more than manifest the simple, if discomforting, reality that different juries may reach different results under any criminal statute. That is one of the consequences we accept under our jury system."

Flexibility of the Law

U.S. law evolves and changes along with the norms of society, technology, and the growth and expansion of commerce in the United States and the world. The following quote by Judge Jerome Frank discusses the value of the adaptability of law:

Law must be stable and yet it cannot stand still.

Roscoe Pound
Interpretations of Legal History (1923)

> The law always has been, is now, and will ever continue to be, largely vague and variable. And how could this be otherwise? The law deals with human relations in their most complicated aspects. The whole confused, shifting helter-skelter of life parades before it—more confused than ever, in our kaleidoscopic age.
>
> Men have never been able to construct a comprehensive, eternalized set of rules anticipating all possible legal disputes and formulating in advance the rules which would apply to them. Situations are bound to occur which were never contemplated when the original rules were made. How much less is such a frozen legal system possible in modern times?

The constant development of unprecedented problems requires a legal system capable of fluidity and pliancy. Our society would be straightjacketed were not the courts, with the able assistance of the lawyers, constantly overhauling the law and adapting it to the realities of ever-changing social, industrial, and political conditions; although changes cannot be made lightly, yet rules of law must be more or less impermanent, experimental and therefore not nicely calculable.

Much of the uncertainty of law is not an unfortunate accident; it is of immense social value.[5]

Landmark Law

Brown v. Board of Education

When states ratified the Constitution of the United States of America in 1788, they created a democratic form of government and granted certain rights to the people. But all persons were not treated equally because many people, including drafters of the Constitution, such as Thomas Jefferson, owned African American slaves. It was more than 75 years before the Civil War was fought between the northern states and the southern Confederate states over the preservation of the Union and slavery. Slavery was abolished by the **Thirteenth Amendment** to the Constitution in 1865. In addition, the **Fourteenth Amendment** of 1868 provided that no state shall "deny to any person within its jurisdiction the equal protection of the laws." The original intent of this amendment was to guarantee equality to freed African Americans.

But equality was denied to African Americans for years to come. This included discrimination in housing, transportation, education, jobs, service at restaurants, and other activities. In 1896, the U.S. Supreme Court decided the case of ***Plessy v. Ferguson***. In that case, the state of Louisiana had a law that provided for separate but equal accommodations for African American and white railway passengers. An African American passenger challenged the state law. The Supreme Court held that the "separate but equal" state law did not violate the Equal Protection Clause of the Fourteenth Amendment. The "separate but equal" doctrine was then applied to all areas of life, including public education. Thus, African American and white children attended separate schools, often with unequal results.

It was not until 1954 that the U.S. Supreme Court decided a case that challenged the separate but equal doctrine as it applied to public elementary and high schools. In ***Brown v. Board of Education***, a consolidated case that challenged the separate school systems of four states—Kansas, South Carolina, Virginia, and Delaware—the Supreme Court decided to revisit the separate but equal doctrine announced by its forbearers in another century. This time, a unanimous Supreme Court, in an opinion written by Chief Justice Earl Warren, reversed prior precedent and held that the separate but equal doctrine violated the Equal Protection Clause of the Fourteenth Amendment to the Constitution. In its opinion, the Court stated:

> We cannot turn the clock back to 1868 when the Amendment was adopted, or even to 1896 when *Plessy v. Ferguson* was written. Today, education is perhaps the most important function of state and local governments.
>
> We conclude that in the field of public education the doctrine of "separate but equal" has no place. Separate educational facilities are inherently unequal. Therefore, we hold that the plaintiffs and others similarly situated for whom actions have been brought are, by reason of the segregation complained of, deprived of the equal protection of the laws guaranteed by the Fourteenth Amendment.

After *Brown v. Board of Education* was decided, it took court orders as well as federal army enforcement to integrate many of the public schools in this country. The *Brown v. Board of Education* case demonstrates that one Supreme Court case can overrule prior Supreme Court cases to promote justice. *Brown v. Board of Education of Topeka*, 347 U.S. 483, 74 S.Ct. 686, 1954 U.S. Lexis 2094 (U.S. Sup.Ct.) ■

Schools of Jurisprudential Thought

The philosophy or science of the law is referred to as **jurisprudence**. There are several different philosophies about how the law developed, ranging from the classical natural theory to modern theories of law and economics and critical legal studies. Classical legal philosophies can be grouped into the following major categories:

jurisprudence
The philosophy or science of law.

- ***The Natural Law School.*** The **Natural Law School** of jurisprudence postulates that the law is based on what is "correct." Natural law philosophers emphasize

> The law is not a series of calculating machines where definitions and answers come tumbling out when the right levers are pushed.
>
> William O. Douglas
> *The Dissent, A Safeguard of Democracy (1948)*

a **moral theory of law**—that is, law should be based on morality and ethics. Natural law is "discovered" by humans through the use of reason and choosing between good and evil. Documents such as the U.S. Constitution, the Magna Carta, and the United Nations Charter reflect this theory.

- ***The Historical School.*** The **Historical School** of jurisprudence believes that the law is an aggregate of social traditions and customs that have developed over the centuries. It believes that changes in the norms of society will gradually be reflected in the law. To these legal philosophers, the law is an evolutionary process. Thus, historical legal scholars look to past legal decisions (precedent) to solve contemporary problems.
- ***The Analytical School.*** The **Analytical School** of jurisprudence maintains that the law is shaped by logic. Analytical philosophers believe that results are reached by applying principles of logic to the specific facts of the case. The emphasis is on the logic of the result rather than on how the result is reached.
- ***The Sociological School.*** The **Sociological School** of jurisprudence asserts that the law is a means of achieving and advancing certain sociological goals. The followers of this philosophy, known as *realists*, believe that the purpose of law is to shape social behavior. Sociological philosophers are unlikely to adhere to past law as precedent.
- ***The Command School.*** The philosophers of the **Command School** of jurisprudence believe that the law is a set of rules developed, communicated, and enforced by the ruling party rather than a reflection of the society's morality, history, logic, or sociology. This school maintains that the law changes when the ruling class changes.

Contemporary Trend

Modern Schools of Jurisprudential Thought

Two schools of jurisprudence have recently been developed by legal thinkers:

- ***The Critical Legal Studies School.*** The **Critical Legal Studies School** proposes that legal rules are unnecessary and are used as an obstacle by the powerful to maintain the status quo. Critical legal theorists (the "Crits") argue that legal disputes should be solved by applying arbitrary rules that are based on broad notions of what is "fair" in each circumstance. Under this theory, subjective decision making by judges would be permitted.
- ***The Law and Economics School.*** The **Law and Economics School** (or the **"Chicago School,"** named after the University of Chicago, where it was first developed) believes that promoting market efficiency should be the central goal of legal decision making. For example, proponents of law and economics theory suggest that the practice of appointing counsel, free of charge, to prisoners who bring civil rights cases should be abolished. If a prisoner cannot find a lawyer who will take the case on a contingency-fee basis or *pro bono* (free of charge), it probably means that the case is not worth bringing. ■

Concept Summary *Schools of Jurisprudential Thought*

School	Philosophy
Natural Law	Postulates that law is based on what is "correct." It emphasizes a moral theory of law—that is, law should be based on morality and ethics.
Historical	Believes that the law is an aggregate of social traditions and customs.
Analytical	Maintains that the law is shaped by logic.
Sociological	Asserts that the law is a means of achieving and advancing certain sociological goals.

Command	Believes that the law is a set of rules developed, communicated, and enforced by the ruling party.
Critical Legal Studies	Maintains that legal rules are unnecessary and that legal disputes should be solved by applying arbitrary rules based on fairness.
Law and Economics	Believes that promoting market efficiency should be the central concern of legal decision making.

History of American Law

When the American colonies were first settled, the English system of law was generally adopted as the system of jurisprudence. This was the foundation from which American judges developed a common law in America.

English Common Law

English **common law** was developed by judges who issued their opinions when deciding cases. The principles announced in these cases became *precedent* for later judges deciding similar cases. The English common law can be divided into cases decided by the law courts, equity courts, and merchant courts.

common law
Law developed by judges who issued their opinions when deciding cases. The principles announced in these cases became precedent for later judges deciding similar cases.

Law Courts Prior to the Norman Conquest of England in 1066, each locality in England was subject to local laws as established by the lord or chieftain in control of the local area. There was no countrywide system of law. After 1066, William the Conqueror and his successors to the throne of England began to replace the various local laws with one uniform system of law. To accomplish this, the king or queen appointed loyal followers as judges in all local areas. These judges were charged with administering the law in a uniform manner in courts that were called **law courts**. Law at that time tended to emphasize the form (legal procedure) over the substance (merit) of a case. The only relief available at law courts was a monetary award for damages.

law court
Courts established where judges were to administer the law in a uniform manner.

Chancery (Equity) Courts Because of the unfair results and the limited remedy available in the law courts, a second set of courts—the **Court of Chancery** (or **equity court**)—was established. These courts were under the authority of the lord chancellor. Persons who believed that the decision of the law court was unfair or believed that the law court could not grant an appropriate remedy could seek relief in the Court of Chancery. Rather than emphasize legal procedure, the Chancery Court inquired into the merits of the case. The chancellor's remedies were called *equitable remedies* because they were shaped to fit each situation. Equitable order and remedies of the Court of Chancery took precedence over the legal decisions and remedies of the law courts.

Two things most people should never see made: sausages and laws.

An old saying

Court of Chancery
The first form of appellate courts where people went to if they felt the decision of the law court was unfair.

Merchant Courts As trade developed in the Middle Ages, the merchants who traveled about England and Europe developed certain rules to solve their commercial disputes. These rules, known as the "law of merchants," or the **Law Merchant**, were based on common trade practices and usage. Eventually, a separate set of courts was established to administer these rules. This court was called the **merchant court**. In the early 1900s, the merchant court was absorbed into the regular law court system of England.

Merchant Court
Early European courts established to administer the rules of trade.

Adoption of English Common Law in America

All the states of the United States of America except Louisiana base their legal systems primarily on the English *common law*. In the United States, the law, equity, and merchant courts have been merged. Thus, most U.S. courts permit the aggrieved party to seek both law and equitable orders and remedies.

The importance of common law to the American legal system is described in the following excerpt from Justice Douglas's opinion in the 1841 case *Penny v. Little*:

> The common law is a beautiful system, containing the wisdom and experiences of ages. Like the people it ruled and protected, it was simple and crude in its infancy and became enlarged, improved, and polished as the nation advanced in civilization, virtue, and intelligence. Adapting itself to the conditions and circumstances of the people and relying upon them for its administration, it necessarily improved as the condition of the people was elevated. The inhabitants of this country always claimed the common law as their birthright, and at an early period established it as the basis of their jurisprudence.[6]

International Law

The Civil Law System

One of the major legal systems that has developed in the world in addition to the Anglo-American common law system is the **Romano-Germanic civil law system**. This legal system, which is commonly called the **civil law**, dates to 450 B.C., when Rome adopted the Twelve Tables, a code of laws applicable to the Romans. A compilation of Roman law, called the *Corpus Juris Civilis* (the Body of Civil Law), was completed in A.D. 534. Later, two national codes—the French Civil Code of 1804 (the Napoleonic Code) and the German Civil Code of 1896—became models for countries that adopted civil codes.

In contrast to the Anglo-American common law, in which laws are created by the judicial system as well as by congressional legislation, the Civil Code and parliamentary statutes that expand and interpret it are the sole sources of the law in most civil law countries. Thus, the adjudication of a case is simply the application of the code or the statutes to a particular set of facts. In some civil law countries, court decisions do not have the force of law.

Many countries in Europe still follow the civil law system. ■

Eiffel Tower, Paris, France.

Sources of Law in the United States

In the more than 200 years since the founding of the United States and adoption of the English common law, the lawmakers of this country have developed a substantial body of law. The *sources of modern law* in the United States are discussed in the paragraphs that follow.

Constitutions

The **Constitution of the United States of America** is the *supreme law of the land.* This means that any law—whether federal, state, or local—that conflicts with the U.S. Constitution is unconstitutional and, therefore, unenforceable.

Constitution of the United States of America
The supreme law of the United States.

The principles enumerated in the Constitution are extremely broad because the founding fathers intended them to be applied to evolving social, technological, and economic conditions. The U.S. Constitution is often referred to as a "living document" because it is so adaptable.

The U.S. Constitution established the structure of the federal government. It created the following three branches of government and gave them the following powers:

- ***Legislative (Congress).*** Power to make (enact) the law.
- ***Executive (president).*** Power to enforce the law.
- ***Judicial (courts).*** Power to interpret and determine the validity of the law.

The Constitution of the United States is not a mere lawyers' document: it is a vehicle of life, and its spirit is always the spirit of age.

Woodrow Wilson
Constitutional Government in the United States (1927)

Powers not given to the federal government by the Constitution are reserved for the states. States also have their own constitutions. These are often patterned after the U.S. Constitution, although many are more detailed. State constitutions establish the legislative, executive, and judicial branches of state government and establish the powers of each branch. Provisions of state constitutions are valid unless they conflict with the U.S. Constitution or any valid federal law.

Treaties

The U.S. Constitution provides that the president, with the advice and consent of two-thirds of the Senate, may enter into **treaties** with foreign governments. Treaties become part of the supreme law of the land. With increasing international economic relations among nations, treaties will become an even more important source of law that will affect business in the future.

treaty
A compact made between two or more nations.

Codified Law

Statutes are written laws that establish certain courses of conduct that must be adhered to by covered parties. The U.S. Congress is empowered by the Commerce Clause and other provisions of the U.S. Constitution to enact *federal statutes* to regulate foreign and interstate commerce. Federal statutes include antitrust laws, securities laws, bankruptcy laws, labor laws, equal employment opportunity laws, environmental protection laws, consumer protection laws, and such. State legislators enact *state statutes.* State statutes include corporation laws, partnership laws, workers' compensation laws, the Uniform Commercial Code, and the like. The statutes enacted by the legislative branches of the federal and state governments are organized by topic into code books. This is often called *codified law.*

statute
Written law enacted by the legislative branch of the federal and state governments that establishes certain courses of conduct that must be adhered to by covered parties.

State legislatures often delegate lawmaking authority to local government bodies, including cities and municipalities, countries, school districts, water districts, and such. These governmental units are empowered to adopt **ordinances**. Examples of ordinances are traffic laws, local building codes, and zoning laws. Ordinances are also codified.

ordinance
Laws enacted by local government bodies such as cities and municipalities, countries, school districts, and water districts.

Executive Orders

The executive branch of government, which includes the president of the United States and state governors, is empowered to issue **executive orders**. This power is derived from express delegation from the legislative branch and is implied from the U.S. Constitution

executive order
An order issued by a member of the executive branch of the government.

U.S. Congress, Washington, DC. The U.S. Congress, which is a bicameral system made up of the U.S. Senate and the U.S. House of Representatives, creates federal law by enacting statutes. Each state has two senators and is allocated a certain number of representatives based on population.

and state constitutions. For example, when the United States is at war with another country, the president of the United States usually issues executive orders prohibiting U.S. companies from selling goods or services to that country.

Regulations and Order of Administrative Agencies

The legislative and executive branches of federal and state governments are empowered to establish **administrative agencies** to enforce and interpret statutes enacted by Congress and state legislatures. Many of these agencies regulate business. For example, Congress has created the Securities and Exchange Commission (SEC) and the Federal Trade Commission (FTC), among others.

administrative agencies
Agencies (such as the Securities and Exchange Commission or the Federal Trade Commission) that the legislative and executive branches of federal and state governments are empowered to establish.

Congress or the state legislatures usually empower these agencies to adopt **administrative rules and regulations** to interpret the statutes that the agency is authorized to enforce. These rules and regulations have the force of law. Administrative agencies usually have the power to hear and decide disputes. Their decisions are called *orders*. Because of their power, administrative agencies are often informally referred to as the "fourth branch of government."

Contemporary Trend

Department of Homeland Security

On September 11, 2001, the World Trade Center buildings in New York City were destroyed, and the Pentagon in Washington, DC, was damaged by terrorist attacks. After the attacks, President George W. Bush issued an executive order creating the Office of Homeland Security. The president called for the office to be made into a Cabinet-level agency. Congress responded by enacting the **Homeland Security Act of 2002**, which created the Cabinet-level **Department of Homeland Security (DHS)**. The creation of the DHS is the largest government reorganization in over 50 years.

The act placed 22 existing federal agencies with more than 180,000 employees under the umbrella of the DHS. The DHS is the second-largest government agency, after the Department of Defense. The DHS contains the Bureau of Customs and Border Protection, the Bureau of Citizenship and Immigration Services, the U.S. Secret Service, the Federal

Emergency Management Agency, the Federal Computer Incident Response Center, the National Domestic Preparedness Office, the U.S. Coast Guard, and portions of the Federal Bureau of Investigation, Treasury Department, Commerce Department, Justice Department, and other federal government agencies.

The mission of the DHS is to prevent domestic terror attacks, reduce vulnerability to terror attacks, minimize the harm caused by such attacks, and assist in the recovery if a terrorist attack occurs. The DHS provides services in the following critical areas: (1) border and transportation security, including protecting airports, seaports, and borders, and providing immigration and visa processing; (2) chemical, biological, radiological, and nuclear countermeasures, including metering the air for biological agents and developing vaccines and treatments for biological agents; (3) information analysis and infrastructure protection, including protection of communications systems, power grids, transportation networks, telecommunications, and cyber systems; and (4) emergency preparedness and response to terrorist incidents, including training first responders and coordinating government disaster relief. ■

Judicial Decisions

When deciding individual lawsuits, federal and state courts issue **judicial decisions**. In these written opinions, the judge or justice usually explains the legal reasoning used to decide the case. These opinions often include interpretations of statutes, ordinances, administrative regulations, and the announcement of legal principles used to decide the case. Many court decisions are printed (reported) in books that are available in law libraries.

judicial decision
A decision about an individual lawsuit issued by federal and state courts.

Doctrine of Stare Decisis Based on the common law tradition, past court decisions become **precedent** for deciding future cases. Lower courts must follow the precedent established by higher courts. That is why all federal and state courts in the United States must follow the precedents established by U.S. Supreme Court decisions.

precedent
A rule of law established in a court decision. Lower courts must follow the precedent established by higher courts.

The courts of one jurisdiction are not bound by the precedent established by the courts of another jurisdiction, although they may look to each other for guidance. For example, state courts of one state are not required to follow the legal precedent established by the courts of another state.

Adherence to precedent is called **stare decisis** ("to stand by the decision"). The doctrine of *stare decisis* promotes uniformity of law within a jurisdiction, makes the court system more efficient, and makes the law more predictable for individuals and businesses. A court may later change or reverse its legal reasoning if a new case is presented to it and change is warranted. The doctrine of *stare decisis* is discussed in the following excerpt from Justice Musmanno's decision in *Flagiello v. Pennsylvania*:

stare decisis
Latin: "to stand by the decision." Adherence to precedent.

> Without stare decisis, there would be no stability in our system of jurisprudence. Stare decisis channels the law. It erects lighthouses and flies the signal of safety. The ships of jurisprudence must follow that well-defined channel which, over the years, has been proved to be secure and worthy.[7]

Priority of Law in the United States

As mentioned previously, the U.S. Constitution and treaties take precedence over all other laws in the United States. Federal statutes take precedence over federal regulations. Valid federal law takes precedence over any conflicting state or local law. State constitutions rank as the highest state law. State statutes take precedence over state regulations. Valid state law takes precedence over local laws.

Concept Summary Sources of Law in the United States

Source of Law	Description
Constitutions	The U.S. Constitution establishes the federal government and enumerates its powers. Powers not given to the federal government are reserved to the states. State constitutions establish state governments and enumerate their powers.
Treaties	The president, with the advice and consent of the Senate, may enter into treaties with foreign countries.
Codified law: statutes and ordinances	Statutes are enacted by Congress and state legislatures. Ordinances are enacted by municipalities and local government agencies. They establish courses of conduct that covered parties must follow.
Administrative agency rules and regulations	Administrative agencies are created by the legislative and executive branches of government. They may adopt rules and regulations that regulate the conduct of covered parties.
Executive orders	Issued by the president and governors of states, executive orders regulate the conduct of covered parties.
Judicial decisions	Courts decide controversies. In doing so, a court issues decisions that state the holding of the case and the rationale the court used in reaching that decision.

Red Square, Moscow, Russia. The legal heritages of countries differ considerably. After the fall of communism, Russia adopted capitalism. New laws have been enacted to allow for the private ownership of property, to provide for the enforcement of contracts, and to otherwise support trade and commerce.

Terms and Concepts

Law

Law is a body of rules of action or conduct that has binding legal force. Laws must be obeyed by citizens subject to sanction or legal consequences.

Functions of the Law

1. Keep the peace
2. Shape moral standards
3. Promote social justice
4. Maintain the status quo
5. Facilitate orderly change
6. Facilitate planning
7. Provide a basis for compromise
8. Maximize individual freedom

Flexibility and Fairness of the Law

1. ***Flexibility.*** The law must be flexible to meet social, technological, and economic changes in the United States and the rest of the world.
2. ***Fairness.*** Although the U.S. legal system is one of the fairest and most democratic systems of law, abuses of process and mistakes in the application of the law do occur.

Schools of Jurisprudential Thought

1. ***Natural Law School.*** This school postulates that law is based on what is "correct." It emphasizes a moral theory of law—that is, law should be based on morality and ethics.
2. ***Historical School.*** This school believes that law is an aggregate of social traditions and customs.
3. ***Analytical School.*** This school maintains that law is shaped by logic.
4. ***Sociological School.*** This school asserts that the law is a means of achieving and advancing certain sociological goals.
5. ***Command School.*** This school believes that the law is a set of rules developed, communicated, and enforced by the ruling party.
6. ***Critical Legal Studies School.*** This school maintains that legal rules are unnecessary and that legal disputes should be solved by applying arbitrary rules based on fairness.
7. ***Law and Economics School.*** This school believes that promoting market efficiency should be the central concern of legal decision making.

Foundation of American Law

The English common law (judge-made law) forms the basis of the legal systems of most states in this country. Louisiana bases its laws on the French civil code.

Sources of Law in the United States

1. ***Constitutions.*** The U.S. Constitution establishes the federal government and enumerates its powers. Powers not given to the federal government are reserved to the states. State constitutions establish state governments and enumerate their powers.
2. ***Treaties.*** The president, with the advice and consent of the Senate, may enter into treaties with foreign countries.
3. ***Codified law.*** *Statutes* are enacted by the federal Congress and state legislatures. *Ordinances* are passed by municipalities and local government bodies. They establish courses of conduct that must be followed by covered parties.
4. ***Administrative agency regulations and orders.*** Administrative agencies are created by the legislative and executive branches of government. They may adopt administrative regulations and issue orders.

5. ***Executive orders.*** Issued by the president and governors of states, executive orders regulate the conduct of covered parties.
6. ***Judicial decisions.*** Federal and state courts decide controversies. In doing so, they issue decisions that state the holding of each case and the reasoning used by the court in reaching its decision.

Doctrine of *Stare Decisis*

This doctrine provides for the adherence to precedent. *Stare decisis* means "to stand by the decision."

Internet Exercises and Case Questions

Working the Web Internet Exercises

Visit the Web sites listed below for more information about the topics covered in this chapter:

1. For a broad overview of legal history, visit **jurist.law.pitt.edu/sg_hist.htm**.
2. To better understand the conceptual differences between law and equity, see **www.law.cornell.edu/topics/equity.html**.
3. For a working definition of basic legal categories, visit *The Columbia Encyclopedia*, Sixth Edition, 2001, at **www.bartleby.com/65/co/commonla.html**.
4. The Shidler Center for Law, Commerce & Technology, University of Washington Law, provides online information about Internet issues, biotechnology, electronic commerce, and technology news in the Northwest. Visit **www.law.washington.edu/lct**.
5. Check out the latest developments at the Business Law—Committee on Cyberspace Law home page, at **www.abanet.org/buslaw/cyber/home.html**.

Legal Environment Case

1.1 Fairness of the Law In 1909, the state legislature of Illinois enacted a statute called the "Woman's 10-Hour Law." The law prohibited women who were employed in factories and other manufacturing facilities from working more than 10 hours per day. The law did not apply to men. W. C. Ritchie & Co., an employer, brought a lawsuit that challenged the statute as being unconstitutional in violation of the Equal Protection Clause of the Illinois constitution. In upholding the statute, the Illinois supreme court stated:

> *It is known to all men (and what we know as men we cannot profess to be ignorant of as judges) that woman's physical structure and the performance of maternal functions place her at a great disadvantage in the battle of life; that while a man can work for more than 10 hours a day without injury to himself, a woman, especially when the burdens of motherhood are upon her, cannot; that while a man can work standing upon his feet for more than 10 hours a day, day after day, without injury to himself, a woman cannot; and that to require a woman to stand upon her feet for more than 10 hours in any one day and perform severe manual labor while thus standing, day after day, has the effect to impair her health, and that as weakly and sickly women cannot be mothers of vigorous children.*
>
> *We think the general consensus of opinion, not only in this country but in the civilized countries of Europe, is, that a working day of not more than 10 hours for women is justified for the following reasons: (1) the physical organization of women, (2) her maternal function, (3) the rearing and education of children, (4) the maintenance of the home; and these conditions are, so far, matters of general knowledge that the courts will take judicial cognizance of their existence.*
>
> *Surrounded as women are by changing conditions of society, and the evolution of employment which environs them, we agree fully with what is said by the Supreme Court of Washington in the Buchanan case; "law is, or ought to be, a progressive science."*

Is the statute fair? Would the statute be lawful today? Should the law be a "progressive science"? *W.C. Ritchie & Co. v. Wayman, Attorney for Cook County, Illinois*, 91 N.E. 695, 1910 Ill. Lexis 1958 (Ill.)

Ethics in Business

1.2 In 1975, after the war in Vietnam, the U.S. government discontinued draft resignation for men in this country. In 1980, after the Soviet Union invaded Afghanistan, President Jimmy Carter asked Congress for funds to reactivate draft registration. President Carter suggested that both males and females be required to register. Congress allocated funds only for the registration of males. Several men who were subject to draft registration brought a lawsuit that challenged the law as being unconstitutional in violation of the Equal Protection Clause of the U.S. Constitution. This clause states that the government must have a significant reason for treating people differently because of their gender. The U.S. Supreme Court upheld the constitutionality of the draft registration law, reasoning as follows:

> *The question of registering women for the draft not only received considerable national attention and was the subject of wide-ranging public debate, but also was extensively considered by Congress in hearings, floor debate, and in committee. The foregoing clearly establishes that the decision to exempt women from registration was not the "accidental by-product of a traditional way of thinking about women."*
>
> *This is not a case of Congress arbitrarily choosing to burden one of two similarly situated groups, such as would be the case with an all-black or all-white, or an all-Catholic or all-Lutheran, or an all-Republican or all-Democratic registration. Men and women are simply not similarly situated for purposes of a draft or registration for a draft.*

Justice Marshall dissented, stating that "The Court today places its imprimatur on one of the most potent remaining public expressions of 'ancient canards about the proper role of women.' It upholds a statute that requires males but not females to register for the draft, and which thereby categorically excludes women from a fundamental civil obligation. I dissent." *Rostker, Director of the Selective Service v. Goldberg*, 453 U.S. 57, 101 S.Ct. 2646, 1981 Lexis 126 (U.S. Sup.Ct.)

Ethics Issues

1. What does the Equal Protection Clause provide?
2. Was the decision in this case fair?
3. Has the law been a "progressive science" in this case?
4. Is it ethical for males, but not females, to have to register for the draft?

Endnotes

1. *The Spirit of Liberty*, 3rd ed. (New York: Alfred A. Knopf, 1960).
2. "Introduction," *The Nature of Law: Readings in Legal Philosophy*, ed. M. P. Golding (New York: Random House, 1966).
3. *Black's Law Dictionary*, 5th ed. (St. Paul, MN: West, 1979).
4. 447 U.S. 10, 100 S.Ct. 1999, 1980 U.S. Lexis 127 (U.S. Sup.Ct.).
5. *Law and the Modern Mind* (New York: Brentano's, 1930).
6. 4 Ill. 301, 1841 Ill. Lexis 98 (Ill.).
7. 208 A.2d 193, 1965 Pa. Lexis 442 (Pa.).

2 Court Systems and Jurisdiction

"I was never ruined but twice; once when I lost a lawsuit, and once when I won one."

—Voltaire

Chapter Objectives

After studying this chapter, you should be able to:

1. Describe the state court systems.
2. Describe the federal court system.
3. Compare the jurisdiction of state and federal courts.
4. List and describe the types of decisions that are issued by the U.S. Supreme Court.
5. Define standing to sue and venue.

Chapter Contents

- State Court Systems
- Federal Court System
- U.S. Supreme Court
- Subject Matter Jurisdiction of Courts
- Personal Jurisdiction of Courts

There are two major court systems in the United States: (1) the federal court system and (2) the court system of the 50 states and the District of Columbia. Each of these systems has jurisdiction to hear different types of lawsuits.

This chapter discusses the various court systems and the jurisdiction of courts to hear and decide cases.

Supreme Court of the United States, Washington, DC. The highest court in the land is the Supreme Court of the United States, located in Washington, DC. The Supreme Court's unanimous and majority decisions are precedent for all the other courts in the country.

State Court Systems

Each state and the District of Columbia has a separate court system. Most state court systems include the following: *limited-jurisdiction trial courts*, *general-jurisdiction trial courts*, *intermediate appellate courts*, and a *supreme court*.

Limited-Jurisdiction Trial Courts

State **limited-jurisdiction trial courts**, which are sometimes referred to as **inferior trial courts**, hear matters of a specialized or limited nature. In many states, traffic courts, juvenile courts, justice-of-the-peace courts, probate courts, family law courts, and courts that hear misdemeanor criminal law cases and civil cases involving lawsuits under a certain dollar amount are examples of such courts. Because these courts are trial courts, evidence can be introduced and testimony given. Most limited-jurisdiction courts keep records of their proceedings. Their decisions can usually be appealed to general-jurisdiction courts or appellate courts.

limited-jurisdiction trial court
A court that hears matters of a specialized or limited nature.

Many states have also created **small claims courts** to hear civil cases involving small dollar amounts (e.g., $5,000 or less). Generally, the parties must appear individually and cannot have lawyers represent them. The decisions of small claims courts are often appealable to general-jurisdiction trial courts or appellate courts.

small claims court
A court that hears civil cases involving small dollar amounts.

General-Jurisdiction Trial Courts

general-jurisdiction trial court
A court that hears cases of a general nature that are not within the jurisdiction of limited-jurisdiction trial courts. Testimony and evidence at trial are recorded and stored for future reference.

Every state has a **general-jurisdiction trial court**. These courts are often referred to as **courts of record** because the testimony and evidence at trial are recorded and stored for future reference. They hear cases that are not within the jurisdiction of limited-jurisdiction trial courts, such as felony cases, civil cases over a certain dollar amount, and so on. Some states divide their general-jurisdiction courts into two divisions: one for criminal cases and another for civil cases. Evidence and testimony are given at general-jurisdiction trial courts. The decisions handed down by these courts are appealable to intermediate appellate courts or the state supreme court, depending on the circumstances.

Intermediate Appellate Courts

intermediate appellate court
An intermediate court that hears appeals from trial courts.

In many states, **intermediate appellate courts** (also called **appellate courts** or **courts of appeals**) hear appeals from trial courts. They review the trial court record to determine whether there have been any errors at trial that would require reversal or modification of the trial court's decision. Thus, the appellate court reviews either pertinent parts or the whole trial court record from the lower court. No new evidence or testimony is permitted. The parties usually file legal *briefs* with the appellate court, stating the law and facts that support their positions. Appellate courts usually grant a brief oral hearing to the parties. Appellate court decisions are appealable to the state's highest court. In sparsely populated states that do not have intermediate appellate courts, trial court decisions can be appealed directly to the state's highest court.

Highest State Court

state supreme court
The highest court in a state court system; it hears appeals from intermediate state courts and certain trial courts.

Each state has a highest court in its court system. Most states call this highest court the **state supreme court**. Some states use other names for their highest court. The function of a state's highest court is to hear appeals from intermediate state courts and certain trial courts. No new evidence or testimony is heard. The parties usually submit pertinent parts of or the entire lower court record for review. The parties also submit legal briefs to the court and are usually granted a brief oral hearing. Decisions of state supreme courts are final, unless a question of law is involved that is appealable to the U.S. Supreme Court.

Exhibit 2.1 portrays a typical state court system.

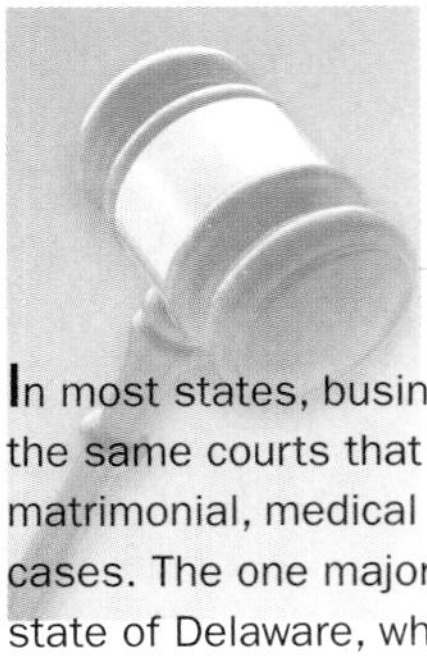

Contemporary Trend

Specialized Courts Hear Commercial Disputes

In most states, business and commercial disputes are heard by the same courts that hear and decide criminal, landlord–tenant, matrimonial, medical malpractice, and other non-business-related cases. The one major exception to this standard has been the state of Delaware, where a special Chancery Court hears and decides business litigation. This court, which deals mainly with cases involving corporate government disputes, has earned a reputation for its expertise in handling and deciding corporate matters. Perhaps the existence of this special court and a corporation code that tends to favor corporate management are the primary reasons that more than 60 percent of the corporations listed on the New York Stock Exchange are incorporated in Delaware.

Businesses tend to favor special commercial courts because the judges presiding over them are expected to have the expertise to handle complex commercial lawsuits. The courts are also expected to be more efficient in deciding business-related cases, thus saving time and money for the parties. Other states are also establishing courts that specialize in commercial matters. ■

Exhibit 2.1

Typical State Court System

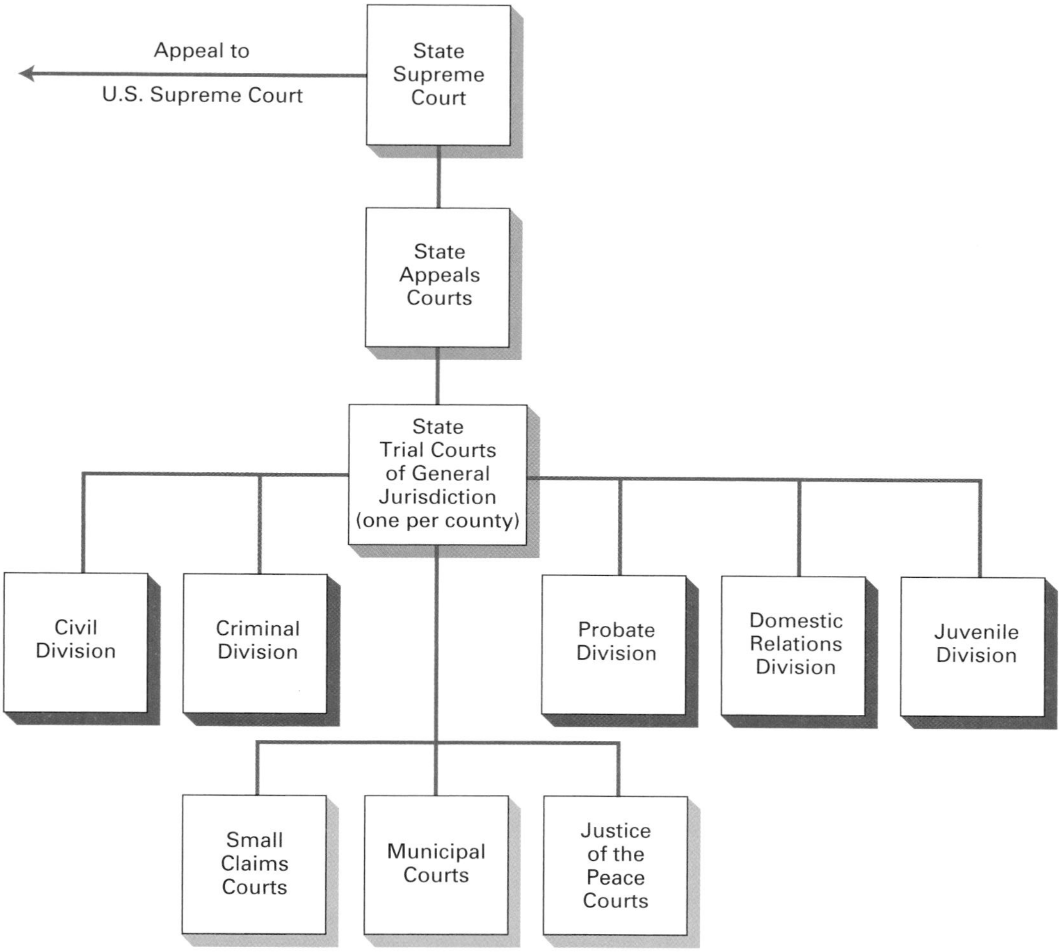

Courthouse, St. Louis, Missouri. State courts hear and decide the majority of cases in this country.

Federal Court System

Article III of the U.S. Constitution provides that the federal government's judicial power is vested in one "Supreme Court." This court is the **U.S. Supreme Court**. The Constitution also authorized Congress to establish "inferior" federal courts. Pursuant to this power, Congress has established special federal courts, the U.S. district courts, and the U.S. Courts of Appeals. Federal judges are appointed for life by the president, with the advice and consent of the Senate (except bankruptcy court judges, who are appointed for 14-year terms).

Special Federal Courts

special federal courts
Federal courts that hear matters of specialized or limited jurisdiction.

The **special federal courts** established by Congress have limited jurisdiction. They include the following:

- ***U.S. tax court.*** Hears cases involving federal tax laws.
- ***U.S. claims court.*** Hears cases brought against the United States.
- ***U.S. Court of International Trade.*** Hears cases involving tariffs and international commercial disputes.
- ***U.S. bankruptcy court.*** Hears cases involving federal bankruptcy laws.

U.S. District Courts

U.S. district courts
The federal court system's trial courts of general jurisdiction.

The **U.S. district courts** are the federal court system's trial courts of general jurisdiction. There is at least one federal district court in each state and the District of Columbia, although heavily populated states have more than one district court. The geographical area served by each court is referred to as a *district*. There are presently 96 federal district courts. The federal district courts are empowered to impanel juries, receive evidence, hear testimony, and decide cases. Most federal cases originate in federal district courts.

U.S. Courts of Appeals

U.S. Courts of Appeals
The federal court system's intermediate appellate courts.

The **U.S. Courts of Appeals** are the federal court system's intermediate appellate courts. There are 13 circuits in the federal court system. The first 12 are geographical. Eleven are designated by numbers, such as the "First Circuit," "Second Circuit," and so on. The geographical area served by each court is referred to as a *circuit*. The 12th circuit court is located in Washington, DC, and is called the "District of Columbia Circuit."

As an appellate court, each of these courts hears appeals from the district courts located in its circuit as well as from certain special courts and federal administrative agencies. The court reviews the record of the lower court or administrative agency proceedings to determine whether there has been any error that would warrant reversal or modification of the lower court decision. No new evidence or testimony is heard. The parties file legal briefs with the court and are given a short oral hearing. Appeals are usually heard by a three-judge panel. After a decision is rendered by the three-judge panel, a petitioner can request a review *en banc* by the full court.

Court of Appeals for the Federal Circuit
A court of appeals in Washington, DC, that has special appellate jurisdiction to review the decisions of the claims court, the Patent and Trademark Office, and the Court of International Trade.

The 13th court of appeals was created by Congress in 1982. It is called the **Court of Appeals for the Federal Circuit** and is located in Washington, DC.[1] This court has special appellate jurisdiction to review the decision of the claims court, the Patent and

Trademark Office, and the Court of International Trade. This court was created to provide uniformity in the application of federal law in certain areas, particularly patent law.

Exhibit 2.2 shows the 13 U.S. Courts of Appeals.

Exhibit 2.2

Federal Circuit Courts

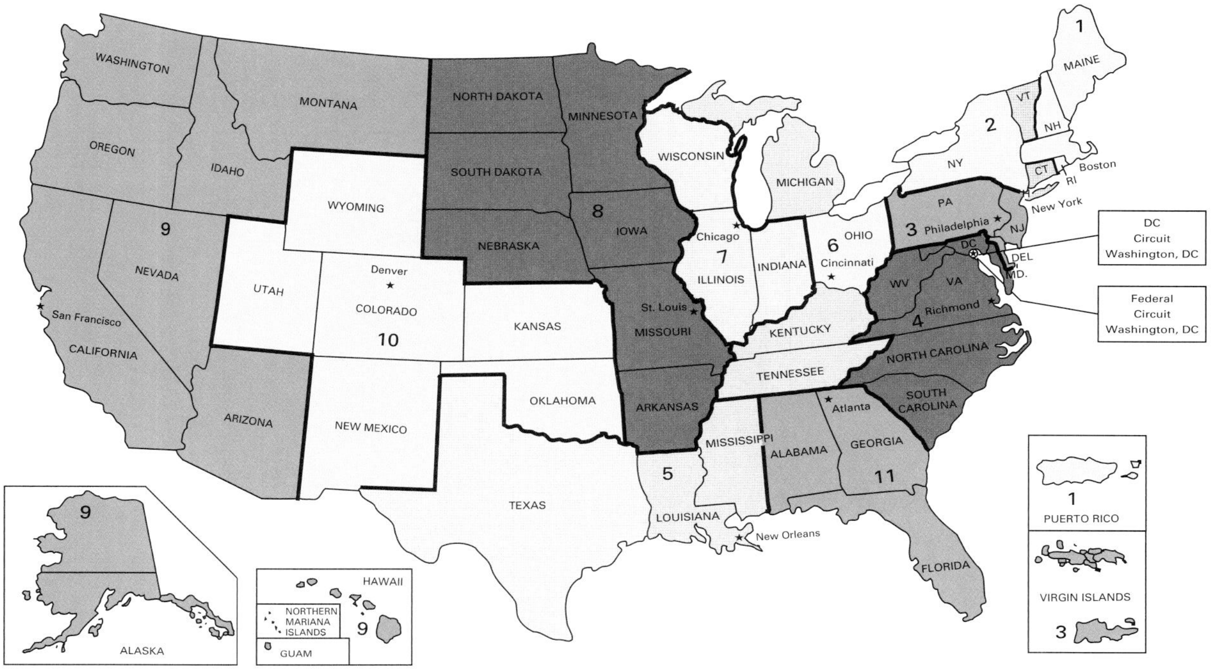

U.S. Supreme Court

The highest court in the land is the **U.S. Supreme Court**, located in Washington, DC. The Court is composed of nine justices who are nominated by the president and confirmed by the Senate. The president appoints one justice as *chief justice*, who is responsible for the administration of the Supreme Court. The other eight justices are *associate justices*.

U.S. Supreme Court
The highest court in the land, created by Article III of the U.S. Constitution. It is located in Washington, DC.

The Supreme Court, which is an appellate court, hears appeals from U.S. Courts of Appeals and, under certain circumstances, from federal district courts, special federal courts, and the highest state courts. No new evidence or testimony is heard. As with other appellate courts, the lower court record is reviewed to determine whether there has been an error that warrants a reversal or modification of the decision. Legal briefs are filed, and the parties are granted a brief oral hearing. The Supreme Court's decision is final.

The federal court system is illustrated in Exhibit 2.3.

Decisions by the U.S. Supreme Court

The U.S. Constitution gives Congress the authority to establish rules for the appellate review of cases by the Supreme Court, except in the rare case in which mandatory review is required. Congress has given the Supreme Court discretion to decide what cases it will hear.[2]

Exhibit 2.3

Federal Court System

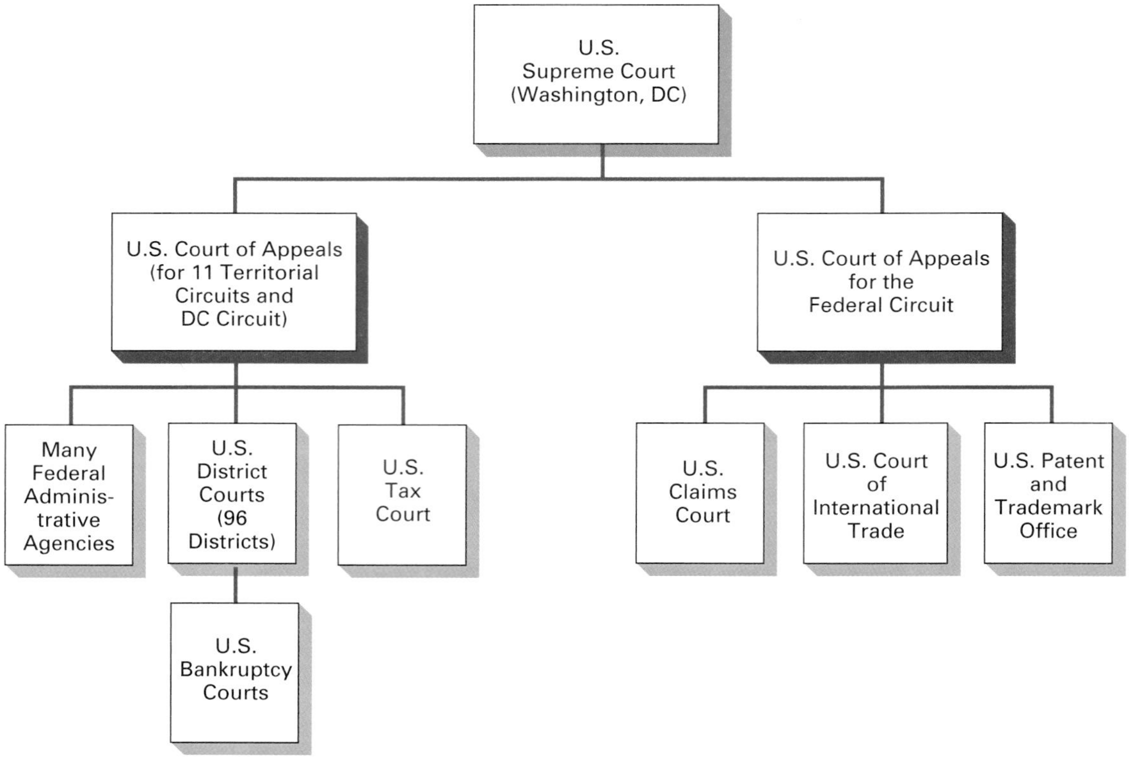

petition for certiorari
A petition asking the Supreme Court to hear a case.

writ of certiorari
An official notice that the Supreme Court will review a case.

Sancho: But if this is hell, why do we see no lawyers?

Clarindo: They won't receive them, lest they bring lawsuits here.

Sancho: If there are no lawsuits here, hell's not so bad.

Lope de Vega
The Star of Seville, Act 3, Scene 2

A petitioner must file a **petition for certiorari** asking the Supreme Court to hear the case. If the Court decides to review a case, it will issue a **writ of certiorari**. Because the Court issues only about 100 opinions each year, writs are granted only in cases involving constitutional and other important issues.

Each justice of the Supreme Court, including the chief justice, has an equal vote. The Supreme Court can issue the following types of decisions:

- ***Unanimous decision.*** If all the justices voting agree as to the outcome and reasoning used to decide a case, it is a unanimous opinion. Unanimous decisions are precedent for later cases. For example, suppose all nine justices hear a case, and all nine agree as to the outcome (e.g., the petitioner wins) and the reason why (e.g., the Equal Protection Clause of the U.S. Constitution had been violated); this is a unanimous decision. This unanimous decision becomes precedent for later cases.
- ***Majority decision.*** If a majority of the justices agree as to the outcome and reasoning used to decide a case, it is a majority opinion. Majority decisions are precedent for later cases. For example, if all nine justices hear a case, and five of them agree as to the outcome (e.g., the petitioner wins) and all these five justices agree to the same reason why (e.g., the Equal Protection Clause of the U.S. Constitution has been violated), it is a majority opinion. The majority opinion becomes precedent for later cases and has the same force of law as a unanimous decision. The remaining four justices' vote for the respondent has no legal effect whatsoever. Remember: A majority decision occurs if five, six, seven, or eight justices vote for the same outcome for the same reason.
- ***Plurality decision.*** If a majority of the justices agree as to the outcome of a case but not as to the reasoning for reaching the outcome, it is a plurality opinion. A plurality decision settles the case but is not precedent for later cases. For example, if all nine

justices hear a case, and five of them agree as to the outcome (e.g., the petitioner wins), but not all of these five agree to the reason why—let's suppose three base their vote on a violation of the Equal Protection Clause and two base their vote on a violation of the Freedom of Speech Clause of the U.S. Constitution—this is a plurality decision. Five justices have agreed to the same outcome, but those five have not agreed to the same reason. The petitioner wins his or her case, but the decision is not precedent for later cases. The remaining four justices' vote for the respondent has no legal effect whatsoever.

- ***Tie decision.*** Sometimes the Supreme Court sits without all nine justices being present. This could happen because of illness, conflict of interest, or a justice not having been confirmed to fill a vacant seat on the Court. If there is a tie vote, the lower court decision is affirmed. Such votes are not precedent for later cases. For example, suppose a petitioner won her case at the Court of Appeals. At the U.S. Supreme Court, only eight justices hear the case. Suppose four justices vote for the petitioner, and four justices vote for the respondent. This is a tie vote. The petitioner remains the winner because she won at the Court of Appeals. The decision of the Supreme Court sets no precedent for later cases.
- ***Concurring and Dissenting Opinions.*** A justice who agrees with the outcome of a case, but not the reason proffered by other justices, can issue a *concurring opinion* that sets forth his or her reasons for deciding the case. A justice who does not agree with a decision can file a *dissenting opinion* that sets forth the reasons for his or her dissent.

Contemporary Trend

"I'll Take You to the U.S. Supreme Court!"

In reality, the chance of ever having your case heard by the highest court is slim to none. Each year, more than 7,000 petitioners ask the Supreme Court to hear their cases. These petitioners usually pay big law firms from $30,000 to $100,000 or more to write the appeal petition. In recent years, the Supreme Court has accepted only fewer than 100 of these cases for full review each term.

Each of the nine Supreme Court justices has three law clerks—recent law school graduates usually chosen from the elite law schools across the country—who assist them. The justices rarely read the appellate petitions but instead delegate this task to their law clerks. A clerk then writes a short memorandum, discussing the key issues raised by the appeal, and recommends to the justices whether they should grant or deny a review. The justices meet once a week to discuss what cases merit review. The votes of four justices are necessary to grant an appeal and schedule an oral argument before the Court ("rule of four"). Written opinions by the justices are usually issued many months later.

So what does it take to win a review by the Supreme Court? The U.S. Supreme Court usually decides to hear cases involving major constitutional questions such as freedom of speech, freedom of religion, equal protection, and due process. The Court, therefore, rarely decides day-to-day legal issues such as breach of contract, tort liability, or corporations law, unless they involve more important constitutional or federal law questions. So the next time you hear someone say, "I'll take you to the U.S. Supreme Court!" just say, "Not!" ■

Subject Matter Jurisdiction of Courts

Federal courts and state courts each have jurisdiction to hear and decide certain types of cases. The **subject matter jurisdiction** of federal and state courts are discussed in the following paragraphs.

subject matter jurisdiction Jurisdiction over the subject matter of a lawsuit.

Jurisdiction of Federal Courts

Article III, Section 2 of the U.S. Constitution sets forth the jurisdiction of federal courts. Federal courts have *limited jurisdiction* to hear cases involving:

federal question
A case arising under the U.S. Constitution, treaties, or federal statutes and regulations.

diversity of citizenship
A case between (1) citizens of different states, (2) a citizen of a state and a citizen or subject of a foreign country, and (3) a citizen of a state and a foreign country where a foreign country is the plaintiff.

1. ***Federal questions.*** **Federal questions** are cases arising under the U.S. Constitution, treaties, and federal statutes and regulations. There is no dollar-amount limit on federal question cases that can be brought in federal court.[3]
2. ***Diversity of citizenship.*** **Diversity of citizenship** cases occur between (a) citizens of different states, (b) a citizen of a state and a citizen or subject of a foreign country, and (c) a citizen of a state and a foreign country where a foreign country is the plaintiff. A corporation is considered to be a citizen of the state in which it is incorporated and in which it has its principal place of business. The reason for providing diversity of citizenship jurisdiction was to prevent state court bias against nonresidents. The federal court must apply the appropriate state's law in deciding the case. The dollar amount of the controversy must exceed $75,000.[4] If this requirement is not met, action must be brought in the appropriate state court.

exclusive jurisdiction
Jurisdiction held by only one court.

Federal courts have **exclusive jurisdiction** to hear cases involving federal crimes, antitrust, bankruptcy; patent and copyright cases; suits against the United States; and most admiralty cases. State courts cannot hear these cases.

Concept Summary Jurisdiction of Federal Courts

Type of Jurisdiction	Description
Federal question	Cases arising under the U.S. Constitution, treaties, and federal statutes and regulations. There is no dollar-amount limit in federal question cases.
Diversity of citizenship	Cases between (i) citizens of different states, (ii) a citizen of a state and a citizen or subject of a foreign country, and (iii) a citizen of a state and a foreign country where a foreign country is the plaintiff. Federal courts must apply the appropriate state law in such cases. The controversy must exceed $75,000 for the federal court to hear the case.

Jurisdiction of State Courts

State courts have jurisdiction to hear cases that federal courts do not have jurisdiction to hear. These usually involve state law, such as real estate law, corporation law, partnership law, limited liability company law, contract law, sales and lease contracts, negotiable instruments, and other state law subject matters.

concurrent jurisdiction
Jurisdiction shared by two or more courts.

State courts have **concurrent jurisdiction** with federal courts to hear cases involving diversity of citizenship and federal questions over which federal courts do not have exclusive jurisdiction (e.g., cases involving federal securities laws). If a case involving concurrent jurisdiction is brought by a plaintiff in federal court, the case remains in federal court. If the plaintiff brings a case involving concurrent jurisdiction in state court, the defendant can either let the case be decided by the state court or can remove the case to federal court. If a case does not qualify to be brought in federal court, it must be brought in the appropriate state court.

Exhibit 2.4 illustrates the jurisdiction of federal and state courts.

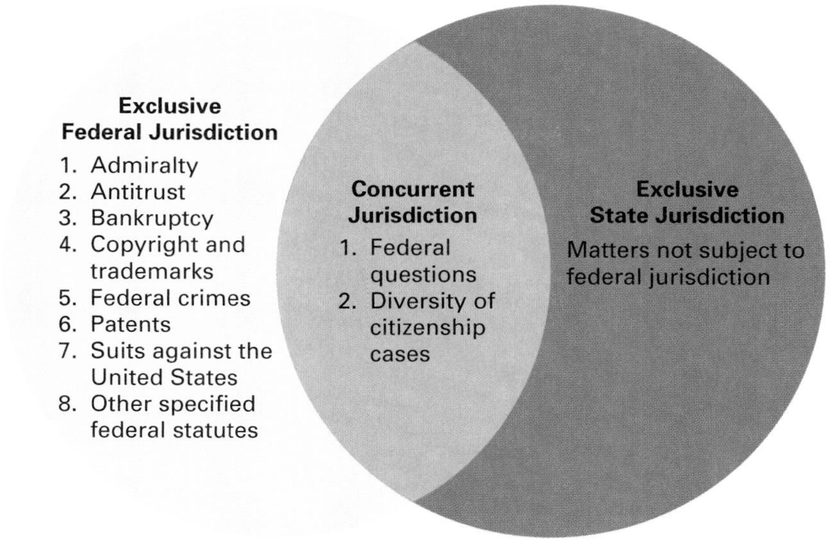

Exhibit 2.4

Jurisdiction of Federal and State Courts

Personal Jurisdiction of Courts

Not every court has the authority to hear all types of cases. First, to bring a lawsuit in a court, the plaintiff must have *standing to sue*. In addition, the court must have *personal jurisdiction* to hear the case, and the case must be brought in the proper *venue*. These topics are discussed in the following paragraphs.

Standing to Sue

To bring a lawsuit, a plaintiff must have **standing to sue**. This means the plaintiff must have some stake in the outcome of the lawsuit. For example, suppose Linda's friend Jon is injured in an accident caused by Emily. Jon refuses to sue. Linda cannot sue Emily on Jon's behalf because she does not have an interest in the result of the case.

standing to sue
A plaintiff's stake in the outcome of a lawsuit.

A few states now permit investors to invest money in a lawsuit for a percentage return of any award of judgment. Courts hear and decide actual disputes involving specific controversies. Hypothetical questions will not be heard, and trivial lawsuits will be dismissed.

In Personam Jurisdiction

Jurisdiction over the person is called **in personam jurisdiction**, or **personal jurisdiction**. A *plaintiff*, by filing a lawsuit with a court, gives the court in personam jurisdiction over himself or herself. The court must also have in personam jurisdiction over the *defendant*, which is usually obtained by having a summons served to that person within the territorial boundaries of the state (i.e., **service of process**). Service of process is usually accomplished by personal service of the summons and complaint on the defendant. If this is not possible, alternative forms of notice, such as mailing of the summons or publication of a notice in a newspaper, may be permitted. A corporation is subject to personal jurisdiction in the state in which it is incorporated, has its principal office, and is doing business. A party who disputes the jurisdiction of a court can make a *special appearance* in that court to argue against imposition of jurisdiction. Service of process is not permitted during such an appearance.

in personam jurisdiction
Jurisdiction over the parties to a lawsuit.

service of process
Service of a summons on a defendant to obtain personal jurisdiction over him or her.

In Rem and Quasi In Rem Jurisdiction

in rem jurisdiction
Jurisdiction to hear a case because of jurisdiction over the property of the lawsuit.

A court may have jurisdiction to hear and decide a case because it has jurisdiction over the property of the lawsuit. This is called **in rem jurisdiction** ("jurisdiction over the thing"). For example, a state court would have jurisdiction to hear a dispute over the ownership of a piece of real estate located within the state. This is so even if one or more of the disputing parties live in another state or states.

quasi in rem jurisdiction
Jurisdiction allowed a plaintiff who obtains a judgment in one state to try to collect the judgment by attaching property of the defendant located in another state.

Sometimes a plaintiff who obtains a judgment against a defendant in one state will try to collect the judgment by attaching property of the defendant that is located in another state. This is permitted under **quasi in rem**, or **attachment jurisdiction**.[5]

Concept Summary Personal and In Rem Jurisdiction

Type of Jurisdiction	Description
In personam jurisdiction	The court must have jurisdiction over the parties to a lawsuit. The plaintiff submits to the jurisdiction of the court by filing the lawsuit there. Personal jurisdiction is obtained over the defendant through service of process to that person.
In rem jurisdiction	A court may have jurisdiction to hear and decide a case because it has jurisdiction over the property at issue in the lawsuit (e.g., real property located in the state).
Quasi in rem jurisdiction	A plaintiff who obtains a judgment against a defendant in one state may utilize the court system of another state to attach property of the defendant's that is located in the second state.

Long-Arm Statutes

long-arm statute
A statute that extends a state's jurisdiction to nonresidents who were not served a summons within the state.

In most states, a state court can obtain jurisdiction over persons and businesses located in another state or country through the state's **long-arm statute**. Such a statute extends a state's jurisdiction to nonresidents who were not served a summons within the state. The nonresident must have had some *minimum contact* with the state.[6] In addition, the maintenance of the suit must uphold the traditional notions of fair play and substantial justice.

The exercise of long-arm jurisdiction is generally permitted over nonresidents who have (1) committed torts within the state (e.g., caused an automobile accident in the state), (2) entered into a contract either in the state or that affects the state (and allegedly breached the contract), or (3) transacted other business in the state that allegedly caused injury to another person.

forum-selection clause
A contract provision that designates a certain court to hear any dispute concerning nonperformance of the contract.

Parties to a contract may include a **forum-selection clause** that designates a certain court to hear any dispute concerning nonperformance of the contract.

The following case illustrates the application of a forum-selection clause.

Case 2.1
Forum-Selection Clause

U.S. SUPREME COURT
Carnival Cruise Lines, Inc. v. Shute

499 U.S. 585, 111 S. Ct. 1522, 1991 U.S. Lexis 2221 Supreme Court of the United States

Background and Facts

Mr. and Mrs. Shute, residents of the state of Washington, purchased passage for a seven-day cruise on the *Tropicale*, a cruise ship operated by Carnival Cruise Lines, Inc. (Carnival). They paid the fare to the travel agent, who forwarded the payment to Carnival's headquarters in Miami, Florida. Carnival prepared the tickets and sent them to the Shutes. Each ticket consisted of five pages, including contract terms. The ticket contained a forum-selection clause that designated the state of Florida as the forum for any lawsuits arising under or in connection with the ticket and cruise. The Shutes boarded the *Tropicale* in Los Angeles, which set sail for Puerto Vallarta, Mexico. While the ship was on its return voyage and in international waters off the Mexican coast, Mrs. Shute was injured when she slipped on a deck mat during a guided tour of the ship's galley. Upon return to Washington, she filed a negligence lawsuit against Carnival in U.S. district court in Washington, seeking damages. Carnival filed a motion for summary judgment, contending that the lawsuit could be brought only in a court located in the state of Florida. The district court granted Carnival's motion. The Court of Appeals reversed, holding that Mrs. Shute could sue Carnival in Washington. Carnival appealed to the U.S. Supreme Court.

Issue

Is the forum-selection clause in the Carnival Cruise Lines ticket enforceable?

In the Language of the Court

As an initial matter, we do not adopt the court of appeals' determination that a nonnegotiated forum-selection clause in a form ticket contract is never enforceable simply because it is not the subject of a bargaining. Including a reasonable forum clause in form contract of this kind may well be permissible for several reasons. First, a cruise line has a special interest in limiting the fora in which it potentially could be subject to suit. Because a cruise ship typically carries passengers from many locales, it is not unlikely that a mishap on a cruise could subject the cruise line to litigation in several different fora.

Additionally, a clause establishing the forum for dispute resolution has the salutary effect of dispelling any confusion where suits arising from the contract must be brought and defended, sparing litigants the time and expense of pretrial motions to determine the correct forum, and conserving judicial resources that otherwise would be devoted to deciding those motions. Finally, it stands to reason that passengers who purchase tickets containing a forum clause like that at issue in this case benefit in form of reduced fares reflecting the savings that the cruise line enjoys by limiting the fora in which it may be sued.

Decision and Remedy

The U.S. Supreme Court held that the forum-selection clause in Carnival's ticket was fair and reasonable and therefore enforceable against Mrs. Shute. If she wished to sue Carnival, she must do so in a court in the state of Florida, not in a court in the state of Washington. The U.S. Supreme Court reversed the decision of the Court of Appeals.

Business and Ethics Questions

1. Should forum-selection clauses be enforced? Why or why not?
2. Did Carnival Cruise Lines act ethically by placing the forum-selection clause in its tickets?
3. Do forum-selection clauses serve any legitimate business purpose? Explain.

Venue

Venue requires lawsuits to be heard by the court with jurisdiction nearest the location in which the incident occurred or where the parties reside.

venue
A concept that requires lawsuits to be heard by the court with jurisdiction that is nearest the location in which the incident occurred or where the parties reside.

Consider This Example Harry, a Georgia resident, commits a felony crime in Los Angeles County, California. The California superior court located in Los Angeles is the proper venue because the crime was committed there, the witnesses are probably from the area, and so on.

Occasionally, pretrial publicity may prejudice jurors located in the proper venue. In such cases, a *change of venue* may be requested so that a more impartial jury can be found. The courts generally frown upon *forum shopping* (i.e., looking for a favorable court without a valid reason).

Islamic mosque, Samarkan, Uzbekistan. Each country has its own national courts that hear and decide legal disputes in that country. This photo is of an Islamic mosque in the country of Uzbekistan.

Terms and Concepts

State Court Systems

1. ***Limited-jurisdiction trial court.*** These state courts hear matters of a specialized or limited nature (e.g., misdemeanor criminal matters, traffic tickets, civil matters under a certain dollar amount). Many states have created small claims courts that hear small-dollar-amount civil cases (e.g., under $5,000) where the parties cannot be represented by lawyers.
2. ***General-jurisdiction trial court.*** These state courts hear cases of a general nature that are not within the jurisdiction of limited-jurisdiction trial courts.
3. ***Intermediate appellate court.*** These state courts hear appeals from state trial courts. The appellate court reviews the trial court record in making its decision. No new evidence is introduced at this level.
4. ***Highest state court.*** Each state has a highest court in its court system. This court hears appeals from appellate courts and, where appropriate, trial courts. This court reviews the record in making its decision. No new evidence is introduced at this level. Most states call this court the supreme court.

Federal Court System

1. ***Special federal courts.*** These federal courts have specialized or limited jurisdiction. They include:
   a. *U.S. tax court.* This court hears cases involving federal tax laws.
   b. *U.S. claims court.* This court hears cases brought against the United States.
   c. *U.S. Court of International Trade.* This court hears cases involving tariffs and international commercial disputes.
   d. *U.S. bankruptcy courts.* This court hears cases involving federal bankruptcy law.
2. ***U.S. districts courts.*** These federal trial courts of general jurisdiction hear cases not within the jurisdiction of specialized courts. There is at least one U.S. district court per state: More

populated states have several district courts. The area serviced by one of these courts is called a *district*.

3. ***U.S. Courts of Appeals.*** These intermediate federal appellate courts hear appeals from district courts located in their circuits and, in certain instances, from special federal courts and federal administrative agencies. There are 12 geographic circuits in this country. Eleven serve areas that are comprised of several states, and another is located in Washington, DC. A 13th circuit court—the Court of Appeals for the Federal Circuit—is located in Washington, DC, and it reviews patent, trademark, and international trade cases.
4. ***U.S. Supreme Court.*** This is the highest court of the federal court system. It hears appeals from the circuit courts and, in some instances, from special courts and U.S. district courts. The Court, which is located in Washington, DC, is composed of nine justices, one of whom is named chief justice.

5. ***Decisions by the U.S. Supreme Court:***

   a. *Writ of certiorari.* To have a case heard by the. U.S. Supreme Court, a petitioner must file a *petition for certiorari* with the Court. If the Court decides to hear the case, it will issue a *writ of certiorari*.

   b. *Voting by the U.S. Supreme Court:*

      i. *Unanimous decision.* In this type of decision, all the justices agree as to the outcome and reasoning used to decide the case. The decision becomes precedent.

      ii. *Majority decision.* In this type of decision, a majority of the justices agree as to the outcome and reasoning used to decide the case. The decision becomes precedent.

      iii. *Plurality decision.* In this type of decision, a majority of the justices agrees as to the outcome but not as to the reasoning. The decision is not precedent.

      iv. *Tie decision.* If there is a tie vote, the lower court's decision stands. The decision is not precedent.

      v. *Concurring opinion.* A justice who agrees as to the outcome of the case but not the reasoning used by other justices may write a concurring opinion, setting forth his or her reasoning.

      vi. *Dissenting opinion.* A justice who disagrees with the outcome of a case may write a dissenting opinion, setting forth his or her reasoning for dissenting.

Jurisdiction of Federal and State Courts

1. ***Jurisdiction of federal courts.*** Federal courts may hear the following cases:

   a. *Federal question.* These are cases arising under the U.S. Constitution, treaties, and federal statutes and regulations. There is no dollar-amount limit in federal question cases.

   b. *Diversity of citizenship.* These are cases between (i) citizens of different states, (ii) a citizen of a state and a citizen or subject of a foreign country, and (iii) a citizen of a state and a foreign country where a foreign country is the plaintiff. Federal courts must apply the appropriate state law in such cases. The controversy must exceed $75,000 for the federal court to hear the case.

2. ***Jurisdiction of state courts.*** State courts hear some cases that may be heard by federal courts.

   a. *Exclusive jurisdiction.* Federal courts have exclusive jurisdiction to hear cases involving federal crimes, antitrust, and bankruptcy; patent and copyright cases; suits against the United States; and most admiralty cases. State courts may not hear these matters.

   b. *Concurrent jurisdiction.* State courts have concurrent jurisdiction to hear cases involving diversity of citizenship cases and federal question cases over which the federal courts do not have exclusive jurisdiction. The defendant may have the case removed to federal court.

Standing to Sue, Jurisdiction, and Venue

1. ***Standing to sue.*** To bring a lawsuit, the plaintiff must have some stake in the outcome of the lawsuit.
2. ***Subject matter jurisdiction.*** The court must have jurisdiction over the subject matter of the lawsuit. Each court has limited jurisdiction to hear only certain types of cases.
3. ***In personam jurisdiction (or personal jurisdiction).*** The court must have jurisdiction over the parties to a lawsuit. The plaintiff submits to the jurisdiction of the court by filing the lawsuit

there. Personal jurisdiction is obtained over the defendant through service of process to that person.

4. ***In rem jurisdiction.*** A court may have jurisdiction to hear and decide a case because it has jurisdiction over the property at issue in the lawsuit (e.g., real property located in the state).
5. ***Quasi in rem jurisdiction (or attachment jurisdiction).*** A plaintiff who obtains a judgment against a defendant in one state may utilize the court system of another state to attach property of the defendant located in the second state.
6. ***Long-arm statutes.*** These statutes permit a state to obtain personal jurisdiction over an out-of-state defendant as long as the defendant had the requisite minimum contact with the state. The out-of-state defendant may be served process outside the state in which the lawsuit has been brought.
7. ***Venue.*** A case must be heard by the court that has jurisdiction nearest to where the incident at issue occurred or where the parties reside. A *change of venue* will be granted if prejudice would occur because of pretrial publicity of another reason.
8. ***Forum-selection clause.*** A forum-selection clause in a contract designates the court that will hear any disputes that arise out of the contract.

Internet Exercises and Case Questions

Working the Web Internet Exercises

1. The site **guide.lp.findlaw.com/10fedgov/judicial/appeals_courts.html** contains links to each of the federal judicial circuits. Find your jurisdiction and review the cases available there. What is the oldest case you can find? The most recent? Now look at state court cases available in your state and apply the same two questions to them.
2. Go to the U.S. Supreme Court site, **www.supremecourtus.gov**. Find a case from your state that has recently been appealed to the Court. Outline the procedural steps involved in the process of appealing a case to the Supreme Court.

Legal Environment Cases

2.1 Federal Question Nutrilab, Inc., manufactures and markets a product known as "Starch Blockers." The purpose of the product is to block the human body's digestion of starch as an aid in controlling weight. On July 1, 1982, the U.S. FDA classified Starch Blockers as a drug and requested that it be removed from the market until the FDA approved of its use. The FDA claimed that it had the right to classify new products as drugs and prevent their distribution until their safety is determined. Nutrilab disputed the FDA's decision and wanted to bring suit to halt the FDA's actions. Do the federal courts have jurisdiction to hear this case? *Nutrilab, Inc. v. Schweiker*, 713 F.2d 335, 1983 U.S. App. Lexis 25121 (7th Cir.)

2.2 Jurisdiction James Clayton Allison, a resident of the state of Mississippi, was employed by the Tru-Amp Corporation as a circuit breaker tester. As part of his employment, Allison was sent to inspect, clean, and test a switch gear located at the South Central Bell Telephone Facility in Brentwood, Tennessee. On August 26, 1988, he attempted to remove a circuit breaker manufactured by ITE Corporation (ITE) from a bank of breakers, when a portion of the breaker fell off. The broken piece fell behind a switching bank and, according to Allison, caused an electrical fire and explosion. Allison was severely burned in the accident. Allison brought suit against ITE in a Mississippi state court, claiming more than $50,000 in damages. Can this suit be removed to federal court? *Allison v. ITE Imperial Corp.*, 729 F. Supp. 45, 1990 U.S. Dist. Lexis 607 (S.D. Miss.)

2.3 In Personam Jurisdiction Saul and Elaine Kozuck borrowed money from the Peoples Trust Company of Bergen County, New Jersey, and cosigned a promissory note promising to repay the money. When Peoples Trust contacted the Kozucks about payment, they denied liability on the ground that the bank had improperly filled in the due date on the note. Peoples Trust filed suit against the Kozucks in a New Jersey state court. A process server went to the Kozucks' home in New Jersey to serve the summons. The process server rang the bell at the home, and a woman appeared at the upstairs window. The process server asked her if she was Mrs. Kozuck, and the woman replied in the affirmative. When the process server identified himself, the woman denied that she was Mrs. Kozuck and refused to come out of the house. The process server told the woman that he would leave the papers in the mailbox if she refused to open the door. When the woman did not reappear, the process server placed the summons in the mailbox and left. Is the service of process good? *Peoples Trust Co. v. Kozuck*, 236 A.2d 630, 1967 N.J. Super. Lexis 389 (N.J. Super.)

Ethics in Business

2.4 One day, Joshua Gnaizda, a three-year-old, received what he (or his mother) thought was a tantalizing offer in the mail from Time, Inc. The front of the envelope contained a see-through window that revealed the following statement: "Joshua Gnaizda, I'll give you this versatile new calculator watch free just for opening this envelope before Feb. 15, 1985." Beneath the offer was a picture of the calculator watch itself. When Joshua's mother opened the envelope, she realized that the see-through window had not revealed the full text of Time's offer. Not viewable through the see-through window were the following words: "And mailing this Certificate today." The certificate required Joshua to purchase a subscription to *Fortune* magazine in order to receive the free calculator watch. Joshua (through his father, a lawyer) sued Time in a class action, seeking compensatory damages in an amount equal to the value of the calculator watch and $15 million in punitive damages. The trial court dismissed the lawsuit as being too trivial for the court to hear. Joshua appealed. *Harris v. Time, Inc.*, 191 C.A.3d 449, 237 Cal. Rptr. 584, 1987 Cal.App. Lexis 1617 (Cal. App.)

Ethics Issues

1. What law did Gnaizda assert had been violated?
2. Did Time, Inc., act ethically? Explain.
3. Did Joshua's father act ethically in suing for $15 million?
4. Should Joshua be permitted to bring his lawsuit against Time, Inc? Why or why not?

Endnotes

1. Federal Courts Improvement Act of 1982. Public Law 97-164, 96 Stat. 25, 28 U.S.C. Sections 1292 and 1295.
2. Effective September 25, 1988, mandatory appeals were all but eliminated, except for reapportionment cases and cases brought under the Civil Rights Act and the Voting Rights Act, antitrust laws, and the Presidential Election Campaign Fund Act.
3. Prior to 1980, there was a minimum dollar amount controversy requirement of $10,000 to bring a federal question action in federal court. This minimum amount was eliminated by the Federal Question Jurisdictional Amendment Act of 1980, Public Law 96-486.
4. The amount was raised from $50,000 to $75,000 by the 1996 Federal Courts Improvement Act.
5. Under the Full Faith and Credit Clause of the U.S. Constitution, a judgment of a court in one state must be given "full faith and credit" by the courts of another state (Article IV, Section 1).
6. *International Shoe Co. v. Washington*, 326 U.S. 310, 66 S.Ct. 154, 1945 U.S. Lexis 1447 (U.S. Sup.Ct.).

3

Alternative, Judicial, and Online Dispute Resolution

"We're the jury, dread our fury!"

—William S. Gilbert
Trial by Jury

Chapter Objectives

After studying this chapter, you should be able to:

1. Describe the pretrial litigation process.
2. Describe how a case proceeds through trial.
3. Describe how a trial court decision is appealed.
4. Describe how e-filings are used in court.
5. Explain the use of arbitration and other nonjudicial methods of alternate dispute resolution.

Chapter Contents

- Pretrial Litigation Process
- Dismissals and Pretrial Judgments
- Settlement Conference
- Trial
- Appeal
- Alternative Dispute Resolution

The process of bringing, maintaining, and defending a lawsuit is called **litigation.** Litigation is a difficult, time-consuming, and costly process that must comply with complex procedural rules. Although it is not required, most parties employ a lawyer to represent them when they are involved in a lawsuit.

Several forms of *nonjudicial* dispute resolution have developed in response to the expense and difficulty of bringing a lawsuit. These methods, collectively called **alternative dispute resolution**, are being used more and more often to resolve commercial and e-commerce disputes.

This chapter discusses the judicial litigation process and alternative dispute resolution.

Courthouse, Baltimore, Maryland. Parties to a dispute can use the court system to have their dispute decided.

Pretrial Litigation Process

The bringing, maintaining, and defense of a lawsuit are generally referred to as the *litigation process*, or **litigation**. The pretrial litigation process can be divided into the following major phases: *pleadings, discovery, dismissals and pretrial judgments,* and *settlement conference*. Each of these phases is discussed in the paragraphs that follow.

litigation
The process of bringing, maintaining, and defending a lawsuit.

The Pleadings

The paperwork that is filed with the court to initiate and respond to a lawsuit is referred to as the **pleadings**. The major pleadings are the *complaint*, the *answer*, the *cross-complaint*, and the *reply*.

pleadings
The paperwork that is filed with the court to initiate and respond to a lawsuit.

plaintiff
The party who files a complaint.

complaint
The document a plaintiff files with the court and serves on the defendant to initiate a lawsuit.

Complaint and Summons To initiate a lawsuit, the party who is suing (the **plaintiff**) must file a **complaint** with the proper court. The complaint must name the parties to the lawsuit, allege the ultimate facts and law violated, and contain a "prayer for relief" for a remedy to be awarded by the court. The complaint can be as long as necessary, depending on the case's complexity. A sample complaint appears in Exhibit 3.1.

Exhibit 3.1

Sample Complaint

In the United States District Court for the District of Idaho

John Doe
Plaintiff

v.

Jane Roe

Defendant

Civil No. 2-1001

COMPLAINT

The plaintiff, by and through his attorney, alleges:

1. The plaintiff is a resident of the State of Idaho, the defendant is a resident of the State of Washington, and there is diversity of citizenship between the parties.
2. The amount in controversy exceeds the sum of $75,000, exclusive of interest and costs.
3. On January 10, 2004, plaintiff was exercising reasonable care while walking across the intersection of Sun Valley Road and Main Street, Ketchum, Idaho, when defendant negligently drove her car through a red light at the intersection and struck plaintiff.
4. As a result of the defendant's negligence, plaintiff has incurred medical expenses of $104,000 and suffered severe physical injury and mental distress.

WHEREFORE, plaintiff claims judgment in the amount of $1,000,000, interest at the maximum legal rate, and costs of this action.

By ______________________

Edward Lawson
Attorney for Plaintiff
100 Main Street
Ketchum, Idaho

summons

A court order directing a defendant to appear in court and answer a complaint.

Once a complaint has been filed with the court, the court issues a **summons**, a court order directing the defendant to appear in court and answer the complaint. The complaint and summons are served on the defendant by a sheriff, another government official, or a private process server.

answer

A defendant's written response to a plaintiff's complaint that is filed with the court and served on the plaintiff.

Answer The defendant must file an **answer** to the plaintiff's complaint. The defendant's answer is filed with the court and served on the plaintiff. In the answer, the defendant admits or denies the allegations contained in the plaintiff's complaint. A judgment will be entered against a defendant who admits all the allegations in the complaint. The case will proceed if the defendant denies all or some of the allegations. If the defendant does not answer the complaint, a *default judgment* is entered against him or her. A default judgment establishes the defendant's liability. The plaintiff then has only to prove damages.

Pieces of evidence, each by itself insufficient, may together constitute a significant whole and justify by their combined effect a conclusion.

Lord Wright
Grant v. Australian Knitting Mills, Ltd. (1936)

In addition to answering the complaint, a defendant's answer can assert *affirmative defenses*. For example, if a complaint alleges that the plaintiff was personally injured by the defendant, the defendant's answer could state that he or she acted in self-defense. Another affirmative defense would be an assertion that the plaintiff's lawsuit is barred because the *statute of limitations* (i.e., the time within which to bring the lawsuit) has expired.

cross-complaint

A document filed by the defendant against the plaintiff to seek damages or some other remedy.

Cross-Complaint and Reply A defendant who believes that he or she has been injured by a plaintiff can file a **cross-complaint** against the plaintiff in addition to an answer. In the cross-complaint, the defendant (now the *cross-complainant*) sues the plaintiff (now the *cross-defendant*) for damages or some other remedy. The original plaintiff must file a

reply (answer) to the cross-complaint. The reply, which can include affirmative defenses, must be filed with the court and served on the original defendant.

reply
A document filed by the original plaintiff to answer the defendant's cross-complaint.

Concept Summary Pleadings

Type of Pleading	Description
Complaint	A *complaint* is a document filed by the plaintiff with the court and served with a *summons* on the defendant. It sets forth the basis of the lawsuit.
Answer	An *answer* is a document filed by the defendant with the court and served on the plaintiff. It usually denies most allegations of the complaint.
Cross-complaint and reply	A *cross-complaint* is a document filed and served by the defendant if he or she countersues the plaintiff. The defendant is the cross-complainant, and the plaintiff is the cross-defendant. The cross-defendant must file and serve a *reply* (answer).

Intervention and Consolidation

If other persons have an interest in a lawsuit, they may **intervene** and become parties to the lawsuit. For instance, a bank that has made a secured loan on a piece of real estate can intervene in a lawsuit between parties who are litigating ownership of the property.

intervention
The act of others to join as parties to an existing lawsuit.

If several plaintiffs have filed separate lawsuits stemming from the same fact situation against the same defendant, the court can **consolidate** the cases into one case if it would not cause undue prejudice to the parties. Suppose, for example, that a commercial airplane crashes, killing and injuring many people. The court could consolidate all the lawsuits against the defendant airplane company.

consolidation
The act of a court to combine two or more separate lawsuits into one lawsuit.

Internet Law & Online Commerce

E-Filings

When litigation ensues, the clients, lawyers, and judges involved in the case are usually buried in papers. These papers include pleadings, interrogatories, documents, motions to the court, briefs, and memorandums; the list goes on and on. By the time a case is over, reams of paper are stored in dozens, if not hundreds, of boxes. In addition, court appearances, for no matter how small the matter, must be made in person. For example, lawyers often wait hours for a 10-minute scheduling or other conference with the judge. The time it takes to drive to and from court, which may amount to hours, also has to be taken into account.

Today, because of the Internet and other technologies, a virtual courthouse is being developed. Technology allows for the electronic filing—**e-filing**—of pleadings, briefs, and other documents related to a lawsuit. E-filing includes using CD-ROMs for briefs, scanning evidence and documents into a computer for storage and retrieval, and e-mailing correspondence and documents to the court and the opposing council. Scheduling and other conferences with the judge or opposing counsel are held via telephone conferences and e-mail.

Many courts have instituted e-filing. In come courts, e-filing is now mandatory. Companies such as Microsoft and LexisNexis have developed systems to manage e-filing of court documents. ■

Statute of Limitations

statute of limitations
A statute that establishes the period during which a plaintiff must bring a lawsuit against a defendant.

A **statute of limitations** establishes the period during which a plaintiff must bring a lawsuit against a defendant. If a lawsuit is not filed within this time period, the plaintiff loses his or her right to sue. A statute of limitations begins to "run" at the time the plaintiff first has the right to sue the defendant (e.g., when the accident happens, when the breach of contract occurs).

Federal and state governments have established statutes of limitations for each type of lawsuit. Most are from one to four years, depending on the type of lawsuit. For example, a one-year statute of limitations is common for ordinary negligence actions. Thus, if on July 1, 2006, Otis negligently causes an automobile accident in which Cha-Yen is injured, Cha-Yen has until July 1, 2007, to bring a negligence lawsuit against Otis. If she waits longer than that, she loses her right to sue him.

Ethics in Business

Statute of Limitations

Kristi Norgart McBride lived with her husband in Santa Rosa, California. Kristi suffered from manic-depressive mental illness (now called bipolar disorder). In this disease, the person cycles between manic (ultrahappy, expansive, extroverted) episodes and depressive episodes. The disease is often treated with prescription drugs. In April 1984, Kristi attempted suicide. A psychiatrist prescribed an antianxiety drug. In May 1985, Kristi attempted suicide again by overdosing on drugs. The doctor prescribed Halcion, a hypnotic drug, and added Darvocet-N, a mild narcotic analgesic. On October 16, after descending into a severe depression, Kristi committed suicide by overdosing on Halcion and Darvocet-N. On October 16, 1991, exactly six years after Kristi's death, Leo and Phyllis Norgart, Kristi's parents, filed a lawsuit against the Upjohn Company, the maker of Halcion, for wrongful death based on Upjohn's alleged failure to warn of the unreasonable dangers of taking Halcion. The trial court granted Upjohn's motion for summary judgment based on the fact that the one-year statute of limitations for wrongful death actions had run. The court of appeals reversed, and Upjohn appealed to the supreme court of California.

The California supreme court noted that the statute of limitations has a purpose to protect defendants from the stale claims of dilatory plaintiffs. It has a related purpose to stimulate plaintiffs to assert fresh claims against defendants in a diligent fashion. The court stated that under the statute of limitations, a plaintiff must bring a cause of action from wrongful death within one year of accrual; this means that the date of accrual of a cause of action for wrongful death is the date of death. The Norgarts had to bring the cause of action of wrongful death within one year of accrual. The court stated, "They did not do so. Pursuant to this rule, the Norgarts were too late, exactly five years too late." The court held that the defendant, the Upjohn Company, was entitled to judgment as a matter of law, based on the fact that the one-year statute of limitations for wrongful death actions had run out, thus barring the plaintiff's lawsuit. *Norgart v. The Upjohn Company*, 21 Cal.4th 383, 87 Cal.Rpt. 2nd 453, 1999 Cal. Lexis 5308 (Cal.)

Ethics Issues

1. What is the public policy behind having statutes of limitations?
2. Was it ethical for the Upjohn Company to avoid facing the merits of the lawsuit by asserting the one-year statute of limitations? Explain. ■

Discovery

discovery
A legal process during which each party engages in various activities to discover facts of the case from the other party and witnesses prior to trial.

The legal process provides for a detailed pretrial procedure called **discovery**. During discovery, each party engages in various activities to discover facts of the case from the other party and witnesses prior to trial. Discovery serves several functions, including preventing surprises, allowing parties to thoroughly prepare for trial, preserving evidence, saving court time, and promoting the settlement of cases. The major forms of discovery are as follows:

1. ***Depositions.*** A **deposition** is the oral testimony given by a party or witness prior to trial. The person giving the deposition is called the **deponent**. Each *party* to the lawsuit must give a deposition, if called upon by the other party to do so. The deposition of a *witness* can be given voluntarily or pursuant to a subpoena (court order). The deponent can be required to bring documents to the deposition. Most depositions are taken at the office of one of the attorneys. The deponent is placed under oath and then orally asked questions by one or both of the attorneys. The questions and answers are recorded in written form by a court reporter. Depositions can also be videotaped. The deponent is given an opportunity to correct his or her answers prior to signing the deposition. Depositions are used to preserve evidence (e.g., if the deponent is deceased, ill, or not otherwise available at trial) and impeach testimony given by witnesses at trial.

deposition
Oral testimony given by a party or witness prior to trial. The testimony is given under oath and is transcribed.

deponent
The party that gives a deposition.

2. ***Interrogatories.*** **Interrogatories** are written questions that one of the parties to a lawsuit submits to the other party. The questions can be very detailed, and certain documents may be attached to the answers. A party is required to answer the interrogatories in writing within a specified time period (e.g., 60 to 90 days). An attorney usually helps with the preparation of the answers. The answers are signed under oath.

interrogatories
Written questions submitted by one party to another party. The questions must be answered in writing within a stipulated time.

3. ***Production of documents.*** Often, particularly in complex business cases, a substantial portion of the lawsuit may be based on information contained in documents (e.g., memorandums, correspondence, company records). One party to a lawsuit may request that the other party produce all documents that are relevant to the case prior to trial. This is called **production of documents**. If the documents sought are too voluminous to be moved or are in permanent storage, or if their movement would disrupt the ongoing business of the party who is to produce them, the requesting party may be required to examine the documents at the other party's premises.

production of documents
A request by one party to another party to produce all documents relevant to the case prior to trial.

4. ***Physical and mental examination.*** In cases that concern the physical or mental condition of a party, a court can order the party to submit to certain **physical or mental examinations** to determine the extent of the alleged injuries. This would occur, for example, where the plaintiff has been injured in an accident and is seeking damages for physical injury and mental distress.

physical or mental examination
A court-ordered physical or mental examination of a party to a lawsuit prior to trial where injuries are alleged that could be verified or disputed by such examination.

Concept Summary Discovery

Form of Discovery	Description
Deposition	Oral testimony given by a *deponent*, either a party or witness. Depositions are transcribed.
Interrogatories	Written questions submitted by one party to the other party. They must be answered within a specified period of time.
Production of documents	Copies of all relevant documents obtained by a party to a lawsuit from another party, upon order of the court.
Physical and mental examination	Examination of a party upon order of the court where injuries are alleged that could be verified or disputed by such examination.

Dismissals and Pretrial Judgments

pretrial motion
A motion a party can make to try to dispose of all or part of a lawsuit prior to trial.

There are several **pretrial motions** that parties to a lawsuit can make to try to dispose of all or part of a lawsuit prior to trial. The two major pretrial motions are discussed in the following paragraphs.

Motion for Judgment on the Pleadings

motion for judgment on the pleadings
A motion that alleges that if all the facts presented in the pleadings are taken as true, the party making the motion will win the lawsuit when the proper law is applied to these asserted facts.

A **motion for judgment on the pleadings** can be made by either party once the pleadings are complete. This motion alleges that if all the facts presented in the pleadings are true, the party making the motion will win the lawsuit when the proper law is applied to these facts. In deciding this motion, the judge cannot consider any facts outside the pleadings.

Motion for Summary Judgment

motion for summary judgment
A motion that asserts that there are no factual disputes to be decided by the jury; in such a case, the judge can apply the proper law to the undisputed facts and decide the case without a jury. These motions are supported by affidavits, documents, and deposition testimony.

The trier of fact (i.e., the jury or, if there is no jury, the judge) determines factual issues. A **motion for summary judgment** asserts that there are no factual disputes to be decided by the jury and that the judge should apply the relevant law to the undisputed facts to decide the case. Motions for summary judgment, which can be made by either party, are supported by evidence outside the pleadings. Affidavits from the parties and witnesses, documents (e.g., a written contract between the parties), depositions, and such are common forms of evidence. If, after examining the evidence, the court finds no factual dispute, it can decide the issue or issues raised in the summary judgment motion. This may dispense with the entire case or with part of the case. If the judge finds that a factual dispute exists, the motion will be denied, and the case will go to trial.

Courthouse, Santa Barbara, California. State courts decide the majority of lawsuits in the United States.

Settlement Conference

Federal court rules and most state court rules permit the court to direct the attorneys or parties to appear before the court for a **settlement conference** or **pretrial hearing**. One of the major purposes of such hearings is to facilitate the settlement of the case. Pretrial conferences are often held informally in the judge's chambers. If no settlement is reached, the pretrial hearing is used to identify the major trial issues and other relevant factors. More than 90 percent of all cases are settled before they go to trial.

settlement conference
A hearing before the trial in order to facilitate the settlement of a case. Also called a *pretrial hearing*.

Contemporary Trend

Cost–Benefit Analysis of a Lawsuit

In lawsuits, each party is responsible for paying its own attorneys' fees, whether the party wins or loses. This is called the "American rule." The court can award lawyers' fees to the winning party as a statute may so provide, the parties have so agreed (e.g., in a contract), or the losing party has acted maliciously or pursued a frivolous case.

An attorney in a civil or criminal lawsuit can represent his or her client on an hourly or project-fee basis. Hourly fees usually range from $100 to $500 per hour, depending on the type of case, the expertise of the lawyer, and the locality of the lawsuit. In a civil lawsuit, plaintiffs' lawyers often work under a *contingency fee arrangement*, where the lawyer receives a percentage of the amount recovered for the plaintiff upon winning or settling the case. Contingency fees normally range from 20 to 50 percent of the award or settlement, with the average being about 35 percent. Lawyers for defendants in civil lawsuits are normally paid on an hourly basis.

The choice of whether to bring or defend a lawsuit should be analyzed like any other business decision. This includes performing a **cost–benefit analysis** of the lawsuit. For the plaintiff, it may be wise not to sue. For the defendant, it may be wise to settle. The following factors should be considered in deciding whether to bring or settle a lawsuit:

- The probability of winning or losing
- The amount of money to be won or lost
- Lawyers' fees and other costs of litigation
- Loss of time by managers and other personnel
- The long-term effects on the relationship and reputation of the parties
- The amount of prejudgment interest provided by law
- The aggravation and psychological costs associated with a lawsuit
- The unpredictability of the legal system and the possibility of error
- Other factors peculiar to the parties and lawsuit ■

Trial

Pursuant to the Seventh Amendment to the U.S. Constitution, a party to an action at law is guaranteed the right to a *jury trial* in a federal court.[1] Most state constitutions contain a similar guarantee for state court actions. If either party requests a jury, the trial will be by jury. If both parties waive their right to a jury, the trial will occur without a jury. The judge sits as the **trier of fact** in nonjury trials. At the time of trial, each party usually submits to the judge a *trial brief* that contains legal support for its side of the case.

trier of fact
The jury in a jury trial; the judge where there is not a jury trial.

Phases of a Trial

A trial can last for less than one day to many months, depending on the type and complexity of the case. A typical trial is divided into the following stages:

1. ***Jury selection.*** The pool of the potential jurors is usually selected from voter or automobile registration lists. Individuals are selected to hear specific cases through a

process called **voir dire** ("to speak the truth"). Lawyers for each party and the judge can ask prospective jurors questions to determine whether they would be biased in their decisions. Biased jurors can be prevented from sitting on a particular case. Once the appropriate number of jurors is selected (usually 6 to 12 jurors), they are *impaneled* to hear the case and are sworn in. The trial is ready to begin. A jury can be *sequestered* (i.e., separated from family and others) in important cases. Jurors are paid minimal fees for the service.

voir dire
A process whereby prospective jurors are asked questions by the judge and attorneys to determine whether they would be biased in their decisions.

2. ***Opening statements.*** Each party's attorney is allowed to make an **opening statement** to the jury. In opening statements, an attorney usually summarizes the main factual and legal issues of the case and describes why he or she believes the client's position is valid. The information given in this statement is not considered as evidence.

opening statement
A factual summary presented by both the plaintiff and defendant at the beginning of a trial.

3. ***The plaintiff's case.*** A plaintiff bears the **burden of proof** to persuade the trier of fact of the merits of his or her case. This is called the **plaintiff's case**. The plaintiff's attorney will call witnesses to give testimony. After a witness has been sworn in, the plaintiff's attorney examines (i.e., questions) the witness. This is called *direct examination*. Documents and other evidence can be introduced through each witness. After the plaintiff's attorney has completed his or her questions, the defendant's attorney can question the witness. This is called *cross-examination*. The defendant's attorney can ask questions only about the subjects that were brought up during the direct examination. After the defendant's attorney completes his or her questions, the plaintiff's attorney can ask questions of the witness. This is called *redirect examination*.

burden of proof
A standard of persuasion the plaintiff must meet in order to win their case.

4. ***The defendant's case.*** The **defendant's case** proceeds after the plaintiff has concluded his or her case. The defendant's case must (1) rebut the plaintiff's evidence, (2) prove any affirmative defenses asserted by the defendant, and (3) prove any allegations contained in the defendant's cross-complaint. The defendant's witnesses are examined in much the same way as the plaintiff's attorney cross-examines each witness. This is followed by redirect and recross-examination.
5. ***Rebuttal and rejoinder.*** After the defendant's attorney has completed calling witnesses, the plaintiff's attorney can call witnesses and put forth evidence to rebut the defendant's case. This is called a *rebuttal*. The defendant's attorney can call additional witnesses and introduce other evidence to counter the rebuttal. This is called the *rejoinder*.
6. ***Closing arguments.*** At the conclusion of the presentation of the evidence, each party's attorney is allowed to make a *closing argument* to the jury. Each attorney tries to convince the jury to render a verdict for his or her client by pointing out the strengths in the client's case and the weaknesses in the other side's case. Information given by the attorneys in their closing statements is not evidence.
7. ***Jury instructions.*** Once the closing arguments are completed, the judge reads **jury instructions** (or **charges**) to the jury. These instructions inform the jury about what law to apply when they decide the case. For example, in a criminal trial, the judge will read the jury the statutory definition of the crime charged. In an accident case, the judge will read the jury the legal definition of *negligence*.

jury instructions
Instructions given by the judge to the jury that informs them of the law to be applied in the case.

8. ***Jury deliberation.*** The jury then retires to the jury room to deliberate its findings. This can take from a few minutes to many weeks. After deliberation, the jury assesses penalties in criminal cases.
9. ***Entry of judgment.*** After the jury has returned its **verdict**, in most cases, the judge will enter **judgment** to the successful party, based on the verdict. This is the official decision of the court. The court may, however, overturn the verdict if it finds bias or jury misconduct. This is called a *judgment notwithstanding the verdict,* or *judgment n.o.v.,* or **j.n.o.v.** In a civil case, the judge may reduce the amount of monetary damages awarded by the jury if he or she finds the jury to have been biased, emotional, or inflamed. This is called *remittitur*. The trial court usually issues a *written memorandum*

verdict
A decision made by the jury based on evidence presented in trial.

judgement
The final decision made by the judge, usually based on the jury's verdict.

setting forth the reasons for the judgment. The memorandum, together with the trial transcript and evidence introduced at trial, constitutes the permanent *record* of the trial court proceeding.

In the following case, the court was asked to grant a judgment notwithstanding the verdict.

Case 3.1

Judgment Notwithstanding the Verdict

Ferlito v. Johnson & Johnson Products, Inc.
771 F.Supp. 196, 1991 U.S. Dist. Lexis 11747
United States District Court, Eastern District, Michigan

Background and Facts

Susan and Frank Ferlito were invited to a Halloween party. They decided to attend as "Little Bo Peep" (Mrs. Ferlito) and her little sheep (Mr. Ferlito). Mrs. Ferlito constructed a lamb costume for her husband by gluing cotton batting manufactured by Johnson & Johnson Products, Inc., to a suit of long underwear. She used the same cotton batting to fashion a headpiece, complete with ears. The costume covered Mr. Ferlito from his head to his ankles, except for his face and hands, which were blackened with paint. At the party, Mr. Ferlito attempted to light a cigarette with a butane lighter. The flame passed close to his left arm, and the cotton batting ignited. He suffered burns over one-third of his body. The Ferlitos sued Johnson & Johnson to recover damages, alleging that Johnson & Johnson had failed to warn them of the ignitability of cotton batting. The jury returned a verdict for Mr. Ferlito in the amount of $555,000 and for Mrs. Ferlito in the amount of $70,000. Johnson & Johnson filed a motion for judgment notwithstanding the verdict (j.n.o.v.).

Issue

Should defendant Johnson & Johnson's motion for j.n.o.v. be granted?

In the Language of the Court

Both plaintiffs testified that they knew that cotton batting burns when it is exposed to flame. Susan Ferlito testified that the idea for the costume was hers alone. As described on the product's package, its intended uses are for cleansing, applying medications, and infant care. Plaintiffs' showing that the product may be used for decorative purposes failed to demonstrate the foreseeability of an adult male encapsulating himself from head to toe in cotton batting and then lighting up a cigarette.

If after reviewing the evidence the trial court is of the opinion that reasonable minds could not come to the result reached by the jury, then the motion for j.n.o.v. should be granted. In the instant action, no jury could find that J&J's failure to warn of the flammability of cotton batting was a proximate cause of plaintiffs' injuries.

Decision and Remedy

The trial court granted defendant Johnson & Johnson's motion for j.n.o.v. By doing so, the court vacated the verdict entered by the jury in favor of Mr. and Mrs. Ferlito. The court of appeals affirmed the grant of j.n.o.v.

Business and Ethics Questions

1. Should trial courts have the authority to enter a j.n.o.v., or should jury verdicts always be allowed to stand? Explain your answer.
2. Did the Ferlitos act ethically in suing Johnson & Johnson in this case? Were they responsible for their own injuries?
3. What would have been the business implications had Johnson & Johnson been found liable?

Appeal

In a civil case, either party can **appeal** the trial court's decision once a *final judgment* is entered. Only the defendant can appeal in a criminal case. The appeal is made to the appropriate appellate court. A *notice of appeal* must be filed within a prescribed time after

appeal
To ask an appellate court to overturn a decision after the trial court's final judgment has been entered.

appellant
The appealing party in an appeal. Also known as *petitioner*.

appellee
The responding party in an appeal. Also known as *respondent*.

judgment is entered (usually within 60 to 90 days). The appealing party is called the **appellant**, or **petitioner**. The responding party is called the **appellee**, or **respondent**. The appellant is often required to post a bond (e.g., one and one-half times the judgment) on appeal.

The parties may designate all or relevant portions of the trial record to be submitted to the appellate court for review. The appellant's attorney may file an *opening brief* with the court that sets forth legal research and other information to support his or her contentions on appeal. The appellee can file a *responding brief*, answering the appellant's contentions. Appellate courts usually permit brief oral arguments at which each party's attorney is heard.

An appellate court will reverse a lower court decision if it finds an *error of law* in the record. An error of law occurs if the jury was improperly instructed by the trial court judge, prejudicial evidence was admitted at trial when it should have been excluded, prejudicial evidence was obtained through an unconstitutional search and seizure, and the like. An appellate court will not reverse a *finding of fact* unless such finding is unsupported by the evidence or is contradicted by the evidence.

Alternative Dispute Resolution

alternative dispute resolution (ADR)
Methods of resolving disputes other than litigation.

The use of the court system to resolve business and other disputes can take years and cost thousands, if not millions, of dollars in legal fees and expenses. In commercial litigation, the normal business operations of the parties are often disrupted. To avoid or lessen these problems, businesses are increasingly turning to methods of **alternative dispute resolution (ADR)** and other aids to resolving disputes. The most common form of ADR is *arbitration*. Other forms of ADR are *mediation, conciliation, minitrial, fact-finding,* and using a *judicial referee*.

Arbitration

arbitration
A form of ADR in which the parties choose an impartial third party to hear and decide the dispute.

arbitration clause
A clause in a contract that requires disputes arising out of the contract to be submitted to arbitration.

In **arbitration**, the parties choose an impartial third party to hear and decide the dispute. This neutral party is called the *arbitrator*. Arbitrators are usually selected from members of the American Arbitration Association (AAA) or another arbitration association. Labor union agreements, franchise agreements, leases, and other commercial contracts often contain **arbitration clauses** that require disputes arising out of the contract to be submitted to arbitration. If there is no arbitration clause, the parties can enter into a *submission agreement* whereby they agree to submit a dispute to arbitration after the dispute arises.

Evidence and testimony are presented to the arbitrator at a hearing held for this purpose. Less formal evidentiary rules are usually applied in arbitration hearings than at court. After the hearing, the arbitrator reaches a decision and enters an *award*. The parties often agree in advance to be bound by the arbitrator's decision and award. If the parties have not so agreed, the arbitrator's award can be appealed to court. The court gives great deference to the arbitrator's decision.

Federal Arbitration Act (FAA)
A federal statute that provides for the enforcement of most arbitration agreements.

Uniform Arbitration Act
A statute adopted by states that promotes the arbitration of disputes at the state level.

Congress enacted the **Federal Arbitration Act** to promote the arbitration of disputes.[2] About half of the states have adopted the **Uniform Arbitration Act**. This act promotes the arbitration of disputes at the state level. Many federal and state courts have instituted programs to refer legal disputes to arbitration or another form of ADR.

Federal Arbitration Act

The **Federal Arbitration Act (FAA)** was originally enacted in 1925 to reverse the long-standing judicial hostility to arbitration agreements that had existed at English common law and had been adopted by American courts. The act provides that arbitration agreements involving commerce are valid, irrevocable, and enforceable contracts, unless some grounds exist at law or equity (e.g., fraud, duress) to revoke them. The FAA permits one party to obtain a court order to compel arbitration if the other party has failed, neglected, or refused to comply with an arbitration agreement.

Since the FAA's enactment, the courts have wrestled with the problem of which types of disputes should be arbitrated. Breach of contract cases, tort claims, and such are clearly candidates for arbitration if there is a valid arbitration agreement. In addition, the U.S. Supreme Court has enforced arbitration agreements that call for the resolution of disputes arising under federal statutes. The Supreme Court has stated, "By agreeing to arbitrate a statutory claim, a party does not forgo the substantive rights afforded by the statute, it only submits to their resolution in an arbitral, rather than a judicial, forum."[3]

Mediation and Conciliation

In **mediation**, the parties choose a neutral third party to act as the mediator of the dispute. Unlike an arbitrator, a mediator does not make a decision or an award. Instead, the mediator acts as a conveyor of information between the parties and assists them in trying to reach a settlement of the dispute. A mediator often meets separately with each of the parties. A settlement agreement is reached if the mediator is successful. If not, the case proceeds to trial. In **conciliation**, the parties choose an interested third party, the *conciliator*, to act as the mediator.

mediation
A form of ADR in which the parties choose a *neutral* third party to act as the mediator of the dispute.

conciliation
A form of mediation in which the parties choose an *interested* third party to act as the mediator of the dispute.

Minitrial

A *minitrial* is a session, usually lasting a day or less, in which the lawyers for each side present their cases to representatives of each party who have authority to settle the dispute. In many cases, the parties hire a neutral person (e.g., a retired judge) to preside over the minitrial. Following the presentations, the parties meet to try to negotiate a settlement.

Kyoto, Japan. Japan nurtures the attitude that confrontation should be avoided. In Japan, a country with about half the population of the United States, there are only one-fiftieth of the lawyers as in the United States. In Japan, no class actions or contingency fee arrangements are allowed. Plaintiffs must pay their lawyers an up-front fee of up to 8 percent of the damages sought, plus a nonrefundable filing fee to the court of 0.5 percent of the damages sought. No discovery is permitted. Even if the plaintiff wins the lawsuit, damage awards are low. Most legal disputes in Japan are settled or decided by private arbitrators.

Fact-Finding

Fact-finding is a process whereby the parties hire a neutral person to investigate the dispute. The *fact-finder* reports his or her findings to the adversaries and may recommend a basis for settlement.

Judicial Referee

If the parties agree, the court may appoint a *judicial referee* to conduct a private trial and render a judgment. Referees, who are often retired judges, have most of the powers of a trial judge, and their decisions stand as judgments of the court. The parties usually reserve their right to appeal.

Terms and Concepts

Pleadings

A pleading is paperwork that initiates and responds to a lawsuit. Pleadings include:

1. ***Complaint.*** A complaint is filed by the plaintiff with the court and served with a summons on the defendant. It sets forth the basis of the lawsuit.
2. ***Answer.*** An answer is filed by the defendant with the court and served on the plaintiff. It usually denies most allegations of the complaint.
3. ***Cross-complaint.*** A cross-complaint is filed and served by the defendant if he or she countersues the plaintiff. The defendant is the cross-complainant, and the plaintiff is the cross-defendant. The cross-defendant must file and serve a reply (answer).
4. ***Intervention.*** A person who has an interest in a lawsuit may intervene and become a party to the lawsuit.
5. ***Consolidation.*** Separate cases against the same defendant arising from the same incident may be consolidated by the court into one case if doing so would not cause prejudice to the parties.

Discovery

Discovery is the pretrial litigation process for discovering facts of the case from the other party and witnesses. Discovery consists of:

1. ***Depositions.*** Oral testimony is given by a deponent, either a party or witness. Depositions are transcribed.
2. ***Interrogatories.*** Written questions are submitted by one party to the other party. They must be answered within a specified period of time.
3. ***Production of documents.*** A party to a lawsuit may obtain copies of all relevant documents from the other party.
4. ***Physical and mental examination.*** Examinations of a party are permitted upon order of the court where injuries are alleged that could be verified or disputed by such examination.

Dismissals and Pretrial Judgments

1. ***Motion for summary judgment on the pleadings.*** This type of motion alleges that if all facts as pleaded are true, the moving party would win the lawsuit. No facts outside the pleadings may be considered.
2. ***Motion for summary judgment.*** This type of motion alleges that there are no factual disputes, so the judge may apply the law and decide the case without a jury. Evidence outside the pleadings may be considered (e.g., affidavits, documents, depositions).

Settlement Conference

The settlement conference occurs prior to trial between the parties in front of the judge to facilitate the settlement of the case. Also called the *pretrial hearing*. If a settlement is not reached, the case proceeds to trial.

Phases of a Trial

1. ***Jury selection.*** Jury selection occurs through a process called *voir dire*. Biased jurors are dismissed and replaced.
2. ***Opening statements.*** The parties' lawyers make opening statements, which are not evidence.
3. ***The plaintiff's case.*** The plaintiff bears the burden of proof. The plaintiff calls witnesses and introduces evidence to try to prove his or her case.
4. ***The defendant's case.*** The defendant calls witnesses and introduces evidence to rebut the plaintiff's case and to prove affirmative defenses and cross-complaints.
5. ***Rebuttal and rejoinder.*** The plaintiff and defendant may call additional witnesses and introduce additional evidence.
6. ***Closing arguments.*** The parties' lawyers make closing arguments, which are not evidence.
7. ***Jury instructions.*** The judge reads instructions to the jury as to what law the jurors are to apply to the case.
8. ***Jury deliberation.*** The jury retires to the jury room and deliberates until it reaches a *verdict*.
9. ***Entry of judgment.*** The judge may:
   a. Enter the verdict reached by the jury as the court's *judgment*.
   b. Grant a motion for *judgment n.o.v.* if the judge finds that the jury was biased. This means that the jury's verdict does not stand.
   c. Order *remittitur* (reduction) of any damages awarded if the judge finds the jury to have been biased or emotional.

Appeal

Both parties in a civil suit and the defendant in a criminal trial may appeal the decision of the trial court. *Notice of appeal* must be filed within a specified period of time. The appeal must be made to the appropriate appellate court.

Alternative Dispute Resolution (ADR)

ADR is a *nonjudicial* means of solving legal disputes. ADR usually saves time and the expense of costly litigation.

Types of ADR

1. ***Arbitration.*** In arbitration, an impartial third party, called the arbitrator, hears and decides the dispute. The arbitrator makes no award: The award is appealable to a court if the parties have not given up this right. Arbitration is designated by the parties pursuant to:
   a. *Arbitration clause*. This clause is an agreement contained in a contract that stipulates that any dispute arising out of the contract will be arbitrated.
   b. *Submission agreement*. This is an agreement to submit a dispute to arbitration after the dispute arises.
2. ***Mediation.*** A neutral third party, called a *mediator*, may assist the parties in trying to reach a settlement of their dispute. The mediator does not make an award.
3. ***Conciliation.*** An interested third party, called a *conciliator*, may assist the parties in trying to reach a settlement of their dispute. The conciliator does not make an award.
4. ***Minitrial.*** A minitrial is a short session in which the lawyers for each side present their cases to representatives of each party who have the authority to settle the dispute.
5. ***Fact-finding.*** The parties may hire a neutral third person, called a *fact-finder*, to investigate the dispute and report his or her findings to the parties.
6. ***Judicial referee.*** With consent of the parties, the court appoints a judicial referee (usually a retired judge or lawyer) to conduct a private trial and render a judgment. The judgment stands as the judgment of the court and may be appealed to the appropriate appellate court.

Internet Exercises and Case Questions

Working the Web Internet Exercise

1. At the International Chamber of Commerce (ICC) Web site, **www.iccwbo.org/court/english/news_archives/2001/adr.asp**, you will find information about rules and procedures for settlement of international commercial disputes. Under what circumstances would you advise a client to elect ICC arbitration rules as compared with AAA rules?

Legal Environment Cases

3.1 Long-Arm Statute Sean O'Grady, a professional boxer, was managed by his father, Pat. Sean was a contender for the world featherweight title. On January 30, 1978, Pat entered into a contract with Magna Verde Corporation, a Los Angeles–based business, to copromote a fight between Sean and the current featherweight champion. The fight was scheduled to take place on February 5, 1978, in Oklahoma City, Oklahoma. To promote the fight, Pat O'Grady scheduled a press conference for January 30, 1978. At the conference, Pat was involved in a confrontation with a sportswriter named Brooks. He allegedly struck Brooks in the face. Brooks brought suit against Pat O'Grady and Magna Verde Corporation in an Oklahoma state court. Court records showed that the only contact Magna Verde had with Oklahoma was that a few of its employees had taken several trips to Oklahoma in January 1978 to plan the title fight. The fight was never held. Oklahoma has a long-arm statute. Magna Verde was served by mail and made a special appearance in Oklahoma state court to argue that Oklahoma does not have personal jurisdiction over it. Does Oklahoma have jurisdiction over Magna Verde Corporation? *Brooks v. Magna Verde Corp.*, 619 P.2d 1271, 1980 Okla. Civ. App. Lexis 118 (Okla. App.)

3.2 Minimum Contacts The National Enquirer, Inc., is a Florida corporation with it principal place of business in Florida. It publishes the *National Enquirer*, a national weekly newspaper with a total circulation of more than 5 million copies. About 600,000 copies are sold in California. On October 9, 1979, the *Enquirer* published an article about Shirley Jones, an entertainer. Jones, a California resident, filed a lawsuit in California state court against the *Enquirer* and its president, who was a resident of Florida. The suit sought damages for alleged defamation, invasion of privacy, and intentional infliction of emotional distress. Are the defendants subject to suit in California? *Calder v. Jones*, 465 U.S. 783, 104 S.Ct. 1482, 1984 U.S. Lexis 41 (U.S. Sup.Ct.)

3.3 Physical Examination Robert Schlagenhauf worked as a bus driver for the Greyhound Corporation. One night, the bus he was driving rear-ended a tractor-trailer. Seven passengers on the bus who were injured sued Schlagenhauf and Greyhound for damages. The complaint alleged that Greyhound was negligent for allowing Schlagenhauf to drive a bus when it knew that his eyes and vision "were impaired and deficient." The plaintiffs petitioned the court to order Schlagenhauf to be medically examined concerning these allegations. Schlagenhauf objected to the examination. Who wins? *Schlagenhauf v. Holder*, 379 U.S. 104, 85 S.Ct. 234, 1964 U.S. Lexis 152 (U.S. Sup.Ct.)

3.4 Interrogatories Cine Forty-Second Street Theatre Corporation operates a movie theater in New York City's Times Square area. Cine filed a lawsuit against Allied Artists Pictures Corporation, alleging that Allied Artists and local theater owners had illegally attempted to prevent Cine from opening its theater, in violation of federal antitrust law. The suit also alleged that once Cine opened the theater, the defendants conspired with motion picture distributors to prevent Cine from exhibiting first-run, quality films. Attorneys for Allied Artists served a set of written questions concerning the lawsuit on Cine. Does Cine have to answer these questions? *Cine Forty-Second Street Theatre Corp. v. Allied Artists Pictures Corp.*, 602 F.2d 1062, 1979 U.S. App. Lexis 13586 (2d Cir.)

3.5 Judgment n.o.v. On November 9, 1964, Mr. Simblest was driving a car that collided with a fire engine at an intersection in Burlington, Vermont. The accident occurred on a night on which a power blackout left most of the state without lights. Mr. Simblest, who was injured in the accident, sued the driver of the fire truck for damages. During the trial, Simblest testified that when he entered the intersection, the traffic light was green in his favor. All the other witnesses testified that the traffic light had gone dark at least 10 minutes before the accident. Simblest testified that the accident was caused by the fire truck's failure to use any warning lights or sirens. Simblest's testimony was contradicted by four witnesses, who testified that the fire truck had used both its lights and sirens. The jury found that the driver of the fire truck had been negligent and rendered a verdict for Simblest. The defense made a motion for judgment n.o.v. Who wins? *Simblest v. Maynard*, 427 F.2d 1, 1970 U.S. App. Lexis 9265 (2d Cir.)

3.6 Arbitration AMF Incorporated and Brunswick Corporation both manufacture electric and automatic bowling center equipment. In 1983, the two companies became involved in a dispute over whether Brunswick had advertised certain automatic scoring devices in a false and deceptive manner. The two parties settled the dispute by signing an agreement that any future problems between them involving advertising claims would be submitted to the National Advertising Council for arbitration. In March 1985, Brunswick advertised a new product, Armor Plate 3000, a synthetic laminated material used to make bowling lanes. Armor Plate 3000 competed with wooden lanes produced by AMF. Brunswick's advertisements claimed that bowling centers could save up to $500 per lane per year in maintenance and repair costs if they switched to Armor Plate 3000 from wooden lanes. AMF disputed this claim and requested arbitration. Is the arbitration agreement enforceable? *AMF Incorporated v. Brunswick Corp.*, 621 F.Supp. 456, 1985 U.S. Dist. Lexis 14205 (E.D. N.Y.)

Ethics in Business

3.7 Dennis and Francis Burnham were married in 1976 in West Virginia. In 1977, the couple moved to New Jersey, where their two children were born. In July 1987, The Burnhams decided to separate. Mrs. Burnham, who intended to move to California, was to have custody of the children. Mr. Burnham agreed to file for divorce on grounds of "irreconcilable differences." In October 1987, Mr. Burnham threatened to file for divorce in New Jersey on grounds of "desertion." After unsuccessfully demanding that Mr. Burnham adhere to the prior agreement, Mrs. Burnham brought suit for divorce in California state court in early January 1988. In late January, Mr. Burnham visited California on a business trip. He then visited his children in the San Francisco Bay area, where his wife resided. He took the older child to San Francisco for the weekend. Upon returning the child to Mrs. Burnham's home, he was served with a California court summons and a copy of Mrs. Burnham's divorce petition. He then returned to New Jersey. Mr. Burnham made a special appearance in the California court and moved to quash the service of process. *Burnham v. Superior Court of California*, 495 U.S. 604, 110 Sect. 2105, 1990 U.S. Lexis 2700 (U.S. Sup.Ct.)

Ethics Issues

1. What is the legal issue of this case?
2. Did Mr. Burnham act ethically in trying to quash the service of process?
3. Did Mrs. Burnham act ethically in having Mr. Burnham served on his visit to California?
4. Is the service of process good?

Endnotes

1. There is no right to a jury trial for actions in equity (e.g., injunctions, specific performance).
2. 9 U.S.C. Section 1 *et seq.*
3. *Gilmer v. Interstate/Johnson Lane Corporation*, 500 U.S. 20, 111 S.Ct. 1647, 1991 U.S. Lexis 2529 (U.S. Sup.Ct.).

4

Constitutional Law for Business and E-Commerce

"We the People of the United States, in Order to form a more perfect Union, establish justice, insure domestic Tranquility, provide for the common defense, promote the general Welfare, and secure the Blessings of Liberty to ourselves and our Posterity, do ordain and establish this Constitution for the United States of America."

—Preamble to the Constitution of the United States of America

Chapter Objectives

After studying this chapter, you should be able to:

1. Describe the concept of federalism and the doctrine of separation of powers.
2. Define and apply the Supremacy Clause of the U.S. Constitution.
3. Explain the federal government's authority to regulate foreign commerce and interstate commerce.
4. Explain how speech is protected by the First Amendment.
5. Explain the doctrines of equal protection and due process.

Chapter Contents

- Constitution of the United States of America
- Supremacy Clause
- Commerce Clause
- Bill of Rights
- Freedom of Speech
- Freedom of Religion
- Equal Protection Clause
- Due Process Clause
- Privileges and Immunities Clause

Prior to the American Revolution, each of the 13 original colonies operated as a separate sovereignty under the rule of England. In September 1774, representatives of the colonies met as a Continental Congress. In 1776, the colonies declared independence from England, and the American Revolution ensued.

This chapter examines the major provisions of the U.S. Constitution and the amendments that have been adopted to the Constitution. Of particular importance, this chapter discusses how these provisions affect the operations of business in this country. The Constitution, with amendments, is set forth as Appendix B to this book.

New York City, New York. The Constitution of the United States of America establishes the structure of the federal government, delegates powers to the federal government, and guarantees certain fundamental rights.

Constitution of the United States of America

In 1778, the Continental Congress formed a *federal government* and adopted the *Articles of Confederation.* The Articles of Confederation created a federal Congress composed of representatives of the 13 new states. The Articles of Confederation was a particularly weak document that gave limited power to the newly created federal government. For example, it did not provide Congress with the power to levy and collect taxes, to regulate commerce with foreign countries, or to regulate interstate commerce among the states.

The *Constitutional Convention* was convened in Philadelphia in May 1787. The primary purpose of the Convention was to strengthen the federal government. After substantial debate, the delegates agreed to a new **U.S. Constitution**. The constitution was reported to Congress in September 1787. State ratification of the Constitution was completed in 1788. Many amendments, including the **Bill of Rights**, have been added to the Constitution since that time.

The U.S. Constitution serves two major functions:

1. It creates the three branches of the federal government (i.e., the executive, legislative, and judicial branches) and allocates powers to these branches.
2. It protects individual rights by limiting the government's ability to restrict those rights.

U.S. Constitution
The fundamental law of the United States of America. It was ratified by the states in 1788.

Bill of Rights
The first ten amendments to the U.S. Constitution.

The nation's armour of defense against the passions of men is the Constitution. Take that away, and the nation goes down into the field of its conflicts like a warrior without armour.

Henry Ward Beecher
Proverbs from Plymouth Pulpit (1887)

The Constitution itself provides that it may be amended to address social and economic changes. Some important constitutional concepts are discussed in the following paragraphs.

Federalism and Delegated Powers

federalism
The U.S. form of government, in which the federal government and the 50 state governments share powers.

enumerated powers
Certain powers delegated to the federal government by the states.

Our country's form of government is referred to as **federalism**. That means that the federal government and the 50 state governments share powers.

When the states ratified the Constitution, they *delegated* certain powers to the federal government. They are called **enumerated powers**. The federal government is authorized to deal with national and international affairs. Any powers that are not specifically delegated to the federal government by the Constitution are reserved to the state governments. State governments are empowered to deal with local affairs.

Doctrine of Separation of Powers

legislative branch
The part of the U.S. government that consists of Congress (the Senate and the House of Representatives).

executive branch
The part of the U.S. government that consists of the president and vice president.

judicial branch
The part of the U.S. government that consists of the Supreme Court and other federal courts.

As mentioned previously, the federal government is divided into three branches:

1. ***Legislative branch.*** Article I of the Constitution established the **legislative branch** of government. This branch is bicameral; that is, it consists of the Senate and the House of Representatives. Collectively, they are referred to as *Congress*.[1] Each state has two senators. The number of representatives to the House of Representatives is determined according to the population of each state. The current number of representatives is determined from the 2000 census.
2. ***Executive branch.*** Article II of the Constitution established the **executive branch** of government by providing for the election of the president and vice president. The president is not elected by popular vote but instead is selected by the *electoral college*, whose representatives are appointed by state delegations.[2]
3. ***Judicial branch.*** Article III of the Constitution established the **judicial branch** of the government by establishing the Supreme Court and providing for the creation of the federal courts by Congress.[3]

Checks and Balances

checks and balances
A system through which the U.S. Constitution prevents any one of the three branches of the government from becoming too powerful.

Certain **checks and balances** are built into the Constitution to ensure that no one branch of the federal government becomes too powerful. Some of the checks and balances in our system of government are as follows:

1. The judicial branch has authority to examine the acts of the other two branches of government and determine whether those acts are constitutional.[4]
2. The executive branch can enter into treaties with foreign governments only with the advice and consent of the Senate.
3. The legislative branch is authorized to create federal courts and determine their jurisdiction and to enact statutes that change judicially made law.

Concept Summary Basic Constitutional Concepts

Concept	Description
Federalism	The Constitution created the federal government. The federal government and the 50 state governments and Washington, DC, share powers in this country.

Delegated powers	When the states ratified the Constitution, they delegated certain powers to the federal government. These are called *enumerated powers*.
Reserved powers	Those powers not granted to the federal government by the Constitution are reserved to the states.
Separation of Powers	Each branch of the federal government has separate powers. These powers are: a. The legislative branch has power to make the law. b. The executive branch has power to enforce the law. c. The judicial branch has power to interpret the law.
Checks and Balances	Certain checks and balances are built into the Constitution to ensure that no one branch of the federal government becomes too powerful.

Supremacy Clause

The **Supremacy Clause** establishes that the federal Constitution, treaties, federal laws, and federal regulations are the supreme law of the land.[5] State and local laws that conflict with valid federal law are unconstitutional. The concept of federal law taking precedence over state or local law is commonly called the **preemption doctrine**.

Supremacy Clause
A clause of the U.S. Constitution that establishes that the federal Constitution, treaties, federal laws, and federal regulations are the supreme law of the land.

Congress may expressly provide that a particular federal statute *exclusively* regulates a specific area or activity. No state or local law regulating the area or activity is valid if there is such a statute. More often, though, federal statutes do not expressly provide for exclusive jurisdiction. In these instances, state and local governments have *concurrent jurisdiction* to regulate the area or activity. However, any state or local law that "directly and substantially" conflicts with valid federal law is preempted under the Supremacy Clause.

preemption doctrine
The concept that federal law takes precedence over state or local law.

The following case demonstrates the application of the Supremacy Clause.

Case 4.1
Supremacy Clause

U.S. SUPREME COURT

Geier v. American Honda Motor Company, Inc.

529 U.S. 861, 120 S.Ct. 1913, 2000 U.S. Lexis 3425 Supreme Court of the United States

Background and Facts

In 1987, the U.S. Department of Transportation, a federal administrative agency, adopted the Federal Motor Vehicle Safety Standard, which required automobile manufacturers to equip 10 percent of their 1987 vehicles with passive restraints, including automatic seat belts or air bags. In 1992, Alexis Geier, driving a 1987 Honda Accord automobile in the District of Columbia, collided with a tree and was seriously injured. The car was equipped with manual shoulder and lap belts that were buckled up at the time of the accident; the car was not equipped with air bags, however. Geier sued the car's manufacturer, the American Honda Motor Company, Inc., to recover damages under the District of Columbia's tort law, alleging that American Honda had negligently and defectively designed the car because it lacked a driver's-side air bag. The trial court dismissed Geier's lawsuit, finding that the District of Columbia's tort law conflicted with the federal passive restraint safety standard and was therefore preempted under the Supremacy Clause of the U.S. Constitution. The Court of Appeals affirmed. Geier appealed to the U.S. Supreme Court.

Geier v. American Honda Motor Company, Inc.

529 U.S. 861, 120 S.Ct. 1913, 2000 U.S. Lexis 3425 Supreme Court of the United States

(continued)

Issue

Does the federal passive restraint safety standard preempt the District of Columbia's common law tort law?

In the Language of the Court

In effect, the petitioner Geier's tort action depends upon his claim that the manufacturer had a duty to install an air bag when it manufactured the 1987 Honda Accord. Such a state law—i.e., a rule of state tort law imposing such a duty—by its terms would have required manufacturers of all similar cars to install air bags rather than other passive restraint systems, such as automatic belts or passive interiors. It would have required all manufacturers to have installed air bags in respect to the entire District of Columbia–related portion of their 1987 new car fleet, even though the federal safety standard at that time required only 10 percent of a manufacturer's nationwide fleet be equipped with any passive restraint device at all. Regardless, the language of the federal passive restraint standard is clear enough. The federal standard sought a gradually developing mix of alternative passive restraint devices for safety-related reasons. The rule of state tort law for which petitioner Geier argues would stand as an "obstacle" to the accomplishment of that objective. And the federal statute foresees the application of ordinary principles of preemption in cases of actual conflict. Hence the tort action is preempted.

Decision and Remedy

The U.S. Supreme Court held that the federal passive restraint safety standard preempted the District of Columbia's tort law under which petitioner Geier sued. The U.S. Supreme Court affirmed the dismissal of Geier's lawsuit against American Honda.

Business and Ethics Questions

1. What would be the consequences if there were no Supremacy Clause? Explain.
2. Do you think American Honda owed a duty to equip all its 1987 vehicles with air bags, even though federal law did not require that?
3. Do laws ever protect—rather than harm—businesses? Do you think defendant American Honda would say there are too many laws in this case?

Commerce Clause

Commerce Clause
A clause of the U.S. Constitution that grants Congress the power "to regulate commerce with foreign nations, and among the several states, and with Indian tribes."

The **Commerce Clause** of the U.S. Constitution grants Congress the power "to regulate commerce with foreign nations, and among the several states, and with Indian tribes."[6] Because this clause authorizes the federal government to regulate commerce, it has a greater impact on business than any other provision in the Constitution. Among other things, this clause is intended to foster the development of a national market and free trade among the states.

Federal Regulation of Interstate Commerce

interstate commerce
Commerce that moves between states or that affects commerce between states.

The Commerce Clause gives the federal government the authority to regulate **interstate commerce**. Originally, the courts interpreted this clause to mean that the federal government could only regulate commerce that moved *in* interstate commerce. The modern rule, however, allows the federal government to regulate activities that *affect* interstate commerce.

Under the *effects on interstate commerce test*, the regulated activity does not itself have to be in interstate commerce. Thus, any local (*intrastate*) activity that has an effect on interstate commerce is subject to federal regulation. Theoretically, this test subjects a substantial amount of business activity in the United States to federal regulation.

For example, in the famous case *Wickard, Secretary of Agriculture v. Filburn*,[7] a federal statute limited the amount of wheat that a farmer could plant and harvest for home

St. Ignace, Michigan. The U.S. Constitution gives the federal government the authority to regulate commerce with Indian tribes. The Sault Ste. Marie Tribe of Chippewa Indians owns and operates casinos in Northern Michigan pursuant to federal laws.

consumption. Filburn, a farmer, violated the law. The U.S. Supreme Court upheld the statute on the grounds that it prevented nationwide surpluses and shortages of wheat. The Court reasoned that wheat grown for home consumption would affect the supply of wheat available in interstate commerce.

In several recent cases, the U.S. Supreme Court has held that the federal government had enacted statutes beyond its Interstate Commerce Clause powers. For example, in *United States v. Lopez*, the Supreme Court invalidated the Gun-Free School Zone Act, a federal statute that made it a crime to knowingly posses a firearm in a school zone.[8] The Court found that there was no commercial activity that was being regulated.

The federal government's authority to enact federal statutes pursuant to the Interstate Commerce Clause was at issue in the following case.

> The American Constitution is, so far as I can see, the most wonderful work ever struck off at a given time by the brain and purpose of man.
>
> W.E. Glastone
>
> *Kin Beyond Sea (1878)*

Case 4.2
Interstate Commerce Clause

U.S. SUPREME COURT

Reno, Attorney General of the United States v. Condon, Attorney General of South Carolina

528 U.S. 141, 120 S.Ct. 666, 2000 U.S. Lexis 503 Supreme Court of the United States

Background and Facts

State departments of motor vehicles (DMVs) register automobiles and issue driver's licenses. State DMVs require automobile owners and drivers to provide personal information, including name, address, telephone number, vehicle description, Social Security number, medical information, and a photograph, as a condition for registering an automobile or obtaining a driver's license. Many states' DMVs sold this personal information to individuals, advertisers, and businesses. These sales generated significant revenues for the states.

After receiving thousands of complaints from individuals whose personal information had been sold, the Congress of the

Reno, Attorney General of the United States v. Condon, Attorney General of South Carolina

528 U.S. 141, 120 S.Ct. 666, 2000 U.S. Lexis 503 Supreme Court of the United States

(continued)

United States enacted the Driver's Privacy Protection Act of 1994 (DPPA), 18 U.S.C. Sections 2721–2775. This federal statute prohibits a state from selling the personal information of a person unless the state obtains that person's affirmative consent to do so. South Carolina sued the United States, alleging that the federal government violated the Commerce Clause by adopting the DPPA. The district court and the Court of Appeals held for South Carolina. The U.S. Supreme Court granted review.

Issue

Was the Driver's Privacy Protection Act properly enacted pursuant to the Interstate Commerce Clause power granted to the federal government by the U.S. Constitution?

In the Language of the Court

The United States asserts that the DPPA is a proper exercise of Congress's authority to regulate interstate commerce under the Commerce Clause. The United States bases its Commerce Clause argument on the fact that the personal, identifying information that the DPPA regulates is a thing in interstate commerce, and that the sale or release of that information in interstate commerce is therefore a proper subject of congressional regulation. We agree with the United States' contention.

The motor vehicle information which the States have historically sold is used by insurers, manufacturers, direct marketers, and others engaged in interstate commerce to contact drivers with customized solicitations. The information is also used in the stream of interstate commerce by various public and private entities for matters related to interstate motoring. Because drivers' information, is, in this context, an article of commerce, its sale or release into the interstate stream of business is sufficient to support congressional regulation.

Decision and Remedy

The U.S. Supreme Court held that Congress had the authority under the Commerce Clause to enact the federal Driver's Privacy Protection Act. The Supreme Court reversed the decisions of the district court and Court of Appeals that held in favor of South Carolina.

Business and Ethics Questions

1. How often do you think one government (the federal government) saves people from the intrusiveness of another government (state or local government)?
2. Was it ethical for the states to sell the personal information of automobile owners and drivers?
3. Who were the winners from this decision? Who were the losers?

State and Local Laws Cannot Unduly Burden Interstate Commerce

The states did not delegate all power to regulate business to the federal government. They retained the power to regulate *intrastate* and much interstate business activity that occurs within their borders. This is commonly referred to as states' **police power**.

police power
The power of states to regulate private and business activity within their borders.

Police power permits states (and, by delegation, local governments) to enact laws to protect or promote *public health, safety, morals, and general welfare*. This includes the authority to enact laws that regulate the conduct of business. Zoning ordinances, state environmental laws, corporation and partnership laws, and property laws are enacted under this power.

State and local laws cannot **unduly burden interstate commerce**. If they do, they are unconstitutional because they violate the Commerce Clause. For example, if the federal government has chosen not to regulate an area that it has the power to regulate (*dormant Commerce Clause*) but the state does regulate it, the state law cannot unduly burden interstate commerce.

unduly burden interstate commerce
To place too heavy a burden on interstate commerce. States may enact laws that protect or promote the public health, safety, morals, and general welfare, as long as the law does not unduly burden interstate commerce.

Consider This Example Each state has enacted a corporations code that regulates the establishment and operations of corporations in that state. Assume that one state's corporations code permits only corporations from that state, but from no other state, to conduct business in that state. This state law would unduly burden interstate commerce and would be unconstitutional.

International Law

Foreign Commerce Clause

The Commerce Clause of the U.S. Constitution gives the federal government the *exclusive power* to regulate commerce with foreign nations. Direct and indirect regulation of **foreign commerce** by state or local governments that discriminates against foreign commerce violates the Foreign Commerce Clause and is therefore unconstitutional.

Consider These Examples The state of Michigan is the home of General Motors Corporation, Ford Motor Company, and Chrysler Corporation, the three largest automobile manufacturers in the United States. Suppose the Michigan state legislature enacts a law that imposes a 100 percent tax on any automobile imported from a foreign country that is sold in Michigan but does not impose the same tax on domestic automobiles sold in Michigan. The Michigan tax violates the Foreign Commerce Clause and is therefore unconstitutional and void. If, on the other hand, Michigan enacts a law that imposes a 100 percent tax on all automobiles sold in Michigan, domestic and foreign, the law does not discriminate against foreign commerce and therefore does not violate the Foreign Commerce Clause. The federal government could enact a 100 percent tax on all foreign automobiles but not domestic automobiles sold in the United States, and that law would be valid, however. ■

Golden Pavilion, Kyoto, Japan.

Bill of Rights

The U.S. Constitution provides that it may be amended. In 1791, the 10 amendments that are commonly referred to as the Bill of Rights were approved by the states and became part of the U.S. Constitution. The Bill of Rights guarantees certain fundamental rights to natural persons and protects these rights from intrusive government action. Most of these rights have also been found applicable to so-called artificial persons (i.e., corporations).

In addition to the Bill of Rights, 17 other **amendments** have been added to the Constitution. These amendments cover a variety of things. For instance, they have

amendments
Additions to the U.S. Constitution that add to natural person's fundamental rights.

abolished slavery, prohibited discrimination, authorized the federal income tax, given women the right to vote, and specifically recognized that persons 18 years of age and older have the right to vote.

Due Process Clause of the Fourteenth Amendment
Limited intrusive actions by state and local governments.

Originally, the Bill of Rights limited intrusive action by the *federal government* only. Intrusive actions by state and local governments were not limited until the **Due Process Clause of the Fourteenth Amendment** was added to the Constitution in 1868. The Supreme Court has applied the **incorporation doctrine** and held that most of the fundamental guarantees contained in the Bill of Rights are applicable to state and local government action. The amendments to the Constitution that are most applicable to business are discussed in the paragraphs that follow.

Freedom of Speech

freedom of speech
The right to engage in oral, written, and symbolic speech protected by the First Amendment.

One of the most honored freedoms guaranteed by the Bill of Rights is the **freedom of speech** of the First Amendment. Many other constitutional freedoms would be meaningless without it. The First Amendment's Freedom of Speech Clause protects speech only, not conduct. The U.S. Supreme Court places speech into three categories: *fully protected*, *limited protected*, and *unprotected speech*.

Fully Protected Speech

Fully protected speech is speech that the government cannot prohibit or regulate. Political speech is an example of such speech. For example, the government could not enact a law that forbids citizens from criticizing the current administration. The First Amendment protects oral, written, and symbolic speech.

I disapprove of what you say, but I will defend to the death your right to say it.

Voltaire

Protest, Los Angeles. The Freedom of Speech Clause of the First Amendment to the U.S. Constitution protects the right to engage in political speech.

Limited Protected Speech

The Supreme Court has held that certain types of speech have only *limited protection* under the First Amendment. The government cannot forbid this type of speech, but it can subject this speech to **time, place**, and **manner restrictions**. The following types of speech are accorded limited protection:

1. ***Offensive speech.*** **Offensive speech** is a speech that offends many members of society. (It is not the same as obscene speech, however.) The Supreme Court has held that offensive speech may be restricted by the government under time, place, and manner restrictions. For example, the Federal Communications Commission (FCC) can regulate the use of offensive language on television by limiting such language to time periods when children would be unlikely to be watching (e.g., late at night).

offensive speech
Speech that is offensive to many members of society. It is subject to time, place, and manner restrictions.

2. ***Commercial speech.*** **Commercial speech**, such as advertising, was once considered unprotected by the First Amendment. The Supreme Court's landmark decision in *Virginia State Board of Pharmacy v. Virginia Citizens Consumer Council, Inc.*[9] changed this rule. In that case, the Supreme Court held that a state statute prohibiting a pharmacist from advertising the price of prescription drugs was unconstitutional because it violated the Freedom of Speech Clause. However, the Supreme Court held that commercial speech is subject to proper time, place, and manner restrictions. For example, a city can prohibit billboards along its highways for safety and aesthetic reasons as long as other forms of advertising (e.g., print media) are available.

commercial speech
Speech used by businesses, such as advertising. It is subject to time, place, and manner restrictions.

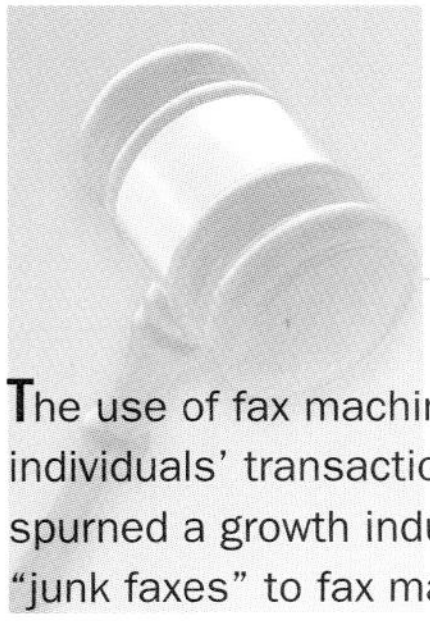

Ethics in Business

Commercial Speech

The use of fax machines has made the conduct of business and individuals' transactions more efficient. However, faxes have also spurned a growth industry that sends unsolicited advertising "junk faxes" to fax machines all over the country. The recipients of these junk faxes complained to the government that these faxes tied up their fax machines and cost them money to receive and process. In order to regulate this practice, Congress enacted a provision in the Telephone Consumer Protection Act of 1991 (TCPA) that outlaws junk faxes. Fax.com, Inc., which provides promotional services to clients, continued to transmit unsolicited advertisements to fax machines of potential customers after the TCPA was enacted. In response to numerous consumer complaints, the U.S. government sued Fax.com for violating the TCPA. Fax.com argued in defense that the TCPA's regulation of unsolicited faxes violated its free speech rights under the First Amendment to the U.S. Constitution. The U.S. government argued that junk faxes were commercial speech that it could regulate in this manner. The U.S. district court held that the TCPA violated Fax.com's free speech rights and dismissed the government's lawsuit. The U.S. government appealed.

The Court of Appeals held that unsolicited advertising faxes—junk faxes—constituted commercial speech. The court cited legislative history of the passage of the TCPA as well as evidence from the district court, which proved that unsolicited junk faxes caused recipients of these faxes substantial costs and time loss. The Court of Appeals held that the federal government's enactment of the TCPA, which prohibits junk faxes, was a constitutional time, place, and manner regulation of commercial speech and did not violate Fax.com's free speech rights. The court stated, "There is a substantial governmental interest in protecting the public from the cost shifting and interference caused by unwanted fax advertisements." The Court of Appeals held that the TCPA's prohibition against unsolicited advertising faxes was a lawful constitutional regulation of commercial speech. *Fax.com, Inc. v. United States of America*, 323 F.3d 649, 2003 U.S. App. Lexis 5469 (8th Cir.)

Ethics Issues

1. Was Fax.com making profits from its endeavors? Did it shift costs to the recipients of its junk faxes?
2. Did Fax.com act ethically in sending unsolicited junk faxes to unsuspecting parties? ■

Unprotected Speech

unprotected speech
Speech that is not protected by the First Amendment and may be forbidden by the government.

The Supreme Court has held that the following types of speech are **unprotected speech**; they are not protected by the First Amendment and may be totally forbidden by the government:

1. Dangerous speech (including such things as yelling "fire" in a crowded theater when there is no fire)
2. Fighting words that are likely to provoke a hostile or violent response from an average person[10]
3. Speech that incites the violent or revolutionary overthrow of the government; the mere abstract teaching of the morality and consequences of such action is protected[11]
4. Defamatory language[12]
5. Child pornography[13]
6. Obscene speech[14]

obscene speech
Speech that (1) appeals to the prurient interest, (2) depicts sexual conduct in a patently offensive way, and (3) lacks serious literary, artistic, political, or scientific value.

The definition of **obscene speech** is quite subjective. One Supreme Court justice stated, "I know it when I see it."[15] In *Miller v. California*, the Supreme Court determined that speech is obscene when:

1. The average person, applying contemporary community standards, would find that the work, taken as a whole, appeals to the prurient interest.
2. The work depicts or describes, in a patently offensive way, sexual conduct specifically defined by the applicable state law.
3. The work, taken as a whole, lacks serious literary, artistic, political, or scientific value.[16]

The Constitution of the United States is not a mere lawyers' document: It is a vehicle of life, and its spirit is always the spirit of the age.

Woodrow Wilson
Constitutional Government in the United States 69 (1927)

States are free to define what constitutes obscene speech. Movie theaters, magazine publishers, and so on are often subject to challenges that the materials they display or sell are obscene and therefore not protected by the First Amendment.

The following case demonstrates the application of the Freedom of Speech Clause.

U.S. SUPREME COURT

United States v. Playboy Entertainment Group, Inc.

529 U.S. 803, 120 S.Ct. 1878, 2000 U.S. Lexis 3427 Supreme Court of the United States

Case 4.3
Free Speech

Background and Facts

Many entertainment companies, including Playboy Entertainment Group, Inc., produce and distribute sexually explicit adult entertainment features for transmission over cable television stations. These shows are usually offered on a pay-per-view subscription service basis. Cable operators provide viewers with a converter box that attaches to the television set and scrambles these sexually explicit materials so they can only be viewed by subscribers who pay the subscription fee. However, with analog television sets, there often occurs "signal bleed" of either a blurred visual image or muted audio transmission of these materials. Digital television eliminates the signal bleed problem.

To address the signal bleed problem. Congress enacted Section 505 of the Telecommunications Act of 1998, which requires cable operators not to transmit sexually explicit materials during the hours from 6:00 A.M. to 10:00 P.M. if the signal bleed problem can occur.

Playboy Entertainment Group, Inc., a cable operator of Playboy Television and Spice, two adult entertainment cable television networks, sued the federal government, alleging that Section 505 violated its free speech rights guaranteed by the U.S. Constitution. The district court declared Section 505 unconstitutional. The court found it feasible to allow cable operators to block individual cable boxes in the home, and therefore Section 505 was an overly broad restriction on content-based speech. The U.S. Supreme Court agreed to hear the case on direct appeal.

Issue

Is Section 505 an overly broad restriction on content-based speech that violates the free speech rights of Playboy Entertainment Group, Inc.?

In the Language of the Court

As this case has been litigated, the programming is not alleged to be obscene, adults have a constitutional right to view it.

The effect of the federal statute on the protected speech is now apparent. It is evident that the only reasonable way for a substantial number of cable operators to comply with the letter of Section 505 is to "time channel", which silences the protected speech for two-thirds of the day in every home in a cable service area, regardless of the presence or likely presence of children or of the wishes of the viewers. According to the District Court, 30 to 50 percent of all adult programming is viewed by households prior to 10 P.M., when the safeharbor period begins. To prohibit this much speech is a significant restriction of communication between speakers and willing adult listeners, communication which enjoys First Amendment protection.

Cable systems have the capacity to block unwanted channels on a household-by-household basis. Simply put, targeted blocking is less restrictive than banning, and the Government cannot ban speech if targeted blocking is a feasible and effective means of furthering its compelling interests. If a less restrictive means is available for the Government to achieve its goals, the Government must use it.

Decision and Remedy

The U.S. Supreme Court held that Section 505 was an overly broad restriction on legal content-based speech and was therefore an unconstitutional violation of free speech rights. The Supreme Court affirmed the judgment of the district court.

Business and Ethics Questions

1. Do you think that Section 505 was an overly broad restriction on free speech rights? Why or why not?
2. Why do you think Congress enacted Section 505 rather than require each home to choose to individually block the challenged programming?
3. What economic consequences did the Supreme Court's ruling have for Playboy Entertainment and other adult entertainment cable companies?

Internet Law & Online Commerce

Broad Free Speech Rights Granted in Cyberspace

Once or twice a century, a new medium comes along that presents new problems for applying freedom of speech rights. This time it is the Internet. In 1996, Congress enacted the ***Computer Decency Act***, which made it a felony to knowingly make "indecent" or "patently offensive" materials available on computer systems, including the Internet, to persons under 18 years of age. Immediately, more than 50 cyberspace providers and users filed a lawsuit challenging the act as a violation of their free speech rights granted under the First Amendment to the Constitution. The U.S. district court agreed with the plaintiffs and declared the act an unconstitutional violation of the Freedom of Speech Clause.

On appeal, the U.S. Supreme Court agreed and held that the act was an unconstitutional violation of free speech rights. The Supreme Court concluded that the Internet allows an individual to reach an audience of millions at almost no cost, setting it apart from TV, radio, and print media, which are prohibitively expensive to use. The Court stated, "As the most participatory form of mass speech yet developed, the Internet deserves the highest protection from government intrusion." The Court declared emphatically that the Internet must be given the highest possible level of First Amendment free speech protection.

Proponents of the act argued that it was necessary to protect children from indecent materials. The Supreme Court reasoned that limiting the content on the Internet to what is suitable for a child resulted in unconstitutionally limiting adult speech. The Court noted that children are far less likely to trip over indecent material on the Internet than on TV or radio because the information must be actively sought out on the Internet. The Court noted that less obtrusive means for protecting children are available, such as requiring parents to regulate their children's access to materials on the Internet and placing filtering and blocking software on computers to control what their children see on the Internet. It still remains a crime under existing laws to transmit obscene materials over the Internet. *Reno v. American Civil Liberties Union*, 521 U.S. 844, 117 S.Ct. 2329, 1997 U.S. Lexis 4037 (U.S. Sup.Ct.) ■

Freedom of Religion

The U.S. Constitution requires federal, state, and local governments to be neutral toward religion. The First Amendment contains two separate religion clauses, the *Establishment Clause* and the *Free Exercise Clause*. These two clauses are discussed in the following paragraphs.

Establishment Clause

Establishment Clause
A clause to the First Amendment that prohibits the government from either establishing a state religion or promoting one religion over others.

The **Establishment Clause** prohibits the government from either establishing a state religion or promoting one religion over others. Thus, it guarantees that there will be no state-sponsored religion. The Supreme Court used this clause as its reason for ruling that an Alabama statute that authorized a one-minute period of silence in school for "meditation or voluntary prayer" was invalid.[17] The Court held that the statute endorsed religion.

Free Exercise Clause

Free Exercise Clause
A clause to the First Amendment that prohibits the government from interfering with the free exercise of religion in the United States.

The **Free Exercise Clause** prohibits the government from interfering with the free exercise of religion in the United States. Generally, this clause prevents the government from enacting laws that either prohibit or inhibit individuals from participating in or practicing their chosen religions. For example, in *Church of Lukumi Babalu Aye, Inc. v. City of Hialeah, Florida*,[18] the U.S. Supreme Court held that a city ordinance that prohibited ritual sacrifices of animals (chickens) during church services violated the Free Exercise Clause and that such sacrifices should be allowed. Of course, this right to be free from government intervention in the practice of religion is not absolute. For example, human sacrifices are unlawful and are not protected by the First Amendment.

Concept Summary *Freedom of Religion*

Clause	Description
Establishment Clause	Prohibits the government from either establishing a government-sponsored religion or promoting one religion over other religions.
Free Exercise Clause	Prohibits the government from enacting laws that either prohibit or inhibit individuals from participating in or practicing their chosen religions.

Equal Protection Clause

Fourteenth Amendment
An amendment added to the U.S. Constitution in 1868 that contains the Due Process, Equal Protection, and Privileges and Immunities clauses.

The **Fourteenth Amendment** was added to the U.S. Constitution in 1868. Its original purpose was to guarantee equal rights to all persons after the Civil War. The provisions of the Fourteenth Amendment prohibit discriminatory and unfair action by the government. Several of these provisions—namely, the *Equal Protection Clause*, the *Due Process Clause*, and the *Privileges and Immunities Clause*—have important implications for business.

The Equal Protection Clause is discussed in this section. The Due Process Clause and the Privileges and Immunities Clause are discussed in following sections.

Federal, State, and Local Government Action

Equal Protection Clause
A clause that provides that a state cannot "deny to any person within its jurisdiction the equal protection of the laws."

The **Equal Protection Clause** provides that a state cannot "deny to any person within its jurisdiction the equal protection of the laws." Although this clause expressly applies to state and local government action, the Supreme Court has held that it also applies to federal government action.

This clause prohibits state, local, and federal governments from enacting laws that classify and treat "similarly situated" persons differently. Artificial persons, such as corporations, are also protected. Note that this clause is designed to prohibit invidious discrimination: It does not make the classification of individuals unlawful per se.

Standards of Review

The Supreme Court has adopted three different standards for reviewing equal protection cases:

1. ***Strict scrutiny test.*** Any government activity or regulation that classifies persons based on a *suspect class* (i.e., **race**) is reviewed for lawfulness using a **strict scrutiny test**. Under this standard, most government classifications of persons based on race are found to be unconstitutional. For example, a government rule that permitted persons of one race but not of another race to receive government benefits such as Medicaid would violate this test. However, an affirmative action program that gives racial minorities a "plus factor" when considered for public university admission is lawful, as long as it does not constitute a quota system.

strict scrutiny test
A test that is applied to classifications based on race.

2. ***Intermediate scrutiny test.*** The lawfulness of government classifications based on *protected classes* other than race (such as **sex** or **age**) are examined using an **intermediate scrutiny test**. Under this standard, the courts determine whether the government classification is "reasonably related" to a legitimate government purpose. For example, a rule prohibiting persons over a certain age from military combat would be lawful, but a rule prohibiting persons over a certain age from acting as government engineers would not be. With regard to a person's gender, the U.S. Supreme Court has held that the federal government can require males, but not females, to register with the military for a possible draft.

intermediate scrutiny test
A test that is applied to classifications based on protected classes other than race (e.g., sex or age).

3. ***Rational basis test.*** The lawfulness of all government classifications that do not involve suspect or protected classes is examined using a **rational basis test**. Under this test, the courts will uphold government regulation as long as there is a justifiable reason for the law. This standard permits much of the government regulation of business. For example, providing government subsidies to farmers but not to those in other occupations is permissible.

rational basis test
A test that is applied to classifications not involving a suspect or protected class.

The Equal Protection Clause was at issue in the following case.

Case 4.4
Affirmative Action

U.S. SUPREME COURT

Grutter v. Bollinger and the University of Michigan Law School

539 U.S. 306, 123 S.Ct. 2325, 2003 U.S. Lexis 4800 Supreme Court of the United States

Background and Facts

Barbara Grutter, a Caucasian resident of the state of Michigan, applied to the Law School of the University of Michigan, a state government–supported institution, in 1996, with a 3.8 undergraduate grade point average and a 161 LSAT score. The Law School received 3,500 applications for a class of 350 students. The Law School used race as one of the factors in considering applicants for admission to law school. The race minority applicants, defined as blacks, Hispanics, and Native Americans, were considered as a "plus factor" in considering their applications to law school. Caucasians and Asians were not given such a plus factor. Evidence showed that the Law School accepted approximately 35 percent of minority applicants, but that if race was not considered in admissions, only 10 percent of those applicants would have been admitted.

Grutter v. Bollinger and the University of Michigan Law School

539 U.S. 306, 123 S.Ct. 2325, 2003 U.S. Lexis 4800 Supreme Court of the United States

(continued)

When the Law School rejected Grutter's application, she brought a class action lawsuit against the Law School of the University of Michigan, alleging that its use of a minority's race as a plus factor in admissions violated the Equal Protection Clause of the Fourteenth Amendment to the U.S. Constitution. The district court held in favor of plaintiff Grutter, finding that the Law School's use of race as a factor in admissions violated the Equal Protection Clause. The Court of Appeals reversed. The U.S. Supreme Court granted certiorari to hear the appeal.

Issue

Does the University of Michigan Law School's use of race as a plus factor in accepting minority applicants for admission to the Law School violate the Equal Protection Clause of the Fourteenth Amendment to the U.S. Constitution?

In the Language of the Court

The Equal Protection Clause provides that no State shall "deny to any person within its jurisdiction the equal protection of the laws." Racial classifications imposed by government must be analyzed by a reviewing court under strict scrutiny. When race-based action is necessary to further a compelling governmental interest, such an action does not violate the constitutional guarantee of equal protection so long as the narrow-tailoring requirement is also satisfied. Universities occupy a special niche in our constitutional tradition. In order to cultivate a set of leaders with legitimacy in the eyes of the citizenry, it is necessary that the path to leadership be visibly open to talented and qualified individuals of every race and ethnicity.

To be narrowly tailored, a race-conscious admissions program cannot use a quota system. Instead, a university may consider race or ethnicity only as a "plus" in a particular applicant's file. We find that the Law School's admissions program bears the hallmark of a narrowly tailored plan. Universities cannot establish quotas for members of certain racial groups or put members of those groups on separate admissions tracks. Nor can universities insulate applicants who belong to certain racial or ethnic groups from the competition for admission. Universities can, however, consider race or ethnicity more flexibly as a "plus" factor in the context of individualized consideration of each and every applicant.

The Law School's goal of attaining a critical mass of underrepresented minority students does not transform its program into a quota. Here, the Law School engages in a highly individualized, holistic review of each applicant's file, giving serious consideration to all the ways an applicant might contribute to a diverse educational environment. The Law School affords this individualized consideration to applicants of all races. We agree that, in the context of its individualized inquiry into the possible diversity contributions of all applicants, the Law School's race conscious admissions program does not unduly harm nonminority applicants.

We take the Law School at its word that it would like nothing better than to find a race-neutral admissions formula and will terminate its race-conscious admissions program as soon as practicable. We expect that 25 years from now, the use of racial preferences will no longer be necessary to further the interest approved today.

Decision and Remedy

The U.S. Supreme Court held that the University of Michigan Law School's policy of using race as a plus factor in admitting minority applicants furthers a compelling state interest and is narrowly tailored to accomplish that interest. The Supreme Court affirmed the decision of the Court of Appeals that held that the Law School's race-conscious admissions policy does not violate the Equal Protection Clause of the Fourteenth Amendment to the U.S. Constitution.

Business and Ethics Questions

1. What is the difference between the U.S. Supreme Court's decision in this case and its decision in the *Gratz v. Bollinger* and *the Regents of the University of Michigan* case? Explain.
2. Is it socially responsible for the University of Michigan Law School to consider a minority applicant's race as a plus factor in its admissions decisions?
3. Is anyone hurt by the University of Michigan Law School's race-conscious admissions policy? Explain.

Due Process Clause

Due Process Clause

A clause that provides that no person shall be deprived of "life, liberty, or property" without due process of the law.

The Fifth and Fourteenth Amendments to the U.S. Constitution both contain **Due Process Clauses**. These clauses provide that no person shall be deprived of "life, liberty, or property" without due process of the law. The Due Process Clause of the Fifth

Amendment applies to federal government action; that of the Fourteenth Amendment applies to state and local government action. It is important to understand that the government is not prohibited from taking a person's life, liberty, or property. However, the government must follow due process to do so. There are two categories of due process: *substantive* and *procedural.*

Substantive Due Process

The **substantive due process** category of due process requires that government statutes, ordinances, regulations, or other laws be clear on their face and not overly broad in scope. The test of whether substantive due process is met is whether a "reasonable person" could understand the law to be able to comply with it. Laws that do not meet this test are declared *void for vagueness.* Suppose, for example, that a city ordinance made it illegal for persons to wear "clothes of the opposite sex." Such an ordinance would be held unconstitutional as void for vagueness because a reasonable person could not clearly determine whether his or her conduct violates the law.

substantive due process
A type of due process that requires that government statutes, ordinances, regulations, or other laws be clear on their face and not overly broad in scope.

Procedural Due Process

The **procedural due process** form of due process requires that the government give a person proper *notice* and *hearing* of legal action before that person is deprived of his or her life, liberty, or property. For example, if the federal government or a state government brings a criminal lawsuit against a defendant, the government must notify the person of its intent (by charging the defendant with a crime) and provide the defendant with a proper hearing (a trial).

If the government wants to take a person's home by **eminent domain** to build a highway, the government must (1) give the homeowner sufficient notice of its intention and (2) provide a hearing. Under the **Just Compensation Clause** of the Fifth Amendment, the government must pay the owner just compensation for taking the property. Oftentimes, a lawsuit is brought for a court to determine just compensation.

procedural due process
A type of due process that requires that the government give a person proper notice and hearing of the legal action before that person is deprived of his or her life, liberty, or property.

United States Post Office, Alhambra, California. The United States is the world's leading democracy. The country, however, has had many blemishes on its citizens' constitutional rights. For example, during World War II, Japanese Americans were involuntarily placed in camps. During the McCarthy hearings of the 1950s, citizens who were communists or associated with communists were "blackballed" from their occupations, most notably in the film industry. It was not until the mid-1960s that equal opportunity laws outlawed discrimination in the workplace based on race and sex.

Privileges and Immunities Clause

The purpose of the U.S. Constitution is to promote nationalism. If the states were permitted to enact laws that favored their residents over out-of-state residents, the concept of nationalism would be defeated. Both Article IV of the Constitution and the Fourteenth Amendment contain a **Privileges and Immunities Clause** that prohibit states from enacting laws that unduly discriminate in favor of their residents. For example, a state cannot enact a law that prevents residents of other states from owning property or businesses in that state. Only invidious discrimination is prohibited. Thus, state universities are permitted to charge out-of-state residents higher tuition than in-state residents. Note that this clause applies only to citizens; it does not protect corporations.

Privileges and Immunities Clause
A clause that prohibits states from enacting laws that unduly discriminate in favor of their residents.

Terms and Concepts

The U.S. Constitution

The Constitution consists of 7 articles and 26 amendments. It establishes the three branches of the federal government, enumerates their powers, and provides important guarantees of individual freedom. The Constitution was ratified by the states in 1788.

Basic Constitutional Concepts

1. ***Federalism.*** The Constitution created the federal government. The federal government and the 50 state governments share powers in this country.
2. ***Delegated powers.*** When the states ratified the Constitution, they delegated certain powers to the federal government. These are called *enumerated powers.*
3. ***Reserved powers.*** Those powers not granted to the federal government by the Constitution are reserved to the states.
4. ***Separation of powers.*** Each branch of the federal government has separate powers. These powers are:
   a. The legislative branch has power to make the law.
   b. The executive branch has power to enforce the law.
   c. The judicial branch has power to interpret the law.
5. ***Checks and balances.*** Certain checks and balances are built into the Constitution to ensure that no one branch of the federal government becomes too powerful.

The Supremacy Clause

The Supremacy Clause stipulates that the U.S. Constitution, treaties, and federal law (statutes and regulations) are the *supreme law of the land.* State and local laws that conflict with valid federal law are unconstitutional. This is called the *preemption doctrine.*

The Commerce Clause

1. ***Commerce Clause.*** The Commerce Clause authorizes the federal government to regulate commerce with foreign nations, among the states, and with Indian tribes.
2. ***Interstate commerce.*** Under the broad *effects test*, the federal government may regulate any activity (even intrastate commerce) that *affects* interstate commerce.
3. ***Undue burden on interstate commerce.*** Any state or local law that causes an undue burden on interstate commerce is unconstitutional as a violation of the Commerce Clause.

The Bill of Rights

The Bill of Rights consists of the first 10 amendments to the Constitution, which establish basic individual rights. The Bill of Rights was ratified in 1791.

Freedom of Speech

1. ***Freedom of Speech Clause.*** The Freedom of Speech Clause of the First Amendment guarantees that the government shall not infringe on a person's right to speak. It protects oral, written, and symbolic speech. This right is not absolute—that is, some speech is not protected, and other speech is granted only limited protection.
2. ***Fully protected speech.*** Fully protected speech cannot be prohibited or regulated by the government.
3. ***Limited protected speech.*** The following types of speech are granted only limited protection under the Freedom of Speech Clause (i.e., subject to governmental *time, place, and manner restrictions*):
   a. Offensive speech
   b. Commercial speech
4. ***Unprotected speech.*** The following speech is not protected by the Freedom of Speech Clause:
   a. Dangerous speech
   b. Fighting words
   c. Speech that advocates the violent overthrow of the government
   d. Defamatory language
   e. Child pornography
   f. Obscene speech

Freedom of Religion

There are two religion clauses in the First Amendment:

1. ***Establishment Clause.*** The Establishment Clause prohibits the government from establishing a state religion or promoting religion.
2. ***Free Exercise Clause.*** The Free Exercise Clause prohibits the government from interfering with the free exercise of religion. This right is not absolute; for example, human sacrifices are forbidden.

Equal Protection Clause

The Equal Protection Clause prohibits the government from enacting laws that classify and treat "similarly situated" persons differently. This standard is not absolute, and the government can treat persons differently in certain situations. The U.S. Supreme Court has applied the following tests to determine whether the Equal Protection Clause has been violated:

1. ***Strict scrutiny test.*** This test applies to *suspect classes* (e.g., race, national origin).
2. ***Intermediate scrutiny test.*** This test applies to other *protected classes* (e.g., sex, age).
3. ***Rational basis test.*** This test applies to government classifications that do not involve a suspect or protected class.

Due Process Clause

The Due Process Clause provides that no person shall be deprived of "life, liberty, or property" without due process. There are two categories of due process:

1. ***Substantive due process.*** Substantive due process requires that laws be clear on their face and not overly broad in scope. Laws that do not meet this test are *void for vagueness.*
2. ***Procedural due process.*** Procedural due process requires that the government give a person proper *notice* and *hearing* before that person is deprived of his or her life, liberty, or property. An owner must be paid *just compensation* if the government takes his or her property.

Privileges and Immunities Clause

The Privileges and Immunities Clause prohibits states from enacting laws that unduly discriminate in favor of their residents over residents of other states.

Internet Exercises and Case Questions

Working the Web Internet Exercises

Visit **www.infoctr.edu/fwl**, the Web site for the Federal Law Locator. Try the following:

1. Check on the product safety record for selected products at the U.S. Consumer Product Safety Commission site (e.g., "Pokemon Balls Recalled by Burger King").
2. Find and compare the U.S. Constitution to the Washington State Constitution, at **www.access.wa.gov.** How are they similar? How are they different?
3. Locate the municipal code for your city. Find the law on loitering in public places. Is it constitutional?
4. Find and review the USA Patriot Act of 2001. Is it constitutional?

Legal Environment Cases

4.1 Separation of Powers In 1951, a dispute arose between steel companies and their employees about the terms and conditions that should be included in a new labor contract. At the time, the United States was engaged in a military conflict in Korea that required substantial steel resources from which to make weapons and other military goods. On April 4, 1952, the steelworkers' union gave notice of a nationwide strike called to begin at 12:01 A.M. on April 9. The indispensability of steel as a component in weapons and other war materials led President Dwight D. Eisenhower to believe that the proposed strike would jeopardize the national defense and that governmental seizure of the steel mills was necessary in order to ensure the continued availability of steel. Therefore, a few hours before the strike was to begin, the president issued Executive Order 10340, which directed the secretary of commerce to take possession of most of the steel mills and keep them running. The steel companies obeyed the order under protest and brought proceedings against the president. Was the seizure of the steel mills constitutional? *Youngstown Co. v. Sawyer, Secretary of Commerce*, 343 U.S. 579, 72 S.Ct. 863, 1952 U.S. Lexis 2625 (U.S. Sup.Ct.)

4.2 Commerce Clause The Heart of Atlanta Motel, located in the state of Georgia, had 216 rooms available to guests. The motel was readily accessible to interstate highways 75 and 85 and to state highways 23 and 41. The motel solicited patronage from outside the state of Georgia through various national advertising media, including magazines of national circulation, and it maintained more than 50 billboards and highway signs within the state. Approximately 75 percent of the motel's registered guests were from out of state. Congress enacted the Civil Rights Act of 1964, which made it illegal for public accommodations to discriminate against guests based on their race. Prior to that, the Heart of Atlanta Motel had refused to rent rooms to blacks. After the act was passed, it alleged that it intended to continue not to rent rooms to blacks. The owner of the motel brought an action to have the Civil Rights Act of 1964 declared unconstitutional, alleging that Congress, in passing the act, had exceeded its powers to regulate commerce under the Commerce Clause of the U.S. Constitution. Who wins? *Heart of Atlanta Motel v. United States*, 379 U.S. 241, 85 S.Ct. 348, 1964 U.S. Lexis 2187 (U.S. Sup.Ct.)

4.3 Commerce and Supremacy Clauses In 1972, Congress enacted a federal statute, called the Ports and Waterways Safety Act, that established uniform standards for the operation of boats on inland waterways in the United States. The act coordinated its provisions with those of foreign countries so that there was a uniform body of international rules that applied to vessels that traveled between countries. Pursuant to the act, a federal rule was adopted that regulated the design, length, and size of oil tankers, some of which traveled the waters of the Puget Sound area in the state of Washington. Oil tankers from various places entered Puget Sound to bring crude oil to refineries located in Washington. In 1975, the state of Washington enacted a statute that established different designs, smaller lengths, and smaller sizes for oil tankers serving Puget Sound than allowed by the federal law. Oil tankers used by the Atlantic Richfield Company (ARCO) to bring oil into Puget Sound met the federal standards but not the state standards. ARCO sued to have the state statute declared unconstitutional. Who wins? *Ray, Governor of Washington v. Atlantic Richfield Co.*, 435 U.S. 151, 98 S.Ct. 988, 1978 U.S. Lexis 18 (U.S. Sup.Ct.)

4.4 Undue Burden on Interstate Commerce Most trucking firms, including Consolidated Freightways Corporation, use 65-foot-long "double" trailer trucks to ship commodities on the highway system across the United States. Almost all states permit these vehicles on their highways. The federal government does not regulate the length of trucks that can use the nation's highways. The state of Iowa enacted a statute that restricts the length of trucks that can use highways in the state to 55 feet. This means that if Consolidated wants to move goods through Iowa, it must either use smaller trucks or detach the double trailers and shuttle them through the state separately. Its only other alternative is to divert its 65-foot doubles around Iowa. Consolidated filed suit against Iowa, alleging that the state statute was unconstitutional. Is it? *Kassel v. Consolidated Freightways Corporation*, 450 U.S. 662, 101 S.Ct. 1309, 1981 U.S. Lexis 17 (U.S. Sup.Ct.)

4.5 Privileges and Immunities Clause During the 1970s, a period of a booming economy in Alaska, many residents of other states moved there in search of work. Construction work on the Trans-Alaska Pipeline was a major source of employment. In 1972, the Alaska legislature enacted an act titled the "Local Hire" Statute. This act required employers to hire Alaska residents in preference to nonresidents. Is this statute constitutional? *Hicklin* *v. Orbeck, Commissioner of the Department of Labor of Alaska*, 437 U.S. 518, 98 S.Ct. 2482, 1978 U.S. Lexis 36 (U.S. Sup.Ct.)

4.6 Commercial Speech The city of San Diego, California, enacted a city zoning ordinance that prohibited outdoor advertising display signs—including billboards. On-site signs at a business location were exempted from this rule. The city based the restriction on traffic safety and aesthetics. Metromedia, Inc., a company in the business of leasing commercial billboards to advertisers, sued the city of San Diego, alleging that the zoning ordinance was unconstitutional. Is it? *Metromedia, Inc. v. City of San Diego*, 453 U.S. 490, 101 S.Ct. 2882, 1981 U.S. Lexis 50 (U.S. Sup.Ct.)

4.7 Substantive Due Process On February 20, 1978, the village of Hoffman Estates, Illinois, enacted an ordinance regulating drug paraphernalia. The ordinance made it unlawful for any person "to sell any items, effect, paraphernalia, accessory or thing which is designed or marketed for use with illegal cannabis or drugs as defined by Illinois Revised Statutes, without obtaining a license therefore." The license fee was $150. A violation was subject to a fine of not more than $500. The Flipside, a retail store located in the village, sold a variety of merchandise, including smoking accessories, clamps, roach clips, scales, water pipes, vials, cigarette rolling papers, and other items. On May 30, 1978, instead of applying for a license, Flipside filed a lawsuit against the village, alleging that the ordinance was unconstitutional as a violation of substantive due process because it was overly broad and vague. Who wins? *Village of Hoffman Estates v. Flipside, Hoffman Estates, Inc.* 455, U.S. 489, 102 S.Ct. 1186, 1982 U.S. Lexis 78 (U.S. Sup.Ct.)

4.8 Equal Protection Clause The state of Alabama enacted a statute that imposed a tax on premiums earned by insurance companies. That statute imposed a 1 percent tax on domestic insurance companies (i.e., insurance companies that were incorporated in Alabama and had their principal office in the state). The statute imposed a 4 percent tax on the premiums earned by out-of-state insurance companies that sold insurance in Alabama. Out-of-state insurance companies could reduce the premium tax by 1 percent by investing at least 10 percent of their assets in Alabama. Domestic insurance companies did not have to invest any of their assets in Alabama. Metropolitan Life Insurance Company, an out-of-state insurance company, sued the state of Alabama, alleging that the Alabama statute violated the Equal Protection Clause of the U.S. Constitution. Who wins? *Metropolitan Life Insurance Co. v. Ward, Commissioner of Insurance of Alabama*, 470 U.S. 869, 105 S.Ct. 1676, 1985 U.S. Lexis 80 (U.S. Sup.Ct.)

Ethics in Business

4.9 The Raiders are a professional football team and a National Football League (NFL) franchise. Each NFL franchise is independently owned. Al Davis was an owner and the managing general partner of the Raiders. The NFL establishes schedules, negotiates television contracts, and otherwise promotes NFL football, including conducting the Super Bowl each year. The Raiders play home and away games against other NFL teams.

Up until 1982, the Raiders played their home games in Oakland, California. The owners of the Raiders decided to move the team from Oakland to Los Angeles, California, to take advantage of the greater seating capacity of the Los Angeles Coliseum, the larger television market of Los Angeles, and other economic factors. The renamed team was to be known as the Los Angeles Raiders. The city of Oakland brought an eminent domain proceeding in court to acquire the Raiders as a city-owned team. *California v. Oakland Raiders*, 174 C.A. 3d 414, 220 Cal. Rptr. 153, 1985 Cal. App. Lexis 2751 (Cal. App.)

Ethics Issues

1. What does the doctrine of eminent domain provide?

2. Can the city of Oakland acquire the Raiders through eminent domain?

3. Is it socially responsible for a professional sports team to move to another location?

Endnotes

1. To be elected to Congress, an individual must be a U.S. citizen, either naturally born or granted citizenship. To serve in the Senate, a person must be 30 years of age or older. To serve in the House of Representatives, a person must be 25 years of age or older.
2. To be president, a person must be 35 years of age or older and a natural citizen of the United States. By amendment to the Constitution (Amendment XXII), a person can serve only two full terms as president.
3. Federal court judges and justices are appointed by the president with the consent of the Senate.
4. The principle that the U.S. Supreme Court is the final arbiter of the U.S. Constitution evolved from *Marbury v. Madison*, 5 U.S. 137, 1803 U.S. Lexis 352 (U.S. Sup.Ct.). In that case, the Supreme Court held that a judiciary statute enacted by Congress was unconstitutional.
5. Article VI, Section 2.
6. Article I, Section 8, clause 3.
7. 317 U.S. III, 63 S.Ct. 82, 1942 U.S. Lexis 1046 (U.S. Sup.Ct.).
8. 514 U.S. 549, 115 S.Ct. 1624, 1995 U.S. Lexis 3039 (U.S. Sup.Ct.).
9. 425 U.S. 748, 96 S.Ct. 1817, 1976 U.S. Lexis 55 (U.S. Sup.Ct.).
10. *Chaplinsky v. New Hampshire*, 315 U.S. 568, 62 S.Ct. 766, 1942 U.S. Lexis 851 (U.S. Sup.Ct.).
11. *Brandenburg v. Ohio*, 395 U.S. 444, 89 S.Ct. 1827, 1969 U.S. Lexis 1367 (U.S. Sup.Ct.).

12. *Beauharnais v. Illinois*, 343 U.S. 250, 72 S.Ct. 725, 1952 U.S. Lexis 2799 (U.S. Sup.Ct.).
13. *New York v. Ferber*, 458 U.S. 747, 102 S.Ct. 3348, 1982 U.S. Lexis 12 (U.S. Sup.Ct.).
14. *Roth v. United States*, 354 U.S. 476, 77 S.Ct. 1304, 1957 U.S. Lexis 587 (U.S. Sup.Ct.).
15. Justice Stewart in *Jacobellis v. Ohio*, 378 U.S. 184, 84 S.Ct. 1676, 1946 U.S. Lexis 822 (U.S. Sup.Ct.).
16. 413 U.S. 15, 93 S.Ct. 2607, 1973 U.S. Lexis 149 (U.S. Sup.Ct.).
17. *Wallace v. Jaffree*, 472 U.S. 38, 105 S.Ct 2479, 1985 U.S. Lexis 91 (U.S. Sup.Ct.).
18. 508 U.S. 520, 113 S.Ct. 2217, 1993 U.S. Lexis 4022 (U.S. Sup.Ct.).

5 International and World Trade Law

"International law, or the law that governs between nations has, at times, been like the common law within states, a twilight existence during which it is hardly distinguishable from morality or justice, till at length the imprimatur of a court attests its jural quality."

—Justice Cardozo
New Jersey v. Delaware, 291 U.S. 361, 54 S.Ct. 407, 1934 U.S. Lexis 973

Chapter Objectives

After studying this chapter, you should be able to:

1. Describe the federal government's power under the Foreign Commerce Clause and the Treaty Clause of the U.S. Constitution.
2. List and describe the sources of international law.
3. Describe the functions and governance of the United Nations.
4. Describe the North American Free Trade Agreement (NAFTA) and other regional economic organizations.
5. Describe the World Trade Organization (WTO) and explain how its dispute resolution procedure works.

Chapter Contents

- The United States and Foreign Affairs
- Sources of International Law
- The United Nations
- Regional International Organizations
- The World Trade Organization (WTO)
- National Courts Decide International Disputes

international law
Law that governs affairs between nations and that regulates transactions between individuals and businesses of different countries.

International law, important to both nations and businesses, has many unique features. First, there is no single legislative source of international law. All countries of the world and numerous international organizations are responsible for enacting international law. Second, there is no single world court that is responsible for interpreting international law. There are, however, several courts or tribunals that hear and decide international legal disputes of parties that agree to appear before them. Third, there is no world executive branch that can enforce international law. Thus, nations do not have to obey international law enacted by other countries or international organizations. Because of these uncertainties, some commentators question whether international law is really "law."

As technology and transportation bring nations closer together and American and foreign firms increase their global activities, international law will become even more important to governments and businesses. This chapter introduces the main concepts of international law and discusses the sources of international law and the organizations responsible for its administration.

Nepal. Many countries of the world are not democracies like the United States. The Kingdom of Nepal, for example, is a monarchy.

The United States and Foreign Affairs

The U.S. Constitution divides the power to regulate the internal affairs of the United States between the federal and state governments. On the international level, however, the Constitution gives most of the power to the federal government. Two constitutional provisions establish this authority:

Foreign Commerce Clause
A clause of the U.S. Constitution that vests Congress with the power "to regulate commerce with foreign nations."

Treaty Clause
A clause of the U.S. Constitution that states the president "shall have the power. . . to make treaties, provided two-thirds of the senators present concur."

- ***Foreign Commerce Clause.*** Article I, Section 8, clause 3—the **Foreign Commerce Clause**—vests Congress with the power "to regulate commerce with foreign nations."
- ***Treaty Clause.*** Article II, Section 2, clause 2—the **Treaty Clause**—states that the president "shall have power, by and with the advice and consent of the Senate, to make treaties, provided two-thirds of the senators present concur."

The Constitution does not vest exclusive power over foreign affairs in the federal government, but any state or local law that unduly burdens foreign commerce is unconstitutional under the Foreign Commerce Clause. Under the Treaty Clause, only the federal government can enter into treaties with foreign nations. Under the Supremacy Clause of the Constitution, treaties become part of the "law of the land," and conflicting state or local law is void. The president is the agent of the United States in dealing with foreign countries.

In the following case, the U.S. Supreme Court struck down a state law as violating the Constitution.

Case 5.1

Foreign Affairs

U.S. SUPREME COURT

Crosby, Secretary of Administration and Finance of Massachusetts v. National Foreign Trade Council

530 U.S. 363, 120 S.Ct. 2288, 2000 U.S. Lexis 4153 Supreme Court of the United States

Background and Facts

The military regime of the country of Myanmar (called Burma prior to 1989) has been accused of major civil rights violations, including using forced and child labor, imprisoning and torturing political opponents, and harshly repressing ethnic minorities. These inhumane actions have been condemned by human rights organizations around the world. The state legislators in the state of Massachusetts were so appalled at these actions that in June 1996, they enacted a state statute banning the state government from purchasing goods and services from any company that did business with Myanmar.

In the meantime, the U.S. Congress enacted a federal statute that delegated power to the president of the United States to regulate U.S. dealings with Myanmar. The federal statute (1) banned all aid to the government of Myanmar except for humanitarian assistance, (2) authorized the president to impose economic sanctions against Myanmar, and (3) authorized the president to develop a comprehensive multilateral strategy to bring democracy to Myanmar.

The National Foreign Trade Council—a powerful Washington, DC–based trade association with more than 500 member companies—filed a lawsuit against Massachusetts to have the state law declared unconstitutional. The council argued that the Massachusetts "anti-Myanmar" statute was preempted by the Supremacy Clause of the U.S. Constitution, which makes federal law the "supreme law of the land" and gives the federal government the power to regulate foreign affairs. The district court and Court of Appeals ruled in favor of the council. Massachusetts appealed to the U.S. Supreme Court.

Issue

Did the Massachusetts anti-Myanmar state statute violate the Supremacy Clause of the U.S. Constitution?

In the Language of the U.S. Supreme Court

Within the sphere defined by Congress, then, the federal statute has placed the president in a position with as much discretion to exercise economic leverage against Burma, with an eye toward national security, as our law will admit. And it is just this plenitude of executive authority that we think controls the issue of preemption here. The president has been given this authority not merely to make a political statement but to achieve a political result, and the fullness of his authority shows the importance in the congressional mind of reaching that result. It is simply implausible that Congress would have gone to such lengths to empower the president if it had been willing to compromise his effectiveness by deference to every provision of state statute or local ordinance that might, if enforced, blunt the consequences of discretionary presidential action.

We find it unlikely that Congress intended both to enable the president to protect national security by giving him the flexibility to suspend or terminate federal sanctions and simultaneously to allow Massachusetts to act at odds with the president's judgment of what national security requires. And that is just what the Massachusetts Burma law would do in imposing a different, state system of economic pressure against the Burmese political regime.

Decision and Remedy

The U.S. Supreme Court held that the Massachusetts anti-Myanmar law conflicted with federal law and was therefore preempted by the Supremacy Clause of the Constitution. The Supreme Court affirmed the decisions of the district court and Court of Appeals in favor of the council.

Business and Ethics Questions

1. Should the federal government have sole power to regulate the foreign affairs of the United States? Or should the states share in this power?
2. Do you think companies that have goods manufactured in Myanmar violate any ethical principles? Explain.
3. Did the Massachusetts anti-Myanmar law have any economic implications for business? What would have been the consequences if the U.S. Supreme Court had held that the Massachusetts anti-Myanmar statute was lawful?

Sources of International Law

sources of international law
Those things that international tribunals rely on in settling international disputes.

The **sources of international law** are those things that international tribunals rely on in deciding international disputes. **Article 38(1) of the Statute of the International Court of Justice** lists the following four sources of international law: *treaties and conventions, custom, general principles of law,* and *judicial decisions and teachings*. Most courts rely on the hierarchy suggested by this list; that is, treaties and conventions are turned to before custom, and so on. Each of these sources of law is discussed in the following paragraphs.

Treaties and Conventions

treaties
The first source of international law, consisting of agreements or contracts between two or more nations that are formally signed by an authorized representative and ratified by the supreme power of each nation.

convention
A treaty that is sponsored by an international organization.

Treaties and conventions are the equivalents of legislation at the international level. A **treaty** is an agreement or a contract between two or more nations that is formally signed by an authorized representative and ratified by the supreme power of each nation. *Bilateral treaties* are between two nations; *multilateral treaties* involve more than two nations. **Conventions** are treaties that are sponsored by international organizations, such as the United Nations. Conventions normally have many signatories.

Treaties and conventions address such matters as human rights, foreign aid, navigation, commerce, and the settlement of disputes. Most treaties are registered with and published by the United Nations.

Custom

custom
The second source of international law, created through consistent, recurring practices between two or more nations over a period of time that have become recognized as binding.

Custom between nations is an independent source of international law. Custom describes a practice followed by two or more nations when dealing with each other. It may be found in official government statements, diplomatic correspondence, policy statements, press releases, speeches, and the like. Two elements must be established to show that a practice has become a custom:

1. Consistent and recurring action by two or more nations over a considerable period of time.
2. Recognition that the custom is binding—that is, followed because of legal obligation rather than courtesy.

International customs evolve as mores, technology, forms of government, political parties, and other factors change throughout the world. Customs that have been recognized for some period of time are often codified in treaties.

General Principles of Law

general principles of law
The third source of international law, consisting of principles of law recognized by civilized nations. These are principles of law that are common to the national law of the parties to the dispute.

Courts and tribunals that decide international disputes frequently rely on **general principles of law** that are recognized by civilized nations. These are principles of law that are common to the *national* law of the parties to the dispute. They may be derived from constitutions, statutes, regulations, common law, or other sources of national law. In some cases, however, the countries' laws may differ concerning the matter in dispute.

Judicial Decisions and Teachings

judicial decisions and teachings
The fourth source of international law, consisting of judicial decisions and writings of the most qualified legal scholars of the various nations involved in the dispute.

A fourth source of law to which international tribunals can refer is **judicial decisions and teachings** of the most qualified scholars of the various nations involved in the dispute. Although international courts are not bound by the doctrine of *stare decisis* and may decide each case on its own merits, the courts often refer to their own past decisions for guidance. Court decisions of national courts do not create precedent for international courts.

The United Nations

One of the most important international organizations is the **United Nations (UN)**, which was created by a multilateral treaty on October 24, 1945.[1] Most countries of the world are members of the UN. The goals of the UN, which is headquartered in New York City, are to maintain peace and security in the world, promote economic and social cooperation, and protect human rights (see Exhibit 5.1).

United Nations (UN)
An international organization created by multilateral treaty in 1945 to promote social and economic cooperation among nations and to protect human rights.

Exhibit 5.1
Selected Provisions from the Charter of the United Nations

Our respective Governments, through representatives assembled in the city of San Francisco, who have exhibited their full powers found to be in good and due form, have agreed to the present Charter of the United Nations and do hereby establish an international organization to be known as the United Nations.

Chapter 1. Purposes and Principles

Article 1 The Purposes of the United Nations are:

(1) To maintain international peace and security, and to that end: to take effective collective measures for the prevention and removal of threats to the peace, and for the suppression of acts of aggression or other breaches of the peace, and to bring about by peaceful means, and in conformity with the principles of justice and international law, adjustment or settlement of international disputes or situations which might lead to a breach of the peace;

(2) To develop friendly relations among nations based on respect for the principle of equal rights and self-determination of peoples, and to take other appropriate measures to strengthen universal peace;

(3) To achieve international co-operation in solving international problems of an economic, social, cultural, or humanitarian character, and in promoting and encouraging respect for human rights and for fundamental freedoms for all without distinction as to race, sex, language, or religion; and

(4) To be a centre for harmonizing the actions of nations in the attainment of these common ends.

Governance of the UN

The UN is governed by:

- **The General Assembly**, composed of all member nations. As the legislative body of the UN, it adopts resolutions concerning human rights, trade, finance and economics, and other matters within the scope of the UN Charter. Although restrictions have limited force, they are usually enforced through persuasion and the use of economic and other sanctions.
- **The Security Council**, composed of 15 member nations, 5 of which are permanent members (China, France, Russia, the United Kingdom, and the United States), and 10 other countries chosen by the members of the General Assembly to serve two-year terms. The council is primarily responsible for maintaining international peace and security and has authority to use armed forces.
- **The Secretariat**, which administers the day-to-day operations of the UN. It is headed by the *secretary-general*, who is elected by the General Assembly. The secretary-general may refer matters that threaten international peace and security to the Security Council and use his office to help solve international disputes.

When Kansas and Colorado have a quarrel over the water in the Arkansas River they don't call out the National Guard in each state and go to war over it. They bring a suit in the Supreme Court of the United States and abide by the decision. There isn't a reason in the world why we cannot do that internationally.

Harry S. Truman
Speech, 1945

Bhutan. Even the smallest countries of the world, such as Bhutan, a Buddhist nation in Asia, are members of the United Nations.

The International Court of Justice

International Court of Justice (ICJ)
The judicial branch of the United Nations that is located in The Hague, the Netherlands. Also called the *World Court*.

The **International Court of Justice (ICJ),** also called the **World Court,** is located in The Hague, the Netherlands. It is the judicial branch of the UN. Only nations, not individuals or businesses, may have cases decided by this court. The ICJ may hear cases that nations refer to it as well as cases involving treaties and the UN Charter. A nation may seek redress on behalf of an individual or a business that has a claim against another country. The ICJ is composed of 15 judges who serve nine-year terms; not more than 2 judges may be from the same nation. A nation that is a party to a dispute before the ICJ may appoint 1 judge on an ad hoc basis for that case.

UN Agencies

The UN is composed of various autonomous agencies that deal with a wide range of economic and social problems. These include UNESCO (United Nations Educational, Scientific, and Cultural Organization), UNICEF (United Nations International Children's Emergency Fund), the IMF (International Monetary Fund), the World Bank, and IFAD (International Fund for Agricultural Development).

International Law

International Monetary Fund (IMF)

The **International Monetary Fund (IMF)**, an agency of the United Nations, was established by treaty in 1945 to help promote the world economy following the Great Depression of the 1930s and the end of World War II in 1945. The IMF comprises more than 180 countries that are each represented on the board of directors, which makes the policy decisions of the IMF. The day-to-day operations of the IMF are run by the executive committee, which is composed of the United States, the United Kingdom, Japan, Germany, France, China, Russia, and Saudi Arabia and 16 other countries elected from countries other than those already named. The IMF is funded by monetary contributions of member nations, assessed based on the size of each nation's economy. The IMF's headquarters is located in Washington, DC.

The primary function of the IMF is to promote sound monetary, fiscal, and macroeconomic policies worldwide by providing assistance to needy countries. The IMF examines a country's economy as a whole, its currency accounts, inflation, balance of payments with other countries, employment, consumer and business spending, and other factors to determine whether the country needs assistance. The IMF responds to financial crises around the globe by providing short-term loans to member countries to help them weather problems caused by unstable currencies, to balance payment problems, and to recover from the economic policies of past governments. For example, the IMF has played a financial role in helping eastern and central European countries recover since the collapse of the Soviet Union. In return for such financial assistance, a country must agree to meet certain monetary, fiscal, employment, inflation, and other goals established by the IMF. ■

Laos.

International Law

World Bank

The **World Bank** is a United Nations agency that comprises more than 180 member nations. The World Bank is financed by contributions from developed countries, with the United States, the United Kingdom, Japan, Germany, and France being its main contributors. The World Bank has employees located in its headquarters in Washington, DC, and regional offices throughout

(continued)

International Law (continued)

Morocco.

the world. Each member country is represented on a board of governors that meets to determine how the bank's funds will be distributed. The executive directors, comprising directors from the 5 largest donor countries and 19 directors elected by the other countries, is responsible for the conduct of the bank's general operations.

The World Bank provides money to developing countries to fund projects for humanitarian purposes and to relieve poverty. The World Bank provides funds to build roads, construct dams and water projects, establish hospitals and provide medical assistance, develop agriculture, and provide funds for humanitarian aid. The World Bank provides outright grants of funds to developing countries for such projects, and it makes long-term low-interest-rate loans to these countries. The bank routinely grants debt relief for these loans. ■

Regional International Organizations

There are several significant regional organizations whose members have agreed to work together to promote peace and security as well as economic, social, and cultural development. The most important of these organizations are discussed in the following paragraphs.

The European Union

European Union (Common Market)
An international regional organization that comprises many countries of Western Europe and that was created to promote peace and security, plus economic, social, and cultural development.

One of the most important international regional organizations is the **European Union (EU),** formerly called the **European Community,** or **Common Market.** The EU was created in 1957 and is composed of many countries of western and eastern Europe, including Austria, Belgium, Cyprus (the Greek part), Denmark, Estonia, Finland, France, Germany, Greece, Hungary, Ireland, Italy, Latvia, Lithuania, Luxembourg, Malta, Netherlands, Poland, Portugal, Slovakia, Slovenia, Spain, Sweden, The Czech Republic, and the United Kingdom of Great Britain and Northern Ireland. The EU represents more than 400 million people and a gross community product that exceeds that of the United States, Canada, and Mexico combined.

The EU's **Council of Ministers** is composed of representatives from each member country, who meet periodically to coordinate efforts to fulfill the objectives of the treaty. The council votes on significant issues and changes to the treaty. Some matters require unanimity, whereas others require only a majority vote. The member nations have surrendered substantial sovereignty to the EU. The EU **commission**, which is independent of member nations, acts in the best interests of the union. The member nations have delegated substantial powers to the commission, including authority to enact legislation and to take enforcement actions to ensure member compliance with the treaty.

We need to have the spirit of science in international affairs, to make the conduct of international affairs the effort to find the right solution, the just solution of international problems, not the effort by each nation to get the better of other nations, to do harm to them when it is possible.

Linus Carl Pauling
No More War (1958)

The EU treaty creates open borders for trade by providing for the free flow of capital, labor, goods, and services among member nations. Under the EU, customs duties have been eliminated among member nations. Common customs tariffs have been established for EU trade with the rest of the world. A single monetary unit, the euro, and a common monetary policy have been introduced. An EU central bank, equivalent to the U.S. Federal Reserve Board, has been established.

A unanimous vote of existing EU members is needed to admit a new member. Other non-member European countries are expected to apply for and be admitted as members of the EU.

A map of the EU is shown in Exhibit 5.2.

Exhibit 5.2

Map of European Union (EU) Countries

European Union (EU). The EU is a regional trading block comprised of 25 countries of Western and Eastern Europe. The EU treaty creates open borders for trade by providing for the free flow of capital, labor, goods, and services among member nations.

North American Free Trade Agreement (NAFTA)

North American Free Trade Agreement (NAFTA)
A treaty that has removed or reduced tariffs, duties, quotas, and other trade barriers between the United States, Canada, and Mexico.

In 1990, Mexico asked the United States to set up a two-country trade pact. Negotiations between the two countries began. Canada joined the negotiations, and on August 12, 1992, the **North American Free Trade Agreement (NAFTA)** was signed by the leaders of the three countries. The treaty creates a free-trade zone stretching from the Yukon to the Yucatan, bringing together more than 400 million people in the three countries.

NAFTA eliminates or reduces most of the duties, tariffs, quotas, and other trade barriers between Mexico, the United States, and Canada. Agriculture, automobiles, computers, electronics, energy and petrochemicals, financial services, insurance telecommunications, and many other industries are affected. The treaty contains a safety valve: A country can reimpose tariffs if an import surge from one of the other nations hurts its economy or workers. Like other regional trading agreements, NAFTA allows the bloc to discriminate against outsiders and to cut deals among themselves. NAFTA also includes special protection for favored industries with a lot of lobby muscle. Thus, many economists assert that NAFTA is not a "free trade" pact but a *managed trade* agreement.

NAFTA forms a supernational trading region that more effectively competes with Japan and the EU. Consumers in all three countries began to pay lower prices on a wide variety of goods and services as trade barriers fell and competition increased. Critics contend that NAFTA shifted American jobs—particularly blue-collar jobs—south of the border, where Mexican wage rates are about one-tenth of those in the United States. Environmentalists criticize the pact for not doing enough to prevent and clean up pollution in Mexico.

A map of the NAFTA countries is shown in Exhibit 5.3.

Exhibit 5.3

Map of North American Free Trade Agreement (NAFTA) Countries

International Law

Free Trade Area of the Americas (FTAA)

The leaders of 34 of North, Central, and South America nations have met to discuss the possibility of creating the **Free Trade Area of the Americas (FTAA)**. The FTAA would be an extension of NAFTA, which currently exists between Canada, Mexico, and the United States. The proposed FTAA would include all the countries of North, Central, and South America and would extend from Alaska in the north to Argentina in the south.

The FTAA would eliminate or reduce trade barriers among its member nations and create a trading zone of more than 800 million people, where trade of over $12 trillion could flourish between seamless economic borders. Negotiations for the creation of the FTAA are conducted with the United States and Brazil co-chairing the process.

The FTAA is supported by the United States and most large U.S. corporations. The FTAA is not without its American critics, however. Labor unions fear loss of jobs, and environmentalists envision more loss of rain forests and further destruction of the environment caused by economic advancement. Brazil and several other nations have also voiced reservations. ■

Latin, Central, and South American Economic Communities

Countries of Latin America and the Caribbean have established several regional organizations to promote economic development and cooperation. These include (1) the **Central American Common Market**, composed of Costa Rica, El Salvador, Guatemala,

Mission Church, Santa Barbara, California.

Honduras, Nicaragua, and Panama; (2) the **MERCOSUR Common Market**, created by Argentina, Brazil, Paraguay, and Uruguay; (3) the **Caribbean Community**, whose member countries are Barbados, Belize, Dominica, Grenada, Jamaica, St. Kitts-Nevis-Anguilla, St. Lucia, St. Vincent, and Trinidad-Tobago; and (4) the **Andean Common Market (ANCOM)**, whose current members are Bolivia, Colombia, Ecuador, and Venezuela.

Mexico, the largest industrialized country in Latin America and the Caribbean, has entered into a free trade agreement with all the countries of Central America as well as Chile, Colombia, and Venezuela.

Asian Economic Communities

Only when the world is civilized enough to keep promises will we get any kind of international law.
Julius Henry Cohen

In 1967, the **Association of South East Asian Nations (ASEAN)** was created. The countries that belong to ASEAN are Brunei Darussalam, Cambodia, Indonesia, Laos, Malaysia, Myanmar, the Philippines, Singapore, Thailand, and Vietnam. ASEAN is a cooperative association of diverse nations.

Two of the world's largest countries, Japan and China, do not belong to any significant economic communities. However, although not a member of ASEAN, Japan has been instrumental in providing financing for the countries that make up that organization. China also works closely with the countries of ASEAN and is a potential member of ASEAN.

African Economic Communities

Several regional economic communities have been formed in Africa. They include (1) the **Economic Community of West African States (ECOWAS)**, created by Dahomey, Gambia, Ghana, Guinea-Bissau, Ivory Coast, Liberia, Mali, Mauritania, Niger, Nigeria, Senegal, Sierra Leone, Togo, and Upper Volta; (2) the **Economic and Customs Union of Central Africa**, composed of Cameroon, Central African Republic, Chad, Congo, and

Gabon; and (3) the **East African Community (EAC)**, created by Kenya, Tanzania, and Uganda. In 1991, 51 African countries of the **Organization of African Unity** signed a **Treaty Establishing the African Economic Community**. This wide-ranging treaty with its large organization of countries is expected to wield more power than the smaller African regional organizations.

Middle Eastern Economic Communities

One of the most well-known economic organizations is the **Organization of Petroleum Exporting Countries (OPEC)**. OPEC consists of 11 oil-producing and exporting countries from Africa, Asia, the Middle East, and South America. The member nations are Algeria, Indonesia, Iran, Iraq, Kuwait, Libya, Nigeria, Qatar, Saudi Arabia, United Arab Emirates, and Venezuela. OPEC sets quotas on the output of oil production by member nations. The **Gulf Cooperation Council** was established by Bahrain, Kuwait, Oman, Qatar, Saudi Arabia, and the United Arab Emirates to establish an economic trade area.

Regional Courts

Various treaties have created regional courts to handle disputes among member nations. For example, most regional economic organizations have established courts to enforce provisions of their respective treaties and to solve disputes among member nations. Regional courts, however, usually do not have mechanisms to enforce their judgments.

The World Trade Organization (WTO)

In 1995, the **World Trade Organization (WTO)** was created as part of the Uruguay Round of trade negotiations on the *General Agreement on Tariffs and Trade (GATT)*. GATT is a multilateral treaty that established trade agreements and limits tariffs and trade restrictions among its more than 130 member nations.

World Trade Organization (WTO) An international organization of more than 130 member nations created to promote and enforce trade agreements among member nations.

The WTO is an international organization whose headquarters is located in Geneva, Switzerland. WTO members have entered into many trade agreements among themselves, including international agreements on investments, sale of goods, provision of services, intellectual property, licensing, tariffs, subsidies, and the removal of trade barriers.

The WTO, which has been referred to as the "Supreme Court of Trade," has become the world's most important trade organization. The WTO has jurisdiction to enforce the most important and comprehensive trade agreements in the world among its more than 130 member nations. Many herald the WTO as a much-needed world court that can peaceably solve trade disputes among nations.

International Law

China Joins the WTO

For the past 50 years, China and the United States have pursued divergent paths. China became the world's largest communist country and the United States the leading democracy. China maintained its agricultural base, while the United States pursued industrialization. Most of China's businesses were state owned, while those in the United States were privately owned under a capitalist system. For over a decade, these two countries engaged in on-again, off-again trade negotiations. Then, in November 1999, they formed a landmark trade pact. In exchange for being granted the right to import most goods and services into

(continued)

International Law (continued)

Beijing, China.

the United States, China, which had substantially restricted imports into its country, agreed to open its markets to foreign goods and services.

The China–U.S. trade agreement was a prelude to China's trade agreements with other countries. These trade agreements supported China's application to join the WTO. In 2002, China became a member of the WTO. China's entry into the WTO makes it a full partner in the world's trading system.

China's entry into the WTO is not without critics. In the United States, labor unions complain that U.S. manufacturing jobs will be lost to China, and environmentalists complain that little is being done to protect the environment from an industrialized economy the size of China's. In China, workers at state-owned enterprises might lose their jobs to foreign capitalist companies that can produce goods and services more efficiently, and China's already impoverished farmers may be harmed by cheap farm products being imported from other countries. ■

WTO Dispute Resolution

One of the primary functions of the WTO is to hear and decide trade disputes between member nations. Before the creation of the WTO, GATT governed trade disputes between signatory nations. This system was inadequate because any member nation that was found to have violated any GATT trade agreement could itself veto any sanctions imposed by GATT's governing body. The WTO solved this problem by adopting a "judicial" mode of dispute resolution to replace GATT's more politically based one: A member nation that believes that another member nation has breached one of these agreements can initiate a proceeding to have the WTO hear and decide the dispute.

The dispute is first heard by a three-member **panel** of the WTO, which issues a "panel report." The members of the panel are professional judges from member nations. The report is the decision of the panel and contains its findings of fact and law and orders a remedy if a violation has been found. The report is then referred to the **dispute settlement body** of the WTO. This body is required to adopt the panel report unless the body, by consensus, agrees not to adopt it. Because each member nation has a representative on this settlement body, it can be presumed that panel reports will automatically be adopted because the winning nation to the dispute will almost assuredly vote to adopt it. This is a radical change from the former GATT settlement procedure. Under GATT, unanimity was required to enforce a panel report, and the losing party usually voted to block the implementation of a panel's findings against it. One of the most important features of the WTO is the elimination of this blocking power of member nations.

panel
A group of three WTO judges that hears trade disputes between member nations and issues a "panel report."

dispute settlement body
A board composed of one representative from each WTO member nation that reviews panel reports.

The WTO creates an **appellate body** to which a party can appeal a decision of the dispute settlement body. This appeals court is composed of seven professional justices selected from member nations. Appeals are heard by panels composed of three members of the appellate body. Appeals are limited to issues of law, not fact. The entire dispute proceeding is completed within 9 months when a panel report is not appealed and within 12 months when there is an appeal. A shortened period is available if the parties agree or if there is an urgent matter that must be decided quickly.

appellate body
A panel of seven judges selected from WTO member nations that hears and decides appeals from decisions by the dispute settlement body.

If a violation of a trade agreement is found, the general report and appellate decision can order the offending nation to cease from engaging in the violating practice and to pay damages to the other party. If the offending nation refuses to abide by the order, the WTO can order retaliatory trade sanctions (e.g., tariffs) by other member nations against the noncomplying nation.

International Law

The International Criminal Court

In the twentieth century, the world witnessed horrible war crimes and crimes against humanity. Most of these crimes were conducted with impunity, and the perpetrators of these crimes went unpunished. To address this problem, at a meeting in 1998, the majority of the countries of the world adopted the **Rome Treaty**, which created the **International Criminal Court (ICC)**. The ICC has authority to prosecute individuals accused of genocide, war crimes, and crimes against humanity. The ICC may prosecute nationals located in the more than 100 countries that have ratified the treaty. The ICC has complementary jurisdiction with the national courts of a country. That is, a nation's courts will have first jurisdiction to criminally prosecute its own national who is suspected of genocide, war crimes, or crimes against humanity. If the nation is unwilling or unable to genuinely prosecute, the ICC can then prosecute the accused national.

The ICC is located in The Hague in the Netherlands. The tribunal came into force on July 1, 2003, and it may prosecute crimes committed after that date. The ICC is comprised of a Pre-Trial Division that investigates alleged crimes and issues indictments, a Trial Division that conduct the criminal trial, and an Appeals Division that hears appeals of decisions of the Trial Division. The judges of these courts are selected by ICC member nations. ICC rules guarantee the accused substantial rights, including the presumption of innocence and the right to have charges proved beyond a reasonable doubt. The accused also has the rights to counsel, to present evidence, and to remain silent.

The creation and operation of the ICC will assure the world that many perpetrators of the worst crimes against humanity will not go unpunished. However, the ICC does not have complete worldwide jurisdiction because only nationals of

(continued)

International Law (continued)

Cambodia.

countries that have ratified the Rome Treaty are subject to prosecution by the ICC. China, the United States, and Iraq are three countries that have not ratified the Rome Treaty. The United States stated that it did not ratify the treaty because it already had laws in place to punish the crimes subject to prosecution by the ICC. ■

National Courts Decide International Disputes

national courts
The courts of individual nations.

The majority of cases involving international law disputes are heard by **national courts** of individual nations. This is primarily the case for commercial disputes between private litigants that do not qualify to be heard by an international court. Some countries have specialized courts that hear international commercial disputes. Other countries permit such disputes to proceed through their regular court systems. In the United States, commercial disputes between U.S. companies and foreign governments or parties may be brought in federal district court.

Judicial Procedure

choice of forum clause
A clause is an international contract that designates which nation's court has jurisdiction to hear a case arising out of the contract. Also known as a *forum-selection clause*.

choice of law clause
A clause in an international contract that designates which nation's laws will be applied in deciding a dispute.

A party seeking judicial resolution of an international dispute faces several problems, including which nation's courts will hear the case and what law should be applied to the case. Jurisdiction is often a highly contested issue. Absent an agreement providing otherwise, a case involving an international dispute will be brought in the national court of the plaintiff's home country.

Many international contracts contain a **choice of forum** (or **forum-selection**) **clause** that designates which nation's court has jurisdiction to hear a case arising out of contract. In addition, many contracts also include a **choice of law clause** that designates which nation's laws will be applied in deciding the case. Absent these two clauses, and without the parties agreeing to these matters, an international dispute may never be resolved.

Concept Summary International Contract Clauses

Clause	Description
Forum-selection	A clause that designates the judicial or arbitral forum that will hear and decide a case.
Choice of law	A clause that designates the law to be applied by the court or arbitrator in deciding a case.

The Act of State Doctrine

A general principle of international law is that a country has absolute authority over what transpires *within* its own territory. In furtherance of this principle, the **act of state doctrine** states that judges of one country cannot question the validity of an act committed by another country within that other country's own borders. In *United States v. Belmont*,[2] the U.S. Supreme Court declared, "Every sovereign state must recognize the independence of every other sovereign state; and the courts of one will not sit in judgment upon the acts of the government of another, done within it own territory." This restraint on the judiciary is justified under the doctrine of separation of powers and permits the executive branch of the federal government to arrange affairs with foreign governments.

act of state doctrine
A doctrine that states that judges of one country cannot question the validity of an act committed by another country within that other country's borders. It is based on the principle that a country has absolute authority over what transpires within its own territory.

Consider This Example Suppose the country of Cuba outlaws the practice of all religions in that country. Paul, a Christian who is a citizen of and living in the United States, disagrees with Cuba's law. Paul brings a lawsuit against Cuba in U.S. district court, arguing to the court that the Cuban law should be declared illegal. The U.S. district court will apply the act of state doctrine and dismiss Paul's lawsuit. The U.S. court will rule that Cuba's law is an act of that state (country) and that a U.S. court does not have authority to hear and decide Paul's case.

The Doctrine of Sovereign Immunity

One of the oldest principles of international law is the **doctrine of sovereign immunity**. Under this doctrine, *countries* are granted immunity from suits in courts in other countries. For example, if a U.S. citizen wanted to sue the government of China in a U.S. court, he or she could not (subject to certain exceptions).

doctrine of sovereign immunity
A doctrine that states that countries are granted immunity from suits in courts of other countries.

Originally, the United States granted absolute immunity to foreign governments from suits in U.S. courts. In 1952, the United States switched to the principle of *qualified*, or *restricted, immunity*, which was eventually codified in the **Foreign Sovereign Immunities Act of 1976 (FSIA).**[3] This act now exclusively governs suits against foreign nations in the United States, whether in federal or state court. Most Western nations have adopted the principle of restricted immunity. Other countries still follow the doctrine of absolute immunity.

Foreign Sovereign Immunities Act
An act that exclusively governs suits against foreign nations that are brought in federal or state courts in the United States. It codifies the principle of *qualified*, or *restricted, immunity*.

Exceptions The FSIA provides that a foreign country is not immune from lawsuits in U.S. courts in the following two situations:

1. The foreign country has waived its immunity, either explicitly or by implication
2. The action is based on a commercial activity carried on in the United States by the foreign country or carried on outside the United States but causing a direct effect in the United States

What constitutes "commercial activity" is the most litigated aspect of the FSIA. If it is commercial activity, the foreign sovereign is subject to suit in the United States; if it is not, the foreign sovereign is immune from suit in this country.

My nationalism is intense internationalism. I am sick of the strife between nations or religions.
Gandhi

Consider These Examples The president of the country of Argentina is visiting the United States on a diplomatic mission to meet with the president of the United States to discuss political and economic issues. Suppose that while in Washington, DC, the president of Argentina negligently injures a U.S. citizen. The doctrine of sovereign immunity protects the president of Argentina from being sued by the injured party in state or federal courts in the United States.

If the country of Argentina sells bonds to investors in the United States to raise money, then Argentina is involved in commercial activity in the United States. If Argentina defaults and does not pay the U.S. investors back their money, the investors can sue Argentina in U.S. courts, under the commercial activity exception to the doctrine of sovereign immunity, to recover the unpaid money.[4]

Concept Summary *Act of State and Sovereign Immunity Doctrines Compared*

Doctrine	Description
Act of state	A doctrine that states that an act of a government in its *own country* is not subject to suit in a foreign country's courts.
Sovereign immunity	A doctrine that states that an act of a government in a *foreign country* is not subject to suit in the foreign country. Some countries provide absolute immunity, and other countries (such as the United States) provide limited immunity.

International Arbitration

As an alternative to litigation, the parties to an international contract may agree that any dispute that arises between them regarding the transaction will be decided through mandatory arbitration. **Arbitration** is a nonjudicial method of dispute resolution whereby a neutral third party decides the case. The parties agree to be bound by the arbitrator's decision. Generally, arbitration is faster, less expensive, less formal, and more private than litigation.

arbitration
A nonjudicial method of dispute resolution whereby a neutral third party decides the case.

arbitration clause
A clause contained in many international contracts that stipulates that any dispute between the parties concerning the performance of the contract will be submitted to an arbitrator or arbitration panel for resolution.

An **arbitration clause** should specify the arbitrator or the means of selecting the arbitrator. Several organizations conduct international arbitrations, including the American Arbitration Association, the International Chamber of Commerce, the International Center for the Settlement of Investment Disputes, and the United Nations Commission on International Trade Law. International arbitrators are usually businesspeople or lawyers experienced in worldwide commercial transactions. An arbitration clause should also specify the law to be applied by the arbitrator. Arbitration clauses are appearing in an increasing number of international contracts.

An arbitrator issues an *award*, not a judgment. An arbitrator does not have the power to enforce the award it renders. Therefore, if the losing party refuses to pay the award, the winning party must petition a court to enforce the award. More than 50 countries that conduct the bulk of worldwide commercial transactions are signatories to the **United Nations Convention on the Recognition and Enforcement of Foreign Arbitral Awards.**[5] The United States adopted the convention in 1970 and amended the Federal Arbitration Act to reflect this international law.[6] The recipient of an arbitral award subject to the convention can attach property of the loser that is located in any country that is a signatory to the convention.

International Law

Jewish Law and the Torah

Jewish law, which has existed for centuries, is a complex legal system based on ideology and theology of the Torah. The Torah prescribes comprehensive and integrated rules of religious, political, and legal life that together form Jewish thought. Jewish law is decided by rabbis who are scholars of the Torah and other Jewish scriptures. Rabbinic jurisprudence, known as ***Halakhah***, is administered by rabbi-judges sitting as the ***Beis Din***, Hebrew for the "house of judgment." As a court, the *Beis Din* has roots that go back 3,000 years.

Today, Jews are citizens of countries worldwide. As such, they are subject to the criminal and civil laws of their host countries. But no matter where they live, Jews abide by the principles of the Torah in many legal matters, such as marriage, divorce, inheritance, and other family matters. Thus, the legal principles embedded in the Torah coexist with the secular laws of Jews' home countries.

The rabbinical judges tend to be actively involved in cases. True to its roots, the *Beis Din* is more a search for the truth than it is an adversarial process. ■

Israel.

International Law

Islamic Law and the Koran

Approximately 20 percent of the world's population is Muslim. Islam is the principal religion of Afghanistan, Algeria, Bangladesh, Egypt, Indonesia, Iran, Iraq, Jordan, Kuwait, Libya, Malaysia, Mali, Mauritania, Morocco, Niger, North Yemen, Oman, Pakistan, Qatar, Saudi Arabia, Somalia, South Yemen, Sudan, Syria, Tunisia, Turkey, and the United Arab Emirates. *Islamic law* (or *Shari'a*) is the only law in Saudi Arabia. In other Islamic countries, the *Shari'a* forms the basis of family law but coexists with other laws.

The Islamic law system is derived from the Koran, the Sunnah (decisions and sayings of the prophet Muhammad), and reasonings by Islamic scholars. By the tenth century A.D., Islamic scholars had decided that no further improvement of the divine law could be made, closed the door of *ijtihad* (independent reasoning), and froze the evolution of Islamic law at that point. Islamic law prohibits *riba*, or the making of unearned or unjustified profit. Making a profit from the sale of goods or the provision of services is permitted. The most

Uzbekistan.

(continued)

International Law

(continued)

notable consequence of *riba* is that the payment of interest on loans is forbidden. To circumvent this result, the party with the money is permitted to purchase the item and resell it to the other party at a profit or to advance the money and become a trading partner who shares in the profits of the enterprise.

Today, Islamic law is primarily used in the areas of marriage, divorce, and inheritance and to a limited degree in criminal law. To resolve the tension between *Shari'a* and the practice of modern commercial law, the *Shari'a* is often ignored in commercial transactions. ■

International Law

Hindu Law—*Dharmasastra*

Over 20 percent of the world's population is Hindu. Most Hindus live in India, where they make up 80 percent of the population. Others live in Burma, Kenya, Malaysia, Pakistan, Singapore, Tanzania, and Uganda. *Hindu law* is a religious law. As such, individual Hindus apply this law to themselves, regardless of their nationality or place of domicile.

Classical Hindu law rests neither on civil codes nor on court decisions, but on the works of private scholars that were passed along for centuries by oral tradition and eventually were recorded in the *smitris* (law books). Hindu law—called *dharmasastra* in Sanskrit (that is, the doctrine of proper behavior)—is linked to the divine revelation of Veda (the holy collection of Indian religious songs, prayers, hymns, and sayings written between 2000 and 1000 B.C.). Most Hindu law is concerned with family matters and the law of succession.

After India became a British colony, British judges applied a combination of Hindu law and common law in solving cases. This Anglo-Hindu law, as it was called, was ousted when India gained its independence. In the mid-1950s, India codified Hindu law by enacting the Hindu Marriage Act, the Hindu Minority and Guardianship Act, the Hindu Succession Act, and the Hindu Adoptions and Maintenance Act. Outside India, Anglo-Hindu law applies in most other countries populated by Hindus. ■

Nepal.

Terms and Concepts

Sources of International Law

1. ***Treaties and conventions.*** Treaties are agreements between nations that are formally ratified by the supreme power of each signatory nation. Conventions are treaties that are sponsored by international organizations (e.g., the United Nations).
2. ***Custom.*** Customs are practices followed by two or more nations over a period of time when dealing with each other.
3. ***General principles of law.*** General principles of law are common to the nations of the parties involved in a dispute.

4. ***Judicial decision and teachings.*** Judicial decisions of national courts and teachings of the most qualified legal scholars of the nations of the parties involved in a dispute are used to resolve the legal dispute.

The United States and Foreign Affairs

The following two provisions in the U.S. Constitution establish the federal government's authority to regulate international affairs:

1. ***Foreign Commerce Clause.*** This clause vests Congress with the power "to regulate commerce with foreign nations."
2. ***Treaty Clause.*** This clause gives the U.S. president the authority to enter into treaties with foreign nations, subject to a two-thirds vote of the Senate.

The United Nations

Governance of the United Nations. The UN is an international organization located in New York City. Most countries of the world are members. Its goals are to maintain peace and security in the world, promote economic and social cooperation, and protect human rights.

Regional Economic Organizations

1. European Union (EU)
2. Central American Common Market
3. MERCOSUR Common Market
4. Caribbean Community
5. Andean Common Market (ANCOM)
6. Economic Community of West African States (ECOWAS)
7. Economic and Customs Union of Central Africa
8. East African Community (EAC)
9. African Economic Community
10. Organization of Petroleum Exporting Countries (OPEC)
11. Gulf Cooperation Council
12. Association of South East Asian Nations (ASEAN)
13. North American Free Trade Agreement (NAFTA)

World Trade Organization

The World Trade Organization is an international organization located in Geneva, Switzerland. Many countries of the world are members. Its goals are to limit tariff and trade restrictions and to provide a mechanism for resolving trade disputes among its member nations.

Principle of Judicial Restraint

National courts are limited by two principles of judicial restraint:

1. ***Act of state doctrine.*** This doctrine states that judges of one country cannot question the validity of an act committed by another country *within* that other country's borders.
2. ***Doctrine of sovereign immunity.*** This doctrine states that countries are granted immunity from suits in courts in other countries. Some countries provide for *absolute immunity*, and other countries (such as the United States) provide *qualified*, or *restricted*, immunity.

   Exceptions: The United States provides that a foreign country is not immune from lawsuits in U.S. court if:

   a. The foreign country has *waived* its immunity.

   b. The foreign country has engaged in *commercial activity* in the United States or outside the United States that causes a direct effect in the United States.

Internet Exercises and Case Questions

Working the Web Internet Exercises

1. Go to Hieros Gamos, at **www.hg.org**. It is a huge international law site that contains laws from 230 countries in more than 50 languages. Look at the list of countries and review the legal structure of Afghanistan.
2. Go to **http://www.travel.state.gov/law/info/judicial/judicial_2515.html.** Check on the procedures for enforcement of judgments in foreign countries. Why are there no treaties or conventions that make enforcement of U.S. judgments easier?
3. Survey the alternative dispute resolution (ADR) material at **search.info.usaid.gov**. What are some of the particular advantages to using ADR in other countries?

Legal Environment Cases

5.1 Act of State Doctrine Prior to 1918, the Petrograd Metal Works, a Russian corporation, deposited a large sum of money with August Belmont, a private banker doing business in New York City under the name August Belmont & Co. (Belmont). In 1918, the Soviet government nationalized the corporation and appropriated all its property and assets wherever situated, including the deposit account with Belmont. As a result, the deposit became the property of the Soviet government. In 1933, the Soviet government and the United States entered into an agreement to settle claims and counterclaims between them. As part of the settlement, it was agreed that the Soviet government would take no steps to enforce claims against American nationals (including Belmont) and assigned all such claims to the United States. The United States brought an action against the executors of Belmont's estate to recover the money originally deposited with Belmont by Petrograd Metal Works. Who owns the money? *United States v. Belmont*, 301 U.S. 324, 57 S.Ct. 758, 1937 U.S. Lexis 293 (U.S. Sup.Ct.)

5.2 Act of State Doctrine Banco Nacional de Costa Rica is a bank wholly owned by the government of Costa Rica. It is subject to the rules and regulations adopted by the minister of finance and the central bank of Costa Rica. In December 1980, the bank borrowed $40 million from a consortium of private banks located in the United Kingdom and the United States. The bank signed promissory notes, agreeing to repay the principal plus interest on the loan in four equal installments due on July 30, August 30, September 30, and October 30, 1981. The money was to be used to provide export financing of sugar and sugar products from Costa Rica. The loan agreements and promissory notes were signed in New York City, and the loan proceeds were tendered to the bank there.

On July 30, 1981, the bank paid the first installment on the loan. The bank did not, however, make the other three installment payments and defaulted on the loan. The lending banks sued the bank in U.S. district court in New York to recover the unpaid principal and interest. The bank alleged in defense that on August 27, 1981, the minister of finance and the central bank of Costa Rica had issued a decree forbidding the repayment of loans by the bank to private lenders, including the lending banks in this case. This action was taken because Costa Rica was having trouble servicing debts to foreign creditors. The bank alleged that the act of state doctrine prevented the plaintiffs from recovering on their loans to the bank. Who wins? *Libra Bank Limited v. Banco Nacional de Costa Rica*, 570 F.Supp. 870, 1983 U.S. Dist. Lexis 14677 (S.D. N.Y.)

5.3 Forum Selection Clause Zapata Off-Shore Company is a Houston, Texas–based American corporation that engages in drilling oil wells throughout the world. Unterweser Reederei, GMBH, is a German corporation that provides ocean shipping and towing services. In November 1967, Zapata requested bids from companies to tow its self-elevating drilling rig *Chaparral* from Louisiana to a point off Ravenna, Italy, in the Adriatic Sea, where Zapata had agreed to drill certain wells. Unterweser submitted the lowest bid and was requested to submit a proposed contract to Zapata, which it did. The contract submitted by Unterweser contained the following provision: "Any dispute arising must be treated before the London Court of Justice." Zapata executed the contract without deleting or modifying this provision.

On January 5, 1968, Unterweser's deep sea tug *Bremen* departed Venice, Louisiana, with the *Chaparral* in tow, bound for Italy. On January 9, while the flotilla was in international waters in the middle of the Gulf of Mexico, a severe storm arose. The sharp roll of the *Chaparral* in Gulf waters caused portions of it to break off and fall into the sea, seriously damaging the *Chaparral*. Zapata instructed the *Bremen* to tow the *Chaparral*, to Tampa, Florida, the nearest port of refuge, which it did. On January 12, Zapata filed suit against Unterweser and the *Bremen* in U.S. district court in Florida, alleging negligent towing and breach of contract. The defendants asserted that suit can be brought only in the London Court of Justice. Who is correct? *M/S Bremen and Unterweser Reederei, GMBH v. Zapata Off-Shore Company*, 407 U.S. 1, 92 S.Ct. 1907, 1972 U.S. Lexis 114 (U.S. Sup.Ct.)

5.4 International Arbitration Alberto-Culver Company is an American company that is incorporated in Delaware and has its principal office in Illinois. It manufactures and distributes toiletries and hair care products in the United States and other countries. Fritz Scherk owned three interrelated businesses organized under the laws of Germany and Liechtenstein that were engaged in the manufacture of toiletries. After substantial negotiations, in February 1969, Alberto-Culver entered into a contract with Scherk to purchase his three companies, along with all rights held by those companies to trademarks in cosmetic goods. The contract contained a number of express warranties whereby Scherk guaranteed the sole and unencumbered ownership of these trademarks. The contract also contained a clause that provided that "any controversy or claim that shall arise out of this agreement or breach thereof" was to be referred to arbitration before the International Chamber of Commerce in Paris, France. The transaction closed in June 1969 in Geneva, Switzerland.

Nearly one year later, Alberto-Culver allegedly discovered that the trademark rights purchased under the contract were subject to substantial encumbrances that threatened to give other parties superior rights to the trademarks and to restrict or preclude Alberto-Culver's use of them. Alberto-Culver sued Scherk in U.S. district court in Illinois, alleging fraudulent misrepresentation in violation of Section 10(b) of the federal Securities Exchange Act of 1934. Scherk asserted in defense that the case was subject to mandatory arbitration in Paris. Who is correct? *Scherk v. Alberto-Culver Co.*, 417 U.S. 506, 94 S.Ct. 2249, 1974 U.S. Lexis 73 (U.S. Sup.Ct.)

Ethics in Business

5.5 Nigeria, an African nation, while in the midst of a boom period due to oil exports, entered into $1 billion of contracts with various countries to purchase huge quantities of Portland cement. Nigeria was going to use the cement to build and improve the country's infrastructure. Several of the contracts were with American companies, including Texas Trading & Milling Corporation (Texas Trading). Nigeria substantially overbought cement, and the country's docks and harbors became clogged with ships waiting to unload. Unable to accept delivery of the cement it had bought, Nigeria repudiated many of its contracts, including the one with Texas Trading. When Texas Trading sued Nigeria in a U.S. district court to recover damages for breach of contract, Nigeria asserted in defense that the doctrine of sovereign immunity protected it from liability. *Texas Trading & Milling Corp. v. Federal Republic of Nigeria*, 647 F.2d 300, 1981 U.S. App. Lexis 14231 (2d Cir.)

Ethics Issues

1. What does the doctrine of sovereign immunity provide?

2. Does the doctrine of sovereign immunity promote or hinder ethical conduct?

3. Did Nigeria act ethically in asserting the doctrine of sovereign immunity to try to avoid liability on its contracts?

4. Who wins? Why?

Endnotes

1. The Charter of the United Nations was entered into force on October 24, 1945; it was adopted by the United States on October 24, 1945 (59 Stat. 1031, T.S. 993, 3 Bevans 153, 1976 Y.B.U.N. 1043).
2. 301 U.S. 324, 57 S.Ct. 758, 1937 U.S. Lexis 293 (U.S. Sup.Ct.).
3. 28 U.S.C. Sections 1602–1611.
4. *Republic of Argentina v. Weltover, Inc.*, 504 U.S. 607, 112 S.Ct. 2160, 1992 U.S. Lexis 3542 (U.S. Sup.Ct.).
5. 21 U.S.T. 2517, T.I.A.S. 6997.
6. 9 U.S.C. Sections 201–208.

6

Torts

"Negligence in not actionable unless it involves the invasion of legally protected interest, the violation of a right. Proof of negligence in the air, so to speak, will not do."

—C. J. Cardozo
Palsgraf v. Long Island Railroad Co., 248 N.Y. 339, 162 N.E. 99, 1928 N.Y. Lexis 1269

Chapter Objectives

After studying this chapter, you should be able to:

1. List and describe intentional torts against persons and against property.
2. List and explain the elements necessary to prove negligence.
3. Describe the business torts of unfair competition, disparagement, and fraud.
4. Describe and apply the doctrine of strict liability.

Chapter Contents

- Intentional Torts Against Persons
- Intentional Torts Against Property
- Unintentional Torts (Negligence)
- Special Negligence Doctrines
- Defenses Against Negligence
- Strict Liability

Tort is the French word for a "wrong." Tort law protects a variety of injuries and provides remedies for them. Under tort law, an injured party can bring a *civil lawsuit* to seek compensation for a wrong done to the party or to the party's property. Many torts have their origin in common law. The courts and legislatures have extended tort law to reflect changes in modern society.

tort
A wrong. There are three categories of torts: (1) intentional torts, (2) unintentional torts (negligence), and (3) strict liability.

Tort damages are monetary damages that are sought from the offending party. They are intended to compensate the injured party for the injury suffered. Such injury may consist of past and future medical expenses, loss of wages, pain and suffering, mental distress, and other damages caused by the defendant's tortious conduct. If the victim of a tort dies, his or her beneficiaries can bring a *wrongful death action* to recover damages from the defendant. *Punitive damages*, which are awarded to punish the defendant, may be recovered in intentional tort and strict liability cases. Other remedies, such as injunctions, may be available, too.

This chapter discusses various tort laws, including intentional torts, negligence, and strict liability.

Roadside Memorial. Exposition Boulevard, Los Angeles, California. Automobile accidents cause thousands of deaths each year. Few of us can pass one of these familiar roadside memorials without thinking about the pain and suffering of the occupants of the vehicle and their surviving loved ones.

Intentional Torts Against Persons

The law protects a person from unauthorized touching, restraint, or other contact. In addition, the law protects a person's reputation and privacy. Violations of these rights are actionable as torts. **Intentional torts** against persons are discussed in the paragraphs that follow.

intentional tort
A category of torts that requires that the defendant possessed the intent to do the act that caused the plaintiff's injuries.

Assault

Assault is (1) the threat of immediate harm or offensive contact or (2) any action that arouses reasonable apprehension of imminent harm. Actual physical contact is unnecessary. Threats of future harm are not actionable. For example, suppose a 6-foot 5-inch, 250-pound male makes a fist and threatens to punch a 5-foot, 100-pound woman. If the woman is afraid that the man will physically harm her, she can sue him for assault. If she

assault
(1) The threat of immediate harm or offensive contact or (2) any action that arouses reasonable apprehension of imminent harm. Actual physical contact is unnecessary.

is a black-belt karate champion and laughs at the threat, there is no assault because the threat does not cause any apprehension.

Battery

battery
Unauthorized and harmful or offensive physical contact with another person. Direct physical contact is not necessary.

Battery is unauthorized and harmful or offensive physical contact with another person. Basically, the interest protected here is each person's reasonable sense of dignity and safety. For example, intentionally hitting someone is considered battery because it is harmful. Note that there does not have to be direct physical contact between the victim and the perpetrator. If an injury results, throwing a rock, shooting an arrow or a bullet, knocking off a hat, pulling a chair out from under someone, and poisoning a drink are all instances of actionable battery. The victim need not be aware of the harmful or offensive contact (e.g., it may take place while the victim is asleep). Assault and battery often occur together, although they do not have to (e.g., the perpetrator hits the victim on the back of the head without any warning).

Transferred Intent Doctrine Sometimes a person acts with the intent to injure one person but actually injures another. The *doctrine of transferred intent* applies to such situations. Under this doctrine, the law transfers the perpetrator's intent from the target to the actual victim of the act. The victim can then sue the defendant.

False Imprisonment

false imprisonment
The intentional confinement or restraint of another person without authority or justification and without that person's consent.

The intentional confinement or restraint of another person without authority or justification and without that person's consent constitutes **false imprisonment.** The victim may be restrained or confined by physical force, barriers, threats of physical harm, or the perpetrator's false assertion of legal authority (i.e., *false arrest*). A threat of future harm or moral pressure is not considered false imprisonment. The false imprisonment must be complete. For example, merely locking one door to a building when other exits are not locked is not false imprisonment. In such a case, a person is not obliged to risk danger or an affront to his or her dignity by attempting to escape.

merchant protection statutes
Statutes that allow merchants to stop, detain, and investigate suspected shoplifters without being held liable for false imprisonment if (1) there are reasonable grounds for suspicion, (2) suspects are detained for only a reasonable time, and (3) investigations are conducted in a reasonable manner. Also known as the *shopkeeper's privilege*.

Merchant Protection Statutes Shoplifting causes substantial losses to merchants each year. Almost all states have enacted **merchant protection statutes,** also known as the **shopkeeper's privilege**. These statutes allow merchants to stop, detain, and investigate suspected shoplifters without being held liable for false imprisonment if:

1. There are reasonable grounds for the suspicion.
2. Suspects are detained for only a reasonable time.
3. Investigations are conducted in a reasonable manner.

Ethics in Business

Wal-Mart Loses False Imprisonment Case

On Christmas Eve of 1995, LaShawna Goodman went to a local Wal-Mart store in Obelika, Alabama, to do some last-minute holiday shopping and brought along her two young daughters and a telephone she had purchased earlier at Wal-Mart to exchange. She presented the telephone and receipt to a Wal-Mart employee, who took the telephone. Unable to find another telephone she wanted, Goodman retrieved the previously purchased telephone from the employee, bought another item, and left. Outside, Ms. Goodman was stopped by Wal-Mart security personnel and was accused of stealing the phone. Goodman offered to show the Wal-Mart employees the original receipt, but the Wal-Mart employees detained her and called the police. Ms. Goodman was handcuffed in front of her children. Wal-Mart filed criminal charges against Ms. Goodman.

At the criminal trial, Ms. Goodman was acquitted of all charges. Now it was Ms. Goodman's turn: She filed a civil lawsuit against Wal-Mart Stores, Inc., to recover damages for falsely accusing her of stealing the telephone. Ms. Goodman presented her evidence. Wal-Mart asserted the defense that it was within its rights to have detained Ms. Goodman as it did and to have prosecuted Ms. Goodman based on its investigation. Wal-Mart asserted that the merchant protection statute protected its actions in this case.

The jury did not accept Wal-Mart's plea that it had acted reasonably. The jury rejected Wal-Mart's defenses, including the shopkeeper's privilege and its allegations that it had not maliciously prosecuted her. The jury determined that Ms. Goodman should be awarded $200,000 in compensatory damages for her suffering. The jury then decided that Wal-Mart had acted so badly in this case that it tacked on punitive damages to its award to Ms. Goodman just to teach Wal-Mart a lesson.

The Supreme Court of Alabama upheld liability, the award of $200,000 in compensatory damages, and an award of $600,000 in punitive damages. *Wal-Mart Stores, Inc. v. Goodman.* 789 So.2d 166, 2000 Ala. Lexis 548 (Ala.)

Ethics Issues

1. Did Wal-Mart act responsibly in this case? Should it have filed criminal charges against Ms. Goodman?
2. Do you think Wal-Mart presented sufficient evidence to be protected by the merchant protection statutes? ■

Misappropriation of the Right to Publicity

Each person has the exclusive legal right to control and profit from the commercial use of his or her name and personality during his or her lifetime. This is a valuable right, particularly to well-known persons such as sports figures and movie stars. Any attempt by another person to appropriate a living person's name or identity for commercial purposes is actionable. The wrongdoer is liable for the **tort of misappropriation of the right to publicity** (also called the **tort of appropriation**). In such cases, the plaintiff can (1) recover the unauthorized profits made by the offending party and (2) obtain an injunction against further unauthorized use of his or her name or identity. Many states provide that the right to publicity survives a person's death and may be enforced by the deceased's heirs.

tort of misappropriation of the right to publicity
An attempt by another person to appropriate a living person's name or identity for commercial purposes.

Consider This Example Brad Pitt is a famous movie star. If an advertising agency places Brad Pitt's likeness (e.g., photo) on a billboard advertising a product without Brad Pitt's permission, it has engaged in the tort of misappropriation of the right to publicity. Brad Pitt could sue and recover the profits made by the offending party as well as an injunction to prevent unauthorized use of his likeness by the offending party.

Invasion of the Right to Privacy

The law recognizes each person's right to live his or her life without being subjected to unwarranted and undesired publicity. A violation of this right constitutes the tort of **invasion of the right to privacy**. If a fact is public information, there is no claim to privacy. However, a fact that was once public (e.g., commission of a crime) may become private after the passage of time.

Consider These Examples Secretly taking photos of another person with a cell-phone camera in a men's or women's locker room would constitute invasion of the right to privacy. Reading someone else's mail, wiretapping someone's telephone, and reading someone else's e-mail without authorization to do so are also examples of invasion of the right to privacy.

Placing someone in a "false light" constitutes an invasion of privacy. For example, sending an objectionable telegram to a third party and signing another's name would place the purported sender in a false light in the eyes of the receiver. Falsely attributing beliefs or acts to another can also form the basis of a lawsuit.

Defamation of Character

A person's reputation is a valuable asset. Therefore, every person is protected from false statements made by others during his or her lifetime. This protection ends upon a person's death. The tort of **defamation of character** requires a plaintiff to prove that (1) the defendant made an *untrue statement of fact* about the plaintiff and (2) the statement was intentionally or accidentally *published* to a third party. In this context, *publication* simply means that a third person heard or saw the untrue statement. It does not just mean appearance in newspapers, magazines, or books.

defamation of character
False statement(s) made by one person about another. In court, the plaintiff must prove that (1) the defendant made an untrue statement of fact about the plaintiff and (2) the statement was intentionally or accidentally published to a third party.

slander
Oral defamation of character.

libel
A false statement that appears in a letter, newspaper, magazine, book, photograph, movie, video, and so on.

The name for an oral defamatory statement is **slander.** A false statement that appears in a letter, newspaper, magazine, book, photograph, movie, video, and the like is called **libel.** Most courts hold that defamatory statements in radio and television broadcasts are considered libel because of the permanency of the media.

The publication of an untrue statement of fact is not the same as the publication of an opinion. The publication of opinions is usually not actionable. For example, the statement "My lawyer is lousy" is an opinion. Because defamation is defined as an untrue statement of fact, truth is an absolute defense to a charge of defamation.

Public Figures as Plaintiffs In *New York Times Co. v. Sullivan*,[1] the U.S. Supreme Court held that *public officials* cannot recover for defamation unless they can prove that the defendant acted with "actual malice." Actual malice means that the defendant made the false statement knowingly or with reckless disregard of its falsity. This requirement has since been extended to *public figure* plaintiffs such as movie stars, sports personalities, and other celebrities.

Disparagement Business firms rely on their reputation and the quality of their products and services to attract and keep customers. That is why state unfair-competition laws protect businesses from disparaging statements made by competitors or others. A disparaging statement is an untrue statement made by one person or business about the products, services, property, or reputation of another business.

product disparagement
False statements about a competitor's products, services, property, or business reputation.

To prove **disparagement**, which is also called **product disparagement, trade libel**, or **slander of title**, the plaintiff must show that the defendant (1) made an untrue statement about the plaintiff's products, services, property, or business reputation; (2) published that untrue statement to a third party; (3) knew the statement was not true; and (4) made the statement maliciously (i.e., with intent to injure the plaintiff).

Contemporary Trend

Eminem Not Liable for Slander

Eminem is a famous white rapper who has won a Grammy award for his music in the movie *8-Mile* in which he starred. Eminem's lyrics often contain references to his personal experiences. In the song "Brain Damage," a song from his 1999 CD *The Slim Shady LP*, Eminem sang lyrics he had written, which read in part:

> I was harassed daily by this fat kid named DeAngelo Bailey,
> He banged my head against the urinal till he broke my nose.
> Soaked my clothes in blood.
> Grabbed me and choked my throat.

DeAngelo Bailey sued Eminem for $1 million, alleging that the lyrics were untrue and slanderous. Eminem's mother publicly defended her son's account of the bullying by Bailey. After hearing all the evidence, Judge Deborah Servitto wrote:

> Mr. Bailey complains that his rap is trash
> So he's seeking compensation in the form of cash.
> Bailey thinks he's entitled to some money gain
> Because Eminem used his name in vain.
> The lyrics are stories no one would take as fact
> They're an exaggeration of a childish act.
> It is therefore this court's ultimate position
> That Eminem is entitled to summary disposition.

Judge Servitto ruled in favor of Eminem. *Bailey v. Eminem*, 2003 Michigan Trial Court. ■

Intentional Misrepresentation (Fraud)

One of the most pervasive business torts is **intentional misrepresentation.** This tort is also known as **fraud**, or **deceit**. It occurs when a wrongdoer deceives another person out of money, property, or something else of value. A person who has been injured by an intentional misrepresentation can recover damages from the wrongdoer. The elements required to find fraud are:

intentional misrepresentation
Intentionally defrauding another person out of money, property, or something else of value.

1. The wrongdoer made a false representation of material fact.
2. The wrongdoer had knowledge that the representation was false and intended to deceive the innocent party.
3. The innocent party justifiably relied on the misrepresentation.
4. The innocent party was injured.

Item 2, which is called *scienter*, includes situations in which the wrongdoer recklessly disregards the truth in making a representation that is false. Intent or recklessness can be inferred from the circumstances.

He that's cheated twice by the same man, is an accomplice with the Cheater.

Thomas Fuller
Gnomologia (1732)

Intentional Infliction of Emotional Distress

In some situations, a victim may suffer mental or emotional distress without first being physically harmed. The *Restatement (Second) of Torts* provides that a person whose *extreme and outrageous* conduct intentionally or recklessly causes severe emotional distress to another is liable for that emotional distress.[2] This is called the tort of **intentional infliction of emotional distress,** or the **tort of outrage**. The plaintiff must prove that the defendant's conduct was "so outrageous in character and so extreme in degree as to go beyond all possible bounds of decency, and to be regarded as atrocious and utterly intolerable in a civilized society."[3] An indignity, an annoyance, rough language, or an occasional inconsiderate or unkind act does not constitute outrageous behavior. However, repeated annoyances or harassment coupled with threats are considered outrageous.

intentional infliction of emotional distress
A tort that says a person whose extreme and outrageous conduct intentionally or recklessly causes severe emotional distress to another person is liable for that emotional distress. Also known as the *tort of outrage*.

The tort does not require any publication to a third party or physical contact between the plaintiff and defendant. For example, a credit collection agency making harassing telephone calls to a debtor every morning between 1:00 and 5:00 A.M. is outrageous conduct.

The mental distress suffered by the plaintiff must be severe. Many states require that this mental distress be manifested by some form of physical injury, discomfort, or illness, such as nausea, ulcers, headaches, or miscarriage. This requirement is intended to prevent false claims. Some states have abandoned this requirement. The courts have held that shame, humiliation, embarrassment, anger, fear, and worry constitute severe mental distress.

The tort of intentional infliction of emotional distress was asserted in the following case.

Case 6.1 Intentional Infliction of Emotional Distress

Roach v. Stern
675 N.Y.S.2d 133, 1998 N.Y.App. Div. Lexis 7998 Supreme Court, Appellate Division, New York

Background and Facts

Howard Stern is a famous television talk-show host who emceed an irreverent daily show on the radio. The show was syndicated by Infinity Broadcasting, Inc. (Infinity), and was listened to by millions of people across the country. Deborah Roach, a self-described topless dancer and cable-access television host, was a perennial guest on the Howard Stern radio show. She was famous for her stories about encounters with aliens. Roach died of a drug overdose at the age of 27. Roach's sister, Melissa Driscoll, had Roach's body cremated and gave a portion of the remains to Roach's close friend Chaunce Hayden. Driscoll said she did so with the understanding that Hayden would "preserve and honor said remains in an appropriate and private manner."

(continued)

Roach v. Stern

675 N.Y.S.2d 133, 1998 N.Y.App. Div. Lexis 7998 Supreme Court, Appellate Division, New York

(continued)

On July 18, Hayden brought a box containing Roach's cremated remains to Stern's radio show. Hayden said she did so as a memorial to Roach because "the only happiness Debbie had was the Howard Stern show." Thereafter, Stern, Hayden, and other participants in the broadcast played with Roach's ashes and made crude comments about the remains. The radio show was videotaped and later broadcast on a national cable television station. Roach's sister and brother sued Stern, Infinity, and Hayden to recover damages for intentional infliction of emotional distress. The trial dismissed the complaint. The plaintiffs appealed.

Issue

Did the plaintiffs sufficiently plead a cause of action to recover damages for the intentional infliction of emotional distress?

In the Language of the Court

Upon our review of the allegations in the case at bar, we conclude that the Supreme Court erred in determining that the element of outrageous conduct was not satisfied as a matter of law. Although the defendants contend that the conduct at issue was not particularly shocking, in light of Stern's reputation for vulgar humor and Tay's actions during her guest appearances on his program, a jury might reasonably conclude that the manner in which Tay's remains were handled for entertainment purposes and against the express wishes of her family, went beyond the bounds of decent behavior.

Decision and Remedy

The court held that the complaint and the facts of the case as pleaded sufficiently stated a cause of action to recover damages for intentional infliction of emotional distress. The supreme court reversed the judgment of the trial court and reinstated the case against Stern and Infinity.

Business and Ethics Questions

1. Should the tort of intentional infliction of emotional distress be recognized by the law? What difficulties arise in trying to apply this tort?
2. Was Stern's and the other participants' conduct on the radio show tasteless? Did it amount to "outrageous conduct" for which legal damages should be awarded?
3. Will the fact that Stern and Infinity were found liable have a chilling effect on future broadcasts?

Malicious Prosecution

malicious prosecution
A situation in which when a lawsuit is frivolous, the original defendant can sue the original plaintiff. In the second lawsuit, the defendant then becomes the plaintiff and vice versa.

Businesses and individuals often believe they have a reason to sue someone to recover damages or other remedies. If the plaintiff has a legitimate reason to bring the lawsuit and does so, but the plaintiff does not win the lawsuit, he or she does not have to worry about being sued by the person whom he or she sued. But a losing plaintiff does have to worry about being sued by the defendant in a second lawsuit for **malicious prosecution** if certain elements are met. In a lawsuit for malicious prosecution, the original defendant sues the original plaintiff. In this second lawsuit, which is a *civil* action for damages, the original defendant is the plaintiff, and the original plaintiff is the defendant. To succeed in a malicious prosecution lawsuit, the courts require the plaintiff to prove all the following:

- The plaintiff in the original lawsuit (now the defendant) instituted or was responsible for instituting the original lawsuit.
- There was no *probable cause* for the first lawsuit; that is, it was a frivolous lawsuit.
- The plaintiff in the original action brought it with *malice*. (Caution: This is a very difficult element to prove.)
- The original lawsuit was terminated in favor of the original defendant (now the plaintiff).
- The current plaintiff suffered injury as a result of the original lawsuit.

The courts do not look favorably on malicious prosecution lawsuits because they feel such lawsuits inhibit the original plaintiff's incentive to sue.

Intentional Torts Against Property

There are two general categories of property: real property and personal property. *Real property* consists of land and anything permanently attached to that land. *Personal property* consists of things that are movable, such as automobiles, books, clothes, pets, and such. The law recognizes certain torts against real and personal property. These torts are discussed in the paragraphs that follow.

Thoughts much too deep for tears subdue the Court When I assumpsit bring, and godlike waive a tort.

J. L. Adolphus
The Circuiteers (1885)

Trespass to Land

Interference with an owner's right to exclusive possession of land constitutes the tort of **trespass to land.** There does not have to be any interference with the owner's use or enjoyment of the land; the ownership itself is what counts. Thus, unauthorized use of another person's land is trespass even if the owner is not using it. Actual harm to the property is not necessary.

trespass to land
A tort that interferes with an owner's right to exclusive possession of land.

Examples of trespass to land include entering another person's land without permission, remaining on the land of another after permission to do so has expired (e.g., a guest refuses to leave), or causing something or someone to enter another's land (e.g., one person builds a dam that causes another person's land to flood). A person who is pushed onto another's land or enters that land with good reason is not liable for trespass. For example, a person may enter onto another person's land to save a child or a pet from harm.

Trespass to and Conversion of Personal Property

The tort of **trespass to personal property** occurs when one person injures another person's personal property or interferes with that person's enjoyment of his or her personal property. The injured party can sue for damages. For example, breaking another's car window is trespass to personal property.

trespass to personal property
A tort that occurs when one person injures another person's personal property or interferes with that person's enjoyment of his or her personal property.

Depriving a true owner of the use and enjoyment of his or her personal property by taking over such property and exercising ownership rights over it constitutes the tort of **conversion of personal property**. Conversion also occurs when someone who originally is given possession of personal property fails to return it (e.g., fails to return a borrowed car). The rightful owner can sue to recover the property. If the property was lost or destroyed, the owner can sue to recover its value.

Pier, Santa Monica, California. Who would be liable if the rollercoaster broke, causing injury to a rider?

unintentional tort
A doctrine that says a person is liable for harm that is the foreseeable consequence of his or her actions. Also called *negligence*.

Negligence is the omission to do something which a reasonable man would do, or doing something which a prudent and reasonable man would not do.

B. Anderson
Blyth v. Birmingham Waterworks Co. (1856)

Unintentional Torts (Negligence)

Under the doctrine of **unintentional tort,** commonly referred to as **negligence**, a person is liable for harm that is a *foreseeable consequence* of his or her actions. *Negligence* is defined as "the omission to do something which a reasonable man would do, or doing something which a prudent and reasonable man would not do."[4]

To be successful in a negligence lawsuit, the plaintiff must prove that (1) the defendant owed a *duty of care* to the plaintiff, (2) the defendant *breached this duty* of care, (3) the plaintiff suffered *injury*, and (4) the defendant's negligent act *caused* the plaintiff's injury. Each of these elements is discussed in the paragraphs that follow.

Concept Summary *Elements of Negligence*

1. The defendant owed a *duty of care* to the plaintiff.
2. The defendant *breached this duty*.
3. The plaintiff suffered *injury*.
4. The defendant's negligent act was the *actual cause* (or *causation in fact*) of the plaintiff's injuries.
5. The defendant's negligent act was the *proximate cause* (or *legal cause*) of the plaintiff's injuries. The defendant is liable only for the *foreseeable* consequences of his or her negligent act.

Duty of Care

duty of care
The obligation we all owe each other not to cause any unreasonable harm or risk of harm.

To determine whether a defendant is liable for negligence, it must first be ascertained whether the defendant owed a **duty of care** to the plaintiff. *Duty of care* refers to the obligation people owe each other—that is, the duty not to cause any unreasonable harm or risk of harm. For example, each person owes a duty to drive his or her car carefully, not to push or shove on escalators, not leave a skateboard on the sidewalk, and the like. Businesses owe a duty to make safe products, not to cause accidents, and so on.

No court has ever given, nor do we think ever can give, a definition of what constitutes a reasonable or an average man.

Lord Goddard C.J.R v. McCarthy (1954)

The courts decide whether a duty of care is owed in specific cases by applying a *reasonable person standard*. Under this test, the courts attempt to determine how an *objective, careful, and conscientious person would have acted in the same circumstances* and then measure the defendant's conduct against that standard. The defendant's subjective intent ("I did not mean to do it") is immaterial in assessing liability. Certain impairments do not affect the reasonable person standard. For example, there is no reasonable alcoholic standard.

Defendants with a particular expertise or competence are measured against a *reasonable professional standard*. This standard is applied in much the same way as the reasonable person standard. For example, a brain surgeon is measured against a reasonable brain surgeon standard rather than a lower reasonable physician standard. Children are generally required to act as a *reasonable child* of similar age and experience would act.

Ethics in Business

Ouch! The Coffee's Too Hot!

Studies have shown that people care less about how good their coffee tastes than whether it is hot. So restaurants, coffee shops, and other sellers make their coffee hot. McDonald's, however, discovered that it was in hot water for making its coffee too hot. Consider this case.

Stella Liebeck, an 81-year-old resident of Albuquerque, New Mexico, visited a drive-through window of a McDonalds' restaurant with her grandson. Her grandson, the driver of the vehicle, placed the order. When it came, he handed a hot cup of coffee to Liebeck. As her grandson drove away from the drive-through window, Liebeck took the lid off the coffee cup she held in her lap. The coffee spilled all over Liebeck, who suffered third-degree burns on her legs, groin, and buttocks. She required medical treatment, was hospitalized, and suffered permanent scars from the incident.

Liebeck sued McDonald's for selling coffee that was too hot and for failing to warn her of the danger of the hot coffee it served. McDonald's rejected Liebeck's pretrial offer to settle the case for $300,000 and went to trial.

At trial, McDonald's denied that it had been negligent and asserted that Liebeck's own negligence—opening a hot coffee cup on her lap—caused her injuries. The jury heard evidence that McDonald's enforces a quality-control rule requiring its restaurants and franchises to serve coffee at 180 to 190 degrees Fahrenheit. Evidence showed that this was 10 to 30 degrees hotter than coffee served by competing restaurant chains and approximately 40 to 50 degrees hotter than normal home-brewed coffee.

Based on this evidence, the jury concluded that McDonald's had acted recklessly and awarded Liebeck $200,000 compensatory damages (reduced by $40,000 for her own negligence) and $2.7 million punitive damages. After the trial court judge reduced the amount of punitive damages to $480,000, the parties reached an out-of-court settlement for an undisclosed amount. Because of this case, McDonald's and other purveyors of coffee have reduced the temperature at which they sell coffee and have placed warnings on their coffee cups.

Ethics Issues

1. Do you think McDonald's acted recklessly?
2. Was an award of punitive damages warranted? Explain.

Breach of Duty

Once a court finds that the defendant actually owed the plaintiff a duty of care, it must determine whether the defendant breached that duty. A **breach of the duty of care** is a failure to exercise care. In other words, it is a failure to act as a reasonable person would act. A breach of this duty may consist of either an action (e.g., throwing a lit match on the ground in a forest and causing a fire) or a failure to act when there is a duty to act (e.g., a firefighter refusing to put out a fire). Generally, passersby are not expected to rescue others gratuitously to save them from harm.

breach of the duty of care
A failure to exercise care or to act as a reasonable person would act.

Case 6.2 Negligence

Wilhelm v. Flores

133 S.W.3d 726, 2003 Tex.App. Lexis 9335
Court of Appeals of Texas

Background and Facts

Curtis R. Wilhelm owned beehives and kept the hives on property he owned. John Black, who operated a honeybee business, contracted to purchase some beehives from Wilhelm. Black employed Santos Flores, Sr., to help him pick up the beehives from Wilhelm. Black provided Flores with a protective suit to wear while picking up the beehives. Neither Wilhelm nor Black informed Flores of the danger of working with bees. After picking up beehives from Wilhelm's home, Black and Flores drove to remote property owned by Wilhelm to pick up other beehives. Flores opened the veil on his protective suit. After loading one beehive onto the truck, Flores started staggering and yelling for help. Flores sustained several bee stings, suffered an anaphylactic shock reaction, and died before an ambulance could reach him. Flores's wife and children sued Wilhelm and Black for negligence for failing to warn Flores of the dangers of working with beehives and the possibility of dying of anaphylactic shock if stung by a bee. The jury found Wilhelm and Black each 50 percent liable and awarded $1,591,000 to the plaintiffs. Wilhelm appealed.

Issue

Did Wilhelm act negligently by failing to warn Flores of the dangers of working with beehives?

In the Language of the Court

Whether a legal duty exists is a threshold question of law for the court to decide from the facts surrounding the occurrence in question. The plaintiffs' allegations of negligence included failure to provide proper instructions. We examine whether the plaintiffs established a duty to warn of the dangerousness of bees. Foreseeability is the foremost and dominant consideration. There must be sufficient evidence indicating that the defendant knew or should have known that the harm would eventually befall the victim. An expert witness testified that bees are probably the number one cause of insect deaths. Appellant Wilhelm himself testified that he was an expert concerning insects, with a degree in entomology. At the time of this incident, Wilhelm had owned beehives for about five years. Accordingly, we hold that there is sufficient evidence to support the jury's verdict and that such verdict is not manifestly unreasonable or unjust.

Decision and Remedy

The court of appeals held that Wilhelm owed a duty of care to warn Flores of the dangers of working with beehives and was negligent in not doing do. The court of appeals affirmed the award of damages to Flores's estate.

Business and Ethics Questions

1. Should failure to warn be a basis for a negligence lawsuit? Explain.
2. Do you think Wilhelm should have been held liable? Explain.
3. Should businesses carry liability insurance to protect against lawsuit judgments? Explain.

Case 6.3 Negligence

James v. Meow Media, Inc.
300 F.3d 683, 2002 U.S. App. Lexis 16185
United States Court of Appeals, Sixth Circuit

Background and Facts

Michael Carneal was a 14-year-old freshmen student at Heath High School in Paducah, Kentucky. Carneal regularly played violent interactive video and computer games "Doom," "Quake," "Castle Wolfenstein," "Rampage," "Nightmare Creatures," "Mech Warrior," "Resident Evil," and "Final Fantasy." These games involved the player shooting virtual opponents with computer guns and other weapons. Carneal also watched videotaped movies, including one called *The Basketball Diaries*, in which a high-school student protagonist dreams of killing his teacher and several of his fellow classmates. On December 1, 1997, Carneal took a .22 caliber pistol and five shotguns into the lobby of Heath High School and shot several of his fellow students, killing three and wounding many others. The three students killed were Jessica James, Kayce Steger, and Nicole Hadley.

The parents of the three dead children ("James") sued the producers and distributors of the violent video games and movies that Carneal had watched previous to the shooting. The parents sued to recover damages for wrongful death, alleging that the defendants had been negligent in producing and distributing such games and movies to Carneal. The U.S. district court applied Kentucky law and held that the defendants did not owe or breach a duty to the plaintiffs and therefore were not liable for negligence. The plaintiffs appealed.

Issue

Did the defendant video and movie producers and distributors owe a duty of care to the plaintiffs by selling and licensing violent video games and movies to Carneal, who killed the three children?

In the Language of the Court

Kentucky courts have held that the determination of whether a duty of care exists is whether the harm to the plaintiff resulting from the defendant's negligence was "foreseeable." Kentucky courts have struggled with the formless nature of this inquiry. Our inquiry is whether the deaths of James, Steger, and Hadley were the reasonably foreseeable result of the defendants' creation and distribution of their games, movie, and Internet sites.

It appears simply impossible to predict that these games, movie, and Internet sites would incite a young person to violence. We find that it is simply too far a leap from shooting characters on a video screen (an activity undertaken by millions) to shooting people in a classroom (an activity undertaken by a handful, at most) for Carneal's actions to have been reasonably foreseeable to the manufacturers of the media that Carneal played and viewed. Carneal's reaction was not a normal reaction. Indeed, Carneal is not a normal person. Individuals are generally entitled to assume that third parties will not commit intentional criminal acts.

Decision and Remedy

The Court of Appeals held that the defendant video game and movie producers and distributors did not owe a duty of care to the plaintiffs by selling and licensing violent video games and movies to Carneal, who murdered the three children.

Business and Ethics Questions

1. How does the court define *foreseeability*? Did the court use a narrow, middle, or broad interpretation of foreseeability in deciding this case? Explain.
2. Do producers and distributors of video games and movies owe a duty of care to society not to produce and distribute violent games and movies?
3. What would have been the consequences for the video game and movie industries if the court had held in favor of the plaintiffs? Explain.

In the first case, the court found the defendants liable for negligence. In the second case, the court held that the defendants were not liable for negligence.

Injury to Plaintiff

injury
Personal injury or damage that the plaintiff must suffer to his or her property to recover monetary damages for the defendant's negligence.

Even though a defendant's act may have breached a duty of care owed to the plaintiff, this breach is not actionable unless the plaintiff suffers **injury.** For example, say a business's negligence causes an explosion and fire to occur at its factory at night. No one is injured, and there is no damage to the neighbors' property. The negligence is not actionable.

The damages recoverable depend on the effect of the injury on the plaintiff's life or profession. Suppose two men injure their hands when a train door malfunctions. The first man is a professional basketball player. The second is a college professor. The first man can recover greater damages than the second.

Actual Cause

The defendant's negligent act must be the **causation in fact**, or **actual cause,** of the plaintiff's injuries. For example, suppose a corporation negligently pollutes the plaintiff's drinking water. The plaintiff dies of a heart attack unrelated to the polluted water. Although the corporation has acted negligently, it is not liable for the plaintiff's death. There were a negligent act and an injury, but there was no cause-and-effect relationship between them. If, instead, the plaintiff had died from the pollution, there would have been causation in fact, and the polluting corporation would have been liable. If two (or more) persons are liable for negligently causing the plaintiff's injuries, both (or all) can be held liable to the plaintiff if each of their acts is a substantial factor in causing the plaintiff's injuries.

actual cause
The actual cause of negligence. A person who commits a negligent act is not liable unless causation in fact can be proven. Also called *causation in fact*.

Proximate Cause

Under the law, a negligent party is not necessarily liable for all damages set in motion by his or her negligent act. Based on public policy, the law establishes a point along the damage chain after which the negligent party is no longer responsible for the consequences of his or her actions. This limitation on liability is referred to as **proximate cause,** or **legal cause**. The general test or proximate cause is *foreseeability*. A negligent party who is found to be the actual cause—but not the proximate cause—of the plaintiff's injuries is not liable to the plaintiff. Situations are examined on a case-by-case basis.

The classical articulation of the doctrine of proximate cause appears in the famous *Palsgraf* case that follows.

proximate cause
A point along a chain of events caused by a negligent party after which that party is no longer legally responsible for the consequences of his or her actions. Also called *legal cause*.

Landmark Law

Palsgraf v. The Long Island Railroad Company

The landmark case establishing the doctrine of proximate cause is *Palsgraf v. The Long Island Railroad Company*, a New York case decided in 1921. Helen Palsgraf was standing on the platform, waiting for a passenger train. The Long Island Railroad Company owned and operated the trains and employed the station guards. As a man carrying a package wrapped in a newspaper tried to board the moving train, railroad guards tried to help him. In doing so, the package was dislodged from the man's arm, fell to the railroad tracks, and exploded. The package contained hidden fireworks. The explosion shook the railroad platform, causing a scale located on the platform to fall on Helen Palsgraf, injuring her. She sued the railroad for negligence. Justice Cardoza eloquently addressed the issue of proximate cause:

> The conduct of the defendant's guard, if a wrong in its relation to the holder of the package, was not a wrong in its relation to the plaintiff, standing far away. Relatively to her it was not negligence at all. Nothing in the situation gave notice that the falling package had in it the potency of peril to persons thus removed. Negligence is not actionable unless it involves the invasion of a legally protected interest, the violation of a right. Proof of negligence in the air, so to speak, will not do. In every instance, before negligence can be predicated of a given act, back of the act must be sought and found a duty to the individual complaining, the observance of which would have averted or avoided the injury.
>
> The argument for the plaintiff is built upon the shifting meanings of such words as "wrong" and "wrongful," and shares their instability. What the plaintiff must show is "a wrong" to herself, i.e., a violation of her own right, and not merely a wrong to some one else, nor conduct "wrongful" because unsocial. The risk reasonably to be perceived defines the duty to be obeyed, and risk imports relation; it is risk to another or to others within the range of apprehension. Here, by concession, there was nothing in the situation to suggest to the most cautious mind that the parcel wrapped in newspaper would spread wreckage through the station. If the guard had thrown it down knowingly and willfully, he would not have threatened the plaintiff's safety, so far as appearances could warn him. His conduct would not have involved, even then, an unreasonable probability of invasion of her bodily security. Liability can be no greater where the act is inadvertent.

(continued)

Landmark Law
(continued)

Negligence, like risk, is thus a term of relation. Negligence in the abstract, apart from things related, is surely not a tort, if indeed it is understandable at all. One who seeks redress at law does not make out a cause of action by showing without more that there has been damage to his person. If the harm was not willful, he must show that the act as to him had possibilities of danger so many and apparent as to entitle him to be protected against the doing of it though the harm was unintended.

Justice Cardoza denied Palsgraf's recovery, finding that the railroad was not the proximate cause of her injuries. *Palsgraf v. The Long Island Railroad Company,* 248 N.Y. 339, 162 N.E. 99, 1928 N.Y. Lexis 1269 (N.Y.) ■

Special Negligence Doctrines

The courts have developed many *special negligence doctrines*. The most important of them are discussed in the paragraphs that follow.

Professional Malpractice

professional malpractice
The liability of a professional who breaches his or her duty of ordinary care.

Professionals, such as doctors, lawyers, architects, accountants, and others, owe a duty of ordinary care in providing their services. This duty is known as the *reasonable professional standard.* A professional who breaches this duty of care is liable for any injury his or her negligence causes. This liability is commonly referred to as **professional malpractice.** For example, a doctor who amputates a wrong leg is liable for *medical malpractice.* A lawyer who fails to file a document with the court on time, causing the client's case to be dismissed, is liable for *legal malpractice.* An accountant who fails to use reasonable care, knowledge, skill, and judgment when providing auditing and other accounting services to a client is liable for *accounting malpractice.*

Professionals who breach this duty are liable to their patients or clients. They may also be liable to some third parties.

Negligent Infliction of Emotional Distress

negligent infliction of emotional distress
A tort that permits a person to recover for emotional distress caused by the defendant's negligent conduct.

Some jurisdictions have extended the tort of emotional distress to include the **negligent infliction of emotional distress.** The most common examples of this involve bystanders who witness the injury or death of a loved one that is caused by another's negligent conduct. Under this tort, the bystander, even though not personally physically injured, can sue the negligent party for his or her own mental suffering.

Generally, to be successful in this type of case, the plaintiff must prove that (1) a relative was killed or injured by the defendant, (2) the plaintiff suffered severe emotional distress, and (3) the plaintiff's mental distress resulted from a sensory and contemporaneous observance of the accident. Some states require that the plaintiff's mental distress be manifested by some physical injury; other states have eliminated this requirement.

Consider This Example A father is driving his young daughter to school in his automobile when another driver negligently runs a red light and hits their automobile. Suppose that the young daughter dies from her injuries, and the father is uninjured. The father suffers severe emotional distress because of the loss of his daughter and manifests this distress by suffering physically. In this case, the father can sue the driver for negligence (1) to recover for his daughter's death and (2) for negligent infliction of emotional distress to recover damages for the severe distress he suffers.

Negligence per Se

Statutes often establish duties owed by one person to another. The violation of a statute that proximately causes an injury is **negligence per se.** The plaintiff in such an action must prove that (1) a statute existed, (2) the statute was enacted to prevent the type of injury suffered, and (3) the plaintiff was within a class of persons meant to be protected by the statute.

negligence per se
A tort in which the violation of a statute or an ordinance constitutes the breach of the duty of care.

Consider This Example Most cities have ordinances that place the responsibility for fixing public sidewalks in residential areas on the homeowners whose homes front the sidewalks. A homeowners is liable if he or she fails to repair a damaged sidewalk in front of his or her home and a pedestrian trips and is injured because of the damage. The injured party does not have to prove that the homeowner owed the duty because the statute establishes that.

Res Ipsa Loquitur

If a defendant is in control of a situation in which a plaintiff has been injured and has superior knowledge of the circumstances surrounding the injury, the plaintiff might have difficulty proving the defendant's negligence. In such a situation, the law applies the doctrine of **res ipsa loquitur** (Latin for "the thing speaks for itself"). This doctrine raises a presumption of negligence and switches the burden to the defendant to prove that he or she was not negligent. *Res ipsa loquitur* applies in cases in which the following elements are met:

1. The defendant had exclusive control of the instrumentality or situation that caused the plaintiff's injury.
2. The injury would not have ordinarily occurred but for someone's negligence.

res ipsa loquitur
A tort in which the presumption of negligence arises because (1) the defendant was in exclusive control of the situation and (2) the plaintiff would not have suffered injury but for someone's negligence. The burden switches to the defendant(s) to prove that they were not negligent.

Consider These Examples Haeran goes in for major surgery and is given anesthesia to put her to sleep during the operation. Sometime after the operation, it is discovered that a surgical instrument was left in Haeran during the operation. She suffers severe injury because of the left-in instrument. Haeran would be hard-pressed to identify which doctor or nurse had been careless and left the instrument in her body. In this case, the court can apply the doctrine of *res ipsa loquitur* and place the presumption of negligence on the defendants. Any defendant who can prove that he or she did not leave the instrument in Haeran escapes liability; any defendant who does not disprove his or her negligence is liable. Other typical *res ipsa loquitur* cases involve commercial airplane crashes, falling elevators, and the like.

Good Samaritan Laws

Good Samaritan law
A statute that relieves medical professionals from liability for negligence when they stop and render aid to victims in emergency situations.

In the past, liability exposure made many doctors, nurses, and other medical professionals reluctant to stop and render aid to victims in emergency situations, such as highway accidents. Almost all states have enacted **Good Samaritan laws** that relieve medical professionals from liability for injury caused by their ordinary negligence in such circumstances. Good Samaritan laws protect medical professionals only from liability for their *ordinary negligence*, not for injuries caused by their gross negligence or reckless or intentional conduct. Most Good Samaritan laws protect licensed doctors and nurses and laypersons who have been certified in CPR. Laypersons not trained in CPR are not generally protected by Good Samaritan statutes—that is, they are liable for injuries caused by their ordinary negligence in rendering aid.

Every unjust decision is a reproach to the law or the judge who administers it. If the law should be in danger of doing injustice, then equity should be called in to remedy it. Equity was introduced to mitigate the rigour of the law.

Lord Denning
M. R. Re Vandervell's Trusts (1974)

Consider This Example Sam is injured in an automobile accident and is unconscious in his automobile alongside the road. Doctor Pamela Heathcoat, who is driving by the scene of the accident, stops, pulls Sam from the burning wreckage, and administers first aid. In doing so, Pamela negligently breaks Sam's shoulder. If Pamela's negligence is ordinary negligence, she is not liable to Sam because the Good Samaritan law protects her from liability; if Pamela was grossly negligent or reckless in administering aid to Sam, she is liable to him for the injuries she caused. It is a question of fact for the jury to decide whether a doctor's conduct was ordinary negligence or gross negligence or recklessness. If Cathy, a layperson not trained in CPR, had rendered aid to Sam and caused Sam injury because of her ordinary negligence, the Good Samaritan law would not protect her, and she would be liable to Sam.

Dram Shop Acts

dram shop act
A statute that makes taverns and bartenders liable for injuries caused to or by patrons who are served too much alcohol.

Many states have enacted **dram shop acts** that make a tavern and bartender civilly liable for injuries caused to or by patrons who are served too much alcohol. The alcohol must be either served in sufficient quantity to make the patron intoxicated or served to an already intoxicated person. Both the tavern and the bartender are liable to third persons injured by the patron and for injuries suffered by the patron. They are also liable for injuries caused by or to minors served by the tavern, regardless of whether the minors are intoxicated.

Guest Statutes

guest statute
A statute that provides that if a driver of a vehicle voluntarily and without compensation gives a ride to another person, the driver is not liable to the passenger for injuries caused by the driver's ordinary negligence.

Many states have enacted **guest statutes,** which provide that if a driver voluntarily and without compensation gives a ride in a vehicle to another person (e.g., a hitchhiker), the driver is not liable to the passenger for injuries caused by the driver's ordinary negligence. However, if the passenger pays compensation to the driver, the driver owes a duty of ordinary care to the passenger and will be held liable. The driver is always liable to the passenger for wanton and gross negligence—for example, injuries caused because of excessive speed.

Fireman's Rule

Under the **fireman's rule**, a firefighter who is injured while putting out a fire may not sue the party whose negligence caused the fire. This rule has been extended to police officers and other government workers. The bases for this rule are (1) people might not call for help if they could be held liable; (2) firefighters, police officers, and other such workers receive special training for their jobs; and (3) these workers have special medical and retirement programs that are paid for by the public.

"Danger Invites Rescue" Doctrine

The law recognizes a **"danger invites rescue" doctrine**. Under this doctrine, a rescuer who is injured while going to someone's rescue can sue the person who caused the dangerous situation. For example, a passerby who is injured while trying to rescue children from a fire set by an arsonist can bring a civil suit against the arsonist.

Social Host Liability

Several states have adopted the **social host liability** rule. This rule provides that a social host is liable for injuries caused by guests who are served alcohol at a social function (e.g., birthday party, wedding reception) and later cause injury because they are intoxicated. The injury may be to a third person or to the guest himself or herself. The alcohol served at the social function must be the cause of the injury. A few states have adopted statutes that relieve social hosts from such liability.[5]

social host liability
A rule that provides that social hosts are liable for injuries caused by guests who become intoxicated at a social function. States vary as to whether they have this rule in effect.

Liability of Landowners

Owners and renters of real property owe certain duties to protect visitors from injury while on the property. A landowner's and tenant's liability generally depends on the status of the visitor. Visitors fall into the following categories:

1. ***Invitees and licensees.*** An *invitee* is a person who has been expressly or impliedly invited onto the owner's premises for the *mutual benefit* of both parties (e.g., guests invited for dinner, the mail carrier, customers of a business). A licensee is a person who, *for his or her own benefit*, enters onto the premises with the express or implied consent of the owner (e.g., an Avon representative, salespersons, Jehovah's Witnesses). An owner owes a **duty of ordinary care** to invitees and licensees. An owner is liable if he or she negligently causes injury to an invitee or a licensee. For example, a homeowner is liable if she leaves a garden hose across the walkway on which an invitee or a licensee trips and is injured.
2. ***Trespassers.*** A *trespasser* is a person who has no invitation, permission, or right to be on another's property. Burglars are a common type of trespasser. Generally, an owner does not owe a duty of ordinary care to a trespasser. For example, if a trespasser trips and injures himself on a bicycle the owner negligently left out, the owner is not liable. An owner does owe a **duty not to willfully or wantonly injure a trespasser.** Thus, an owner cannot set traps to injure trespassers.

duty or ordinary care
The duty an owner owes an invitee or a licensee to prevent injury or harm when the invitee or licensee steps on the owner's premises.

duty not to willfully or wantonly injure
The duty an owner owes a trespasser to prevent intentional injury or harm to the trespasser when the trespasser is on his or her premises.

A few states have eliminated the invitee-licensee-trespasser distinction. These states hold that owners and renters owe a duty of ordinary care to all persons who enter upon the property.

Liability of Common Carriers and Innkeepers

The common law holds common carriers and innkeepers to a higher standard of care than it does most other businesses. Common carriers and innkeepers owe a **duty of utmost care**—rather than a duty of ordinary care—to their passengers and guests. For example, innkeepers must provide security for their guests. The concept of utmost care is applied on a case-by-case basis. Obviously, a large hotel must provide greater security to guests than a "mom-and-pop" motel. Some states and cities have adopted specific statutes and ordinances relating to this duty.

duty of utmost care
A duty of care that goes beyond ordinary care that says common carriers and innkeepers have a responsibility to provide security to their passengers or guests.

In the following case, the court found that a landowner had engaged in *willful and wanton conduct*, and it awarded punitive damages.

Case 6.4
Innkeepers' Liability

Matthias v. Accor Economy Lodging, Inc. and Motel 6 Operating L.P.

347 F.3d 672, 2003 U.S.App. Lexis 21299 United States Court of Appeals, Seventh Circuit

Background and Facts

The defendants, Accor Economy Lodging, Inc., and Motel 6 Operating L.P. (hereinafter referred to as Motel 6) operate the Motel 6 nationwide chain of motels and hotels. One of these hotels is in downtown Chicago. In 1998, EcoLab, an extermination service that the motel used, discovered bedbugs in several rooms in the motel and recommended that it be hired to spray every room, for which EcoLab would charge the motel $500 total, but the motel refused. The next year, bedbugs were again discovered in a room, but EcoLab was hired to spray just that room. By the spring of 2000, the motel had given refunds to several guests bitten by bedbugs in their rooms. The motel manager looked at several rooms and found bedbugs. Further incidents of guests being bitten by bedbugs led the motel's manager to recommend that the motel be closed while every room was sprayed, but Motel 6 refused. The infestation continued, and several of the rooms were placed on "Do not rent, bugs in room" status.

In November 2000, Burl Matthias and Desiree Matthias, brother and sister, checked in to the Motel 6 in downtown Chicago. They were given Room 514, even though it was on the "Do not rent, bugs in room" list. That night, 190 of the motel's 191 rooms were rented. That night, the Matthiases were severely bitten by bedbugs. The Matthiases sued Motel 6 to recover damages, alleging that it had engaged in willful and wanton conduct. The jury agreed and awarded each plaintiff $5,000 in compensatory damages and $186,000 in punitive damages. Motel 6 appealed.

Issue

Was Motel 6 liable for willful and wanton conduct that supported the award of punitive damages of $186,000 to each plaintiff?

In the Language of the Court

Although bedbug bites are not as serious as the bites of some other insects, they are painful and unsightly. Motel 6 could not have rented any rooms at the prices it charged had it informed guests that the risk of being bitten by bedbugs was appreciable. Its failure to warn guests or to take effective measures to eliminate the bedbugs amounted to fraud and probably to battery as well. There was, in short, sufficient evidence of "willful and wanton conduct" to permit an award of punitive damages in this case.

But what amount? The term "punitive damages" implies punishment, and a standard principle of penal theory is that "the punishment should fit the crime." All things considered, we cannot say that the award of punitive damages was excessive, albeit the precise number chosen by the jury was arbitrary. It is probably not a coincidence that $5,000 + $186,000 = $191,000/191 = $1,000: i.e., $1,000 per room in the motel.

Decision and Remedy

The Court of Appeals held that Motel 6's willful and wanton conduct warranted the trial court's award of $186,000 in punitive damages to each defendant. The Court of Appeals affirmed the judgment of the district court.

Business and Ethics Questions

1. Define *punitive damages*. Why are they awarded?
2. Did Motel 6 act ethically in this case? Explain.
3. Does the possibility of an award of punitive damages make businesses act more responsibly?

Defenses Against Negligence

A defendant in a negligence lawsuit may raise several defenses to the imposition of liability. These defenses are discussed in the following paragraphs.

Superseding, or Intervening, Event

superseding event
An intervening event that causes injuries. A defendant is not liable for injuries caused by such events for which he or she is not responsible.

Under negligence, a person is liable only for foreseeable events. Therefore, an original negligent party can raise a **superseding, or intervening, event** as a defense to liability. For example, assume that an avid golfer negligently hits a spectator with a golf ball, knocking the spectator unconscious. While lying on the ground waiting for an ambulance to come, the spectator is struck by a bolt of lightning and killed. The golfer is liable for the injuries caused by the golf ball. He is not liable for the death of the spectator, however, because the lightning bolt was an unforeseen intervening event.

Assumption of the Risk

If a plaintiff knows of and voluntarily enters into or participates in a risky activity that results in injury, the law recognizes that the plaintiff assumed, or took on, the risk involved. Thus, the defendant can raise the defense of **assumption of the risk** against the plaintiff. This defense assumes that the plaintiff (1) had knowledge of the specific risk and (2) voluntarily assumed that risk. For example, under this theory, a race-car driver assumes the risk of being injured or killed in a crash.

In the following case, the court had to decide whether the plaintiff had assumed the risk.

assumption of the risk
A defense a defendant can use against a plaintiff who knowingly and voluntarily enters into or participates in a risky activity that results in injury.

Lilya v. The Greater Gulf State Fair, Inc.

855 So.2d 1049, 2003 Ala. Lexis 57 Supreme Court of Alabama

Case 6.5

Assumption of the Risk

Background and Facts

The Greater Gulf State Fair, Inc., operated the Gulf State Fair in Mobile County, Alabama. One of the events at the fair was a mechanical bull ride for which participants paid money to ride the mechanical bull. A mechanical bull is a ride in which the rider sits on a motorized device shaped like a real bull, and the ride simulates a real bull ride as the mechanical bull turns, twists, and bucks. The challenge is to stay on the bull and not be thrown off the bull. A large banner above the ride read "Rolling Thunder."

John Lilya and a friend watched as a rider was thrown from the mechanical bull. Lilya also watched as his friend paid and rode the bull but was also thrown off. Lilya then paid the $5 admission charge and signed a release agreement that stated: "I acknowledge that riding a mechanical bull entails known and unanticipated risks which could result in physical or emotional injury, paralysis, death, or damage to my self, to property, or to third parties. I expressly agree and promise to accept and assume all of the risks existing in this activity. My participation in this activity is purely voluntary, and I elect to participate in spite of the risks."

Lilya boarded the mechanical bull and was immediately thrown off onto a soft pad underneath the bull. Lilya reboarded the bull for a second ride. The bull ride began again and became progressively faster, spinning and bucking to the left and right until Lilya fell off the bull. On the fall, Lilya landed on his head and shoulders, and he suffered a fractured neck. Lilya sued Gulf State Fair to recover damages for his severe injuries. The trial court granted summary judgment to Gulf State Fair, finding that Lilya had voluntarily assumed an open and obvious danger. Lilya appealed.

Issue

Was riding a mechanical bull an open and obvious danger for which Lilya had voluntarily assumed the risk when he rode the mechanical bull?

In the Language of the Court

As the landowner, Gulf State Fair would owe Lilya, its invitee, the duty to use reasonable care. The owner of the premises has no duty to warn an invitee of open and obvious defects in the premises which the invitee is aware of or should be aware of in the exercise of reasonable care. Here, the only evidence of danger stemming from the mechanical bull ride is the most open and obvious characteristic of the ride: the possibility of falling off the mechanical bull. Lilya was aware that the two riders who had ridden the mechanical bull immediately before he rode it had fallen off. He noticed the thick floor mat, and he knew that the mat was there to protect riders when they fell. Also, he signed a release explicitly stating that riding the mechanical bull involved inherent risks and that the risks included falling off or being thrown from the bull which could result in head, neck, and back injuries. Additionally, the very name of the ride—"Rolling Thunder"—hanging on a banner above the ride, gives a somewhat graphic indication of what is the very nature of bull riding: an extremely turbulent ride the challenge of which is to hang on and not fall off. The entertainment value—and, indeed, the concept—of bull riding becomes meaningless without the inherent possibility of falling off. "Violenti non fit injuria" (a person who knowingly and voluntarily risks danger cannot recover for any resulting injury).

Decision and Remedy

The supreme court of Alabama held that riding a mechanical bull and being thrown and injured by the bull is an open and obvious danger and that Lilya had voluntarily assumed the risk when he rode the bull and was thrown and injured. The supreme court affirmed the trial court's grant of summary judgment in favor of Gulf State Fair.

Business and Ethics Questions

1. Do you think the doctrine of assumption of the risk should be recognized by the law? Explain.
2. Did Gulf State Fair act ethically by making money from such a dangerous activity as mechanical bull riding?
3. Give several examples of sports or other activities that rely on the doctrine of assumption of the risk.

Contributory Negligence

contributory negligence
A doctrine that says a plaintiff who is partially at fault for his or her own injury cannot recover against the negligent defendant.

Sometimes a plaintiff is partially liable for causing his or her own injuries. Under the common law doctrine of **contributory negligence,** a plaintiff who is partially at fault for his or her own injury cannot recover against the negligent defendant. Many states follow this rule.

Consider This Example Suppose a driver who is driving over the speed limit negligently hits and injures a pedestrian who is jaywalking. Suppose the jury finds that the driver is 80 percent responsible for the accident and the jaywalker is 20 percent responsible. The pedestrian suffered $100,000 in injuries. Under the doctrine of contributory negligence, the pedestrian cannot recover any damages from the driver.

Last Clear Chance Rule There is one major exception to the doctrine of contributory negligence: The defendant has a duty under the law to avoid the accident if at all possible. This rule is known as the **last clear chance rule**. For example, a driver who sees a pedestrian walking across the street against a "Don't Walk" sign must avoid hitting him or her if possible. When deciding cases involving this rule, the courts consider the attentiveness of the parties and the amount of time each had to respond to the situation.

Comparative Negligence

comparative negligence
A doctrine under which damages are apportioned according to fault.

The application of the doctrine of contributory negligence could reach an unfair result where a party only slightly at fault for his or her injuries could not recover from an otherwise negligent defendant. Many states have replaced the doctrine of contributory negligence with the doctrine of **comparative negligence.** Under this doctrine, damages are apportioned according to fault.

When the comparative negligence rule is applied to the previous example, the result is much fairer. The plaintiff-pedestrian who was 20 percent at fault for causing his own injuries can recover 80 percent of his damages (or $80,000) from the defendant-driver. This is an example of *pure comparative negligence*.

Several states have adopted *partial comparative negligence*, which provides that a plaintiff must be less than 50 percent responsible for causing his or her own injuries to recover under comparative negligence; otherwise, contributory negligence applies.

Strict Liability

strict liability
Liability without fault.

Strict liability, another category of torts, is *liability without fault*. That is, a participant in a covered activity will be held liable for any injuries caused by the activity, even if he or she was not negligent. This doctrine holds that (1) there are certain activities that can place the public at risk of injury even if reasonable care is taken, and (2) the public should have some means of compensation if such injury occurs.

Strict liability was first imposed for *abnormally dangerous activities*, such as crop dusting, blasting, fumigation, burning of fields, storage of explosives, and the keeping of wild animals as pets.

In the following case, the court imposed strict liability.

Case 6.6
Strict Liability

Cook v. Whitsell-Sherman

796 N.E.2d 271, 2003 Ind. Lexis 793 Supreme Court of Indiana

Background and Facts

Tamara Cook owned a 100-pound Rottweiler dog named Maggie. Maggie had never demonstrated any aggressive or violent tendencies. Cook went out of town and left Maggie in the care of Marva and Joseph Hart. When Kenneth Whitsell-Sherman was delivering mail as a letter carrier for the U.S. Postal Services to the Harts' home, the Harts were on the sidewalk outside their yard, and their eight-year-old daughter was several feet away, holding Maggie on a leash. Maggie broke free and bit Whitsell-Sherman on the left hand, causing injuries. Whitsell-Sherman sued Cook to recover damages, based on an Indiana statute that made dog owners strictly liable for pets who injured postal carriers. The trial court found Cook strictly liable and awarded Whitsell-Sherman $87,000 in damages. The court of appeals reversed, and Whitsell-Sherman appealed.

Issue

Is the owner of a dog strictly liable for injuries caused by the dog biting a postal carrier?

In the Language of the Court

At the time Maggie bit Whitsell-Sherman, Cook was Maggie's owner but not her custodian. Cook argues that the statute does not apply to her in this situation because at the time of the incident she was not in possession of the dog. Indiana law was intended to alter the common law negligence framework if the victim is a letter carrier. In this case, the statute reflects a policy choice that the dog's owner and keeper should bear the loss rather than the injured public employee. Accordingly, Cook is subject to strict liability for Maggie's biting Whitsell-Sherman.

Decision and Remedy

The Indiana supreme court held that Indiana law made a dog owner strictly liable to mail carriers for injuries caused by their dog biting a mail carrier and upheld the liability of Maggie's owner. The supreme court held that the damages were incorrectly calculated by the trial court and remanded the case for a proper determination of damages.

Business and Ethics Questions

1. Describe the doctrine of strict liability. How does it differ from the doctrine of negligence? Explain.
2. Did Cook act ethically by trying to avoid liability in this case?
3. Does household liability insurance cover injuries caused by the homeowner's pet?

Nepal. Each country has developed its own liability laws. Individuals conducting business in foreign countries must be aware of the liability laws of those countries.

Terms and Concepts

Intentional Torts Against Persons

1. ***Assault.*** Assault is the threat of immediate harm or offensive contact, or any action that arouses reasonable apprehension of imminent harm.
2. ***Battery.*** Battery is unauthorized and harmful or offensive physical contact with another person.
   a. *Transferred intent doctrine.* If a person intends to injure one person but actually harms another person, the law transfers the perpetrator's intent from the target to the actual victim.
3. ***False imprisonment.*** False imprisonment is intentional confinement or restraint of another person without authority or justification and without that person's consent.
   a. *Merchant protection statutes.* Merchant protection statutes permit businesses to stop, detain, and investigate suspected shoplifters (and not be held liable for false imprisonment) if the following requirements are met:
      i. There are reasonable grounds for the suspicion.
      ii. Suspects are detained for only a reasonable time.
      iii. Investigations are conducted in a reasonable manner.
4. ***Defamation of character.*** Defamation of character occurs when the defendant makes an untrue statement of fact about the plaintiff that is published to a third party. Truth is an absolute defense.
   a. There are two types of defamation:
      i. *Slander.* Slander is oral defamation.
      ii. *Libel.* Libel is written defamation.
   b. *Public figure plaintiffs.* With public figure plaintiffs, the additional element of *malice* must be proven.
5. ***Misappropriation of the right to publicity.*** This tort involves appropriating another person's name or identity for commercial purposes without that person's consent. Also called the tort of appropriation.
6. ***Invasion of privacy.*** This tort involves unwarranted and undesired publicity of a private fact about a person. The fact does not have to be untrue. Truth is not a defense.
7. ***Intentional infliction of emotional distress.*** This tort involves extreme and outrageous conduct intentionally or recklessly done that causes severe emotional distress. Some states require that the mental distress be manifested by physical injury. Also known as the *tort of outrage.*
8. ***Malicious prosecution.*** A successful defendant in a prior lawsuit can sue the plaintiff if the first lawsuit was frivolous.

Intentional Torts Against Property

1. ***Trespass to land.*** This tort involves interference with a landowner's right to exclusive possession of his or her land.
2. ***Trespass to personal property.*** This tort involves a person injuring another person's personal property or interfering with that person's enjoyment of his or her property.
3. ***Conversion of personal property.*** Taking over another person's personal property and depriving him or her of the use and enjoyment of the property is called conversion of personal property.

Negligence

The omission to do something which a reasonable man would do, or doing something which a prudent and reasonable man would not do."

Elements of Negligence

To establish negligence, the plaintiff must prove:

1. The defendant owed a *duty of care* to plaintiff.

2. The defendant *breached this duty*.
3. The plaintiff suffered *injury*.
4. The defendant's negligent act *caused* the plaintiff's injury. Two types of causation must be shown:
   a. *Causation in fact (or actual cause).* The defendant's negligent act was the actual cause of the plaintiff's injury.
   b. *Proximate cause (or legal cause).* The defendant is liable only for the *foreseeable* consequences of his or her negligent act.

Professional Malpractice

Doctors, lawyers, architects, accountants, and other professionals owe a duty of ordinary care in providing their services. They are judged by a *reasonable professional standard*. Professionals who breach this duty are liable to clients and some third parties for *professional malpractice*.

Special Negligence Doctrines

1. ***Negligent infliction of emotional distress.*** A person who witnesses a close relative's injury or death may sue the negligent party who caused the accident to recover damages for any emotional distress suffered by the bystander. To recover for *negligent infliction of emotional distress*, the plaintiff must prove:
   a. A relative was killed or injured by the defendant.
   b. The plaintiff suffered severe emotional distress.
   c. The plaintiff's mental distress resulted from a sensory and contemporaneous observance of the accident. Some states require that the mental distress be manifested by physical injury.
2. ***Negligence per se.*** A statute or an ordinance establishes the duty of care. A violation of the statute or ordinance constitutes a breach of this duty of care.
3. ***Res ipsa loquitur.*** A presumption of negligence is established if the defendant had exclusive control of the instrumentality or situation that caused the plaintiff's injury and the injury would not have ordinarily occurred but for someone's negligence. The defendants may rebut this presumption.
4. ***Good Samaritan laws.*** These laws relieve doctors and other medical professionals from liability for ordinary negligence when rendering medical aid in emergency situations.
5. ***Dram shop acts.*** These state statutes make taverns and bartenders liable for injuries caused to or by patrons who are served too much alcohol and cause injury to themselves or others.
6. ***Guest statutes.*** These statutes provide that a driver of a vehicle is not liable for ordinary negligence to passengers he or she gratuitously transports. The driver is liable for gross negligence.
7. ***Fireman's rule.*** Firefighters, police officers, and other government employees who are injured in the performance of their duties cannot sue the person who negligently caused the dangerous situation that caused the injury.
8. ***"Danger invites rescue" doctrine.*** A person who is injured while going to someone's rescue may sue the person who caused the dangerous situation.
9. ***Social host liability.*** Some states make social hosts liable for injuries caused by guests who are served alcohol at a social function and later cause injury because they are intoxicated.
10. ***Liability of Landowners.*** Landowners (and tenants) owe the following duties to persons who come upon their property:
    a. *Invitees.* Landowners owe a duty of ordinary care to invitees.
    b. *Licensees.* Landowners owe a duty of ordinary care to licensees.
    c. *Trespassers.* Landowners owe a duty not to willfully and wantonly injure trespassers.
11. ***Liability of common carriers and innkeepers.*** Common carriers and innkeepers owe a *duty of utmost care*, rather than the duty of ordinary care, to protect their passengers and patrons from injury.

Defenses Against Negligence

1. ***Superseding event.*** A superseding event is an intervening event caused that caused the plaintiff's injuries; it relieves the defendant from liability.

2. ***Assumption of the risk.*** A defendant is not liable for the plaintiff's injuries if the plaintiff had knowledge of a specific risk and voluntarily assumed that risk.
3. ***Plaintiff partially at fault.*** States have adopted one of the following two rules that affect a defendant's liability if the plaintiff was partially at fault for causing his or her own injuries:
   a. *Contributory negligence.* A plaintiff cannot recover anything from the defendant under contributory negligence.
   b. *Comparative negligence.* Damages are apportioned according to the parties' fault under comparative negligence.

Business Torts

1. ***Entering business without a license.*** The law requires that persons obtain a license from the government prior to entering certain businesses or professions.
2. ***Palming off.*** A company that passes off its products or services as those of another company is said to be palming off.
3. ***Disparagement.*** Disparagement is an untrue statement about the products, services, property, or reputation of a business. Also called *product disparagement, trade libel*, or *slander of title*.
4. ***False advertising.*** Section 43(a) of the Lanham Act, a federal law, prohibits false and misleading advertising. State laws also prohibit false and misleading advertising.
5. ***Intentional misrepresentation.*** A wrongdoer who commits this tort defrauds another person of money, property, or something else of value. Also known as *fraud* or *deceit*. The following elements must be shown:
   a. The wrongdoer made a false representation of material fact.
   b. The wrongdoer had knowledge that the representation was false and intended to deceive the innocent party.
   c. The innocent party justifiably relied on the misrepresentation.
   d. The innocent party was injured.

Tort Damages

1. ***Actual damages.*** Actual damages include compensation for personal injury, pain and suffering, emotional distress, and other injuries caused by the defendant's tortious conduct.
2. ***Punitive damages.*** Punitive damages are recoverable against a defendant for intentional or egregious conduct. They are awarded to punish the defendant, to deter the defendant from similar conduct in the future, and to set an example for others. The plaintiff may keep these damages.

Strict Liability

In strict liability, liability is assessed on defendants without regard to fault. Strict liability applies to *abnormally dangerous activities* and certain products.

WWW Internet Exercises and Case Questions

Working the Web Internet Exercises

1. Find a state court case opinion that relates to intentional torts. See, for example, a state-based plaintiffs' trial lawyers' association site (**www.wstla.org**), or, at the national level, the Association of Trial Lawyers of America (**www.atla.org**), or the ABA Tort and Insurance Practice Section (**www.abanet.org/tips/thebrief.html**).
2. Find a medical malpractice case. For the viewpoint of the defense, see **www.dri.org**. For the insurance industry's view, see **www.ircweb.org**.

Check the following site as a starting point for the questions below: **http://www.law.cornell.edu/wex/index.php/Tort**.

3. Find a state court case that establishes the rule in your jurisdiction on social host liability.
4. Find the statute in your jurisdiction that contains the Good Samaritan rule.
5. Find the statute in your jurisdiction that contains the innkeepers' liability law.

Legal Environment Cases

6.1 Intentional Tort September 16, 1975, the Baltimore Orioles professional baseball team was at Boston's Fenway Park to play the Boston Red Sox. Ross Grimsley was a pitcher for the visiting Baltimore club. During one period of the game, Grimsley was warming up in the bullpen, throwing pitches to a catcher. During this warmup, Boston spectators in the stands heckled Grimsley. After Grimsley had completed warming up and the catcher had left from behind the plate in the bullpen, Grimsley wound up as if he were going to throw the ball in his hand at the plate, and then he turned and threw the ball at one of the hecklers in the stand. The ball traveled at about 80 miles an hour, passed through a wire fence protecting the spectators, missed the heckler that Grimsley was aiming at, and hit another spectator, David Manning, Jr., causing injury. Manning sued Grimsley and the Baltimore Orioles. Are the defendants liable? *Manning v. Grimsley*, 643 F.2d 20, 1981 U.S. App. Lexis 19782 (1st Cir.)

6.2 Merchant Protection Statute At about 7:30 P.M. on September 8, 1976, Deborah A. Johnson entered a Kmart store located in Madison, Wisconsin, to purchase some diapers and several cans of motor oil. She took her small child along to enable her to purchase the correct size diapers, carrying the child in an infant seat that she had purchased at Kmart two or three weeks previously. A large Kmart price tag was still attached to the infant seat. Johnson purchased the diapers and oil and some children's clothes. She was in a hurry to leave because it was 8:00 P.M., her child's feeding time, and she hurried through the checkout lane. She paid for the diapers, the oil, and the clothing. Just after leaving the store, she heard someone ask her to stop. She turned around and saw a Kmart security officer. He showed her a badge and asked her to come back into the store, which she did. The man stated, "I have reason to believe that you have stolen this car seat." Johnson explained that she had purchased the seat previously. She demanded to see the manager, who was called to the scene. When Johnson pointed out that the seat had cat hairs, food crumbs, and milk stains on it, the man said, "I'm really sorry, there's been a terrible mistake. You can go." Johnson looked at the clock, which read 8:20 P.M., when she left. Johnson sued Kmart for false imprisonment. Is Kmart liable? *Johnson v. Kmart Enterprises, Inc.*, 297 N.W.2d 74, 1980 Wisc.App. Lexis 3197 (Wis. App.)

6.3 Trespass A. C. Wade operated a liquor store in Cordele, Georgia. Because the store had been burglarized on several occasions and money had been stolen from a cigarette vending machine, Wade booby-trapped the machine with dynamite, with the intent to scare away thieves when they tried to steal money from the vending machine. Robert McKinsey, a 16-year-old, was killed when the dynamite attached to the vending machine exploded while McKensey was burglarizing the liquor store. Mrs. Ella McKinsey, Robert's mother, although admitting her son was committing a crime at the time he was killed, brought action for damages against Wade for the wrongful death of her son. Who wins? *McKinsey v. Wade*, 220 SE.2d 30, 1975 Ga.App. Lexis 1264 (Ga.)

6.4 Negligence In January 1984, George Yanase was a paying guest at the Royal Lodge-Downtown Motel in San Diego, California. Yanase was a member of the Automobile Club of Southern California. The Auto Club publishes a "Tourbook" in which it lists hotels and motels and rates the quality of their services, including the cleanliness of rooms, quality of the restaurant, level of personal service, and the like. Yanase had selected the Royal from the Tourbook. On the night of his stay at the Royal, Yanase was shot in the parking lot adjacent to the motel and died as a result of his injuries. Yanase's widow sued the Auto Club for negligence. Is the Auto Club liable? *Yanase v. Automobile Club of Southern California*, 212 Cal.App.3d 468, 260 Cal.Rptr. 513, 1989 Cal.App. Lexis 746 (Cal. App.)

6.5 Causation In February 1973, W. L. Brown purchased a new large Chevrolet truck from Days Chevrolet. The truck had been manufactured by General Motors Corporation. On March 1, 1973, an employee of Brown's was operating the truck when it ceased to function in rush-hour traffic on Interstate Highway 75 in the Atlanta suburbs. A defect within the alternator caused a complete failure of the truck's electrical system. The defect was caused by General Motors's negligence in manufacturing the truck. When the alternator failed to operate, the truck came to rest in the right-hand lane of two north-bound lanes of freeway traffic. Because of the electrical failure, no blinking lights could be used to warn traffic of the danger. The driver, however, tried to motion traffic around the truck. Some time later, when the freeway traffic had returned to normal, the large Chevrolet truck was still motionless on the freeway. At approximately 6:00 P.M., a panel truck approached the stalled truck in the right-hand lane of traffic at freeway speed. Immediately behind the panel truck, Mr. Davis, driving a Volkswagen fastback, was unable to see the stalled truck. At the last moment, the driver of the panel truck saw the stalled truck and swerved into another lane to avoid it. Mr. Davis drove his Volkswagen into the stalled truck at freeway speed, causing his death. Mr. Davis's wife brought a wrongful death action based on negligence against General Motors. Was there causation linking the negligence of the defendant to the fatal accident? *General Motors Corporation v. Davis*, 223 S.E.2d 825, 1977 Ga.App. Lexis 1961 (Ga. App.)

6.6 Negligence per Se On March 21, 1980, Julius Ebanks set out from home in East Elmhurst, Queens, New York, en route to his employment in the downtown district of Manhattan. When Ebanks reached the Bowling Green subway station, he boarded an escalator owned and operated by the New York City Transit Authority. While the escalator was ascending, Ebanks's left foot became caught in a two-inch gap between the escalator step on which he was standing and the side wall of the escalator. Ebanks was unable to free himself. When he reached the top of the escalator, he was thrown to the ground, fracturing his hip and causing other serious injuries. The two-inch gap exceeded the three-eighths-inch standard required by the city's building code. Ebanks sued the Transit Authority to recover damages for his injuries. Who wins? *Ebanks v. New York City Transit Authority*, 70 N.Y.2d. 621, 518 N.Y.S.2d 776, 1987 N.Y. Lexis 17294 (N.Y. App.)

6.7 Liability of Landowners George and Beverly Wagner owned a 1.6-acre parcel of land on which they operated "Bowag Kennels," which catered to training, boarding, and caring for show dogs. The property was entirely surrounded by land owned by Ruben Shiling and W. Dale Hess. In August 1964, Shiling and Hess granted the Wagners an easement right-of-way over their land that connected the kennel to Singer Road, a public road. Singer Road was a rural, unlit two-lane road running through a wooded area. The right-of-way was an unpaved, unlit, narrow road that crossed an uninhabited wooded area leading to Bowag Kennels. On numerous occasions, unauthorized motorcyclists drove on the right-of-way. On several occasions, the bikers had loud parties along the right-of-way. In September 1982, the Wagners stretched a large metal chain between two poles at the entrance of the right-of-way. The Wagners testified that they marked the chain with reflectors and signs. Just before midnight on October 2, 1982, William E. Doehring, Jr., and his passenger, Kelvin Henderson, drove their motorcycle off Singer Road and turned onto the right-of-way. The motorcycle they were riding was not equipped with a headlight, and the riders were not wearing helmets. Doehring and Henderson had not been granted permission by the Wagners or Shiling or Hess to use the right-of-way. The motorcycle struck the chain, and the riders were thrown off. Doehring died several hours later at a hospital. Doehring's father filed a wrongful death and survival action against the Wagners. Who Wins? *Wagner v. Doehring*, 553 A.2d 684, 1989 Md. Lexis 29 (Md. App.)

6.8 Liability of Common Carrier The Southern California Rapid Transit District (RTD) is a public common carrier that operates public buses throughout the Los Angeles area. Carmen and Carla Lopez were fare-paying passengers on an RTD bus when a group of juveniles began harassing them and other passengers. When the bus driver was notified of this problem, he failed to take any precautionary measures and continued to operate the bus. The juveniles eventually physically assaulted Carmen and Carla, who were injured. The RTD was aware of a history of violent attacks on its bus line. Carmen and Carla sued RTD to recover damages for their injuries. Who wins? *Lopez v. Southern California Rapid Transit District*, 40 Cal.3d 780, 221 Cal.Rptr. 840, 1985 Cal. Lexis 434 (Cal.)

6.9 Emotional Distress On August 10, 1983, Gregory and Demetria James, brother and sister, were riding their bicycles north on 50th Street in Omaha, Nebraska. Spaulding Street intersects 50th Street. A garbage truck owned by Watts Trucking Service, Inc., and driven by its employee, John Milton Lieb, was backing up into the intersection of 50th and Spaulding streets. The truck backed into the intersection, through a stop sign, and hit and ran over Demetria, killing her. Gregory helplessly watched the entire accident but was not in danger himself. As a result of watching his sister's peril, Gregory suffered severe emotional distress. Gregory sued Watts and Lieb to recover damages for his emotional distress. Who wins? *James v. Watts Trucking Service, Inc.*, 375 N.W.2d 109, 1985 Neb. Lexis 1209 (Neb.)

6.10 Defense On the night of June 13, 1975, the New York Yankees professional baseball team played the Chicago White Sox at Shea Stadium, New York. Elliot Maddox played center field for the Yankees that night. It had rained the day before, and the previous night's game had been canceled because of bad weather. On the evening of June 13, the playing field was still wet, and Maddox commented on this fact several times to the club's manager but continued to play. In the ninth inning, when Maddox was attempting to field a ball in center field, he slipped on a wet spot, fell, and injured his right knee. Maddox sued the City of New York, which owned Shea Stadium; the Metropolitan Baseball Club, Inc., as lessee; the architect; the consulting engineer; and the American League. Maddox alleged that the parties were negligent in causing the field to be wet and that the injury ended his professional career. Who win? *Maddox v. City of New York*, 496 N.Y.S.2d 726, 1985 N.Y. Lexis 17254 (N.Y. App.)

Ethics in Business

6.11 Radio Station KHJ was a successful Los Angeles broadcaster of rock music that commanded a 48 percent market share of the teenage audience in the Los Angeles area. KHJ was owned and operated by RKO General, Inc. In July 1973, KHJ inaugurated a promotion titled "The Super Summer Spectacular." As part of this promotion, KHJ had a disc jockey known as "The Real Don Steel" ride around the Los Angeles area in a conspicuous red automobile. Periodically KHJ would announce to its radio audience Steele's location. The first listener to thereafter locate Steel and answer a question received a cash prize and participated in a brief interview on the air with Steele. On July 16, 1973, one KHJ broadcast identified Steele's next destination as Canoga Park. Robert Sentner, 17 years old, heard the broadcast and immediately drove to Canoga Park. Marsha Baime, 19 years old, also heard the broadcast and drove to Canoga Park. By the time Sentner and Baime located Steele, someone else had already claimed the prize. Without the knowledge of the other, Sentner and Baime each decided to follow Steele to the next destination and to be first to "find him."

Steele proceeded onto the freeway. For the next few miles, Sentner and Baime tried to jockey for position closest to the Steele vehicle, reaching speeds of up to 80 miles per hour. There is no evidence that the Steele vehicle exceeded the speed limit. When Steele left the freeway at the Westlake off-ramp, Sentner and Baime tried to follow. In their attempts to do so, they knocked another vehicle, driven by Mr. Weirum, into the center divider of the freeway, where it overturned. Mr. Weirum died in the accident. Baime stopped to report the accident. Sentner, after pausing momentarily to relate the tragedy to a passing police officer, got back into his car, pursued and successfully located Steele, and collected the cash prize. The wife and children of Mr. Weirum brought a wrongful death negligence action against Sentner, Baime, and RKO General. *Weirum v. RKO General, Inc.*, 15 Cal.3d 40, 123 Cal.Rptr. 468, 175 Cal. Lexis 220 (Cal.)

Ethics Issues

1. What legal theory did the plaintiffs assert had been violated by the defendant?

2. Did Sentner and Baime act negligently? Are they liable?

3. Did RKO General, Inc., act responsibly? Explain.

4. Did RKO General, Inc.'s, conduct amount to negligence? Why or why not?

Endnotes

1. 376 U.S. 254, 84 S.Ct. 710, 1964 U.S. Lexis 1655 (U.S. Sup.Ct.).
2. *Restatement (Second) of Torts*, Section 46.
3. *Restatement (Second) of Torts*, Section 46, comment d.
4. Justice B. Anderson, *Blyth v. Birmingham Water Works Co.*, 11 Exch. 781, 784 (1856).
5. For example, see Cal. Civil Code, Section 1714(c).

7

Strict Liability and Product Liability

"A manufacturer is strictly liable in tort when an article he places on the market, knowing that it is to be used without inspection for defects, proves to have a defect that causes injury to a human being."

—Greenman v. Yuba Power Product Inc., 59 Cal.2d 57, 27 Cal.Rptr. 697, 1963 Cal. Lexis 140

Chapter Objectives

After studying this chapter, you should be able to:

1. Describe and distinguish among the several legal theories of product liability.
2. Define strict liability.
3. Identify and describe defects in manufacture and design.
4. Identify and describe the defects of failure to warn and failure to provide adequate packaging.
5. Describe the damages recoverable in a product liability lawsuit.

Chapter Contents

- Negligence and Fault
- Strict Liability
- Defect in Manufacture
- Defect in Design
- Failure to Warn
- Defect in Packaging
- Defenses to Product Liability

If a product defect causes injury to purchasers, lessees, users, or bystanders, the injured party may be able to recover for his or her injuries under certain tort theories, including negligence, misrepresentation, and the modern theory of strict liability. The liability of manufacturers, sellers, lessors, and others for injuries caused by defective products is commonly referred to as **product liability.**

product liability
The liability of manufacturers, sellers, and others for the injuries caused by defective products.

The various tort principles that permit injured parties to recover damages caused by defective products are discussed in this chapter.

Restaurant, Sault Ste. Marie, Michigan. The sellers of goods, including food, can be held liable under the doctrines of negligence and strict liability for injuries caused by the products they sell.

Negligence and Fault

Depending on the circumstances of the case, persons who are injured by defective products may be able to recover damages under the tort theories of *negligence* and *misrepresentation*. Both of these theories require the defendant to be *at fault* for causing the plaintiff's injuries. These theories are discussed in the paragraphs that follow.

Negligence

A person injured by a defective product may bring an action for **negligence** against the negligent party. To be successful, the plaintiff must prove that the defendant breached a duty of due care to the plaintiff that caused the plaintiff's injuries. Failure to exercise due care includes failing to assemble a product carefully, negligent product design, negligent inspection or testing of the product, negligent packaging, failure to warn of the dangerous propensities of the product, and such. It is important to note that in a negligence lawsuit, only a party who was actually negligent is liable to the plaintiff.

negligence
A tort related to defective products in which the defendant has breached a duty of due care and caused harm to the plaintiff.

The plaintiff and the defendant do not have to be in privity of contract.[1] For example, in the landmark case *MacPherson v. Buick Motor Co.*,[2] the court held that an injured consumer could recover damages from the manufacturer of a product even though the consumer was not in a contract with the manufacturer from whom he had purchased the product. The plaintiff generally bears the difficult burden of proving that the defendant was negligent.

Consider This Example Assume that the purchaser of a motorcycle is injured in an accident. The accident occurred because a screw was missing from the motorcycle. How does the buyer prove who was negligent? Was it the manufacturer, who left the screw out during the assembly of the motorcycle? Was it the retailer, who negligently failed to discover the missing screw while preparing the motorcycle for sale? Was it the mechanic, who failed to replace the screw after repairing the motorcycle? Negligence remains a viable, yet difficult, theory on which to base a product liability action.

In the following case, the court held a defendant manufacturer liable for negligence in a product liability lawsuit.

Case 7.1
Product Liability

Benedi v. McNeil-P.P.C., Incorporated

66 F.3d 1378, 1985 U.S. App. Lexis 28061 United States Court of Appeals, Fourth Circuit

Background and Facts

Antonio Benedi consumed three to four glasses of wine a night during the week and sometimes more on the weekend. On February 5, 1993, Benedi began taking Extra-Strength Tylenol in normal doses for flu-like aches. On February 10, 1993, Benedi was admitted to the hospital in a coma and near death due to liver and kidney failure. On the night of February 12, 1993, Benedi underwent an emergency liver transplant. Because of the transplant, Benedi would have to undergo kidney dialysis in the future. Blood tests performed shortly after Benedi's admission to the hospital revealed that he suffered from acetaminophen (Tylenol) toxicity, which is caused by the combination of Tylenol and too much alcohol. The bottle from which Benedi took the Tylenol did not contain a warning of the dangers of the combination of Tylenol and excessive alcohol consumption. Benedi sued McNeil-P.P.C., Incorporated (McNeil), the manufacturer of Tylenol, for negligent failure to warn. The jury found McNeil negligent and awarded Benedi $7,850,000 in compensatory damages. McNeil appealed.

Issue

Is McNeil liable for negligent failure to warn?

In the Language of the Court

At trial, Benedi called two liver disease specialists who both testified that a warning of the possible danger to heavy drinkers from combining alcohol and acetaminophen should have been place on the Tylenol label since the mid-1980s. These experts described exactly how the alcohol–acetaminophen mixture can become a toxin in the liver. They cited numerous treatises and articles published in medical journals prior to 1993 that described the increased risk of liver injury when acetaminophen is combined with alcohol. One of plaintiff's experts referred to sixty reports that McNeil had received by the end of 1992 documenting cases of liver injury associated with combining therapeutic doses of Tylenol with alcohol. Because Benedi's experts presented sufficient evidence on the issue of causation, the district judge properly submitted that issue to the jury. It was the jury's role to assess the weight and credibility of the evidence, and the jury found that Benedi proved causation. We find that ample evidence existed from which a reasonable jury should find for Benedi.

Decision and Remedy

The Court of Appeals affirmed the jury's verdict awarding plaintiff Benedi $7,850,000 against McNeil for negligent failure to warn.

Note: In the summer of 1993 (after Benedi's injury), McNeil included a warning on Tylenol that persons who regularly consume three or more alcoholic drinks a day should consult a physician before using Tylenol.

Business and Ethics Questions

1. What elements are necessary to prove negligence? Do you think that McNeil was negligent in this case? Do you think jurors are sophisticated enough to evaluate and judge scientific evidence.
2. Did McNeil act ethically in failing to put a warning on Tylenol? Do you think a warning was warranted?
3. What will be the implication of this case to manufacturers of pain-killing drugs? Will consumers be better off because of this decision? Explain.

Misrepresentation

A buyer or lessee who is injured because a seller or lessor fraudulently misrepresented the quality of a product can sue the seller or lessor for the tort of **intentional misrepresentation,** or **fraud**. Recovery is limited to persons who were injured because they relied on the misrepresentation.

intentional misrepresentation
A situation in which a seller or lessor fraudulently misrepresents the quality of a product and a buyer is injured thereby. Also called *fraud*.

Intentional misrepresentation occurs where a seller or lessor either (1) affirmatively misrepresents the quality of a product or (2) conceals a defect in it. Because most reputable manufacturers, sellers, and lessors do not intentionally misrepresent the quality of their products, fraud is not often used as the basis for product liability actions.

Strict Liability

In the landmark case *Greenmun v. Yuba Power Products, Inc.*,[3] the California supreme court adopted the **doctrine of strict liability in tort** as a basis for product liability actions. Most states have now adopted this doctrine as a basis for product liability actions. The doctrine of strict liability removes many of the difficulties for the plaintiff associated with other theories of product liability. The remainder of this chapter examines the scope of the strict liability doctrine.

Liability Without Fault

Unlike negligence, strict liability does not require the injured persons to prove that the defendant breached a duty of care. **Strict liability** is **liability without fault**. A seller can be found strictly liable even though he or she has exercised all possible care in the preparation and sale of his or her product.

strict liability
A tort doctrine that makes manufacturers, distributors, wholesalers, retailers, and others in the chain of distribution of a defective product liable for the damages caused by the defect, *irrespective of fault*.

The doctrine of strict liability applies to sellers and lessors of products who are engaged in the business of selling and leasing products. Casual sales and transactions by nonmerchants are not covered. Thus, a person who sells a defective product to a neighbor in a casual sale is not strictly liable if the product causes injury.

Strict liability applies only to products, not to services. In hybrid transactions involving both services and products, the dominant element of the transaction dictates whether strict liability applies. For example, in a medical operation that requires a blood transfusion, the operation would be the dominant element, and strict liability would not apply. Strict liability may not be disclaimed.

All in the Chain of Distribution Are Liable

All parties in the **chain of distribution** of a defective product are **strictly liable** for the injuries caused by that product. Thus, all manufacturers, distributors, wholesalers, retailers, lessors, and subcomponent manufacturers may be sued under the **doctrine of strict liability in tort**. This view is based on public policy. Lawmakers presume that sellers and lessors will insure against the risk of a strict liability lawsuit and spread the cost to their consumers by raising the price of products.

chain of distribution
All manufacturers, distributors, wholesalers, retailers, lessors, and subcomponent manufacturers involved in a transaction.

Consider This Example Suppose a subcomponent manufacturer produces a defective tire and sells it to a truck manufacturer. The truck manufacturer places a defective tire on one of its new-model trucks. The truck is distributed by a distributor to a retail dealer. Ultimately, the retail dealer sells the truck to a buyer. The defective tire causes an accident in which the buyer is injured. All the parties in the tire's chain of distribution can be sued by the injured party; in this case, the liable parties are the subcomponent manufacturer, the truck manufacturer, the distributor, and the retailer.

A defendant who has not been negligent but who is made to pay a strict liability judgment can bring a separate action against the negligent party in the chain of distribution to recover its losses. In the preceding example, for instance, the retailer could sue the manufacturer to recover the strict liability judgment assessed against it.

Exhibit 7.1 compares the doctrines of negligence and strict liability.

Exhibit 7.1

Negligence and Strict Liability Compared

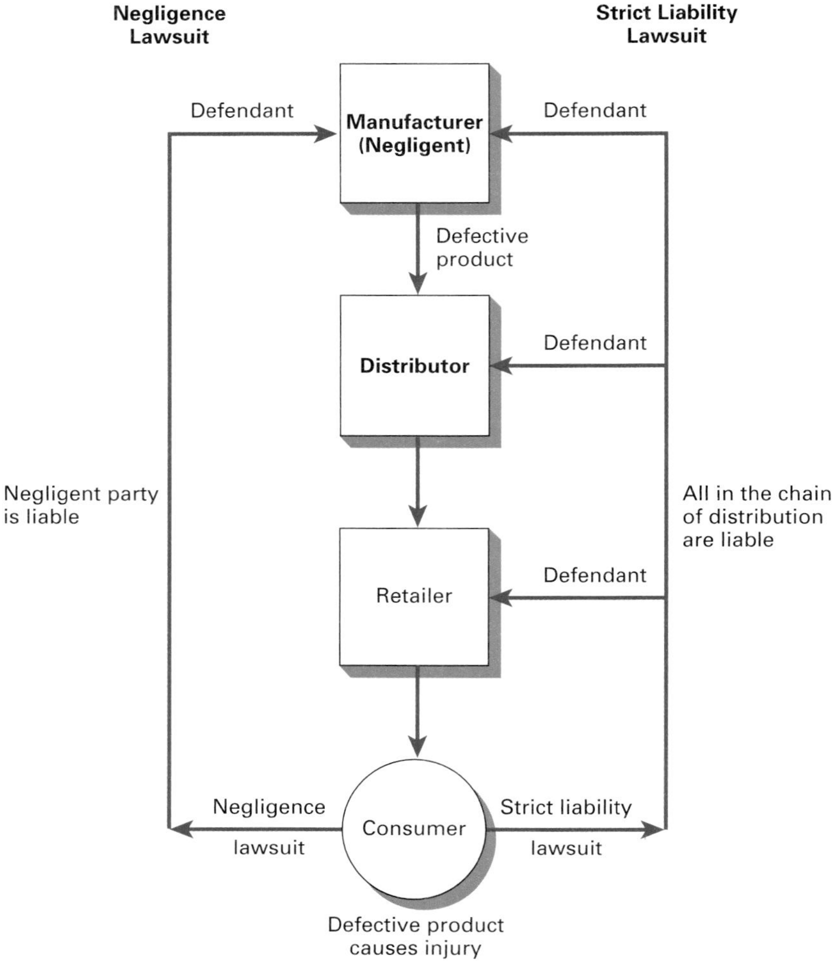

Contemporary Trend

Strict Liability

The recognized articulation of the doctrine of strict liability in tort is found in **Section 402A** of the ***Restatement (Second) of Torts***, which provides:

1. One who sells any product in a defective condition unreasonably dangerous to the user or consumer or to his property is subject to liability for physical harm thereby caused to the ultimate user or consumer, or to his property, if

   a. the seller is engaged in the business of selling such a product, and

   b. it is expected to and does reach the user or consumer without substantial change in the condition in which it is sold.

2. The rule stated in Subsection (1) applies although

   a. the seller has exercised all possible care in the preparation and sale of his product, and

b. the user or consumer had not bought the product from or entered into any contractual relation with the seller.

In 1997, the American Law Institute (ALI) adopted the ***Restatement (Third) of Torts: Product Liability***. This new *Restatement* includes the following definition of *defect*:

> A product is defective when, at the time of sale or distribution, it contains manufacturing defect, is defective in design, or is defective because of inadequate instructions or warnings.
>
> A product:
>
> a. contains a manufacturing defect when the product departs from its intended design even though all possible care was exercised in the preparation and marketing of the product;
>
> b. is defective in design when the foreseeable risks of harm posed by the product could have been reduced or avoided by the adoption of a reasonable alternative design by the seller or other distributor, or a predecessor in the commercial chain of distribution, and the omission of the alternative design renders the product not reasonably safe;
>
> c. is defective because of inadequate instructions or warnings when the foreseeable risks of harm posed by the product could have been reduced or avoided by the provision of reasonable instructions or warnings by the seller or other distributor, or a predecessor in the commercial chain of distribution, and the omission of the instructions or warnings renders the product not reasonably safe. ■

Parties Who Can Recover for Strict Liability

Because strict liability is a tort doctrine, privity of contract between the plaintiff and the defendant is not required. In other words, the doctrine applies even if the injured party had no contractual relations with the defendant. Under strict liability, sellers and lessors are liable to the ultimate user or consumer. Users include the purchaser or lessee, family members, guests, employees, customers, and persons who passively enjoy the benefits of the product (e.g., passengers in automobiles).

Most jurisdictions have judicially or statutorily extended the protection of strict liability to bystanders. The courts have stated that bystanders should be entitled to even greater protection than consumers or users. This is because consumers and users have the chance to inspect for defects and to limit their purchases to articles manufactured by reputable manufacturers and sold by reputable retailers, whereas bystanders do not have the same opportunity.

Damages Recoverable for Strict Liability

The damages recoverable in a strict liability action vary by jurisdiction. Damages for personal injuries are recoverable in all jurisdictions that have adopted the doctrine of strict liability, although some jurisdictions limit the dollar amount of the award. Property damage is recoverable in most jurisdictions, but economic loss (e.g., lost income) is recoverable in only a few jurisdictions. **Punitive damages,** which are monetary damages awarded to punish the defendant, are generally allowed if the plaintiff can prove that the defendant either intentionally injured him or her or acted with reckless disregard for his or her safety.

punitive damages
Monetary damages that are awarded to punish a defendant who either intentionally or recklessly injured the plaintiff.

Defective Product

To recover for strict liability, the injured party must first show that the product that caused the injury was somehow *defective*. (Remember that the injured party does not have to prove who caused the product to become defective.) Plaintiffs can allege multiple **product defects** in one lawsuit. A product can be found to be defective in many ways. The most common types of defects are *defects in manufacturer, design*, and *failure to warn*. These defects are discussed in the following paragraphs.

product defect
Something wrong, inadequate, or improper in the manufacture, design, packaging, warning, or safety measures of a product.

Defect in Manufacture

defect in manufacture

A defect that occurs when the manufacturer fails to (1) properly assemble a product, (2) properly test a product, or (3) adequately check the quality of a product.

A **defect in manufacture** occurs when the manufacturer fails to (1) properly assemble a product, (2) properly test a product, or (3) adequately check the quality of a product.

Consider This Example American Ladder Company designs, manufacturers, and sells ladders. American Ladder Company manufacturers a ladder, but a worker at the company fails to put one of the screws in the ladder that would support one of the steps of the ladder. The ladder is sold to Weingard Distributor, a wholesaler, which sells it to Reynolds Hardware Store, which sells the ladder to Heather, a consumer. When Heather is on the ladder painting her house, the step breaks because of the missing screw, and Heather falls and is injured. The missing screw is an example of a defect in manufacture. Under the doctrine of strict liability, American Ladder Company, Weingard Distributor, and Reynolds Hardware Store are liable to Heather.

The following case is a classic example involving a defect in manufacture.

Case 7.2

Defect in Manufacture

Shoshone Coca-Cola Bottling Co. v. Dolinski

420 P.2d 855, 1966 Nev. Lexis 260 Supreme Court of Nevada

Background and Facts

Leo Dolinski purchased a bottle of Squirt, a soft drink, from a vending machine at a Sea and Ski plant, his place of employment. Dolinski opened the bottle and consumed part of its contents. He immediately became ill. Upon examination, it was found that the bottle contained the decomposed body of a mouse, mouse hair, and mouse feces. Dolinski visited a doctor and was given medicine to counteract nausea. Dolinski suffered physical and mental distress from consuming the decomposed mouse and thereafter possessed an aversion to soft drinks. The Shoshone Coca-Cola Bottling Company (Shoshone) had manufactured and distributed the Squirt bottle. Dolinski sued Shoshone, basing his lawsuit on the doctrine of strict liability. The state of Nevada had not previously recognized the doctrine of strict liability. However, the trial court adopted the doctrine of strict liability, and the jury returned a verdict in favor of the plaintiff. Shoshone appealed.

Issue

Should the state of Nevada judicially adopt the doctrine of strict liability? If so, was there a defect in the manufacture of the Squirt bottle that caused the plaintiff's injuries?

In the Language of the Court

In our view, public policy demands that one who places upon the market a bottled beverage in a condition dangerous for use must be held strictly liable to the ultimate user for injuries resulting from such use, although the seller has exercised all reasonable care. Our acceptance of strict tort liability against the manufacturer and distributor of a bottled beverage does not mean that the plaintiff is relieved of the burden of proving a case. He must still establish that his injury was caused by a defect in the product and that such defect existed when the product left the hands of the defendant.

In the case at hand, Shoshone contends that insufficient proof was offered to establish that the mouse was in the bottle of "Squirt" when it left Shoshone's possession. The plaintiff offered the expert testimony of a toxicologist who examined the bottle and contents on the day the plaintiff drank from it. It was his opinion that the mouse "had been dead for a long time" and that the dark stains (mouse feces) that he found on the bottom of the bottle must have been there before the liquid was added. The jury apparently preferred the latter evidence that traced cause to the defendant.

Decision and Remedy

The supreme court of Nevada adopted the doctrine of strict liability and held that the evidence supported the trial court's finding that there was a defect in manufacture. The supreme court affirmed the trial court's decision in favor of plaintiff Dolinski.

Business and Ethics Questions

1. Should the courts adopt the theory of strict liability? Why or why not?
2. Was it ethical for Shoshone to argue that it was not liable to Dolinski?
3. Should all in the chain of distribution of a defective product—even parties that are not responsible for the defect—be held liable under the doctrine of strict liability? Or should liability be based only on fault?

Defect in Design

A **defect in design** can support a strict liability action. Design defects that have supported strict liability awards include toys that are designed with removable parts that could be swallowed by children, machines and appliances designed without proper safeguards, and trucks and other vehicles designed without a warning device to let people know that the vehicle is backing up.

defect in design
A defect that occurs when a product is improperly designed.

In evaluating the adequacy of a product's design, the courts apply a risk-utility analysis and consider the gravity of the danger posed by the design, the likelihood that injury will occur, the availability and cost of producing a safer alternative design, the social utility of the product, and other factors.

The following design defect case demonstrates the application of a risk-utility analysis.

Case 7.3 Defect in Design

Lakin v. Senco Products, Inc.

925 P.2d 107, 1996 Ore. App. Lexis 1466
Court of Appeals of Oregon

Background and Facts

Senco Products, Inc. (Senco), manufactures and markets a variety of pneumatic nail guns, including the SN325 nail gun, which discharges 3.25-inch nails. The SN325 uses special nails designed and sold by Senco. The SN325 will discharge a nail only if two trigger mechanisms are activated; that is, the user must both squeeze the nail gun's finger trigger and press the nail gun's muzzle against a surface, activating the bottom trigger, or safety. The SN325 can fire up to nine nails per second if the trigger is continuously depressed and the gun is bounced along the work surface, constantly reactivating the muzzle safety/trigger.

On December 1, 1990, John Lakin was using a Senco SN325 nail gun to help build a new home. When attempting to nail two-by-fours under the eaves of the garage, Lakin stood on tiptoe and raised a two-by-four over his head. As he held the board in position with his left hand and the nail gun in his right hand, he pressed the nose of the SN325 up against the board, depressed the safety, and pulled the finger trigger to fire the nail into the board. The gun fired the first nail and then, in a phenomenon known as "double firing," immediately discharged an unintended second nail that struck the first nail. The gun recoiled violently backward toward Lakin and, with Lakin's finger still on the trigger, came into contact with his cheek. That contact activated the safety/trigger, causing the nail gun to fire a third nail. This third nail went through Lakin's cheekbone and into his brain.

The nail penetrated the frontal lobe of the right hemisphere of Lakin's brain, blocked a major artery, and caused extensive tissue damage. Lakin was unconscious for several days and ultimately underwent multiple surgeries. He suffers permanent brain damage and is unable to perceive information from the left hemisphere of the brain. He also suffers partial paralysis of the left side of his body. Lakin has undergone a radical personality change and is prone to violent outbursts. He is unable to obtain employment. Lakin's previously warm and loving relationship with his wife and four children has been permanently altered. He can no longer live with his family and instead resides in a supervised group home for brain-injured persons. Lakin and his wife sued Senco for strict liability based on design defect. The trial court found Senco liable and awarded $5,323,413 to Lakin, $876,000 to his wife, and $4 million in punitive damages against Senco. Senco appealed.

Issue

Is Senco liable to Lakin for strict liability based on a design defect in the SN325 that allowed it to double fire?

In the Language of the Court

The evidence disclosed that the SN325 double-fired once in every 15 firings. Defendant rushed the SN325's production in order to maintain its position in the market, modifying an existing nail gun model so that it could shoot longer nails, without engaging in additional testing to determine whether the use of longer nails in that model would increase the prevalence of double fire. A reasonable juror could plausibly infer that conscious profit/market share motives underlay the failure to engage in adequate product research development and testing.

After reviewing the entire record, we conclude that the amount of damages awarded was within the range that a rational juror would be entitled to award. Before John Lakin's injury, defendant knew from numerous complaints that it was highly probable that the SN325 would "double fire." Thus, it was foreseeable—indeed, highly likely given the SN325 recoil and "bump fire" potential—that serious injury could occur to someone when the nail gun double fired.

Decision and Remedy

The court of appeals applied a risk-utility analysis and held that the SN325 was defectively designed. The court affirmed the award of damages to Lakin and his wife.

(continued)

Lakin v. Senco Products, Inc.

925 P.2d 107, 1996 Ore. App. Lexis 1466 Court of Appeals of Oregon

(continued)

Business and Ethics Questions

1. Do you think the utility served by the nine-nail-per-second SN325 outweighed its risk of personal injury?
2. Did Senco act in conscious disregard of safety factors when it designed, manufactured, and sold the SN325 nail gun?
3. Do you think the award of punitive damages was warranted in this case?

Crashworthiness Doctrine

Often when an automobile is involved in an accident, the driver or passengers are not injured by the blow itself. Instead, they are injured when their bodies strike something inside their own automobile (e.g., the dashboard or the steering wheel). This is commonly referred to as the "second collision." The courts have held that automobile manufacturers are under a duty to design automobiles to take into account the possibility of this second collision. This is called the **crashworthiness doctrine.** Failure to design an automobile to protect occupants from foreseeable dangers caused by a second collision subjects the manufacturer and dealer to strict liability.

crashworthiness doctrine
A doctrine that says automobile manufacturers are under a duty to design automobiles so they take into account the possibility of harm from a person's body striking something inside the automobile in the case of a car accident.

Ethics in Business

Design Defect in Pool Equipment

On June 1, 2000, Lorenzo Peterson was swimming in a swimming pool with a friend at an apartment complex. Lorenzo watched as his friend swam to the bottom of the pool, slid an unattached drain cover away, and then slid it back. Lorenzo thought his friend had hidden something inside the drain, so he swam to the bottom of the pool. Lorenzo slid the drain cover aside and stuck his arm inside the drain. The 300 to 400 pounds of pull of the drain pump held Lorenzo trapped underwater. At least seven people tried to free Lorenzo, to no avail. When the police arrived, they broke down the door to the pool equipment room and turned off the drain pump.

Lorenzo was trapped underwater for 12 minutes, which left him irreversibly brain damaged. Lorenzo, through his relatives, sued Sta-Rite Industries, Inc., the manufacturer of the drain, under the doctrine of strict liability to recover damages for Lorenzo's injuries. The plaintiff alleged that the underwater pool drain was defectively designed because it did not contain a shutoff mechanism. Evidence at trial showed that Sta-Rite's drain covers are designed to screw down, but often a drain cover becomes loose. Further evidence showed that there had been more than 20 prior suction-entrapment accidents involving Sta-Rite's drain covers and pumps.

Previously, experts had designed a pool drain pump with a mechanism that would automatically shut off a pool drain pump when it detected that it was pulling more than it should. Sta-Rite did not install such safety features on its drain pumps, however. After hearing the evidence, including seeing a video of a typical day in the life of Lorenzo after the accident, the jury took less than two hours to return a verdict against Sta-Rite. The jury found that a design defect existed in Sta-Rite's pool drain equipment and awarded Lorenzo $32 million for past and future medical expenses and $72 million for pain and suffering. *Sta-Rite Industries, Inc. v. Peterson*, 837 So.2d 988, 2003 Fla.App. Lexis 1673 (2003)

Ethics Issues

1. Do you think Sta-Rite acted unethically in its conduct? Why or why not?
2. Was the award of $104 million warranted? Explain. ■

Failure to Warn

Certain products are inherently dangerous and cannot be made any safer and still accomplish the task for which they are designed. For example, certain useful drugs cause side effects, allergies, and other injuries to some users. Many machines and appliances include dangerous moving parts that, if removed, would defeat the purpose of the machine or appliance. Manufacturers and sellers of such products are under a *duty to warn* users about such a product's propensities. A proper and conspicuous warning placed on the product insulates the manufacturer and others in the chain of distribution from strict liability. **Failure to warn** of these dangerous propensities is a defect that will support a strict liability action.

failure to warn
A defect that occurs when a manufacturer does not place a warning on the packaging of products that could cause injury if the danger is unknown.

Consider This Example The Universal Drug Corporation develops a new drug that has tremendous success in preventing and treating a certain type of cancer. However, the drug has a 3 percent probability of causing an increased risk of heart disease in patients who take the drug. The drug cannot be made any safer and still have its cancer treatment effects. The Universal Drug Corporation owes a duty to warn potential users of its new drug of these heart-related risks. If it fails to do so, and a user suffers a heart attack because of use of the drug, the Universal Drug Corporation would be held strictly liable for failure to warn.

Defect in Packaging

Manufacturers owe a duty to design and provide safe packages for their products. This duty requires manufacturers to provide packages and containers that are tamperproof or that clearly indicate whether they have been tampered with. Certain manufacturers, such as drug manufacturers, owe a duty to place their products in containers that cannot be opened by children. A manufacturer's failure to meet this duty—a **defect in packaging**—subjects the manufacturer and others in the chain of distribution of the product to strict liability.

In the following case, the court had to decide whether there was defective packaging.

defect in packaging
A defect that occurs when a product has been placed in packaging that is insufficiently tamperproof.

Case 7.4 Defect in Packaging

Elsroth v. Johnson & Johnson

700 F.Supp. 151, 1988 U.S. Dist. Lexis 13167 United States District Court, S.D. New York

Background and Facts

On February 4, 1986, Harriet Notarnicola purchased a box of Extra-Strength Tylenol capsules from a Bronxville, New York, grocery owned by The Great Atlantic & Pacific Tea Co. (A&P). The Tylenol was manufactured by McNeil Consumer Products Co., a division of McNeilab, Inc. (McNeil), under the name Johnson & Johnson. Diane Elsroth was visiting her boyfriend, Michael Notarnicola, for a week at the home of Michael's parents. Late on the night of February 7, Diane complained of a headache. Michael went to the kitchen, opened the box and plastic container of Extra-Strength Tylenol purchased by his mother, Harriet, at the A&P store, and returned with two capsules and a glass of water for Diane. A short time after ingesting the capsules, Diane retired. Her dead body was found the next day. The medical examiner concluded that the Tylenol capsules ingested by Diane were contaminated by a lethal does of potassium cyanide. The murder remains unsolved, but evidence shows that the Tylenol bottle had been tampered with after the product left the manufacturer's control. An unknown third party purchased the Tylenol, breached the packaging, substituted cyanide for some of the medicine contained in several of the gelatin capsules, somehow resealed the container and box in such a way that the tampering was not readily detectable, and placed the contaminated box on the shelf of the A&P store. John Elsroth, administrator of Diane's estate, brought a strict liability action against McNeil and A&P, seeking $1 million in compensatory damages and $92 million in punitive damages.

(continued)

Elsroth v. Johnson & Johnson

700 F.Supp. 151, 1988 U.S. Dist. Lexis 13167 United States District Court, S.D. New York

(continued)

Issue

Was there a defect in packaging that would support an action for strict liability?

In the Language of the Court

Following issuance of the rule, the makers of Tylenol have marketed the product in tamper-resistant packaging with the following features: (1) a foil seal glued to the mouth of the container or bottle, (2) a "shrink seal" around the neck and cap of the container, and (3) a sealed box (the end flaps of which are glued shut) in which the product and container are placed. As one McNeil official put it, tampering by "the Rembrandt kind of criminal" could not be prevented by this type of packaging. McNeil was also operating under the constraint, as recognized by the Food and Drug Administration (FDA), that no packaging could prevent this kind of "exotic" tampering—tamperproof packaging is not possible.

The packaging alternative designed by McNeil employed not one, not two, but three of the tamper-resistant features. When all of these factors are thrown into the mix, we find, as a matter of law, that under a utility/risk analysis this packaging was in a condition reasonably contemplated by the ultimate consumer and was not unreasonably dangerous for its intended use. If there are better tamper-resistant features available that would be feasible for use here, plaintiff has not described them. We return, however, to the fundamental premise: no packaging can boast of being tamperproof.

Decision and Remedy

The court held that there was not a defect in packaging. The defendants were therefore not strictly liable for Ms. Elsroth's death.

Business and Ethics Questions

1. Should manufacturers be forced to make tamperproof packaging for their products? Is this possible? What would be the expense?
2. Did any of the parties in the case act unethically?
3. Do you think the plaintiff's seeking $92 million in punitive damages was warranted?

Failure to Provide Adequate Instructions

failure to provide adequate instructions
A defect that occurs when a manufacturer does not provide detailed directions for safe assembly and use of a product.

Sellers are responsible to provide adequate instructions for the safe assembly and use of the products they sell. **Failure to provide adequate instructions** for the safe assembly and use of a product is a defect that subjects the manufacturer and others in the chain of distribution to strict liability.

Other defects include inadequate testing of products, inadequate selection of component parts or material, and improper certification of the safety of a product. The concept of "defect" is an expanding area of the law.

Defenses to Product Liability

Defendants in strict liability or negligence actions may raise several defenses to the imposition of liability. These defenses are discussed in the paragraphs that follow.

Generally Known Dangers

generally known dangers
A defense that acknowledges that certain products are inherently dangerous and are known to the general population to be so.

Certain products are inherently dangerous and are known to the general population to be so. Sellers are not strictly liable for failing to warn of **generally known dangers.** For example, it is a known fact that guns shoot bullets. Manufacturers of guns do not have to place a warning on the barrel of a gun warning of this generally known danger.

Government Contractor Defense

government contractor defense
A defense that says a contractor who was provided specifications by the government is not liable for any defect in the product that occurs as a result of those specifications.

Many defense and other contractors manufacture products (e.g., rockets, airplanes, and such) to government specifications. Most jurisdictions recognize a **government contractor defense** to product liability actions. To establish this defense, a government contractor must prove that (1) the precise specifications for the product were provided by the government, (2) the product conformed to those specifications, and (3) the contractor warned the government of any known defects or dangers of the product.

Consider This Example Assume that an airplane manufacturer becomes a government contractor when it is hired to manufacture a fighter airplane to specifications provided by the U.S. Air Force. If the airplane proves defective because of its design, crashes, and causes injury, the manufacturer can escape from liability by asserting the government contractor defense if the manufacturer either did not know of the defect or knew of the defect and warned the government of the defect.

Assumption of the Risk

Theoretically, the traditional doctrine of **assumption of the risk** is a defense to a product liability action. For this defense to apply, the defendant must prove that (1) the plaintiff knew and appreciated the risk and (2) the plaintiff voluntarily assumed the risk. In practice, the defense assumption of the risk is narrowly applied by the courts.

Misuse of the Product

Sometimes users are injured when they misuse a product. If they bring a product liability action, the defendant-seller may be able to assert the **misuse** as a defense. Whether the defense is effective depends on whether the misuse was foreseeable. The seller is relieved of product liability if the plaintiff has **abnormally misused** the product—that is, if there has been an *unforeseeable misuse* of the product. This reasoning is intended to provide an incentive for manufacturers to design and manufacture safer products.

misuse
A defense that relieves a seller of product liability if the user *abnormally* misused the product. Products must be designed to protect against foreseeable misuse.

Correction of a Product Defect

A manufacturer that produces a defective product and later discovers said defect must (1) notify purchasers and users of the defect and (2) correct the defect. Most manufacturers faced with this situation recall the defective product and either repair the defect or replace the product.

The seller must make reasonable efforts to notify purchasers and users of the defect and the procedure to correct it. Reasonable efforts normally consist of sending letters to known purchasers and users and placing notices in newspapers and magazines of general circulation. If a user ignores the notice and fails to have the defect corrected, the seller may raise this as a defense against further liability with respect to the defect. Many courts have held that reasonable notice is effective even against users who did not see the notice.

Supervening Event

For a seller to be held strictly liable, the product it sells must reach the consumer or user "without substantial change" in its condition. Under the doctrine of **supervening, or intervening, event,** the original seller is not liable if the product is materially altered or modified after it leaves the seller's possession and the alteration or modification causes an injury. A supervening event absolves all prior sellers in the chain of distribution from strict liability.

supervening event
An alteration or modification of a product by a party in the chain of distribution that absolves all prior sellers from strict liability. Also called *intervening event.*

Consider This Example A manufacturer produces a safe piece of equipment. It sells the equipment to a distributor, which removes a safety guard from the equipment. The distributor sells it to a retailer, who sells it to a buyer. The buyer is injured because of the removal of the safety guard. The manufacturer can raise the defense of supervening event against the imposition of liability. However, the distributor and retailer are strictly liable for the buyer's injuries.

Ethics in Business

General Motors Liable for Design Defect

On Christmas Eve, Patricia Anderson was driving her Chevrolet Malibu automobile, which was manufactured by the General Motors Corporation (GM), home from church. Her four young children, ages one through nine, and a neighbor, were also in the car. The Chevy Malibu was stopped at a stoplight at 89th Place and Figueroa Street in Los Angeles when a drunken driver plowed his car into the back of the Malibu at 50 to 70 mph. The Malibu burst into flames as its gas tank ruptured and ignited. Although no one died in the crash, the occupants of the Malibu were severely burned. Many required substantial and multiple skin grafts.

The two injured women and four injured children sued GM for product liability. They alleged that the fuel tank of the Chevy Malibu was defectively designed and placed too close to the rear bumper. GM countered that the tragic accident was the fault of the drunken driver who struck the Malibu. The accident victims produced evidence which showed that GM knew that the car's fuel-tank design was unsafe but had not changed the design because of the cost. The Chevy Malibu was one of GM's A-class cars, which also included the Pontiac Grand Am, the Oldsmobile Cutlass, and the Chevrolet Monte Carlo, all of which had similar fuel-tank designs. The plaintiffs produced GM memos that said it would cost GM $8.59 per vehicle to produce and install a safer fuel tank design but that it would cost the company only an estimated $2.40 per car to not fix the cars and pay damages to injured victims.

After a 10-week trial, the jurors returned a verdict of $107 million in compensatory damages to the plaintiffs for injuries, disfigurement, and pain and suffering caused to them by the accident. The jury than tacked on $4.9 billion as punitive damages to punish GM. This was the largest amount ever awarded in a personal-injury lawsuit. After the trial, one juror stated: "We're just like the numbers. Statistics. That's something that is wrong."

GM asked the trial judge to throw out the trial. GM claimed that the jury was prejudiced by repetitive personal attacks on GM as a "soulless company" and its lawyers as "hired guns" who consumed "cappuccinos and designer muffins." GM did not convince the judge that such animosity influenced the jury.

In its posttrial motions, GM argued that the award of damages, specifically the $4.9 billion in punitive damages, was the result of bias and prejudice of the jury and asked the trial court judge to reduce the award of damages. This the trial court judge did do: He let the compensatory damage award stand but reduced the award of punitive damages to $1 billion.

Ethics Issues

1. Did GM's "cost–benefit" memos have much bearing on the outcome of the lawsuit? Explain.
2. Do you think GM deserved to be punished with punitive damages? Was the amount of punitive damages awarded appropriate? Explain. ■

Statute of Limitations and Statute of Repose

statute of limitations
A statute that requires an injured person to bring an action within a certain number of years from the time that he or she was injured by the defective product.

statue of repose
A statute that limits the seller's liability to a certain number of years from the date when the product was first sold.

Most states have **statues of limitations** that require an injured person to bring an action within a certain number of years from the time that he or she was injured by a defective product. This limitation period varies from state to state. Failure to bring action within the appropriate time relieves the defendant of liability.

In most jurisdictions, the statute of limitation does not begin to run until the plaintiff suffers an injury. This subjects sellers and lessors to exposure for an unspecified period of time because a defective product may not cause an injury for years, or even decades, after it was sold. Because this may be unfair to the seller, some states have enacted **statutes of repose.** Statutes of repose limit the seller's liability to a certain number of years from the date when the product was first sold. The period of repose varies from state to state.

Concept Summary Statute of Limitations and Statute of Repose

Statute	Begins to Run
Statute of limitations	When the plaintiff suffers injury
Statute of repose	When the product is first sold

Contributory Negligence and Comparative Fault

Sometimes a person who is injured by a defective product is negligent and contributes to his or her own injuries. The defense of **contributory negligence** bars an injured plaintiff from recovering from the defendant in a negligence action. However, this doctrine generally does not bar recovery in strict liability actions.

Many states have held that the doctrine of **comparative fault** (or **comparative negligence**) applies to strict liability actions. Under this doctrine, a plaintiff who is contributorily negligent for his or her injuries is responsible for a *proportional share* of damages. In other words, the damages are apportioned between the plaintiff and the defendant.

contributory negligence

A defense that says a person who is injured by a defective product but has been negligent and has contributed to his or her own injuries cannot recover from the defendant.

comparative fault

A doctrine that applies to strict liability actions that says a plaintiff who is contributorily negligent for his or her injuries is responsible for a proportional share of the damages. Also called *comparative negligence*.

Consider This Example Suppose an automobile manufacturer produces a car with a hidden defect, and a consumer purchases the car from an automobile dealer. Assume that the consumer is injured in an automobile accident in which the defect is found to be 75 percent responsible for the accident, and the consumer's own reckless driving is found to be 25 percent responsible. The plaintiff suffers $1 million worth of injuries. Under the doctrine of *contributory negligence*, the plaintiff would recover nothing from the defendants. Under the doctrine of *comparative negligence*, the plaintiff would recover $750,000 from the defendants.

Concept Summary *Contributory Negligence and Comparative Fault*

Doctrine	Description
Contributory negligence	A person who is partially responsible for causing his or her own injuries may not recover anything from the manufacturer or seller of a defective product that caused the remainder of the person's injuries.
Comparative fault	A person who is partially responsible for causing his or her own injuries is responsible for a proportional share of the damages. The manufacturer or seller of the defective product is responsible for the remainder of the plaintiff's damages. Also called *comparative negligence*.

London, England. Most industrialized countries and many other countries have well-developed product liability law based on negligence, but few have adopted the doctrine of strict liability.

Terms and Concepts

Misrepresentation

In a case of misrepresentation, a seller or lessor fraudulently misrepresents the quality of a product, and the plaintiff relies on the misrepresentation and is injured thereby.

Negligence

In a case of negligence, a seller or lessor breaches his or her duty of due care by producing a defective product that causes injury to the plaintiff. Privity of contract between the seller or lessor and the plaintiff is not required.

Strict Liability in Tort

A manufacturer or seller who sells a defective product is liable to the ultimate user who is injured thereby. All in the chain of distribution are liable, irrespective of fault. Sometimes called *vertical liability*.

The Concept of Defect

1. Defect in manufacture
2. Defect in design
3. Failure to warn
4. Defect in packaging
5. Failure to provide adequate instructions for assembly of a product
6. Other defects

Defenses to Product Liability

A manufacturer or seller is not liable for damages caused by a product it manufactures or sells if one of the following defenses applies:

1. ***Supervening event.*** The product was materially altered or modified after it left the seller's possession, and the alteration or modification caused an injury. Also called *intervening event*.
2. ***Generally known dangers.*** A seller is not liable for failing to warn about inherent dangers in products that are known to the general population.
3. ***Government contractor defense.*** A manufacturer produces a product (1) to the precise specifications for the product that were provided by the government, (2) the product conformed to those specifications, and (3) the contractor warned the government of any known defects or dangers of the product.
4. ***Correction of a defect.*** A manufacturer or seller who learns about a defect in a product it has sold notifies purchasers and users of the defect and corrects the defect.
5. ***Assumption of the risk.*** The plaintiff knew and appreciated the risk and voluntarily assumed the risk.
6. ***Misuse of the product:***
   a. *Abnormal misuse.* The seller is not liable for injuries caused by the abnormal misuse of a product by the plaintiff. Also called *unforeseeable misuse*.
   b. *Foreseeable misuse.* The seller is liable for injuries caused by the foreseeable misuse of a product. The manufacturer must design products to be safe for foreseeable misuses.

Statutes of Limitations and Repose

1. ***Statute of limitations.*** An injured person must bring a product liability lawsuit within a specified period of time after being injured by a defective product.
2. ***Statute of repose.*** A person must bring a product liability lawsuit within a specified period of time after a defective product was first purchased or leased.

Contributory Negligence and Comparative Fault

1. ***Contributory negligence.*** A person who is partially responsible for causing his or her own injuries may not recover anything from the manufacturer or seller of a defective product that caused the remainder of the person's injuries.
2. ***Comparative fault.*** A person who is partially responsible for causing his or her own injuries is responsible for a proportional share of the damages. The manufacturer or seller of the defective product is responsible for the remainder of the plaintiff's damages. Also called *comparative negligence.*

Internet Exercises and Case Questions

Working the Web Internet Exercises

1. Find the statistics on the most frequent type of product liability cases filed in your jurisdiction. Start with "Consumer Product-Related Statistics," at **www.cpsc.gov/library/data.html**.
2. What is the statute of limitations on product liability in your jurisdiction for strict liability? See *Restatement (Third) of Torts* Section 402A, at **www.ali.org/ali/Tortpl.htm**. See also **www.law.cornell.edu/topics/products_liability.html**, which contains an overview of products liability law, with links to key primary and secondary sources.
3. Does your state have a statute of repose for product liability cases?

Legal Environment Cases

7.1 Strict Liability Jeppesen and Company produces charts that graphically display approach procedures for airplanes landing at airports. These charts are drafted from tabular data supplied by the Federal Aviation Administration (FAA), a federal agency of the U.S. government. By law, Jeppesen cannot construct charts that include information different from that supplied by the FAA. On September 8, 1973, the pilot of an airplane owned by World Airways was on descent to land at the Cold Bay, Alaska, airport. The pilot was using an instrument approach procedure chart published by Jeppesen. The airplane crashed into a mountain near Cold Bay, killing all six crew members and destroying the aircraft. Evidence showed that the FAA data did not include the mountain. The heirs of the deceased crew members and World Airways brought a strict liability action against Jeppesen. Does the doctrine of strict liability apply to this case? Is Jeppesen liable? *Brockeshy v. Jeppesen and Company*, 767 F.2d 1288, 1985, U.S. App. Lexis 21290 (9th Cir.)

7.2 Failure to Warn The Emerson Electric Co. manufactured and sold a product called the Weed Eater XR-90. The Weed Eater was a multipurpose weed-trimming and brush-cutting device. It consisted of a handheld gasoline-powered engine connected to a long drive shaft, at the end of which could be attached various tools for cutting weeds and brush. One such attachment was a 10-inch circular sawblade capable of cutting through growth up to 2 inches in diameter. When this sawblade was attached to the Weed Eater, approximately 270 degrees of blade edge were exposed when in use. The owner's manual contained the following warning: "Keep children away. All people and pets should be kept at a safe distance from the work area, at least 30 feet, especially when using the blade." Donald Pearce, a 13-year-old boy, was helping his uncle clear an overgrown yard. The uncle was operating a Weed Eater XR-90 with the circular sawblade attachment. When Pearce stopped to pick up something off the ground about 6 to 10 feet behind and slightly to the left of where his uncle was operating the Weed Eater, the sawblade on the Weed Eater struck something near the ground. The Weed Eater kicked back to the left and cut off Pearce's right arm to the elbow. Pearce, through his mother, Charlotte Karns, sued Emerson to recover damages under strict liability. Is Emerson liable? *Karns v. Emerson Electric Co.*, 817 F.2d 1452, 1987 U.S. App. Lexis 5608 (10th Cir.)

7.3 Crashworthiness Doctrine At 11 P.M. on April 10 1968, Verne Prior, driving on U.S. 101 under the influence of alcohol and drugs at a speed of 65 to 85 miles per hour, crashed his 1963 Chrysler into the left rear of a 1962 Chevrolet station wagon stopped on the shoulder of the freeway because of a flat tire. Christine Smith was sitting in the passenger seat of the parked car when the accident occurred. In the crash, the Chevrolet station wagon was knocked into a gully, where its fuel tank ruptured. The vehicle caught fire, and Smith suffered severe burn injuries. The Chevrolet station wagon was manufactured by General Motors Corporation. Evidence showed that the fuel tank was located in a vulnerable position in the back of the station wagon, outside the crossbars of the frame. Evidence further showed that if the fuel tank had been located underneath the body of the station wagon, between the crossbars of the frame, it would have been well protected in the collision. Smith sued General Motors for strict liability. Was the Chevrolet station wagon a defective product? *Smith v. General Motors Corporation*, 42 C.A.3d 1, 116 Cal.Rptr. 575, 1974 Cal.App. Lexis 1199 (Cal. App.)

7.4 Failure to Warn Virginia Burke purchased a bottle of "Le Domaine" champagne that was manufactured by Almaden Vineyards, Inc. At home, she removed the wine seal from the top of the bottle but did not remove the plastic cork. She set the bottle on the counter, intending to serve it in a few minutes. Shortly thereafter, the plastic cork spontaneously ejected from the bottle, ricocheted off the wall, and struck Burke in the lens of her eyeglasses, shattering the lens and driving pieces of glass into her eye. The champagne bottle did not contain any warning of this danger. Evidence showed that Almaden had previously been notified of the spontaneous ejection of the cork from its champagne bottles. Burke sued Almaden to recover damages for strict liability. *Burke v. Almaden Vineyards, Inc.*, 86 C.A.3d 768, 150 Cal.Rptr. 419, 1978 Cal. App. Lexis 2123 (Cal. App.)

7.5 Assumption of Risk Lillian Horn was driving her Chevrolet station wagon, which was designed and manufactured by General Motors Corporation, down Laurel Canyon Boulevard in Los Angeles, California. Horn swerved to avoid a collision when a car coming toward her crossed the center line and was coming at her. In doing so, her hand knocked the horn cap off the steering wheel, which exposed the area underneath the horn cap, including the three sharp prongs that had held the horn cap to the steering wheel. A few seconds later, when her car hit an embankment, Horn's face was impaled on the three sharp exposed prongs, causing her severe facial injuries. Horn sued General Motors for strict liability. General Motors asserted the defense of assumption of the risk against Horn. Who wins? *Horn v. General Motors Corporation*, 17 C.3d 359, 131 Cal.Rptr. 78, 1976 Cal. Lexis 283 (Cal.)

7.6 Misuse The Wilcox-Crittendon Company manufactured harnesses, saddles, bridles, leads, and other items commonly used for horses, cattle, and other ranch and farm animals. One such item was a stallion or cattle tie, a five-inch-long iron hook with a one-inch ring at one end. The tongue on the ring opened outward to allow the hook to be attached to a rope or another object. In 1964, a purchasing agent for United Airlines, who was familiar with this type of hook because of earlier experiences on a farm, purchased one of these hooks from Keystone Brothers, a harness and saddlery wares outlet located in San Francisco, California. Four years later, on March 28, 1968, Edward Dosier, an employee of United Airlines, was working to install a new grinding machine at a United Airlines maintenance plant. As part of the installation process, Dosier attached the hook to a 1,700-pound counterweight and raised the counterweight into the air. While the counterweight was suspended in the air, Dosier reached under the counterweight to retrieve a missing bolt. The hook broke, and the counterweight fell and crushed Dosier's arm. Dosier sued Wilcox-Crittendon for strict liability. Who wins? *Dosier v. Wilcox-Crittendon Company*, 45 Cal.App.3d. 74, 119 Cal.Rptr. 135, 1975 Cal.App. Lexis 1665 (Cal. App.)

Ethics in Business

7.7 Celestino Luque lived with his cousins Harry and Laura Dunn in Milbrae, California. The Dunns purchased a rotary lawn mower from Rhoads Hardware. The lawn mower was manufactured by Air Capital Manufacturing Company and was distributed by Garehime Corporation. On December 4, 1965, neighbors asked Luque to mow their lawn. While Luque was cutting the lawn, he noticed a small carton in the path of the lawn mower. Luque left the lawn mower in a stationary position with its motor running and walked around the side of the lawn mower to remove the carton. As he did so, he slipped on the wet grass and fell backward. Luque's left hand entered the unguarded hole of the lawn mower and was caught in its revolving blade, which turns at 175 miles per hour and 100 revolutions per second. Luque's hand was severely mangled and lacerated. The word *Caution* was printed above the unguarded hole on the lawn mower. Luque sued Rhoads Hardware, Air Capital, and Garehime Corporation for strict liability. The defendants argued that strict liability does not apply to *patent* (obvious) defects. *Luque v. McLean, Trustee*, 8 Cal.3d 135, 104 Cal.Rptr. 443, 1972 Cal. Lexis 245 (Cal.)

Ethics Issues

1. What legal concept did the plaintiff assert was violated?
2. Was it ethical for the defendants to argue that they were not liable for patent defects?
3. Would patent defects ever be corrected if the defendant's contention was accepted by the court?
4. Who wins this case? Why?

Endnotes

1. *Restatement (Second) of Torts*, Section 395.
2. 111 N.E. 1050, 217 N.Y. 382, 1916 N.Y. Lexis 1324 (N.Y. App.)
3. 59 Cal.2d Cal.Rptr. 697, 1963 Cal. Lexis 140 (Cal.)

8

Business and Online Crimes

"In our complex society the accountant's certificate and the lawyer's opinion can be instruments for inflicting pecuniary loss more potent than the chisel or the crowbar."

— Justice Blackman, Dissenting Opinion.
Ernst & Ernst v. Hochfelder, 425 U.S. 185 (1976)

Chapter Objectives

After studying this chapter, you should be able to:

1. Define crime and list the essential elements of a crime.
2. Describe criminal procedure, including arrest, indictment, arraignment, and the criminal trial.
3. Define major white-collar crimes, such as embezzlement, bribery, and criminal fraud.
4. Explain the constitutional safeguards provided by the Fourth, Fifth, Sixth, and Eighth Amendments to the U.S. Constitution.
5. List and describe laws involving computer and Internet crimes.

Chapter Contents

For members of society to peacefully coexist and commerce to flourish, people and their property must be protected from injury by other members of society. Federal, state, and local governments' **criminal laws** are intended to accomplish this by providing an incentive for persons to act reasonably in society and imposing penalties on persons who violate them.

The United States has one of the most advanced and humane criminal law systems in the world. It differs from any other criminal law systems in several respects. A person charged with a crime in the United States is *presumed innocent until proven guilty*. The *burden of proof* is on the government to prove that the accused is guilty of the crime charged. Further, the accused must be found guilty "beyond a reasonable doubt." Conviction requires unanimous jury vote. Under many other legal systems, a person accused of a crime is presumed guilty unless the person can prove he or she is not. A person charged with a crime in the United States is also provided with substantial constitutional safeguards during the criminal justice process.

This chapter discusses crime, criminal procedure, crimes affecting business, white-collar crime, computer and Internet crime, inchoate crime, international crime, criminal penalties, and constitutional safeguards afforded criminal defendants.

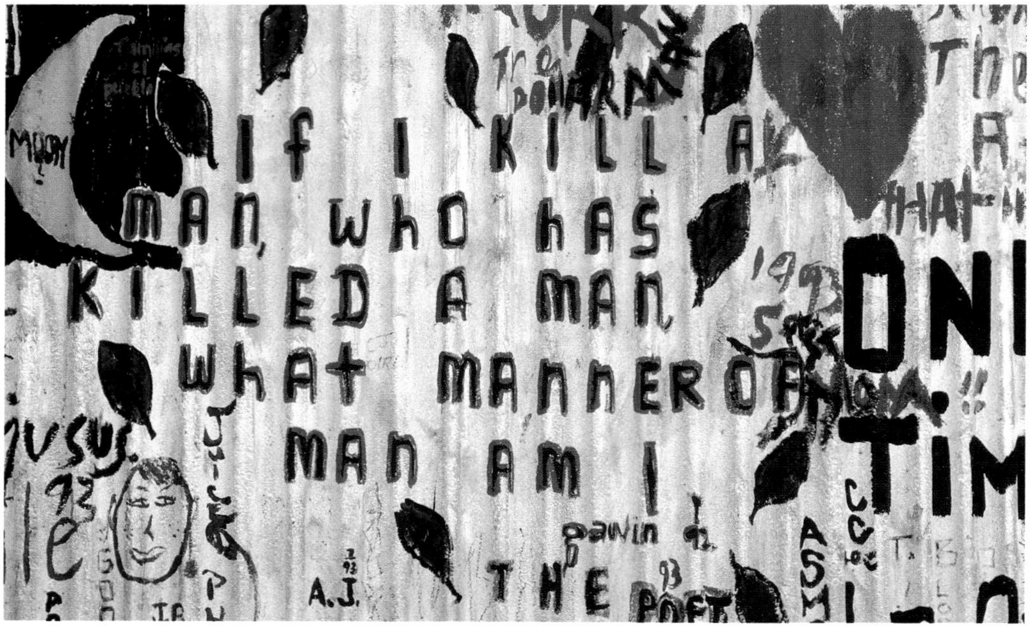

Homeless Person's Poet Wall, Los Angeles, California. Should the death penalty be permitted in the United States?

Definition of Crime

crime
A violation of a statute for which the government imposes a punishment.

A **crime** is defined as any act done by an individual in violation of those duties that he or she owes to society and for the breach of which the law provides that the wrongdoer shall make amends to the public. Many activities have been considered crimes through the ages, whereas other crimes are of recent origin.

Penal Codes and Regulatory Statutes

penal codes
A collection of criminal statutes.

Statutes are the primary source of criminal law. Most states have adopted comprehensive **penal codes** that define in detail the activities considered to be crimes within their jurisdictions and the penalties that will be imposed for their commission. A comprehensive federal criminal code defines federal crimes.[1] In addition, state and federal **regulatory statutes** often provide for criminal violations and penalties. The state and federal legislatures are continually adding to the list of crimes.

The penalty for committing a crime may consist of the imposition of a fine, imprisonment, both, or some other form of punishment (e.g., probation). Generally, imprisonment is imposed to (1) incapacitate the criminal so he or she will not harm others in society, (2) provide a means to rehabilitate the criminal, (3) deter others from similar conduct, and (4) inhibit personal retribution by the victim.

regulatory statutes
Statutes, such as environmental laws, securities laws, and antitrust laws, that provide for criminal violations and penalties.

Parties to a Criminal Action

In a criminal lawsuit, the government (not a private party) is the *plaintiff*. The government is represented by a lawyer called the *prosecutor*. The accused, which is usually an individual or a business, is the *defendant*. The accused is represented by a *defense attorney*. If the accused cannot afford a defense lawyer, the government will provide one free of charge.

Law cannot persuade, where it cannot punish.

Thomas Fuller
Gnomologia (1732)

Classification of Crimes

All crimes can be classified in one of the following categories.

Felonies **Felonies** are the most serious kinds of crimes. Felonies include crimes that are *mala in se*; that is, they are inherently evil. Most crimes against persons (e.g., murder, rape) and certain business-related crimes (e.g., embezzlement, bribery) are felonies in most jurisdictions. Felonies are usually punishable by imprisonment. In some jurisdictions, certain felonies (e.g., first-degree murder) are punishable by death. Federal law[2] and some state laws require mandatory sentencing for specified crimes. Many statutes define different degrees of crimes (e.g., first-, second-, and third-degree murder). Each degree earns different penalties. Serious violations of regulatory statutes are also felonies.

felony
The most serious type of crime; inherently evil crime. Most crimes against the person and some business-related crimes are felonies.

Misdemeanors **Misdemeanors** are less serious than felonies. They are crimes *mala prohibita*; that is, they are not inherently evil but are prohibited by society. Many crimes against property, such as robbery, burglary, and less serious violations of regulatory statutes, are included in this category. Misdemeanors carry lesser penalties than felonies. They are usually punishable by fines and/or imprisonment for one year or less.

misdemeanor
A less serious crime; not inherently evil but prohibited by society. Many crimes against property are misdemeanors.

Violations Crimes such as traffic violations, jaywalking, and such are neither felonies nor misdemeanors. These crimes, which are called **violations**, are generally punishable by fines. Occasionally, a few days of imprisonment are imposed for a violation.

violation
A crime that is neither a felony nor a misdemeanor that is usually punishable by a fine.

Concept Summary Classification of Crimes

Classification	Description
Felony	The most serious kinds of crime. Felonies are *mala in se* (inherently evil), and they are usually punishable by imprisonment.
Misdemeanor	A crime that is less serious than felonies. Misdemeanors are *mala prohibita* (prohibited by society), and they are usually punishable by fine and/or imprisonment for less than one year.
Violation	A crime that is neither a felony nor a misdemeanor. Violations are generally punishable by a fine.

Elements of a Crime

The following two elements must be proven for a person to be found guilty of most crimes:

actus reus
"Guilty act"—the actual performance of a criminal act.

1. ***Criminal act.*** The defendant must have actually performed the prohibited act. The actual performance of the criminal act is called the **actus reus** (guilty act). Killing someone without legal jurisdiction is an example of *actus reus*. Sometimes, the omission of an act constitutes the requisite *actus reus*. For example, a crime has been committed if a taxpayer who is under a legal duty to file a tax return fails to do so. However, merely thinking about committing a crime is not a crime because no action has been taken.

mens rea
"Evil intent"—the possession of the requisite state of mind to commit a prohibited act.

2. ***Criminal intent.*** To be found guilty of a crime, the accused must be found to have possessed the requisite state of mind (i.e., specific or general intent) when the act was performed. This is called the **mens rea** (evil intent). *Specific intent* is found where the accused purposefully, intentionally, or with knowledge commits a prohibited act. *General intent* is found where there is a showing of recklessness or a lesser degree of mental culpability. The individual criminal statutes state whether the crime requires a showing of specific or general intent. Juries may infer an accused's intent from the facts and circumstances of the case. There is no crime if the requisite *mens rea* cannot be proven. Thus, no crime is committed if a person accidentally injures another person.

non-intent crime
"A crime that imposes criminal liability without a finding of *mens rea* (intent).

Most states provide for certain **non-intent crimes**. The crime of *involuntary manslaughter* is often imposed for reckless conduct. For example, if a driver of an automobile drives too fast (e.g., 20 miles over the speed limit) on a city street and hits and kills a pedestrian, the driver will most likely be found guilty of the crime of involuntary manslaughter and be sentenced to jail.

Concept Summary Elements of an Intent Crime

Element	Description
actus rea	Guilty act
mens rea	Evil intent

Criminal Acts as the Basis for Tort Actions

The magnitude of a crime is proportionate to the magnitude of the injustice which prompts it. Hence, the smallest crimes may be actually the greatest.

Aristotle
The Rhetoric, Bk. 1, Ch. XIV

An injured party may bring a *civil tort action* against a wrongdoer who has caused the party injury during the commission of a criminal act. Civil lawsuits are separate from the government's criminal action against the wrongdoer. In many cases, a person injured by a criminal act will not sue the criminal to recover civil damages. This is because the criminal is often *judgment proof*—that is, the criminal does not have the money to pay a civil judgment.

Concept Summary Civil and Criminal Law Compared

Issue	Civil Law	Criminal Law
Party who brings the action	The plaintiff	The government
Trial by jury	Yes, except actions for equity	Yes
Burden of proof	Preponderance of the evidence	Beyond a reasonable doubt

Jury vote	Judgment for plaintiff requires specific jury vote	Conviction requires unanimous jury vote (e.g., 9 of 12 jurors)
Sanctions and penalties	Monetary damages and equitable remedies (e.g., injunction, specific performance)	Imprisonment, capital punishment, fine, probation

Ethics in Business

Martha Stewart Guilty of a Crime

Martha Stewart is an icon of fine living. Through her company, Martha Stewart Living Omnimedia, Inc. (Omnimedia), Stewart built a business conglomerate involved in publishing magazines and cookbooks, selling clothing and home-based merchandise, and producing a syndicated television program. She and her business became so successful that when the company went public in 1999, Stewart became an instant billionaire.

In 2003, Stewart's friend Sam Waksal, the primary owner of ImClone Systems Inc. (ImClone), received news that the U.S. Food and Drug Administration (FDA) had not given approval for ImClone to market a cancer-fighting drug. Waksal received this information one day before the news would be made public. Waksal and a number of his family members tried to sell their ImClone stock through a securities broker named Peter E. Bacanovic. Bacanovic was also Martha Stewart's stockbroker, and Stewart was a shareholder of ImClone. Bacanovic had his assistant, Douglas Faneuil, notify Stewart of Waksal's activities. Stewart sold her ImClone stock at $58 per share. When the FDA's negative decision regarding the anticancer drug was released, ImClone stock fell in value. Stewart saved $45,000 by selling her ImClone stock early.

When the U.S. Government investigated the substantial selling activity in ImClone stock prior to the public announcement of the FDA's adverse ruling, they netted the Waksal family *and* Martha Stewart. Sam Waksal pleaded guilty to insider trading and was sent to jail. When the federal government questioned Stewart about her sale of ImClone stock, she said that she had a prior $60 "sell order" (to sell the stock if it ever dropped to $60). Although both Bacanovic and Faneuil first corroborated this story, eventually Faneuil reached a plea bargain with the government and became a witness. He then told the government that the $60 sell order story was a lie and cover-up.

The U.S. Government brought criminal charges against Stewart for criminal conspiracy, lying to the federal government, and obstruction of justice. Stewart pleaded the Fifth Amendment and did not testify at trial. The government called many witnesses, including Faneuil and several of Stewart's friends to whom she had talked to about the ImClone stock sale. One witness testified that Stewart told her that Stewart knew of Waksal's trading before she sold her ImClone stock and then stated, "Isn't it nice to have brokers who tell you these things?" The jury returned a verdict of guilty on all charges. On the day the judgment was announced, Stewart's Omnimedia stock plummeted, and Stewart lost about $100 million in one day. Stewart served four and a half months in jail. *United States v. Stewart* (2004)

Ethics Issues

1. Did Stewart act ethically in this case?
2. Why do you think Stewart sold her ImClone stock to save only $45,000?

Criminal Procedure

The procedure for initiating and maintaining a criminal action is quite detailed. It includes both pretrial procedures and the actual trial.

Arrest

Before the police can arrest a person for the commission of a crime, they usually must obtain an **arrest warrant** based on a showing of probable cause. *Probable cause* is defined as the substantial likelihood that the person either committed or is about to commit a crime. If there is no time for the police to obtain a warrant (e.g., if the police arrive during the

arrest warrant
A document for a person's detainment based on a showing of probable cause that the person committed a crime.

commission of a crime, when a person is fleeing from the scene of a crime, when it is likely that evidence will be destroyed), the police may still arrest the suspect. *Warrantless arrests* are also judged by the probable cause standard.

After a person is arrested, he or she is taken to the police station to be booked. *Booking* is the administrative procedure for recording the arrest, fingerprinting, and so on.

In the following case, the U.S. Supreme Court held that a police officer may make a warrantless arrest pursuant to a minor criminal offense.

Case 8.1
Arrest

U.S. SUPREME COURT

Atwater v. Lago Vista, Texas

532 U.S. 318, 121 S. Ct. 1536, 2001 U.S. Lexis 3366
Supreme Court of the United States

Background and Facts

Texas law requires that front-seat drivers and passengers wear seat belts and that a driver secure any small child riding in front. In March 1997, Gail Atwater was driving her pickup truck in Lago Vista, Texas, with her three-year-old son and five-year-old daughter in the front seat. None of them were wearing seat belts. Bart Turek, a Lago Vista police officer, observed the seat belt violation and pulled Atwater over. A friend of Atwater's arrived at the scene and took charge of the children. Turek handcuffed Atwater, placed her in his squad car, and drover her to the police station. Atwater was booked, her mug shot was taken, and she was placed in a jail cell for about one hour, until she was released on $310 bond. Atwater ultimately pleaded no contest to the misdemeanor seatbelt offenses and paid a $50 fine. Atwater sued the City of Lago Vista and the police officer for compensatory and punitive damages for allegedly violating her Fourth Amendment right to be free from unreasonable seizure. The district court ruled against Atwater, and the Court of Appeals affirmed. The U.S. Supreme Court granted certiorari to hear the appeal.

Issue

Does the Fourth Amendment permit police to make a warrantless arrest pursuant to a minor criminal offense?

In the Language of the Court

There is no support for Atwater's position in this Court's cases. Both the legislative tradition of granting warrantless misdemeanor arrest authority and the judicial tradition of sustaining such statutes against constitutional attack are buttressed by legal commentary that, for more than a century now, has almost uniformly recognized the constitutionality of extending warrantless arrest power to misdemeanors without limitation to breaches of the peace. If an officer has probable cause to believe that an individual has committed even a very minor criminal offense in his presence, he may, without violating the Fourth Amendment, arrest the offender.

Decision and Remedy

The U.S. Supreme Court held that the Fourth Amendment permits police officers to make a warrantless arrest pursuant to a minor criminal offense. The Supreme Court affirmed the judgments of the district court and the Court of Appeals.

Business and Ethics Questions

1. Did you agree with the U.S. Supreme Court's decision in this case? Why or why not?
2. Did the police officer act ethically in this case? Should he have used more discretion?
3. What would be the consequences if the Supreme Court had held in favor of Atwater?

Indictment or Information

Accused persons must be formally charged with a crime before they can be brought to trial. This is usually done through the issuance of a *grand-jury indictment* or a *magistrate's information statement*.

Evidence of serious crimes, such as murder, is usually presented to a *grand jury*. Most grand juries comprise between 6 and 24 citizens who are charged with evaluating the evidence presented by the government. Grand jurors sit for a fixed period of time, such as one year. If the grand jury determines that there is sufficient evidence to hold the accused for trial, it issues an **indictment**. Note that the grand jury does not determine guilt. If an indictment is issued, the accused will be held for later trial.

For lesser crimes (e.g., burglary, shoplifting), the accused will be brought before a *magistrate* (judge). A magistrate who finds that there is enough evidence to hold the accused for trial will issue an **information**.

The case against the accused is dismissed if neither an indictment nor an information is issued.

indictment
The charge of having committed a crime (usually a felony), based on the judgment of a grand jury.

information
The charge of having committed a crime (usually a misdemeanor), based on the judgment of a judge (magistrate).

Arraignment

If an indictment or information is issued, the accused is brought before a court for an **arraignment** proceeding, during which the accused is (1) informed of the charges against him or her and (2) asked to enter a *plea*. The accused may plead *guilty*, *not guilty*, or *nolo contendere*. A plea of *nolo contendere* means that the accused agrees to the imposition of a penalty but does not admit guilt. A *nolo contendere* plea cannot be used as evidence of liability against the accused at a subsequent civil trial. Corporate defendants often enter this plea. The government has the option of accepting a *nolo contendere* plea or requiring the defendant to plead guilty or not guilty.

arraignment
A hearing during which the accused is brought before a court and is (1) informed of the charges against him or her and (2) asked to enter a plea.

Plea Bargaining

Sometimes the accused and the government enter into a **plea bargaining agreement**. The government engages in plea bargaining to save costs, avoid the risks of a trial, and prevent further overcrowding of the prisons. This type of arrangement allows the accused to admit to a lesser crime than charged. In return, the government agrees to impose a lesser penalty or sentence than might have been obtained had the case gone to trial.

plea bargain
A situation in which the accused admits to a lesser crime than charged. In return, the government agrees to impose a lesser sentence than might have been obtained had the case gone to trial.

The Criminal Trial

At a criminal trial, all jurors must *unanimously* agree before the accused is found *guilty* of the crime charged. If even one juror disagrees (i.e., has reasonable doubt) about the guilt of the accused, the accused cannot be found guilty of the crime charged. If all the jurors agree that the accused did not commit the crime, the accused is found *not guilty* of the crime charged. After trial, the following rules apply:

- If the defendant if found guilty, he or she may appeal.
- If the defendant is found not guilty, the government cannot appeal.
- If the jury cannot come to a unanimous decision about the defendant's guilt one way or the other, the jury is considered a **hung jury**. The government may choose to retry the case before a new judge and jury.

There can be no equal justice where the kind of trial a man gets depends on the amount of money he has.

J. Black
Griffin v. Illinois (1956)

hung jury
A jury that cannot come to a unanimous decision about a defendant's guilt. In the event of a hung jury, the government may choose to retry the case.

Internet Law & Online Commerce

Cyber Crimes

The Internet and Information Age ushered in a whole new world for education, business, and consumer transactions. But with it followed a new rash of cyber crimes. Prosecutors and courts wrestled over how to apply existing laws written in a nondigital age to new Internet-related abuses.

In 1996, Congress responded by enacting the **Information Infrastructure Protection Act (IIP Act)**. In this federal law, Congress addressed computer-related crimes as distinct offenses. The IIP Act provides protection for any computer attached to the Internet.

(continued)

Internet Law & Online Commerce (continued)

The IIP Act makes it a federal crime for anyone to intentionally access and obtain information from a protected computer without authorization. The IIP Act does not require that the defendant accessed a protected computer for commercial benefit. Thus, persons who transmit a computer virus over the Internet or hackers who trespass into Internet-connected computers may be criminally prosecuted under the IIP Act. Even merely observing data on a protected computer without authorization is sufficient to meet the requirement that the defendant has accessed a protected computer. Criminal penalties for violating the IIP Act include imprisonment for up to 10 years and fines.

The IIP Act gives the federal government a much-needed weapon for directly prosecuting cyber-crooks, hackers, and others who enter, steal, destroy, or look at others' computer data without authorization. ■

Common Crimes

Many crimes are committed against property. These crimes often involve the theft, misappropriation, or fraudulent taking of property. Many of the most important crimes against business property are discussed in the following paragraphs.

Robbery

robbery
The taking of personal property from another person by use of fear or force.

In common law, **robbery** is defined as the taking of personal property from another person or business by the use of fear or force. For example, if a robber threatens to physically harm a storekeeper unless that victim surrenders the contents of the cash register, it is robbery. If a criminal pickpockets somebody's wallet, it is not robbery because there has been no use of force or fear. Robbery with a deadly weapon is generally considered aggravated robbery (or armed robbery) and carries a harsher penalty.

Burglary

burglary
The taking of personal property from another's home, office, commercial, or other type of building.

In common law, **burglary** is defined as "breaking and entering a dwelling at night" with the intent to commit a felony. Modern penal codes have broadened this definition to include daytime thefts from offices and commercial and other buildings. In addition, the "breaking in" element has been abandoned by most modern definitions of burglary. Thus, unauthorized entry of a building through an unlocked door is sufficient. Aggravated burglary (or armed burglary) carries stiffer penalties.

Larceny

larceny
The taking of another's personal property other than from his or her person or building.

In common law, **larceny** is defined as the wrongful and fraudulent taking of another person's personal property. Most personal property—including tangible property, trade secrets, computer programs, and other business property—is subject to larceny. The stealing of automobiles and car stereos, pickpocketing, and such are larceny. Neither the use of force nor the entry of a building is required. Some states distinguish between grand larceny and petit larceny, based on the value of the property taken.

Theft

Some states have dropped the distinctions among the crimes of robbery, burglary, and larceny. Instead, these states group such crimes under the general crime of **theft**. Most of these states distinguish between grand theft and petit theft, based on the value of the property taken.

Receiving Stolen Property

It is a crime for a person to (1) knowingly **receive stolen property** and (2) intend to deprive the rightful owner of that property. Knowledge and intent can be inferred from the circumstances. The stolen property can be any tangible property (e.g., personal property, money, negotiable instruments, stock certificates).

receiving stolen property
A person's (1) knowingly receiving stolen property and (2) intending to deprive the rightful owner of that property.

Arson

In common law, **arson** is defined as the malicious or willful burning of the dwelling of another person. Modern penal codes have expanded this definition to include the burning of all types of private, commercial, and public buildings. Thus, in most states, an owner who burns his or her own building to collect insurance proceeds can be found liable for arson. If arson is found, the insurance company does not have to pay proceeds of any insurance policy on the burned property.

arson
The willful or malicious burning of another's building.

Extortion

The crime of **extortion** involves the obtaining of property from another, with his or her consent, induced by wrongful use of actual or threatened force, violence, or fear. For example, extortion occurs when a person threatens to expose something about another person unless that other person gives money or property. The truth or falsity of the information is immaterial. Extortion of private persons is commonly referred to as **blackmail**. Extortion of public officials is called **extortion "under color of official right."**

extortion
A threat to expose something about another person unless that other person gives money or property. Often referred to as *blackmail*.

The Bahamas. Certain countries provide bank secrecy laws that protect the identity of depositors from disclosure. The Bahamas has such a law, and many of its chartered "banks" are no more than lawyers' offices in office buildings. Who do you think uses these bank accounts?

White-Collar Crimes

Certain types of crime are prone to being committed by businesspersons. These crimes are often referred to as **white-collar crimes**. These crimes usually involve cunning and deceit rather than physical force. Many of the most important white-collar crimes are discussed in the paragraphs that follow.

Forgery

forgery
The fraudulent making or altering of a written document that affects the legal liability of another person.

The crime of **forgery** occurs if a written document is fraudulently made or altered and that change affects the legal liability of another person. Counterfeiting, falsifying public records, and materially altering legal documents are examples of forgery. One of the most common forms of forgery is signing another person's signature to a check or changing the amount of a check. Note that signing another person's signature without the intent to defraud is not forgery. For example, forgery has not been committed if one spouse signs the other spouse's payroll check for deposit in a joint checking or savings account at the bank.

Embezzlement

embezzlement
The fraudulent conversion of property by a person to whom that property was entrusted.

Unknown in common law, the crime of **embezzlement** is not a statutory crime. Embezzlement is the fraudulent conversion of property by a person to whom that property was entrusted. Typically, embezzlement is committed by an employer's employees, agents, or representatives (e.g., accountants, lawyers, trust officers, treasurers). Embezzlers often try to cover their tracks by preparing false books, records, or entries.

The key element here is that the stolen property was *entrusted* to the embezzler. This differs from robbery, burglary, and larceny, where property is taken by someone not entrusted with the property. For example, embezzlement has been committed if a bank teller absconds with money that was deposited by depositors. The employer (the bank) entrusted the teller to take deposits from its customers.

Bribery

bribery
A crime in which one person gives another person money, property, favors, or anything else of value for a favor in return. Often referred to as a *payoff* or *kickback*.

Bribery is one of the most prevalent forms of white-collar crime. A bribe can be money, property, favors, or anything else of value. The crime of commercial bribery prohibits the payment of bribes to private persons and businesses. This type of bribe is often referred to as a **kickback** or **payoff**. Intent is a necessary element of this crime. The offeror of a bribe commits the crime of bribery when the bribe is tendered. The offeree is guilty of the crime of bribery when he or she accepts the bribe. The offeror can be found liable for the crime of bribery even if the person to whom the bribe is offered rejects the bribe.

Consider This Example Harriet Landers is the purchasing agent for the ABC Corporation and is in charge of purchasing equipment to be used by the corporation. Neal Brown, the sales representative of a company that make equipment that can be used by the ABC Corporation, offers to pay her a 10 percent kickback if she buys equipment from him. She accepts the bribe and orders the equipment. Both parties are guilty of bribery.

In common law, the crime of bribery is defined as the giving or receiving of anything of value in corrupt payment for an "official act" by a public official. Public officials include legislators, judges, jurors, witnesses at trial, administrative agency personnel, and other government officials. Modern penal codes also make it a crime to bribe public officials. For example, a developer who is constructing an apartment building cannot pay the building inspector to overlook a building code violation.

International Law

Foreign Corrupt Practices Act

It is well known that the payment of bribes is pervasive in conducting international business. To prevent U.S. companies from engaging in this type of conduct, the U.S. Congress enacted the **Foreign Corrupt Practices Act of 1977 (FCPA)** [15 U.S.C. Section 78m]. The FCPA makes it illegal for U.S. Companies or their officers, directors, agents, or employees to bribe a foreign official, a foreign political party official, or a candidate for foreign political office. A bribe is illegal only where it is meant to influence the awarding of new business or the retention of a continuing business activity.

The FCPA imposes criminal liability where a person pays the illegal bribe himself or herself, or supplies a payment to a third party or an agent, knowing that it will be used as a bribe. A firm can be fined up to $2 million, and an individual can be fined up to $100,000 and imprisoned for up to five years for violations of the FCPA.

The 1988 amendments to the FCPA created two defenses. One excuses a firm or person charged with bribery under the FCPA if the firm or person can show that the payment was lawful under the written laws of that country. The other allows a defendant to show that a payment was a reasonable and bona fide expenditure related to the furtherance or execution of a contract. This latter exemption is difficult to interpret.

Some people argue that U.S. Companies are placed at a disadvantage in international markets where commercial bribery is commonplace and firms from other countries are not hindered by laws similar to the FCPA. ■

St. Petersburg, Russia.

Criminal Fraud

criminal fraud

A crime that involves obtaining title to property through deception or trickery. Also known as *false pretenses* or *deceit*.

Obtaining title to property through deception or trickery constitutes the crime of **false pretenses**. This crime is commonly referred to as **criminal fraud**, or **deceit**.

Consider This Example Bob Anderson, a stockbroker, promises Mary Greenberg, a prospective investor, that he will use any money she invests to purchase interests in oil wells. Based on this promise. Ms. Greenberg decides to make the investment. Mr. Anderson never intended to invest the money. Instead, he used the money for his personal needs. This is criminal fraud.

There are some frauds so well conducted that it would be stupidity not to be deceived by them.

C. C. Colton
Lacon, Vol. 1 (1820)

Mail and Wire Fraud Federal law prohibits the use of mails or wires (e.g., telegraphs, telephone, Internet) to defraud another person. These crimes are called **mail fraud**[3] and **wire fraud**,[4] respectively. The government often prosecutes a suspect under these statutes if there is insufficient evidence to prove the real crime that the criminal was attempting to commit or did commit. The maximum penalty for mail, wire, and Internet fraud is 20 years in prison.

Internet Law & Online Commerce

Cyber Identity Fraud

For centuries, some people—for various purposes, mostly financial in nature—have attempted to take the identities of other persons. Today, taking on the identity of another can be extremely lucrative, earning the spoils of another's credit cards, bank accounts, Social Security benefits, and such. The use of new technology—computers and the Internet—has made such "identity fraud" even easier. But the victim of such fraud is left with funds stolen, a dismantled credit history, and thousands of dollars in costs trying to straighten out the mess. Identity fraud is the fastest-growing financial fraud in America.

To combat such fraud, Congress passed the **Identity Theft and Assumption Deterrence Act of 1998**. This act criminalizes identity fraud, making it a federal felony punishable with prison sentences ranging from 3 to 25 years. The act also appoints a federal administrative agency, the Federal Trade Commission (FTC), to help victims restore their credit and erase the impact of the imposter. Law enforcement officials suggest the following steps to protect against identity fraud: Never put your Social Security number on any document unless it is legally required, obtain and review copies of your credit report at least twice each year, and use safe passwords (e.g., other than family names and birthdays) on bank accounts and other accounts that require personal identification numbers (PINs). ■

Racketeer Influenced and Corrupt Organizations Act (RICO)

Racketeer Influenced and Corrupt Organizations Act (RICO)

A federal act that provides for both criminal and civil penalties for racketeering.

Organized crime has a pervasive influence on many parts of the U.S. economy. In 1980, Congress enacted the Organized Crime Control Act, of which the **Racketeer Influenced and Corrupt Organizations Act (RICO)**[5] is part. Originally, RICO was intended to apply only to organized crime. However, the broad language of the RICO statute has been used against non-organized crime defendants as well. RICO, which provides for both criminal and civil penalties, is one of the most important laws affecting business today.

Criminal RICO RICO makes it a federal crime to acquire or maintain an interest in, use income from, or conduct or participate in the affairs of an enterprise through a pattern of racketeering activity. An *enterprise* is defined as a corporation, a partnership, a sole proprietorship, another business or organization, or the government. *Racketeering activity* consists of a number of specifically enumerated federal and state crimes, including such activities as gambling, arson, robbery, counterfeiting, and dealing in narcotics. Business-related crimes, such as bribery, embezzlement, mail fraud, and wire fraud, are also considered racketeering. To prove a *pattern of racketeering*, at least two of these acts must be committed by the defendant within a 10-year period. For example, committing two different frauds would be considered a pattern.

Individual defendants found criminally liable for RICO violations can be fined up to $25,000 per violation, imprisoned for up to 20 years, or both. In addition, RICO provides for the *forfeiture* of any property or business interests (even interests in a legitimate business) that were gained because of RICO violations. This provision allows the government to recover investments made with monies derived from racketeering activities. The government may also seek civil penalties for RICO violations. These include injunctions, orders of dissolution, reorganization of businesses, and the divestiture of the defendant's interest in an enterprise.

Civil RICO Persons injured by a RICO violation can bring a private *civil* action against the violator to recover injury to business or property. A successful plaintiff may recover *treble damages* (three times actual loss), plus attorneys' fees.

Criminal Conspiracy

A **criminal conspiracy** occurs when two or more persons enter into an agreement to commit a crime. To be liable for a criminal conspiracy, an *overt act* must be taken to further the crime. The crime itself does not have to be committed, however.

criminal conspiracy
A situation in which two or more persons enter into an agreement to commit a crime and an overt act is taken to further the crime.

Consider This Example Two securities brokers agree over the telephone to commit a securities fraud. They also obtain a list of potential victims and prepare false financial statements necessary for the fraud. Because they entered into an agreement to commit a crime and took overt action, the brokers are guilty of the crime of criminal conspiracy, even if they never carry out the securities fraud. The government usually brings criminal conspiracy charges if (1) the defendants have been thwarted in their efforts to commit the substantive crime or (2) there is insufficient evidence to prove the substantive crime.

Ethics in Business

Money Laundering

When criminals make money from illegal activities, they are often faced with the problem of having large sums of money and no record of how that money was earned. This could easily tip off the government to their illegal activities. In order to "wash" the money and make it look as though it was earned legitimately, many criminals purchase legitimate businesses and run the money through those businesses to clean it before the criminal receives the money. The legitimate business has "cooked" books showing faked expenditures and receipts, in which the illegal money is buried. Restaurants, motels, and other cash businesses make excellent money laundries.

To address this problem, the federal government enacted the **Money Laundering Control Act** [18 U.S.C. Section 1957]. This act makes it a crime to:

- Knowingly engage in a *monetary transaction* through a financial institution involving property worth more than $10,000. For example, this would include making deposits, withdrawals, or transactions between accounts or obtaining monetary instruments such as cashiers' checks, money orders, and travelers' checks from a bank or another financial institution.

(continued)

Ethics in Business
(continued)

- Knowingly engage in a *financial transaction* involving the proceeds of an illegal activity. For example, this would include buying real estate, automobiles, personal property, intangible assets, or anything of value with money obtained from illegal activities.

Thus, money laundering itself is now a federal crime. The money that is washed could have been made from illegal gambling operations, drug dealing, fraud, and other crimes, including white-collar crimes. Persons convicted of money laundering can be fined up to $500,000 or twice the value of the property involved, whichever is greater, and sentenced to up to 20 years in federal prison. In addition, violation of the Money Laundering Control Act subjects any property involved in or traceable to the offense to forfeiture to the government.

Ethics Issues

1. How does money laundering work? Give an example.
2. Is it ethical to launder money? Why did Congress make money laundering a crime?

Corporate Criminal Liability

A *corporation* is a fictitious legal person that is granted legal existence by the state only after certain requirements are met. A corporation cannot act on its own behalf. Instead, it must act through *agents*, such as managers, representatives, and employees.

The question of whether a corporation can be held criminally liable has intrigued legal scholars for some time. Originally, under the common law, it was generally held that corporations lacked the criminal mind (*mens rea*) to be held criminally liable. Modern courts, however, impose **corporate criminal liability**. These courts have held that corporations are criminally liable for the acts of their managers, agents, and employees. In any event, because corporations cannot be put in prison, they are usually sanctioned with fines, loss of a license or franchise, and the like.

corporate criminal liability
Criminal liability of a corporation for actions of its officers, employees, or agents.

Corporate directors, officers, and employees are individually liable for crimes they personally commit, whether for personal benefit or on behalf of a corporation. In addition, under certain circumstances, a corporate manager can be held criminally liable for the

The Forbidden City, Beijing, China. Multinational corporations have to obey the criminal laws of all the countries in which they conduct business.

criminal activities of his or her subordinates. To be held criminally liable, the manager must have failed to supervise the subordinate appropriately. This is an evolving area of the law.

Protection Against Unreasonable Search and Seizure

In many criminal cases, the government relies on information obtained from searches of individuals and businesses.

The *Fourth Amendment* to the U.S. Constitution protects persons and corporations from overzealous investigative activities by the government. It protects the rights of the people from **unreasonable search and seizure** by the government. It permits people to be secure in their persons, houses, papers, and effects.

"Reasonable" search and seizure by the government is lawful. A **search warrant** based on probable cause is necessary in most cases. Such a warrant specifically states the place and scope of the authorized search. General searches beyond the specified area are forbidden. *Warrantless searches* are permitted only (1) incident to arrest, (2) where evidence is in "plain view," or (3) where it is likely that evidence will be destroyed. Warrantless searches are also judged by the probable cause standard.

unreasonable search and seizure
Any search and seizure by the government that violates the Fourth Amendment.

search warrant
A warrant issued by a court that authorizes the police to search a designated place for specified contraband, articles, items, or documents. The search warrant must be based on probable cause.

Exclusionary Rule

Evidence obtained from an unreasonable search and seizure is considered tainted evidence ("fruit of a tainted tree"). Under the **exclusionary rule**, such evidence can generally be prohibited from introduction at a trial or an administrative proceeding against the person searched. However, this evidence is freely admissible against other persons. The U.S. Supreme Court created a *good faith exception* to the exclusionary rule.[6] This exception allows evidence otherwise obtained illegally to be introduced as evidence against the accused if the police officers who conducted the unreasonable search reasonably believed they were acting pursuant to a lawful search warrant.

exclusionary rule
A rule that says evidence obtained from an unreasonable search and seizure can generally be prohibited from introduction at a trial or administrative proceeding against the person searched.

The following U.S. Supreme Court cases examine the reach of the Fourth Amendment's protection against unreasonable search and seizure.

Case 8.2
Search

U.S. SUPREME COURT
Kyllo v. United States
533 U.S. 27, 121 S.Ct. 2038, 2001 U.S. Lexis 4487
Supreme Court of the United States

Background and Facts

In 1992, government agents suspected that marijuana was being grown in the home of Danny Kyllo, which was part of a triplex building in Florence, Oregon. Indoor marijuana growth typically requires high-intensity lamps. In order to determine whether an amount of heat was emanating from Kyllo's home consistent with the use of such lamps, federal agents used a thermal imager to scan the triplex. Thermal imagers detect infrared radiation and produce images of the radiation. The scan of Kyllo's home, which was performed from an automobile on the street, showed that the roof over the garage and a side wall of Kyllo's home were "hot." The agents used this scanning evidence to obtain a search warrant authorizing a search of Kyllo's home. During the search, the agents found an indoor growing operation involving more than 100 marijuana plants.

Kyllo was indicted for manufacturing marijuana, a violation of federal criminal law. Kyllo moved to suppress the imaging evidence and the evidence it led to, arguing that it was an unreasonable search that violated the Fourth Amendment to the U.S. Constitution. The trial court disagreed with Kyllo and let the evidence be introduced and considered at trial. Kyllo then entered a conditional guilty plea and appealed the trial court's failure to

(*continued*)

Kyllo v. United States

533 U.S. 27, 121 S.Ct. 2038, 2001 U.S. Lexis 4487
Supreme Court of the United States
(continued)

suppress the challenged evidence. The Court of Appeals affirmed the trial court's decision admitting the evidence. The U.S. Supreme Court granted certiorari to hear the appeal.

Issue

Is the use of a thermal-imaging device aimed at a private home from a public street to detect relative amounts of heat within the home a "search" within the meaning of the Fourth Amendment?

In the Language of the Court

At the very core of the Fourth Amendment stands the right of a man to retreat into his own home and there be free from unreasonable government intrusion. With few exceptions, the question whether a warrantless search of a home is reasonable and hence constitutional must be answered no. On the other hand, the lawfulness of warrantless visual surveillance of a home has still been preserved. In fact we have held that visual observation is no "search" at all. We have applied the test on different occasions in holding that aerial surveillance of private homes and surrounding areas does not constitute a search.

The present case involves officers on a public street engaged in more than naked-eye surveillance of a home. The question we confront today is what limits there are upon this power of technology to shrink the realm of guaranteed privacy. We think that obtaining by sense-enhancing technology any information regarding the interior of the home that could not otherwise have been obtained without physical intrusion into a constitutionally protected area constitutes a search. This assures preservation of that degree of privacy against a government that existed when the Fourth Amendment was adopted. On the basis of this criterion, the information obtained by the thermal imager in this case was the product of a search.

Decision and Remedy

The U.S. Supreme Court held that the use of a thermal-imaging device aimed at a private home from a public street to detect relative amounts of heat within the home is a "search" within the meaning of the Fourth Amendment. The Supreme Court reversed the decision of the Court of Appeals and remanded the case for further proceedings.

Business and Ethics Questions

1. Is the Fourth Amendment's prohibition against unreasonable search and seizure an easy standard to apply? Explain.
2. Did the police act ethically in obtaining the evidence in this case? Did Kyllo act ethically in trying to suppress the evidence?
3. How can the government catch entrepreneurs such as Kyllo? Explain.

Case 8.3
Search and Seizure

U.S. SUPREME COURT

City of Indianapolis v. Edmond

531 U.S. 32, 121 S.Ct. 447, 2000 U.S. Lexis 8084
Supreme Court of the United States

Background and Facts

In August 1998, the police of the city of Indianapolis, Indiana, began to operate vehicle roadblock checkpoints on Indianapolis roads in an effort to interdict unlawful drugs. Once a car had been stopped, police questioned the driver and passengers and conducted an open-view examination of the vehicle from the outside. A narcotics-detection dog walked around outside each vehicle. The police conducted a search and seizure of the occupants and vehicle only if particular suspicion developed from the initial investigation. The overall "hit rate" of the program was approximately 9 percent.

James Edmond and Joel Palmer, each attorneys who had been stopped at one of the Indianapolis checkpoints, filed a lawsuit on behalf of themselves and the class of all motorists who had been stopped or were subject to being stopped at such checkpoints. They claimed that the roadblocks violated the Fourth Amendment to the Constitution. The district court found for Indianapolis, but the Court of Appeals reversed. The U.S. Supreme Court granted certiorari to hear the appeal.

Issue

Does the Indianapolis highway checkpoint program, whereby police, without individualized suspicion, stop vehicles for the primary purpose of discovering and interdicting illegal narcotics, violate the Fourth Amendment to the U.S. Constitution?

In the Language of the Court

The Fourth Amendment requires that searches and seizures be reasonable. A search or seizure is ordinarily unreasonable in the absence of individualized suspicion of wrongdoing. We have recognized only limited circumstances in which the usual rule does not apply. We have upheld brief, suspicionless seizures of motorists at a fixed border patrol checkpoint designed to intercept illegal aliens, *United States v. Martinez-Fuerte*, 428 U.S. 543, 96 S.Ct. 3074 (1976), and at a sobriety checkpoint aimed at removing drunk drivers from the road, *Michigan Dept. of State Police v. Sitz*, 496 U.S. 444, 110 S.Ct. 2481 (1990). In none of these cases, however, did we indicate approval of a checkpoint program whose primary purpose was to detect evidence of ordinary criminal wrongdoing.

We have never approved a checkpoint program whose primary purpose was to detect evidence of ordinary criminal wrongdoing. Because the primary purpose of the Indianapolis narcotics checkpoint program is to uncover evidence of ordinary criminal wrongdoing, the program contravenes the Fourth Amendment. Of course, there are circumstances that may justify a law enforcement checkpoint where the primary purpose would otherwise, but for some emergency, relate to ordinary crime control. For example, the Fourth Amendment would almost certainly permit an appropriate tailored roadblock set up to thwart an imminent terrorist attack or to catch a dangerous criminal who is likely to flee by way of a particular route. The exigencies created by these scenarios are far removed from the circumstances under which authorities might simply stop cars as a matter of course to see if there just happens to be a felon leaving the jurisdiction.

Decision and Remedy

The U.S. Supreme Court held that the Indianapolis general highway checkpoint, whereby police, without individualized suspicion, stopped vehicles for the primary purpose of discovering and interdicting narcotics, was an unreasonable search and seizure in violation of the Fourth Amendment. The Supreme Court affirmed the decision of the Court of Appeals.

Business and Ethics Questions

1. How did the Supreme Court reconcile its decision in this case with its prior decisions in *Martinez-Fuerte* and *Sitz*? Explain.
2. Should the 9 percent of criminals who were caught by the roadblock get off because of the Fourth Amendment?
3. How big of a business is illegal narcotics sales in this country? Should that industry be legalized and taxed? Why or why not?

Searches of Business Premises

Generally, the government does not have the right to search business premises without a search warrant.[7] Certain hazardous and regulated industries—such as sellers of firearms and liquor, coal mines, and the like—are subject to warrantless searches if proper statutory procedures are met.

> The criminal is to go free because the constable has blundered.
>
> C. J. Cardozo
> *People v. Defore* (1926)

Contemporary Trend

Federal Antiterrorism Act

The devastating terrorist attacks on the World Trade Center in New York and the Pentagon in Washington, DC, on September 11, 2001, shocked the world. The attacks were organized and orchestrated by terrorists who crossed nations' borders easily, secretly planned and prepared for the attacks undetected, and financed the attacks using money located in banks in the United States, Great Britain, and other countries. In response, Congress enacted a federal Antiterrorism Act that assists the government in detecting, investigating, and prosecuting terrorists. The bill was signed into law on October 26, 2001. The act contains the following main features:

- ***Special Intelligence Court.*** The act authorizes the Special Intelligence Court to issue expanded wiretap orders and subpoenas to obtain evidence of suspected terrorism.
- ***Nationwide search warrant.*** The act creates a nationwide search warrant to obtain evidence of terrorist activities.
- ***Roving wiretaps.*** The act permits "roving wiretaps" on a person suspected of involvement in terrorism so that any telephone or electronic device used by the person may be monitored.
- ***Detection of noncitizens.*** The act gives the federal government authority to detain a nonresident in the United States for up to seven days without filing charges against that person. Nonresidents who are certified by a court as a threat to national security may be held for up to six months without a trial. ■

Privilege Against Self-Incrimination and Other Protections

The *Fifth Amendment* to the U.S. Constitution provides that no person "shall be compelled in any criminal case to be a witness against himself." Thus, a person cannot be compelled to give testimony against himself or herself, although nontestimonial evidence (e.g., fingerprints, body fluids) may be required. A person who asserts this right is described as having "taken the Fifth." This protection applies to federal cases and is extended to state and local criminal cases through the Due Process Clause of the Fourteenth Amendment.

self-incrimination

The giving of testimony that will likely subject a person to criminal prosecution. The Fifth Amendment states that no person shall be compelled in any criminal case to be a witness against him- or herself.

The protection against **self-incrimination** applies only to natural persons who are accused of crimes. Therefore, artificial persons (such as corporations and partnerships) cannot raise this protection against incriminating testimony.[8] Thus, business records of corporations and partnerships are not generally protected from disclosure, even if they incriminate individuals who work for the business. However, certain "private papers" of businesspersons (such as personal diaries) are protected from disclosure.

Miranda Rights

Most people have not read and memorized the provisions of the U.S. Constitution. The U.S. Supreme Court recognized this fact when it decided the landmark case *Miranda v. Arizona* in 1966.[9] In that case, the Supreme Court held that the Fifth Amendment privilege against self-incrimination is not useful unless a criminal suspect has knowledge of this right. Therefore, the Supreme Court required that the following warning—colloquially called the **Miranda rights**—be read to a criminal suspect before he or she is interrogated by the police or other government officials:

***Miranda* rights**

Rights that a suspect must be informed of before being interrogated, so that the suspect will not unwittingly give up his or her Fifth Amendment right.

- You have the right to remain silent.
- Anything you say can and will used against you.
- You have the right to consult a lawyer and to have a lawyer present with you during interrogation.
- If you cannot afford a lawyer, a lawyer will be appointed free of charge to represent you.

Any statements or confessions obtained from a suspect prior to being read his or her *Miranda* rights can be excluded from evidence at trial. In 2000, the U.S. Supreme Court upheld *Miranda* in *Dickerson v. United States*.[10] The Supreme Court stated, "We do not think there is justification for overruling *Miranda*. *Miranda* has become embedded in routine police practice to the point where the warnings have become part of our national culture."

> At the present time in this country there is more danger that criminals will escape justice than that they will be subjected to tyranny.
>
> J. Holmes Dissenting
> *Kepner v. United States* (1904)

Attorney–Client Privilege and Other Privileges

To obtain a proper defense, an accused person must be able to tell his or her attorney facts about the case without fear that the attorney will be called as a witness against the accused. The **attorney–client privilege** is protected by the Fifth Amendment. Either the client or the attorney can raise this privilege. For the privilege to apply, the information must be told to the attorney in his or her capacity as an attorney, and not as a friend or neighbor or such.

attorney–client privilege

A rule that says a client can tell his or her lawyer anything about the case without fear that the attorney will be called as a witness against the client.

The following privileges have also been recognized under the Fifth Amendment: (1) *psychiatrist/psychologist–patient privilege*, (2) *priest/minister/rabbi–penitent privilege*,

(3) *spouse–spouse privilege*, and (4) *parent–child privilege*. There are some exceptions. For example, a spouse or child who is beaten by a spouse or parent may testify against the accused.

The U.S. Supreme Court has held that there is no accountant–client privilege under federal laws.[11] Thus, an accountant could be called as a witness in cases involving federal securities laws, federal mail or wire fraud, or other federal crimes. Nevertheless, approximately 20 states have enacted special statutes that create an **accountant–client privilege**. An accountant cannot be called as a witness against a client in a court action in a state where these statutes are in effect. Federal courts do not recognize these laws, however.

It is better that ten guilty persons escape, than that one innocent suffer.

Sir William Blackstone
Commentaries on the Laws of England (1809)

Immunity from Prosecution

On occasion, the government may want to obtain information from a suspect who has asserted his or her Fifth Amendment privilege against self-incrimination. The government can often achieve this by offering the suspect **immunity from prosecution**. Immunity from prosecution means that the government agrees not to use against a person granted immunity any evidence given by that person. Once immunity is granted, the suspect loses the right to assert his or her Fifth Amendment privilege. Grants of immunity are often given when the government wants the suspect to give information that will lead to the prosecution of other, more important, criminal suspects. Partial grants of immunity are also available. For example, a suspect may be granted immunity from prosecution for a serious crime, but not a lesser crime, in exchange for information. The suspect must agree to a partial grant of immunity.

immunity from prosecution
A situation in which the government agrees not to use any evidence given by a person granted immunity against that person.

Protection Against Double Jeopardy

The **Double Jeopardy Clause** of the Fifth Amendment protects persons from being tried twice for the same crime. For example, if the state tries a suspect for the crime of murder and the suspect is found not guilty, the state cannot bring another trial against the accused for the same crime. However, if the same criminal act involves several different crimes, the accused may be tried for each of the crimes without violating the Double Jeopardy Clause. Suppose the accused kills two people during a robbery. The accused may be tried for two murders and the robbery.

Double Jeopardy Clause
A clause of the Fifth Amendment that protects persons from being tried twice for the same crime.

If the same act violates the laws of two or more jurisdictions, each jurisdiction may try the accused. For example, if an accused kidnaps a person in one state and brings the victim across a state border into another state, the act violates the laws of two states and the federal government. Thus, three jurisdictions can prosecute the accused without violating the Double Jeopardy Clause.

Right to a Public Jury Trial

The *Sixth Amendment* guarantees certain rights to criminal defendants. These rights are (1) to be tried by an impartial jury of the state or district in which the alleged crime was committed, (2) to confront (cross-examine) the witnesses against the accused, (3) to have the assistance of a lawyer, and (4) to have a speedy trial.[12]

Protection Against Cruel and Unusual Punishment

The *Eighth Amendment* protects criminal defendants from **cruel and unusual punishment**. For example, it prohibits the torture of criminals. However, this clause does not prohibit capital punishment.[13]

Terms and Concepts

Specifics of a Criminal Trial

1. The accused is *presumed innocent until proven guilty.*
2. The plaintiff (the government) bears the *burden of proof.*
3. The government must prove *beyond a reasonable doubt* that the accused is guilty of the crime charged.
4. The accused does not have to testify against him or herself.

Definition of Crime

1. ***Crime.*** A crime is an act done by a person in violation of those duties that he or she owes to society and for the breach of which the law provides a penalty.
2. ***Penal codes.*** Penal codes are state and federal statues that define many crimes. Criminal conduct is also defined in many *regulatory statutes.*
3. ***Parties to a criminal lawsuit:***
   a. *Plaintiff.* The plaintiff is the government, which is represented by the *prosecuting attorney* (or *prosecutor*).
   b. *Defendant.* The defendant is the person or business accused of the crime and is represented by a *defense attorney.*

Classification of Crimes

1. ***Felonies.*** Felonies are the most serious kinds of crimes. They are *mala in se* (inherently evil) and are usually punishable by imprisonment.
2. ***Misdemeanors.*** Misdemeanors are less serious crimes than felonies. They are *mala prohibita* (prohibited by society) and are usually punishable by fine and/or imprisonment for less than one year.
3. ***Violations.*** A violation is neither a felony nor a misdemeanor. It is generally punishable by a fine.

Elements of a Crime

Most crimes require that the following two elements be proven:

1. ***Actus reus.*** Guilty act.
2. ***Mens rea.*** Evil intent.

Pretrial Criminal Procedure

1. ***Arrest.*** An arrest is made pursuant to an *arrest warrant*, based on a showing of "probable cause," or, where permitted, a *warrantless* arrest may be made.
2. ***Indictment or information.*** Grand juries issue *indictments*, and magistrates (judges) issue *informations.* These formally charge the accused with specific crimes.
3. ***Arraignment.*** The accused is informed of the charges against him or her and enters a *plea* in court. The plea may be *not guilty, guilty*, or *nolo contendere.*
4. ***Plea bargaining.*** The government and the accused may negotiate a settlement agreement wherein the accused agrees to admit to a lesser crime than charged.

Criminal Trial and Appeal

1. Criminal trial:
   a. *Conviction.* A guilty verdict requires a unanimous vote of the jury.
   b. *Innocent.* A verdict of innocent requires a unanimous vote of the jury.
   c. *Hung jury.* A hung jury results from a unanimous vote of the jury. The government may prosecute the case again.

1. Appeal:
   a. Defendant. A defendant may appeal his or her conviction.
   b. Plaintiff (government). A plaintiff may not appeal a verdict of innocent.

Crimes Affecting Business

1. ***Robbery.*** Robbery is the taking of personal property from another by fear or force.
2. ***Burglary.*** Burglary is the unauthorized entering of a building to commit a felony.
3. ***Larceny.*** Larceny is the wrongful taking of another's property other than from his or her person or building.
4. ***Theft.*** Theft is the wrongful taking of another's property, whether by robbery, burglary, or larceny.
5. ***Receiving stolen property.*** A person who knowingly receives stolen property with the intent to deprive the rightful owner of that property commits a crime.
6. ***Arson.*** The malicious and willful burning of a building is called arson.
7. ***Extortion.*** Extortion is a threat to expose something about another person unless that person gives up money or property.

White-Collar Crimes

White-collar crimes are prone to be committed by businesspersons; they involve cunning and trickery rather than physical force.

1. ***Forgery.*** Forgery is fraudulently making or altering a written document that affects the legal liability of another person.
2. ***Embezzlement.*** Embezzlement is the fraudulent conversion of property by a person to whom the property was *entrusted*.
3. ***Criminal fraud.*** Criminal fraud involves obtaining title to another's property through deception or trickery. Also called *false pretenses* or *deceit*.
4. ***Mail fraud.*** Mail fraud is the use of mail to defraud another person.
5. ***Wire fraud.*** Wire fraud is the use of wire (telephone, telegraph) to defraud another person.
6. ***Bribery.*** *Bribery* is the offer of payment of money or property or something else of value in return for an unwarranted favor. The payer of a bribe is also guilty of the crime of bribery.
   a. Commercial bribery is the offer of a payment of a bribe to private persons and businesses. This is often referred to as a *kickback* or *payoff*.
   b. Bribery of public officials for an "official act" is a crime.
7. ***Money Laundering Control Act.*** This federal statute makes it a crime to:
   a. Knowingly engage in a *monetary transaction* through a financial institution involving property worth more than $10,000.
   b. Knowingly engage in a *financial transaction* involving the proceeds of an illegal activity.
8. ***Racketeer Influenced and Corrupt Organizations Act (RICO).*** RICO makes it a federal crime to acquire or maintain an interest in, use income from, or conduct or participate in the affairs of an "enterprise" through a "pattern" of "racketeering activity." Criminal penalties include the forfeiture of any property or business interests gained through a RICO violation.

Corporate Criminal Liability

1. Corporate directors, officers, and employees are criminally liable for crimes they commit for personal benefit or on behalf of a corporation.
2. A corporation is criminally liable for crimes committed by directors, officers, and employees while acting on behalf of the corporation.

Fourth Amendment Protection Against Unreasonable Searches and Seizures

The Fourth Amendment protects persons and corporations from *unreasonable searches and seizures*.

1. ***Reasonable searches and seizures.*** Such seizures based on *probable cause* are lawful.
   a. Search warrant. A search warrant stipulates the place and scope of the search.

b. Warrantless search. Warrantless search is permitted only:
   i. Incident to an arrest.
   ii. Where evidence is in plain view.
   iii. Where it is likely that evidence will be destroyed.

2. ***Exclusionary rule.*** Evidence obtained from an unreasonable search and seizure is *tainted evidence* that may not be introduced at a government proceeding against the person searched.
3. ***Business premises.*** Business premises are protected by the Fourth Amendment, except that certain *regulated industries* may be subject in warrantless searches authorized by statute.

Fifth Amendment Privilege Against Self-Incrimination

Privilege against self-incrimination. The Fifth Amendment provides that no person "shall be compelled in any criminal case to be a witness against himself." A person asserting this privilege is said to have "taken the Fifth."

1. ***Nontestimonial evidence.*** This evidence (e.g., fingerprints, body fluids) is not protected.
2. ***Businesses.*** The privilege against self-incrimination applies only to natural persons; businesses cannot assert the privilege.
3. **Miranda** ***rights.*** A criminal suspect must be informed of his or her Fifth Amendment rights before the suspect can be interrogated by the police or government officials.
4. ***Immunity from prosecution.*** Immunity is granted by the government to obtain otherwise privileged evidence. The government agrees not to use the evidence against the person who gave it.
5. ***Attorney–client privilege.*** An accused's lawyer cannot be called as a witness against the accused.
6. ***Other privileges.*** The following privileges have been recognized, with some limitations:
   a. Psychiatrist/psychologist–patient
   b. Priest/minister/rabbi–penitent
   c. Spouse–spouse
   d. Parent–child
7. ***Accountant–client privilege.*** This privilege is not recognized at the federal level. Some states recognize this privilege in state law actions.

Fifth Amendment Protection Against Double Jeopardy

The Fifth Amendment protects persons from being tried twice by the same jurisdiction for the same crime. If an act violates the laws of two or more jurisdictions, each jurisdiction may try the accused.

Sixth Amendment Right to a Public Jury Trial

The Sixth Amendment guarantees criminal defendants the following rights:

1. To be tried by an impartial jury.
2. To confront the witness.
3. To have the assistance of a lawyer.
4. To have a speedy trial.

Eighth Amendment Protection Against Cruel and Unusual Punishment

The Eighth Amendment protects criminal defendants from cruel and unusual punishment. Capital punishment is permitted.

Internet Exercises and Case Questions

Working the Web Internet Exercises

1. Check on the U.S. Department of Justice Web site for information about computer-related crimes: **www.usdoj.gov/criminal**.
2. See **www.hg.org/crime.html** for a comprehensive list of criminal law resources. Find the listing for your jurisdiction and research state laws related to white-collar crime.

Legal Environment Cases

8.1 Criminal Liability of Corporations Representatives of hotels, restaurants, hotel and restaurant supply companies, and other businesses located in Portland, Oregon, organized an association to attract conventions to their city. Members were asked to make contributions equal to 1 percent of their sales to finance the association. To aid collections, hotel members, including Hilton Hotels Corporation, agreed to give preferential treatment to suppliers that paid their assessment and to curtail purchases from those that did not. This agreement violated federal antitrust laws. The United States sued the members of the association, including Hilton Hotels, for the crime of violating federal antitrust laws. Can a corporation be held criminally liable for the acts of its representatives? If so, what criminal penalties can be assessed against the corporations? *United States v. Hilton Hotels Corp.*, 467 F.2d 1000, 1972 U.S. App. Lexis 7414 (9th Cir.)

8.2 Forgery Evidence showed that there was a burglary in which a checkbook belonging to Mary J. Harris, doing business as The Report Department, and a check encoder machine were stolen. Two of the checks from that checkbook were cashed at the Citizens & Southern National Bank branch office in Riverdale, Georgia, by Joseph Leon Foster, who was accompanied by a woman identified as Angela Foxworth. The bank teller who cashed the checks testified that the same man and woman cashed the checks on two different occasions at her drive-up window at the bank and that on both occasions they were in the same car. Each time the teller wrote the license tag number of the car on the back of the check. The teller testified that both times the checks and the driver's license used to identify the woman were passed to her by the man driving and that the man received the money from her. What crime has been committed? *Foster v. State of Georgia*, 387 S.E.2d 637, 1989 Ga.App. Lexis 1456 (Ga. App.)

8.3 Extortion On February 3, 1987, the victim (Mr. X) went to the premises at 42 Taylor Terrace in New Milford, Connecticut, where his daughter and her husband lived. Lisa Percoco, who was Gregory Erhardt's girlfriend, was at the residence. Mr. X and Percoco were in the bedroom, partially dressed, engaging in sexual activity, when Erhardt entered the room and photographed them. He then informed Mr. X that unless he procured $5,000 and placed it in a mailbox at a designated address by 8 P.M. that night, Erhardt would show the photographs to Mr. X's wife. Mr. X proceeded to make telephone arrangements for the procurement and placement of the money according to Erhardt's instructions. If the money were paid, what crime would have been committed? *State of Connecticut v. Erhardt*, 533 A.2d 188, 1989 Conn.App. Lexis 21 (Conn. App.)

8.4 Criminal Fraud In 1978, Miriam Marlowe's husband purchased a life insurance policy on his own life, naming his wife as the beneficiary. After Marlowe's husband died in a swimming accident in July 1981, she received payment on the policy. Marlowe later met John Walton, a friend of a friend. He convinced her and her representative that he had a friend who worked for the State Department and had access to gold in Brazil and that the gold could be purchased in Brazil for $100 an ounce and sold in the United States for $300 an ounce. Walton convinced Miriam to invest $25,000. Instead of investing the money in gold in Brazil, Walton opened an account at Tracy Collins Bank in the name of Jeffrey McIntyre Roberts and deposited Miriam's money in the account. He later withdrew the money in cash. What crime is Walton guilty of? *State of Utah v. Roberts*, 711 P. 2d 235, 1985 Utah Lexis 872 (Utah)

8.5 Bribery In 1979, the city of Peoria, Illinois, received federal funds from the Department of Housing and Urban Development (HUD) to be used for housing rehabilitation assistance. The city of Peoria designated United Neighborhoods, Inc. (UNI), a corporation, to administer the funds. Arthur Dixon was UNI's executive director, and James Lee Hinton was its housing rehabilitation coordinator. In these capacities, they were responsible for contracting with suppliers and tradespeople to provide the necessary goods and services to rehabilitate the houses. Evidence showed that Dixon and Hinton used their positions to extract 10 percent payments back on all contracts they awarded. What crime have they committed? *Dixon and Hinton v. United States*, 465 U.S. 482, 104 S.Ct. 1172, 1984 U.S. Lexis 35 (U.S. Sup.Ct.)

8.6 Administrative Search Lee Stuart Paulson owned the liquor license for My House, a bar in San Francisco. The California Department of Alcoholic Beverage Control is the administrative agency that regulates bars in that state. The California Business and Professions Code, which the department administers, prohibits "any kind of illegal activity on licensed premises." On February 11, 1988, an anonymous informer tipped the department that narcotics sales were occurring on the premises of My House and that the narcotics were kept in a safe behind the bar on the premises. A special department investigator entered the bar during its hours of operations, identified himself, and informed Paulson that he was conducting an inspection. The investigator, who did not have a search warrant, opened the safe without seeking Paulson's consent. Twenty-two bundles of cocaine, totaling 5.5 grams, were found in the safe. Paulson was arrested. At his criminal trial, Paulson challenged the lawfulness of the search. Was the warrantless search of the safe a lawful search? *People v. Paulson*, 216 Cal.App.3d 1480, 265 Cal.Rptr. 579, 1990 Cal.App. Lexis 10 (Cal. App.)

8.7 Search Warrant The Center Art Galleries–Hawaii sells artwork. Approximately 20 percent of its business involves art by Salvador Dalí. The federal government, which suspected the center of fraudulently selling forged Dalí artwork, obtained identical search warrants for six locations controlled by the center. The warrants commanded the executing officer to seize items that were "evidence of violations of federal criminal law." The warrants did not describe the specific crimes suspected and did not stipulate that only items pertaining to the sale of Dalí's work could be seized. There was no evidence of any criminal activity unrelated to that artist. Is the search warrant valid? *Center Art Galleries–Hawaii, Inc. v. United States*, 875 F.2d 747, 1989 U.S. App. Lexis 6983 (9th Cir.)

8.8 Privilege Against Self-Incrimination John Doe is the owner of several sole-proprietorship businesses. In 1980, during the course of an investigation of corruption in awarding county and municipal contracts, a federal grand jury served several subpoenas on John Doe, demanding the production of certain business records. The subpoenas demanded the production of the following records: (1) general ledgers and journals, (2) invoices, (3) bank statements and canceled checks, (4) financial statements, (5) telephone-company records, (6) safe-deposit box records, and (7) copies of tax returns. John Doe filed a motion in federal court, seeking to quash the subpoenas, alleging that producing these business records would violate his Fifth Amendment privilege of not testifying against himself. Do the records have to be disclosed? *United States v. John Doe*, 465 U.S. 605, 104 S.Ct. 1237, 1984 Lexis 169 (U.S. Sup.Ct.)

Ethics in Business

8.9 In 1980, Ronald V. Cloud purchased the Cal-Neva Lodge, a hotel and casino complex located in the Lake Tahoe area near the California–Nevada border, for $10 million. Cloud was a sophisticated 68-year-old entrepreneur who was experienced in buying and selling real estate and had real estate holdings valued at more than $65 million. He also had experience in banking and finance, having been the founder and chairman of Continental National Bank of Fresno. After two years of mounting operation losses, Cloud closed the Cal-Neva Lodge and actively began seeking a new buyer. In December 1984, Cloud met with Jon Perroton and orally agreed to transfer the lodge to Perroton for approximately $17 million. On January 2, 1985, Perroton met with an executive of Hibernia Bank (Hibernia) to discuss a possible loan to finance the purchase of the lodge. Perroton made multiple false representations and presented false documents to obtain a $20 million loan from Hibernia. In particular, Perroton misrepresented the sale price for the lodge ($27.5 million) and stated that $7.5 million had already been paid to Cloud. An escrow account was opened with Transamerica Title Company (Transamerica).

On January 15, 1985, Cloud and his attorney and Perroton met at Transamerica to sign mutual escrow instructions. Cloud reviewed the instructions and noticed that the sale price and down payment figures were incorrectly stated at $27.5 million and $7.5 million, respectively, and that the Hibernia loan was for $20 million, almost $3 million above what he knew to be the true sale price. Cloud signed the escrow instructions. Later, Cloud signed a settlement statement containing the same false figures and signed a grant deed to the property. The sale closed on January 23, 1985, with Hibernia making the $20 million loan to Perroton. Subsequently, when the loan went into default, Continental Insurance Company (Continental) paid Hibernia its loss of $7.5 million on the bank's blanket bond insurance policy. The United States sued Cloud for aiding and abetting a bank fraud in violation of federal law (18 U.S.C. Sections 2 and 1344). The jury convicted Cloud of the crime and ordered him to make restitution of $7.5 million to Continental. Cloud appealed.

Ethics Issues

1. Did the buyer, Ronald V. Cloud, act ethically in this case?
2. Did Cloud commit criminal fraud? Explain.
3. Did Cloud act ethically in this case? Explain.
4. Is Cloud guilty of aiding and abetting a bank fraud?

Endnotes

1. Title 18 of the U.S. Code contains the federal criminal code.
2. Sentencing Reform Act of 1984, 18 U.S.C. Section 3551 *et seq.*
3. 18 U.S.C. Section 1341.
4. 18 U.S.C. Section 1343.
5. 18 U.S.C. Sections 1961–1968.
6. *United States v. Leon*, 468 U.S. 897, 104 S.Ct. 3405, 82 1984 U.S. Lexis 153 (U.S. Sup.Ct.).
7. *Marshall v. Barlow's Inc.*, 436 U.S. 307, 98 S.Ct. 1816, 1978 U.S. Lexis 26 (U.S. Sup.Ct.).
8. *Bellis v. United States*, 417 U.S. 85, 94 S.Ct. 2179, 1974 U.S. Lexis 58 (U.S. Sup.Ct.).
9. 384 U.S. 436, 86 S.Ct. 1603, 1996 U.S. Lexis 2817 (U.S. Sup.Ct.).
10. 530 U.S. 428, 120 S.Ct. 2326, 2000 U.S. Lexis 23 (U.S. Sup.Ct.).
11. 409 U.S. 322, 93 S.Ct. 611, 1973 U.S. Lexis 23 (U.S. Sup.Ct.).
12. The Speedy Trial Act requires that a criminal defendant be brought to trial within 70 days after indictment [18 U.S.C. Section 316(c)(1)]. Continuances may be granted by the court to serve the "ends of justice."
13. *Baldwin v. Alabama*, 472 U.S. 372, 105 S.Ct. 2727, 1985 U.S. Lexis 106 (U.S. Sup.Ct.).

9

Internet Law and Intellectual Property

"The Congress shall have the power . . . to promote the Progress of Science and useful Arts, by securing for limited Times to Authors and Inventors the exclusive Right to their respective Writings and Discoveries."

—Article I, Section 8, clause 8 of the U.S. Constitution

Chapter Objectives

After studying this chapter, you should be able to:

1. Describe the business tort of misappropriating a trade secret.
2. Describe how an invention can be patented under federal patent laws and the penalties for patent infringement.
3. List the writings that can be copyrighted and describe the penalties for copyright infringement.
4. Define trademark and service mark and describe the penalties for trademark infringement.
5. Describe the Internet and the use of domain names and Web sites.

Chapter Contents

- Trade Secrets
- Patents and Cyber Patents
- Copyrights and Software Copyrights
- Trademarks and Online Commerce
- The Internet
- Domain Names

intellectual property rights
Rights, such as patents, copyrights, trademarks, trade secrets, trade names, and domain names, that are very valuable business assets. Federal and state laws protect intellectual property rights from misappropriation and infringement.

The U.S. economy is based on the freedom of ownership of property. In addition to real estate and personal property, **intellectual property rights** have value to both business and individuals. This is particularly the case in the modern era of the Information Age, computers, and the Internet.

Trade secrets form the basis of many successful businesses, and they are protected from misappropriation. Federal law provides protections for intellectual property rights, such as patents, copyrights, and trademarks. In addition, businesses and individuals may register domain names to use on the Internet. Anyone who infringes on these rights may be stopped from doing so and is liable for damages.

This chapter discusses the protection of trade secrets, patents, copyrights, trademarks, and information technology.

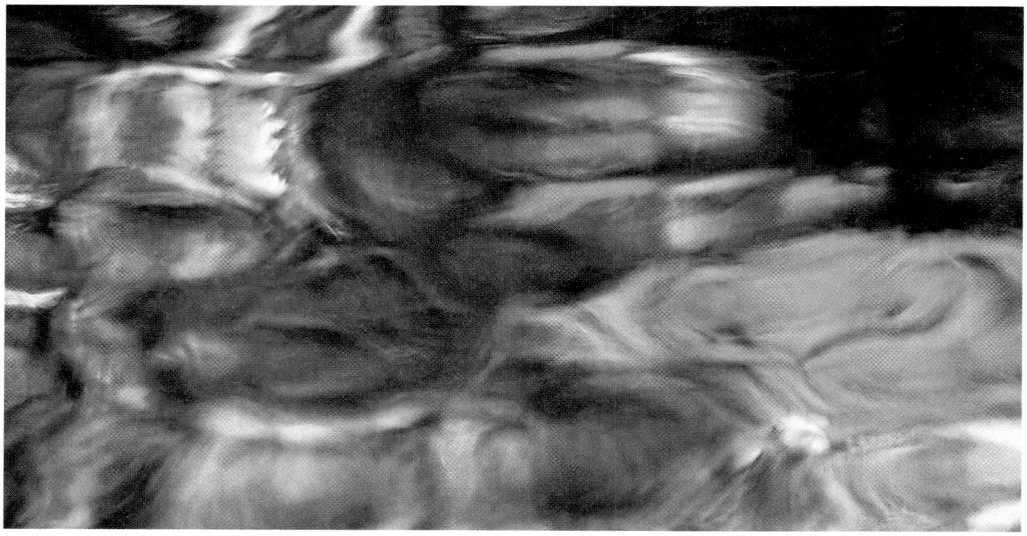

Reflecting Pool, Los Angeles County Museum of Art. Photographs such as this one, titled "Colorful Dream," are copyrighted.

Trade Secrets

trade secret
A product formula, pattern, design, compilation of data, customer list, or other business secret.

Many businesses are successful because their **trade secrets** set them apart from their competitors. Trade secrets may be product formulas, patterns, designs, compilations of data, customer lists, or other business secrets. Many trade secrets either do not qualify to be—or simply are not—patented, copyrighted, or trademarked. Many states have adopted the **Uniform Trade Secrets Act** to give statutory protection to trade secrets.

State unfair competition laws allow the owner of a trade secret to bring a lawsuit for *misappropriation* against anyone who steals a trade secret. For the lawsuit to be actionable, the defendant (often an employee of the owner or a competitor) must have obtained the trade secret through unlawful means, such as theft, bribery, or industrial espionage. No tort has occurred if there is no misappropriation. For example, a competitor can lawfully discover a trade secret by performing reverse engineering (i.e., taking apart and examining a rival's product).

The owner of a trade secret is obliged to take all reasonable precautions to prevent that secret from being discovered by others. Such precautions include fencing in buildings, placing locks on doors, hiring security guards, and the like. If the owner fails to take such actions, the secret is no longer subject to protection under state unfair competition laws.

Generally, a successful plaintiff in a trade secret action can (1) recover the profits made by the offender from the use of the trade secret, (2) recover for damages, and (3) obtain an injunction prohibiting the offender from divulging or using the trade secret.

Internet Law & Online Commerce

The Economic Espionage Act

Stealing of trade secrets exposes the offender to a civil lawsuit by the injured party to recover economic damages. In addition, the enactment by Congress of the federal **Economic Espionage Act of 1996** [18 U.S.C. Sections 1831–1839] makes it a federal crime to steal another's trade secrets. Under the Espionage Act, it is a federal crime for any person to convert a trade secret to his or her benefit or for the benefit of others, knowing or intending that the act would cause injury to the owner of the trade secret. The definition of *trade secret* under the Espionage Act is very broad and parallels the definition used under the civil laws of misappropriating a trade secret.

One of the major reasons for the passage of the Espionage Act was to address the ease of stealing trade secrets through computer espionage and using the Internet. For example, hundreds of pages of confidential information can be downloaded onto a small computer disk, placed in a pocket, and taken from the legal owner. In addition, computer hackers can crack into a company's computers and steal customer lists, databases, formulas, and other trade secrets. The Espionage Act is a very important weapon in addressing and penalizing computer and Internet espionage.

The Espionage Act provides for severe criminal penalties. An organization can be fined up to $5 million per criminal act and $10 million if the criminal act was committed to benefit a foreign government. The act imposes prison terms on individuals of up to 15 years per criminal violation, which can be increased to 25 years per violation if the criminal act was done with the intent to benefit a foreign government. ■

Patents and Cyber Patents

When drafting the Constitution of the United States of America, the founders of the United States provided for protection of the work of inventors and writers. Article I, Section 8 of the constitution provides, "The Congress shall have Power . . . to promote the Progress of Science and useful Arts, by securing for limited Times to Authors and Inventors the exclusive Right to their respective Writings and Discoveries."

Federal Patent Statute

Pursuant to the express authority granted in the U.S. Constitution, Congress enacted the **Federal Patent Statue of 1952.**[1] This law is intended to provide an incentive for inventors to invent and make their inventions public and to protect patented inventions from infringement. Federal patent law is exclusive; there are no state patent laws. Applications for patents must be filed with the **United States Patent and Trademark Office (PTO)** in Washington, DC. The U.S. Court of Appeals for the Federal Circuit in Washington, DC, was created in 1982 to hear patent appeals. The court was established to promote uniformity in patent law.

Federal Patent Statute of 1952
A federal statute that establishes the requirements for obtaining a patent and protects patented inventions from infringement.

In 1995, in order to bring the U.S. patent system into harmony with the systems of the majority of other developed nations, Congress made the following important changes in U.S. patent law:

1. Patents for inventions are valid for *20 years* (instead of the previous term of 17 years). Design patents are valid for 14 years.
2. The patent term begins to run from the date the patent application is *filed* (instead of when the patent is issued, as was previously the case).

After the patent period runs out, the invention or design enters the *public domain*, which means that anyone can produce and sell the invention without paying the prior patent holder.

The United States still follows the *first-to-invent rule* rather than the *first-to-file rule* followed by some other countries. Thus, in the United States, the first person to invent an item or process is given patent protection over another party who is first to file a patent application.

Patenting an Invention

To be patented, an invention must be *novel, useful*, and *nonobvious*. In addition, only certain subject matters can be patented. Patentable subject matters include (1) machines; (2) processes; (3) compositions of matter; (4) improvements to existing machines, processes, or compositions of matter; (5) designs for an article of manufacture; (6) asexually reproduced plants; and (7) living material invented by a person. Abstractions and scientific principles cannot be patented unless they are part of the tangible environment. For example, Einstein's Theory of Relativity ($E = mc^2$) cannot be patented.

> The patent system added the fuel of interest to the fire of genius.
>
> Abraham Lincoln
> *Lectures on Discoveries, Inventions, and Improvements* (1859)

A *patent application* must contain a written description of the invention and be filed with the PTO in Washington, DC. Patent applications are complicated. An inventor should hire a patent attorney to assist in obtaining a patent for an invention. If a patent is granted, the invention is assigned a patent number. Patent holders usually affix the word *patent* or *pat.* and the patent number to the patented article. If a patent application is filed but a patent has not yet been issued, the applicant usually places the words *patent pending* on the article. Any party can challenge either the issuance of a patent or the validity of an existing patent.

In the following case, the U.S. Supreme Court had to decide whether the subject matter was patentable.

U.S. SUPREME COURT

Case 9.1

Patent

J.E.M. Ag Supply, Inc., d.b.a. Farm Advantage, Inc. v. Pioneer Hi-Bred International, Inc.

534 U.S. 124, 122 S.Ct. 593, 2001 U.S. Lexis 10949
Supreme Court of the United States

Background and Facts

Pioneer Hi-Bred International, Inc. (Pioneer), holds patents that cover the company's inbred and hybrid corn and corn seed products. A hybrid plant patent protects the plant, its seeds, variants, mutants, and modifications of the hybrid. Pioneer sells its patented hybrid seeds under a limited label license that provides: "License is granted solely to produce grain and/or forage." The license states that it "does not extend to the use of seed from such crop or the progeny thereof for propagation or seed multiplication."

J.E.M. Ag Supply, Inc., doing business as Farm Advantage, Inc., purchased patented hybrid seeds from Pioneer in bags bearing this license agreement. Farm Advantage created seed from the hybrid corn products it grew from Pioneer's patented hybrid seed. Pioneer sued Farm Advantage, alleging that Farm Advantage had infringed its patent. Farm Advantage filed a counterclaim of patent invalidity, arguing that Pioneer hybrid plant seed patents are not patentable subject matter. The U.S. district court granted summary judgment to Pioneer, and the Court of Appeals affirmed. The U.S. Supreme Court agreed to hear Farm Advantage's appeal.

Issue

Are sexually reproducing hybrid plants patentable subject matter?

In the Language of the Court

The text of 35 U.S.C. Section 101 provides "Whoever invents or discovers any new and useful process, machine, manufacture, or composition of matter, or any new and useful improvement thereof, may obtain a patent therefor, subject to the conditions and requirements of this title." As this Court recognized over 20 years ago in *Diamond v. Chakrabarty*, 447 U.S. at 308 (1980), the language of Section 101 is extremely broad. Congress plainly contemplated that the patent laws would be given wide scope. This Court thus concluded in Chakrabarty that living things were patentable under Section 101, and held that a manmade micro-organism fell within the scope of the statute.

It has been the unbroken practice of the PTO since to confer patents for plants. To obtain patent protection, a plant breeder must show that the plant he has developed is new, useful, and non-obvious. Petitioner Farm Advantage essentially asks us to deny utility patent protection for sexually reproduced plants because it was unforeseen in 1930 that such plants could receive protection under Section 101. Denying patent protection under Section 101 simply because such coverage was thought technologically infeasible in 1930, however, would be inconsistent with the forward-looking perspective of the utility patent statute. As we noted in Chakrabarty, "Congress employed broad general language in drafting Section 101 precisely because new types of inventions are often unforeseeable."

Decision and Remedy

The U.S. Supreme Court held that sexually reproducing hybrid plants are patentable subject matter. The Supreme Court affirmed the judgment of the Court of Appeals.

Business and Ethics Questions

1. Do you think sexually reproducing hybrid plants should be patentable subject matter? Why or why not?
2. Did Farm Advantage act ethically in this case? Explain.
3. What are the economic implications of the U.S. Supreme Court's decision in this case?

One-Year "On Sale" Doctrine

Under the **one-year "on sale" doctrine**, also called the **public use doctrine**, a patent may not be granted if the invention was used by the public for more than one year prior to the filing of the patent application. This doctrine forces inventors to file their patent applications at the proper time.

one-year "on sale" doctrine A doctrine that says a patent may not be granted if the invention was used by the public for more than one year prior to the filing of the patent application.

Consider This Example Suppose Cindy Parsons invents a new invention on January 1. She allows the public to use this invention and does not file a patent application until February of the following year. The inventor has lost the right to patent her invention.

The American Inventors Protection Act

In 1999, Congress enacted the **American Inventors Protection Act**. This statute does the following:

- Permits an inventor to file a **provisional application** with the PTO, pending the preparation and filing of a final and complete patent application. This part of the law grants "provisional rights" to an inventor for three months, pending the filing of a final application.
- Requires the PTO to issue a patent within three years after the filing of a patent application unless the applicant engages in dilatory activities.
- Provides that non-patent holders may challenge a patent as being overly broad by requesting a contested reexamination of the patent application by the PTO. This provides that the reexamination will be within the confines of the PTO; the decision of the PTO can be appealed to the U.S. Court of Appeals for the Federal Circuit in Washington, DC.

Internet Law & Online Commerce

Cyber Business Plans Are Patentable

Federal patent law recognizes four categories of innovation: (1) machines, (2) articles of manufacture, (3) compositions, and (4) processes. For centuries, most patents involved tangible inventions, such as the telephone and the light bulb. Next, chemical, polymer, and biotechnology patents were granted. Now, the computer and the Internet have added to what can be patented.

(continued)

Signature Financial Group, Inc. (Signature), filed for and was granted a patent for a computerized accounting system that determines share prices through a series of mathematical calculations and is then used to manage mutual funds [U.S. Patent No. 5,193,056]. State Street Bank, another financial institution that wanted to offer a similar mutual fund investment program to clients, sued to have Signature's patent declared invalid. Signature defended, arguing that its intangible financial business model was a "process" that was protected under federal patent law. The U.S. Court of Appeals for the Federal Circuit upheld the patent as a "practical application of a mathematical, algorithm, formula, or calculation, because it produces a useful, concrete and tangible result."

Taking the lead from the *State Street* case, many persons and businesses have filed for and received patents for business and financial models that are used over the Internet. Critics contend that Congress did not intend to grant patents for intangible processes when it enacted federal patent law. Business plan patent holders counter that the trend reflects a necessary evolution in patent law and claim that business plan patterns are to the Internet Age what machine patents were to the Industrial Age. *State Street Bank & Trust Co. v. Signature Financial Group, Inc.*, 149 F.3d 1368, 1998 U.S. App. Lexis 16869 (Fed. Cir.) ■

Patent Infringement

patent infringement
Unauthorized use of another's patent. A patent holder may recover damages and other remedies against a patent infringer.

Patent holders own exclusive rights to use and exploit their patents. **Patent infringement** occurs when someone makes unauthorized use of another's patent. In a suit for patent infringement, a successful plaintiff can recover (1) money damages equal to a reasonable royalty rate on the sale of the infringed articles, (2) other damages caused by the infringement (such as loss of customers), (3) an order requiring the destruction of the infringing article, and (4) an injunction preventing the infringer from such action in the future. The court has the discretion to award up to treble damages if the infringement was intentional.

Ethics in Business

Patent Infringement

In 1967, Robert Kearns, a professor at Wayne State University in Detroit, Michigan, patented his design for the electronic intermittent-speed windshield wiper for automobiles and other vehicles. He peddled his invention around to many automobile manufacturers but never reached a licensing deal with any of them. In 1969, automobile manufacturers began producing cars using Kearns's intermittent-speed windshield wiper invention. Virtually all cars sold in the United States today now have these wipers as standard equipment. Kearns filed patent infringement lawsuits against virtually all automobile manufacturers.

The Ford case went to trial first. Ford alleged that Kearns's patents were not valid because of obviousness and prior art. The jury disagreed with Ford, decided that Kearns's patents were valid, and ordered Ford to pay $5.2 million, plus interest, for patent infringement. In 1990, Ford settled by paying Kearns $10.2 million and agreeing to drop all appeals. This represented 50¢ per Ford vehicle that used the wiper system.

In the Chrysler case, Kearns fired his lawyers and represented himself. Kearns won a second victory: In 1991, the jury found that Chrysler had infringed Kearns's patents and awarded him $11.3 million. Kearns received over $21 million from Chrysler, which amounted to 90¢ for every vehicle sold by Chrysler with the wiper system.

In 1993 and 1994, courts dismissed Kearns's lawsuits against 23 other automobile manufacturers, including General Motors, Porsche, Nissan, Toyota, and Honda because Kearns failed to comply with court orders to disclose documents. These ended Kearns's legal battle with the automobile industry.

Ethics Issues

1. Do you think that intermittent-speed windshield wipers were obvious when Kearns invented them?
2. Did the automobile manufacturers that used Kearns' invention without paying him act ethically? Explain. ■

Copyrights and Software Copyrights

Article I, Section 8 of the Constitution of the United States of America authorizes Congress to enact statutes to protect the works of writers for limited times.

Pursuant to this authority, Congress has enacted copyright laws. The **Copyright Revision Act of 1976** currently governs copyright law.[2] The act establishes the requirements for obtaining a copyright and protects copyrighted works from infringement. Federal copyright law is exclusive; there are no state copyright laws. Federal copyright law protects the works of authors and other creative persons from the unauthorized use of their copyrighted materials and provides a financial incentive for authors to write, thereby increasing the number of creative works available in society.

Copyright Revision Act of 1976
A federal statute that (1) establishes the requirements for obtaining a copyright and (2) protects copyrighted works from infringement.

Only *tangible writings*—writings that can be physically seen—are subject to copyright registration and protection. The term *writing* has been broadly defined to include books, periodicals, and newspapers; lectures, sermons, addresses, and poems; musical compositions; plays, motion pictures, and radio and television productions; maps; works of art, including paintings, drawings, sculptures, jewelry, glassware, tapestries, and lithographs; architectural drawings and models; photographs, including prints, slides, and filmstrips; greeting cards and picture postcards; photoplays, including feature films, cartoons, newsreels, travelogues, and training films; and sound recordings published in the form of tapes, cassettes, and compact discs.

Registration of Copyrights

To be protected under federal copyright law, a work must be the original work of the author. A copyright is created when an author produces his or her work. For example, when a student writes a term paper for her class, she owns a copyright to her work.

Published and unpublished works may be registered with the **United States Copyright Office** in Washington, DC. Registration is permissive and voluntary and can be effected at any time during the term of the copyright.

In 1989, the United States signed the **Berne Convention**, an international copyright treaty. This law eliminated the need to place the symbol © or the word "copyright" or "copr." on a copyrighted work.

The **Sonny Bono Copyright Term Extension Act of 1998** granted individuals copyright protection for their life plus 70 years. For example, if an author writes a novel at age 25 and she dies when she is 85, the copyright on her novel applies for the remaining 60 years of her life, and her heirs have copyright protection for an additional 70 years beyond the author's life. Copyrights owned by businesses are protected for 95 years from the year of first publication or for 120 years from the year of creation, whichever is shorter. After the copyright period runs out, the work enters the *public domain*, which means that anyone can publish the work without paying the prior copyright holder.

Copyrighting Software

In 1980, Congress enacted the **Computer Software Copyright Act**,[3] which amended the Copyright Act of 1976. The 1980 amendments included computer programs in the list of tangible items protected by copyright law. The creator of a copyrightable software program obtains automatic copyright protection. The Registrar of Copyright is authorized to accept and record any document pertaining to computer software and to issue a *certificate of recordation* to the recorder.

The law in respect to literature ought to remain upon the same footing as that which regards the profits of mechanical inventions and chemical discoveries.

William Wordsworth
Letter (1838)

Exhibit 9.1

Poem Qualifies for Copyright

Like oceans, we have spent
this time together before.
In gallery slave pits you fed me
water and removed my slivers.
Riding Ch'u dynasty chariots
we perished on Mongol swords.
We toiled rocks in chains
and built Stonehenge,
drank with King Arthur
and danced with Black Elk.
We fled, hand-in-hand, dodging
Hitler's bullets, and
I carried you over the border
to have our baby in freedom.
During past full moons, the sun set
the seas in orbit
and as driftwood we tumbled
onto the shores of Los Angeles.
Another life together, my love?

Henry Cheeseman

Congress passed the **Semiconductor Chip Protection Act of 1984** to provide greater protection of the hardware components of a computer.[4] This law protects masks that are used to create computer chips. A *mask* is an original layout of software programs that is used to create a semiconductor chip. This act is sometimes referred to as the "Mask Work Act." Notice on the work is optional but when used must contain the words *mask work* or the symbol *M* or (M) and the name of the owner.

Copyright Infringement

copyright infringement

A situation in which a party copies a substantial and material part of the plaintiff's copyrighted work without permission. A copyright holder may recover damages and other remedies against the infringer.

Copyright infringement occurs when a party copies a substantial and material part of the plaintiff's copyrighted work without permission. The copying does not have to be either word for word or the entire work. A successful plaintiff can recover (1) the profit made by the infringer from the copyright infringement, (2) damages suffered by the plaintiff, (3) an order requiring the impoundment and destruction of the infringing works, and (4) an injunction preventing the infringer from doing so in the future. The court, in its discretion, can award statutory damages up to $150,000 for willful infringement in lieu of actual damages.

Internet Law & Online Commerce

The NET Act: Criminal Copyright Infringement

In 1997, Congress enacted the **No Electronic Theft Act (NET Act)**, which criminalizes certain copyright infringement. The NET Act prohibits any person from willfully infringing a copyright for the purpose of either commercial advantage or financial gain, or by reproduction or distribution, even without commercial advantage or financial gain, including by electronic means, where the retail value of the copyrighted work exceeds $1,000. Criminal penalties for violating the act include imprisonment for up to one year and fines of up to $100,000.

The NET Act adds a new law for the federal government to criminally attack copyright infringement and curb digital piracy. ■

The Fair Use Doctrine

The copyright holder's rights in a work are not absolute. The law permits certain limited unauthorized use of copyrighted material under the **fair use doctrine**. The following uses are protected under this doctrine: (1) quotation of the copyrighted work for review or criticism or in a scholarly or technical work, (2) use in a parody or satire, (3) brief quotation in a news report, (4) reproduction by a teacher or student of a small part of the work to illustrate a lesson, (5) incidental reproduction of a work in a newsreel or broadcast of an event being reported, and (6) reproduction of a work in a legislative or judicial proceeding. The copyright holder cannot recover for copyright infringement where fair use is found.

fair use doctrine
A doctrine that permits certain limited use of a copyright by someone other than the copyright holder without the permission of the copyright holder.

In the following case, the court had to decide whether there was copyright infringement or fair use.

Case 9.2

Fair Use

Newton v. Beastie Boys
349 F.3d 591, 2003 U.S. App. Lexis 22635
United States Court of Appeals, Ninth Circuit

Background and Facts

James W. Newton, Jr., is an accomplished avant-garde jazz composer and flutist. In 1978, Newton wrote a composition for the song "Choir," a piece for flute and voice that incorporated elements of African-American gospel music. Newton owns the copyright to the composition "Choir." In 1992, the Beastie Boys, a rap and hip-hop group, used six seconds of Newton's "Choir" composition in their song "Pass the Mic" without obtaining a license from Newton to do so. Newton sued the Beastie Boys for copyright infringement. The Beastie Boys defended, arguing that their use of six seconds of Newton's song was fair use. The district court found that the Beastie Boys's use of Newton's composition was *de minimis* and therefore fair use. The district court granted summary judgment in favor of the Beastie Boys, and Newton appealed.

Issue

Does the incorporation of a short segment of a copyrighted musical composition into a new musical recording constitute fair use, or is it copyright infringement?

In the Language of the Court

The dispute between Newton and Beastie Boys centers around the copyright implications of the practice of "sampling," a practice now common to many types of popular music. Sampling entails the incorporation of short segments of prior sound recordings into new recordings. For an unauthorized use of a copyrighted work to be actionable, there must be substantial similarity between the plaintiff's and defendant's works. This means that even where the fact of copying is conceded, no legal consequences will follow from that fact unless the copying is substantial. The focus on the sample's relation to the plaintiff's work as a whole embodies the fundamental question in any infringement action: whether so much is taken that the value of the original is sensibly diminished. When viewed in relation to Newton's composition as a whole, the sampled portion is neither quantitatively nor qualitatively significant. Quantitatively, the three-note sequence appears only once in Newton's composition. When played, the segment lasts six seconds and is roughly two percent of the four-and-a-half-minute "Choir." Beastie Boys' use of the "Choir" composition was *de minimis*. We hold today that Beastie Boys' use of a brief segment of the "Choir" composition is not sufficient to sustain a claim for copyright infringement.

Decision and Remedy

The Court of Appeals held that the Beastie Boys's *de minimis* sampling of Newton's "Choir" composition constituted fair use and not copyright infringement. The Court of Appeals affirmed the district court's grant of summary judgment in favor of the Beastie Boys.

Business and Ethics Questions

1. Should sampling be allowed as fair use? Why or why not?
2. Did the Beastie Boys act ethically when they used part of Newton's "Choir" composition in their song?
3. Has the use of sampling become a big part of today's music recordings? Why do you think recording artists engage in sampling?

Ethics in Business

Copyright Infringement

Elvis Presley became a musical icon during a career that spanned more than 20 years, until he died on August 16, 1977. Many companies and individuals own copyrights to Presley's songs, lyrics, photographs, movies, and appearances on TV shows. Millions of dollars of these copyrighted materials are sold or licensed annually.

Passport Video produced a video documentary titled *The Definitive Elvis*, comprising 16 one-hour episodes. The producers interviewed more than 200 people regarding virtually all aspects of Elvis's life. Passport sold the videos commercially for a profit. Approximately 5 to 10 percent of the videos were composed of copyrighted music and appearances of Presley on TV and in movies owned by copyright holders other than Passport. Passport did not obtain permission to use those copyrighted works. Elvis Presley Enterprises, Inc., and other companies and individuals that owned copyrights to the Presley works used by Passport sued Passport for copyright infringement. Passport defended, arguing that its use of the copyrighted materials was fair use. The U.S. district court held in favor of the plaintiff copyright holders and enjoined Passport from further distribution of its documentary videos. Passport appealed.

The U.S. Court of Appeals held that Passport's use of the copyrighted Elvis Presley materials was not fair use but instead constituted copyright infringement. The Court of Appeals stated, "The King is dead. His legacy, and those who wish to profit from it, remain very much alive." The Court of Appeals held that Passport's use of others' copyrighted materials was for commercial use rather than for a nonprofit purpose. The court rejected Passport's claim that the videos consisted of scholarly research that would be protected as fair use. The court found that Passport's use of the copyrighted material caused market harm to the copyright holders because it would act as a substitute for the original copyrights and thus deny the copyright holders of the value of their copyrights. The Court of Appeals denied Passport's claim of fair use and affirmed the district court's judgment that enjoined Passport from distributing its videos containing these copyrighted materials. *Elvis Presley Enterprises, Inc. v. Passport Video*, 349 F.3d 622, 2003 U.S. App. Lexis 22775 (9th Cir.)

Ethics Issues

1. How valuable do you think the copyrights to Elvis Presley songs, movies, and TV appearances are?
2. What law did Elvis Presley Enterprises, Inc., assert was violated?
3. What was Passport Video's defense?
4. Did Passport Video act ethically in this case? Do you think Passport Video knew it was engaging in copyright infringement? ■

Internet Law & Online Commerce

Encryption Technology

The Internet makes it easier than ever before for people to illegally copy and distribute copyrighted works. To combat this, software and entertainment companies have developed "wrappers" and encryption technology to protect their copyrighted works from unauthorized access. Not to be outdone, software pirates and other Internet users have devised ways to crack these wrappers and protection devices. Software and entertainment companies have lobbied Congress to enact legislation to make the cracking of their wrappers and selling of technology to do so illegal. In response, Congress has enacted the **Digital Millennium Copyright Act (DMCA)** [17 U.S.C. 1201], which does the following:

- Prohibits unauthorized access to copyrighted *digital* works by circumventing the wrapper or encryption technology that protects the intellectual property. This "black box" protection prohibits simply accessing the protected information and does not require that the accessed information be misused.
- Prohibits the manufacture and distribution of technologies, products, or services primarily designed for the purpose of circumventing wrappers or encryption technology protecting *digital* works. However, multipurpose devices that can be used in ways other than for cracking wrappers or encryption technology can be manufactured and sold without violating the DMCA.

Thus, for digital protected works, the DMCA makes it illegal to merely access the copyrighted material by breaking through the digital wrapper or encryption technology that protects the work.

Congress granted exceptions to DMCA liability to (1) software developers to achieve compatibility of their software with the protected work; (2) federal, state, and local law enforcement agencies conducting criminal investigations; (3) parents who are protecting children from pornography or other harmful materials available on the Internet; (4) Internet users who are identifying and disabling cookies and other identification devices that invade their personal privacy rights; and (5) nonprofit libraries, educational institutions, and archives that access a protected work to determine whether to acquire the work.

The DMCA imposes civil and criminal penalties. A successful plaintiff in a civil action can recover actual damages from first-time offenders and treble damages from repeat offenders, costs and attorneys' fees, an order for the destruction of illegal products and devices, and an injunction against future violations by the offender. As an alternative to actual damages, a plaintiff can recover statutory damages of not less than $2,500 and up to $25,000 per act of circumvention. The following criminal penalties can be assessed for willful violations committed for "commercial advantage" or "private financial gain": First-time violators can be fined up to $500,000 and imprisoned for up to 5 years; subsequent violators can be fined up to $1 million and imprisoned for up to 10 years. ■

Trademarks and Online Commerce

Businesses often develop company names, as well as advertising slogans and commercial logos, to promote the sale of their goods and services. Companies such as Nike, Microsoft, Louis Vuitton, and McDonald's spend millions of dollars annually to gain market recognition from consumers. The U.S. Congress has enacted trademark laws to provide legal protection for these names, slogans, and logos.

Federal Lanham Trademark Act

In 1946, Congress enacted the **Lanham Act**[5] to provide federal protection to trademarks, service marks, and other marks. This act, as amended, is intended to (1) protect the owner's investment and goodwill in a **mark** and (2) prevent consumers from being confused as to the origin of goods and services.

Lanham Act (as amended)
A federal statute that (1) establishes the requirements for obtaining a federal mark and (2) protects marks from infringement.

mark
The collective name for trademarks, service marks, certification marks, and collective marks that all can be trademarked.

Trademarks are registered with the United States PTO in Washington, DC. The original registration of a mark is valid for 10 years and can be renewed for an unlimited number of 10-year periods. The registration of a trademark, which is given nationwide effect, serves as constructive notice that the mark is the registrant's personal property. The registrant is entitled to use the registered trademark symbol ® in connection with a registered trademark or service mark. Use of the symbol is not mandatory. Note that the frequently used notations TM and SM have no legal significance.

An applicant can register a mark if it has been used in commerce (e.g., actually used in the sale of goods or services). An applicant can also register a mark six months prior to its proposed use in commerce, but if the mark is not used within this period, the applicant loses the mark. A party other than the registrant can submit an opposition to a proposed registration of a mark or the cancellation of a previously registered mark.

Marks That Can Be Trademarked

The word **mark** collectively refers to *trademarks, service marks, certification marks*, and *collective marks*. The following types of marks can be trademarked:

- ***Trademarks.*** A **trademark** is a distinctive mark, symbol, name, word, motto, or device that identifies the *goods* of a particular business. For example, the words *Chevrolet, Coca-Cola*, and *IBM* are trademarks.
- ***Service marks.*** A **service mark** is used to distinguish the *services* of the holder from those of its competitors. The trade names *United Airlines, Marriott Hotels*, and *Weight Watchers* are examples of service marks.
- ***Certification marks.*** A **certification mark** is a mark that is used to certify that goods and services are of a certain quality or originate from particular geographical areas (for example, wines from the *Napa Valley* of California or *Florida* oranges). The

trademark
A distinctive mark, symbol, name, word, motto, or device that identifies the goods of a particular business.

service mark
A mark that distinguishes the services of the holder from those of its competitors.

owner of the mark is usually a nonprofit corporation that licenses producers that meet certain standards or conditions to use the mark.

- ***Collective marks.*** A **collective mark** is a mark used by cooperatives, associations, and fraternal organizations. *Boy Scouts of America* is an example of a collective mark.

Certain marks cannot be registered. They include (1) the flag or coat of arms of the United States, any state, municipality, or foreign nation; (2) marks that are immoral or scandalous; (3) geographical names standing alone (e.g., "South"); (4) surnames standing alone (note that a surname can be registered if it is accompanied by a picture or fanciful name, such as *Smith Brothers' Cough Drops*); and (5) any mark that resembles a mark already registered with the federal PTO.

Napa Valley, California. This certification mark designates California cheese manufacturers.

Distinctiveness of a Mark

To qualify for federal protection, a mark must be **distinctive** or have acquired a "**secondary meaning**." For example, marks such as *Xerox* and *Acura* are *distinctive*. Nike, Inc., has trademarked its *Just Do It* slogan, which has taken on a secondary meaning. Words that are *descriptive* but have no secondary meaning cannot be trademarked. For example, the word *cola* alone could not be trademarked.

distinctive

A brand name that is unique and fabricated.

secondary meaning

An ordinary term that has become a brand name.

Trademark Infringement

The owner of a mark can sue a third party for the unauthorized use of the mark. To succeed in a **trademark infringement** case, the owner must prove that (1) the defendant infringed the plaintiff's mark by using it in an unauthorized manner and (2) such use is likely to cause confusion, mistake, or deception of the public as to the origin of the goods or services. A successful plaintiff can recover (1) the profits made by the infringer through the unauthorized use of the mark, (2) damages caused to the plaintiff's business and reputation, (3) an order requiring the defendant to destroy all goods containing the unauthorized mark, and (4) an injunction preventing the defendant from such infringement in the future. The court has discretion to award up to treble damages where intentional infringement is found.

trademark infringement
Unauthorized use of another's mark. The holder may recover damages and other remedies from the infringer.

Trade Dress

Section 43(a) of the Lanham Act protects certain forms of **trade dress**. This consists of the "look and feel" of a product, a product's packaging, or a service establishment. The area of trade dress protection is an evolving area of the law.

In the following case, the U.S. Supreme Court found infringing copying of trade dress.

Case 9.3
Trade Dress

U.S. SUPREME COURT
Two Pesos, Inc. v. Taco Cabana, Inc.
505 U.S. 763, 112 S.Ct. 2753, 1992 U.S. Lexis 4533
Supreme Court of the United States

Background and Facts

Since 1976, Taco Cabana, Inc. (Taco Cabana), had operated a chain of fast-food Mexican restaurants in Texas. Its restaurants provided a festive eating atmosphere of interior dining and patio areas decorated with artifacts, bright colors, paintings, and murals. The exterior of its buildings had a vivid color scheme, using top border paint and neon stripes. Bright awnings and umbrellas continued the theme. Beginning in 1985, Two Pesos, Inc. (Two Pesos), opened a chain of competing Mexican fast-food restaurants in Texas. When Two Pesos adopted a motif similar to Taco Cabana's, Taco Cabana sued Two Pesos, alleging trade dress infringement in violation of Section 43(a) of the Lanham Act. Two Pesos argued that Taco Cabana's trade dress should not be protected because it had not yet acquired a secondary meaning. The U.S. district court found that Taco Cabana's trade dress was protected. The Court of Appeals affirmed. Two Pesos appealed to the U.S. Supreme Court.

Issue

Does a restaurant design have to have acquired a secondary meaning before it is protected as trade dress under Section 43(a) of the Lanham Act?

In the Language of the Court

Trade dress is the total image of the business. Taco Cabana's trade dress may include the shape and general appearance of the exterior restaurant, the identifying sign, the interior kitchen floor plan, the decor, the menu, the equipment used to serve food, the servers' uniforms and other features reflecting on the total image of the restaurant. The trade dress of a product is essentially its total image and overall appearance. The user of a trade dress should be able to maintain what competitive position it has and continue to seek wider identification among potential customers.

We see no basis for requiring secondary meaning for inherently distinctive trade dress protection. Adding a secondary meaning requirement could have anticompetitive effects, creating particular burdens on the start-up of small companies. It would present special difficulties for a business, such as Taco Cabana, that seeks to start a new product in a limited area and then expand into new markets. Denying protection for inherently distinctive trade dress until after secondary meaning has been established would allow a competitor, which has not adopted a distinctive trade dress of its own, to appropriate the originator's dress in other markets and to deter the originator from expanding into and competing in these areas.

Decision and Remedy

The Supreme Court held that distinctive trade dress is protectable under the Lanham Act without proof that it has acquired a secondary meaning. The Supreme Court affirmed the decision of the Court of Appeals.

Business and Ethics Questions

1. Should trade dress be protected under the Lanham Act? Why or why not?
2. Did Two Pesos act ethically in copying Taco Cabana's trade dress?
3. Does the Supreme Court decision in this case have a pro- or anticompetitive effect on business? Explain.

Generic Names

Most companies promote their trademarks and service marks to increase the public's awareness of the availability and quality of their products and services. At some point in time, however, the public may begin to treat the mark as a common name to denote the type of product or service being sold, rather than as the trademark or trade name of an individual seller. A trademark that becomes a common term for a product line or type of service is called a **generic name**. Once a trademark becomes a generic name, the term loses its protection under federal trademark law because it has become *descriptive* rather than *distinctive* (see Exhibit 9.2).

generic name
A term for a mark that has become a common term for a product line or type of service and therefore has lost its trademark protection.

Exhibit 9.2
Generic Names
Reprinted with permission of Xerox Corporation.

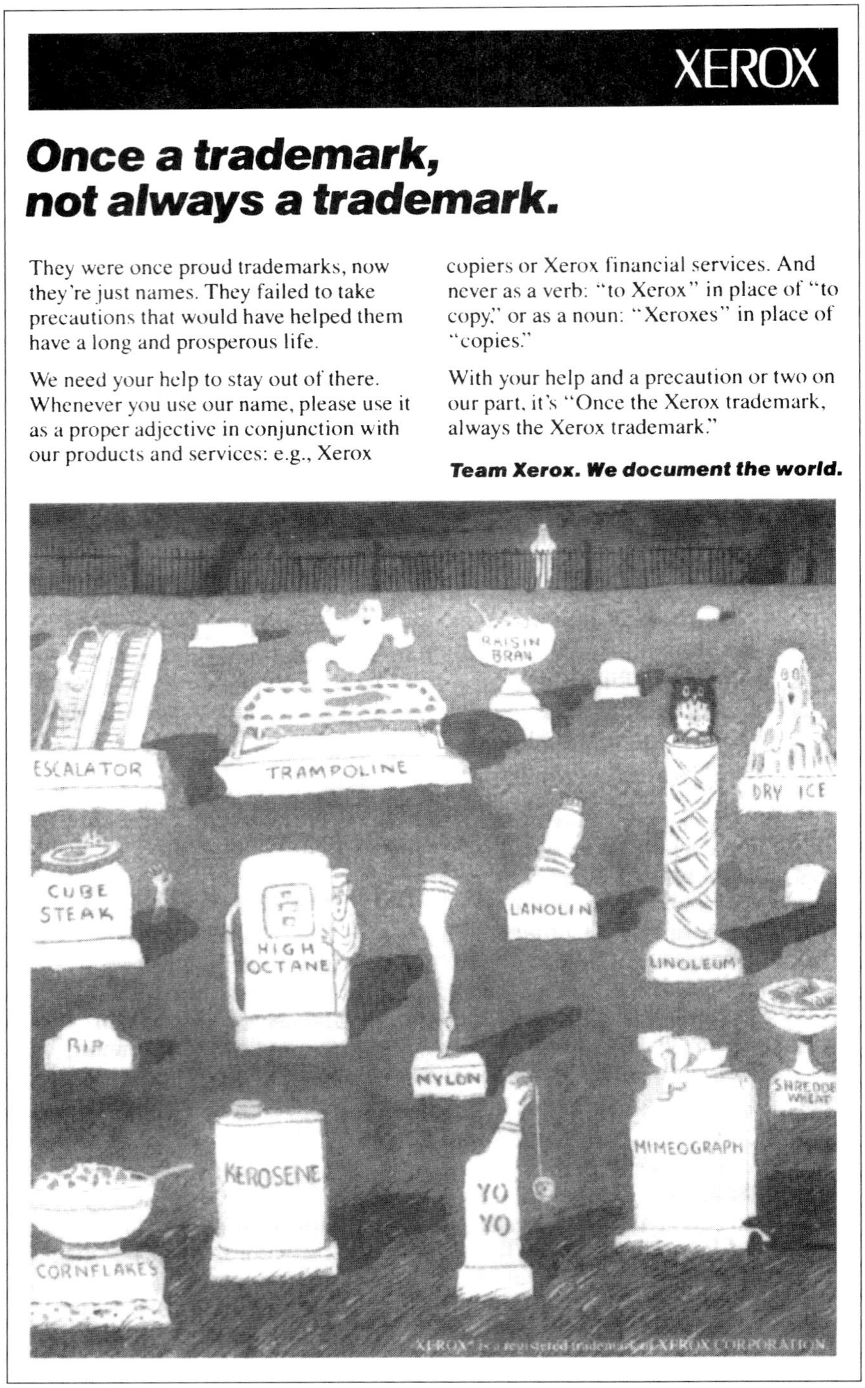

Concept Summary Types of Intellectual Property Protected by Federal Law

Type	Subject Matter	Term
Patent	Inventions (e.g., machines; processes compositions of matter; designs for articles of manufacture; and improvements to existing machines, processes). Invention must be: 1. Novel 2. Useful 3. Nonobvious *Public use doctrine*: Patent will not be granted if the invention was used in the public for more than one year prior to the filing of the patent application.	Patents on articles of manufacture and processes: 20 years; design patents: 14 years.
Copyright	Tangible writing (e.g., books, magazines, newspapers, lectures, operas, plays, screenplays, musical compositions, maps, works of art, lithographs, photographs, postcards, greeting cards, motion pictures, newsreels, sound recordings, computer programs, and mask works fixed to semiconductor chips). Writing must be the original work of the author. *Fair use doctrine:* It permits use of copyrighted material without consent for limited uses (e.g., scholarly work, parody or satire, and brief quotation in news reports).	Author (individual registrant): life of author plus 70 years. Work for hire (business registrant): the shorter of either 120 years from the date of creation or 95 years from the date of first. publication.
Trademark	Marks (e.g., name, symbol, word, logo, or device). Marks include trademarks, service marks, certification marks, and collective marks. Marks must be distinctive or have acquired a secondary meaning. *Generic name:* A mark that becomes a common term for a product line or type of service loses its protection under federal trademark law.	Original registration: 10 years. Renewal registration: unlimited number of renewals for 10-year terms.

Federal Dilution Act

Companies that own trademarks often spend millions of dollars each year advertising and promoting the quality of the goods and services sold under their names. Many of these become household names that are recognized by millions of consumers, such as Coca-Cola, McDonald's, Microsoft, and Nike.

Traditional trademark law protected these marks where an infringer used the mark and confused consumers as to the source of the goods or services. For example, if a knock-off company sold athletic shoes and apparel under the name "Nike," there would be trademark infringement.

Federal Dilution Act
A federal statute that protects famous marks from dilution, erosion, blurring, or tarnishing.

Often, however, a party would use a name similar to, but not exactly identical to, a holder's trademark. Congress enacted the **Federal Dilution Act of 1995** to protect *famous marks* from *dilution*. The Federal Dilution Act provides that owners of marks have a valuable property right in their marks that should not be *eroded, blurred, tarnished*, or *diluted* in any way by another. The Federal Dilution Act has three fundamental requirements:

1. The mark must be famous.
2. The use by the other party must be commercial.
3. The use must cause dilution of the distinctive quality of the mark.

Dilution is broadly defined as the lessening of the capacity of a famous mark to identify and distinguish its holder's goods and services, regardless of the presence or absence of competition between the owner of the mark and the other party. For example, if someone other than Nike had a Web site at the address **www.nikeathletes.com**, it would be unlawful dilution.

Hong Kong. These counterfeit knock-off goods are an example of how companies' trademarks and copyrights are being infringed around the world. Knock-off goods cause a huge monetary loss to the owners' intellectual property rights.

The Internet

Internet
A collection of millions of computers that provide a network of electronic connections between computers.

The **Internet**, or **Net**, is a collection of millions of computers that provide a network of electronic connections between the computers. There are hundreds of millions of computers connected to the Internet. The Internet's evolution helped usher in the Information Age of today. Individuals and businesses use the Internet for communication of information and data.

E-Mail

electronic mail (e-mail)
Electronic written communication between individuals using computers connected to the Internet.

Electronic mail, or **e-mail**, is one of the most widely used applications for communication over the Internet. Using e-mail, individuals around the world can instantaneously communicate in electronic writing with one another. Each person can have an e-mail address that identifies him or her by a unique address. E-mail will continue to grow in use in the future as it replaces some telephone and paper correspondence and increases new communication between persons.

World Wide Web

The **World Wide Web** consists of millions of computers that support a standard set of rules for the exchange of information called Hypertext Transfer Protocol (HTTP). Web-based documents are formatted using common coding languages. Businesses and individuals can hook up to the Web by registering with a server such as American Online (AOL).

World Wide Web
An electronic collection of millions of computers that support a standard set of rules for the exchange of information.

Individuals and businesses can have their own Web sites. A Web site is composed of electronic documents known as Web pages. Web sites and pages are stored on servers throughout the world, which are operated by **Internet service providers (ISPs)**. They are viewed by using Web browsing software such as Microsoft Internet Explorer and Netscape Navigator. Each Web site has a unique online address.

The Web has made it extremely attractive to conduct commercial activities online. Companies such as Amazon.com and eBay are e-commerce powerhouses that sell all sorts of goods and services. Existing brick-and-mortar companies, such as Wal-Mart, Merrill Lynch, and Dell Computers, sell their goods and services online as well. E-commerce over the Web will continue to grow dramatically each year.

In the following case, the court addressed the liability of an ISP.

Case 9.4
Internet

John Doe v. GTE Corporation
347 F.3d 655, 2003 U.S. App. Lexis 21345
United States Court of Appeals, Seventh Circuit

Background and Facts

Someone secretly took video cameras into the locker room and showers of the Illinois State football team. Visual tapes and audio showing these undressed players were displayed at the Web site **univ.youngstuds.com** operated by Franco Productions. The Internet name concealed the name of the person responsible. GTE Corporation, an ISP, provided a high-speed connection and storage space on its server so that the content of the Web site could be assessed. The nude images passed over GTE's network between Franco Productions and its customers. The football players sued Franco Productions and GTE for monetary damages. Franco Productions defaulted when it could not be located. Franco Productions was ordered to pay over $500 million in damages, though there is little hope of collection. The U.S. district court dismissed the case against GTE. The football players appealed.

Issue

Is GTE Corporation, as the ISP, liable for damages to the plaintiff football players?

In the Language of the Court

The district court's order dismissing the complaint rests on 47 U.S.C. Section 230(c)(1), a part of the federal Communications Decency Act of 1996. This subsection provides: "No provider or user of an interactive computer service shall be treated as the publisher or speaker of any information provided by another information content provider." Just as the telephone company is not liable as an aider and abetter for tapes or narcotics sold by phone, and the Postal Service is not liable for tapes sold (and delivered) by mail, so a web host cannot be classified as an aider and abetter of criminal activities conducted through access to the Internet. GTE is not a "publisher or speaker" as Section 230(c)(1) uses those terms. Therefore, GTE cannot be liable under any state-law theory to the persons harmed by Franco's material.

Decision and Remedy

The Court of Appeals held that GTE Corporation, as an ISP, was not liable for the nude videos of the football players transmitted over its system by Franco Productions. The Court of Appeals

(continued)

John Doe v. GTE Corporation

347 F.3d 655, 2003 U.S. App. Lexis 21345
United States Court of Appeals, Seventh Circuit
(continued)

affirmed the district court's order, dismissing the plaintiff football players' lawsuit against GTE.

Business and Ethics Questions

1. Why do you think Congress enacted Section 230(c)(1)? Explain.
2. Did the owner of Franco Productions act ethically in this case?
3. Will the taking and posting on the Internet of unconsented to photographs of others escalate? Explain.

Domain Names

domain name
A unique name that identifies an individual's or company's Web site.

Most businesses conduct e-commerce by using Web sites that can be located on the Internet. Each Web site is identified by a unique Internet **domain name**. For example, the domain name for the publisher of this book is **www.prenhall.com**. Domain names can be registered. Domain names can be registered at Network Solutions, Inc.'s, Web site, which is located at **www.networksolutions.com**, as well as at other sites. An applicant must complete a registration form, which can be done online. It costs less than $50 to register a domain name for one year, and the fee may be paid by credit card online.

The most commonly used top-level extensions for domain names are:

- ***.com.*** This extension represents the word *commercial* and is the most widely used extension in the world. Most businesses prefer a .com domain name because it is a highly recognized business symbol.
- ***.net.*** This extension represents the word *network*, and it is most commonly used by ISPs, Web-hosting companies, and other business that are directly involved in the infrastructure of the Internet. Some businesses also choose domain names with a .net extension.
- ***.org.*** This extension represents the word *organization* and is primarily used by non-profit groups and trade associations.
- ***.info.*** This extension signifies a resource Web site. It is an unrestricted global name that may be used by businesses, individuals, and organizations.
- ***.biz.*** This extension is used for small-business Web sites.
- ***.us.*** This extension is for U.S. Web sites. Many businesses choose this extension, which is a relatively new extension.
- ***.cc.*** This extension was originally the country code for Coco Keeling Islands, but it is now unrestricted and may be registered by anyone from any country. It is often registered by businesses.
- ***.bz.*** This extension was originally the country code for Belize, but it is now unrestricted and may be registered by anyone from any country. It is commonly used by small businesses.
- ***.name.*** This new extension is for individuals, who can use it to register personalized domain names.

- ***.museum.*** This extension enables museums, museum associations, and museum professionals to register Web sites.
- ***.coop.*** This extension represents the word *cooperative* and may be used by cooperative associations around the world.
- ***.aero.*** This extension is exclusively reserved for the aviation community. It enables organizations and individuals in that community to reserve Web sites.
- ***.pro.*** This extension is available to professionals, such as doctors, lawyers, consultants, and other professionals.
- ***.edu.*** This extension is for educational institutions.

Internet Law & Online Commerce

Electronic Communications Privacy Act

E-mail, computer data, and other electronic communications are sent daily by millions of people using computers and the Internet. Recognizing how the use of computer and electronic communications raise special issues of privacy, the federal government enacted the **Electronic Communications Privacy Act (ECPA)**. The ECPA makes it a crime to intercept an "electronic communication" at the point of transmission, while in transit, when stored by a router or server, or after receipt by the intended recipient. An electronic communication includes any transfer of signals, writings, images, sounds, data, or intelligence of any nature. The ECPA makes it illegal to access stored e-mail as well as e-mail in transmission.

The ECPA provides that the following parties may access stored electronic communications without violating the law:

1. The party or entity providing the electronic communication service. The primary example would be an employer who can access stored e-mail communications of employees using the employer's service.
2. Government and law enforcement entities that are investigating suspected illegal activity. Disclosure would be required only pursuant to a validly issued warrant.

The ECPA provides for criminal penalties. In addition, the ECPA provides that an injured party may sue for civil damages for violations of the ECPA. ■

International Law

International Protection of Intellectual Property Rights

For centuries, national patent, copyright, and trademark laws defined the rights of inventors, authors, and businesses. These laws offered protection within a country's borders but not in other countries. Beginning in the late 1800s, countries began entering into treaties and conventions with other countries that provided international protection of intellectual property rights. Several of these treaties are:

1. ***Paris Convention.*** This international treaty protects patents and trademarks.
2. ***Berne Convention.*** This international treaty protects copyrights.
3. ***WIPO Copyright Treaty.*** This international treaty protects copyrights to computer programs and data compilations.
4. ***WIPO Phonogram Treaty.*** This international treaty gives performers and producers the exclusive right to broadcast, reproduce, and distribute copies of their performances. ■

Arc de Triumphe, Paris, France

Terms and Concepts

Trade Secrets

1. ***Trade secret.*** A *trade secret* is a product formula, pattern, design, compilation of data, customer list, or other business secret that makes a business successful. The owner of a trade secret must take reasonable precautions to prevent its trade secret from being discovered by others.
2. ***Misappropriation of a trade secret.*** Obtaining another's trade secret through unlawful means such as theft, bribery, or espionage is a tort. A successful plaintiff can recover profits, damages, and an injunction against the offender.
3. ***The Economic Espionage Act.*** This federal statute makes it a crime for any person to convert a trade secret for his or her benefit or for someone else's, knowing or intending to cause injury to the owners of the trade secret.

Patents

Patent law is exclusively federal law; there are no state patent laws.

1. ***Patent.*** Patentable subject matter includes inventions such as machines; processes; compositions of matter; improvements to existing machines, processes, or compositions of matter; designs for articles of manufacture; asexually reproduced plants; and living matter invented by a person.

   To be patented, an invention must be:

   a. Novel

   b. Useful

   c. Nonobvious
2. ***Business plans.*** In *State Street Bank & Trust Co. v. Signature Financial Group, Inc.*, the U.S. Court of Appeals held that business plans are patentable.
3. ***Patent application.*** An application containing a written description of an invention must be filed with the *U.S. Patent and Trademark Office (PTO)* in Washington, DC.
4. ***Term.*** Patents are valid for 20 years.

5. ***Public use doctrine.*** A patent may not be granted if the invention was used by the public for more than one year prior to the filing of the patent application.
6. ***Patent infringement.*** Patent infringement is the unauthorized use of another's patent. The patent holder may recover damages and other remedies against the infringer.
7. ***The American Inventors Protection Act.*** This federal statute does the following:
   a. Permits the inventor to file a *provisional application* with the U.S. PTO, pending the filing of a final patent application.
   b. Requires the PTO to issue a patent within three years after the filing of a patent application.
8. ***Patent appeals.*** Patent appeals are heard by the *U.S. Court of Appeals for the Federal Circuit* in Washington, DC.

Copyrights

Copyright law is exclusively federal law; there are no state copyright laws.

1. ***Copyright.*** Only tangible writings can be copyrighted. These include books, newspapers, addresses, musical compositions, motion pictures, works of art, architectural plans, greeting cards, photographs, sound recordings, computer programs, and mask works fixed in semiconductor chips.
2. ***Requirements for copyright.*** A writing must be the original work of the author.
3. ***Copyright registration.*** Copyright registration is permissive and voluntary. Published and unpublished works may be registered with the *U.S. Copyright Office* in Washington, DC. Registration itself does not create the copyright.
4. ***Term.*** Copyrights are for the following terms:
   a. Individual holder. Life of the author plus 70 years.
   b. Corporate holder. Either 120 years from the date of creation or 95 years from the date of publication, whichever is shorter.
5. ***Copyright infringement.*** Copyright infringement is the copying of a substantial and material part of a copyrighted work without the holder's permission. The copyright holder may recover damages and other remedies against the infringer.
6. ***Fair use doctrine.*** This doctrine permits use of copyrighted material without the consent of the copyright holder for limited uses (e.g., scholarly work, parody or satire, brief quotation in news reports).
7. ***No Electronic Theft Act (NET Act).*** This federal statute makes it a crime for a person to willfully infringe a copyright exceeding $1,000 in retail value.
8. ***Digital Millennium Copyright Act (DMCA).*** This federal statute, enacted in 1998, provides civil and criminal penalties that:
   a. Prohibit the manufacture and distribution of technologies, products, or services primarily designed for the purpose of circumventing wrappers or encryption protection.
   b. Prohibit unauthorized *access* to copyrighted digital works by circumventing the wrapper or encryption technology that protects the intellectual property.

Trademarks and Service Marks

1. ***Mark.*** A mark is a trade name, symbol, word, logo, design, or device that distinguishes the owner's goods or services. Marks are often referred to collectively as trademarks. Types of marks are:
   a. Trademark. This type of mark identifies goods of a particular business.
   b. Service mark. This type of mark identifies services of a particular business.
   c. Certification mark. This type of mark certifies that goods or services are of a certain quality or origin.
   d. Collective mark. A collective mark is used by cooperatives, associations, and fraternal organizations.
2. ***Requirements for a trademark.*** The mark must either (a) be *distinctive* or (b) have acquired a *secondary meaning*. The mark must have been used in commerce or the holder must intend to use the mark in commerce and actually do so within six months after registering the mark.
3. ***Trademark registration.*** Marks are registered with the *U.S. Patent and Trademark Office* in Washington, DC.

4. ***Term.*** The original registration of a mark is valid for 10 years and can be renewed for an unlimited number of 10-year periods.
5. ***Trademark infringement.*** Trademark infringement is the unauthorized use of another's registered mark. The mark holder may recover damages and other remedies from the infringer.
6. ***Trade dress.*** Trade dress protection involves the look and feel of a product, a product's packaging, or a service establishment.
7. ***Generic name.*** A mark that becomes a common term for a product line or type of service loses its protection under federal trademark law.
8. ***Federal Trademark Dilution Act of 1995.*** This federal statue protects famous marks from dilution. A violation of the act requires that marks be famous, the use by the other party was commercial, and the use caused dilution of the distinctive quality of the mark.

Internal Protection of Intellectual Property Rights

1. ***Paris Convention.*** This international treaty protects patents and trademarks.
2. ***Berne Convention.*** This international treaty protects copyrights.
3. ***WIPO Copyright Treaty.*** This international treaty protects copyrights on computer programs and data compilations.
4. ***WIPO Phonogram Treaty.*** This international treaty gives performers and producers the exclusive right to broadcast, reproduce, and distribute copies of their performances.

The Internet and World Wide Web

1. ***Internet.*** The Internet is a collection of millions of computers that provides a network of electronic connections between computers.
2. ***World Wide Web.*** The Web is an electronic connection of computers that support a standard set of rules for the exchange of information called Hypertext Transfer Protocol (HTTP).
3. ***Electronic mail (e-mail).*** E-mail is electronic written communication between individuals using computers connected to the Internet.

Domain Name

1. ***Domain name.*** A domain name is a unique name that identifies an individual's or company's Web site.
2. ***Domain name registration.*** Domain names are registered by filing the appropriate form with a domain name regulation service and paying the appropriate fee.

Electronic Privacy

The *Electronic Communications Privacy Act* is a federal statute that makes it a crime to intercept an electronic communication at the point of transmission, while in transit, when stored by a router or server, or after receipt by the intended recipient.

Internet Exercises and Case Questions

Working the Web Internet Exercises

1. Research the Web to determine whether your state has adopted the Uniform Trade Secrets Act. Visit the Trade Secrets home page, at **www.execpc.com/~mhallign**.
2. The site **www.uspto.gov** contains information about the federal copyright registration system. Does the most recent copyright law require authors to use the copyright notice on printed material in order to protect it from infringement?
3. What is the current duration of a U.S. patent? What was the duration of a U.S. patent under previous law, and why was it changed? See **www.uspto.gov**.
4. Visit **www.wipo.int** and outline the process for international registration of a patent.

Legal Environment Cases

9.1 Trade Secret CRA-MAR Video Center, Inc., sells electronic equipment and videocassettes, as does its competitor, Koach's Sales Corporation. Both CRA-MAR and Koach's purchased computers from Radio Shack. CRA-MAR used its computer to store customer lists, movie lists, personnel files, and financial records. Because the computer was new to CRA-MAR, Randall Youts, Radio Shack's salesman and programmer, agreed to modify CRA-MAR's programs when needed, including the customer list program. At one point, CRA-MAR decided to send a mailing to everyone on its customer list. The computer was unable to perform the function, so Youts took the disks containing the customer lists to the Radio Shack store to work on the program. Somehow Koach's came into possession of CRA-MAR's customer lists and sent advertising mailings to the parties on the list. When CRA-MAR discovered this fact, it sued Koach's, seeking an injunction against any further use of its customer lists. Is a customer list a trade secret that can be protected from misappropriation? *Koach's Sales Corp. v. CRA-MAR Video Center, Inc.*, 478 N.E.2d 110, 1985 Ind.App. Lexis 2432 (Ind.App.)

9.2 Patent In 1968, Patent No. 3,397,928 (928) was issued to Edward M. Galle, an executive of Hughes Tool Company. Galle assigned the patent, and other related patents, to Hughes. The patent was for an O-ring rubber seal that was used to seal bearings in the cone of a rock bit that rotated to drill holes in rocks. Rock bits were used to drill oil wells. Hughes did not license its 928 patent, which was a substantial commercial success. Smith International, Inc., was Hughes's major competitor in this industry. Between 1971 and 1984, Smith made more than 460,000 rock bits (reaping sales of about $1.3 billion) that contained rubber seals that infringed on Hughes's patents. Hughes sued Smith for patent infringement and requested $1.2 billion in lost royalties and interest. Smith offered $20 million to $60 million in settlement. The case went to trial, and the court found Smith liable for patent infringement. How much should Hughes be awarded in damages? *Smith International Inc. v. Hughes Tool Co.*, 229 U.S.P.Q. 81, 1986 U.S. Dist. Lexis 2847 (Fed. Cir.)

9.3 Copyright When Spiro Agnew resigned as vice president of the United States, President Richard M. Nixon appointed Gerald Ford as vice president. In 1974, amid growing controversy surrounding the Watergate scandal, President Nixon resigned, and Vice President Ford acceded to the presidency. As president, Ford pardoned Nixon for any wrongdoing regarding the Watergate affair and related matters. Ford served as president until he was defeated by Jimmy Carter in the 1976 presidential election. In 1973, Ford entered into a contract with Harper & Row, Publishers, Inc., to publish his memoirs in book form. The memoirs were to contain significant unpublished materials concerning the Watergate affair and Ford's personal reflections on that time in history. The publisher instituted security measures to protect the confidentiality of the manuscript. Several weeks before the book was to be released, an unidentified person secretly brought a copy of the manuscript to Victor Navasky, editor of *The Nation*, a weekly political commentary magazines. Navasky, knowing that his possession of the purloined manuscript was not authorized, produced a 2,250-word piece titled "The Ford Memoirs" and published it in the April 3, 1979, issue of *The Nation*. Verbatim quotes of between 300 and 400 words from Ford's manuscript, including some of the most important parts, appeared in the article. Harper & Row sued the publishers of *The Nation* for copyright infringement. Who wins? *Harper & Row, Publishers, Inc. v. Nation Enterprises*, 471 U.S. 539, 105 S.Ct. 2218, 1985 U.S. Lexis 17 (U.S. Sup.Ct.)

9.4 Copyright The Sony Corporation of America manufactures videocassette recorders (VCRs) that can be used to videotape programs and films that are shown on television and cable stations. VCRs are used by consumers and others to videotape both copyrighted and uncopyrighted works. The primary use for VCRs is by consumers for "time-shifting"—that is, taping a television program for viewing at a more convenient time. Universal City Studios, Inc., and Walt Disney Productions hold copyrights on a substantial number of motion-picture and audiovisual works that are shown on television and cable stations, which pay them a fee to do so. Some of Universal's and Disney's copyrighted works have been copied by consumers using Sony's VCRs. Universal and Disney sued Sony, seeking an injunction against the sale of VCRs by Sony. Is Sony liable for contributory copyright infringement? *Sony Corp. of America v. University City Studios, Inc.*, 464 U.S. 417, 104 S.Ct. 774, 1984 U.S. Lexis 19 (U.S. Sup.Ct.)

9.5 Fair Use Doctrine In the dark days of 1977, when the City of New York teetered on the brink of bankruptcy, on the television screens of America there appeared an image of a top-hatted Broadway showgirl, backed by an advancing phalanx of dancers, chanting: "I-I-I-I-I-I Love New Yo-o-o-o-o-o-rk." As an ad campaign for an ailing city, it was an unparalleled success. Crucial to the campaign was a brief but exhilarating musical theme written by Steve Karmin called "I Love New York." Elsmere Music, Inc., owned the copyright to the music. The success of the campaign did not go unnoticed. On May 20, 1978, the popular weekly variety program *Saturday Night Live* (*SNL*) performed a comedy sketch over National Broadcasting Company's (NBC's) network. In the sketch, the cast of *SNL*, portraying the mayor and members of the chamber of commerce of the biblical city of Sodom, were seen discussing Sodom's poor public image with out-of-towners and its effect on the tourist trade. In an attempt to recast Sodom's image in a more positive light, a new advertising campaign was revealed, with the highlight of the campaign being a song "I Love Sodom," sung a cappella by a chorus line of *SNL* regulars to the tune of "I Love New York." Elsmere Music did not see the humor of the sketch and sued NBC for copyright infringement. Who wins? *Elsmere Music, Inc. v. National Broadcasting Co., Inc.*, 623 F.2d 252, 1980 U.S. App. Lexis 16820 (2d Cir.)

9.6 Trademark Clairol Incorporated manufactures and distributes hair tinting, dyeing, and coloring preparations. In 1956, Clairol embarked on an extensive advertising campaign to promote the sale of its "Miss Clairol" hair-coloring preparations that included advertisement in national magazines, on outdoor billboards, on radio and television, in mailing pieces, and on point-of-sale display materials to be used by retailers and beauty salons. The advertisements prominently displayed the slogans "Hair Color So Natural Only Her Hairdresser Knows for Sure" and "Does She or Doesn't She?" Clairol registered these slogans as trademarks. During the next decade, Clairol spent more than

$22 million for advertising materials, resulting in more than a billion separate audio and visual impressions using the slogans. Roux Laboratories, Inc., a manufacturer of hair-coloring products and a competitor of Clairol's, filed an opposition to Clairol's registration of the slogans as trademarks. Do the slogans qualify for trademark protection? *Roux Laboratories, Inc. v. Clairol Inc.*, 427 F.2d 823, 1970 CCPA Lexis 344 (Cust.Pat.App.)

9.7 Trademark Since 1972, Mead Data Central, Inc., has provided computer-assisted legal research services to lawyers and others under the trademark "Lexis." Lexis is based on *lex*, the Latin word for law, and *IS*, for information systems. Through extensive sales and advertising, Mead has made Lexis a strong mark in the computerized legal research field, particularly among lawyers. However, Lexis is recognized by only 1 percent of the general population, with almost half of this 1 percent being attorneys. Toyota Motor Corporation has for many years manufactured automobiles, which it markets in the United States through its subsidiary Toyota Motor Sales, U.S.A., Inc. On August 24, 1987, Toyota announced a new line of luxury automobiles to be called Lexus. Toyota planned on spending almost $20 million for marketing and advertising Lexus during the first nine months of 1989. Mead filed suit against Toyota, alleging that Toyota's use of the name Lexus violated New York's antidilution statute and would cause injury to the business reputation of Mead and a dilution of the distinctive quality of the Lexis mark. Who wins? *Mead Data Central, Inc. v. Toyota Motor Sales, U.S.A., Inc.*, 875 F.2d 1026, 1989 U.S. App. Lexis 6644 (2d Cir.)

9.8 Generic Name The Miller Brewing Company, a national brewer, produces a reduced-calorie beer called Miller Lite. Miller began selling beer under this name in the 1970s and has spent millions of dollars promoting the Miller Lite brand name on television, in print, and via other forms of advertising. Since July 11, 1980, Falstaff Brewing Corporation has been brewing and distributing a reduced-calorie beer called "Falstaff Life." Miller brought suit under the Lanham Act, seeking an injunction to prevent Falstaff from using the term *Lite*. Is the term *Lite* a generic name that does not qualify for trademark protection? *Miller Brewing Co. v. Falstaff Brewing Corp.*, 655 F.2d 5, 1981 U.S. App. Lexis 11345 (1st Cir.)

Ethics in Business

9.9 Integrated Cash Management Services, Inc. (ICM), designs and develops computer software programs and systems for banks and corporate financial departments. ICM's computer programs and systems are not copyrighted, but they are secret. After Alfred Sims Newlin and Behrouz Vafa completed graduate school, they were employed by ICM as computer programmers. They worked at ICM for several years, writing computer programs. In March 1987, they left ICM to work for Digital Transactions, Inc. (DTI). Before leaving ICM, however, they copied certain ICM files onto computer disks. Within two weeks of starting to work at DTI, they created prototype computer programs that operated in substantially the same manner as comparable ICM programs and were designed to compete directly with ICM's programs. ICM sued Newlin, Vafa, and DTI for misappropriation of trade secrets. *Integrated Cash Management Services, Inc. v. Digital Transactions, Inc.*, 920 F.2d 171, 1990 U.S. App. Lexis 20985 (2d Cir.)

Ethics Issues

1. What law does Integrated Cash Management Services allege was violated? Explain the elements of this law.
2. Did Alfred Sims Newlin and Behrouz Vafa act ethically in this case?
3. Are the defendants liable? Explain.

Endnotes

1. 35 U.S.C. Section 10 *et seq.*
2. 17 U.S.C. Section 101 *et seq.*
3. 17 U.S.C. Section 101.
4. 17 U.S.C. Sections 901–914.
5. 15 U.S.C. Section 1114 *et seq.*

10

Ethics and Social Responsibility of Business

"Ethical considerations can no more be excluded from the administration of justice, which is the end and purpose of all civil laws, than one can exclude the vital air from his room and live."

—John F. Dillon
Laws and Jurisprudence of England and American Lecture I (1894)

Chapter Objectives

After studying this chapter, you should be able to:

1. Describe how law and ethics intertwine.
2. Describe the moral theories of business ethics.
3. Describe the theories of the social responsibility of business.
4. Describe corporate social audits.
5. Examine how international ethical standards differ from country to country.

Chapter Contents

- Ethics and the Law
- Business Ethics
- Social Responsibility of Business

Businesses organized in the United States are subject to its laws. They are also subject to the laws of other countries in which they operate. In addition, businesspersons owe a duty to act ethically in the conduct of their affairs, and businesses owe a social responsibility not to harm society.

Although much of the law is based on ethical standards, not all ethical standards have been enacted as law. The law establishes a minimum degree of conduct expected by persons and businesses in society. Ethics demands more. This chapter discusses business ethics and the social responsibility of business.

Myanmar. Some companies refuse to do business with Myanmar because of allegations that its military-led government engages in humanitarian violations.

Ethics and the Law

ethics

A set of moral principles or values that governs the conduct of an individual or a group.

Sometimes the rule of law and the golden rule of **ethics** demand the same response by the person confronted with a problem. For example, federal and state laws make bribery unlawful. A person violates the law if he or she bribes a judge for a favorable decision in a case. Ethics would also prohibit this conduct.

The law may permit something that would be ethically wrong.

Consider This Example Occupational safety laws set standards for emissions of dust from toxic chemicals in the workplace. Suppose a company can reduce the emissions below the legal standard by spending additional money. The only benefit from the expenditure would be better employee health. Ethics would require the extra expenditure; the law would not.

Ethics precede laws as man precedes society.

Jason Alexander
Philosophy for Investors (1979)

Another alternative occurs where the law demands certain conduct but a person's ethical standards are contrary.

Consider This Example Federal law prohibits employees from hiring certain illegal alien workers. Suppose an employer advertises the availability of a job and receives no response except from a person who cannot prove he or she is a citizen of this country or does not possess a required visa. The worker and his or her family are destitute. Should the employer hire him or her? The law says no, but ethics says yes (see Exhibit 10.1).

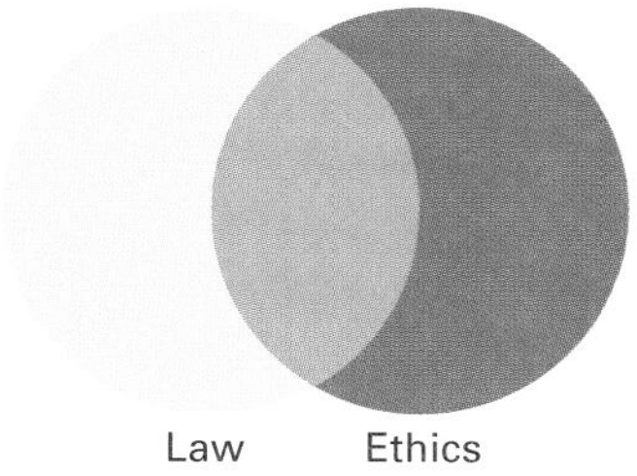

Exhibit 10.1
Law and Ethics

Business Ethics

How can ethics be measured? The answer is very personal: What is considered ethical by one person may be considered unethical by another. However, there do seem to be some universal rules about what conduct is ethical and what conduct is not. The following discussion highlights five major theories of ethics.

> He who seeks equality must do equity.
>
> Joseph Story
> *Equity Jurisprudence* (1836)

Ethical Fundamentalism

Under **ethical fundamentalism**, a person looks to an *outside source* for ethical rules or commands. This may be a book (e.g., the Bible or the Koran) or a person (e.g., Karl Marx). Critics argue that ethical fundamentalism does not permit people to determine right and wrong for themselves. Taken to an extreme, the result could be considered unethical under most other moral theories. For example, a literal interpretation of the maxim "an eye for an eye" would permit retaliation.

ethical fundamentalism
A theory of ethics in which a person looks to an outside source for ethical rules or commands.

Ethics in Business

Qui Tam *Lawsuit*

The Bayer Corporation (Bayer) is a U.S. subsidiary corporation of giant German-based Bayer A.G. Bayer is a large pharmaceutical company that produces prescription drugs, including its patented antibiotic Cipro. Bayer sold Cipro to private health providers and hospitals, including Kaiser Permanente Medical Care Program, the largest health maintenance organization in the United States. Bayer also sold Cipro to the federal government's Medicaid program, which provides medical insurance to the poor. Federal law contains a "best price" rule that prohibits companies that sell drugs to Medicaid to charge Medicaid a price higher than the lowest price for which it sells the drug to private purchasers.

In the spring of 1995, Kaiser told Bayer that it would not purchase Cipro from Bayer—and would switch to a competitor's antibiotics—unless Bayer reduced the price of Cipro. Bayer's executives came up with a plan whereby Bayer would put a private label on its Cipro and not call it Cipro and then sell the antibiotic to Kaiser at a 40 percent discount. Thus, Bayer continued to charge Medicaid the full price for Cipro, while giving Kaiser a 40 percent discount through a private labeling program. One of Bayer's executives who negotiated this deal with Kaiser was corporate account manager George Couto.

Everything went well for Bayer until Couto attended a mandatory ethics training class at Bayer at which a video of Helge Wehmeier, then company chief executive, was shown. When the video stated that Bayer employees were to obey not only "the letter of the law but the spirit of the law as well," some of the Bayer executives laughed. Later that day, Couto attended a staff meeting at which it was disclosed that Bayer kept $97 million from Medicaid by using the discounted private labeling program for Kaiser and other health care companies. Two days later, Couto wrote a memorandum to his boss, questioning the legality of the private label program in light of Medicaid's "best price" law.

(continued)

Ethics in Business
(continued)

When he received no response to his memo, Couto contacted a lawyer. Couto filed a ***Qui tam* lawsuit** under the Federal **False Claims Act**—also known as the **Whistle-Blower statute**—which permits private parties to sue companies for fraud on behalf of the government. The riches: The whistle-blower can be awarded up to 25 percent of the amount recovered on behalf of the federal government, even if the informer has been a co-conspirator in perpetrating the fraud.

Once the case was filed, the U.S. Department of Justice took over the case, as allowed by law, and filed criminal as well as civil charges against Bayer. After discovery was taken, Bayer pleaded guilty to one criminal felony and agreed to pay federal and state governments $257 million to settle the civil and criminal cases. Couto, age 39, died of pancreatic cancer three months prior to the settlement. Couto was awarded $34 million, which was to go to his three children. *United States v. Bayer Corporation*.

Ethics Issues

1. Was it very difficult for the Bayer executives to devise the private labeling plan to cheat the federal government?
2. Did Couto act ethically in this case? Should a fraudulent co-conspirator be allowed to recover an award under the Whistle-Blower statute? Explain.

Utilitarianism

utilitarianism
A moral theory that dictates that people must choose the action or follow the rule that provides the greatest good to society.

Utilitarianism is a moral theory with origins in the works of Jeremy Bentham (1748–1832) and John Stuart Mill (1806–1873). This moral theory dictates that people must choose the actions or follow the rule that provides the *greatest good to society*. This does not mean the greatest good for the greatest number of people. For instance, if one action would increase the good of 25 people 1 unit each, and an alternative action would increase the good of 1 person 26 units, the latter action should be taken.

Utilitarianism has been criticized because it is difficult to estimate the "good" that will result from different actions, it is hard to apply in an imperfect world, and it treats morality as if it were an impersonal mathematical calculation.

Consider This Example A company is trying to determine whether it should close an unprofitable plant located in a small community. Utilitarianism would require that the benefits to shareholders from closing the plant be compared to the benefits to employees, their families, and others in the community in keeping it open.

The ethics of a fast-food restaurant chain were raised in the following case.

Case 10.1
Business Ethics

Bradley v. McDonald's Corporation
2003 U.S.Dist. Lexis 15202 United States District Court, Southern District of New York

Background and Facts

McDonald's Corporation operates the largest fast-food restaurant chain in the United States and the world. It produces such famous food as the "Big Mac" hamburger, chicken "McNuggets," the egg "McMuffin," French fries, shakes, and other foods. A McDonald's survey showed that 22% of its customers are "Super Heavy Users," meaning that they eat at McDonald's at least 10 times or more a month. Super Heavy Users account for approximately 75% of McDonald's sales. The survey also found that 72% of McDonald's customers were "Heavy Users," meaning they ate at McDonald's at least once a week.

Jazlym Bradley consumed McDonald's foods her entire life during school lunch breaks and before and after school, approximately five times per week, ordering two meals per day. When Bradley was 19 years old, she sued McDonald's Corporation for causing her obesity and health problems associated with obesity.

Plaintiff Bradley sued McDonald's in U.S. district court for violating the New York Consumer Protection Act, which prohibits deceptive and unfair acts and practices. She alleged that McDonald's misled her, through its advertising campaigns and other publicity, that its food products were nutritious, of a beneficial nutritional nature, and easily part of a healthy lifestyle if consumed on a daily basis. The plaintiff sued on behalf of herself and a class of minors residing in New York State who purchased and consumed McDonald's products. McDonald's filed a motion with the district court to dismiss the plaintiff's complaint.

Issue

Did the plaintiff state a case against McDonald's for deceptive and unfair acts and practices in violation of the New York Consumer Protection Act?

In the Language of the Court

It is well-known that fast food in general, and McDonald's products in particular, contain high levels of cholesterol, fat, salt and sugar, and that such attributes are bad for one. The plaintiff therefore either knew or should have known enough of the critical facts of her injury that her claims accrued upon being injured. The complaint does specify how often the plaintiff ate at McDonald's. Jazlyn Bradley is alleged to have "consumed McDonald's foods her entire life during school lunch breaks and before and after school, approximately five times per week, ordering two meals per day."

What the plaintiff has not done, however, is to address the role that a number of other factors other than diet may come to play in obesity and the health problems of which the plaintiff complains. In order to allege that McDonald's products were a significant factor in the plaintiff's obesity and health problems, the complaint must address these other variables and, if possible, eliminate them or show that a McDiet is a substantial factor despite these other variables. Similarly, with regards to plaintiff's health problems that she claims resulted from her obesity, it would be necessary to allege that such diseases were not merely hereditary or caused by environmental or other factors. Without this additional information, McDonald's does not have sufficient information to determine if its foods are the cause of the plaintiff's obesity, or if instead McDonald's foods are only a contributing factor.

Decision and Remedy

The district court granted defendant McDonald's motion to dismiss the plaintiff's complaint.

Note: Because of this case and other threatened obesity-related litigation, fast-food franchisors introduced salads, low-fat fare, and low-carb offerings to their menus.

Business and Ethics Questions

1. What is the purpose of consumer protection laws?
2. Do you think McDonald's has a duty to warn consumers of the dangers of eating its fast food? Do parents owe a duty to their children not to let them eat fast food too often?
3. What would have been the effect on McDonald's and other fast-food companies if the plaintiff had won her lawsuit against McDonald's? Explain.

Kantian Ethics

Immanuel Kant (1724–1804) is the best-known proponent of **duty ethics**, also called **Kantian ethics**. Kant believed that people owe moral duties that are based on *universal* rules. For example, keeping a promise to abide by a contract is a moral duty even if that contract turns out to be detrimental to the obligated party. Kant's philosophy is based on the premise that people can use reasoning to reach ethical decisions. His ethical theory would have people behave according to the *categorical imperative* "Do unto others as you would have them do unto you."

Kantian ethics
A moral theory that says that people owe moral duties that are based on universal rules, such as the categorical imperative "Do unto others as you would have them do unto you." Also called *duty ethics*.

The universal rules of Kantian ethics are based on two important principles: (1) consistency— that is, all cases are treated alike, with no exceptions—and (2) reversibility—that is, the actor must abide by the rule he or she uses to judge the morality of someone else's conduct. Thus, if you are going to make an exception for yourself, that exception becomes a universal rule that applies to all others. For example, if you rationalize that it is all right for you to engage in deceptive practices, it is all right for competitors to do so also. A criticism of Kantian ethics is that it is difficult to reach a consensus as to what the universal rules should be.

In the following case, a company alleged that a competitor had engaged in false advertising.

Case 10.2

Comparative Advertising

Pizza Hut, Inc. v. Papa John's International, Inc.

227 F.3d 489, 2000 U.S.App. Lexis 23444
United States Court of Appeals, Fifth Circuit

Background and Facts

Papa John's International, Inc., is the third-largest pizza chain in the United States, with more than 2,050 locations. In May 1995, Papa John's adopted a new slogan—"Better ingredients. Better Pizza."—and applied for and received a federal trademark for this slogan. Papa John's spent over $300 million building customer recognition and goodwill for this slogan. The slogan has appeared on millions of signs, shirts, menus, pizza boxes, napkins, and other items, and it has regularly appeared as the tag line at the end of Papa John's radio and television advertisements.

Pizza Hut, Inc., is the largest pizza chain in the United States, with more than 7,000 restaurants. On May 1, 1997, Pizza Hut launched a new advertising campaign in which it declared "war" on poor-quality pizza. The advertisements touted the "better taste" of Pizza Hut's pizza and "dared" anyone to find a better pizza. A few weeks later, Papa John's launched a comparative advertising campaign that touted the superiority of Papa John's pizza over Pizza Hut's pizza. Papa John's claimed it had superior sauce and dough to Pizza Hut. Many of these advertisements were accompanied by Papa John's slogan "Better Ingredients. Better Pizza."

In 1998, Pizza Hut filed a civil action in federal district court, charging Papa John's with false advertising in violation of Section 43(a) of the federal Lanham Act. The district court found that Papa John's slogan "Better Ingredients. Better Pizza." standing alone, was mere puffery and did not constitute false advertising. The district court found, however, that Papa John's claims of superior sauce and dough were misleading and that Papa John's slogan "Better Ingredients. Better Pizza." became tainted because it was associated with these misleading statements. The district court enjoined Papa John's from using the slogan "Better Ingredients. Better Pizza." Papa John's appealed.

Issue

Is Papa John's slogan, "Better Ingredients. Better Pizza." false advertising?

In the Language of the Court

Essential to any claim under Section 43(a) of the Lanham Act is a determination whether the challenged statement is one of fact—actionable under Section 43(a)—or one of general opinion—not actionable under Section 43(a). One form of non-actionable statements of general opinion under Section 43(a) of the Lanham Act has been referred to as "puffery." We think that non-actionable "puffery" comes in at least two possible forms: (1) an exaggerated, blustering, and boasting statement upon which no reasonable buyer would be justified in relying; or (2) a general claim of superiority over comparable products that is so vague that it can be understood as nothing more than a mere expression of opinion. Prosser and Keeton on the Law of Torts (5th edition) define "puffing" as a "seller's privilege to lie his head off, so long as he says nothing specific, on the theory that no reasonable man would believe him, or that no reasonable man would be influenced by such talk."

We now turn to consider the case before us. Reduced to its essence, the question is whether the evidence established that Papa John's slogan "Better Ingredients. Better Pizza." is misleading and violative of Section 43(a) of the Lanham Act. Bisecting the slogan "Better Ingredients. Better Pizza.," it is clear that the assertion by Papa John's that it makes a "Better Pizza." is a general statement of opinion regarding the superiority of its product over all others. This simple statement, "Better Pizza.," epitomizes the exaggerated advertising, blustering and boasting by a manufacturer upon which no consumer would reasonably rely. Consequently, it appears indisputable that Papa John's assertion "Better Pizza." is non-actionable puffery.

Moving next to consider the phrase "Better Ingredients.," the same conclusion holds true. Like "Better Pizza.," it is typical puffery. The word "better," when used in this context is unquantifiable. What makes one food ingredient "better" than another comparable ingredient, without further description, is wholly a matter of individual taste or preference not subject to scientific quantification. Indeed, it is difficult to think of any product, or any component of any product, to which the term "better," without more quantifiable, is quantifiable. Thus, it is equally clear that Papa John's assertion that it uses "Better Ingredients." is one of opinion not actionable under the Lanham Act.

Consequently, the slogan as a whole is a statement of non-actionable opinion. Thus, there is no legally sufficient basis to support the jury's finding that the slogan is a "false or misleading" statement of fact.

Decision and Remedy

The Court of Appeals held that the Papa John's trademarked slogan "Better Ingredients. Better Pizza." was mere puffery and a statement of opinion that was not false advertising and did not violate Section 43(a) of the Lanham Act. The Court of Appeals reversed the judgment of the district court and remanded the case to the district court for entry of judgment for Papa John's.

Business and Ethics Questions

1. What is false advertising? What is puffery? How do they differ?
2. Do businesses sometimes make exaggerated claims about their products? Are consumers smart enough to see through companies' puffery?
3. If the Court of Appeals had found in favor of Pizza Hut, what would have been the effect on advertising in this country? Explain.

Rawls's Social Justice Theory

John Locke (1632–1704) and Jean-Jacques Rousseau (1712–1778) proposed a **social contract** theory of morality. Under this theory, each person is presumed to have entered into a social contract with all others in society to obey moral rules that are necessary for people to live in peace and harmony. This implied contract states, "I will keep the rules if everyone else does." These moral rules are then used to solve conflicting interests in society.

The leading proponent of the modern social justice theory is John Rawls, a contemporary philosopher at Harvard University. Under **Rawls's *social justice theory***, fairness is considered the essence of justice. The principles of justice should be chosen by persons who do not yet know their station in society—thus, their "veil of ignorance" would permit the fairest possible principles to be selected. For example, the principle of equal opportunity would be promulgated by people who would not yet know if they were in a favored class. As a caveat, Rawls also proposes that the least advantaged in society must receive special assistance to allow them to realize their potential.

Rawls's theory of social justice is criticized for two reasons. First, establishing the blind "original position" for choosing moral principles is impossible in the real world. Second, many persons in society would choose not to maximize the benefit to the least advantaged persons in society.

Rawls's social contract
A moral theory that says each person is presumed to have entered into a social contract with all others in society to obey moral rules that are necessary for people to live in peace and harmony.

The notion that a business is clothed with a public interest and has been devoted to the public use is little more than a fiction intended to beautify what is disagreeable to the sufferers.

Justice Holmes
Tyson & Bro-United Theatre Ticket Officers v. Banton (1927)

Ethics in Business

Enron Corporation Plunges into Bankruptcy

By the year 2000, the Enron Corporation, a Houston-based energy company, had become the sixth-largest corporation in America. Its rise to this status was meteoric, and the company's stock was trading at over $90 per share. The company's main business was brokering energy between buyers and sellers. It also engaged in building huge energy projects worldwide, as well as speculating in oil and gas futures on the world's commodities markets. Enron spread its money around by making large political campaign donations to presidential candidates and members of the U.S. Congress.

But all was not well with the corporation. Enron had created hundreds of partnerships, many located in offshore tax havens. These partnerships were used to borrow money from banks and other creditors and to engage in speculative business dealings. Enron booked its investments and money from these partnerships as assets, but the debts of these partnerships and much of the self-dealing with and among them were not reported on Enron's consolidated financial statements. Enron executives purposefully created this maze of entities to perpetrate accounting fraud. Thus, the company looked profitable when in fact it was not. Enron was able to run this charade for years before the bubble finally burst.

In 2002, reporters and securities analysts began investigating Enron's financial empire. As rumors of Enron's "creative accounting" reached the public, the price of its stock began to fall. Many of its top executives sold their Enron shares before the stock price plummeted. Investors who did not have inside information were not so lucky; they lost their investments as the price of Enron stock tumbled to less than 50 cents per share.

The Securities and Exchange Commission (SEC), a federal government agency, announced that it was investigating the Enron affair. Officers and employees at Enron began to shred thousands of documents relevant to the investigation. Andersen LLP, one of the "Big Five" accounting firms in the United States, had been Enron's auditor for years. Andersen was making between $2 million and $4 million per month providing auditing and other services to Enron. Andersen's malpractice or fraud contributed to Enron's being able to conceal its fraud from the investing public. Several of Andersen's partners in the Houston office who were responsible for auditing Enron also shredded thousands of documents pertaining to the Enron audits. Once alerted, the court issued an injunction prohibiting the destruction of any more documents by Enron or Andersen.

In late 2002, Enron Corporation filed for Chapter 11 bankruptcy. By that time, billions of dollars of shareholder wealth had been wiped out. Enron's employees, who had their pension funds invested in Enron stock, saw their dreams of a comfortable retirement evaporate. And bond holders, banks, suppliers, and other creditors lost billions of dollars in unpaid debts. Enron was the largest company in America ever to file for bankruptcy. Some parts of it were sold to other energy companies, but the majority of its businesses were worthless. Andersen LLP unraveled, was sued criminally by the U.S. government, and eventually went out of business.

The Enron debacle is one of the grossest examples of corporate greed and fraud in America.

Ethics Issues

1. Did the Enron executives act ethically by using offshore, "off-balance-sheet" partnerships to hide Enron's liabilities?
2. Did the Enron executives and Andersen partners act ethically in shredding documents? ■

Ethical Relativism

ethical relativism
A moral theory that holds that individuals must decide what is ethical based on their own feelings as to what is right or wrong.

Ethical relativism holds that individuals must decide what is ethical based on their own feelings as to what is right or wrong. Under this moral theory, if a person meets his or her own moral standard in making a decision, no one can criticize him or her for it. Thus, there are no universal ethical rules to guide a person's conduct. This theory has been criticized because action that is usually thought to be unethical (e.g., committing fraud) would not be unethical if the perpetrator thought it was in fact ethical. Few philosophers advocate ethical relativism as an acceptable moral theory.

Concept Summary Theories of Ethics

Theory	Description
Ethical fundamentalism	Persons look to an outside source (e.g., Bible or Koran) or central figure for ethical guidelines.
Utilitarianism	Persons choose the alternative that would provide the greatest good to society.
Kantian ethics	A set of universal rules establishes ethical duties. The rules are based on reasoning and require (1) consistency in application and (2) reversibility.
Rawls's social justice theory	Moral duties are based on an implied social contract. Fairness is justice. The rules are established from an original position of a "veil of ignorance."
Ethical relativism	Individuals decide what is ethical based on their own feelings as to what is right or wrong.

Vietnam. Many U.S. multinational corporations "outsource" the manufacture of goods to workers in foreign countries. The goods are then imported into the United States and sold to consumers. Are there any ethical problems with this practice?

Social Responsibility of Business

Businesses do not operate in a vacuum. Decisions made by businesses have far-reaching effects on society. In the past, many business decisions were based solely on a cost–benefit analysis and how they affected the "bottom line." Such decisions, however, may cause negative externalities for others. For example, the dumping of hazardous wastes from a manufacturing plant into a river affects the homeowners, farmers, and others who use the river's waters. Thus, corporations are considered to owe some degree of **social responsibility** for their actions. Four theories of the social responsibility of business are discussed in the following paragraphs.

The ultimate justification of the law is to be found, and can only be found, in moral considerations.

Lord MacMillan
Law and Other Things (1937)

Maximizing Profits

The traditional view of the social responsibility of business is that business should **maximize profits** for shareholders. This view, which dominated business and the law during the nineteenth century, holds that the interests of other constituencies (e.g., employees, suppliers, residents of the communities in which businesses are located) are not important in and of themselves.

maximizing profits
A theory of social responsibility that says a corporation owes a duty to take actions that maximize profits for shareholders.

In the famous case *Dodge v. Ford Motor Company*,[1] a shareholder sued the car company when Henry Ford introduced a plan to reduce the price of cars so that more people would be put to work and more people could own cars. The shareholders alleged that such a plan would not increase dividends. Mr. Ford testified, "My ambition is to employ still more men, to spread the benefits of this industrial system to the greatest number, to help them build up their lives and their homes." The court sided with the shareholders and stated:

> [Mr. Ford's] testimony creates the impression that he thinks the Ford Motor company has made too much money, has had too large profits and that, although large profits might still be earned, a sharing of them with the public, by reducing the price of the output of the company, ought to be undertaken.
>
> There should be no confusion of the duties which Mr. Ford conceives that he and the stockholders owe to the general public and the duties which in law he and his codirectors owe to protesting, minority stockholders. A business corporation is organized and carried on primarily for the profit of the stockholders. The powers of the directors are to be employed for that end. The discretion of directors is to be exercised in the choice of means to attain that end and does not extend to a change in the end itself, to the reduction of profits, or to the nondistribution of profits among stockholders in order to devote them to other purposes.

Public policy: That principle of the law which holds that no subject can lawfully do that which has a tendency to be injurious to the public or against the public good.

Lord Truro
Egerton v. Brownlow (1853)

Milton Friedman, who won the Nobel Prize in economics when he taught at the University of Chicago, advocated this theory. Friedman asserted that in a free society, "there is one and only one social responsibility of business—to use its resources and engage in activities designed to increase its profits as long as it stays within the rules of the game, which is to say, engages in open and free competition without deception and fraud."[2]

In the following case, one company was accused of knocking off another company's product design.

Case 10.3
Knock-Offs

U.S. SUPREME COURT
Wal-Mart Stores, Inc. vs. Samara Brothers, Inc.
529 U.S. 205, 123 S.Ct. 1339, 2000 U.S. Lexis 2197
Supreme Court of the United States

Background and Facts

Samara Brothers, Inc. (Samara), is a designer and manufacturer of children's clothing. The core of Samara's business is its annual new line of spring and summer children's garments. Samara sold its clothing to retailers, which in turn sold the clothes to consumers. Wal-Mart Stores, Inc. (Wal-Mart), operates a large chain of budget warehouse stores that sell thousands of items at low prices. In 1995, Wal-Mart contacted one of its suppliers, Judy-Philippine, Inc. (JPI), about the possibility of making a line of children's clothes just like Samara's successful line. Wal-Mart sent photographs of Samara's children's clothes to JPI (the name "Samara" was readily discernible on the labels of the garments) and directed JPI to produce children's clothes exactly like those in the photographs. JPI produced a line of children's clothes for Wal-Mart that copied the designs, colors, and patterns of Samara's clothing. Wal-Mart then sold this line of children's clothing in its stores, making a gross profit of over $1.15 million on these clothes sales during the 1996 selling season.

Samara discovered that Wal-Mart was selling the knock-off clothes at a price that was lower than Samara's retailers were paying Samara for its clothes. After sending unsuccessful cease-and-desist letters to Wal-Mart, Samara sued Wal-Mart, alleging that Wal-Mart had stolen Samara's trade dress (i.e., look and feel) in violation of Section 43(a) of the Lanham Act. Although not finding that Samara's clothes had acquired a secondary meaning in the minds of the public, the district court held in favor of Samara and awarded damages. The Court of Appeals affirmed. Wal-Mart appealed to the U.S. Supreme Court.

Issue

Must a product's design have acquired a secondary meaning before it is protected as trade dress?

In the Language of the Court

The Lanham Act, in Section 43(a), gives a producer a cause of action for the use by any person of "any word, term, name, symbol, or device, or any combination thereof which is likely to cause confusion as to the origin, sponsorship, or approval of his or her goods." The text of Section 43(a) provides little guidance as to the circumstances under which unregistered trade dress may be protected. It does require that a producer show that the allegedly infringing feature is likely to cause confusion with the product for which protection is sought. In an action for infringement of unregistered trade dress a product's design is protectible only upon a showing of secondary meaning.

Decision and Remedy

The U.S. Supreme Court held that a product's design has to have acquired a secondary meaning in the public's eye before it is protected as trade dress under Section 43(a) of the Lanham Act. The Supreme Court reversed the decision of the Court of Appeals.

Business and Ethics Questions

1. What is trade dress? Should it have been protected in this case?
2. Even though Wal-Mart's conduct was ruled legal, was it ethical?
3. Before reading this case, had you heard or read about Samara's children's clothing?

Moral Minimum

moral minimum
A theory of social responsibility that says a corporation's duty is to make a profit while avoiding harm to others.

Some proponents of corporate social responsibility argue that a corporation's duty is to *make a profit while avoiding causing harm to others*. This theory of social responsibility is called the **moral minimum.** Under this theory, as long as business avoids or corrects the social injury it causes, it has met its duty of social responsibility. For instance, a corporation that pollutes the waters and then compensates those whom it injures has met its moral minimum duty of social responsibility.

The legislative and judicial branches of government have established laws that enforce the moral minimum of social responsibility on corporations. For example, occupational safety laws establish minimum safety standards for protecting employees from injuries in the workplace. Consumer protection laws establish safety requirements for products and make manufacturers and sellers liable for injuries caused by defective products. Other laws establish similar minimum standards for conduct for business in other areas.

Stakeholder Interest

Businesses have relationship with all sorts of people other than their stockholders, including employees, suppliers, customers, creditors, and the local community. Under the **stakeholder interest** theory of social responsibility, a corporation must consider the effects its actions have on these *other stakeholders*. For example, a corporation would violate the stakeholder interest theory if it viewed employees solely as a means of maximizing stockholder wealth.

stakeholder interest
A theory of social responsibility that says a corporation must consider the effects its actions have on persons other than its stockholders.

This theory is criticized because it is difficult to harmonize the conflicting interests of stakeholders. For example, in closing a plant, certain stakeholders may benefit (e.g., stockholders, creditors) while other stakeholders may not (e.g., current employees, the local community).

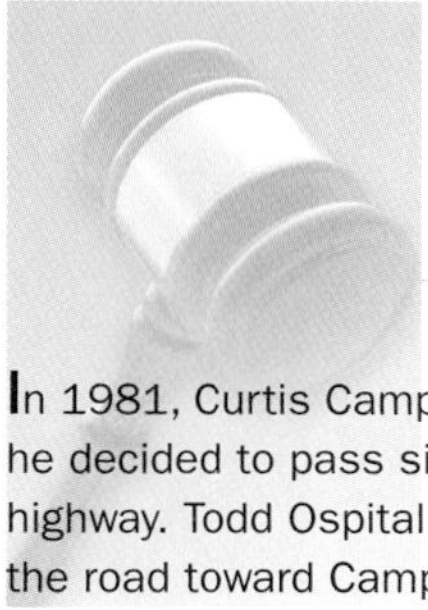

Ethics in Business

State Farm: Not Such a Good Neighbor

In 1981, Curtis Campbell was driving with his wife in Utah when he decided to pass six vans traveling ahead of him on a two-lane highway. Todd Ospital, who was driving on the opposite side of the road toward Campbell, swerved to avoid a collision with Campbell and collided with an automobile driven by Robert Slusher. Ospital was killed, Slusher was rendered permanently disabled, and the Campbells escaped unscathed. Early investigations determined that Campbell had made an unsafe pass and had caused the crash. Ospital's heirs and Slusher sued Campbell for wrongful death and injuries, respectively. Campbell's insurance company, State Farm Mutual Automobile Insurance Company (State Farm), declined offers by Ospital's estate and Slusher to settle their claims for the insurance policy limit of $50,000 and took the case to trial. The jury determined that Campbell was 100 percent at fault and returned a judgment for $185,000.

Campbell reached a settlement with Ospital's and Slusher's attorneys whereby Campbell agreed to pursue a bad faith tort action against State Farm, and Ospital's estate and Slusher would receive 90 percent of any verdict against State Farm. One and one-half years after the initial judgment, State Farm paid all of the $185,000 judgment against Campbell, even though it exceeded the $50,000 policy limit. The bad faith tort case went to trial against State Farm in a Utah trial court. At trial, evidence was introduced that State Farm had a policy to take many cases to trial even though they could be settled within the insurance policy limits. The jury held against State Farm and awarded Campbell $2.6 million in compensatory damages and $145 million in punitive damages. The trial court judge reduced compensatory damages to $1 million and punitive damages to $25 million. The Utah Supreme Court reinstated the $145 million punitive damage award. State Farm appealed to the U.S. Supreme Court.

The issue on appeal was whether an award of $145 million in punitive damages, where compensatory damages are $1 million, was excessive and a violation of the Due Process Clause of the Fourteenth Amendment to the Constitution of the United States.

The U.S. Supreme Court noted that while states possess discretion over the imposition of punitive damages, it is well established that there are procedural and substantive constitutional limitations on these awards. The Due Process Clause of the Fourteenth Amendment prohibits the imposition of grossly excessive or arbitrary punishments on a tortfeasor. This case was neither close nor difficult. It was an error to reinstate the jury's $145 million punitive damages award.

The Supreme Court stated that this case was used as a platform to expose and punish the perceived deficiencies of State Farm's operations throughout the country. The Utah supreme court's opinion made explicit that State Farm was being condemned for its nationwide policies rather than for the conduct directed toward the Campbells. The Utah court awarded punitive damages to punish and deter conduct that bore no relation to the Campbells' harm. A defendant's dissimilar acts, independent from the acts on which liability was premised, may not serve as the basis for punitive damages. A defendant should be punished for the conduct that harmed the plaintiff, not for being an unsavory individual or business. The Court concluded that due process does not permit courts, in the calculation of punitive damages, to adjudicate the merits of other parties' hypothetical claims against a defendant, under the guise of the reprehensibility analysis.

The Supreme Court stated that few awards exceeding a single-digit ratio between punitive and compensatory damages, to a significant degree, will satisfy due process. In a previous case, the Supreme Court concluded that an award of more than four times the amount of compensatory damages might be close to the line of constitutional impropriety (*BMW of North America, Inc. v. Gore*, 517 U.S. 559, 116 S.Ct. 1589, 1996 U.S. Lexis 3390). While these ratios are not binding, they are instructive. Single-digit multipliers are more likely to comport with due process, while still achieving the state's goals of deterrence and retribution, than awards with ratios in the range of 500 to 1, or, in this case, of 145 to 1.

(continued)

Ethics in Business

(continued)

The Court concluded that because there are no rigid benchmarks that a punitive damages award may not surpass, ratios greater than those previously upheld by the Court may comport with due process where a particularly egregious act has resulted in only a small amount of economic damages.

The U.S. Supreme Court held that an award of $145 million in punitive damages where compensatory damages were $1 million was excessive and violated the Due Process Clause of the Fourteenth Amendment to the U.S. Constitution. The U.S. Supreme Court reversed the decision of the Utah supreme court and remanded the case for proceedings consistent with the U.S. Supreme Court's opinion.

Ethics Issues

1. What is the purpose of punitive damages? What is the protection afforded by the Due Process Clause? Explain.
2. Did Campbell act ethically in this case? Did State Farm act ethically in this case? ■

Corporate Citizenship

corporate citizenship
A theory of responsibility that says a business has a responsibility to do good.

The **corporate citizenship** theory of social responsibility argues that business has a responsibility to do good. That is, business is responsible for helping to solve social problems that it did little, if anything, to cause. For example, under this theory, corporations owe a duty to subsidize schools and help educate children.

This theory contends that corporations owe a duty to promote the same social goals as do individual members of society. Proponents of this "do good" theory argue that corporations owe a debt to society to make it a better place and that this duty arises because of the social power bestowed on them. That is, this social power is a gift from society and should be used to good ends.

A major criticism of this theory is that the duty of a corporation to do good cannot be expanded beyond certain limits. There is always some social problem that needs to be addressed, and corporate funds are limited. Further, if this theory were taken to its maximum limit, potential shareholders might be reluctant to invest in corporations.

Concept Summary *Theories of Social Responsibility*

Theory	Description
Maximizing profits	To maximize profits for stockholders.
Moral minimum	To avoid causing harm and to compensate for harm caused.
Stakeholder interest	To consider the interests of all stakeholders, including stockholders, employees, customers, suppliers, creditors, and the local community.
Corporate citizenship	To do good and solve social problems.

Ethics in Business

Sarbanes-Oxley Act Prompts Public Companies to Adopt Code of Ethics

In the late 1990s and early 2000s, many large corporations in the United States were found to have engaged in massive financial frauds. Many of these frauds were perpetrated by the chief executive officers and other senior officers of the companies. Financial officers, such as chief financial officers and controllers, were also found to have been instrumental in creating these frauds. In response, Congress enacted the **Sarbanes-Oxley Act of 2002**, which makes certain conduct illegal and establishes criminal penalties for violations.

In addition, the Sarbanes-Oxley Act prompts companies to encourage senior offices of public companies to act ethically in their dealings with shareholders, employees, and other constituents. **Section 406** of the Sarbanes-Oxley Act requires a public company to disclose whether it has adopted a **code of ethics** for senior financial officers, including its principal financial officer and principal accounting officer. In response, public companies have adopted codes of ethics for their senior financial officers. Many public companies have included all officers and employees in the coverage of their codes of ethics.

A typical code of ethics is illustrated in Exhibit 10.2.

Ethics Issues

1. Do you think the Sarbanes-Oxley Act will be effective in promoting ethical conduct by officers and directors? Explain.
2. Can ethics be mandated? In other words, will crooks still be crooks? ■

Exhibit 10.2

Code of Ethics

Big Cheese Corporation
Code of Ethics

Big Cheese Corporation's mission includes the promotion of professional conduct in the practice of general management worldwide. Big Cheese's Chief Executive Officer (CEO), Chief Financial Officer (CFO), corporate Controller, and other employees of the finance organization and other employees of the corporation hold an important and elevated role in the corporate governance of the corporation. They are empowered and uniquely capable to ensure that all constituents' interests are appropriately balanced, protected, and preserved.

This Code of Ethics embodies principles to which we are expected to adhere and advocate. The CEO, CFO, finance organization employees, and other employees of the corporation are expected to abide by this Code of Ethics and all business conduct standards of the corporation relating to areas covered by this Code of Ethics. Any violation of the Code of Ethics may result in disciplinary action, up to and including termination of employment. All employees will:

- Act with honesty and integrity, avoiding actual or apparent conflicts of interest in their personal and professional relations.
- Provide stakeholders with information that is accurate, fair, complete, timely, objective, relevant, and understandable, including in our filings with and other submissions to the U.S. Securities and Exchange Commission.
- Comply with rules and regulations of federal, state, provincial, and local governments and other appropriate private and public regulatory agencies.
- Act in good faith, responsibly, with due care, competence, and diligence, without misrepresenting materials facts or allowing one's independent judgment to be subordinated.
- Respect the confidentiality of information acquired in the course of one's work, except when authorized or otherwise legally obligated to disclose. Confidential information acquired in the course of one's work will not be used for personal advantage.
- Share knowledge and maintain professional skills important and relevant to stakeholders' needs.
- Proactively promote and be an example of ethical behavior as a responsible partner among peers, in the work environment and the community.
- Achieve responsible use, control, and stewardship over all Big Cheese's assets and resources that are employed or entrusted to us.
- Not unduly or fraudulently influence, coerce, manipulate, or mislead any authorized audit or interfere with any auditor engaged in the performance of an internal or independent audit of Big Cheese's financial statements or accounting books and records.

If you are aware of any suspected or known violations of this Code of Ethics or other Big Cheese policies or guidelines, you have a duty to promptly report such concerns either to your manager, another responsible member of management, a Human Resources representative, or the Director of Compliance or the 24-hour Business Conduct Line.

If you have a concern about a questionable accounting or auditing matter and wish to submit the concern confidentially or anonymously, you may do so by sending an e-mail to (bc.codeofethics@bigcheese.cc) or calling the Business Conduct Line's 24-hour number at 1-888-666-BIGC (2442).

Big Cheese will handle all inquiries discretely and make every effort to maintain, within the limits allowed by law, the confidentiality of anyone requesting guidance or reporting questionable behavior and/or a compliance concern.

It is Big Cheese's intention that this Code of Ethics to be its written code of ethics under Section 406 of the Sarbanes-Oxley Act of 2002 complying with the standards set forth in Securities and Exchange Commission Regulation S-K Item 406.

International Law

United Nations Code of Conduct for Transnational Corporations

Respect for National Sovereignty

Transnational corporations shall respect the national sovereignty of the countries in which they operate and the right of each state to exercise its permanent sovereignty over its natural wealth and resources.

Transnational corporations should carry out their activities in conformity with the development policies, objectives and priorities set out by the governments of the countries in which they operate and work seriously toward making a positive contribution to the achievement of such goals at

(continued)

International Law (continued)

Louang-Phrabang, Laos.

the national and, as appropriate, the regional level, within the framework of regional integration programs. Transnational corporations should cooperate with the governments of the countries in which they operate with a view to contributing to the development process and should be responsive to requests for consultation in this respect, thereby establishing mutually beneficial relations with these countries.

Adherence to Sociocultural Objectives and Values
Transnational corporations should respect the social and cultural objectives, values, and traditions of the countries in which they operate. While economic and technological development is normally accompanied by social change, transnational corporations should avoid practices, products or services which cause detrimental effects on cultural patterns and socio-cultural objectives as determined by governments. For this purpose, transnational corporations should respond positively to requests for consultations from governments concerned.

Respect for Human Rights and Fundamental Freedoms
Transnational corporations shall respect human rights and fundamental freedoms in the countries in which they operate. In their social and industrial relations, transnational corporations shall not discriminate on the basis of race, color, sex, religion, language, social, national, and ethnic origin or political or other opinion. Transnational corporations shall conform to government policies designed to extend quality of opportunity and treatment.

Abstention from Corrupt Practices

Transnational corporations shall refrain, in their transactions, from the offering, promising or giving of any payment, gift, or other advantage to or for the benefit of a public official as consideration for performing or refraining from the performance of his duties in connection with those transactions. ■

Terms and Concepts

Ethics

Ethics is a set of moral principles on values that governs the conduct of an individual or a group.

Moral Theories

1. ***Ethical fundamentalism.*** Under this moral theory, persons look to an outside source (e.g., Bible, Koran) or a central figure to set ethical guidelines.

2. ***Utilitarianism.*** Under this moral theory, persons choose the alternative that would provide the greatest good to society.
3. ***Kantian ethics.*** Under this moral theory, a set of universal rules establishes ethical duties. The rules are based on reasoning and require (1) consistency in application and (2) reversibility.
4. ***Rawls's social justice theory.*** Under this moral theory, moral duties are based on an implied social contract. Fairness is justice. The rules are established from an original position of a "veil of ignorance."
5. ***Ethical relativism.*** Under this moral theory, individuals decide what is ethical based on their own feelings of what is right or wrong.

Theories of Social Responsibility

1. ***Maximizing profits.*** The goal of this theory is to maximize profits for shareholders.
2. ***Moral minimum.*** The goal of this theory is to make a profit and avoid harm and to compensate for harm caused.
3. ***Stakeholder interests.*** The goal of this theory is to consider the interests of stakeholders other than shareholders, such as employees, suppliers, customers, creditors, and the local community.
4. ***Corporate citizenship.*** The goal of this theory is to do good and help solve social problems.

Corporate Social Audit

A social audit is an audit of a corporation by independent auditors that examines how well employees have adhered to the company's code of ethics and how well the company has met its duty of social responsibility.

Internet Exercises and Case Questions

Working the Web Internet Exercises

1. Find the list titled "Baby Boomer Sports Injuries" at **www.cpsc.gov**. What is the ethical duty of the companies that sell sports equipment to consumers in this age bracket?
2. Locate the Drudge Report at **www.drudgereport.com**. What is the ethical basis for the press to report on topics such as consumer fraud, arrests, and trials of notorious criminals, questionable tax policies, and so on?
3. Locate and review the story on the use of torture and drugs to interrogate captured suspected terrorists at **www.washingtonpost.com./wp-dyn/articles/A59631-2004 may27.htm**. Is it constitutional? Is it ethical?

Ethics in Business

10.1 The Johns-Manville Corporation was a profitable company that made a variety of building and other products. It was a major producer of asbestos, which was used for insulation in buildings and for a variety of other uses. It has been medically proven that excessive exposure to asbestos causes asbestosis, a fatal lung disease. Thousands of employees of the company and consumers who were exposed to asbestos and contracted this fatal disease sued the company for damages. In 1983, the lawsuits were being filed at a rate of more than 400 per week.

As a response, the company filed for reorganization bankruptcy. It argued that if it did not, an otherwise viable company that provided thousands of jobs and served a useful purpose in this country would be destroyed, and that without the declaration of bankruptcy, a few of the plaintiffs who first filed their lawsuits would win awards of hundreds of millions of dollars, leaving nothing for the remainder of the plaintiffs. Under the bankruptcy court's protection, the company was restructured to survive. As part of the release from bankruptcy, the company contributed money to a fund to pay current and future claimants. The fund is not large enough to pay all injured persons the full amount of their claims. *In re Johns-Manville Corporation*, 36 B.R. 727, 1984 Bankr. Lexis 6384 (Bankr. S.D.N.Y.)

Ethics Issues

1. The Johns-Manville Corporation filed for reorganization bankruptcy. What effect does this have on injured plaintiffs?

2. Was it ethical for Johns-Manville to declare bankruptcy? Did it meet its duty of social responsibility in this case?

3. If you were a member of the board of directors of Johns-Manville, would you have voted to place the company in bankruptcy? Why or why not?

Endnotes

1. 170 N.W. 668, 1919 Mich. Lexis 720 (Mich.)
2. Milton Friedman, "The Social Responsibility of Business Is to Increase Its Profits," *New York Times Magazine*, September 13, 1970.

PART III / The Contract and E-Commerce Environment

11

Formation of Traditional and Online Contracts

"The movement of the progressive societies has hitherto been a movement from status to contract."

—Sir Henry Maine
Ancient Law, Chapter 5

Chapter Objectives

After studying this chapter, you should be able to:

1. List the elements necessary to form a valid contract.
2. Describe and distinguish among valid, void, voidable, and unenforceable contracts.
3. Define offer and acceptance.
4. Define consideration and analyze whether contracts are lacking in consideration.
5. Identify illegal contracts that are contrary to statutes and that violate public policy.

Chapter Contents

- Definition of Contract
- Classification of Contracts
- Agreement
- Consideration
- Capacity to Contract
- Legality

Contracts are the basis of many of our daily activities. They provide the means for individuals and businesses to sell and otherwise transfer property, services, and other rights. The purchase of goods, such as books and automobiles, is based on sales contracts; the hiring of employees is based on service contracts; and the lease of an apartment is based on a rental contract. The list is almost endless. Without enforceable contracts, commerce would collapse.

Contracts are voluntarily entered into by parties. The terms of a contract become **private law** between the parties. One court has stated, "The contract between parties is the law between them and the courts are obliged to give legal effect to such contracts according to the true interests of the parties."[1]

This chapter introduces you to the study of contract law. Such topics as the definition of *contract* and the requirements for forming a contract are discussed.

Marrakech, Morocco. In many parts of the world, the parties usually engage in negotiations that involve substantial posturing prior to agreeing on a final price.

Definition of Contract

A *contract* is an agreement that is enforceable by a court of law or equity. A simple and widely recognized definition of *contract* is provided by the *Restatement (Second) of Contracts:* "A contract is a promise or set of promises for the breach of which the law gives a remedy or the performance of which the law in some way recognizes a duty."[2]

Parties to a Contract

Every contract involves at least two parties. The **offeror** is the party who makes an offer to enter into a contract. The **offeree** is the party to whom the offer is made (Exhibit 11.1). In making an offer, the offeror promises to do—or to refrain from doing—something. The offeree then has the power to create a contract by accepting the offeror's offer. A contract is created if the offer is accepted. No contract is created if the offer is not accepted.

offeror
A party who makes an offer to enter into a contract.

offeree
A party to whom an offer to enter into a contract is made.

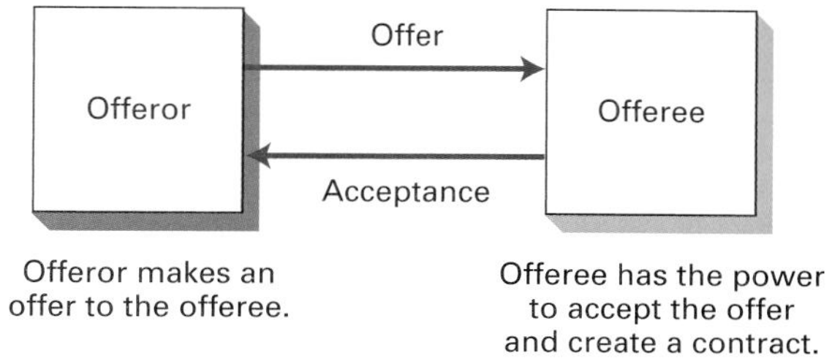

Exhibit 11.1
Parties to a Contract

Contemporary Trend

The Evolution of the Modern Law of Contracts

The use of contracts originally developed in ancient times. The common law of contracts developed in England around the fifteenth century. American contract law evolved from the English common law.

At first, the United States adopted a *laissez-faire* approach to the law of contracts. The central theme of this theory was *freedom of contract*. The parties (such as consumers, shopkeepers, farmers, and traders) generally dealt with one another face-to-face, had equal knowledge and bargaining power, and had the opportunity to inspect the goods prior to sales. Contract terms were openly negotiated. There was little, if any, government regulation of the right to contract. This "pure," or **"classical," law of contracts** produced objective rules, which, in turn, produced certainty and predictability in the enforcement of contracts. It made sense until the Industrial Revolution.

The Industrial Revolution changed many of the underlying assumptions of pure contract law. For example, as large corporations developed and gained control of crucial resources, the traditional balance of parties' bargaining power shifted: Large corporations now had the most power. The chain of distribution for goods also changed because (1) buyers did not have to deal face-to-face with sellers and (2) there was not always an opportunity to inspect the goods prior to sale.

Eventually, sellers began using *form contracts* that offered their goods to buyers on a take-it-or-leave-it basis. The majority of contracts in this country today are form contracts. Automobile contracts, mortgage contracts, sales contracts for consumer goods, and such are examples of form contracts.

Both federal and state governments have enacted statutes intended to protect consumers, debtors, and others from unfair contracts. In addition, the courts have developed certain common law legal theories that allow some oppressive or otherwise unjust contracts to be avoided. Today, under this **modern law of contracts,** there is substantial government regulation of the right to contract. ■

Classifications of Contracts

There are several types of contracts. Each differs somewhat in formation, enforcement, performance, and discharge. The different types of contracts are discussed in the following paragraphs.

Bilateral and Unilateral Contracts

Contracts are either *bilateral* or *unilateral*, depending on what the offeree must do to accept the offeror's offer. A contract is **bilateral** if the offeror's promise is answered with the offeree's promise of acceptance. In other words, a bilateral contract is a "promise for a promise." This exchange of promises creates an enforceable contract. No act of performance is necessary to create a bilateral contract.

bilateral contract
A contract entered into by way of exchange of promises of the parties; "a promise for a promise."

A contract is **unilateral** if the offeror's offer can be accepted only by the performance of an act by other offeree. There is no contract until the offeree performs the requested act. An offer to create a unilateral contract cannot be accepted by a promise to perform. It is a "promise for an act."

unilateral contract
A contract in which the offeror's offer can be accepted only by the performance of an act by the offeree; a "promise for an act."

Consider This Example Suppose Mary Douglas, the owner of the Chic Dress Shop, says to Peter Jones, a painter, "If you promise to paint my store by July 1, I will pay you $3,000." Peter promises to do so. A bilateral contract was created at the moment Peter promised to paint the dress shop (a promise for a promise). If Peter fails to paint the store, he can be sued for whatever damages result from his breach of contract. Similarly, Peter can sue Mary if she refused to pay him after he has performed as promised.

However, if Mary had said, "If you paint my shop by July 1, I will pay you $3,000," the offer would have created a unilateral contract. The offer can be accepted only by the painter's performance of the requested act. If Peter does not paint the shop by July 1, there has been no acceptance, and the painter cannot be sued for damages.

No cause of action arises from a bare promise.

Legal Maxim

Problems can arise if the offeror in a unilateral contract attempts to revoke an offer after the offeree has begun performance. Generally, an offer to create a unilateral contract can be revoked by the offeror any time prior to the offeree's performance of the requested act. However, the offer cannot be revoked if the offeree has begun or has substantially completed performance. For example, suppose Alan Matthews tells Sherry Levine that he will pay her $5,000 if she finished the Boston Marathon. Alan cannot revoke the offer once Sherry starts running the marathon.

Express and Implied-in-Fact Contracts

An *actual contract* (as distinguished from a quasi-contract, which is discussed later in this chapter) may be either *express* or *implied-in-fact*.

express contract
An agreement that is expressed in written or oral words.

implied-in-fact contracts
A contract in which agreement between parties has been inferred from their conduct.

Express contracts are stated in oral or written words. Examples of such contracts include an oral agreement to purchase a neighbor's bicycle and a written agreement to buy an automobile from a dealership.

Implied-in-fact contracts are implied from the conduct of the parties. Implied-in-fact contracts leave more room for questions. The following elements must be established to create an implied-in-fact contract:

1. The plaintiff provided property or services to the defendant.
2. The plaintiff expected to be paid by the defendant for the property or services and did not provide the property or services gratuitously.
3. The defendant was given an opportunity to reject the property or services provided by the plaintiff but failed to do so.

In the following case, the court had to decide whether the plaintiffs could sue a defendant for breach of an implied-in-fact contract.

Case 11.1

Implied-in-Fact Contract

Wrench LLC v. Taco Bell Corporation
256 F.3d 446, 2001 U.S.App. Lexis 15097
United States Court of Appeals, Sixth Circuit

Background and Facts

Thomas Rinks and Joseph Shields created the "Psycho Chihuahua" cartoon character, which they promote, market, and license through their company, Wrench LLC. The Psycho Chihuahua is a clever, feisty cartoon character dog with an attitude; a self-confident, edgy, cool dog who knows what he wants and will not back down. In June 1996, Rink and Shields attended a licensing trade show in New York City, where they were approached by two Taco Bell employees, Rudy Pollak, a vice president, and Ed Alfaro, a creative services manager. Taco Bell owns and operates a nationwide chain of fast-food Mexican restaurants.

Pollak and Alfaro expressed interest in the Psycho Chihuahua character for Taco Bell advertisements because they thought his character would appeal to Taco Bell's core consumers, males aged 18 to 24. Pollak and Alfaro obtained some Psycho Chihuahua materials to take back with them to Taco Bell's headquarters.

Later, Alfaro contacted Rinks and asked him to create art boards combining Psycho Chihuahua with the Taco Bell name and image. Rinks and Shields prepared art boards and sent them to Alfaro, along with Psycho Chihuahua T-shirts, hats, and stickers. Alfaro showed these materials to Taco Bell's vice president of brand management as well as to Taco Bell's outside advertising agency. Alfaro tested the Psycho Chihuahua marketing concept with focus groups. Rinks suggested to Alfaro that instead of using the cartoon version of Psycho Chihuahua in its advertisements, Taco Bell should use a live Chihuahua dog manipulated by computer graphic imaging, who had the personality of Psycho Chihuahua and a love for Taco Bell food. In early March 1997, Rinks and Shields gave a formal presentation of this concept to Taco Bell's marketing department. One idea presented by Rinks and Shields was a commercial in which a male Chihuahua dog passed by a female Chihuahua dog in order to get to Taco Bell food. Taco Bell did not enter into an express contract with Wrench LLC, Rinks, or Shields.

On March 18, 1997, Taco Bell hired a new outside advertising agency, Chiat/Day. Taco Bell gave Chiat/Day materials received from Rinks and Shields regarding Psycho Chihuahua. On June 2, 1997, Chiat/Day proposed using a Chihuahua in Taco Bell commercials. One commercial had a male Chihuahua passing up a female Chihuahua to get to a person seated on a bench eating Taco Bell food. Chiat/Day said that it conceived the idea by itself. In July 1997, Taco Bell aired its first Chihuahua commercial in the United States, and it became an instant success and the basis of its advertising. Taco Bell paid nothing to Wrench LLC or to Rinks and Shields. Plaintiffs Wrench LLC, Rinks, and Shields sued defendant Taco Bell to recover damages for breach of an implied-in-fact contract. On this issue, the district court agreed with the plaintiffs. The decision was appealed.

Issue

Do the plaintiffs Wrench LLC, Rinks, and Shields state a cause of action for the breach of an implied-in-fact contract?

In the Language of the Court

The district court found that appellants produced sufficient evidence to create a genuine issue of material fact regarding whether an implied-in-fact contract existed between the parties. On appeal, Taco Bell argues that this conclusion was erroneous, and asserts that the record contains no evidence of an enforceable contract. We agree with the district court's finding that appellants presented sufficient evidence to survive summary judgment on the question of whether an implied-in-fact contract existed under Michigan law.

Decision and Remedy

The U.S. Court of Appeals held that the plaintiffs had stated a proper cause of action against defendant Taco Bell for breach of an implied-in-fact contract. The Court of Appeals remanded the case for trial.

Business and Ethics Questions

1. What does the doctrine of implied-in-fact contract provide? Explain.
2. Did Taco Bell act ethically in this case? Did Chiat/Day act ethically in this case?
3. Do you think there was an implied-in-fact contract in this case? If so, what damages should be awarded to the plaintiffs?

Quasi-Contracts (Implied-in-Law Contracts)

The equitable doctrine of **quasi-contract,** also called **implied-in-law contract,** allows a court to award monetary damages to a plaintiff for providing work or services to a defendant even though no actual contract existed between the parties. Recovery is generally based on the reasonable value of the services received by the defendant.

quasi-contract
An equitable doctrine whereby a court may award monetary damages to a plaintiff for providing work or services to a defendant even though no actual contract existed. Also called an *implied-in-law contract.*

This doctrine is intended to prevent *unjust enrichment* and *unjust detriment.* A quasi-contract is imposed where (1) one person confers a benefit on another who retains the benefit and (2) it would be unjust not to require that person to pay for the benefit received.

Consider This Example Heather is driving her automobile when she is involved in a serious automobile accident in which she is knocked unconscious. She is rushed to Metropolitan Hospital, where the doctors and other staff perform the necessary medical procedures to save her life. Heather comes out of her coma and, after recovering, is released from the hospital. Subsequently, Metropolitan Hospital sends Heather a bill for its services. The charges are reasonable. Under the doctrine of quasi-contract, Heather is responsible for any charges that are not covered by her insurance coverage.

Formal and Informal Contracts

formal contract
A contract that requires a special form or method of creation.

Contracts may be classified as either *formal* or *informal*. **Formal contracts** are contracts that require a special form or method of creation. The following are formal contracts:

- ***Negotiable instruments.*** Negotiable instruments, which include checks, drafts, notes, and certificates of deposit, are special forms of contracts recognized by the Uniform Commercial Code (UCC). They require a special form and language for their creation and must meet certain requirements for their transfer.
- ***Letters of credit.*** A letter of credit is an agreement by the issuer of the letter to pay a sum of money upon the receipt of an invoice and other documents. Letters of credit are governed by the UCC.
- ***Recognizances.*** In a recognizance, a party acknowledges in court that he or she will pay a specified sum of money if a certain event occurs. A bail bond is an example of a recognizance.
- ***Contracts under seal.*** This type of contract is one to which a seal (usually a wax seal) is attached. Although no state currently requires contracts to be under seal, a few states provide that no consideration is necessary if a contract is made under seal.

informal contract
A contract that is not formal. Valid informal contracts are fully enforceable and may be sued upon if breached.

All contracts that do not qualify as formal contracts are called **informal contracts** (or **simple contracts**). The term is a misnomer. Valid informal contracts (e.g., leases, sales contracts, service contracts) are fully enforceable and may be sued upon if breached. They are called informal contracts only because no special form or method is required for their creation.

Valid, Void, Voidable, and Unenforceable Contracts

Contract law places contracts in the following categories:

valid contract
A contract that meets all the essential elements to establish a contract; a contract that is enforceable by at least one of the parties.

1. ***Valid contract.*** A **valid contract** meets all the essential elements to establish a contract. In other words, it must (1) consist of an agreement between the parties, (2) be supported by legally sufficient consideration, (3) be between parties with contractual capacity, and (4) accomplish a lawful object. Valid contracts are enforceable by at least one of the parties.

void contract
A contract that has no legal effect; a nullity.

2. ***Void contract.*** A **void contract** has no legal effect. It is as if no contract had ever been created. For example, a contract to commit a crime is void. If a contract is void, neither party is obligated to perform, and neither party can enforce the contract.

voidable contract
A contract in which one or both parties have the option to avoid their contractual obligations. If a contract is avoided, both parties are released from their contractual obligations.

3. ***Voidable contract.*** A **voidable contract** is one in which at least one party has the *option* to avoid his or her contractual obligations. If the contract is avoided, both parties are released from their obligations under the contract. If the party with the option chooses to ratify the contract, both parties must fully perform their obligations. With certain exceptions, contracts may be avoided by minors; insane persons; intoxicated

persons; persons acting under duress, undue influence, or fraud; and cases involving mutual mistake.

4. ***Unenforceable contract.*** With an **unenforceable contract,** there is some legal defense to the enforcement of the contract. For example, if a contract is required to be in writing under the Statute of Frauds but is not, the contract is unenforceable. The parties may voluntarily perform a contract that is unenforceable.

unenforceable contract
A contract in which the essential elements to create a valid contract are met but there is some legal defense to the enforcement of the contract.

Executed and Executory Contracts

A completed contract—that is, one that has been fully performed on both sides—is called an **executed contract.** A contract that has not been performed on both sides is called an **executory contract.** Contracts that have been fully performed by one side but not by the other are classified as executory contracts.

executed contract
A contract that has been fully performed on both sides; a completed contract.

executory contract
A contract that has not been fully performed by either or both sides.

Consider These Examples (1) Suppose Elizabeth Andres signs a contract to purchase a new Jaguar automobile from Ace Motors. She has not yet paid for the car, and Ace Motors has not yet delivered it. This is an executory contract. (2) Assume that the car was paid for, but Ace Motors has not yet delivered the car. Here, the contract is executed by Elizabeth but is executory as to Ace Motors. This is an executory contract. (3) Assume that Ace Motors now delivers the car to Elizabeth. The contract has been fully performed by both parties. It is an executed contract.

Concept Summary Classifications of Contracts

Formation	1. **Bilateral contract.** A promise for a promise. 2. **Unilateral contract.** A promise for an act. 3. **Express contract.** A contract expressed in oral or written words. 4. **Implied-in-fact contract.** A contract inferred from the conduct of the parties. 5. **Quasi-contract.** A contract implied by law to prevent unjust enrichment. 6. **Formal contract.** A contract that requires a special form or method of creation. 7. **Informal contract.** A contract that requires no special form or method of creation.
Enforceability	1. **Valid contract.** A contract that meets all the essential elements of establishing a contract. 2. **Void contract.** A contract that has no legal effect. 3. **Voidable contract.** A contract for which a party has the option of voiding or enforcing the contract. 4. **Unenforceable contract.** A contract that cannot be enforced because of a legal defense.
Performance	1. **Executed contract.** A contract that is fully performed on both sides. 2. **Executory contract.** A contract that is not fully performed by one or both parties.

Requirements of a Contract

For a contract to be enforceable, the following four basic requirements must be met:

1. ***Agreement.*** To have an enforceable contract, there must be an agreement between the parties.
2. ***Consideration.*** The promise must be supported by a bargained-for consideration that is legally sufficient.
3. ***Contractual capacity.*** The parties to a contract must have contractual capacity.
4. ***Lawful object.*** The object of the contract must be lawful.

The following text discusses these requirements in greater detail.

Agreement

agreement
The manifestation by two or more persons of the substance of a contract.

offeror
The party who makes an offer.

offeree
The party to whom an offer is made.

Agreement is the manifestation by two or more persons of the substance of a contract. It requires an *offer* and an *acceptance*. The process of reaching an agreement usually proceeds as follows. Prior to entering into a contract, the parties may engage in preliminary negotiations about price, time of performance, and such. At some point during these negotiations, one party makes an **offer.** The person who makes the offer is called the **offeror,** and the person to whom the offer is made is called the **offeree.** The offer sets forth the terms under which the offeree is willing to enter into the contract. The offeree has the power to create an agreement by accepting the offer.

Requirements of an Offer

offer
The manifestation of willingness to enter into a bargain, so made as to justify another person in understanding that his assent to that bargain is invited and will conclude it.

Section 24 of the *Restatement (Second) of Contracts* defines an **offer** as "the manifestation of willingness to enter into a bargain, so made as to justify another person in understanding that his assent to that bargain is invited and will conclude it." The following three elements are required for an offer to be effective:

1. The offeror must *objectively intend* to be bound by the offer.
2. The terms of the offer must be definite or reasonably *certain.*
3. The offer must be *communicated* to the offeree.

The terms of an offer must be clear enough for the offeree to be able to decide whether to accept or reject the terms of the offer. If the terms are indefinite, the courts cannot enforce the contract or determine an appropriate remedy for its breach.

A contract is a mutual promise.
William Paley
The Principles of Moral and Political Philosophy (1784)

Generally, an offer (and contract) must contain the following terms: (1) identification of the parties, (2) identification of the subject matter and quantity, (3) consideration to be paid, and (4) time of performance. Complex contracts usually state additional terms.

The making of an offer is shown in Exhibit 11.2.

Exhibit 11.2
Offer

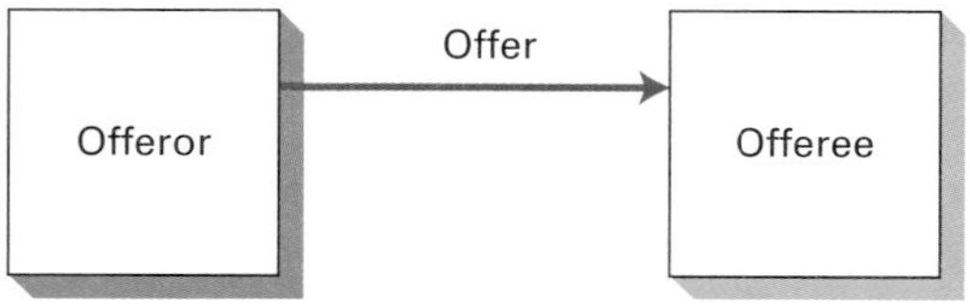

Offeror makes an offer to the offeree.

Objective Intent

The intent to enter into a contract is determined by asking whether a reasonable person viewing the circumstances would conclude that the parties intended to be legally bound. Therefore, no valid contract results from preliminary negotiations. For example, a question such as "Are you interested in selling your building for $2 million?" is not an offer. It is an invitation to make an offer or an invitation to negotiate. However, the statement, "I will buy your building for $2 million" is a valid offer because it indicates the offeror's present intent to contract.

The meaning of words varies according to the circumstances of and concerning which they are used.

Judge Blackburn
Allgood v. Blake (1873)

Auctions

At an auction, the seller offers goods for sale through an auctioneer. Unless otherwise expressly stated, an auction is considered an **auction with reserve;** that is, it is an invitation to make an offer. The seller retains the right to refuse the highest bid and withdraw the goods from sale. A contract is formed only when the auctioneer strikes the gavel down or indicates acceptance by some other means. The bidder may withdraw his or her bid prior to that time.

If an auction is expressly announced to be an **auction without reserve,** the participants reverse the roles: The seller is the offeror, and the bidders are the offerees. The seller must accept the highest bid and cannot withdraw the goods from sale. A seller who sets a minimum bid has to sell the item only if the highest bid is equal to or greater than the minimum bid.

In the following case, the court addressed the issue of an auction.

auction with reserve
An auction in which the seller retains the right to refuse the highest bid and withdraw the goods from sale. Unless expressly stated otherwise, an auction is an auction with reserve.

auction without reserve
An auction in which the seller expressly gives up his or her right to withdraw the goods from sale and must accept the highest bid.

Case 11.2 Auction

Lin v. The.TV Corporation International

999 Cal.App.4th 684, 121 Cal.Rptr.2d 323, 2002 Cal. App. Lexis 4315 Supreme Court of California

Background and Facts

The island nation of Tuvalu was awarded the top-level domain name "tv." Thus, Tuvalu controlled who could use domain names with the suffix "tv" on the Internet. For example, if a person named Jones acquired the suffix tv, her domain name on the Internet would be "jones.tv." Tuvalu hired The.TV Corporation International, a California corporation doing business under the name dotTV, to sell Internet names bearing the top-level domain name "tv." In April 2000, dotTV posted the name "golf.tv" for sale on its Web site, to be sold to the highest bidder. Je Ho Lim, a resident of South Korea, submitted the highest bid of $1,010 and authorized dotTV to charge his credit card for the amount of the bid. dotTV sent the following e-mail to Lim, confirming the sale:

> DotTV—The New Frontier on the Internet
> E-Mail Invoice for Domain Registration
> NAME: Je Ho Lim
> Congratulations!
> You have won the auction for the following domain name:
> DOMAIN NAME: - -golf
> SUBSCRIPTION LENGTH: 2 years, starts from activation date
> Amount (US$): $1,010 (first year registration fee)
> Please remember that the annual registration fee increases by 5 annually.
> You have the guaranteed right to renew the registration indefinitely.
> dotTV expects to charge your card and activate the registered domain name by May 15, 2000.
> See ya on the new frontier of the Internet!
> Lou Kerner CEO, dotTV Corporation www.TV

Shortly thereafter, dotTV sent another e-mail to Lim that stated "we have decided to release you from your bid" and that Lim should disregard the prior e-mail because of "an e-mail error that occurred." Later, dotTV publicly offered the domain name "golf.tv" with a beginning bid of $1 million. DotTV claimed that its original e-mail to Lim concerned a different domain name, "- -golf," instead of "golf." Lim countered that characters such as two dashes ("- -") are not recognized on the Internet and, therefore, the name "- -golf" is an invalid domain name. When dotTV refused to transfer the domain name "golf.tv" to Lim, Lim sued dotTV for breach of contract. The trial court dismissed Lim's case against dotTV. Lim appealed.

(continued)

Issue

Did Lim properly state a cause of action for breach of contract against dotTV?

In the Language of the Court

Defendant put the name "Golf.tv" up for public auction, and plaintiff bid on that name and no other. That was an offer and acceptance, and formed a contract. The distinction between "Golf.tv" and "- -Golf.tv" comes from the acceptance e-mail sent by defendant. Certainly the hyphens preceding the name "golf" could not defeat the existence of an already formed contract. Defendant was accepting plaintiff's bid; it plainly was not making a counteroffer, particularly since, according to the pleading, the name "- -Golf" did not "compute"; it did not qualify as a domain name. The e-mail must be read as an acknowledgment of plaintiff's winning bid and acceptance of the contract.

Decision and Remedy

The court of appeals held that plaintiff Lim had properly pleaded a cause of action against defendant dotTV for breach of contract and reinstated Lim's case against dotTV.

Business and Ethics Questions

1. Explain the difference between an auction with reserve and an auction without reserve. Which is presumed if there is no statement to the contrary?
2. Did dotTV act ethically in this case? Why you think dotTV reneged on its e-mail confirmation to Lim?
3. Are Internet domain names valuable? How do you register an Internet domain name?

Termination of Offers

An offer may be terminated by the following acts of the parties:

revocation
Withdrawal of an offer by the offeror, which terminates the offer.

rejection
Express words or conduct by the offeree that rejects an offer. Rejection terminates the offer.

counteroffer
A response by an offeree that contains terms and conditions different from or in addition to those of the offer. A counteroffer terminates the offer.

1. ***Revocation of an offer by the offeror.*** Under the common law, an offeror may **revoke** (i.e., withdraw) an offer anytime prior to its acceptance by the offeree. Generally, an offer can be so revoked even if the offeror promised to keep the offer open for a longer time. The revocation may be communicated to the offeree by the offeror or by a third party and made by (1) the offeror's express statement (e.g., "I hereby withdraw my offer") or (2) an act of the offeror that is inconsistent with the offer (e.g., selling the goods to another party). Most states provide that the revocation is not effective until it is actually received by the offeree or the offeree's agent.
2. ***Rejection of an offer by the offeree.*** An offer is terminated if the offeree **rejects** it. Any subsequent attempt by the offeree to accept the offer is ineffective and is construed as a new offer that the original offeror (now the offeree) is free to accept or reject. A rejection may be evidenced by the offeree's express words (oral or written) or conduct. Generally, a rejection is not effective until it is actually received by the offeror.
3. ***Counteroffer by the offeror.*** A **counteroffer** by the offeree simultaneously terminates the offeror's offer and creates a new offer. For example, suppose that Fei Jia says to Harold Brown, "I will sell you my house for $700,000." Brown says, "I think $700,000 is too high; I will pay you $600,000." Brown has made a counteroffer. The original offer is terminated, and the counteroffer is a new offer that Jia is free to accept or reject.

Offers are also terminated by operation of law (Exhibit 11.3).

Exhibit 11.3
Termination of an Offer by Operation of Law

Action	Description
Destruction of the subject matter	The subject matter of the offer is destroyed prior to acceptance through no fault of either party.
Death or incompetence	Either the offeror or the offeree dies or is deemed incompetent prior to acceptance of the offer.
Supervening illegality	Prior to the acceptance of an offer, the object of the offer is made illegal by statute, regulation, court decision, or other law.
Lapse of time	An offer terminates upon the expiration of a stated time in the offer. If no time is stated, the offer terminates after a "reasonable time."

Contemporary Trend
Option Contracts

An offeree can prevent the offeror from revoking his or her offer by paying the offeror compensation to keep the offer open for an agreed-upon period of time. This payment is called an **option contract.** In other words, the offeror agrees not to sell the property to anyone but the offeree during the option period. The death or incompetence of either party does not terminate an option contract unless the contract is for the performance of a personal service.

Consider This Example Anne Mason offers to sell a piece of real estate to Harold Greenberg for $1 million. Greenberg wants time to make a decision, so he pays Mason $20,000 to keep her offer open to him for six months. At any time during the option period, Greenberg may exercise his option and pay Mason the $1 million purchase price. If Greenberg lets the option expire, however, Mason may keep the $20,000 and sell the property to someone else. ■

Acceptance

Acceptance is a manifestation of assent by the offeree to the terms of the offer in a manner invited or required by the offer, as measured by the objective theory of contracts. Recall that generally (1) unilateral contracts can be accepted only by the offeree's performance of the required act, and (2) a bilateral contract can be accepted by an offeree who promises to perform (or, where permitted, by performance of) the requested act.

The offeree's acceptance must be **unequivocal.** For an acceptance to exist, the offeree must accept the terms as stated in the offer. This is called the **mirror image rule.** Generally, "a grumbling acceptance" is a legal acceptance. For example, a response such as "Okay, I'll take the car, but I sure wish you would make me a better deal" creates an enforceable contract. An acceptance is equivocal if certain conditions are added to the acceptance. For example, suppose the offeree had responded, "I accept, but only if you repaint the car red." There is no acceptance in this case.

The acceptance of an offer is illustrated in Exhibit 11.4.

acceptance
A manifestation of assent by the offeree to the terms of an offer in a manner invited or required by the offer, as measured by the objective theory of contracts (Section 50 of the *Restatement (Second) of Contracts*).

mirror image rule
A rule that states that in order for there to be an acceptance, the offeree must accept the terms as stated in the offer.

Exhibit 11.4
Acceptance

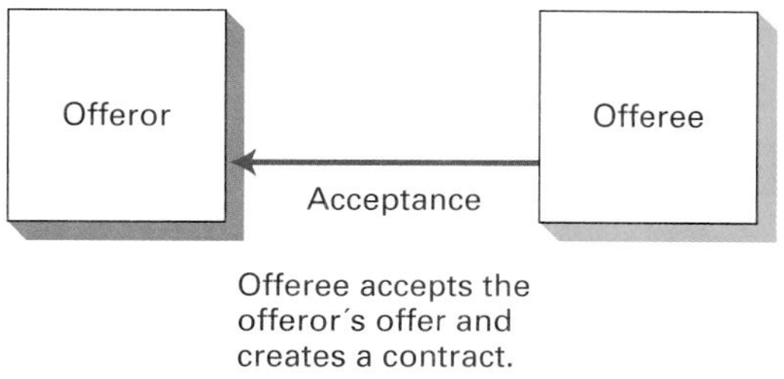

Mailbox Rule

Under the common law of contracts, acceptance of a bilateral contract occurs at the time the offeree *dispatches* the acceptance by an authorized means of communication. This is called the **acceptance-upon-dispatch rule** or, more commonly, the **mailbox rule.** Under this rule, the acceptance is effective when it is dispatched, even if it is lost in transmission. If an offeree first dispatches a rejection and then sends an acceptance, the mailbox rule does not apply to the acceptance.

The problem of lost acceptances can be minimized by expressly altering the mailbox rule. The offeror can do this by stating in the offer that acceptance is effective only upon actual receipt of the acceptance.

mailbox rule
A rule that states that an acceptance is effective when it is dispatched, even if it is lost in transmission.

Consideration

consideration
Something of legal value given in exchange for a promise.

Consideration is a necessary element for the existence of a contract. Consideration is defined as a thing of value given in exchange for a promise. Consideration can come in many forms. The most common types consist of either a tangible payment (e.g., money or property) or the performance of an act (e.g., providing legal services). Less-usual forms of consideration include the forbearance of a legal right (e.g., accepting an out-of-court settlement in exchange for dropping a lawsuit) and noneconomic forms of consideration (e.g., refraining from "drinking, using tobacco, swearing, or playing cards or billiards for money"[3] for a specified time period).

Written contracts are presumed to be supported by consideration. This is a rebuttable presumption that may be overcome by sufficient evidence. A few states provide that contracts made under seal cannot be challenged for lack of consideration.

Consideration consists of two elements: (1) Something of *legal value* must be given (e.g., either a legal benefit must be received or legal detriment must be suffered) and (2) there must be a *bargained-for exchange*. Each of these is discussed in the paragraphs that follow.

Legal Value

legal value
Support for a contract that consists of either (1) the promisee suffering a legal detriment or (2) the promisor receiving a legal benefit.

In a consideration, something of **legal value** must be given. Under the modern law of contracts, a contract is considered supported by legal value if (1) the promise suffers a *legal detriment* or (2) the promisor receives a *legal benefit*.

Consider This Example Suppose the Dallas Cowboys contract with a tailor to have the tailor make uniforms for the team. The tailor completes the uniforms, but the team manager thinks the color is wrong and refuses to allow the team to wear them. Here, there has been no benefit to either the manager or the players. However, the tailor has suffered a legal detriment (time spent making the uniforms). Under the modern rule of contracts, there is sufficiency of consideration, and the contract is enforceable.

Bargained-for Exchange

bargained-for exchange
An exchange that parties engage in that leads to an enforceable contract.

gift promise
A promise that is unenforceable because it lacks consideration.

To be enforceable, a contract must arise from a **bargained-for exchange.** In most business contracts, the parties engage in such exchanges. The commercial setting in which business contracts are formed leads to this conclusion.

Gift promises, also called **gratuitous promises**, are unenforceable because they lack consideration. To change a gift promise into an enforceable promise, the promise must offer to do something in exchange—that is, consideration—for the promise. For instance, suppose Mrs. Colby promised to give her son $10,000 and then rescinded the promise. The son would have no recourse because it was a gift promise that lacked consideration. However, if Mrs. Colby promised her son $10,000 for getting an "A" in his business law course and the son performed as required, the contract would be enforceable.

A completed gift promise cannot be rescinded for lack of consideration. For example, on May 1, Mr. Smith promises to give his granddaughter $10,000 on June 1. If on June 1 Mr. Smith actually gives the $10,000 to his granddaughter, it is a completed gift promise. Mr. Smith cannot thereafter recover the money from his granddaughter, even if the original promise lacked consideration.

The following case involves gifts.

Case 11.3
Completed Gift

Cooper v. Smith
800 N.E.2d 372, 2003 Ohio App. Lexis 5446
Court of Appeals of Ohio

Background and Facts

In May 2001, Lester Cooper suffered serious injuries that caused him to be hospitalized for an extended period of time. While he was hospitalized, Julie Smith, whom Cooper had met the year before, and Janet Smith, Julie's mother, made numerous trips to visit him. Although Julie was married to another man at the time, a romantic relationship developed between Cooper and Julie. While in the hospital, Cooper proposed marriage to Julie, and she accepted. Julie obtained a divorce from her husband in October 2001. Cooper ultimately received an $180,000 settlement for his injuries.

After being released from the hospital, Cooper moved into Janet's house and lived with Janet and Julie. Over the next couple months, Cooper purchased a number of items for Julie, including a diamond engagement ring, a car, a computer, a tanning bed, and horses. At Julie's request, Cooper paid off Janet's car. Cooper also paid for various improvements to Janet's house, such as having a new furnace installed and having wood flooring laid in the kitchen. By December 2001, the settlement money had run out, and Julie had not yet married Cooper. In the summer of 2002, Julie and Cooper had a disagreement, and Cooper moved out of the house. Julie returned the engagement ring to Cooper. Cooper sued Julie and Janet to recover the gifts or the value of the gifts he had given them. The magistrate who heard the case dismissed Cooper's case, and the trial court affirmed the dismissal of the case. Cooper appealed.

Issue

Can Cooper recover the gifts or the value of the gifts he gave to Julie and Janet Smith?

In the Language of the Court

Unless the parties have agreed otherwise, the donor is entitled to recover the engagement ring (or its value) if the marriage does not occur, regardless of who ended the engagement. While we are willing to imply a condition concerning the engagement ring, we are unwilling to do so for other gifts given during the engagement period. Unlike the engagement ring, the other gifts have no symbolic meaning. Rather, they are merely "tokens of love and affection" which the donor bore for the donee. Many gifts are made for reasons that sour with the passage of time. Unfortunately, gift law does not allow a donor to recover/revoke a gift simply because his or her reasons for giving it have soured.

Generally, a completed gift is absolute and irrevocable. If we were to imply a condition on gifts given during the engagement period, then every gift the donor gave, no matter how small or insignificant, would be recoverable. We believe the best approach is to treat gifts exchanged during the engagement period (excluding the engagement ring) as absolute and irrevocable gifts unless the donor has expressed intent that the gift be conditioned on the subsequent marriage. Cooper offered no evidence establishing that he gave the gifts on the express condition that they be returned to him if the engagement ended. Thus, the gifts are irrevocable gifts and Cooper is not entitled to their return.

Decision and Remedy

The court of appeals held that the gifts made by Cooper to Julie (other than the engagement ring) and to Janet were irrevocable gifts that he could not recover simply because his engagement with Julie ended. The court of appeals affirmed the judgment of the trial court, allowing Julie and Janet Smith to keep these gifts.

Business and Ethics Questions

1. Should the return of an engagement ring and other gifts made during the engagement period be treated differently than a gift when the engagement is broken off? Explain.
2. Did Julie and Janet Smith act ethically in keeping the gifts Cooper had given them? Did Cooper act ethically in trying to get the gifts back?
3. Does the no-fault rule regarding the return of engagement rings upon the termination of an engagement save court expenses? Explain.

Contracts Lacking Consideration

Some contracts seem as if they are supported by consideration even though they are not. Exhibit 11.5 lists promises that lack consideration and are therefore unenforceable.

Capacity to Contract

Generally, the law presumes that the parties to a contract have the requisite **contractual capacity** to enter into the contract. However, certain persons do not have this capacity. They include minors, mentally incompetent persons, and intoxicated persons. Both the

Exhibit 11.5

Promises Lacking Consideration

Type of Consideration	Description of Promise
Illegal consideration	A promise to refrain from doing an illegal act. For example, statements such as "I will burn your house down unless you agree to pay me $10,000," to which the homeowner out of fear agrees, are void.
Illusory promise	A promise in which one or both parties can choose not to perform their obligations. For example, a contract that provides that one of the parties has to perform only if he or she chooses to do so is an illusory contract.
Moral obligation	A promise made out of a sense of moral obligation, honor, love, or affection. (Some states enforce these types of contracts.)
Preexisting duty	A promise based on the preexisting duty of the promisee to perform. For example, a police offer cannot demand a payment from someone to save that person from becoming a victim of a crime.
Past consideration	A promise based on the past performance of the promisee. For example, an employee who has worked for a company for 30 years is retiring. The president of the company says, "Because you were such a loyal employee, the company will pay you a bonus of $25,000." The company refuses to pay the $25,000. The contract is unenforceable because it is based on past consideration.

common law of contracts and many state statutes protect persons who lack contractual capacity from having contracts enforced against them. The party asserting incapacity, or his or her guardian, conservator, or other legal representative bears the burden of proof.

Minors: The Infancy Doctrine

Minors do not always have the maturity, experience, or sophistication needed to enter into contracts with adults. States have enacted statutes that specify the *age of majority*. The most prevalent age of majority is 18 years for both males and females. Any age below the statutory age of majority is called the *period of minority*.

infancy doctrine
A doctrine that allows minors to disaffirm (cancel) most contracts they have entered into with adults.

disaffirmance
The act of a minor to rescind a contract under the infancy doctrine. Disaffirmance may be done orally, in writing, or by the minor's conduct.

To protect minors, the law recognizes the **infancy doctrine,** which allows minors to **disaffirm** (or **cancel**) most contracts they have entered into with adults. A minor's right to disaffirm a contract is based on public policy. The reasoning is that minors should be protected from unscrupulous behavior of adults.

Under the infancy doctrine, a minor has the option of choosing whether to enforce the contract (i.e., the contract is **voidable** by a minor). The adult party is bound to the minor's decision. If both parties to the contract are minors, both parties have the right to disaffirm the contract.

A minor may disaffirm a contract at any time prior to reaching the age of majority plus a "reasonable time." The designation of a reasonable time is determined on a case-by-case basis.

Disaffirmance If a minor's contract is executory and neither party has performed, the minor can simply disaffirm the contract: There is nothing to recover because neither party has given the other party anything of value.

> The right of a minor to disaffirm his contract is based upon sound public policy to protect the minor from his own improvidence and the overreaching of adults.
>
> Justice Sullivan
> *Star Chevrolet v. Green* (1985)

If the minor has transferred consideration—money, property, or other valuables—to the competent party before disaffirming the contract, the minor must be restored to the same position he or she was in before entering into the contract. This is usually done by returning the consideration to the minor. If the consideration has been sold or has depreciated in value, the competent party must pay the minor the cash equivalent.

Generally, a minor is obligated only to return the goods or property he or she has received from the adult in the condition they are in at the time of disaffirmance.

Most states provide that the minor must put the adult in status quo upon disaffirmance of the contract if (1) the minor's intentional or grossly negligent conduct caused the loss of value to the adult's property or (2) the minor misrepresented his or her age when entering into the contract.

Consider These Examples Peter is a 16-year-old minor who purchases a used automobile from Nancy, an adult, for $15,000 cash. Jane does not inquire about Peter's age. The age of majority is 18 years old. When Peter is 17 years old, his own negligence causes an automobile accident in which the automobile suffers $10,000 of damage and is worth only $5,000 after the accident. Peter can disaffirm the contract and recover $15,000 from Jane. Jane receives the damaged automobile worth $5,000.

However, if Peter would have lied about his age to Jane at the time of purchase, Peter could still disaffirm the contract and give Jane the damaged automobile worth $5,000, but Jane would only have to return $5,000 to Peter.

Ratification If a minor does not disaffirm a contract either during the period of minority or within a reasonable time after reaching the age of majority, the contract is considered **ratified** (accepted). This means that the minor (who is now an adult) is bound by the contract; the right to disaffirm the contract has been lost.

ratification
An act of a minor after the minor has reached the age of majority by which he or she accepts a contract entered into when he or she was a minor.

Necessaries of Life Minors are obligated to pay for the **necessaries of life** that they contract for. Otherwise, many adults would refuse to sell such items to them. There is no standard definition of what is a *necessary of life*, but items such as food, clothing, shelter, medical services, and the like are generally understood to fit this category. Goods and services such as automobiles, tools of trade, education, and vocational training have also been found to be necessaries of life in some situations.

Mentally Incompetent Persons

Mental incapacity may arise because of mental illness, brain damage, mental retardation, senility, and the like. The law protects people suffering from substantial mental incapacity from enforcement of contracts against them because such persons may not understand the consequences of their actions in entering into a contract.

The law has developed the following two standards concerning contracts of mentally incompetent persons:

1. ***Adjudged insane.*** In certain cases, a relative, a loved one, or another interested party may institute a legal action to have someone declared legally (i.e., adjudged) insane. If, after hearing the evidence at a formal judicial or administrative hearing, the person is **adjudged insane,** the court will make that person a ward of the court and appoint a guardian to act on that person's behalf. If a person has been adjudged insane, any contract entered into by that person is *void*. That is, no contract exists. The court-appointed guardian is the only one who has the legal authority to enter into contracts on behalf of the person.
2. ***Insane but not adjudged insane.*** If a person is **insane but has not been adjudged insane,** any contracts that person enters into are voidable by the insane person. Unless the other party does not have contractual capacity, he does not have the option to void the contract.

adjudged insane
Determined to be insane by a proper court or administrative agency. A contract entered into by a person adjudged insane is void.

insane but not adjudged insane
Insane but not adjudged insane by a court or an administrative agency. A contract entered into by such person is generally voidable. Some states hold that such a contract is void.

A person who has dealt with an insane person must place that insane person in status quo if the contract is either void or voided by the insane person. Most states hold that a party who did not know he or she was dealing with an insane person must be placed in status quo upon avoidance of the contract. Insane persons are liable in quasi-contract to pay the reasonable value for necessaries of life they receive.

Intoxicated Persons

intoxicated person
A person who is under contractual incapacity because of ingestion of alcohol or drugs to the point of incompetence.

Most states provide that a contract entered into by an **intoxicated person** is voidable by that person. The intoxication may occur because of alcohol or drugs. The contract is not voidable by the other party if that party had contractual capacity.

Under the majority rule, a contract is voidable only if the person was so intoxicated when the contract was entered into that he or she was incapable of understanding or comprehending the nature of the transaction. In most states, this rule holds even if the intoxication was self-induced. The amount of alcohol or drugs that a person must consume to be considered legally intoxicated to disaffirm contracts varies from case to case. The factors that are considered include the user's physical characteristics and his or her ability to "hold" intoxicants.

A person who disaffirms a contract based on intoxication generally must be returned to the status quo. In turn, the intoxicated person generally must return the consideration received under the contract to the other party and make restitution that returns the other party to status quo. After becoming sober, an intoxicated person can ratify the contracts he or she entered into while intoxicated. Intoxicated persons are liable in quasi-contract to pay the reasonable value for necessaries of life they receive.

Legality

One requirement to have an enforceable contract is that the object of the contract must be **lawful.** Most contracts that individuals and businesses enter into are **lawful contracts** that are enforceable. These include contracts for the sale of goods, services, real property, intangible rights, the lease of goods, property leases, licenses, and other contracts.

illegal contract
A contract that has an illegal object. Such contracts are *void*.

Some contracts have an illegal object. A contract with an illegal object is *void* and is therefore unenforceable. Such contracts are called **illegal contracts.** Because illegal contracts are void, the parties cannot sue for nonperformance. Further, if an illegal contract is executed, the court will generally leave the parties where it finds them. The burden of proving that a contract is unlawful rests on the party who asserts its illegality.

Illegality—Contracts Contrary to Statutes

Both federal and state legislatures have enacted statutes that prohibit certain types of conduct. Contracts to perform an activity that is prohibited by statute are illegal contracts. Such contracts include gambling contracts, contracts that provide for usurious rates of interest, and contracts that violate Sabbath laws and licensing statutes.

Illegality—Contracts Contrary to Public Policy

contract contrary to public policy
A contract that has a negative impact on society or interferes with the public's safety and welfare.

Certain contracts are illegal because they are **contrary to public policy.** Although *public policy* eludes a precise definition, the courts have held contracts to be contrary to public policy if they have a negative impact on society or interfere with the public's safety and welfare. Such contracts include immoral contracts, contracts in restraint of trade, certain covenants not to compete, and some exculpatory clauses.

In the following case, the court had to decide the lawfulness of a contract.

Case 11.4

Lawfulness of a Contract

Ryno v. Tyra
752 S.W.2d 148, 1988 Tex.App Lexis 1646
Court of Appeals of Texas

Background and Facts

R. D. Ryno, Jr., owned Bavarian Motors, an automobile dealership in Fort Worth, Texas. On March 5, 1981, Lee Tyra discussed purchasing a 1980 BMW M-1 from Ryno for $125,000. Ryno then suggested a double-or-nothing coin flip, to which Tyra agreed. If the seller Ryno won the coin flip, Tyra would have to pay $250,000 for the car; if the buyer Tyra won the coin flip, he would get the car for free. When Tyra won the coin flip, Ryno said, "It's yours," and handed Tyra the keys and German title to the car. Tyra drove away in the car. This suit ensued as to the ownership of the car. The trial court held in favor of Tyra. Ryno appealed.

Issue

Was there an illegal contract? Who owns the car?

In the Language of the Court

Ryno complains that the trial court erred in granting Tyra judgment because the judgment enforces a gambling contract. We find there was sufficient evidence to sustain the jury finding that Ryno intended to transfer to Tyra his ownership interest in the BMW at the time he delivered the documents, keys, and possession of the automobile to Tyra. We agree with appellant Ryno that his wager with Tyra was unenforceable. The trial court could not have compelled Ryno to honor his wager by delivering the BMW to Tyra. However, Ryno did deliver the BMW to Tyra and the facts incident to that delivery are sufficient to establish a transfer by gift of the BMW from Ryno to Tyra.

Decision and Remedy

Tyra, the patron at the car dealership who won the coin toss, owns the car. The appellate court found that there was an illegal contract and left the parties where it found them—that is, with Tyra in possession of the car. The court of appeals affirmed the trial court's judgment in favor of Tyra.

Business and Ethics Questions

1. Should the court have lent its resources to help Ryno recover the car?
2. Did Ryno act ethically in this case?
3. What is the moral of this story if you ever win anything in an illegal gambling contract?

Licensing Statutes

All states have **licensing statutes** that require members of certain professions and occupations to be licensed by the state in which they practice. Lawyers, doctors, real estate agents, insurance agents, certified public accountants, teachers, contractors, hairdressers, and such are among them. In most instances, a **license** is granted to a person who demonstrates that he or she has the proper schooling, experience, and moral character required by the relevant statute. Sometimes a written examination is also required. Generally, unlicensed persons cannot recover payment for services that a regulatory statute requires a licensed person to provide.

licensing statute
A statute that requires a person or business to obtain a license from the government prior to engaging in a specified occupation or activity.

Consider This Example State law provides that legal services can be provided only by lawyers who have graduated from law school and passed the appropriate bar exam. Nevertheless, Jackie Yu, a first-year law student, agrees to draft a will for Randy McCabe for a $150 fee. Because Ms. Yu is not licensed to provide legal services, she has violated a regulatory statute. She cannot enforce the contract and recover payment from Mr. McCabe.

Covenants Not to Compete

Employment contracts often contain noncompete clauses that prohibit an employee from competing with his or her employer for a certain time period after leaving the employment. This agreement is called a covenant not to compete clause, or a **noncompete clause.**

noncompete clause
An agreement whereby a person agrees not to engage in a specified business or occupation within a designated geographical area for a specified period of time following sale of the business or termination of employment.

A covenant not to compete that is ancillary to an employment contract is lawful if it is reasonable in three aspects: (1) the line of business protected, (2) the geographical area protected, and (3) the duration of the restriction. A covenant that is found to be unreasonable is not enforceable as written. The reasonableness of covenants not to compete is examined on a case-by-case basis. If a covenant not to compete is unreasonable, the courts may either refuse to enforce it or change it so that it is reasonable. Usually, the courts choose the first option.

Consider This Example Suppose Karen Ma is the chief financial officer (CFO) of Aszic Software in San Diego, California. In her employment contract with Aszic, Karen agrees that when her employment with Aszic ends, she will not accept a job as CFO of another software company in the state of California for a 10-year period. This covenant not to compete is reasonable in the line of business protected but is unreasonable in geographical scope and duration. It will not be enforced by the courts as written. The covenant not to compete would be reasonable and enforceable if it prohibited Ms. Ma from accepting a job as CFO of a software company in the city of San Diego for 5 years.

A covenant not to compete that is not *ancillary* to a legitimate employment contract is void as against public policy because the noncompete clause is not protecting a legitimate business interest.

Exculpatory Clauses

exculpatory clause
A contractual provision that relieves one (or both) parties to a contract from tort liability for ordinary negligence.

An **exculpatory clause** is a contractual provision that relieves one or both parties to the contract from tort liability. Exculpatory clauses can relieve a party of liability for ordinary negligence. They cannot be used in situations involving willful conduct, intentional torts, fraud, recklessness, or gross negligence. Exculpatory clauses are often found in leases, sales contracts, ticket stubs to sporting events, parking lot tickets, services contracts, and the like. Such clauses do not have to be reciprocal (i.e., one party may be relieved of tort liability while the other party is not).

Generally, the courts do not favor exculpatory clauses unless both parties have equal bargaining power. The courts are willing to permit competent parties of equal bargaining power to establish which of them bears the risk.

Freedom of contract begins where equality of bargaining power begins.
Oliver Wendell Holmes, Jr.

Consider This Example Trent Anderson voluntarily enrolled in a parachute jump course and signed a contract containing an exculpatory clause that relieved the parachute center of liability. After receiving proper instruction, he jumped from an airplane. Unfortunately, Trent was injured when he could not steer his parachute toward the target area. He sued the parachute center for damages, but the court enforced the exculpatory clause, reasoning that parachute jumping did not involve an essential service and that there was no decisive advantage in bargaining power between the parties.

Exculpatory clauses that either affect the *public interest* or result from superior bargaining power are usually found to be void as against public policy. Although the outcome varies with the circumstances of the case, the greater the degree that the party serves the general public, the greater the chance that the exculpatory clause will be struck down as illegal. The courts will consider such factors as the type of activity involved and the relative bargaining power, knowledge, experience, and sophistication of the parties, as well as other relevant factors. For example, exculpatory clauses used by many doctors and hospitals have been struck down as against public policy.

Finland. International trade is often governed by contracts between businesses or parties from different nations.

Terms and Concepts

Definition of *Contract*

"A promise or set of promises for the breach of which the law gives a remedy or the performance of which the law in some way recognizes a duty."

Parties to a Contract

1. ***Offeror.*** An offeror is a party who makes an offer to enter into a contract.
2. ***Offeree.*** An offeree is a party to whom an offer is made.

Formation

1. ***Bilateral contract.*** A bilateral contract is a promise for a promise.
2. ***Unilateral contract.*** A unilateral contract is a promise for an act.
3. ***Express contract.*** An express contract is a contract expressed in oral or written words.
4. ***Implied-in-fact contract.*** An implied-in-fact contract is a contract implied from the conduct of the parties.
5. ***Quasi-contract.*** A quasi-contract is a contract implied by law to prevent unjust enrichment and unjust detriment.

Enforceability

1. ***Valid contract.*** A valid contract meets all the essential elements to establish a contract.
2. ***Void contract.*** No contract exists with a void contract.
3. ***Voidable contract.*** With a voidable contract, one or both parties have the option of voiding or enforcing the contract.
4. ***Unenforceable contract.*** An unenforceable contract is a contract that cannot be enforced because of a legal defense.

Performance

1. ***Executed contract.*** An executed contract is a contract that is fully performed on both sides.
2. ***Executory contract.*** An executory contract is a contract that is not fully performed by one or both parties.

Requirements of a Contract

1. Agreement
2. Consideration
3. Contractual capacity
4. Lawful object

Offer

1. ***Offer.*** An offer is a manifestation by one party of a willingness to enter into a contract.
2. ***Offeror.*** An offeror is a party who makes an offer.
3. ***Offeree.*** An offeree is a party to whom an offer is made. This party has the power to create an agreement by accepting the terms of the offer.

Requirements of an Offer

1. ***Objection intent.*** The intent to enter into a contract is determined by the *objective theory of contracts*—that is, whether a reasonable person viewing the circumstances would conclude that the parties intended to be legally bound.
2. ***Definite terms.*** The terms of an offer must be definite so that the agreement between them can be determined. Reasonable terms (e.g., price, time for performance) may be *implied.*
3. ***Communication.*** An offer must be communicated to the offeree by the offeror.

Termination of an Offer by Action of the Parties

1. ***Revocation.*** The offeror may *revoke* (withdraw) an offer any time prior to its acceptance by the offeree.
2. ***Rejection.*** An offer is terminated if the offeree rejects the offer through his or her words or conduct.
3. ***Counteroffer.*** A counteroffer by the offeree terminates the offeror's offer (and creates a new offer).

Termination of an Offer by Operation of Law

1. ***Lapse of time.*** An offer terminates upon the expiration of a stated time in the offer. If no time is stated, the offer terminates after a "reasonable time."
2. ***Destruction of the subject matter.*** An offer terminates if the subject matter of the offer is destroyed prior to acceptance through no fault of either party.
3. ***Death or incompetence.*** The death or incompetence of either the offeror or the offeree prior to acceptance terminates the offer.
4. ***Supervening illegality.*** If, prior to the acceptance of an offer, the object of the offer is made illegal by statute, regulation, court decision, or other law, the offer terminates.

Acceptance

Acceptance is manifestation of assent by the offeree to the terms of the offer. The offeree's acceptance of the offer creates a contract.

1. ***Mirror image rule.*** Under the common law of contracts, the offeror must accept the terms offered by the offeror to create a contract. Any changes in terms by the offeree constitutes a counteroffer, not an acceptance.
2. ***Mailbox rule.*** Unless otherwise provided in an offer, acceptance is effective when it is dispatched by the offeree.

Consideration

Consideration is a thing of value given in exchange for a promise. It may be tangible or intangible property, performance of a service, forbearance of a legal right, or another thing of value.

Requirements of Consideration

1. ***Legal value.*** Something of legal value must be given to make a contract valid. Either (a) the promisee must suffer a *legal detriment* or (b) the promisor must receive a *legal benefit.*
2. ***Bargained-for exchange.*** A contract must arise from a bargained-for exchange. *Gift promises* (or gratuitous promises) are unenforceable because they lack consideration.

Contracts That Lack Consideration

The following contracts are unenforceable because they lack consideration:

1. ***Illusory promise.*** If one or both parties to a contract can choose not to perform their contractual duties, the contract is based on an illusory promise and lacks consideration.
2. ***Moral obligation.*** A promise made out of a sense of moral obligation, honor, or love and affection causes a contract to lack consideration.
3. ***Part consideration.*** A promise that is based on a party's past consideration causes a contract to lack consideration.
4. ***Preexisting duty.*** A promise to perform an act or do something that a person is already under an obligation to do causes a contract to lack consideration.

Minors

1. ***Infancy doctrine.*** Minors under that age of majority may *disaffirm* (cancel) most contracts they have entered into with adults. Such a contract is *voidable* by the minor but not by the adult.
2. ***Disaffirmance.*** A minor must disaffirm a contract within a reasonable time after reaching the age of majority.
3. ***Competent party's duty of restitution.*** If a minor disaffirms a contract, the adult must place the minor in status quo by returning the value of the consideration that the minor paid.
4. ***Minor's duty upon disaffirmance:***
   a. *General rule.* Generally, upon disaffirmance of a contract, a minor owes a duty to return the consideration to the adult in whatever condition it is in at the time of disaffirmance.
   b. *Exceptions.* A minor owes a duty to place the adult in status quo by returning the value of the consideration paid by the adult at the time of contracting if the minor (1) misrepresented his or her age or (2) intentionally or with gross negligence caused the loss to the adult's property.
5. ***Ratification.*** If a minor does not disaffirm a contract during the period of minority or within a reasonable time after reaching the age of majority, the contract is *ratified* (accepted).
6. ***Necessaries of life.*** Minors are obligated to pay the reasonable value for necessaries of life (e.g., food, clothing, shelter).

Mentally Incompetent Persons

1. ***Adjudged insane.*** Contracts by persons who have been adjudged insane are *void.* That is, such a contract cannot be enforced by either the sane or insane party.
2. ***Insane but not adjudged insane.*** Contracts by persons who are insane but have not been adjudged insane are *voidable* by the insane person but not by the competent party to the contract.
3. ***Duty of restitution.*** A person who has dealt with an insane person must place the insane person in status quo by returning the value of the consideration paid by the insane person at the time of contracting. Most states place the same duty on insane persons when they void a contract.
4. ***Necessaries of life.*** Insane persons are obligated to pay the reasonable value for necessaries of life.

Intoxicated Persons

1. ***Intoxicated persons.*** Contracts by intoxicated persons are *voidable* by the intoxicated person but not by the competent party to the contract.
2. ***Duty of restitution.*** Each party owes a duty to place the other party in status quo by returning the value of the consideration paid by the other party at the time of contracting.
3. ***Necessaries of life.*** Intoxicated persons are obliged to pay the reasonable value for necessaries of life.

Effect of Illegality

An illegal contract is *void*. Therefore, the parties cannot sue for nonperformance. If the contract has been executed, the court will *leave the parties where it finds them.*

1. ***Contracts contrary to statutes.*** Contracts that violate statutes are illegal, void, and unenforceable.
2. ***Contracts contrary to public policy.*** Contracts that violate public policy are illegal, void, and unenforceable.

Licensing Statutes

Licensing statutes are enacted to protect the public. Unlicensed persons cannot recover payment for providing services that a licensed person is required to provide.

Covenants Not to Compete

A covenant not to compete, also called a *noncompete clause*, is a contract that provides that a seller of a business or an employee will not engage in a similar business or occupation within a specified geographical area for a specified time following the sale of the business or termination of employment. These contracts are illegal if they are *unreasonable* in scope, area, or time. Reasonable noncompete clauses are legal and enforceable.

Exculpatory Clauses

Exculpatory clauses are contract clauses that relieve one or both of the parties to the contract from tort liability for ordinary negligence. Exculpatory clauses that affect public interests, result from superior bargaining power, or attempt to relieve a person of the liability for intentional torts, fraud, recklessness, or gross negligence are illegal. Reasonable exculpatory clauses between parties of equal bargaining power are legal.

Internet Exercises and Case Questions

Working the Web Internet Exercises

1. Go to **www.findlaw.com** and review the extensive material on contracts. Determine the statute of limitations on written contracts in your jurisdiction.
2. Visit **http://cori.missouri.edu**. Use this site to aid in drafting specific types of contracts and/or clauses. Test your ability by visiting the site and searching for employment agreements with noncompete clauses.
3. To review the basic elements of a contract, visit **http://law.freeadvice.com/general_practice/contract_law/binding_contract.htm**.
4. See the extensive overview of contract law at the Contracts 101 page (by Craig Smith of Santa Barbara College of Law), **www.west.net/~smith/contracts.htm**. Review the Policing the Bargain page.

Legal Environment Cases

11.1 Objective Theory of Contracts On July 24, 1973, Warren Treece appeared before the Washington State Gambling Commission to testify on an application for a license to distribute punchboards. During his testimony, Treece made the following statement: "I'll put a hundred thousand dollars to anyone to find a crooked board. If they find it, I'll pay it." The next day, Vernon Barnes watched a television news report of the proceeding and heard Treece's statement. He also read a newspaper report of the hearings that quoted Treece's statement. A number of years earlier, while employed as a bartender, Barnes had obtained two fraudulent punchboards. When Barnes presented the two crooked punchboards to Treece and demanded payment of the $100,000, Treece refused to pay. Did Treece's statement form the basis for an enforceable contract? *Barnes v. Treece*, 549 P.2d 1152, 1976 Wash.App. Lexis 1418 (Wash. App.)

11.2 Essential Terms Ben Hunt and others operated a farm under the name S. B. H. Farms. Hunt went to McIlroy Bank and Trust and requested a loan to build hog houses, buy livestock, and expand farming operations. The bank agreed to loan S. B. H. Farms $175,000, for which short-term promissory notes were signed by Hunt and the other owners of S. B. H. Farms. At that time, oral discussions were held with the bank officer regarding long-term financing of S. B. H.'s farming operations. No dollar amount, interest rate, or repayment terms were discussed. When the owners of S. B. H. Farms defaulted on the promissory notes, the bank filed for foreclosure on the farm and other collateral. S. B. H. Farms counterclaimed for $750,000 damages, alleging that the bank had breached its oral contract to provide long-term financing. Was there an oral contract for long-term financing? *Hunt v. McIlroy Bank and Trust*, 616 S.W.2d 759, 1981 Ark.App. Lexis 716 (Ark. App.)

11.3 Counteroffer Glende Motor Company, an automobile dealer that sold new cars, leased premises from certain landlords. In October 1979, fire destroyed part of the leased premises, and Glende restored the leasehold premises. The landlords received payment of insurance proceeds for the fire. Glende sued the landlords to recover the insurance proceeds. On May 7, 1982, 10 days before the trial was to begin, the defendants jointly served on Glende a document titled "Offer to Compromise Before Trial," which was a settlement offer of $190,000. On May 16, Glende agreed to the amount of the settlement but made it contingent upon the execution of a new lease. On May 17, the defendants notified Glende that they were revoking the settlement offer. Glende thereafter tried to accept the original settlement offer. Has there been a settlement of the lawsuit? *Glende Motor Company v. Superior Court*, 159 Cal.App.3d 389, 205 Cal.Rptr. 682 Cal.App. Lexis 2435 (Cal. App.)

11.4 The Mailbox Rule William Jenkins and Nathalie Monk owned a building in Sacramento, California. In 1979, they leased the building to Tuneup Masters for five years. The lease provided that Tuneup Masters could extend the lease for an additional five years if it gave written notice of its intention to do so by certified or registered mail at least six months prior to the expiration of the term of the lease, which was August 1, 1983.

On July 29, 1983, Larry Selditz, vice president of Tuneup Masters, prepared a letter exercising the option, prepared and sealed an envelope with the letter in it, prepared U.S. Postal Service Form 3800 and affixed the certified mail sticker on the envelope, and had his secretary deliver the envelope to the Postal Service annex located on the ground floor of the office building. Postal personnel occupied the annex only between the hours of 9 A.M. and 10 A.M. At the end of each day, between 5 P.M. and 5:15 P.M., a postal employee picked up outgoing mail. The letter to the landlords was lost in the mail. The landlords thereafter refused to renew the lease and brought an unlawful detainer action against Tuneup Masters. Was the notice renewing the option effective? *Jenkins v. Tuneup Masters*, 190 Cal.App.3d 1, 235 Cal.Rptr. 214, 1987 Cal.App. Lexis 1475 (Cal. App.)

11.5 Consideration When John W. Frasier died, he left a will that devised certain of his community and separate property to his wife, Lena, and their three children. These devises were more valuable to Lena than just her interest in the community property that she would otherwise have received without the will. The devise to her, however, was conditioned upon the filing of a waiver by Lena of her interest in the community property, and if she failed to file the waiver, she would then receive only her interest in the community property and nothing more. Lena hired her brother, D. L. Carter, an attorney, to represent her. Carter failed to file the waiver on Lena's behalf, thus preventing her from receiving her inheritance under the will. Instead, she received her interest in the community property, which was $19,358 less than she would have received under the will. Carter sent Lena the following letter:

> *This is to advise and confirm our agreement—that in the event the J. W. Frasier estate case now on appeal is not terminated so that you will receive settlement equal to your share of the estate as you would have done if your waiver had been filed in the estate in proper time, I will make up any balance to you in payments as suits my convenience and will pay interest on your loss at 6%.*

The appeal was decided against Lena. When she tried to enforce the contract against Carter, he alleged that the contract was not enforceable because it was not supported by valid consideration. Who wins? *Frasier v. Carter*, 437 P.2d 32, 1968 Ida. Lexis 249 (Idaho)

11.6 Preexisting Duty Robert Chuckrow Construction Company was employed as the general contractor to build a Kenney Shoe Store. Chuckrow employed Ralph Gough to perform the carpentry work on the store. The contract with Gough stipulated that he was to provide all labor, materials, tools, equipment, scaffolding, and other items necessary to complete the carpentry work. On May 15, 1965, Gough's employees erected 38 trusses at the job site. The next day, 32 of the trusses fell off the building. The reason for the trusses' falling was unexplained, and evidence showed that it was not due to Chuckrow's fault or a deficiency in the building plans. Chuckrow told Gough that he would pay him to erect the trusses and continue to work. When the job was complete, Chuckrow paid Gough the original contract price but refused to pay him for the additional cost of reerecting the trusses. Gough sued Chuckrow for this expense. Can Gough recover? *Robert Chuckrow Construction Company v. Gough*, 159 S.E.2d 469, 1968 Ga.App. Lexis 1007 (Ga. App.)

11.7 Infancy Doctrine Charles Edwards Smith, a minor, purchased an automobile from Bobby Floars Toyota on August 15, 1973. Smith executed a security agreement to finance part of the balance due on the purchase price, agreeing to pay off the balance in 30 monthly installments. On September 25, 1973, Smith turned 18, which was the age of majority. Smith made 10 monthly payments after turning 18. He then decided to disaffirm the contract and stopped making the payments. Smith claimed that he could disaffirm the contract entered into when he was a minor. Toyota argued that Smith had ratified the contract since attaining the age of majority. Who is correct? *Bobby Floars Toyota, Inc. v. Smith*, 269 S.E.2d 320, 1980 N.C.App. Lexis 3263 (N.C. App.)

11.8 Illegal Contract In 1972, Jordanos', Inc., suspected and accused one of its employees, Arthur T. Allen, of theft. The union to which Allen belonged negotiated an oral contract with Jordanos' whereby Allen agreed to accept a permanent layoff if Jordanos' would not report the suspected theft to the state's unemployment agency, so that Allen could collect unemployment benefits. Jordanos' agreed. It is a crime for an employer and employee to withhold relevant information from the state's unemployment agency. Jordanos' subsequently reported the suspected theft to the state's unemployment agency, and Allen was denied unemployment benefits. Allen sued Jordanos' for damages for breach of contract. Can Allen recover against Jordanos'? *Allen v. Jordanos', Inc.*, 52 Cal.App. 3d 160, 125 Cal.Rptr. 31, 1975 Cal.App. Lexis 1442 (Cal. App.)

11.9 Covenant Not to Compete Gerry Morris owned a silk screening and lettering shop in Tucson, Arizona. On April 11, 1974, Morris entered into a contract to sell the business to Alfred and Connie Gann. The contract contained the following covenant not to compete: "Seller agrees not to enter into silk screening or lettering shop business within Tucson and a 100-mile radius of Tucson, for a period of ten (10) years from the date of this Agreement and will not compete in any manner whatsoever with buyers, and seller further agrees that he will refer all business contacts to buyers." Morris opened a silk screening and lettering business in competition with the Ganns and in violation of the noncompete clause. The Ganns brought this action against Morris for breach of contract and to enforce the covenant not to compete. Is the covenant not to compete valid and enforceable in this case? *Gann v. Morris*, 596 P.2d 43, 1979 Ariz.App. Lexis 487 (Ariz. App.)

11.10 Exculpatory Clause Grady Perkins owned the Raleigh Institute of Cosmetology, and Ray Monk and Rovetta Allen were employed as instructors at the institute. The school trained students to do hair styling and coloring, cosmetology, and other beauty services. The students received practical training by providing services to members of the public under the supervision of the instructors. On March 28, 1985, Francis I. Alston went to the institute to have her hair colored and styled by a student who was under the supervision of Monk and Allen. Before receiving any services, Alston signed a written release form that released the institute and its employers from liability for their negligence. While coloring Alston's hair, the student negligently used a chemical that caused Alston's hair to fall out. Alston sued the institute, Perkins, Monk, and Allen for damages. The defendants asserted that the release form signed by Alston barred her suit. Is the exculpatory clause valid? *Alston v. Monk*, 373 S.E.2d 463, 1988 N.C.App. Lexis 987 (N.C. App.)

Ethics in Business

11.11 On Sunday, October 6, 1974, the Lewiston Lodge of Elks sponsored a golf tournament at the Fairlawn Country Club in Poland, Maine. For promotional purposes, Marcel Motors, an automobile dealership, agreed to give any golfer who shot a hole-in-one a new 1974 Dodge Colt. Fliers advertising the tournament were posted in the Elks Club and sent to potential participants. On the day of the tournament, a 1974 Dodge Colt was parked near the clubhouse, with one of the posters conspicuously displayed on the vehicle. Alphee Chenard, Jr., who had seen the promotional literature regarding the hole-in-one offer, registered for the tournament and paid the requisite entrance fee. While playing the thirteenth hole of the golf course, and in the presence of the other members of his foursome, Chenard shot a hole-in-one. When Marcel Motors refused to tender the automobile, Chenard sued for breach of contract. *Chenard v. Marcel Motors*, 387 A.2d 596, 1978 Me. Lexis 911 (Maine)

Ethics Issues

1. Was the contract a bilateral or a unilateral contract?
2. Was it ethical for Marcel Motors to refuse to give the automobile to Chenard?
3. Who wins? Why?

Endnotes

1. *Rebstock v. Birthright Oil & Gas Co.*, 406 So.2d 636, 1981 La.App. Lexis 5242 (La. App.).
2. *Restatement (Second) of Contracts*, Section 1.
3. *Hamer v. Sidway*, 124 N.Y. 538, 27 N.E. 256, 1891 N.Y. Lexis 1396 (N.Y.).

12

Performance of Contracts and Remedies for Breach

"Contracts must not be sports of an idle hour, mere matters of pleasantry and badinage, never intended by the parties to have any serious effect whatsoever."

—Lord Stowell
Dalrymple v. Dalrymple, 2 Hag.Con. 54, at 105 (1811)

Chapter Objectives

After studying this chapter, you should be able to:

1. Explain the genuineness of assent.
2. List and describe the contracts that must be in writing under the Statute of Frauds.
3. Describe the performance of a contract.
4. Describe compensatory, consequential, and liquidated damages.
5. Define the equitable remedies of specific performance, reformation, and injunction.

Chapter Contents

- Genuineness of Assent
- Statute of Frauds—Writing Requirement
- Third-Party Rights
- Promises of Performance
- Discharge of Performance
- Breach of Contract
- Monetary Damages
- Equitable Remedies

Once a contract is formed, the parties owe a duty to perform the contract. Certain defenses or events may discharge a party's duty to perform. If a party has an enforceable duty to perform but fails to do so, there is a breach of contract. The nonbreaching party can sue to recover certain remedies, including monetary damages or nonmonetary remedies, depending on the circumstances of the case.

This chapter covers the topics of genuineness of assent, the writing requirements of the Statute of Frauds, contract performance, discharge of performance, breach of contract, and remedies for breach of contract.

Hong Kong, China. International contracts between businesses located in different countries make the global economy possible.

Genuineness of Assent

genuineness of assent
The requirement that a party's assent to a contract be genuine. Genuineness of assent is an issue in the areas of mistake, misrepresentation, duress, and undue influence.

One of the primary defenses to the enforcement of a contract is that the assent of one or both of the parties to the contract was not genuine or real. **Genuine assent** may be missing because a party entered into a contract based on *mistake, fraudulent misrepresentation, duress*, or *undue influence*. These defenses are discussed in the following paragraphs.

Mistake

rescission
An action to undo a contract.

mutual mistake of fact
A mistake made by both parties concerning a material fact that is important to the subject matter of the contract.

A **mistake** occurs when one or both of the parties has an erroneous belief about the subject matter, value, or some other aspect of a contract. Mistakes may be either *unilateral* or *mutual*. The law permits **rescission** of some contracts made in mistake.

Mutual Mistake of Fact Either party may rescind a contract if there has been a **mutual mistake of a past or existing material fact**. A material fact is one that is important to the subject matter of the contract. An ambiguity in a contract may constitute a mutual mistake of a material fact. An ambiguity occurs when a word or term in a contract is susceptible to more than one logical interpretation. If there has been a mutual mistake, the contract may be rescinded on the ground that no contract has been formed because there has been no "meeting of the minds" between the parties.

Consider This Example In the celebrated case of *Raffles v. Wichelhaus*,[1] which has become better known as the case of the good ship *Peerless*, the parties agreed on a sale of cotton that was to be delivered from Bombay by the ship. However, there were two ships named *Peerless*, and each party, in agreeing to the sale, was referring to a different ship. Because the sailing time of the two ships was materially different, neither party was willing to agree to shipment by the other *Peerless*. The court ruled that there was no binding contract because each party had a different ship in mind when entering into the contract.

Mutual Mistake of Value A **mutual mistake of value** exists if both parties know the object of the contract but are mistaken as to its value. Here, the contract remains enforceable by either party because the identity of the subject matter of the contract is not at issue. If the rule were different, almost all contracts could later be rescinded by the party who got the "worst" of the deal.

mutual mistake of value
A mistake that occurs when both parties know the object of the contract but are mistaken as to its value.

Consider This Example Suppose Eileen Spencer cleans her attic and finds a painting of a tomato soup can. She has no use for the painting, so she offers to sell it to Fred Lee for $100. Fred, who likes the painting, accepts the offer and pays Eileen $100. It is later discovered that the painting is worth $1 million because it was painted by Andy Warhol. Neither party knew this at the time of contracting. It was a mistake of value. Eileen cannot recover the painting.

Unilateral Mistake **Unilateral mistakes** occur when only one party is mistaken about a material fact regarding the subject matter of the contract. In most cases, however, the mistaken party will not be permitted to rescind the contract. The contract will be enforced on its terms.

unilateral mistake
A situation in which only one party is mistaken about a material fact regarding the subject matter of a contract.

Consider This Example Suppose Trent Anderson wants to purchase a car from the showroom floor. He looks at several models. Although he decides to purchase a car with a sunroof, he does not tell the salesman about this preference. The model named in the contract he signs does not have this feature, although he believes it does. Mr. Anderson's unilateral mistake will not relieve him of his contractual obligation to purchase the car.

Duress

Duress occurs when one party threatens to do some wrongful act unless the other party enters into a contract. If a party to a contract has been forced into making the contract, the assent is not voluntary. Such contracts are not enforceable against the innocent party.

The threat to commit physical harm or extortion unless someone enters into a contract constitutes duress; so does a threat to bring (or not drop) a criminal lawsuit. This is so even if the criminal lawsuit is well founded. However, a threat to bring (or not drop) a civil lawsuit does not constitute duress unless such a suit is frivolous or brought in bad faith.

duress
A situation that occurs when one party threatens to do a wrongful act unless the other party enters into a contract.

Undue Influence

The courts may permit the rescission of a contract based on the equitable doctrine of **undue influence.** Undue influence occurs when one person (the dominant party) takes advantage of another person's mental, emotional, or physical weakness and unduly persuades that person (the servient party) to enter into a contract. The persuasion by the wrongdoer must overcome the free will of the innocent party. A contract that is entered into because of undue influence is voidable by the innocent party. Wills are often challenged as having been made under undue influence.

undue influence
A situation that occurs when one person takes advantage of another person's mental, emotional, or physical weakness and unduly persuades that person to enter into a contract; the persuasion by the wrongdoer must overcome the free will of the innocent party.

If there is a confidential relationship between persons—such as a lawyer and a client, a doctor and a patient, a psychiatrist and a patient—any contract made by the servient party that benefits the dominant party is presumed to be entered into under undue influence. This rebuttable presumption can be overcome through proper evidence.

Consider This Example Mr. Johnson, 70 years old, has a stroke and is partially paralyzed. He is required to use a wheelchair, and he needs constant nursing care. Prior to his stroke, Mr. Johnson had executed a will, leaving his property upon his death equally to his four grandchildren. Edward, a licensed nurse, is hired to care for Mr. Johnson on a daily basis, and Mr. Johnson relies on Edward's care. Edward works for Mr. Johnson for two years before Mr. Johnson passes away. It is discovered that Mr. Johnson executed a new will three months before he died, leaving all his property to Edward. If it is shown that Edward has used his dominant and fiduciary position to unduly influence Mr. Johnson to change his will, the will is invalid. If no undue influence is shown, the second will is valid, and Edward will receive the property left to him by Mr. Johnson in the will.

The meaning of words varies according to the circumstances of and concerning which they are used.

Justice Blackburn
Allgood v. Blake (1873)

Ethics in Business

Fraud

A misrepresentation occurs when an assertion is made that is not in accord with the facts. An intentional misrepresentation occurs when one person consciously decides to induce another person to rely and act on a misrepresentation. Intentional misrepresentation is commonly referred to as **fraudulent misrepresentation**, or **fraud**. When fraudulent misrepresentation is used to induce another to enter into a contract, the innocent party's assent to the contract is not genuine, and the contract is voidable by the innocent party. The innocent party can either rescind the contract and obtain restitution or enforce the contract and sue for contract damages.

To prove fraud, the following elements must be shown:

1. The wrongdoer made a false representation of material fact.
2. The wrongdoer intended to deceive the innocent party.
3. The innocent party justifiably relied on the misrepresentation.
4. The innocent party was injured.

Each of these elements is discussed in the following paragraphs:

- ***Material misrepresentation of fact.*** A misrepresentation may occur by words (oral or written) or by the conduct of the party. To be actionable as fraud, the misrepresentation must be of a past or existing *material fact*. This means that the misrepresentation must have been a significant factor in inducing the innocent party to enter into the contract. It does not have to have been the sole factor. Statements of opinion or predictions about the future generally do not form the basis for fraud.
- ***Intent to deceive.*** To prove fraud, the person making the misrepresentation must have either had knowledge that the representation was false or made it without sufficient knowledge of the truth. This is called **scienter** ("guilty mind"). The misrepresentation must have been made with the intent to deceive the innocent party. Intent can be inferred from the circumstances.
- ***Reliance on the misrepresentation.*** A misrepresentation is not actionable unless the innocent party to whom the misrepresentation was directed acted on it. Further, an innocent party who acts in reliance on the misrepresentation must justify his or her reliance. Justifiable reliance is generally found unless the innocent party knew that the misrepresentation was false or was so extravagant as to be obviously false. For example, reliance on a statement such as "This diamond ring is worth $10,000, but I'll sell it to you for $100" would not be justified.
- ***Injury to the innocent party*** To recover damages, the innocent party must prove that the fraud caused economic injury. The measure of damages is the difference between the value of the property as represented and the actual value of the property. This measure of damages gives the innocent party the "benefit of the bargain." In the alternative, the buyer can rescind the contract and recover the purchase price.

Although the law permits a victim of fraud to rescind the contract and recover damages from the wrongdoer, often the wrongdoer cannot be found or the money has been spent.

Ethics Issues

1. What does the element of *scienter* require? Explain.
2. Is it easy to spot fraud? Explain. ■

Statute of Frauds—Writing Requirement

Today, every state has enacted a **Statute of Frauds** that requires certain types of contracts to be in *writing*. This statute is intended to ensure that the terms of important contracts are not forgotten, misunderstood, or fabricated.

Statute of Frauds
A state statute that requires certain types of contracts to be in writing.

Generally, an *executory contract* that is not in writing even though the Statute of Frauds requires it to be is unenforceable by either party. (If the contract is valid in all other respects, however, it may be voluntarily performed by the parties.) The Statute of Frauds is usually raised by one party as a defense to the enforcement of a contract by the other party. If an oral contract that should have been in writing under the Statute of Frauds is already executed, neither party can seek to rescind the contract on the ground of noncompliance with the Statute of Frauds, however.

Contracts that are required to be in writing under the Statute of Frauds are discussed in the following paragraphs.

Contracts Involving Interests in Land

To be enforceable, any contract that transfers an ownership interest in **real property** must be in writing under the Statute of Frauds. Real property includes the land itself, buildings, trees, soil, minerals, timber, plants, crops, fixtures, and things permanently affixed to the land or buildings. Certain personal property that is permanently affixed to the real property—for example, built-in cabinets in a house—are *fixtures* that are considered part of the real property.

real property
Land itself, as well as buildings, trees, soil, minerals, timber, plants, crops, and other things permanently affixed to the land.

Other contracts that transfer an ownership interest in land must be in writing under the Statute of Frauds. These interests include the following:

- ***Mortgages.*** Borrowers often give a lender an interest in real property as security for the repayment of a loan. This must be done through the use of a written **mortgage** or **deed of trust**.
- ***Leases.*** A **lease** is the transfer of the right to use real property for a specified period of time. Most Statutes of Frauds require leases for a term of more than one year to be in writing.
- ***Life estates.*** On some occasions, a person is given a **life estate** in real property. This means that the person has an interest in the land for the person's lifetime, and the interest will be transferred to another party on that person's death. A life estate is an ownership interest that must be in writing under the Statute of Frauds.
- ***Easements.*** An **easement** is a given or required right to use another person's land without owning or leasing it. Easements may be either express or implied. Express easements must be in writing to be enforceable, whereas implied easements need not be written.

Statute of frauds: That unfortunate statute, the misguided application of which has been the cause of so many frauds.

Bacon, V. C.
Morgan v. Worthington (1878)

The courts have developed the equitable doctrine of **part performance.** This doctrine allows the court to order an oral contract to be specifically performed if performance is necessary to avoid injustice. For this doctrine to apply, courts require that the purchaser either pay part of the purchase price and take possession of the property or make valuable improvements on the land.

part performance
An equitable doctrine that allows the court to order an oral contract for the sale of land or transfer of another interest in real property to be specifically performed if it has been partially performed and performance is necessary to avoid injustice.

The following case applies the doctrine of part performance.

Case 12.1
Statute of Frauds

Sutton v. Warner
12 Cal.App.4th 415, 15 Cal.Rptr.2d 632, 1993 Cal.App. Lexis 22
California Court of Appeals

Background and Facts

In 1983, Arlene and Donald Warner inherited a one-third interest in a home at 101 Molimo Street in San Francisco. The Warners bought out the other heirs and obtained a $170,000 loan on the property. Donald Warner and Kenneth Sutton were friends. In January 1984, Donald Warner proposed that Sutton and his wife purchase the residence. His proposal included a $15,000 down payment toward the purchase price of $185,000. The Suttons were to pay all the mortgage payments and real estate taxes on the property for five years, and at any time during the five-year period, they could purchase the house. All this was agreed to orally. The Suttons paid the down payment and cash payments equal to the monthly mortgage ($1,881) to the Warners. They paid the annual property taxes on the house. The Suttons also made improvements to the property. In July 1998, the Warners reneged on the sales/option agreement. At that time, the house had risen in value to between $250,000 and $320,000. The Suttons sued for specific performance of the sales agreement. The Warners defended, alleging that the oral promise to sell real estate had to be in writing under the Statute of Frauds and was therefore unenforceable. The trial court applied the equitable doctrine of part performance and ordered specific performance. The Warners appealed.

Issue

Does the equitable doctrine of part performance make this oral contract for the sale of real property enforceable even though the statute of frauds may apply?

In the Language of the Court

The doctrine of part performance by purchaser is a well-recognized exception to the Statute of Frauds as applied to contracts for the sale of real property. The question here, then, is whether the continued possession of the property by the Suttons and their other actions are sufficiently related to the option contract to constitute part performance. The trial court responded in the affirmative. After entering the oral agreement, the Suttons made a $15,000 down payment and increased their monthly payments to the Warners from the original monthly rental payment to payments in the precise amount of the variable mortgage payments due under the $170,000 loan. They reimbursed the Warners for property taxes in the sum of $800 every six months.

Although it was disputed whether the dollar value of improvements made by the Suttons in reliance upon the oral agreement constituted "substantial" improvements, it is undisputed that many of the improvements—such as painting the interior of the house and the installation of a toilet and entry lamp—were done by the Suttons' own labor. The trial court found that these actions were unequivocally related to the purchase agreement.

The actions taken by the Suttons in reliance upon the oral agreement, when considered together with the Warners' admission that there was an oral agreement of some duration, satisfy both elements of the part performance doctrine.

Decision and Remedy

The appellate court held that the doctrine of part performance applied and that the Statute of Frauds did not prevent the enforcement of the oral contract to sell the real estate.

Business and Ethics Questions

1. What purposes are served by the Statute of Frauds? Explain.
2. Did the Warners act ethically in this case? Did the Statute of Frauds give them a justifiable reason not to go through with the deal?
3. Should important business contracts be put in writing? Why or why not?

One-Year Rule

one-year rule
A rule that says an executory contract that cannot be performed by its own terms within one year of its formation must be in writing.

According to the Statute of Frauds, an executory contract that cannot be performed by its own terms within one year of its formation must be in writing. This **one-year rule** is intended to prevent disputes about contract terms that may otherwise occur toward the end of a long-term contract. If the performance of a contract is possible within the one-year period, the contract may be oral.

The extension of an oral contract might cause the contract to violate the Statute of Frauds. For example, suppose the owner of a Burger King franchise hires Eugene Daly as a manager for 6 months. This contract may be oral. Assume that after 3 months, the owner and manager agree to extend the contract for an additional 11 months. At the time of the extension, the contract would be for 14 months (the 3 left on the contract plus 11 added by the extension). The modification would have to be in writing because it exceeds the one-year rule.

Guaranty Contract

A **guaranty contract** occurs when one person agrees to answer for the debts or duties of another person. Guaranty contracts are required to be in writing under the Statute of Frauds.

In a guaranty situation, there are at least three parties and two contracts (see Exhibit 12.1). The *first contract*, which is knows as the **original**, or **primary**, **contract**, is between the debtor and the creditor. It does not have to be in writing (unless another provision of the Statute of Frauds requires it to be). The *second contract*, called the **guaranty contract**, is between the person who agrees to pay the debt if the primary debtor does not (i.e., the **guarantor**) and the original creditor. The guarantor's liability is secondary because it does not arise unless the party primarily liable fails to perform.

guaranty contract
A promise in which one person agrees to answer for the debts or duties of another person. It is contract between the guarantor and the original creditor.

guarantor
A person who agrees to pay a debt if the primary debtor does not.

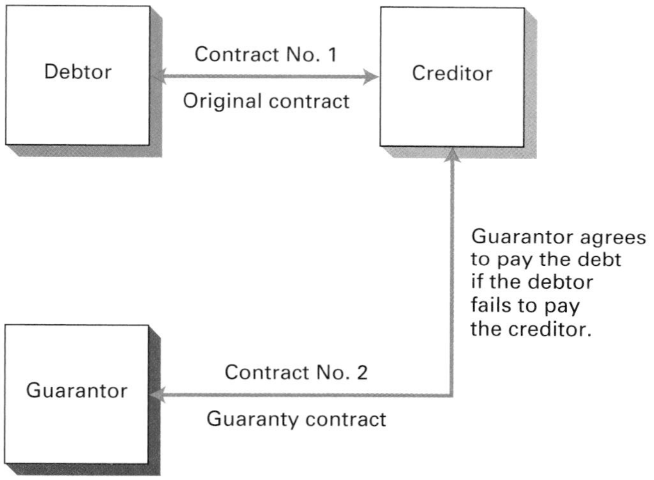

Exhibit 12.1
Guaranty Contract

Consider This Example Wei Wang, a recent college graduate, offers to purchase a new automobile on credit from a Mercedes-Benz automobile dealership. Because Wei, a student, does not have a credit history, the dealer will agree to sell the car to her only if there is a guarantor. Wei's father signs the guaranty contract. He becomes responsible for any payments his daughter fails to make.

Contracts for the Sale of Goods

Section 201 of the **Uniform Commercial Code (UCC)** is the basic Statute of Frauds provision for sales contracts. It requires that contracts for the sale of goods costing *$500 or more* be in writing to be enforceable.[2] If the contract price of an original sales contract is below $500, it does not have to be in writing under the **UCC Statute of Frauds**, but if a modification of the contract increases the sales price to $500 or more, the *modification* has to be in writing to be enforceable.

UCC Statute of Frauds
A statute that says that contracts for the sale of goods costing $500 or more must be in writing.

Consider This Example Echo enters into an oral contract to sell James her used car for $10,000, with the delivery date to be May 1. When May 1 comes and James tenders $10,000 to Echo, Echo refused to sell her car to James. The contract will not be enforced against Echo because it was an oral contract for the sale of goods costing $500 or more, and it should have been in writing.

To break an oral agreement which is not legally binding is morally wrong.

Talmud
Bava Metzi'a

Agents' Contracts

Many state Statutes of Frauds require that *agents' contracts* to sell real property covered by the Statute of Frauds be in writing to be enforceable. This requirement is often referred to as the **equal dignity rule.**

equal dignity rule

A rule that says agents' contracts to sell property covered by the Statute of Frauds must be in writing to be enforceable.

Consider This Example Suppose Barney Berkowitz hires Cynthia Lamont, a licensed real estate agent, to sell his house. Because a contract to sell real estate must be in writing pursuant to the Statute of Frauds, the equal dignity rule requires the agents' contract to be in writing as well. Some state Statutes of Frauds expressly list the agents' contracts that must be in writing.

Formality of the Writing

Many written commercial contracts are long, detailed documents that have been negotiated by the parties and drafted and reviewed by their lawyers. Other written contracts are preprinted forms that are prepared in advance to be used in recurring situations.

However, a written contract does not have to be either drafted by a lawyer or formally typed to be legally binding. Generally, the law only requires a writing containing the essential terms of the parties' agreement. Any writing—including letters, telegrams, invoices, sales receipts, handwritten agreements written on scraps of paper, and such—can be an enforceable contract under this rule.

A verbal contract isn't worth the paper it's written on.

Samuel Goldwyn

Required Signature

The Statute of Frauds and the UCC require a written contract, whatever its form, to be signed *by the party against whom enforcement is sought*. The signature of the person who is enforcing the contract is not necessary. Thus, a written contract may be enforceable against one party but not the other party.

Generally, the signature may appear anywhere on the writing. In addition, it does not have to be a person's full legal name. For example, the person's last name, first name, nickname, initials, seal, stamp, engraving, or other symbol or mark (e.g., an *X*) that indicates the person's intent can be binding. The signature may be affixed by an authorized agent.

Parol Evidence Rule

By the time a contract is reduced to writing, the parties usually have engaged in prior or contemporaneous discussions and negotiations or exchanged prior writings. Any oral or written words outside the *four corners* of the written contract are called **parol evidence**. *Parol* means "word."

The **parol evidence rule** states that if a written contract is a complete and final statement of the parties' agreement (i.e., a **complete integration**), any prior or contemporaneous oral or written statements that alter, contradict, or are in addition to the terms of the written contract are inadmissible in any court proceeding concerning the contract.

parol evidence rule

A rule that says if a written contract is a complete and final statement of the parties' agreement, any prior or contemporaneous oral or written statements that alter, contradict, or are in addition to the terms of the written contract are inadmissible in court regarding a dispute over the contract.

The parties to a written contract may include a clause stipulating that the oral contract is a complete integration and the exclusive expression of their agreement and that parol evidence may not be introduced to explain, alter, contradict, or add to the terms of the contract. This type of clause, called a **merger**, or **integration**, **clause**, expressly reiterates the parol evidence rule.

merger clause

A clause in a contract that stipulates that it is a complete integration and the exclusive expression of the parties' agreement.

Third-Party Rights

Third parties acquire rights under other people's contracts in two situations: first, as *assignees* to whom rights are subsequently transferred, and second, as *intended third-party*

International Law

Chinese *Chops* and Japanese *Hankos* as Signatures

Americans, Europeans, and many others in the world use their personal hand-applied signatures on legal documents. In Japan, China, and other countries of Asia, however, individuals often do not use their hand-applied signatures to sign legal documents. Instead, they follow the age-old tradition of using a stamp as their signature. The stamp is a character or set of characters carved onto the end of a cylinder-shaped piece held in a person's hand. The characters are carved onto one end of the cylinder. The owner places this end in ink and then applies this end to the document to be signed, leaving an imprint that serves as the owner's signature. In Japan, this cylinder is called a *hanko*; in China it is called a *chop*. *Hankos* and *chops* are registered with the government. *Hankos* and *chops* can be made of ivory, jade, agate, gold, animal's horn, wood, or even plastic.

In societies that use personal signatures, if a signature is suspected of being forged, the victim can hire handwriting experts and use modern technology to prove it is not his or her signature. In Japan, China, and other countries where *hankos* and *chops* are used, it is much more difficult to prove forgery because anyone in possession of another's *hanko* or *chop* can apply it. Some people predict the demise of the *hanko* and *chop* because of the possible problem of fraud and the increased use of hand-applied signatures by younger persons in countries used to using the *hanko* and *chop*. Others predict that the rich tradition of using a *hanko* or *chop* will continue. ■

Beijing, China.

beneficiaries to whom the contracting parties intended to give rights under the contract at the time of contracting.

Assignment

In many cases, the parties to a contract can transfer their rights under the contract to other parties. The transfer of contractual rights is called an **assignment of rights**, or just an **assignment.** The party who owes the duty of performance is called the *obligor*. The party owed a right under the contract is called the *obligee*. An obligee who transfers a right to

assignment
The transfer of contractual rights by an obligee to another party.

receive performance is called an **assignor.** The party to whom a right has been transferred is called the **assignee.** The assignee can assign the right to yet another person (called a **subsequent assignee**, or **subassignee**).

assignor
An obligee who transfers a right.

assignee
A party to whom a right has been transferred.

Consider This Example Suppose the owner of a clothing store purchases $50,000 worth of goods on credit from a manufacturer. Payment is due in 120 days. Assume that the manufacturer needs cash before that period expires, so he sells his right to collect the money to a factor for $46,000. If the store owner is given proper notice of the assignment, he must pay $50,000 to the factor. The manufacturer is the assignor, and the factor is the assignee.

Generally, no formalities are required for a valid assignment of rights. Although the assignor often uses the word *assign*, other words or terms, such as *sell, transfer, convey, give*, and the like, are sufficient to indicate an intent to transfer a contract right.

Intended Beneficiaries

When the parties enter into a contract, they can agree that the performance of one of the parties should be rendered to or directly benefit a third party. Under such circumstances, the third party is called an **intended third-party beneficiary**. An intended third-party beneficiary can enforce the contract against the party who promised to render performance.

intended beneficiary
A third party who is not in privity of contract but who has rights under the contract and can enforce the contract against the obligor.

Consider This Example Fred Richards hires a lawyer to draft his will. He directs the lawyer to leave all his property to his best friend, Shari Silverman. Assume that Mr. Richards dies and the lawyer's negligence in drafting the will causes it to be invalid. Consequently, Mr. Richards's distant relatives receive the property under the state's inheritance statute. Ms. Silverman can sue the lawyer for damages because she was the intended beneficiary of the will.

Promises of Performance

In contracts, parties make certain promises to each other. These promises may be classified as *covenants* or *conditions*. The differences between them are discussed in the following paragraphs.

Covenants

A **covenant** is an unconditional promise to perform. Nonperformance of a covenant is a breach of contract that gives the other party the right to sue. For example, if Medcliff Corporation borrows $100,000 from a bank and signs a promissory note to repay this amount plus 10 percent interest in one year, this promise is a covenant. That is, it is an unconditional promise to perform.

covenant
An unconditional promise to perform.

Conditions of Performance

A conditional promise (or qualified promise) is not as definite as a covenant. The promisor's duty to perform (or not perform) arises only if the **condition** does (or does not) occur. However, it becomes a covenant if the condition is met.

condition
A qualification of a promise that becomes a covenant if it is met.

Generally, contractual language such as *if, on condition that, provided that, when, after, as soon as*, and the like indicates a condition. A single contract may contain numerous conditions that trigger or excuse performance. There are two types of conditions: *conditions precedent* and *conditions subsequent*.

Conditions Precedent If a contract requires the occurrence (or nonoccurrence) of an event before a party is obligated to perform a contractual duty, there is a **condition precedent**. The happening (or nonhappening) of the event triggers the contract or duty of performance. If the event does not (or does) occur, no duty to perform arises because there is a failure of condition.

condition precedent
A condition that requires the occurrence of an event before a party is obligated to perform a duty under a contract.

Consider This Example Suppose E. I. duPont offers Joan Andrews a job as an industrial engineer upon her graduation from college. If Ms. Andrews graduates, the condition has been met. If the employer refuses to hire Ms. Andrews at that time, she can sue the employer for breach of contract. However, if Ms. Andrews does not graduate, duPont is not obligated to hire her because there has been a failure of condition.

Conditions Subsequent A **condition subsequent** exists when a contract provides that the occurrence or nonoccurrence of a specific event automatically excuses the performance of an existing duty to perform. For example, many employment contracts include a clause that permits the employer to terminate the contract if the employee fails a drug test.

condition subsequent
A condition that, if it occurs, automatically excuses the performance of an existing contractual duty to perform.

Concept Summary Types of Conditions

Type of Condition	Description
Condition precedent	A specified event must occur (or not occur) before a party is obligated to perform contractual duties.
Condition subsequent	The occurrence (or nonoccurrence) of a specified event excuses the performance of an existing contractual duty to perform.

Discharge of Performance

A party's duty to perform under a contract may be discharged by *mutual agreement* of the parties, by *impossibility of performance*, or by *commercial impracticability*. These methods of discharge are discussed in the paragraphs that follow.

Discharge by Agreement

In many situations, the parties to a contract mutually decide to discharge their contractual duties. The different types of mutual agreements are as follows:

- ***Mutual rescission.*** If a contract is wholly or partially executory on both sides, the parties can agree to rescind (i.e., cancel) the contract. **Mutual rescission** requires the parties to enter into a second agreement that expressly terminates the first one.
- ***Novation.*** A **novation agreement** (commonly called a **novation**) substitutes a third party for one of the original contracting parties. The new substituted party is obligated to perform the contract. All three parties must agree to the substitution. In a novation, the exiting party is relieved of liability on the contract.

novation
An agreement that substitutes a new party for one of the original contracting parties and relieves the existing party of liability on the contract.

accord and satisfaction
The settlement of a contract dispute.

- ***Accord and satisfaction.*** The parties to a contract may agree to settle a contract dispute through an **accord and a satisfaction.** An agreement whereby the parties agree to accept something different in satisfaction of the original contract is called an **accord**. The performance of an accord is called a **satisfaction**. Satisfaction of an accord discharges both the original contract and the accord. If an accord is not satisfied when it is due, the aggrieved party may enforce either (1) the accord or (2) the original contract.

force majeure clause
A clause in a contract in which the parties specify certain events that will excuse nonperformance.

Force Majeure Clause The parties may agree in a contract that certain events will excuse nonperformance of the contract. These clauses are called **force majeure clauses.** Usually, force majeure clauses excuse nonperformance caused by natural disasters such as floods, tornadoes, earthquakes, and such. Modern clauses often excuse performance due to labor strikes, shortages of raw materials, and the like.

Discharge by Impossibility

impossibility of performance
Nonperformance that is excused if a contract becomes impossible to perform; it must be objective impossibility, not subjective.

Under certain circumstances, the nonperformance of contractual duties is excused (i.e., discharged) because of **impossibility of performance**, or **objective impossibility**. Impossibility of performance occurs if a contract becomes impossible to perform. The impossibility must be objective impossibility ("it cannot be done") rather than subjective impossibility ("I cannot do it"). The following types of objective impossibility excuse nonperformance:

1. The death or incapacity of the promisor prior to the performance of a personal service contract. For example, if a professional athlete dies prior to or during a contract period, her contract with the team is discharged.
2. The destruction of the subject matter of a contract prior to performance. For instance, if a building is destroyed by fire, the lessees are discharged from further performance unless otherwise provided in the lease.
3. A supervening illegality makes performance of the contract illegal. For example, suppose an art dealer contracts to purchase native art found in a foreign country. The contract is discharged if the foreign country enacts a law forbidding native art from being exported from the country before the contract is performed.

Commercial Impracticability

commercial impracticability
Nonperformance that is excused if an extreme or unexpected development or expense makes it impractical for the promisor to perform.

Many states recognize the doctrine of **commercial impracticability** as an excuse of nonperformance of contracts. Commercial impracticability excuses performance if an unforeseeable event makes it impractical for the promisor to perform. This doctrine has not yet been fully developed by the courts. It is examined on a case-by-case basis.

Consider This Example A utility company enters into a contract to purchase uranium for its nuclear-powered generator from a uranium supplier at a fixed price of $1 million per year for five years. Suppose a new uranium cartel is formed worldwide, and the supplier must pay $4 million for uranium to supply the utility with each year's supply. In this case, the court would likely allow the supplier to rescind its contract with the utility based on commercial impracticability. Note that it is not impossible for the supplier to supply the uranium.

Ethics in Business

Unconscionable Contracts

The general rule of freedom of contracts holds that if (1) the object of a contract is lawful and (2) the other elements for the formation of a contract are met, the courts will enforce a contract according to its terms. Although it is generally presumed that parties are capable of protecting their own interest when contracting, it is a fact of life that dominant parties sometimes take advantage of weaker parties. As a result, some otherwise lawful contracts are so oppressive or manifestly unfair that they are unjust. To prevent the enforcement of such contracts, the courts developed the equitable **doctrine of unconscionability**, which is based on public policy. A contract found to be unsconscionable under this doctrine is called an **unconscionable contract**, or a **contract of adhesion**.

The courts are given substantial discretion in determining whether a contract or contract clause is unconscionable. There is no single definition of *unconscionability*. The doctrine may not be used merely to save a contracting party from a bad bargain. The following elements must be shown to prove that a contract or clause in a contract is unconscionable:

1. The parties possessed severely unequal bargaining power.
2. The dominant party unreasonably used its unequal bargaining power to obtain oppressive or manifestly unfair contract terms.
3. The adhering party had no reasonable alternative.

Unconscionable contracts are sometimes found where there is a consumer contract that takes advantage of uneducated, poor, or elderly people who have been persuaded to enter into an unfair contract. This often involves door-to-door sales and sales over the telephone.

If the court finds that a contract or contract clause is unconscionable, it may (1) refuse to enforce the contract, (2) refuse to enforce the unconscionable clause but enforce the remainder of the contract, or (3) limit the applicability of any unconscionable clause so as to avoid any unconscionable result. The appropriate remedy depends on the facts and circumstances of each case. Note that because unconscionability is a matter of law, the judge may opt to decide the case without a jury trial.

Consider This Example Suppose a door-to-door salesperson sells a poor family a freezer full of meat and other foods for $3,000, with monthly payments for 60 months at 20 percent interest. If the actual cost of the freezer and the food is $1,000, this contract could be found to be unconscionable. In this case, the court could rewrite the contract to conscionable terms, or it could enforce only part or none of the contract against the purchaser.

Ethics Issues

1. Define *unconscionable contract*.
2. What public policy is served by the doctrine of unconscionability of contracts? Explain. ■

Breach of Contract

If a contractual duty has not been discharged (i.e., terminated) or excused (i.e., relieved of legal liability), the contracting party owes an absolute duty (i.e., covenant) to perform the duty. There are three types of performance of a contract: (1) *complete performance*, (2) *substantial performance* (or minor breach), and (3) *inferior performance* (or material breach). These concepts are discussed in the following paragraphs.

An honest man's word is as good as his bond.

Don Quixote

Complete Performance

Most contracts are discharged by the **complete**, or **strict**, **performance** of the contracting parties. Complete performance occurs when a party to a contract renders performance exactly as required by the contract. A fully performed contract is called an **executed contract**. The *tender of performance* also discharges a party's contractual obligations. *Tender* is an unconditional and absolute offer by a contracting party to perform his or her obligations under the contract.

complete performance
A type of performance that occurs when a party to a contract renders performance exactly as required by the contract; it discharges that party's obligations under the contract.

Consider This Example Suppose Ashley's Dress Shops, Inc., contracts to purchase dresses from a dress manufacturer for $25,000. Ashley's has performed its obligation under the contract once it tenders the $25,000 to the manufacturer. If the manufacturer fails to deliver the dresses, Ashley's can sue it for breach of contract.

Substantial Performance: Minor Breach

substantial performance
Performance by a contracting party that deviates only slightly from complete performance.

Substantial performance occurs when there has been a **minor breach** of contract. In other words, it occurs when a party to a contract renders performance that deviates only slightly from complete performance. The nonbreaching party may either (1) convince the breaching party to elevate his or her performance to complete performance, (2) deduct the cost to repair the defect from the contract price and remit the balance to the breaching party, or (3) sue the breaching party to recover the cost to repair the defect if the breaching party has already been paid.

Consider This Example Suppose Donald Trump contracts with Big Apple Construction Co. to have Big Apple construct an office building for $50 million. The architectural plans call for installation of three-ply windows in the building. Big Apple constructs the building exactly to plan except that it installs two-ply windows. There has been substantial performance. It would cost $300,000 to install the correct windows. If Big Apple agrees to replace the windows, its performance is elevated to complete performance, and Trump must remit the entire contract price. However, if Trump has to hire someone else to replace the windows, he may deduct this cost of repair from the contract price and remit the difference to Big Apple.

Inferior Performance: Material Breach

material breach
A breach that occurs when a party renders inferior performance of his or her contractual duties.

inferior performance
Performance that occurs when a party fails to perform express or implied contractual obligations that impair or destroy the essence of a contract.

A **material breach** of a contract occurs when a party fails to perform certain express or implied obligations that impair or destroy the essence of the contract. When a material breach occurs, it is called **inferior performance**. Because there is no clear line between a minor breach and a material breach, determination is made on a case-by-case basis. Where there has been a material breach of a contract, the nonbreaching party has two choices:

1. The nonbreaching party may *rescind* the contract, seek restitution of any compensation paid under the contract to the breaching party, and be discharged from any further performance under the contract.
2. The nonbreaching party may treat the contract as being in effect and sue the breaching party to recover *damages*.

Consider This Example Suppose a university contracts with a general contractor to build a new three-story building with classroom space for 1,000 students. However, the completed building can support the weight of only 500 students because the contractor used inferior materials. The defect cannot be repaired without rebuilding the entire structure. Because this is a material breach, the university may rescind the contract and require removal of the building. The university is discharged of any obligations under the contract and is free to employ another contractor to rebuild the building. Alternatively, the university could accept the building and deduct from the contract price damages caused by the defect.

In the following case, the court found a breach of contract.

Case 12.2
Breach of Contract

Chodos v. West Publishing Company, Inc.
292 F.3d 992, 2002 U.S. App. Lexis 10823
United States Court of Appeals, Ninth Circuit

Background and Facts

Rafael Chodos is a California attorney who specializes in the law of fiduciary duty, which includes a party's obligation to act honestly and with loyalty when performing his or her legal duties to another. In early 1995, Chodos sent a detailed proposal and table of contents to Bancroft-Whitney, the leading publisher of legal texts, to write a treatise on fiduciary duties. The editors at Bancroft-Whitney were enthusiastic about the proposal and sent Chodos a standard-form "author agreement" that set forth the terms of the publishing contract. Chodos was to be paid 15 percent of the gross revenues from the sales of the treatise. Chodos and Bancroft-Whitney signed the agreement.

From July 1995 through June 1998, Chodos wrote the manuscript. He significantly limited the time spent on his law practice and spent over 3,600 hours writing the manuscript. During this time, Chodos worked with editors of Bancroft-Whitney in developing and editing the manuscript. In mid-1996, West Publishing Group purchased Bancroft-Whitney, and the two companies merged. The Bancroft-Whitney editors, now employed by West, continued to work with Chodos on editing and developing the manuscript. In June 1998, Chodos submitted the final manuscript to West. During the fall of 1998, West editors suggested changes to the manuscript, which Chodos completed. In December 1998, West sent Chodos a letter, apologizing for delays in publication and assuring him publication would take place in the first quarter of 1999.

In February 1999, Chodos received a letter from West's marketing department, stating that West had decided not to publish Chodos's manuscript because it did not "fit with [West's] current product mix" and because of concerns about its "market potential." West admitted, however, that the manuscript was of "high quality" and that its decision was not due to any literary shortcomings of Chodos's work. Chodos filed a lawsuit against West, alleging breach of contract. The U.S. district court granted summary judgment in favor of West. Chodos appealed.

Issue

Did West Publishing breach the author agreement it had with Chodos?

In the Language of the Court

The uncontroverted evidence in this case is that Chodos worked diligently in cooperation with West—indeed with West's encouragement—to produce a work that met the highest professional standard, and that he was successful in that venture. His performance was induced by an agreement that permitted rejection of the completed manuscript only for deficiencies in "form and content." Chodos thus labored to complete a work of high quality with the expectation that, if he did so, it would be published. He devoted thousands of hours of labor to the venture, and passed up substantial professional opportunities, only for West to decide that due to the vagaries of its internal reorganizations and changes in its business strategies or in the national economy or the market for legal treaties, his work, albeit admittedly of high quality, was for naught. It would be inequitable, if not unconscionable, for an author to be forced to bear this considerable burden solely because of his publisher's change of management, its poor planning, or its inadequate financial analyses at the time it entered into the contract, or even because of an unexpected change in the marketplace. Moreover, to allow a publisher to escape its contractual obligations for these reasons would be directly contrary to both the language and the spirit of the standard Author Agreement.

In sum, we reject the district court's determination that West acted within its discretion afforded it by the Author Agreement when it decided not to publish Chodos's manuscript. Because West concedes that the manuscript was of high quality and that it declined to publish it solely for commercial reasons rather than because of any defect in its form and content, we hold as a matter of law that West breached its agreement with Chodos.

Decision and Remedy

The U.S. Court of Appeals held as a matter of law that West Publishing had breached its contract with Chodos. The Court of Appeals reversed the district court's summary judgment in favor of West, remanded the case to the district court to enter summary judgment as to liability in Chodos's favor, and ordered further proceedings consistent with the opinion of the Court of Appeals.

Business and Ethics Questions

1. Should a court enforce the terms of a contract literally? Or should the court give contracts a broad interpretation, as requested by West Publishing?
2. Did West Publishing act ethically in this case? Should it have read Chodos's treatise on fiduciary duty before terminating its contract with Chodos?
3. If West Publishing wanted to reserve the right to terminate its contract with Chodos based on changes in its own marketing strategy, company reorganization, or changes in the marketplace, how should West have done so? What amount of money should West have paid Chodos?

Monetary Damages

A nonbreaching party may recover **monetary damages** from a breaching party. Monetary damages are available whether the breach was minor or material. Several types of monetary damages may be awarded. These include *compensatory*, *consequential*, and *liquidated damages*, which are discussed in the following paragraphs.

monetary damages
Financial damages that a nonbreaching party may recover from a breaching party whether the breach was minor or material.

Compensatory Damages

Compensatory damages are intended to compensate a nonbreaching party for the loss of a bargain. In other words, they place the nonbreaching party in the same position as if the contract had been fully performed by restoring the "benefit of the bargain."

compensatory damages
A remedy intended to compensate a nonbreaching party for the loss of a bargain; these damages place the nonbreaching party in the same position as if the contract had been fully performed by restoring the "benefits of the bargain."

Consider This Example Suppose Lederle Laboratories enters into a written contract to employ a manager for three years at a salary of $6,000 per month. Before work is to start, the manager is informed that he will not be needed. This is a material breach of contract. Assume that the manager finds another job, but it pays only $5,000 a month. The manager may recover $1,000 per month for 36 months ($36,000 total) from Lederle Laboratories as compensatory damages. These damages place the manager in the same situation as if the contract with Lederle had been performed.

Consequential Damages

consequential damages
Foreseeable damages that arise from circumstances outside a contract. In order to be liable for these damages, the breaching party must know or have reason to know that the breach will cause special damages to the other party.

In addition to compensatory damages, a nonbreaching party can sometimes recover **special**, or **consequential**, **damages** from the breaching party. Consequential damages are *foreseeable* damages that arise from circumstances outside the contract. To be liable for consequential damages, the breaching party must know or have reason to know that the breach will cause special damages to the other party.

Consider This Example Suppose Soan-Allen Co., a wholesaler, enters into a contract to purchase 1,000 men's suits for $150 each from Fabric Manufacturing Co., a manufacturer. Prior to contracting, the wholesaler tells the manufacturer that the suits will be resold to retailers for $225. The manufacturer breaches the contract by failing to manufacture the suits. The wholesaler cannot get the suits manufactured by anyone else in time to meet his contracts. He can recover $75,000 of lost profits on the resale contracts (1,000 suits × $75 profit) as consequential damages from the manufacturer because the manufacturer knew of this special damage to Soan-Allen Co. if it breached the contract.

Liquidated Damages

liquidated damages
An agreement by the parties in advance that sets the amount of damages recoverable in case of breach

Under certain circumstances, the parties to a contract may agree in advance to the amount of damages payable upon a breach of contract. These are called **liquidated damages.** To be lawful, the actual damages must be difficult or impracticable to determine, and the liquidated amount must be reasonable in the circumstances. An enforceable liquidated damage clause is an exclusive remedy even if actual damages are later determined to be different.

A liquidated damage clause is considered a **penalty** if actual damages are clearly determinable in advance or the liquidated damages are excessive or unconscionable. If a liquidated damage clause is found to be a penalty, it is unenforceable. The nonbreaching party may then recover actual damages.

Concept Summary *Types of Monetary Damages*

Type of Damage	Description
Compensatory	Damages that compensate a nonbreaching party for the loss of a bargain. These damages place the nonbreaching party in the same position as if the contract had been fully performed.
Consequential	Damages that compensate a nonbreaching party for foreseeable special damages. The breaching party must have known or should have known that these damages would result from the breach.
Liquidated	An agreement by the parties in advance that sets the amount of damages recoverable in case of breach. These damages are lawful if they do not cause a penalty.

Mitigation of Damages

If a contract has been breached, the law places a duty on the innocent nonbreaching party to take reasonable efforts to mitigate (i.e., avoid and reduce) the resulting damages. The extent of **mitigation** required depends on the type of contract involved. For example, if an employer breaches an employment contract, the employee owes a duty to mitigate damages by trying to find substitute employment. The employee is only required to accept comparable employment. The courts consider such factors as compensation, rank, status, job description, and geographical location in determining the comparability of jobs.

mitigation of damages
A nonbreaching party is under a legal duty to avoid or reduce damages caused by a breach of contract.

Consider This Example Suppose Shou-Yi Kang is employed as the chief financial officer (CFO) by Imperial Corporation. The corporate office where Ms. Kang works is in Irvine, California, a 15-minute commute from her home to work. Ms. Kang's employment contract with Imperial is for $200,000 salary per year. With three years left on the contract, Imperial breaches the contract and wrongfully discharges Ms. Kang. Legally, Imperial owes Ms. Kang $600,000 in damages.

However, Ms. Kang is under a legal duty to mitigate these damages. If Ms. Kang locates a job as CFO of a comparable company at $200,000 per year for three years, but the job is in Las Vegas, Nevada, she does not have to take the job. If she locates a CFO position at a comparable company in Irvine for three years, but the pay is $150,000, she does not have to take the job. If she locates a job as a financial analyst, a lower position than CFO, at a comparable company in Irvine and at $200,000 salary per year for three years, she does not have to take the job. If Ms. Kang finds a job as CFO at a comparable company located in Irvine for three years at $200,000 salary per year, but her commute to work would take 35 minutes rather than 15 minutes, the court would consider this reasonable and require Ms. Kang to mitigate damages.

Equitable Remedies

Equitable remedies are available if there has been a breach of contract that cannot be adequately compensated through a legal remedy. They are also available to prevent unjust enrichment. The most common equitable remedies are *specific performance, reformation,* and *injunction.*

equitable remedies
Remedies that may be awarded by a judge where there has been a breach of contract and either (1) the legal remedy is not adequate or (2) the judge wants to prevent unjust enrichment.

Specific Performance

An award of **specific performance** orders the breaching party to *perform* the acts promised in the contract. The courts have the discretion to award this remedy if the subject matter of the contract is unique. This remedy is available to enforce land contracts because every piece of real property is considered to be unique. Works of art, antiques, items of sentimental value, rare coins, stamps, heirlooms, and such also fit the requirement for uniqueness. Most other personal property does not. Specific performance of personal service contracts is not granted because the courts would find it difficult or impracticable to supervise or monitor performance of these contracts.

specific performance
A remedy that orders the breaching party to perform the acts promised in the contract. Specific performance is usually awarded in cases in which the subject matter is unique, such as in contracts involving land, heirlooms, paintings, and the like.

Consider This Example Patel contracts to purchase a piece of vacant real property on the shore of a lake from Heather, its owner. Heather and Patel sign a written contract agreeing to a purchase price of $500,000. Patel wants to build his dream house on this property. Heather later refuses to sell the property to Patel. Patel can bring a lawsuit against Heather and obtain an award of specific performance from the court that orders Heather to sell the property to Patel.

Reformation

reformation
An equitable doctrine that permits the court to rewrite a contract to express the parties' true intentions.

Reformation is an equitable doctrine that permits the court to rewrite a contract to express the parties' true intentions. For example, suppose a clerical error is made during the typing of a contract, and both parties sign the contract without discovering the error. If a dispute later arises, the court can reform the contract to correct the clerical error to read as the parties originally intended.

Injunction

injunction
A court order that prohibits a person from doing a certain act.

An **injunction** is a court order that prohibits a person from doing a certain act. To obtain an injunction, the requesting party must show that he or she will suffer irreparable injury if the injunction is not issued.

Consider This Example Suppose a professional football team enters into a five-year employment contract with a "superstar" quarterback. During this five-year period, the quarterback breaches the contract and enters into a contract to play for a competing team. Here, the first team can seek an injunction to prevent the quarterback from playing for the other team.

Concept Summary *Equitable Remedies*

Type of Equitable Remedy	Description
Specific performance	A court orders the breaching party to perform the acts promised in the contract. The subject matter of the contract must be unique.
Reformation	A court rewrites the contract to express the parties' true intentions. Reformation is usually used to correct clerical errors.
Injunction	A court prohibits a party from doing a certain act. Injunctions are available in contract actions only in limited circumstances.

Ethics in Business

Intentional Interference with Contractual Relations

A party to a contract may sue any third person who intentionally interferes with the contract and causes that party injury. This tort, which is known as the tort of **intentional interference with contractual relations**, usually arises when a third party induces a contracting party to breach a contract with another party. Punitive damages can be awarded because this is an intentional tort. Consider the following case.

Ricardo E. Brown, Jr., known as "Kurupt," was an unknown teenage rap singer who lived with his father. In 1989, Lamont Brumfield, a promoter of young rappers, "discovered" Kurupt. Lamont introduced his brother Kenneth Brumfield, who owned a music publishing business, to Kurupt. Beginning in 1990, Lamont produced demos for Kurupt, set up photo shoots, booked him to sing at many clubs, and paid for Kurupt's clothing and personal and living expenses. Kurupt lived with Lamont after Kurupt's father kicked him out of the house. In 1991, Lamont obtained recording work for Kurupt with the rap group SOS. In November 1991, Kurupt signed an exclusive recording agreement with Lamont's company, an exclusive publishing agreement with Kenneth's company, and a management agreement with Kenneth for an initial term of three years, with an additional option term. These contracts gave Kurupt 7 percent royalties on sales. The Brumfields spent at least $65,000 to support and promote Kurupt, often borrowing money from family and friends to do so.

Andre Young, known as Dr. Dre, invited Lamont, Kenneth, and Kurupt to a picnic, where he introduced them to Marion Knight, the owner of Death Row Records, Inc. The Brumfields and Kurupt made it clear to Dr. Dre and Knight that the Brumfields had exclusive contracts with Kurupt. After Kurupt performed at the picnic, Dr. Dre invited Kurupt to his house to record songs for Dr. Dre's album *Chronic*. In December 1992, *Chronic* was released by Death Row Records, Inc., and sold millions of copies. The Brumfields continued to promote Kurupt and to take care of his living expenses. When Dr. Dre invited Kurupt to go on tour to promote the *Chronic* album, Kurupt told the Brumfields that he was going to visit family in Philadelphia but instead went on tour for four weeks. In 1993, Kurupt worked on another Death Row Records album. In May 1994, Kenneth exercised his option and renewed his management agreement with Kurupt. Despite the multimillion-dollar profit of the *Chronic* album, the Brumfields were paid nothing by Death Row Records. At the end of 1994, Death Row moved Kurupt out of the condominium he shared with Lamont and into a house. While cleaning out the condominium, Lamont found papers showing that Death Row Records had paid Kurupt advances commencing in April 1993.

The evidence showed that Kurupt had breached the contracts he had with the Brumfields and had earned approximately $1.5 million in royalties from Death Row Records for his work on the *Chronic* album and many other albums. The court held that there was evidence that Death Row Records had caused Kurupt to breach these contracts and was therefore liable for the tort of intentional interference with a contract.

The court held that defendant Death Row Records, Inc., had committed the tort of intentionally interfering with the contracts that the Brumfields had with rapper Kurupt. The court awarded $5,519,000 to the Brumfields, including $1.5 million in punitive damages to Lamont and $1 million in punitive damages to Kenneth. The judgment of the superior court was upheld by the court of appeals of California. *Brumfield v. Death Row Records, Inc.*, 2003 Cal.App. Unpub. Lexis 7843 (Cal. App.)

Ethics Issues

1. What does the tort of intentional interference with contractual relations provide? Explain.
2. Did the principals of Death Row Records act ethically in this case?
3. What purpose is served by an award of punitive damages? Explain. ■

Tibet, China. Many areas of the world are trying to preserve historical cultural values while at the same time develop business and trade.

Terms and Concepts

Mutual Mistakes

1. ***Mutual mistake of fact.*** With this type of mistake, both parties are mistaken about the essence or object of the contract. Either party may rescind the contract.
2. ***Mutual mistake of value.*** With this type of mistake, both parties know the object of the contract but are mistaken as to its value. Neither party may rescind the contract.

Unilateral Mistakes

A unilateral mistake occurs when only one party is mistaken about a material fact regarding the subject matter of the contract. The mistaken party is not permitted to rescind the contract.

Duress

Duress occurs when one party threatens to do some wrongful act unless the other party enters into a contract. A contract entered into under duress cannot be enforced.

Types of duress:

1. Physical duress
2. Extortion

Undue Influence

Undue influence occurs when one person takes advantage of another person's mental, emotional, or physical weakness and unduly persuades that person to enter into a contract. A contract entered into under undue influence cannot be enforced.

1. ***Elements of undue influence:***
   a. A fiduciary or confidential relationship existed between the dominant and servient parties.
   b. The dominant party unduly used his or her influence to persuade the servient party to enter into a contract.
2. ***Presumption.*** If there is a confidential relationship between persons, any contract by the servient party that benefits the dominant party is presumed to be entered into under undue influence. This is a *rebuttable presumption.*

Fraud

Fraudulent misrepresentation occurs when a person intentionally makes an assertion that is not in accord with the facts. Also called *fraud.*

1. ***Elements of fraud:***
   a. The wrongdoer made a false representation of material fact.
   b. The wrongdoer intended to deceive the innocent party.
   c. The innocent party justifiably relied on the misrepresentation.
   d. The innocent party was injured.
2. ***Legal consequences if fraudulent misrepresentation is found.*** The innocent party may:
   a. Rescind the contract and obtain restitution, or
   b. Enforce the contract and sue for damages

Writing Requirement

Statute of Frauds. The Statute of Frauds is a state statute that requires the following contracts to be in writing:

1. ***Contracts involving the transfer of interests in real property.*** This includes contracts for the sale of land, buildings, and items attached to land, mortgages, leases for a term of more than one year, and express easements.
   a. Part performance exception. This exception permits the specific enforcement of oral contracts for the sale of land when they have been partially performed to avoid injustice.
2. ***Contracts that cannot be performed within one year of their formation.***
3. ***Guaranty contracts.*** These contracts occur when one person promises to answer for the debts of another person.
4. ***Contracts for the sale of goods costing $500 or more.*** [UCC Section 201]
5. ***Agents' contracts to sell real estate.***

Sufficiency of the Writing

1. ***Formality of the writing.*** A written contract does not have to be formal or drafted by a lawyer to be enforceable. Informal contracts, such as handwritten notes, letters, invoices, and the like, are enforceable contracts.
2. ***Required signature.*** The party against whom enforcement of a contract is sought must have signed the contract. The signature may be the person's full legal name, last name, first name, nickname, initials, or other symbol or mark.

The Parol Evidence Rule

1. ***Parol evidence.*** Parol evidence consists of any oral or written words that are outside the four corners of a written contract.
2. ***Parol evidence rule.*** This rule provides that if a written contract is a complete integration, any prior contemporaneous oral or written statements are inadmissible as evidence to alter or contradict the terms of the written contract.
3. ***Merger clause.*** A clause that may be included in a contract that expressly reiterates the parol evidence rule. Also called an *integration clause*.

Assignment

1. ***Assignment.*** Transfer of contractual rights by a party to a contract to a third person is called assignment.
2. ***Assignor.*** An assignor is a contract party who assigns the contractual rights.
3. ***Assignee.*** An assignee is a third person to whom contract rights are assigned. The assignee "stands in the shoes of the assignor" and is entitled to performance of the contract by the obligor.

Intended Beneficiaries

A third person who is owed performance under other parties' contract is an intended beneficiary. A person who is to be rendered performance gratuitously under a contract, such as a beneficiary of a life insurance policy, may sue the promisor for nonperformance.

Covenants

A covenant is an unconditional promise to perform. Nonperformance of a covenant is a breach of contract that gives the other party the right to sue.

Conditions of Performance

The promisor's duty to perform or not perform arises only if a certain condition does or does not occur. Also called a *qualified promise*. There are two types:

1. ***Condition precedent.*** This condition requires the occurrence or nonoccurrence of an event before a party is obligated to perform.
2. ***Condition subsequent.*** This condition provides that the occurrence or nonoccurrence of a specific event automatically excuses performance under a contract.

Discharge by Agreement

1. ***Mutual rescission.*** The parties may mutually agree to rescind an executory contract.
2. ***Novation.*** The parties may agree to the substitution of a third party for one of the original parties. The existing party is relieved of liability, and the entering party is obligated to perform the contract.
3. ***Accord and satisfaction.*** The parties may agree to settle a contract dispute. The *satisfaction* of the *accord* discharges the original contract.
4. ***Force majeure clause.*** The parties may stipulate in a contract what events will excuse performance.

Discharge by Impossibility

1. ***Impossibility of performance.*** A contract may be objectively impossible to perform because of an event.
2. ***Commercial impracticability.*** A contract may be impractical for the promisor to perform because of an event.

Unconscionable Contracts

Contracts that are oppressively unfair or unjust are called unconscionable. Also called *contracts of adhesion*.

1. ***Elements of unconscionable contracts:***
   a. The parties possessed severely unequal bargaining power.
   b. The dominant party unreasonably used its power to obtain oppressive or manifestly unfair contract terms.
   c. The adhering party had no reasonable alternative.
2. ***Remedies for unconscionability.*** Where a contract or contract clause is found to be unconscionable, the court may do one of the following:
   a. Refuse to enforce the contract.
   b. Refuse to enforce the unconscionable clause but enforce the remainder of the contract.
   c. Limit the applicability of an unconscionable clause so as to avoid any unconscionable result.

Breach of Contract

1. ***Complete performance.*** When a party renders performance exactly as required by the contract, that party's contractual duties are discharged.
2. ***Substantial performance.*** When a party renders performance that deviates only slightly from complete performance, there is a *minor breach* and the nonbreaching party may recover damages caused by the breach.
3. ***Inferior performance.*** When a party fails to perform express or implied contractual duties that impair or destroy the essence of the contract, there is a *material breach* and the nonbreaching party may either (1) rescind the contract and recover restitution or (2) affirm the contract and recover damages.

Monetary Damages

1. ***Compensatory damages.*** Compensatory damages compensate a nonbreaching party for the loss of a contract. They restore the "benefit of the bargain" to the nonbreaching party as if the contract had been fully performed.
2. ***Consequential damages.*** Consequential damages are foreseeable damages that arise from circumstances outside the contract and of which the breaching party either knew or had reason to know. Also called *special damages*.
3. ***Liquidated damages.*** Liquidated damages are damages payable upon breach of contract that are agreed on in advance by the contracting parties. Liquidated damages substitute for actual damages. A liquidated damage clause is considered a *penalty* if actual damages are clearly determinable in advance or the liquidated damages are excessive or unconscionable.

Mitigation of Damages

The law places a duty on a nonbreaching party to take reasonable efforts to avoid or reduce the resulting damages from a breach of contract. To mitigate a breach of an employment contract, the nonbreaching party must only accept "comparable" employment.

Equitable Remedies

Equitable remedies are available if the nonbreaching party cannot be adequately compensated by a legal remedy or to prevent unjust enrichment.

1. ***Specific performance.*** Specific performance is a court order that requires the breaching party to perform his or her contractual duties. It is available only if the subject matter of the contract is *unique*.
2. ***Reformation.*** Reformation permits the court to rewrite a contract to express the parties' true intention. It is available to correct clerical and mathematical errors.
3. ***Injunction.*** An injunction is a court order that prohibits a person from doing a certain act. The requesting party must show that he or she will suffer irreparable injury if the injunction is not granted.

Intentional Interference with Contractual Relations

When this tort is committed, a third party intentionally interferes with another party's contract and induces the other party to that contract to breach it, causing the nonbreaching party injury.

Internet Exercises and Case Questions

Working the Web Internet Exercises

1. For an interesting case involving genuineness of assent, go to **www.legalwa.org,** click on the Washington State Supreme and Appellate Court decisions and search for *Barnes v. Treece, 15 Wn. App. 437.*
2. While common law contract principles have general application, many contracts are regulated on an industry-wide basis, by state statutes. See **http://www.law.cornell.edu/wex/index.php/Contracts** for examples.
3. For an overview of defenses to contract claims, see **www.west.net/~smith/contracts.htm**.
4. A good case can be lost because of a statute of limitations. These statutes vary by state and by type of claim. See **www.nolo.com/encyclopedia/articles/cm/timely.html** for a summary of the statutes; find your state law at the site.
5. Additional online contract cases can be found at **http://eric_goldman.tripod.com/resources/onlinecontractcases.htm**.

Legal Environment Cases

12.1 Mutual Mistake Ron Boskett, a part-time coin dealer, purchased a dime purportedly minted in 1916 at the Denver mint for nearly $450. The fact that the D on the coin signified Denver mintage made the coin rare and valuable. Boskett sold the coin to Beachcomber Coins, Inc., a retail coin dealer, for $500. A principal of Beachcomber examined the coin for 15 to 45 minutes prior to its purchase. Soon thereafter, Beachcomber received an offer of $700 for the coin, subject to certification of its genuineness by the American Numismatic Society. When this organization labeled the coin counterfeit, Beachcomber sued Boskett to rescind the purchase of the coin. Can Beachcomber rescind the contract? *Beachcomber Coins, Inc. v. Boskett*, 400 A.2d 78, 1979 N.J.Super. Lexis 659 (N.J.)

12.2 Fraud Robert McClure owned a vehicle salvage and rebuilding business. He listed the business for sale and had a brochure printed that described the business and stated that during 1981, the business grossed $581,117 and netted $142,727. Fred H. Campbell saw the brochure and inquired about buying the business. Campbell hired a CPA to review McClure's business records and tax returns, but the CPA could not reconcile them with the income claimed for the business in the brochure. When Campbell asked McClure about the discrepancy, McClure stated that the business records and tax returns did not accurately reflect the cash flow or profits of the business because it was such a high-cash operation that much of the cash was not being reported to the Internal Revenue Service on tax returns. McClure signed a warranty that stated that the true income of the business was as represented in the brochure. Campbell bought the business based on these representations. However, the business, although operated in substantially the same manner as when owned by McClure, failed to yield a net income similar to that warranted by McClure. Evidence showed that McClure's representations were substantially overstated. Campbell sued McClure for damages for fraud. Who wins? *Campbell v. McClure*, 182 Cal.App.3d 806, 227 Cal.Rptr. 450, 1986 Cal.App. Lexis 1751 (Cal. App.)

12.3 Undue Influence Conrad Schaneman, Sr., had eight sons and five daughters. He owned four 80-acre farms in the Scottsbluff area of Nebraska. Conrad was born in Russia and could not read or write English. Prior to 1974, all of his children had frequent contact with Conrad and helped with his needs. In 1974, his eldest son, Lawrence, advised the other children that he would henceforth manage his father's business affairs. On March 18, 1975, after much urging by Lawrence, Conrad deeded the farm to Lawrence for $23,500. Evidence showed that at the time of the sale, the reasonable fair market value of the farm was between $145,000 and $160,000. At the time of the conveyance, Conrad was more than 80 years old; had deteriorated in health; suffered from heart problems, diabetes, and high and uncontrollable blood sugar levels; weighed almost 300 pounds; had difficulty breathing; could not walk more than 15 feet; and had to have a jack hoist life him into and out of the bathtub. He was for all purposes an invalid, relying on Lawrence for most of his personal needs, transportation, banking, and other business matters. After Conrad died, the conservators of the estate brought an action to cancel the deed transferring the farm to Lawrence. Can the conservators cancel the deed? *Schaneman v. Schaneman*, 291 N.W.2d 412, 1980 Neb. Lexis 823 (Neb.)

12.4 Statute of Frauds In 1955, Robert Briggs and his wife purchased a home located at 167 Lower Orchard Drive, Levittown, Pennsylvania. They made a $100 down payment and borrowed the balance of $11,600 on a 30-year mortgage. In late 1961, when the Briggs family was behind on mortgage payments, it entered into an oral contract to sell the house to Winfield and Emma Sackett if the Sacketts would pay the three months' arrearages on the loan and agree to make the future payments on the mortgage. Mrs. Briggs and Mrs. Sackett were sisters. The Sacketts paid the arrearages, moved into the house, and had lived there continuously. In 1976, Robert Briggs filed an action to void the oral contract as in violation of the Statute of Frauds and evict the Sacketts from the house. Who wins? *Briggs v. Sackett*, 418 A.2d 586, 1980 Pa.Super. Lexis 2034 (Pa. App.)

12.5 Guaranty Contract On May 17, 1979, David Brown met with Stan Steele, a loan officer with the bank of Idaho (now First Interstate Bank), to discuss borrowing $5,000 from the bank to start a new business. After learning that he did not qualify for the loan on the basis of his own financial strength, Brown told Steele that his former employers, James and Donna West of California, might be willing to guarantee the payment of the loan. On May 18, 1979, Steele talked to Mr. West, who orally stated on the telephone that he would personally guarantee the loan to Brown. Based on this guarantee, the bank loaned Brown $5,000. The bank sent a written guarantee to Mr. and Mrs. West for their signature, but it was never returned to the bank. When Brown defaulted on the loan, the bank filed suit against the Wests to recover on their guarantee contract. Are the Wests liable? *First Interstate Bank of Idaho, N.A. v. West*, 693 P.2d 1053, 1984 Ida. Lexis 600 (Idaho)

12.6 Condition Shumann Investments, Inc., hired Pace Construction Corporation, a general contractor, to build "Outlet World of Pasco County." In turn, Pace hired OBS Company, Inc., a subcontractor, to perform the framing, drywall, insulation, and stucco work on the project. The contract between Pace and OBS stipulated: "Final payment shall not become due unless and until the following conditions precedent to final payment have been satisfied . . . (c) receipt of final payment for subcontractor's work by contractor from owner." When Shumann refused to pay Pace, Pace refused to pay OBS. OBS sued Pace to recover payment. Who wins? *Pace Construction Corporation v. OBS Company, Inc.*, 531 So.2d 737, 1988 Fla.App. Lexis 4020 (Fla. App.)

12.7 Damages Raquel Welch was a movie actress who appeared in about 30 films between 1965 and 1980. She was considered a sex symbol, and her only serious dramatic role was as a roller derby queen in *Kansas City Bomber*. About 1980, Michael Phillips and David Ward developed a film package based on the John Steinbeck novella *Cannery Row*. In early 1981, Metro-Goldwyn-Mayer Film Co. (MGM) accepted to produce the project and entered into a contract with Welch to play the leading female character, a prostitute named Suzy. At 40 years old, Welch relished the chance to redirect her career toward more serious roles. Welch was to receive $250,000 from MGM, with payment being divided into weekly increments during filming. Filming began on December 1, 1980. On December 22, 1980, MGM fired Welch and replaced her with another actress, Debra Winger. Welch sued MGM to recover the balance of $194,444 that remained unpaid under the contract. Who wins? *Welch v. Metro-Goldwyn-Mayer Film Co.*, 207 Cal.App.3d 164, 254 Cal.Rptr. 645, 1988 Cal.App. Lexis 1202 (Cal. App.)

12.8 Damages On August 28, 1979, Ptarmigan Investment Company, a partnership, entered into a contract with Gundersons, Inc., a South Dakota corporation in the business of golf course construction. The contract provided that Gundersons would construct a golf course for Ptarmigan for a contract price of $1,294,129. Gundersons immediately started work and completed about one-third of the work by late November 1979, when bad weather forced cessation of most work. Ptarmigan paid Gundersons for the work to that date. In the spring of 1980, Ptarmigan ran out of funds and was unable to pay for the completion of the golf course. Gundersons sued Ptarmigan and its individual partners to recover the lost profits that it would have made on the remaining two-thirds of the contract. Can Gundersons recover these lost profits as damages? *Gundersons, Inc. v. Ptarmigan Investment Company*, 678 P.2d 1061, 1983 Colo.App. Lexis 1133 (Colo. App.)

12.9 Liquidated Damages In December 1974, H. S. Perlin Company, Inc. (Perlin), and Morse Signal Devices of San Diego entered into a contract whereby Morse agreed to provide burglar and fire alarm service to Perlin's coin and stamp store. Perlin paid $50 per month for this service. The contract contained a liquidated damage clause by Perlin based on Morse's failure of service. During the evening of August 25, 1980, a burglary occurred at Perlin's store. Before entering the store, the burglars cut a telephone line that ran from the burglar system in Perlin's store to Morse's central location. When the line was cut, a signal indicated the interruption of service at Morse's central location. Inexplicably, Morse took no further steps to investigate the interruption of service at Perlin's store. The burglars stole stamps and coins with a wholesale value of $958,000, and Perlin did not have insurance against this loss. Perlin sued Morse to recover damages. Is the liquidated damage clause enforceable? *H. S. Perlin Company, Inc. v. Morse Signal Devices of San Diego*, 209 Cal.App.3d 1289, 258 Cal.Rptr. 1, 1989 Cal.App. Lexis 400 (Cal. App.)

12.10 Specific Performance Liz Claiborne, Inc., is a large maker of women's better sportswear in the United States and a well-known name in fashion, with sales of more than $1 billion a year. Claiborne distributes its products through 9,000 retail outlets in the United States. Avon Products, Inc., is a major producer of fragrances, toiletries, and cosmetics, with sales of more than $3 billion a year. Claiborne, which desired to promote its well-known name on perfumes and cosmetics, entered into a joint venture with Avon whereby Claiborne would make available its name, trademarks, and marketing experience, and Avon would engage in the procurement and manufacture of the fragrances, toiletries, and cosmetics. The parties would equally share the financial requirements of the joint venture. In 1986, its first year of operation, the joint venture had sales of more than $16 million. In the second year, sales increased to $26 million, making it one of the fastest-growing fragrance and cosmetic lines in the country. In 1987, Avon sought to uncouple the joint venture. Avon thereafter refused to procure and manufacture the line of fragrances and cosmetics for the joint venture. When Claiborne could not obtain the necessary fragrances and cosmetics from any other source for the fall/Christmas season, Claiborne sued Avon for breach of contract, seeking specific performance of the contract by Avon. Is specific performance an appropriate remedy in this case? *Liz Claiborne, Inc. v. Avon Products, Inc.*, 530 N.Y.S.2d 425, 141 A.D.2d 329, 1988 N.Y.App.Div.Lexis 6423 (N.Y.Sup. App.)

12.11 Injunction In 1982, Anita Baker, a then-unknown singer, signed a multiyear recording contract with Beverly Glen Music, Inc. Baker recorded a record album for Beverly Glen that was moderately successful. After having some difficulties with

Beverly Glen, Baker was offered a considerably more lucrative contract by Warner Communications, Inc. Baker accepted the Warner offer and informed Beverly Glen that she would not complete her contract because she had entered into an agreement with Warner. Beverly Glen sued Baker and Warner and sought an injunction to prevent Baker from performing as a singer for Warner. Is an injunction an appropriate remedy in this case? *Beverly Glen Music, Inc. v. Warner Communications, Inc.*, 178 Cal.App.3d 1142, 224 Cal.Rptr. 260, 1986 Cal.App. Lexis 2729 (Cal. App.)

Ethics in Business

12.12 The First Baptist Church of Moultrie, Georgia, invited bids for the construction of a music, education, and recreation building. The bids, which were to be opened on May 15, 1986, were to each be accompanied by a bid bond of 5 percent of the bid amount. Barber Contracting Company submitted a bid in the amount of $1,860,000. A bid bond in the amount of 5 percent of the bid—$93,000—was issued by The American Insurance Company. The bids were opened by the church on May 15, 1986, as planned, and Barber's was the lowest bid.

On May 16, 1986, Albert W. Barber, the president of Barber Contracting Company, informed the church that its bid was in error and should have been $143,120 higher. The error was caused in totaling the materials costs on Barber's estimate worksheets. The church had not been provided these worksheets. On May 20, 1986, Barber sent a letter to the church, stating that it was withdrawing its bid. The next day, the church sent a construction contract to Barber, containing the original bid amount. When Barber refused to sign the contract and refused to do the work for the original contract price, the church signed a contract with the second-lowest bidder, H & H Construction and Supply Company, Inc., to complete the work for $1,919,272. The church sued Barber Contracting Company and The American Insurance Company, seeking to recover the amount of the bid bond. *First Baptist Church of Moultrie v. Barber Contracting Co.*, 377 S.E.2d 717, 1989 Ga.App. Lexis 25 (Ga. App.)

Ethics Issues

1. Did Barber act ethically in trying to get out of the contract?
2. Did the church act ethically in trying to enforce Barber's bid?
3. Who wins? Why?

Endnotes

1. 159 Eng.Rep. 376 (1864).
2. UCC Section 2-201(1).

13

Sales and Lease Contracts

"Commercial law lies within a narrow compass, and is far purer and freer from defects than any other part of the system."

—Henry Peter Brougham
House of Commons, February 7, 1828

Chapter Objectives

After studying this chapter, you should be able to:

1. Define sales contracts governed by Article 2 of the UCC.
2. Define lease contracts governed by Article 2A of the UCC.
3. Describe the formation and performance of sales and lease contracts.
4. List and describe the remedies for the breach of sales and lease contracts.
5. List and describe express and implied warranties.

Chapter Contents

- Article 2 (Sales)
- Article 2A (Leases)
- Formation of Sales and Lease Contracts
- Risk of Loss
- Performance and Remedies
- Warranties

In 1949, the National Conference of Commissioners on Uniform State Laws, a body of legal scholars, promulgated the **Uniform Commercial Code (UCC)**. The UCC, a model act that is divided into articles, sets forth uniform rules that govern many commercial transactions. Before the UCC can become law in a state, that state must enact the UCC as its commercial law statute. Every state (except Louisiana, which has adopted only parts of the UCC) has enacted the UCC as a commercial statute. Many states have enacted the UCC verbatim, while several states have modified the UCC upon adoption. The UCC is continually being revised to reflect changes in modern commercial practices and technology.

Article 2 (Sales) of the UCC governs the *sale* of personal property. **Article 2A (Leases)** of the UCC governs the *lease* of personal property. These articles provide clear rules for the formation and performance of sales and lease contracts. This chapter discusses sales and lease contracts governed by Article 2 and Article 2A of the UCC.

Automobile. Many automobiles are sold, while others are leased. The provisions of Article 2 of the UCC apply to sales contracts, while the provisions of Article 2A of the UCC apply to lease contracts.

Article 2 (Sales)

All states except Louisiana have adopted some version of **Article 2 (Sales)** of the UCC. Article 2 is also applied by federal courts to sales contracts governed by federal law. Article 2 has recently been revised. This article, referred to as **Revised Article 2**, has been adopted by some states.

What Is a Sale?

Article 2 of the UCC applies to transactions in goods [UCC 2–102]. All states have held that Article 2 applies to the sale of goods. A **sale** consists of the passing of title from a seller to a buyer for a price [UCC 2–106(1)]. For example, the purchase of a computer is a sale subject to Article 2, whether the computer was paid for by cash, credit card, or another form of consideration (see Exhibit 13.1).

sale
The passing of title from a seller to a buyer for a price.

Exhibit 13.1
Sales Transaction

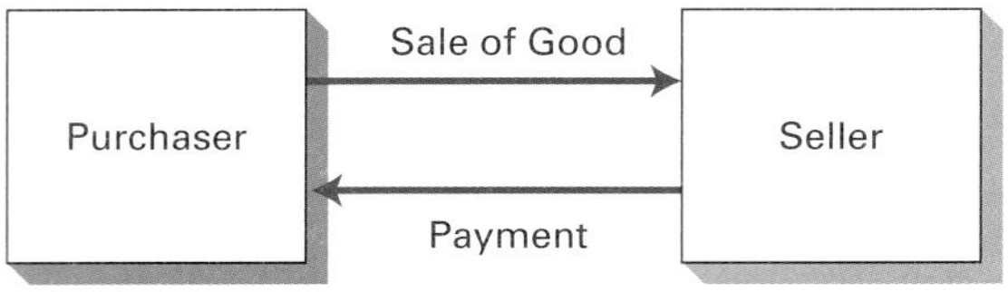

What Are Goods?

goods
Tangible things that are movable at the time of their identification to the contract.

Goods are defined as tangible things that are movable at the time of their identification to the contract [UCC 2–105(1)]. Specially manufactured goods and the unborn young of animals are examples of goods. Certain items are not considered goods and are not subject to Article 2. They include:

1. Money and intangible items, such as stocks, bonds, and patents, are not tangible goods.
2. Real estate is not a tangible good because it is not movable [UCC 2–105(1)]. Minerals, structures, growing crops, and other things that are severable from real estate may be classified as goods subject to Article 2, however. For example, the sale and removal of a chandelier in a house is a sale of goods subject to Article 2 because its removal would not materially harm the realty. The sale and removal of the furnace, however, would be a sale of real property because its removal would cause material harm [UCC 2–107(2)].

Who Is a Merchant?

merchant
A person who (1) deals in the goods of the kind involved in the transaction or (2) by his or her occupation holds himself or herself out as having knowledge or skill peculiar to the goods involved in the transaction.

Generally, Article 2 of the UCC applies to all sales contracts, whether they involve merchants or not. However, Article 2 contains several provisions that either apply only to merchants or impose a greater-than-usual duty on merchants. UCC 2–104(1) defines a **merchant** as (1) a person who deals in the goods of the kind involved in the transaction or (2) a person who by his or her occupation holds himself or herself out as having knowledge or skill peculiar to the goods involved in the transaction. For example, a sporting goods dealer is a merchant with respect to sporting goods but is not if he sells his lawn mower to a neighbor. The courts disagree as to whether farmers are merchants within this definition.

Rodeo Drive, Beverly Hills, California. Businesses offer a variety of goods for sale based on contracts subject to the Uniform Commercial Code (UCC).

Article 2A (Leases)

Personal property leases are a billion-dollar industry. Consumer leases of automobiles or equipment and commercial leases of such items as aircraft and industrial machinery fall into this category. In the past, these transactions were governed by a combination of common law principles, real estate law, and reference to Article 2. Some of these legal rules and concepts do not quite fit lease transactions.

Article 2A of the UCC was promulgated in 1987. This article, which is cited as the **Uniform Commercial Code—Leases**, directly addresses personal property leases [UCC 2A–101]. It establishes a comprehensive, uniform law covering the formation, performance, and default of leases in goods [UCC 2A–102, 2A–103(h)].

Article 2A (Leases)
An article of the UCC that governs the lease of goods.

Article 2A is similar to Article 2. In fact, many Article 2 provisions were changed to reflect leasing terminology and practices that carried over to Article 2A.

Definition of Lease

A **lease** is a transfer of the right to the possession and use of the named goods for a set term in return for certain consideration [UCC 2A–103(1)(i)(x)]. The leased goods can be anything from a hand tool leased to an individual for a few hours to a complex line of industrial equipment leased to a multinational corporation for a number of years.

In ordinary lease, the **lessor** is the person who transfers the right of possession and use of goods under a lease [UCC 2A–103(1)(p)]. The **lessee** is the person who acquires the right to possession and use of goods under a lease [UCC 2A-103(1)(n)].

lease
A transfer of the right to the possession and use of the named goods for a set term in return for certain consideration.

lessor
The person who transfers the right of possession and use of goods under a lease.

lessee
The person who acquires the right to possession and use of goods under a lease.

Consider This Example Dow Chemical Company decides to lease robotic equipment to manufacture most of its products. Ingersoll-Rand Corporation, which manufactures robotic equipment, enters into a lease contract to lease robotic equipment to Dow Chemical. Ingersoll-Rand is the lessor, and Dow Chemical is the lessee (see Exhibit 13.2).

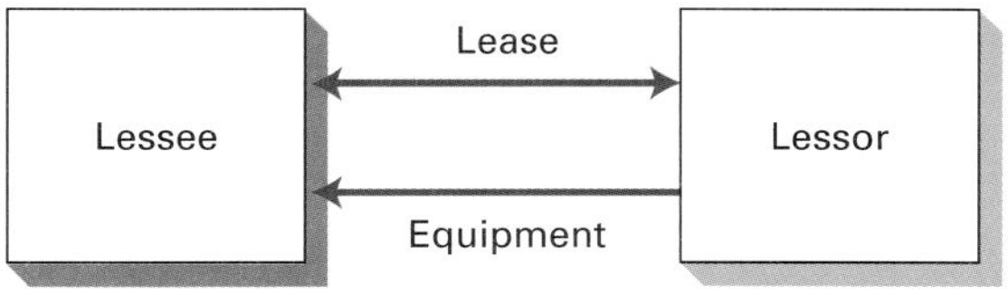

Exhibit 13.2
Lease

Formation of Sales and Lease Contracts

As with general contracts, the formation of sales and lease contracts requires an offer and an acceptance. The UCC-established rules for each of these elements often differ considerably from common law.

A contract for the sale or lease of goods may be made in any manner sufficient to show agreement, including conduct by both parties that recognizes the existence of a contract [UCC 2–204(1), 2A–204(1)]. Under the UCC, an agreement sufficient to constitute a contract for the sale or lease of goods may be found even though the moment of its making is undetermined [UCC 2–204(2), 2A–204(2)].

Open Terms

Sometimes the parties to a sale or lease contract leave open a major term in the contract. The UCC is tolerant of open terms. According to UCC 2–204(3) and 2A–204(3), a contract does not fail because of indefiniteness if (1) the parties intended to make a contract and (2) there is a reasonably certain basis for giving an appropriate remedy. In effect, certain **open terms** are permitted to be "read into" a sales or lease contract. This rule is commonly referred to as the **gap-filling rule**.

gap-filling rule
A rule that says an open term can be "read into" a contract.

Some examples of terms that are commonly left open are:

- ***Open price term.*** If a sales contract does not contain a specific price (**open price term**), a "reasonable price" is implied at the time of delivery. The contract may provide that a price is to be fixed by a market rate (e.g., a commodities market), as set or recorded by a third person or agency (e.g., a government agency), or by another standard, either upon delivery or on a set date. If the agreed-upon standard is unavailable when the price is to be set, a reasonable price is implied at the time of delivery of the goods [UCC 2–305(1)].

  A seller or buyer who reserves the right to fix a price must do so in good faith [UCC 2–305(2)]. When one of the parties fails to fix an open price term, the other party may opt either (1) to treat the contract as canceled or (2) to fix a reasonable price for the goods [UCC 2–305(3)].
- ***Open payment term.*** If the parties to a sales contract do not agree on payment terms, payment is due at the time and place at which the buyer is to receive the goods. If delivery is authorized and made by way of document of title, payment is due at the time and place at which the buyer is to receive the document of title, regardless of where the goods are to be received [UCC 2–310].
- ***Open delivery term.*** If the parties to a sales contract do not agree to the time, place, and manner of delivery of the goods, the place of delivery is the seller's place of business. If the seller does not have a place of business, delivery is to be made at the seller's residence. If identified goods are located at some other place, and both parties know of this fact at the time of contracting, that place is the place of delivery [UCC 2–308].

  Where the goods are to be shipped but the shipper is not named, the seller is obligated to make the shipping arrangements. Such arrangements must be made in good faith and within limits of commercial reasonableness [UCC 2–311(2)].
- ***Open time term.*** If the parties to a sales contract do not set a specific time of performance for any obligation under the contract, the contract must be performed within a reasonable time. If the sales contract provides for successive performance over an unspecified period of time, the contract is valid for a reasonable time [UCC 2–309].
- ***Open assortment term.*** If the assortment of goods to a sales contract is left open, the buyer is given the option of choosing those goods. For example, suppose Macy's contracts to purchase 1,000 dresses from Liz Claiborne, Inc. The contract is silent as to the assortment of colors of the dresses. The buyer may pick the assortment of colors for the dresses from the seller's stock. The buyer must make the selection in good faith and within limits set by commercial reasonableness [UCC 2–311(2)].

The foundation of justice is good faith.

Cicero
De Officiis, Bk. I, Ch. VII
(106–43 B.C.)

Contemporary Trend

UCC "Firm Offer" Rule

Recall that the common law of contracts allows the offeror to revoke an offer any time prior to its acceptance. The only exception allowed by the common law is an *option contract* (i.e., where the offeree pays the offeror consideration to keep the offer open).

The UCC recognizes another exception, which is called the **firm offer rule**. This rule states that a *merchant* who (1) offers to buy, sell, or lease goods and (2) gives a written and signed assurance on a separate form that the offer will be held open cannot revoke the offer for the time stated or, if no time is stated, for a reasonable time. The maximum amount of time permitted under this rule is three months [UCC 2–205, 2A–205].

Consider This Example On June 1, a merchant-seller offers to sell a Mercedes-Benz to a buyer for $60,000. The merchant-seller signs a written assurance to keep that offer open until August 30. On July 1, the merchant-seller sells the car to another buyer. On August 21, the original offeree tenders $60,000 for the car. The merchant-seller is liable to the original offeree for breach of contract. ■

Acceptance

Both common law and the UCC provide that a contract is created when the offeree (i.e., the buyer or lessee) sends an acceptance to the offeror, not when the offeror receives the acceptance. For example, a contract is made when the acceptance letter is delivered to the post office. The contract remains valid even if the post office loses the letter.

Unless otherwise unambiguously indicated by language or circumstance, an offer to make a sales or lease contract may be accepted in any manner and by any reasonable medium of acceptance [UCC 2–206(1)(a), 2A–206(1)]. Applications of this rule are discussed in the following paragraphs.

Contemporary Trend

Nonmerchant: Proposed Additional Terms

If one or both parties to a sales contract are nonmerchants, any additional terms are considered **proposed additions** to the contract. The proposed additions do not constitute a counteroffer or extinguish the original offer. If the offeree's proposed additions are accepted by the original offeror, they become part of the contract. If they are not accepted, the sales contract is formed on the basis of the terms of the original offer [UCC 2–207(2)].

Consider This Example A salesperson at a Lexus dealership offers to sell a top-of-the-line coupe to a buyer for $47,000. The buyer replies, "I accept your offer, but I would like to have a satellite radio in the car." The satellite radio is a proposed addition to the contract. If the salesperson agrees, the contract between the parties consists of the terms of the original offer plus the additional term regarding the satellite radio. If the salesperson rejects the proposed addition, the sales contract consists of the terms of the original offer because the buyer made a definite expression of acceptance. ■

Accommodation Shipment

A shipment of nonconforming goods does not constitute an acceptance if the seller reasonably notifies the buyer that the shipment is offered only as an **accommodation** to the buyer [UCC 2–206(1)(b)]. For example, suppose a buyer offers to purchase 500 red candles from a seller. The seller's red candles are temporarily out of stock. The seller sends the buyer 500 green candles and notifies the buyer that these candles are being sent as an accommodation. The seller has not accepted (or breached) the contract. The accommodation is a counteroffer from the seller to the buyer. The buyer is free either to accept or to reject the counteroffer.

accommodation
A shipment that is offered to the buyer as a replacement for the original shipment when the original shipment cannot be filled.

Contemporary Trend

Merchants: "Battle of the Forms"

When merchants negotiate sales contracts, they often exchange preprinted forms; these "boilerplate" forms usually contain terms that favor the drafter. Thus, an offeror who sends a standard form contract as an offer to the offeree may receive an acceptance drafted on the offeree's own form contract. This scenario—commonly called the **battle of the forms**—raises important

(continued)

Contemporary Trend
(Continued)

questions: Is there a contract? If so, what are its terms? The UCC provides guidance in answering these questions.

Under UCC 2–207(2), if both parties are merchants, any additional terms contained in an acceptance become part of the sales contract unless (1) the offer expressly limits acceptance to the terms of the offer, (2) the additional terms materially alter the terms of the original contract, or (3) the offeror notifies the offeree that he or she objects to the additional terms within a reasonable time after receiving the offeree's modified acceptance.

The most important point in the battle of the forms is that there is no contract if the additional terms so materially alter the terms of the original offer that the parties cannot agree on the contract. This fact-specific determination is made by the courts on a case-by-case basis. ■

UCC Statute of Frauds

UCC Statute of Frauds
A rule that requires all contracts for the sale of goods costing $500 or more and lease contracts involving payments of $1,000 or more to be in writing.

The UCC includes **Statute of Frauds** provisions that apply to all sales and lease contracts. All contracts for the sale of goods costing $500 or more and lease contracts involving payments of $1,000 or more must be in writing [UCC 2–201(1), 2A–201(1)]. The writing must be sufficient to indicate that a contract has been made between the parties. Except as discussed in the paragraphs that follow, the writing must be signed by the party against whom enforcement is sought or by his or her authorized agent or broker. If a contract that falls within these parameters is not written, it is unenforceable.

Consider This Example A seller orally agrees to sell her computer to a buyer for $550. When the buyer tenders the purchase price, the seller asserts the Statute of Frauds and refuses to sell the computer to him. The seller is correct. The contract must be in writing to be enforceable because the contract price for the computer exceeds $499.99.

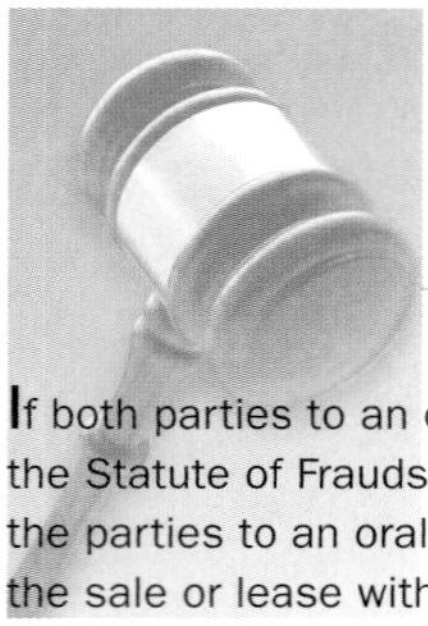

Contemporary Trend
UCC Written Confirmation Rule

If both parties to an oral sale or lease contract are merchants, the Statute of Frauds requirement can be satisfied if (1) one of the parties to an oral agreement sends a written confirmation of the sale or lease within a reasonable time after contracting and (2) the other merchant does not give written notice of an objection to the contract within 10 days after receiving the confirmation. This situation is true even though the party receiving the written confirmation has not signed it. The only stipulations are that the confirmation be sufficient and that the party to whom it was sent have reason to know its contents [UCC 2–201(2)].

Consider This Example A merchant-seller in Chicago orally contracts by telephone to sell goods to a merchant-buyer in Phoenix for $25,000. Within a reasonable time after contracting, the merchant-seller sends a sufficient written confirmation to the buyer. The buyer, who has reason to know the contents of the confirmation, fails to object to the contents of the confirmation in writing within 10 days after receiving it. The Statute of Frauds has been met, and the buyer cannot thereafter raise it against enforcement of the contract. ■

Concept Summary Comparison of Contract Law and the Law of Sales

Topic	Common Law of Contracts	UCC Law of Sales
Definiteness	Contract must contain all the material terms of the parties' agreement.	The UCC gap-filling rule permits terms to be implied if the parties intended to make a contract [UCC 2–204].
Irrevocable offers	Option contracts.	Option contracts. Firm offers by merchants to keep an offer open are binding up to three months without any consideration [UCC 2–205].
Counteroffers	Acceptance must be a mirror image of the offer. A counteroffer rejects and terminates the offer.	Additional terms of an acceptance become part of the contract if (1) they do not materially alter the terms of the offer and (2) the offeror does not object within a reasonable time after reviewing the acceptance [UCC 2–207].
Statute of Frauds	Writing must be signed by the party against whom enforcement is sought.	Writing may be enforced against a party who has not signed it if (1) both parties are merchants, (2) one party sends a written confirmation of oral agreement within a reasonable time after contracting, and (3) the other party does not give written notice of objection within 10 days after receiving the confirmation [UCC 2–201].

Identification of Goods

The identification of goods is rather simple. It means distinguishing the goods named in a contract from the seller's or lessor's other goods. The seller or lessor retains the risk of loss of the goods until he or she identifies them to a sales or lease contract. Further, UCC 2–401(1) and 2–501 prevent title to goods from passing from the seller to the buyer unless the goods are identified to the sales contract. In a lease transaction, title to the leased goods remains with the lessor or a third party. It does not pass to the lessee.

Passage of Title

Once the goods that are the subject of a contract exist and have been identified, title to the goods may be transferred from the seller to the buyer. Under UCC 2–401(1), **title** to goods passes from the seller to the buyer in any manner and on any conditions explicitly agreed upon by the parties. If the parties do not agree to a specific time, title passes to the buyer when and where the seller's performance with reference to the physical delivery is completed. This point in time is determined by applying the following rules [UCC 2–401(2)]:

title
Legal, tangible evidence of ownership of goods.

shipment contract
A contract that requires the seller to ship the goods to the buyer via a common carrier.

- ***Shipment contract.*** A **shipment contract** requires the seller to ship the goods to the buyer via a common carrier. The seller is required to (1) make proper shipping arrangements and (2) deliver the goods into the carrier's hands. Title passes to the buyer at the time and place of shipment [UCC-2–401(2)(a)].

destination contract

A contract that requires the seller to deliver the goods either to the buyer's place of business or to another destination specified in the sales contract.

- ***Destination contract.*** A **destination contract** requires the seller to deliver the goods either to the buyer's place of business or to another destination specified in the sales contract. Title passes to the buyer when the seller tenders delivery of the goods at the specified destination [UCC 2–401(2)(b)].

Risk of Loss

In the case of sales contracts, common law placed the risk of loss of goods on the party who had title to the goods. Article 2 of the UCC rejects this notion and allows the parties to a sales contract to agree among themselves who will bear the risk of loss if the goods subject to the contract are lost or destroyed. If the parties do not have a specific agreement concerning the assessment of the risk of loss, the UCC mandates who will bear the risk.

Carrier Cases

Unless otherwise agreed, goods that are shipped via carrier (e.g., railroad, ship, truck) are considered to be sent pursuant to a *shipment contract* or a *destination contract.* Absent any indication to the contrary, sales contracts are presumed to be shipment contracts rather than destination contracts.

Shipment Contracts The risk of loss passes to the buyer when the seller delivers the conforming goods to the carrier. The buyer bears the risk of loss of the goods during transportation [UCC 2–509(1)(a)].

Shipment contracts are created in two ways. The first requires the use of the term *shipment contract.* The second requires the use of one of the following delivery terms: *F.O.B.*, *F.A.S.*, or *C.I.F.* (see the following "Contemporary Trend" box).

Destination Contracts A destination contract requires the seller to bear the risk of loss of the goods during their transportation. Thus, with the exception of a no-arrival, no-sale contract, the seller is required to replace any goods lost in transit. The buyer does not have to pay for destroyed goods. The risk of loss does not pass until the goods are tendered to the buyer at the specified destination [UCC 2–509(1)(b)].

Unless otherwise agreed, destination contracts are created in two ways. The first method requires the use of the term *destination contract.* The alternative method requires the use of the following delivery terms: *F.O.B. place of destination*, *ex-ship*, or *no-arrival, no-sale contract.*

Contemporary Trend

Shipping Terms

The following are commonly used shipping terms:

- **F.O.B. (free on board) point of shipment** (e.g., F.O.B. Anchorage, Alaska) requires the seller to arrange to ship goods and put the goods in the carrier's possession. The seller bears the expense and risk of loss until this is done [UCC 2–319(1)(a)].
- **F.A.S. (free alongside) or F.A.S. *vessel*, *port of shipment*** (e.g., F.A.S. *The Gargoyle*, New Orleans) requires the seller to deliver and tender the goods alongside the named vessel

or on the dock designated and provided by the buyer. The seller bears the expense and risk of loss until this is done [UCC 2–319(2)(a)].

- **C.I.F. (cost, insurance, and freight) and C. & F. (cost and freight)** are pricing terms that indicate the cost for which the seller is responsible. These terms require the seller to bear the expense and the risk of loss of loading the goods on the carrier [UCC 2–320(1)(3)].
- **F.O.B. *place of destination*** (e.g., F.O.B. Miami, Florida) requires the seller to bear the expense and risk of loss until the goods are tendered to the buyer at the place of destination [UCC 2–319(1)(b)].
- **Ex-ship (from the carrying vessel)** requires the seller to bear the expense and risk of loss until the goods are unloaded from the ship at its port of destination [UCC 2–322(1)(b)].
- **No-arrival, no-sale contract** requires the seller to bear the expense and risk of loss of the goods during transportation. However, the seller is under no duty to deliver replacement goods to the buyer because there is no contractual stipulation that the goods will arrive at the appointed destination [UCC 2–324(a)(b)]. ■

No Movement of Goods

Sometimes a sales contract stipulates that the buyer is to pick up the goods, either at the seller's place of business or another specified location. This type of arrangement raises a question: Who bears the risk of loss if the goods are destroyed or stolen after the contract date and before the buyer picks up the goods from the seller? The UCC provides two different rules for this situation. One applies to *merchant-sellers* and the other to *nonmerchant-sellers* [UCC 2–509(3)]:

- ***Merchant-seller.*** If the seller is a merchant, the risk of loss does not pass to the buyer until the goods are received. In other words, a merchant-seller bears the risk of loss between the time of contracting and the time the buyer picks up the goods. For example, on June 1, Tyus Motors, a merchant, contracts to sell a new automobile to a consumer. Tyus Motors keeps the car for a few days after contracting to prep it. During this period, the car is destroyed by fire. Under the UCC, Tyus Motors bears the risk of loss because of its merchant status.
- ***Nonmerchant-seller.*** Nonmerchant-sellers pass the risk of loss to the buyer upon "tender of delivery" of the goods. Tender of delivery occurs when the seller (1) places or holds the goods available for the buyer to take delivery and (2) notifies the buyer of this fact. For example, June 1, a nonmerchant contracts to sell his automobile to his next-door neighbor. Delivery of the car is tendered on June 3, and the buyer is notified of this. The buyer tells the seller he will pick up the car in a few days. The car is destroyed by fire before the buyer picks it up. In this situation, the buyer bears the risk of loss because (1) the seller is a nonmerchant and (2) delivery was tendered on June 3. If the car were destroyed on June 2—that is, before delivery was tendered—the seller would bear the risk of loss.

The law is not a series of calculating machines where definitions and answers come tumbling out when the right levers are pushed.

William O. Douglas
The Dissent A Safeguard of Democracy (1948)

International Law

International Trade Terms

Trade abbreviations, such as F.O.B., C.I.F., etc., are widely used in international contracts. The most widely used trade terms are those published by the International Chamber of Commerce. Called *Incoterms*, they are well known throughout the world. Their use in international sales is encouraged by trade councils, courts, and international lawyers. The United Nations Convention on Contracts for the International Sale of Goods (CISG) allows parties to incorporate trade terms of their choosing.

Parties who adopt the *Incoterms* or any other trade terms in their international contracts should make sure they express their desire clearly. For example, a contract might refer to F.O.B. (*Incoterms 1990*) or C.I.F. (*U.S. UCC*). ■

Singapore.

Lease Contracts

The parties to a lease contract may agree as to who will bear the risk of loss of the goods if they are lost or destroyed. If the parties do not so agree, the UCC supplies the following rules for risk of loss:

1. In the case of an ordinary lease, the risk of loss is retained by the lessor. [UCC 2A–219].
2. If a tender of delivery of goods fails to conform to the lease contract, the risk of loss remains with the lessor or supplier until cure or acceptance [UCC 2A–220(1)(a)].

Insuring Against Loss of Goods

To protect against financial loss that would occur if goods were damaged, destroyed, lost, or stolen, the parties to sales and lease contracts should purchase insurance against such loss. If the goods are then lost or damaged, the insured party receives reimbursement from the insurance company for the loss.

To purchase insurance, a party must have an *insurable interest* in the goods. A seller has an insurable interest in goods as long as he or she retains title or has a security interest in the goods. A lessor retains an insurable interest in the goods during the term of the lease. A buyer or lessee obtains an insurable interest in the goods when they are identified in the sales or lease contract. Both the buyer and seller or the lessee and lessor can have an insurable interest in the goods at the same time [UCC 2–501, 2A–218].

To obtain and maintain proper insurance coverage on goods, a contacting party should:

- Determine the value of goods subject to the sales or lease contract.
- Purchase insurance from a reputable insurance company to cover the goods subject to the contract.
- Maintain the insurance by paying the premiums when they are due.
- Immediately file the proper claim and supporting documentation with an insurance company if the goods are damaged, destroyed, lost, or stolen.

Ethics in Business

Sales of Goods by Nonowners

Sometimes people sell goods even though they do not hold valid title to them. The UCC anticipated many of the problems this situation could cause and established the following rules.

Void Title and Lease: Stolen Goods In a case in which a buyer purchases goods or a lessee leases goods from a thief who has stolen them, the purchaser does not acquire title to the goods, and the lessee does not acquire any leasehold interest in the goods. The real owner can reclaim the goods from the purchaser or lessee [UCC 2–403(1)]. This is called **void title**.

Consider This Example Suppose someone steals a truckload of Sony television sets that are owned by Sears. The thief resells the televisions to City-Mart, which does not know that the goods were stolen. If Sears finds out where the televisions are, it can reclaim them. Because the thief had no title in the goods, title was not transferred to City-Mart. City-Mart's only recourse is against the thief, if he or she can be found.

Voidable Title: Sales or Lease of Goods to Good Faith Purchasers for Value A seller or lessor has **voidable title** to goods if the goods were obtained by fraud, if a check is later dishonored, or if he or she impersonates another person. A person with voidable title to goods can transfer good title to a **good faith purchaser for value** or a **good faith subsequent lessee**. A good faith purchaser or lessee for value is someone who pays sufficient consideration or rent for the goods to the person he or she honestly believes has good title to those goods [UCC 2–201(1), 1–201(44)(d)]. The real owner cannot reclaim goods from such a purchaser [UCC 2–403(1)].

Consider This Example Suppose a person buys a Rolex watch from his neighbor for nearly fair market value. It is later discovered that the seller obtained the watch from a jewelry store with a "bounced check." The jewelry store cannot reclaim the watch because the second purchaser purchased the watch in good faith and for value.

Assume instead that the purchaser bought the watch from a stranger for far less than fair market value. It is later discovered that the seller obtained the watch from a jewelry store by fraud. The jewelry store can reclaim the watch because the second purchaser was not a good faith purchaser for value.

Entrustment Rule The rule found in UCC 2–403(2) holds that if an owner **entrusts** the possession of his or her goods to a merchant who deals in goods of that kind, the merchant has the power to transfer all rights (including title) in the goods to a **buyer in the ordinary course of business**. The real owner cannot reclaim the goods from the buyer.

Consider This Example Kim Jones brings her computer to The Computer Store to be repaired. The Computer Store both sells and services computers. Jones leaves (entrusts) her computer at the store until it is repaired. The Computer Store sells her computer to Harold Green. Green, a buyer in the ordinary course of business, acquires title to the computer. Jones cannot reclaim the computer from Green. Her only recourse is against The Computer Store.

The entrustment rule also applies to leases. If a lessor entrusts the possession of his or her goods to a lessee who is a merchant who deals in goods of that kind, the merchant-lessee has the power to transfer all the lessor's and lessee's rights in the goods to a buyer or sublessee in the ordinary course of business [UCC 2A–305(2)].

Ethics Issues

1. What is the public policy underlying the void title rule concerning stolen goods? Explain.
2. What purpose does the good faith purchaser in value rule serve? Explain.
3. Does the entrustment rule place the risk of loss on the proper party? Explain. ■

Performance and Remedies

Tender of delivery, or the transfer and delivery of goods to the buyer or lessee in accordance with a sales or lease contract, is the seller's or lessor's basic obligation [UCC 2–301]. Tender of delivery requires the seller or lessor to (1) put and hold conforming goods at the buyer's or lessee's disposition and (2) give the buyer or lessee any notification reasonably necessary to enable delivery of goods. The parties may agree as to the time, place, and manner or delivery. If there is no special agreement, tender must be made at a reasonable hour, and the goods must be kept available for a reasonable period of time.

tender of delivery
The obligation of a seller to transfer and deliver goods to a buyer in accordance with a sales contract.

Perfect Tender Rule

The seller or lessor is under a duty to deliver conforming goods. If the goods or tender of delivery fails in any respect to conform to the contract, the buyer or lessee may opt either (1) to reject the whole shipment, (2) to accept the whole shipment, or (3) to reject part and accept part of the shipment. This option is referred to as the **perfect tender rule** [UCC 1–601, 2A–509].

perfect tender rule
A rule that says if the goods or tender of a delivery fail in any respect to conform to the contract, the buyer may opt either (1) to reject the whole shipment, (2) to accept the whole shipment, or (3) to reject part and accept part of the shipment.

Consider This Example A sales contract requires the seller to deliver 100 shirts to a buyer. When the buyer inspects the delivered goods, it is discovered that 80 shirts conform to the contract and 20 shirts do not conform. Pursuant to the perfect tender rule, the buyer may reject the entire shipment. If the buyer accepts nonconforming goods, the buyer may seek remedies against the seller.

Payment

A proceeding may be perfectly legal and may yet be opposed to sound commercial principles.

L. J. Lindley
Verner v. General and Commercial Trust (1894)

Goods that are accepted must be paid for [UCC 2–607(1)]. Unless the parties to a contract agree otherwise, payment is due from a buyer when and where the goods are delivered, even if the place of delivery is the same as the place of shipment. Buyers often purchase goods on credit extended by the seller. A lessee must pay lease payments in accordance with the lease contract [UCC 2A–516(1)].

Seller's and Lessor's Remedies

Various remedies are available to sellers and lessors if a buyer or lessee breaches a contract. These remedies are set forth in Exhibit 13.3.

Exhibit 13.3 Seller's and Lessor's Remedies

Possession of Goods at Time of Buyer's Breach	Seller's or Lessor's Remedies
Goods in the possession of the seller	1. Withhold delivery of the goods [UCC 2–703(a), 2A–523(1)(c)]. 2. Demand payment in cash if the buyer is insolvent [UCC 2–702(1), 2A–525(1)]. 3. Resell or re-lease the goods and recover the difference between the contract or lease price and the resale or re-lease price [UCC 2–706, 2A–527]. 4. Sue for breach of contract and recover as damages either: a. The difference between the market price and contract price [UCC 2–708(1), 2A–528(1)] or b. Lost profits [UCC 2–708(2), 2A–528(2)]. 5. Cancel the contract [UCC 2–703(f), 2A–523(1)(a)].
Goods in the possession of a carrier or bailee	1. Stop goods in transit [UCC 2–705(1), 2A–526(1)]. a. Carload, truckload, planeload, or larger shipment if the buyer is solvent. b. Any size shipment if the buyer is insolvent.
Goods in the possession of the buyer	1. Sue to recover the purchase price or rent [UCC 2–709(1), 2A–529(1)]. 2. Reclaim the goods [UCC 2–507(2), 2A–525(2)]. a. The seller delivers goods in cash sale, and the buyer's check is dishonored. b. The seller delivers goods in a credit sale, and the goods are received by an insolvent buyer.

Buyer's and Lessee's Remedies

The UCC provides a variety of remedies to a buyer or lessee upon the seller's or lessor's breach of a sales or lease contract. These remedies are set forth in Exhibit 13.4.

Exhibit 13.4
Buyer's and Lessee's Remedies

Situation	Buyer's or Lessee's Remedy
Seller or lessor refuses to deliver the goods or delivers nonconforming goods that the buyer or lessee does not want.	1. Reject nonconforming goods [UCC 2–601, 2A–509]. 2. Revoke acceptance of nonconforming goods [UCC 2–608, 2A–517(1)]. 3. Cover [UCC 2–712, 2A–518]. 4. Sue for breach of contract and recover damages [UCC 2–713, 2A–519]. 5. Cancel the contract [UCC 2–711(1), 2A–508(1)(a)].
Seller or lessor tenders nonconforming goods and buyer or lessee accepts them.	1. Sue for ordinary damages [UCC 2–714(1), 2A–516(1)]. 2. Deduct damages from the unpaid purchase or rent price [UCC 2–714(1), 2A–516(1)].
Seller or lessor refuses to deliver the goods and buyer or lessee wants them.	1. Sue for specific performance [UCC 2–716(1), 2A–521(1)]. 2. Replevy the goods [UCC 2–716(3), 2A–521(3)]. 3. Recover the goods from an insolvent seller or lessor [UCC 2–502, 2A–522].

Agreements Affecting Remedies

The parties to a sales or lease contract may agree on remedies in addition to or in substitution for the remedies provided by the UCC. For example, the parties may limit the buyer's or lessee's remedies to repair and replacement of defective goods or parts or to the return of the goods and repayment (refund) of the purchase price or rent.

Convenience is the basis of mercantile law.

Lord Mansfield
Medcalf v. Hall (1782)

The UCC permits parties to a sales or lease contract to establish in advance the damages that will be paid upon a breach of the contract. Such preestablished damages, called **liquidated damages,** substitute for actual damages. In a sales or lease contract, liquidated damages are valid if they are reasonable in light of the anticipated or actual harm caused by the breach [UCC 2–718(1), 2A–504].

liquidated damages
Damages that will be paid upon a breach of contract and that are established in advance.

Ethics in Business
Unconscionable Contract

UCC Article 2 (Sales) and Article 2A (Leases) have adopted the equity doctrine of **unconscionability**. Under this doctrine, a court may determine as a matter of law that a contract is unconscionable. To prove unconscionability, there must be proof that the parties had substantial unequal bargaining power, that the dominant party misused its power in contracting, and that it would be manifestly unfair or oppressive to enforce the contract. This sometimes happens when a dominant party uses a preprinted form contract and the terms of the contract are unfair or oppressive.

If a court finds that a contract or any clause in a contract is unconscionable, the court may refuse to enforce the contract, it may enforce the remainder of the contract without the unconscionable clause, or it may so limit the application of any unconscionable clause as to avoid any unconscionable result [UCC 2–302, 2A–108]. Unconscionability is sometimes found in a consumer lease if the consumer has been induced by unconscionable conduct to enter into the lease. The doctrine of unconscionability also applies to Web contracts.

Ethics Issues

1. Does the doctrine of unconscionability encourage ethical behavior? Explain.
2. Is the doctrine of unconscionability necessary? Explain. ■

Warranties

The doctrine of *caveat emptor*—let the buyer beware—governed the law of sales and leases for centuries. Finally, the law recognized that consumers and other purchasers and lessees of goods needed greater protection. Article 2 of the UCC establishes certain **warranties** that apply to the sale of goods. Article 2A of the UCC establishes warranties that apply in lease transactions.

warranty
A seller's or buyer's express or implied assurance to a buyer or lessee that the goods sold or leased meet certain quality standards.

Warranties are the buyer's or lessee's assurance that the goods meet certain standards. Warranties, which are based on contract law, may be either *expressly* stated or *implied* by law. If the seller or lessor fails to meet a warranty, the buyer or lessee can sue for breach of warranty.

Express Warranty

express warranty
A warranty that is created when a seller or lessor makes an affirmation that the goods he or she is selling or leasing meet certain standards of quality, description, performance, or condition.

Express warranties, which are the oldest form of warranty, are created when a seller or lessor affirms that the goods he or she is selling or leasing meet certain standards of quality, description, performance, or condition [UCC 2–313(1), 2A–210(1)]. Express warranties can be either written, oral, or inferred from the seller's conduct.

Sellers and lessors are not required to make such warranties. Generally, express warranties are made to entice consumers and others to buy or lease their products. That is why these warranties are often in the form of advertisements, brochures, catalogs, pictures, illustrations, diagrams, blueprints, and so on.

Express warranties are created when the seller or lessor indicates that the goods will conform to:

1. All *affirmations of fact or promise* made about them (e.g., statements such as "This car will go 100 miles per hour" or "This house paint will last at least five years")
2. Any *description* of them (e.g., terms such as *Idaho potatoes* and *Michigan cherries*)
3. Any *model* or *sample* of them (e.g., a model oil drilling rig or a sample of wheat taken from a silo)

Statements of Opinion Many express warranties arise during the course of negotiations between a buyer and a seller (or lessor and lessee). The seller's or lessor's **statements of opinion** (i.e., **puffing**) or commendation of the goods do not create an express warranty [UCC 2–313(2)]. It is often difficult to determine whether the seller's statement is an affirmation of fact (which creates an express warranty) or a statement of opinion (which does not create a warranty). An affirmation of the *value* of goods does not create an express warranty [UCC 2–313(2)].

Consider These Examples A used car salesperson's statement such as "This is the best used car available in town" does not create an express warranty because it is an opinion and mere puffing. However, a statement such as "This car has been driven only 20,000 miles" is an express warranty because it is a statement of fact. Statements such as "This painting is worth a fortune" or "Others would gladly pay $20,000 for this car" do not create an express warranty because they are statements of value and of fact.

Implied Warranty of Merchantability

implied warranty of merchantability
Unless properly disclosed, a warranty that is implied that sold or leased goods are fit for the ordinary purpose for which they are sold or leased, and other assurances.

If the seller or lessor of a good is a merchant with respect to goods of that kind, the sales contract contains an **implied warranty of merchantability** unless it is properly disclaimed [UCC 2–314(1), 2A–212(1)]. This requires the following standards to be met:

- ***The goods must be fit for the ordinary purposes for which they are used.*** For example, a chair must be able to safely perform the function of a chair. For example, if a normal-sized person sits in a chair that has not been tampered with, and the chair collapses, there has been a breach of the implied warranty of merchantability. If, however, the same person is injured because he or she uses the chair as a ladder and it tips over, there is no breach of implied warranty because serving as a ladder is not the ordinary purpose of a chair.

- ***The goods must be adequately contained, packaged, and labeled.*** The implied warranty of merchantability applies to the milk bottle as well as to the milk inside the bottle.
- ***The goods must be of an even kind, quality, and quantity within each unit.*** All the goods in a carton, package, or box must be consistent.
- ***The goods must conform to any promise or affirmation of fact made on the container or label.*** The goods can be used safely in accordance with the instructions on the package or label.
- ***The quality of the goods must pass without objection in the trade.*** Other users of the goods should not object to their quality.
- ***Fungible goods must meet a fair average or middle range of quality.*** To be classified as a certain grade, grain or ore must meet the average range of quality of that grade.

Note that the implied warranty of merchantability does not apply to sales or leases by nonmerchants or casual sales. For example, the implied warranty of merchantability applies to the sale of a lawn mower that is sold by a merchant who is in the business of selling lawn mowers. It does not apply when one neighbor sells a lawn mower to another neighbor.

The following case raised the issue of implied warranty of merchantability.

Case 13.1 Implied Warranty of Merchantability

Denny v. Ford Motor Company

639 N.Y.S. 2d 250, 87 N.Y.2d 248, 1995 N.Y. Lexis 4445

Court of Appeals of New York

Background and Facts

Nancy Denny purchased a Bronco II, a small utility vehicle that was manufactured by Ford Motor Company. Denny testified that she purchased the Bronco for use on paved city and suburban streets and not for off-road use. On June 9, 1986, when Denny was driving the vehicle on a paved road, she slammed on the brakes in an effort to avoid a deer that had walked directly into her motor vehicle's path. The Bronco II rolled over, and Denny was severely injured. Denny sued Ford Motor Company to recover damages for breach of the implied warranty of merchantability.

Denny alleged that the Bronco II presented a significantly higher risk of occurrence of rollover accidents than did ordinary passenger vehicles. Denny introduced evidence at trial that showed that the Bronco II had a low stability index because of its high center of gravity, narrow tracks, and shorter wheel base, as well as the design of its suspension system. Ford countered that the Bronco II was intended as an off-road vehicle and was not designed to be used as a conventional passenger automobile on paved streets. The trial court found Ford liable and awarded Denny $1.2 million in damages. Ford appealed.

Issue

Did Ford Motor Company breach the implied warranty of merchantability?

In the Language of the Court

Plaintiff introduced a Ford marketing manual that predicted many buyers would be attracted to the Bronco II because utility vehicles were suitable to "contemporary lifestyles" and were "considered fashionable" in some suburban areas. According to this manual, the sales presentation of the Bronco II should take into account the vehicle's "suitability for commuting and for suburban and city driving." Additionally, the vehicle's ability to switch between two-wheel and four-wheel drive would "be particularly appealing to women who may be concerned about driving in snow and ice with their children." Plaintiff testified that the perceived safety benefits of its four-wheel drive capacity was what

(*continued*)

Denny v. Ford Motor Company

639 N.Y.S. 2d 250, 87 N.Y.2d 248, 1995 N.Y. Lexis 4445
Court of Appeals of New York
(*continued*)

attracted her to the Bronco II. She was not at all interested in its off-road use.

The law implies a warranty by a manufacturer that places its product on the market that the product is reasonably fit for the ordinary purpose for which it was intended. If it is, in fact, defective and not reasonably fit to be used for its intended purpose, the warranty is breached. Plaintiff's proof focused on the sale of Bronco II for suburban driving and everyday road travel. Plaintiff also adduced proof that the Bronco II's design characteristics made it unusually susceptible to rollover accidents when used on paved roads. All of this evidence was useful in showing that routine highway and street driving was the "ordinary purpose" for which the Bronco II was sold and that it was not "fit"—or safe—for that purpose. Thus, under the evidence in this case, a rational fact finder could have concluded that the vehicle was not safe for the "ordinary purpose" of daily driving for which it was marketed and sold.

Decision and Remedy

The court of appeals held that Ford had breached the implied warranty of merchantability and upheld the jury award for the plaintiff.

Business and Ethics Questions

1. Should the law impose an *implied* warranty of merchantability in the sale of goods? What is the public policy underlying this implied warranty?
2. Did Ford act ethically in defending that the Bronco II was sold only as an off-road vehicle? Was this argument persuasive?
3. What are the business implications of this decision? Do you think that utility vehicles such as the Bronco II have a higher rollover danger than normal passenger automobiles?

Implied Warranty of Fitness for Human Consumption The common law implied a special warranty—the **implied warranty of fitness for human consumption**—to food products. The UCC incorporates this warranty, which applies to food and drink consumed on or off the premises, within the implied warranty of merchantability. Restaurants, grocery stores, fast-food outlets, and vending-machine operators are all subject to this warranty. States use one of the following two tests in determining whether there has been a breach of the implied warranty of fitness for human consumption:

implied warranty of fitness for human consumption
A warranty that applies to food or drink consumed on or off the premises of restaurants, grocery stores, fast-food outlets, and vending machines.

foreign substance test
A test to determine merchantability based on foreign objects that are found in food.

consumer expectation test
A test to determine merchantability based on what the average consumer would expect to find in food products.

- ***Foreign substance test.*** Under the **foreign substance test,** a food product is unmerchantable if a foreign object in that product causes injury to a person. For example, the warranty would be breached if an injury were caused by a nail in a cherry pie. If an injury were caused by a cherry pit in the pie, the pie would not be unmerchantable.
- ***Consumer expectation test.*** The majority of states have adopted the modern **consumer expectation test** to determine the merchantability of food products. For example, under this implied warranty, if a person is injured by a chicken bone while eating fried chicken, the injury is not actionable. However, the warranty would be breached if a person were injured by a chicken bone while eating a chicken salad sandwich. This is because a consumer would expect that the food preparer would have removed all bones from the chicken.

Implied Warranty of Fitness for a Particular Purpose

warranty of fitness for a particular purpose
A warranty that arises when a seller or lessor warrants that goods will meet the buyer's or lessee's expressed needs.

The UCC contains an implied **warranty of fitness for a particular purpose.** This implied warranty is breached if the goods do not meet the buyer's or lessee's expressed needs. The warranty applies to both merchant and nonmerchant sellers and lessors.

The warranty of fitness for a particular purpose is implied at the time of contracting if:

1. The seller or lessor has reason to know the particular purpose for which the buyer is purchasing the goods or the lessee is leasing the goods.

Santa Monica, California. The law implies a warranty that the food restaurants serve is fit for human consumption.

2. The seller or lessor makes a statement that the goods will serve this purpose.
3. The buyer or lessee relies on the seller's or lessor's skill and judgment and purchases or leases the goods [UCC 2–315, 2A–213].

Consider This Example Susan Logan wants to buy lumber to build a house, so she goes to Winter's lumber yard. Logan describes to Winter the house she intends to build. She also tells Winter that she is relying on him to select the right lumber. Winter selects the lumber, and Logan buys it and builds the house. Unfortunately, the house collapses because the lumber was not strong enough to support it. Logan can sue Winter for breach of the implied warranty of fitness for a particular purpose.

Concept Summary *Express and Implied Warranties of Quality*

Type of Warranty	How Created	Description
Express warranty	Made by the seller or lessor.	Affirms that goods meet certain standards of quality, description, performance, or condition [UCC 2–313(1), 2A–210(1)].
Implied warranty of merchantability	Implied by law if the seller or lessor is a merchant.	Implies that the goods: 1. Are fit for the ordinary purposes for which they are used 2. Are adequately contained, packaged, and labeled 3. Are of an even kind, quality, and quantity within each unit 4. Conform to any promise or affirmation of fact made on the container or label 5. Pass without objection in the trade

(continued)

Concept Summary (Continued)

		6. Meet a fair, average, or middle range of quality for fungible goods [UCC 2–314(1), 2A–212(1)]
Implied warranty of fitness for a particular purpose.	Implied by law.	Implies that goods are fit for the purpose for which the buyer or lessee acquires the goods if: 1. The seller or lessor has reason to know the particular purpose for which the goods will be used 2. The seller or lessor makes a statement that the goods will serve that purpose, and 3. The buyer or lessee relies on the statement and buys or leases the goods [UCC 2–315, 2A–213]

Warranty Disclaimer

warranty disclaimer
Statements that negate express and implied warranties.

Warranties can be **disclaimed** or limited. If an *express warranty* is made, it can be limited only if the **warranty disclaimer** and the warranty can be reasonably construed with each other.

All implied warranties of quality may be disclaimed by expressions such as *as is, with all faults*, or other language that makes it clear to the buyer that there are no implied warranties. This type of disclaimer is often included in sales contracts for used products. If the preceding language is not used, disclaimers of the *implied warranty of merchantability* must specifically mention the term *merchantability*. These disclaimers may be oral or written.

The *implied warranty of fitness for a particular purpose* may be disclaimed in general language, without specific use of the term *fitness*. For example, language such as "There are no warranties that extend beyond the description on the fact hereof" is sufficient to disclaim the fitness warranty. The disclaimer must be in writing.

conspicuous
A requirement that warranty disclaimers be noticeable to the average person.

Written disclaimers must be conspicuously displayed to be valid. The courts construe **conspicuous** as noticeable to a reasonable person [UCC 2–316, 2A–214]. For example, a heading printed in capitals or typeface that is larger or in a different style than the rest of the body of a sales or lease contract will be considered to be conspicuous. Different-color type is also considered conspicuous.

Ethics in Business

Magnuson-Moss Warranty Act

In 1975, Congress enacted the **Magnuson-Moss Warranty Act**, which covers written warranties related to *consumer* products.[1] This federal act is administered by the Federal Trade Commission (FTC). Commercial and industrial transactions are not governed by the act.

The act does not require a seller or lessor to make express written warranties. However, sellers and lessors that do make certain express warranties are subject to the provisions of the act. If a seller or lessor chooses to make an express warranty, the Magnuson-Moss Warranty Act requires that the warranty be labeled as either "full" or "limited."

To qualify as a **full warranty**, the warrantor must guarantee free repair or replacement of the defective product. The warrantor must indicate whether there is a time limit on the full warranty (e.g., "full 36-month warranty"). **In a limited warranty**, the warrantor limits the scope of a full warranty in some way (e.g., a return of the purchase price or replacement or such). The fact that the warranty is full or limited must be conspicuously displayed and be made in "understandable language."

A consumer may bring a civil action against a defendant for violating the provisions of the act. A successful plaintiff can recover damages, attorneys' fees, and other costs incurred in bringing the action. The act authorizes warrantors to establish an informal dispute resolution procedure. The procedure must be conspicuously described in the written warranty.

The act does not create any implied warranties. If does, however, modify the state law of implied warranties in one crucial respect: Sellers or lessors who make express written warranties related to consumer products are forbidden from disclaiming or modifying the implied warranties of merchantability and fitness for a particular purpose. A seller or lessor may set a time limit on implied warranties, but this time limit must correspond to the duration of any express warranty.

Ethics Issues

1. Why was the Magnuson-Moss Warranty Act enacted? Explain.
2. Does the Magnuson-Moss Warranty Act promote ethical conduct by sellers and lessors of goods? Explain. ■

Internet Law & Online Commerce

Warranty Disclaimers in Software Licenses

Most software companies license their software to users. A software license is a complex contract that contains the terms of the license. Most software licenses contain warranty disclaimer and limitation on liability clauses that limit the licenser's liability if the software malfunctions. Disclaimer of warranty and limitation on liability clauses that are included in a typical software license appear below. ■

SOFTWARE.COM, INC.
LIMITATION AND WAIVERS OF WARRANTIES, REMEDIES, AND CONSEQUENTIAL DAMAGES

Limited Warranty. Software.com, Inc. warrants that (a) the software will perform substantially in accordance with the accompanying written materials for a period of 90 days from the date of receipt, and (b) any hardware accompanying the software will be free from defects in materials and workmanship under normal use and service for a period of one year from the date of the receipt. Any implied warranties on the software and hardware are limited to 90 days and one (1) year, respectively. Some states do not allow limitations on duration of an implied warranty, so the above limitation may not apply to you.

Customer Remedies. Software.com, Inc.'s entire liability and your exclusive remedy shall be, at Software.com, Inc.'s option, either (a) return of the price paid or (b) repair or replacement of the software or hardware that does not meet Software.com, Inc.'s Limited Warranty and that is returned to Software.com, Inc. with a copy of your receipt. This Limited Warranty is void if failure of the software or hardware has resulted from accident, abuse, or misapplication. Any replacement software will be warranted for the remainder of the original warranty or 30 days, whichever is longer. These remedies are not available outside the United States of America.

No Other Warranties. Software.com, Inc. disclaims all other warranties, either express or implied, including but not limited to implied warranties of merchantability and fitness for a particular purpose, with respect to the software, the accompanying written materials, and any accompanying hardware. This Limited Warranty gives you specific legal rights. You may have others, which vary from state to state.

No Liability for Consequential Damages. In no event shall Software.com, Inc. or its suppliers be liable for any damages whatsoever (including, without limitation, damages for loss of business profits, business interruption, loss of business information, or other pecuniary loss) arising out of the use of or inability to use this Software.com, Inc. product, even if Software.com, Inc. has been advised of the possibility of such damages. Because some states do not allow the exclusion or limitation of liability for consequential or incidental damages, the above limitation may not apply to you.

Terms and Concepts

Article 2 (Sales)

Article 2 of the UCC applies to transactions in goods [UCC 2–102].

1. ***Goods.*** Goods are tangible things that are movable at the time of their identification in a sales contract [UCC 2–105(1)].

2. ***Scope of Article 2.*** Article 2 applies to all sales contracts, whether they involve merchants or not.

Article 2A, Leases

Article 2A of the UCC applies to personal property leases of goods [UCC 2A-101].

1. ***Lease.*** A lease is a transfer of the right to the possession and use of the named goods for a set term in return for certain consideration.
2. ***Parties to a lease:***
   a. *Lessor.* A lessor is a person who transfers the right of possession and use of goods [UCC 2A–103(1)(p)].
   b. *Lessee.* A lessee is a person who acquires the right to possession and use of goods [UCC 2A-103(1)(n)].

Offer

Open terms. If the parties leave open a major term in a sales or lease contract, the UCC permits the following terms to be read into the contract:

1. Price term
2. Payment term
3. Delivery term
4. Time term
5. Assortment term

These are commonly called *gap-filling rules* [UCC 2–204(3), 2A–204(3)].

Firm Offer Rule

The firm offer rule is a UCC rule which says that a merchant who (1) makes an offer to buy, sell, or lease goods and (2) assures the other party in a separate writing that the offer will be held open cannot revoke the offer for the time stated or, if no time is stated, for a reasonable time [UCC 2–205, 2A–205].

Additional Terms Permitted

The UCC permits an acceptance of a sales contract to contain additional terms and still to act as an acceptance rather than a counteroffer in certain circumstances. The following UCC rules apply [UCC 2–207(2)]:

1. ***One or both parties are nonmerchants.*** In this situation, the additional terms are considered proposed additions to the contract. If the offeree's proposed terms are accepted by the offeror, they become part of the contract. If they are not accepted, the sales contract is formed on the basis of the terms of the original offer.
2. ***Both parties are merchants.*** In this situation, the additional terms contained in the acceptance become part of the sales contract *unless* (1) the offer expressly limits the acceptance to the terms of the offer, (2) the additional terms materially alter the original contract, or (3) the offeror notifies the offeree that he or she objects to the additional terms within a reasonable time after receiving the offeree's modified acceptance. There is no contract if the additional terms so materially alter the terms of the original offer that the parties cannot agree on the contract.

Statute of Frauds

The UCC Statute of Frauds requires contracts for the sale of goods costing $500 or more and lease contracts involving payments of $1,000 or more to be in writing [UCC 2–201(1), 2A–201(1)].

Written Confirmation Rule

If both parties to an oral sales or lease contract are merchants, the Statute of Frauds requirements are satisfied if (1) one of the parties sends a *written confirmation* of the sale to the other within a reasonable time after contracting and (2) the merchant does not give written notice of an objection to the contract within 10 days after receiving the confirmation [UCC 2–201(2)].

Identification

Identification distinguishes the goods named in a contract from the seller's or lessor's other goods [UCC 2–501(1)].

Passage of Title

1. ***Passage of title by agreement.*** The title to goods of a sales contract passes from the seller to the buyer in any manner and on any condition explicitly agreed upon by the parties.
2. ***Passage of title where there is no agreement.*** If the parties have no agreement as to the passage of title, title passes according to the following UCC rules [UCC 2–401(2)]:
   a. *Shipment contract.* With this type of contract, the seller must ship the goods to the buyer via a common carrier. Title passes to the buyer at the time and place of shipment.
   b. *Destination contract.* With this type of contract, the seller must deliver the goods to the buyer's place of business or other designated destination. Title passes to the buyer when the seller tenders delivery of the goods at the specified destination.
3. ***Passage of title in lease contracts.*** Title to the leased goods remains with the lessor or a third party. Title does not pass to the lessee.

Risk of Loss: Sales Contracts

1. ***Agreement.*** The parties to a sales contract may agree among themselves as to who will bear the risk of loss if the goods are lost or destroyed.
2. ***No agreement.*** If the parties do not have a specific agreement concerning the assessment of risk of loss, the UCC mandates who will bear the risk [UCC 2–509].
3. ***Carrier cases: Movement of goods.***
   a. *Shipment contract.* The risk of loss passes to the buyer when the seller delivers conforming goods to a carrier. The buyer bears the risk of loss during transportation.
   b. *Destination contract.* The risk of loss does not pass to the buyer until the goods are tendered to the buyer at the designated destination. The seller bears the risk of loss during transportation.
4. ***Shipping terms.*** Sales contracts often contain the following shipping terms:
   a. F.O.B. (free on board) *point of shipment*
   b. F.A.S. (free alongside) or F.A.S. *vessel, part of shipment*
   c. C.I.F. (cost, insurance, and freight) and C. & F. (cost and freight)
   d. F.O.B. *place of destination*
   e. Ex-ship (from the carrying vessel)
   f. No arrival, no sale contract
5. ***No movement of goods.*** If the buyer is to pick up the goods from the seller's place of business or other specified location, the following UCC rules apply:
   a. *Merchant-seller.* If the seller is a merchant, the risk of loss does not pass to the buyer until the goods are received by the buyer. The merchant-seller bears the risk of loss between the time of contracting and the time the buyer picks up the goods.
   b. *Nonmerchant-seller.* If the seller is a nonmerchant, risk of loss passes to the buyer upon tender of delivery of the goods by the seller (i.e., the seller holds the goods available for the buyer to take delivery).

Risk of Loss: Lease Contracts

1. ***Agreement.*** The parties to a lease contract may agree as to who will bear the risk of loss of the goods if they are lost or destroyed.
2. ***No agreement.*** If the parties do not have an agreement concerning the assessment of risk of loss, the following UCC rules for risk of loss apply [UCC 2A–219, 2A–220]:
   a. *Ordinary lease.* In this type of lease, the risk of loss is retained by the lessor.
   b. *Breach of contract.* If a tender of delivery of goods fails to conform to the lease contract, the risk of loss remains with the lessor or supplier until acceptance or cure.

Sales by Nonowners

If a person sells goods that he or she does not hold valid title to, the buyer acquires rights in the goods under the UCC [UCC 2–403].

1. ***Void title and lease: Stolen goods.*** A thief acquires no title to goods he or she steals. A person who purchases stolen goods does not acquire title to the goods. Any such title is called *void title.* The real owner can reclaim the goods from the purchaser. The purchaser's recourse is to recover from the thief.
2. ***Voidable title sale or lease of goods to good faith purchasers for value.*** If goods are obtained through fraud, by writing a check that is later dishonored or by impersonating another person, the perpetrator acquires *voidable title* to the goods. If the perpetrator sells or leases the goods to a *good faith to purchaser* or *lessee for value*—a person who pays sufficient consideration or rent for the goods and honestly believes that the seller or lessor has good title to the goods—the buyer or lessor acquires good title to the goods. The real owner's recourse is against the perpetrator who acquired the goods from him or her.
3. ***Entrustment rule.*** If an owner entrusts possession of his or her goods to a merchant who deals in goods of that kind (e.g., for repair) and the merchant sells those goods to a *buyer in the ordinary course of business* (e.g., a customer of the merchant), the buyer acquires title to the goods. The real owner's recourse is against the merchant who sold his or her goods. This rule is called the *entrustment rule.*

Tender of Delivery

Tender of delivery requires the seller or lessor to (1) put and hold *conforming goods* at the buyer's or lessee's disposition and (2) give the buyer and lessee any notification reasonably necessary to enable the buyer or lessee to take delivery of the goods [UCC 2–503(1), 2A–508(1)].

1. ***Perfect tender rule.*** The seller or lessor is under a duty to deliver *conforming goods* to the buyer or lessee. If the goods or tender of delivery fails in any respect to conform to the contract, the buyer or lessee may opt to (1) reject the whole shipment, (2) accept the whole shipment, or (3) reject part and accept part of the shipment [UCC 2–601, 2A–509].
2. ***Payment.*** Goods that are accepted by the buyer or lessee must be paid for in accordance with the terms of the sales or lease contract. Unless otherwise agreed, payment or rent is due when and where the goods are delivered [UCC 2–310, 2A–516(1)].

Agreements Affecting Remedies

1. ***Limitations on remedies.*** The parties to a sales or lease contract may agree on remedies in addition to or in substitution for the remedies provided by Article 2 or Article 2A of the UCC [UCC 2–719(1), 2A–503(1)].
2. ***Liquidated damages.*** The parties to a sales or lease contract may establish in advance the damages that will be paid upon a breach of the contract [UCC 2–718(1), 2A–504].

Unconscionable Sales and Lease Contracts

If a sales or lease contract or any clause in it is *unconscionable*, the court may either refuse to enforce the contract or limit the application of the unconscionable clause [UCC 2–302, 2A–108].

Express Warranty

An express warranty is affirmation by a seller or lessor that the goods he or she is selling or leasing meet certain standards of quality, description, performance, or condition.

Implied Warranty of Merchantability

1. ***Implied warranty of merchantability.*** This warranty is implied by law in sales and lease transactions, and it requires that the goods:
   a. Be fit for the ordinary purposes for which they are used
   b. Be adequately contained, packaged, and labeled
   c. Be of an even kind, quality, and quantity within each unit
   d. Conform to any promise or affirmation of fact made on the container or label
   e. Pass without objection in the trade
   f. Meet a fair or middle range of quality if the goods are fungible

2. ***Implied warranty of fitness for human consumption.*** This warranty is implied by law, and it requires that food products be fit for human consumption. The UCC incorporates this warranty within the implied warranty of merchantability. States apply one of the two following tests.
   a. *Foreign substance test.* A food is unmerchantable if a foreign object in the food caused the plaintiff's injury.
   b. *Consumer expectation test.* A food is unmerchantable if an object in the food that a consumer would not expect to be there caused the plaintiff's injury.

Implied Warranty of Fitness for a Particular Purpose

An implied warrant of fitness for a particular purpose is a warranty by a seller or lessor that the goods will meet the buyer's or lessee's expressed needs.

Warranty Disclaimers

1. ***Express warranties.*** These warranties can be limited if the warranty and disclaimer can be reasonably construed with each other.
2. ***Implied warranties.***
   a. *Disclaimer.* Implied warranties can be disclaimed by expressions such as *as is, with all faults*, or other such language. If such language is not used, implied warranties are disclaimed as follows:
      i. *Implied warranty of merchantability.* This oral or written disclaimer mentions the word *merchantability.*
      ii. *Implied warranty of fitness for a particular purpose.* This is a written disclaimer of general language.
3. ***Conspicuousness.*** Written disclaimers must be conspicuously displayed to be enforceable.

Magnuson-Moss Warranty Act

This federal statute covers written warranties that apply to *consumer* products.

1. ***Full and limited warranties.*** If a good costs more than $10 and the warrantor makes an express warranty, the warranty must be labeled *full* or *limited*:
   a. *Full warranty.* A full warranty guarantees free repair or replacement of a defective product. A time limit may be placed on the warranty.
   b. *Limited warranty.* A limited warranty limits the scope of a full warranty in some way (e.g., return of the purchase price).
2. ***Limitation on disclaiming implied warranties.*** If a seller or lessor makes an express warranty, he or she cannot disclaim or modify the implied warranties of merchantability and fitness for a particular purpose. A time limit may be placed on implied warranties but must correspond to the duration of the express warranty.

Internet Exercises and Case Questions

Working the Web Internet Exercises

1. Find the major differences in the rules of contract formation under the common law and UCC Article 2. Visit "Legal Information Institute (LII): Sales Law" at **www.law.cornell.edu/topics/sales.html**.
2. Find UCC Article 2 as adopted in your jurisdiction. Review the seller's remedies under UCC 2–703. See **www.law.cornell.edu/uniform/vol7.html**.
3. Visit "Legal Information Institute (LII): Remedies" at **www.law.cornell.edu/topics/remedies.html** and "Legal Information Institute (LII): Commercial Law" at **www.law.cornell.edu/topics/commercial.html**, which includes information on consumer credit, damages, debtors and creditors, injunctions, and remedies.
4. UCC Article 2 provides for disclaimers of warranties. Find the provisions of the Magnuson-Moss Warranty Act and review the various disclaimers. Do you think disclaimers are a good idea? See "Legal Information Institute (LII): Sales" at **www.law.cornell.edu/topics/sales.html** for a summary of the warranties under UCC Article 2.

Legal Environment Cases

13.1 Unconscionable Contract Jane Wilson leased a Toyota pickup truck from World Omni Leasing, Inc. (Omni). Wilson had experience in business and had signed contracts before. In the past, Wilson had read the contracts before signing them. When signing the contract for the lease of the truck, however, Wilson did not take the opportunity to read the lease. However, she signed a statement declaring that she had read and understood the lease. The lease contained a provision that made Wilson responsible for payments on the truck even if the truck was destroyed. Several months after leasing the truck, Wilson was involved in a two-vehicle collision. The pickup truck was destroyed. Omni demanded to be paid for the balance of the lease. Wilson refused, claiming that the lease was unconscionable. Is the lease unconscionable? *Wilson v. World Omni Leasing, Inc.*, 540 So.2d 713, 1989 Ala. Lexis 41 (Ala.)

13.2 Firm Offer Gordon Construction Company (Gordon) was a general contractor in the New York City area. Gordon planned on bidding for the job of constructing two buildings for the Port Authority of New York. In anticipation of its own bid, Gordon sought bids from subcontractors. On April 22, 1963, E. A. Coronis Associates (Coronis), a fabricator of structured steel, sent a signed letter to Gordon. The letter quoted a price for work on the Port Authority project and stated that the price could change, based on the amount of steel used. The letter contained no information other than the price Coronis would charge for the job. On May 27, Gordon was awarded the Port Authority project. On June 1, Coronis sent Gordon a telegram, withdrawing its offer. Gordon replied that it expected Coronis to honor the price quoted in its April 22 letter. When Coronis refused, Gordon sued. Gordon claimed that Coronis was attempting to withdraw a firm offer. Who wins? *E. A. Coronis Associates v. Gordon Construction Co.*, 216 A.2d 246, 1966 N.J. Super. Lexis 368 (N.J. Super.)

13.3 Battle of the Forms Dan Miller was a commercial photographer who had taken a series of photographs that had appeared in the *New York Times*. *Newsweek* magazine wanted to use the photographs. When a *Newsweek* employee named Dwyer phoned Miller, he was told that 72 images were available. Dwyer said that he wanted to inspect the photographs and offered a certain sum of money for each photo *Newsweek* used. The photos were to remain Miller's property. Miller and Dwyer agreed to the price and the date for delivery. *Newsweek* sent a courier to pick up the photographs. Along with the photos, Miller gave the courier a delivery memo that set out various conditions for the use of the photographs. The memo included a clause that required *Newsweek* to pay $1,500 each if any of the photos were lost or destroyed. After *Newsweek* received the package, it decided it no longer needed Miller's work. When Miller called to have the photos returned, he was told that they had all been lost. Miller demanded that *Newsweek* pay him $1,500 for each of the 72 lost photos. Assuming that the court finds Miller and *Newsweek* to be merchants, are the clauses in the delivery memo part of the sales contract? *Miller v. Newsweek, Inc.*, 660 F.Supp.852, 1987 U.S.Dist. Lexis 4338 (D. Del.)

13.4 Open Terms Alvin Cagle was a potato farmer in Alabama who had had several business dealings with H.C. Schmieding Produce Co. (Schmieding). Several months before harvest, Cagle entered into an oral sales contract with Schmieding. The contract called for Schmieding to pay the market price at harvest time for all the red potatoes that Cagle grew on his 30-acre farm. Schmieding asked that the potatoes be delivered during the normal harvest months. As Cagle began harvesting his red potatoes, he contacted Schmieding to arrange delivery. Schmieding told the farmer that no contract had been formed because the terms of the agreement were too indefinite. Cagle demanded that Schmieding buy his crop. When Schmieding refused, Cagle sued to have the contract enforced. Has a valid sales contract been formed? *H.C. Schmieding Produce Co. v. Cagle*, 529 So.3d 243, 1988 Ala. Lexis 284 (Ala.)

13.5 Stolen Goods John Torniero was employed by Micheals Jewelers, Inc. (Micheals). During the course of his employment, Torniero stole pieces of jewelry, including several diamond rings, a sapphire ring, a gold pendant, and several loose diamonds. Over a period of several months, Torniero sold individual pieces of the stolen jewelry to G&W Watch and Jewelry Corporation (G&W). G&W had no knowledge of how Torniero obtained the jewels. Torniero was arrested when Micheals discovered the thefts. After Torniero admitted that he had sold the stolen jewelry to G&W, Michaels attempted to recover it from G&W. G&W claimed title to the jewelry as a good faith purchaser for value. Micheals challenged G&W's claim to title in court. Who wins? *United States v. Micheals Jewelers, Inc.* 42 UCC Rep.Serv. 141, 1985 U.S.Dist. Lexis 15142 (D.C. Conn.)

13.6 Entrustment Rule Fuqua Homes, Inc. (Fuqua), is a manufacturer of prefabricated houses. MMM was a partnership created by two men named Kirk and Underhill. MMM operated as a dealer of prefabricated homes. On seven occasions before the disputed transactions occurred, MMM had ordered homes from Fuqua. In early 1977, MMM was contacted by Kenneth Ryan. Ryan wanted to purchase a 55-foot modular home. MMM called Fuqua and ordered a prefabricated home that met Ryan's specifications. Fuqua delivered the home to MMM and retained a security interest in it until MMM paid the purchase price. MMM installed the house on Ryan's property and collected full payment from Ryan. Kirk and Underhill then disappeared, taking Ryan's money with them. Fuqua was never paid for the prefabricated home it had manufactured. Ryan had no knowledge of the dealings between MMM and Fuqua. Fuqua claimed title to the house based on its security interest. Who has title to the home? *Fuqua Homes, Inc. v. Evanston Bldg. & Loan Co.*, 370 N.E.2d 780, 1977 Ohio App. Lexis 6968 (Ohio App.)

13.7 Risk of Loss In 1982, Martin Silver ordered two rooms of furniture from Wycombe, Meyer & Co., Inc. (Wycombe), a manufacturer and seller of custom-made furniture. On February 23, 1982, Wycombe sent invoices to Silver, advising him that the furniture was ready for shipment. Silver tendered payment in full for the goods and asked that one room of furniture be shipped immediately and that the other be held for shipment on a later date. Before any instructions were received as to the second room of furniture, it was destroyed in a fire. Silver and his insurance company attempted to recover the money he paid for the destroyed furniture. Wycombe refused to return the payment, claiming that the risk of loss was on Silver. Who wins? *Silver v. Wycombe, Meyer & Co., Inc.*, 477 N.Y.S.2d 288, 1984 N.Y.Misc. Lexis 3319 (N.Y. City Civ. Ct.)

13.8 Right to Cover Kent Nowlin Construction, Inc. (Nowlin), was awarded a contract by the state of New Mexico to pave a number of roads. After Nowlin was awarded the contract, it entered into an agreement with Concrete Sales & Equipment Rental Company, Inc. (C&E). C&E was to supply 20,000 tons of paving material to Nowlin. Nowlin began paving the roads, anticipating C&E's delivery of materials. On the delivery date, however, C&E shipped only 2,099 tons of paving materials. Because Nowlin had a deadline to meet, the company contracted with Gallup Sand and Gravel Company (Gallup) for substitute material. Nowlin sued C&E to recover the difference between the higher price it had to pay Gallup for materials and the contract price C&E had agreed to. C&E claims that it is not responsible for Nowlin's increased costs. Who wins? *Concrete Sales & Equipment Rental Company, Inc. v. Kent Nowlin Construction, Inc.*, 746 P.2d 645, 1987 N.M. Lexis 3808 (N.M.)

13.9 Implied Warranty of Merchantability Geraldine Maybank took a trip to New York City to visit her son and her two-year-old grandson. She borrowed her daughter's camera for the trip. Two days before leaving for New York, Maybank purchased a package of G.T.E. Sylvania Blue Dot flash cubes at a Kmart store, owned by the S.S. Kresge Company. On the carton of the package were words to the effect that each bulb was safety coated. Upon arriving in New York, Maybank decided to take a picture of her grandson. She opened the carton of flash cubes and put one on the camera. When Maybank pushed down the lever to take a picture, the flash cube exploded. The explosion knocked her glasses off and caused cuts to her left eye. Maybank was hospitalized for eight days. Maybank sued S.S. Kresge Company. Who wins? *Maybank v. S. S. Kresge Company*, 266 S.E.2d 409, 1980 N.C.App. Lexis 2927 (N.C. App.)

13.10 Implied Warranty of Fitness for Human Consumption Tina Keperwes went to a Publix Supermarket (Publix) in Florida and bought a can of Doxsee brand clam chowder. Keperwes opened the can of soup and prepared it at home. While eating the chowder, she bit down on a clam shell and injured one of her molars. Keperwes filed suit against Publix and Doxsee for breach of an implied warranty. In the lawsuit, Keperwes alleged that the clam chowder "was not fit for use as food, but was defective, unwholesome, and unfit for human consumption" and "was in such condition as to be dangerous to life and health." At the trial, Doxsee's general manager testified as to the state-of-the-art methods Doxsee uses in preparing its chowder. Are Publix and Doxsee liable for the injury to Keperwes's tooth? *Keperwes v. Publix Supermarkets. Inc.*, 534 So.2d 872, 1988 Fla.App. Lexis 5306 (Fla. App.)

Ethics in Business

13.11 In 1974, Alex Abatti was the sole owner of A&M Produce Company (A&M), a small farming company located in California's Imperial Valley. Although Abatti had never grown tomatoes, he decided to do so. He sought the advice of FMC Corporation (FMC), a large, diversified manufacturer of farming and other equipment, as to what kind of equipment he would need to process the tomatoes. An FMC representative recommended a certain type of machine, which A&M purchased from FMC pursuant to a form sales contract provided by FMC. Within the fine print, the contract contained one clause that disclaimed any warranty liability by FMC and a second clause that stated that FMC would not be liable for consequential damages if the machine malfunctioned.

A&M paid $10,680 down toward the $32,041 purchase price, and FMC delivered and installed the machine. A&M immediately began experiencing problems with the machine. It did not process the tomatoes quickly enough. Tomatoes began piling up in front of the belt that separated the tomatoes for weight-sizing. Overflow tomatoes had to be sent through the machine at least twice, causing damage to them. Fungus spread through the damaged crop. Because of these problems, the machine had to be continually started and stopped, which significantly reduced processing speed.

A&M tried on several occasions to get additional equipment from FMC, but on each occasion, its request was rejected. Because of the problems with the machine, on June 17, 1974, A&M closed its tomato operation. A&M finally stated, "Let's call the whole thing off," and offered to return the machine if FMC would refund A&M's down payment. When FMC rejected this offer and demanded full payment of the balance due, A&M sued to recover its down payment and damages. It alleged breach of warranty caused by defect in the machine. In defense, FMC pointed to the fine print of the sales contract, stating that the buyer waived any rights to sue it for breach of warranty or to recover consequential damages from it. *A&M Produce Co. v. FMC Corp.*, 135 Cal.App.3d 473, 186 Cal.Rptr. 114, 1982 Cal.App. Lexis 1922 (Cal. App.).

Ethics Issues

1. Was it ethical for FMC to include waiver of liability and waiver of consequential damage clauses in its form contract?
2. Did A&M act morally in signing the contract and then trying to get out from under its provisions?
3. Legally, are the waiver clauses so unconscionable as to not be enforced?

Endnote

1. 15 U.S.C. Sections 2301–2312.

14

Online Commerce and E-Contracts

"Through the use of chat rooms, any person with a phone line can become a town crier with a voice that resonates farther than it could from any soapbox. Through the use of Web pages, mail exploders, and newsgroups, the same individual can become a pamphleteer."

—Justice Stevens
Reno v. American Civil Liberties Union (1997)

Chapter Objectives

After studying this chapter, you should be able to:

1. Describe e-mail and Web contracts.
2. Describe the process for obtaining Internet domain names and the procedure for arbitrating Internet name disputes.
3. Define license and the parties to a licensing agreement.
4. Describe the provisions of the Electronic Signature in Global and National Commerce Act for e-commerce.
5. Describe the Uniform Computer Information Transactions Act (UCITA).

Chapter Contents

- The Internet and World Wide Web
- Domain Names
- E-Contracts
- E-Licensing

In the late 1990s and early 2000s, the use of the Internet and the World Wide Web, and the sale of goods and services through **e-commerce**, exploded. Large and small businesses began selling goods and services over the Internet through Web sites and registered domain names. Consumers and businesses can purchase almost any good or service they want over the Internet, using such sites as Amazon.com, eBay, and others. In addition, software and information may be licensed either by physically purchasing the software or information and installing it on a computer or by merely downloading the software or information directly into the computer.

e-commerce
The sale of goods and services by computer over the Internet.

Many legal scholars and lawyers argued that traditional rules of contract law do not adequately meet the needs of Internet transactions and software and information licensing. These concerns led to an effort to create new contract law for electronic transactions. After much debate, the National Conference of Commissioners on Uniform State Laws developed the **Uniform Computer Information Transactions Act (UCITA)**. This model act provides uniform and comprehensive rules for contracts involving computer information transactions and software and information licenses.

This chapter covers the registration of domain names and the operation of Web businesses and explains how the UCITA and other laws regulate the creation, transfer, and enforcement of e-commerce and informational rights licensing contracts.

Online commerce. The development of electronic commerce has required courts to apply existing contract law to online commerce transactions and spurred the federal Congress and state legislatures to enact new laws to govern the formation and enforcement of e-contracts.

The Internet and World Wide Web

The **Internet,** or **Net**, is a collection of millions of computers that provide a network of electronic connections between the computers. The Internet began in 1969 when the U.S. Department of Defense created electronic communications for military and national defense purposes. Building on this start, in the 1980s, the National Science Foundation, the federal government's main scientific and technical agency, established the Net to facilitate high-speed communications among research centers at academic and research institutions around the world.

Internet
A collection of millions of computers that provide a network of electronic connections between computers.

Eventually, individuals and businesses began using the Internet for communication of information and data. In 1980, there were fewer than 250 computers hooked to the Internet. Growth was rapid in the late 1990s and in the early 2000s, and today there are several hundred million computers connected to the Internet. The Internet's evolution helped usher in the Information Age of today.

The World Wide Web

World Wide Web
An electronic connection of millions of computers that support a standard set of rules for the exchange of information.

The **World Wide Web** consists of millions of computers that support a standard set of rules for the exchange of information called Hypertext Transfer Protocol (HTTP). Web-based documents are formatted using common coding languages such as Hypertext Markup Language (HTML) and Java. Businesses and individuals can hook up to the Web by registering with a server such as America Online (AOL) or other servers.

Individuals and businesses can have their own Web sites. A Web site is composed of electronic documents known as Web pages. Web sites and pages are stored on servers throughout the world, which are operated by **Internet service providers (ISP)**. They are viewed by using Web browsing software such as Microsoft Internet Explorer and Netscape Navigator. Each Web site has a unique online address. Web pages can contain a full range of multimedia content, including text, images, video, sound, and animation. Web pages can include references, called *hyperlinks*, or *links*, to other Web pages or sites.

The Web has made it extremely attractive to conduct commercial activities online. Companies such as Amazon.com and eBay are e-commerce powerhouses that sell all sorts of goods and services. Existing brick-and-mortar companies, such as Wal-Mart, Merrill Lynch, and Dell Computers, sell their goods and services online as well. E-commerce over the Web will continue to grow dramatically each year.

Electronic Mail

electronic mail (e-mail)
Electronic written communication between individuals using computers connected to the Internet.

Electronic mail, or **e-mail**, is one of the most widely used applications for communication over the Internet. Using e-mail, individuals around the world can instantaneously communicate with one another in electronic writing. Each person can have an e-mail address that identifies him or her by a unique address. E-mail will continue to grow in use in the future as it replaces some telephone and paper correspondence and increases new communication between persons.

Cambodia. The Internet and World Wide Web are available throughout the world.

Domain Names

Most businesses conduct e-commerce by using Web sites that can be located on the Internet under domain names. Each Web site is identified by a unique Internet **domain name**. For example, the domain name for the publisher of this book is **www.prenhall.com**. Some of the top-level suffixes for domain names are *.com* for commercial use, *.net* for networks, *.org* for organizations, and *.edu* for educational institutions.

domain name
A unique name that identifies an individual's or company's Web site.

Domain names can be registered. The first step in registering a domain name is to determine whether any other party owns the name. For this purpose, InterNIC maintains a "Whois" database that contains the domain names that have been registered. The InterNIC Web site is located online at **internic.net**. Domain names can also be registered at Network Solutions, Inc., Web site, which is located at **www.networksolutions.com**, as well as at other sites. An applicant must complete a registration form, which can be done online. It costs less than $50 to register a domain name for one year, and the fee may be paid by credit card online.

The most commonly used top-level extensions for domain names are:

- ***.com.*** This extension represents the word *commercial* and is the most widely used extension in the world. Most businesses prefer a .com domain name because it is a highly recognized business symbol.
- ***.net.*** This extension represents the word *network*, and it is most commonly used by ISPs, Web-hosting companies, and other businesses that are directly involved in the infrastructure of the Internet. Some businesses also choose domain names with a .net extension.
- ***.org.*** This extension represents the word *organization* and is primarily used by nonprofit groups and trade associations.
- ***.info.*** This extension signifies a resource Web site. It is an unrestricted global name that may be used by businesses, individuals, and organizations.
- ***.biz.*** This extension is used for small-business Web sites.
- ***.us.*** This extension is for U.S. Web sites. Many businesses choose this extension, which is a relatively new extension.
- ***.cc.*** This extension was originally the country code for Coco Keeling Islands, but it is now unrestricted and may be registered by anyone from any country. It is often registered by businesses.
- ***.bz.*** This extension was originally the country code for Belize, but it is now unrestricted and may be registered by anyone from any country. It is commonly used by small businesses.
- ***.name.*** This new extension is for individuals, who can use it to register personalized domain names.
- ***.museum.*** This extension enables museums, museum associations, and museum professionals to register Web sites.
- ***.coop.*** This extension represents the word *cooperative* and may be used by cooperative associations around the world.
- ***.aero.*** This extension is exclusively reserved for the aviation community. It enables organizations and individuals in that community to reserve Web sites.
- ***.pro.*** This extension is available to professionals, such as doctors, lawyers, consultants, and other professionals.
- ***.edu.*** This extension is for educational institutions.

It will be of little avail to the people, that the laws are made by men of their own choice, if the laws be so voluminous that they cannot be read, or so incoherent that they cannot be understood.

Alexander Hamilton
The Federalist Papers (1788)

Internet Law & Online Commerce

Domain Name Anticybersquatting Act

In November 1999, the U.S. Congress enacted, and the president signed, the **Anticybersquatting Consumer Protection Act** [15 U.S.C. § 1125(d)]. The act was specifically aimed at cybersquatters who register Internet domain names of famous companies and people and hold them hostage by demanding ransom payments from the famous company or person. In the past, trademark law was of little help in this area, either because the famous person's name was not trademarked or because, even if the name was trademarked, trademark law required distribution of goods or services to find infringement, and most cybersquatters did not distribute goods or services but merely sat on the Internet domain names. The 1999 act has two fundamental requirements: (1) The name must be famous and (2) the domain name must have been registered in bad faith. Thus, the law prohibits the act of cybersquatting itself if it is done in *bad faith*.

The first issue in applying the statute is whether the domain name is someone else's famous name. Trademarked names qualify; nontrademarked names—such as those of famous actors, actresses, singers, sports stars, politicians, and such—are also protected. In determining bad faith, the law provides that courts may consider the extent to which the domain name resembles the holder's name or the famous person's name, whether goods or services are sold under the name, the holder's offer to sell or transfer the name, and whether the holder has acquired multiple Internet domain names of famous companies and persons.

The act provides for issuance of cease-and-desist orders and injunctions by the court. In addition, the law adds monetary penalties: A plaintiff has the option of seeking statutory damages of between $1,000 and $300,000 in lieu of proving damages. The Anticybersquatting Consumer Protection Act gives owners of trademarks and persons with famous names a new weapon to attack the kidnapping of Internet domain names by cyberpirates.

For example, the Academy Award–winning actress Julia Roberts won back the domain name **Juliaroberts.com** because it had been registered in bad faith by another party. The singer Sting was not so lucky because the word *sting* is generic, allowing someone else to register and keep the domain name **sting.com**. ■

In the following case, the court applied the federal anticybersquatting act.

Case 14.1
Cybersquatting

E. & J. Gallo Winery v. Spider Webs Ltd.
286 F.3d 270, 2002 U.S. App. Lexis 5928
United States Court of Appeals, Fifth Circuit

Background and Facts

Ernest & Julio Gallo Winery (Gallo) is a famous maker of wines that is located in California. The company registered the trademark "Ernest & Julio Gallo" in 1964 with the United States Patent and Trademark Office. The company has spent over $500 million promoting its brand name and has sold more than four billion bottles of wine. Its name has taken on a secondary meaning as a famous trademark name. In 1999, Steve, Pierce, and Fred Thumann created Spider Webs Ltd., a limited partnership, to register Internet domain names. Spider Webs registered more than 2,000 Internet domain names, including ernestandjuliogallo.com. Spider Webs was in the business of selling domain names. Gallo filed suit against Spider Webs Ltd. and the Thumanns, alleging violation of the federal Anticybersquatting Consumer Protection Act (ACPA). The district court held in favor of Gallo and ordered Spider Webs to transfer the domain name **ernestandjuliogallo.com** to Gallo. Spider Webs Ltd. appealed.

Issue

Did Spider Webs Ltd. and the Thumanns act in bad faith in registering the Internet domain name **ernestandjuliogallo.com**?

In the Language of the Court

Spider Webs does not appeal the holdings that Gallo had a valid registration in its mark, that the mark is famous and distinctive, and that the domain name registered by Spider Webs is identical or confusingly similar to Gallo's mark. However, Spider Webs argues that they did not act with a "bad faith intent to profit," as required by the ACPA.

Spider Webs has no intellectual property rights or trademark in the name "ernestandjuliogallo," aside from its registered domain name. The domain name does not contain the name of Spider Webs or any of the other defendants. Spider Web had no prior use (or any current use) of the domain in connection with the bona fide offering of goods or services.

Steve Thumann admitted that the domain name was valuable and that they hoped Gallo would contact them so that they could "assist" Gallo in some way. There is uncontradicted evidence that Spider Webs was engaged in commerce in the selling of domain names and that they hoped to sell this domain name some day.

There was evidence presented that Gallo's mark is distinctive and famous. Further, Gallo registered the mark, which is a family name, thirty-eight years ago, and other courts have found that "Gallo" has clearly become associated with wine in the United States such that its evolution to 'secondary meaning' status may not be seriously questioned. The circumstances of this case all indicate that Spider Webs knew Gallo had a famous mark in which Gallo had built up goodwill, and that they hoped to profit from this by registering "ernestandjuliogallo.com" and waiting for Gallo to contact them so they could "assist" Gallo. In sum, the factors strongly support a finding of bad faith.

Decision and Remedy

The Court of Appeals held that the name Ernest and Julio Gallo was a famous trademark name and that Spider Web Ltd. and the Thumanns had acted in bad faith when they registered the Internet domain name **ernestandjulio.com**. The Court of Appeals upheld the district court's decision, ordering the defendants to transfer the domain name to plaintiff E. & J. Gallo Winery.

Business and Ethics Questions

1. Should Congress have enacted the ACPA? Does it really protect consumers? Explain.
2. Did the defendants act ethically in registering so many Internet domain names? What was the motive of the defendants?
3. How valuable is a company's trademark name? Does the ACPA protect that value? Explain.

Internet Law & Online Commerce

Armani Outmaneuvered for Domain Name

G. A. Modefine S.A. is the owner of the famous "Armani" trademark, under which it produces and sells upscale and high-priced apparel. The Armani label is recognized worldwide. But Modefine was surprised when it tried to register for the domain name **armani.com** and found that it had already been taken. Modefine brought an arbitration action in the World Intellectual Property Organization (WIPO), an international arbitration and mediation center, against the domain name owner to recover the **armani.com** domain name. To win, Modefine had to prove that the domain name was identical or confusingly similar to its trademark, the owner who registered the name did not have a legitimate interest in the name, and the owner registered the name in bad faith.

The person who owned the domain name, Anand Ramnath Mani, appeared at the proceeding and defended his ownership rights. The arbitrator found that Modefine's trademark and Mr. Mani's domain name were identical but held that Mr. Mani had a legitimate claim to the domain name. The arbitrator wrote that it is "common practice for people to register domain names which are based upon initials and a name, acronyms or otherwise variants of their full names." The court rejected Modefine's claim that Mr. Mani's offer to sell the name for $1,935 constituted bad faith. The arbitrator ruled against Modefine and permitted Mr. Mani to own the domain name **armani.com**. *G. A. Modefine S. A. v A. R. Mani*, 2001 WIPO, No. D2001–0537 ■

E-Contracts

E-mail and the Web have exploded as means of personal and business communication. In the business environment, e-mail and the Web are sometimes the methods used to negotiate and agree on contract terms and to send and agree to a final contract. Are e-mail and Web contracts enforceable? Assuming that all the elements to establish a contract are present, an **e-mail** or **Web contract** is valid and enforceable. The main problem in a lawsuit seeking to enforce an e-mail or Web contract is evidence, but this problem, which exists in almost all lawsuits, can be overcome by printing out the e-mail or Web contract and its prior e-mail or Web negotiations, if necessary.

e-mail and Web contracts
Contracts entered into by e-mail and over the World Wide Web.

Internet Law & Online Commerce

E-Contracts Writing Requirement

In 2000, the federal government enacted the **Electronic Signature in Global and National Commerce Act**, also known as the **E-Sign Act**. This act is a federal statute enacted by Congress that therefore has national reach. The act is designed to place the world of electronic commerce on a par with the world of paper contracts in the United States.

One of the main features of the act is that it recognizes electronic contracts (e-contracts) as meeting the writing requirement of the Statute of Frauds for most contracts. Statutes of Frauds are state laws that require certain types of contracts to be in writing. The new federal act provides that electronically signed contracts cannot be denied effect because they are in electronic form or delivered electronically. The act also provides that record retention requirements are satisfied if the records are stored electronically.

The federal law was passed with several provisions to protect consumers. First, consumers must consent to receiving electronic records and contracts. Second, to receive electronic records, consumers must be able to demonstrate that they have access to the electronic records. Third, businesses must tell consumers that they have the right to receive hardcopy documents of the transaction. ■

Internet Law & Online Commerce

E-Signatures

In the past, signatures were hand-applied by the person signing the document. No more. In the electronic commerce world, it is now "What is your mother's maiden name?" "Slide your smart card in the sensor," or "Look into the iris scanner." But are electronic signatures sufficient to form an enforceable contract? In 2000, the federal government stepped into the breach and enacted the **Electronic Signature in Global and National Commerce Act**.

One of the main features of this federal law is that it recognizes an *electronic signature*, or *e-signature*. This act gives an e-signature the same force and effect as a pen-inscribed signature on paper. The act is technology neutral, however, in that the law does not define or decide which technologies should be used to create a legally binding signature in cyberspace. Loosely defined, a *digital signature* is some electronic method that identifies an individual. The challenge is to make sure that someone who uses a digital signature is the person he or she claims to be. The act provides that a digital signature can basically be verified in one of three ways:

1. By something the signatory knows, such as a secret password, pet's name, and so forth
2. By something a person has, such as a smart card, which looks like a credit card and stores personal information
3. By biometrics, which uses a device that digitally recognizes fingerprints or the retina or iris of the eye

The verification of electronic signatures is creating a need for the use of scanners and methods for verifying personal information. ■

E-Licensing

Uniform Computer Information Transactions Act (UCITA)
A model state law that creates contract law for the licensing of information technology rights.

Much of the new cyberspace economy is based on electronic contracts and the licensing of computer information. E-commerce created problems for forming contracts over the Internet, enforcing e-commerce contracts, and providing consumer protection. To address these problems, in 1999, the National Conference of Commissioners on Uniform State Laws (a group of lawyers, judges, and legal scholars) drafted the **Uniform Computer Information Transactions Act (UCITA)**. This is a model act that establishes a uniform and comprehensive set of rules that govern the creation, performance, and enforcement of computer information transactions. A computer information transaction is an agreement

Russia. Electronic commerce has made it possible to shop online and purchase goods from around the world.

to create, transfer, or license computer information or information rights [UCITA § 102(a)(11)].

The UCITA does not become law until a state's legislature enacts it as a state statute. States have adopted the UCITA or laws similar to the UCITA as their law for computer transactions and the licensing of informational rights.

Unless displaced by the UCITA, state law and equity principles, including principal and agent law, fraud, duress, mistake, trade secret law, and other state laws, supplement the UCITA [UCITA § 114]. Any provisions of the UCITA that are preempted by federal law are enforceable to the extent of the preemption [UCITA § 105(a)].

Licensing

Intellectual property and information rights are an extremely important asset of many individuals and companies. Patents, trademarks, copyrights, trade secrets, data, software programs, and such constitute valuable intellectual property and information rights.

The owners of intellectual property and information rights often wish to transfer limited rights in the property or information to parties for specified purposes and limited duration. The agreement that is used to transfer such limited rights is called a **license**, which is defined as follows [UCITA § 102(a)(40)]:

> License means a contract that authorizes access to, or use, distribution, performance, modification, or reproduction of, information or informational rights, but expressly limits the access or uses authorized or expressly grants fewer than all rights in the information, whether or not the transferee has title to a licensed copy. The term includes an access contract, a lease of a computer program, and a consignment of a copy.

license
A contract that transfers limited rights in intellectual property and informational rights.

The parties to a license are the licensor and the licensee. The **licensor** is the party who owns the intellectual property or information rights and obligates him- or herself to transfer rights in the property or information to the licensee. The **licensee** is the party who is granted limited rights in or access to the intellectual property or information rights [UCITA §§ 102 (a)(41), 102 (a)(42)]. A licensing arrangement is illustrated in Exhibit 14.1.

licensor
The owner of intellectual property or informational rights who transfer rights in the property or information to the licensee.

licensee
The party who is granted limited rights in or access to intellectual property or informational rights owned by the licensor.

Exhibit 14.1
Licensing Arrangement

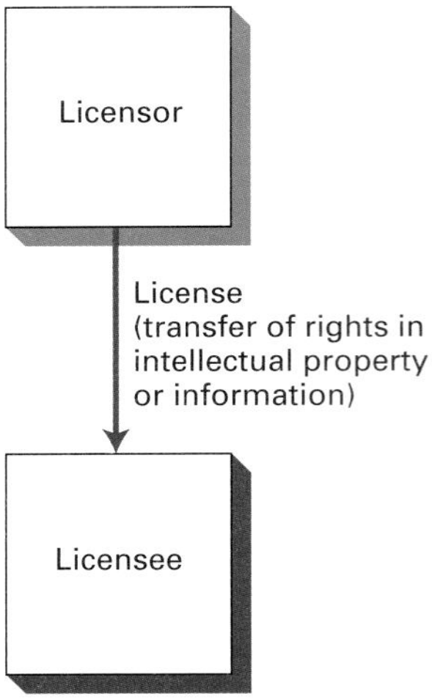

A license grants the contractual rights expressly described in the license and the right to use any information rights within the licensor's control that are necessary to exercise the expressly described rights [UCITA § 307(a)].

exclusive license
A license that grants the licensee exclusive rights to use informational rights for a specified duration.

A license can grant the licensee the exclusive rights to use the information. An **exclusive license** means that for the specified duration of the license, the licensor will not grant to any other person rights in the same information [UCITA § 307(f)(2)].

Licensing Agreement

licensing agreement
A detailed and comprehensive written agreement between a licensor and licensee that sets forth the express terms of their agreement.

The licensor and licensee usually enter into a written **licensing agreement** that expressly states the terms of their agreement. Licensing agreements tend to be very detailed and comprehensive contracts. This is primarily because of the nature of the subject matter and the limited uses granted in the intellectual property or informational rights.

Internet Law & Online Commerce

Counteroffers Ineffectual Against Electronic Agents

In today's e-commerce, many sellers use electronic agents to sell goods and services. An *electronic agent* is any telephonic or computer system that has been established by a seller to accept orders. Voice mail and Web page order systems are examples of electronic agents.

In the past, when humans dealt with each other face-to-face, by telephone, or in writing, their negotiations might have consisted of an exchange of several offers and counteroffers until agreed-upon terms were reached and a contract was formed. Each new counteroffer extinguished the previous offer and became a new viable offer. Most electronic agents do not have the ability to evaluate and accept counteroffers or to make counteroffers. The UCITA recognizes this limitation and provides that a contract is formed if an individual takes action that causes the electronic agent to cause performance or promise benefits to the individual. Thus, counteroffers are not effective against electronic agents [UCITA § 206(a)].

Consider This Example "Birdie" is an electronic ordering system for placing orders for electronic information sold by the Green Company, a producer of computer software and electronic information. Freddie Calloway dials the Green Company's toll-free telephone number and orders new software for $1,000, using the Birdie voice mail electronic ordering system. Freddie enters the product code and description, his mailing address and credit card information, and other data needed to complete the transaction, but at the end of the order, he states, "I will accept this software if, after two weeks of use, I am satisfied with the software." Because Freddie has placed the order with an electronic agent, Freddie has ordered the software, and his counteroffer is ineffectual. ■

Breach of License Agreements

The parties to a contract for the licensing of information owe a duty to perform the obligations stated in the contract. If a party fails to perform as required, there is a breach of the contract. Breach of contract by one party to a licensing agreement gives the non-breaching party certain rights, including the right to recover damages or other remedies [UCITA § 701].

Each party to a license agreement expects to receive due performance from the other party. If any reasonable grounds arise prior to the performance date that make one party think that the other party might not deliver performance when due, the aggrieved party may demand adequate assurance of due performance from the other party. Until such assurance is received, the aggrieved party may, if commercially reasonable, suspend performance until assurance is received. Failure to provide assurance within 30 days permits the aggrieved party to repudiate the contract [UCITA § 708].

If the licensor tenders a copy that is a material breach of the contract, the non-breaching party to whom tender is made may either (1) refuse the tender, (2) accept the tender, or (3) accept any commercially reasonable units and refuse the rest [UCITA § 704].

If a licensee has accepted tender of a copy where the nonconformity is a material breach, the licensee may later revoke his or her acceptance if (1) acceptance was made because discovery was difficult at the time of tender but was then later discovered or (2) the nonconformity was discovered at the time of tender but the licensor agreed to cure the defect, and the defect has not been reasonably cured [UCITA § 707].

Our legal system faces no theoretical dilemma but a single continuous problem: how to apply to ever changing conditions the never changing principles of freedom.

Earl Warren

Internet Law & Online Commerce

Consumers Saved from Electronic Errors

The UCITA provides that a consumer is not bound by his or her unilateral electronic error if the consumer:

1. Promptly upon learning of the error notifies the licensor of the error
2. Does not use or receive any benefit from the information, or make the information or benefit available to a third party
3. Delivers all copies of the information to the licensor or destroys all copies of the information, pursuant to reasonable instructions from the licensor
4. Pays all shipping, reshipping, and processing costs of the licensor [UCITA § 217]

The UCITA does not relieve a consumer of his or her electronic error if the other party provides a reasonable method to detect and correct or avoid the error. Thus, many sellers establish methods whereby the buyer must verify the information and purchase order a second time before an electronic order is processed. This procedure strips the consumer of the defense of UCITA Section 217. Section 217 of the UCITA applies only to consumers who make electronic errors in contracting. Electronic errors by nonconsumers are handled under the common law of contracts or the Uniform Commercial Code (UCC), whichever applies.

Consider This Example Kai, a consumer, intends to order 10 copies of a video game over the Internet from Cybertendo, a video game producer. In fact, Kai makes an error and orders 110 games. The electronic agent maintaining Cybertendo's Web site's ordering process electronically disburses 110 games. The next morning, Kai discovers his mistake and immediately e-mails Cybertendo, describing the mistake and offering to return or destroy the copies at his expense. When Kai receives the games, he returns the 110 copies unused. Under the UCITA, Kai has no contract obligation for 110 copies but bears the cost of returning them to Cybertendo or destroying them if Cybertendo instructs him to do so. However, if Cybertendo's Web site's electronic ordering system had asked Kai to confirm his order of 110 copies of the purchase order and Kai had confirmed the original order of 110 copies, Kai would have had to pay for the 110 copies, even if his confirmation had been in error. ■

Remedies

> You must remember that some things that are legally right are not morally right.
>
> Abraham Lincoln

The UCITA provides certain *remedies* to an aggrieved party upon the breach of a licensing agreement. A party may not recover more than once for the same loss, and his or her remedy (other than liquidated damages) may not exceed the loss caused by the breach [UCITA § 801]. The UCITA provides that a cause of action must be commenced within one year after the breach was or should have been discovered, but not more than five years after the breach actually occurred [UCITA § 805]. Remedies are discussed in the following paragraphs.

Cancellation

cancellation
The termination of a contract by a contracting party upon the material breach of the contract by the other party.

If there has been a material breach of a contract that has not been cured or waived, the aggrieved party may cancel the contract. **Cancellation** is effective when the canceling party notifies the breaching party of the cancellation. Upon cancellation, the breaching party in possession or control of copies, information, documentation, or other materials that are the property of the other party must use commercially reasonable efforts to return them or hold them for disposal on instructions from the other party. All obligations that are executory on both sides at the time of cancellation are discharged [UCITA §§ 802(a), 802(b)].

Upon cancellation of a license, the licensor has the right to have all copies of the licensed information returned by the licensee and to prevent the licensee from continuing to use the licensed information.

Licensor's Damages

licensor's damages
Monetary damages that a licensee causes by breaching a contract. The licensor may sue and recover these damages.

If a licensee breaches a contract, the licensor may recover **licensor's damages.** The licensor may sue and recover from the licensee monetary damages caused by the breach, plus any consequential and incidental damages [UCITA § 808]. A licensor can recover *lost profits* caused by the licensee's failure to accept or complete performance of the contract. Lost profits is a proper measure of damages in this case because the licensor has effectively unlimited capability to make access available to others so there will be no license to substitute to reduce damages owed by the breaching licensee.

Consider This Example iSuperSoftware.com licenses a master disk of its software program to Distributors, Inc., to make and distribute 10,000 copies of the software. This is a nonexclusive license, and the license fee is $1 million. It costs iSuperSoftware.com $15 to produce the disk. If Distributors, Inc., refuses the disk and breaches the contract, iSuperSoftware.com can recover $1 million less $15 as damages for the profits lost on the transaction.

Licensor's Right to Cure

right to cure
A right that a licensor has to make amends under certain conditions after breaching a contract.

Unlike the common law of contracts, the UCITA provides that a licensor has the **right to cure** a breach of a license in certain circumstances. A breach of contract may be cured if (1) the time of performance of the contract has not expired and the licensor makes conforming performance within the time of performance; (2) the time of performance has expired but the licensor had reasonable grounds to believe the performance would be acceptable, in which case the licensor has a reasonable time to make conforming performance; or (3) the licensor makes conforming performance before the licensee cancels the contract. In all three situations, the licensor must reasonably notify the licensee of the intent to cure [UCITA § 703(a)].

Internet Law & Online Commerce
Electronic Self-Help

Just like normal contracts, electronic licenses can be breached by licensees. If such a breach occurs, the licensor can resort to remedies provided in the UCITA. Sections 815 and 816 of the UCITA provide that a licensor can resort to electronic self-help if a breach occurs—for example, if the licensee fails to pay the license fee. Such electronic self-help can consist of activating disabling bugs and time bombs that have been embedded in the software or information that will prevent the licensee from further using the software or information.

Section 816 provides that a licensor is entitled to use electronic self-help only if the following requirements are met:

1. The licensee must specifically agree to the inclusion in the license of self-help as a remedy. There must be a specific self-help option to which the licensee assents.
2. The licensor must give the licensee at least 15 days' notice prior to the disabling action. The notice period allows the licensee to make lawful adjustments to minimize the effects of the licensor's self-help or to seek a judicial remedy to combat the use of the self-help.
3. The licensor may not use self-help if it would cause a breach of the peace, risk personal injury, cause significant damage or injury to information other than the licensee's information, result in injury to the public health or safety, or cause grave harm to national security.

A licensor who violates these provisions and uses self-help improperly is liable for damages. This liability cannot be disclaimed. ■

Licensee's Damages

When a licensor breaches a contract, the licensee may sue and recover monetary damages from the licensor. The amount of the damages depends on the facts of the situation. This is called the **licensee's damages.** Upon the licensor's breach, the licensee may either (1) cover by purchasing other electronic information from another source and recover the difference between the value of the promised performance from the licensor and the cost of cover or (2) not cover and recover the value of the performance from the licensor. **Cover** involves engaging in a commercially reasonable substitute transaction. The licensee may obtain an award of consequential and incidental damages in either case. A licensee cannot obtain excessive or double recovery [UCITA § 809].

licensee's damages
Monetary damages that a licensee may sue and recover from a licensor when the licensor breaches a contract.

cover
A licensee's right to engage in a commercially reasonable substitute transaction after the licensor has breached the contract.

Consider This Example Auction.com is an Internet company that operates an online auction service. Auction.com enters into a contract with MicroHard, Inc., a software producer, for a site license to use MicroHard, Inc.'s software. Auction.com agrees to pay $500,000 as an initial license fee and $10,000 per month for the license duration of three years. Before Auction.com pays any money under the license, MicroHard, Inc., breaches the contract and does not deliver the software. Auction.com covers by licensing commercially similar software from another software company for the payment of a $600,000 initial licensing fee and $11,000 per month for the license duration of three years. Under the facts of this case, Auction.com can recover $100,000 for the increased initial fee and $36,000 for the increased monthly costs from MicroHard, Inc., for breach of contract.

Limitations of Remedies

The UCITA provides that the parties to an agreement may limit the remedies available for breach of the contract. This is done by including provisions in the contract. Remedies may be restricted to the return of copies and repayment of the licensing fee or limited to the repair or replacement of the nonconforming copies. Limitations of remedies in licenses subject to the UCITA are enforceable unless they are unconscionable [UCITA § 803].

In the following case, the court upheld a limitation-on-remedies clause in a software license.

Case 14.2 Limitation of Remedies

M.A. Mortenson Company, Inc. v. Timberline Software Corporation

970 P.2d 803, 1999 Wash.App. Lexis 185
Court of Appeals of Washington

Background and Facts

The Timberline Software Corporation (Timberline) produces software programs that contractors use to prepare bids to do work on construction projects. The M. A. Mortenson Company (Mortenson), a contractor, had been using Timberline software for some time without any problem. In 1993, Timberline introduced an advanced version of its bidding software program called *Precision*. Mortenson, as the licensee, entered into a license agreement with Timberline, the licensor, to license the use of the Precision software. Timberline delivered the software to Mortenson, and a Timberline representative installed the software on Mortenson's computer. The software license agreement contained the following terms, which were printed on the outside of the envelope in which the software disks were packaged and on the inside cover of the user's manual, and they also appeared on the introductory computer screen each time the software program was executed:

> Carefully read the following terms and conditions before using the programs. Use of the programs indicates your acknowledgement that you have read this license, understand it, and agree to be bound by its terms and conditions. If you do not agree to these terms and conditions, promptly return the programs and user manuals to the place of purchase and your purchase price will be refunded. You agree that your use of the program acknowledges that you have read this license, understand it, and agree to be bound by its terms and conditions.
>
> Limitation of remedies and liability. Neither Timberline nor anyone else who has been involved in the creation, production or delivery of the programs or user manuals shall be liable to you for any damages of any type, including but not limited to, any lost profits, lost savings, loss of anticipated benefits, or other incidental or consequential damages arising out of the use or inability to sue such programs, whether arising out of contract, negligence, strict tort, or under any warranty, or otherwise, even if Timberline has been advised of the possibility of such damages or for any other claim by any other party. Timberline's liability for damages in no event shall exceed the license fee paid for the right to use the programs.

On December 2, 1993, Mortenson used the Precision software and prepared a bid to do contracting work for the Harborview Hospital project. While preparing the bid, the program aborted at lease five times before Mortenson's employees finished the bid. Subsequently, Mortenson claimed that its bid was $2 million under what it should have been had the Precision software program worked correctly. Mortenson sued Timberline to recover consequential damages, arguing that the Precision software had calculated an inaccurate bid. Timberline defended, alleging that the limitation-of-remedies clause in the software license prevented Mortenson's lawsuit. Mortenson countered that the limitation-of-remedies clause was unconscionable and therefore unenforceable. The trial court granted summary judgment to Timberline and dismissed the lawsuit. Mortenson appealed.

Issue

Was the limitation-of-remedies clause in the Timberline software license unconscionable?

In the Language of the Court

We hold that the terms of the present license agreement are part of the contract as formed between the parties. We find that Mortenson's installation and use of the software manifested its assent to the terms of the license and that it is bound by all terms of the license that are not found to be illegal or unconscionable.

Considering all the circumstances surrounding the transaction in this case, the limitations clause is not unconscionable. The introductory screen warned that use of the program was subject to a license. This warning placed Mortenson on notice that use of the software was governed by a license. Mortenson had reasonable opportunity to learn and understand the terms of the agreement. The limitation provision was not hidden in a maze of fine print but appeared in all capital letters. Finally, such limitations provisions are widely used in the computer software industry.

Decision and Remedy

The court of appeals held that the limitation-of-remedies clause in the software license was conspicuous and not unconscionable and that it therefore prohibited Mortenson's lawsuit to recover consequential damages from Timberline. The court of appeals affirmed the trial court's grant of summary judgments to Timberline that dismissed the case.

Business and Ethics Questions

1. What does the doctrine of unconscionability provide? Does this doctrine serve any useful purpose?
2. Did Timberline act ethically when it included a limitation-of-remedies clause in its software license?
3. What would be the business consequences if limitation-of-remedies clauses in software licenses were all held to be *per se* illegal?

Tibet, China. The use of the Internet is expanding around the globe. Chinese is the second-most-used language on the Internet.

Terms and Concepts

The Internet and World Wide Web

1. ***Internet.*** A collection of millions of computers that provide a network of electronic connections between computers.
2. ***World Wide Web.*** An electronic connection of computers that support a standard set of rules for the exchange of information called Hypertext Transfer Protocol (HTTP).
3. ***Electronic mail (e-mail).*** Electronic written communication between individuals using computers connected to the Internet.
4. ***E-mail contracts.*** Contracts that are formed electronically over the Internet using e-mail.

Electronic Privacy

Electronic Communications Privacy Act. A federal statute that makes it a crime to intercept an electronic communication at the point of transmission, while in transit, when stored by a router or server, or after receipt by the intended recipient.

Internet Domain Names

1. ***Domain name.*** A unique name that identifies an individual's or a company's Web site.
2. ***Internet Corporation for Assigned Names and Numbers (ICANN).*** ICANN is responsible for regulating the issuance of domain names on the Internet. ICANN approves registrars of domain names.
3. ***Domain name registration.*** One registers a domain name by filing the appropriate form with a domain name registration service and paying the appropriate fee.

Anticybersquatting Act

The *Anticybersquatting Consumer Protection Act (ACPA)* is a federal statute that permits a court to issue cease-and-desist orders and injunctions and to award monetary damages against anyone who has registered a domain name (1) of a famous name and (2) in bad faith.

Uniform Computer Information Transactions Act (UCITA)

The *Uniform Computer Information Transactions Act (UCITA)* is a model act issued by the National Conference of Commissioners on Uniform State Laws that establishes a uniform and comprehensive set of rules that governs the creation, performance, and enforcement of computer information transactions.

1. ***Adoption of UCITA by states.*** The UCITA does not become law until a state's legislature enacts it as a state statute.

Licensing of Information Rights

1. ***License.*** A license is a contract that transfers limited rights in intellectual property and informational rights.
2. ***Licensor.*** A licensor is the owner of intellectual property or information rights who transfers rights in the property or information to the licensee.
3. ***Licensee.*** A licensee is the party who is granted limited rights or access to intellectual property or information rights owned by the licensor.
4. ***Licensing agreement.*** A licensing agreement is a detailed and comprehensive written agreement between a licensor and licensee that sets forth the express terms of their agreement.
5. ***Access contract.*** An access contract is a type of license that grants the licensee access to the licensed information for an agreed-upon time or number of uses.

Electronic Signature in Global and National Commerce Act

The *Electronic Signature in Global and National Commerce Act*, also known as the *E-Sign Act*, is a federal statute that recognizes the validity of electronic contracts and electronic signatures.

1. ***Writing.*** The E-sign Act provides that electronic contracts meet the writing requirement of the Statute of Frauds for most contracts.
2. ***Record retention.*** The E-Sign Act provides that record retention requirements are satisfied if the records are stored electronically.
3. ***Electronic signatures.*** The E-Sign Act recognizes and gives electronic signatures, or e-signatures, the same force and effect as a pen-inscribed signature on paper. The act is technology neutral in that the law does not define or decide which technologies should be used to create a legally binding signature in cyberspace.

Counteroffer Rule

Counteroffers are not effective against electronic agents because most electronic agents do not have the ability to evaluate and accept counteroffers or make counteroffers.

Electronic Errors

The UCITA provides that a *consumer* is not bound by his or her unilateral electronic errors if the consumer:

1. Promptly upon learning of the error notifies the other party of the error.
2. Does not use or receive any benefit from the information or make the information or benefit available to a third party.
3. Delivers all copies of the information to the third party or destroys all copies of the information, pursuant to reasonable instructions from the other party.
4. Pays all shipping, reshipping, and processing costs of the other party.

Electronic Self-Help

If an electronic license has been breached by a licensee, the licensor can resort to electronic self-help such as activating disabling bugs and time bombs that have been embedded in the software or information that will prevent the licensee from further using the software or information. A licensor is entitled to use electronic self-help only if the following requirements are met:

1. The licensee specifically agrees to the inclusion in the license of self-help as a remedy.
2. The licensor must give the licensee at least 15 days' notice prior to the disabling action.
3. The licensor may not use self-help if it would cause a breach of the peace, risk personal injury, cause significant damage or injury to information other than the licensee's information, result in injury to the public health or safety, or cause grave harm to national security.

Internet Exercises and Case Questions

Working the Web Internet Exercises

1. For a discussion of the Federal Dilution Act, featuring Barbie, Elvis, and Coca-Cola, see **cyber.law.harvard.edu/property/respect/antibarbie.html**.
2. For an overview of the Electronic Signature in Global and National Commerce Act, explore the law review article "Are Online Business Transactions Executed by Electronic Signatures Legally Binding?" at **www.law.duke.edu/journals/dltr/Articles/2001dltr0005.html**.
3. Domain name dispute resolution procedures are presented in great detail at **http://www.arbforum.com/domains/UDRP/index.asp**. Check this site for everything from an overview to sample pleading forms.

Legal Environment Cases

14.1 Domain Name Francis Net, a freshman in college and a computer expert, browses Web sites for hours each day. One day she thinks to herself, "I can make money registering domain names and selling them for a fortune." She has recently seen an advertisement for Classic Coke, a cola drink produced and marketed by the Coca-Cola Company. The Coca-Cola Company has a famous trademark on the term *Classic Coke* and has spent millions of dollars advertising this brand and making the term famous throughout the United States and the rest of the world. Francis goes to the Web site **www.networksolutions.com**, an Internet domain name registration service, to see if the Internet domain name **classicoke.com** has been taken. She discovers that it is available, so she immediately registers the Internet domain name **classicoke.com** for herself and pays the $70 registration fee with her credit card. Coca-Cola Company decides to register the Internet domain name **classicoke.com**, but when it checks at Network Solutions, Inc.'s, Web site, it discovers that Francis Net has already registered the Internet domain name. Coca-Cola Company contacts Francis, who demands $500,000 for the name. Coca-Cola Company sues Francis to prevent Francis from using the Internet domain name classiccoke.com and to recover it from her under the federal ACPA. Who wins?

14.2 E-Mail Contract The Litle Steel Company is a small steel fabricator that makes steel parts for various metal machine shop clients. When Litle Steel Company receives an order from a client, it must locate and purchase 10 tons of a certain grade of steel to complete the order. The Litle Steel Company sends an e-mail message to West Coast Steel Company, a large steel company, inquiring about the availability of 10 tons of the described grade of steel. West Coast Steel Company replies by e-mail that it has available the required 10 tons of steel and quotes $450 per ton. The Litle Steel Company's purchasing agent replies by e-mail that the Litle Steel Company will purchase the 10 tons of described steel at the quoted price of $450 per ton. The e-mails are signed electronically by the Litle Steel Company's purchasing agent and the selling agent of West Coast Steel Company. When the steel arrives at the Litle Steel Company's plant, the Litle Steel Company rejects the shipment, claiming the defense of the Statute of Frauds. The West Coast Steel Company sues the Litle Steel Company for damages. Who wins?

14.3 Contract Einstein Financial Analysts, Inc. (EFA), has developed an electronic database that has recorded the number of plastic pails manufactured and sold in the United States since plastic was first invented. Using this data, and a complicated patented software mathematical formula developed by EFA, a user can predict with 100 percent accuracy (historically) how the stock of each of the companies of the Dow Jones Industrial Average will perform on any given day of the year. William Buffet, an astute billionaire investor, wants to increase his wealth, so he enters into an agreement with EFA whereby he is granted the sole right to use the EFA data (updated daily) and its financial model for the next five years. Buffet pays EFA $100 million for the right to the data and mathematical formula. After using the data and software formula for one week, Buffet discovers that EFA has also transferred the right to use the EFA plastic pail database and software formula to his competitor. Buffet sues EFA. What type of arrangement has EFA and Buffet entered into? Who wins?

14.4 License An Internet firm called Info.com, Inc., licenses computer software and electronic information over the Internet. Info.com has a Web site, **info.com**, where users can license Info.com software and electronic information. The Web site is operated by an electronic agent; a potential user enters Info.com's Web site and looks at available software and electronic information that is available from Info.com. Mildred Hayward pulls up the Info.com Web site on her computer screen and decides to order a certain type of Info.com software. Hayward enters the appropriate product code and description;

her name, mailing address, and credit card information; and other data needed to complete the order for a three-year license at $300 per month; the electronic agent has Hayward verify all the information a second time. When Hayward has completed verifying the information, she types at the end of her order, "I accept this electronic software only if after I have used it for two months I still personally like it." Info.com's electronic agent delivers a copy of the software to Hayward, who downloads the copy of the software onto her computer. Two weeks later Hayward sends the copy of the software back to Info.com, stating, "Read our contract: I personally don't like this software; cancel my license." Info.com sues Hayward to recover the license payments for three years. Who wins?

14.5 Electronic Signature David Abacus uses the Internet to place an order to license software for his computer from Inet.License, Inc. (Inet), through Inet's electronic Web site ordering system. Inet's Web page order form asks David to type in his name, mailing address, telephone number, e-mail address, credit card information, computer location information, and personal identification number. Inet's electronic agent requests that David verify the information a second time before it accepts the order, which David does. The license duration is two years, at a license fee of $300 per month. Only after receiving the verification of information does Inet's electronic agent place the order and send an electronic copy of the software to David's computer, where he installs the new software program. David later refuses to pay the license fees due Inet because he claims his electronic signature and information were not authentic. Inet sues David to recover the license fees. Is David's electronic signature enforceable against him?

14.6 License Tiffany Pan, a consumer, intends to order three copies of a financial software program from iSoftware, Inc. Tiffany, using her computer, enters iSoftware's Web site, **isoftware.com**, and places an order with the electronic agent that takes orders for the Web site. The license provides for a duration of three years at $300 per month for each copy of the software program. Tiffany enters the necessary product code and description; her name, mailing address, and credit card information; and other data necessary to place the order. When the electronic order form prompts Tiffany to enter the number of copies of the software program she is ordering, Tiffany mistakenly types in "30." ISoftware's electronic agent places the order and ships 30 copies of the software program to Tiffany. When Tiffany receives the 30 copies of the software program, she ships them back to iSoftware with a note stating, "Sorry, there has been a mistake. I only meant to order 3 copies of the software, not 30." When iSoftware bills Tiffany for the license fees for the 30 copies, Tiffany refuses to pay. ISoftware sues Tiffany to recover the license fees for 30 copies. Who wins?

14.7 License Silvia Miofsky licenses a software program from Accura.com, Inc., to sort information from a database to be used in Silvia's financial planning business. The license is for three years, and the license fee is $500 per month. The new software program from Accura.com will be run in conjunction with other software programs and databases used by Silvia in her business. The licensing agreement between Accura.com and Silvia and the label on the software package state that the copy of the licensed software program has been tested by Accura.com and will run without error. Silvia installs the copy of Accura.com's software, but every fifth or sixth time the program is run, it fails to operate properly and shuts down Silvia's computer and other programs. Silvia sends the software, marked *defective*, back to Accura.com. When Accura.com bills Silvia for the unpaid license fees for the three years of the license, Silvia refuses to pay. Accura.com sues Silvia to recover the license fees under the three-year license. Who wins?

14.8 License Metatag, Inc., is a developer and distributor of software and electronic information rights over the Internet. Metatag produces a software program called Virtual 4-D Links; a user of the program merely types in the name of the city and address anywhere in the world, and the computer transports the user there and creates a four-dimensional space and a sixth sense unknown to the world before. The software license is nonexclusive, and Metatag licenses its Virtual 4-D Link to millions of users worldwide. Nolan Bates, who has lived alone with his mother too long, licenses the Virtual 4-D Link program for five years for a $350 per month license fee. Bates uses the program for two months before his mother discovers why he has had a smile on his face lately. Bates, upon his mother's urging, returns the Virtual 4-D Link software program to Metatag, stating that he is canceling the license. Metatag sues Bates to recover the unpaid license fees. Who wins?

Ethics in Business

14.9 BluePeace.org is a new environmental group that has decided that expounding its environmental causes over the Internet is the best and most efficient way to spend its time and money to advance its environmental causes. To draw attention to its Web sites, BluePeace.org comes up with catchy Internet domain names. One is **macyswearus.org**, another is **exxonvaldezesseals.org**, and another is **generalmotorcrashesdummies.org**. The **macyswearus.org** Web site first shows beautiful women dressed in mink fur coats sold by Macy's Department Stores and then goes into graphic photos of minks being slaughtered and skinned and made into coats. The **exxonvaldezesseals.org** Web site first shows a beautiful, pristine bay in Alaska, with the *Exxon Valdez* oil tanker quietly sailing through the waters, and then it shows photos of the ship breaking open and spewing forth oil and then seals who are gooed with oil, suffocating and dying on the shoreline. The Web site **generalmotorscrashesdummies.org** shows a General Motors automobile involved in normal crash tests with dummies followed by photographs of automobile accident scenes where people and children lie bleeding and dying after an accident involving General Motors automobiles. Macy's Department Stores, the Exxon Oil Company, and the General Motors Corporation sue BluePeace.org for violating the federal Anticybersquatting Consumer Protection Act (ACPA).

Ethics Issues

1. What does the ACPA provide? Explain the law.
2. Has BluePeace.org acted unethically in this case? Explain.
3. Who wins? Why?

15

Entrepreneurship, Sole Proprietorships, and Partnerships

"One of the must fruitful source of ruin to men of the world is the recklessness or want of principle of partners, and it is one of the perils to which every man exposes himself who enters into partnership with another."

—V. C. Malins
Mackay v. Douglas (1872)

Chapter Objectives

After studying this chapter, you should be able to:

1. Define sole proprietorship and describe the liability of a sole proprietor.
2. Define general partnership and describe how general partnerships are formed.
3. Explain the tort and contract liability of general partners.
4. Define limited partnership and describe how limited partnerships are formed.
5. Explain the tort and contract liability of general and limited partners.

Chapter Contents

- Entrepreneurship
- Sole Proprietorship
- General Partnership
- Limited Partnership

A person who wants to start a business must decide whether the business should operate as one of the major forms of business organization—*sole proprietorship, general partnership, limited partnership, limited liability partnership, limited liability company*, or *corporation*—or under some other available legal business form. The selection depends on many factors, including the ease and cost of formation, the capital requirements of the business, the flexibility of management decisions, government restrictions, the extent of personal liability, tax considerations, and the like.

Large businesses and transnational businesses, such as Intel Corporation, General Motors Corporation, and ExxonMobile Corporation, usually operate as corporations.

This chapter discusses entrepreneurship, sole proprietorships, general partnerships, and limited partnerships. Corporations, limited liability partnerships, limited liability companies, franchising, and other forms of business are discussed in following chapters.

University of Southern California campus. Many of today's students will become tomorrow's entrepreneurs.

Entrepreneurship

entrepreneur
A person who forms and operates a new business either by him- or herself or with others.

An **entrepreneur** is a person who forms and operates a new business. An entrepreneur may start the business by him- or herself or cofound the business with others. Most businesses started by entrepreneurs are small, although some grow into substantial organizations. For example, Bill Gates started Microsoft Corporation, which grew into the giant software and Internet company. Michael Dell started Dell Inc. as a mail-order business; it has become a leader in computer sales. Entrepreneurs in this country and elsewhere around the world create new businesses daily that hire employees, provide new products and services, and make economies of countries grow.

Entrepreneurial Forms of Conducting Business

Entrepreneurs contemplating starting a business have many options when choosing the legal form in which to conduct the business. Each of these forms of business has advantages and disadvantages for the entrepreneur. The major forms for conducting businesses and professions are:

> It is when merchants dispute about their own rules that they invoke the law.
>
> J. Brett
> *Robinsone v. Mollett* (1875)

1. Sole proprietorship
2. General partnership
3. Limited partnership
4. Limited liability partnership
5. Limited liability company
6. Corporation

Certain requirements must be met to form and operate each of these forms of business.

Sole Proprietorship

A **sole proprietorship** is the simplest form of business organization. The owner is the business. There is no separate legal entity. Sole proprietorships are the most common form of business organization in the United States. Many small businesses—and a few large ones—operate in this way.

sole proprietorship
A form of business in which the owner is actually the business; the business is not a separate legal entity.

There are several major advantages to operating a business as a sole proprietorship. They include the following:

1. Forming a sole proprietorship is easy and does not cost a lot.
2. The owner has the right to make all management decisions concerning the business, including those involving hiring and firing employees.
3. The sole proprietor owns all of the business and has the right to receive all of the business's profits.
4. A sole proprietorship can be easily transferred or sold if and when the owner desires to do so; no other approval (such as from partners or shareholders) is necessary.

There are important disadvantages to this business form, too. For example, (1) the sole proprietor's access to the capital is limited to personal funds plus any loans he or she can obtain, and (2) the sole proprietor is legally responsible for the business's contracts and the torts he or she or any of his or her employees commit in the course of employment.

Creation of a Sole Proprietorship

It is easy to create a sole proprietorship. There are no formalities, and no federal or state government approval is required. Some local governments require all businesses, including sole proprietorships, to obtain licenses to do business within the city. If no other form of business organization is chosen, the business is by default a sole proprietorship.

Contemporary Trend

d.b.a.—"Doing Business As"

A sole proprietorship can operate under the name of the sole proprietor or a *trade name*. For example, the author of this book can operate a sole proprietorship under the name "Henry R. Cheeseman" or under a trade name such as "The Big Cheese." Operating under a trade name is commonly designated as **d.b.a. (doing business as)** (e.g., Henry R. Cheeseman, doing business as "The Big Cheese").

Most states require any business that operates under a trade name to file a **fictitious business name statement (or certificate of trade name)** with the appropriate government agency. The statement must contain the name and address of the applicant, the trade name, and the address of the business. Most states also require notice of the trade name to be published in a newspaper of general circulation serving the area in which the applicant does business.

These requirements are intended to disclose the real owner's name to the public. Noncompliance can result in a fine. Some states prohibit violators from maintaining lawsuits in the state's courts. ■

Personal Liability of Sole Proprietors

A sole proprietor bears the risk of loss of the business; that is, the owner will lose his or her entire capital contribution if the business fails. In addition, the sole proprietor has *unlimited personal liability* (see Exhibit 15.1). Therefore, creditors may recover claims against the business from the sole proprietor's personal assets (e.g., home, automobile, bank accounts).

Exhibit 15.1
Sole Proprietorship

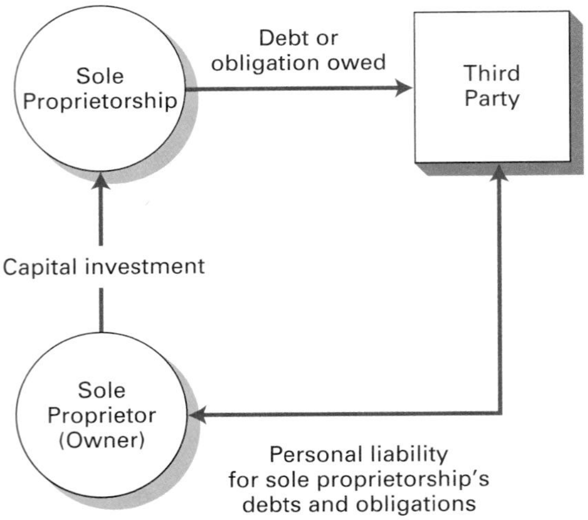

Consider This Example Suppose Kathan Perek opens the clothing store "The Clothing Store" and operates it as a sole proprietorship. Perek files the proper statement and publishes the necessary notice of the use of the trade name. Perek contributes $25,000 of his personal funds to the business and borrows $100,000 in the name of the business from a bank. Assume that after several months, Perek closes the business because it was unsuccessful. At the time it is closed, the business has no assets, owes the bank $100,000, and owes rent, trade credit, and other debts of $25,000. Here, Perek is personally liable to pay the bank and all the debts from his personal assets.

In the following case, the court addressed the liability of a sole proprietorship.

Case 15.1
Sole Proprietorship

Vernon v. Schuster, d/b/a Diversity Heating and Plumbing
688 N.E.2d 1172, 1997 Ill. Lexis 482
Supreme Court of Illinois

Background and Facts

James Schuster was a sole proprietor doing business as (d/b/a) "Diversity Heating and Plumbing." Diversity Heating was in the business of selling, installing, and servicing heating and plumbing systems. George Vernon and others (Vernon) owned a building that needed a new boiler. In November 1989, Vernon hired Diversity Heating to install a new boiler in the building. Diversity Heating installed the boiler and gave a warranty that the boiler would not crack for 10 years. On October 20, 1993, James Schuster died. On that date, James's son, Jerry Schuster, inherited his father's business and thereafter ran the business as a sole proprietorship under the d/b/a "Diversity Heating and Plumbing." In February 1994, the boiler installed in Vernon's building broke and could not be repaired. Vernon demanded that Jerry Schuster honor the warranty and replace the boiler. When Jerry Schuster refused to do so, Vernon had the boiler replaced at the cost of $8,203 and sued Jerry Schuster to recover this amount for breach of warranty. The trial court dismissed Vernon's complaint, but the appellate court reinstated the case. Jerry Schuster appealed to the supreme court of Illinois.

Issue

Is Jerry Schuster liable for the warranty made by his father?

In the Language of the Court

Common identity of ownership is lacking when one sole proprietorship succeeds another. It is well settled that a sole proprietorship has no legal identity separate from that of the individual who owns it. The sole proprietor may do business under a fictitious name if he or she chooses. However, doing business under another name does not create an entity distinct from the person operating the business. The individual who does business as a sole proprietor under one or several names remains one person, personally liable for all his or her obligations. There is generally no continuity of existence because on the death of the sole proprietor, the sole proprietorship obviously ends.

In this case, therefore, it must be remembered that "Diversity Heating" has no legal existence. Diversity Heating was only a pseudonym for James Schuster. Once he died, Diversity Heating ceased to exist. Now, Diversity Heating is only a pseudonym for the defendant, Jerry Schuster. Once sole proprietor James Schuster died, he could not be the same sole proprietor as defendant Jerry Schuster who became a sole proprietor after his father's death. James Schuster and Jerry Schuster, one succeeding the other, cannot be the same entity. Even though defendant Jerry Schuster inherited Diversity Heating from his father, defendant would not have continued his father's sole proprietorship, but rather would have started a new sole proprietorship.

Decision and Remedy

The Illinois supreme court held that Jerry Schuster, as a sole proprietor, was not liable for the warranty previously made by his father, who was also a sole proprietor. The supreme court reversed the decision of the appellate court.

Business and Ethics Questions

1. Is a sole proprietorship a separate legal entity? Explain.
2. Did Jerry Schuster act unethically by failing to honor the warranty made by his father?
3. Do you think many busines*ses are run as sole proprietorships? What are the benefits and detriments of doing so?

General Partnership

General, or *ordinary*, *partnerships* have been recognized since ancient times. The English common law of partnerships governed early U.S. partnerships. The individual states expanded the body of partnership law.

A **general partnership**, or partnership, is a voluntary association of two or more persons for carrying on a business as co-owners for profit. The formation of a partnership creates certain rights and duties among partners and with third parties. These rights and duties are established in the partnership agreement and by law. **General partners**, or **partners**, are personally liable for the debts and obligations of the partnership (see Exhibit 15.2).

general partnership
An association of two or more persons to carry on as co-owners of a business for profit [UPA § 6(1)].

Exhibit 15.2
General Partnership

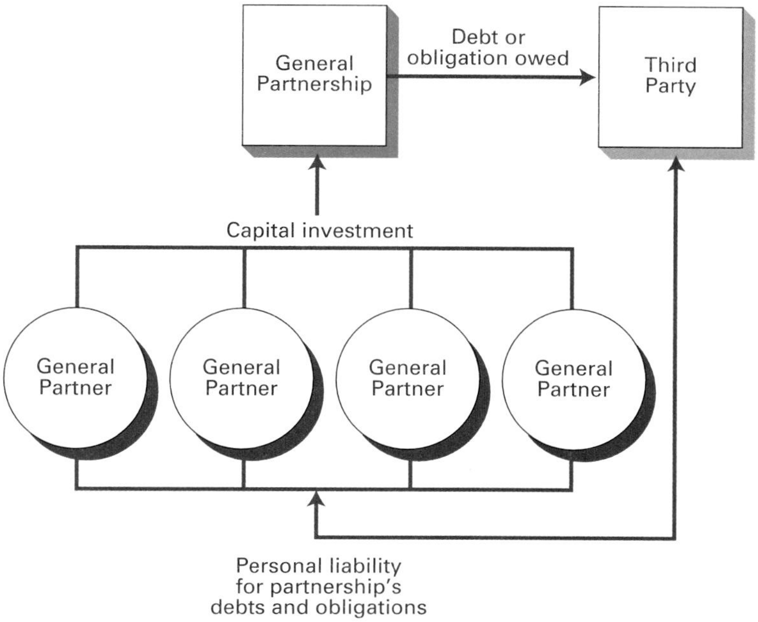

Uniform Partnership Act (UPA)

Uniform Partnership Act (UPA)
A model act that codifies partnership law. Most states have adopted the UPA in whole or in part.

In 1914, the National Conference of Commissioners on Uniform State Laws (a group of lawyers, judges, and legal scholars) promulgated the **Uniform Partnership Act (UPA)**. The UPA codifies partnership law. Its goal was to establish consistent partnership law that was uniform throughout the United States. The UPA has been adopted in whole or in part by 48 states,[1] the District of Columbia, Guam, and the Virgin Islands. Because it is so important, the UPA forms the basis of the study of general partnership in this chapter.

The UPA covers most problems that arise in the formation, operations, and dissolution of ordinary partnerships. Other rules of law or equity govern if there is no applicable provision of the UPA [UPA § 5].

The UPA adopted the *entity theory* of partnership, which considers partnerships as separate legal entities. As such, partnerships can hold title to personal and real property, transact business in the partnership name, and the like.

General Partnership Name

An ordinary partnership can operate under the names of any one or more of the partners or under a fictitious business name. If the partnership operates under a fictitious name, it must file a *fictitious business name statement* with the appropriate government agency and publish a notice of the name in a newspaper of general circulation where the partnership does business. The name selected by the partnership cannot indicate that it is a corporation (e.g., it cannot contain the term *Inc.*) and cannot be similar to the name used by any existing business entity.

Formation of a General Partnership

A business must meet four criteria to qualify as a partnership under the UPA [UPA § 6(1)]. It must be (1) an association of two or more persons (2) carrying on a business (3) as co-owners (4) for profit. Partnerships are voluntary associations of two or more persons. All partners must agree to the participation of each co-partner. A person cannot be forced to be a partner or to accept another person as a partner. The UPA definition of *person* includes natural persons, partnerships (including limited partnerships), corporations, and other associations. A business—trade, occupation, or profession—must be carried on. The organization or venture must have a profit motive in order to qualify as a partnership, even though the business does not actually have to make a profit.

The partner of my partner is not my partner.
Legal maxim

A general partnership may be formed with little or no formality. Co-ownership of a business is essential to create a partnership. The most important factor in determining co-ownership is whether the parties share the business's profits and management responsibility.

Receipt of a share of business profits is prima facie evidence of a partnership because nonpartners are usually not given the right to share in the business's profits. No inference of the existence of a partnership is drawn if profits are received in payment of (1) a debt owed to a creditor in installments or otherwise; (2) wages owed to an employee; (3) rent owed to a landlord; (4) an annuity owed to a widow, widower, or representative of a deceased partner; (5) interest owed on a loan; or (6) consideration for the sale of goodwill of a business [UPA § 7]. An agreement to share losses of a business is strong evidence of a partnership.

The right to participate in the management of a business is important evidence for determining the existence of a partnership, but it is not conclusive evidence because the right to participate in management is sometimes given to employees, creditors, and others.

It is compelling evidence of the existence of a partnership if a person is given the right to share in profits, losses, and management of a business.

The General Partnership Agreement

The agreement to form a partnership may be oral, written, or implied from the conduct of the parties. It may even be created inadvertently. No formalities are necessary, although a few states require general partnerships to file certificates of partnership with an appropriate government agency. Partnerships that exist for more than one year or are authorized to deal in real estate must be in writing under the Statute of Frauds.

It is good practice for partners to put their partnership agreement in writing. A written document is important evidence of the terms of the agreement, particularly if a dispute arises among the partners.

partnership agreement
A written partnership agreement that the partners sign. Also called *articles of partnership*.

A written partnership agreement is called a **partnership agreement**, or **articles of partnership**. The partners can agree to almost any terms in their partnership agreement, except terms that are illegal. The articles of partnership can be short and simple or long and complex. If the agreement fails to provide for an essential term or contingency, the provisions of the UPA control. Thus, the UPA acts as a gap-filling device to the partners' agreement.

In the following case, the court had to decide whether a partnership had been created.

Case 15.2
General Partnership

Vohland v. Sweet
435 N.E. 2d 860, 1982 Ind.App. Lexis 1145
Court of Appeals of Indiana

Background and Facts

Norman E. Sweet began working for Charles Vohland as an hourly employee at a garden nursery owned by Vohland in 1956, when he was a youngster. Upon completion of military service (from 1958 to 1960), Sweet resumed his former employment. In 1963, Charles Vohland retired, and his son Paul Vohland (Vohland) commenced what became known as Vohland's Nursery, the business of which was landscape gardening. Vohland purchased the interests of his brothers and sisters in the nursery. At that time, Sweet's status changed: He was to receive a 20 percent share of the net profit of the business after all expenses were paid, including labor, supplies, plants, and other expenses. Sweet contributed no capital to the enterprise. The compensation was paid on an irregular basis; every several weeks, Vohland and Sweet would sit down, compute the income received and expenses paid, and Sweet would be issued a check for 20 percent of the balance. No Social Security or income taxes were withheld from Sweet's checks.

Vohland and Sweet did not enter into a written agreement. No partnership income tax returns were filed by the business. Sweet's tax returns declared that he was a self-employed salesman. He paid self-employment Social Security taxes. Vohland handled all the finances and books of the nursery and borrowed money from the bank solely in his own name for business purposes. Vohland made most of the sales for the business. Sweet managed the physical aspects of the nursery, supervised the care of the nursery stock, and oversaw the performance of the contracts for customers. Sweet testified that in the early 1970s, Vohland told him:

> He was going to take me in and that I wouldn't have to punch a time clock anymore, that I would be on a commission basis and that I would be—have more of an interest in the business if I had an interest in the business. He referred to it as a "piece of the action."

Vohland denied having made this statement. Sweet brought an action for dissolution of the alleged partnership and for an accounting. He sought payment for 20 percent of the business's inventory. The trial court held in favor of Sweet and awarded him $58,733. Vohland appealed.

Issue

Did Vohland and Sweet enter into a general partnership?

In the Language of the Court

"Commission" was used to refer to Sweet's share of the profits, and the receipt of a share of the profits is prima facie evidence of a partnership. Though evidence is conflicting, there is evidence that the payments were not wages, but a share of the profit of a partnership. It can readily be inferred from the evidence most favorable to support the judgment that the parties intended a community of interest in any increment in the value of the capital and in the profit. Absence of contribution to capital is not controlling, and contribution of labor and skill will suffice. There is evidence from which it can be inferred that

(continued)

Vohland v. Sweet

435 N.E. 2d 860, 1982 Ind.App. Lexis 1145 Court of Appeals of Indiana

(continued)

the parties intended to do the things that amount to the formation of a partnership, regardless of how they may later characterize the relationship.

Decision and Remedy

The court of appeals held that a general partnership had been created between Vohland and Sweet. The court of appeals affirmed the decision of the trial court in favor of Sweet.

Business and Ethics Questions

1. Do you think a partnership was formed in this case? Should all partnership agreements be required to be in writing?
2. Do you think either party acted unethically in this case?
3. What are the economic consequences of founding a partnership?

Right to Participate in Management

management of partnerships
The running of a partnership. Unless otherwise agreed, each partner has a right to participate in the management of the partnership and has an equal vote on partnership matters.

In the absence of an agreement to the contrary, all partners have equal rights in the **management** and conduct of the partnership business. In other words, each partner has one vote, regardless of the proportional size of his or her capital contribution or share in the partnership's profits. Under the UPA, a simple majority decides most ordinary partnership matters [UPA § 18]. If the vote is tied, the action being voted on is considered to be defeated. The partners may agree to modify the majority rule by delegating management responsibility to a committee of partners or to a managing partner.

Right to an Accounting

action for an accounting
A formal judicial proceeding in which the court is authorized to (1) review the partnership and the partners' transactions and (2) award each partner his or her share of the partnership assets.

Partners are not permitted to sue the partnership or other partners at law. Instead, they are given the right to bring an **action for an accounting** against other partners. An *accounting* is a formal judicial proceeding in which the court is authorized to (1) review the partnership and the partners' transactions and (2) award each partner his or her share of the partnership assets [UPA § 24]. It results in a monetary judgment for or against partners, according to the balance struck.

General Partners' Rights to Share in Profits

Unless otherwise agreed, the UPA mandates that a partner has the right to an equal share in the partnership's profits and losses [UPA § 18(a)]. Partnership agreements often provide that profits and losses are to be allocated in proportion to the partners' capital contributions. The right to share in the profits of the partnership is considered to be the right to share in the earnings from the investment of capital.

For example, suppose LeAnn Pearson and Mark Butler form a partnership. Pearson contributes $75,000 capital, and Butler contributes $25,000 capital. They do not have an agreement as to how profits or losses are to be shared. Assume that the partnership makes $100,000 in profits. Under the UPA, Pearson and Butler share the profits equally—$50,000 each.

Where a partnership agreement provides for the sharing of profits but is silent as to how losses are to be shared, losses are shared in the same proportion as profits. The reverse is not true, however. If a partnership agreement provides for the sharing of losses but is silent as to how profits are to be shared, profits are shared equally.

Expressly providing how profits and losses are to be shared by partners can increase the benefits to partners. For example, partners with high incomes from other sources can benefit most from the losses generated by a partnership.

Tort Liability

While acting on partnership business, a partner or an employee of the partnership may commit a tort that causes injury to a third person. This tort could be caused by a negligent act, a breach of trust (such as embezzlement from a customer's account), a breach of fiduciary duty, defamation, fraud, or another intentional tort. The partnership is liable if the act is committed while the person is acting within the ordinary course of partnership business or with the authority of his or her co-partners.

Under the UPA, partners are **jointly and severally liable** for torts and breaches of trust [UPA § 15(a)]. This is so even if a partner did not participate in the commission of the act. This type of liability permits a third party to sue one or more of the partners separately. Judgment can be collected only against the partners who are sued. The partnership and partners who are made to pay tort liability may seek indemnification from the partner who committed the wrongful act. A release of one partner does not discharge the liability of other partners.

joint and several liability
Liability of partners for tort liability of the partnership in which the plaintiff can sue one or more of the partners separately. If successful, the plaintiff can recover the entire amount of the judgment from any or all of the defendant-partners.

Consider This Example Suppose Nicole, Jim, and Maureen form a partnership. Assume that Jim, while on partnership business, causes an automobile accident that injures Kurt, a pedestrian. Kurt suffers $100,000 in injuries. Kurt, at his option, can sue Nicole, Jim, or Maureen separately, or any two of them, or all of them.

The court applied the doctrine of joint and several liability in the following case.

Case 15.3
Tort Liability

Zuckerman v. Antenucci
478 N.Y.S,2d 578, 1984 N.Y.Misc. Lexis 3283
Supreme Court of New York

Background and Facts

Jose Pena and Joseph Antenucci were both medical doctors who were partners in a medical practice. Both doctors treated Elaine Zuckerman during her pregnancy. Her son, Daniel Zuckerman, was born with severe physical problems. Elaine, as Daniel's mother and natural guardian, brought a medical malpractice suit against both doctors. The jury found that Pena was guilty of medical malpractice but that Antenucci was not. The amount of the verdict totaled $4 million. The trial court entered judgment against Pena but not against Antenucci. The plaintiffs made a posttrial motion for judgment against both defendants.

Issue

Is Antenucci jointly and severally liable for the medical malpractice of his partner, Pena?

In the Language of the Court

A partnership is liable for the tortious act of a partner, and a partner is jointly and severally liable for tortious acts chargeable to the partnership. When a tort is committed by the partnership, the wrong is imputable to all of the partners jointly and severally, and an action may be brought against all or any of them in their individual capacities or against the partnership as an entity. Therefore, even though the jury found that defendant Antenucci was not guilty of any malpractice in his treatment of the patient, but that defendant Pena, his partner, was guilty of malpractice in his treatment of the patient, they were then both jointly and severally liable for the malpractice committed by defendant Pena by operation of law.

Decision and Remedy

The court held that both partners were jointly and severally liable for the judgment. The supreme court reversed the decision of the trial court and held that Antenucci was liable for the tort of his partner Pena.

Business and Ethics Questions

1. What is joint and several liability? How does it differ from joint liability?
2. Is it ethical for a partner to deny liability for torts of other partners?
3. What types of insurance should a partnership purchase? Why?

Contract Liability

As a legal entity, a partnership must act through its agents—that is, its partners. Contracts entered into with suppliers, customers, lenders, or others on the partnership's behalf are binding on the partnership.

joint liability
Partners' liability for contracts and debts of the partnership in which a plaintiff must name the partnership and all of the partners as defendants in a lawsuit.

Under the UPA, partners are **jointly liable** for the contracts and debts of the partnership [UPA § 15 (b)]. This means that a third party who sues to recover on a partnership contract or debt must name all the partners in a lawsuit. If such a lawsuit is successful, the plaintiff can collect the entire amount of the judgment against any or all of the partners. If the third party's suit does not name all the partners, the judgment cannot be collected against any of the partners or the partnership assets. Similarly, releasing any partner from the lawsuit releases them all.

A partner who is made to pay more than his or her proportionate share of contract liability may seek **indemnification** from the partnership and from those partners who have not paid their share of the loss.

Concept Summary *Personal Liability of General Partners*

Issue	Joint Liability	Joint and Several Liability
Type of lawsuit	Contract action.	Tort action.
Defendants	Plaintiff must name all partners as defendants.	Plaintiff can sue partners individually.
Recovery	If successful, the plaintiff can recover the judgment against all or any of the defendants.	If successful, the plaintiff can recover the judgment against all or any of the named defendants.
Indemnification	A partner who pays a judgment can recover contributions from other partners for their share of the judgment.	A partner who pays a judgment can recover contributions from other partners for their share of the judgment.

Liability of Incoming Partners

A new partner who is admitted to a partnership is liable for the existing debts and obligations (*antecedent debts*) of the partnership only to the extent of his or her capital contribution. The new partner is personally liable for debts and obligations incurred by the partnership after becoming a partner.

Consider This Example Bubble.com is a general partnership with four partners. On May 1, Frederick is admitted as a new general partner by investing $100,000 capital contribution. As of May 1, Bubble.com owes $800,000 of debt. After Frederick becomes a partner, the general partnership borrows $1 million of new debt. If the general partnership goes bankrupt and out of business still owing both debts, Frederick's capital contribution of $100,000 will go toward paying the $800,000 of existing debt owed by the partnership when he joined the partnership, but he is not personally liable for that debt. However, Frederick is personally liable for the $1 million of unpaid debt that the partnership borrowed after he became a partner.

Dissolution of a General Partnership

The duration of a partnership can be a fixed term (e.g., five years) or until a particular undertaking is accomplished (e.g., until a real estate development is completed), or it can be an unspecified term. A partnership with a fixed duration is called a **partnership for a term**. A partnership with no fixed duration is called a **partnership at will**.

The **dissolution** of a partnership is "the change in the relation of the partners caused by any partner ceasing to be associated in the carrying on of the business" [UPA § 29]. A partnership that is formed for a specific time (e.g., five years) or purpose (e.g., the completion of a real estate development) dissolves automatically upon the expiration of the time or the accomplishment of the objective. Any partner of a partnership at will (i.e., one without a stated time or purpose) may rightfully withdraw and dissolve the partnership at any time.

dissolution
"The change in the relation of the partners caused by any partner ceasing to be associated in the carrying on of the business" [UPA § 29].

Unless the partnership is continued, the **winding up** of the partnership follows its dissolution. The process of winding up consists of the liquidation (sale) of partnership assets and the distribution of the proceeds to satisfy claims against the partnership. The surviving partners have the right to wind up the partnership. If a surviving partner performs the winding up, he or she is entitled to reasonable compensation for his or her services [UPA § 18(f)].

winding up
The process of liquidating a partnership's assets and distributing the proceeds to satisfy claims against the partnership.

Wrongful Dissolution

A partner has the *power* to withdraw and dissolve a partnership at any time, whether it is a partnership at will or a partnership for a term. A partner who withdraws from a partnership at will has the *right* to do so and is therefore not liable for dissolving the partnership. A partner who withdraws from a partnership for a term prior to the expiration of the term does not have the right to dissolve the partnership. The partner's action causes a **wrongful dissolution** of the partnership. The partner is liable for damages caused by the wrongful dissolution of the partnership.

wrongful dissolution
A situation in which a partner withdraws from a partnership without having the right to do so at that time.

Consider This Example Ashley, Vivi, Qixia, and Tina form a general partnership called "Four Divas Clothing" to operate an upscale woman's clothing store. The partnership has a stated term of five years. After one year, Ashley decides to quit the partnership. Because Ashley has the power to quit the partnership, when she does so, the four-partner partnership dissolves. Ashley does not have the right to quit the partnership, and her action causes the wrongful dissolution of the partnership. She is liable for any damages caused by her wrongful dissolution of the partnership.

Notice of Dissolution

The dissolution of a partnership terminates the partners' actual authority to enter into contracts or otherwise act on behalf of the partnership. Notice of dissolution must be given to certain third parties. The degree of notice depends on the relationship of the third party with the partnership [UPA § 35]:

1. Third parties who have actually dealt with the partnership must be given *actual notice* (verbal or written) of dissolution or have acquired knowledge of the dissolution from another source.
2. Third parties who have not dealt with the partnership but have knowledge of it must be given either actual or *constructive notice* of dissolution. Constructive notice consists of publishing a notice of dissolution in a newspaper of general circulation serving the area where the business of the partnership was regularly conducted.

3. Third parties who have not dealt with the partnership and do not have knowledge of it do not have to be given notice.

If proper notice is not given to a required third party after the dissolution of a partnership and a partner enters into a contract with the third party, liability may arise on the grounds of *apparent authority*.

Distribution of Assets

After a partnership's assets have been liquidated and reduced to cash, the proceeds are distributed to satisfy claims against the partnership. The debts are satisfied in the following order [UPA § 40(b)]:

1. Creditors (except partners who are creditors)
2. Creditor-partners
3. Capital contributions
4. Profits

The partners can agree to change the priority of **distribution of assets** among themselves. If the partnership cannot satisfy its creditors' claims, the partners are personally liable for the partnership's debts and obligations [UPA §§ 40(d), 40(f)].

After the proceeds are distributed, the partnership automatically terminates. Termination ends the legal existence of the partnership [UPA § 30].

Continuation of a General Partnership After Dissolution

The surviving or remaining partners have the right to continue a partnership after dissolution. It is good practice for the partners in a partnership to enter into a *continuation agreement* that expressly sets forth the events that allow for continuation of the partnership, the amount to be paid to outgoing partners, and other details.

When a partnership is continued, the old partnership is dissolved, and a new partnership is created. The new partnership is composed of the remaining partners and any new partners admitted to the partnership. The creditors of the old partnership become creditors of the new partnership and have equal status with the creditors of the new partnership [UPA § 41].

Contemporary Trend

Right of Survivorship

A partner is a co-owner with the other partners of a partnership's specific property as a *tenant in partnership* [UPA § 25(1)]. This is a special legal status that exists only in a partnership. Upon the death of a partner, the deceased partner's right in specific partnership property vests in the remaining partner or partners—it does not pass to his or her heirs or next of kin. This is called the **right of survivorship**. Upon the death of the last surviving partner, the rights in specific partnership property vest in the deceased partner's legal representative [UPA § 25(2)C]. The *value* of the deceased partner's interest in the partnership passes to his or her beneficiaries or heirs upon his or her death, however.

Consider This Example Jaime, Harold, Shou-Ju, and Jesus form a general partnership to operate a new restaurant. After their first restaurant is successful, they expand until the partnership owns 100 restaurants. At that time, Jaime dies. None of the partnership assets transfer to Jaime's heirs; for example, the heirs do not get 25 of the restaurants. Instead, under the right of survivorship, they inherit Jaime's ownership interest, and his heirs now have the right to receive Jaime's one-quarter of the partnership's profits each year. ■

Limited Partnership

Limited partnerships are statutory creations that have been used since the Middle Ages. They include both general (manager) and limited (investor) partners. Today, all states have enacted statutes that provide for the creation of limited partnerships. In most states, these partnership are called **limited partnerships**, or **special partnerships**. Limited partnerships are used for such business ventures as investing in real estate, drilling oil and gas wells, investing in movie productions, and the like.

limited partnership
A type of partnership that has two types of partners: (1) general partners and (2) limited partners.

general partners
Partners in a limited partnership who invest capital, manage the business, and are personally liable for partnership debts.

limited partners
Partners in a limited partnership who invest capital but do not participate in management and are not personally liable for partnership debts beyond their capital contributions.

General and Limited Partners

Limited partnerships have two types of partners: (1) **general partners**, who invest capital, manage the business, and are personally liable for partnership debts, and (2) **limited partners**, who invest capital but do not participate in management and are not personally liable for partnership debts beyond their capital contributions (see Exhibit 15.3).

Exhibit 15.3
Limited Partnership

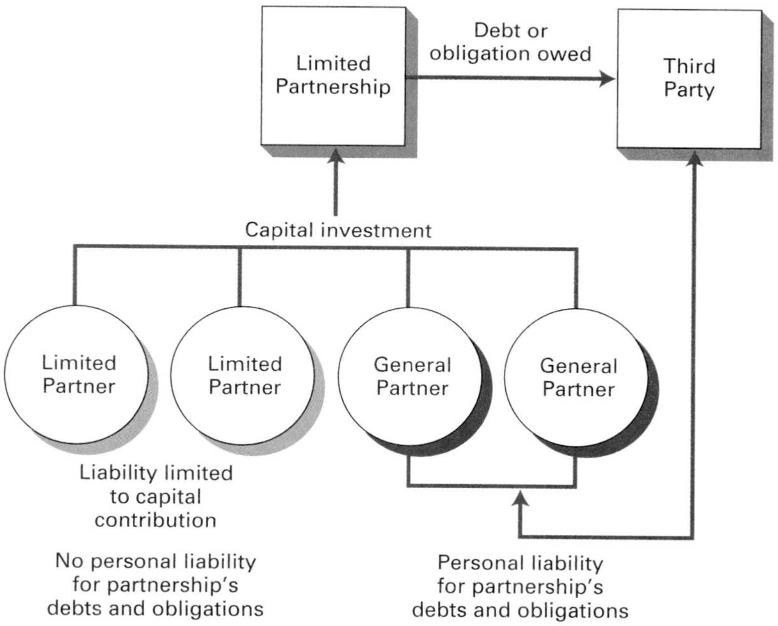

A limited partnership must have one or more general partners and one or more limited partners [RULPA § 101(7)]. There are no upper limits on the number of general or limited partners allowed in a limited partnership. Any person may be a general or limited partner. This includes natural persons, partnership, limited partnerships, trusts, estates, associations, and corporations. A person may be both a general and a limited partner in the same limited partnership.

The RULPA permits a corporation to be the sole general partner of a limited partnership. Where this is permissible, it affects the liability of the limited partnership. This is because the limited partners are liable only to the extent of their capital contributions, and the corporation acting as general partner is liable only to the extent of its assets.

The Revised Uniform Limited Partnership Act

In 1916, the National Conference of Commissioners on Uniform State Laws, a group composed of lawyers, judges, and legal scholars, promulgated the **Uniform Limited Partnership Act (ULPA)**. The ULPA contains a uniform set of provisions for the formation, operation, and dissolution of limited partnerships. Most states originally enacted this law.

In 1976, the National Conference of Commissioners on Uniform State Laws promulgated the **Revised Uniform Limited Partnership Act (RULPA)**, which provides a more modern comprehensive law for the formation, operation, and dissolution of limited partnerships. This law supersedes the ULPA in the states that have adopted it. The RULPA provides the basic foundation for the discussion of limited partnership law in the following paragraphs.

Revised Uniform Limited Partnership Act (RULPA)
A 1976 revision of the ULPA that provides a more modern, comprehensive law for the formation, operation, and dissolution of limited partnerships.

Windmills Near Palm Springs, California. Many businesses, such as these windmills, are operated as limited partnerships.

Formation of a Limited Partnership

The creation of a limited partnership is formal and requires public disclosure. The entity must comply with the statutory requirements of the RULPA or other state statutes.

Under the RULPA, two or more persons must execute and sign a **certificate of limited partnership** [RULPA §§ 201, 206]. The certificate must contain the following information:

certificate of limited partnership
A document that two or more persons must execute and sign that makes the limited partnership legal and binding.

1. Name of the limited partnership
2. General character of the business
3. Address of the principal place of business and name and address of the agent to receive service of legal process
4. Name and business address of each general and limited partner
5. Latest date on which the limited partnership is to dissolve
6. Amount of cash, property, or services (and description of property or services) contributed by each partner, and any contributions of cash, property, or services promised to be made in the future
7. Any other matters that the general partners determine to include

The certificate of limited partnership must be filed with the secretary of state of the appropriate state and, if required by state law, with the county recorder in the county or counties in which the limited partnership carries on business. The limited partnership is formed when the certificate of limited partnership is filed.

Defective Formation

Defective formation occurs when (1) a certificate of limited partnership is not properly filed, (2) there are defects in a certificate that is filed, or (3) some other statutory requirement for the creation of a limited partnership is not met. If there is a substantial defect in the creation of a limited partnership, persons who thought they were limited partners can find themselves as general partners.

Partners who erroneously but in good faith believe they have become limited partners can escape liability as general partners by either (1) causing the appropriate certificate of limited partnership (or certificate of amendment) to be filed or (2) withdrawing from any future equity participation in the enterprise and causing a certificate showing this withdrawal to be filed. Nevertheless, the limited partner remains liable to any third party who transacts business with the enterprise before either certificate is filed if the third person believed in good faith that the partner was a general partner at the time of the transaction [RULPA § 304].

Limited Partnership Agreement

Although not required by law, the partners of a limited partnership often draft and execute a **limited partnership agreement** (also called the **articles of limited partnership**) that sets forth the rights and duties of the general and limited partners; the terms and conditions regarding the operation, termination, and dissolution of the partnership; and so on. Where there is no such agreement, the certificate of limited partnership serves as the articles of limited partnership.

limited partnership agreement
A document that sets forth the rights and duties of the general and limited partners; the terms and conditions regarding the operation, termination, and dissolution of the partnership; and so on.

It is good practice to establish voting rights in the limited partnership agreement or certificate of limited partnership. The limited partnership agreement can provide which transactions must be approved by which partners (i.e., general, limited, or both). General and limited partners may be given unequal voting rights.

A limited partnership agreement may specify how profits and losses from the limited partnership are to be allocated among the general and limited partners. If there is no such agreement, the RULPA provides that profits and losses from a limited partnership are shared on the basis of the value of the partner's capital contribution [RULPA § 503]. A limited partner is not liable for losses beyond his or her capital contribution.

Liability of General and Limited Partners

The general partners of a limited partnership have **unlimited liability** for the debts and obligations of the limited partnerships. Thus, general partners have unlimited **personal liability** for the debts and obligations of the limited partnership. This liability extends to debts that cannot be satisfied with the existing capital of the limited partnership.

personal liability of general partners
The liability of general partners of a limited partnership. General partners of a limited partnership have unlimited personal liability for the debts and obligations of the general partnership.

Generally, limited partners have **limited liability** for the debts and obligations of the limited partnership. Limited partners are liable only for the debts and obligations of the limited partnership up to their capital contributions and are not personally liable for the debts and obligations of the limited partnership.

limited liability of limited partners
The liability of limited partners of a limited partnership. Limited partners of a limited partnership have liability limited to only their capital contribution to the limited partnership; limited partners are not personally liable for the debts and obligations of the limited partnership.

Consider This Example Gertrude and Gerald are the general partners of a limited partnership called Real Estate Development, Ltd. Lin, Leopold, Lonnie, and Lawrence are limited partners of the limited partnership and have each invested $100,000 in the limited partnership. Real Estate Development, Ltd., borrows $2 million from City Bank. After six months, the limited partnership goes bankrupt, still owing City Bank $2 million. In this case, the four limited partners each lose their $100,000 capital investment but are not personally liable for the $2 million debt owed by the limited partnership to City Bank. The two general partners, however, are each personally liable to City Bank for the limited partnership's unpaid $2 million loan to City Bank.

Participation in Management

Under partnership law, general partners have the right to manage the affairs of the limited partnership. On the other hand, as a trade-off for limited liability, limited partners give up their right to participate in the control and management of the limited partnership. This means, in part, that limited partners have no right to bind the partnership to contracts or other obligations.

Under the RULPA, a limited partner is liable as a general partner if his or her participation in the control of the business is substantially the same as that of a general partner, but the limited partner is liable only to persons who reasonably believed him or her to be a general partner [RULPA § 303(a)].

Consider This Example Laura is an investor limited partner in a limited partnership. At some time after she becomes a partner, Laura does not think that the general partners are doing a very good job at managing the affairs of the limited partnership, so she participates in the management of the limited partnership. While doing so, a bank loans $1 million to the limited partnership, believing that Laura is a general partner because of her involvement in the management of the limited partnership. If the limited partnership defaults on the $1 million loan owed to the bank, Laura will be treated as a general partner and be held personally liable for the loan along with the general partners of the limited partnership.

Assume that in the prior example, the general partners of the limited partnership vote to make Laura, a limited partner, president of the limited partnership. Laura therefore has two distinct relationships with the limited partnership: first, as an investor limited partner and second, as a manager (president) of the limited partnership. In this case, Laura can lawfully participate in the management of the limited partnership without losing the limited liability shield granted by her limited partner status.

Dissolution of a Limited Partnership

A limited partnership may be dissolved and its affairs wound up just like an ordinary partnership. The RULPA establishes rules for the dissolution and winding up of limited partnerships. Upon the dissolution and the commencement of the winding up of a limited partnership, a **certificate of cancellation** must be filed by the limited partnership with the secretary of state of the state in which the limited partnership is organized [RULPA § 203].

certificate of cancellation
A document that is filed with the secretary of state upon the dissolution of a limited partnership.

Distribution of Assets

After the assets of a limited partnership have been liquidated, the proceeds must be distributed. The RULPA provides the following order of distribution of partnership assets upon the winding up of a limited partnership [RULPA § 804]:

1. *Creditors* of the limited partnership, including partners who are creditors (except for liabilities for distributions)
2. *Partners* with respect to:
   a. Unpaid distributions
   b. Capital contributions
   c. The remainder of the proceeds

The partners may provide in the limited partnership agreement for a different distribution among the partners, but the creditors must retain their first priority.

Advertisement, China. In many parts of the world, long-term relationships must be developed before parties will conduct business with one another.

Terms and Concepts

Entrepreneurial Forms of Conducting Business

Entrepreneurs may choose to conduct business using any of the following forms:

1. Sole proprietorship
2. General partnership
3. Limited partnership
4. Limited liability partnership (LLP)
5. Limited liability company (LLC)
6. Corporation

Sole Proprietorship

Sole proprietorship is a form of business in which the owner and the business are one. The business is not a separate legal entity.

1. ***Business name.*** A sole proprietorship can operate under the name of the sole proprietor or a *trade name*. Operating under a trade name is commonly designated as *d.b.a. (doing business as)*. If a trade name is used, a *fictitious business name statement* must be filed with the appropriate state government office.
2. ***Personal liability of sole proprietors.*** A sole proprietor is personally liable for the debts and obligations of the sole proprietorship.

General Partnership

1. ***Uniform Partnership Act (UPA).*** The UPA is a model act that codifies partnership law. Most states have adopted all or part of the UPA.
2. ***Entity theory of partnerships.*** This theory holds that partnerships are *separate legal entities* that can hold title to personal and real property, transact business in the partnership name, and the like.

Formation of General Partnerships

1. ***General partnership.*** A general partnership is an association of two or more persons to carry on as co-owners of a business for profit.
2. ***Partnership name.*** A general partnership can operate under the names of any one or more of the partners or under a fictitious business name.

General Partnership Agreement

A general partnership agreement is an agreement establishing a general partnership. It sets forth terms of the partnership. It is good practice to have a written partnership agreement that the partners sign.

Tort Liability of General Partners

1. ***Tort.*** A tort occurs when a partner causes injury to a third party by his or her negligent act, breach of trust, breach of fiduciary duty, or intentional tort.
2. ***Partnership liability.*** A partnership is liable to third persons who are injured by torts committed by a partner while he or she is acting within the ordinary course of partnership business.
3. ***Joint and several liability of partners.*** Partners are *personally liable* for torts committed by partners acting on partnership business. This liability is *joint and several*, which means that the plaintiff can sue *one or more* of the partners separately. If successful, the plaintiff can recover the entire amount of the judgment from any or all of the defendant-partners.

Contract Liability of General Partners

1. ***Partners' contract authority.*** A contract entered into by a partner with a third party on behalf of a partnership is binding on the partnership.
2. ***Partnership liability.*** A partnership is liable for contracts entered into on its behalf by partners acting with express, implied, or apparent authority, or where unauthorized contracts have been ratified by the partners.

Liability of Incoming General Partners

A new partner who is admitted to a partnership is liable for the existing debts and obligations (*antecedent debts*) of the partnership only to the extent of his or her capital contribution. The new partner is personally liable for debts and obligations incurred by the partnership after becoming a partner.

Dissolution of General Partnerships

Dissolution is a change in the relationship of the partners caused by any partner ceasing to be associated in the carrying on of the business.

1. ***Wrongful dissolution.*** Wrongful dissolution occurs when a partner withdraws from a partnership without having the *right* to do so at the time. The partner is liable for damages caused by the wrongful dissolution of the partnership.
2. ***Notice of dissolution of general partnerships:***
   a. *Notice of dissolution of partners.* Notice of dissolution must be given to all partners. If a partner who has not received notice of dissolution enters into a contract on behalf of the partnership in the course of partnership business, the contract is binding on all the partners.
   b. *Notice of dissolution to third parties.* The following notice must be given to third parties when a partnership has been dissolved other than by operation of law:
      i. ***Actual notice.*** Actual notice must be given to third parties who have actually dealt with the partnership.
      ii. ***Constructive notice.*** Constructive notice must be given to third parties who have not dealt with the partnership but have knowledge of it. Constructive notice is given by publishing a notice of dissolution in a newspaper of general circulation serving the area where the business of the partnership is conducted.

iii. ***No notice.*** Parties who have not dealt with the partnership and do not have knowledge of it do not have to be given notice.

Continuation of a Partnership After Dissolution

The surviving or remaining partners are given the right to continue the partnership after dissolution. When a partnership is continued, the old partnership is dissolved, and a new partnership is created.

1. ***Continuation agreement.*** A continuation agreement is a document that expressly sets forth the events that allow for continuation of the partnership, the amount to be paid to outgoing partners, and other details.
2. ***Creditors' status.*** The creditors of the old partnership become creditors of the new partnership and have equal status with the creditors of the new partnership.

Limited Partnerships

1. ***Limited partnerships.*** A limited partnership is a special form of partnership that has both limited and general partners.
   a. ***General partners.*** General partners in a limited partnership invest capital, manage the business, and are personally liable for partnership debts.
   b. ***Limited partners.*** Limited partners in a limited partnership invest capital but do not participate in management and are not personally liable for partnership debts beyond their capital contributions.
2. ***Corporation as sole general partner.*** A corporation may be the sole general partner of a limited partnership. Shareholders of corporations are liable only up to their capital contributions.

Formation of Limited Partnerships

1. ***Certificate of limited partnership.*** A certificate of limited partnership is a document that two or more persons must execute and sign that establishes a limited partnership. The certificate of limited partnership must be filed with the secretary of state of the appropriate state.
2. ***Limited partnership agreement.*** A limited partnership agreement is a document that sets forth the rights and duties of general and limited partners; the terms and conditions regarding the operation, termination, and dissolution of the partnership; and so on.
3. ***Defective formation.*** Defective formation occurs when (a) a certificate of limited partnership is not properly filed, (b) there are defects in a certificate that is filed, or (c) some other statutory requirement for the creation of a limited partnership is not met. A limited partner may be held liable as a general partner if a limited partner is defectively formed.
4. ***Share of profit and losses.*** Unless otherwise agreed, profits and losses from a limited partnership are shared on the basis of the value of the partners' capital contributions. A limited partner is not liable for losses beyond his or her capital contribution. The limited partnership agreement may specify how profits and losses are to be allocated among the general and limited partners.

Liability of General and Limited Partners

1. ***General partners.*** General partners of a limited partnership have *unlimited personal liability* for the debts and obligations of the limited partnership.
2. ***Limited partners.*** Limited partners of a limited partnership are liable only for the debts and obligations of the limited partnership up to their capital contributions.
3. ***Limited partner and management.*** Limited partners have no right to participate in the management of the partnership. A limited partner is *liable as a general partner* if his or her participation in the control of the business is substantially the same as that of a general partner, but the limited partner is liable only to persons who reasonably believed him or her to be a general partner.

Internet Exercises and Case Questions

Working the Web Internet Exercises

1. Review the materials at **smallbusiness.findlaw.com/business-structure/partnership.html**. Compare this information with the text discussion of partnerships. Can you see why lawyers generally advise business clients *not* to do business in a partnership form?
2. A large, rambling, and self-consciously offbeat site is the Lectric Law Library, **www.lectlaw.com/bus.html**. There you will find a business law section with numerous items of interest, including an overview of (business) partnership law, with links to key primary and secondary sources.
3. A checklist of questions about partnership can be found at **www.nolo.com/lawcenter/faqs/detail.cfm/objectID/D2C7200B-28A8-49FB-9EA5E2B7E7F15CB5**. Use it as a self-test.
4. Study the provisions of the Uniform Limited Partnership Act at **www.law.upenn.edu/bll/ulc/ulpa/final2001.htm**.

Legal Environment Cases

15.1 General Partnership In early 1986, Thomas Smithson, a house builder and small-scale property developer, decided that a certain tract of undeveloped land in Franklin, Tennessee, would be extremely attractive for development into a subdivision. Smithson contacted the owner of the property, Monsanto Chemical Company, and was told that the company would sell the property at the "right price."

Smithson did not have the funds with which to embark unassisted in the endeavor, so he contacted Frank White, a co-owner of the Andrews Realty Company, and two agents of the firm, Dennis Devrow and Temple Ennis. Smithson showed them a sketch map with the proposed layout of the lots, roads, and so forth. Smithson testified that they all orally agreed to develop the property together, and in lieu of a financial investment, Smithson would oversee the engineering of the property. Subsequently, H. R. Morgan was brought into the deal to provide additional financing.

Smithson later discovered that White had contacted Monsanto directly. When challenged about this, White assured Smithson that he was still "part of the deal" but refused to put the agreement in writing. White, Devrow, Ennis, and Morgan purchased the property from Monsanto. They then sold it to H. A. H. Associates, a corporation, for a $184,000 profit. When they refused to pay Smithson, he sued to recover an equal share of the profits. Was a partnership formed between Smithson and the defendants? *Smithson v. White*, 1988 Tenn.App. Lexis 221 (Tenn. App.)

15.2 Fiduciary Duty Edgar and Selwyn Husted, attorneys, formed Husted and Husted, a law partnership. Herman McCloud, who was the executor of his mother's estate, hired them as attorneys for the estate. When taxes were due on the estate, Edgar told McCloud to make a check for $18,000 payable to the Husted and Husted Trust Account and that he would pay the IRS from this account. There was no Husted and Husted trust account. Instead, Edgar deposited the check into his own personal account and converted the funds to his own personal use. When Edgar's misconduct was uncovered, McCloud sued the law firm for conversion of estate funds. Is the partnership liable for Edgar's actions? *Husted v. McCloud*, 436 N.E.2d 341, 1982 Ind.App. Lexis 1244 (Ind. App.)

15.3 Tort Liability Thomas McGrath was a partner in the law firm Torbenson, Thatcher, McGrath, Treadwell & Schoonmaker. At approximately 4:30 P.M. on February 11, 1980, McGrath went to a restaurant-cocktail establishment in Kirkland, Washington. From that time until about 1:00 A.M. he imbibed considerable alcohol while socializing and discussing personal and firm-related business. After 1:00 A.M. McGrath did not discuss firm business but continued to socialize and drink until approximately 1:45 A.M., when he and Frederick Hayes, another bar patron, exchanged words. Shortly thereafter, the two encountered each other outside, and after another exchange, McGrath shot Hayes. Hayes sued McGrath and the law firm for damages. Who is liable? *Hayes v. Torbenson, Thatcher, McGrath, Treadwell & Schoonmaker*, 749 P.2d 178, 1988 Wash.App. Lexis 27 (Wash. App.)

15.4 Notice of Dissolution In 1976, Leonard Sumter, Sr., entered into a partnership agreement with his son, Michael T. Sumter, to conduct a plumbing business in Shreveport, Louisiana, under the name Sumter Plumbing Company. On June 18, 1976, the father, on behalf of the partnership, executed a credit application with Thermal Supply of Louisiana, Inc., for an open account to purchase supplies on credit. From that date until the spring of 1980, the Sumters purchased plumbing supplies from Thermal on credit and paid their bills without fail. Both partners and one employee signed for supplies at Thermal. In May 1980, the partnership was dissolved and all outstanding debts to Thermal were paid in full. The Sumters did not, however, notify Thermal that the partnership had been dissolved.

A year later, the son decided to reenter the plumbing business. He used the name previously used by the former partnership, listed the same post office address for billing purposes, and hired the employee of the former partnership who signed for supplies at Thermal. The father decided not to become involved in this venture. The son began purchasing supplies on credit from Thermal on the open credit account of the former partnership. Thermal was not informed that he was operating a new business. When the son defaulted on payments to Thermal, it sued the original partnership to recover the debt. Is the father liable for these debts? *Thermal Supply of Louisiana, Inc. v. Sumter*, 452 So.2d 312, 1984 La.App. Lexis 8975 (La. App.)

15.5 Liability of General Partners Pat McGowan, Val Somers, and Brent Robertson were general partners of Vermont Place, a limited partnership formed on January 20, 1984, for the purpose of constructing duplexes on an undeveloped tract of land in Fort Smith, Arkansas. The general partners appointed McGrowan and his company, Advance Development Corporation, to develop the project, including contracting with materials people, mechanics and other suppliers. None of the limited partners took part in the management or control of the partnership.

On September 3, 1984, Somers and Robertson discovered that McGowan had not been paying the suppliers. They removed McGowan from the partnership and took over the project. The suppliers sued the partnership to recover the money owed them. The partnership assets were not sufficient to pay all their claims. Who is liable to the suppliers? *National Lumber Company v. Advance Development Corporation*, 732 S.W. 2d 840, 1987 Ark. Lexis 2225 (Ark.)

15.6 Liability of Limited Partners Union Station Associates of New London (USANL) is a limited partnership formed under the laws of Connecticut. Allen M. Schultz, Anderson Nolter Associates, and the Lepton Trust were limited partners. The limited partners did not take part in the management of the partnership. The National Railroad Passenger Association (NRPA) entered into an agreement to lease part of a railroad facility from USANL. NRPA sued USANL for allegedly breaching the lease and also named the limited partners as defendants. Are the limited partners liable? *National Railroad Passenger Association v. Union Station Associates of New London*, 643 F.Supp. 192 1986 U.S.Dist. Lexis 22190 (D. D.C.)

15.7 Liability of Limited Partners Brookwood Fund (Brookwood) was a limited partnership that was formed to invest in securities. The original certificate of limited partnership, which was filed with the Westchester County, New York, clerk on April 24, 1984, listed Kenneth Stein as the general partner and Barbara Stein as the limited partner. Between May and August 1987, additional investors joined Brookwood as limited partners. However, no certificate amending the original certificate was filed to reflect the newly admitted limited partners. The newly added partners conducted themselves at all times as limited partners.

The partnership purchased a securities on margin (i.e., it borrowed a percentage of the purchase of the securities) from the securities firms of Sloate, Weisman, Murray & Co., Inc. (Sloate), and Bear Stearns & Co., Inc. (Bear Stearns). On October 19, 1987, the stock market crashed, causing many of the securities that Brookwood purchased to go down in value. The securities firms made margin calls on Brookwood to pay more money to cover the losses. When the margin calls were not met, Sloate and Bear Stearns immediately initiated arbitration proceedings to recover the balance of $1,849,183 allegedly due after Brookwood's accounts were liquidated. On October 28, 1987, Brookwood filed a certificate amending the original certificate of limited partnership to reflect the recently added limited partners.

Upon receiving the notice of arbitration, the recently added limited partners renounced their interest in the profits of the limited partnership. Can these limited partners be held individually liable for the partnership debts owed to Sloate and Bear Stearns? *8 Brookwood Fund v. Bear Stearns & Co., Inc.* 539 N.Y.S.2d 411, 1989 N.Y.App.Dist. Lexis 4208 (N.Y. A.D.)

15.8 Liability of Limited Partners Virginia Partners, Ltd. (Virginia Partners), a limited partnership organized under the laws of Florida, conducted business in Kentucky but failed to register as a foreign limited partnership as required by Kentucky law. On August 2, 1980, Robert Day was tortiously injured in Garrard County, Kentucky, by a negligent act of Virginia Partners. At the time of the accident, Day was a bystander observing acid being injected into an abandoned oil well by Virginia Partners. The injury occurred when a polyvinyl chloride (PVC) valve failed, causing a hose to rupture from its fitting and spray nitric acid on Day, severely injuring him. Day sued Virginia Partners and its limited partners to recover damages. Are the limited partners liable? *Virginia Partners, Ltd. v. Day*, 738 S.W.2d 837, 1987 Ky.App. Lexis 564 (Ky. App.)

15.9 Liability of Partners Raugust-Mathwig, Inc., a corporation, was the sole general partner of a limited partnership. Calvin Raugust was the major shareholder of this corporation. The three limited partners were (1) Cal-Lee Trust, (2) W. J. Mathwig, Inc., and (3) W. J. Mathwig, Inc., and Associates. All three of the limited partners were valid corporate entities. Although the limited partnership agreement was never executed and a certificate of limited partnership was not filed with the state, the parties opened a bank account and began conducting business.

On May 9, 1973, John Molander, an architect, entered into an agreement with the limited partnership to design a condominium complex and professional office building to be located in Spokane, Washington. The contract was signed on behalf of the limited partnership by its corporate general partner. Molander provided substantial architectural services to the partnership, but neither project was completed because of a lack of financing. Molander sued the limited partnership, its corporate general partner, the corporate limited partners, and Calvin Raugust individually to recover payments allegedly due him. Whom can Molander recover against? *Molander v. Raugust-Mathwig, Inc.*, 722 P.2d 103, 1986 Wash.App. Lexis 2992 (Wash. App.)

Ethics in Business

15.10 Robert K. Powers and Lee M. Solomon were among other limited partners of the Cosmopolitan Chinook Hotel (Cosmopolitan), a limited partnership. On October 25, 1972, Cosmopolitan entered into a contract to lease and purchase neon signs from Dwinell's Central Neon (Dwinell's). The contract identified Cosmopolitan as a "partnership" and was signed on behalf of the partnership, "R. Powers, President." At the time the contract was entered into, Cosmopolitan had taken no steps to file its certificate of limited partnership with the state as required by limited partnership law. The certificate was not filed with the state until several months after the contract was signed. When Cosmopolitan defaulted on payments due under the contract, Dwinell's sued Cosmopolitan and its general limited partners. The limited partners asserted that they were not liable. *Dwinell's Central Neon v. Cosmopolitan Chinook Hotel*, 587 P.2d 191, 1978 Wash.App. Lexis 2735 (Wash. App.)

Ethics Issues

1. What are the consequences if a certificate of limited partnership is not filed? Explain.
2. Did the limited partners act ethically in denying liability on the contract?
3. Are the limited partners liable? Explain.

Endnote

1. Georgia and Louisiana have not adopted the UPA. These states have enacted their own partnership statutes.

16

Corporate Formation, Financing, and Multinational Corporations

"The biggest corporation, like the humblest private citizen, must be held to strict compliance with the will of the people."

—Theodore Roosevelt
Speech (1902)

Chapter Objectives

After studying this chapter, you should be able to:

1. Define corporation and list the major characteristics of a corporation.
2. Describe the process of forming a corporation.
3. Describe common stock, preferred stock, and debt securities.
4. Explain how corporations are acquired through mergers and tender offers.
5. Describe the organization and operation of multinational corporations.

Chapter Contents

corporation
A fictitious legal entity that is created according to statutory requirements.

Corporations are the most dominant form of business organization in the United States, generating over 85 percent of the country's gross business receipts. Corporations range in size from one owner to thousands of owners. Owners of corporations are called *shareholders*.

Corporations were first formed in medieval Europe. Great Britain granted charters to certain trading companies from the 1500s to the 1700s. The English law of corporations applied in most of the colonies until 1776. After the War of Independence, the states of the United States developed their own corporations law.

Originally, corporate charters were individually granted by state legislatures. In the late 1700s, however, the states began enacting *general corporations statutes* that permitted corporations to be formed without the separate approval of the legislature. Today, most corporations are formed pursuant to general corporations laws of the states.

Most of the largest businesses in the United States are operated as corporations. Corporations can acquire other corporations through mergers and tender offers. Many multinational corporations have global operations. The formation, financing, and termination of corporations, mergers and acquisitions of corporations and the global operation of multinational corporations are discussed in this chapter.

Kracow, Poland. Commercial opportunities for multinational corporations will increase as new markets open up around the world.

Nature of the Corporation

corporations codes
State statutes that regulate the formation, operation, and dissolution of corporations.

Corporations can be created only pursuant to the laws of the state of incorporation. These statutes—commonly referred to as **corporations codes**—regulate the formation, operation, and dissolution of corporations. The state legislature may amend its corporate statute at any time. Such changes may require the corporation's articles of incorporation to be amended.

The courts interpret state corporations statutes to decide individual corporate and shareholder disputes. As a result, a body of common law has evolved concerning corporate and shareholder rights and obligations.

The Corporation as a Legal "Person"

A corporation is a separate *legal entity* (or *legal person*) for most purposes. Corporations are treated, in effect, as artificial persons created by the state that can sue or be sued in their own names, enter into and enforce contracts, hold title to and transfer property, and be found civilly and criminally liable for violations of law. Because corporations cannot be put in prison, the normal criminal penalty is the assessment of a fine, loss of a license, or other sanction.

Characteristics of Corporations

limited liability of shareholders
A general rule of corporate law that provides that generally shareholders are liable only to the extent of their capital contributions for the contracts and debts of their corporation and are not personally liable for the contracts and debts of the corporation.

Corporations have the following unique characteristics:

1. ***Limited liability of shareholders.*** As separate legal entities, corporations are liable for their own contracts and debts. Generally, shareholders have only **limited liability**. That is, they are liable only to the extent of their capital contributions and do not have personal liability for the corporation's contracts and debts (see Exhibit 16.1).

Exhibit 16.1
Corporation

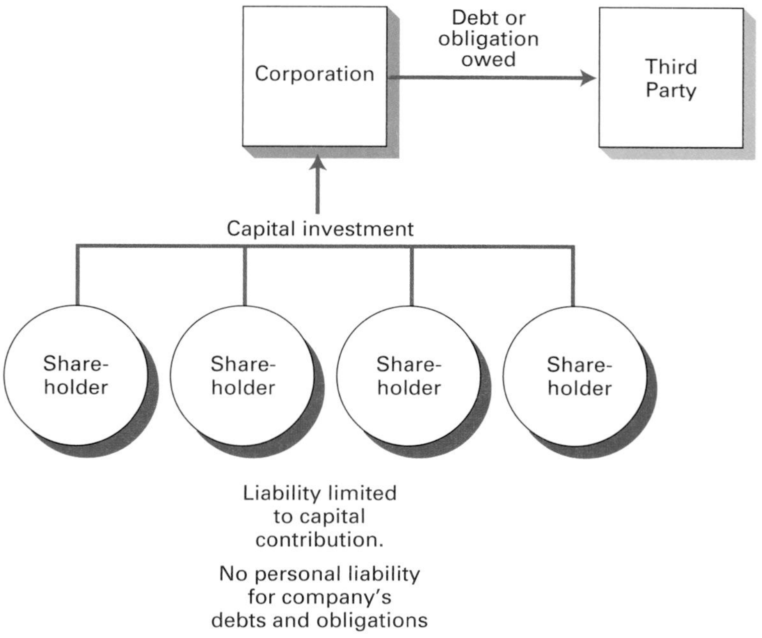

   For example, Tina, Vivi, and Qixia each contribute $100,000 capital and form IT.com, Inc., a corporation. The corporation borrows $1 million from State Bank. One year later, IT.com, Inc., goes bankrupt and defaults on the $1 million loan owed to State Bank. At that time, IT.com, Inc., has only $50,000 cash left, which State Bank recovers. Tina, Vivi, and Qixia each lose their $100,000 capital contribution. However, Tina, Vivi, and Qixia are not personally liable for the $950,000 still owed to State Bank. State Bank must absorb this loss.
2. ***Free transferability of shares.*** Corporate shares are freely transferable by shareholders via sale, assignment, pledge, or gift unless they are issued pursuant to certain exemptions from securities registration. Shareholders may agree among themselves on restrictions on the transfer of shares. National securities markets, such as the New York Stock Exchange and NASDAQ, have been developed for the organized sale of securities.
3. ***Perpetual existence.*** Corporations exist in perpetuity unless a specific duration is stated in the corporation's articles of incorporation. The existence of a corporation can

be voluntarily terminated by the shareholders. Corporations may be involuntarily terminated by the corporation's creditors if an involuntary petition for bankruptcy against the corporation is granted. The death, insanity, or bankruptcy of a shareholder, a director, or an officer of the corporation does not affect its existence.

4. ***Centralized management.*** The *board of directors* makes policy decisions concerning the operation of the corporation. The members of the board of directors are elected by the shareholders. The directors, in turn, appoint corporate *officers* to run the corporation's day-to-day operations. Together, the directors and the officers form the corporate "management."

Revised Model Business Corporation Act (RMBCA)

The Committee on Corporate Laws of the American Bar Association first drafted the **Model Business Corporation Act (MBCA)** in 1950. This act was intended to provide a uniform law regulating the formation, operation, and termination of corporations.

Revised Model Business Corporation Act (RMBCA)
A 1984 revision of the MBCA that arranged the provisions of the act more logically, revised the language to be more consistent, and made substantial changes in the provisions.

In 1984, the committee completely revised the MBCA and issued the **Revised Model Business Corporation Act (RMBCA)**. Certain provisions of the RMBCA have been amended since 1984. The RMBCA arranges the provisions of the act more logically, revises the language of the act to be more consistent, and makes substantial changes in the provisions of the model act. Many states have adopted all or part of the RMBCA. The RMBCA serves as the basis for the discussion of corporations law in this book.

There is no general federal corporations law governing the formation and operation of private corporations. Many federal laws regulate the operation of private corporations, however. These include federal securities laws, labor laws, antitrust laws, consumer protection laws, environmental protection laws, bankruptcy laws, and the like. These federal statutes are discussed in other chapters in this book.

Profit and Not-for-Profit Corporations

profit corporation
A corporation created to conduct a business for profit that can distribute profits to shareholders in the form of dividends.

Private corporations may be classified as either for profit or not-for-profit. **Profit corporations** are created to conduct a business for profit and can distribute profits to shareholders in the form of dividends. Most private corporations fit this definition.

Not-for-profit corporations are formed for charitable, educational, religious, or scientific purposes. Although not-for-profit corporations may make a profit, they are prohibited by law from distributing this profit to their members, directors, or officers. About a dozen states have enacted the **Model Nonprofit Corporation Act**, which governs the formation, operation, and termination of nonprofit corporations. All other states have their own individual statutes that govern the formation, operation, and dissolution of such corporations.

Publicly Held and Closely Held Corporations

publicly held corporation
A corporation that has many shareholders and whose securities are often traded on national stock exchanges.

Publicly held corporations have many shareholders. Often, they are large corporations with hundreds or thousands of shareholders whose shares are traded on organized securities markets. IBM Corporation and General Motors Corporation are examples of publicly held corporations. The shareholders rarely participate in the management of such corporations.

closely held corporation
A corporation owned by one or a few shareholders.

A **closely held** (or **close**) **corporation** is one whose shares are owned by a few shareholders who are often family members, relatives, or friends. Frequently, the shareholders are involved in the management of the corporation. The shareholders sometimes enter into buy-and-sell agreements that prevent outsiders from becoming shareholders.

Corporate Powers

A corporation has the same basic rights to perform acts and enter into contracts as a physical person [RMBCA § 3.02]. A corporation's **express powers** are found in (1) the U.S. Constitution, (2) state constitutions, (3) federal statutes, (4) state statutes, (5) articles of incorporation, (6) bylaws, and (7) resolutions of the board of directors. Corporation statutes normally state the express powers granted to the corporation.

express powers
Powers given to a corporation by (1) the U.S. Constitution, (2) state constitutions, (3) federal statutes, (4) state statutes, (5) articles of incorporation, (6) bylaws, and (7) resolutions of the board of directors.

Generally, a corporation has the power to purchase, own, lease, sell, mortgage, or otherwise deal in real and personal property; make contracts; lend money; borrow money; incur liabilities; issue notes, bonds, and other obligations; invest and reinvest funds; sue and be sued in its corporate name; make donations for the public welfare or for charitable, scientific, or educational purposes; and the like. RMBCA § 3.02 provides a list of express corporate powers.

Corporations formed under general incorporation laws cannot engage in certain business, such as banking, insurance, or operating public utilities. A corporation must obtain a corporate charter under special incorporation statutes and receive approval of special government administrative agencies before engaging in these businesses.

Neither the governing laws nor the corporate documents can anticipate every act necessary for a corporation to carry on its business. **Implied powers** allow a corporation to exceed its express powers in order to accomplish its corporate purpose. For instance, a corporation has the implied power to open a bank account, reimburse its employees for expenses, engage in advertising, purchase insurance, and the like.

implied powers
Powers beyond express powers that allow a corporation to accomplish its corporate purpose.

Incorporation Procedures

Corporations are creatures of statute. Thus, the organizers of a corporation must comply with the state's corporations code to form a corporation. Although relatively similar, the procedure for *incorporating* a corporation varies somewhat from state to state. The procedure for incorporating a corporation is discussed in the following paragraphs.

Selecting a State for Incorporating a Corporation

A corporation can be incorporated in only one state, even though it can do business in all other states in which it qualifies to do business. In choosing a state for incorporation, the incorporators, directors, and/or shareholders must consider the corporations law of the states under consideration.

For the sake of convenience, most corporations (particularly small ones) choose the state in which the corporation will be doing most of its business as the state for incorporation. Large corporations generally opt to incorporate in the state with the laws that are most favorable to the corporation's internal operations (e.g., Delaware).

The corporation is, and must be, the creature of the state, into its nostrils the state must breathe the breath of a fictitious life for otherwise it would be no animated body but individualistic dust.

Frederic Wm. Maitland
Introduction to Gierke, Political Theories of the Middle Ages

Domestic, Foreign, and Alien Corporations

A corporation is a **domestic corporation** in the state in which it is incorporated. It is a **foreign corporation** in all other states and jurisdictions. For example, suppose a corporation is incorporated in Texas and does business in Montana. The corporation is a domestic corporation in Texas and a foreign corporation in Montana.

domestic corporation
A corporation in the state in which it was formed.

foreign corporation
A corporation in any state or jurisdiction other than the one in which it was formed.

A state can require a foreign corporation to *qualify* to conduct intrastate commerce within the state. Where a foreign corporation is required to qualify to do intrastate commerce in a state, it must obtain a *certificate of authority* from the state [RMBCA § 15.01(a)]. This requires the foreign corporation to file certain information with the secretary of state, pay the required fees, and appoint a registered agent for service of process.

alien corporation
A corporation that is incorporated in another country.

An **alien corporation** is a corporation that is incorporated in another country. In most instances, alien corporations are treated as foreign corporations.

Concept Summary Types of Corporations

Type of Corporation	Description
Domestic	A corporation is a domestic corporation in the state in which it is incorporated.
Foreign	A corporation is a foreign corporation in states other than the one in which it is incorporated.
Alien	A corporation is an alien corporation in the United States if it is incorporated in another country.

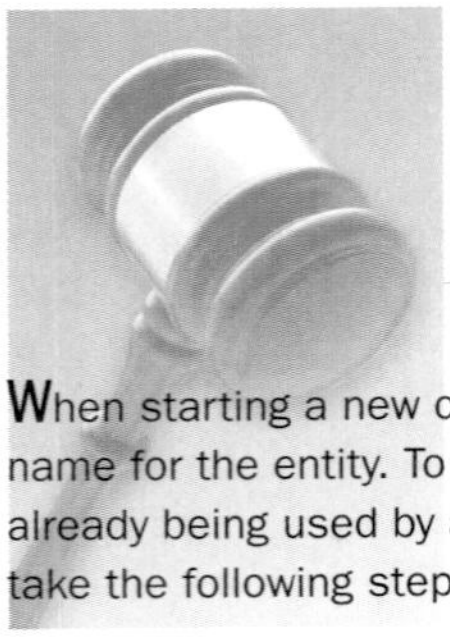

Contemporary Trend
Selecting a Corporate Name

When starting a new corporation, the organizers must choose a name for the entity. To ensure that the name selected is not already being used by another business, the organizers should take the following steps [RMBCA § 4.01]:

1. Choose a name (and alternative names) for the corporation. The name must contain the words *corporation*, *company*, *incorporated*, or *limited* or an abbreviation of one of these words (i.e., *Corp., Co., Inc., Ltd.*).
2. Make sure that the name chosen does not contain any word or phrase that indicates or implies that the corporation is organized for any purpose other than those stated in the articles of incorporation. For example, a corporate name cannot contain the work *Bank* if it is not authorized to conduct the business of banking.
3. Determine whether the name selected is federally trademarked by another company and is therefore unavailable for use. Trademark lawyers and specialized firms will conduct trademark searches for a fee.
4. Determine whether the chosen name is similar to other non-trademarked names and is therefore unavailable for use. Lawyers and specialized firms will conduct such searches for a fee.
5. Determine whether the name selected is available as a domain name on the Internet. If the domain name is already owned by another person or business, the new corporation cannot use this domain name to conduct e-commerce over the Internet. Therefore, it may be advisable to select another corporate name. ■

Articles of Incorporation

articles of incorporation
The basic governing documents of a corporation. These documents must be filed with the secretary of state of the state of incorporation.

The **articles of incorporation** (or **corporate charter**) are the basic governing documents of a corporation. They must be drafted and filed with, and approved by, the state before the corporation can be officially incorporated. Under RMBCA, the articles of incorporation must include [RMBCA § 2.02(a)]:

1. The name of the corporation
2. The number of shares the corporation is authorized to issue
3. The address of the corporation's initial registered office and the name of the initial registered agent
4. The name and address of each incorporator

The articles of incorporation may also include provisions concerning (1) the period of duration (which may be perpetual), (2) the purpose or purposes for which the corporation is organized, (3) limitation or regulation of the powers of the corporation, (4) regulation of

ARTICLES OF INCORPORATION
OF
THE BIG CHEESE CORPORATION

ONE: The name of this corporation is:

THE BIG CHEESE CORPORATION

TWO: The purpose of this corporation is to engage in any lawful act or activity for which a corporation may be organized under the General Corporation Law of California other than the banking business, the trust company business, or the practice of a profession permitted to be incorporated by the California Corporations Code.

THREE: The name and address in this state of the corporation's initial agent for service of process is:

Nikki Nguyen, Esq.
1000 Main Street
Suite 800
Los Angeles, California 90010

FOUR: This corporation is authorized to issue only one class of shares which shall be designated common stock. The total number of shares it is authorized to issue is 1,000,000 shares.

FIVE: The names and addresses of the persons who are appointed to act as the initial directors of this corporation are:

Shou-Yi Kang	100 Maple Street Los Angeles, California 90005
Frederick Richards	200 Spruce Road Los Angeles, California 90006
Jessie Qian	300 Palm Drive Los Angeles, California 90007
Richard Eastin	400 Willow Lane Los Angeles, California 90008

SIX: The liability of the directors of the corporation from monetary damages shall be eliminated to the fullest extent possible under California law.

SEVEN: The corporation is authorized to provide indemnification of agents (as defined in Section 317 of the Corporations Code) for breach of duty to the corporation and its stockholders through bylaw provisions or through agreements with the agents, or both, in excess of the indemnification otherwise permitted by Section 317 of the Corporations Code, subject to the limits on such excess indemnification set forth in Section 204 of the Corporations Code.

IN WITNESS WHEREOF, the undersigned, being all the persons named above as the initial directors, have executed these Articles of Incorporation.

Dated: January 2, 2007

Exhibit 16.2

Articles of Incorporation

the affairs of the corporation, or (5) any provision that would otherwise be contained in the corporation's bylaws.

Exhibit 16.2 illustrates sample articles of incorporation.

The articles of incorporation can be amended to contain any provision that could have been lawfully included in the original document. After the amendment is approved by the shareholders, the corporation must file *articles of amendment* with the secretary of state [RMBCA § 10.06].

Registered Agent

The articles of incorporation must identify a **registered office** with a designated **registered agent** (either an individual or a corporation) in the state of incorporation [RMBCA § 5.01]. The registered office does not have to be the same as the corporation's place of business. A statement of change must be filed with the secretary of state of the state of incorporation if either the registered office or the registered agent is changed.

registered agent
A person or corporation that is empowered to accept service of process on behalf of a corporation.

The registered agent is empowered to accept service of process on behalf of the corporation. For example, if someone were suing the corporation, the complaint and summons would be served on the registered agent. If no registered agent is named or the registered agent cannot be found at the registered office with reasonable diligence, service may be made by mail or alternative means.

Contemporary Trend

Close Corporation

Many of the formal rules in state corporations statutes are designed to govern the management of large, publicly held corporations. These rules may not be relevant for regulating the management of **close corporations**—that is, corporations formed by entrepreneurs with few shareholders who often work for the corporation and manage its day-to-day operations.

The **Model Statutory Close Corporation Supplement (Supplement)** was added to the RMBCA to permit entrepreneurial corporations to choose to be **close corporations**. Only corporations with 50 or fewer shareholders may elect statutory close corporation (SCC) status. To choose this status, two-thirds of the shares of each class of the corporation must approve the election. The articles of incorporation must contain a statement that the corporation is a statutory close corporation, and the share certificates must conspicuously state that the shares have been issued by a statutory close corporation.

A close corporation may dispense with some of the formalities of operating a corporation. For example, if all the shareholders approve, a close corporation may operate without a board of directors, and the articles of incorporation should contain a statement to that effect. The powers and affairs of the corporation are then managed by the shareholders. A close corporation need not adopt bylaws if the provisions required by law to be contained in bylaws are contained in the articles of incorporation or a shareholders' agreement. The corporation need not hold annual shareholders' meetings unless one or more shareholders demand in writing that such meetings be held. The shareholders may enter into a shareholders' agreement about how the corporation will be managed. In effect, the shareholders can treat the corporation as a partnership for governance purposes [Supp. § 20(b)(3)]. Selecting statutory close corporation status does not affect the limited liability of shareholders [Supp. § 25]. ■

Corporate Bylaws

bylaws
A detailed set of rules adopted by the board of directors after a corporation is incorporated that contains provisions for managing the business and the affairs of the corporation.

In addition to the articles of incorporation, corporations are governed by their **bylaws**. Either the incorporators or initial directors can adopt the bylaws of the corporation. The bylaws are much more detailed than are the articles of incorporation. Bylaws may contain any provisions for managing the business and affairs of the corporation that are not inconsistent with law or the articles or incorporation [RMBCA § 2.06]. They do not have to be filed with any government official. The bylaws are binding on directors, officers, and shareholders of the corporation.

The bylaws govern the internal management structure of the corporation. For example, they typically specify the time and place of the annual shareholders' meeting, how special meetings of shareholders are called, the time and place of annual and monthly board of directors' meetings, how special meetings of the board of directors are called, the notice required for meetings, the quorum necessary to hold a shareholders' or board of directors' meeting, the required vote necessary to enact a corporate matter, the corporate officers and their duties, the committees of the board of directors and their duties, where the records of the corporation are kept, directors' and shareholders' inspection rights of corporate records, the procedure for transferring shares of the corporation, and such. Sample provisions of corporate bylaws are set forth in Exhibit 16.3.

The board of directors has the authority to amend the bylaws unless the articles of incorporation reserve that right for the shareholders. The shareholders of the corporation have the absolute right to amend the bylaws even though the bylaws may also be amended by the board of directors.

Exhibit 16.3
Bylaws

BYLAWS
of
THE BIG CHEESE CORPORATION (EXCERPTS)

ARTICLE I Offices

Section 1. Principal Executive Office. The corporation's principal executive office shall be fixed and located at such place as the Board of Directors (herein called the "Board") shall determine. The Board is granted full power and authority to change said principal executive office from one location to another.

Section 2. Other Offices. Branch or subordinate offices may be established at any time by the Board at any place or places.

ARTICLE II Shareholders

Section 1. Annual Meetings. The annual meetings of shareholders shall be held on such date and at such time as may be fixed by the Board. At such meetings, directors shall be elected and any other proper business may be transacted.

Section 2. Special Meetings. Special meetings of the shareholders may be called at any time by the Board, the Chairman of the Board, the President, or by the holders of shares entitled to cast not less than ten percent of the votes at such meeting. Upon request in writing to the Chairman of the Board, the President, any Vice President or the Secretary by any person (other than the Board) entitled to call a special meeting of shareholders, the officer forthwith shall cause notice to be given to the shareholders entitled to vote that a meeting will be held at a time requested by the person or persons calling the meeting, not less than thirty-five nor more than sixty days after the receipt of the request. If the notice is not given within twenty days after receipt of the request, the persons entitled to call the meeting may give the notice.

Section 3. Quorum. A majority of the shares entitled to vote, represented in person or by proxy, shall constitute a quorum at any meeting of shareholders. If a quorum is present, the affirmative vote of a majority of the shares represented and voting at the meeting (which shares voting affirmatively also constitute at least a majority of the required quorum) shall be the act of the shareholders, unless the vote of a greater number or voting by classes is required by law or by the Articles, except as provided in the following sentence. The shareholders present at a duly called or held meeting at which a quorum is present may continue to do business until adjournment, notwithstanding the withdrawal of enough shareholders to leave less than a quorum, if any action taken (other than adjournment) is approved by at least a majority of the shares required to constitute a quorum.

ARTICLE III Directors

Section 1. Election and term of office. The directors shall be elected at each annual meeting of the shareholders, but if any such annual meeting is not held or the directors are not elected there at, the directors may be elected at any special meeting of shareholders held for that purpose. Each director shall hold office until the next annual meeting and until a successor has been elected and qualified.

Section 2. Quorum. A majority of the authorized number of directors constitutes a quorum of the Board for the transaction of business. Every act or decision done or made by a majority of the directors present at a meeting duly held at which a quorum is present shall be regarded as the act of the Board, unless a greater number be required by law or by the Articles. A meeting at which a quorum is initially present may continue to transact business notwithstanding the withdrawal of directors, if any action taken is approved by at least a majority of the required quorum for such meeting.

Section 3. Participation in Meetings by Conference Telephone. Members of the Board may participate in a meeting through use of conference telephone or similar communications equipment, so long as all members participating in such meeting can hear one another.

Section 4. Action Without Meeting. Any action required or permitted to be taken by the Board may be taken without a meeting if all members of the board shall individually or collectively consent in writing to such action. Such consent or consents shall have the same effect as a unanimous vote of the Board and shall be filed with the minutes of the proceedings of the Board.

Corporate Seal

Most corporations adopt a *corporate seal* [RMBCA § 3.02(2)]. Generally, the seal is a design that contains the name of the corporation and the date of incorporation. It is imprinted by the corporate secretary on certain legal documents (e.g., real estate deeds) that are signed by corporate officers or directors. The seal is usually affixed by using a metal stamp.

Organizational Meeting

An **organizational meeting** of the initial directors of the corporation must be held after the articles of incorporation are filed. At this meeting, the directors must adopt the bylaws, elect corporate officers, and transact such other business as may come before the meeting [RMBCA §2.05]. The last category includes such matters as accepting share subscriptions, approving the form of the stock certificate, authorizing the issuance of the shares, ratifying or adopting promoters' contracts, authorizing the reimbursement of promoters' expenses, selecting a bank, choosing an auditor, forming committees of the board of directors, fixing the salaries of officers, hiring employees, authorizing the filing of applications for government licensees to transact the business of the corporation, and empowering corporate officers to enter into contracts on behalf of the corporation. Exhibit 16.4 contains sample corporate resolutions from an organizational meeting of a corporation.

organizational meeting
A meeting that must be held by the initial directors of a corporation after the articles of incorporation are filed.

MINUTES OF FIRST MEETING
OF
BOARD OF DIRECTORS
OF
THE BIG CHEESE CORPORATION
January 2, 2007
10:00 A.M.

The Directors of said corporation held their first meeting on the above date and at the above time pursuant to required notice.

The following Directors, constituting a quorum of the Board of Directors, were present at such meeting:

Shou-Yi Kang
Frederick Richards
Jessie Quian
Richard Eastin

Upon motion duly made and seconded, Shou-Yi was unanimously elected Chairman of the meeting and Frederick Richards was unanimously elected Secretary of the meeting.

1. Articles of Incorporation and Agent for Service of Process

The Chairman stated that the Articles of Incorporation of the Corporation were filed in the office of the California Secretary of State. The Chairman presented to the meeting a certified copy of the Articles of Incorporation. The Secretary was directed to insert the copy in the Minute Book. Upon motion duly made and seconded, the following resolution was unanimously adopted:

RESOLVED, that the agent named as the initial agent for service of process in the Articles of Incorporation of this corporation is hereby confirmed as this corporation's agent for the purpose of service of process.

2. Bylaws

The matter of adopting Bylaws for the regulation of the affairs of the corporation was next considered. The Secretary presented to the meeting a form of Bylaws, which was considered and discussed. Upon motion duly made and seconded, the following recitals and resolutions were unanimously adopted:

WHEREAS, there has been presented to the directors a form of Bylaws for the regulation of the affairs of this corporation; and

WHEREAS, it is deemed to be in the best interests of this corporation that said Bylaws be adopted by this Board of Directors as the Bylaws of this corporation;

NOW, THEREFORE, BE IT RESOLVED, that Bylaws in the form presented to this meeting are adopted and approved as the Bylaws of this corporation until amended or repealed in accordance with applicable law.

RESOLVED FURTHER, that the Secretary of this corporation is authorized and directed to execute a certificate of the adoption of said Bylaws and to enter said Bylaws as so certified in the Minute Book of this corporation, and to see that a copy of said Bylaws is kept at the principal executive or business office of this corporation in California.

3. Corporate Seal

The secretary presented for approval a proposed seal of the corporation. Upon motion duly made and seconded, the following resolution was unanimously adopted:

RESOLVED, that a corporate seal is adopted as the seal of this corporation in the form of two concentric circles, with the name of this corporation between the two circles and the state and date of incorporation within the inner circle.

4. Stock Certificate

The Secretary presented a proposed form of stock certificate for use by the corporation. Upon motion duly made and seconded, the following resolution was unanimously adopted:

RESOLVED, that the form of stock certificate presented to this meeting is approved and adopted as the stock certificate of this corporation.

The secretary was instructed to insert a sample copy of the stock certificate in the Minute Book immediately following these minutes.

5. Election of officers

The Chairman announced that it would be in order to elect officers of the corporation. After discussion and upon motion duly made and seconded, the following resolution was unanimously adopted:

RESOLVED, that the following persons are unanimously elected to the offices indicated opposite their names

Title	Name
Chief Executive Officer	Shou-Yi Kang
President	Frederick Richards
Secretary and Vice President	Jessie Quian
Treasurer	Richard Eastin

There being no further business to come before the meeting, on motion duly made, seconded and unanimously carried, the meeting was adjourned.

Exhibit 16.4
Minutes

Contemporary Trend
S Corporation

A C corporation is a corporation that does not qualify to or does not elect to be taxed as an S corporation. Any corporation with more than 75 shareholders is automatically a C corporation. A C corporation must pay federal income tax at the corporate level. In addition, if a C corporation distributes its profits to shareholders in the form of dividends, the shareholders must pay personal income tax on the dividends. This causes *double taxation*: one tax paid at the corporate level and another paid at the shareholder level.

In 1982, Congress enacted the **Subchapter S Revision Act** [26 U.S.C. §§ 6242 *et seq.*]. The act allows some corporations and their shareholders to avoid double taxation by electing to be S corporations.

If a corporation elects to be taxed as an **S corporation**, it pays no federal income tax at the corporate level. As in a partnership, the corporation's income or loss flows to the shareholders' individual income tax returns. Thus, this election is particularly advantageous if (1) the corporation is expected to have losses that can be offset against other income of the shareholders or (2) the corporation is expected to make profits and the shareholders' income tax brackets are lower than the corporation's. Profits are taxed to the shareholders even if the income is not distributed. The shares retain other attributes of the corporate form, including limited liability.

Election to be an S Corporation Corporations that meet the following criteria can elect to be taxed as S corporations:

1. The corporation must be a domestic corporation.
2. The corporation cannot be a member of an affiliated group of corporations.
3. The corporation can have no more than 75 shareholders.
4. Shareholders must be individuals, estates, or certain trusts. Corporations and partnerships cannot be shareholders.
5. Shareholders must be citizens or residents of the United States. Nonresident aliens cannot be shareholders.
6. The corporation cannot have more than one class of stock. Shareholders do not have to have equal voting rights.

An S corporation election is made by filing *form 2553* with the Internal Revenue Service (IRS). The election can be rescinded by shareholders who collectively own at least a majority of the shares of the corporation. However, if the election is rescinded, another S corporation election cannot be made for five years. ■

Financing the Corporation

A corporation needs to finance the operation of its business. The most common way to do this is by selling *equity securities* and *debt securities*. **Equity securities** (or **stocks**) represent ownership rights in the corporation. Equity securities can be *common stock* and *preferred stock*. These are discussed in the following paragraphs.

equity securities
Representation of ownership rights to a corporation. Also called stocks.

Common Stock

Common stock is an equity security that represents the residual value of a corporation. Common stock has no preferences. That is, creditors and preferred shareholders must receive their required interest and dividend payments before common shareholders receive anything. Common stock does not have a fixed maturity date. If the corporation is liquidated, the creditors and preferred shareholders are paid the value of their interests first, and the common shareholders are paid the value of their interest (if any) last. Corporations may issue different classes of common stock [RMBCA § 6.01(a), 6.01(b)].

common stock
A type of equity security that represents the *residual* value of the corporation.

Persons who own common stock are called **common stockholders**. A common stockholder's investment in the corporation is represented by a *common stock certificate*. Common stockholders have the right to elect directors and to vote on mergers and other important matters. In return for their investment, common stockholders receive *dividends* declared by the board of directors.

common stockholder
A person who owns common stock.

Par Value and No Par Shares Common shares are sometimes categorized as either par or no par. *Par share* is a value assigned to common shares by the corporation, usually in the articles of incorporation, which sets the lowest price at which the shares may be issued by the corporation. It does not affect the market value of the shares. Most shares that are issued by corporations are *no par shares*. No par shares are not assigned a par value. The RMBCA has eliminated the concept of par value.

Preferred Stock

preferred stock
A type of equity security that is given certain preferences and rights over common stock.

preferred stockholder
A person who owns preferred stock.

Preferred stock is an equity security that is given certain *preferences and rights over common stock* [RMBCA § 6.01(c)]. The owners of preferred stock are called **preferred stockholders**. Preferred stockholders are issued *preferred stock certificates* to evidence their ownership interest in the corporation.

Preferred stock can be issued in classes or series. One class of preferred stock can be given preferences over another class of preferred stock. Like common stockholders, preferred stockholders have limited liability. Preferred stockholders generally are not given the right to vote for the election of directors or such. However, they are often given the right to vote if there is a merger or if the corporation has not made the required dividend payments for a certain period of time (e.g., three years).

Preferences Preferences of preferred stock must be set forth in the articles of incorporation. Preferred stock may have any or all of the following preferences or rights:

dividend preference
The right to receive a fixed dividend at stipulated periods during the year (e.g., quarterly).

- ***Dividend preference.*** A **dividend preference** is the right to receive a *fixed dividend* at set periods during the year (e.g., quarterly). The dividend rate is usually a set percentage of the initial offering price. For example, suppose a stockholder purchases $10,000 of a preferred stock that pays an 8 percent dividend annually. The stockholder has the right to receive $800 each year as a dividend on the preferred stock.

liquidation preference
The right to be paid a stated dollar amount if the corporation is dissolved and liquidated.

- ***Liquidation preference.*** The right to be paid before common stockholders if the corporation is dissolved and liquidated is called a **liquidation preference**. A liquidation preference is normally a stated dollar amount. For example, a corporation issues a preferred stock that has a liquidation preference of $200. This means that if the corporation is dissolved and liquidated, the holder of each preferred share will receive at least $200 before the common shareholders receive anything. Note that because the corporation must pay its creditors first, there may be insufficient funds to pay this preference.

cumulative preferred stock
Stock that provides that any missed dividend payments must be paid in the future to the preferred shareholders before the common shareholders can receive any dividends.

- ***Cumulative dividend right.*** Corporations must pay a preferred dividend if they have the earnings to do so. **Cumulative preferred stock** provides that any missed dividend payments must be paid in the future to preferred shareholders before the common shareholders can receive any dividends. The amount of unpaid cumulative dividends is called dividend *arrearages*. Usually, arrearages can be accumulated for only a limited period of time (e.g., three years). If the preferred stock is **noncumulative**, there is no right of accumulation. In other words, the corporation does not have to pay any missed dividends.

participating preferred stock
Stock that allows the stockholder to participate in the profits of the corporation along with the common stockholders.

- ***Right to participate in profits.*** **Participating preferred stock** allows a stockholder to participate in the profits of the corporation along with the common stockholders. Participation is in addition to the fixed dividend paid on preferred stock. The terms of participation vary widely. Usually, the common stockholders must be paid a certain amount of dividends before participation is allowed. **Nonparticipating preferred stock** does not give the holder a right to participate in the profits of the corporation beyond the fixed dividend rate. Most preferred stock falls into this category.

convertible preferred stock
Stock that permits the stockholders to convert their shares into common stock.

- ***Conversion right.*** **Convertible preferred stock** permits the stockholders to convert their shares into common stock. The terms and exchange rate of the conversion are established when the shares are issued. The holders of the convertible preferred stock usually exercise this option if the corporation's common stock significantly increases in value. Preferred stock without a conversion feature is called **nonconvertible preferred stock**. Nonconvertible stock is more common.

This list of preferences and rights is not exhaustive [RMBCA § 6.01(d)]. Corporations may establish other preferences and rights for preferred stock.

Redeemable Preferred Stock

Redeemable preferred stock (or **callable preferred stock**) permits a corporation to redeem (i.e., buy back) the preferred stock at some future date. The terms of the redemption are established when the shares are issued. Corporations usually redeem the shares when the current interest rate falls below the dividend rate of the preferred shares. Preferred stock that is not redeemable is called **nonredeemable preferred stock**. Nonredeemable stock is more common.

redeemable preferred stock
Stock that permits the corporation to buy back the preferred stock at some future date.

Authorized, Issued, and Outstanding Shares

The number of shares provided for in a corporation's articles of incorporation is called **authorized shares** [RMBCA § 6.01]. The shareholders may vote to amend the articles of incorporation to increase this amount. Authorized shares that have been sold by the corporation are called **issued shares**. Not all authorized shares have to be issued at the same time. Authorized shares that have not been issued are called *unissued shares*. The board of directors can vote to issue unissued shares at any time without shareholder approval.

A corporation is permitted to repurchase its own shares. Repurchased shares are commonly called **treasury shares**. Treasury shares cannot be voted by the corporation, and dividends are not paid on them. Treasury shares can be reissued by the corporation. The shares that are in shareholder hands, whether originally issued or reissued treasury shares, are called **outstanding shares**. Only outstanding shares have the right to vote.

authorized shares
The number of shares provided for in a corporation's articles of incorporation.

issued shares
Shares that have been sold by a corporation.

Concept Summary Types of Shares

Type of Share	Description
Authorized	Shares authorized in the corporation's articles of incorporation.
Issued	Shares sold by the corporation.
Treasury	Shares repurchased by the corporation. They do not have the right to vote.
Outstanding	Issued shares minus treasury shares. These shares have the right to vote.

Debt Securities

A corporation often raises funds by issuing debt securities [RMBCA § 3.02(7)]. **Debt securities** (also called **fixed income securities**) establish a debtor–creditor relationship in which the corporation borrows money from the investor to whom the debt security is issued. The corporation promises to pay interest on the amount borrowed and to repay the principal at some stated maturity date in the future. The corporation is the *debtor*, and the holder is the *creditor*. The three classifications of debt securities are:

debt securities
Securities that establish a debtor–creditor relationship in which the corporation borrows money from the investor to whom the debt security is issued.

1. ***Debenture.*** A **debenture** is a *long-term* (often 30 years or more), *unsecured* debt instrument that is based on the corporation's general credit standing. If the corporation encounters financial difficulty, unsecured debenture holders are treated as general creditors of the corporation (i.e., they are paid only after the secured creditors' claims are met).

debenture
A long-term unsecured debt instrument that is based on the corporation's general credit standing.

bond
A long-term debt security that is secured by some form of collateral.

2. ***Bond.*** A **bond** is a *long-term* debt security that is *secured* by some form of *collateral* (e.g., real estate, personal property). Thus, bonds are the same as debentures except that they are secured. Secured bondholders can foreclose on the collateral in the event of nonpayment of interest, principal, or other specified events.

note
A debt security with a maturity of five years or less.

3. ***Note.*** A **note** is a *short-term* debt security with a maturity of five years or less. Notes can be either *unsecured* or *secured*. They usually do not contain a conversion feature. They are sometimes made redeemable.

indenture agreement
A contract between a corporation and a holder that contains the terms of a debt security.

Indenture Agreement The terms of a debt security are commonly contained in a contract between the corporation and the holder known as an **indenture agreement** (or simply an **indenture**). The indenture generally contains the maturity date of the debt security, the required interest payment, the collateral (if any), rights of conversion into common or preferred stock, call provisions, any restrictions on the corporation's right to incur other indebtedness, the rights of holders upon default, and such. It also establishes the rights and duties of the indenture trustee. Generally, a trustee is appointed to represent the interest of the debt security holders. Bank trust departments often serve in this capacity.

Concept Summary Debt Instruments

Debt Instruments	Description
Debenture	A *long-term, unsecured* debt instrument that is based on the corporation's general credit rating.
Bond	A *long-term* debt security that is *secured* by some form of property. The property securing the bond is called *collateral*. In the event of nonpayment of interest or principal or other specified events, bondholders can foreclose on and obtain the collateral.
Note	A *short-term* debt instrument with a maturity of five years or less. Notes can be either unsecured or secured.

Medina, Fez, Morocco. The global expansion of trade requires that businesses consider the cultural differences of the countries in which they wish to conduct business.

Mergers and Acquisitions

Corporations may agree to friendly acquisitions or combinations of one another. This is usually accomplished through a merger. An acquisition of a corporation can also be made through a hostile tender offer. Mergers and tender offers are discussed in the following paragraphs.

Merger

A **merger** occurs when one corporation is absorbed into another corporation and ceases to exist. The corporation that continues to exist is called the *surviving corporation*. The other corporation, which ceases to exist, is called the *merged corporation* [RMBCA § 11.01]. The surviving corporation gains all the rights, privileges, powers, duties, obligations, and liabilities of the merged corporation. Title to property owned by the merged corporation transfers to the surviving corporation, without formality or deeds. The shareholders of the merged corporation receive stock or securities of the surviving corporation or other consideration, as provided in the plan of merger.

merger
A situation in which one corporation is absorbed into another corporation and ceases to exist.

Suppose, for example, that Corporation A and Corporation B merge and it is agreed that Corporation A will absorb Corporation B. Corporation A is the surviving corporation. Corporation B is the merged corporation. A symbolic representation of this merger is A + B = A (see Exhibit 16.5).

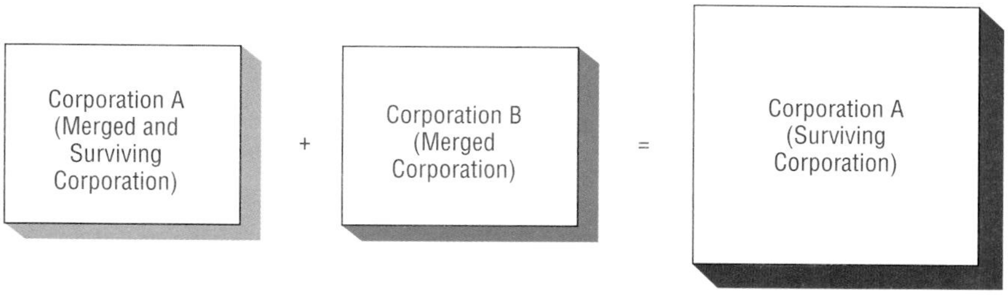

Exhibit 16.5
Merger

Required Approvals for a Merger

An ordinary merger requires (1) the recommendation of the board of directors of each corporation and (2) an affirmative vote of the majority of shares of each corporation that is entitled to vote [RMBCA § 11.03]. The articles of incorporation or corporate bylaws can require the approval of a *supramajority*, such as 80 percent of the voting shares.

The approval of the surviving corporation's shareholders is not required if the merger increases the number of voting shares of the surviving corporation by 20 percent or less.

The approved *articles of merger* must be filed with the secretary of state. The state normally issues a *certificate of merger* to the surviving corporation after all the formalities are met and the requisite fees are paid.

Short-Form Merger If one corporation (called the *parent corporation*) owns 90 percent or more of the outstanding stock of another corporation (known as the *subsidiary corporation*), a **short-form merger** procedure may be followed to merge the two corporations. The short-form merger procedure is simpler than an ordinary merger because neither the approval of the shareholders of either corporation nor the approval of the board of directors of the subsidiary corporation is needed. All that is required is the approval of the board of directors of the parent corporation [RMBCA § 11.04].

short-form merger
A merger between a parent corporation and a subsidiary corporation that does not require the vote of the shareholders of either corporation or the board of directors of the subsidiary corporation.

Dissenting Shareholder Appraisal Rights

dissenting shareholder appraisal right
The right of shareholders who object to a proposed merger, share exchange, or sale or lease of all or substantially all of the property of a corporation to have their shares valued by the court and receive cash payment of this value from the corporation.

Specific shareholders sometimes object to a proposed ordinary or short-form merger, even though the transaction received the required approvals. Objecting shareholders are provided a statutory right to dissent and obtain payment of the fair value of their shares [RMBCA § 13.02]. This is referred to as a **dissenting shareholder appraisal right**, or **appraisal right**. Shareholders have no other recourse unless the transaction is unlawful or fraudulent.

The corporation must notify shareholders of the existence of their appraisal rights before the transaction can be voted on. To obtain appraisal rights, a dissenting shareholder must (1) deliver written notice of his or her intent to demand payment of his or her shares to the corporation before the vote is taken and (2) not vote his or her shares in favor of the proposed action. The shareholder must deposit his or her share certificates with the corporation. Shareholders who fail to comply with these statutory procedures lose their appraisal rights.

As soon as the proposed action is taken, the corporation must pay each dissenting shareholder the amount the corporation estimates to be the fair value of his or her shares, plus accrued interest. If the dissenter is dissatisfied, the corporation must petition the court to determine the fair value of the shares.

After a hearing, the court will issue an order declaring the fair value of the shares. Appraisers may be appointed to help in determining this value. Court costs and appraisal fees are usually paid by the corporation. However, the court can assess these costs against the dissenters if they acted arbitrarily, vexatiously, or in bad faith.

tender offer
An offer that an acquirer makes directly to a target corporation's shareholders in an effort to acquire the target corporation.

target corporation
The corporation that is proposed to be acquired in a tender offer situation.

tender offeror
A party that makes a tender offer.

Tender Offer

Recall that a merger requires the approval of the board of directors of the corporation that is to be acquired. If the board of directors of the target corporation does not agree to the merger or acquisition, the acquiring corporation can make a **tender offer** for the shares directly to the shareholders of the **target corporation**. The shareholders each make an individual decision about whether to sell their shares to the **tender offeror** (see Exhibit 16.6). Such offers are often referred to as *hostile tender offers.*

Exhibit 16.6
Tender Offer

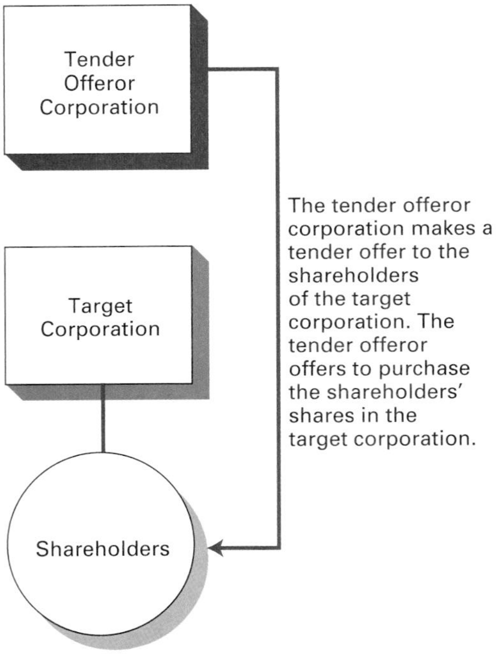

The tender offeror's board of directors must approve the offer, although the shareholders do not have to approve. The offer can be made for all or a portion of the shares of the target corporation.

In a tender offer, the tendering corporation and the target corporation retain their separate legal status. However, a successful tender offer is sometimes followed by a merger of the two corporations.

The Williams Act

Prior to 1968, tender offers were not federally regulated. However, securities that were issued in conjunction with such offers had to be registered with the SEC or qualify for an exemption from registration. Tender offers made with cash were not subject to any federal disclosure requirements.

In 1968, Congress enacted the **Williams Act** as an amendment to the Securities Exchange Act of 1934.[1] This act specifically regulates all tender offers, whether they are made with securities, cash, or other consideration, and it establishes certain disclosure requirements and antifraud provisions.

Williams Act
A 1968 amendment to the Securities Exchange Act of 1934 that specifically regulates all tender offers.

The Williams Act does not require the tender offeror to notify either the management of the target company or the SEC until the offer is made. Detailed information regarding the terms, conditions, and other information concerning the tender offer must be disclosed at that time.

A shareholder who tenders his or her shares has the absolute right to withdraw them at any time prior to the closing of the tender offer. Dissenting shareholder appraisal rights are not available.

Section 14(e) of the Williams Act prohibits fraudulent, deceptive, and manipulative practices in connection with a tender offer. Violations of this section may result in civil charges brought by the SEC or criminal charges brought by the Justice Department. The courts have implied a private civil cause of action under Section 14(e). Therefore, a shareholder who has been injured by a violation of Section 14(e) can sue the wrongdoer for damages.

Section 14(e) of the Williams Act
A provision of the Williams Act that prohibits fraudulent, deceptive, and manipulative practices in connection with a tender offer.

Fighting a Tender Offer

The incumbent management of the target of a hostile tender offer may not want the corporation taken over by the tender offeror. Therefore, it may engage in varied activities to impede and defeat the tender offer. Some of the strategies and tactics used by incumbent management in defending against hostile tender offers are as follows:

1. ***Persuasion of shareholders.*** Media campaigns are organized to convince shareholders that the tender offer is not in their best interests.
2. ***Delaying lawsuits.*** Lawsuits are filed, alleging that the tender offer violates securities laws, antitrust laws, or other laws. The time gained by this tactic gives management the opportunity to erect or implement other defensive maneuvers.
3. ***Selling a crown jewel.*** Such assets as profitable divisions or real estate that are particularly attractive to outside interests—that is, **crown jewels**—are sold. This tactic makes the target corporation less attractive to the tender offeror.
4. ***Adopting a poison pill.*** Poison pills are defensive strategies that are built into the target corporation's articles of incorporation, corporate bylaws, or contracts and leases. For example, contracts and leases may provide that they will expire if the ownership of the corporation changes hands. These tactics make the target corporation more expensive to the tender offeror.

crown jewel
A valuable asset of a target corporation that a tender offeror particularly wants to acquire in a tender offer.

5. ***White knight merger.*** White knight mergers are mergers with friendly parties—that is, parties that promise to leave the target corporation and/or its management intact.
6. ***Pac-Man (or reverse) tender offer.*** The target corporation makes a **tender offer** on the tender offeror. Thus, the target corporation tries to purchase the tender offeror.
7. ***Issuing additional stock.*** Placing additional stock on the market increases the number of outstanding shares that the tender offeror must purchase in order to gain control of the target corporation.
8. ***Creating an employee stock ownership plan (ESOP).*** A company creates an ESOP and places a certain percentage of the corporation's securities (e.g., 15 percent) in it. The ESOP is then expected to vote the shares it owns against the potential acquirer in a proxy contest or tender offer because the beneficiaries (i.e., the employees) have a vested interest in keeping the company intact.
9. ***Flip-over and flip-in rights plans.*** These plans provide that existing shareholders of the target corporation may convert their shares for a greater amount (e.g., twice the value) of shares of the acquiring corporation (*flip-over rights plan*) or debt securities of the target company (*flip-in rights plan*). Rights plans are triggered if the acquiring firm acquires a certain percentage (e.g., 20 percent) of the shares of the target corporation. They make it more expensive for the acquiring firm to take over the target corporation.
10. ***Greenmail and standstill agreements.*** Most tender offerors purchase a block of stock in the target corporation before making an offer. Occasionally, the tender offeror will agree to give up its tender offer and agree not to purchase any further shares if the target corporation agrees to buy back the stock at a premium over fair market value. This payment is called **greenmail**. The agreement of the tender offeror to abandon its tender offer and not purchase any additional stock is called a *standstill agreement*.

The usual trade and commerce is cheating all round by consent.
Thomas Fuller
Gnomologia (1732)

greenmail
The purchase by a target corporation of its stock from an actual or perceived tender offeror at a premium.

There are many other strategies and tactics that target companies initiate and implement in defending against a tender offer.

State Antitakeover Statutes

state antitakeover statutes
Statutes enacted by state legislatures that protect from hostile takeovers corporations incorporated in or doing business in the state.

Many states have enacted **antitakeover statutes** that are aimed at protecting from hostile takeovers corporations that are either incorporated in or do business within the state.

In the following case, the U.S. Supreme Court held that a state antitakeover statute was constitutional.

Case 16.1 Antitakeover Statute

U.S. SUPREME COURT

CTS Corporation v. Dynamics Corporation of America

481 U.S. 69, 107 S.Ct. 1637, 1987 U.S. Lexis 1811

Supreme Court of the United States

Background and Facts

On March 4, 1986, Indiana enacted the Control Share Acquisitions Chapter. This act covers corporations that (1) are incorporated in Indiana and have at least 100 shareholders, (2) have their primary place of business or substantial assets in Indiana, and (3) have either 10 percent of their shareholders in Indiana or 10 percent of their shares owned by Indiana residents. The act provides that if an entity acquires 20 percent or more of the voting shares of a covered corporation, the acquirer loses voting rights to those shares unless a majority of the disinterested shareholders of the acquired corporation vote to restore such voting rights. The acquirer can request that such vote be held within 50 days after its acquisition. If the shareholders do not restore the voting rights, the target corporation may redeem the shares from the acquirer at fair market value, but it is not required to do so.

On March 10, 1986, Dynamics Corporation of America (Dynamics), a Delaware corporation, announced a tender offer for one million shares of CTS Corporation, an Indiana corporation covered by the act. The purchase of these shares would have brought Dynamics's voting interest in CTS to 27.5 percent. Dynamics sued in federal court, alleging that Indiana's Control Share Acquisitions Chapter was unconstitutional. The U.S. district court held for Dynamics. The Court of Appeals affirmed. CTS appealed.

Issue

Does the Indiana Control Share Acquisitions Chapter conflict with the Williams Act or violate the Commerce Clause of the U.S. Constitution by unduly burdening interstate commerce?

In the Language of the U.S. Supreme Court

It is entirely possible for entities to comply with both the Williams and the Indiana acts. The statute now before the court protects the independent shareholder against the contending parties. Thus, the Indiana act furthers a basic purpose of the Williams Act, placing investors on an equal footing with the takeover bidder. The Indiana Act operates on the assumption that independent shareholders faced with tender offers often are at a disadvantage. By allowing such shareholders to vote as a group, the act protects them from the coercive aspects of some tender offers. Under the Indiana Act, the shareholders as a group could reject the offer although individual shareholders might be inclined to accept it. The desire of the Indiana legislature to protect shareholders of Indiana corporations from this type of coercive offer does not conflict with the Williams Act. Rather, it furthers the federal policy of investor protection.

Decision and Remedy

The U.S. Supreme Court held that the Indiana Control Share Acquisitions Chapter neither conflicted with the Williams Act nor violated the Commerce Clause of the U.S. Constitution. The Supreme Court reversed the decision of the Court of Appeals.

Business and Ethics Questions

1. Should states be permitted to adopt antitakeover statutes? Why or why not? Whom do you think these statutes actually protect?
2. Is it ethical for a target corporation's management to assert a state antitakeover statute?
3. What are the economic effects of a state antitakeover statute?

International Law

The Exon-Florio Law

The **Exon-Florio Law** of 1988 [50 U.S.C. § 2170], as amended, mandates that the president of the United States suspend, prohibit, or dismantle the acquisition of U.S. businesses by foreign investors if there is credible evidence that the foreign investor might take action that threatens to impair the "national security."

The act applies to mergers, acquisitions, takeovers, stock purchases, asset purchases, joint ventures, and proxy contests that would result in foreign control of U.S. businesses engaged in interstate commerce in the United States. The U.S. business could be a corporation, a partnership, a sole proprietorship, or another business. The size of the U.S. operation is irrelevant.

Exon-Florio and the regulations adopted thereunder do not define the term *national security*. The Treasury Department has interpreted the term broadly to include not only defense contractors but also technology and other businesses. The term *control* includes any investment exceeding 10 percent ownership in a U.S. business by a foreign investor.

When a foreign investor proposes to acquire an interest in a U.S. business, it may voluntarily notify the U.S. government of its intention. If the president finds a threat to the national security, the acquisition may be prohibited. If the foreign investor does not notify the U.S. government and completes the acquisition, it remains indefinitely subject to divestment if the president subsequently determines that the acquisition threatens the national security. The president's decision is not subject to judicial review. ■

The Great Wall, China.

Dissolution of the Corporation

The life of a corporation may be terminated voluntarily or involuntarily. The methods for dissolving and terminating corporations are discussed in the following paragraphs.

Voluntary Dissolution

voluntary dissolution
Dissolution of a corporation that has begun business or issued shares upon recommendation of the board of directors and a majority vote of the shares entitled to vote.

A corporation can be **voluntarily dissolved**. If the corporation has not commenced business or issued any shares, it may be dissolved by a vote of the majority of the incorporators or initial directors [RMBCA § 14.01]. After that, the corporation can be voluntarily dissolved if the board of directors recommends dissolution and a majority of shares entitled to vote (or a greater number, if required by the articles of incorporation or bylaws) votes for dissolution as well. For a voluntary dissolution to be effective, *articles of dissolution* must be filed with the secretary of state of the state of incorporation. A corporation is dissolved upon the effective date of the articles of dissolution.

Administrative Dissolution

administrative dissolution
Involuntary dissolution of a corporation that is ordered by the secretary of state if the corporation has failed to comply with certain procedures required by law.

The secretary of state can obtain **administrative dissolution** of a corporation if (1) it failed to file an annual report, (2) it failed for 60 days to maintain a registered agent in the state, (3) it failed, for 60 days after a change of its registered agent, to file a statement of such change with the secretary of state, (4) it did not pay its franchise fee, or (5) the period of duration stated in the corporation's articles of incorporation has expired [RMBCA § 14.20]. Administrative dissolution is simple. If the corporation does not cure the default within 60 days of being notified of it, the secretary of state issues a *certificate of dissolution* that dissolves the corporation.

Judicial Dissolution

A corporation can be involuntarily dissolved by a judicial proceeding. **Judicial dissolution** can be instituted by the attorney general of the state of incorporation if the corporation (1) procured its articles of incorporation through fraud or (2) exceeded or abused the authority conferred on it by law. If a court judicially dissolves a corporation, it enters a *decree of dissolution* that specifies the date of dissolution [RMBCA § 14.33].

judicial dissolution
Dissolution of a corporation by a court proceeding instituted by the state.

Winding Up, Liquidation, and Termination

A dissolved corporation continues its corporate existence but may not carry on any business except as required to **wind up and liquidate** its business and affairs [RMBCA § 14.05].

winding up and liquidation
The process by which a dissolved corporation's assets are collected, liquidated, and distributed to creditors, shareholders, and other claimants.

In a voluntary dissolution, the liquidation is usually carried out by the board of directors. If (1) the dissolution is involuntary or (2) the dissolution is voluntary but the directors refuse to carry out the liquidation, a court-appointed receiver carries out the winding up and liquidation of the corporation.

Termination occurs only after the winding up of the corporation's affairs, the liquidation of its assets, and the distribution of the proceeds to the claimants. The liquidated assets are paid to claimants according to the following priority: (1) expenses of liquidation and creditors according to their respective liens and contract rights, (2) preferred shareholders according to their liquidation preferences and contract rights, and (3) common stockholders.

The dissolution of a corporation does not impair any rights or remedies available against the corporation or its directors, officers, or shareholders for any right or claim existing or incurred prior to dissolution.

Multinational Corporations

In the past, the size, power, and range of activities of corporations were limited. This changed at the beginning of the twentieth century, when corporations won the right to own the stock in each other. National corporate networks soon followed. Eventually, parent corporations, mostly American, expanded these networks overseas by setting up subsidiary corporations under the laws of other countries. These international networks are made up of companies of different nationalities that constitute a single economic unit connected by shareholding, managerial control, or contractual agreement. A corporation that operates in more than one country is called a **multinational corporation**.

multinational corporation
A corporation that operates in more than one country.

Consider These Examples The Ford Motor Company is an example of a national multinational firm. Organized in the United States at the beginning of the twentieth century, Ford has always viewed the entire world as its market. The company's policy is for the American parent to own and control all of its overseas subsidiaries. Ford's 10 European subsidiaries are all owned entirely by the American parent. The Mitsubishi Group is another example of this organizational format. It is actually made up of several Japanese companies that use joint directors' meetings to coordinate their activities in Japan and overseas.

The Royal Dutch/Shell Group is an example of an international multinational corporation. In 1907, the Dutch and British parents each formed a wholly owned holding company in their respective countries. Each then transferred the ownership of the operating subsidiary to the holding company and exchanged shares in the holding companies. The management and operation of the two companies were organized to function as a single economic unit. Unilever, Dunlop, Pirelli, and VFW/Fokker also operate under an international multinational umbrella.

International Law

Multinational Corporation: International Branch Office

A corporation can conduct business in another country by using a **branch office**. A branch office is not a separate legal entity but is merely an office of the corporation. The corporation is therefore liable for the contracts of the branch office and is also liable for the torts committed by personnel of the branch office. There is no liability shield between the corporation and the branch office.

Consider This Example General Motors Corporation, a U.S. corporation incorporated under the laws of Delaware, opens a branch office in Delhi, India, to sell its automobiles there. If an employee at the branch office in India negligently injures an Indian citizen in India while on a test drive, General Motors Corporation in the United States is wholly liable for the injured person's damages. ■

Conducting International Business Using a Branch Office

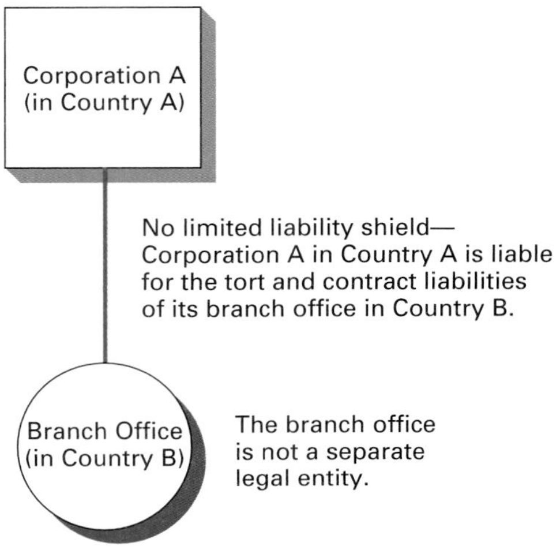

International Law

Multinational Corporation: International Subsidiary Corporation

A corporation can conduct business in another country by using a **subsidiary corporation**. The subsidiary corporation is organized under the laws of the foreign country. The **parent corporation** usually owns all or the majority of the subsidiary corporation. A subsidiary corporation is a separate legal entity. Therefore, the parent corporation is not liable for the contracts of or torts committed by the subsidiary corporation. There is a liability shield between the parent corporation and the subsidiary corporation.

Conducting International Business Using a Subsidiary Corporation

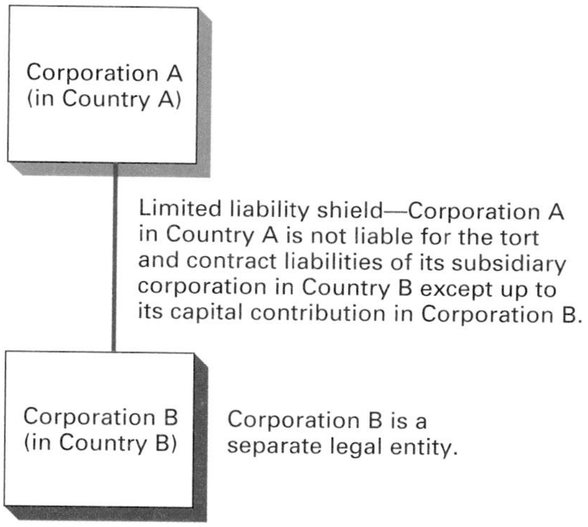

Consider This Example General Motors Corporation, a U.S. corporation incorporated under the laws of Delaware, forms a subsidiary corporation called General Motors-India Corporation, an Indian corporation formed under the laws of India, to sell automobiles in India. General Motors Corporation is the parent corporation, and General Motors-India Corporation is the subsidiary corporation. If an employee of General Motors-India Corporation negligently injures an Indian citizen while on a test drive, only General Motors-India Corporation is liable; General Motors Corporation in the United States is not liable other than that it may lose its capital contribution in General Motors-India Corporation. ■

Terms and Concepts

Nature of the Corporation

1. ***Corporation.*** A legal entity created pursuant to the laws of the state of incorporation.
2. ***Corporations codes.*** State statutes that govern the formation, operation, and dissolution of corporations.

The Corporation as a Legal "Person"

A corporation is a separate legal entity—an *artificial person*—that can own property, sue and be sued, enter into contracts, and such.

Characteristics of Corporations

1. ***Limited liability of shareholders.*** Shareholders are liable for the debts and obligations of the corporation only to the extent of their capital contributions.
2. ***Free transferability of shares.*** Shares of a corporation are freely transferable by shareholders unless they are expressly restricted.
3. ***Perpetual existence.*** Corporations exist in perpetuity unless a specific duration is stated in the corporation's articles of incorporation.
4. ***Centralized management.*** The *board of directors* of the corporation makes policy decisions for the corporation. Corporate *officers* appointed by the board of directors run the corporation's day-to-day operations. Together, the directors and officers form the corporation's "management."

Revised Model Business Corporation Act

1. ***Model Business Corporation Act (MBCA).*** A model act drafted in 1950 that was intended to provide a uniform law for the regulation of corporations.

2. ***Revised Model Business Corporation Act (RMBCA).*** A revision of the MBCA promulgated in 1984 that arranged the provisions of the model act more logically, revised the language to be more consistent, and made substantial changes that modernized the provisions of the act.

Classifications of Corporations

1. ***Domestic corporation.*** A domestic corporation is a corporation in the state in which it is incorporated.
2. ***Foreign corporation.*** A foreign corporation is a corporation in any state other than the one in which it is incorporated. A domestic corporation often transacts business in states other than its state of incorporation; hence it is a foreign corporation in these other states. A foreign corporation must obtain a *certificate of authority* from these other states in order to transact intrastate business in those states.
3. ***Alien corporation.*** An alien corporation is a corporation that is incorporated in another country. Alien corporations are treated as foreign corporations for most purposes.

Incorporation Procedures

1. ***Incorporation.*** Incorporation is the process of incorporating (forming) a new corporation.
2. ***Corporations code.*** Corporations are creatures of statute; they can be formed only if certain statutory formalities contained in the state's corporations code are followed.
3. ***Selecting a state of incorporation.*** A corporation can be incorporated in only one state, although it can conduct business in other states.
4. ***Corporate name.*** A corporate name selected for a new corporation must be distinguishable from existing corporate names. A corporate name may be reserved for a limited period of time while the corporation is being formed.

Articles of Incorporation

The articles of incorporation are the basic governing documents of a corporation. They must be filed with the secretary of state of the state of incorporation. They are a public document and are also called the *corporate charter*.

1. ***Information to be set forth in the articles of incorporation.*** The corporations code of each state sets out the information that must be included in a corporation's articles of incorporation. Additional information may be included in the articles of incorporation, as deemed necessary or desirable by the incorporators.
2. ***Amending the articles of incorporation.*** The articles of incorporation can be amended to contain any provision that could have been lawfully included in the original articles of incorporation. After an amendment is approved by the shareholders, the corporation must file *articles of amendment* with the secretary of state.

Corporate Bylaws

Bylaws are a detailed set of rules that are adopted by the board of directors after a corporation is formed that contain provisions for managing the business and affairs of the corporation. This document does not have to be filed with the secretary of state.

Organizational Meeting

An organizational meeting must be held by the initial directors of a corporation after the articles of incorporation are filed. At this meeting, the directors adopt the bylaws, elect corporate officers, ratify promoters' contracts, adopt a corporate seal, and transact such other business as may come before the meeting.

Authorized, Issued, and Outstanding Shares

1. ***Authorized shares.*** The number of shares provided for in the articles of incorporation is called the authorized shares. The shareholders may amend the articles of incorporation to increase this amount.

2. ***Issued shares.*** Authorized shares that have been sold by a corporation are called issued shares.
3. ***Unissued shares.*** Authorized shares that have not been sold by a corporation are called unissued shares.
4. ***Treasury shares.*** Treasury shares are issued shares that have been repurchased by the corporation. They may be resold by the corporation.
5. ***Outstanding shares.*** Outstanding shares are shares that are in shareholder hands, whether originally issued or reissued treasury shares. Only outstanding shares have the right to vote.

Financing the Corporation

Equity securities, also called stocks, are securities that represent the ownership rights to a corporation. Equity securities consist of *common stock* and *preferred stock.*

Common Stock

Common stock is a type of equity security that represents the *residual value* of the corporation. Common stock has no preferences, and its shareholders are paid dividends and assets upon liquidation only after creditors and preferred shareholders have been paid.

1. ***Common stockholder.*** A person who owns common stock is called a common shareholder.
2. ***Common stock certificate.*** A common stock certificate is a document that represents the common shareholders' investment in the corporation.
3. ***Par value.*** A corporation assigns a par value to common shares to set the lowest price at which the shares may be issued by the corporation. *No par shares* are not assigned a par value. The RMBCA has eliminated the concept of par value.

Preferred Stock

Preferred stock is a type of equity security that is given certain preferences and rights over common stock.

1. ***Preferred stockholder.*** A preferred stockholder is a person who owns preferred stock.
2. ***Preferred stock certificate.*** A preferred stock certificate is a document that represents the preferred stockholders' investment in the corporation.
3. ***Preferences and rights.*** Preferred stock may have any or all of the following preferences or rights:
   a. *Dividend preference.* This is the right to receive a fixed dividend at stipulated periods during the year (e.g., quarterly).
   b. *Liquidation preference.* This is the right to be paid a stated dollar amount if the corporation is dissolved and liquidated. The corporation must pay its creditors first, however.
   c. *Cumulative dividend right. Cumulative preferred* stock is stock that provides that any missed dividend payments must be paid in the future to the preferred shareholders before the common shareholders can receive any dividends.
   d. *Right to participate in profits. Participating preferred stock* is preferred stock that allows the stockholder to participate in the profits of the corporation along with the common stockholders on an expressly stated basis.
   e. *Conversion right. Convertible preferred* stock is preferred stock that permits stockholders to convert their shares into common stock at a stipulated conversion price.
4. ***Redeemable preferred stock.*** Redeemable preferred stock may be bought back by the corporation at a specified price at some future date. It is also called *callable preferred stock.*

Debt Securities

Debt securities establish a *debtor–creditor* relationship in which the corporation borrows money from the investor to whom the debt security is issued.

1. ***Debenture.*** A debenture is a *long-term, unsecured debt* instrument that is based on a corporation's general credit rating.

2. ***Bond.*** A bond is a *long-term* debt security that is *secured* by some form of property. The property securing the bond is called *collateral*. In the event of nonpayment of interest, principal, or other specified events, bondholders can foreclose on and obtain the collateral.
3. ***Note.*** A note is a *short-term* debt instrument with a maturity of five years or less. It can either be unsecured or secured.

Merger

A merger occurs when one corporation is absorbed into another corporation and ceases to exist. The corporation that continues to exist after a merger is called the *surviving corporation*. The corporation that is absorbed in the merger and ceases to exist as a separate entity is called the *merged corporation*.

Required Approvals for a Merger

1. ***Required approvals.*** An ordinary merger requires (a) the recommendation of the board of directors of each corporation and (b) an affirmative vote of the majority of shares of each corporation that are entitled to vote (unless greater vote is required).
2. ***No shareholders' vote required.*** The approval of the surviving corporation's shareholders is not required if the merger increases the number of voting shares of the surviving corporation by 20 percent or less.
3. ***Articles of merger.*** A document must be filed with the secretary of state when a merger is completed.

Short-Form Mergers

A short-form merger is a merger between a *parent corporation* and a *subsidiary corporation* in which the parent corporation owns 90 percent or more of the subsidiary corporation.

1. ***Required approval.*** Only the approval of the board of directors of the parent corporation is required to effectuate a short-form merger. The votes of the shareholders of either corporation and the board of directors of the subsidiary corporation are not required.

Dissenting Shareholder Appraisal Rights

Shareholders have a statutory right to object to a proposed merger, share exchange, or sale or lease of all or substantially all of the property of a corporation to have their shares valued by the court and receive cash payment of this value from the corporation.

1. ***Procedures.*** The corporation must notify shareholders of their appraisal rights. To obtain appraisal rights, a shareholder must (a) deliver written notice to the corporation of his or her intent to demand payment of his or her shares before the vote is taken and (b) not vote his or her shares in favor of the proposed action.
2. ***Fair value.*** If a shareholder does not accept the value offered by the corporation, the court will determine the *fair value* of the shares. The court may hire appraisers to assist in making this determination. Costs of this proceeding are usually borne by the corporation.

Tender Offer

A tender off is an offer that an acquirer makes directly to a *target corporation's shareholders* in an effort to acquire or gain control of the target corporation.

1. ***Tender offeror.*** A party that makes a tender offer is called the tender offeror.
2. ***Target corporation.*** The corporation that is proposed to be acquired in a tender offer situation is called the target corporation.
3. ***The Williams Act.*** This federal statute regulates all tender offers. The SEC is empowered to administer the Williams Act.
4. ***Antifraud provision.*** *Section 14(e)* of the Williams Act prohibits fraudulent, deceptive, and manipulative practices in connection with a tender offer.

Fighting a Tender Offer

The management of a target corporation often takes one or more of the following steps to try to defeat a hostile tender offer:

1. Persuade the shareholders not to tender their shares.
2. File delaying lawsuits (e.g., antitrust lawsuits).

3. Sell the *crown jewel* (e.g., a valuable asset that the tender offeror is particularly interested in acquiring).
4. Adopt *poison pills* (e.g., contract provisions that make contracts and leases expire).
5. Find a *white knight* to purchase the corporation in a friendly acquisition.
6. Conduct a *Pac-Man tender offer* (i.e., a reverse tender offer to acquire the tender offeror).
7. Issue additional stock to friendly parties.
8. Create an *employee stock ownership plan (ESOP)* and issue stock to the ESOP.
9. Adopt *flip-over* and *flip-in rights plans* that make it more expensive for the tender offeror to acquire shares.
10. Pay *greenmail* by purchasing the shares held by the tender offeror at a premium. In this way, the target corporation can obtain a *standstill agreement* whereby the offeror agrees not to purchase shares of the target corporation for a stipulated period of time.

The target corporation may also engage in other strategies and tactics that make it more difficult for a tender offeror to complete its tender offer.

State Antitakeover Statutes

State legislatures enact state antitakeover statutes to protect from hostile takeovers corporations that are either incorporated in or doing business within the state.

WWW Internet Exercises and Case Questions

Working the Web Internet Exercises

1. Create a hypothetical corporation by preparing articles of incorporation, bylaws, and a shareholder agreement, using forms suitable for your state. For a list of state corporation statutes, see **www.law.cornell.edu/topics/state_statutes.html#corporations**.
2. Prepare minutes of the organizational meeting for your newly formed corporation. See Findlaw's compilation of state corporation and business forms, at **www.findlaw.com/11stategov/indexcorp.html**.
3. Using your state's database of corporations, find the last field annual report of a local corporation and determine who the officers are and who is designated as the registered agent for service of process. See "Legal Information Institute: Corporations," at **www.law.cornell.edu/topics/corporations.html**. See also "The Corporate Library," at **www.thecorporatelibrary.com**.
4. Assume that you have decided to form a not-for-profit corporation. What other steps do you need to take to properly create such an entity? See "Locating U.S. Corporation Records Online: Finding Secretaries of State Contact Information," at **www.internet-prospector.org/secstate.html**.
5. Research your own state law on antitakeover statutes. Compile examples. See **www.law.cornell.edu/topics/state_statutes.html#corporations**.
6. Find state statutes that control the distribution of corporate assets at termination for not-for-profit corporations. How does this differ from the rules in for-profit corporations? See **www.law.cornell.edu/topics/state_statutes.html#corporations**.

Legal Environment Cases

16.1 Legal Entity Jeffrey Sammak was the owner of a contracting business known as Senaco. In the early part of 1980, Sammak decided to enter the coal reprocessing business. In April 1980, Sammak attended the "Coal Show" in Chicago, Illinois, at which he met representatives of the Deister Co., Inc. (Deister). Deister was incorporated under the laws of Pennsylvania. Sammak began negotiating with Deister to purchase equipment to be used in his coal reprocessing business. Deister sent Sammak literature guaranteeing a certain level of performance for the equipment. On April 3, 1981, Sammak purchased the equipment. After the equipment was installed, Sammak became dissatisfied with its performance. Sammak believed that Deister breached an express warranty, and he wanted to sue. Can a suit be brought against a corporation such as Deister? *Blackwood Coal v. Deister Co., Inc.*, 626 F.Supp. 727, 1985 U.S.Dist. Lexis 12767 (E.D. Pa.)

16.2 Limited Liability of Shareholders Joseph M. Billy was an employee of the USM Corporation (USM), a publicly held corporation. On October 21, 1976, Billy was at work when a 4,600-pound ram from a vertical boring mill broke loose and crushed him to death. Billy's widow brought suit against USM, alleging that the accident was caused by certain defects in the manufacture and design of the vertical boring mill and the two moving parts directly involved in the accident, a metal lifting arm and the 4,600-pound ram. If Mrs. Billy's suit is successful, can the shareholders of USM be held personally liable for any judgment against USM? *Billy v. Consolidated Mach. Tool. Corp.*, 412 N.E.2d 934, 51 N.Y.2d 152, 1980 N.Y. Lexis 2638 (N.Y. App.)

16.3 Corporation William O'Donnel and Vincent Marino worked together as executives of a shipping container repair company known as Marine Trailers. Marine Trailers's largest customer was American Export Lines (American Export). When American Export became unhappy with the owners of Marine Trailers, it let O'Donnel and Mario know that if they formed their own company, American Exports would give them its business. O'Donnel and Marino decided to take American Exports's suggestion, and they bought the majority of shares of a publicly traded corporation known as Marine Repair Service, Inc. (Repair Services). O'Donnel and Marino operated Repair Services as a container repair company at the Port of New York. The company prospered, expanding to five other states and overseas. O'Donnel and Marino's initial $12,000 investment paid off. Ten years after buying the company, each man was earning over $150,000 a year in salary alone. What type of corporation is Repair Service? *O'Donnel v. Marine Repair Services, Inc.*, 530 F.Supp. 1199, 1982 U.S. Dist. Lexis 10456 (S.D. N.Y.)

16.4 Corporation Hutchinson Baseball Enterprises, Inc. (Hutchinson, Inc.), was incorporated under the laws of Kansas on August 31, 1980. Among the purposes of the corporation, according to its bylaws, were to "promote, advance, and sponsor baseball, which shall include Little League and Amateur baseball in the Hutchinson, Kansas, area." The corporation was involved in a number of activities, including leasing a field for American Legion teams, furnishing instructors as coaches for Little League teams, conducting a Little League camp, and leasing a baseball field to a local junior college for a nominal fee. Hutchinson, Inc., raised money through ticket sales to amateur baseball games, concessions, and contributions. Any profits were used to improve the playing fields. Profits were never distributed to the corporation's directors or members. What type of corporation is Hutchinson, Inc.? *Hutchinson Baseball Enterprises, Inc. v. Commissioner of Internal Revenue,* 696 F.2d 757, 1982 U.S. App. Lexis 23179 (10th Cir.)

16.5 Corporation In November 1979, Elmer Balvik and Thomas Sylvester formed a partnership, named Weldon Electric, for the purpose of engaging in the electrical contracting business. Balvik contributed $8,000 and a vehicle worth $2,000, and Sylvester contributed $25,000 to the partnership's assets. The parties operated the business as a partnership until 1984, when they decided to incorporate. Stock was issued to Balvik and Sylvester in proportion to their partnership ownership interests, with Sylvester receiving 70 percent and Balvik 30 percent of the stock. Balvik and his wife and Sylvester and his wife were the four directors of the corporation. Sylvester was elected president of the corporation. Balvik was vice president. The corporation's bylaws stated that "sales of shares of stock by any shareholder shall be as set forth in a 'Buy Sell Agreement' entered into by the shareholders." What type of corporation is Weldon Electric? *Balvik v. Sylvester*, 411 N.W.2d 383, 1987 N.D. Lexis 392 (ND)

16.6 Corporation Leo V. Mysels was the president of Florida Fashions of Interior Design, Inc. (Florida Fashions). Florida Fashions, which was a Pennsylvania corporation, had never registered to do business in the state of Florida. In 1973, while acting in the capacity of a salesman for the corporation, Mysels took an order for goods from Francis E. Barry. The transaction took place in Florida. Barry paid Florida Fashions for the goods ordered. When Florida Fashions failed to perform its obligations under the sales agreement, Barry brought suit in Florida. What type of corporation was Florida Fashions in regard to the state of Pennsylvania and to the state of Florida? Can Florida Fashions defend itself in a lawsuit? *Mysels v. Barry*, 332 So.2d 38, 1976 Fla.App. Lexis 14344 (Fla. App.)

16.7 Preferred Stock On June 24, 1970, Commonwealth Edison Co. (Commonwealth Edison), through its underwriters, sold one million shares of preferred stock at an offering price of $100 per share. Commonwealth Edison wanted to issue the stock with a dividend rate of 9.26 percent, but its major underwriter, First Boston Corporation (First Boston), advised that a rate of 9.44 percent should be paid. According to First Boston, a shortage of investment funds existed, and a higher dividend rate was necessary for a successful stock issue. Commonwealth Edison's management was never happy with the high dividend rate being paid on this preferred stock. On April 2, 1971, Commonwealth Edison's vice chairman was quoted in the report of the annual meeting of the corporation as saying, "We were disappointed at the 9.44 percent dividend rate on the preferred stock we sold last August, but we expect to refinance it when market conditions make it feasible." On March 20, 1972, Commonwealth Edison, pursuant to the terms under which the stock was sold, bought back the one million shares of preferred stock at a price of $110 per share. What type of preferred stock is this? *The Franklin Life Insurance Company v. Commonwealth Edison Company*, 451 F.Supp. 602, 1978 U.S.Dist. Lexis 17604 (S.D. Ill.)

16.8 Debt Security United Financial Corporation of California (United Financial) was incorporated in the state of Delaware on May 8, 1959. United Financial owned the majority of a California savings and loan association as well as three insurance agencies. In 1960, the original investors in United Financial decided to capitalize on an increase in investor interest in savings and loans. In June 1960, the first public offering of United Federal stock was made. The stock was sold on a unit basis, with 60,000 units being offered. Each unit consisted of two shares of United Financial stock and one $100, 5 percent interest-bearing debenture bond. This initial offering was a success. It provided $7.2 million to the corporation, of which $6.2 million was distributed as a return of capital to the original investors. What is the difference between the stock offered for sale by United Financial and the debenture bonds? *Jones v. H.F. Ahmanson & Company*, 1 Cal. 3d 93, 81 Cal.Rptr. 592, 1969 Cal. Lexis 195 (Cal.)

16.9 Dissenting Shareholder Appraisal Rights Over a period of several years, the Curtiss-Wright Corporation (Curtiss-Wright) purchased 65 percent of the stock of Dorr-Oliver Incorporated (Dorr-Oliver). In early 1979, Curtiss-Wright's board of directors decided that a merger with Dorr-Oliver would be beneficial to Curtiss-Wright. The board voted to approve a merger of the two companies and to pay $23 per share to the stockholders of Dorr-Oliver. The Dorr-Oliver board and 80 percent of Dorr-Oliver's shareholders approved the merger. The merger became effective on May 31, 1979. John Bershad, a minority shareholder of Dorr-Oliver, voted against the merger but thereafter tendered his 100 shares and received payment of $2,300. Bershad subsequently sued, alleging that the $23 per share paid to Dorr-Oliver shareholders was grossly inadequate. Can Bershad obtain minority shareholder appraisal rights? *Bershad v. Curtiss-Wright Corporation,* 535 A.2d 840, 1987 Del. Lexis 1313 (Del.)

16.10 Tender Offer On October 30, 1981, Mobil Corporation (Mobil) made a tender offer to purchase up to 40 million outstanding common shares of stock in Marathon Oil Company (Marathon) for $85 per share in cash. It further stated its intentions to follow the purchase with a merger of the two companies. Mobil was primarily interested in acquiring Marathon's oil and mineral interests in certain properties, including the Yates Field. Marathon directors immediately held a board meeting and determined to find a white knight. Negotiations developed between Marathon and United States Steel Corporation (U.S. Steel). On November 18, 1981, Marathon and U.S. Steel entered into an agreement whereby U.S. Steel would make a tender offer for 30 million common shares of Marathon stock at $125 per share, to be followed by a merger of the two companies.

The Marathon–U.S. Steel agreement was subject to the following two conditions: (1) U.S. Steel was given an irrevocable option to purchase 10 million authorized but unissued shares of Marathon common stock for $90 per share (or 17 percent of Marathon's outstanding shares), and (2) U.S. Steel was given an option to purchase Marathon's interest in oil and mineral rights in Yates Field for $2.8 billion (Yates Field option). The latter option could be exercised only if U.S. Steel's offer did not succeed and if a third party gained control of Marathon. Evidence showed that Marathon's interest in the Yates Field was worth up to $3.6 billion. Marathon did not give Mobil either of these two options. Mobil sued, alleging that these two options violated Section 14(e) of the Williams Act. Who wins? *Mobil Corporation v. Marathon Oil Company*, 669 F.2d 366, 1981 U.S.App. Lexis 14958 (6th Cir.)

Ethics in Business

16.11 MCA, Inc. (MCA), a corporate holding company, owned 92 percent of the stock of Universal Pictures Company (Universal) and 100 percent of the stock of Universal City Studios, Inc. (Universal City). On March 25, 1966, these two subsidiaries merged pursuant to Delaware's short-form merger statute. The minority shareholders of Universal were offered $75 per share for their shares. Francis I. DuPont & Company and other minority shareholders (Plaintiffs) rejected the offer and then perfected their dissenting shareholder appraisal rights. On March 29, 1973, the appraiser filed a final report in which he found the value of Universal stock to be $91.47 per share. Both parties filed exceptions to this report.

The parties' ultimate disagreement, of course, was over the value of the stock. Plaintiffs submitted that the true value was $131.89 per share; the defendant said it was $52.36. The computations were as follows:

Plaintiffs

Value Factor	Value	Weight	Result
Earnings	$129.12	70%	$ 90.38
Market	144.36	20	28.87
Assets	126.46	10	12.64
		Value per share	**$131.89**

Defendants

Value Factor	Value	Weight	Result
Earnings	$51.93	70%	$36.35
Dividends	41.66	20	8.33
Assets	76.77	10	7.68
		Value per share	**$52.36**

Appraiser

Value Factor	Value	Weight	Result
Earnings	$92.89	80%	$74.31
Assets	85.82	20	17.16
		Value per share	**$91.47**

The defendant took exception to the appraiser's failure to find that, in the years prior to the merger, the industry was declining and that Universal was ranked near its bottom. And it argued that Universal was in the business of producing and distributing feature motion pictures for theatrical exhibition. It contended that such business, generally, was in a severe decline at the time of merger and that Universal, in particular, was in a vulnerable position because it had failed to diversify, its feature films were of low commercial quality, and, unlike other motion picture companies, substantially all of its film library had already been committed to distributors for television exhibition. In short, defendant pictured Universal as a weak "wasting asset" corporation in a sick industry with poor prospects for revival.

The stockholders saw a different company. They said that Universal's business was indeed the production and distribution of features films, but not merely for theatrical exhibition. They argued that there was a dramatic increase in the television market for such feature films at the time of the merger. This new market, they contended, gave great new value to a fully amortized film library and significantly enhanced the value of Universal's current and future productions. They equated the television market to the acquisition of a new and highly profitable business whose earnings potential was just beginning to be realized at the time of the merger. Finally, said Plaintiffs, the theatrical market itself was recovering in 1966. Thus, they painted the portrait of a well-situated corporation in a rejuvenated industry. *Francis I. Du Pont & Company v. Universal City Studios, Inc.*, 312 A.2d 344, 1973 Del.Ch. Lexis 123 (Del. Ch.)

Ethics Issues

1. Describe dissenting shareholders appraisal rights.
2. Did the parties act ethically in arriving at their proposed values of the company? Explain.
3. What is the value of the minority shareholders' shares of Universal Pictures Company?

Endnote

1. 15 U.S.C. Section 78n(a).

17

Corporate Directors, Officers, Shareholders, and Corporate Liability

> "Corporation, n. An ingenious device for obtaining individual profit without individual responsibility."
>
> —Ambrose Bierce
> The Devil's Dictionary (1911)

Chapter Objectives

After studying this chapter, you should be able to:

1. Describe the functions of shareholders, directors, and officers in managing the affairs of a corporation.
2. Describe a director's and an officer's duty of care and the business judgment rule.
3. Describe a director's and an officer's duty of loyalty and how this duty is breached.
4. Describe how the Sarbanes-Oxley Act affects corporate governance.
5. Describe corporate liability.

Chapter Contents

- Shareholders
- Board of Directors
- Corporate Officers
- Liability of Directors and Officers
- Corporate Criminal Liability

Shareholders, directors, and officers have different rights in managing a corporation. The shareholders elect the directors and vote on other important issues affecting the corporation. The directors are responsible for making policy decisions and employing officers. The officers are responsible for the corporation's day-to-day operations.

As a legal entity, a corporation can be held liable for the acts of its directors and officers and for authorized contracts entered into on its behalf. The directors and officers of a corporation have certain rights and owe certain duties to the corporation and its shareholders. A director or an officer who breaches any of these duties can be held personally liable to the corporation, to its shareholders, or to third parties. Insurance is available against certain of these losses. Except in a few circumstances, shareholders do not owe a fiduciary duty to other shareholders or the corporation.

This chapter discusses the rights, duties, and liability of corporate shareholders, directors, and officers.

Mandalay, Myanmar. Many companies in the United States and other countries do not do business in or with companies from Myanmar. This is because of alleged human rights violations by the military government of Myanmar.

Shareholders

A corporation's shareholders own the corporation (see Exhibit 17.1). Nevertheless, they are not agents of the corporation (i.e., they cannot bind the corporation to any contracts), and the only management duties they have are the right to vote on matters such as the election of directors and the approval of fundamental changes in the corporation.

Shareholders' Meetings

annual shareholders' meeting
A meeting of the shareholders of a corporation that must be held annually by the corporation to elect directors and to vote on other matters.

Annual shareholders' meetings are held to elect directors, choose an independent auditor, or take other actions. These meetings must be held at the times fixed in the corporation's bylaws. If a meeting is not held within either 15 months of the last annual meeting or 6 months after the end of the corporation's fiscal year, whichever is earlier, a shareholder may petition the court to order the meeting held.

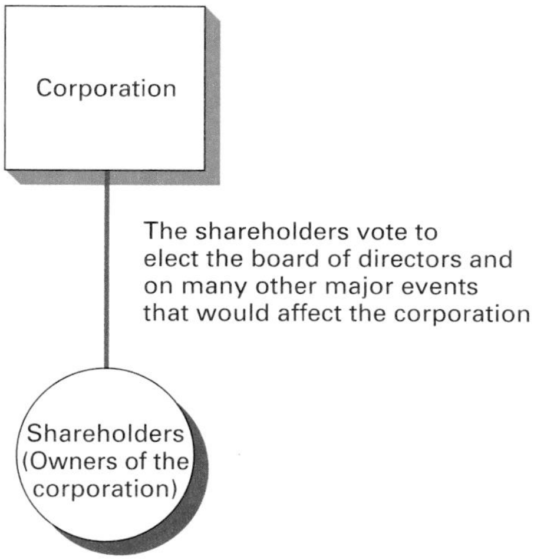

Exhibit 17.1
Shareholders

Special shareholders' meetings may be called by the board of directors, the holders of at least 10 percent of the voting shares of the corporation, or any other person authorized to do so by the articles of incorporation or bylaws (e.g., the president) [RMBCA § 7.02]. Special meetings may be held to consider important or emergency issues, such as a merger or consolidation of the corporation with one or more other corporations, the removal of directors, amendment of the articles of incorporation, or dissolution of the corporation.

special shareholders' meetings
Meetings of shareholders that may be called to consider and vote on important or emergency issues, such as a proposed merger or amending the articles of incorporation.

Any act that can be taken at a shareholders' meeting can be taken without a meeting if all the corporate shareholders sign a written consent approving the action.

Notice of Meetings A corporation is required to give the shareholders written *notice* of the place, day, and time of annual and special meetings. For a special meeting, the purpose of the meeting must also be stated. Only matters stated in the notice of a special meeting can be considered at the meeting. The notice, which must be given not fewer than 10 days or more than 50 days before the date of the meeting, may be given in person or by mail [RMBCA § 7.05]. If the required notice is not given or is defective, any action taken at the meeting is void.

Proxies

Shareholders do not have to attend a shareholders' meeting to vote. Shareholders may vote by *proxy*; that is, they can appoint another person (the proxy) as their agent to vote at the shareholders' meeting. The proxy may be directed exactly how to vote the shares or may be authorized to vote the shares at his or her discretion. Proxies may be in writing or posted online. The written document itself is called the **proxy** (or **proxy card**). Unless otherwise stated, a proxy is valid for 11 months.

proxy
A written document that a shareholder signs to authorize another person to vote his or her shares at the shareholders' meetings in the event of the shareholder's absence.

Quorum and Vote Required

Unless otherwise provided in a corporation's articles of incorporation, if a majority of shares entitled to vote are represented at the meeting in person or by proxy, there is a **quorum** to hold the meeting. Once a quorum is present, the withdrawal of shares does not affect the quorum of the meeting.

quorum
The required number of shares that must be represented in person or by proxy to hold a shareholders' meeting. The RMBCA establishes a majority of outstanding shares as a quorum.

The affirmative *vote* of the majority of the *voting* shares represented at a shareholders' meeting constitutes an act of the shareholders for actions other than for the election of directors [RMBCA § 7.25(c)].

Consider This Example Suppose there are 20,000 shares of a corporation outstanding. Assume that a shareholders' meeting is duly called to amend the articles of incorporation and that 10,001 shares are represented at the meeting. A quorum is present because a majority of the shares entitled to vote are represented. Suppose that 5,001 shares are voted in favor of the amendment. The amendment passes. In this example, just over 25 percent of the shares of the corporation bound the other shareholders to the action taken at the shareholders' meeting.

supramajority voting requirement
A requirement that a greater than majority of shares constitutes a quorum of the vote of the shareholders.

The articles of incorporation or the bylaws of a corporation can require a greater than majority of shares to constitute a quorum or the vote of the shareholders [RMBCA § 7.27]. This is called a **supramajority voting requirement** (or **supermajority**). Such votes are often required to approve mergers, consolidation, the sale of substantially all the assets of a corporation, and such.

Straight (Noncumulative) Voting

straight voting
A voting method in which each shareholder votes the number of shares he or she owns on candidates for each of the positions open.

Unless otherwise stated in a corporation's articles of incorporation, voting for the election of directors is by the **straight voting** method. This voting method is quite simple: Each shareholder votes the number of shares he or she owns on candidates for each of the positions open for election. Thus, a majority shareholder can elect the entire board of directors.

Consider This Example Assume that a corporation has 10,000 outstanding shares. Erin Caldwell owns 5,100 shares (or 51 percent), and Michael Rhodes owns 4,900 shares (49 percent). Suppose that three directors of the corporation are to be elected. Caldwell casts 5,100 votes each for her chosen candidates. Rhodes votes 4,900 shares for each of his chosen candidates, who are different from those favored by Caldwell. Each of the three candidates whom Caldwell voted for wins, with 5,100 votes.

Cumulative Voting

cumulative voting
A voting method in which a shareholder can accumulate all of his or her votes and vote them all for one candidate or split them among several candidates.

The law does not permit the stockholders to create a sterilized board of directors.

Judge Collins
Mason v. Curtis (1918)

A corporation's articles of incorporation may provide for **cumulative voting** for the election of directors. Under this method, a shareholder can accumulate all of his or her votes and vote them all for one candidate or split them among several candidates. This means that each shareholder is entitled to multiply the number of shares he or she owns by the number of directors to be elected and cast the product for a single candidate or distribute the product among two or more candidates [RMBCA § 7.28]. Cumulative voting gives a minority shareholder a better opportunity to elect someone to the board of directors.

Consider This Example Suppose Lisa Monroe owns 1,000 shares. Assume that four directors are to be elected to the board. Under cumulative voting, Monroe can multiply the number of shares she owns by the number of directors to be elected. She can take the resulting number of votes (4,000) and cast them all for one candidate or split them. Examples of cumulative voting are set forth in Exhibit 17.2.

Preemptive Rights

preemptive rights
Rights that give existing shareholders the option of subscribing to new shares being issued in proportion to their current ownership interests.

A corporation's articles of incorporation can grant shareholders preemptive rights. **Preemptive rights** give existing shareholders the option of subscribing to new shares being issued by the corporation in proportion to their current ownership interests [RMBCA § 6.30]. Such a purchase can prevent a shareholder's interest in the corporation from being *diluted*. Shareholders are given a reasonable period of time (such as 30 days) to exercise their preemptive rights. If a shareholder does not exercise his or her preemptive rights during this time, the shares can then be sold to anyone.

Exhibit 17.2
Cumulative Voting

Formula for Cumulative Voting. A shareholder can use the following formula to determine whether or not he or she owns a sufficient number of shares to elect a director to the board of directors using cumulative voting:

$$\frac{S \times T}{D+1} + 1 = X$$

where X is the number of shares needed by a shareholder to elect a director to the board, S is the number of shares that actually vote at the shareholders' meeting, T is the number of directors the shareholder wants to elect, and D is the number of directors to be elected at the shareholders' meeting.

Example 1 Suppose there are 9,000 outstanding shares of a corporation. Shareholder 1 owns 1,000 shares, Shareholder 2 owns 4,000 shares, and Shareholder 3 owns 4,000 shares. Assume nine directors are to be elected to the board of directors. All the shares are voted. Under cumulative voting, does Shareholder 1 have enough votes to elect a director to the board? The answer is yes:

$$\frac{9{,}000 \times 1}{9+1} + 1 = 901$$

Example 2 If a board of directors is divided into classes and elected by staggered elections, the ability of a minority shareholder to elect a director to the board is diminished. Suppose in Example 1 that the corporation staggered the election of the board of directors so that three directors are elected each year to serve three-year terms. How many shares would a shareholder have to own to elect a director to the board?

$$\frac{9{,}000 \times 1}{3+1} + 1 = 2{,}251$$

Because of the staggered election of the board of directors, Shareholder 1 (who owns 1,000 shares) would not be able to elect a director to the board without the assistance of another shareholder.

Consider This Example Suppose that the ABC Corporation has 10,000 outstanding shares and that Linda Norton owns 1,000 shares (10 percent). Assume that the corporation plans to raise more capital by issuing another 10,000 shares of stock. With preemptive rights, Norton must be offered the option to purchase 1,000 of the 10,000 new shares before they are offered to the public. If she does not purchase them, her ownership in the corporation will be diluted from 10 percent to 5 percent.

Contemporary Trend

Agreements Restricting the Transfer of Shares

Generally, shareholders have the right to transfer their shares. Shareholders may enter into agreements with one another to prevent unwanted persons from becoming owners of the corporation [RMBCA § 6.27]. The following are the two most common forms of agreements:

- ***Right of first refusal.*** A **right of first refusal** is an *agreement* entered into by shareholders whereby they grant each other the right of first refusal to purchase shares they are going to sell. A selling shareholder must offer his or her shares for sale to the other parties to the agreement before selling them to anyone else. If the shareholders do not exercise their right of first refusal, the selling shareholder is free to sell his or her shares to another party. A right of first refusal may be granted to the corporation as well.
- ***Buy-and-sell agreement.*** A **buy-and-sell agreement** is one entered into by shareholders that requires selling shareholders to sell their shares to the other shareholders or to the corporation at the price specified in the agreement. The price of the shares is normally determined by a formula that considers, among other factors, the profitability of the corporation. The purchase of shares of a deceased shareholder pursuant to a buy-and-sell agreement is often funded by proceeds from life insurance. ■

Dividends

Profit corporations operate to make a profit. The objective of the shareholders is to share in those profits, either through capital appreciation, the receipt of dividends, or both. **Dividends** are paid at the discretion of the board of directors [RMBCA § 6.40]. The directors are responsible for determining when, where, how, and how much will be paid in dividends. They may opt to retain the profits in the corporation to be used for corporate purposes instead of as dividends. This authority cannot be delegated to a committee of the board of directors or to officers of the corporation.

dividend
A distribution of profits of the corporation to shareholders.

When a corporation declares a dividend, it sets a date, usually a few weeks prior to the actual payment, that is called the *record date*. Persons who are shareholders on that date are entitled to receive the dividend, even if they sell their shares before the payment date. Once declared, a cash or property dividend cannot be revoked. Shareholders can sue to recover declared but unpaid dividends.

Derivative Lawsuits

If a corporation is harmed by someone, the directors of the corporation have the authority to bring an action on behalf of the corporation against the offending party to recover damages or other relief. If the corporation fails to bring the lawsuit, shareholders have the right to bring the lawsuit on behalf of the corporation. This is called a **derivative action**, or **derivative lawsuit** [RMBCA § 7.40].

derivative lawsuit
A lawsuit a shareholder brings against an offending party on behalf of the corporation when the corporation fails to bring the lawsuit. Also called a *derivative action*.

A shareholder can bring a derivative action if he or she (1) was a shareholder of the corporation at the time of the act complained of; (2) fairly and adequately represents the interests of the corporation; and (3) made a written demand on the corporation to take suitable actions and either the corporation rejected the demand or 90 days have expired from the date of the demand.

A derivative lawsuit will be dismissed by the court if either a majority of independent directors or a panel of independent persons appointed by the court determines that the lawsuit is not in the best interests of the corporation. This decision must be reached in good faith and only after conducting a reasonable inquiry.

If a shareholder derivative action is successful, any award goes into the corporate treasury. The plaintiff-shareholder is entitled to recover payment for reasonable expenses, including attorneys' fees, incurred in bringing and maintaining the derivative action. Any settlement of a derivative action requires court approval.

Piercing the Corporation Veil

Shareholders of a corporation generally have **limited liability** (i.e., they are liable for the debts and obligations of the corporation only to the extent of their capital contributions), and they are not personally liable for the debts and obligations of the corporation. However, if a shareholder or shareholders dominate a corporation and misuse it for improper purposes, a court of equity can *disregard the corporate entity* and hold the shareholders of a corporation personally liable for the corporation's debts and obligations. This doctrine is commonly referred to as **piercing the corporate veil**. It is often resorted to by unpaid creditors who are trying to collect from shareholders a debt owed by the corporation. The piercing the corporate veil doctrine is also called the *alter ego doctrine* because the corporation has become the *alter ego* of the shareholder.

piercing the corporate veil
A doctrine that says if a shareholder dominates a corporation and uses it for improper purposes, a court of equity can disregard the corporate entity and hold the shareholder personally liable for the corporation's debts and obligations.

Courts will pierce the corporate veil if (1) the corporation has been formed without sufficient capital (i.e., *thin capitalization*) or (2) separateness has not been maintained between the corporation and its shareholders (e.g., commingling of personal and corporate assets, failure to hold required shareholders' meetings, failure to maintain corporate records and books). The courts examine this doctrine on a case-by-case basis.

The piercing the corporate veil doctrine was raised in the following case.

Case 17.1 Piercing the Corporate Veil

Kinney Shoe Corp. v. Polan
939 F.2d 209, 1991 U.S.App. Lexis 15304
United States Court of Appeals, Fourth Circuit

Background and Facts

In 1984, Lincoln M. Polan formed Industrial Realty Company (Industrial), a West Virginia corporation. Polan was the sole shareholder of Industrial. Although a certificate of incorporation was issued, no organizational meeting was held, and no officers were elected. Industrial issued no stock certificates because nothing was ever paid in to the corporation. Other corporate formalities were not observed. Polan, on behalf of Industrial, signed a lease to sublease commercial space in a building controlled by Kinney Shoe Corporation (Kinney). The first rental payment to Kinney was made out of Polan's personal funds, and no further payments were made on the lease. Kinney filed suit against Industrial and obtained a judgment of $66,400 for unpaid rent. When the amount was unpaid by Industrial, Kinney sued Polan individually and sought to pierce the corporate veil to collect from Polan. The district court held for Polan. Kinney appealed.

Issue

Is Polan personally liable for Industrial's debts?

In the Language of the Court

Kinney seeks to pierce the corporate veil of Industrial so as to hold Polan personally liable on the sublease debt. The Supreme Court of Appeals of West Virginia has set forth a two prong test to be used in determining whether to pierce a corporate veil in a breach of contract case. This test raises two issues: first, is the unity of interest and ownership such that the separate personalities of the corporation and the individual shareholder no longer exist; and second, would an equitable result occur if the acts are treated as those of the corporation alone.

The district court found that the two prong test had been satisfied. The court concluded that Polan's failure to carry out the corporate formalities with respect to Industrial, coupled with Industrial's gross undercapitalization, resulted in damage to Kinney. We agree. It is undisputed that Industrial was not adequately capitalized. Actually, it had no paid in capital. Polan had put nothing into this corporation, and it did not observe any corporate formalities. Polan was obviously trying to limit his liability by setting up a paper curtain constructed of nothing more than Industrial's certificate of incorporation. These facts present the classic scenario for an action to pierce the corporate veil so as to reach the responsible party and produce an equitable result.

Decision and Remedy

The Court of Appeals pierced the corporate veil and held Polan personally liable on Industrial's debt to Kinney. The Court of Appeals reversed the district court's judgment.

Business and Ethics Questions

1. Is the doctrine of piercing the corporate veil needed? Should parties such as Kinney bear the risk of dealing with corporations such as Industrial?
2. Is it ethical for persons to form corporations to avoid personal liability? Should this be allowed?
3. What is the risk if corporate formalities are not observed? Explain.

Internet Law & Online Commerce

Corporations Codes Recognize Electronic Communications

Most state corporations codes have been amended to permit the use of electronic communications to shareholders and among directors. For example, the Delaware general corporation law recognizes the following uses of electronic technology:

- Delivery of notices to stockholders may be made electronically if the stockholder consents to the delivery of notice in this form.
- Proxy solicitation for shareholder votes may be made by electronic transmission.
- The shareholder list of a corporation that must be made available during the 10 days prior to a stockholder meeting may be made available either at the principal place of business of the corporation or by posting the list on an electronic network.

(continued)

Internet Law & Online Commerce (continued)

- Stockholders who are not physically present at a meeting may be deemed present, participate in, and vote at the meeting by electronic communication; a meeting may be held solely by electronic communication, without a physical location.
- The election of directors of the corporation may be held by electronic transmission.
- Directors' actions by unanimous consent may be taken by electronic transmission.

The use of electronic transmissions, electronic networks, and communications by e-mail will make the operation and administration of corporate affairs more efficient. ■

Shareholder Resolution

At times, shareholders may wish to submit issues for a vote to other shareholders. The Securities Exchange Act of 1934 and SEC rules adopted thereunder permit a shareholder to submit a resolution to be considered by other shareholders if (1) the shareholder has owned at least 1,000 shares of the corporation's stock for at least two years and (2) the resolution does not exceed 550 words. Such **shareholder resolutions** are usually made when the corporation is soliciting proxies from its shareholders.

shareholder resolution

A resolution that may be submitted by a shareholder who meets certain ownership requirements to other shareholders for a vote. Many shareholder resolutions concern social issues.

If management does not oppose the resolution, it may be included in the proxy materials issued by the corporation. Even if management is not in favor of the resolution, the shareholder has the right to have the shareholder resolution included in the corporation's proxy materials if it (1) relates to the corporation's business, (2) concerns a *policy issue* (and not the day-to-day operations of the corporation), and (3) does not concern the payment of dividends. The SEC rules on whether a resolution can be submitted to shareholders.

Shareholder resolutions have recently been presented concerning protecting the environment, reducing global warming, preventing the overcutting of the rain forests in Brazil, and prohibiting U.S. corporations from purchasing goods manufactured in developing countries under poor working conditions, including the use of forced and child labor.

Most shareholder resolutions have a slim chance of being enacted because large-scale investors usually support management. They can, however, cause a corporation to change the way it does business. For example, to avoid the adverse publicity such issues can create, some corporations voluntarily adopt the changes contained in shareholder resolutions. Others negotiate settlements with the sponsors of resolutions to get the measures off the agenda before the annual shareholders' meetings.

Ethics in Business

Shareholder Resolution

The E. I. DuPont de Nemours and Company (DuPont), organized under the laws of the state of Delaware, is one of the largest chemical and consumer products companies in the world. DuPont has manufacturing and production facilities located in many foreign countries. Several of these countries have been criticized because child labor and forced labor are alleged to be used to produce goods in those countries.

At its annual meeting in April 2001, the International Brotherhood of Teamsters General Fund, owner of 90 shares of DuPont common stock, proposed the following shareholder resolution to the shareholders of DuPont:

The shareholder resolution for the adoption of international workplace standards was defeated by an overwhelming majority of DuPont shareholders at the annual meeting.

Ethics Issues

1. Why do you think the International Brotherhood of Teamsters introduced this shareholder resolution?
2. Do you think the reasons DuPont asserted for recommending that its shareholders vote against the proposal were legitimate? Explain. ■

Stockholder Proposal on International Workplace Standards

RESOLVED: *That the Board of Directors of E. I. du Pont de Nemours and Company (Du Pont) shall adopt, implement and enforce the workplace Code of Conduct (Code) as based on the International Labor Organization's (ILO) Conventions on workplace human rights, which include:*

- *No use of child labor.*
- *No discrimination or intimidation in employment.*
- *All workers have the right to form and join unions and to bargain collectively.*
- *No use of forced labor.*

Stockholder's (Teamster's) Statement in Support of the Proposal:

The Teamsters, in support of its proposal, provided the following statement in Du Pont's annual Proxy Statement submitted to Du Pont shareholders.

As a global institution, Du Pont and its international operations and sourcing arrangements are exposed to sundry risks. Adoption of this proposal manages the risk of being a party to serious human rights violations in the workplace. Du Pont operates or has business relationships in a number of countries, including China, Indonesia, and Thailand, where the U.S. State Department, Amnesty International, and Human Rights Watch indicate law and public policy do not adequately protect human rights. To wit: Forced labor, illegal child labor, and violence against women.

The success of Du Pont's operations depends on consumer and governmental good will. Brand name is a significant asset. Du Pont benefits from adopting and enforcing the Code ensuring that it isn't associated with human rights violations. This protects Du Pont's brand names and its relationships with customers and the numerous governments under which Du Pont operates and with which it does business.

Position of the Board of Directors in Opposition to the Proposal

In response, Du Pont included the following statement in the Proxy Statement, recommending that Du Pont shareholders vote against the shareholder resolution.

Du Pont is committed to conducting its business affairs with the highest ethical standards, and works diligently to be a respected corporate citizen throughout the world. The company has had in place for many years an Ethics Policy, Mission Statement and Code of Business Conduct addressing many of the issues covered in the standards proposed for adoption. These corporate policies are applicable to all employees in all Du Pont businesses around the world.

The company is supportive of the general intent of the proposal and similar international workplace standards suggested by other organizations for adoption. The company reviews on an ongoing basis codes offered by other organizations, and examines its own policies and practices in light of the provisions of the proposed codes. The company also meets with advocates of codes to explore issues of mutual concern. These efforts will continue. The company therefore believes adoption of the proposed code is unnecessary.

Board of Directors

The **board of directors** of a corporation is responsible for formulating the *policy decisions* affecting the management, supervision, control, and operation of the corporation (see Exhibit 17.3) [RMBCA § 8.01]. Such policy decisions include deciding what business or businesses the corporation should be engaged in, selecting and removing the top officers of the corporation, determining the capital structure of the corporation, declaring dividends, and the like.

board of directors
A panel of decision makers whose members are elected by the shareholders of a corporation.

Exhibit 17.3
Board of Directors

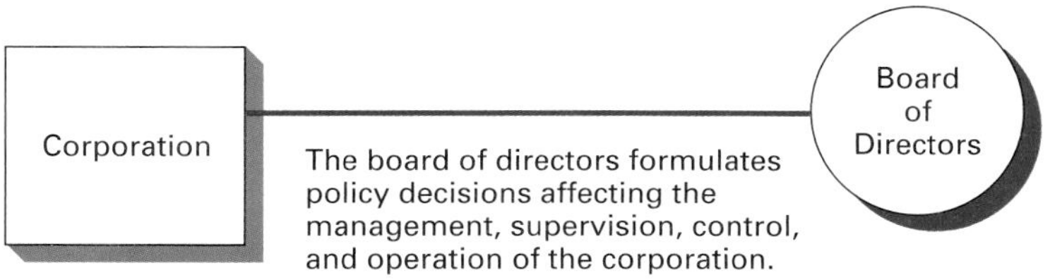

The board may initiate certain actions that require shareholders' approval. These actions are initiated when the board of directors adopts a *resolution* that approves a transaction and recommends that it be submitted to the shareholders for a vote. Examples of such transactions include mergers, sale of substantially all of the corporation's assets outside the course of ordinary business operations, amendment of the articles of incorporation, and the voluntary dissolution of the corporation.

Corporate directors are required to have access to the corporation's books and records, facilities, and premises, as well as any other information affecting the operation of the corporation. This right of inspection is absolute. It cannot be limited by the articles of incorporation, the bylaws, or board resolution.

inside director
A member of a board of directors who is also an officer of the corporation.

outside director
A member of a board of directors who is not an officer of the corporation.

Boards of directors are typically composed of inside and outside directors. An **inside director** is a person who is also an officer of the corporation. For example, the president of a corporation often sits as a director of the corporation.

An **outside director** is a person who sits on the board of directors of a corporation but is not an officer of that corporation. Outside directors are often officers and directors of other corporations, bankers, lawyers, professors, and others. Outside directors are often selected for their business knowledge and expertise.

Director's Term of Office

The director is really a watch-dog, and the watch-dog has no right, without the knowledge of his master, to take a sop from a possible wolf.

L.J. Bowen
Re The North Australian Territory Co. Ltd. (1891)

The term of a director's office expires at the next annual shareholders' meeting following his or her election, unless terms are staggered. The RMBCA allows boards of directors that consist of nine or more members to be divided into two or three classes (each class to be as nearly equal in number as possible) that are elected to serve *staggered terms* of two or three years [RMBCA § 8.06]. The specifics of such an arrangement must be outlined in the articles of incorporation.

Consider This Example Suppose a board of directors consists of nine directors. The board can be divided into three classes of three directors each, each class to be elected to serve a three-year term. Only three directors of the nine-member board would come up for election each year. This nine-member board could also be divided into two classes of five and four directors, each class to be elected to two-year terms.

Meetings of the Board of Directors

The directors of a corporation can act only as a board. They cannot act individually on the corporation's behalf. Every director has the right to participate in any meeting of the board of directors. Each director has one vote. Directors cannot vote by proxy.

Regular meetings of the board of directors are held at the times and places established in the bylaws. Such meetings can be held without notice. The board can call *special meetings* as provided in the bylaws [RMBCA § 8.20(a)]. These meetings are usually convened for such reasons as issuing new shares, considering proposals to merge with other corporations, adopting maneuvers to defend against hostile takeover attempts, and the like.

The board of directors may act without a meeting if all the directors sign written consents that set forth the actions taken. The RMBCA permits meetings of the board to be held via conference calls.

quorum
The number of directors necessary to hold a meeting of the board of directors or transact business of the board.

Quorum and Voting Requirement A simple majority of the number of directors established in the articles of incorporation or bylaws usually constitutes a **quorum** for transacting business. However, the articles of incorporation and the bylaws may increase this number. If a quorum is present, the approval or disapproval of a majority of the quorum binds the entire board. The articles of incorporation or the bylaws can require a greater than majority of directors to constitute a quorum or the vote of the board.

Committees of the Board of Directors

committees of the board of directors
Committees created by a board of directors that are comprised of designated members of the board who are delegated certain powers to act on behalf of the board of directors.

In the current complex business world, the demands on directors have increased. To help handle this increased workload, boards of directors have turned to creating **committees** of their members to handle specific duties. Board members with special expertise or interests are appointed to the various committees.

Unless the articles of incorporation or bylaws provide otherwise, the board of directors may create committees of the board and delegate certain powers to those committees [RMBCA § 8.25]. All members of these committees must be directors. An act of a committee pursuant to delegated authority is the act of the board of directors.

Committees commonly appointed by the board of directors include:

- ***Executive committee.*** This committee has authority to (1) act on certain matters on behalf of the board during the interim period between board meetings and (2) conduct preliminary investigations of proposals on behalf of the full board. Most members of the committee are inside directors because it is easier for them to meet to address corporate matters.
- ***Audit committee.*** This committee hires independent public accountants and supervises the audit of the financial records of the corporation.
- ***Nominating committee.*** This committee nominates the management slate of directors to be submitted for shareholder vote.
- ***Compensation committee.*** This committee approves management compensation, including salaries, bonuses, stock option plans, fringe benefits, and such.
- ***Investment committee.*** This committee is responsible for investing and reinvesting the funds of the corporation.
- ***Litigation committee.*** This committee reviews and decides whether to pursue requests by shareholders for the corporation to sue persons who have allegedly harmed the corporation.

The following powers cannot be delegated to committees but must be exercised by the board itself: (1) declaring dividends, (2) initiating actions that require shareholders' approval, (3) appointing members to fill vacancies on the board, (4) amending the bylaws, (5) approving a plan of merger that does not require shareholder approval (short-form merger), and (6) authorizing the issuance of shares.

Ethics in Business

Sarbanes-Oxley Act Imposes Duties on Audit Committee

During the late 1990s and early 2000s, many corporations engaged in accounting fraud to report inflated earnings or to conceal losses. It was often management who perpetrated this accounting fraud, which was not detected by the board of directors. Sometimes members of the board of directors conspired or participated in the accounting fraud. In response, Congress enacted the federal **Sarbanes-Oxley Act of 2002**. This act placed certain responsibilities on a corporation's **audit committee**.

A public company must have an audit committee. Members of the audit committee must be members of the board of directors and must be independent—that is, not employed or receive compensation from the company or any of its subsidiaries for services other than as a board member and member of the audit committee. These board members are called *outside* board members because they are not employees (e.g., president, CEO) of the corporation. At least one member of the audit committee must be a financial expert, based on either education or prior experience, so as to understand generally accepted accounting principles, preparation of financial statements, and audit committee functions.

The audit committee is responsible for the appointment, payment of compensation, and oversight of public accounting firms employed to audit the company. The audit committee must preapprove all audit and permissible nonaudit services to be performed by a public accounting firm. The audit committee has authority to employ independent legal counsel and other advisors.

The act requires public companies to establish and maintain adequate internal controls and procedures for financial reporting. The act required public companies to prepare an assessment of the effectiveness of its internal quality controls at the end of each fiscal year. These internal audits are supervised by the audit committee.

Ethics Issues

1. Who are outside directors? How do they differ from inside directors? Do you think outside directors are more important than inside directors? Explain.
2. Will the requirement of having only independent outside directors on the audit committee help prevent accounting fraud? Explain. ■

Corporate Officers

officers
Employees of a corporation who are appointed by the board of directors to manage the day-to-day operations of the corporation.

The board of directors has the authority to appoint the **officers** of the corporation. The officers are elected by the board of directors at such time and by such manner as prescribed in the corporation's bylaws. The directors can delegate certain management authority to the officers of the corporation (see Exhibit 17.4).

Exhibit 17.4
Corporate Officers

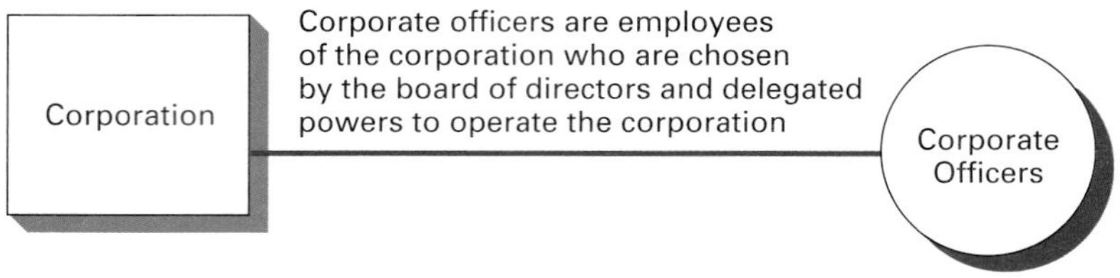

At a minimum, most corporations have the following officers: (1) a president, (2) one or more vice presidents, (3) a secretary, and (4) a treasurer. The bylaws or the board of directors can authorize duly appointed officers the power to appoint assistant officers. The same individual may simultaneously hold more than one office in the corporation [RMBCA § 8.40]. The duties of each officer are specified in the bylaws of the corporation.

Officers and agents of a corporation have such authority as may be provided in the bylaws of the corporation or as determined by resolution of the board of directors. As agents, officers have the authority to bind a corporation to contracts; this authority is derived from express authority, implied authority, and apparent authority.

Concept Summary *Management of a Corporation*

Group	Function
Shareholders	Owners of the corporation. They vote on the directors and other major actions to be taken by the corporation.
Board of directors	Responsible for making policy decisions and employing the major officers for the corporation. It also makes recommendations regarding actions to be taken by the shareholders.
Officers	Responsible for the day-to-day operation of the corporation. Includes acting as agents for the corporation, hiring other officers and employees, and the like.

Ethics in Business

Sarbanes-Oxley Act Improves Corporate Governance

During the late 1990s and early 2000s, the U.S. economy was wracked by a number of business and accounting scandals. Companies such as Enron, Tyco, and Worldcom engaged in fraudulent conduct, leading to the conviction of many corporate officers of financial crimes. Many of these companies went bankrupt, causing huge losses to their shareholders, employees, and creditors. Boards of directors were complacent, not keeping a watchful eye over the conduct of their officers and employees.

In response, Congress enacted the federal **Sarbanes-Oxley Act of 2002**. This act establishes far-reaching new rules regarding corporate governance. The goals of the Sarbanes-Oxley Act are to improve corporate governance rules, eliminate conflicts of interest, and instill confidence in investors and the public that management will run public companies in the best interests of all constituents.

Several major provisions of the act are:

- ***CEO and CFO certification.*** The CEO and CFO of a public company must file a statement accompanying each annual and quarterly report, certifying that the signing officer has reviewed the report, based on the officer's knowledge that the report does not contain any untrue statement of a material fact or omit to state a material fact that would make the statement misleading and that the financial statement and disclosures fairly present, in all material aspects, the operation and financial condition of the company. A knowing and willful violation is punishable for up to 20 years in prison and a fine of not more than $5 million.
- ***Reimbursement of bonuses and incentive pay.*** If a public company is required to restate its financial statements because of material noncompliance with financial reporting requirements, the CEO and CFO must reimburse the company for any bonuses, incentive pay, or securities trading profits made because of the noncompliance.
- ***Prohibition on personal loans.*** The act prohibits public companies from making personal loans to its directors or executive officers.
- ***Tampering with evidence.*** The act makes it a crime for any person to knowingly alter, destroy, mutilate, conceal, or create any document to impair, impede, influence, or obstruct any federal investigation. A violation is punishable for up to 20 years in prison and a monetary fine.
- ***Bar from acting as an officer or a director.*** The Securities and Exchange Commission (SEC), a federal government agency, may issue an order prohibiting any person who has committed securities fraud from acting as an officer or a director of a public company.

Although the Sarbanes-Oxley Act applies only to public companies, private companies and nonprofit organizations are also influenced by the act's accounting and corporate governance rules.

Ethics Issues

1. Will the CEO and CFO certification requirement reduce corporate fraudulent conduct? Explain.
2. Will the Sarbanes-Oxley Act encourage ethical behavior by corporate officers and directors? ■

Liability of Directors and Officers

A corporation's directors and officers owe the **fiduciary duties** of trust and confidence to the corporation and its shareholders. More specifically, they owe the (1) *duty of loyalty* and (2) *duty of care*. Each of these is discussed in detail in the paragraphs that follow.

fiduciary duties
The duties of obedience, care, and loyalty owed by directors and officers to their corporation and its shareholders.

Duty of Loyalty

The **duty of loyalty** requires directors and officers to subordinate their personal interests to those of the corporation and its shareholders. Justice Benjamin Cardozo defined this duty of loyalty as follows:

duty of loyalty
A duty that directors and officers have not to act adversely to the interests of the corporation and to subordinate their personal interests to those of the corporation and its shareholders.

> [A corporate director or officer] owes loyalty and allegiance to the corporation—a loyalty that is undivided and an allegiance that is influenced by no consideration other than the welfare of the corporation. Any adverse interest of a director [or officer] will be subjected to a scrutiny rigid and uncompromising. He may not profit at the expense of his corporation and in conflict with its rights; he may not for personal gain divert unto himself the opportunities that in equity and fairness belong to the corporation.
>
> Many forms of conduct permissible in a workaday world for those acting at arm's length are forbidden to those bound by fiduciary ties. Not honesty alone, but the punctilio of an honor the most sensitive, is then the standard of behavior. As to this there has developed a tradition that is unbending and inveterate.[1]

If a director or an officer breaches his or her duty of loyalty and makes a secret profit on a transaction, the corporation can sue the director or officer to recover the secret profit. Some of the most common breaches of the duty of loyalty are:

- ***Usurping a corporate opportunity.*** Directors and officers may not personally usurp (steal) a corporate opportunity for themselves. **Usurping a corporate opportunity** constitutes a violation of a director's or an officer's duty of loyalty. If usurping is proven, the corporation can (1) acquire the opportunity from the director or officer and (2) recover any profits made by the director or officer.

The following elements must be shown to prove usurping:

1. The opportunity was presented to the director or officer in his or her corporate capacity.
2. The opportunity is related to or connected with the corporation's current or proposed business.
3. The corporation has the financial ability to take advantage of the opportunity.
4. The corporate officer or director took the corporate opportunity for him- or herself.

However, the director or officer is personally free to take advantage of a corporate opportunity if it was fully disclosed and presented to the corporation and the corporation rejected it.

- ***Self-dealing.*** Under the RMBCA, a contract or transaction with a corporate director or officer is voidable by the corporation if it is unfair to the corporation [RMBCA § 8.31]. Contracts of a corporation to purchase property from, sell property to, or make loans to corporate directors or officers where the directors or officers have not disclosed their interest in the transaction are often voided under this standard. Contracts or transactions with corporate directors or officers are enforceable if their interest in the transaction has been disclosed to the corporation and the disinterested directors or the shareholders have approved the transaction.
- ***Competing with the corporation.*** Directors and officers cannot engage in activities that *compete* with the corporation unless full disclosure is made and a majority of the disinterested directors or shareholders approve the activity. The corporation can recover any profits made by nonapproved competition and any other damages caused to the corporation.

> It appears to me that the atmosphere of the temple of Justice is polluted by the presence of such things as companies.
>
> L.J. James
> *Wilson v. Church* (1879)

- ***Making a secret profit.*** If a director or an officer breaches his or her duty of loyalty and makes a secret profit on a transaction, the corporation can sue the director or officer to recover the secret profit. For example, suppose Maxine Chambers is the purchasing agent for the Roebolt Corporation. Her duties require her to negotiate and execute contracts to purchase office supplies and equipment for the corporation. Assume that Bruce Nevel, a computer salesperson, pays Chambers a $10,000 kick-back to purchase computers needed by the Roebolt Corporation. The Roebolt Corporation can sue and recover the $10,000 secret profit from Chambers.

Duty of Care

The **duty of care** requires corporate directors and officers to use *care and diligence* when acting on behalf of the corporation. To meet this duty, the directors and officers must discharge their duties (1) in good faith, (2) with the care that an *ordinary prudent person* in a like position would use under similar circumstances, and (3) in a manner he or she reasonably believes to be in the best interests of the corporation [RMBCA §§ 8.30(a), 8.42(a)].

duty of care
A duty that corporate directors and officers have to use care and diligence when acting on behalf of the corporation.

A director or an officer who breaches this duty of care is personally liable to the corporation and its shareholders for any damages caused by the breach. Such breaches, which are normally caused by **negligence**, often involve a director's or an officer's failure to (1) make a reasonable investigation of a corporate matter, (2) attend board meetings on a regular basis, (3) properly supervise a subordinate who causes a loss to the corporation

negligence
Failure of a corporate director or officer to exercise the duty of care while conducting the corporation's business.

through embezzlement and such, or (4) keep adequately informed about corporate affairs. *Breaches* are examined by the courts on a case-by-case basis.

The Business Judgment Rule The determination of whether a corporate director or officer has met his or her duty of care is measured as of the time the decision is made; the benefit of hindsight is not a factor. Therefore, the directors and officers are not liable to the corporation or its shareholders for honest mistakes of judgment. This is called the **business judgment rule**. Were it not for the protection afforded by the business judgment rule, many high-risk but socially desirable endeavors might not be undertaken.

business judgment rule
A rule that says directors and officers are not liable to the corporation or its shareholders for honest mistakes of judgment.

Consider This Example Suppose that after conducting considerable research and investigation, the directors of a major automobile company decide to produce a large and expensive SUV vehicle. Three years later, when the SUV is introduced to the public for sale, few of the SUVs are sold because of the public's interest in buying smaller, less expensive automobiles caused by a recession in the economy and an increase in gasoline prices. Because this was an honest mistake of judgment on the part of corporate management, their judgment is shielded by the business judgment rule.

The court had to decide whether directors were protected by the business judgment rule in the following case.

Case 17.2
Business Judgment Rule

Smith v. Van Gorkom
488 A.2d 858, 1985 Del. Lexis 421
Supreme Court of Delaware

Background and Facts

Trans Union Corporation (Trans Union) was a publicly traded, diversified holding company that was incorporated in Delaware. Its principal earnings were generated by its railcar leasing business. Jerome W. Van Gorkom was a Trans Union officer for more than 24 years, its CEO for more than 17 years, and the chairman of the board of directors for 2 years. Van Gorkom, a lawyer and certified public accountant, owned 75,000 shares of Trans Union. He was approaching 65 years of age and mandatory retirement. Trans Union's board of directors was composed of 10 members—5 inside directors and 5 outside directors.

In September 1980, Van Gorkom decided to meet with Jay A. Pritzker, a well-known corporate takeover specialist and a social acquaintance of Van Gorkom's, to discuss the possible sale of Trans Union to Pritzker. Van Gorkom met Pritzker at Pritzker's home on Saturday, September 13, 1980. He did so without consulting Trans Union's board of directors. At this meeting, Van Gorkom proposed a sale of Trans Union to Pritzker at a price of $55 per share. The stock was trading at about $38 in the market. On Monday, September 15, Pritzker notified Van Gorkom that he was interested in the $55 cash-out merger proposal. Van Gorkom, along with two inside directors, privately met with Pritzker on September 16 and 17. After meeting with Van Gorkom on Thursday, September 18, Pritzker notified his attorney to begin drafting the merger documents.

On Friday, September 19, Van Gorkom called a special meeting of Trans Union's board of directors for the following day. The board members were not told the purpose of the meeting. At the meeting, Van Gorkom disclosed the Pritzker offer and described its terms in a 20-minute presentation. Neither the merger agreement nor a written summary of the terms of agreement was furnished to the directors. No valuation study as to the value of Trans Union was prepared for the meeting. After two hours, the board voted in favor of the cash-out merger with Pritzker's company at $55 per share for Trans Union's stock. The board also voted not to solicit other offers. The merger agreement was executed by Van Gorkom during the evening of September 20 at a formal social event he hosted for the opening of the Chicago Lyric Opera's season. Neither he nor any other director read the agreement prior to its signing and delivery to Pritzker.

Trans Union's board of directors recommended that the merger be approved by its shareholders and distributed proxy materials to the shareholders stating that the $55 per share price for their stock was fair. In the meantime, Trans Union's board of directors took steps to dissuade two other possible suitors who showed an interest in purchasing Trans Union. On February 10, 1981, 69.9 percent of the shares of Trans Union stock was voted in favor of the merger. The merger was consummated. Alden Smith and other Trans Union shareholders sued Van Gorkom and the other directors for damages. The plaintiffs alleged that the defendants were negligent in their conduct in selling Trans Union to Pritzker. The Delaware court of chancery held in favor of the defendants. The plaintiffs appealed.

Issue

Did Trans Union's directors breach their duty of care?

(*continued*)

Smith v. Van Gorkom

488 A.2d 858, 1985 Del. Lexis 421

Supreme Court of Delaware

(continued)

In the Language of the Court

In the specific context of a proposed merger of domestic corporations, a director has a duty, along with his fellow directors, to act in an informed and deliberate manner in determining whether to approve an agreement of merger. The directors (1) did not adequately inform themselves as to Van Gorkom's role in forcing the sale of the company and in establishing the per share purchase price; (2) they were uninformed as to the intrinsic value of the company and (3) given these circumstances, at a minimum, they were grossly negligent in approving the sale of the company upon two hours' consideration, without prior notice, and without the exigency of a crisis or emergency.

Without any documents before them concerning the proposed transaction, the members of the board were required to rely entirely upon Van Gorkom's 20-minute oral presentation of the proposal. No written summary of the terms of the merger was presented; the directors were given no documentation to support the adequacy of $55 price per share for sale of the company; and the board had before it nothing more than Van Gorkom's statement of his understanding of the substance of an agreement that he admittedly had never read, or that any member of the board had ever seen. Thus, the record compels the conclusion that the board lacked valuation information to reach an informed business judgment as to the fairness of $55 per share for sale of the company. We conclude that Trans Union's board was grossly negligent in that it failed to act with informed reasonable deliberation in agreeing to the Pritzker merger proposal.

Decision and Remedy

The supreme court of Delaware held that the defendant directors had breached their duty of care. The supreme court reversed the judgment of the court of chancery and remanded the case to the court of chancery to conduct an evidentiary hearing to determine the fair value of the shares represented by the plaintiffs' class. If that value was higher than $55 per share, the difference was to be awarded to the plaintiffs as damages.

Business and Ethics Questions

1. What does the business judgment rule provide? Is this a good rule? Explain.
2. Do you think Van Gorkom and the other directors had the shareholders' best interests in mind? Were the plaintiff-shareholders being greedy?
3. Is there any liability exposure for sitting on a board of directors?

Concept Summary *Fiduciary Duties of Corporation Directors and Officers*

Duty	Description	Violation
Duty of loyalty	Duty to subordinate personal interests to those of the corporation and its shareholders.	Acts of disloyalty. Such acts include unauthorized: 1. Self-dealing with the corporation. 2. Usurping of a corporate opportunity. 3. Competition with the corporation. 4. Making of a secret profit that belongs to the corporation.
Duty of care	Duty to use care and diligence when acting on behalf of the corporation. This duty is discharged if an officer or a director acts: 1. In good faith. 2. With the care that an ordinary prudent person in a like position would use under similar circumstances. 3. In a manner he or she reasonably believes to be in the best interests of the corporation.	Acts of negligence and mismanagement. Such acts include failure to: 1. Make a reasonable investigation of a corporate matter. 2. Attend board meetings on a regular basis. 3. Properly supervise a subordinate who causes a loss to the corporation. 4. Keep adequately informed about corporate matters. 5. Take other actions necessary to discharge duties.

Contemporary Trend

Indemnification and D&O Insurance Protection

Directors and officers of corporations are sometimes personally named in lawsuits that involve actions they have taken on behalf of the corporation. Such lawsuits are often brought by disgruntled shareholders or third parties who claim they have suffered damages because of the director's or officer's negligence or other conduct.

Directors and officers can protect themselves against personal liability by making sure the corporation does the following:

- ***Purchases directors' and officers' liability insurance (D&O insurance).*** Corporations can purchase D&O insurance from private insurance companies by paying an annual premium for the insurance. The insurance company is required to defend a corporate director or officer who has been sued in his or her corporate capacity. The insurance company is also required, subject to the terms of the insurance coverage, to pay the litigation costs incurred in defending the lawsuit (e.g., attorneys' fees, court costs) and any judgments or settlement costs. Most D&O policies contain deductible clauses and maximum coverage limits [RMBCA § 8.57].
- ***Provides indemnification.*** Corporations may provide that directors and officers who are sued in their corporate capacities will be **indemnified** by the corporation for the costs of the litigation as well as any judgments or settlements stemming from the lawsuit. Indemnification means that the corporation—and not the director or officer personally—pays these costs. The RMBCA provides that a court may order indemnification if a director or an officer is found to be fairly and reasonably entitled to such indemnification [RMBCA §§ 8.54, 8.56(1)]. ■

Corporate Criminal Liability

Corporate directors, officers, employees, and agents are personally liable for the crimes they commit while acting on behalf of the corporation. Criminal law sanctions include fines and imprisonment.

Under the law of agency, a corporation is liable for the crimes committed by its directors, officers, employees, or agents while acting within the scope of their employment.

Japan. Multinational corporations have grown to immense size and power in recent years. For example, the Mitsubishi Group of Japan operates subsidiary corporations in many nations of the world.

Because a corporation cannot be placed in prison, the criminal penalty imposed on a corporation is usually the assessment of a monetary fine or the loss of some legal privilege (such as a license).

Terms and Concepts

Rights of Shareholders

Ownership rights. Shareholders of a corporation own the corporation.

Shareholder Meetings

1. ***Annual shareholders' meeting.*** This meeting of the shareholders of a corporation must be held annually by the corporation to elect directors and to vote on other matters.
2. ***Special shareholders' meeting.*** Such a meeting of shareholders may be called to consider and vote on important or emergency matters, such as a proposed merger, amending the articles of incorporation, and so forth.

Proxies

1. ***Proxy.*** Shareholders may appoint another person (the *proxy*) as their agent to vote their shares at shareholders' meetings.
2. ***Proxy card.*** A proxy card, also called a *proxy*, is a document that a shareholder signs that authorizes another person to vote his or her shares at a shareholders' meeting.

Voting Requirements

1. ***Quorum.*** A quorum is the required number of shares that must be represented in person or by proxy in order to hold a shareholders' meeting. The RMBCA establishes a majority of outstanding shares as a quorum.
2. ***Vote required for elections other than for directors.*** The affirmative vote of the *majority* of the voting shares represented at a shareholders' meeting constitutes an act of the shareholders for actions other than for the election of directors.
3. ***Supramajority voting requirement.*** The articles of incorporation or bylaws of a corporation can require a greater than majority of shares to constitute quorum or the vote of the shareholders (e.g., 80 percent).
4. ***Voting methods for electing directors:***
   a. *Straight (noncumulative) voting.* Unless otherwise stated, each shareholder votes the number of shares he or she owns on candidates for each of the positions open for election. The candidate or candidates with the most votes win the open position or positions.
   b. *Cumulative voting.* The articles of incorporation may provide for cumulative voting. Under this method, a shareholder is entitled to multiply the number of shares he or she owns by the number of directors to be elected and cast the product for a single candidate or distribute the product among two or more candidates.

Preemptive Rights

Preemptive rights give existing shareholders the option of subscribing to new shares being issued by the corporation in proportion to their current ownership interest.

Dividends

1. ***Directors' authority to pay dividends.*** The board of directors has the discretion to pay *dividends* to shareholders or *retain earnings* for use by the corporation.
2. ***Record date.*** When a corporation declares a dividend, it sets a date, usually a few weeks prior to the actual payment, that establishes the *record date* for payment of the dividend. Shareholders as of that date will be paid the dividend.

Derivative Lawsuits

A shareholder may bring a derivative lawsuit on behalf of the corporation against an offending party who has injured the corporation when the directors of the corporation fail to bring the suit. The shareholders must make a written *demand* upon the corporation to bring the lawsuit, and then the corporation either may reject it or 90 days may expire without the corporation's bringing the requested lawsuit.

Liability of Shareholders

Limited liability. Shareholders of corporations generally have *limited liability*. That is, they are liable for the debts and obligations of the corporation only to the *extent of their capital contributions* to the corporation.

Disregard of the Corporate Entity

Shareholders may be found *personally liable* for the debts and obligations of the corporation under the *piercing the corporate veil* doctrine. Courts can *disregard the corporate entity* and hold shareholders personally liable for the debts and obligations of the corporations if (a) the corporation has been formed without sufficient capital (*thin capitalization*) or (b) separateness has not been maintained between the corporation and its shareholders (e.g., commingling of personal and corporate assets, failure to hold required shareholders' meetings). This is also called the *alter ego doctrine*.

Shareholder Proposals

A shareholder proposal may be submitted by a shareholder or group of shareholders to be considered and voted upon by the corporation's shareholders. Most shareholder proposals concern social issues (e.g., protection of the environment, discontinuation of the manufacture and sale of dangerous products).

1. ***Inclusion in proxy materials.*** If management does not oppose a proposal, it may be included in the proxy materials issued by the corporation. If management opposes the shareholder proposal, the SEC rules on whether the proposal must be submitted to the shareholders in the corporation's proxy materials.
2. ***Requirements.*** To be included in the corporation's proxy materials, a shareholder proposal must (a) not violate federal or state law, (b) relate to the corporation's business, (c) concern policy issues (and not the day-to-day operations of the corporation), and (d) not concern the payment of dividends.

Rights of Directors

1. ***Board of directors.*** The board of directors is a panel of decision makers for a corporation; its members are elected by the shareholders.
2. ***Policy decisions.*** The directors of a corporation are responsible for formulating the *policy* decisions affecting the corporation, such as deciding what businesses to engage in, determining the capital structure of the corporation, selecting and removing top officers of the corporation, and the like.
3. ***Resolution.*** The board of directors can adopt a resolution that approves a transaction that requires shareholder vote and recommend it to shareholders.

Selecting Directors

1. ***Inside director.*** An inside director is a member of the board of directors who is also an officer of the corporation.
2. ***Outside director.*** An outside director is a member of the board of directors who is not an officer of the corporation.

Term of Office

1. ***Annual term.*** The term of a director's office expires at the next annual shareholders' meeting following his or her election, unless terms are staggered.
2. ***Staggered terms.*** If a board of directors consists of nine or more members, it may be divided into two or three *classes* (each class to be as nearly equal in number as possible), and classes can be elected to serve *staggered terms* for two or three years.

Meetings of the Board of Directors

1. ***Regular meeting.*** A regular meeting of the board of directors is held at the time and place scheduled in the bylaws.
2. ***Special meeting.*** A special meeting of the board of directors may be convened to discuss an important or emergency matter, such as a proposed merger or a hostile takeover attempt.
3. ***Quorum.*** A simple *majority* of the number of directors established in the articles of incorporation or bylaws constitutes a quorum for transacting business.
4. ***Vote.*** The approval or disapproval of a *majority* of the quorum binds the entire board.

Committees of the Board of Directors

Unless the articles of incorporation or bylaws provide otherwise, the board of directors may create committees of its members and delegate certain powers to those committees. The most common committees are:

1. ***Executive committee.*** This committee has authority to (1) act on certain matters during the interim period between board meetings and (2) conduct preliminary investigations of proposals on behalf of the board.
2. ***Audit committee.*** This committee recommends independent public accountants and supervises the audit of the financial records of the corporation by the accountants.
3. ***Nominating committee.*** This committee nominates the management slate of directors to be submitted for shareholder vote.
4. ***Compensation committee.*** This committee approves management compensation, including salaries, bonuses, stock option plans, fringe benefits, and such.
5. ***Investment committee.*** This committee is responsible for investing and reinvesting the funds of the corporation.
6. ***Litigation committee.*** This committee reviews and decides whether to pursue requests by shareholders for the corporation to sue persons who have allegedly harmed the corporation.

Officers

Officers are employees of the corporation who are appointed by the board of directors to manage *day-to-day operations* of the corporation.

Duty of Loyalty

Directors and officers have a duty not to act adversely to the interests of the corporation and to subordinate their personal interests to those of the corporation and its shareholders.

These are common examples of breaches of the duty of loyalty:

1. ***Self-dealing.*** The corporation may void any transaction with a director or an officer if it is *unfair to the corporation*. This usually involves undisclosed self-dealing by a director or an officer with the corporation.
2. ***Usurping a corporate opportunity.*** A director or an officer may not personally *usurp* (*steal*) an opportunity that belongs to the corporation. The corporation can acquire the opportunity from the director or officer and recover any profits made by the director or officer.
3. ***Competing with the corporation.*** Directors and officers may not compete with their corporation unless the competitive activity has been fully disclosed to the corporation and approved by a majority of disinterested directors or shareholders.

Duty of Care

Corporate directors and officers have a duty to use care and diligence when acting on behalf of the corporation. This duty is discharged if they perform their duties (a) in good faith, (b) with the care that an *ordinary prudent person* in a like position would use under similar circumstances, and (c) in a manner they reasonably believe to be in the best interests of the corporation.

1. ***Negligence.*** Failure of a corporate director or officer to exercise this duty of care when conducting the corporation's business is called negligence.
2. ***Business judgment rule.*** This rule says that directors and officers are not liable to the corporation or its shareholders for honest mistakes of judgment.

Internet Exercises and Case Questions

Working the Web Internet Exercises

1. Find your state statute on indemnification for corporate officers and directors. Why do you think this concept was included in the statute? See **www.law.cornell.edu/topics/corporations.html** for an overview of corporations law with links to key primary and secondary sources.
2. Review the sample indemnification agreement at **http://contracts.onecle.com/type/11.shtml**.
3. For more coverage of the background on directors and officers liability, see **www.trafalgar-intl.com/d&o.htm**.
4. Go to **lawcrawler.findlaw.com**. Type in the search term *piercing the corporate veil*. Note how many articles are written from the perspective of an attorney representing a small business owner against claims seeking personal assets.

Legal Environment Cases

17.1 Shareholder Meeting Ocilla Industries, Inc. (Ocilla), owned 40 percent of the stock of Direct Action Marketing, Inc. (Direct Action). Direct Action was a New York corporation that specialized in the marketing of products through billing inserts. In 1985, Ocilla helped place Howard Katz and Joseph Esposito on Direct Action's five-member board of directors. A dispute between Ocilla and the two directors caused Ocilla to claim that Katz and Esposito wanted excess remuneration in exchange for leaving the board at the end of their terms. As a result, no shareholders' meeting was held between September 19, 1986, and January 27, 1988. Under the Model Business Corporations Act, can Ocilla compel Direct Action to hold the meeting earlier? *Ocilla Industries, Inc. v. Katz*, 677 F.Supp. 1291, 1987 U.S.Dist. Lexis 12741 (E.D. N.Y.)

17.2 Special Shareholder Meeting Jack C. Schoenholtz was a shareholder and member of the board of directors of Rye Psychiatric Hospital Center, Inc. (Rye Hospital). The hospital was incorporated in 1973. By 1977, a split had developed in the board of directors concerning the operation of the facility. Three directors stood on one side of the dispute and three directors on the other. In an attempt to break the deadlock, Schoenholtz, who owned over 10 percent of the corporation's voting stock, asked the corporation's secretary to call a special meeting of the shareholders. In response, the secretary sent a notice to the shareholders stating that a special meeting of the shareholders would be held on November 12, 1982, "for the purpose of electing directors." The meeting was held as scheduled. Some stockholders brought suit, claiming that the special shareholders' meeting was not called properly. Who wins? *Rye Psychiatric Hospital Center, Inc. v. Schoenholtz*, 476 N.Y.S.2d 339, 1984 N.Y.App.Div. Lexis 17818 (N.Y. App.)

17.3 Proxy George Gibbons, William Smith, and Gerald Zollar were all shareholders in GRG Operating, Inc. (GRG). On May 13, 1983, Zollar contributed $1,000 of his own funds so that the corporation could begin to do business. In exchange for this contribution, Gibbons and Smith both granted Zollar the right to vote their shares of GRG stock. They gave Zollar a signed form that stated that "Gibbons and Smith, for a period of 10 years from the date hereof, appoint Zollar as their proxy. This proxy is solely intended to be an irrevocable proxy." A year after the agreement was signed, Gibbons and Smith wanted to revoke their proxies. Can they? *Zollar v. Smith*, 710 S.W.2d 155, 1986 Tx.App. Lexis 12900 (Tex. App.)

17.4 Right to Inspect Records On July 20, 1983, Helmsman Management Services, Inc. (Helmsman), became a 25 percent stockholder of A&S Consultants, Inc. (A&S), a Delaware corporation. Helmsman paid $50,000 for its interest in A&S. At the time of the stock purchase, Helmsman was also a customer of A&S, paying the company for the use of a computer software program. Since 1983, Helmsman verified A&S's billings by a periodic review of certain A&S books and records. In January 1986, Helmsman conducted a review of A&S's records over a six-day period. The review showed that A&S had never paid any dividends on the stock held by Helmsman and that Helmsman had never received notice of A&S's stockholder meetings. Suspecting that A&S was being mismanaged, Helmsman sent a letter to A&S asking to inspect all A&S's records. The letter stated several purposes for the inspection, including to (1) determine the reasons for nonpayment of dividends and (2) gain information to be used in determining how to vote in stockholders' elections. Under the Model Business Corporations Act, should Helmsman's request be honored? *Helmsman Management Services, Inc. v. A&S Consultants, Inc.*, 525 A.2d 160, 1987 Del.Ch. Lexis 397 (Del. Ch.)

17.5 Dividends Gay's Super Markets, Inc. (Super Markets), was a corporation formed under the laws of the state of Maine.

Hannaford Bros. Company held 51 percent of the corporation's common stock. Lawrence F. Gay and his brother Carrol were both minority shareholders in Super Markets. Lawrence Gay was also the manager of the corporation's store at Machias, Maine. On July 5, 1971, he was dismissed from his job. At the January 1972 meeting of Super Markets's board of directors, a decision was made not to declare a stock dividend for 1971. The directors cited expected losses from increased competition and the expense of opening a new store as reasons for not paying a dividend. Lawrence Gay claims that the reason for not paying a dividend was to force him to sell his shares in Super Markets. Lawrence sued to force the corporation to declare a dividend. Who wins? *Gay v. Gay's Super Markets, Inc.*, 343 A.2d 577, 1975 Me. Lexis 391 (Maine Sup.)

17.6 Duty of Loyalty Edward Hellenbrand ran a comedy club known as the Comedy Cottage in Rosemont, Illinois. The business was incorporated, with Hellenbrand and his wife as the corporation's sole shareholders. The corporation leased the premises in which the club was located. In 1978, Hellenbrand hired Jay Berk as general manager of the club. In 1980, Berk was made vice president of the corporation and given 10 percent of its stock. Hellenbrand experienced health problems and moved to Nevada, leaving Berk to manage the daily affairs of the business. In June 1984, the ownership of the building where the Comedy Cottage was located changed hands. Shortly thereafter, the club's lease on the premises expired. Hellenbrand instructed Berk to negotiate a new lease. Berk arranged a month-to-month lease but had the lease agreement drawn up in his name instead of that of the corporation. When Hellenbrand learned of Berk's move, he fired him. Berk continued to lease the building in his own name and opened his own club there, known as the Comedy Company, Inc. Hellenbrand sued Berk for an injunction to prevent Berk from leasing the building. Who wins? *Comedy Cottage, Inc. v. Berk* 495 N.E.2d 1006, 1986 Ill.App. Lexis 2486 (Ill. App.)

17.7 Duty of Loyalty Lawrence Gaffney was the president and general manager of Ideal Tape Company (Ideal). Ideal, which was a subsidiary of Chelsea Industries, Inc. (Chelsea), was engaged in the business of manufacturing pressure-sensitive tape. In 1975, Gaffney recruited three other Ideal executives to join him in starting a tape manufacturing business. The four men remained at Ideal for the two years it took them to plan the new enterprise. During this time, they used their positions at Ideal to travel around the country to gather business ideas, recruit potential customers, and purchase equipment for their business. At no time did they reveal to Chelsea their intention to open a competing business. In November 1977, the new business was incorporated as Action Manufacturing Company (Action). When executives at Chelsea discovered the existence of the new venture, Gaffney and the others resigned from Chelsea. Chelsea sued them for damages. Who wins? *Chelsea Industries, Inc. v. Gaffney*, 449 N.E.2d 320, 1983 Mass. Lexis 1413 (Mass. Sup.)

17.8 Derivative Shareholder Lawsuit In 1948, four brothers—Monnie, Mechel, Merko, and Sam Dotlich—formed a partnership to run a heavy equipment rental business. By 1957, the company had been incorporated as Dotlich Brothers, Inc. Each brother owned 25 percent of the corporation's stock, and each served on the board of directors. In 1951, the business acquired a 56-acre tract of land in Speedway, Indiana. This land was held in the name of Monnie Dotlich. Each of the brothers was aware of this agreement. By 1976, the corporation had purchased six other pieces of property, all of which were held in Monnie's name. Sam Dotlich was not informed that Monnie was the record owner of these other properties. In 1976, Sam discovered this irregularity and requested that the board of directors take action to remedy the situation. When the board refused to do so, Sam initiated a lawsuit on behalf of the corporation. Can Sam bring this lawsuit? *Dotlich v. Dotlich*, 475 N.E.2d 331, 1985 Ind.App. Lexis 2233 (Ind. App.)

17.9 Piercing the Corporate Veil M. R. Watters was the majority shareholder of several closely held corporations, including Wildhorn Ranch, Inc. (Wildhorn). All these businesses were run out of Watters's home in Rocky Ford, Colorado. Wildhorn operated a resort called the Wildhorn Ranch Resort in Teller County, Colorado. Although Watters claimed that the ranch was owned by the corporation, the deed for the property listed Watters as the owner. Watters paid little attention to corporate formalities, holding corporate meetings at his house, never taking minutes of these meetings, and paying the debts of one corporation with the assets of another. During August 1986, two guests of Wildhorn Ranch Resort drowned while operating a paddleboat at the ranch. The family of the deceased guests sued for damages. Can Watters be held personally liable? *Geringer v. Wildhorn Ranch, Inc.*, 706 F.Supp. 1442, 1988 U.S.Dist. Lexis 15701 (D. Colo.)

Ethics in Business

17.10 Jon-T Chemicals, Inc. (Chemicals), was an Oklahoma corporation engaged in the fertilizer and chemicals business. John H. Thomas was its majority shareholder and its president and board chairman. In April 1971, Chemicals incorporated Jon-T Farms, Inc. (Farms), as a wholly owned subsidiary to engage in the farming and land-leasing business. Chemicals invested $10,000 to establish Farms. All the directors and officers of Farms were directors and officers of Chemicals, and Thomas was its president and board chairman. In addition, Farms used offices, computers, and accountants of Chemicals without paying a fee, and Chemicals paid the salary of Farms's only employee. Chemicals made regular informal advances to pay Farms's expenses. These payments reached $7.5 million by January 1975.

Thomas and Farms engaged in a scheme whereby they submitted fraudulent applications for agricultural subsidies from the federal government under the Uplands Cotton Program. As a result of these applications, the Commodity Credit Corporation, a government agency, paid over $2.5 million in subsidies to Thomas and Farms. After discovering the fraud, the federal government obtained criminal convictions against Thomas and Farms. In a separate civil action, the federal government obtained a $4.7 million judgment against Thomas and Farms, finding them jointly and severally liable for the tort of fraud. Farms declared bankruptcy, and Thomas was unable to pay the judgment. Because Thomas and Farms were insolvent, the federal government sued Chemicals to recover the judgment. *United States of America v. Jon-T Chemicals, Inc.*, 768 F.2d 686, 1985 U.S.App. Lexis 21255 (5th Cir.)

Ethics Issues

1. What does the doctrine of piercing the corporate veil provide? Explain.
2. Did Thomas act ethically in this case?
3. Was Farms the alter ego of Chemicals, permitting the United States to pierce the corporate veil and recover the judgment from Chemicals?

Endnote

1. *Meinhard v. Salmon*, 164 N.E.2d 545, 546, 1928 N.Y. Lexis 830 (N.Y. App.)

18

Limited Liability Companies and Special Forms of Business

"It has been uniformly laid down in this Court, as far back as we can remember, that good faith is the basis of all mercantile transactions."

—J. Buller
Salomons v. Nisson (1788)

Chapter Objectives

After studying this chapter, you should be able to:

1. Define limited liability company (LLC) and describe the benefits of an LLC.
2. Define limited liability partnership (LLP) and describe the benefits of an LLP.
3. Define franchise and describe the various forms of franchises.
4. Define licensing and describe how intellectual property is licensed.
5. Describe international agreements and strategic alliances used in global commerce.

Chapter Contents

- Limited Liability Company (LLC)
- Limited Liability Partnership (LLP)
- Franchise
- License
- Joint Venture
- Strategic Alliance

Owners may choose to operate a business as a **limited liability company (LLC)**. The use of LLCs as a form of conducting business in the United States is of rather recent origin. The use of this new form of business grew quickly, with all the states having enacted LLC statues by 1998. One of the main attributes of an LLC is that its owners have limited liability. Most LLC laws are quite similar, although some differences do exist between these state statutes.

Most states have enacted laws that permit certain types of professionals, such as accountants, lawyers, and doctors, to operate as **limited liability partnerships (LLPs)**. The owners of LLPs have limited liability.

Franchising is an important method for distributing goods and services to the public. Franchising today is used in many other forms of business.

Special forms of business are often used in domestic and international commerce. **Licensing** permits one business to use another business' trademarks, service marks, trade names, and other intellectual property in selling goods or services. **Joint ventures** allow two or more businesses to combine their resources to pursue a single project or transaction. **Strategic alliances** are often used to enter foreign markets.

This chapter discusses LLCs, LLPs, franchises, licensing, joint ventures, and strategic alliances.

London, England. The limited liability company form of business is used in the United States and countries of Europe and Latin America.

Limited Liability Company (LLC)

A **limited liability company (LLC)** is an unincorporated business entity that combines the most favorable attributes of general partnerships, limited partnerships, and corporations. An LLC may elect to be taxed as a partnership, the owners can manage the business, and the owners have limited liability. Many entrepreneurs who begin new businesses choose the LLC as their legal form for conducting business.

limited liability company (LLC)
An unincorporated business entity that combines the most favorable attributes of general partnerships, limited partnerships, and corporations.

LLCs are creatures of state law, not federal law. LLCs can only be created pursuant to the laws of the state in which the LLC is being organized. These statutes, commonly referred to as **limited liability company codes**, regulate the formation, operation, and dissolution of LLCs. A state legislature may amend its LLC statute at any time. The courts interpret state LLC statutes to decide LLC and member disputes.

An LLC is a separate *legal entity* (or legal person) distinct from its members [ULLCA § 201]. Limited liability companies are treated as artificial persons who can sue or be sued, enter into and enforce contracts, hold title to and transfer property, and be found civilly and criminally liable for violations of law.

The Uniform Limited Liability Company Act

Uniform Limited Liability Company Act (ULLCA)
A model act that provides comprehensive and uniform laws for the formation, operation, and dissolution of LLCs.

In 1995, the National Conference of Commissioners on Uniform State Laws (a group of lawyers, judges, and legal scholars) issued the **Uniform Limited Liability Company Act (ULLCA)**. The ULLCA codifies LLC law. Its goal is to establish comprehensive LLC law that is uniform throughout the United States. The ULLCA covers most problems that arise in the formation, operation, and termination of LLCs. The ULLCA is not law unless a state adopts it as its LLC statute. Many states have adopted all or part of the ULLCA as their LLC law. Because it is so important, the ULLCA forms the basis of the study of LLCs in this chapter.

Taxation of LLCs

Morality cannot be legislated, but behavior can be regulated. Judicial decrees may not change the heart, but they can restrain the heartless.

Martin Luther King, Jr.
Strength to Love (1963)

Under the Internal Revenue Code and regulations adopted by the Internal Revenue Service (IRS), for federal income tax purposes, an LLC is taxed as a partnership unless it elects to be taxed as a corporation. Thus, an LLC is not taxed at the entity level, but its income or losses "flow through" to the members' individual income tax returns. This avoids double taxation. Most LLCs accept the default status of being taxed as a partnership instead of electing to be taxed as a corporation.

Powers of an LLC

An LLC has the same powers as an individual to do all things necessary or convenient to carry on its business or affairs. These include the power to own and transfer personal property; sell, lease, and mortgage real property; make contracts and guarantees; borrow and lend money; issue notes and bonds; sue and be sued; and take other actions to conduct the affairs and business of the LLC [ULLCA § 112].

Contemporary Trend

DreamWorks SKG, LLC

Steven Spielberg, Jeffrey Katzenberg, and David Geffen formed **Dream Works SKG**, which is a major movie and recording production company. Spielberg's fame and money came from directing films, Katzenberg had been a leading executive at Disney, and Geffen built and sold a major record company. These multimillionaire, multimedia giants combined their talents to form a formidable entertainment company.

DreamWorks was formed as a Delaware LLC. The organizers chose an LLC because it is taxed as a partnership, and the profits (or losses) flow directly to the owners, but as with a corporation, the owners are protected from personal liability beyond their capital contributions.

DreamWorks issued several classes of interests. The three principals put up $100 million ($33.3 million each) for **"SKG" stock**, which grants the principals 100 percent voting control and 67 percent of the firm's profits. In addition, each principal has multiyear employment contracts plus other benefits.

DreamWorks raised the other $900 million of its $1 billion capital from other investors, who received one-third of future profits. The other investors were issued the following classes of stock:

Class	Investment
A	Outside investors. Class A stock was sold to big investors with over $20 million to invest. Microsoft's cofounder, Paul Allen, purchased $500 million of Class A stock. Class A investors got seats on the board of directors.
S	Outside investors. Class S stock was issued for smallish, "strategic" investments with other companies for cross-marketing purposes.
E	Employees. Employees were granted the right to participate in an employee stock purchase plan. ■

Members' Limited Liability

The owners of LLCs are usually called **members.** The general rule is that members are not personally liable to third parties for the debts, obligations, and liabilities of an LLC beyond their capital contributions. Members are said to have **limited liability** (see Exhibit 18.1). The debts, obligations, and liabilities of an LLC, whether arising from contracts, torts, or otherwise, are solely those of the LLC [ULLCA § 303(a)].

member
An owner of an LLC.

limited liability
The liability of LLC members for the LLC's debts, obligations, and liabilities only to the extent of their capital contributions.

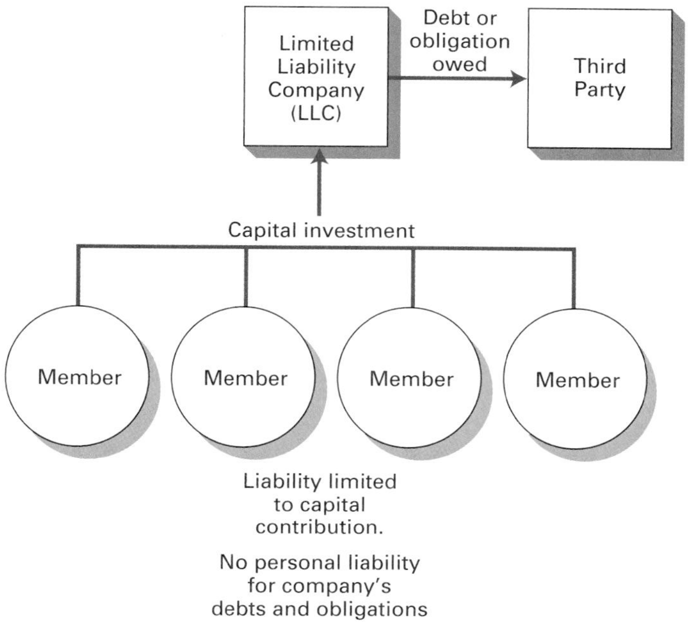

Exhibit 18.1
Limited Liability Company (LLC)

Consider This Example Jasmin, Shou-Yi, and Vanessa form an LLC, and each contributes $25,000 in capital. The LLC operates for a period of time, during which it borrows money from banks and purchases goods on credit from suppliers. After some time, the LLC experiences financial difficulty and goes out of business. If the LLC fails with $500,000 in debts, each of the members will lose her capital contribution of $25,000 but will not be personally liable for the rest of the unpaid debts of the LLC.

The failure of an LLC to observe the usual company formalities is not ground for imposing personal liability on the members of the LLC [ULLCA § 303(b)]. For example, if the LLC does not keep minutes of the company's meetings, the members do not become personally liable for the LLC's debts.

In the following case, the court addressed the issue of the limited liability of a member of an LLC.

Case 18.1
Limited Liability Company

Page v. Roscoe, LLC
497 S.E.2nd 422, 1998 N.C.App. Lexis 169
Court of Appeals of North Carolina

Background and Facts

Dale C. Bone was a member of Roscoe, LLC, an LLC organized under the laws of North Carolina. In August 1994, Roscoe, LLC, purchased two acres of land near the town of Apex, North Carolina. In January 1995, Apex approved Roscoe, LLC's, plan to construct and operate a propane gas bulk storage and distribution facility on the land. This use was permitted under Apex's zoning ordinance. In April 1995, Daylene Page and other homeowners in the area sued

(continued)

Page v. Roscoe, LLC

497 S.E.2nd 422, 1998 N.C.App. Lexis 169
Court of Appeals of North Carolina
(continued)

Roscoe, LLC, and Dale C. Bone, alleging that the gas storage facility, if constructed, would constitute a nuisance. In December 1995, after the trial court denied the plaintiffs' motion to obtain a preliminary injunction against construction of the facility, the plaintiffs dismissed the lawsuit. Subsequently, Bone sued the plaintiffs for sanctions to recover attorneys' fees he had spent in defending against the plaintiffs' lawsuit. The trial court ordered the plaintiffs to pay Bone's attorneys' fees. The plaintiffs appealed.

Issue

Were the sanctions warranted against the plaintiffs for naming an individual member of an LLC in the lawsuit they brought against the LLC?

In the Language of the Court

We do find that the allegations against Bone individually are not well-grounded in law. N.C.Gen.Stat. § 57C-3-30 (1993) provides in pertinent part:

a. A person who is a member or manager, or both, of a limited liability company is not liable for the obligations of a limited liability company solely by reason of being a member or manager or both, and does not become so by participating in whatever capacity, in the management or control of the business.

b. A member of a limited liability company is not a proper party to proceedings by or against a limited liability company.

Therefore, under the above statute, it was improper to name an individual member of a limited liability company as a party defendant. The naming of Bone as an individual defendant was not well-grounded in law.

Decision and Remedy

The court of appeals held that Bone, as a member of Roscoe, LLC, was not liable as a matter of law for the acts of the LLC and had therefore been improperly named as a defendant in the lawsuit filed by the plaintiffs. The plaintiffs were held liable for sanctions and were required to pay Bone's attorneys' fees that he had expended in defending against the plaintiffs' lawsuit. The court of appeals affirmed the trial court's judgment in favor of Bone.

Business and Ethics Questions

1. Should members of an LLC be released from personal liability for the debts and obligations incurred by the LLC?
2. Did the plaintiff homeowners act ethically in naming Bone as a defendant? Why do you think they named Bone as a defendant?
3. Is this case good precedent for businesspersons wishing to conduct business as LLCs?

Liability of an LLC

The great can protect themselves, but the poor and humble require the arm and shield of the law.

Andrew Jackson

An LLC is liable for any loss or injury caused to anyone as a result of a wrongful act or an omission by a member, a manager, an agent, or an employee of the LLC who commits the wrongful act while acting within the ordinary course of business of the LLC or with authority of the LLC [ULLCA § 302].

Consider This Example Sable, Silvia, and Samantha form the SSS, LLC, to own and operate a business. Each member contributes $10,000 capital. While on LLC business, Sable drives her automobile and accidentally hits and injures Damon. Damon can recover damages for his injuries from Sable personally because she committed the negligent act. Damon can also recover damages from the SSS, LLC, because Sable was acting within the scope of the ordinary business of the LLC when the accident occurred. Silvia and Samantha have limited liability only up to their capital contributions in the SSS, LLC.

Liability of a Tortfeasor

A person who intentionally or unintentionally (negligently) causes injury or death to another person is called a **tortfeasor**. A tortfeasor is personally liable to persons he or she injures and to the heirs of persons who die because of his or her conduct. This rule applies to members and managers of LLCs. Thus, if a member or manager of an LLC negligently causes injury or death to another person, he or she is personally liable to the injured person or the heirs of a deceased person.

Liability of Managers

Managers of LLCs are not personally liable for the debts, obligations, and liabilities of the LLC they manage [ULLCA § 303(a)].

Consider This Example An LLC that does real estate development hires Sarah Goldstein, a nonmember, to be its president. While acting within the scope of her LLC authority, Sarah signs a loan agreement whereby the LLC borrows $1 million from a bank to complete the construction of an office building. If the LLC subsequently suffers financial difficulty and defaults on the bank loan, Sarah is not personally responsible for the loan. The LLC is liable for the loan, but Sarah is not because she is the manager of the LLC.

Formation of an LLC

Forming an LLC is very similar to organizing a corporation. Two or more persons (which include individuals, partnerships, corporations, and associations) may form an LLC for any lawful purpose. To form an LLC, **articles of organization** must be filed with the appropriate state office, usually the secretary of state's office (see Exhibit 18.2). The articles of organization must state the LLC's name, duration, and other information required by

articles of organization
A formal document that must be filed with the secretary of state to form an LLC.

Exhibit 18.2
Articles of Organization

ARTICLES OF ORGANIZATION
FOR FLORIDA LIMITED LIABILITY COMPANY

ARTICLE I - NAME

The name of the Limited Liability Company is
iCitrusSystems.com

ARTICLE II - ADDRESS

The mailing address and street address of the principal office of the Limited Liability Company is

3000 Dade Boulevard
Suite 200
Miami Beach, Florida 33139

ARTICLE III - DURATION

The period of duration for the Limited Liability Company shall be
50 years

ARTICLE IV - MANAGEMENT

The Limited Liability Company is to be managed by a manager and the name and address of such manager is

Susan Escobar
1000 Collins Avenue
Miami Beach, Florida 33141

____
Thomas Blandford

____
Pam Rosales

te or that the organizers deem important to include. The name of an LLC must ain the words *Limited Liability Company* or the abbreviation *L.L.C.* or *L.C.*

perating Agreement

the re
managers, and th

Members of an LLC may enter into an **operating agreement** that regulates the affairs of the company and the conduct of its business and governs relations among the members, the managers, and the company [ULLCA § 103(a)]. The operating agreement may be amended by the approval of all members, unless otherwise provided in the agreement. The operating agreement and amendments may be oral but are usually written.

Contemporary Trend

Why Operate a Business as an LLC?

Why should an LLC be used instead of an S corporation or a partnership? S corporations and partnerships are subject to many restrictions and adverse consequences that do not exist with an LLC. Some differences are:

- S corporations cannot have shareholders other than estates, certain trusts, and individuals (who cannot be nonresident aliens). S corporations can have no more than 75 shareholders and one class of stock and may not own more than 80 percent of another corporation. LLCs have no such restrictions.
- In a general partnership, the partners are personally liable for the obligations of the partnership. Members of LLCs have limited liability.
- A limited partnership must have at least one general partner who is personally liable for the obligations of the partnership (although this partner can be a corporation). Limited partners are precluded from participating in the management of the business. An LLC provides limited liability to all members, even though they participate in management of the business. ■

Management of an LLC

member-managed LLC
An LLC that has not designated that it is a manager-managed LLC in its article of organization. The members have the right to manage the LLC.

manager-managed LLC
An LLC that has designated in its articles of organization that it is a manager-managed LLC. The members and nonmembers who are designated managers control the management of the LLC.

An LLC can be either a **member-managed LLC** or a **manager-managed LLC**. An LLC is a member-managed LLC unless it is designated as a manager-managed LLC in its articles of organization [ULLCA § 203(a)(b)]. The distinctions between these two are:

- ***Member-managed LLC.*** In this type of LLC, the members of the LLC have the right to manage the LLC.
- ***Manager-managed LLC.*** In this type of LLC, the members designate a manager or managers to manager the LLC, and by doing so they delegate their management rights to the manager or managers, the designated manager or managers have the authority to manage the LLC, and the members no longer have the right to manage the LLC. A manager may be a member of an LLC or a nonmember.

Whether an LLC is a member-managed or manager-managed LLC has important consequences on the right to bind the LLC to contracts and on determining the fiduciary duties owed by members to the LLC. These important distinctions are discussed in the paragraphs that follow.

Member-Managed LLC In a member-managed LLC, each member has equal rights in the management of the business of the LLC, irrespective of the size of his or her capital contribution. Any matter relating to the business of the LLC is decided by a majority vote of the members [ULLCA § 404(a)].

Consider This Example Allison, Jaeson, Stacy, Lan-Wei, and Ivy form NorthWest.com, LLC. Allison contributes $100,000 capital, and the other four members each contributes $25,000 capital. When deciding whether to add another line of products to the business, Stacy, Lan-Wei, and Ivy vote to add the line, and Allison and Jaeson vote against it. The line of new products is added to the LLC's business because three members voted yes while two members voted no. It does not matter that the two members who voted no contributed $125,000 in capital collectively versus $75,000 in capital contributed by the three members who voted yes.

Manager-Managed LLC In a manager-managed LLC, the members and nonmembers who are designated managers control the management of the LLC. The members who are not managers have no rights to manage the LLC unless otherwise provided in the operating agreement. In a manager-managed LLC, each manager has equal rights in the management and conduct of the company's business. Any matter relating to the business of the LLC may be exclusively decided by the managers by a majority vote of the managers [ULLCA § 403(b)].

Laws too gentle are seldom obeyed; too severe, seldom executed.

Benjamin Franklin
Poor Richard's Almanack (1756)

A manager must be appointed by a vote of a majority of the members; managers may also be removed by a vote of the majority of the members [ULLCA § 404(b)(3)].

Certain actions cannot be delegated to managers but must be voted on by all members of the LLC. These include (1) amending the articles of organization, (2) amending the operating agreement, (3) admitting new members, (4) consenting to dissolve the LLC, (5) consenting to merge the LLC with another entity, and (6) selling, leasing, or disposing of all or substantially all of the LLC's property [ULLCA § 404(c)].

Concept Summary *Management of an LLC*

Type of LLC	Description
Member-managed LLC	The members do not designate managers to manage the LLC. The LLC is managed by its members.
Manager-managed LLC	The members designate certain members or nonmembers to manage the LLC. The LLC is managed by the designated managers; nonmanager members have no right to manage the LLC.

Agency Authority to Bind an LLC to Contracts

The designation of an LLC as member-managed or manager-managed is important in determining who has authority to bind the LLC to contracts. The following rules apply:

- ***Member-managed LLC.*** In a member-managed LLC, all members have agency authority to bind the LLC to contracts. For example, if Theresa, Artis, and Yolanda form a member-managed LLC, each one of them can bind the LLC to a contract with a third party such as a supplier, purchaser, landlord, and others.
- ***Manager-managed LLC.*** In a manager-managed LLC, the managers have authority to bind the LLC to contracts, but nonmanager members cannot bind the LLC to contracts. For example, Alexis, Derek, Ashley, and Sadia form an LLC. They designate the LLC as a manager-managed LLC and name Alexis and Ashley as the managers. Alexis, a manager, enters into a contract to purchase goods from a supplier for the LLC. Derek, a nonmanager member, enters into a contract to lease equipment on behalf of the LLC. The LLC is bound to the contract entered into by Alexis, a manager, but is not bound to the contract entered into by Derek, a nonmanager member.

It is the spirit and not the form of law that keeps justice alive.

Earl Warren
The Law and the Future (1955)

An LLC is bound to contracts that members or managers have properly entered into on its behalf in the ordinary course of business [ULLCA § 301].

Concept Summary Agency Authority to Bind an LLC to Contracts

Type of LLC	Agency Authority
Member-managed LLC	All members have agency authority to bind the LLC to contracts.
Manager-managed LLC	The managers have authority to bind the LLC to contracts; the nonmanager members cannot bind the LLC to contracts.

Duty of Loyalty Owed to an LLC

duty of loyalty
A duty owed by a member of a member-managed LLC and a manager of a manager-managed LLC to be honest in his or her dealings with the LLC and to not act adversely to the interests of the LLC.

A member of a member-managed LLC and a manager of a manager-managed LLC owe a *fiduciary* **duty of loyalty** to the LLC. This means that these parties must act honestly in their dealings with the LLC. The duty of loyalty includes the duty not to usurp the LLC's opportunities, make secret profits, secretly deal with the LLC, secretly compete with the LLC, or represent any interests adverse to those of the LLC [ULLCA § 409(b)].

Consider These Examples Ester, Yi, Maria, and Enrique form the member-managed LLC BigBusiness.com, LLC, which conducts online auctions over the Internet. Ester secretly starts a competing business to conduct online auctions over the Internet. Ester is liable for breaching her duty of loyalty to the LLC with Yi, Maria, and Enrique. Ester is liable for any secret profits she made, and her business will be shut down.

Suppose that instead, Ester, Yi, Maria, and Enrique designated their LLC as a manager-managed LLC and named Ester and Yi managers. In this case, only the managers owe a duty of loyalty to the LLC, but nonmanager members do not. Therefore, Ester and Yi, the named managers, could not compete with the LLC; Maria and Enrique, nonmanager members, could compete with the LLC without any legal liability.

Dissolution of an LLC

Unless the operating agreement provides otherwise, a member has the *power* to withdraw from both an at-will LLC and a term LLC [ULLCA § 602(a)]. The disassociation of a member from an at-will LLC is not wrongful unless the power to withdraw is eliminated in the operating agreement [ULLCA § 602(b)]. The disassociation of a member from a term LLC before the expiration of the specified term is wrongful. A member who wrongfully disassociates him- or herself from an LLC is liable to the LLC and to the other members for any damages caused by his or her **wrongful disassociation** [ULLCA § 602(c)].

wrongful disassociation
Disassociation that occurs when a member withdraws from (1) a term LLC prior to the expiration of the term or (2) an at-will LLC when the operating agreement eliminates a member's power to withdraw.

Continuation of an LLC

At the expiration of the term of a term LLC, some of its members may want to continue the LLC. At the expiration of its term, a term LLC can be continued in two situations. First, the members of the LLC may vote prior to the expiration date to continue the LLC for an additional specified term. This requires the unanimous vote of all the members and the filing of an amendment to the articles of organization with the secretary of state, stating this fact. Second, absent the unanimous vote to continue the term LLC, the LLC may be continued as an at-will LLC by a simple majority vote of the members of the LLC [ULLCA § 411(b)].

Limited Liability Partnership (LLP)

Many states have enacted legislation to permit the creation of **limited liability partnership (LLPs)**. In an LLP, there does not have to be a general partner who is personally liable for the debts and obligations of the partnership. Instead, *all* partners are limited partners who stand to lose only their capital contributions should the partnership fail. None of the partners is personally liable for the debts and obligations of the partnership beyond his or her capital contribution (see Exhibit 18.3).

limited liability partnership (LLP) A special form of partnership in which all partners are limited partners and there are no general partners.

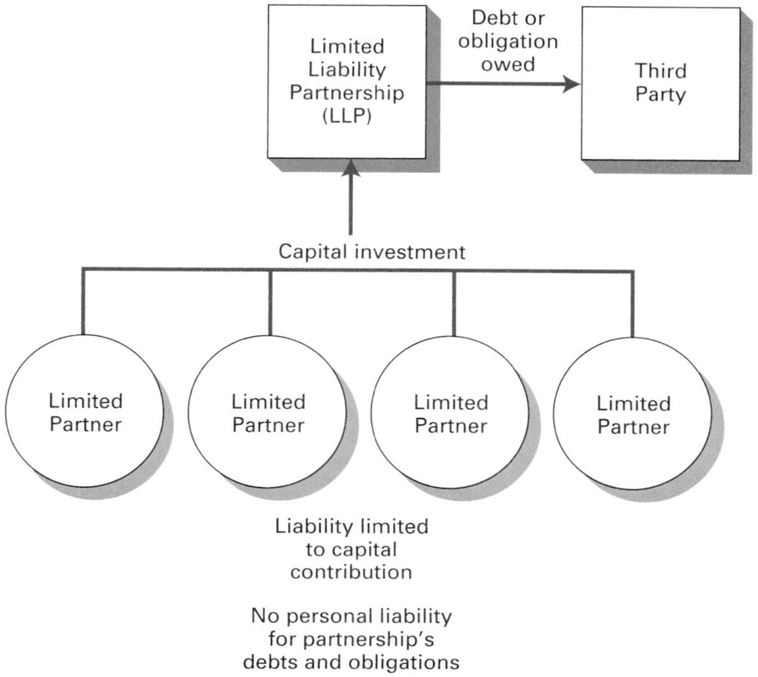

Exhibit 18.3 Limited Liability Partnership (LLP)

In most states, the law restricts the use of LLPs to certain types of professionals, such as accountants, lawyers, and doctors. Nonprofessionals cannot use the LLP form of partnership.

LLPs enjoy the "flow-through" tax benefit of other types of partnerships—that is, there is no tax paid at the partnership level, and all profits and losses are reported on the individual partners' income tax returns.

Consider This Example Suppose Shou-Yi, Patricia, Ricardo, and Namira, each a lawyer, form an LLP called "Shou-Yi Namira LLP" to provide legal services. While providing legal services to the LLP's client Multi Motors, Inc., Patricia commits legal malpractice (negligence). This malpractice causes Multi Motors, Inc., a huge financial loss. In this case, Multi Motors, Inc., can sue and recover against Patricia, the negligent party, and against Shou-Yi Namira LLP. Shou-Yi, Ricardo, and Namira can lose their capital contributions in Shou-Yi Namira LLP but are not personally liable for the damages caused to Multi Motors, Inc. Patricia is personally liable to Multi Motors, Inc., because she was the negligent party.

Articles of Partnership

LLPs must be created formally by filing **articles of partnership** with the secretary of state of the state in which the LLP is organized. This is a public document. The LLP is a

domestic LLP in the state in which it is organized. The LLP law of the state governs the operation of the LLP. An LLP may do business in other states, however. To do so, the LLP must register as a **foreign LLP** in any state in which it wants to conduct business.

Liability Insurance Required

In most states, LLP law restricts the use of LLPs to certain types of professionals, such as accountants and lawyers. Many state laws require LLPs to carry a minimum of $1 million of liability insurance that covers negligence, wrongful acts, and misconduct by partners or employees of the LLP. This requirement guarantees that injured third parties will have compensation to recover for their injuries and is a quid pro quo for permitting partners to have limited liability.

Contemporary Trend

Accounting Firms Operate as LLPs

Prior to the advent of the LLP form of doing business, accounting firms operated as general partnerships. The general partners were therefore personally liable for the debts and obligations of the general partnership. In large accounting firms, this personal liability was rarely imposed because the partnership usually carried sufficient liability insurance to cover most awards to third-party plaintiffs in lawsuits.

In the 1980s and 1990s, accounting firms were hit with many large court judgments. These cases were brought in conjunction with the failure of large commercial banks and other large firms that accountants had audited. Many of these firms failed because of fraud by their major owners and officers. The shareholders and creditors of these failed companies sued the auditors, alleging that the auditors had been negligent in not catching the fraud. Many juries agreed and awarded large awards against the accounting firms. Sometimes an accounting firm's liability insurance was not enough to cover the judgment, thus imposing personal liability on partners.

In the 1990s, state legislatures created a new form of business, the LLP. This entity was particularly created for accountants, lawyers, and other professionals to offer their services under an umbrella of limited liability. The partners of an LLP have limited liability up to their capital contributions; the partners do not have personal liability for the debts and liabilities of the LLP, however.

Once LLPs were permitted by law, all of the Big Five accounting firms changed their status from general partnerships to LLPs. The signs and letterhead of each Big Five accounting firm prominently announces that the firm is an LLP. Many accounting firms other than the Big Five have also changed over to LLP status, as have many law firms. ■

Franchise

franchise
An agreement that is established when one party (the *franchisor*) licenses another party (the *franchisee*) to use the franchisor's trade name, trademarks, commercial symbols, patents, copyrights, and other property in the distribution and selling of goods and services.

A **franchise** is established when one party (the **franchisor**, or **licensor**) licenses another party (the *franchisee*, or *licensee*) to use the franchisor's trade name, trademarks, commercial symbols, patents, copyrights, and other property in the distribution and selling of goods and services. Generally, the franchisor and the franchisee are established as separate corporations. The term *franchise* refers to both the agreement between parties and the franchise outlet.

There are several advantages to franchising, such as (1) the franchisor can reach lucrative new markets, (2) the franchisee has access to the franchisor's knowledge and resources while running an independent business, and (3) consumers are assured of uniform product quality.

A typical franchise arrangement is illustrated in Exhibit 18.4.

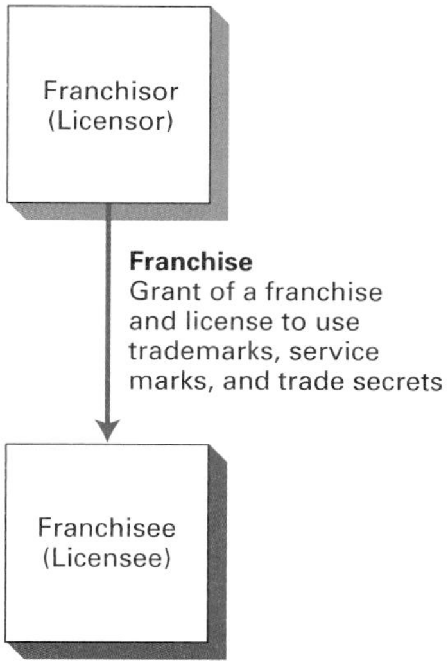

Exhibit 18.4
Franchise

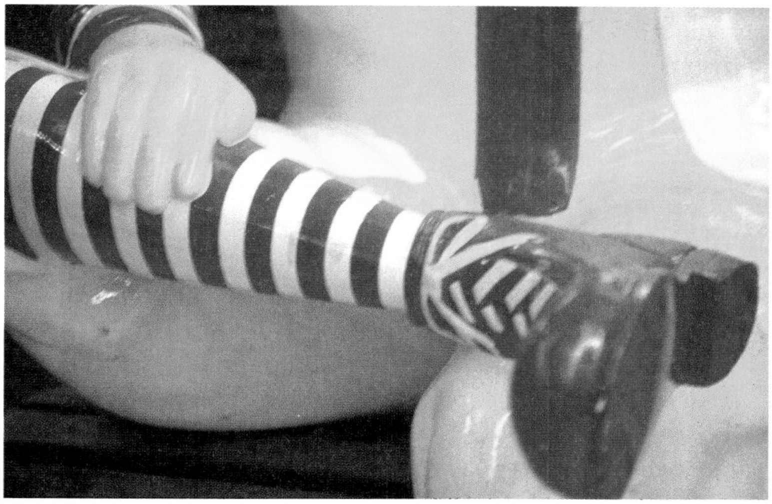

Franchise outlet. Franchising is a major form of business in the United States.

Types of Franchises

There are four basic forms of franchises:

- ***Distributorship franchise.*** In a **distributorship franchise**, the franchisor manufactures a product and licenses a retail dealer to distribute the product to the public. For example, the Ford Motor Company manufactures automobiles and franchises independently owned automobile dealers (franchisees) to sell them to the public.
- ***Processing plant franchise.*** In a **processing plant franchise**, the franchisor provides a secret formula or the like to the franchisee. The franchisee then manufactures the product at its own location and distributes it to retail dealers. For example, the Coca-Cola Corporation, which owns the secret formulas for making Coca-Cola and other soft drinks, licenses regional bottling companies to manufacture and distribute soft drinks under the "Coca-Cola" and other brand names.
- ***Chain-style franchise.*** In a **chain-style franchise**, the franchisor licenses the franchisee to make and sell its products or services to the public from a retail outlet serving an exclusive geographical territory. Most fast-food franchises use this form. For example, the Pizza Hut Corporation franchises independently owned restaurant franchises to make and sell pizza to the public under the "Pizza Hut" name.

- *Area franchise.* In an **area franchise**, the franchisor authorizes the franchisee to negotiate and sell franchises on behalf of the franchisor. The area franchisee is called a **subfranchisor** (see Exhibit 18.5). An area franchise is granted for a certain designated geographical area, such as a state, a region, or another agreed-upon area.

Exhibit 18.5
Area Franchise

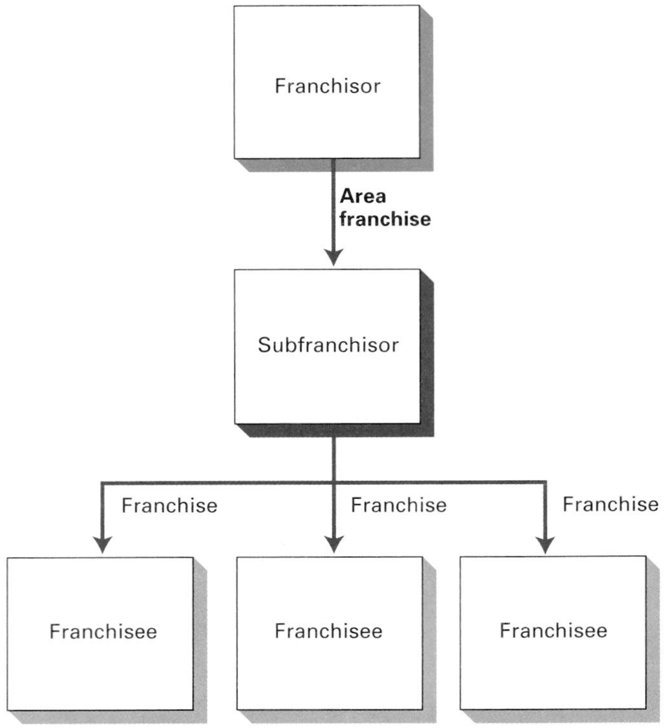

Area franchises are often used when a franchisor wants to enter a market in another country. For example, if Starbucks wanted to enter the country of Vietnam to operate its coffee shops, it could grant an area franchise to a Vietnamese company, which would then choose the individual franchises in that country.

Trademarks and Trade Secrets

A franchisor's ability to maintain the public's perception of the quality of the goods and services associated with its trade name, **trademarks**, and **service marks** is the essence of its success. Most franchisors license the use of their trade names, trademarks, and service marks to their franchisees.

trademarks and service marks
A distinctive mark, symbol, name, word, motto, or device that identifies the goods or services of a particular franchisor.

Franchisor's are often owners of **trade secrets**, including product formulas, business plans and models, and other ideas. Franchisors license and disclose many of their trade secrets to franchisees.

trade secrets
Ideas that make a franchise successful but that do not qualify for trademark, patent, or copyright protection.

The Franchise Agreement

A prospective franchisee must apply to the franchisor for a franchise. The application often includes detailed information about the applicant's previous employment, financial and educational history, credit status, and so on. If an applicant is approved, the parties enter into a **franchise agreement** that sets forth the terms and conditions of the franchise. Most states have enacted a Statute of Frauds that requires franchise agreements to be in writing.

franchise agreement
An agreement that a franchisor and franchisee enter into that sets forth the terms and conditions of the franchise.

Liability of Franchisor and Franchisee

If a franchise is properly organized and operated, the franchisor and franchisee are separate legal entities. Therefore, the franchisor deals with the franchisee as an *independent contractor*.

Franchisees are liable on their own contracts and are liable for their own torts (e.g., negligence). Franchisors are liable for their own contracts and torts. Generally, neither party is liable for the contracts or torts of the other.

Consider These Examples Suppose that the McDonald's Corporation, a fast-food restaurant franchisor, grants a restaurant franchise to Tina Corporation. Tina Corporation opens the franchise restaurant. One day, a customer at the franchise spills a chocolate shake on the floor. The employees at the franchise fail to clean up the spilled shake, and one hour later another customer slips on the spilled shake and suffers severe injuries. The injured customer can recover damages from the franchisee, Tina Corporation, because it was negligent. It cannot recover damages from the franchisor, McDonald's Corporation.

Now suppose that the McDonald's Corporation, the franchisor, grants a franchise to Gion Corporation, the franchisee. McDonald's Corporation enters into a loan agreement with City Bank, whereby it borrows $100 million. Gion Corporation, the franchisee, is not liable on the loan. McDonald's Corporation, the franchisor and debtor, is liable on the loan.

In the case that follows, the court found the franchisee directly liable for its own negligent conduct.

Case 18.2 Franchisee's Liability

Cislaw v. Southland Corporation

4 Cal.App.4th 1384, 6 Cal.Rptr.2d 386, 1992 Cal.App. Lexis 375
Court of Appeals of California

Background and Facts

The Southland Corporation (Southland) owned the "7-Eleven" trademark and licenses franchisees to operate convenience stores using this trademark. Each franchise was independently owned and operated. The franchise agreement stipulated that the franchisee was an independent contractor authorized to make all inventory, employment, and operational decisions for the franchise.

Timothy Cislaw, 17 years old, died of respiratory failure on May 10, 1984. His parents filed a wrongful death action against the franchise and Southland, alleging that Timothy's death resulted from his consumption of Djarum Specials (clove cigarettes) sold at a Costa Mesa, California, 7-Eleven franchise store. The Costa Mesa 7-Eleven was franchised to Charles Trujillo and Patricia Colwell-Trujillo. After answering the complaint, Southland moved for summary judgment, arguing that it was not liable for the alleged tortious conduct of its franchisee because the franchisee was an independent contractor. The plaintiffs alleged that the franchisee was Southland's agent and therefore Southland was liable for its agent's alleged negligence of selling the clove cigarettes to their son. The trial court granted Southland's motion. The Cislaws appealed.

Issue

Was the Costa Mesa franchisee an agent of Southland?

In the Language of the Court

In this field of franchise agreements, the question of whether the franchisee is an independent contractor or an agent is ordinarily one of fact, depending on whether the franchisor exercises complete or substantial control over the franchisee. The agreement recites that the franchisees are independent contractors, and two provisions give the Trujillos the right to make all inventory, employment, and operational decisions.

Colwell-Trujillo said that, as provided under the franchise agreement, she exercised "full and complete control over" the store's employees and "any and all labor relations," including "hiring, firing, disciplining, compensation and work schedules." She attested, "I could purchase whatever inventory I chose and from whomever I wanted and I did so." Colwell-Trujillo stated, "Southland had no control over my decision to sell or not sell clove cigarettes at the store. It was my sole decision to sell clove cigarettes. In no way did Southland ever advertise, promote, or merchandise the clove cigarettes sold in my store."

Decision and Remedy

The court of appeals held that the Costa Mesa 7-Eleven franchise was not an agent of Southland but was an independent contractor. The court of appeals affirmed the judgment of the trial court.

Business and Ethics Questions

1. Should franchisors be automatically held liable for the tortious conduct of their franchisees? Why or why not?
2. Did the Cislaws act ethically in suing Southland?
3. How careful must a franchisor be to retain enough control to protect the quality of the goods and services sold by its franchisees but not to retain too much control so as to become liable for the actions of its franchisees?

Apparent Agency

If a franchisee is the *actual* or *apparent agent* of the franchisor, the franchisor is responsible for the torts and contracts the franchise commits or enters into within the scope of the agency. Franchisors very seldom appoint franchisees as their agents.

apparent agency
An agency that arises when a franchisor creates the appearance that a franchisee is its agent when in fact an actual agency does not exist.

Apparent agency is created when a franchisor leads a third person into believing that the franchisee is its agent. For example, a franchisor and franchisee who use the same trade name and trademarks and make no effort to inform the public of their separate legal status may find themselves in such a situation. However, mere use of the same name does not automatically make the franchisor liable for the franchisee's actions. The court's decision about whether an apparent agency has been created depends on the facts and circumstances of the case.

In the following case, the court found that a franchisee was the apparent agent of the franchisor, thereby making the franchisor liable for the tortious conduct of the franchisee.

Case 18.3
Apparent Agency

Holiday Inns, Inc. v. Shelburne
576 So.2d 322, 1991 Fla.App. Lexis 585
District Court of Appeals of Florida

Background and Facts

Holiday Inns, Inc. (Holiday Inns), is a franchisor that licenses franchisees to operate hotels using its trademarks and service marks. Holiday Inns licensed Hospitality Venture to operate a franchised hotel in Fort Pierce, Florida. The Rodeo Bar, which had a reputation as the "hottest bar in town," was located in the hotel.

The Fort Pierce Holiday Inn and Rodeo Bar did not have sufficient parking, so security guards posted in the Holiday Inn parking lot required Rodeo Bar patrons to park in vacant lots that surrounded the hotel but that were not owned by the hotel. The main duty of the guards was to keep the parking lot open for hotel guests. Two unarmed security guards were on duty on the night in question. One guard was drinking on the job, and the other was an untrained temporary fill-in.

The record disclosed that although the Rodeo Bar had a capacity of 240 people, the bar regularly admitted 270 to 300 people, with 50 to 75 people waiting outside. Fights occurred all the time in the bar and the parking lots, and often there were three or four fights a night. Police reports involving 58 offenses, including several weapons charges and battery and assault charges, had been filed during the previous 18 months.

On the night in question, the two groups involved in the altercation did not leave the Rodeo Bar until closing time. According to the record, these individuals exchanged remarks as they moved toward their respective vehicles in the vacant parking lots adjacent to the Holiday Inn. Ultimately, a fight erupted. The evidence shows that during the course of physical combat, Mr. Carter shot David Rice, Scott Turner, and Robert Shelburne. Rice died from his injuries.

Rice's heirs, Turner, and Shelburne, sued the franchisee, Hospitality Venture, and the franchisor, Holiday Inns, for damages. The trial court found Hospitality Venture negligent for not providing sufficient security to prevent the foreseeable incident that took the life of Rice and injured Turner and Shelburne. The court also found that Hospitality Venture was the apparent agent of Holiday Inns, and therefore Holiday Inns was vicariously liable for its franchisee's tortious conduct. Turner was awarded $3,825,000 for his injuries, Shelburne received $1 million, and Rice's interests were awarded $1 million. Hospitality Venture and Holiday Inns appealed.

Issue

Are the franchisee and the franchisor liable?

In the Language of the Court

There was testimony that Holiday Inns, Inc., gave Hospitality Venture, the franchisee, use of the Holiday Inns, Inc., logo and made the franchisee part of the corporation's reservation system. In fact, Holiday Inns, Inc.'s standard sign was displayed in front of the Fort Pierce Holiday Inn in order to draw customers through name recognition. Clearly, this evidence shows that Holiday Inns, Inc., represented to the public that this particular hotel was a part of the national chain of Holiday Inns and that it could find a certain level of service and safety at its hotel and bar.

Clearly, on the question of reliance, the jury had a right to conclude that appellees believed exactly what Holiday Inns, Inc., wanted them to believe—that the Fort Pierce Holiday Inn and its Rodeo Bar were part of Holiday Inns' system. For these reasons, the evidence supported the jury's finding that Hospitality Venture was the apparent agent of Holiday Inns, Inc., and was acting within the scope of its apparent authority.

Decision and Remedy

The court of appeals held that the franchisee was negligent and that the franchisee was the apparent agent of the franchisor. The court of appeals affirmed the judgment of the trial court.

Business and Ethics Questions

1. What does the doctrine of apparent agency provide? How does it differ from actual agency?
2. Did Hospitality Venture act ethically in denying liability? Did Holiday Inns act ethically in denying liability?
3. Why do you think the plaintiffs included Holiday Inns as a defendant in their lawsuit? Do you think the damages that were awarded were warranted?

International Law

International Franchising

The international market presently offers a great opportunity for U.S. franchisors to expand their businesses. Many U.S. franchisors view international expansion as their number-one priority. However, in addition to providing lucrative new markets, international franchising also poses difficulties and risks.

The expansion into other countries through franchising means that U.S. franchisors can expand internationally without the huge capital investments that would be required if they tried to penetrate these markets with company-owned stores or branches. In addition, a foreign franchisee will know things about the cultural and business traditions of the foreign country that the franchisor will not. Consequently, the franchisee will be better able to serve the consumers and customers in the particular market.

Foreign franchising is not without difficulties, however. For example, the host country's laws may differ from U.S. laws. Foreign cultures may also require different advertising, marketing, and promotional approaches. In addition, the franchisor may be subjecting itself to government regulation in the host country. Finally, different dispute settlement procedures may be in place that will have to be used if there is a dispute between the U.S. franchisor and the foreign franchisee.

In addition to U.S. franchisors' expanding into other countries, foreign franchisors also view the United States as a potential market. This will provide an opportunity for U.S. entrepreneurs to become franchisees for foreign franchisors. ■

Tokyo, Japan.

License

Licensing is an important business arrangement in both domestic and international markets. **Licensing** occurs when one business or party that owns trademarks, service marks, trade names, and other intellectual property (the licensor) contracts to permit another business or party (the licensee) to use its trademarks, service marks, trade names, and other intellectual property in the distribution of goods, services, software, and digital information. A licensing arrangement is illustrated in Exhibit 18.6.

licensing
A business arrangement that occurs when the owner of intellectual property (the *licensor*) contracts to permit another party (the *licensee*) to use the intellectual property.

Consider This Example The Walt Disney Company owns the merchandising rights to "Winnie the Pooh" stories and all the characters associated with the Winnie the Pooh stories. The Walt Disney Company enters into an agreement whereby it permits the Beijing Merchandising Company, a business formed under Chinese law, to manufacture and distribute a line of clothing, children's toys, and other items bearing the likeness of the Winnie the Pooh characters. This is a license. The Walt Disney Company is the licensor, and the Beijing Merchandising Company is the licensee.

Exhibit 18.6
Licensing

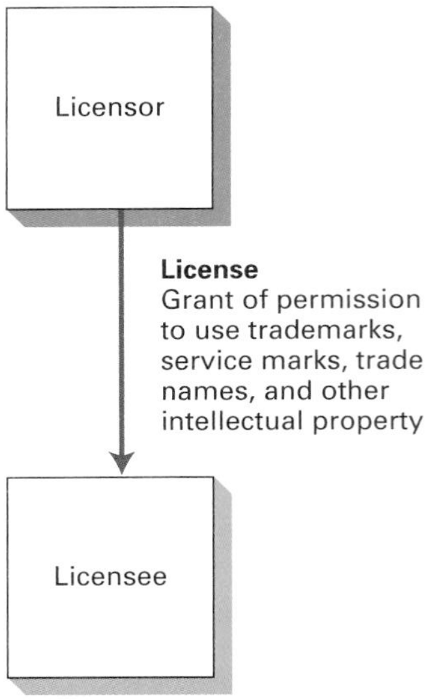

Joint Venture

joint venture
An arrangement in which two or more business entities combine their resources to pursue a single project or transaction.

A **joint venture** is an arrangement in which two or more business entities combine their resources to pursue a single project or transaction. The parties to a joint venture are called **joint venturers**. Joint ventures resemble partnerships, except that partnerships are usually formed to pursue ongoing business operations rather than to focus on a single project or transaction.

Unless otherwise agreed, joint venturers have equal rights to manage the joint venture. Joint venturers owe each other the fiduciary duties of loyalty and care. If a joint venturer violates these duties, it is liable for the damages the breach causes.

International Law

Chinese–U.S. International Joint Venture

Beijing, China.

Starbucks Coffee has been a tremendous success in the United States. Beginning with a single outlet in Seattle, Washington, Starbucks Coffee Company has expanded Starbucks coffee shops across the United States. The company expanded in the United States through company-owned stores.

When Starbucks wanted to enter overseas markets, however, it realized it could not expand solely through company-owned outlets. This was because (1) government restrictions in some countries prohibit 100 percent ownership of a business by a foreign investor and (2) the company lacked the business expertise and knowledge necessary to enter many foreign markets. To enter foreign markets, Starbucks turned to joint ventures.

For example, Starbucks is expanding its operations in China by using a 50–50 joint venture with Shanghai President Coffee Corporation, a Chinese company. ■

Strategic Alliance

A **strategic alliance** is an arrangement between two or more companies in the same industry whereby they agree to ally themselves to accomplish a designated objective. A strategic alliance allows the companies to reduce risks, share costs, combine technologies, and extend their markets. For example, companies often enter into strategic alliances when they decide to expand internationally into foreign countries.

strategic alliance
An arrangement between two or more companies in the same industry whereby they agree to ally themselves to accomplish a designated objective.

Strategic alliances do not have the same protection as mergers, joint ventures, or franchising, and sometimes they are dismantled. Consideration must always be given to the fact that a strategic alliance partner is also a potential competitor.

Internet Law & Online Commerce

Strategic Internet Alliances in China

Leading Internet companies in the United States have eyed the China market for its tremendous growth potential. But China prohibits complete ownership of Internet companies in China by foreigners. In addition, the legendary Chinese "connections" method of conducting business places another hurdle in the way of foreign companies wishing to do business there. So what is the main way to tap into this Internet market? Strategic alliances.

A major strategic alliance by U.S. companies in China was their tie-in and investment in China.com. China.com is a Chinese-language Web portal backed by investments by U.S. companies TimeWarner, Inc., Sun Microsystems, and Nortel Networks. China.com became China's largest Internet company when it went public in 1999. Intel Corp., another major U.S. company, has aligned itself with Sohu.com, a Chinese Internet company located in Beijing. CMGI Inc., a U.S. Internet holding company, has joined with Pacific Century Cyber-Works (PCCW), a Hong Kong company, to sell Web content and e-commerce services to the exploding Chinese Internet market from its base in Hong Kong.

The Chinese government has permitted these strategic alliances. Based on the communist government's rules in China and a culture that favors business connections, U.S. Internet companies will continue to enter the Chinese Internet market through strategic alliances with Chinese Internet firms. These strategic alliances bring together the expertise of all the parties. ■

Terms and Concepts

Limited Liability Company (LLC)

1. ***Limited liability company (LLC).*** The LLC is a special form of unincorporated business entity that combines the tax benefits of a partnership with the limited personal liability of a corporation.
2. ***Members.*** Owners of an LLC are called members.
3. ***Articles of organization.*** The articles of organization is a document that owners of an LLC must execute, sign, and file with the secretary of state of the appropriate state to form an LLC.
4. ***Operating agreement.*** An operating agreement is an agreement entered into among members that governs the affairs and business of an LLC and the relations among partners, managers, and the LLC.

5. ***Taxation.*** An LLC does not pay federal income taxes unless it elects to do so. If an LLC is taxed as a partnership, the income and losses of the LLC flow onto individual members' federal income tax returns.
6. ***Member-managed and manager-managed LLC.*** An LLC can be either a *member-managed LLC* or a *manager-managed LLC.* An LLC is a member-managed LLC unless it is designated as a manager-managed LLC.
   a. *Member-managed LLC.* All members of the LLC have agency authority to bind the LLC to contracts.
   b. *Manager-managed LLC.* Only the designated managers have authority to bind the LLC to contracts.

Limited Liability Partnership (LLP)

The LLP is a form of business in which there does not have to be a general partner who is personally liable for debts and obligations of the partnership. All partners are limited partners and stand to lose only their capital contributions should the partnership fail. LLPs are formed by accountants and other professionals, as allowed by LLP law.

1. ***Partners.*** Owners of an LLP are called partners.
2. ***Articles of partnership.*** The articles of partnership is a document that the partners of an LLP must execute, sign, and file with the secretary of state of the appropriate state to form an LLP.
3. ***Taxation.*** An LLP does not pay federal income taxes unless it elects to do so. If an LLP is taxed as a partnership, the income and losses of the LLP flow onto individual partners' federal income tax returns.

Franchise

A franchise is established when one party licenses another party to use the franchisor's trade name, trademarks, commercial symbols, patents, copyrights, and other property in the distribution and selling of goods and services.

1. ***Franchisor.*** The party who does the licensing in a franchising arrangement is called the *franchisor*, or *licensor*.
2. ***Franchisee.*** The party who is licensed by the franchisor in a franchise arrangement is called the *franchisee*, or *licensee*.

Types of Franchises

1. ***Distributorship franchise.*** In this type of franchise, the franchisor manufactures a product and licenses a retail franchisee to distribute the product to the public.
2. ***Processing plant franchise.*** In this type of franchise, the franchisor provides a secret formula or process to the franchisee, and the franchisee manufactures the product and distributes it to retail dealers.
3. ***Chain-style franchise.*** In this type of franchise, the franchisor licenses the franchisee to make and sell its products or distribute its services to the public from a retail outlet serving an exclusive territory.
4. ***Area franchise.*** In this type of franchise, the franchisor authorizes the franchisee to negotiate and sell franchises on behalf of the franchisor in designated areas. The area franchisee is called a *subfranchisor*.

The Franchise Agreement

A franchise agreement is an agreement that the franchisor and the franchisee enter into that sets forth the terms and conditions of the franchise (e.g., quality control standards, covenant-not-to-compete).

Franchise: Trademarks and Trade Secrets

1. ***Trademarks and service marks.*** Trademarks and service marks are distinctive marks, symbols, names, words, mottos, or devices that identify the goods or services of a particular franchisor.
2. ***Licensing of marks.*** A franchisor *licenses* the use of its trademarks and service marks to a franchisee in the franchise agreement.

3. ***Trade secrets.*** Trade secrets are ideas, formulas, and methods of doing business that make a franchise successful but do not qualify for trademark, patent, or copyright protection.

Franchise: Contract and Tort Liability

Franchisors and franchisees are liable for their own contracts and torts.

1. ***Independent contractor.*** An independent contractor is a separately organized and operated business that is not the agent of another party with which its does business. This is the typical franchisor–franchisee arrangement. There is no agency relationship, so neither party is liable for the other's contracts or torts.
2. ***Actual agency.*** An actual agency is an arrangement in which a franchisor expressly or implicitly by its conduct makes a franchisee its agent. The franchisor is liable for the contracts entered into and torts committed by the franchisee while acting within the scope of the agency.
3. ***Apparent agency.*** An apparent agency arises when a franchisor creates the appearance that a franchisee is its agent when in fact an actual agency does not exist. The franchisor is liable for the contracts entered into and torts committed by the franchisee acting as an apparent agent.

License

A license is a business arrangement that occurs when the owner of intellectual property (the *licensor*) contracts to permit another party (the *licensee*) to use the intellectual property.

1. ***Licensor.*** The licensor is the party that owns intellectual property and grants a license.
2. ***Licensee.*** The licensee is the party that receives a license.

Joint Venture

1. ***Joint venture.*** A joint venture is an arrangement in which two or more business entities combine their resources to pursue a single project or transaction.
2. ***Joint venturer.*** A party to a joint venture is called a joint venturer.

Strategic Alliance

A strategic alliance is an arrangement between two or more companies in the same industry whereby they agree to ally themselves to accomplish a designated objective.

Internet Exercises and Case Questions

Working the Web Internet Exercises

1. Review business associations at **jurist.law.pitt.edu/sg_bus.htm**. to determine why the LLC is an increasingly popular form of doing business.
2. Check your state statute on LLCs. How many persons are required to form an LLC? Try **www.4inc.com/llcfaq.htm**.
3. For an overview of partnerships and LLCs in the context of a state law, see "Florida's New Partnership Law," at **www.law.fsu.edu/journals/lawreview/issues/232/larson.html**.
4. Review the FTC cases of alleged abusive practices of franchisors at **www.ftc.gov/bcp/franchise/1999-2000cases.htm**. How would you advise a franchise client to protect against such practices? For information on federal law regarding franchising, see **www.ftc.gov/bcp/franchise/netfran.htm**.
5. Franchising makes extensive use of licensing of intellectual property, especially trademarks and trade secrets. Use the Web sites listed below to find examples of licensing agreements and the disputes they can sometimes produce:
   - The Trade Secrets home page, at **http://my.execpc.com/~mhallign/index.html**
   - All About Trademarks, at **www.ggmark.com**
   - Intellectual Property Digital Library, at **ipdl.wipo.int**
   - Intellectual Property Mall, at **http://www.piercelaw.edu/TFIELD/ipbasics.htm**
   - JurisNotes.Com, a source for all aspects of intellectual property law, at **www.jurisnotes.com**

Legal Environment Cases

18.1 Liability of Members Harold, Jasmine, Caesar, and Yuan form Microhard.com, LLC, a limited liability company, to sell computer hardware and software over the Internet. Microhard.com, LLC, hires Heather, a recent graduate of the University of Chicago and a brilliant software designer, as an employee. Heather's job is to design and develop software that will execute a computer command when the computer user thinks of the next command he or she wants to execute on the computer. Using Heather's research, Microhard.com, LLC, develops the "Third Eye" software program that does this. Microhard.com, LLC, sends Heather to the annual Comdex Computer Show in Las Vegas, Nevada, to unveil this revolutionary software. Heather goes to Las Vegas, and while there, she rents an automobile to get from the hotel to the computer show and to meet interested buyers at different locations in Las Vegas. While Heather is driving from her hotel to the site of the Comdex Computer Show, she negligently causes an accident in which she runs over Harold Singer, a pedestrian. Singer, who suffers severe personal injuries, sues Microhard.com, LLC, Heather, Harold, Jasmine, Caesar, and Yuan to recover monetary damages for his injuries. Who is liable?

18.2 Liability of Members Isabel, Koshi, and Winchester each contribute $50,000 capital and form an LLC called Fusion Restaurant, LLC, which operates an upscale restaurant serving "fusion" cuisine, combining foods from cultures around the world. Fusion Restaurant, LLC, as a business, borrows $1 million from Melon Bank for operating capital. Isabel, Koshi, and Winchester are so busy cooking, serving, and running the restaurant that they forget to hold members' meetings, keep minute books, or otherwise observe any usual company formalities for the entire first year of business. After this one year of hard work, Fusion Restaurant, LLC, suffers financial difficulties and defaults on the $1 million bank loan from Melon Bank. Melon Bank sues Fusion Restaurant, LLC, Isabel, Koshi, and Winchester to recover the unpaid bank loan. Who is liable?

18.3 Member-Managed LLC Jennifer, Martin, and Edsel form an LLC called Big Apple, LLC, to operate a bar in New York City. Jennifer, Martin, and Edsel are member-managers of the LLC. One of Jennifer's jobs as a member-manager is to drive the LLC's truck and pick up certain items of supply for the bar each Wednesday. On the way back to the bar one Wednesday after picking up the supplies for that week, Jennifer negligently runs over a pedestrian, Tilly Tourismo, on a street in Times Square. Tilly is severely injured and sues Big Apple, LLC, Jennifer, Martin, and Edsel to recover monetary damages for her injuries. Who is liable?

18.4 Contract Liability Maria, Richard, and Dakota form an LLC called Ummmmm, LLC, to operate a spa in Santa Fe, New Mexico. Each member contributes $100,000 in capital to start the LLC. Ummmmm, LLC, is a member-managed LLC. Maria enters into a contract on behalf of the LLC in which she contracts to have a new hot tub installed at the spa by Hot Tubs, Inc., for $80,000. Hot Tubs, Inc., installs the hot tub and sends a bill for $80,000 to Ummmmm, LLC. When Ummmmm, LLC, fails to pay the bill, Hot Tub, Inc., sues Ummmmm, LLC, to recover the unpaid $80,000. Is Ummmmm, LLC, liable?

18.5 Manager-Managed LLC Juan, Min-Yi, and Chelsea form Unlimited, LLC, a limited liability company that operates a chain of women's retail clothing stores that sell eclectic women's clothing. The company is a manager-managed LLC, and Min-Yi has been designated in the articles of organization filed with the secretary of state as the manager of Unlimited, LLC. Min-Yi sees a store location on Rodeo Drive in Beverly Hills, California, that she thinks would be an excellent location for an Unlimited Store. Min-Yi enters into a five-year lease on behalf of Unlimited, LLC, with Landlord, Inc., the owner of the store building, to lease the store at $100,000 rent per year. While visiting Chicago, Chelsea sees a store location on North Michigan Avenue in Chicago that she thinks is a perfect location for an Unlimited store. Chelsea enters into a five-year lease on behalf of Unlimited, LLC, with Real Estate, Inc., the owner of the store building, to lease the store location at $100,000 rent per year. Is Unlimited, LLC, bound to either of these leases?

18.6 Duty of Loyalty Ally is a member and a manager of the manager-managed LLC called Movers & You, LLC, a moving company. Movers & You, LLC's main business is moving large corporations from old office space to new office space in other buildings. After Ally has been a member-manager of Movers & You, LLC, for several years, she decides to join her friend Lana and form another LLC, called Lana & Me, LLC. This new LLC provides moving services that move large corporations from old office space to new office space. Ally becomes a member-manager of Lana & Me, LLC, while retaining her member-manager position at Movers & You, LLC. Ally does not disclose her new position at Lana & Me, LLC, to the other members or managers of Movers & You, LLC. Several years later, the other members of Movers & You, LLC, discover Ally's other ownership and management position at Lana & Me, LLC. Movers & You, LLC, sues Ally to recover damages for her working at Lana & Me, LLC. Is Ally liable?

18.7 Franchise Agreement Libby-Broadway Drive-In, Inc. (Libby), is a corporation licensed to operate a McDonald's fast-food franchise restaurant by the McDonald's System, Inc. (McDonald's). Libby was granted a license to operate a McDonald's in Cleveland, Ohio, and was granted an exclusive territory in which McDonald's could not grant another franchise. The area was described as "bound on the north by the south side of Miles Avenue, on the west and south side by Turney Road, on the east by Warrensville Center Road." In December 1976, McDonald's granted a franchise to another franchisee to operate a McDonald's restaurant on the west side of Turney Road. Libby sued McDonald's, alleging a breach of the franchise agreement. Is McDonald's liable? *Libby-Broadway Drive-In, Inc. v. McDonald's System, Inc.*, 391 N.E. 2d 1, 1979 Ill.App. Lexis 2698 (Ill. App.)

18.8 Tort Liability The Seven-Up Company (Seven-Up) is a franchisor that licenses local bottling companies to manufacture, bottle, and distribute soft drinks using the "7-Up" trademark. The Brooks Bottling Company (Brooks) was a Seven-Up franchisee that bottled and sold 7-Up soft drinks to stores in Michigan. Under the franchise agreement, the franchisee was required to purchase the 7-Up syrup from Seven-Up, but it could purchase its bottles, cartons, and other supplies from independent suppliers if Seven-Up approved the design of those articles.

Brooks used cartons designed and manufactured by Olinkraft, Inc., using a design that Seven-Up had approved. Sharon Proos

Kosters, a customer at a Meijers Thrifty Acres Store in Holland, Michigan, removed a cardboard carton containing six bottles of 7-Up from a grocery store shelf, put it under her arm, and walked toward the checkout counter. As she did so, a bottle slipped out of the carton, fell on the floor, and exploded, causing a piece of glass to strike Kosters in her eye as she looked down; she was blinded in that eye. Evidence showed that the 7-Up carton was designed to be held from the top and was made without a strip on the side of the carton that would prevent a bottle from slipping out if held underneath. Kosters sued Seven-Up to recover damages for her injuries. Is Seven-Up liable? *Kosters v. Seven-Up Company*, 595 F.2d 347, 1979 U.S.App. Lexis 15945 (6th Cir.)

18.9 Trademark Ramada Inns, Inc. (Ramada Inns), is a franchisor that licenses franchisees to operate motor hotels using the "Ramada Inns" trademarks and service marks. In August 1977, the Gadsden Motor Company (Gadsden), a partnership, purchased a motel in Attalla, Alabama, and entered into a franchise agreement with Ramada Inns to operate it as a Ramada Inns motor hotel. In 1982, the motel began receiving poor ratings from Ramada Inns inspectors, and Gadsden fell behind on its monthly franchise fee payments. Despite proddings from Ramada Inns, the motel never met Ramada Inns's operational standards again. On November 17, 1983, Ramada Inns properly terminated the franchise agreement, citing quality deficiencies and Gadsden's failure to pay past-due franchise fees. The termination notice directed Gadsden to remove any materials or signs identifying the motel as a Ramada Inns. Gadsden continued using Ramada Inns's signage, trademarks, and service marks inside and outside the motel. In September 1984, Ramada Inns sued Gadsden for trademark infringement. Who wins? *Ramada Inns, Inc. v. Gadsden Motel Company*, 804 F.2d 1562, 1986 U.S. App. Lexis 34279 (11th Cir.)

Ethics in Business

18.10 Angela, Yoko, Cherise, and Serena want to start a new business that designs and manufactures toys for children. At a meeting where the owners want to decide what type of legal form to use to operate the business, Cherise states:

> *We should use a limited liability company to operate our business because this form of business provides us, the owners, with a limited liability shield, which means that if the business gets sued and loses, we the owners are not personally liable to the injured party except up to our capital contribution in the business.*

The others agree and form an LLC called Fuzzy Toys, LLC, to conduct the member-managed business. Each of the four owners contributes $50,000 as her capital contribution to the LLC. Fuzzy Toys, LLC, purchases $800,000 of liability insurance from Allied Insurance Company and starts business. Fuzzy Toys, LLC, designs and produces "Heidi," a new toy doll and female action figure. The new toy doll is an instant success, and Fuzzy Toys, LLC, produces and sells millions of these female action figures. After a few months, however, the LLC starts getting complaints that one of the parts of the female action figure is breaking off quite regularly, and some children are swallowing the part. The concerned member-managers of Fuzzy Toys, LLC, issue an immediate recall of the female action figure, but before all the dolls are returned for a refund, Catherine, a seven-year-old child, swallows the toy's part and is severely injured. Catherine, through her mother, sues Fuzzy Toys, LLC, Allied Insurance Company, Angela, Yoko, Cherise, and Serena to recover damages for product liability. At the time of suit, Fuzzy Toys, LLC, has $200,000 of assets. The jury awards Catherine $10 million for her injuries.

Ethics Issues

1. What is the liability of members for an LLC's debts and obligations? Explain.
2. Who is liable to Catherine and for how much? How much does Catherine recover?
3. Did Angela, Yoko, Cherise, and Serena act ethically in using an LLC as the form of business for conducting their toy business? Explain.

19

Agency Law

"Let every eye negotiate for itself, and trust no agent."

—William Shakespeare
Much Ado About Nothing (1598)

Chapter Objectives

After studying this chapter, you should be able to:

1. Define agency.
2. Identify and define a principal–independent contractor relationship.
3. List and describe the agent's duties to the principal and the principal's duties to the agent.
4. Describe the principal's and agent's liability on third-party contracts.
5. Identify and describe the principal's liability for the tortious conduct of an agent.

Chapter Contents

- Agency
- Formation of an Agency
- Principal's and Agent's Duties
- Contract Liability to Third Parties
- Tort Liability to Third Parties
- Independent Contractor
- Termination of an Agency

If businesspeople had to personally conduct all their business, the scope of their activities would be severely curtailed. Partnerships would not be able to operate; corporations could not act through managers and employees; and sole proprietorships would not be able to hire employees. The use of agents (or agency), which allows one person to act on behalf of another, solves this problem.

There are many examples of agency relationships. They include a salesperson who sells goods for a store, an executive who works for a corporation, a partner who acts on behalf of a partnership, an attorney who is hired to represent a client, a real estate broker who is employed to sell a house, and so on. Agency is governed by a large body of common law, known as **agency law**. This law, which is a mixture of contract law and tort law, is discussed in this chapter.

agency law
The large body of common law that governs agency; a mixture of contract law and tort law.

Agency

Agency relationships are formed by the mutual consent of a principal and an agent. Section 1(1) of the *Restatement (Second) of Agency* defines agency as a *fiduciary relationship* "which results from the manifestation of consent by one person to another that the other shall act in his behalf and subject to his control, and consent by the other so to act." The *Restatement (Second) of Agency* is the reference source for the rules of agency. A party who employs another person to act on his or her behalf is called a **principal**. A party who agrees to act on behalf of another is called an **agent**. The principal–agent relationship is commonly referred to as an **agency**. This relationship is depicted in Exhibit 19.1.

principal
A party who employs another person to act on his or her behalf.

agent
A party who agrees to act on behalf of another.

agency
A principal–agent relationship: the fiduciary relationship "which results from the manifestation of consent by one person to another that the other shall act in his behalf and subject to his control, and consent by the other so to act."

Exhibit 19.1
Principal–Agent Relationship

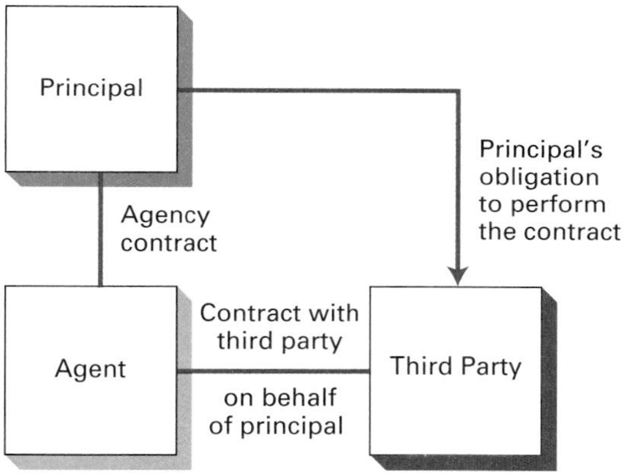

Persons Who Can Initiate an Agency Relationship

Any person who has the capacity to contract can appoint an agent to act on his or her behalf. Generally, persons who lack **contractual capacity**, such as insane persons and minors, cannot appoint an agent. However, the court can appoint a legal guardian or another representative to handle the affairs of insane persons, minors, and others who lack capacity to contract. With court approval, these representatives can enter into enforceable contracts on behalf of the persons they represent.

An agency can be created only to accomplish a lawful purpose. Agency contracts that are created for illegal purposes or are against public policy are void and unenforceable. For example, a principal cannot hire an agent to kill another person. Some agency relationships are prohibited by law. For example, unlicensed agents cannot be hired to perform the duties of certain licensed professionals (e.g., doctors, lawyers).

Employer–Employee Relationship

employer–employee relationship
A relationship that results when an employer hires an employee to perform some form of physical service.

An **employer–employee relationship** exists when an employer hires an employee to perform some form of physical service. For example, a welder on General Motors Corporation's assembly line is employed in an employer–employee relationship because he performs a physical task.

An employee is not an agent unless he or she is specifically empowered to enter into contracts on the principal employer's behalf. Employees may only enter into contracts that are within the scope of their employment. The welder in the previous example is not an agent because he cannot enter into contracts on behalf of General Motors Corporation. If the company empowered him to enter into contracts, he would become an agent.

Principal–Agent Relationship

principal–agent relationship
A relationship in which an employer hires an employee and gives that employee authority to act and enter into contracts on his or her behalf.

A **principal–agent relationship** is formed when an employer hires an employee and gives that employee authority to act and enter into contracts on his or her behalf. The extent of this authority is governed by an express agreement between the parties and implied from the circumstances of the agency. For example, the president of a corporation usually has the authority to enter into major contracts on the corporation's behalf, and a supervisor on a corporation's assembly line may have the authority only to purchase the supplies necessary to keep the line running.

Concept Summary Types of Employment Relationships

Type of Relationship	Description
Employer–employee	The employer has the right to control the physical conduct of the employee.
Principal–agent	The agent has authority to act on behalf of the principal as authorized by the principal and implied from the agency. An employee is often the agent of his or her employer.

Principal–Independent Contractor Relationship

independent contractor
A person or business that is not an employee and is employed by a principal to perform a certain task on his or her behalf.

Principals often employ outsiders—that is, persons and businesses that are not employees—to perform certain tasks on their behalf. These persons and businesses are called **independent contractors**. For example, doctors, dentists, consultants, stockbrokers, architects, certified public accountants, real estate brokers, and plumbers are examples of professions and trades that commonly act as independent contractors. An independent contractor who is a professional, such as a lawyer, is called a *professional agent*.

A principal can authorize an independent contractor to enter into contracts. Principals are bound by the authorized contracts of their independent contractors. For example, if a client authorizes an attorney to settle a case within a certain dollar amount and the attorney does so, the settlement agreement is binding.

Formation of an Agency

An agency and the resulting authority of an agent can arise in any of these four ways: (1) express agency, (2) implied agency, (3) apparent agency, and (4) agency by ratification. Each of these types of agencies is discussed in the paragraphs that follow.

Express Agency

Express agency is the most common form of agency. In an express agency, the agent has the authority to contract or otherwise act on the principal's behalf, as expressly stated in the agency agreement. In addition, the agent may also possess certain implied or apparent authority to act on the principal's behalf (as discussed later in this chapter).

express agency
An agency that occurs when a principal and an agent expressly agree to enter into an agency agreement with each other.

Express agency occurs when a principal and an agent expressly agree to enter into an agency agreement with each other. Express agency contracts can be either oral or written, unless the Statute of Frauds stipulates that they must be written. For example, in most states, a real estate broker's contract to sell real estate must be in writing.

If a principal and an agent enter into an **exclusive agency contract**, the principal cannot employ any agent other than the exclusive agent. If the principal does so, the exclusive agent can recover damages from the principal. If an agency is not an exclusive agency, the principal can employ more than one agent to try to accomplish a stated purpose. When multiple agents are employed, the agencies with all the agents terminate when any one of the agents accomplishes the stated purpose.

exclusive agency contract
A contract a principal and an agent enter into that says the principal cannot employ any agent other than the exclusive agent.

Power of Attorney A **power of attorney** is one of the most formal types of express agency agreements. It is often used to give an agent the power to sign legal documents, such as deeds to real estate, on behalf of the principal. There are two kinds of powers of attorney: *general*, which confers broad power on the agent to act in any matters on the principal's behalf, and *special*, which limits the agent to those acts specifically enumerated in an agreement. The agent is called an *attorney-in-fact* even though he or she does not have to be a lawyer. Powers of attorney must be written. Usually, they must be notarized.

power of attorney
An express agency agreement that is often used to give an agent the power to sign legal documents on behalf of the principal.

Implied Agency

In many situations, a principal and an agent do not expressly create an agency. Instead, the agency is implied from the conduct of the parties. This type of agency is referred to as **implied agency**. The extent of the agent's authority is determined from the facts and circumstances of the particular situation. Implied authority can be conferred by industry custom, prior dealing between the parties, the agent's position, the acts deemed necessary to carry out the agent's duties, and other factors the court deems relevant. Implied authority cannot conflict with express authority or with stated limitations on express authority.

implied agency
An agency that occurs when a principal and an agent do not expressly create an agency, but it is inferred from the conduct of the parties.

Incidental Authority Often, even an express agency agreement does not provide enough detail to cover all contingencies that may arise in the future regarding the performance of the agency. In this case, the agent possesses certain implied authority to act. This implied authority is sometimes referred to as *incidental authority*.

Certain emergency situations may arise in the course of an agency. If the agent cannot contact the principal for instructions, the agent has implied emergency powers to take all actions reasonably necessary to protect the principal's property and rights.

Apparent Agency

Apparent agency (or **agency by estoppel**) arises when a principal creates the appearance of an agency that in actuality does not exist. Where an apparent agency is established, the principal is estopped from denying the agency relationship and is bound to contracts entered into by the apparent agent while acting within the scope of the apparent agency. Note that it is the principal's actions—not the agent's—that create an apparent agency.

apparent agency
Agency that arises when a principal creates the appearance of an agency that in actuality does not exist.

Consider This Example Suppose Georgia Pacific, Inc., interviews Albert Iorio for a sales representative position. Mr. Iorio, accompanied by Jane Franklin, the national sales manager, visits retail stores located in the open sales territory. While visiting one store, Jane tells the store manager, "I wish I had more sales reps like Albert." Nevertheless, Albert is not hired. If Albert later enters into contracts with the store on behalf of Georgia Pacific and Jane has not controverted the impression of Albert she left with the store manager, the company will be bound to the contract.

Contemporary Trend

Apparent Agency

Franchising has become a major form of conducting business in the United States. In a franchise agreement, one company (called the *franchisor*) licenses another company (called the *franchisee*) to use its trade name, trademarks and service marks, and trade secrets. Many fast-food restaurants, gasoline stations, motels and hotels, and other businesses operate in this fashion.

The franchisor and franchisee are independently owned businesses. A principal–agent relationship usually is not created by the franchise. If no express or implied agency is created, the franchisor would not normally be civilly liable for the tortious conduct (e.g., negligence) of the franchisee. Liability could be imposed on the franchisor, however, if an apparent agency is shown. Consider the following case.

The Howard Johnson Company (HJ) operates a chain of hotels, motels, and restaurants across the United States. Approximately 75 percent of the HJ motor lodges are owned and operated by franchisees that are licensed by HJ to do business under the "Howard Johnson" trade name and trademarks. The rest are company owned.

Orlando Executive Part, Inc. (OEP), is a corporate franchisee that owns and operates an HJ motor lodge franchise in Orlando, Florida. The motor lodge is part of a complex known as "Howard Johnson's Plaza," located off Interstate 4. The motor lodge contains approximately 300 guest rooms in six separate buildings.

P.D.R. (name withheld by the court), a 35-year-old married woman and mother of a small child, worked as a supervisor for a restaurant chain. Her work occasionally required her to travel and stay overnight in Orlando. On October 22, 1975, P.D.R. stopped to stay at the HJ motor lodge in Orlando. At approximately 9:30 P.M., P.D.R. registered for her previously reserved room at the lodge. The registration form did not inform her that the hotel was an HJ franchisee. P.D.R. parked her car in the motor lodge parking lot and proceeded with her suitcase to her ground-floor room in Building A, which was located directly behind the registration office. P.D.R. then went back to her car to get some papers. After obtaining the papers from her car, P.D.R. returned to Building A. As she proceeded down an interior hallway of the building toward her room, she was accosted by a man she had previously seen standing behind the registration office. The man struck her in the throat and neck and choked her until she became semiconscious. When P.D.R. fell to the floor, her assailant sat on top of her and stripped her of her jewelry. He than dragged her down the hallway and beneath a secluded stairway, where he brutally beat her. The assailant then disappeared into the night and has never been identified.

P.D.R. suffered serious physical and psychological injury, including memory loss, mental confusion, and an inability to tolerate and communicate with people. P.D.R. suffers permanent injury that requires expensive, long-term medical and psychiatric treatment. P.D.R. brought a tort action against OEP and HJ and sought actual and punitive damages against both of them.

Negligence of the Independent Contractor

The jury had little trouble finding that OEP had breached its duty of care and was liable. Evidence showed that other criminal activity had occurred previously on the premises but that OEP had failed to warn guests, including P.D.R., of the danger. In fact, OEP management actively discouraged criminal investigations by the sheriff's deputies, thus minimizing any deterrent effect they may have had. Further evidence showed that the dark and secluded stairwell area where P.D.R. was dragged was a security hazard that should have been boarded up or better lit.

Liability of the Principal

The jury also found HJ liable to P.D.R. under the doctrine of **apparent agency**. The appellate court stated: "While OEP might not be HJ's agent for all purposes, the signs, national advertising, uniformity or building design and color schemes allow the public to assume that this and other similar motor lodges are under the same ownership. An HJ official testified that it was the HJ marketing strategy to appear as a chain that sells a product across the nation." The court continued, "There was sufficient evidence for the jury to reasonably conclude that HJ represented to the traveling public that it could expect a particular level of service at a Howard Johnson Motor Lodge. The uniformity of signs, design and color schemes easily leads the public to believe that each motor lodge is under common ownership or conforms to common standards, and the jury could find they are intended to do so." The appellate court upheld an award of $750,000 compensatory damages against OEP and HJ jointly. *Orlando Executive Park, Inc. v. P.D.R.*, 402 So.2d 442, 1981 Fla. App. Lexis 20565 (Fla. App.) ■

Agency by Ratification

Agency by ratification occurs when (1) a person misrepresents himself or herself as another's agent when, in fact, he or she is not and (2) the purported principal ratifies (accepts) the unauthorized act. In such cases, the principal is bound to perform, and the agent is relieved of any liability for misrepresentation.

agency by ratification
An agency that occurs when (1) a person misrepresents him- or herself as another's agent when in fact he or she is not and (2) the purported principal ratifies the unauthorized act.

Consider This Example Bill Levine sees a house for sale and thinks his friend Sherry Maxwell would want it. Bill Levine enters into a contract to purchase the house from the seller and signs the contract "Bill Levine, agent for Sherry Maxwell." Because Bill is not Sherry Maxwell's agent, she is not bound to the contract. However, if Sherry agrees to purchase the house, there is an agency by ratification. The ratification "relates back" to the moment Bill Levine entered into the contract. Upon ratification of the contract, Sherry Maxwell is obligated to purchase the house.

Concept Summary Formation of Agency Relationships

Type of Agency	Definition	Enforcement of the Contract
Express	Authority is expressly given to the agent by the principal.	Principal and third party are bound to the contract.
Implied	Authority is implied from the conduct of the parties, custom and usage of trade, or act incidental to carrying out the agent's duties.	Principal and third party acts are bound to the contract.
Apparent	Authority created when the principal leads a third party into believing that the agent has authority.	Principal and third party are bound to the contract.
By ratification	Acts of the agent committed outside the scope of his or her authority.	Principal and third party are not bound to the contract unless the principal ratifies the contract.

Principal's and Agent's Duties

The principal and the agent owe each other certain duties. These duties are discussed in the paragraphs that follow.

Principal's Duty of Compensation

A principal owes a **duty to compensate** an agent for services provided. Usually, the agency contract (whether written or oral) specifies the compensation to be paid. The principal must pay this amount either upon the completion of the agency or at some other mutually agreeable time.

duty to compensate
A duty that a principal owes to pay an agreed-upon amount to the agent either upon the completion of the agency or at some other mutually agreeable time.

If there is no agreement as to the amount of compensation, the law implies a promise that the principal will pay the agent the customary fee paid in the industry. If the compensation cannot be established by custom, the principal owes a duty to pay the reasonable value of the agent's services.

There is no duty to compensate a gratuitous agent. However, gratuitous agents who agree to provide their services free of charge may be paid voluntarily.

Certain types of agents traditionally perform their services on a *contingency-fee* basis. Under this type of arrangement, the principal owes a duty to pay the agent the agreed-upon contingency fee only if the agency is completed. For example, real estate brokers, finders, lawyers, and salespersons often work on this basis.

Principal's Duties of Reimbursement and Indemnification

In carrying out an agency, an agent may spend his or her own money on the principal's behalf. Unless otherwise agreed, the principal owes a **duty to reimburse** the agent for all such expenses if they were (1) authorized by the principal, (2) within the scope of the agency, and (3) necessary to discharge the agent's duties in carrying out the agency. For example, a principal must reimburse an agent for authorized business trips taken on the principal's behalf.

A principal also owes a **duty to indemnify** the agent for any losses the agent suffers because of the principal. This duty usually arises where an agent is held liable for the principal's misconduct. For example, suppose an agent enters into an authorized contract with a third party on the principal's behalf, the principal fails to perform on the contract, and the third party recovers a judgment against the agent. The agent can recover indemnification of this amount from the principal.

Principal's Duty of Cooperation

Unless otherwise agreed, the principal owes a **duty to cooperate** with and assist the agent in the performance of the agent's duties and the accomplishment of the agency. For example, unless otherwise agreed, a principal who employs a real estate agent to sell her house owes a duty to allow the agent to show the house to prospective purchasers during reasonable hours.

Agent's Duty of Performance

An agent who enters into a contract with a principal has two distinct obligations: (1) performing the lawful duties expressed in the contract and (2) meeting the standards of reasonable care, skill, and diligence implicit in all contracts. Collectively, these duties are referred to as the agent's **duty of performance**.

duty of performance
An agent's duty to a principal that includes (1) performing the lawful duties expressed in the contract and (2) meeting the standards of reasonable care, skill, and diligence implicit in all contracts.

Normally, an agent is required to render the same standard of care, skill, and diligence that a fictitious reasonable agent in the same occupation would render in the same locality and under the same circumstances. For example, a general medical practitioner in a rural area would be held to the standard of a reasonable general practitioner in rural areas. That standard might be different for a general medical practitioner in a big city. In some professions, such as accounting, a national standard of performance (such as the "generally accepted accounting principle") is imposed. If an agent holds himself or herself as possessing higher-than-customary skills, the agent will be held to this higher standard of performance. For example, a lawyer who claims to be a specialist in securities law will be held to a reasonable specialist-in-securities-law standard.

An agent who does not perform his or her express duties or fails to use the standard degree of care, skill, or diligence is liable to the principal for breach of contract. An agent who has negligently (or intentionally) failed to perform properly is also liable in tort.

Agent's Duty of Notification

In the course of an agency, the agent usually learns information that is important to the principal. This information may come from third parties or other sources. The agent's duty to notify the principal of such information is called the **duty of notification**. The agent is liable to the principal for any injuries resulting from a breach of this duty.

Imputed Knowledge Most information learned by an agent in the course of an agency is **imputed** to the principal. This means that the principal is assumed to know what the agent knows. This is so even if the agent does not tell the principal certain relevant information.

imputed knowledge
Information that is learned by an agent that is attributed to the principal.

Agent's Duty of Accountability

Unless otherwise agreed, an agent owes a duty to maintain an accurate accounting of all transactions undertaken on the principal's behalf. This **duty of accountability** includes keeping records of all property and money received and expended during the course of the agency. A principal has a right to demand an accounting from the agent at any time, and the agent owes a legal duty to make the accounting. This duty also requires the agent to (1) maintain a separate account for the principal and (2) use the principal's property in an authorized manner.

duty of accountability
A duty that an agent owes to maintain an accurate accounting of all transactions undertaken on the principal's behalf.

Any property, money, or other benefit received by the agent in the course of an agency belongs to the principal. For example, all secret profits received by the agent are the property of the principal. If an agent breaches the agency contract, the principal can sue the agent to recover damages caused by the breach. The court can impose a *constructive trust* on any secret profits or property purchased with secret profits for the benefit of the principal.

Ethics in Business

Agent's Duty of Loyalty

Because the agency relationship is based on trust and confidence, an agent owes the principal a **duty of loyalty** in all agency-related matters. Thus, an agent owes a fiduciary duty not to act adversely to the interests of the principal. If this duty is breached, the agent is liable to the principal. The most common types of breaches of loyalty by an agent are discussed here:

- ***Self-dealing.*** Agents are generally prohibited from undisclosed self-dealing with the principal. For example, a real estate agent who is employed to purchase real estate for a principal cannot secretly sell his own property in the transaction. However, the deal is lawful if the principal agrees to buy the property after the agent discloses his or her ownership.
- ***Usurping an opportunity.*** An agent cannot usurp an opportunity that belongs to the principal. For example, a third-party offer to an agent must be conveyed to the principal. The agent cannot appropriate the opportunity for himself or herself unless the principal rejects it after due consideration. Opportunities to purchase real estate, businesses, products, ideas, and other property are subject to this rule.
- ***Competing with the principal.*** Agents are prohibited from competing with the principal during the course of an agency unless the principal agrees to the competition. The reason for this rule is that an agent cannot meet his or her duty of loyalty when his or her personal interests conflict with the principal's interests. If the parties have not entered into an enforceable covenant-not-to-compete, an agent is free to compete with the principal once the agency has ended.
- ***Misuse of confidential information.*** In the course of an agency, the agent often acquires confidential information about the principal's affairs (e.g., business plans, technological innovations, customer lists, trade secrets). The agent is under a legal duty not to disclose or misuse such information either during or after the course of the agency. There is no prohibition against using general information, knowledge, or experience acquired during the course of the agency.
- ***Dual agency.*** An agent cannot meet a duty of loyalty to two parties who have conflicting interests. Dual agency occurs when an agent acts for two or more different principals in the same transaction. This practice is generally prohibited unless all the parties involved in the transaction agree to it. If an agent acts as an undisclosed dual agent, he or she must forfeit all compensation received in the transaction. Some agents, such as middlemen and finders, are not considered dual agents. This is because they only bring interested parties together; they do not take part in any negotiations.

Ethics Issues

1. Describe an agent's fiduciary duty of loyalty.
2. What remedies should be imposed against an agent who breaches his or her loyalty to the principal?

Contract Liability to Third Parties

A principal who authorizes an agent to enter into a contract with a third party is liable on the contract. Thus, the third party can enforce the contract against the principal and recover damages from the principal if the principal fails to perform it.

The agent can also be held liable on the contract in certain circumstances. Imposition of such liability depends on whether the agency is classified as (1) *fully disclosed*, (2) *partially disclosed*, or (3) *undisclosed*.

Fully Disclosed Agency

fully disclosed agency
An agency in which the contracting third party knows (1) that the agent is acting for a principal and (2) the identity of the principal.

A **fully disclosed agency** results if the third party entering into the contract knows (1) that the agent is acting as an agent for a principal and (2) the actual identity of the principal. The third party has the requisite knowledge if the principal's identity is disclosed to the third party by either the agent or some other source.

In a fully disclosed agency, the contract is between the principal and the third party. Thus, the principal, who is called a *fully disclosed principal*, is liable on the contract. The agent, however, is not liable on the contract because the third party relied on the principal's credit and reputation when the contract was made. An agent is liable on the contract if he or she guarantees that the principal will perform the contract.

The agent's signature on a contract entered into on the principal's behalf is important. It can establish the agent's status and, therefore, his or her liability. For instance, in a fully disclosed agency, the agent's signature must clearly indicate that he or she is acting as an agent for a specifically identified principal. Examples of proper signatures include "Allison Adams, agent for Peter Perceival," "Peter Perceival, by Allison Adams, agent," and "Peter Perceival, by Allison Adams."

Consider This Example Poran Kawamara decides to sell her house and hires Mark Robbins, a real estate broker, to list and sell the house for a price of $1 million. They agree that Mark will disclose the existence of the agency and the identity of the principal to interested third parties. This is a fully disclosed agency. Mark shows the house to Heather, a prospective buyer, and discloses to Heather that he is acting as an agent for Poran. Heather makes an offer for the house at the $1 million asking price. Mark signs the contract with Heather on behalf of Poran by signing "Mark Robbins, agent for Poran Kawamara." Poran is liable on the contract with Heather, but Mark is not liable on the contract with Heather.

Partially Disclosed Agency

partially disclosed agency
An agency in which the contracting third party knows that the agent is acting for a principal but does not know the identity of the principal.

A **partially disclosed agency** occurs if the agent discloses his or her agency status but does not reveal the principal's identity and the third party does not know the principal's identity from another source. The nondisclosure may be because (1) the principal instructs the agent not to disclose his or her identity to the third party or (2) the agent forgets to tell the third party the principal's identity. In this kind of agency, the principal is called a *partially disclosed principal.*

In a partially disclosed agency, both the principal and the agent are liable on third-party contracts. This is because the third party must rely on the agent's reputation, integrity, and credit because the principal is unidentified. If the agent is made to pay the contract, the agent can sue the principal for indemnification. The third party and the agent can agree to relieve the agent's liability. A partially disclosed agency can be created either expressly or by mistake.

Consider These Examples Assume that a principal employs an agent to purchase a business on its behalf. The principal and agent expressly agree that the agent will disclose the existence of the agency to third parties but will not disclose the identity of the principal. The agent finds a business that is for sale, and he discloses to the seller that he is acting as an agent but does not disclose the identity of the principal. The seller agrees to sell the business, and the agent signs "Allison Adams, agent." Here, there is a partially disclosed agency. The principal is liable on the contract with the third-party seller; the agent is also liable on the contract with the third-party seller.

If instead a principal and an agent agree that the agent will represent the principal to purchase a business and that the agent will disclose the existence of the agency and the identity of the principal to third parties, this is a fully disclosed agency. Suppose the agent finds a suitable business for the principal and contracts to purchase the business on behalf of the principal, but the agent mistakenly signs the contract with the third party "Allison Adams, agent." This is a partially disclosed agency. The principal is liable on the contract with the third party, but the agent is also liable.

Undisclosed Agency

An **undisclosed agency** occurs when the third party is unaware of either the existence of an agency or the principal's identity. The principal is called an *undisclosed principal*. Undisclosed agencies are lawful. They are often used when the principal feels that the terms of a contract would be changed if his or her identity were known. For example, a wealthy person may use an undisclosed agency to purchase property if he thinks the seller would raise the price of the property if his identity were revealed.

undisclosed agency
An agency in which the contracting third party does not know of either the existence of the agency or the principal's identity.

In an undisclosed agency, both the principal and the agent are liable on the contract with the third party. This is because the agent, by not divulging that he or she is acting as an agent, becomes a principal to the contract. The third party relies on the reputation and credit of the agent in entering into the contract. If the principal fails to perform the contract, the third party can recover against the principal of the agent. If the agent is made to pay the contract, he or she can recover indemnification from the principal. An undisclosed agency can be created either expressly or by mistake.

Consider These Examples Assume that The Walt Disney Company wants to open a new theme park in Chicago but needs to first acquire land for the park. Disney employs an agent to work on its behalf to acquire the needed property, with an express agreement that the agent will not disclose the existence of the agency to a third-party seller. If a seller agrees to sell the needed land, and the agent signs her name "Allison Adams," without disclosing the existence of the agency, it is an undisclosed agency. Disney is liable on the contract with the third-party seller and so is the agent.

Suppose instead that Disney hires an agent to purchase land on its behalf and they agree that the agent will represent Disney in a fully disclosed agency—that is, the agent is to disclose the existence of the agency and the identity of the principal to the third-party seller. If the agent locates a third-party seller who is willing to enter into a contract to sell the land, but the agent mistakenly signs the contract "Allison Adams," without disclosing the agency to the third party, it is an undisclosed agency. Disney is liable on the contract with the third-party seller, and the agent is also liable.

Agent Exceeding the Scope of Authority

implied warranty of authority
An implied guarantee that an agent who enters into a contract on behalf of another party has the authority to do so.

ratification
A principal's acceptance of an agent's unauthorized contract.

An agent who enters into a contract on behalf of another party impliedly warrants that he or she has the authority to do so. This is called the agent's **implied warranty of authority**. If the agent exceeds the scope of his or her authority, the principal is not liable on the contract unless the principal **ratifies** it. The agent, however, is liable to the third party for breaching the implied warranty of authority. To recover, the third party must show (1) reliance on the agent's representation and (2) ignorance of the agent's lack of status.

Consider This Example Suppose Sam, Sara, Satchel, Samantha, and Simone form a rock band called SSSS. SSSS is a voluntary association without any legal status. Sam enters into a contract with Rocky's Musical Instruments to purchase instruments and equipment for the band on credit and signs the contract "Sam, for SSSS." When SSSS fails to pay the debt, Rocky's can sue Sam and recover. Sam must pay the debt because he breached his implied warranty of authority when he acted as an agent for a *nonexistent principal*; that is, the purported principal was not a legal entity on which liability could be imposed.

Concept Summary Contract Liability of Principals and Agents to Third Parties

Type of Agency	Principal Liable	Agent Liable
Fully disclosed	Yes	No, unless the agent (1) acts as a principal or (2) guarantees the performance of the contract
Partially disclosed	Yes	Yes, unless the third party relieves the agent's liability
Undisclosed	Yes	Yes
Nonexistent	No, unless the principal ratifies the contract	Yes, the agent is liable for breaching the implied warranty of authority

Grand Hotel, Mackinac Island, Michigan. This hotel, as the employer, is liable for injuries caused by the negligent acts of its employees that are committed while the employees are acting within their scope of employment.

Tort Liability to Third Parties

A principal and an agent are each personally liable for their own tortious conduct. The principal is liable for the tortious conduct of an agent who is acting within the scope of his or her authority. The agent, however, is liable for the tortious conduct of the principal only if he or she directly or indirectly participates in or aids and abets the principal's conduct.

The courts have applied a broad and flexible standard in interpreting scope of authority in the context of employment. Although other factors may also be considered, the courts rely on the following factors to determine whether an agent's conduct occurred within the scope of his or her employment:

- Was the act specifically requested or authorized by the principal?
- Was it the kind of act that the agent was employed to perform?
- Did the act occur substantially within the time period of employment authorized by the principal?
- Did the act occur substantially within the location of employment authorized by the employer?
- Was the agent advancing the principal's purpose when the act occurred?

Where liability is found, tort remedies are available to the injured party. These remedies include recovery for medical expenses, lost wages, pain, and suffering, emotional distress, and, in some cases, punitive damages. As discussed in the following paragraphs, the three main sources of tort liability for principals and agents are misrepresentation, negligence, and intentional torts.

An agent's scope of authority was at issue in the following case.

Case 19.1 Tort Liability

Edgewater Motels, Inc. v. Gatzke and Walgreen Co.
277 N.W.2d 11, 1979 Minn. Lexis 1381
Supreme Court of Minnesota

Background and Facts

Arlen Gatzke (Gatzke) was a district manager for the Walgreen Company (Walgreen). In August 1979, Gatzke was sent to Duluth, Minnesota, to supervise the opening of a new Walgreen store. In Duluth, Gatzke stayed at the Edgewater Motel (Edgewater). While in Duluth, Gatzke was "on call" 24 hours a day to other Walgreen stores located in his territory. About midnight on the evening of August 23, 1979, Gatzke, after working 17 hours that day, went with several other Walgreen employees to a restaurant and bar to drink. Within 1 hour's time, Gatzke had consumed three doubles and one single brandy Manhattan. About 1:30 A.M., he went back to the Edgewater Motel and filled out his expense report. Soon thereafter, a fire broke out in Gatzke's motel room. Gatzke escaped, but the fire spread and caused extensive damage to the motel. Evidence showed that Gatzke smoked two packs of cigarettes a day. An expert fire reconstruction witness testified that the fire started from a lit cigarette in or next to the wastepaper basket in Gatzke's room. Edgewater sued Gatzke, and Walgreen. The parties stipulated that the damage to the Edgewater Motel was $330,360. The jury returned a verdict against defendants Gatzke and Walgreen. The court granted Walgreen's posttrial motion for judgment notwithstanding the verdict. Plaintiff Edgewater and defendant Gatzke appealed.

Issue

Was Gatzke's act of smoking within his "scope of employment," making his principal, the Walgreen Company, vicariously liable for his negligence?

(continued)

Edgewater Motels, Inc. v. Gatzke and Walgreen Co.
277 N.W.2d 11, 1979 Minn. Lexis 1381
Supreme Court of Minnesota
(continued)

In the Language of the Court

After careful consideration of the issue we are persuaded by the reasoning of the courts that hold that smoking can be an act within an employee's scope of employment. It seems only logical to conclude that an employee does not abandon his employment as a matter of law while temporarily acting for his personal comfort when such activities involve only slight deviations from work that are reasonable under the circumstances. We hold that an employer can be held vicariously liable for his employee's negligent smoking of a cigarette if he was otherwise acting in the scope of his employment at the time of the negligent act.

The record contains a reasonable basis from which a jury could find that Gatzke was involved in serving his employer's interests at the time he was at the bar. Gatzke testified that, while at the Bellows, he discussed the operation of the newly opened Walgreen's store with other Walgreen employees. Additionally, the record indicates that Gatzke was an executive type of employee who had no set working hours. He considered himself a 24-hour-a-day man; his room at the Edgewater Motel was his "office away from home." It was therefore also reasonable for the jury to determine that the filling out of his expense account was done within authorized time and space limits of his employment.

Decision and Remedy

The state supreme court held that Gatzke's negligent act of smoking was within the scope of his employment while acting as an employee of the Walgreen Company. The supreme court reinstated the verdict awarding damages to plaintiff Edgewater Motels, Inc.

Business and Ethics Questions

1. Should smoking cigarettes be held to be within an employee's scope of employment? Why or why not?
2. Do employers owe a duty to police the personal habits of their employees?
3. Because of the dangers of smoking, would employers be justified in hiring only nonsmokers as employees?

Negligence

Principals are liable for the negligent conduct of agents acting within the scope of their employment. This liability is based on the common law doctrine of **respondeat superior** ("let the master answer"), which, in turn, is based on the legal theory of *vicarious liability* (liability without fault). In other words, the principal is liable because of his or her employment contract with the negligent agent, not because the principal was personally at fault.

respondeat superior
A rule that says an employer is liable for the tortious conduct of its employees or agents while they are acting within the scope of its authority.

This doctrine rests on the principle that if someone (i.e., the principal) expects to derive certain benefits from acting through others (i.e., an agent), that person should also bear the liability for injuries caused to third persons by the negligent conduct of an agent who is acting within the scope of his or her employment.

Frolic and Detour

Agents sometimes do things during the course of their employment to further their own interests rather than the principal's. For example, an agent might take a detour to run a personal errand while on assignment for the principal. This is commonly referred to as a **frolic and detour**. Negligence actions stemming from frolic and detour are examined on a case-by-case basis. Agents are always personally liable for their tortious conduct in such situations. Principals are generally relived of liability if the agent's frolic and detour is substantial. However, if the deviation is minor, the principal is liable for the injuries caused by the agent's tortious conduct.

frolic and detour
A situation in which an agent does something during the course of his or her employment to further his or her own interests rather than the principal's.

Consider This Example A salesperson stops home for lunch while on an assignment for his principal. While leaving his home, the agent hits and injures a pedestrian with his automobile. The principal would be liable if the agent's home were not too far out of the way from the agent's assignment. However, the principal would not be liable if an agent who is supposed to be on assignment to Los Angeles flies to San Francisco to meet a friend and is involved in an accident. The facts and circumstances of each case determine its outcome.

The "Coming and Going" Rule

Under the common law, a principal is generally not liable for injuries caused by its agents and employees while they are on their way to or from work. This **"coming and going" rule** applies even if the principal supplies the agent's automobile or other transportation or pays for gasoline, repairs, and other automobile operating expenses. This rule is quite logical. Because principals do not control where their agents and employees live, they should not be held liable for tortious conduct of agents on their way to and from work.

"coming and going" rule
A rule that says a principal is generally not liable for injuries caused by its agents and employees while they are on their way to and from work.

Dual-Purpose Mission

Sometimes, a principal requests that an agent run errands or conduct other acts on its behalf while the agent is on personal business. In this case, the agent is on a **dual-purpose mission**. That is, he or she is acting partly for himself or herself and partly for the principal. Most jurisdictions hold both the principal and the agent liable if the agent injures someone while on such a mission.

dual-purpose mission
An errand or another act that a principal requests of an agent while the agent is on his or her own personal business.

Consider This Example Suppose a principal asks an employee to drop off a package at a client's office on the employee's way home. If the employee negligently injures a pedestrian while on this dual-purpose mission, the principal is liable to the pedestrian.

Intentional Torts

Intentional torts include such acts as assault, battery, false imprisonment, and other intentional conduct that cause injury to another person. A principal is not liable for the intentional torts of agents and employees that are committed outside the principal's scope of business. For example, if an employee attends a sporting event after working hours and gets into a fight with another spectator at the event, the employer is not liable.

However, a principal is liable under the doctrine of vicarious liability for intentional torts of agents and employees committed within the agent's scope of employment. The courts generally apply one of the following tests in determining whether an agent's intentional torts were committed within the agent's scope of employment:

- ***The motivation test.*** Under the **motivation test**, if the agent's motivation in committing the intentional tort is to promote the principal's business, the principal is liable for any injury caused by the tort. However, if the agent's motivation in committing the intentional tort was personal, the principal is not liable, even if the tort took place during business hours or on business premises. For example, a principal is not liable if his agent was motivated by jealousy to beat up someone on the job who dated her boyfriend.

motivation test
A test that says if the agent's motivation in committing an intentional tort is to promote the principal's business, then the principal is liable for any injury caused by the tort.

work-related test

A test that says if an agent commits an intentional tort within a work-related time or space, the principal is liable for any injury caused by the agent's intentional tort.

- ***Work-related test.*** Some jurisdictions have rejected the motivation test as too narrow. These jurisdictions apply the **work-related test** instead. Under this test, if an agent commits an intentional tort within a work-related time or space—for example, during working hours or on the principal's premises—the principal is liable for any injuries caused by the agent's intentional torts. Under this test, the agent's motivation is immaterial.

In the following case, the court applied the work-related test in determining whether an employer was liable for an agent's intentional tort.

Case 19.2

Intentional Tort

Desert Cab Inc. v. Marino

823 P.2d 898, 1992 Nev. Lexis 6

Supreme Court of Nevada

Background and Facts

On October 6, 1986, Maria Marino, a cab driver with Yellow-Checkered Cab Company (Yellow Cab), and James Edwards, a cab driver with Desert Cab Inc. (Desert Cab), parked their cabs at the taxicab stand at the Sundance Hotel and Casino in Las Vegas to await fares. Marino's cab occupied the first position in the line, and Edwards's cab occupied the third. As Marino stood alongside her cab, conversing with the driver of another taxi, Edwards began verbally harassing her from inside his cab. When Marino approached Edwards to inquire as to the reason for the harassment, a verbal argument ensued. Edwards jumped from his cab, grabbed Marino by her neck and shoulders, began choking her, and threw her in front of his taxicab. A bystander pulled Edwards off Marino and escorted her back to her cab. Marino sustained injuries that rendered her unable to work for a time. Edwards was convicted of misdemeanor assault and battery. Marino brought a personal injury action against Desert Cab. The jury found Desert Cab liable and awarded Marino $65,000. Desert Cab appealed.

Issue

Is Desert Cab liable for the intentional tort of its employee?

In the Language of the Court

This district court admitted into evidence the judgment of Edwards' misdemeanor assault and battery conviction. The court found this evidence to conclusively prove Edwards' civil liability to Marino. Edwards' judgment of conviction provides conclusive evidence of his civil liability to Marino.

A finding that Edwards committed a wrongful act by attacking Marino is a prerequisite to imposing liability upon Desert Cab. In order to find Desert Cab liable, Marino still had to establish that Desert Cab was "responsible" for Edwards' conduct. Desert Cab could be found "responsible" only if Marino proved that the attack arose out of the course and scope of Edwards' employment with Desert Cab. We affirm the judgment of the district court.

Decision and Remedy

The appellate court held that Desert Cab was liable for the intentional tort committed by its employee.

Business and Ethics Questions

1. Should employers be held liable for the intentional torts of their employees?
2. Did Desert Cab act ethically in denying liability?
3. Should employers give prospective employees psychological examinations to determine whether they have any dangerous propensities?

Misrepresentation

intentional misrepresentation

An agent's untrue statement that he or she knows is not true. Also called *fraud* or *deceit*.

Intentional misrepresentations are also known as **fraud** or **deceit**. They occur when an agent makes statements that he or she knows are not true. An *innocent misrepresentation* occurs when an agent negligently makes a misrepresentation to a third party.

A principal is liable for the intentional and innocent misrepresentations made by an agent acting within the scope of employment. The third party can either (1) rescind the contract with the principal and recover any consideration paid or (2) affirm the contract and recover damages.

Consider This Example Assume that (1) a car salesman is employed to sell the principal's car and (2) the principal tells the agent that the car was repaired after it was involved in a major accident. If the agent intentionally tells the buyer that the car was never involved in an accident, the agent has made an intentional misrepresentation. Both the principal and the agent are liable for this misrepresentation.

Concept Summary *Tort Liability of Principals and Agents to Third Parties*

Agent's Conduct	Agent Liable	Principal Liable
Negligence	Yes	The principal is liable under the doctrine of *respondeat superior* if the agent's negligent act was committed within his or her scope of employment.
Intentional tort	Yes	Motivation test: The principal is liable if the agent's motivation in committing the intentional tort was to promote the principal's business.
	Yes	Work-related test: The principal is liable if the agent committed the intentional tort within work-related time and space.
Misrepresentation	Yes	The principal is liable for the intentional and innocent misrepresentations made by an agent acting within the scope of his or her authority.

Independent Contractor

Principals often employ outsiders—that is, persons and businesses that are not employees—to perform certain tasks on their behalf. These persons and businesses are called **independent contractors**. For example, lawyers, doctors, dentists, consultants, stockbrokers, architects, certified public accountants, real estate brokers, and plumbers are examples of people who commonly act as independent contractors. The party that employs an independent contractor is called a **principal**.

Consider This Example Jin is a lawyer who has her own law firm and specializes in real estate law. Raymond, a real estate developer, hires Jin to represent him in the purchase of land. Raymond is the principal, and Jin is the independent contractor.

A principal–independent contractor relationship is depicted in Exhibit 19.2.

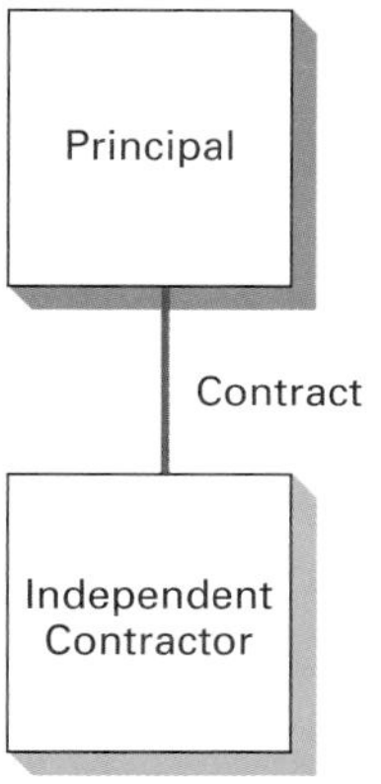

Exhibit 19.2

Principal–Independent Contractor Relationship

Factors for Determining Independent Contractor Status

independent contractor
"A person who contracts with another to do something for him who is not controlled by the other nor subject to the other's right to control with respect to his physical conduct in the performance of the undertaking" [*Restatement (Second) of Agency*].

Section 2 of the *Restatement (Second) of Agency* defines an **independent contractor** as "a person who contracts with another to do something for him who is not controlled by the other nor subject to the other's right to control with respect to his physical conduct in the performance of the undertaking." Independent contractors usually work for a number of clients, have their own offices, hire employees, and control the performance of their work.

The crucial factor in determining whether someone is an independent contractor or an employee is the *degree of control* the principal has over the agent. Critical factors in determining independent contractor status include:

- Whether the worker is engaged in a distinct occupation or an independently established business
- The length of time the agent has been employed by the principal
- The amount of time that the agent works for the principal
- Whether the principal supplies the tools and equipment used in the work
- The method of payment, whether by time or by the job
- The degree of skill necessary to complete the task
- Whether the worker hires employees to assist him or her
- Whether the employer has the right to control the manner and means of accomplishing the desired result

If an examination of these factors shows that the principal asserts little control, the person is an independent contractor. Substantial control indicates an employer–employee relationship. Labeling someone an "independent contractor" is only one factor in determining whether independent contractor status exists.

Liability for an Independent Contractor's Contracts

A principal can authorize an independent contractor to enter into contracts. Principals are bound by the authorized contracts of their independent contractors. For example, suppose a client hires a lawyer as an independent contractor to represent her in a civil lawsuit against a defendant to recover monetary damages. If the client authorizes the lawyer to settle a case within a certain dollar amount and the lawyer does so, the settlement agreement is binding.

If an independent contractor enters into a contract with a third party on behalf of the principal without express or implied authority from the principal to do so, the principal is not liable on the contract.

Liability for an Independent Contractor's Torts

Generally, a principal is not liable for the torts of its independent contractors. Independent contractors are personally liable for their own torts. The rationale behind this rule is that principals do not control the means by which the results are accomplished.

Consider This Example Qixia hires Harold, a lawyer and an independent contractor, to represent her in a court case. While driving to the courthouse to represent Qixia at trial, Harold negligently causes an automobile accident in which Mildred is severely injured. Harold is liable to Mildred because he caused the accident. Qixia is not liable to Mildred because Harold was an independent contractor when he caused the accident.

Ethics in Business

Principal Liable for Repo Man's Tort

Yvonne Sanchez borrowed money from MBank El Paso (MBank) to purchase an automobile. She gave MBank a security interest in the vehicle to secure the loan. When Sanchez defaulted on the loan, MBank hired El Paso Recovery Service, an independent contractor, to repossess the automobile. The two men who were dispatched to Sanchez's house found the car parked in the driveway and hooked it to a tow truck. Sanchez demanded that they cease their efforts and leave the premises, but the men nonetheless continued with the repossession. Before the men could tow the automobile into the street, Sanchez jumped into the car, locked the doors, and refused to leave. The men towed the car at a high rate of speed to the repossession yard. They parked the car in the fenced repossession yard, with Sanchez inside, and padlocked the gate. Sanchez was left in the repossession lot with a Doberman Pinscher guard dog loose in the yard. Later, she was rescued by the police. The law prohibits the repossession of a vehicle if a breach of peace would occur. Sanchez filed suit against MBank, alleging that it was liable for the tortious conduct of El Paso Recovery Service. The trial court granted summary judgment to MBank, but the court of appeals reversed. MBank appealed.

The supreme court of Texas held that MBank, the principal, was liable for the tortious conduct of El Paso Recovery Service, an independent contractor. The court held that the act of repossessing an automobile from a defaulting debtor is an inherently dangerous activity and a nondelegable duty. The court concluded that El Paso Recovery Service had breached the peace in repossessing the car from Sanchez and caused her physical and emotional harm. The court held that MBank, the principal, could not escape liability by hiring an independent contractor to do this task. The court found MBank liable to Sanchez. *MBank El Paso, N.S. v. Sanchez*, 836 S.W.2d 151, 1992 Tex. Lexis 97 (Tex.)

Ethics Issues

1. Did the independent contractor act responsibly in this case?
2. Should the principal bank have been held liable in this case? Why or why not?

Lighthouse, Straits of Mackinac. Common carriers, such as freighters and other ships that carry goods for others, are independent contractors. Risk of loss of goods depends on the shipping terms used in the shipping contract.

Termination of an Agency

An agency contract is similar to other contracts in that it can be terminated either by an act of the parties or by operation of law. These different methods of termination are discussed next. Note that once an agency relationship is terminated, the agent can no longer represent the principal or bind the principal to contracts.

Termination by Acts of the Parties

The parties to an agency contract can terminate the agency contract by agreement or by their actions. The four methods of termination of an agency relationship by acts of the parties are:

1. ***Mutual agreement.*** As with any other contract, the parties to an agency contract can mutually agree to terminate their agreement. By doing so, the parties relieve each other of any further rights, duties, obligations, or powers provided for in the agency contract. Either party can propose the termination of an agency contract.
2. ***Lapse of time.*** Agency contracts are often written for a specific period of time. The agency terminates when the specified time period elapses. Suppose, for example, that the principal and agent enter into an agency contract "beginning January 1, 2006, and ending December 31, 2008." The agency automatically terminates on December 31, 2008. If the agency contract does not set forth a specific termination date, the agency terminates after a reasonable time has elapsed. The courts often look to the custom of an industry in determining the reasonable time for the termination of an agency.
3. ***Purpose achieved.*** A principal can employ an agent for the time it takes to accomplish a certain task, purpose, or result. Such agencies automatically terminate when they are completed. For example, suppose a principal employs a licensed real estate broker to sell his house. The agency terminates when the house is sold and the principal pays the broker the agreed-upon compensation.
4. ***Occurrence of a specified event.*** An agency contract can specify that the agency exists until a specified event occurs. The agency terminates when the specified event happens. For example, if a principal employs an agent to take care of her dog until she returns from a trip, the agency terminates when the principal returns from the trip.

Termination by Operation of Law

Agency contracts can be **terminated by operation of law** as well as by agreement. The six methods of terminating an agency relationship by operation of law are:

1. ***Death.*** The death of either the principal or the agent terminates an agency relationship. This rule is based on the old legal principle that because a dead person cannot act, no one can act for him or her. Note that an agency terminates even if one party is unaware of the other party's death. An agent's actions that take place after the principal's death do not bind the principal's estate.
2. ***Insanity.*** The insanity of either the principal or the agent generally terminates an agency relationship. A few states have modified this rule to provide that a contract entered into by an agent on behalf of an insane principal is enforceable if (1) the insane person has not been adjudged insane, (2) the third party does not have knowledge of the principal's insanity at the time of contracting, and (3) the enforcement of the contract will prevent injustice.
3. ***Bankruptcy.*** An agency relationship is terminated if the principal is declared bankrupt. Bankruptcy requires the filing of a petition for bankruptcy under the federal bankruptcy law. With few exceptions, neither the appointment of a state court receiver nor the principal's financial difficulties or insolvency terminates the agency relationship. The agent's bankruptcy usually does not terminate an agency unless the agent's credit standing is important to the agency relationship.
4. ***Impossibility.*** An agency relationship terminates if a situation arises that makes its fulfillment impossible. The following circumstances can lead to termination on this ground:
   - ***The loss or destruction of the subject matter of the agency.*** For example, assume that a principal employs an agent to sell his horse, but the horse dies before it is sold. The agency relationship terminates at the moment the horse dies.

- ***The loss of a required qualification.*** For example, suppose a principal employs a licensed real estate agent to sell her house, and the real estate agent's license is revoked. The agency terminates at the moment the license is revoked.
- ***A change in the law.*** For example, suppose that a principal employs an agent to trap alligators. If a law is passed that makes trapping alligators illegal, the agency contract terminates when the law becomes effective.

5. ***Changed circumstances.*** An agency terminates when there is an unusual change in circumstances that would lead the agent to believe that the principal's original instructions should no longer be valid. For example, a principal employs a licensed real estate agent to sell a farm for $100,000. The agent thereafter learns that oil has been discovered on the property and makes it worth $1 million. The agency terminates because of this change in circumstances.
6. ***War.*** The outbreak of a war between the principal's country and the agent's country terminates an agency relationship between the parties. Such an occurrence usually makes the performance of the agency contract impossible.

Notification Required at the Termination of an Agency

If an agency is terminated by agreement between the parties, the principal is under a duty to give certain third parties notification of the termination. Unless otherwise required, the notice can be from the principal or some other source (e.g., the agent). If an agency terminates by operation of law, there is no duty to notify third parties about the termination, however.

The termination of an agency extinguishes an agent's actual authority to act on the principal's behalf. However, if the principal fails to give the proper notice of termination to a third party, the agent still has apparent authority to bind the principal to contracts with these third parties. If this happens, the contract is enforceable against the principal. The principal's only recourse is against the agent to recover damages caused by these unauthorized contracts.

The following notification requirements must be met:

- ***Parties who dealt with the agent.*** Direct notice of termination must be given to all persons with whom the agent dealt. Although the notice may be either written or oral, it is better practice to give written notice.
- ***Parties who have knowledge of the agency.*** The principal must give direct or constructive notice to any third party who has knowledge of the agency but with whom the agent has not dealt. Direct notice is often in the form of a letter. Constructive notice usually consists of placing a notice of the termination of the agency in a newspaper serving the relevant community. This notice is effective even against persons who do not see it.
- ***Parties who have no knowledge of the agency.*** Generally, a principal is not obligated to give notice of termination to strangers who have no knowledge of the agency. However, a principal who has given the agent written authority to act but fails to recover the writing upon termination of the agency may be liable to strangers who later rely on this writing and deal with the agent. The laws of most states provide that this liability can be avoided by giving constructive notice (e.g., newspaper announcement) of the termination of the agency.

The foundation of Justice is good faith.

Cicero
De Officiis, Bk. 1, Ch. VII

Wrongful Termination of an Agency or Employment Contract

Generally, agency and employment contracts that do not specify a definite time for their termination can be terminated at will by either the principal or the agent without liability to the other party. When a principal terminates an agency contract, it is called a

revocation of authority. When an agent terminates an agency, it is called a **renunciation of authority**.

Unless an agency is irrevocable, both the principal and the agent have an individual power to unilaterally terminate any agency contract. Note that having the power to terminate an agency agreement is not the same as having the right to terminate it. The unilateral termination of an agency contract may be wrongful. If the principal's or agent's termination of an agency contract breaches the contract, the other party can sue for damages for **wrongful termination**.

wrongful termination
The termination of an agency contract in violation of the terms of the agency contract. In this situation, the nonbreaching party may recover damages from the breaching party.

Consider This Example A principal employs a licensed real estate agent to sell his house. The agency contract gives the agent an exclusive listing for three months. After one month, the principal unilaterally terminates the agency. The principal has the power to do so, and the agent can no longer act on behalf of the principal. However, because the principal did not have the right to terminate the contract, the agent can sue him and recover damages (i.e., lost commission) for wrongful termination.

Warsaw, Poland. Agents are often used to facilitate international commerce.

Terms and Concepts

The Nature of Agency

1. ***Agency.*** A fiduciary relationship that results from the manifestation of consent by one person to act on behalf of another person with that person's consent.
2. ***Parties:***
   a. *Principal.* A principal is a party who employs another person to act on his or her behalf.
   b. *Agent.* An agent is a party who agrees to act on behalf of another person.

Employer-Employee Relationship

In this type of relationship, an employer hires an employee to perform some form of physical service. An employee is not an agent unless the principal authorizes him or her to enter into contracts on the principal's behalf.

Principal–Agent Relationship

In this type of relationship, an employer hires an employee and authorizes the employee to enter into contracts on the employer's behalf.

Principal–Independent Contractor Relationship

In this type of relationship, the principal employs a person who is not an employee of the principal. The independent contractor has authority only to enter into contracts authorized by the principal.

Agency Relationships

1. ***Express agency.*** In this type of relationship, the principal and agent expressly agree in words to enter into an agency agreement. The agency contract may be oral or written unless the Statute of Frauds requires it to be in writing.
2. ***Implied agency.*** In this type of relationship, an agency is implied (inferred) from the conduct of the parties.
3. ***Apparent agency.*** This type of relationship arises when a principal creates the appearance of an agency that in actuality does not exist. Also called *agency by estoppel.*
4. ***Agency by ratification.*** This type of relationship occurs when a person misrepresents him- or herself as another's agent when he or she is not and the purported principal ratifies (accepts) the unauthorized act.

Principal's Duties

1. ***Duty of compensation.*** A principal must pay the agent agreed-upon compensation. If there is no agreement as to compensation, the principal must pay what is customary in the industry, or if there is no custom, then the reasonable value of the services.
2. ***Duties of reimbursement and indemnification.*** A principal must *reimburse* an agent for all expenses paid that were authorized by the principal, within the scope of the agency, and necessary to discharge the agent's duties. The principal must *indemnify* the agent for any losses suffered because of the principal's misconduct.
3. ***Duty of cooperation.*** A principal must cooperate with and assist an agent in the performance of the agent's duties and the accomplishment of the agency.

Agent's Duties

1. ***Duty of performance.*** An agent owes a duty to perform the lawful duties expressed in the agency contract with reasonable care, skill, and diligence.
2. ***Duty of notification.*** An agent owes a duty to notify the principal of any information he or she learns that is important to the agency. Information learned by the agent in the course of the agency is *imputed* to the principal.
3. ***Duty of accountability.*** An agent must maintain an accurate accounting of all transactions undertaken on the principal's behalf. A principal may demand an accounting from the agent at any time.
4. ***Duty of loyalty.*** An agent owes a duty not to act adversely to the interests of the principal. The most common breaches of loyalty are:
   a. *Self-dealing.* An agent cannot deal with the principal unless his or her position is disclosed and the principal agrees to deal with the agent.
   b. *Usurping an opportunity.* An agent cannot usurp (take) an opportunity belonging to the principal as his or her own.
   c. *Competing with the principal.* An agent is prohibited from competing with the principal during the course of an agency unless the principal agrees to the competition.
   d. *Misuse of confidential information.* An agent is under a legal duty not to disclose or misuse confidential information learned within the course of an agency.
   e. *Dual agency.* An agent cannot act on behalf of two different principals in the same transaction unless the principals agree.

Contract Liability to Third Parties

1. ***Fully disclosed agency.*** In this type of agency, the third party entering into the contract knows that the agent is acting for a principal and knows the identity of the principal. The principal is liable on the contract; the agent is not liable on the contract.
2. ***Partially disclosed agency.*** In this type of agency, the third party knows that the agent is acting for a principal but does not know the identity of the principal. Both the principal and the agent are liable on the contract.
3. ***Undisclosed agency.*** In this type of agency, the third party does not know that the agent is acting for a principal. Both the principal and the agent are liable on the contract.

Tort Liability to Third Parties

Principals are liable for the *tortious conduct* of an agent who is acting within the *scope of his or her authority*. Liability is imposed for misrepresentation, negligence, and intentional torts.

1. ***Negligence.*** Principals are liable for the negligent conduct of agents acting within the scope of their employment. Special negligence doctrines include:
   a. *Frolic and detour.* A principal is generally relieved of liability if an agent's negligent act occurred on a substantial frolic and detour from the scope of employment.
   b. *"Coming and going" rule.* A principal is not liable if an agent's tortious conduct occurred while on the way to or from work.
   c. *Dual-purpose mission.* If an agent is acting on his or her own behalf and on behalf of the principal, both the principal and agent are generally liable for the agent's tortious conduct.
2. ***Intentional torts.*** States apply one of the following rules:
   a. *Motivation test.* The principal is liable if an agent's intentional tort was committed to promote the principal's business.
   b. *Work-related test.* The principal is liable if an agent's intentional tort was committed within a work-related time or space.

   Agents are personally liable for their own tortious conduct.
3. ***Misrepresentation.*** A principal is liable for intentional and innocent misrepresentations made by an agent acting within the scope of his or her employment.

Independent Contractor

Generally, principals are not liable for the tortious conduct of independent contractors. Independent contractors are personally liable for their own torts.

Termination of an Agency by the Acts of the Parties

The following *acts of the parties* terminate agency contracts:

1. ***Mutual agreement.*** Parties may mutually agree to terminate an agency contract.
2. ***Lapse of time.*** The stipulated time period of an agency may expire.
3. ***Purpose achieved.*** The stipulated purpose of an agency may be achieved.
4. ***Occurrence of a specified event.*** A stipulated event may occur.

Termination of an Agency by Operation of Law

Agency contracts can be terminated by *operation of law.* This includes the following methods:

1. ***Death.*** The death of either the principal or the agent terminates an agency.
2. ***Insanity.*** Insanity of either the principal or the agent terminates an agency.
3. ***Bankruptcy.*** Bankruptcy of the principal terminates an agency.
4. ***Impossibility.*** A situation that makes the performance of the agency contract impossible terminates an agency.
5. ***Changed circumstances.*** An unusual circumstance that leads the agent to believe that the principal's original instructions are no longer valid terminates an agency.
6. ***War.*** Outbreak of war between the principal's country and the agent's country terminates an agency.

Notification of Termination

If an agency is terminated by agreement between the parties, the principal must notify third parties as follows:

1. ***Parties who dealt with the agent.*** Direct notice must be given to these parties.
2. ***Parties who have knowledge of the agency.*** Direct or constructive (e.g., public notice in newspapers) notice must be given to these parties.
3. ***Parties who have no knowledge of the agency.*** No notice needs to be given to these parties.

If the proper notice of the termination of the agency is not given, the agent has *apparent authority* to bind the principal to contracts.

The principal and agent both have the *power* to terminate an agency at any time. After termination, the agent can no longer act on behalf of the principal. The terminating party may not, however, have had the *right* to terminate the agency and may be held liable for damages caused by *wrongful termination* of the agency.

Wrongful Termination of an Agency Contract

If an agency is for an agreed-upon term or purpose, the *unilateral termination* of the agency contract by either the principal or the agent constitutes the *wrongful termination* of the agency. The breaching party is liable to the other party for damages caused by the breach.

Internet Exercises and Case Questions

Working the Web Internet Exercises

1. Visit Nolo Press at **www.nolo.com/category/ic_home.html** to find general information regarding the classification of independent contractors versus employees.
2. One way to create an agency is to execute a power of attorney. See **smallbiz.biz.findlaw.com/bookshelf/sblg/sblgchp13_f.html** for information and **consumer.pub.findlaw.com/nllg/forms/128.html** for a form.
3. A quick overview of the topic of agency from a practical business perspective can be found at **consumer.pub.findlaw.com/newcontent/consumerlaw/chp2_h.html**. See also "Legal Information Institute: Agency," at **www.law.cornell.edu/topics/agency.html**.
4. Agency law is very important and widely used in international business ventures. For an example of how the law is applied in another country, Iran, see **www.nourlaw.com/guide_to_iranian_market/Agency.html**.

Legal Environment Cases

19.1 Creation of an Agency Renaldo, Inc., d/b/a Baker Street, owns and operates a nightclub in Georgia. On the evening in question, plaintiff Ginn became "silly drunk" at the nightclub and was asked by several patrons and the manager to leave the premises. The police were called, and Ginn left the premises. When Ginn realized that his jacket was still in the nightclub, he attempted to reenter the premises. He was met at the door by the manager, who refused him admittance. When Ginn persisted, an unidentified patron, without the approval of the manager, pushed Ginn, who lost his balance and fell backward. To break his fall, Ginn put his hand against the doorjamb. The unidentified patron slammed the door on Ginn's hand and held it shut for several minutes. Ginn, who suffered severe injuries to his right hand, sued the nightclub for damages. Was the unidentified patron an agent of the nightclub? *Ginn v. Renaldo, Inc.,* 359 S.E.2d 390, 1987 Ga.App. Lexis 2023 (Ga. App.)

19.2 Independent Contractor The Butler Telephone Company, Inc. (Butler), contracted with Sandidge Construction Company to lay 18 miles of telephone cable in a rural area. In the contract, Butler reserved the right to inspect the work for compliance with the terms of the contract. Butler did not control how Sandidge performed the work. Johnnie Carl Pugh, an employee of Sandidge, was killed on the job when the sides to an excavation in which he was working caved in on top of him. Evidence disclosed that the excavation was not properly shored and sloped and that it violated general safety standards. Pugh's parents and estate brought a wrongful death action against Butler. Is Butler liable? *Pugh v. Butler Telephone Company, Inc.,* 512So.2d 1317, 1987 Ala. Lexis 4468 (Ala.)

19.3 Apparent Agency Gene Mohr and James Loyd each owned 50 percent of Tri-County Farm Equipment Company. Tri-County had its depository bank account at First National Bank of Olathe, Kansas. Loyd also personally owned an oil business known as Earthworm Energy, which had its bank account at the State Bank of Stanley. Neither Mohr nor Tri-County had any ownership interest in Earthworm. Mohr did not indicate to the State Bank of Stanley that Loyd had any authority to personally sign checks on behalf of Tri-County. In 1982, Loyd took eight checks that were payable to Tri-County and endorsed and deposited them into Earthworm's account at the State Bank of Stanley. Mohr brought an action for conversion against State Bank of Stanley to recover the amount of the checks. The bank argued in defense that Loyd had apparent authority to deposit the checks in his personal business account. Does Loyd possess apparent authority? *Mohr v. State Bank of Stanley*, 734 P.2d 1071, 1987 Kan. Lexis 297 (Kan.)

19.4 Ratification After Francis Pusateri retired, he met with Gilbert J. Johnson, a stockbroker with E. F. Hutton & Co., Inc., and informed Johnson that he wished to invest in tax-free bonds and money market accounts. Pusateri opened an investment account with E. F. Hutton and checked the box stating that his objective was "tax-free income and moderate growth." During the course of a year, Johnson churned Pusateri's account to make commissions and invested Pusateri's funds in volatile securities and options. Johnson kept telling Pusateri that his account was making money, and the monthly statement from E. F. Hutton did not indicate otherwise. The manager at E. F. Hutton was aware of Johnson's activities but did nothing to prevent them. When Johnson left E. F. Hutton, Pusateri's account—which had been the "laughingstock" of the office—had shrunk from $196,000 to $96,880. Pusateri sued E. F. Hutton for damages. Is E. F. Hutton liable? *Pusateri v. E. F. Hutton & Co., Inc.*, 180 Cal.App.3d 247, 255 Cal.Rptr. 526, 1986 Cal.App. Lexis 1502 (Cal. App.)

19.5 Reasonable Care and Skill Norman R. Barton and his wife decided to vacation in Florida in November 1984. In March 1984, they contacted Wonderful World of Travel, Inc., a travel agency licensed by the state of Ohio, to make the arrangements. They requested a room with a view of the ocean, a kitchenette so they would be saved the expense of dining out, free parking, and a free spa. In August, with the Bartons' approval, the travel agency made reservations at the Beau Rivage motel in Bal Harbour, Florida. The travel agency did not confirm the reservations prior to the Bartons' departure in November. When the Bartons arrived at the motel, they found it closed, chained, and guarded. The only other hotel or motel in the area was a Sheraton, which was almost triple the room cost of the Beau Rivage. The Sheraton overlooked the ocean, but it did not have a kitchenette, free parking, or free spa privileges. The Bartons stayed at the Sheraton. They sued the travel agent upon their return. Is the travel agent liable for the increased costs incurred by the Bartons? *Barton v. Wonderful World of Travel, Inc.*, 502 N.E.2d 715, 1986 Ohio Misc. Lexis 57 (Ohio Mun.)

19.6 Imputed Knowledge On March 31, 1981, Iota Management Corporation entered into a contract to purchase the Bel Air West Motor Hotel in the City of St. Louis from Boulevard Investment Company. The agreement contained the following warranty: "Seller has no actual notice of any substantial defect in the structure of the Hotel or in any of its plumbing, heating, air-conditioning, electrical, or utility systems."

When the buyer inspected the premises, no leaks in the pipes were visible. Iota purchased the hotel for $2 million. When Iota removed some of the walls and ceilings during remodeling, it found evidence of prior repairs to leaking pipes and ducts, as well as devices for catching water (e.g., milk cartons, cookie sheets, buckets). The estimate to repair these leaks was $500,000. Evidence at trial showed that Cecil Lilibridge, who was Boulevard's maintenance supervisor from 1975 until the sale of the hotel in 1981, had actual knowledge of these problems and had repaired some of the pipes. Iota sued Boulevard to rescind the contract. Is Boulevard liable? *Iota Management Corporation v. Boulevard Investment Company*, 731 S.W.2d 399, 1987 Mo.App. Lexis 4027 (Mo. App.)

19.7 Duty of Loyalty Peter Shields was the president and a member of the board of directors of Production Finishing Corporation from 1974 through August 1981. The company provided steel polishing services. It did most, if not all, of the polishing work in the Detroit area, except for that of the Ford Motor Company. (Ford did its own polishing.) Shields discussed this matter with Ford on behalf of Production Finishing on a number of occasions. When Shields learned that Ford was discontinuing its polishing operation, he incorporated Flat Rock Metal and submitted a confidential proposal to Ford that provided that he would buy Ford's equipment and provide polishing services to Ford. It was not until he resigned from Production Finishing that Shields informed the board of directors that he was pursuing the Ford business himself. Production Finishing sued Shields. Did Shields breach his fiduciary duty of loyalty to Production Finishing? *Production Finishing Corporation v. Shields*, 405 N.W.2d 171, 1987 Mich. App. Lexis 2379 (Mich. App.)

19.8 Contract Liability G. Elvin Grinder of Marbury, Maryland, was a building contractor who, prior to May 1, 1973, did business as an individual and traded as "Grinder Construction." Grinder maintained an open account, on his individual credit, with Bryans Road Building & Supply Co., Inc. Grinder would purchase materials and supplies from Bryans on credit and later pay the invoices. On May 1, 1973, G. Elvin Grinder Construction, Inc., a Maryland corporation, was formed, with Grinder personally owning 52 percent of the stock of the corporation. Grinder did not inform Bryans that he had incorporated and continued to purchase supplies on credit from Bryans under the name "Grinder Construction." In May 1978, after certain invoices were not paid by Grinder, Bryans sued Grinder personally to recover. Grinder asserted that the debts were owed by the corporation. Bryans amended its complaint to include the corporation as a defendant. Who is liable to Bryans? *Grinder v. Bryans Road Building & Supply Co., Inc.*, 432 A.2d 453, 1981 Md. Lexis 246 (Md. App.)

19.9 Contract Liability In the spring of 1974, certain residents of Harrisville, Utah, organized Golden Spike Little League for the youngsters of the town. This was an unincorporated association. David Anderson and several other organizers contracted with Smith & Edwards, a sporting goods store, which agreed to give them favorable prices on merchandise. During the course of the summer, parents went into Smith & Edwards and picked up uniforms and equipment for their children and other Little Leaguers. At the end of the summer, Smith & Edwards sent them a bill for $3,900. Fund-raising activities produced only $149, and the organizers refused to pay the difference. Smith & Edwards sued Anderson and the other organizers for the unpaid balance. Are the organizers personally liable for the debt? *Smith & Edwards v. Anderson*, 577 P.2d 132, 1978 Utah Lexis 1269 (Utah)

19.10 Tort Liability Intrastate Radiotelephone, Inc., is a public utility that supplies radiotelephone utility service to the general public for radiotelephones, pocket pagers, and beepers. Robert Kranhold, an employee of Intrastate, was authorized to use his personal vehicle on company business. On the morning of March 9, 1976, when Kranhold was driving his vehicle to Intrastate's main office, he negligently struck a motorcycle being driven by Michael S. Largey, causing severe and permanent injuries to Largey. The accident occurred at the intersection where Intrastate's main office is located. Evidence showed that Kranhold acted as a consultant to Intrastate, worked both in and out of Intrastate's offices, had no set hours of work, often attended meetings at Intrastate's offices, and went to Intrastate's offices to pick things up or drop things off. Largey sued Intrastate for damages. Is Intrastate liable? *Largey v. Radiotelephone, Inc.*, 136 Cal.App.3d 660, 186 Cal.Rptr. 520, 1982 Cal.App. Lexis 2049 (Cal. App.)

Ethics in Business

19.11 The National Biscuit Company (Nabisco) is a corporation that produces and distributes cookies and other food products to grocery stores and other outlets across the nation. In October 1968, Nabisco hired Ronnell Lynch as a cookie salesman-trainee. On March 1, 1969, Lynch was assigned his own sales territory. Lynch's duties involved making sales calls, taking orders, and making sure that shelves of stores in his territory were stocked with Nabisco products. During the period March 1 to May 1, 1969, Nabisco received numerous complaints from store owners in Lynch's territory that Lynch was overly aggressive and taking shelf space for Nabisco products that was reserved for competing brands.

On May 1, 1969, Lynch visited a grocery store that was managed by Jerome Lange. Lynch was there to place previously delivered merchandise on the store's shelves. An argument developed between Lynch and Lange. Lynch became very angry and started swearing. Lange, the store manager, told Lynch to stop swearing or leave the store because children were present. Lynch became uncontrollably angry and went behind the counter and dared Lange to a fight. When Lange refused to fight, Lynch proceeded to viciously assault and batter Lange, causing severe injuries. Lange sued Nabisco. *Lange v. National Biscuit Company*, 211 N.W.2d 783, 1973 Minn. Lexis 1106 (Minn.)

Ethics Issues

1. Was Lynch an agent of Nabisco?
2. Was it ethical for Nabisco to deny liability in this case?
3. Is Nabisco liable for the intentional tort (assault and battery) of its employee, Lynch?
4. Do you think the prior complaints against Lynch had any effect on the decision reached in this case?

20

Employment and Worker Protection Laws

"It is difficult to imagine any grounds, other than our own personal economic predilections, for saying that the contract of employment is any the less an appropriate subject of legislation than are scores of others, in dealing with which this Court has held that legislatures may curtail individual freedom in the public interest."

—Justice Stone
Dissenting Opinion, Morehead v. New York, 298 U.S. 587, 56 S.Ct. 918 (1936)

Chapter Objectives

After studying this chapter, you should be able to:

1. Define employment-at-will doctrine.
2. Explain how state workers' compensation programs work and describe the benefits available.
3. Describe employers' duty to provide safe working conditions under the Occupational Safety and Health Act.
4. Describe the minimum wage and overtime pay rules of the Fair Labor Standards Act.
5. Explain the rules governing private pensions under the Employee Retirement Income Security Act.

Chapter Contents

Before the Industrial Revolution, the doctrine of laissez-faire governed the employment relationship in this country. Generally, this meant that employment was subject to the common law of contracts and agency law. In most instances, employees and employers had somewhat equal bargaining power.

This changed dramatically when the country became industrialized in the late 1800s. For one thing, large corporate employers had much more bargaining power than their employees. For another, the issues of child labor, unsafe working conditions, long hours, and low pay caused concern. Both federal and state legislation were enacted to protect workers' rights. Today, employment law is a mixture of contract law, agency law, and government regulation.

This chapter discusses employment laws, worker safety, immigration laws, and workers' privacy laws.

Mackinac Bridge, Michigan. Workers on this bridge are covered by workers' compensation, occupational safety, and other labor and worker protection laws.

Employment at Will

An employee who is offered an express employment contract for a definite term cannot be discharged in violation of the contract. Employment contracts that cannot be performed within one year must be in writing under most state Statute of Frauds laws. Most employees, however, do not have employment contracts. They are considered **at-will employees.**

at-will employees
Employees who do not have employment contracts.

Under common law, an at-will employee can be discharged by an employer at any time for any reason. This laissez-faire doctrine gave the employer great flexibility in responding to its changing needs. It also caused unfair results for some employees. Today, there are many statutory, contract, public policy, and tort exceptions to the employment-at-will doctrine. These exceptions are discussed in the following paragraphs. An employee who has been **wrongfully discharged** can sue his or her employer for damages and other remedies (reinstatement, back pay, and such).

wrongful discharge
The discharge of an employee in violation of a statute, an employment contract, or public policy, or tortiously. As a result, the employee can recover damages and other remedies.

Exceptions to the Employment-at-Will Doctrine

There are certain exceptions when employers cannot dismiss at-will employees. These exceptions include:

- ***Statutory exception.*** Federal labor laws prohibit employers from discharging employee-members of labor unions in violation of labor laws or collective bargaining agreements.

Title VII and other federal and state antidiscrimination laws prohibit employers from engaging in race, sex, religious, age, handicap, or other forms of discrimination.

implied-in-fact contract
A contract in which agreement between parties has been inferred because of their conduct.

- ***Contract exception.*** In certain situations, an **implied-in-fact contract** can be created between an employer and an employee. For example, a company bulletin, handbook, or personnel policy might mention that employees who do their jobs properly will not be discharged. An employee who is discharged in violation of an implied-in-fact contract can sue the employer for breach of contract.

public policy exception
An exception to the employment-at-will doctrine that states an employee cannot be discharged if such discharge violates the public policy of the jurisdiction.

- ***Public policy exception.*** The **public policy exception** states that an employee cannot be discharged if such discharge violates the public policy of the jurisdiction. Discharging an employee for serving as a juror, refusing to do an act in violation of the law (e.g., refusing to engage in dumping of toxic wastes in violation of environmental protection laws), refusing to distribute defective products, and the like have been held to violate public policy.
- ***Tort exception.*** Wrongful discharge actions can be based on several tort theories. In certain instances, an employee can sue an employer for (1) fraud, (2) intentional infliction of emotional distress, or (3) defamation of character. If an employee is successful in a tort action, he or she may recover punitive damages.

Workers' Compensation

Many types of employment are dangerous, and each year many workers are injured on the job. Under common law, employees who were injured on the job could sue their employers for negligence. This time-consuming process placed the employee at odds with his or her employer. In addition, there was no guarantee that the employee would win the case. Ultimately, many injured workers—or the heirs of deceased workers—were left uncompensated.

workers' compensation acts
Acts that compensate workers and their families if workers are injured in connection with their jobs.

Workers' compensation acts were enacted by states in response to the unfairness of that result. These acts create an administrative procedure for workers to receive compensation for injuries that occur on the job. First, the injured worker files a claim with the appropriate state government agency (often called the workers' compensation board or commission). Next, that entity determines the legitimacy of the claim. If the worker disagrees with the agency's findings, he or she may appeal the decision through the state court system. Workers' compensation benefits are paid according to preset limits established by statute or regulation. The amounts that are recoverable vary from state to state.

Workers' Compensation Insurance

States usually require employers to purchase insurance from private insurance companies or state funds to cover workers' compensation claims. Some states permit employers to self-insure if they demonstrate that they have the ability to pay workers' compensation claims. Many large companies self-insure. Workers can sue an employer in court to recover damages for employment-related injuries if the employer does not carry workers' compensation insurance or does not self-insure if permitted to do so.

Employment-Related Injury

For an injury to be compensable under workers' compensation, the claimant must prove that the injury arose out of and in the course of his or her employment. An accident that occurs while an employee is actively working is clearly within the scope of this rule. Accidents that occur at a company cafeteria or while on a business lunch for an employer are covered. Accidents that happen while the employee is at an off-premises restaurant during his or her personal lunch hour are not covered. Many workers' compensation acts include stress as a compensable work-related injury.

Exclusive Remedy

Workers' compensation is an exclusive remedy. Thus, workers cannot sue their employers in court for damages. There are exceptions to this rule: If workers' compensation is not provided or if an employer intentionally injures a worker, the worker can collect workers' compensation benefits and sue the employer. Workers' compensation acts do not bar injured workers from suing responsible third parties to recover damages.

In the following case, the court had to decide whether an accident was work related.

Case 20.1 Workers' Compensation

Smith v. Workers' Compensation Appeals Board
191 Cal.App.3d 127, 236 Cal.Rptr. 248, 1987 Cal.App. Lexis 1587
Court of Appeals of California

Background and Facts

Ronald Wayne Smith was employed by Modesto High School as a temporary math instructor. In addition, he coached the girls' baseball and basketball teams. The contract under which he was employed stated that he "may be required to devote a reasonable amount of time to other duties" in addition to instructional duties. The teachers in the school system were evaluated once a year regarding both instructional duties and noninstructional duties, including "sponsorship or the supervision of out-of-classroom student activities."

The high school's math club holds an annual end-of-year outing. For the 1983–1984 school year, a picnic was scheduled for June 7, 1984, at the Modesto Reservoir. The students invited their math teachers, including Smith, to attend. The food was paid for by math club members' dues. Smith attended the picnic with his wife and three children. One of the students brought along a windsurfer. Smith watched the students as they used it before and after the picnic. When Smith tried it himself, he fell and was seriously injured. He died shortly thereafter. Mrs. Smith filed a claim for workers' compensation benefits, which was objected to by the employer. The workers' compensation judge denied benefits. The Workers' Compensation Appeals Board affirmed. Mrs. Smith appealed.

Issue

Was Smith engaged in employment-related activities when the accident occurred?

In the Language of the Court

In the instant case, decedent was a temporary instructor at Modesto High. As such, he was more vulnerable to pressure or suggestion that he participate in extracurricular activities to better his chances of being rehired. The math club was an official school club. Notices of meetings to plan the picnic appeared in the school bulletin. The food for the event was paid for out of the math club funds. The school was more than minimally involved in the picnic. Teachers were encouraged to involve themselves in extracurricular activities of the school, thus conferring the benefit of better teacher–student relationships. More importantly, teachers were evaluated on whether they shared equally in the sponsorship or the supervision of out-of-classroom student activities, and decedent had been commended for his participation in this area.

Respondent argues that if this court finds that decedent's attendance at the picnic was required by his employment, then his activities in using the windsurfer were outside the course and scope of his employment. Because attendance at the picnic was an implied requirement of decedent's employment, his accident that resulted from his engaging in the recreational activities that were part and parcel of the picnic's "entertainment" is causally connected to his employment.

Decision and Remedy

The court of appeals held that the decedent's accident was causally connected to his employment for purposes of awarding workers' compensation benefits to his heirs. The court of appeals reversed the decision of the Workers' Compensation Appeals Board and remanded the case for further proceedings.

Business and Ethics Questions

1. Should workers' compensation benefits be awarded only for accidents that occur at the job site? Why or why not?
2. Did the employer act ethically in objecting to the payment of benefits in this case?
3. How costly is workers' compensation for business? Do you think that many fraudulent workers' compensation claims are filed?

Occupational Safety

Occupational Safety and Health Act
A federal act enacted in 1970 that promotes safety in the workplace.

In 1970, Congress enacted the **Occupational Safety and Health Act**[1] to promote safety in the workplace. Virtually all private employers are within the scope of the act, but federal, state, and local governments are exempt. Industries regulated by other federal safety legislation are also exempt.[2] The act also established the **Occupational Safety and Health Administration (OSHA)**, a federal administrative agency within the Department of Labor, that is empowered to enforce the act. The act imposes recordkeeping and reporting requirements on employers and requires them to post notices in the workplace, informing employees of their rights under the act.

Specific and General Duty Standards

OSHA is empowered to adopt rules and regulations to interpret and enforce the Occupational Safety and Health Act. OSHA has adopted thousands of regulations to enforce the safety standards established by the act. These include the following:

specific duty
A duty that an employer has to provide a workplace free from specific hazards (e.g., requirement for a safety guard on a particular type of equipment).

general duty
A duty that an employer has to provide a work environment free from recognized hazards that are causing or are likely to cause death or serious physical harm to employees.

- ***Specific duty standards.*** Many of the OSHA standards address safety problems of a **specific duty** nature. For example, OSHA standards establish safety requirements for equipment (e.g., safety guards), set maximum exposure levels to hazardous chemicals, regulate the location of machinery, establish safety procedures for employees, and the like.
- ***General duty standards.*** The act imposes a **general duty** on an employer to provide a work environment free from recognized hazards that are causing or are likely to cause death or serious physical harm to employees. This is so even if no specific regulation applies to the situation.

OSHA is empowered to inspect places of employment for health hazards and safety violations. If a violation is found, OSHA can issue a *written citation* that requires the employer to abate or correct the situation. Contested citations are reviewed by the Occupational Safety and Health Review Commission. Its decision is appealable to the Federal Circuit Court of Appeals. Employers who violate the act, OSHA rules and regulations, or OSHA citations are subject to both civil and criminal penalties.

Fair Labor Standards Act (FLSA)

Fair Labor Standards Act (FLSA)
A federal act enacted in 1938 to protect workers that prohibits child labor and establishes minimum wage and overtime pay requirements.

In 1938, Congress enacted the **Fair Labor Standards Act (FLSA)** to protect workers.[3] The FLSA applies to private employers and employees engaged in the production of goods for interstate commerce.

Child Labor

The FLSA forbids the use of oppressive child labor and makes it unlawful to ship goods produced by businesses that use oppressive child labor. The Department of Labor has adopted the following regulations that define lawful child labor: (1) children under the age of 14 cannot work except as newspaper deliverers; (2) children ages 14 and 15 may work limited hours in nonhazardous jobs approved by the Department of Labor (e.g., restaurants and gasoline stations); and (3) children ages 16 and 17 may work unlimited hours in nonhazardous jobs. The Department of Labor determines which occupations are hazardous (e.g., mining, roofing, working with explosives). Children who work in agricultural employment and child actors and performers are exempt from these restrictions. Persons age 18 and older may work at any job, whether it is hazardous or not.

Minimum Wage and Overtime Pay Requirements

The FLSA establishes minimum wage and overtime pay requirements for workers. Managerial, administrative, and professional employees are exempt from the act's wage and hour provisions. As outlined in the following paragraphs, the FLSA requires employers to pay covered workers at least the minimum wage for their regular work hours and to provide overtime pay:

- ***Minimum wage.*** The minimum wage is set by Congress and can be changed. As of 2006, it was set at $5.15 per hour. The Department of Labor permits employers to pay less than the minimum wage to students and apprentices. An employer may reduce minimum wages by an amount equal to the reasonable cost of food and lodging provided to employees.
- ***Overtime pay.*** Under the FLSA, an employer cannot require nonexempt employees to work more than 40 hours per week unless they are paid one-and-a-half times their regular pay for each hour worked in excess of 40 hours. Each week is treated separately. For example, if an employee works 50 hours one week and 30 hours the next, the employer owes the employee 10 hours of overtime pay for the first week.

Ethics in Business

Microsoft Violates Employment Law

Microsoft Corporation is the world's largest provider of computer operating systems, software programs, and Internet browsers. The company has grown into a monopoly and made one of its founders, Bill Gates, one of the richest people in the world. But the company was caught nickel-and-diming some of its workers. It all started with an Internal Revenue Service (IRS) investigation.

Microsoft is headquartered in the state of Washington. In addition to having regular employees, Microsoft used the services of other workers classified as *independent contractors* (called *freelancers*) and temporary agency employees (called *temps*). Most of these special employees worked full time for Microsoft, doing jobs that were identical to jobs performed by Microsoft's regular employees. Microsoft paid the special employees by check as outside workers. In 1990, the IRS conducted an employment tax examination and determined that Microsoft had misclassified these special workers as independent contractors and that the workers in these positions needed to be reclassified as "employees" for federal tax purposes.

But the IRS investigation was not the end of the story. Plaintiff Donna Vizcaino and other freelancers sued Microsoft in a class action lawsuit, alleging that they were denied employment benefits, especially employee stock options, that were paid to regular employees. Microsoft contributed 3 percent of an employee's salary to the stock option plan. The court of appeals agreed with the plaintiffs, citing the Internal Revenue Code that requires such stock option plans to be available to all employees. Thus, Microsoft's attempts to define certain full-time employees as freelancers and temps was rebuffed by the courts. *Vizcaino v. United States District Court for the Western District of Washington*, 173 F.3d 713, 1999 U.S.App. Lexis 9057 (9th Cir.)

Ethics Issues

1. Did Microsoft act ethically in this case?
2. Why did Microsoft classify full-time workers as freelancers and temps? Explain. ■

Family and Medical Leave Act

In February 1993, Congress enacted the **Family and Medical Leave Act.**[4] This act guarantees workers unpaid time off from work for medical emergencies. The act, which applies to companies with 50 or more workers as well as federal, state, and local governments, covers about half of the nation's workforce. To be covered by the act, an employee must have worked for the employer for at least one year and have performed more than 1,250 hours of service during the previous 12-month period.

Family and Medical Leave Act
A federal act that guarantees employees unpaid time off for family or medical emergencies.

Covered employees are required to provide up to 12 weeks of unpaid leave during any 12-month period due to:

1. The birth of, and care for, a child
2. The placement of a child with an employee for adoption or in foster care
3. A serious health condition that makes the employee unable to perform his or her duties
4. Care for a spouse, child, or parent with a serious health problem

Leave because of the birth of a child or the placement of a child for adoption or in foster care cannot be taken intermittently unless the employer agrees. Other leaves may be taken on an intermittent basis. The employer may require medical proof of claimed serious health conditions.

An eligible employee who takes leave must, upon returning to work, be restored to either the same or equivalent position with equivalent employment benefits and pay. The restored employee is not entitled to the accrual of seniority during the leave period, however. A covered employer may deny restoration to a salaried employee who is among the highest-paid 10 percent of that employer's employees if the denial is necessary to prevent "substantial and grievous economic injury" to the employer's operations.

Consolidated Omnibus Budget Reconciliation Act (COBRA)

Consolidated Omnibus Budget Reconciliation Act (COBRA)
A federal law that permits employees and their beneficiaries to continue their group health insurance after an employee's employment has ended.

The **Consolidated Omnibus Budget Reconciliation Act of 1985 (COBRA)**[5] provides that an employee of a private employer or the employee's beneficiaries must be offered the opportunity to continue his or her group health insurance after the voluntary or involuntary termination of a worker's employment or the loss of coverage due to certain qualifying events defined in the law. The employer must notify covered employees and their beneficiaries of their rights under COBRA. To continue coverage, a person must pay the required group rate premium. Government employees are subject to parallel provisions found in the Public Health Service Act.

Employee Retirement Income Security Act (ERISA)

Employee Retirement Income Security Act (ERISA)
A federal act designed to prevent fraud and other abuses associated with private pension funds.

Employers are not required to establish pension plans for their employees. If they do, however, they are subject to the recordkeeping, disclosure, and other requirements of the **Employee Retirement Income Security Act (ERISA)**.[6] ERISA is a complex act designed to prevent fraud and other abuses associated with private pension funds. Federal, state, and local government pension funds are exempt from its coverage. ERISA is administered by the Department of Labor and the IRS.

Among other things, ERISA requires pension plans to be in writing and to name a pension fund manager. The plan manager owes a fiduciary duty to act as a "prudent person" in managing the fund and investing its assets. No more than 10 percent of a pension fund's assets can be invested in the securities of the sponsoring employer.

Vesting occurs when an employee has a nonforfeitable right to receive pension benefits. First, ERISA provides for immediate vesting of each employee's own contributions to the plan. Second, it requires employers' contributions to be either (1) completely forfeitable for a set period of up to five years and totally vested after that (*cliff vesting*) or (2) gradually vested over a seven-year period and completely vested after that time.

Immigration Reform and Control Act (IRCA)

The **Immigration Reform and Control Act of 1986 (IRCA)**[7] and the **Immigration Act of 1990**[8] are administered by the U.S. Citizenship and Immigration Services formally the U.S. Immigration and Naturalization Service (INS). These acts make it unlawful for employers to hire illegal immigrants. As of June 1, 1987, all U.S. employers must complete **USCIS Form I-9** for each employee. The form attests that the employer has inspected documents of the employee and has determined that he or she is either a U.S. citizen or otherwise qualified to work in the country (e.g., has a proper work visa). Employers must maintain records and post in the workplace notices of the contents of the law. Violators are subject to both civil and criminal penalties.

Contemporary Trend

Drug Testing and Polygraph Tests

Drug Testing

Drug testing of employees or prospective employees by private and public employers has increased dramatically in the past decade. Employers see drug testing as a way to increase productivity and decrease liability exposure. Job applicants and employees often view drug testing as an invasion of privacy. Although the courts have not been totally consistent in deciding drug-testing cases, several trends have emerged.

Generally, preemployment drug screening has been upheld by the courts. Because job applicants have a lower expectation of privacy than incumbent employees, legal challenges are less likely. Drug testing of incumbent employees by private employers is usually upheld where the employer either has a reasonable suspicion that an employee is impaired or drug testing is required after an accident has occurred.

Polygraph Tests

The **Employee Polygraph Protection Act of 1988** [29 U.S.C. Sections 2001–2009], a federal statute, prohibits most private employers from using polygraph (lie detector) tests, to screen job applicants and employees. Federal and state governments are not covered by the act. Polygraph tests may also be used by employers in matters dealing with the national defense (e.g., certain defense contractors) and security services that hire employees who protect the public health and safety (e.g., guards at electric power plants).

The act requires private employers that are permitted to use polygraph testing to follow certain procedures, including giving notice to the person to be tested, using licensed examiners, and prohibiting certain questions (e.g., those relating to the religion or sexual behavior of the subject). ■

Government Programs

The U.S. government has established several programs that provide benefits to workers and their dependants. Two of these programs, unemployment compensation and Social Security, are discussed in the following paragraphs.

Unemployment Compensation

In 1935, Congress established an unemployment compensation program to assist workers who were temporarily unemployed. Under the **Federal Unemployment Tax Act (FUTA)**[9] and state laws enacted to implement the program, employers are required to pay unemployment contributions (taxes). The tax rate and unemployment wage level are subject to change. Employees do not pay unemployment taxes.

Federal Unemployment Tax Act (FUTA)
A federal act that requires employers to pay unemployment taxes; unemployment compensation is paid to workers who are temporarily unemployed.

State governments administer unemployment compensation programs under general guidelines set by the federal government. Each state establishes its own eligibility requirements and the amount and duration of the benefits. To collect benefits, applicants must be able and available for work and seeking employment. Workers who have been let go because of bad conduct (e.g., illegal activity, drug use on the job) or who voluntarily quit work without just cause are not eligible to receive benefits.

Social Security

Social Security
A federal system that provides limited retirement and death benefits to covered employees and their dependents.

In 1935, Congress established the federal **Social Security** system to provide limited retirement and death benefits to certain employees and their dependents. The Social Security system is administered by the Social Security Administration. Today, Social Security benefits include (1) retirement benefits, (2) survivors' benefits to family members of deceased workers, (3) disability benefits, and (4) medical and hospitalization benefits (Medicare).

Under the **Federal Insurance Contributions Act (FICA),**[10] employees and employers must make contributions (pay taxes) into the Social Security fund. The employer must pay a matching amount. Social Security does not operate like a savings account. Instead, current contributions are used to fund current claims. The employer is responsible for deducting employees' portions from their wages and remitting the entire payment to the IRS.

Under the **Self-Employment Contributions Act,**[11] self-employed individuals must pay Social Security contributions, too. The amount of taxes self-employed individuals must pay is equal to the combined employer–employee amount.

Failure to submit Social Security taxes subjects the violator to interest payments, penalties, and possible criminal liability. Social Security taxes may be changed by an act of Congress.

Vietnam. Workers in many other countries are not accorded the same worker protections as are provided by many state and federal laws in the United States.

Terms and Concepts

Workers' Compensation Acts

These state statutes create an administrative procedure for workers to receive payments for job-related injuries.

1. ***Workers' compensation insurance.*** Most states require employers to carry private or government-sponsored workers' compensation insurance. Some states permit employers to self-insure.

Employment-Related Injury

To be compensable under workers' compensation, a claimant must prove that his or her injury arose out of and in the course of his or her employment.

Exclusive Remedy

Workers' compensation is an exclusive remedy. Thus, workers cannot sue their employers to recover damages for job-related injuries.

1. ***Exceptions to the exclusive-remedy rule.*** Workers may recover damages from their employers for job-related injuries if the employer:
   a. Does not provide workers' compensation
   b. Intentionally causes the worker's injuries
2. ***Lawsuits against third parties.*** Workers' compensation acts do not bar injured workers from suing responsible third parties to recover damages (e.g., the manufacturer of a defective machine that cause a worker's injuries).

Occupational Safety and Health Act

This federal statute requires employers to provide safe working conditions.

1. ***Occupational Safety and Health Administration (OSHA).*** This federal administrative agency administers and enforces the Occupational Safety and Health Act.

Specific and General Duties

1. ***Specific duty standards.*** These are OSHA safety standards for specific equipment (e.g., lathe) or a specific industry (e.g., mining).
2. ***General duty standards.*** These OSHA standards impose a general duty on employers to provide safe working conditions.

Fair Labor Standards Act (FLSA)

This federal statute protects workers.

1. ***Child labor.*** The FLSA forbids the use of illegal child labor. The U.S. Department of Labor defines illegal child labor.
2. ***Minimum wage and overtime pay requirements:***
   a. Minimum wage. The minimum wage is set by Congress and can be changed. The minimum wage, as of 2006, is $5.15 per hour.
   b. Overtime pay. An employer cannot require employees to work more than 40 hours per week unless they are paid 1.5 times their regular pay for each hour worked in excess of 40 hours.

Family and Medical Leave Act

This federal statute guarantees covered workers unpaid time off from work for the birth or adoption of a child, serious health problems of the worker, and serious health problems of a spouse, child, or parent.

Consolidated Omnibus Budget Reconciliation Act (COBRA)

This federal statute requires an employer to offer an employee or the employee's beneficiaries the opportunity to continue health benefits (upon payment of the premium) after termination of employment due to dismissal or death.

Employee Retirement Income Security Act (ERISA)

This federal statute governs the establishment and administration of private pension programs to prevent fraud and other abuses.

Immigration Reform and Control Act (IRCA)

This federal statute prohibits employers from employing illegal immigrants. Employers must require workers to prove that they are U.S. citizens or have proper work visas to work in this country.

Unemployment Compensation

This state and federal program pays compensation to unemployed persons who meet certain qualifying standards. Employers are required to pay unemployment compensation payments to the government to fund the program. Authorized by the *Federal Unemployment Tax Act (FUTA)* and state laws.

Social Security

This federal government program provides limited retirement, disability, and medical and hospitalization to covered employees and their dependents. Employers and employees pay taxes to fund the program.

Internet Exercises and Case Questions

Working the Web Internet Exercises

1. Check the current unemployment rate at the Department of Labor (DOL): **www.dol.gov**. Is it higher or lower than it was one year ago?
2. Find the major laws section of the DOL Web site. Review the provisions of the FLSA relating to minimum wage rates and look up the current minimum wage.
3. What are the requirements for employment under an H-1B visa? Search the DOL site for the answer.

Legal Environment Cases

20.1 Employment Contract The Hyatt Corporation (Hyatt) operates the Hyatt Regency Hotel in Milwaukee, Wisconsin. In May 1980, Hyatt employed Annunzio Ferraro, a former boxer, as a security guard at its Milwaukee hotel. The written employment agreement signed by Ferraro stated, "I agree that my employment may be terminated by this Company at any time without liability for wages or salary except such as may have been earned at the date of such termination." Ferraro was given the Hyatt employee handbook at that time. A paragraph in the 48-page handbook stated: "In order for Hyatt to maintain a desirable level of employee conduct and productivity, Hyatt policies must be enforced. Hyatt policy requires that employees not be dismissed or laid off without just cause."

Ferraro was reprimanded on several occasions for using excessive force and abusive conduct toward guests and female employees. On February 25, 1981, Thomas Koelsch was attempting to visit a guest at the hotel and parked in the hotel employees' parking lot. When Ferraro told Koelsch to leave, and Koelsch did not, a shouting match developed, and Ferraro grabbed Koelsch and attempted to force him back into his car. Hyatt discharged Ferraro on March 18, 1981, because of these incidents. Ferraro sued Hyatt to recover damages for wrongful discharge. Is Ferraro an at-will employee? Who wins? *Ferraro v. Hyatt Corporation*, 368 N.W.2d 666, 1985 Wis. Lexis 2387 (Wis.)

20.2 Wrongful Discharge Ray Palmateer worked for International Harvestor Company (IH) for 16 years. He had risen from a unionized job at an hourly rate to a managerial position on a fixed salary. Palmateer was an at-will employee. He supplied information to local law enforcement authorities that an IH employee was involved in a violation of the Illinois Criminal Code and agreed to assist in the investigation and testify at trial against the employee if called by the prosecuting attorney. Shortly thereafter, Palmateer was discharged by IH. He sued IH to recover damages for retaliatory discharge. Does his complaint state a cause of action for retaliatory discharge? *Palmateer v. International Harvester Company*, 421 N.E.2d 876, 1981 Ill. Lexis 282 (Ill.)

20.3 Workers' Compensation John B. Wilson was employed by the city of Modesto, California, as a police officer. He was a member of the special emergency reaction team (SERT), a tactical unit of the city's police department trained and equipped to handle highly dangerous criminal situations. Membership in SERT was voluntary for police officers. No additional pay or benefits were involved. To be a member of SERT, each officer was required to pass physical tests four times a year. One such test required members to run two miles in 17 minutes. Other tests called for a minimum number of push-ups, pull-ups, and sit-ups. Officers who did not belong to SERT were not required to undergo these physical tests. On June 27, 1984, Wilson completed his patrol shift, changed clothes, and drove to the Modesto Junior College track. While running there, he injured his left ankle. Wilson filed a claim for workers' compensation benefits, which was contested by his employer. Who wins? *Wilson v. Workers' Compensation Appeals Board*, 196 Cal.App.3d 302, 239 Cal.Rptr. 719, 1987 Cal.App. Lexis 2382 (Cal. App.)

20.4 Workers' Compensation Joseph Albanese was employed as a working foreman by Atlantic Steel Company, Inc., for approximately 20 years prior to 1970. His duties included the supervision of plant employees. In 1967, the business was sold to a new owner. In 1969, after the employees voted to unionize, friction developed between Albanese and the workers. Part of the problem was caused by management's decision to eliminate overtime work, which required Albanese to go out into the shop and prod the workers to expedite the work.

Additional problems resulted from the activities of Albanese's direct supervisor, the plant manager. On one occasion in 1968, the manager informed Albanese that the company practice of distributing Thanksgiving turkeys was to be discontinued. In 1969, the manager told Albanese that the company did not intend to give the workers a Christmas bonus. The plant manager also informed Albanese that he did not intend to pay overtime wages to any worker. On each occasion, after Albanese relayed the information to the workers, the plant manager reversed his own decision.

After the last incident, Albanese became distressed and developed chest pains and nausea. When the chest pains became sharper, he went home to bed. Albanese did not work thereafter. He experienced continuing pain, sweatiness, shortness of breath, headaches, and depression. Albanese filed a claim for workers' compensation based on stress. The employer contested the claim. Who wins? *Albanese's Case*, 389 N.E.2d 83, 1979 Mass. Lexis 795 (Mass.)

20.5 Occupational Safety Getty Oil Company (Getty) operated a separation facility where it gathered gas and oil from wells and transmitted them to an outgoing pipeline under pressure. Getty engineers designed and produced a pressure vessel, called a fluid booster, that was to be installed to increase pressure in the system. Robinson, a Getty engineer, was instructed to install the vessel. Robinson picked up the vessel from the welding shop without having it tested. After he completed the installation, the pressure valve was put into operation. When the pressure increased from 300 to 930 pounds per square inch, an explosion occurred. Robinson died from the explosion, and another Getty employee was seriously injured. The secretary of labor issued a citation against Getty for violating the general duty provision for worker safety contained in the Occupational Safety and Health Act. Getty challenged the citation. Who wins? *Getty Oil Company v. Occupational Safety and Health Review Commission*, 530 F.2d 143, 1976 U.S.App. Lexis 11640 (5th Cir.)

20.6 ERISA United Artists was a Maryland corporation doing business in the state of Texas. United Pension Fund (Plan) was a defined-contribution employee pension benefit plan sponsored by United Artists for its employees. Each employee had his or her own individual pension account, but Plan's assets were pooled for investment purposes. Plan was administered by a board of trustees. During the period 1977 through 1986, seven of the trustees used Plan to make a series of loans to themselves. The trustees did not (1) require the borrowers to submit written applications for the subject loans, (2) assess the prospective borrowers' ability to repay the loans, (3) specify a period in which the loans were to be repaid, or (4) call the loans when they remained unpaid. The trustees also charged less than fair market value interest rates for the loans. The secretary of labor sued the trustees, alleging that they had breached their fiduciary duty in violation of ERISA. Who wins? *McLaughlin v. Rowley*, 698 F.Supp. 1333, 1988 U.S.Dist. Lexis 12679 (N.D. Tex.)

20.7 Drug Testing Air traffic controllers are federal government employees who are responsible for directing commercial and private air traffic in this country. They are subject to regulation by the secretary of transportation (Secretary). Secretary adopted a regulation that provides for postaccident urinalysis drug testing of air traffic controllers responsible for the airspace in which an airplane accident has occurred. The National Air Traffic Controllers Association, MEBA/NNU, AFL-CIO, sued, alleging that such drug testing was an unreasonable search and seizure in violation of the Fourth Amendment to the U.S. Constitution. Who wins? *National Air Traffic Controllers Assn., MEBA/NNU, AFL-CIO v. Burnley*, 700 F.Supp. 1043, 1988 U.S.Dist Lexis 15884 (N.D. Cal.)

20.8 Unemployment Benefits Devon Overstreet, who worked as a bus driver for the Chicago Transit Authority (CTA) for over six years, took a sick leave from January 30 to March 15, 1985. Because she had been on sick leave for more than 7 days, CTA required her to take a medical examination. The blood and urine analysis indicated the presence of cocaine. A second test confirmed this finding. On March 20, 1985, CTA suspended her and placed her in the Employee Assistance Program for Substance Abuse for no less than 30 days, with a chance of reassignment to a nonoperating job if she successfully completed the program. The program is an alternative to discharge and is available at the election of the employee. Overstreet filed for unemployment compensation benefits. CTA contested her claim. Who wins? *Overstreet v. Illinois Department of Employment Security*, 522 N.E.2d 185, 1988 U.S.App. Lexis 10091 (Ill. App.)

Ethics in Business

20.9 Whirlpool Corporation (Whirlpool) operated a manufacturing plant in Marion, Ohio, for the production of household appliances. Overhead conveyors transported appliance components throughout the plant. To protect employees from objects that occasionally fell from the conveyors, Whirlpool installed a horizontal wire-mesh guard screen approximately 20 feet above the plant floor. The mesh screen was welded to angle-iron frames suspended from the building's structural steel skeleton.

Maintenance employees spent several hours each week removing objects from the screen, replacing paper spread on the screen to catch grease drippings from the materials on the conveyors, and performing occasional maintenance work on the conveyors. To perform these duties, maintenance employees were usually able to stand on the iron frames, but sometimes they found it necessary to step onto the wire-mesh screen itself. Several employees had fallen partly through the screen. On June 28, 1974, a maintenance employee fell to his death through the guard screen.

On July 4, 1974, two maintenance employees, Virgil Deemer and Thomas Cornwell, met with the plant supervisor to voice their concern about the safety of the screen. Unsatisfied with the supervisor's response, on July 9 they met with the plant safety director and voiced similar concerns. When they asked him for the name, address, and telephone number of the local OSHA office, he told them they "had better stop and think about" what they were doing. The safety director then furnished them with the requested information, and later that day, one of the men contacted the regional OSHA office and discussed the guard screen.

The next day, Deemer and Cornwell reported for the night shift at 10:45 P.M. Their foreman directed the two men to perform their usual maintenance duties on a section of the screen. Claiming that the screen was unsafe, they refused to carry out the directive. The foreman sent them to the personnel office, where they were ordered to punch out without working or being paid for the remaining six hours of the shift. The two men subsequently received written reprimands, which were placed in their employment files.

The secretary of labor filed suit, alleging that Whirlpool's actions constituted discrimination against the two men in violation of the Occupational Safety and Health Act. *Whirlpool Corporation v. Marshall, Secretary of Labor*, 445 U.S. 1, 100 S.Ct. 883, 1980 U.S. Lexis 81, (U.S. Sup.Ct.)

Ethics Issues

1. What law did the workers allege Whirlpool Corporation had violated?
2. Did Whirlpool act ethically in this case?
3. Can employees engage in self-help under certain circumstances under OSHA regulations?
4. Who wins? Why?

Endnotes

1. 29 U.S.C. Sections 553 and 651–678.
2. For example, the Railway Safety Act and the Coal Mine Safety Act regulate workplace safety of railway workers and coal miners, respectively.
3. 29 U.S.C. Sections 201–206.
4. 29 U.S.C. Sections 2601, 2611–2619, and 2651–2654.
5. 26 U.S.C. Sections 1161–1169.
6. 29 U.S.C. Section 1001 *et seq.*
7. 29 U.S.C. Section 1802.
8. 8 U.S.C. Section 1101 *et seq.*
9. 26 U.S.C. Sections 3301–3310.
10. 26 U.S.C. Sections 3101–3125.
11. 26 U.S.C. Sections 1401–1403.

21

Equal Opportunity in Employment

"What people have always sought is equality of rights before the law. For rights that were not open to all equally would not be rights."

—Cicero
De Officiis, Bk. II., Ch. XII

Chapter Objectives

After studying this chapter, you should be able to:

1. Describe the scope of coverage of Title VII of the Civil Rights Act of 1964.
2. Identify race, color, and national origin discrimination that violates Title VII.
3. Identify sex discrimination—including sexual harassment—that violates Title VII.
4. Describe the scope of coverage of the Age Discrimination in Employment Act (ADEA).
5. Describe the protections afforded by the Americans with Disabilities Act (ADA) of 1990.

Chapter Contents

- Equal Employment Opportunity Commission (EEOC)
- Title VII of the Civil Rights Act
- Civil Rights Act of 1866
- Equal Pay Act
- Age Discrimination in Employment Act (ADEA)
- Americans with Disabilities Act (ADA)
- Affirmative Action

Under common law, employers could terminate an employee at any time and for whatever reason. In this same vein, employers were free to hire and promote anyone they chose without violating the law. This often created unreasonable hardship on employees and erected employment barriers to certain minority classes.

Starting in the 1960s, Congress began enacting a comprehensive set of federal laws that eliminated major forms of employment discrimination. These laws, which were passed to guarantee **equal employment opportunity** to all employees and job applicants, have been broadly interpreted by the federal courts, particularly the U.S. Supreme Court. States have also enacted antidiscrimination laws.

equal opportunity in employment
The right of all employees and job applicants (1) to be treated without discrimination and (2) to be able to sue employers if they are discriminated against.

This chapter discusses federal and state equal opportunity in employment laws.

Parking Space for Individuals with Disabilities. Title I of the Americans with Disabilities Act (ADA) requires employers to make reasonable accommodations for individuals with disabilities that do not cause undue hardship to the employer.

Equal Employment Opportunity Commission (EEOC)

The **Equal Employment Opportunity Commission (EEOC)** is a federal agency responsible for enforcing most federal antidiscrimination laws. The members of the EEOC are appointed by the U.S. president. The EEOC is empowered to conduct investigations, interpret the statutes, encourage conciliation between employees and employers, and bring suit to enforce the law. The EEOC can also seek injunctive relief.

Equal Employment Opportunity Commission (EEOC)
A federal administrative agency responsible for enforcing most federal antidiscrimination laws.

Title VII of the Civil Rights Act

After substantial debate, Congress enacted the **Civil Rights Act of 1964**. **Title VII of the Civil Rights Act of 1964** (called the **Fair Employment Practices Act**) was intended to eliminate job discrimination based on the following *protected classes: (1) race, (2) color, (3) national origin, (4) sex,* and *(5) religion.*

Title VII of the Civil Rights Act of 1964
A title of a federal statute enacted to eliminate job discrimination based on five protected classes: *race, color, religion, sex,* and *national origin.*

As amended by the **Equal Employment Opportunity Act of 1972**, Section 703(a)(2) of Title VII provides in pertinent part that:

> It shall be an unlawful employment practice for an employer
>
> (1) to fail or refuse to hire or to discharge any individual, or otherwise to discriminate against any individual with respect to his compensation, terms, conditions, or privileges of employment, because of such individual's race, color, religion, sex, or national origin; or

(2) to limit, segregate, or classify his employees or applicants for employment in any way which would deprive or tend to deprive any individual of employment opportunities or otherwise adversely affect his status as an employee, because of such individual's race, color, religion, sex, or national origin.

Scope of Coverage of Title VII

Title VII of the Civil Rights Act of 1964 applies to (1) employers with 15 or more employees, (2) all employment agencies, (3) labor unions with 15 or more members, (4) state and local governments and their agencies, and (5) most federal government employment. Indian tribes and tax-exempt private clubs are expressly excluded from coverage.[1]

Rights matter most when they are claimed by unpopular minorities.

J. Michael Kirby
Sydney Morning Herald
(November 30, 1985)

Title VII prohibits discrimination in hiring, decisions regarding promotion or demotion, payment of compensation and fringe benefits, availability of job training and apprenticeship opportunities, referral systems for employment, decisions regarding dismissal, work rules, and any other "term, condition, or privilege" of employment. Any employee of covered employers, including undocumented aliens,[2] may bring actions for employment discrimination under Title VII.

Forms of Title VII Actions

Title VII prohibits the following forms of employment discrimination based on any of the five prohibited factors listed previously:

1. ***Disparate-treatment discrimination.*** **Disparate-treatment discrimination** occurs when an employer treats a specific *individual* less favorably than others because of that person's race, color, national origin, sex, or religion. In such situations, the complainant must prove that (1) he or she belongs to a Title VII protected class, (2) he or she applied for and was qualified for the employment position, (3) he or she was rejected despite this, and (4) the employer kept the position open and sought applications from persons with the complainant's qualifications.[3]

   Consider This Example A member of a minority race applies for a promotion to a position advertised as available at his company. The minority applicant, who is qualified for the position, is rejected by the company, which hires a nonminority applicant for the position. The minority applicant sues under Title VII. He has a prima facie case of illegal discrimination. The burden of proof shifts to the employer to prove a nondiscriminatory reason for its decision. If the employer offers a reason, such as saying that the minority applicant lacked sufficient experience, the burden shifts back to the minority applicant to prove that this was just a *pretest* (not the real reason) for the employer's decision.

disparate-treatment discrimination
A type of discrimination that occurs when an employer discriminates against a specific *individual* because of his or her race, color, national origin, sex, or religion.

2. ***Disparate-impact discrimination.*** **Disparate-impact discrimination** occurs when an employer discriminates against an entire protected *class*. Many disparate-impact cases are brought as class action lawsuits. Often, this type of discrimination is proven through statistical data about the employer's employment practices. The plaintiff must demonstrate a *causal link* between the challenged practice and the statistical imbalance. Showing a statistical disparity between the percentage of protected class employees versus the percentage of the population that the protected class makes within the surrounding community is not enough, by itself, to prove discrimination.

   Consider This Example Disparate-impact discrimination occurs when an employer adopts a work rule that is neutral on its face but is shown to cause an adverse impact on a protected class. If an employer has a rule that all applicants for a position of

disparate-impact discrimination
A type of discrimination that occurs when an employer discriminates against an entire *protected class* (e.g., where an employment practice or rule that is neutral on its face causes an adverse impact on a protected class).

executive must be at least 5'8" tall, this looks like a neutral rule because it applies to both males and females. However, because this rule is unrelated to the performance of an executive position and eliminates many more females than males from being hired or promoted to an executive position, it is disparate-impact sex discrimination in violation of Title VII.

In a case involving intentional discrimination, the aggrieved party can recover compensatory damages. A court can award punitive damages against an employer in a case involving an employer's malice or reckless indifference to federally protected rights. The sum of compensatory and punitive damages is capped at up to $50,000 for employers with 100 or fewer employees, $100,000 for employers with 101 to 200 employees, $200,000 for employers with 201 to 500 employees, and $300,000 for employers with more than 500 employees.

Procedure for Bringing a Title VII Action

To bring an action under Title VII, a private complainant must first file a complaint with the EEOC.[4] The EEOC is given the opportunity to sue the employer on the complainant's behalf. If the EEOC chooses not to bring suit, it will issue a *right to sue letter* to the complainant. This gives the complainant the right to sue the employer.

Remedies for Violations of Title VII

A successful plaintiff in a Title VII action can recover back pay and reasonable attorneys' fees. The courts also have broad authority to grant equitable remedies. For instance, the courts can order reinstatement, grant fictional seniority, and issue injunctions to compel the hiring or promotion of protected minorities.

> Racial discrimination in any form and in any degree has no justifiable part whatever in our democratic way of life. It is unattractive in any setting but it is utterly revolting among a free people who have embraced the principles set forth in the Constitution of the United States.
>
> Judge Murphy
> Dissenting opinion, *Korematsu v. U.S.* (1944)

Race, Color, and National Origin Discrimination

Title VII of the Civil Rights Act of 1964 was primarily enacted to prohibit employment discrimination based on *race, color, and national origin*. *Race* refers to broad categories such as black, Caucasian, Asian, and Native American. *Color* refers to the color of a person's skin. *National origin* refers to the country of a person's ancestors or cultural characteristics.

The following case demonstrates race discrimination.

Case 21.1

Race Discrimination

National Association for the Advancement of Colored People, Newark Branch v. Town of Harrison, New Jersey

907 F.2d 1408, 1990 U.S. App. Lexis 11793

United States Court of Appeals, Third Circuit

Background and Facts

The town of Harrison, New Jersey (Harrison), adopted Ordinance 747, which stipulated that "all officers and employees of the Town shall, as a condition of employment, be bona fide residents of the Town." Because of the implementation of this ordinance for years, none of the 51 police officers, 55 firefighters, or 80 nonuniformed employees of the town were black. Although Harrison is a small primarily white community located in Hudson County, New Jersey, it is clearly aligned with Essex County to the west and is considered an extension of the city of Newark, which it abuts. Adjacent counties are within an easy commute of Harrison. Only 0.2 percent of Harrison's population is black. Several blacks who were members of the National Association for the Advancement of Colored People, Newark Branch (NAACP), applied for employment with Harrison but were rejected because they did not meet the residency requirement. The NAACP sued Harrison for race discrimination in violation of Title VII. The U.S. district court dismissed the plaintiff's complaint. The NAACP appealed.

Issue

Does the residency requirement of the town of Harrison violate Title VII of the Civil Rights Act of 1964?

In the Language of the Court

The geographical area from which Harrison draws employees includes its own county of Hudson as well as Bergen, Essex, and Union counties. These four counties have a total civilian labor force of 1,353,555 of which 214,747 are black. By reason of the geographical location and the flow of transportation facilities, Harrison could reasonably be viewed as functionally a component of the city of Newark and a part of Essex County. Newark's population is approximately 60% black. Essex County's civilian labor force totals 391,612 of which 130,397 (or 33.3%) are black. It would be hard to conclude that among the very substantial number of black workers in the four-county labor market there are not large numbers of persons qualified to serve as police officers, firefighters, clerk typists, and laborers.

For all practical purposes, Harrison has no black residents. Thus, to limit employment or applications for employment to residents effectively excludes black persons from employment by the municipality. There is strong evidence that, if the residency requirement were removed, qualified black persons would seek positions with Harrison's municipal government. Thus, Harrison's facially neutral residency requirements have been shown to have a disproportionate impact upon black persons.

Decision and Remedy

The court held that the plaintiffs had established that the ordinance constituted disparate-impact race discrimination in violation of Title VII of the Civil Rights Act of 1964. The court issued an injunction against enforcement of the ordinance.

Business and Ethics Questions

1. Would the same residency requirement rule cause disparate impact discrimination if it were adopted by New York City or Los Angeles? Explain.
2. Did the town of Harrison act ethically when it adopted the residency requirements?
3. Could a private business impose a residency requirement on its employees?

Sex Discrimination

Although the prohibition against **sex discrimination** applies equally to men and women, the overwhelming majority of Title VII sex discrimination cases are brought by women. The old airline practice of ignoring the marital status of male flight attendants but hiring only single female flight attendants is an example of such discrimination.

sex discrimination
Discrimination against a person solely because of his or her sex.

In 1978, the **Pregnancy Discrimination Act** was enacted as an amendment to Title VII.[5] This amendment forbids employment discrimination because of "pregnancy, childbirth, or related medical conditions." Thus, a work rule that prohibits the hiring of pregnant women violates Title VII.

In the following case, the court found sex discrimination in violation of Title VII.

Case 21.2
Sex Discrimination

Barbano v. Madison County
922 F.2d 139, 1990 U.S.App. Lexis 22494
United States Court of Appeals, Second Circuit

Background and Facts

In February 1980, the position of director of the Madison County Veterans Service Agency became vacant. The Madison County Board of Supervisors (Board) appointed a committee of five men to hold interviews. Maureen E. Barbano applied for the position and was interviewed by the committee. Upon entering the interview, Barbano heard someone say, "Oh, another woman." When the interview began, Donald Greene, a committee member, said he would not consider "some woman" for the position. He then asked Barbano personal questions about her plans on having a family and whether her husband would object to her transporting male veterans. Barbano said the questions were irrelevant and discriminatory. No committee member asked Barbano any substantive questions. Ultimately, the Board acted on the committee's recommendation and hired a male candidate. Barbano sued Madison County for sex discrimination in violation of Title VII. The district court held in favor of Barbano and awarded her $55,000 in back pay, prejudgment interest, and attorneys' fees. Madison County appealed.

Issue

Did the defendant engage in sex discrimination in violation of Title VII?

In the Language of the Court

There is little doubt that Greene's statements during the interview were discriminatory. He said he would not consider

(continued)

Barbano v. Madison County

922 F.2d 139, 1990 U.S.App. Lexis 22494
United States Court of Appeals, Second Circuit
(continued)

"some woman" for the position. His questioning Barbano about whether she would get pregnant and quit was also discriminatory, since it was unrelated to a bona fide occupational qualification. Similarly, Greene's questions about whether Barbano's husband would mind if she had to "run around the country with men," and that he would not want his wife to do it, were discriminatory.

Given the discriminatory tenor of the interview, and the acquiescence of the other Committee members to Greene's line of questioning, it follows that the trial court judge could find that those present at the interview, and not merely Greene, discriminated against Barbano. The record before us supports the district court's finding that the Board discriminated in making the hiring decision.

Decision and Remedy

The Court of Appeals held that the defendant, Madison County, had engaged in sex discrimination in violation of Title VII. The Court of Appeals affirmed the district court's decision and award of damages to plaintiff Barbano.

Business and Ethics Questions

1. Why are questions concerning family obligations made illegal by Title VII?
2. Was Greene's conduct morally reprehensible?
3. What actions should employers take to ensure that their interviewers and other personnel understand Title VII and other antidiscrimination laws?

Hong Kong, China. Many foreign countries are granting greater opportunities and protections to females in business. In addition, women are becoming entrepreneurs all over the world.

Sexual Harassment

In the modern work environment, co-workers sometimes become sexually interested or involved with each other voluntarily. On other occasions, though, a co-worker's sexual advances are not welcome.

sexual harassment
Lewd remarks, touching, intimidation, posting of pinups, and other verbal or physical conduct of a sexual nature that occur on the job.

Refusing to hire or promote someone unless he or she has sex with the manager or supervisor is sex discrimination that violates Title VII. Other forms of conduct, such as lewd remarks, touching, intimidation, posting of indecent materials, and other verbal or physical conduct of a sexual nature, constitute **sexual harassment** and violate Title VII.[6]

To determine what conduct creates a hostile work environment, the Supreme Court stated:

> We can say that whether an environment is "hostile" or "abusive" can be determined only by looking at all the circumstances. These may include the frequency of the discriminatory conduct; its severity; whether it is physically threatening or humiliating, or a mere offensive utterance; and whether it unreasonably interferes with an employee's work performance.[7]

In the following case, the U.S. Supreme Court decided that the challenged conduct created a hostile work environment.

Case 21.3
Sexual Harassment

U.S. SUPREME COURT
Harris v. Forklift Systems, Inc.
510 U.S. 17, 114 S.Ct. 367, 1993 U.S. Lexis 7155
Supreme Court of the United States

Background and Facts

Teresa Harris worked as a manager at Forklift Systems, Inc. (Forklift), an equipment rental company, from April 1985 until October 1987. Charles Hardy was Forklift's president. Throughout Harris's time at Forklift, Hardy often insulted her because of her sex and made her the target of unwanted sexual innuendos. Hardy told Harris on several occasions, in the presence of other employees, "You're a woman, what do you know" and "We need a man as the rental manager"; at least once, he told her she was "a dumb ass woman." Again in front of others, he suggested that the two of them "go to the Holiday Inn to negotiate Harris's raise." He made sexual innuendos about Harris's and other women's clothing.

In mid-August 1987, Harris complained to Hardy about his conduct. Hardy said he was surprised that Harris was offended, claimed he was only joking, and apologized. He also promised he would stop, and based on this assurance, Harris stayed on the job. But in early September, Hardy began anew: While Harris was arranging a deal with one of Forklift's customers, he asked her, again in front of other employees, "What did you do, promise the guy some sex Saturday night?" On October 1, Harris collected her paycheck and quit.

Harris then sued Forklift, claiming that Hardy's conduct had created an abusive work environment for her because of her sex. The district court held that because Harris had not suffered severe psychological injury, she could not recover. The Court of Appeals affirmed. Harris appealed to the U.S. Supreme Court.

Issue

Must conduct, to be actionable as abusive work environment harassment, seriously affect the victim's psychological well-being?

In the Language of the U.S. Supreme Court

When the workplace is permeated with discriminatory intimidation, ridicule, and insult, that is sufficiently severe or pervasive to alter the conditions of the victim's employment and create an abusive working environment, Title VII is violated.

A discriminatory abusive work environment, even one that does not seriously affect employees' psychological well-being, can and often will detract from employees' job performance, discourage employees from remaining on the job, or keep them from advancing in their careers. The very fact that the discriminatory conduct was so severe or pervasive that it created a work environment abusive to employees because of their race, gender, religion or national origin offends Title VII's broad rule of workplace equality.

Certainly Title VII bars conduct that would seriously affect a reasonable person's psychological well-being, but the statute is not limited to such conduct. So long as the environment would reasonably be perceived, and is perceived, as hostile or abusive, there is no need for it also to be psychologically injurious.

Decision and Remedy

The Supreme Court held that Title VII does not require a victim to prove that the challenged conduct seriously affected her psychological well-being. The Supreme Court reversed the decision of the Court of Appeals and remanded the case to the district court for trial.

Business and Ethics Questions

1. Should an employer be held liable for sexual harassment committed by one of its employees?
2. What penalty should be assessed against Hardy for his conduct?
3. How can businesses eliminate sexual harassment on the job?

Same-Sex Discrimination

For years, it was unclear whether same-sex sexual harassment and sex discrimination in employment were actionable under Title VII. In 1998, in *Omcale v. Sundowner Offshore Services, Incorporated*,[8] the U.S. Supreme Court held that same-sex discrimination and harassment violated Title VII. Many state and local antidiscrimination laws outlaw same-sex discrimination and harassment in the workplace.

Contemporary Trend

Employer's Defense to a Charge of Sexual Harassment

In two cases, *Faragher v. City of Boca Raton* and *Burlington Industries, Inc. v. Ellerth*, female plaintiffs sued their employers, proving that their supervisors had engaged in unconsented physical touching and verbal sexual harassment. In both cases, the female employee quit her job and sued her employer for sexual harassment in violation of Title VII. In the first case, the employer had never disseminated to its employees a policy against sexual harassment. In the second case, the employer had disseminated to its employees its policy against sexual harassment and had put into place a complaint system that was not used by the female employee. After trials and appeals, the U.S. Supreme Court accepted these two cases for review.

The U.S. Supreme Court, in these two decisions, held that an employer is not strictly liable for sexual harassment. The Supreme Court held that an employer may raise an *affirmative defense* against liability by proving two elements:

1. The employer exercised reasonable care to prevent, and promptly correct, any sexual-harassing behavior.
2. The plaintiff employee unreasonably failed to take advantage of any preventive or corrective opportunities provided by the employer or to otherwise avoid harm.

The defendant employer has the burden of proving this affirmative defense. In determining whether the defense has been proven, a court must consider (1) whether the employer has an antiharassment policy, (2) whether the employer had a complaint mechanism in place, (3) whether employees were informed of the antiharassment policy and complaint procedure, and (4) other factors that the court deems relevant. *Faragher v. City of Boca Raton*, 524 U.S. 775, 118 S.Ct. 2275, 1998 U.S. Lexis 4216 (U.S. Sup.Ct.) and *Burlington Industries, Inc. v. Ellerth*, 524 U.S. 742, 118 S.Ct. 2257, 1998 U.S. Lexis 4217 (U.S. Sup.Ct.) ■

Religious Discrimination

religious discrimination
Discrimination against a person solely because of his or her religion or religious practices.

Title VII prohibits employment discrimination based on a person's religion. Religions include traditional religions, other religions that recognize a supreme being, and religions based on ethical or spiritual tenets. Many **religious discrimination** cases involve a conflict between an employer's work rule and an employee's religious beliefs (e.g., when an employee is required to work on his or her religious holiday).

The right of an employee to practice his or her religion is not absolute. Under Title VII, an employer is under a duty to *reasonably accommodate* the religious observances, practices, or beliefs of its employees if doing so does not cause an *undue hardship* on the employer. The courts must apply these general standards to specific fact situations. In making their decisions, the courts must consider such factors as the size of the employer, the importance of the employee's position, and the availability of alternative workers.

Title VII expressly permits religious organizations to give preference in employment to individuals of a particular religion. For example, if a person applies for a job with a religious organization but does not subscribe to its religious tenets, the organization may refuse to hire that person.

Defenses to a Title VII Action

Title VII and case law recognize the following defenses to a charge of discrimination under Title VII:

- ***Merit.*** Employers can select or promote employees based on *merit*. Merit decisions are often based on work, educational experience, and professionally developed ability tests. To be lawful under Title VII, the requirement must be job related. For example, requiring a person to pass a typing test to be hired as a typist would be lawful. Requiring a person to pass a college-level English composition test to be employed as a maintenance worker would violate Title VII.
- ***Seniority.*** Many employers maintain *seniority* systems that reward long-term employees. Higher wages, fringe benefits, and other preferential treatment (e.g., choice of working hours and vacation schedule) are examples of such rewards. Seniority systems provide an incentive for employees to stay with the company. Such systems are lawful if they are not the result of intentional discrimination.
- ***Bona fide occupational qualification (BFOQ).*** Discrimination based on protected classes (other than race or color) is permitted if it is shown to be a **bona fide occupational qualification (BFOQ)**. To be legal, a BFOQ must be both *job related* and a *business necessity*. For example, allowing only women to be locker room attendants in a women's gym is a valid BFOQ, but prohibiting males from being managers or instructors at the same gym would not a be a BFOQ.

As the following U.S. Supreme Court case shows, BFOQ exceptions are narrowly interpreted by the courts.

bona fide occupational qualification (BFOQ)
Lawful employment discrimination that is based on a protected class (other than race or color) and is *job related* and a *business necessity*. This exception is narrowly interpreted by the courts.

Case 21.4 Bona Fide Occupational Qualification

U.S. SUPREME COURT

International Union, United Automobile, Aerospace and Agricultural Implement Workers of America, UAW v. Johnson Controls, Inc.

499 U.S. 187, 111 S.Ct. 1196, 1991 U.S. Lexis 1715
Supreme Court of the United States

Background and Facts

Johnson Controls, Inc. (Johnson Controls), manufactures batteries. Lead is the primary ingredient in the manufacturing process. Exposure to lead entails health risks, including risk of harm to any fetus carried by a female employee. To protect unborn children from such risk, Johnson Controls adopted an employment rule that prevent pregnant women and women of childbearing age from working at jobs involving lead exposure. Only women who were sterilized or could prove they could not have children were not affected by the rule. Consequently, most female employees were relegated to lower-paying clerical jobs at the company. Several female employees filed a class action suit, challenging Johnson Controls's fetal-protection policy as sex discrimination in violation of Title VII. The district court held that the policy was justified as a bona fide occupational qualification (BFOQ) and granted summary judgment to Johnson Controls, and the Court of Appeals affirmed. The plaintiffs appealed to the U.S. Supreme Court.

Issue

Is Johnson Controls's fetal-protection policy a BFOQ?

In the Language of the U.S. Supreme Court

The bias in Johnson Controls' policy is obvious. Fertile men, but not fertile women, are given a choice as to whether they wish to risk their reproductive health for a particular job. Johnson Controls' fetal-protection policy explicitly discriminates against women on the basis of their sex. The policy excludes women with childbearing capacity from lead-exposed jobs and so creates a facial classification based on gender.

The bona fide occupational qualifications (BFOQ) defense is written narrowly, and this Court has read it narrowly. We have no difficulty concluding that Johnson Controls cannot establish a BFOQ. Fertile women, as far as appears in the record, participate in the manufacture of batteries as efficiently as anyone else. Johnson Controls' professed moral and ethical concerns

(continued)

International Union, United Automobile, Aerospace and Agricultural Implement Workers of America, UAW v. Johnson Controls, Inc.

499 U.S. 187, 111 S.Ct. 1196, 1991 U.S. Lexis 1715
Supreme Court of the United States
(continued)

about the welfare of the next generation do not suffice to establish a BFOQ of female sterility. Decisions about the welfare of future children must be left to the parents who conceive, bear, support, and raise them rather than to the employers who hire those parents.

Decision and Remedy

The U.S. Supreme Court held that Johnson Controls's fetal-protection policy was not a BFOQ. Instead, it was sex discrimination in violation of Title VII. The Supreme Court reversed the decision of the Court of Appeals and remanded the case for further proceedings.

Business and Ethics Questions

1. Should any BFOQ exceptions to Title VII actions be permitted? Why or why not?
2. Should Johnson Controls's moral and ethical concerns about the welfare of the next generation justify its actions?
3. Does Johnson Controls have any tort liability to children who are born injured by exposure to lead? How can Johnson Controls limit such liability?

Concept Summary Title VII of the Civil Rights Act

Covered employers and employment decisions	1. **Employers.** Employers with 15 or more employees for 20 weeks in the current or preceding year, all employment agencies, labor unions with 15 or more members, state and local governments, and most federal agencies. 2. **Employment decisions.** Decisions regarding hiring; promotion; demotion; payment of salaries, wages, and fringe benefits; dismissal; job training and apprenticeships; work rules; or any other *term, condition*, or *privilege* of employment. Decisions to admit partners to a partnership are also covered.
Protected classes	1. **Race.** A broad class of individuals with common characteristics (e.g., black, Caucasian, Asian, Native American). 2. **Color.** The color of a person's skin (e.g., light-skinned person, dark-skinned person). 3. **National origin.** A person's country of origin or national heritage (e.g., Italian, Hispanic). 4. **Sex.** A person's sex, whether male or female. Includes sexual harassment and discrimination against females who are pregnant. 5. **Religion.** A person's religious beliefs. An employer has a duty to reasonably accommodate an employee's religious beliefs if doing so does not cause an undue hardship on the employer.
Types of discrimination	1. **Disparate-treatment discrimination.** Discrimination against a specific individual because that person belongs to a protected class. 2. **Disparate-impact discrimination.** Discrimination in which an employer discriminates against a protected class. A neutral-looking employment rule that causes discrimination against a protected class is disparate-impact discrimination.
Defenses	1. **Merit.** Job-related experience, education, or unbiased employment test. 2. **Seniority.** Length of time an employee has been employed by the employer. Intentional discrimination based on seniority is unlawful.

	3. **Bona fide occupational qualification (BFOQ).** Discrimination based on sex, religion, or national origin is permitted if it is a valid BFOQ for the position. Qualification based on race or color is not a permissible BFOQ.
Remedies	1. The court may order the payment of back pay, issue an injunction awarding reinstatement, grant fictional seniority, or order some other equitable remedy. 2. The court can award compensatory damages in cases of intentional discrimination. The court can award punitive damages in cases involving an employer's malice or reckless indifference to federally protected rights.

Civil Rights Act of 1866

The **Civil Rights Act of 1866** was enacted after the Civil War. **Section 1981** of this act states that all persons "have the same right . . . to make and enforce contracts . . . as is enjoyed by white persons."[9] This law was enacted to give African Americans, just freed from slavery, the same right to contract as Caucasians. Section 1981 expressly prohibits racial discrimination; it has also been held to forbid discrimination based on national origin.

Civil Rights Act of 1866
A federal statute enacted after the Civil War that says all persons "have the same right . . . to make and enforce contracts . . . as is enjoyed by white persons." It prohibits racial and national origin employment discrimination.

Employment decisions are covered by Section 1981 because the employment relationship is contractual. Although most racial and national origin employment discrimination cases are brought under Title VII, there are two reasons that a complainant would bring the action under Section 1981: (1) A private plaintiff can bring an action without going through the procedural requirements of Title VII, and (2) there is no cap on the recovery of compensatory or punitive damages.

Equal Pay Act

Discrimination often takes the form of different pay scales for men and women performing the same job. The **Equal Pay Act of 1963** protects both sexes from pay discrimination based on sex.[10] This act covers all levels of private-sector employees and state and local government employees. Federal workers are not covered, however.

Equal Pay Act of 1963
A federal statute that protects both sexes from pay discrimination based on sex. It extends to jobs that require equal skill, equal effort, equal responsibility, and similar working conditions.

The act prohibits disparity in pay for jobs that require *equal skill* (i.e., equal experience), *equal effort* (i.e., mental and physical exertion), *equal responsibility* (i.e., supervision and accountability), or *similar working conditions* (e.g., dangers of injury, exposure to the elements). To make this determination, the courts examine the actual requirements of jobs to determine whether they are equal and similar. If two jobs are determined to be equal and similar, an employer cannot pay disparate wages to members of different sexes.

Employees can bring a private cause of action against an employer for violating the act. Back pay and liquidated damages are recoverable. In addition, the employer must increase the wages of the discriminated-against employee to eliminate the unlawful disparity of wages. The wages of other employees may not be lowered.

Criteria That Justify a Differential in Wages The Equal Pay Act expressly provides four criteria that justify a differential in wages. These defenses include payment systems that are based on

God . . . hath made of one blood all nations of men for to dwell on the face of the earth.
Bible, Acts 17:26

- Seniority
- Merit (as long as there is some identifiable measurement standard)

- Quantity or quality of product (commission, piecework, or quality-control–based payment systems are permitted)
- "Any factor other than sex" (including shift differentials, i.e., night versus day shifts)

The employer bears the burden of proving these defenses.

Age Discrimination in Employment Act (ADEA)

Age Discrimination in Employment Act (ADEA) of 1967
A federal statute that prohibits age discrimination practices against employees who are 40 and older.

Some employers have discriminated against employees and prospective employees based on their age. Primarily, employers have often refused to hire older workers. The **Age Discrimination in Employment Act (ADEA)**, which prohibits certain *age discrimination* practices, was enacted in 1967.[11]

The ADEA covers nonfederal employers with at least 20 employees, labor unions with at least 25 members, and all employment agencies. State and local government employees except those in policy-making positions are covered, as are employees of certain sectors of the federal government.

Older Workers Benefit Protection Act (OWBPA)
A federal statute that prohibits age discrimination in employee benefits.

The ADEA prohibits age discrimination in all employment decisions, including hiring, promotions, payment of compensation, and other terms and conditions of employment. The **Older Workers Benefit Protection Act (OWBPA)** amended the ADEA to prohibit age discrimination with regard to employee benefits. Employers cannot use employment advertisements that discriminate against applicants covered by the ADEA. The same defenses that are available in a Title VII action are also available in an ADEA action.

Protected Age Categories

Originally, the ADEA prohibited employment discrimination against persons between the ages of 40 and 65. In 1978, its coverage was extended to persons up to the age of 70. Further amendments completely eliminated an age ceiling, so the ADEA now applies to employees who are 40 and older. As a result, covered employers cannot establish mandatory retirement ages for their employees.

Because persons under 40 are not protected by the ADEA, an employer can maintain an employment policy of hiring only workers who are 40 years of age or older without violating the ADEA. However, the employer could not maintain an employment practice whereby it hired only persons 50 years of age and older because it would discriminate against persons age 40 to 49.

By what justice can an association of citizens be held together when there is no equality among the citizens?

Cicero
De Re Publia De Legibus J XXXII 49

The ADEA is administered by the EEOC. Private plaintiffs can also sue under the ADEA. A successful plaintiff in an ADEA action can recover back wages, attorneys' fees, and equitable relief, including hiring, reinstatement, and promotion. Where a violation of the ADEA is found, the employer must raise the wages of the discriminated-against employee. It cannot lower the wages of other employees.

Americans with Disabilities Act (ADA)

Americans with Disabilities Act (ADA) of 1990
A federal statute that imposes obligations on employers and providers of public transportation, telecommunications, and public accommodations to accommodate individuals with disabilities.

The **Americans with Disabilities Act (ADA) of 1990,**[12] which was signed into law July 26, 1990, is the most comprehensive piece of civil rights legislation since the Civil Rights Act of 1964. The ADA imposes obligations on employers and providers of public transportation, telecommunications, and public accommodations to accommodate individuals with disabilities.

Title I of the ADA

Title I of the ADA prohibits employment discrimination against qualified individuals with disabilities in regard to job application procedures, hiring, compensation, training, promotion, and termination. Title I covers employers with 15 or more employees. The United States, corporations wholly owned by the United States, and bona fide tax-exempt private membership clubs are exempt from Title I coverage.

Title I of the ADA
A title of a federal statute that prohibits employment discrimination against qualified individuals with disabilities in regard to job application procedures, hiring, compensation, training, promotion, and termination.

Title I requires an employer to make reasonable accommodations to individuals with disabilities that do not cause undue hardship to the employer. **Reasonable accommodations** may include making facilities readily accessible to individuals with disabilities, providing part-time or modified work schedules, acquiring equipment or devices, modifying examination and training materials, and providing qualified readers or interpreters.

Employers are not obligated to provide accommodations that would impose an **undue burden**. This means actions that would require significant difficulty or expense. Factors such as the nature and cost of accommodation, the overall financial resources of the employer, and the employer's type of operation are considered by the EEOC and the courts. Obviously, what may be a significant difficulty or expense for a smaller employer may not be an undue hardship for a large employer.

Qualified Individual with a Disability

A **qualified individual with a disability** is a person who, with or without reasonable accommodation, can perform the essential functions of the job that person desires or holds. A person with a disability is someone who (1) has a physical or mental impairment that substantially limits one or more of his or her major life activities, (2) has a record of such impairment, or (3) is regarded as having such impairment. Mental retardation, paraplegia, schizophrenia, cerebral palsy, epilepsy, diabetes, muscular dystrophy, multiple sclerosis, cancer, infection with HIV (human immunodeficiency virus), and visual, speech, and hearing impairments are covered under the ADA. A current user of illegal drugs or an alcoholic who uses alcohol or is under the influence of alcohol at the workplace is not covered. However, recovering alcoholics and former users of illegal drugs are protected.

qualified individual with a disability
A person who (1) has a physical or mental impairment that substantially limits one or more of his or her major life activities, (2) has a record of such impairment, or (3) is regarded as having such impairment.

Forbidden Conduct

Title I of the ADA limits an employer's ability to inquire into or test for an applicant's disabilities. Title I forbids an employer from asking a job applicant about the existence, nature, and severity of a disability. An employer may, however, inquire about the applicant's ability to perform job-related functions. Preemployment medical examinations are forbidden before a job offer. Once a job offer has been made, an employer may require a medical examination and may condition the offer on the examination results, as long as all entering employees are subject to such an examination. The information obtained must be kept confidential.

All about me may be silence and darkness, yet within me, in the spirit, is music and brightness, and color flashes through all my thoughts.

Helen Keller
The Open Door (1957)

Procedure and Remedies

Title I of the ADA is administered by the EEOC. An aggrieved individual must first file a charge with the EEOC, which may take action against the employer or permit the individual to pursue a private cause of action. Relief can take the form of an injunction, hiring or reinstatement (with back pay), payment of attorneys' fees, and recovery of compensatory and punitive damages (subject to the same caps as Title VII damages).

In the following case, the U.S. Supreme Court was called upon to interpret and apply the ADA.

Case 21.5
Americans with Disabilities Act

U.S. SUPREME COURT
PGA Tour, Inc. v. Martin
532 U.S. 661, 121 S.Ct. 1879, 2001 U.S. Lexis 4115
Supreme Court of the United States

Background and Facts

The PGA Tour, Inc., is a nonprofit entity that sponsors professional golf tournaments. The PGA has adopted a set of rules that apply to its golf tour. One rule requires golfers to walk the course during PGA-sponsored tournaments. Casey Martin is a talented amateur golfer who won many high school and university golf championships. Martin has been affected with Klippel-Trenaunay-Weber Syndrome, a degenerative circulatory disorder that obstructs the flow of blood from his right leg to his heart. The disease is progressive and has atrophied his right leg. Walking causes Martin pain, fatigue, and anxiety, with significant risk of hemorrhaging.

When Martin turned professional, he qualified for the PGA Tour. He made a request to use a golf cart while playing in PGA tournaments. When the PGA denied his request, Martin sued the PGA for violation of the Americans with Disabilities Act (ADA) for not making reasonable accommodations for his disability. The district court sided with Martin and ordered the PGA to permit Martin to use a golf cart, and the Court of Appeals affirmed. The U.S. Supreme Court agreed to hear the PGA's appeal.

Issue

Does the ADA require the PGA Tour, Inc., to accommodate Casey Martin, a professional golfer with a disability, by permitting him to use a golf cart while playing in PGA-sponsored golf tournaments?

In the Language of the U.S. Supreme Court

As an initial matter, we observe that the use of carts is not itself inconsistent with the fundamental character of the game of golf. From early on, the essence of the game has been shot-making—using clubs to cause a ball to progress from the teeing ground to a hole some distance away with as few strokes as possible. Golf carts started appearing with increasing regularity on American golf courses in the 1950's. Today they are everywhere. And they are encouraged. For one thing, they often speed up play, and for another, they are great revenue producers.

The force of petitioner PGA Tour's argument is, first of all, mitigated by the fact that golf is a game in which it is impossible to guarantee that all competitors will play under exactly the same conditions or that an individual's ability will be the sole determinant of the outcome. For example, changes in the weather may produce harder greens and more head winds for the tournament leader than for his closest pursuers. A lucky bounce may save a shot or two. Whether such happenstance events are more or less probable than the likelihood that a golfer afflicted with Klippel-Trenaunay-Weber Syndrome would one day qualify for the PGA Tour, they at least demonstrate that pure chance may have a greater impact on the outcome of elite golf tournaments than the fatigue resulting from the enforcement of the walking rule.

Decision and Remedy

The U.S. Supreme Court held that the ADA requires that the PGA Tour, Inc., accommodate Casey Martin, a professional golfer with a disability, by allowing him to use a golf cart while competing in PGA-sponsored professional golf tournaments. The Supreme Court affirmed the judgment of the Court of Appeals.

Business and Ethics Questions

1. Do you agree with the U.S. Supreme Court's decision? Will the decision open a floodgate of similar lawsuits?
2. Was Casey Martin just asking for "fairness," or was he asking for an advantage when competing in professional golf tournaments?
3. Is the PGA Tour a lucrative business? Will the Supreme Court's ruling have any effect on the revenues generated by the PGA Tour?

Affirmative Action

affirmative action
A policy that provides that certain job preferences will be given to minority or other protected-class applicants when an employer makes an employment decision.

Employers often adopt **affirmative action plans** that provide that certain job preferences will be given to members of minority racial and ethnic groups, females, and other protected-class applicants when an employer makes an employment decision. Such plans can be voluntarily adopted by employers, undertaken to settle a discrimination action, or ordered by the courts.

To be lawful, an affirmative action plan must be narrowly tailored to achieve some compelling interest. Employment quotas based on a specified number or percentage of minority applicants or employees are unlawful. If a person's minority status is only one factor of many factors considered in an employment decision, that decision will be considered lawful.

Affirmative action plans are often controversial. Proponents of such plans argue that the plans are necessary to address imbalances in the workforce and to remedy past discrimination against protected classes. Some argue that affirmative action plans cause work hardship on other employees.

Reverse Discrimination

Title VII not only applies to members of minority groups, but it also protects members of majority classes from discrimination. Lawful affirmative action plans have an effect on members of majority classes. The courts have held that this effect is not actionable by the members of the majority class who are affected.

The courts have held, however, that if an affirmative action plan is based on preestablished numbers or percentage quotas for hiring or promoting minority applicants, then it causes illegal **reverse discrimination**. In this case, the members of the majority class may sue under Title VII and recover damages and other remedies for reverse discrimination.

reverse discrimination
Discrimination against a group that is usually thought of as a majority.

State and Local Government Antidiscrimination Laws

Many state and local governments have adopted laws that prevent discrimination in employment. These laws usually include classes protected by federal equal opportunity laws as well as classes of persons not protected by federal laws.

International Law

International Reach of U.S. Antidiscrimination Laws

The **Civil Rights Act of 1991** protects *U.S. citizens*—but not foreign nationals—employed in a foreign country by U.S.-controlled employers. An employer of a U.S. citizen abroad is subject to claims under Title VII in the following two situations:

1. An employer that is incorporated in the United States operates a branch office in a foreign country. Conduct in the branch office is covered by Title VII.
2. A U.S. parent corporation owns a foreign corporation that is incorporated in another country. The foreign-controlled subsidiary is subject to Title VII.

The 1991 act also extends its international reach to disabilities and age discrimination. ■

Japan.

Terms and Concepts

Equal Employment Opportunity Commission (EEOC)

The EEOC is a federal administrative agency responsible for administering, interpreting, and enforcing most federal equal employment opportunity (antidiscrimination) laws.

Title VII of the Civil Rights Act of 1964

This federal statute prohibits job discrimination based on the (1) race, (2) color, (3) religion, (4) sex, or (5) national origin of the job applicant.

Scope of Coverage of Title VII

1. ***Employers subject to Title VII.*** Employers with 15 or more employees for at least 20 weeks in the current or preceding year, all employment agencies, labor unions with 15 or more members, state and local governments, and most federal agencies are subject to Title VII.
2. ***Employment decisions subject to Title VII.*** Decisions regarding hiring; promotion; demotion; payment of salaries, wages, and fringe benefits; job training and apprenticeships; work rules; or any other "term, condition, or privilege of employment" are subject to Title VII.

Forms of Title VII Actions

1. ***Disparate-treatment discrimination.*** This type of discrimination occurs when an employer treats a specific *individual* less favorably than others because of that person's race, color, national origin, sex, or religion.To be successful, the complainant must prove that:
   a. He or she belongs to a Title VII protected class.
   b. He or she applied for and was qualified for the employment position.
   c. He or she was rejected despite these qualifications.
   d. The employer kept the position open and sought applications from persons with the complainant's qualifications.
2. ***Disparate-impact discrimination.*** This type of discrimination occurs when an employer discriminates against an entire protected *class*. It may be proven by statistical data that demonstrate a causal link between the challenged practice and the statistical imbalance. *Neutral employment rules* that have an adverse impact on a protected class constitute disparate-impact discrimination.

Procedure for Bringing a Title VII Action

1. ***Complaint.*** A private complainant must file a complaint with the EEOC. The EEOC then has the opportunity to sue the employer on the complainant's behalf.
2. ***Right to sue letter.*** If the EEOC chooses not to bring suit, it will issue a *right to sue letter* that authorizes the complainant to sue the employer.

Remedies for Violations of Title VII

A successful plaintiff in a Title VII action can recover back pay, compensatory and punitive damages (subject to certain caps, based on the size of the defendant employer), reasonable attorneys' fees, and equitable remedies such as reinstatement, fictional seniority, and injunctions.

Protected Classes Under Title VIII

Employment discrimination based on the following protected classes is forbidden by Title VII:

1. Race
2. Color
3. National origin
4. Sex
5. Religion

Title VII: Race, Color, and National Origin Discrimination

1. ***Race.*** *Race* is a broad class of individuals with common physical characteristics (e.g., black, Caucasian, Asian, Native American).
2. ***Color.*** *Color* refers to the color of a person's skin (e.g., light-skinned person, dark-skinned person).
3. ***National origin.*** *National origin* is a person's country of origin or national heritage (e.g., Italian, Hispanic).

Title VII: Sex Discrimination

1. ***Sex.*** *Sex* refers to a person's sex, whether male or female.
2. ***Pregnancy.*** The *Pregnancy Discrimination Act of 1978* amended Title VII to forbid employment discrimination because of "pregnancy, childbirth, or related medical conditions."
3. ***Sexual harassment.*** Sexual harassment is lewd remarks, touching, intimidation, posting of pinups, and other verbal or physical conduct of a sexual nature that occurs on the job. Sexual harassment that creates *a hostile work environment* violates Title VII.
4. ***Sexual preference.*** Title VII applies to employment discrimination based on sexual preference.

Title VII: Religious Discrimination

Religious discrimination is discrimination solely because of a person's religious beliefs or practices. An employer has a duty to *reasonably accommodate* an employee's religious beliefs if doing so does not cause an *undue hardship* on the employer.

Defenses to a Title VII Action

1. ***Merit.*** Merit includes job-related experience, education, and unbiased employment tests.
2. ***Seniority.*** Seniority is the length of time an employee has been employed by the employer. Intentional discrimination based on seniority is unlawful.
3. ***Bona fide occupational qualification (BFOQ).*** Employment discrimination based on the sex, religion, or national origin of an applicant is permitted if it is a valid *bona fide occupational qualification (BFOQ)* for the position. To be legal, a BFOQ must be *job related* and a *business necessity*. BFOQ exceptions are narrowly interpreted by the courts.

Civil Rights Act of 1866

1. ***Section 1981 of the Civil Rights Act of 1866.*** This federal statute, enacted after the Civil War, states that all persons "have the same right . . . to make and enforce contracts . . . as is enjoyed by white persons."
2. ***Protected class.*** Section 1981 prohibits *race* and *national origin* discrimination concerning employment contracts.
3. ***Remedies.*** A successful plaintiff can recover back pay, equitable remedies, compensatory and punitive damages, and reasonable attorneys' fees. There are no monetary caps on compensatory and punitive damages.

Equal Pay Act

This federal statute forbids pay discrimination for the same job based on the sex of the employee performing the job. There cannot be pay disparity based on sex for jobs that require equal skill, equal effort, equal responsibility, and similar working conditions.

1. ***Criteria that justify a differential in wages.*** The Equal Pay Act stipulates that the following four criteria justify a differential in wages:
   a. Seniority
   b. Merit
   c. Quantity or quality of work (commission, piecework, or quality control-based pay systems)
   d. Any factor other than sex (e.g., night versus day shifts)

Age Discrimination in Employment Act (ADEA)

This federal statute prohibits employment discrimination against applicants and employees who are 40 years of age or older.

1. ***Older Workers Benefit Protection Act (OWBPA).*** This federal statute amended the ADEA to prohibit age discrimination with respect to employment benefits.
2. ***Defenses.*** The same defenses that are available in a Title VII action are also available in an ADEA action.
3. ***Remedies.*** A successful plaintiff can recover back wages, attorneys' fees, and equitable relief, including hiring, reinstatement, and promotion.

Americans with Disabilities Act (ADA) of 1990

This federal statute imposes obligations on employers and providers of public transportation, telecommunications, and public accommodations to accommodate individuals with disabilities.

Title I of the ADA

This federal law prohibits employment discrimination against qualified individuals with disabilities.

1. ***Reasonable accommodation.*** Title I requires employers to make *reasonable accommodations* to accommodate employees with disabilities that do not cause *undue hardship* to the employer.

Title I: Qualified Individual with a Disability

A qualified individual with a disability is a person who (1) has a physical or mental impairment that substantially limits one or more of his or her major life functions, (2) has a record of such impairment, or (3) is regarded as having such impairment.

Title I: Procedure and Remedies

A successful plaintiff can recover back pay, compensatory and punitive damages (subject to certain caps, based on the size of the defendant employer), reasonable attorneys' fees, and equitable remedies, such as hiring, reinstatement, or promotion.

Affirmative Action and Reverse Discrimination

Affirmative action is a policy that provides that certain job preferences will be given to minority or other protected-class applicants when an employer makes an employment decision.

1. ***Lawfulness of affirmative action plans.*** An employer may adopt a voluntary affirmative action plan that uses race or other protected-class status as a "plus factor" in making employment decisions.
2. ***Reverse discrimination.*** Reverse discrimination is discrimination against a person who is a member of a group that is usually thought of as a majority. Very few reverse discrimination lawsuits are successful.

State and Local Government Antidiscrimination Laws

Many state and local governments have adopted laws that prevent discrimination in employment. These laws usually include classes protected by federal equal opportunity laws (e.g., race, color, national origin, sex, religion, age, disability) as well as classes not protected by federal laws (e.g., homosexuals).

Internet Exercises and Case Questions

Working the Web Internet Exercises

1. Review the case *Gupta v. Florida Bd. of Regents* (5/17/2000, No. 98-5392) via the Cornell Discrimination Web site, at **http://www.ca11.uscourts.gov/opinions/searchpage.php.** According to the 11th Circuit Court of Appeals, is it sexual harassment to make comments to co-workers such as "You are looking very beautiful?"
2. Review Congress's statement of purpose in the ADEA. Has this law served to accomplish that purpose? See the U.S. Equal Employment Opportunity Commission site, at **www.eeoc.gov**, and the "Legal Information Institute: Employment Discrimination" site, at

www.law.cornell.edu/ topics/employment_discrimination.html.

3. For a discussion of the courts' definition of *disability*, see "The Supreme Court's Definition of Disability Under the ADA: A Return to the Dark Ages," at **www.law.ua.edu/lawreview/tucker521.htm.**
4. Find the case *PGA Tour, Inc. v. Martin* involving the ADA and a professional golfer. Do you agree with the court's decision? Try the "Legal Information Institute: Employment Discrimination" site, at **www.law.cornell.edu/ topics/employment_discrimination.html.**

Legal Environment Cases

21.1 Equal Pay Act For years, New York law prevented females from working at night. Therefore, Corning Glass Works employed male workers for night inspection jobs and female workers for day inspection jobs. Males working the night shift were paid higher wages than were females who worked the day shift. When the federal Equal Pay Act was enacted, Corning began hiring females for night shift jobs, but it instituted a "red circle" wage rate that permitted previously hired male night shift workers to continue to receive higher wages than newly hired night shift workers. Does this violate the Equal Pay Act? *Corning Glass Works v. Brennan, Secretary of Labor*, 417 U.S. 188, 94 S.Ct. 2223, 1974 U.S. Lexis 62 (U.S. Sup.Ct.)

21.2 Sex Discrimination The Los Angeles Department of Water and Power maintains a pension plan for its employees that is funded by both employer and employee contributions. The plan pays men and women retirees pensions with the same monthly benefits. However, because statistically women on average live several years longer than men, female employees are required to make monthly contributions to the pension fund that are 14.84 percent higher than the contributions required of male employees. Because employee contributions are withheld from paychecks, a female employee takes home less pay than a male employee earning the same salary. Does this practice violate Title VII? *City of Los Angeles Department of Water and Power v. Manhart*, 435 U.S. 702, 98 S.Ct. 1370, 1978 U.S. Lexis 23 (U.S. Sup.Ct.)

21.3 Hostile Work Environment Shirley Huddleston became the first female sales representative of Roger Dean Chevrolet, Inc. (RDC), in West Palm Beach, Florida. Shortly after she began working at RDC, Philip Geraci, a fellow sales representative, and other male employees began making derogatory comments to and about her, expelled gas in her presence, and called her derogatory names. Many of these remarks were made in front of customers. The sales manager of RDC participated in the harassment. On several occasions, Huddleston complained about this conduct to RDC's general manager. Was Title VII violated? *Huddleston v. Roger Dean Chevrolet, Inc.*, 845 F.2d 900, 1988 U.S.App. Lexis 6823 (11th Cir.)

21.4 National Origin Discrimination The Federal Bureau of Investigation (FBI) engaged in a pattern and practice of discrimination against Hispanic FBI agents. Job assignments and promotions were areas that were especially affected. Bernardo M. Perez, a Hispanic, brought a Title VII action against the FBI. Did the FBI violate Title VII? *Perez v. Federal Bureau of Investigation*, 714 F.Supp. 1414, 1989 U.S.Dist. Lexis 8426 (W.D. Tex.)

21.5 Religious Discrimination Trans World Airlines (TWA), an airline, operates a large maintenance and overhaul base for its airplanes in Kansas City, Missouri. Because of its essential role, the stores department at the base must operate 24 hours per day, 365 days per year. The employees at the base are represented by the International Association of Machinists and Aerospace Workers (Union). TWA and Union entered into a collective bargaining agreement that included a seniority system for the assignment of jobs and shifts.

Larry Hardison was hired by TWA to work as a clerk in the stores department. Soon after beginning work, Hardison joined the Worldwide Church of God, which does not allow its members to work from sunset on Friday until sunset on Saturday and on certain religious holidays. Hardison, who had the second-lowest seniority within the stores department, did not have enough seniority to observe his Sabbath regularly. When Hardison asked for special consideration, TWA offered to allow him to take his Sabbath off if he could switch shifts with another employee-union member. None of the other employees would do so. TWA refused Hardison's request for a four-day workweek because it would have to either hire and train a part-time worker to work on Saturdays or incur the cost of paying overtime to an existing full-time worker on Saturdays. Hardison sued TWA for religious discrimination in violation of Title VII. Did TWA's actions violate Title VII? *Trans World Airlines v. Hardison*, 432 U.S. 63, 97 S.Ct. 2264, 1977 U.S. Lexis 115 (U.S. Sup.Ct.)

21.6 Bona Fide Occupational Qualification At the age of 60, Manuel Fragante emigrated from the Philippines to Hawaii. In response to a newspaper ad, Fragante applied for an entry-level civil service clerk job with the City of Honolulu's Division of Motor Vehicles and Licensing. The job required constant oral communication with the public, either at the information counter or on the telephone. Fragante scored the highest of 731 test takers on a written examination that tested word usage, grammar, and spelling. As part of the application process, two civil service employees who were familiar with the demands of the position interviewed Fragante. They testified that his accent made it difficult to understand him. Fragante was not hired for the position, which was filled by another applicant. Fragante sued, alleging national origin discrimination in violation of Title VII. Who wins? *Fragante v. City and County of Honolulu*, 888 F.2d 591, 1989 U.S.App. Lexis 2636 (9th Cir.)

21.7 Age Discrimination Walker Boyd Fite was an employee of First Tennessee Production Credit Association for 19 years. He had attained the position of vice president–credit. During the course of his employment, he never received an unsatisfactory review. On December 26, 1983, at the age of 57, Fite was hospitalized with a kidney stone. On January 5, 1984, while Fite was recovering at home, an officer of First Tennessee called to inform him that he had been retired as of December 31, 1983. A few days later, Fite received a letter stating that he had been retired because of poor job performance. Fite sued First Tennessee for age discrimination. Who wins? *Fite v. First Tennessee Production Credit Association*, 861 F.2d 884, 1988 U.S.App. Lexis 14759 (6th Cir.)

Ethics in Business

21.8 Dianne Rawlinson, 22 years old, was a college graduate whose major course of study was correctional psychology. After graduation, she applied for a position as a correctional counselor (prison guard) with the Alabama Board of Corrections. Her application was rejected because she failed to meet the minimum 120-pound weight requirement of an Alabama statute that also established a height minimum of 5 feet 2 inches. In addition, the Alabama Board of Corrections adopted Administrative Regulation 204, which established gender criteria for assigning correctional counselors to maximum-security prisons for "contact positions." These are correctional counselor positions that require continual close physical proximity to inmates. Under this rule, Rawlinson did not qualify for contact positions with male prisoners in Alabama maximum-security prisons. Rawlinson brought a class action lawsuit against Dothard, who was the director of the Department of Public Safety of Alabama. *Dothard, Director, Department of Public Safety of Alabama v. Rawlinson*, 433 U.S. 321, 97 S.Ct. 2720, 1977 U.S. Lexis 143 (U.S. Sup.Ct.)

Ethics Issues

1. What does the Equal Protection Clause of the U.S. Constitution provide? Explain.
2. What is a bona fide occupational qualification?
3. Does society owe a duty of social responsibility to protect women from dangerous job positions? Or is this "romantic paternalism"?
4. Does either the height–weight requirement or the contact position rule constitute a bona fide occupational qualification that justifies the sexual discrimination in this case?

Endnotes

1. 42 U.S.C. Sections 2000e *et seq*. Other portions of the Civil Rights Act of 1964 prohibit discrimination in housing, education, and other facets of life.
2. *Equal Employment Opportunity Commission v. Tortilleria "La Mejor,"* 758 F.Supp.585, 1991 U.S.Dist. Lexis 5754 (E.D. Cal.).
3. *McDonnell Douglas v. Green*, 411 U.S. 792, 93 S.Ct. 1817, 1973 U.S. Lexis 154 (U.S. Sup.Ct.).
4. In some states, the complaint must be filed with the appropriate state agency rather than the EEOC.
5. 42 U.S.C. Section 2000e(K).
6. *Meritor Savings Bank v. Vinson*, 477 U.S. 57, 106 S.Ct. (U.S. Sup.Ct.).
7. *Harris v. Forklift Systems, Inc.*, 510 U.S. 17, 114 S.Ct. 367, 1993 U.S. Lexis 7155 (U.S. Sup.Ct.).
8. 523 U.S. 75, 118 S.Ct.998, 1998 U.S. Lexis 1599 (U.S. Sup.Ct.).
9. 42 U.S.C. Section 1981.
10. 29 U.S.C. Section 206(d).
11. 29 U.S.C. Sections 621–634.
12. 42 U.S.C. Section 1201 *et seq*.

22

Labor Law

"Strong responsible unions are essential to industrial fair play. Without them the labor bargain is wholly one-sided."

—Louis D. Brandeis

Chapter Objectives

After studying this chapter, you should be able to:

1. Describe how a union is organized.
2. Explain the consequences of an employer's illegal interference with a union election.
3. Describe the process of collective bargaining.
4. Describe employees' rights to strike and picket.
5. Explain state right-to-work laws.

Chapter Contents

- Labor Law
- Organizing a Union
- Collective Bargaining
- Strikes and Picketing
- Internal Union Affairs

Prior to the Industrial Revolution, employees and employers had somewhat equal bargaining power. Once the country became industrialized in the late 1800s, large corporate employers had much more bargaining power than their employees. In response, federal legislation was enacted that gave employees the right to form and join labor unions. Through negotiation with employers, labor unions obtained better working conditions, higher wages, and greater benefits for their members.

This chapter discusses labor unions and labor relations laws.

Washington DC. In the United States, federal labor laws protect the rights of workers to form and join unions and to engage in peaceful strikes and picketing.

Labor Law

In the 1880s, few laws protected workers against employment abuses. The workers reacted by organizing unions in an attempt to gain bargaining strength. Unlike unions in many European countries, unions in the United States did not form their own political party. By the early 1990s, employers used violent tactics against workers who were trying to organize into unions. The courts generally sided with employers in such disputes.

The **American Federation of Labor (AFL)** was formed in 1886, under the leadership of Samuel Gompers. Only skilled craft workers such as silversmiths and artisans were allowed to belong. In 1935, John L. Lewis formed the **Congress of Industrial Organizations (CIO)**. The CIO permitted semiskilled and unskilled workers to become members. In 1955, the AFL and CIO combined to form the **AFL-CIO**. Individual unions (such as the United Auto Workers and United Steel Workers) may choose to belong to the AFL-CIO, but not all unions opt to join.

AFL-CIO
The 1955 combination of the AFL and the CIO.

Today, approximately 12 percent of private-sector wage and salary workers belong to labor unions. Many government employees also belong to unions.

Federal Labor Union Statutes

In the early 1900s, members of the labor movement lobbied Congress to pass laws to protect their rights to organize and bargain with management. During the Great Depression of the 1930s, several statutes were enacted to give workers certain rights and protections. Other statutes have been added since then. The major federal statutes in this area are:

- ***Norris-LaGuardia Act.*** Enacted in 1932, this act stipulates that it is legal for employees to organize.[1]
- ***National Labor Relations Act (NLRA).*** This act, also known as the Wagner Act, was enacted in 1935.[2] The NLRA establishes the right to employees to form, join, and assist labor organizations; to bargain collectively with employers; and to engage in concerted activity to promote these rights.
- ***Labor–Management Relations Act.*** In 1947, Congress enacted the Labor–Management Relations Act (the Taft-Hartley Act).[3] This act (1) expands the activities that labor unions can engage in, (2) gives employers the right to engage in free speech efforts against unions prior to a union election, and (3) gives the president of the United States the right to seek an injunction (for up to 80 days) against a strike that would create a national emergency.
- ***Labor–Management Reporting and Disclosure Act.*** Congress enacted the Labor–Management Reporting and Disclosure Act of 1959 (the Landrum-Griffin Act).[4] This act regulates internal union affairs and establishes the rights of union members.
- ***Railway Labor Act.*** The Railway Labor Act of 1926, as amended in 1934, covers employees of railroad and airline carriers.[5]

No private business monopoly, producer organization or cartel wields the market (and physical) power or commands the discipline over its members which many unions have achieved.

Gottfried Haberler
Economic Growth and Stability (1974)

National Labor Relations Board (NLRB)

The NLRA created the **National Labor Relations Board (NLRB)**. The NLRB is an administrative body composed of five members appointed by the president and approved by the Senate. The NLRB oversees union elections, prevents employers and unions from engaging in illegal and unfair labor practices, and enforces and interprets certain federal labor laws. The decisions of the NLRB are enforceable in court.

National Labor Relations Board (NLRB)
A federal administrative agency that oversees union elections, prevents employers and unions from engaging in illegal and unfair labor practices, and enforces and interprets certain federal labor laws.

Organizing a Union

Section 7 of the NLRA gives employees the right to join together and form a union. Section 7 provides that employees shall have the right to self-organization; to form, join, or assist labor organizations; to bargain collectively through representatives of their own choosing; and to engage in other concerted activities for the purpose of collective bargaining or other mutual aid protection.

Section 7 of the NLRA
A law that gives employees the right to join together and form a union.

The group that the union is seeking to represent—which is called the *appropriate bargaining unit* or *bargaining unit*—must be defined before the union can petition for an election. This group can be the employees of a single company or plant, a group within a single company (e.g., maintenance workers at all of a company's plants), or an entire industry (e.g., nurses at all hospitals in the country). Managers and professional employees may not belong to unions formed by employees whom they manage.

Types of Union Elections

If it can be shown that at least 30 percent of the employees in the bargaining unit are interested in joining or forming a union, the NLRB can be petitioned to investigate and set an election date. The following types of elections are possible:

- ***Contested election.*** Most union elections are contested by the employer. The NLRB is required to supervise all *contested elections*. A simple majority vote (over 50 percent) wins the election. For example, if 51 of 100 employees vote for the union, the union is certified as the bargaining agent for all 100 employees.
- ***Consent election.*** If management does not contest the election, a *consent election* may be held without NLRB supervision.
- ***Decertification election.*** If employees no longer want to be represented by a union, a *decertification election* will be held. Such elections must be supervised by the NLRB.

Union Solicitation on Company Property

If union solicitation is being conducted by employees, an employer may restrict solicitation activities to the employees' free time (e.g., coffee breaks, lunch hours, before and after work). The activities may also be limited to nonworking areas, such as the cafeteria, rest room, or parking lot. Off-duty employees may be barred from union solicitation on company premises, and nonemployees (e.g., union management) may be prohibited from soliciting on behalf of the union anywhere on company property. Employers may dismiss employees who violate these rules.

inaccessibility exception
A rule that permits employees and union officials to engage in union solicitation on company property if the employees are beyond reach of reasonable union efforts to communicate with them.

An exception to this rule applies if the location of the business and the living quarters of the employees place the employees beyond the reach of reasonable union efforts to communicate with them. This so-called **inaccessibility exception** applies to logging camps, mining towns, company towns, and the like.

In the following case, the U.S. Supreme Court addressed the issue of whether an employer had to allow nonemployee union organizers on its property.

Case 22.1
Organizing a Union

U.S. SUPREME COURT
Lechmere, Inc. v. National Labor Relations Board
502 U.S. 527, 112 S.Ct. 841, 1992 U.S. Lexis 555
Supreme Court of the United States

Background and Facts

Lechmere, Inc. (Lechmere), owned and operated a retail store in the Lechmere Shopping Plaza in Newington, Connecticut. Thirteen smaller stores were located between Lechmere's store and the parking lot, which was owned by Lechmere. In June 1987, the United Food and Commercial Workers Union, AFL-CIO (Union), attempted to organize Lechmere's 200 employees, none of whom belonged to a union. After a full-page advertisement in a local newspaper drew little response, nonemployee Union organizers entered Lechmere's parking lot and began placing handbills on windshields of cars parked in the employee section of the parking lot. Lechmere's manager informed the organizers that Lechmere prohibited solicitation or handbill distribution of any kind on the property and asked them to leave. They did so, and Lechmere personnel removed the handbills. Union organizers renewed their handbill effort in the parking lot on several subsequent occasions, but each time, they were asked to leave, and the handbills were removed. Union filed a grievance with the NLRB. The NLRB ruled in favor of Union and ordered Lechmere to allow handbill distribution in the parking lot. The Court of Appeals affirmed. Lechmere appealed to the U.S. Supreme Court.

Issue

May a store owner prohibit nonemployee union organizers from distributing leaflets in a shopping mall parking lot owned by the store?

In the Language of the Court

In practice, nonemployee organizational trespassing had generally been prohibited except where "unique obstacles" prevented nontrespassory methods of communication with the employees. The inaccessibility exception is a narrow one. It does not apply wherever nontrespassory access to employees may be cumbersome or less-than-ideally effective, but only where the location of a plant and the living quarters of the employees place the employees beyond the reach of reasonable union efforts to communicate with them.

Although the employees live in a large metropolitan area (Greater Hartford), that fact does not in itself render them "inaccessible." Their accessibility is suggested by the union's success in contacting a substantial percentage of them directly, via mailings, phone calls, and home visits. In this case, other alternative means of communication were readily available. Thus, signs (displayed, for example, from the public grassy strip adjoining Lechmere's parking lot) would have informed the employees about the union's organizational efforts. Access to employees, not success in winning them over, is the critical issue.

Decision and Remedy

The U.S. Supreme Court held that under the facts of this case, Lechmere could prohibit nonemployee union organizers from distributing leaflets to employees in the store's parking lot. The Supreme Court reversed the decision of the Court of Appeals.

Business and Ethics Questions

1. Should property rights take precedence over a union's right to organize employees?
2. Is it ethical for an employer to deny union organizers access to company property to conduct their organization efforts? Is it ethical for union organizers to demand this as a right?
3. What implications does this case have for business? Is this a pro- or antibusiness decision?

Illegal Interference with an Election

Section 8(a) of the NLRA makes it an **unfair labor practice** for an employer to interfere with, coerce, or restrain employees from exercising their statutory right to form and join unions. Threats of loss of benefits for joining the union, statements such as "I'll close this plant if a union comes in here," and the like are unfair labor practices. Also, an employer may not form a company union.

> **Section 8(a) of the NLRA**
> A law that makes it an *unfair labor practice* for an employer to interfere with, coerce, or restrain employees from exercising their statutory right to form and join unions.

Section 8(b) of the NLRA prohibits unions from engaging in unfair labor practices that interfere with a union election. Coercion, physical threats, and such are unfair labor practices.

Where an unfair labor practice has been found, the NLRB (or the courts) may issue a cease-and-desist order or an injunction to restrain unfair labor practices and may set aside an election and order a new election.

In the following case, the U.S. Supreme Court found that an employer had engaged in an unfair labor practice and ordered a new election.

Case 22.2

Unfair Labor Practice

U.S. SUPREME COURT

National Labor Relations Board v. Exchange Parts Co.

375 U.S. 405, 84 S.Ct. 457, 1964 U.S. Lexis 2263

Supreme Court of the United States

Background and Facts

Exchange Parts Co. (Exchange Parts) was engaged in the business of rebuilding automobile parts in Fort Worth, Texas. Prior to November 1959, its employees were not represented by a union. On November 9, 1959, the International Brotherhood of Boilermakers, Iron Shipbuilders, Blacksmiths, Forgers and Helpers, AFL-CIO (Union), advised Exchange Parts that it was going to conduct a campaign to organize the workers at the plant. After obtaining sufficient support from members of the appropriate bargaining unit, Union petitioned the NLRB to set an election date. After completing its investigation on February 19, 1960, the NLRB issued an order setting March 18, 1960, as the election date. On February 25, 1960, Exchange Parts held a dinner for its employees at which management announced a new company benefit allowing employees to have an extra holiday (their birthday). On March 4, Exchange Parts sent a letter to its employees that announced new increased wages for overtime pay and an extended vacation plan for employees. Union subsequently lost the election. Union filed a complaint with the NLRB, and the NLRB held in favor of Union and ordered a

(*continued*)

National Labor Relations Board v. Exchange Parts Co.

375 U.S. 405, 84 S.Ct. 457, 1964 U.S. Lexis 2263
Supreme Court of the United States
(*continued*)

new election. The Court of Appeals reversed. The NLRB appealed to the Supreme Court.

Issue

Is it an unfair practice for an employer to confer new economic benefits on its employees on the eve of a union election?

In the Language of the Court

The broad purpose of Section 8(a) is to establish the right of employees to organize for mutual aid without employer interference. We have no doubt that it prohibits not only intrusive threats but also conduct immediately favorable to employees that is undertaken with the express purpose of impinging upon their freedom of choice for or against unionization and is reasonably calculated to have that effect. The danger inherent in well-timed increases in benefits is the suggestion of a "fist inside a velvet glove." Employees are not likely to miss the inference that the source of benefits now conferred is also the source from which future benefits must flow and which may dry up if it is not obliged.

We cannot agree with the court of appeals that enforcement of the NRLB's order will have the ironic result of discouraging benefits for labor. The beneficence of an employer is likely to be ephemeral if prompted by a threat of unionization that is subsequently removed. Insulating the right of collective organization from calculated goodwill of this sort deprives employees of little that has lasting value.

Decision and Remedy

The U.S. Supreme Court held that an employer's conferral of benefits on employees on the eve of a union election, in an effort to affect the outcome of that election, is an unfair labor practice. The Supreme Court reversed the decision of the Court of Appeals.

Business and Ethics Questions

1. Should a company be prohibited from taking away (or giving) economic benefits in its fight with a union?
2. Was it ethical for the employer in this case to increase employee benefits on the eve of the union election?
3. Do you think the employer's conduct in this case constituted a "fist in a velvet glove"? Were the benefits conferred in this case likely to be ephemeral?

Collective Bargaining

collective bargaining
The act of negotiating contract terms between an employer and the members of a union.

collective bargaining agreement
The resulting contract from a collective bargaining procedure.

Once a union has been elected, the employer and the union discuss the terms of employment of union members and try to negotiate a contract that embodies these terms. The act of negotiating is called **collective bargaining**, and the resulting contract is called a **collective bargaining agreement**. The employer and the union must negotiate with each other in good faith. Among other things, this prohibits making take-it-or-leave-it proposals.

The subjects of collective bargaining are classified as follows:

- ***Compulsory subjects.*** Wages, hours, and other terms and conditions of employment are compulsory subjects of collective bargaining. Fringe benefits, health benefits, retirement plans, work assignments, safety rules, and the like are included in this category.
- ***Illegal subjects.*** Subjects such as closed shops and discrimination are illegal subjects and may not be negotiated.
- ***Permissive subjects.*** Subjects that are not compulsory or illegal are permissive subjects of collective bargaining. These include such issues as the size and composition of the supervisory force, location of plants, corporate reorganizations, and the like. These subjects may be bargained for if the company and union agree to do so.

Plant Closing Act

Often a company would choose to close a plant without giving its employees prior notice of the closing. To remedy this situation, on August 4, 1988, Congress enacted the **Worker Adjustment and Retraining Notification (WARN) Act**, also called the **Plant Closing Act**.[6] The act, which covers employers with 100 or more employees, requires employers to give their employees 60 days' notice before engaging in certain plant closings or layoffs.

Worker Adjustment and Retraining Notification (WARN) Act
A federal act that requires employers with 100 or more employees to give their employees 60 days' notice before engaging in certain plant closings or layoffs.

If the employees are represented by a union, the notice must be given to the union; if they are not, the notice must be given to the employees individually.

The actions covered by the act are:

- ***Plant closings.*** A plant closing is a permanent or temporary shutdown of a single site that results in a loss of employment of 50 or more employees during any 30-day period.
- ***Mass layoffs.*** A mass layoff is a reduction of 33 percent of the employees or at least 50 employees during any 30-day period.

An employer is exempted from having to give such notice if:

1. The closing or layoff is caused by business circumstances that were not reasonably foreseeable as of the time that the notice would have been required.
2. The business was actively seeking capital or business that, if obtained, would have avoided or postponed the shutdown and the employer in good faith believed that giving notice would have precluded it from obtaining the needed capital or business.

Union Security Agreements

To obtain the greatest power possible, elected unions sometimes try to install a *union security agreement*. The two types of security agreements are:

- ***Union shop.*** Under a **union shop** agreement, an employee must join the union within a certain time period (e.g., 30 days) after being hired. Employees who do not join must be discharged by the employer upon notice from the union. Union members pay union dues to the union. Union shops are lawful.
- ***Agency shop.*** Under an **agency shop** agreement, employees do not have to become union members, but they do have to pay an agency fee (an amount equal to dues) to the union. Agency shops are lawful.

union shop
An establishment in which an employee must join the union within a certain number of days after being hired.

agency shop
An establishment in which an employee does not have to join the union but must pay a fee equal to the union dues.

Upon proper notification by the union, union and agency shop employers are required to (1) deduct union dues and agency fees from employees' wages and (2) forward these dues to the union.

The following case involves the legality of a union security agreement.

Case 22.3 Union Security Agreement

U.S. SUPREME COURT

Marquez v. Screen Actors Guild, Inc.

525 U.S. 33, 119 S.Ct. 292, 1998 U.S. Lexis 7110

Supreme Court of the United States

Background and Facts

The Screen Actors Guild (SAG) is a labor union that represents performers in the entertainment industry. In 1994, Lakeside Productions, an entertainment production company, signed a collective bargaining agreement with SAG, making SAG the exclusive union for performers that Lakeside hired for its productions. The collective bargaining agreement contained a standard "union security clause" providing that any performer who worked for Lakeside must be a member of SAG. Naomi Marquez, a part-time actress, auditioned for a one-line role in a TV episode to be filmed

(continued)

Marquez v. Screen Actors Guild, Inc.

525 U.S. 33, 119 S.Ct. 292, 1998 U.S. Lexis 7110
Supreme Court of the United States
(continued)

by Lakeside and won the part. When Marquez did not pay the $500 membership fee to SAG, Lakeside hired another actress for the part. Marquez sued SAG and Lakeside, alleging that the union security clause was unlawful. The district court held for the defendants, and the Court of Appeals affirmed. The U.S. Supreme Court granted certiorari to hear the appeal.

Issue

Does the union security clause negotiated between Lakeside Productions and the Screen Actors Guild violate federal labor law?

In the Language of the Court

Section 8(a)(3) of the National Labor Relations Act (NLRA), permits unions and employers to negotiate an agreement that requires union "membership" as a condition of employment for all employees. Although Section 8(a)(3) states that unions may negotiate a clause requiring "membership" in the union, an employee can satisfy the membership condition merely by paying to the union an amount equal to the union's initiation fees and dues. In other words, the membership that may be required as a condition of employment is whittled down to its financial core.

Section 8(a)(3) does not permit unions to exact dues or fees from employees for activities that are not germane to collective bargaining, grievance adjustment, or contract administration. Section 8(a)(3) permits unions and employers to require only that employees pay the fees and dues necessary to support the union's activities as the employees' exclusive bargaining representative.

Decision and Remedy

The U.S. Supreme Court held that the union security clause negotiated between Lakeside Productions and SAG was lawful under federal labor law. The U.S. Supreme Court affirmed the judgment of the Court of Appeals.

Business and Ethics Questions

1. What does an exclusive union security clause provide? Under this agreement, must a worker join a labor union? Explain.
2. Did SAG and Lakeside act ethically in this case?
3. Do the decisions of the U.S. Supreme Court regarding union security agreements prevent the "free rider" problem? Explain.

Contemporary Trend

State Right-to-Work Laws

In 1947, Congress amended the Taft-Hartley Act by enacting Section 14(b), which provides: "Nothing in this Act shall be construed as authorizing the execution or application of agreements requiring membership in a labor organization as a condition of employment in any State or Territory in which such execution or application is prohibited by State or Territorial Law." In other words, states can enact **right-to-work laws**—either by constitutional amendment or statute—that outlaw union and agency shops.

If a state enacts a right-to-work law, individual employees cannot be forced to join a union or pay union dues and fees even though a union has been elected by other employees. Right-to-work laws are often enacted by states to attract new businesses to a nonunion and low-wage environment. Unions vehemently oppose the enactment of right-to-work laws because they substantially erode union power.

Today, the following 22 states have enacted right-to-work laws:

Alabama
Arizona
Arkansas
Florida
Georgia
Idaho
Iowa
Kansas
Louisiana
Mississippi
Nebraska
Nevada
North Carolina
North Dakota
Oklahoma
South Carolina
South Dakota
Tennessee
Texas
Utah
Virginia
Wyoming

The remedies for violation of right-to-work laws vary from state to state but usually include damages to persons injured by the violation, injunctive relief, and often criminal penalties. ■

Strikes and Picketing

The NLRA gives union management the right to recommend that the union call a **strike** if a collective bargaining agreement cannot be reached. Before there can be a strike, though, a majority vote of the union's members must agree to the action. In order to support a strike, union members often picket at their employer's place of business. Strikes and picketing are discussed in the following paragraphs.

strike
A cessation of work by union members in order to obtain economic benefits or correct an unfair labor practice.

Picketing

Striking union members often engage in **picketing** in support of their strike. Picketing usually takes the form of the striking employees and union representatives walking in front of the employer's premises carrying signs announcing their strike. It is used to put pressure on an employer to settle a strike. The right to picket is implied from the NLRA.

picketing
The action of strikers walking in front of the employer's premises carrying signs announcing their strike.

Picketing is lawful unless it (1) is accompanied by violence, (2) obstructs customers from entering the employer's place of business, (3) prevents nonstriking employees from entering the employer's premises, or (4) prevents pickups and deliveries at the employer's place of business. An employer may seek an injunction against unlawful picketing.

Secondary Boycott Picketing

Unions sometimes try to bring pressure against an employer by picketing the employer's suppliers or customers. Such **secondary boycott picketing** is lawful only if it is product picketing (i.e., if the picketing is against the primary employer's product). The picketing is illegal if it is directed against the neutral employer instead of the struck employer's product.

secondary boycott picketing
A type of picketing in which unions try to bring pressure against an employer by picketing the employer's suppliers or customers.

Consider This Example Suppose the apple pickers' union in the state of Washington goes on strike against its primary employers, the apple growers. Picketing the apple orchards may do little to draw attention of the strike to the public. Therefore, members of the apple pickers' union may picket grocery stores in metropolitan areas that sell Washington apples. If the signs the picketers carry ask shoppers at the grocery stores not to buy Washington apples, the secondary boycott is lawful. However, it is unlawful if the signs ask customers not to shop at the grocery stores.

Illegal Strikes

Several types of strikes have been held to be illegal and are not protected by federal labor laws. Illegal strikes are:

- ***Violent strikes.*** In violent strikes, striking employees cause substantial damage to property of the employer or a third party. Courts usually tolerate a certain amount of isolated violence before finding that the entire strike is illegal.
- ***Sit-down strikes.*** In sit-down strikes, striking employees continue to occupy the employer's premises. Such strikes are illegal because they deny the employer's statutory right to continue its operations during the strike.
- ***Partial or intermittent strikes.*** In these strikes, employees strike part of the day or workweek and work the other part. This type of strike is illegal because it interferes with the employer's right to operate its facilities at full operation.

Management and union may be likened to that serpent of the fables who on one body had two heads that fighting with poisoned fangs, killed themselves.

Peter Drucker
The New Society (1951)

cooling-off period
A required 60-day period that a union must give an employer before commencing a strike.

- ***Wildcat strikes.*** In wildcat strikes, individual union members go on strike without proper authorization from the union. The courts have recognized that a wildcat strike becomes lawful if it is quickly ratified by the union.
- ***Strikes during the 60-day cooling-off period.*** A mandatory 60-day **cooling off-period** is designed to give the employer and the union time to negotiate a settlement of the union grievances and avoid a strike. Any strike without a proper 60-day notice is illegal.
- ***Strikes in violation of a no-strike clause.*** Strikes that take place in violation of a negotiated no-strike clause—under which an employer gives economic benefits to the union and, in exchange, the union agrees that no strike will be called for a set time—are illegal.

Illegal strikers may be discharged by the employer, with no rights to reinstatement.

Crossover and Replacement Workers

Individual members of a union do not have to honor a strike. They may (1) choose not to strike or (2) return to work after joining the strikers for a time. Employees who choose either of these two options are known as *crossover workers*.

Once a strike begins, the employer may continue operations by using management personnel and hiring *replacement workers* to take the place of the striking employees. Replacement workers can be hired on either a temporary or permanent basis. If replacement workers are given permanent status, they do not have to be dismissed when the strike is over.

Employer Lockout

employer lockout
An act of an employer to prevent employees from entering the work premises when the employer reasonably anticipates a strike.

If an employer reasonably anticipates a strike by some of its employees, it may prevent those employees from entering the plant or premises. This is called an **employer lockout**. For example, in 2004, when the owners of professional hockey teams that belong to the National Hockey League (NHL) anticipated a strike by the professional hockey players' union, the owners locked out the players. The team owners and the union could not reach an agreement, so the 2004–2005 season was cancelled.

Internal Union Affairs

Title I of the Landrum-Griffin Act
Referred to as labor's "bill of rights," a provision of a federal act that gives each union member equal rights and privileges to nominate candidates for union office, vote in elections, and participate in membership meetings.

Unions may adopt **internal union rules** to regulate the operation of the union, acquire and maintain union membership, and the like. The undemocratic manner in which many unions were formulating these rules prompted Congress in 1959 to enact **Title I of the Landrum-Griffin Act**. Title I, which is often referred to as **labor's "bill of rights,"** gives each union member equal rights and privileges to nominate candidates for union office, vote in elections, and participate in membership meetings. It further guarantees union members the right of free speech and assembly, provides for due process (notice and hearing), and permits union members to initiate judicial or administrative action.

A union may discipline members for participating in certain activities, including (1) walking off the job in a nonsanctioned strike, (2) working for wages below union scale, (3) spying for an employer, and (4) any other unauthorized activity that has an adverse economic impact on the union. A union may not punish a union member for participating in a civic duty, such as testifying in court against the union.

London, England. In many countries, labor unions are more powerful and political than they are in the United States. Labor unions are strong in Great Britain and support the Labor Party, a political party, in that country.

Terms and Concepts

Federal Labor Statutes

Federal labor statutes include:

1. ***Norris-LaGuardia Act.*** This act made it legal for employees to organize.
2. ***National Labor Relations Act (NLRA).*** This act established the right of employees to form, join, and assist labor unions. Also called the *Wagner Act.*
3. ***Labor–Management Relations Act.*** This act expanded the activities labor unions could engage in, gave employers free speech rights to oppose unionization, and gave the U.S. president the right to seek injunctions against strikes that would create a national emergency. Also called the *Taft-Hartley Act.*
4. ***Labor–Management Reporting and Disclosure Act.*** Called labor's "bill of rights," this act gives union members the right to nominate candidates for union offices and vote in union elections. Also called the *Landrum-Griffin Act.*
5. ***Railway Labor Act.*** This act governs union rights of railroad and airline employees.

National Labor Relations Board (NLRB)

This federal administrative agency is empowered to administer federal labor law, oversee union elections, and decide labor disputes.

Organizing a Union

1. ***Section 7 of the NLRA.*** This section gives employees the right to join together and form a union.
2. ***Appropriate bargaining union.*** An appropriate bargaining union is a group of employees that a union is seeking to represent.

Types of Union Elections

1. ***Contested election.*** Management may contest a union. The NLRB must supervise this type of election.
2. ***Consent election.*** In a consent election, management does not contest the union election.
3. ***Decertification election.*** This is an election to determine whether the employees want to reject a union as a representative. The NLRB must supervise such an election.

Union Solicitation on Company Property

1. ***Employees.*** An employer may restrict solicitation activities to the employees' free time (e.g., breaks, lunch hours, before and after work).
2. ***Nonemployee union representatives.*** An employer may prohibit solicitation on company property unless the employees cannot otherwise be contacted.

Illegal Interference with an Election

1. ***Section 8(a) of the NLRA.*** This section makes it an unfair labor practice for an *employer* to interfere with, coerce, or restrain employees from exercising their right to form and join unions.
2. ***Section 8(b) of the NLRA.*** This section makes it an unfair practice for a *union* to interfere with a union election.

Collective Bargaining

Collective bargaining is a process whereby a union and an employer negotiate the terms and conditions of employment for the covered employee union members.

1. ***Collective bargaining agreement.*** A collective bargaining agreement is a contract that results from collective bargaining.

Subjects of Collective Bargaining

1. ***Compulsory subjects.*** Compulsory subjects are wages, hours, and other terms and conditions of employment (e.g., vacations, medical benefits).
2. ***Illegal subjects.*** Illegal subjects are subjects that may not be negotiated (e.g., discrimination).
3. ***Permissive subjects.*** Permissive subjects are not compulsory or illegal (e.g., closing of plants).

Union Security Agreements

1. ***Union shop.*** A union shop is an establishment in which an employee must join a union within a certain number of days after being hired.
2. ***Agency shop.*** In an agency shop, employees do not have to join the union but must pay an *agency fee* equal to union dues.

State Right-to-Work Laws

States may enact statutes that make union shops and agency shops illegal. In such a case, individual employees may choose not to join the union.

Strikes

A strike is a cessation of work by union members in order to obtain economic benefits, to correct an unfair labor practice, or to preserve their work. The NLRA gives union employees the right to strike.

Picketing

Striking employees and union organizers may picket—that is, walk around the employer's premises, usually carrying signs, notifying the public of their grievance against the employer.

1. ***Illegal picketing.*** Picketing is illegal if it is accompanied by violence or obstructs customers, nonstriking workers, or suppliers from entering the employer's premises.
2. ***Secondary boycott.*** A secondary boycott is picketing conducted at a third party's premises. *Product picketing* against the products of the struck employer is lawful. A secondary boycott is illegal if it is directed against the neutral employer.

Illegal Strikes

1. ***Violent strike.*** In this type of strike, striking employees cause substantial damage to the employer's or a third party's property.
2. ***Sit-down strike.*** In this type of strike, employees occupy and refuse to leave the employer's premises.
3. ***Partial or intermittent strike.*** In this type of strike, employees strike for only parts of each day or week.

4. ***Wildcat strike.*** A wildcat strike is a strike that is not sanctioned by the union.
5. ***Strike during the 60-day cooling-off period.*** In this type of strike, the union has not given the employer at least 60 days' prior notice of the strike.
6. ***Strike in violation of a no-strike clause.*** This type of strike violates a no-strike clause in a collective bargaining agreement.

Crossover Workers and Replacement Workers

1. ***Crossover worker.*** A crossover worker is an employee who does not honor a strike and either (1) chooses not to strike or (2) returns to work after joining strikers for a time.
2. ***Replacement worker.*** Replacement workers are persons who are hired to take the place of striking workers. The employer may offer these employees permanent positions.

Employer Lockout

An employer may lock employees out of its premises if it reasonably anticipates a strike.

Internal Union Rules

Title I of the Landrum-Griffin Act is a federal law that gives each union member equal rights and privileges to nominate candidates for union office, vote in union elections, and participate in membership meetings. Commonly called *labor's "bill of rights."*

Plant Closings

The *Worker Adjustment and Retraining Notification (WARN) Act* is a federal law that requires employers with 100 or more employees to give their employees 60 days' notice before engaging in certain plant closings or layoffs. Also called the *Plant Closing Act.*

Internet Exercises and Case Questions

Working the Web Internet Exercises

1. For an overview of labor law, see "Labor and Employment Law," at **jurist.law.pitt.edu/sg_lab.htm**.
2. Visit the Web site of one of the largest labor unions at **www.aflcio.org**.
3. Check the current unemployment rate at the Department of Labor: **www.dol.gov**. Is it higher or lower than it was one year ago?

Legal Environment Cases

22.1 Unfair Labor Practice In July 1965, the Teamsters Union (Teamsters) began a campaign to organize the employees at a Sinclair Company (Sinclair) plant. When the president of Sinclair learned of the Teamsters' drive, he talked with all his employees and emphasized the results of a long 1952 strike that he claimed "almost put our company out of business" and expressed worry that the employees were forgetting the "lessons of the past." He emphasized that Sinclair was on "thin ice" financially, that the Teamsters' "only weapon is to strike," and that a strike "could lead to the closing of the plant" because Sinclair had manufacturing facilities elsewhere. He also noted that because of the employees' ages and the limited usefulness of their skills, they might not be able to find reemployment if they lost their jobs. Finally, he sent literature to the employees stating "the Teamsters Union is a strike happy outfit." and that they were under "hoodlum control," and included a cartoon showing the preparation of a grave for Sinclair and other headstones containing the names of the other plants allegedly victimized by unions. The Teamsters lost the election 7 to 6 and then filed an unfair labor practice charge with the NLRB. Did Sinclair violate labor law? *N.L.R.B. v. Gissel Packing Co.,* 395 U.S. 575, 89 S.Ct. 1918, 1969 U.S. Lexis 3172 (U.S. Sup.Ct)

22.2 Right-to-Work Law Mobile Oil Corporation (Mobile) has it headquarters in Beaumont, Texas. It operates a fleet of eight oceangoing tankers that transport its petroleum products from Texas to ports on the East Coast. A typical trip on a tanker from Beaumont to New York took about five days. No more than 10 to 20 percent of the seamen's work time was spent in Texas. The 300 or so seamen who were employed to work on the tankers belong to the Oil Chemical & Atomic Workers International Union, AFL-CIO (Union), which had an agency shop agreement with Mobile. The state of Texas enacted a right-to-work law. Mobile sued Union, claiming that the agency shop agreement was unenforceable because it violated the Texas right-to-work law. Who wins? *Oil, Chemical, & Atomic Workers International Union AFL-CIO v. Mobil Oil Corp.*, 426 U.S. 407, 96 S.Ct. 2140, 1976 U.S. Lexis 106 (U.S. Sup.Ct.)

22.3 Plant Closing Arrow Automotive Industries, Inc. (Arrow), is engaged in the remanufacture and distribution of automobile and truck parts. All its operating plants produced identical product lines. Arrow was planning to open a new facility in Santa Maria, California.

The employees at the Arrow plant in Hudson, Massachusetts, were represented by the United Automobile, Aerospace, and Agricultural Implement Workers of America (Union). The Hudson plant had a history of unprofitable operations. Union called a strike when the existing collective bargaining agreement expired and a new agreement could not be reached. After several months, the board of directors of Arrow voted to close the striking plant. The closing gave Arrow a 24 percent increase in gross profits and freed capital and equipment for the new Santa Maria plant. In addition, the existing customers of the Hudson plant could be serviced by the Spartanburg plant, which at the time was being underutilized. Union filed an unfair labor practice claim with the NLRB. Does Arrow have to bargain with Union over the decision to close a plant? What would have to be done if the Plant Closing Act applied to this situation? *Arrow Automotive Industries, Inc. v. N.L.R.B.*, 853 F.2d 223, 1989 U.S.App. Lexis 10091 (4th Cir.)

22.4 Work Preservation The Frouge Corporation (Frouge) was the general contractor on a housing project in Philadelphia. The carpenter employees of Frouge were represented by the Carpenters' International Union (Union). Traditional jobs of carpenters included taking blank wooden doors and mortising them for doorknobs, routing them for hinges, and beveling them to fit between door jambs. Union had entered into a collective bargaining agreement with Frouge that provided that no member of Union would handle any doors that had been fitted prior to being furnished to the job site. The housing project called for 3,600 doors. Frouge contracted for the purchase of premachined doors that were already mortised, routed, and beveled. When Union ordered its members not to hang the prefabricated doors, the National Woodwork Manufacturers Association filed an unfair labor practice charge against Union with the NLRB. Is Union's refusal to hang prefabricated doors lawful? *National Woodwork Manufacturers Association v. N.L.R.B.*, 386 U.S. 612, 87 S.Ct. 1250, 1967 U.S. Lexis 2858 (U.S. Sup.Ct.)

22.5 Illegal Strike In September 1966, the employees of the Shop Rite Foods, Inc. (Shop Rite), warehouse in Lubbock, Texas, elected United Packinghouse, Food and Allied Workers (Union) as its bargaining agent. Negotiations for a collective bargaining agreement began in late November 1966. In February and March 1967, when an agreement had not yet been reached, Shop Rite found excessive amounts of damage to merchandise in its warehouse and concluded that it was being intentionally caused by dissident employees as a pressure tactic to secure concessions from Shop Rite. Shop Rite notified the Union representative that employees caught doing such acts would be terminated; the Union representative in turn notified the employees.

On March 31, 1967, a Shop Rite manager observed an employee in the flour section—where he had no business being—making quick motions with his hands. The manager found several bags of flour that had been cut. The employee was immediately fired. Another employee (a fellow Union member) led about 30 other employees in an immediate walkout. The company discharged those employees and refused to rehire them. The employees filed a grievance with the NLRB. Can they get their jobs back? *N.L.R.B. v. Shop Rite Foods, Inc.*, 430 F.2d 786, 1970 U.S.App. Lexis 7613 (5th Cir.)

22.6 Employer Lockout The American Ship Building Company (American) operated a shipyard in Chicago, Illinois, where it repaired Great Lakes ships during the winter months when freezing on the Great Lakes rendered shipping impossible. The workers at the shipyard were represented by several unions. On May 1, 1961, the unions notified American of their intention to seek modification of the current collective bargaining agreement when it expired on August 1, 1961. On five previous occasions, agreements had been preceded by strikes (including illegal strikes) that were called just after the ships had arrived in the shipyard for repairs so that the unions increased their leverage in negotiations with the company.

Based on this prior history, American displayed anxiety as to the unions' strike plans and possible work stoppage. On August 1, 1961, after extended negotiations, American and the unions reached an impasse in their collective bargaining. In response, American decided to lay off most of the workers at the shipyard. It sent them the following notice: "Because of the labor dispute which has been unresolved since August 1, 1961, you are laid off until further notice." The unions filed unfair labor practice charges with the NLRB. Are American's actions legal? *American Ship Building Company v. N.L.R.B.*, 380 U.S. 300, 85 S.Ct. 955, 1965 U.S. Lexis 2310 (U.S. Sup.Ct.)

22.7 Replacement Workers The union (Union) member-employees of the Erie Resistor Company (Company) struck Company over the terms of a new collective bargaining agreement that was being negotiated between Company and Union. Company continued production operations during the strike by hiring new hires and crossover union members who were persuaded to abandon the strike and come back to work. Company promised all replacement workers superseniority. This would take the form of adding 20 years to the length of a worker's actual service for the purpose of future layoffs and recalls. Many union members accepted the offer. Union filed an unfair labor practice charge with the NLRB. Is Company's offer of superseniority lawful? *N.L.R.B. v. Erie Resistor Co.*, 373 U.S. 221, 83 S.Ct. 1139, 1963 U.S. Lexis 2492 (U.S. Sup.Ct.)

22.8 Secondary Boycott Safeco Title Insurance Company (Safeco) is a major insurance company that underwrites title insurance for real estate in the state of Washington. Five local title companies acted as insurance brokers that exclusively sold Safeco insurance. In 1972, Local 1001 of the Retail Store Employees Union, AFL-CIO (Union), was elected as the bargaining agent for certain Safeco employees. When negotiations between Safeco and Union reached an impasse, the employees went on strike. Union did not confine its picketing to Safeco's office in Seattle but also picketed each of the five local title companies. The picketers carried signs declaring that Safeco had no contract with Union and distributed handbills asking consumers to support the strike by canceling their Safeco insurance policies. The local title companies filed a complaint with the NLRB. Is the picketing of the neutral title insurance companies lawful? *N.L.R.B. v. Retail Store Employees Union, Local 1001, Retail Clerks International Association, AFL-CIO*, 447 U.S. 607, 100 S.Ct. 2372, 1980 U.S. Lexis 133 (U.S. Sup.Ct.)

Ethics in Business

22.9 On April 23, 1971, the International Association of Machinists and Aerospace Workers, AFL-CIO (Union), began soliciting the employees of Whitcraft Houseboat Division, North American Rockwell Corp. (Whitcraft), to organize a union. On April 26, 27, and 28, Whitcraft management dispersed congregating groups of employees. During these three days, production was down almost 50 percent. On April 28, Whitcraft adopted the following no-solicitation rule and mailed a copy to each employee and posted it around the workplace:

> *As you well know working time is for work. No one will be allowed to solicit or distribute literature during our working time, that is, when he or she should be working. Anyone doing so and neglecting his work or interfering with the work of another employee will be subject to discharge.*

On April 30, a manager of Whitcraft found that two employees of the company were engaged in union solicitation during working hours in a working area. Whitcraft discharged them for violating the no-solicitation rule. *Whitcraft Houseboat Division, North American Rockwell Corporation v. International Association of Machinists and Aerospace Workers,* AFL-CIO, 195 N.L.R.B. 1046 (N.L.R.B.)

Ethics Issue

1. What law did Whitcraft allege was violated by the discharged employees?
2. Did the employees act ethically in this case?
3. Did Whitcraft act ethically in this case?
4. Who wins? Why?

Endnotes

1. 29 U.S.C. Sections 101–110 and 113–115.
2. U.S.C. Sections 151–169.
3. U.S.C. Section 141 *et seq.*
4. U.S.C. Section 401 *et seq.*
5. U.S.C. Sections 151–162 and 181–188.
6. U.S.C. Section 2102.

23

Government Regulation and Administrative Law

"Good government is an empire of laws."

—John Adams
Thoughts on Government (1776)

Chapter Objectives

After studying this chapter, you should be able to:

1. Describe government regulation.
2. Define administrative law.
3. List and explain the functions of administrative agencies.
4. Describe the provisions of the Administrative Procedure Act (APA).
5. Explain the procedure for judicial review of administrative agency decisions.

Chapter Contents

- Administrative Agencies
- Administrative Law
- Judicial Review of Administrative Agency Actions
- Disclosure of Administrative Agency Actions

Federal and state governments enact laws that regulate business. The legislative and executive branches of government have created numerous administrative agencies to assist in implementing and enforcing these laws. The operation of these administrative agencies is governed by a body of **administrative law**. Because of their importance, administrative agencies are informally referred to as the "fourth branch of government."

This chapter examines government regulation of business, administrative agencies, and administrative law.

Baldy Mountain, Sun Valley, Idaho. Federal and state governments regulate the logging, mineral extraction, and recreational uses of government-owned land.

Administrative Agencies

Administrative agencies are created by federal, state, and local governments. They range from large, complex federal agencies, such as the federal Department of Health and Human Resources, to local zoning boards. At the federal government level, the legislative branch (Congress) and the executive branch (the president) have created over 100 administrative agencies. Thousands of other administrative agencies have been created by state and local governments.

administrative agencies
Agencies that the legislative and executive branches of federal and state governments establish.

When Congress enacts a statute, it often creates an administrative agency to administer and enforce the statute (see Exhibit 23.1). When Congress enacts some statutes, it authorizes an existing administrative agency to administer and enforce the new statute. For example, when Congress enacted the Securities Act of 1933 and the Securities Exchange Act of 1934, it created the Securities and Exchange Commission (SEC), a federal administrative agency, to administer and enforce those statutes.

Federal Administrative Agencies

Federal administrative agencies can be created by either the legislative or the executive branch of the federal government. Congress has established many federal administrative agencies. These agencies have broad regulatory powers over key areas of the national economy. An example is the Commodity Futures Trading Commission (CFTC), which regulates the trading in commodities futures contracts. Other federal administrative agencies

federal administrative agencies
Administrative agencies that are part of the executive or legislative branch of federal government.

Exhibit 23.1

Administrative Agency

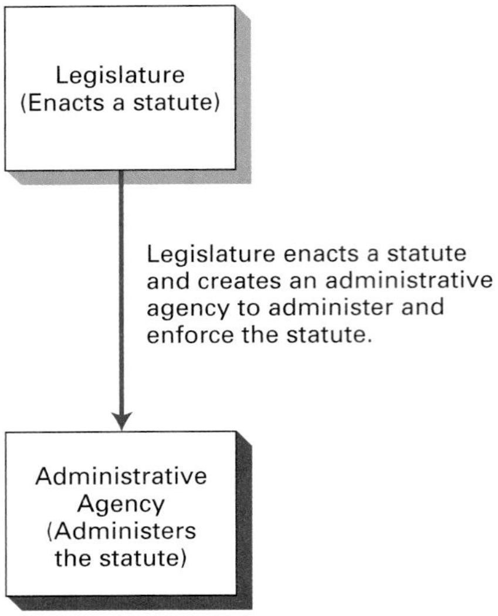

are created by the president to help operate the federal government. These include the Justice Department, the Department of Labor, and the Commerce Department.

State Administrative Agencies

All states have created administrative agencies to enforce and interpret state law. For example, most states have a corporations department to enforce state corporations law, a banking department to regulate the operation of banks, fish and game departments, and workers' compensation boards. **State administrative agencies** also have a profound effect on business. Local governments and municipalities create administrative agencies, such as zoning commissions, to administer local law.

state administrative agencies
Administrative agencies that states create to enforce and interpret state law.

General Government Regulation

Many administrative agencies, and the laws they enforce, regulate businesses and industries collectively. For example, the National Labor Relations Board (NLRB) is empowered to regulate the formation and operation of labor unions in most industries, the Occupational Health and Safety Administration (OSHA) is authorized to formulate and enact safety and health standards for the workplace, and the Consumer Product Safety Commission (CPSC) is empowered to establish mandatory safety standards for products sold in this country.

Specific Government Regulation

The great can protect themselves, but the poor and humble require the arm and shield of the law.
Andrew Jackson

Some administrative agencies, and the laws they enforce, are created to regulate specific industries. For example, the Federal Communications Commission (FCC) regulates the operation of television and radio stations, the Federal Aviation Administration (FAA) regulates commercial airlines, and the Office of the Comptroller of the Currency (OCC) regulates national banks.

Concept Summary Government Regulation of Business

Type of Regulation	Description
General government regulation	Government regulation that applies to many industries (e.g., antidiscrimination laws).
Specific government regulation	Government regulation that applies to a specific industry (e.g., banking laws).

Islamic Mosque, Uzbekistan. Government regulation of business in many countries is influenced by religious principles.

Administrative Law

Administrative law is a combination of substantive and procedural law. *Substantive law* is the law that has been created that the administrative agency enforces. For example, the federal Environmental Protection Agency (EPA) enforces laws that protect the environment. The EPA must follow certain *procedural laws* (e.g., notice, hearing) in enforcing these laws.

administrative law
Substantive and procedural law that governs the operation of administrative agencies.

Administrative Procedure Act (APA)

In 1946, Congress enacted the **Administrative Procedure Act (APA).**[1] This act establishes certain administrative procedures that federal administrative agencies must follow in conducting their affairs. For example, the APA establishes notice and hearing requirements, rules for conducting agency adjudicative actions, and procedures for rule making. Most states have enacted administrative procedural acts that govern state administrative agencies.

Administrative Procedure Act (APA)
A federal act that establishes certain administrative procedures that federal administrative agencies must follow in conducting their affairs.

Administrative Law Judge

Administrative law judges (ALJs) preside over administrative proceedings. They decide questions of law and fact concerning a case. There is no jury. An ALJ is an employee of the administrative agency. Both the administrative agency and the respondent may be

administrative law judge (ALJ)
A judge, presiding over administrative proceedings, who decides questions of law and fact concerning a case.

represented by counsel. Witnesses may be examined and cross-examined, evidence may be introduced, objections may be made, and such.

order
A decision issued by an administrative law judge.

The ALJ's decision is issued in the form of an **order**. The order must state the reasons for the ALJ's decision. The order becomes final if it is not appealed. An appeal consists of a review by the agency. Further appeal can be made to the appropriate federal court (in federal agency actions) or state court (in state agency actions).

Delegation of Powers

delegation doctrine
A doctrine that says when an administrative agency is created, it is delegated certain powers; the agency can use only those legislative, judicial, and executive powers that are delegated to it.

When an administrative agency is created, it is delegated certain powers. The agency has only the legislative, judicial, and executive powers that are delegated to it. This is called the **delegation doctrine**. Thus, an agency can adopt a rule or regulation (a legislative function), prosecute a violation of the statute or rule (an executive function), and adjudicate the dispute (a judicial function). The courts have upheld this combined power of administrative agencies as being constitutional. If an administrative agency acts outside the scope of its delegated powers, it is an unconstitutional act.

Administrative agencies have been delegated legislative powers that consist of substantive rule making, interpretative rule making, issue of statements of policy, and granting of licenses. Administrative agencies have also been delegated certain executive powers and judicial powers. These powers are discussed in the following paragraphs.

Rule Making

substantive rule
A rule issued by an administrative agency that has the force of law and must be adhered to by covered persons and businesses.

Many federal statutes expressly authorize an administrative agency to issue **substantive rules**. A substantive regulation is much like a statute: It has the force of law and must be adhered to by covered persons and businesses. Violators may be held civilly or criminally liable, depending on the rule. All substantive rules are subject to judicial review.

A federal administrative agency that proposes to adopt a substantive rule must follow procedures set forth in the APA.[2] This means the agency must do the following:

1. Publish a general notice of the proposed rule making in the *Federal Register*. The notice must include:
   a. The time, place, and nature of the rule-making proceeding.
   b. The legal authority pursuant to which the rule is proposed.
   c. The terms or substance of the proposed rule or a description of the subject and issues involved.
2. Give interested persons an opportunity to participate in the rule-making process. This may involve oral hearings.
3. Review all written and oral comments. Then the agency announces its *final rule making* in the matter. This procedure is often referred to as *notice-and-comment rule making*, or *informal rule making*.
4. Require, in some instances, *formal rule making*. Here, the agency must conduct a trial-like hearing at which the parties may present evidence, engage in cross-examination, present rebuttal evidence, and such.[3]

interpretive rule
A rule issued by an administrative agency that interprets existing statutory language.

statement of policy
A statement issued by an administrative agency that announces a proposed course of action that the agency intends to follow in the future.

Administrative agencies can issue **interpretive rules** that interpret existing statutory language. Such rules do not establish new laws. Neither public notice nor public participation is required.

Administrative agencies may issue **statements of policy**. These statements announce a proposed course of action that an agency intends to follow in the future. Such statements do not have the force of law. Again, public notice and participation are not required.

In the following case, the U.S. Supreme Court determined the lawfulness of an administrative agency's rule.

Case 23.1 Administrative Agency Rule

U.S. SUPREME COURT

Food and Drug Administration v. Brown & Williamson Tobacco Corporation

529 U.S. 120, 120 S.Ct. 1291, 2000 U.S. Lexis 2195
Supreme Court of the United States

Background and Facts

The Food and Drug Administration (FDA) is a federal administrative agency empowered to administer the Food, Drug, and Cosmetic Act (FDC Act). Pursuant to this act, the FDA can regulate "drugs" and medical "devices." Based on its perceived power under the FDC Act, the FDA enacted a rule regulating tobacco products. The rule:

1. Prohibits the sale of cigarettes and smokeless tobacco to persons younger than 18.
2. Requires retailers to verify through photo identification the age of all purchasers younger than 27.
3. Prohibits the sale of cigarettes in quantities smaller than 20.
4. Prohibits the distribution of free samples.
5. Prohibits sales through self-service displays and vending machines except in adult-only locations.
6. Requires print advertising to appear in black-and-white, text-only format.
7. Prohibits outdoor advertising within 1,000 feet of any public school or playground.
8. Prohibits the distribution of any promotional items, such as t-shirts or hats, bearing the manufacturer's brand.
9. Prohibits a manufacturer from sponsoring any athletic, musical, artistic, or other social or cultural event using its brand name.

A group of tobacco manufacturers and advertisers filed a lawsuit in district court, asserting that the FDA did not have authority to regulate tobacco as a "drug" or "device" that delivered nicotine to the body. The district court certified the issue to the Court of Appeals, which held that the FDC Act did not grant the FDA power to regulate tobacco products. The U.S. Supreme Court granted certiorari to hear the appeal.

Issue

Does the Food, Drug, and Cosmetics Act grant the Food and Drug Administration authority to regulate tobacco products as a "drug" or "device"?

In the Language of the Court

Regardless of how serious the problem an administrative agency seeks to address, however, it may not exercise its authority in a manner that is inconsistent with the administrative structure that Congress enacted into law. Congress has directly addressed the problem of tobacco and health through legislation on six occasions since 1965. When Congress enacted these statutes, the adverse health consequences of tobacco use were well known, as were nicotine's pharmacological effects. Nonetheless, Congress stopped well short of ordering a ban. Instead, it has generally regulated the labeling and advertisement of tobacco products. The inescapable conclusion is that there is no room for tobacco products within the FDC Act's regulatory scheme.

By no means do we question the seriousness of the problem that the FDA has sought to address. The agency has amply demonstrated that tobacco use, particularly among children and adolescents, poses perhaps the single most significant threat to public health in the United States. Nonetheless, no matter how important, conspicuous, and controversial the issue, an administrative agency's power to regulate in the public interest must always be grounded in a valid grant of authority from Congress. And, in our anxiety to effectuate the congressional purpose of protecting the public, we must take care not to extend the scope of the statute beyond the point where Congress indicated it would stop. Reading the FDC Act as a whole, as well as in conjunction with Congress' subsequent tobacco-specific legislation, it is plain that Congress has not given the FDA the authority that it seeks to exercise here.

Decision and Remedy

The U.S. Supreme Court held that the FDA does not have authority under the Food, Drug, and Cosmetics Act to regulate tobacco products as a "drug" or "device." The U.S. Supreme Court affirmed the judgment of the Court of Appeals.

Business and Ethics Questions

1. Did the FDA exceed its delegated authority under the FDC Act by enacting its tobacco product rules?
2. Do you think that the cigarette companies have "bought off" Congress? Explain your answer.
3. Do the state and federal governments have a "stake" in cigarette product sales? What economic effects would a ban on cigarette sales cause to state and federal governments?

Licensing Power

Statutes often require the issuance of a government *license* before a person can enter certain types of industries (e.g., the operation of banks, television and radio stations, commercial airlines) or professions (e.g., doctors, lawyers, dentists, certified public accountants, contractors). Administrative agencies are granted the power to determine whether to grant licenses to applicants.

Applicants must usually submit detailed applications to the appropriate administrative agency. In addition, the agency usually accepts written comments from interested parties and holds hearings on the matter. Courts generally defer to the expertise of administrative agencies in licensing matters.

Judicial Power

Many administrative agencies have the judicial authority to adjudicate cases through an administrative proceeding. Such a proceeding is initiated when an agency serves a complaint on a party the agency believes has violated a statute or an administrative rule or order.

In adjudicating cases, an administrative agency must comply with the Due Process Clause of the U.S. Constitution (and state constitution, where applicable). **Procedural due process** requires the respondent to be given (1) proper and timely notice of the allegations or charges against him or her and (2) an opportunity to present evidence on the matter.

procedural due process
Due process that requires the respondent to be given (1) proper and timely notice of the allegations or charges against him or her and (2) an opportunity to present evidence on the matter.

Executive Power

executive power
Power that administrative agencies are granted, such as the investigation and prosecution of possible violations of statutes, administrative rules, and administrative orders.

Administrative agencies are usually granted **executive powers**, such as the investigation and prosecution of possible violations of statutes, administrative rules, and administrative orders. To perform these functions successfully, the agency must often obtain information from the persons and businesses under investigation as well as from other sources. If the required information is not supplied voluntarily, the agency may issue an administrative subpoena to search the business premises.

administrative subpoena
An order that directs the subject of the subpoena to disclose the requested information.

An administrative agency can issue an **administrative subpoena** to a business or person subject to its jurisdiction. The subpoena directs the party to disclose the requested information to the administrative agency. The administrative agency can seek judicial enforcement of the subpoena if the party does not comply with the subpoena.

Administrative Searches

Sometimes a physical inspection of business premises is crucial to an investigation. Most inspections by administrative agencies are considered "searches" that are subject to the Fourth Amendment of the U.S. Constitution. The Fourth Amendment protects persons (including businesses) from **unreasonable search and seizure**.

unreasonable search and seizure
Any search and seizure by the government that violates the Fourth Amendment.

Searches by administrative agencies are generally considered to be reasonable within the meaning of the Fourth Amendment if:

- The party voluntarily agrees to the search.
- The search is conducted pursuant to a validly issued *search warrant*.
- A warrantless search is conducted in an emergency situation.
- The business is part of a special industry where warrantless searches are automatically considered valid (such as liquor or firearm sales).
- The business is part of a hazardous industry (such as coal mines), and a statute expressly provides for nonarbitrary warrantless searches.

Evidence from an unreasonable search and seizure ("tainted evidence") is inadmissible in court.

In the following case, the U.S. Supreme Court had to decide whether a search of a business by an administrative agency violated the Fourth Amendment.

U.S. SUPREME COURT

New York v. Burger

482 U.S. 691, 197 S.Ct. 2636, 1987 U.S. Lexis 2725
Supreme Court of the United States

Case 23.2

Administrative Search

Background and Facts

Joseph Burger was the owner of a junkyard in Brooklyn, New York. His business consisted, in part, of dismantling automobiles and selling their parts. The state of New York enacted a statute requiring automobile junkyards to keep certain records. The statute authorizes warrantless searches of vehicle dismantlers and automobile junkyards without prior notice. At approximately noon on November 17, 1982, five plainclothes officers of the Auto Crimes Division of the New York City Police Department entered Burger's junkyard to conduct a surprise inspection. Burger did not have either a license to conduct the business or records of the automobiles and vehicle parts on his premises, as required by state law. After conducting an inspection of the premises, the officers determined that Burger was in possession of stolen vehicles and parts. He was arrested and charged with criminal possession of stolen property. Burger moved to suppress the evidence. The New York supreme court and appellate division held the search to be constitutional. The New York court of appeals reversed. New York appealed.

Issue

Does the warrantless search of an automobile junkyard pursuant to a state statute that authorizes such search constitute an unreasonable search and seizure in violation of the Fourth Amendment to the U.S. Constitution?

In the Language of the Court

The Court has long recognized that the Fourth Amendment's prohibition on unreasonable searches and seizures is applicable to commercial premises, as well as to private homes. An expectation of privacy in commercial premises, however, is different from, and indeed less than, a similar expectation in an individual's home. This expectation is particularly attenuated in commercial property employed in "closely regulated" industries. The nature of the regulatory statute reveals that the operation of a junkyard, part of which is devoted to vehicle dismantling, is a closely regulated business in the state of New York. A warrantless inspection of commercial premises may well be reasonable within the meaning of the Fourth Amendment.

The New York regulatory scheme satisfies the three criteria necessary to make reasonable warrantless inspections. First, the state has a substantial interest in regulating the vehicle dismantling and automobile junkyard industry because motor vehicle theft has increased in the state of New York and because the problem of theft is associated with this industry. Second, regulation of the vehicle dismantling industry reasonably serves the state's substantial interest in eradicating automobile theft. It is well established that the theft problem can be addressed effectively by controlling the receiver of, or market in, stolen property. Automobile junkyards and vehicle dismantlers provide the major market for stolen vehicles and vehicle parts. Third, New York law provides a constitutionally adequate substitute for a warrant. The statute informs the operator of a vehicle dismantling business that inspections will be made on a regular basis.

Decision and Remedy

The U.S. Supreme Court held that the New York statute that authorizes warrantless searches of vehicles dismantling businesses and automobile junkyards does not constitute an unreasonable search in violation of the Fourth Amendment to the U.S. Constitution. The Supreme Court reversed the judgment of the New York court of appeals and remanded the case for further proceedings consistent with its decision.

Business and Ethics Questions

1. Should the Fourth Amendment's protection against unreasonable searches and seizures apply to businesses? Why or why not?
2. Was it ethical for the defendant to assert the Fourth Amendment's prohibition against unreasonable searches and seizures?
3. Is auto theft a big business? Will the New York law that regulates vehicle dismantling businesses and junkyards help to alleviate this crime?

Concept Summary *Powers of Administrative Agencies*

Power	Description of Power
1. **Legislative power**	
a. Substantive rule making	Adopting rules that advance the purpose of the statutes that the agency is empowered to enforce. These rules have the force of law. Public notice and participation are required.

b. Interpretive rule making	Adopting rules that interpret statutory language. These rules do not establish new laws. Neither public notice nor participation is required.
c. Statements of policy	Announcing a proposed course of action the agency plans to take in the future. These statements do not have the force of law. Public participation and notice are not required.
d. Licensing	Granting licenses to applicants (e.g., television station licenses, bank charters) and suspending or revoking licenses.
2. **Judicial power**	Adjudicating cases through an administrative proceeding. This includes the power to issue a complaint, hold a hearing by an administrative law judge (ALJ), and issue an order deciding the case and assessing remedies.
3. **Executive power**	Prosecuting violations of statutes and administrative rules and orders. This includes the power to investigate suspected violations, issue administrative subpoenas, and conduct administrative searches.

Katmandu, Nepal. Many other countries do not have administrative law systems as extensive as that of the United States.

Judicial Review of Administrative Agency Actions

Many federal statutes expressly provide for judicial review of administrative agency actions. Where an enabling statute does not provide for review, the Administrative Procedure Act (APA) authorizes judicial review of federal administrative agency actions.[4] The party appealing the decision of an administrative agency is called the **petitioner**.

Decisions of federal administrative agencies may be appealed to the appropriate federal court (see Exhibit 23.2). Decisions of state administrative agencies may be appealed to the proper state court.

Exhibit 23.2

Appeal of a Federal Administrative Agency Action

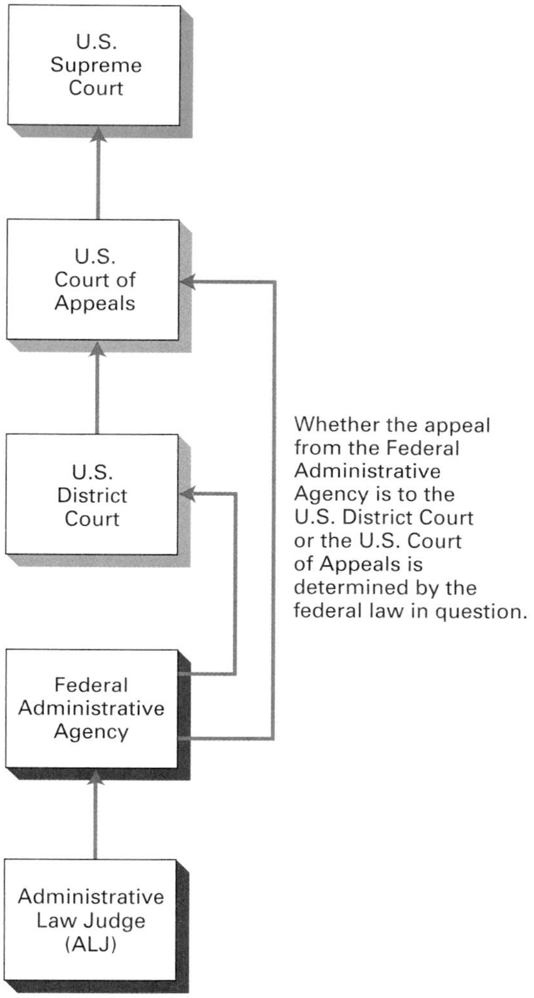

The decision of the administrative agency must be final before judicial review can be sought. (This is called the **final order rule**.) This rule is intended to prevent the disruption of an agency proceeding. For example, an accused party in an administrative agency proceeding cannot appeal to the courts until the agency issues its final ruling in the matter.

final order rule
A rule that says the decision of an administrative agency must be final before judicial review can be sought.

Standards of Judicial Review

Depending on the circumstances, different standards of judicial review apply to questions of law and questions of fact. The standards are:

- ***Question of law.*** If the administrative agency has decided a question of law—such as the interpretation of statutory language—the reviewing court is free to substitute its own judgment for that of the administrative agency.
- ***Question of fact.*** Questions of fact are not easily overturned. The reviewing court usually defers to the agency's fact-finding. The APA specifies three different standards of review for fact-finding by administrative agencies.

An administrative agency's decision can be overturned if it does not meet the appropriate standard of review.

Disclosure of Administrative Agency Actions

Public concern over possible secrecy of administrative agency actions led Congress to enact several statutes that promote public disclosure of federal administrative agency actions and protect parties from overobtrusive agency actions. These statutes are discussed in the paragraphs that follow.

Freedom of Information Act

Freedom of Information Act
A federal act that gives the public access to documents in the possession of federal administrative agencies. There are many exceptions to disclosure.

The **Freedom of Information Act**[5] was enacted to give the public access to most documents in the possession of federal administrative agencies. The act requires federal administrative agencies to publish agency procedures, rules, regulations, interpretations, and other such information in the *Federal Register*. The act also requires agencies to publish quarterly indexes of certain documents. In addition, the act specifies time limits for agencies to respond to requests for information, sets limits on copying charges, and provides for disciplinary action against agency employees who refuse to honor proper requests for information.

For purposes of privacy, the following documents are exempt from disclosure: (1) documents classified by the president to be in the interests of national security; (2) documents that are statutorily prohibited from disclosure; (3) records whose disclosure would interfere with law enforcement proceedings; (4) medical, personnel, and similar files; and (5) documents containing trade secrets or other confidential or privileged information.

Decisions by federal administrative agencies not to publicly disclose documents requested under the act are subject to judicial review in the proper U.S. district court.

Government in the Sunshine Act

Government in the Sunshine Act
A federal act that opens certain federal administrative agency meetings to the public.

The **Government in the Sunshine Act**[6] was enacted to open most federal administrative agency meetings to the public. There are some exceptions to this rule. These include meetings (1) where a person is accused of a crime, (2) concerning an agency's issuance of a subpoena, (3) where attendance of the public would significantly frustrate the implementation of a proposed agency action, and (4) concerning day-to-day operations. Decisions by federal administrative agencies to close a meeting to the public are subject to judicial review in the proper U.S. district court.

Equal Access to Justice Act

Equal Access to Justice Act
A federal act that protects persons from harassment by federal administrative agencies.

Congress enacted the **Equal Access to Justice Act**[7] to protect persons from harassment by federal administrative agencies. Under this act, a private party who is the subject of an unjustified federal administrative agency action can sue to recover attorneys' fees and other costs. The courts have generally held that the agency's conduct must be extremely outrageous before an award will be made under the act. A number of states have similar statutes.

Privacy Act

Privacy Act
A federal act that says federal administrative agencies can maintain only information about an individual that is relevant and necessary to accomplish a legitimate agency purpose.

The federal **Privacy Act**[8] concerns individual privacy. It stipulates that federal administrative agencies can maintain only information about an individual that is relevant and necessary to accomplish a legitimate agency purpose. The act affords individuals the right to have access to agency records concerning themselves and to correct these records. Many states have enacted similar privacy acts.

Concept Summary Public Disclosure of Agency Actions and Protection of Individual Rights

Act	Provision of the Act
Freedom of Information Act	Requires that documents of federal administrative agencies be open to the public; there are certain exemptions from this requirement. The act requires agencies to publish their proceedings, rules, regulations, and other information in the *Federal Register*.
Government in the Sunshine Act	Requires that meetings of federal administrative agencies be open to the public; there are certain exceptions to this requirement.
Equal Access to Justice Act	Gives a private party who was subject to an unjustified federal administrative agency action the right to sue and recover attorneys' fees and costs.
Privacy Act	Requires that federal administrative agencies maintain only information about an individual that is relevant and necessary to accomplish a legitimate agency purpose. Also gives individuals access to these records and a right to correct the records.

Moscow, Russia. For most of the twentieth century, Russia and the other countries of the Soviet Union were governed by communism. Under communism, the government owned much of the property and planned and regulated the economy. With the fall of communism in 1989, the Soviet Union collapsed. Russia and most of the other countries of the dismantled Soviet Union have replaced their planned economies with capitalism.

Terms and Concepts

Government Regulation of Business

1. ***General government regulation.*** General government regulation applies to many industries (e.g., antidiscrimination laws).
2. ***Specific government regulation.*** Specific government regulation applies to a specific industry (e.g., banking laws).

Administrative Agencies

Federal and state legislative and executive branches create *administrative agencies*. They consist of professionals having an area of expertise in a certain area of commerce who interpret and apply designated statutes.

1. ***Administrative rules and regulations.*** Administrative agencies are empowered to adopt rules and regulations that interpret and advance the laws they enforce.
2. ***Administrative Procedure Act (APA).*** The APA is an act that establishes procedures (i.e., notice, hearing, and such) that federal agencies must follow in conducting their affairs. States have enacted their own procedural acts to govern state agencies.

Disclosure of Agency Administrative Actions

1. ***Freedom of Information Act.*** This federal act gives the public access to documents in the possession of federal administrative agencies. There are many exceptions to disclosure.
2. ***Government in the Sunshine Act.*** This federal act opens certain federal administrative agency meetings to the public.
3. ***Equal Access to Justice Act.*** This federal act protects persons from harassment by federal administrative agencies.
4. ***Privacy Act.*** This federal act states that federal administrative agencies can maintain only information about an individual that is relevant and necessary to accomplish a legitimate agency purpose.

Internet Exercises and Case Questions

Working the Web Internet Exercises

1. How does administrative law work? What makes it administrative? An overview of administrative law and procedure is collected at **www.law.fsu.edu/library/admin**.
2. Cases and related materials can be found at **http://www.law.cornell.edu/supct/search/search.html?query=administrative**
3. How often are administrative law cases reviewed by the U.S. Supreme Court? See **supct.law.cornell.edu/supct/cases/adlaw.htm**.

Legal Environment Cases

23.1 Administrative Procedure The Federal Deposit Insurance Corporation (FDIC) insures the deposit accounts of banks up to $100,000. Federal law [12 U.S.C. Section 1818(g)] permits the FDIC to suspend from office any officer of a federally insured bank who is criminally indicted if that person's continued service poses a threat to the interest of the bank's depositors or threatens to impair public confidence in the bank. The statute entitiles suspended bank officers to a hearing before the FDIC within 30 days of a written request and to a final decision within 60 days of the hearing. At the administrative hearing, the officer may submit written material or, at the discretion of the FDIC, oral testimony.

The FDIC suspended James E. Mallen, the president and director of Farmers State Bank in Kanawha, Iowa, upon his indictment for conspiracy to commit mail fraud and for making false statements in violation of federal law. The FDIC issued an order suspending Mallen as president and director. A hearing was scheduled to occur within 19 days after his written request. The FDIC did not permit oral testimony in this case. Mallen sued, alleging that the FDIC's refusal to allow oral testimony at the administrative hearing violated the Due Process Clause to the U.S. Constitution. Is Section 1818(g) constitutional? *Federal Deposit Insurance Corporation v. Mallen*, 486 U.S. 230, 108 S.Ct. 1780, 1988 U.S. Lexis 2477 (U.S. Sup.Ct.)

23.2 Rule Making The Food and Drug Administration (FDA), a federal administrative agency, is charged with enforcing the Food, Drug, and Cosmetics Act. This statute mandates that the FDA limit the amount of "poisonous or deleterious substances" in food. Pursuant to this authority, the FDA established certain "action levels" of unavoidable contaminants, such as aflatoxins, in food. Food producers that sell products that are contaminated above the set action level are subject to enforcement proceedings initiated by the FDA. In announcing these action levels, the FDA did not comply with the notice and comment procedure required for the adoption of a substantive or legislative rule. The FDA argued that the "action levels" are merely interpretive rules or statements of policy that do not require notice and comment. The Community Nutrition Institute, a consortium of consumer public interest groups, sued to require the FDA to follow the notice and comment procedure. Who wins? *Community Nutrition Institute v. Young*, 818 F.2d 943, 1987 U.S.App. Lexis 6385 (D.C. Cir.)

23.3 Rule Making The Federal Communications Commission (FCC) is a federal administrative agency that is empowered to enforce the Communications Act of 1934. This act, as amended, gives the FCC power to regulate broadcasting of radio and television. The act provides that "broadcasting shall not be deemed a common carrier." In *United States v. Midwest Video Corporation* [406 U.S. 649, 92 S.Ct. 1860 (1972)], the U.S. Supreme Court held that the FCC also has the power to regulate cable television.

In May 1976, the FCC promulgated rules requiring cable television operators that have 3,500 or more subscribers to (1) develop a 20-channel capacity, (2) make four channels available for use by public, educational, local, governmental, and leased-access users (with one channel assigned to each), (3) make equipment available for those utilizing these public-access channels, and (4) limit the fees cable operators could charge for their services. Do these rules exceed the statutory authority of the FCC? *Federal Communications Commission v. Midwest Video Corporation*, 440 U.S. 689, 99 S.Ct. 1435, 1979 U.S. Lexis 82 (U.S. Sup.Ct.)

23.4 Administrative Regulation George Carlin, a satiric humorist, recorded a 12-minute monologue called "Filthy Words." He began by referring to his thoughts about "the words you couldn't say on the public airwaves" and then proceeded to list those words, repeating them over and over again in a variety of colloquialisms. At about 2 o'clock in the afternoon, a New York radio station owned by Pacifica Foundation (Pacifica) broadcast Carlin's "Filthy Words" monologue. A father who heard the broadcast while driving with his young son filed a complaint with the FCC, a federal administrative agency charged with regulating broadcasting. The Federal Communications Act forbids the use of "any obscene, indecent, or profane language by means of radio communications." Therefore, the FCC issued an order granting the complaint and informing Pacifica that the order would be considered in future licensing decisions involving Pacifica. Is the FCC regulation legal? *Federal Communications Commission v. Pacifica Foundation*, 438 U.S. 726, 98 S.Ct. 3026, 1978 U.S. Lexis 135 (U.S. Sup.Ct.)

23.5 License The Interstate Commerce Commission (ICC) is a federal administrative agency empowered to regulate motor carriers involved in interstate commerce. Trucking companies must apply to the ICC and obtain a license before they can offer trucking services on a route. The Interstate Commerce Act empowers the ICC to grant an application for a license if it finds that (1) the applicant is fit, willing, and able to properly perform the service proposed and (2) the service proposed is or will be required by the present or future "public convenience or necessity."

Thirteen motor carriers applied to offer trucking services between points in the Southwest and Southeast. After reviewing the applications and extensive written evidence (including the testimony of more than 900 witnesses), the ICC granted licenses to three of the applicants. Arkansas-Best Freight System, Inc., a rejected applicant, brought an action seeking to annul the ICC's order. Should the ICC's grant of the licenses be overturned on appeal? *Brownam Transportation, Inc. v. Arkansas-Best Freight System, Inc.*, 419 U.S. 281, 95 S.Ct. 438, 1974 U.S. Lexis 51 (U.S. Sup.Ct.)

Ethics in Business

23.6 The Federal Mine Safety and Health Act of 1977 requires the secretary of labor to develop detailed mandatory health and safety standards to govern the operation of the nation's mines. The act provides that federal mine inspectors are to inspect underground mines at least four times a year and surface mines at least twice a year to ensure compliance with these standards and to make the following inspections to determine whether previously discovered violations have been corrected. The act also grants mine inspectors "a right of entry to, upon or through any coal or other mine" and states that "no advance notice of an inspection shall be provided to any person."

In July 1978, a federal mine inspector attempted to inspect quarries owned by Waukesha Lime and Stone Company (Waukesha) to determine whether all 25 safety and health violations uncovered during a prior inspection had been corrected. Douglas Dewey, Waukesha's president, refused to allow the inspector to inspect the premises without first obtaining a search warrant. The federal Mine Safety and Health Act authorizes warrantless searches of stone quarries. *Donovan, Secretary of Labor v. Dewey* 452 U.S. 594, 101 S.Ct. 2534, 1980 U.S. Lexis 58 (U.S. Sup.Ct.)

Ethics Issue

1. Are the warrantless searches of stone quarries authorized by the Mine Safety and Health Act constitutional?
2. Did Dewey act ethically in refusing to allow the inspections?

Endnotes

1. 5 U.S.C. Sections 551–706.
2. 5 U.S.C. Section 553.
3. 5 U.S.C. Section 556.
4. 5 U.S.C. Section 702.
5. 5 U.S.C. Section 552.
6. 5 U.S.C. Section 552(b).
7. 5 U.S.C. Section 504.
8. 5 U.S.C. Sections 552(a).

24

Consumer Protection

"I should regret to find that the law was powerless to enforce the most elementary principles of commercial morality."

—Lord Herschell
Reddaway v. Banham (1896), A.C. 199, at p. 209

Chapter Objectives

After studying this chapter, you should be able to:

1. Describe government regulation of food and food additives.
2. Describe government regulation of drugs, cosmetics, and medicinal devices.
3. Explain the coverage of consumer product safety acts.
4. Identify and describe unfair and deceptive business practices.
5. Describe the coverage of consumer credit protection statutes.

Chapter Contents

- Food, Drug, and Cosmetic Safety
- Product Safety
- Unfair and Deceptive Practices
- Debtor Protection Law

Originally, sales transactions in this country were guided by the principle of *caveat emptor* ("let the buyer beware"). To promote the safety of foods, cosmetics, drugs, products, and services, and to prohibit abusive, unfair, and deceptive selling practices, federal and state governments have enacted a variety of statutes that regulate the behavior of businesses that deal with consumers. These laws are collectively referred to as **consumer protection laws**.

This chapter examines consumer protection laws.

consumer protection laws
Federal and state statutes and regulations that promote product safety and prohibit abusive, unfair, and deceptive business practices.

Cattle. The United States Department of Agriculture (USDA), a federal administrative agency, administers and enforces numerous federal statutes that regulate the safety of agricultural and food products.

Food, Drug, and Cosmetic Safety

The federal **Food, Drug, and Cosmetic Act (FDCA)** was enacted in 1938.[1] This act, as amended, regulates the testing, manufacture, distribution, and sale of foods, drugs, cosmetics, and medicinal products and devices in the United States. The **Food and Drug Administration (FDA)** is the federal administrative agency empowered to enforce the FDCA.

Food, Drug, and Cosmetic Act (FDCA)
A federal statute that provides the basis for the regulation of much of the testing, manufacture, distribution, and sale of foods, drugs, cosmetics, and medicinal products.

Food and Drug Administration (FDA)
A federal administrative agency that administers and enforces the federal Food, Drug, and Cosmetic Act (FDCA) and other federal consumer protection laws.

Before certain food additives, drugs, cosmetics, and medicinal devices can be sold to the public, they must receive FDA approval. An applicant must submit an application to the FDA that contains relevant information about the safety and uses of the product. The FDA, after considering the evidence, will either approve or deny the application.

The FDA can seek search warrants and conduct inspections; obtain orders for the seizure, recall, and condemnation of products; seek injunctions; and turn over suspected criminal violations to the U.S. Department of Justice for prosecution.

Regulation of Food

The FDCA prohibits the shipment, distribution, or sale of *adulterated food*. Food is deemed adulterated if it consists in whole or in part of any "filthy, putrid, or decomposed substance" or if it is otherwise "unfit for food." Note that food does not have to be entirely pure to be distributed or sold—it only has to be unadulterated.

The FDCA also prohibits *false and misleading labeling* of food products. In addition, it mandates affirmative disclosure of information on food labels, including the name of the food, the name and place of the manufacturer, a statement of ingredients, and nutrition content. A manufacturer may be held liable for deceptive labeling or packaging.

Contemporary Trend

Food Safety

You take a big bite of a peanut butter sandwich and savor the taste. It has been processed by a food manufacturer and inspected by the federal government, so you think it is pure peanut butter. Not necessarily. Under federal FDA guidelines, peanut butter may contain up to 30 insect fragments per 3 ounces and still be considered "safe" for human consumption.

The FDA has set ceilings, or "action levels," for certain contaminants, or "defects," as the FDA likes to call them, for various foods. Several of these action levels are:

- Golden raisins—35 fly eggs per 8 ounces
- Popcorn—two rodent hairs per pound
- Shelled peanuts—20 insects per 100 pounds
- Canned mushrooms—20 maggots per 3.5 ounces
- Tomato juice—10 fly eggs per 3.5 ounces

The FDA can mount inspections and raids to enforce its action levels. If it finds that the federal tolerance system has been violated, it can seize the offending food and destroy it at the owner's expense.

The courts have upheld the presence of some contamination in food as lawful under the federal FDCA. For example, in one case, the court found that 28 insect parts in 9 pounds of butter did not violate the act. The court stated, "Few foods contain no natural or unavoidable defects. Even with modern technology, all defects in foods cannot be eliminated." *United States v. Capital City Foods, Inc.*, 345 F.Supp. 277, 1972 U.S.Dist. Lexis (N.D. Dist.) ■

Food Labeling

Nutrition Labeling and Education Act
A federal statute that requires food manufacturers to place labels on food that disclose nutritional information about the food.

In 1990, Congress passed a sweeping truth-in-labeling law called the **Nutrition Labeling and Education Act**. This statute requires food manufacturers and processors to provide more nutritional information on most foods and prohibits them from making scientifically unsubstantiated health claims.

The law requires the more than 20,000 food labels found on grocery store shelves to disclose the number of calories derived from fat and the amount of dietary fiber, saturated fat, cholesterol, and a variety of other substances. The law applies to packaged foods as well as fruits, vegetables, and raw seafood. Meat, poultry, and egg products, which are regulated by the Department of Agriculture, are exempt from the act.

The FDA announced final regulations to implement the act. The regulations require food processors to provide uniform information about serving sizes and nutrients on labels of the food products they sell and establish standard definitions for *light, low fat, natural,* and other terms routinely bandied about by food processors.

Regulation of Drugs

The FDCA gives the FDA the authority to regulate the testing, manufacture, distribution, and sale of drugs. The **Drug Amendment to the FDCA**,[2] enacted in 1962, gives the FDA broad powers to license new drugs in the United States. After a new drug application is filed, the FDA holds a hearing and investigates the merits of the application. This process can take many years. The FDA may withdraw approval of any previously licensed drug.

This law requires all users of prescription and nonprescription drugs to receive proper directions for use (including the method and duration of use) and adequate warnings about any related side effects. The manufacture, distribution, or sale of adulterated or misbranded drugs is prohibited.

Ethics in Business

Safety Warnings About Viagra

The anti-impotency drug Viagra is prescribed by doctors to male patients who cannot have or have trouble getting erections, and it helps such men have intercourse. It became successful and is now used by millions of men worldwide. In the United States, the Food and Drug Administration (FDA) approved the drug for use by the general public. After hundreds of deaths of men taking the drug were reported, the FDA investigated and found that men with certain health predispositions may be at risk of death if they take Viagra. Therefore, the FDA required Pfizer, Inc., the manufacturer of Viagra, to place labels on Viagra containers, warning individuals with the following conditions to be careful when taking the drug:

- Men who have had a heart attack or an irregular heartbeat in the past six months
- Men who have a history of cardiac failure or coronary artery disease that has caused angina
- Men who have significant high or low blood pressure

By requiring the new warnings, the FDA hopes men consider these risk factors before taking Viagra.

Ethics Issues

1. Are there risks in taking many of the prescription drugs on the market today? Can you describe one such drug?
2. In applying a cost–benefit analysis to the development and marketing of a drug, when is the point reached where the cost (in injuries, side effects, and deaths) exceeds the benefits to society? Discuss. ■

Regulation of Cosmetics

The FDA's definition of *cosmetics* includes substances and preparations for cleansing, altering the appearance of, and promoting the attractiveness of a person. Eye shadow and other facial makeup products are examples of cosmetics subject to FDA regulation. Ordinary household soap is expressly exempted from this definition.

The FDA has issued regulations that require cosmetics to be labeled, to disclose ingredients, and to contain warnings if they are carcinogenic (i.e., cancer-causing) or otherwise dangerous to a person's health. The manufacture, distribution, or sale of adulterated or misbranded cosmetics is prohibited. The FDA may remove from commerce any cosmetics that contain unsubstantiated claims of preserving youth, increasing virility, growing hair, and such.

Myanmar. Laws of foreign countries differ considerably concerning the regulation of the sale of food.

Regulation of Medicinal Devices

In 1976, Congress enacted the **Medicinal Device Amendment to the FDCA.**[3] This amendment gives the FDA authority to regulate medicinal devices, such as heart pacemakers, kidney dialysis machines, defibrillators, surgical equipment, and other diagnostic, therapeutic, and health devices. The mislabeling of such devices is prohibited. The FDA is empowered to remove "quack" devices from the market.

Product Safety

Consumer Product Safety Act (CPSA)
A federal statute that regulates potentially dangerous consumer products and that created the Consumer Product Safety Commission.

Consumer Product Safety Commission (CPSC)
A federal administrative agency empowered to adopt rules and regulations to interpret and enforce the Consumer Product Safety Act (CPSA).

In 1972, Congress enacted the **Consumer Product Safety Act (CPSA)**[4] and created the **Consumer Product Safety Commission (CPSC)**. The CPSC is an independent federal regulatory agency empowered to (1) adopt rules and regulations to interpret and enforce the CPSA, (2) conduct research on the safety of consumer products, and (3) collect data regarding injuries caused by consumer products.

Because the CPSC regulates potentially dangerous consumer products, it issues product safety standards for consumer products that pose an unreasonable risk of injury. If a consumer product is found to be imminently hazardous—that is, its use can cause an unreasonable risk of death or serious injury or illness—the manufacturer can be required to recall, repair, or replace the product or take other corrective action. Alternatively, the CPSC can seek injunctions, bring actions to seize hazardous consumer products, seek civil penalties for knowing violations of the act or of CPSA rules, and seek criminal penalties for knowing and willful violations of the act or of CPSC rules. A private party can sue for an injunction to prevent violations of the act or of CPSC rules and regulations.

Certain consumer products, including motor vehicles, boats, aircraft, and firearms, are regulated by other government agencies.

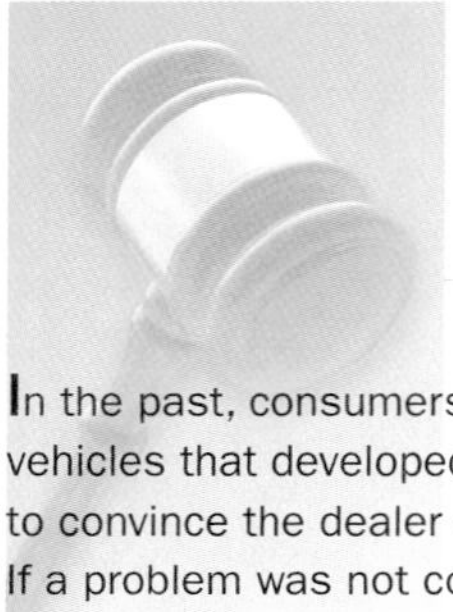

Ethics in Business

Lemon Laws

In the past, consumers who purchased automobiles and other vehicles that developed nagging mechanical problems had to try to convince the dealer or manufacturer to correct the problems. If a problem was not corrected, the consumer's only recourse was to seek redress through costly and time-consuming litigation. Today, most states have enacted **lemon laws**, which give consumers a new weapon in this battle.

Lemon laws provide a procedure for consumers to follow to correct recurring problems in vehicles. Lemon laws establish an administrative procedure that is less formal than a court proceeding. Most of these laws require that an arbitrator decide the dispute between a consumer and a car dealer. Lemon laws stipulate that if the dealer or manufacturer does not correct a recurring defect in a vehicle within a specified number of tries (e.g., four tries) within a specified period of time (e.g., two years), the purchaser can rescind the purchase and recover a full refund of the vehicle's purchase price.

To properly invoke a state's lemon law, a consumer should take the following steps:

- Notify the car dealer immediately of any mechanical or other problems that develop in the vehicle.
- Take the vehicle back to the dealer for the statutory number of times to give the dealer the opportunity to correct the defect.
- File a claim with the appropriate state agency, seeking arbitration of the claim if the defect is not corrected during the number of times and time period established by the state's lemon law.
- Attend the arbitration hearing and present evidence to substantiate the claim that the vehicle suffered from a defect that was not corrected by the dealer or manufacturer within the statutorily prescribed period.

Ethics Issues

1. In general, do you think automobile dealerships are very scrupulous?
2. Are lemon laws needed to protect consumers?

Unfair and Deceptive Practices

The **Federal Trade Commission (FTC) Act** was enacted in 1914.[5] The **Federal Trade Commission (FTC)** was created the following year. The FTC is empowered to enforce the FTC Act as well as other federal consumer protection statutes.

Section 5 of the FTC Act, as amended, prohibits *unfair and deceptive practices*. It has been used extensively to regulate business conduct. Section 5 gives the FTC the authority to bring an administrative proceeding to attack a deceptive or unfair practice. If, after a public administrative hearing, the FTC finds a violation of Section 5, it may order a cease-and-desist order, an affirmative disclosure to consumers, corrective advertising, or the like. The FTC may sue in state or federal court to obtain compensation on behalf of consumers. The decision of the FTC may be appealed to federal court.

Federal Trade Commission (FTC)
A federal administrative agency that is empowered to enforce the Federal Trade Commission (FTC) Act and other federal consumer protection statutes.

Section 5 of the FTC Act
A provision in the FTC Act that prohibits unfair and deceptive practices.

False and Deceptive Advertising

Advertising is false and deceptive under Section 5 of the FTC Act if it (1) contains misinformation or omits important information that is likely to mislead a "reasonable consumer" or (2) makes an unsubstantiated claim (e.g., "This product is 33 percent better than our competitor's"). Proof of actual deception is not required. Statements of opinion and "sales talk" (e.g., "This is a great car") do not constitute false and deceptive advertising.

Bait and Switch

Bait and switch is a type of deceptive advertising under Section 5 of the FTC Act. It occurs when a seller advertises the availability of a low-cost discounted item (the "bait") to attract customers to its store. Once the customers are in the store, however, the seller pressures them to purchase more expensive merchandise (the "switch"). The FTC states that a bait and switch occurs if the seller refuses to show consumers the advertised merchandise, discourages employees from selling the advertised merchandise, or fails to have adequate quantities of the merchandise available.

bait and switch
A type of deceptive advertising that occurs when a seller advertises the availability of a low-cost, discounted item but then pressures the buyer into purchasing more expensive merchandise.

Door-to-Door Sales

Some salespersons sell merchandise and services door-to-door. In some situations, these salespersons use aggressive sales tactics to overcome a consumer's resistance to the sale. To protect consumers from ill-advised decisions, many states have enacted laws that give the consumer a certain number of days to rescind (cancel) a door-to-door sales contract. The usual period is three days. The consumer must send a required notice of cancellation to the seller. An FTC regulation requires the salesperson to permit cancellation of the contract within the stipulated time.

The following is a classic case of false and deceptive advertising.

Case 24.1
False and Deceptive Advertising

U.S. SUPREME COURT

Federal Trade Commission v. Colgate-Palmolive Company

380 U.S. 374, 85 S.Ct. 1035, 1965 U.S. Lexis 2300

Supreme Court of the United States

Background and Facts

The Colgate-Palmolive Co. (Colgate) manufactured and sold a shaving cream called "Rapid Shave." Colgate hired Ted Bates & Company (Bates), an advertising agency, to prepare television commercials designed to show that Rapid Shave could shave the toughest beards. With Colgate's consent, Bates prepared a television commercial that included the sandpaper test. The announcer informed the audience, "To prove Rapid Shave's super-moisturizing power, we put it right from the can onto this tough, dry sandpaper. And off in a stroke."

(continued)

Federal Trade Commission v. Colgate-Palmolive Company

380 U.S. 374, 85 S.Ct. 1035, 1965 U.S. Lexis 2300
Supreme Court of the United States
(*continued*)

While the announcer was speaking, Rapid Shave was applied to a substance that appeared to be sandpaper, and immediately a razor was shown shaving the substance clean. Evidence showed that the substance resembling sandpaper was in fact a simulated prop or "mock-up" made of Plexiglas to which sand had been glued. The Federal Trade Commission (FTC) issued a complaint against Colgate and Bates, alleging a violation of Section 5 of the FTC Act. The FTC held against the defendants. The Court of Appeals reversed. The FTC appealed to the U.S. Supreme Court.

Issue

Did the defendants engage in false and deceptive advertising in violation of Section 5 of the FTC Act?

In the Language of the Court

We agree with the FTC that the undisclosed use of Plexiglas in the present commercial was a material deceptive practice. Respondents claim that it will be impractical to inform the viewing public that it is not seeing an actual test, experiment, or demonstration, but we think it inconceivable that the ingenious advertising world will be unable, if it so desires, to conform to the FTC's insistence that the public be not misinformed.

If it becomes impossible or impracticable to show simulated demonstrations on television in a truthful manner, this indicates that television is not a medium that lends itself to this type of commercial. Similarly unpersuasive is respondents' objection that the FTC's decision discriminates against sellers whose product claims cannot be verified on television without the use of simulation. All methods of advertising do not equally favor every seller. If the inherent limitations of a method do not permit its use in the way a seller desires, the seller cannot by material misrepresentation compensate for those limitations.

Decision and Remedy

The U.S. Supreme Court held that Colgate and Bates had engaged in false and deceptive advertising. The Supreme Court reversed the decision of the Court of Appeals and remanded the case for further proceedings.

Business and Ethics Questions

1. Does the government owe a duty to protect consumers from false and misleading business practices?
2. Did Colgate and Bates act ethically in this case? Do you think the viewing public believed the commercial?
3. Do you think many companies engage in false and deceptive advertising? Can you think of any examples?

Ethics in Business

Do-Not-Call Registry

In 2003, two federal administrative agencies—the **Federal Trade Commission (FTC)** and the **Federal Communications Commission (FCC)**—promulgated administrative rules that created the **"Do-Not-Call" Registry**, on which consumers can place their names and free themselves from most unsolicited commercial telephone calls. A person can place himself or herself on the Do-Not-Call Registry by calling toll-free 888-382-1222 or registering online, at **www.donotcall.gov**. Both wire-connected phones and wireless cell phones can be registered. Telemarketers have three months from the date on which a consumer signs up for the registry to remove the customer's phone number from their sales call list. Customer registration remains valid for five years and can be renewed. Charitable and political organizations are exempt from the registry. Also, there is an "established business relationship" exception that allows businesses to call customers for 10 months after they sell or lease goods or services to that person or conduct a financial transaction with that person. The Do-Not-Call Registry allows consumers to designate specific companies not to call them, including those that otherwise qualify for the established business relationship exemption.

The FTC and FCC found their authority to adopt their coordinated do-not-call rules in several federal statutes. The first is the **Telephone Consumer Protection Act of 1991**, which authorized the FCC to establish a national database of consumers who objected to receiving commercial sales calls. The second is the **Telemarketing and Consumer Fraud and Abuse Prevention Act of 1994**, which authorized the FTC to prohibit sales calls that a reasonable consumer would consider abusive to his or her privacy. And just to wrap things up, after the Do-Not-Call Registry was put in place, in 2003, Congress enacted an **Act to Ratify the Authority of the Federal Trade Commission to Establish a Do-Not-Call Registry**.

Telemarketers, who claimed they would lose substantial business and have to fire millions of workers, sued to have the Do-Not-Call Registry declared unconstitutional as a violation of their constitutional right to free speech. A U.S. district court in Colorado agreed with the telemarketers. On appeal, however, the U.S. Court of Appeals for the Tenth Circuit reversed, holding that the Do-Not-Call Registry did not violate telemarketers' free speech rights. The Court of Appeals held that the Do-Not-Call Registry was narrowly tailored and did not prevent marketers from reaching consumers by direct mail, advertisements, and other lawful methods. The Court stated, "The Do-Not-Call Registry lets consumers avoid unwanted sales pitches that invade the home via telephone." *Mainstream Marketing Services, Inc. v. Federal Trade Commission*, 358 F.3d 1228, 2004 U.S. App. Lexis 2564 (10th Cir.)

Ethics Issues

1. Do many telemarketers act unethically? Explain.
2. Do you think that the Do-Not-Call Registry was warranted? ■

Prague, Czech Republic. The European Union (EU), which comprises 25 countries of Europe, has adopted consumer protection laws to protect consumers in the EU.

Debtor Protection Law

Creditors have been known to engage in various abusive, deceptive, and unfair practices when dealing with consumer-debtors. To protect consumer-debtors from such practices, the federal government has enacted a comprehensive scheme of laws concerning the extension and collection of credit. These laws are discussed in the following sections.

Truth-in-Lending Act

In 1968, Congress enacted the **Truth-in-Lending Act (TILA)** as part of the Consumer Credit Protection Act (CCPA).[6] The TILA, as amended, requires creditors to make certain disclosures to debtors in consumer transactions (e.g., retail installment sales, automobile loans) and real estate loans of any amount on the debtor's principal dwelling.

Truth-in-Lending Act (TILA) A federal statute that requires creditors to make certain disclosures to debtors in consumer transactions.

The TILA covers only creditors that regularly (1) extend credit for goods or services to consumers or (2) arrange such credit in the ordinary course of their business. *Consumer credit* is defined as credit extended to natural persons for personal, family, or household purposes.

Regulation Z A regulation that sets forth detailed rules for compliance with the TILA.

Regulation Z The TILA is administered by the Federal Reserve Board, which has authority to adopt regulations to enforce and interpret the act. **Regulation Z**, which sets forth detailed rules for compliance with the TILA, was adopted under this authority.[7] The TILA and Regulation Z require the following information to be disclosed by the creditor to the consumer-debtor:

- The cash price of the product or service
- The down payment and trade-in allowance
- The unpaid cash price
- The finance charge, including interest, points, and other fees paid for the extension of credit
- The annual percentage rate (APR) of the finance charges
- Charges not included in the finance charge (such as appraisal fees)
- The total dollar amount financed
- The date the finance charge begins to accrue
- The number, amounts, and due dates of payments
- A description of any security interest
- Penalties to be assessed for delinquent payments and late charges
- Prepayment penalties
- Comparative costs of credit (optional)

The uniform disclosures required by the TILA and Regulation Z are intended to help consumers shop for the best credit terms.

Consumer Leasing Act

Consumer Leasing Act (CLA)
An amendment to the TILA that extends the TILA's coverage to lease terms in consumer leases.

Consumers often opt to lease consumer products, such as automobiles, rather than purchase them. The **Consumer Leasing Act (CLA)** extended the TILA's coverage to lease terms in consumer leases.[8] The CLA applies to lessors who engage in leasing or arranging leases for consumer goods in the ordinary course of their business. Casual leases (such as leases between consumers) are not subject to the CLA. Creditors that violate the CLA are subject to the same civil and criminal penalties as provided in the TILA.

Fair Credit and Charge Card Disclosure Act

Fair Credit and Charge Card Disclosure Act
An amendment to the TILA that requires disclosure of certain credit terms on credit- and charge-card solicitations and applications.

The **Fair Credit and Charge Card Disclosure Act of 1988**[9] amended the TILA to require disclosure of credit terms on credit- and charge-card solicitations and applications.

The regulations adopted under the act require that any direct written solicitation to a consumer display, in tabular form, the following information: (1) the APR, (2) any annual membership fee, (3) any minimum or fixed finance charge, (4) any transaction charge for use of the card for purchases, and (5) a statement that charges are due when the periodic statement is received by the debtor.

Equal Credit Opportunity Act

Equal Credit Opportunity Act (ECOA)
A federal statute that prohibits discrimination in the extension of credit based on sex, marital status, race, color, national origin, religion, age, or receipt of income from public assistance programs.

The **Equal Credit Opportunity Act (ECOA)** was enacted in 1975.[10] The ECOA, as amended, prohibits discrimination in the extension of credit based on sex, marital status, race, color, national origin, religion, age, or receipt of income from public assistance programs. The ECOA applies to all creditors that extend or arrange credit in the ordinary course of their business, including banks, savings and loan associations, automobile dealers, real estate brokers, credit-card issuers, and the like.

The creditor must notify the applicant within 30 days regarding the action taken on a credit application. If the creditor takes an *adverse action* (i.e., denies, revokes, or changes the credit terms), the creditor must provide the applicant with a statement containing the specific reasons for the action. If a creditor violates the ECOA, the consumer may bring a civil action against the creditor and recover actual damages (including emotional distress and embarrassment).

Fair Credit Reporting Act (FCRA)

The 1970 Congress enacted the **Fair Credit Reporting Act (FCRA)** as Title VI of the TILA.[11] This act protects consumers who are subjects of a **credit report** by setting out guidelines for consumer reporting agencies—that is, credit bureaus that compile and sell credit reports for a fee. The consumer may request the following information at any time: (1) the nature and substance of all the information in his or her credit file, (2) the sources of this information, and (3) the names of recipients of his or her credit report.

If a consumer challenges the accuracy of pertinent information contained in a credit report, the agency may be compelled to reinvestigate. If the agency cannot find an error despite the consumer's complaint, the consumer may file a 100-word written statement of his or her version of the disputed information. If a consumer reporting agency or user violates the FCRA, the injured consumer may bring a civil action against the violator and recover actual damages. The FCRA also provides for criminal penalties.

Fair Credit Reporting Act (FCRA)
An amendment to the TILA that protects customers who are subjects of a credit report by setting out guidelines for credit bureaus.

credit report
A report that contains information about a person's credit history that can be secured from a credit bureau reporting company.

Fair Debt Collection Practices Act (FDCPA)

In 1977, Congress enacted the **Fair Debt Collection Practices Act (FDCPA)**.[12] This act protects consumer-debtors from abusive, deceptive, and unfair practices used by *debt collectors*. The FDCPA expressly prohibits debt collectors from using certain practices. They are (1) harassing, abusive, or intimidating tactics (e.g., threats of violence and obscene or abusive language), (2) false or misleading misrepresentations (e.g., posing as a police officer or attorney), and (3) unfair or unconscionable practices (e.g., threatening the debtor with imprisonment).

Fair Debt Collection Practices Act (FDCPA)
A federal act that protects consumer-debtors from abusive, deceptive, and unfair practices used by debt collectors.

In some circumstances, the debt collector may not contact the debtor. These situations include the following:

1. At any inconvenient time. The FDCPA provides that convenient hours are between 8:00 A.M. and 9:00 P.M. unless this time is otherwise inconvenient for the debtor (e.g., the debtor works a night shift and sleeps during the day).
2. At inconvenient places, such as at a place of worship or social events.
3. A the debtor's place of employment if the employer objects to such contact.
4. If the debtor is represented by an attorney.
5. If the debtor gives written notice to the debt collector that he or she refuses to pay the debt or does not want the debt collector to contact him or her again.

The FDCPA limits the contact a debt collector may have with third persons other than the debtor's spouse or parents. Such contacts are strictly limited. Unless the court has given its approval, third parties can be consulted only for the purpose of locating the debtor. They can be contacted only once. The debt collector may not inform the third person that the consumer owes a debt that is in the process of collection. A debtor may bring a civil action against a debt collector for intentionally violating the FDCPA.

International Law

United Nations Biosafety Protocol for Genetically Altered Foods

In many countries, the food is not genetically altered. However, many food processors in the United States and elsewhere around the world genetically modify some foods by adding genes from other organisms to help crops grow faster or ward off pests. In the past, food processors did not notify consumers that they were purchasing genetically modified agricultural products. Although companies insist that genetically altered foods are safe, consumers and many countries began to demand that such foods be clearly labeled so that buyers could decide for themselves.

The most concerned countries in the world regarding this issue were in Europe. Led by Germany, many European countries wanted to require genetically engineered food products to be labeled as such and be transported separately from nonaltered agricultural products. Some European countries wanted genetically altered foods to be banned completely. The United States, a major exporter of agricultural products and the leader in the development of biotech foods, argued that these countries were using this issue to erect trade barriers to keep U.S.-produced food products out of their countries in violation of international trade treaties and conventions administered by the World Trade Organization (WTO), which had reduced or eliminated many international trade restrictions.

Tibet, China.

In January 2000, a compromise was reached when 138 countries, including the United States, agreed to the United Nations-sponsored **Biosafety Protocol**. After much negotiation, the countries agreed that all genetically engineered foods would be clearly labeled with the phrase "May contain living modified organisms." This allows consumers to decide on their own whether to purchase such altered food products. In addition, the boxes and containers in which such goods are shipped must also be clearly marked as containing genetically altered food products. ■

Terms and Concepts

Federal Food, Drug, and Cosmetic Act (FDCA)

The FDCA is a federal statute that regulates the testing, manufacture, distribution, and sale of foods, food additives, drugs, cosmetics, and medical products.

Required FDA Approval

1. ***Food and Drug Administration (FDA).*** This federal administrative agency is empowered to interpret and enforce the federal FDCA and other federal consumer protection laws.

2. ***Powers of the FDA.*** The FDA has the power to approve or deny applications by private companies to distribute drugs, food additives, and medical devices to the public.

Regulation of Food, Drugs, and Cosmetics

1. ***Adulterated food.*** The FDA prohibits the shipment, distribution, or sale of *adulterated* or *misbranded* food, drugs, cosmetics, or medical devices.

Other Acts Administered by the FDA

The FDA has authority to administer the following health-related federal statutes and amendments:

1. Pesticide Amendment of 1954
2. Food Additives Amendment of 1958
3. Color Additives Amendment of 1960
4. Animal Drug Amendment of 1968
5. Biologies Act of 1902
6. Public Health Service Act
7. Radiation for Health and Safety of 1968

Consumer Product Safety Act (CPSA)

The CPSA is a federal statute that regulates the safety of consumer products. It created the Consumer Product Safety Commission.

1. ***Consumer Product Safety Commission (CPSC).*** This federal administrative agency is empowered to:
   a. Interpret and enforce the CPSA
   b. Conduct research on safety
   c. Collect data regarding injuries

Consumer Product Safety Statutes Administered by the CPSC

The CPSC also has authority to administer the following federal consumer product safety acts:

1. Consumer Product Safety Act (CPSA)
2. Fair Packaging and Labeling Act
3. Poison Prevention Packaging Act

Section 5 of the Federal Trade Commission Act (FTC Act)

The FTC Act is a federal statute that prohibits unfair and deceptive practices, including false and deceptive advertising, abusive sales tactics, consumer fraud, and other unfair business practices.

1. ***Federal Trade Commission (FTC).*** This federal administrative agency is empowered to enforce the FTC Act and other federal consumer protection statutes.

Truth-in-Lending Act (TILA)

The TILA is a federal statute that requires creditors to make certain disclosures to consumer-debtors in most consumer credit transactions. It mandates disclosure of a single-figure *annual percentage rate (APR)*.

1. ***Regulation Z.*** The Federal Reserve Board adopted Regulation Z to enforce and interpret the TILA.

Consumer Leasing Act (CLA)

The CLA is a federal statute that requires lessors to make disclosures to lessees in most consumer lease transactions.

Fair Credit and Charge Card Disclosure Act of 1988

The Fair Credit and Charge Card Disclosure Act is a federal statute that requires disclosure of certain credit terms to credit-card holders.

Equal Credit Opportunity Act (ECOA)

The ECOA is a federal statute that prohibits discrimination in the extension of credit based on the applicant's sex, marital status, race, color, national origin, religion, age, or receipt of income from public assistance programs.

1. ***Notification.*** The ECOA requires a creditor to notify a consumer-debtor of the reasons for an *adverse action* on a credit report.

Fair Credit Reporting Act (FCRA)

The FCRA is a federal statute that regulates credit reporting agencies and establishes a procedure for a consumer-debtor to have errors in credit reports corrected.

1. ***100-word statement.*** The FCRA permits a consumer-debtor to place a 100-word written statement in his or her credit report file concerning any unresolved dispute. This information must be conveyed to anyone seeking a credit report on the debtor.

Fair Debt Collection Practices Act (FDCPA)

The FDCPA is a federal statute that protects consumer-debtors from abusive, deceptive, and unfair practices used by debt collectors.

1. ***Prohibited contact.*** The FDCPA prohibits or limits the creditor from making certain contact with third parties and the debtor concerning a debt it is trying to collect.

Internet Exercises and Case Questions

Working the Web Internet Exercises

1. Check the Consumer Product Safety Commission site, at **www.cpsc.gov**, for information on window blinds and/or batteries for notebook computers.
2. Review the FDA Enforcement Reports for a detailed list of recent violators. Are any of your favorite foods listed? See the U.S. Food & Drug Administration site, at **www.fda.gov**.
3. Go to the FTC site and find the "Top Ten Dot Cons," at **www.ftc.gov**. See also **www.law.cornell.edu/topics/consumer_credit.html** for an overview of consumer credit law, with links to key primary and secondary sources.

Legal Environment Cases

24.1 Food Regulation Barry Engle owned and operated the Gel Spice Co., Inc. (Gel Spice), which specialized in the importation and packaging of various food spices for resale. All the spices Gel Spice imported were unloaded at a pier in New York City and taken to a warehouse on McDonald Avenue. Storage and repackaging of the spices took place in the warehouse. Between July 1976 and January 1979, the McDonald Avenue warehouse was inspected four times by investigators from the Food and Drug Administration (FDA). The investigators found live rats in bags of basil leaves, rodent droppings in boxes of chili peppers, and mammalian urine in bags of sesame seeds. The investigators produced additional evidence that showed that spices packaged and sold from the warehouse contained insects, rodent excreta pellets, rodent hair, and rodent urine. The FDA brought criminal charges against Engle and Gel Spice. Are they guilty? *United States v. Gel Spice Co., Inc.*, 601 F.Supp. 1205, 1984 U.S. Dist. Lexis 21041 (E.D. N.Y.)

24.2 Regulation of Drugs Dey Laboratories, Inc. (Dey), is a drug manufacturer operating in the state of Texas. In 1983, Dey scientists created an inhalant known as ASI, whose only active ingredient was atropine sulfate. The inhalant was sold to physicians, who then prescribed the medication for patients suffering from asthma, bronchitis, and other pulmonary diseases. In May 1983, Dey filed a new drug application with the Food and Drug Administration (FDA). By September 1983, Dey was advised that its application would not be approved. In spite of the lack of FDA approval, Dey began marketing ASI in November 1983. On August 25, 1985, the United States filed a complaint for forfeiture of all ASI manufactured by Dey. The inhalant was seized, and Dey sued to have the FDA's seizure declared illegal. Who wins? *United States v. Atropine Sulfate 1.0 Mg. (Article of Drug)*, 843 F.2d 860, 1988 U.S. App. Lexis 5819 (5th Cir.)

24.3 Cosmetics Regulation FBNH Enterprises, Inc. (FBNH), was a distributor of a product known as "French Bronze Tablets." The purpose of the tablets was to allow a person to achieve an even tan without exposure to the sun. When ingested, the tablets imparted color to the skin through the use of various ingredients, one of which was canthaxanthin, a coloring agent. Canthaxanthin had not been approved for use by the Food and Drug Administration (FDA) as a coloring additive. The FDA became aware that FBNH was marketing the tablets and that each contained 30 milligrams of canthaxanthin. On

June 16, 1988, the FDA filed a lawsuit seeking the forfeiture and condemnation of eight cases of the tablets in the possession of FBNH. FBNH challenged the government's right to seize the tablets. Who wins? *United States v. Eight Unlabeled Cases of an Article of Cosmetic*, 888 F.2d 945, 1989 U.S. App. Lexis 15589 (2d Cir.)

24.4 Drug Regulation In June 1980, Joseph Wahba had a prescription filled at Zuckerman's Pharmacy (Zuckerman's) in Brooklyn, New York. The prescription was for Lomotil, a drug used to counteract stomach disorders. The pharmacy dispensed 30 tablets in a small, plastic container unequipped with a "child-proof" cap. Joseph took the medicine home, where it was discovered by Wahba's two-year-old son, Mark. Mark opened the container and ingested approximately 20 pills before Mark's mother saw him and stopped him. She rushed him to a hospital but, despite the efforts of the doctors, Mark lapsed into a coma and died. The Wahbas sued H&N Prescription Center, Inc., the company that owned Zuckerman's, for damages. Who wins? *Wahba v. H&N Prescription Center, Inc.*, 539 F.Supp. 352, 1982 U.S. Dist. Lexis 12327 (E.D. N.Y.)

24.5 Truth-in-Lending In June 1979, Elizabeth Valentine purchased a home in Philadelphia, Pennsylvania. In October 1979, she applied for and received a $4,500 home loan from Salmon Building and Loan Association (Salmon) for the purpose of paneling the cellar walls and redecorating the house. Salmon took a security interest in the house as collateral for the loan. Although Valentine was given a disclosure document by Salmon, nowhere on the document were "finance charges" disclosed. The document did not notify Valentine that Salmon had a security interest in the house. In May 1982, Valentine sued Salmon (which had since merged with Influential Savings and Loan Association) to rescind the loan. Who wins? *Valentine v. Influential Savings and Loan Association*, 572 F.Supp. 36, 1983 U.S. Dist. Lexis 15884 (F.D. Pa.)

24.6 Consumer Leasing In April 1986, Joyce Givens entered into a rental agreement with Rent-A-Center, Inc. (Rent-A-Center), whereby she rented a bar and entertainment center. The agreement provided that she must pay in advance to keep the furniture for periods of one week or one month. Givens could terminate the agreement at any time by making arrangements for the furniture's return. Givens made payments between April and August 1986. After that, she failed to make any further payments but continued to possess the property. When Rent-A-Center became aware that Givens had moved and taken the furniture with her, in violation of the rental agreement, it filed a criminal complaint against her. On January 9, 1988, Givens agreed to return the furniture, and Rent-A-Center dropped the charges. After Rent-A-Center recovered the furniture, Givens sued the company, claiming that the agreement she had signed violated the Consumer Leasing Act. Who wins? *Givens v. Rent-A-Center, Inc.*, 720 F.Supp. 160, 1988 U.S. Dist. Lexis 16839 (S.D. Ala.)

24.7 Fair Credit Billing Oscar S. Gray had been an American Express cardholder since 1964. In 1980, Gray used his card to purchase airline tickets costing $9,312. American Express agreed that Gray could pay for the tickets in 12 equal monthly installments. In January and February of 1981, Gray made substantial prepayments of $3,500 and $1,156, respectively. When his March bill arrived, Gray was surprised because American Express had converted the deferred payment plan to a currently due charge, making the entire amount for the tickets due and payable. Gray paid the normal monthly charge under the deferred payment plan and informed American Express by letter dated April 22, 1981, of its error. In the letter, Gray identified himself, his card number, and the nature of the error. Gray did not learn of any adverse action by American Express until almost one year later, on the night of his and his wife's anniversary. When he offered his American Express card to pay for their wedding anniversary dinner, the restaurant informed Gray that American Express had canceled his account and had instructed the restaurant to destroy the card. Gray sued American Express. Did American Express violate the Fair Credit Reporting Act? *Gray v. American Express Company*, 743 F.2d 10, 1984 U.S. App. Lexis 19033 (D.C. Cir.)

24.8 Credit Reporting The San Antonio Retail Merchants Association (SARMA) is a business engaged in selling computerized credit reports. In November 1974, William Daniel Thompson Jr. (Jr.), opened a credit account with Gordon's Jewelers (Gordon's) in San Antonio, listing his Social Security number as 457-68-5778. Jr. subsequently ran up a delinquent account of $77.25 at Gordon's that was subsequently charged off as a bad debt. Gordon's reported the bad debt to SARMA, which placed the information and a derogatory credit rating in Jr.'s file, No. 5867114.

In early 1978, William Douglas Thompson III (III) applied for credit with Gulf Oil and Wards. He listed his Social Security number as 407-86-4065. On February 9, 1978, a worker in the credit department of Gulf accepted file No. 5867114 from SARMA as the credit history of III. Thereafter, SARMA combined the reports of the two men. III was denied credit by both Gulf and Wards on the basis of this erroneous information. It was not until June 1979 that III learned of the mistake. After straightening out the facts with Gordon's, III requested SARMA to correct the error. SARMA took no action on III's complaint for four months. III sued SARMA for violating the Fair Credit Reporting Act. Who wins? *Thompson v. San Antonio Retail Merchants Association*, 682 F.2d 509, 1982 U.S. App. Lexis 16612 (5th Cir.)

24.9 Fair Debt Collection Stanley M. Juras was a student at Montana State University (MSU) from 1972 to 1976. During his years at MSU, Juras took out several student loans from the school under the National Direct Student Loan program. By the time Juras left MSU, he owed the school over $5,000. Juras defaulted on these loans, and MSU assigned the debt to Aman Collection Services, Inc. (Aman), for purposes of collection. Aman obtained a judgment against Juras in a Montana state court for $5,015 on the debt and $1,920 in interest and attorneys' fees. Juras, who by then lived in California, still refused to pay these amounts. On May 5, 1982, a vice president of Aman, Mr. Gloss, telephoned Juras twice in California before 8:00 A.M. Pacific Standard Time. Gloss told Juras that if he did not pay the debt, he would not receive a college transcript. Juras sued Aman, claiming that the telephone calls violated the Fair Debt Collection Practices Act. Gloss testified at trial that he made the calls before 8:00 A.M. because he had forgotten the difference in time zones between California and Aman's offices in South Dakota. Who wins? *Juras v. Aman Collection Services, Inc.*, 829 F.2d 739, 1987 U.S. App. Lexis 12888 (9th Cir.)

Ethics in Business

24.10 Charles of the Ritz Distributing Corporation (Ritz) is a New York corporation that was engaged in the sale and distribution of a product called "Rejuvenescence Cream." The extensive advertising campaign that accompanied the sale of the cream placed emphasis on the supposed rejuvenating powers of the product. The ads claimed that the cream would bring to the user's "skin quickly the clear radiance" and "the petal-like quality and texture of youth." Another advertisement claimed that the product would "restore natural moisture necessary for a live, healthy skin" with the result that "Your face need not know drought years." The Federal Trade Commission (FTC) learned of the ads and asked several experts to investigate the claimed benefits of Rejuvenescence Cream. The experts reported to the FTC that it is impossible for an external application of cosmetics to overcome skin conditions that result from physiological changes occurring with the passage of time. The FTC issued a cease-and-desist order with regard to the advertising. Ritz appealed the FTC's decision to a federal court. *Charles of the Ritz Distributing Corp. v. FTC*, 143 F.2d 676, 1944 U.S. App. Lexis 3172 (2d Cir.)

Ethics Issues

1. Did Ritz act ethically in making its advertising claims?
2. What does Section 5 of the Federal Trade Commission Act provide?
3. Why was Section 5 enacted into law? Explain.
4. Who wins? Why?

Endnotes

1. 21 U.S.C. Section 301.
2. 21 U.S.C. Section 321.
3. 21 U.S.C. Section 360(c) *et seq*.
4. 15 U.S.C. Section 2051.
5. 15 U.S.C. Sections 41–51.
6. 15 U.S.C. Section 1601 *et seq*.
7. 12 C.F.R. 226.
8. 15 U.S.C. Section 1667 *et seq*.
9. 15 U.S.C. Section 1637.
10. 15 U.S.C. Section 1691.
11. 15 U.S.C. Section 1681 *et seq*.
12. 15 U.S.C. Section 1692.

25

Environmental Protection

"All animals are equal but some animals are more equal than others"

—George Orwell
Animal Farm (1945)

Chapter Objectives

After studying this chapter, you should be able to:

1. Describe an environmental impact statement and identify when one is needed.
2. Describe the Clean Air Act and national ambient air quality standards.
3. Describe the Clean Water Act and other water-quality standards.
4. Explain how environmental laws regulate the use of toxic substances and the disposal of hazardous wastes.
5. Describe how the Endangered Species Act protects endangered and threatened species and their habitats.

Chapter Contents

- Environmental Protection
- Air Pollution
- Water Pollution
- Toxic Substances and Hazardous Waste
- Endangered Species
- State Environmental Protection Laws

In producing and consuming products, businesses and consumers generate air pollution, water pollution, and hazardous and toxic wastes that cause harm to the environment and to human health. Pollution has now reached alarming rates in this country and elsewhere in the world. In response, federal and state governments have enacted **environmental protection laws** to contain the levels of pollution and to clean up hazardous waste sites in this country.

This chapter examines environmental laws that are applicable to businesses and individuals.

La Jolla, California. Federal and state governments have enacted many statutes to protect the environment from air, water, and other types of pollution.

Environmental Protection

In the 1970s, the federal government began enacting statutes to protect our nation's air and water from pollution, to regulate hazardous wastes, and to protect wildlife. In many instances, states enacted their own environmental laws that now coexist with federal laws. These laws provide both civil and criminal penalties. **Environmental protection** is one of the most important, and costly, issues facing business and society today.

Environmental Protection Agency (EPA)

Environmental Protection Agency (EPA)
A federal administrative agency created by Congress to coordinate the implementation and enforcement of the federal environmental protection laws.

In 1970, Congress created the **Environmental Protection Agency (EPA)** to coordinate the implementation and enforcement of the federal environmental protection laws. The EPA has broad rule-making powers to adopt regulations to advance the laws that it is empowered to administer. The agency also has adjudicative powers to hold hearings, make decisions, and order remedies for violations of federal environmental laws. In addition, the EPA can initiate judicial proceedings in court against suspected violators of federal environmental laws.

Environmental Impact Statement

National Environmental Policy Act (NEPA)
A federal statute that mandates that the federal government consider the adverse impact a federal government action would have on the environment before the action is implemented.

The **National Environmental Policy Act (NEPA)** became effective January 1, 1970.[1] The NEPA mandates that the federal government consider the "adverse impact" of proposed legislation, rule making, or other federal government action on the environment before the action is implemented.

The NEPA and rules adopted thereunder require that an **environmental impact statement (EIS)** must be prepared for any proposed legislation or major federal action that significantly affects the quality of the human environment. The purpose of the EIS is to provide enough information about the environment to enable the federal government to determine the feasibility of the project. The EIS is also used as evidence in court whenever a federal action is challenged as violating the NEPA or other federal environmental protection laws. Examples of actions that require an EIS include proposals to build a new federally funded highway, to license nuclear plants, and the like.

environmental impact statement (EIS)
A document that must be prepared for any proposed legislation or major federal action that significantly affects the quality of the human environment.

The EIS must (1) describe the affected environment, (2) describe the impact of the proposed federal action on the environment, (3) identify and discuss alternatives to the proposed action, (4) list the resources that will be committed to the action, and (5) contain a cost-benefit analysis of the proposed action and alternative actions. Expert professionals, such as engineers, geologists, and accountants, may be consulted during the preparation of the EIS.

Once an EIS is prepared, it is subject to public review, and the public has 30 days in which to submit comments to the EPA. After the comments have been received and reviewed, the EPA will issue an order that states whether the proposed federal action may proceed. Decisions of the EPA are appealable to the appropriate U.S. Court of Appeals.

Most states and many local governments have enacted laws that require an EIS to be prepared regarding proposed state and local government action as well as private development.

Air Pollution

One of the major problems facing the United States is **air pollution**. The **Clean Air Act** was enacted in 1963 to assist states in dealing with air pollution. The act was amended in 1970 and 1977 and, most recently, by the **Clean Air Act Amendments of 1990**.[2] The Clean Air Act, as amended, provides comprehensive regulation of air quality in this country.

air pollution
Pollution caused by factories, homes, vehicles, and the like that affects the air.

Clean Air Act
A federal statute that provides comprehensive regulation of air quality in the United States.

Sources of Air Pollution

Substantial amounts of air pollution are emitted by *stationary sources* (e.g., industrial plants, oil refineries, public utilities). The Clean Air Act requires states to identify major stationary sources and develop plans to reduce air pollution from these sources. Automobile and other vehicle emissions are one of the major sources of air pollution in this country. In an effort to control emissions from these *mobile sources*, the Clean Air Act requires air pollution controls to be installed on motor vehicles. Emissions standards have been set for automobiles, trucks, buses, motorcycles, and airplanes. In addition, the Clean Air Act authorizes the EPA to regulate air pollution caused by fuel and fuel additives.

National Ambient Air Quality Standards

The Clean Air Act directs the EPA to establish **national ambient air quality standards (NAAQS)** for certain pollutants. These standards are set at two different levels: primary (to protect human beings) and secondary (to protect vegetation, matter, climate, visibility, and economic values). Specific standards have been established for carbon monoxide, nitrogen oxide, sulfur oxide, ozone, lead, and particulate matter.

national ambient air quality standards (NAAQS)
Standards for certain pollutants set by the EPA that protect (1) human beings (primary) and (2) vegetation, matter, climate, visibility, and economic values (secondary).

Although the EPA establishes air quality standards, the states are responsible for their enforcement. The federal government has the right to enforce these air pollution standards if the states fail to do so. Each state is required to prepare a *state implementation plan (SIP)* that sets out how the state plans to meet the federal standards. The EPA has divided each state into *air quality control regions (AQCRs)*. Each region is monitored to ensure compliance.

Nonattainment Areas

nonattainment area
A designated geographical area that does not meet established air quality standards.

Regions that do not meet the air quality standards are designated **nonattainment areas**. Nonattainment areas are classified into one of five categories—(1) marginal, (2) moderate, (3) serious, (4) severe, and (5) extreme—based on the degree to which they exceed the ozone standard. Deadlines are established for areas to meet the attainment level. States must submit compliance plans that (1) identify major sources of air pollution and require them to install pollution control equipment, (2) institute permit systems for new stationary sources, and (3) implement inspection programs to monitor mobile sources. States that fail to develop or implement approved plans are subject to the following sanctions: (1) loss of federal highway funds and (2) limitations on new sources of emissions (e.g., the EPA can prohibit the construction of a new pollution-causing industrial plant in the nonattainment area).

The Clean Air Act was at issue in the following case.

Case 25.1
Clean Air Act

U.S. SUPREME COURT

Whitman, Administrator of Environmental Protection Agency v. American Trucking Association

531 U.S. 457, 121 S. Ct. 903, 2001 U.S. Lexis 1952
Supreme Court of the United States

Background and Facts

Section 109 of the federal Clean Air Act requires the administrator of the EPA, a federal administrative agency, to set NAAQS for air pollutants. Section 109 instructs the EPA to set NAAQS at levels "to protect the public health" with "an adequate margin of safety." Pursuant to Section 109, the EPA issued new standards for ozone and particular matter emitted from the operation of trucks. The American Trucking Association sued the EPA, arguing that the EPA must consider the cost caused to trucking firms before issuing the NAAQS. The EPA argued that it did not have to do so under the statute. The U.S. district court held for the American Trucking Association, but the U.S. Court of Appeals held for the EPA on this issue. The U.S. Supreme Court granted review.

Issue

Under Section 109 of the federal Clean Air Act, must the EPA consider the cost imposed on trucking firms before setting NAAQS for ozone and particulate matter emissions from trucks?

In the Language of the Court

Section 109 instructs the EPA to set primary ambient air quality standards "the attainment and maintenance of which are requisite to protect the public health" with "an adequate margin of safety." This text does not permit the EPA to consider costs in setting the standards. The language is absolute. The EPA, based on the information about health effects contained in the technical criteria documents is to identify the maximum airborne concentration of a pollutant that the public health can tolerate, decrease the concentration to provide an adequate margin of safety, and set the standard at that level. Nowhere are the costs of achieving such a standard made part of that initial calculation.

Respondent argues many more factors than air pollution affect public health. In particular, the economic cost of implementing a very stringent standard might produce losses sufficient to offset the health gains achieved in cleaning the air—for example, by closing down whole industries and thereby impoverishing the workers and consumers dependent upon those industries. That is unquestionably true. Accordingly, to prevail in their present challenge, respondent must show a textual commitment of authority to the EPA to consider costs in setting NAAQS under Section 109. Congress does not alter the fundamental details of a regulatory scheme.

Decision and Remedy

The U.S. Supreme Court held that the statutory language of Section 109 of the Clean Air Act does not require the EPA to consider the cost to trucking firms for implementing the NAAQS set by the EPA. The Supreme Court affirmed the decision of the Court of Appeals in favor of the EPA.

Business and Ethics Questions

1. Do you think the statutory language of Section 109 was clear in this case?
2. Would the "public health" be compromised under the trucking firms' argument? Why did the trucking firms resist the NAAQS set by the EPA?
3. What are the economic consequences of the Supreme Court's ruling? Explain.

Contemporary Trend

Indoor Air Pollution

According to officials of the EPA, the air inside some buildings may be 100 times more polluted than outside air. Doctors increasingly attribute a wide range of symptoms to **indoor air pollution**, or **sick building syndrome**. Indoor air pollution has two primary causes. In an effort to reduce dependence on foreign oil, many recently constructed office buildings were overly insulated and built with sealed windows and no outside air ducts. As a result, no fresh air enters many workplaces. This absence of fresh air can cause headaches, fatigue, and dizziness among workers.

The other chief cause of sick building syndrome, which is believed to affect up to one-third of U.S. office buildings, is hazardous chemicals and construction materials. In the office, these include everything from asbestos to noxious fumes emitted from copy machines, carbonless paper, and cleaning fluids. In the home, radon, an odorless gas that is emitted from the natural breakdown of uranium in soil, poses a particularly widespread danger. Radon gas damages and may destroy lung tissue. The costs of eliminating these conditions can be colossal.

Experts predict that sick building syndrome is likely to spawn a flood of litigation and that a wide range of parties will be sued. Manufacturers, employers, home sellers, builders, engineers, and architects will increasingly be forced to defend themselves against tort and breach of contract actions filed by homeowners, employees, and others affected by indoor air pollution. Insurance companies will undoubtedly be drawn into costly lawsuits stemming from indoor air pollution. ■

Bhutan. Many countries of the world are developing and enforcing laws to protect the environment.

Water Pollution

Water pollution affects human health, recreation, agriculture, and business. Pollution of waterways by industry and humans has caused severe ecological and environmental problems, including making water sources unsafe as drinking water and for fish, birds, and other animals. The federal government has enacted a comprehensive scheme of statutes and regulations to prevent and control water pollution.

water pollution
Pollution of lakes, rivers, oceans, and other bodies of water.

In 1948, Congress enacted the **Federal Water Pollution Control Act (FWPCA)** to regulate water pollution. This act has been amended several times. As amended, it is simply referred to as the **Clean Water Act**.[3] This act is administered by the EPA.

Clean Water Act
A federal statute that establishes water quality standards and regulates water pollution.

Pursuant to the Clean Water Act, the EPA has established water quality standards that define which bodies of water can be used for public drinking water, recreation (such as swimming), propagation of fish and wildlife, and agricultural and industrial uses.

States are primarily responsible for enforcing the provisions of the Clean Water Act and EPA regulations adopted thereunder. If a state fails to do so, the federal government may enforce the act.

Point Sources of Water Pollution

The Clean Water Act authorizes the EPA to establish water pollution control standards for *point sources* of water pollution (i.e., mines, manufacturing plants, paper mills, electric utility plants, municipal sewage plants, other stationary sources of water pollution). Dischargers of pollutants are required to keep records, maintain monitoring equipment, and keep samples of discharges.

Thermal Pollution

thermal pollution
The discharge of heated water or material into waterways, which upsets the ecological balance and decreases the oxygen content.

The Clean Water Act expressly forbids **thermal pollution** because the discharge of heated waters or materials into the nation's waterways may upset the ecological balance; decrease the oxygen content of water; and harm fish, birds, and other animals that use the waterways.[4] Sources of thermal pollution (such as electric utility companies and manufacturing plants) are subject to the provisions of the Clean Water Act and regulations adopted by the EPA.

Wetlands

wetlands
Areas that are inundated or saturated by surface water or groundwater that support vegetation typically adapted for life in such conditions.

Wetlands are defined as areas that are inundated or saturated by surface water or groundwater that support vegetation typically adapted for life in saturated soil conditions. Wetlands include swamps, marshes, bogs, and similar areas that support birds, other animals, and vegetative life. The Clean Water Act forbids the filling or dredging of wetlands unless a permit has been obtained from the **Army Corps of Engineers (Corps)**. The Corps is empowered to adopt regulations and conduct administrative proceedings to enforce the act.

Safe Drinking Water Act

Safe Drinking Water Act
A federal statute that authorizes the EPA to establish national primary drinking water standards.

The **Safe Drinking Water Act**,[5] which was enacted in 1974 and amended in 1986, authorizes the EPA to establish national primary drinking water standards (minimum quality of water for human consumption). The act also prohibits the dumping of wastes into wells used for drinking water. The states are primarily responsible for enforcing the act. If a state fails to do so, the federal government can enforce the act.

The following case involves the definition of *navigable waters* under the Clean Water Act.

U.S. SUPREME COURT

Solid Waste Agency of Northern Cook County, Illinois v. United States Army Corps of Engineers

531 U.S. 159, 121 S.Ct. 675, 2001 U.S. Lexis 640
Supreme Court of the United States

Case 25.2
Clean Water Act

Background and Facts

Section 404 of the federal Clean Water Act regulates the discharge of dredged or fill material into *navigable waters*. The U.S. Army Corps of Engineers (Corps) is authorized to enforce this statute and to issue permits for discharge of dredged or fill material into navigable waters in the United States. The Solid Waste Agency of Northern Cook County, Illinois (Agency), a consortium of 23 suburban Chicago cities and villages, located a 533-acre parcel of real property that was a closed sand and gravel pit mining operation as a proposed disposal site for baled nonhazardous solid waste. Long since abandoned, the old mining site had permanent and seasonal water ponds of varying size and depth that served several species of migrating birds. The ponds were not connected to any water tributary but were filled by rain water and melting snow. When the Corps refused to issue a permit, the Agency sued the Corps, arguing that the Corps had no jurisdiction over the site because it did not contain any *navigable waters*. The district court held for the Corps, and the Court of Appeals affirmed. The U.S. Supreme Court granted review.

Issue

Does the gravel and sand pit contain navigable waters that give the Army Corps of Engineers jurisdiction over the site?

In the Language of the Court

Congress passed the Clean Water Act for the stated purpose of restoring and maintaining the chemical, physical, and biological integrity of the Nation's waters. Relevant here, Section 404 authorizes the U.S. Army Corps of Engineers to regulate the discharge of fill material into "navigable waters," which the statute defines as "the waters of the United States, including the territorial seas." The Corps has interpreted these words to cover the abandoned gravel pit at issue here because it is used as habitat for migratory birds. We thus decline the Corps' invitation to hold that isolated ponds, some only seasonal, wholly located within Illinois, fall under 404's definition of "navigable waters" because they serve as habitat for migratory birds. As counsel for the Corps conceded at oral argument, such a ruling would assume that the use of the word navigable in the statute does not have any independent significance.

Decision and Remedy

The U.S. Supreme Court held that the ponds located on the sand and gravel pit are not navigable waters as defined by Section 404 of the Clean Water Act. Therefore, the U.S. Army Corps of Engineers does not have authority or jurisdiction over these ponds. The U.S. Supreme Court reversed the judgment of the Court of Appeals.

Business and Ethics Questions

1. Do you think that the U.S. Supreme Court properly interpreted the term *navigable waters* as used in Section 404 of the Clean Water Act?
2. Did the petitioner Solid Waste Agency act ethically in placing a waste disposal site on an area where the habitat of several migrating birds could be destroyed?
3. In the United States, has a proper balance been struck between the protection of the environment and the ability of businesses to operate without too much burden from these laws? Explain.

Ocean Protection

The **Marine Protection, Research, and Sanctuaries Act**,[6] enacted in 1972, extended environmental protection to the oceans. It (1) requires a permit for dumping wastes and other foreign materials into ocean waters and (2) establishes marine sanctuaries in ocean waters as far seaward as the edge of the continental shelf and in the Great Lakes and their connecting waters.

Marine Protection, Research, and Sanctuaries Act
A federal statute that extends limited environmental protection to the oceans.

The Clean Water Act authorizes the U.S. government to clean up oil spills and spills of other hazardous substances in ocean waters within 12 miles of the shore and on the continental shelf and to recover the cleanup costs from responsible parties.

In the past, there have been several major oil spills from oil tankers in ocean waters off the coast of the United States. These oil spills have caused significant damage to sea life,

Oil Pollution Act
A federal statute that requires the oil industry to take measures to prevent oil spills and to readily respond to clean up oil spills.

animal life, and human life, and to their habitats. In response, Congress enacted the federal **Oil Pollution Act** of 1990,[7] which is administered by the U.S. Coast Guard. This act requires the oil industry to adopt procedures and contingency plans to readily respond to and clean up oil spills. A tanker owner-operator must prove that it is fully insured to cover any liability that may occur from an oil spill. The act also requires oil tankers to have double hulls by 2015.

Ethics in Business

Illegal Dumping of Pollutants

Mark Irby was plant manager of a wastewater treatment plant. The records show that Irby ordered employees of the plant to bypass the treatment system after-hours and to discharge approximately 500,000 gallons of raw untreated sewage and partially treated sludge sewage at least twice a week for two years into the Reedy River. The court found that these discharges caused environmental damage. Irby was charged with criminal violation of the Clean Water Act. The jury convicted him of six criminal violations of the act, and the district court sentenced him to the maximum allowable jail sentence of 33 months. Irby challenged his sentence.

The Court of Appeals held that Irby had exercised decision-making authority in directing the employees of the wastewater treatment plant to discharge the untreated sewage into the Reedy River. The court also held that the offense resulted in an ongoing, continuous, and repetitive discharge of pollutants into the environment, thus justifying the imposition of the 33 months of jail time. The court stated, "There was absolutely no acceptance of responsibility in this case. No remorse whatsoever was shown by Irby." *United States v. Irby*, 944 F.2d 902, 1991 U.S.App. Lexis 27736 (4th Cir.)

Ethics Issues

1. Did Irby act ethically in this case?
2. What is the incentive for businesses and organizations to avoid environmental laws?

Gitchie Manitou Shores, Lake Huron, Upper Peninsula, Michigan. Federal environmental laws protect the nation's waters from pollution.

Toxic Substances and Hazardous Waste

Many chemicals used for agriculture, industry, and mining contain **toxic substances** that cause cancer, birth defects, and other health-related problems in human beings, as well as injury or death to birds, fish, other animals, and vegetation. Many chemical compounds that are used in the manufacture of products are toxic (e.g., PCBs, asbestos). Hundreds of new chemicals and chemical compounds that may be toxic are discovered each year.

Wastes, which often contain hazardous substances that can harm the environment or pose a danger to human health, are generated by agriculture, mining, industry, other businesses, and households. Wastes consist of garbage, sewage, industrial discharges, old equipment, and such. The mishandling and disposal of **hazardous wastes** can cause air, water, and land pollution.

toxic substances
Chemicals used for agricultural, industrial, and mining uses that cause injury to humans, birds, fish, other animals, and vegetation.

hazardous waste
Solid waste that may cause or significantly contribute to an increase in mortality or serious illness or pose a hazard to human health or the environment if improperly managed.

Toxic Substances Control

In 1976, Congress enacted the **Toxic Substances Control Act**[8] and gave the EPA authority to administer the act. The act requires the EPA to identify **toxic air pollutants** that cause serious illness or death to humans. So far, more than 200 chemicals have been listed as toxic, including asbestos, mercury, vinyl chloride, benzene, beryllium, and radionuclides.

The act requires the EPA to establish standards for toxic chemicals and requires stationary sources to install equipment and technology to control emissions of toxic substances. EPA standards for toxic substances are set without regard to economic or technological feasibility. The act requires manufacturers and processors to test new chemicals to determine their effects on human health and the environment and to report the results to the EPA before they can be marketed.

The EPA may limit or prohibit the manufacture and sale of toxic substances, and it can remove them from commerce if it finds that they pose an imminent hazard or an unreasonable risk of injury to human health or the environment. The EPA also requires special labeling of toxic substances.

Toxic Substances Control Act
A federal statute that authorizes the EPA to regulate toxic substances.

toxic air pollutants
Air pollutants that cause serious illness or death to humans.

Insecticides, Fungicides, and Rodenticides

Farmers and ranchers use chemical pesticides, herbicides, fungicides, and rodenticides to kill insects, weeds, and pests. Evidence shows that the use of some of these chemicals on food, and their residual accumulation in soil, poses health hazards. In 1947, Congress enacted the **Insecticide, Fungicide, and Rodenticide Act**, which gave the federal government authority to regulate pesticides and related chemicals. This act, which was substantially amended in 1972,[9] is administered by the EPA. Under the act, pesticides must be registered with the EPA before they can be sold. The EPA may suspend the registration of a registered pesticide that it finds poses an imminent danger or emergency.

Insecticide, Fungicide, and Rodenticide Act
A federal statute that requires pesticides, herbicides, fungicides, and rodenticides to be registered with the EPA; the EPA may deny, suspend, or cancel registration.

Hazardous Waste

The disposal of hazardous wastes sometimes causes **land pollution**. In 1976, Congress enacted the **Resource Conservation and Recovery Act (RCRA)**,[10] which regulates the disposal of new hazardous wastes. This act, which has been amended several times, authorizes the EPA to regulate facilities that generate, treat, store, transport, and dispose

land pollution
Pollution of the land that is generally caused by hazardous waste being disposed of in an improper manner.

Resource Conservation and Recovery Act (RCRA)
A federal statute that authorizes the EPA to regulate facilities that generate, treat, store, transport, and dispose of hazardous wastes.

of hazardous wastes. States have primary responsibility for implementing the standards established by the act and EPA regulations.

The RCRA defines *hazardous waste* as a solid waste that may cause or significantly contribute to an increase in mortality or serious illness or pose a hazard to human health or the environment if improperly managed. The EPA has designated as hazardous substances that are toxic, radioactive, or corrosive or that ignite, and it can add to the list of hazardous wastes as needed.

The EPA also establishes standards and procedures for the safe treatment, storage, disposal, and transportation of hazardous wastes. Under the act, the EPA is authorized to regulate underground storage facilities, such as underground gasoline tanks.

Contemporary Trend

Superfund

In 1980, Congress enacted the **Comprehensive Environmental Response, Compensation, and Liability Act (CERCLA)**, which is commonly called the **Superfund** [42 U.S.C. Sections 9601–9675]. The act, which was significantly amended in 1986, is administered by the EPA. The act gave the federal government a mandate to deal with hazardous wastes that have been spilled, stored, or abandoned. The Superfund provides for the creation of a government fund to finance the cleanup of hazardous waste sites (hence the name *Superfund*). The fund is financed through taxes on chemicals, feedstocks, motor fuels, and other products that contain hazardous substances.

The Superfund requires the EPA to (1) identify sites in the United States where hazardous wastes have been disposed, stored, abandoned, or spilled and (2) rank these sites regarding their severity of risk. When it ranks the sites, the EPA considers factors such as the types of hazardous waste, the toxicity of the wastes, the types of pollution (air, water, land, or other pollution), the number of people potentially affected by the risk, and other factors. The hazardous waste sites with the highest ranking are put on the National Priority List. The sites on this list receive first consideration for cleanup. The EPA has the authority to clean up hazardous priority or nonpriority sites quickly to prevent fire, explosion, contamination of drinking water, or other imminent danger.

The EPA can order a responsible party to clean up a hazardous waste site. If that party fails to do so, the EPA can clean up the site and recover the cost of the cleanup. The Superfund imposes strict liability—that is, liability without fault. The EPA can recover the cost of the cleanup from (1) the generator who deposited the wastes, (2) the transporter of the wastes to the site, (3) the owner of the site at the time of the disposal, and (4) the current owner and operator of the site. The Superfund permits states and private parties who clean up hazardous waste sites to seek reimbursement from the fund. ■

Nuclear Waste

Nuclear-powered fuel plants create radioactive wastes that maintain a high level of *radioactivity*. Radioactivity can cause injury and death to humans and other life and can also cause severe damage to the environment. Accidents, human error, faulty construction, and such all can be causes of **radiation pollution**.

radiation pollution
Emissions from radioactive wastes that can cause injury and death to humans and other life and can cause severe damage to the environment.

Nuclear Regulatory Commission (NRC)
A federal agency that licenses the construction and opening of commercial nuclear power plants.

The **Nuclear Regulatory Commission (NRC)**, which was created by Congress in 1977, licenses the construction and opening of commercial nuclear power plants. It continually monitors the operation of nuclear power plants and may close a plant if safety violations are found.

The EPA is empowered to set standards for radioactivity in the environment and to regulate the disposal of radioactive waste. The EPA also regulates thermal pollution from nuclear power plants and emissions from uranium mines and mills.

The **Nuclear Waste Policy Act of 1982**[11] mandated that the federal government select and develop a permanent site for the disposal of nuclear wastes.

Seal, Monterey, California. Endangered species of birds, fish, and other animals are protected by federal and state environmental laws.

Endangered Species

Many species of animals are endangered or threatened with extinction. The reduction of certain species of wildlife may be caused by environmental pollution, real estate development, or hunting. The **Endangered Species Act** was enacted in 1973.[12] The act, as amended, protects *endangered* and *threatened* species of animals. The secretary of the interior is empowered to declare a form of wildlife as *endangered* or *threatened*. The act requires the EPA and the Department of Commerce to designate *critical habitats* for each endangered and threatened species. Real estate and other development in these areas is prohibited or severely limited. The secretary of commerce is empowered to enforce the provisions of the act as to marine species.

Endangered Species Act
A federal statute that protects endangered and threatened species of animals.

In addition, the Endangered Species Act, which applies to both the government and private persons, prohibits the taking of any endangered species, where *taking* is defined as an act intended to "harass, harm, pursue, hunt, shoot, wound, kill, trap, capture, or collect" an endangered animal.

Numerous other federal laws protect wildlife. These include (1) the Migratory Bird Treaty Act, (2) the Bald Eagle Protection Act, (3) the Wild Free-Roaming Horses and Burros Act, (4) the Marine Mammal Protection Act, (5) the Migratory Bird Conservation Act, (6) the Fishery Conservation and Management Act, (7) the Fish and Wildlife Coordination Act, and (8) the National Wildlife Refuge System. Many states have also enacted statutes that protect and preserve wildlife.

Good government is an empire of laws.

John Adams
Thoughts on Government (1776)

The following classic case illustrates the application of the Endangered Species Act.

Case 25.3 Endangered Species Act

U.S. SUPREME COURT

Tennessee Valley Authority v. Hill, Secretary of the Interior

437 U.S. 153, 98 S.Ct. 2279, 1978 U.S. Lexis 33

Supreme Court of the United States

Background and Facts

The Tennessee Valley Authority (TVA) is a wholly owned public corporation of the United States. It operates a series of dams, reservoirs, and water projects that provide electric power, irrigation, and flood control to areas in several southern states. In 1967, with appropriations from Congress, the TVA began construction of the Tellico Dam on the Little Tennessee River. When completed, the dam would impound water covering 16,500 acres,

(*continued*)

Tennessee Valley Authority v. Hill, Secretary of the Interior

437 U.S. 153, 98 S.Ct. 2279, 1978 U.S. Lexis 33
Supreme Court of the United States
(continued)

thereby converting the river's shallow, fast-flowing waters into a deep reservoir over 30 miles in length. Construction of the dam continued until 1977, when it was completed.

In 1973, a University of Tennessee ichthyologist found a previously unknown species of perch called the *Percina (Imostoma) Tansai*—or "snail darter"—in the Little Tennessee River. After further investigation, it was determined that approximately 10,000 to 15,000 of these three-inch, tannish-colored fish existed in the river's waters that would be flooded by the operation of the Tellico Dam. The snail darter was not found anywhere else in the world. It feeds exclusively on snails and requires substantial oxygen, both supplied by the fast-moving waters of the Little Tennessee River. The impounding of the water behind the Tellico Dam would destroy the snail darter's food and oxygen supplies, thus causing its extinction. Evidence was introduced showing that the TVA could not, at that time, successfully transplant the snail darter to any other habitat.

Also in 1973, Congress enacted the Endangered Species Act, which authorizes the secretary of the interior to declare species of animal life "endangered" and to identify the "critical habitats" of these creatures. When a species or its habitat is so listed, Section 7 of the act mandates that the secretary take such action as is necessary to ensure that actions of the federal government do not jeopardize the continued existence of such endangered species. The secretary declared the snail darter an endangered species and the area that would be affected by the Tellico Dam its critical habitat.

Congress continued to appropriate funds for the construction of the dam, which was completed at a cost of over $100 million. In 1976, a regional association of biological scientists, a Tennessee conservation group, and several individuals filed an action seeking to enjoin the TVA from closing the gates of the dam and impounding the water in the reservoir on the grounds that those actions would violate Section 7 of the act by causing the extinction of the snail darter. The district court held in favor of the TVA. The Court of Appeals reversed and remanded the case with instructions to the district court to issue a permanent injunction halting the operation of the Tellico Dam. The TVA appealed to the U.S. Supreme Court.

Issue

Would the TVA be in violation of the Endangered Species Act if it operated the Tellico Dam?

In the Language of the Court

It may seem curious to some that the survival of a relatively small number of 3-inch fish among all the countless millions of species extant would require the permanent halting of a virtually completed dam for which Congress has expended more than $100 million. We conclude, however, that the explicit provisions of the Endangered Species Act required precisely this result.

One would be hard pressed to find a statutory provision whose terms were any plainer than those in Section 7 of the Endangered Species Act. Its very words affirmatively command all federal agencies to ensure that actions authorized, funded, or carried out by them do not jeopardize the continued existence of an endangered species or result in the destruction or modification of habitat of such species. This language admits no exception. Nonetheless, petitioner TVA urges that the Act cannot reasonably be interpreted as applying to a federal project that was well under way when Congress passed the Endangered Species Act of 1973. To sustain that position, however, we would be forced to ignore the ordinary meaning of plain language.

Examination of the language, history, and structure of the legislation under review here indicates beyond doubt that Congress intended endangered species to be afforded the highest of priorities. As it was passed, the Endangered Species Act of 1973 represented the most comprehensive legislation for the preservation of endangered species ever enacted by any nation. Virtually all dealings with endangered species, including taking, possession, transportation, and sale, were prohibited.

Decision and Remedy

The U.S. Supreme Court held that the Endangered Species Act prohibited the impoundment of the Little Tennessee River by the Tellico Dam. The Supreme Court affirmed the decision of the Court of Appeals that enjoined the operation of the dam.

Eventually, after substantial research and investigation, it was determined that the snail darter could live in another habitat that was found for it. After the snail darter was removed, at government expense, to this new location, the TVA was permitted to close the gates of the Tellico Dam and begin its operation.

Business and Ethics Questions

1. Should the law protect endangered species? Why or why not?
2. Did the TVA act ethically in this case by completing construction of the dam?
3. Do you think the cost of constructing the Tellico Dam ($100 million) should have been considered by the Court in reaching its decision?

State Environmental Protection Laws

Many state and local governments have enacted statutes and ordinances to protect the environment. For example, most states require that an EIS or a report be prepared for any proposed state action. In addition, under their police power to protect the health, safety, and welfare of their residents, many states require private industry to prepare EISs for proposed developments.

Some states have enacted special environmental statutes to protect unique areas within their boundaries. For example, Florida has enacted laws to protect the Everglades, and California has enacted laws to protect its Pacific Ocean coastline.

International Law

Kyoto Protocol

For decades, scientists have been concerned that *greenhouse gases*—particularly from carbon dioxide created by burning coal, oil, and gas—are causing a global warming effect and creating a hole in the ozone layer around the earth. In 1997, after much debate, many countries of the world met in Kyoto, Japan, and proposed the **Kyoto Protocol**, an international treaty to reduce greenhouse gases. The deal almost fell apart, but in 2001, 178 countries agreed to abide by the rules of the Kyoto Protocol.

The Kyoto Protocol calls for the reduction of greenhouse gases worldwide to 5.2 percent below 1990 levels, with this goal to be reached by 2012. The protocol originally set targets for 39 industrialized countries; however, developing nations are not covered by the initial emission control standards. The protocol calls for member nations to create a $400 million fund to help developing nations adopt technology to reduce greenhouse gases. The United States was not a signatory to the Kyoto Protocol but instead chose to adopt its own laws to control greenhouse gas emissions. ■

Tibet, China.

Terms and Concepts

Environmental Protection

Federal and state governments have enacted environmental protection statutes to control pollution and to penalize those who violate these statutes.

Environmental Protection Agency (EPA)

The EPA is a federal administrative agency created in 1970 that is empowered to implement and enforce federal environmental protection statutes. The EPA can adopt regulations to interpret and enforce the laws it is authorized to administer.

National Environmental Policy Act (NEPA)

The NEPA is a federal statute that mandates that the federal government consider the *adverse impact* a federal government action would have on the environment before the action is implemented.

Environmental Impact Statement (EIS)

An EIS is a document that must be prepared for all proposed legislation or major federal action that significantly affects the quality of the human environment. The EIS must (1) describe the affected environment, (2) describe the impact of the proposed federal action on the environment, (3) identify and discuss alternatives to the proposed action, (4) list the resources that will be committed to the action, and (5) contain a cost–benefit analysis of the proposed action and alternative actions.

Air Pollution

Air pollution is pollution caused by factories, homes, vehicles, and the like that affects the air.

Clean Air Act

The Clean Air Act is a federal statute enacted in 1963 and amended several times that regulates air pollution.

National Ambient Air Quality Standards (NAAQS)

NAAQS are standards for certain pollutants set by the EPA that protect (1) human beings (*primary*) and (2) vegetation, matter, climate, visibility, and economic values (*secondary*).

1. ***Nonattainment areas.*** These regions do not meet federal air quality standards. They are classified into one of five categories—(1) marginal, (2) moderate, (3) serious, (4) severe, and (5) extreme—based on the degree to which they exceed federal air quality standards. States that fail to develop or implement an approved plan to correct deficiencies are subject to sanctions.

Stationary Sources of Air Pollution

Stationary sources of air pollution are sources such as industrial plants, oil refineries, and public utilities.

1. ***Pollution controls for stationary sources.*** Stationary sources are required to install pollution control equipment.

Mobile Sources of Air Pollution

Mobile sources of air pollution are sources such as automobiles, trucks, buses, motorcycles, and airplanes.

1. ***Pollution controls for mobile sources.*** The Clean Air Act requires air pollution controls to be installed on automobiles and other sources of mobile air pollution.

Water Pollution

Water pollution is pollution of lakes, rivers, oceans, and other bodies of water.

Clean Water Act

The *Federal Water Pollution Control Act (FWPCA)* of 1948 is a federal statute that regulates water pollution. As amended, it is called the *Clean Water Act*.

Point Sources of Water Pollution

Point sources are sources of water pollution such as paper mills, manufacturing plants, electric utility plants, and sewage plants.

1. ***Pollution controls for point sources.*** Point sources are required to install pollution control equipment.

Thermal Pollution

Thermal pollution occurs when heated water or material is discharged into waterways that upsets the ecological balance and decreases the oxygen content. Thermal pollution is subject to the provisions of the Clean Water Act.

Wetlands

Wetlands are areas that are inundated or saturated by surface water or groundwater that support vegetation typically adapted for life in such conditions. The Clean Water Act forbids the filling or dredging of wetlands unless a permit has been obtained from the *Army Corps of Engineers*.

Safe Drinking Water

The *Safe Drinking Water Act of 1974* authorizes the EPA to establish national minimum quality of water standards for human consumption. States are primarily responsible for enforcing the act. If a state fails to do so, the federal government can enforce the act.

Ocean Dumping

The *Marine Protection, Research, and Sanctuaries Act of 1972* is a federal statute that extends environmental protection to oceans. It requires a permit for dumping wastes and other foreign materials into ocean waters.

Oil Spills

The Clean Water Act authorizes the U.S. government to clean up oil spills and spills of other hazardous substances in ocean waters within 12 miles of the shore and on the continental shelf. The act authorizes the federal government to recover the cleanup costs from responsible parties.

Toxic Substances

Toxic substances are chemicals used for agricultural, industrial, and mining uses that cause injury to humans, birds, fish, other animals, and vegetation.

Toxic Substances Control Act

The *Toxic Substances Control Act* is a federal statute that requires manufacturers and processors to test new chemicals to determine their effects on human health and the environment before the EPA will allow them to be marketed. The EPA requires special labeling of toxic substances.

Federal Insecticide, Fungicide, and Rodenticide Act

The Federal Insecticide, Fungicide, and Rodenticide Act is a federal statute that requires pesticides, herbicides, fungicides, and rodenticides to be registered with the EPA. The EPA may deny, suspend, or cancel registration.

Hazardous Waste

Hazardous waste is solid waste that may cause or significantly contribute to an increase in mortality or serious illness or pose a hazard to human health or the environment if improperly managed.

1. ***Land pollution.*** Pollution of the land that is generally caused by hazardous waste being disposed of in an improper manner.

Resource Conservation and Recovery Act (RCRA)

The Resource Conservation and Recovery Act (RCRA) is a federal statute that authorizes the EPA to regulate facilities that generate, treat, store, transport, and dispose of hazardous wastes.

Comprehensive Environmental Response, Compensation, and Liability Act (Superfund)

The Comprehensive Environmental Response, Compensation, and Liability Act is a federal statute that gives the federal government a mandate to deal with hazardous wastes that have been spilled, stored, or abandoned. This act is commonly called Superfund.

1. ***Hazardous waste sites.*** Superfund requires the EPA to identify sites in the United States where hazardous wastes have been disposed, stored, spilled, or abandoned, and to rank these sites regarding their severity of risk.
2. ***Superfund.*** Superfund created a fund to finance the cleanup of hazardous waste sites (hence the name *Superfund*). The fund is financed through taxes on chemicals, feedstocks, motor fuels, and other products that contain hazardous substances.
3. ***Liability for cleanup costs.*** The EPA can order a responsible party to clean up a hazardous waste site. If that party fails to do so, the EPA can clean up the site and recover the cost of the cleanup from the responsible party or parties. Superfund imposes *strict liability* (liability without fault). Liability is *joint and several* (i.e., a party who is only partially responsible may be liable for all the cleanup costs).

Nuclear Waste

Nuclear waste is radioactive waste generated by nuclear-powered fuel plants.

1. ***Radioactive pollution.*** Emissions from radioactive wastes can cause injury and death to humans and other life and can cause severe damage to the environment.
2. ***Nuclear Regulatory Commission (NRC).*** The NRC is a federal agency that licenses the construction and opening of commercial nuclear power plants. The NRC may deny or remove a license.
3. ***Nuclear Waste Policy Act of 1982.*** This federal statute says that the federal government must select and develop a permanent site for the disposal of nuclear wastes.

Endangered Species Act

The Endangered Species Act is a federal statute that protects endangered and threatened species of animals.

1. ***Critical habitat.*** The act requires the EPA to designate critical habitats for each endangered and threatened species.
2. ***Taking.*** The act prohibits the taking (e.g., hunting, trapping, harming) of any endangered species.

State Environmental Protection Laws

Many state and local governments have enacted statutes and ordinances to protect the environment. States and local governments are entitled to set pollution control standards that are stricter than federal requirements.

Internet Exercises and Case Questions

Working the Web Internet Exercises

1. Find the EPA Superfund toxic waste cleanup sites in your state. See the U.S. Environmental Protection Agency site, at **www.epa.gov**.
2. Compare the positions of Greenpeace, the Sierra Club, and others on drilling in the Arctic National Wildlife Refuge:
   - Greenpeace: **www.greenpeace.org**
   - National Audubon Society: **www.audubon.org**
   - Natural Resources Defense Council: **www.nrdc.org**
   - Sierra Club: **www.sierraclub.org**
   - Earth Watch Institute: **www.earthwatch.org**
   - World Environment Law: **www.hg.org/environ.html**
3. Is your state home to any of the animals protected by the Endangered Species Act? Which ones? See the Earthjustice legal defense site, at **www.earthjustice.org**, and the Environmental Defense site, at **www.edf.org**.

Legal Environment Cases

25.1 Environmental Impact Statement The U.S. Forest Service is responsible for managing the country's national forests for recreational and other purposes. This includes issuing special-use permits to private companies to operate ski areas on federal lands. Sandy Butte is a 6,000-foot mountain located in the Okanogan National Forest in Okanogan County, Washington. Sandy Butte, like the Methow Valley it overlooks, is a pristine, unspoiled, sparsely populated area located within the North Cascades National Park. Large populations of mule deer and other animals exist in the park.

In 1978, Methow Recreation, Inc. (MRI), applied to the Forest Service for a special-use permit to develop and operate its proposed Early Winters Ski Resort on Sandy Butte and a 1,165-acre parcel of private land it had acquired adjacent to the national forest. The proposed development would make use of approximately 3,900 acres of Sandy Butte to provide up to 16 ski lifts capable of accommodating 10,500 skiers at one time. Is an environmental impact statement required? *Robertson v. Methow Valley Citizens Council*, 490 U.S. 332, 109 S.Ct. 1835, 1989 U.S. Lexis 2160 (U.S. Sup.Ct.)

25.2 Clean Air Act Pilot Petroleum Associates, Inc., and various affiliated companies distribute gasoline to retail gasoline stations in the state of New York. Pilot owns some of these stations and leases them out to individual operators who are under contract to purchase gasoline from Pilot. At various times during 1984, the EPA took samples of gasoline from five different service stations to which Pilot had sold unleaded gasoline. These samples showed that Pilot had delivered "unleaded gasoline that contained amounts of lead in excess of that permitted by the Clean Air Act and EPA regulations." The United States brought criminal charges against Pilot for violating the act and EPA regulations and sought fines from Pilot. Who wins? *United States v. Pilot Petroleum Associates, Inc.*, 712 F.Supp. 1077, 1989 U.S.Dist. Lexis 6119 (E.D. N.Y.)

25.3 Rule Making Placer mining is a method used to mine for gold in the streambeds of Alaska. The miner removes soil, mud, and clay from the streambed, places it in an onsite sluice box, and separates the gold from the other matter by forcing water through the paydirt. The water in the sluice box is discharged into the stream, causing aesthetic and water-quality impacts on the water both in the immediate vicinity and downstream. Toxic metals, including arsenic, cadmium, lead, zinc, and copper, are found in higher concentrations in streams where mining occurs than in nonmining streams.

In 1988, after public notice and comment, the EPA issued rules that require placer miners to use the best practical control technology (BPCT) to control discharges of nontoxic pollutants and the best available control technology (BACT) to control discharges of toxic pollutants. The BACT standard requires miners to construct settling ponds and recycle water through these ponds before discharging the water into the streambed. This method requires substantial expenditure. The Alaska Miners Association challenged the EPA's rule making. Who wins? *Rybachek v. U.S. Environmental Protection Agency*, 904 F.2d 1276, 1990 U.S.App. Lexis 7833 (9th Cir.)

25.4 Wetlands Leslie Salt Company owned a 153-acre tract of undeveloped land south of San Francisco. The property abuts the San Francisco National Wildlife Refuge and lies approximately one-quarter mile from Newark Slough, a tidal arm of San Francisco Bay. Originally, the property was pasture land. The first change occurred in the early 1900s, when Leslie's predecessors constructed facilities to manufacture salt on the property. They excavated pits and created large, shallow, watertight basins on the property. Salt production on the property was stopped in 1959. The construction of a sewer line and public roads on and around the property created ditches and culverts on the property. Newark Slough is connected to the property by these culverts, and tidewaters reach the property. Water accumulates in the ponds, ditches, and culverts, providing wetland vegetation to wildlife and migratory birds. Fish live in the ponds on the property. In 1985, Leslie started to dig a ditch to drain the property and began construction to block the culvert that connected the property to the Newark Slough. The Army Corps of Engineers issued a cease-and-desist order against Leslie. Leslie challenged the order. Who wins? *Leslie Salt Co. v. United States*, 896 F.2d 354, 1990 U.S.App. Lexis 1524 (9th Cir.)

25.5 Clean Water Act Reserve Mining Company owned and operated a mine in Minnesota, on the shores of Lake Superior, and it produced hazardous waste. In 1947, Reserve obtained a permit from the state of Minnesota to dump its wastes into Lake Superior. The permits prohibited discharges that would "result in any clouding or discoloration of the water outside the specific discharge zone" or "result in any material adverse affects on public water supplies." Reserve discharged its wastes into Lake Superior for years, until it reached 67,000 tons per day in the early 1970s. Evidence showed that the discharges caused discoloration of surface waters outside the zone of discharge and contained carcinogens that adversely affected public water supplies. The United States sued Reserve for engaging in unlawful water pollution. Who wins? *United States v. Reserve Mining Co.*, 543 F.2d 1210, 1976 U.S.App. Lexis 6503 (8th Cir.)

25.6 Hazardous Waste Douglas Hoflin was the director of the Public Works Department for Ocean Shores, Washington. From 1975 to 1982, the department purchased 3,500 gallons of paint for road maintenance. As painting jobs were finished, the 55-gallon drums that had contained the paint were returned to the department's yard. Paint contains hazardous substances such as lead. When 14 of the drums were discovered to still contain unused paint, Hoflin instructed employees to haul the paint drums to the city's sewage treatment plant and bury them. The employees took the drums, dug a hole on the grounds of the treatment plant, and dumped the drums in. Some of the drums were rusted and leaking. The hole was not deep enough, so the employees crushed the drums with a front-end loader to make them fit. The refuse was then covered with sand. Almost two years later, one of the city's employees reported the incident to state authorities, who referred the matter to the EPA. Investigation showed that the paint had contaminated the soil. The United States brought criminal charges against Hoflin for aiding and abetting the illegal dumping of hazardous waste. Who wins? *United States v. Hoflin*, 880 F.2d 1033, 1989 U.S.App. Lexis 10169 (9th Cir.)

25.7 Nuclear Waste Metropolitan Edison Company owns and operates two nuclear-fueled power plants at Three Mile

Island near Harrisburg, Pennsylvania. Both power plants were licensed by the NRC after extensive proceedings and investigations, including the preparation of the required environmental impact statements. On March 28, 1979, when one of the power plants was shut down for refueling, the other plant suffered a serious accident that damaged the reactor. The governor of Pennsylvania recommended an evacuation of all pregnant women and small children, and many area residents did leave their homes for several days. As it turned out, no dangerous radiation was released.

People Against Nuclear Energy (PANE), as association of area residents who opposed further operation of either nuclear power plant at Three Mile Island, sued to enjoin the plants from reopening. They argued that the reopening of the plants would cause severe psychological health damage to persons living in the vicinity and serious damage to the stability and cohesiveness of the community. Are these reasons sufficient to prevent the reopening of the nuclear power plants? *Metropolitan Edison Co. v. People Against Nuclear Energy*, 460 U.S. 766, 103 S.Ct. 1556, 1983 U.S. Lexis 21 (U.S. Sup.Ct.)

25.8 Endangered Species The red-cockaded woodpecker is a small bird that lives almost exclusively in old pine forests throughout the southern United States. Its survival depends on a very specialized habitat of pine trees that are at least 30, if not 60, years old, in which they build their nests and forage for insects. The population of this bird decreased substantially between 1978 and 1987 as pine forests were destroyed by clear-cutting. The secretary of the interior has named the red-cockaded woodpecker as an endangered species.

The Forest Service, which is under the authority of the secretary of agriculture, manages federal forests and is charged with duties to provide recreation, protect wildlife, and provide timber. To accomplish the charge of providing timber, the Forest Service leases national forest lands to private companies for lumbering. The Forest Service proposed leasing several national forests in Texas, where the red-cockaded woodpecker lives, to private companies for lumbering. The Sierra Club sued, seeking to enjoin the Forest Service from leasing these national forests for lumbering. Who wins? *Sierra Club v. Lyng, Secretary of Agriculture*, 694 F.Supp. 1260, 1990 U.S.Dist. Lexis 9203 (E.D. Tex.)

Ethics in Business

25.9 The state of Michigan owns approximately 57,000 acres of land that comprise the Pigeon River County State Forest in southwestern Michigan. On June 12, 1977, Shell Oil Company applied to the Michigan Department of Natural Resources (DNR) for a permit to drill 10 exploratory oil wells in the forest. Roads had to be constructed to reach the proposed drill sites. Evidence showed that the only sizable elk herd east of the Mississippi River annually used the forest as its habitat and returned to this range every year to breed. Experts testified that elk avoid roads, even when there is no traffic, and that the construction of the roads and wells would destroy the elk's habitat. Michigan law prohibits activities that adversely affect natural resources. The West Michigan Environmental Action Council sued the DNR, seeking to enjoin the DNR from granting the drilling permits to Shell. *West Michigan Environmental Action Council, Inc. v. Natural Resources Commission*, 275 N.W.2d 538, 1979 Mich. Lexis 347 (Mich.)

Ethics Issues

1. What law did the plaintiff West Michigan Environmental Action Council allege was violated?
2. Did Shell Oil Company act socially responsibly in this case?
3. Who wins? Why?

Endnotes

1. 42 U.S.C. Sections 4321–4370d.
2. 42 U.S.C. Sections 7401–7671q.
3. 33 U.S.C. Sections 1251–1367.
4. 33 U.S.C. Section 1254(t).
5. 21 U.S.C. Sections 349 and 300f–300j-25.
6. 16 U.S.C. Section 1431 *et seq.* and 1401–1445.
7. 33 U.S.C. Sections 2701–2761.
8. 15 U.S.C. Sections 2601–2692.
9. 7 U.S.C. Section 135 *et seq.*
10. 42 U.S.C. Sections 6901–6986.
11. 42 U.S.C. Sections 10101–10270.
12. 16 U.S.C. Sections 1531–1544.

26

Antitrust Law

"While competition cannot be created by statutory enactment, it can in large measure be revived by changing the laws and forbidding the practices that killed it, and by enacting laws that will give it heart and occasion again. We can arrest and prevent monopoly."

—Woodrow Wilson
Speech (August 7, 1912)

Chapter Objectives

After studying this chapter, you should be able to:

1. Describe the enforcement of federal antitrust laws.
2. Describe the horizontal and vertical restraints of trade that violate Section 1 of the Sherman Act.
3. Identify acts of monopolization that violate Section 2 of the Sherman Act.
4. Explain how the lawfulness of mergers is examined under Section 7 of the Clayton Act.
5. Apply Section 5 of the Federal Trade Commission Act to antitrust cases.

Chapter Contents

- Federal Antitrust Laws
- Restraints of Trade: Section 1 of the Sherman Act
- Monopolization: Section 2 of the Sherman Act
- Mergers: Section 7 of the Clayton Act
- Tying Arrangements: Section 3 of the Clayton Act
- Price Discrimination: Section 2 of the Clayton Act
- Unfair Methods of Competition: Section 5 of the Federal Trade Commission Act
- Exemptions from Antitrust Laws
- State Antitrust Laws

The U.S. economic system was built on the theory of freedom of competition. After the Civil War, however, the American economy changed from a rural and agricultural economy to an individualized and urban one. Many large industrial trusts were formed during this period. These arrangements resulted in a series of monopolies in basic industries such as oil and gas, sugar, cotton, and whiskey.

Because the common law could not deal effectively with these monopolies, Congress enacted a comprehensive system of **antitrust laws** to limit anticompetitive behavior. Almost all industries, businesses, and professions operating in the United States were affected. Although many states have also enacted antitrust laws, most actions in this area are brought under federal law.

antitrust laws
A series of laws enacted to limit anticompetitive behavior in almost all industries, businesses, and professions operating in the United States.

This chapter discusses antitrust laws.

Oriole Park, Baltimore, Maryland. In 1922, the U.S. Supreme Court held that professional baseball was exempt from antitrust laws because baseball was not engaged in interstate commerce.

Federal Antitrust Laws

The **Sherman Act**, enacted in 1890, made certain restraints of trade and monopolistic acts illegal. Both the **Clayton Act** and the **Federal Trade Commission Act (FTC Act)** were enacted in 1914. The Clayton Act regulates mergers and prohibits certain exclusive dealing arrangements. The FTC Act prohibits unfair methods of competition. The **Robinson-Patman Act**, which prohibits price discrimination, was enacted in 1930.

Antitrust Enforcement

The federal antitrust statutes are broadly drafted to reflect the government's enforcement policy and to allow it to respond to economic, business, and technological changes. Each administration that occupies the White House adopts an enforcement policy for antitrust laws. From the 1940s through the 1970s, antitrust enforcement was quite stringent. During the 1980s, government enforcement of antitrust laws was more relaxed. During the 2000s, antitrust enforcement increased.

Federal antitrust laws provide for both government and private lawsuits.

Government Actions

The federal government is authorized to bring actions to enforce federal antitrust laws. Government enforcement of federal antitrust laws is divided between the Antitrust Division of the Department of Justice and the Bureau of Competition of the Federal Trade Commission (FTC).

The Sherman Act is the only major antitrust act with *criminal* sanctions. Intent is the prerequisite for criminal liability under this act. Penalties for individuals include fines of up to $350,000 per violation and up to three years in prison; corporations may be fined up to $10 million per violation.[1]

The government may seek *civil* damages, including treble damages, for violations of antitrust laws.[2] Broad remedial powers allow the courts to order a number of civil remedies, including orders for divestiture of assets, cancellation of contracts, liquidation of businesses, licensing of patents, and such. Private parties cannot intervene in public antitrust actions brought by the government.

> The notion that a business is clothed with a public interest and has been devoted to the public use is little more than a fiction intended to beautify what is disagreeable to the sufferers.
>
> Holmes, Jr.
> *Tyson & Bro-United Theatre Ticket Offices v. Banton* (1927)

Private Actions

Section 4 of the **Clayton Act** permits any person who suffers antitrust injury in his or her business or on his or her property to bring a *private civil action* against the offenders.[3] Consumers who have to pay higher prices because of an antitrust violation have recourse under this provision.[4] To recover damages, plaintiffs must prove that they suffered *antitrust injuries* caused by the prohibited act. The courts have required that consumers must have dealt *directly* with the alleged violators to have standing to sue; indirect injury resulting from higher prices being passed on is insufficient.

Successful plaintiffs may recover **treble damages** (i.e., triple the amount of the damages), plus reasonable costs and attorneys' fees. Damages may be calculated as lost profits, an increase in the cost of doing business, or a decrease in the value of tangible or intangible property caused by the antitrust violation. This rule applies to all violations of the Sherman Act, the Clayton Act, and the Robinson-Patman Act. Only actual damages—not treble damages—may be recovered for violations of the FTC Act.

A private plaintiff has four years from the date on which an antitrust injury occurred to bring a private civil treble damages action. Only damages incurred during this four-year period are recoverable. This statute is *tolled* (i.e., does not run) during a suit by the government.

> People of the same trade seldom meet together, even for merriment and diversion, but that the conversation ends in a conspiracy against the public, or in some contrivance to raise prices.
>
> Adam Smith
> *The Wealth of Nations* (1776)

Effect of a Government Judgment

A government judgment against a defendant for an antitrust violation may be used as prima facie evidence of liability in a private civil treble damages action. Antitrust defendants often opt to settle government-brought antitrust actions by entering a plea of *nolo contendere* in a criminal action or a *consent decree* in a government civil action. These pleas usually subject the defendant to penalty without an admission of guilt or liability.

Section 16 of the **Clayton Act** permits the government or a private plaintiff to obtain an injunction against anticompetitive behavior that violates antitrust laws.[5] Only the FTC may obtain an injunction under the FTC Act.

Restraints of Trade: Section 1 of the Sherman Act

In 1890, Congress enacted the **Sherman Antitrust Act**. The purpose of the act was to outlaw anticompetitive behavior. The Sherman Act has been called the "Magna Carta of

Section 1 of the Sherman Act
A provision that prohibits *contracts*, *combinations*, and *conspiracies* in restraint of trade.

free enterprise."[6] **Section 1 of the Sherman Act** is intended to prohibit certain concerted anticompetitive activities. It provides that:

> Every contract, combination in the form of trust or otherwise, or conspiracy, in restraint of trade or commerce among the several states, or with foreign nations, is hereby declared to be illegal. Every person who shall make any contract or engage in any combination or conspiracy hereby declared to be illegal shall be deemed guilty of a felony.[7]

In other words, Section 1 outlaws **contracts, combinations**, and **conspiracies** in restraint of trade. Thus, it applies to unlawful conduct by two or more parties. The agreement may be written, oral, or inferred from the conduct of the parties. The two tests the U.S. Supreme Court has developed for determining the lawfulness of a restraint—the *rule of reason* and the *per se rule*—are discussed in the following paragraphs.

Rule of Reason

rule of reason
A rule that holds that only unreasonable restraints of trade violate Section 1 of the Sherman Act. The court must examine the pro- and anticompetitive effects of the challenged restraint.

If Section 1 of the Sherman Act were read literally, it would prohibit almost all contracts. In the landmark case *Standard Oil Company of New Jersey v. United States*,[8] the Supreme Court adopted the **rule of reason** standard for analyzing Section 1 cases. This rule holds that only *unreasonable restraints of trade* violate Section 1 of the Sherman Act. Reasonable restraints are lawful. The courts examine the following factors in applying the rule of reason:

- The pro- and anticompetitive effects of the challenged restraint
- The competitive structure of the industry
- The firm's market share and power
- The history and duration of the restraint
- Other relevant factors

Per Se Rule

***per se* rule**
A rule that is applicable to those restraints of trade considered inherently anticompetitive. Once this determination is made, the court will not permit any defenses or justifications to save it.

The Supreme Court adopted the ***per se* rule**, which is applicable to those restraints of trade considered inherently anticompetitive. No balancing of pro- and anticompetitive effects is necessary in such cases: The restraint is automatically in violation of Section 1 of the Sherman Act. Once a restraint is characterized as a *per se* violation, no defenses or justifications for the restraint will save it, and no further evidence need be considered. Restraints that are not characterized as *per se* violations are examined under the rule of reason.

Concept Summary Restraints of Trade: Section 1 of the Sherman Act

Rule	Description
Rule of reason	Requires a balancing of pro- and anticompetitive effects of the challenged restraint. Restraints that are found to be unreasonable are unlawful and violate Section 1 of the Sherman Act. Restraints that are found to be reasonable are lawful and do not violate Section 1 of the Sherman Act.
Per se rule	Applies to restraints that are inherently anticompetitive. No justification for the restraint is permitted. Such restraints automatically violate Section 1 of the Sherman Act.

Horizontal Restraints of Trade

A **horizontal restraint of trade** occurs when two or more competitors at the *same level of distribution* enter into a contract, combination, or conspiracy to restrain trade (see Exhibit 26.1). Many horizontal restraints fall under the *per se* rule; others are examined under the rule of reason. The most common forms of horizontal restraint are discussed in the following paragraphs.

horizontal restraint of trade
A restraint of trade that occurs when two or more competitors at the *same level of distribution* enter into a contract, combination, or conspiracy to restrain trade.

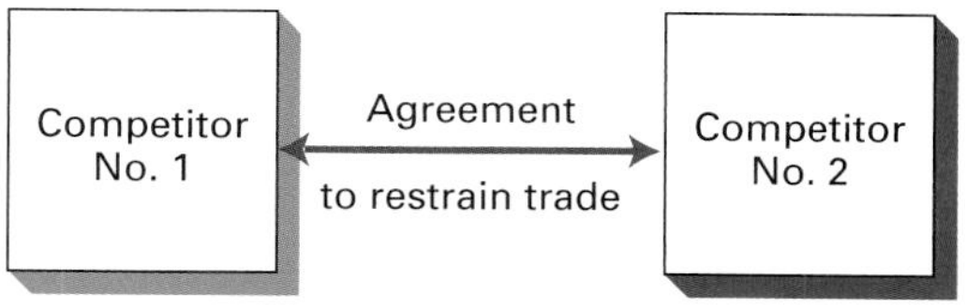

Exhibit 26.1
Horizontal Restraint of Trade

Price-Fixing Horizontal **price-fixing** occurs when competitors in the same line of business agree to set the price of goods or services they sell. Price-fixing is defined as raising, depressing, fixing, pegging, or stabilizing the price of a commodity or service. Illegal price-fixing includes setting minimum or maximum prices or fixing the quantity of a product or service to be produced or provided. Although most price-fixing agreements occur between sellers, an agreement among buyers to set the price they will pay for goods or services is also price-fixing. The plaintiff bears the burden of proving a price-fixing agreement.

Price-fixing is a *per se* violation of Section 1 of the Sherman Act. No defenses or justifications of any kind—such as "the price-fixing helps consumers or protects competitors from ruinous competition"—can prevent the *per se* rule from applying.

price-fixing
A horizontal restraint of trade that occurs when competitors in the same line of business agree to set the price of the goods or services they sell. It includes raising, depressing, fixing, pegging, or stabilizing the price of a commodity or service.

Consider These Examples If the three largest automobile manufacturers agreed among themselves as to what prices to charge automobile dealers for this year's models, this would be sellers' illegal *per se* price-fixing. If the same automobile manufacturers agreed among themselves as to what price they would pay to purchase tires from tire manufacturers, this would be buyers' illegal *per se* price-fixing.

Ethics in Business

The Department of Justice Flunks the Ivy League Schools

For years, the administrators of the Ivy League schools (Brown, Columbia, Cornell, Dartmouth, Harvard, Princeton, the University of Pennsylvania, and Yale) and the Massachusetts Institute of Technology (M.I.T.) met annually to trade information about student applicants seeking admission and scholarships at their universities. The universities then divided up the applicants and agreed to offer scholarships to the students they thought would attend their schools; scholarships were not offered to those less likely to attend. The schools defended this practice as preventing "overlap"—that is, certain students getting scholarship offers from many schools and other applicants receiving no scholarship offers.

The U.S. Department of Justice sued the universities, alleging that they had engaged in the horizontal restraint of trade of price-fixing, in violation of Section 1 of the Sherman Act.

The Department of Justice lawyers pointed to what they learned in Economics 101 and asserted that this collegiate cartel was no different from any other cartel: It denied customers (students) the right to "comparison shop" just as they would for other services.

The eight Ivy League schools agreed to settle the case with the Department of Justice. Under the terms of the consent decree, the schools agreed not to share financial aid information or discuss future tuition levels with other schools. M.I.T. chose to fight the case in court and lost. The court found M.I.T. guilty of price-fixing and enjoined the challenged practices. *United States v. Brown University*, 5 F.3d 658, 1993 U.S.App. Lexis 23895 (3d Cir.)

Ethics Issues

1. Do you think the schools acted ethically in this case?
2. Did their "overlap" argument justify their actions? ■

division of markets
A horizontal restraint of trade in which competitors agree that each will serve only a designated portion of the market.

Division of Markets Competitors who agree that each will serve only a designated portion of the market are engaging in a **division of markets** (or **market sharing**), which is a *per se* violation of Section 1 of the Sherman Act. Each market segment is considered a small monopoly served only by its designated "owner." Horizontal market-sharing arrangements include division by geographical territory, customers, and products.

Consider These Examples Suppose three national breweries agreed among themselves that each one would be assigned one-third of the country as its geographical "territory," and each agreed not to sell beer in the other two companies' territories. This would be a *per se* illegal geographical division of markets. If the three largest sellers of media software agreed that each could only sell media software to one designated media software purchaser and not to any other media software purchasers, this would be a *per se* illegal product division of markets.

group boycott
A horizontal restraint of trade in which two or more competitors at one level of distribution agree not to deal with others at another level of distribution.

Group Boycotts A **group boycott** (or **refusal to deal**) occurs when two or more competitors at one level of distribution agree not to deal with others at a different level of distribution. Although in the past the U.S. Supreme Court has held that group boycotts were *per se* illegal, recent Supreme Court decisions have held that only certain group boycotts are *per se* illegal. Others are to be examined under the rule of reason. Nevertheless, most group boycotts are found to be illegal.

Consider These Examples A boycott would occur if a group of television manufacturers agreed not to sell their products to certain discount retailers (see Exhibit 26.2). A boycott would also occur if a group of rental car companies agreed not to purchase Chrysler automobiles for their fleets (see Exhibit 26.3).

Exhibit 26.2
Group Boycott by Sellers

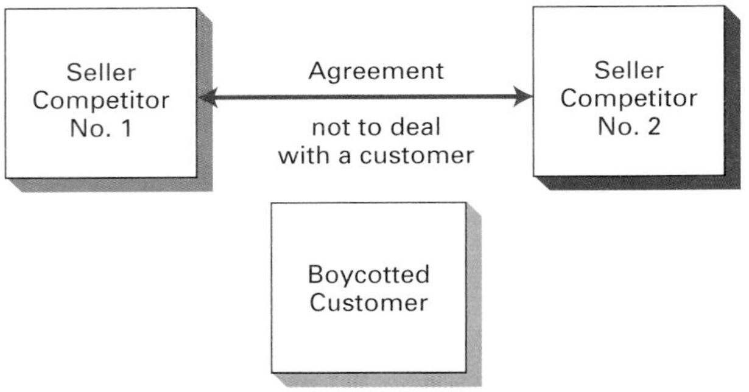

Exhibit 26.3
Group Boycott by Purchasers

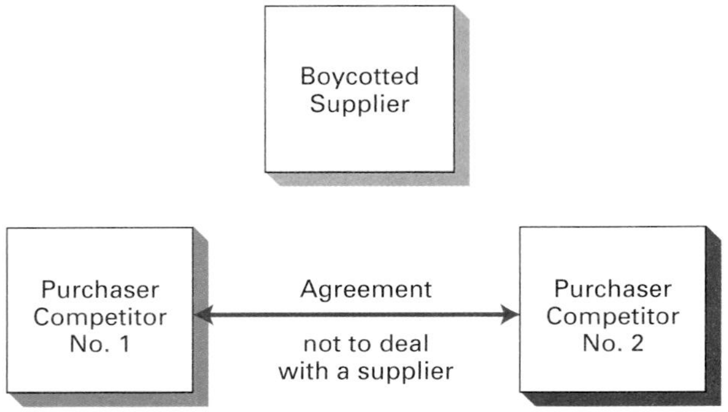

Other Horizontal Agreements Some agreements entered into by competitors at the same level of distribution—including trade association activities and rules, exchange of non-price information, participation in joint ventures, and the like—are examined using the rule of reason. Reasonable restraints are lawful; unreasonable restraints violate Section 1 of the Sherman Act.

Vertical Restraints of Trade

A **vertical restraint of trade** occurs when two or more parties on *different levels of distribution* enter into a contract, combination, or conspiracy to restrain trade (see Exhibit 26.4). The Supreme Court has applied both the *per se* rule and the rule of reason in determining the legality of vertical restraints of trade under Section 1 of the Sherman Act. The most common forms of vertical restraint are discussed in the following paragraphs.

vertical restraint of trade
A restraint of trade that occurs when two or more parties on *different levels of distribution* enter into a contract, combination, or conspiracy to restrain trade.

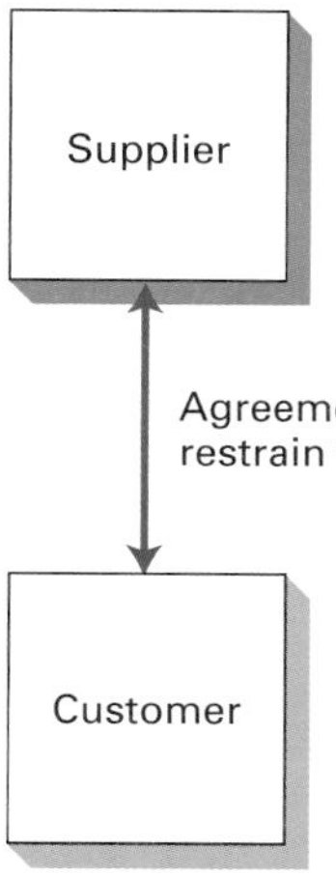

Exhibit 26.4
Vertical Restraint of Trade

Resale Price Maintenance **Resale pricing maintenance** (or **vertical price-fixing**) occurs when a party at one level of distribution enters into an agreement with a party at another level to adhere to a price schedule that either sets or stabilizes prices. For example, a computer manufacturer that sells its computers only to retailers that agree to resell them at the prices set by the manufacturer is engaged in this practice.

Setting *minimum* resale prices is a *per se* violation of Section 1 of the Sherman Act as an unreasonable restraint of trade.[9]

resale price maintenance
A vertical restraint of trade that occurs when a party at one level of distribution enters into an agreement with a party at another level to adhere to a price schedule that either sets or stabilizes prices. Resale price maintenance is a *per se* violation of Section 1 of the Sherman Act.

Consider This Example Integral Camera Corporation manufactures digital cameras and sets a *minimum* price below which the cameras cannot be sold by retailers (e.g., the cameras cannot be sold for less then $1,000 by retailers). This constitutes *per se* illegal minimum resale price maintenance.

In the following case, the Supreme Court had to decide whether the setting of a *maximum* resale price was a *per se* violation of Section 1 of the Sherman Act.

Case 26.1 Resale Price Maintenance

U.S. SUPREME COURT
State Oil Company v. Khan
522 U.S. 3, 118 S.Ct. 275, 1997 U.S. Lexis 6705
Supreme Court of the United States

Background and Facts

Barkat U. Khan and his corporation entered into an agreement with State Oil Company to lease and operate a gas station and convenience store owned by State Oil. The agreement provided that Khan would obtain his station's gasoline supply from State Oil. The agreement provided that Khan could charge any price for the gasoline he sold to the station's customers, but if the price charged was higher than State Oil's suggested retail price, the excess was to be rebated to State Oil; Khan could choose to sell gasoline for less than State Oil's suggested retail price. Khan sued State Oil, alleging that the maximum resale price required by State Oil was a *per se* violation of Section 1 of the Sherman Act. The district court entered summary judgment for State Oil, but the Court of Appeals reversed and held that the maximum resale price set by State Oil was a *per se* violation of Section 1. The Court of Appeals cited a previous U.S. Supreme Court case—*Albrecht v. Herald Co.*, 390 U.S. 145 (1968)—which held that the setting of maximum resale prices was a *per se* violation of Section 1. State Oil appealed to the U.S. Supreme Court.

Issue

Is the setting of a maximum resale price by a supplier a *per se* violation of Section 1 of the Sherman Act?

In the Language of the U.S. Supreme Court

We find it difficult to maintain that vertically-imposed maximum prices could harm consumers or competition to the extent necessary to justify their *per se* invalidation. Although we have acknowledged the possibility that maximum pricing might mask minimum pricing, we believe that such conduct can be appropriately recognized and punished under the rule of reason. Indeed, both courts and antitrust scholars noted that Albrecht's rule may actually harm consumers and manufacturers. After reconsidering Albrecht's rationale and the substantial criticism the decision has received, we conclude that there is insufficient economic justification for per se invalidation of vertical maximum price fixing.

In overruling *Albrecht*, we of course do not hold that all vertical maximum price fixing is per se lawful. Instead, vertical maximum price fixing, like the majority of commercial arrangements subject to the antitrust laws, should be evaluated under the rule of reason. In our view, rule-of-reason analysis will effectively identify those situations in which vertical maximum price fixing amounts to anticompetitive conduct.

Decision and Remedy

The U.S. Supreme Court reversed *Albrecht*. The Supreme Court held that the setting of a maximum resale price is not a *per se* violation of Section 1 of the Sherman Act, but instead its legality must be analyzed using the rule of reason test. The Supreme Court remanded the current case for trial, using the new rule-of-reason standard.

Business and Ethics Questions

1. How often do you think the U.S. Supreme Court reverses itself? Do you think it should have done so in this case?
2. Was the State Oil contract that set a maximum resale price in this case lawful under the rule-of-reason standard?
3. How will this decision affect suppliers and the retailers they sell to? Explain.

nonprice vertical restraints
Vertical restraints of trade that are unlawful under Section 1 of the Sherman Act if their anticompetitive effects outweigh their procompetitive effects.

Nonprice Vertical Restraints The legality of **nonprice vertical restraints** of trade under Section 1 of the Sherman Act is examined using the rule of reason.[10] Nonprice restraints are unlawful under this analysis if their anticompetitive effects outweigh their procompetitive effects. Nonprice vertical restraints include situations in which a manufacturer assigns exclusive territories to retail dealers or limits the number of dealers that may be located in a certain territory.

Defenses to Section 1 of the Sherman Act

The courts have recognized several defenses to alleged violations of Section 1 of the Sherman act. These defenses are:

1. ***Unilateral refusal to deal.*** The U.S. Supreme Court has held that a firm can unilaterally choose not to deal with another party without being liable under Section 1 of the

Sherman Act. A **unilateral refusal to deal** is not a violation of Section 1 because there is no concerted action with others. This rule was announced in *United States v. Colgate & Co.* and is therefore often referred to as the "**Colgate doctrine**."[11]

unilateral refusal to deal
A unilateral choice by one party not to deal with another party. This does not violate Section 1 of the Sherman Act because there is not concerted action.

Consider This Example If Louis Vuitton, a maker of expensive women's clothing, shoes, handbags, and accessories, refuses to sell its merchandise to Wal-Mart stores, this a lawful unilateral refusal to deal.

2. ***Conscious parallelism.*** If two or more firms act the same, but no concerted action is shown, there is no violation of Section 1 of the Sherman Act. This doctrine is often referred to as **conscious parallelism**. Thus, if two competing manufacturers of a similar product both separately reach an independent decision not to deal with a retailer, there is no violation of Section 1 of the Sherman Act. The key is that each of the manufacturers acted on its own.

conscious parallelism
A doctrine that states that if two or more firms act the same, but no concerted action is shown, there is no violation of Section 1 of the Sherman Act.

Consider This Example If Louis Vuitton, Gucci, and Chanel, makers of expensive women's clothing, shoes, handbags, and accessories, each independently make a decision not to sell their products to Wal-Mart, this is lawful conscious parallelism. There is no violation of Section 1 of the Sherman Act because the parties did not agree with one another in making their decisions.

3. ***Noerr doctrine.*** The ***Noerr* doctrine** holds that two or more persons may petition the executive, legislative, or judicial branch of the government or administrative agencies to enact laws or to take other action without violating the antitrust laws. The rationale behind this doctrine is that the right to petition the government has precedence because it is guaranteed by the Bill of Rights.[12] For example, General Motors and Ford could collectively petition Congress to pass a law that would limit the import of foreign automobiles into this country.

Noerr doctrine
A doctrine that says two or more persons may petition the executive, legislative, or judicial branch of the government or administrative agencies to enact laws or take other action without violating the antitrust laws.

There is an exception to this doctrine. Under, the *"sham" exception*, petitioners are not protected if their petition or lawsuit is baseless—that is, if a reasonable petitioner or litigant could not realistically expect to succeed on the merits of the petition or lawsuit. If the protection of the Noerr doctrine is lost, an antitrust action may be maintained against the parties who had asserted its protection.

Contemporary Trend

Trade Association Members Avoid Antitrust Liability

Trade associations are organizations that are formed by industry members to promote the industry, provide education to members, formulate rules for self-regulation of the industry, and conduct lobbying and other activities.

Trade associations usually hold annual and other meetings that industry members attend. To avoid antitrust problems, attendees should avoid sharing and discussing certain information with each other. Here are some activities they should avoid:

- They should not discuss or exchange price information about current or future sales to customers.
- They should not agree to share or split customers or geographical areas.
- They should not agree to operate only during agreed-upon hours. ■

Monopolization: Section 2 of the Sherman Act

Section 2 of the Sherman Act
A provision that prohibits the act of monopolization and attempts or conspiracies to monopolize trade.

By definition, monopolies have the ability to affect the price of goods and services. **Section 2 of the Sherman Act** was enacted in response to widespread concern about the power generated by this type of anticompetitive activity. Section 2 of the Sherman Act prohibits the act of monopolization. It provides that:

> Every person who shall monopolize, or attempt to monopolize, or combine or conspire with any other person or persons, to monopolize any part of the trade or commerce among the several States, or with foreign nations, shall be deemed guilty of a felony.[13]

Proving that a defendant is in violation of Section *2* means proving that the defendant (1) possesses monopoly power in the relevant market and (2) engaged in a willful act of monopolization to acquire or maintain the power. Each of these elements is discussed in the following paragraphs.

Defining the Relevant Market

Identifying the relevant market for a Section 2 action requires defining the relevant product or service market and geographical market. The definition of the relevant market often determines whether the defendant has monopoly power. Consequently, this determination is often litigated.

relevant product or service market
A relevant market that includes substitute products or services that are reasonably interchangeable with the defendant's products or services.

The **relevant product or service market** generally includes substitute products or services that are reasonably interchangeable with the defendant's products or services. Defendants often try to make their market share seem smaller by arguing for a broad definition of the product or service market. Plaintiffs, on the other hand, usually argue for a narrow definition.

Consider These Examples If the Anheuser-Busch Corporation, which is the largest beer producer in the United States, were sued by the government for violating Section 2 of the Sherman Act, the government would argue that the relevant product market is beer sales. Anheuser-Busch, on the other hand, would argue that the relevant product market is all alcoholic beverages, or even all drinkable beverages.

relevant geographical market
A relevant market that is defined as the area in which the defendant and its competitors sell the product or service.

The **relevant geographical market** is usually defined as the area in which the defendant and its competitors sell the product or service. This may be a national, regional, state, or local area, depending on the circumstances.

Consider These Examples If the Coca-Cola Corporation is sued by the government for violating Section 2 of the Sherman Act, the relevant geographical market would be the nation. If the largest owner of automobile dealerships in south Florida were sued for violating Section 2, the geographical market would be the counties of south Florida.

Monopoly Power

monopoly power
The power to control prices or exclude competition, measured by the market share the defendant possesses in the relevant market.

For an antitrust action to be sustained, the defendant must possess **monopoly power** in the relevant market. Monopoly power is defined by the courts to be the power to control prices or exclude competition. The courts generally apply the following guidelines: Market share above 70 percent is monopoly power; market share under 20 percent is not monopoly power. Otherwise, the courts generally prefer to examine the facts and circumstances of each case before making this determination.

Willful Act of Monopolizing

Section 2 of the Sherman Act outlaws the **act of monopolizing**, not monopolies. Any act that otherwise violates any other antitrust law (such as illegal restraints of trade in violation of Section 1 of the Sherman Act) is an act of monopolizing that violates Section 2. When coupled with monopoly power, certain otherwise lawful acts have been held to constitute an act of monopolizing. For example, *predatory pricing*—that is, pricing below average or marginal cost—that is intended to drive out competition has been held to violate Section 2.[14]

act of monopolizing
A required act for there to be a violation of Section 2 of the Sherman Act. Possession of monopoly power without such act does not violate Section 2.

Concept Summary: Monopolization: Section 2 of the Sherman Act

Element	Description
Relevant product or service market	The market that includes substitute products or services that are reasonably interchangeable with the defendant's products or services.
Relevant geographical market	The geographical area in which the defendant and its competitors sell the product or service.
Monopoly power	The power to control prices or exclude competition. If the defendant does not possess monopoly power, it cannot be held liable for monopolization. If the defendant possesses monopoly power, the court will determine whether the monopolist has engaged in an act of monopolizing.
Act of monopolizing	The defendant must have engaged in a willful act of monopolizing trade or commerce in the relevant market.

Defenses to Monopolization

Only two narrow defenses to a charge of monopolizing have been recognized: (1) *innocent acquisition* (e.g., acquisition because of superior business acumen, skill, foresight, or industry) and (2) *natural monopoly* (e.g., a small market that can support only one competitor, such as a small-town newspaper). If a monopoly that fits into one of these categories exercises its power in a predatory or exclusionary way, the defense is lost.

A monopoly granted either to an individual or to a trading company has the same effect as a secret in trade or manufacture. The monopolists, by keeping the market constantly understocked, by never fully supplying the effectual demand, sell their commodities much above the natural price, and raise their emoluments greatly above their natural rate.

Adam Smith
Wealth of Nations (1776)

Attempts and Conspiracies to Monopolize

Firms that *attempt* or *conspire* to monopolize a relevant market may be found liable under Section 2 of the Sherman Act. A single firm may be found liable for monopolizing or attempting to monopolize. Two or more firms may be found liable for conspiring to monopolize.

Internet Law & Online Commerce

United States v. Microsoft Corporation

In less than 30 years, Microsoft Corporation grew from a startup company into the world's largest software company, whose products touch the lives of virtually everyone who uses a personal computer. Microsoft dominates the software market with its Windows operating system, which is used on most of the world's personal computers.

(continued)

Internet Law & Online Commerce
(*continued*)

Netscape, a competing company, developed its Navigator Internet Web browser, and by 1994, it controlled over 80 percent of that market. Microsoft began a campaign to defeat Netscape. Microsoft developed its own browser, called *Explorer*, and attached it to its Windows operating system for free. Microsoft warned Apple, a manufacturer of personal computers, that it would cancel Microsoft's all-important Office software unless Apple used Explorer; Apple capitulated and made Explorer its Web browser. Microsoft muscled AOL into offering Explorer in return for a small placement on the Windows desktop if it would not offer Netscape anywhere on its online service. AOL agreed. Microsoft gave Compaq, a maker of personal computers, a lower price for Windows in return for placing a Microsoft icon for the Explorer Web browser on Compaq's computers.

After investigating, the U.S. government and 19 states sued Microsoft in a civil antitrust case. After a nine-month trial and four months of failed settlement negotiations, the U.S. district court held that Microsoft had used predatory and anticompetitive conduct to illegally maintain its monopoly in the Windows operating system in violation of Section 2 of the Sherman Act. The judge issued an order that prohibited Microsoft from engaging in such conduct in the future and ordered that Microsoft be split into two separate companies: one company to own the operating systems such as Windows, and a second company to own software, Internet browsers, and other computer applications.

Microsoft appealed. On appeal, the U.S. Court of Appeals upheld the finding that Microsoft had engaged in monopolization in violation of Section 2, but it ruled that Microsoft did not have to be broken up. The case was remanded for further proceedings.

A new district court judge ordered Microsoft Corporation to refrain from engaging in coercive practices and to make some of the code for its operating systems available to other software companies under reasonable licensing arrangements so that they could design their software to be used in conjunction with Microsoft's operating system. Many commentators believe that Microsoft basically "won" this case. *United States v. Microsoft Corporation,* 2002 U.S.Dist. Lexis 22864 (District Court, D.C.) ■

Concept Summary The Sherman Act

Section	Description
1	Prohibits contracts, combinations, and conspiracies in restraint of trade. To violate Section 1, the restraint must be found to be reasonable under either of two tests: 1. Rule of reason 2. *Per se* rule Requires the concerted action of two or more parties.
2	Prohibits the act of monopolizing and attempts or conspiracies to monopolize. Can be violated by the conduct of one firm.

Mergers: Section 7 of the Clayton Act

Section 7 of the Clayton Act
A provision that says it is unlawful for a person or business to acquire the stock of assets of another "where in any line of commerce or in any activity affecting commerce in any section of the country, the effect of such acquisition may be substantially to lessen competition or to tend to create a monopoly."

In the late 1800s and early 1900s, *mergers* led to an increased concentration of wealth in the hands of a few wealthy individuals and large corporations. In response, in 1914, Congress enacted **Section 7 of the Clayton Act**, which gave the federal government the power to prevent anticompetitive mergers. Originally, Section 7 of the Clayton Act applied only to stock mergers. The *Celler-Kefauver Act*, which was enacted in 1950, widened Section 7's scope to include asset acquisitions.

Today, Section 7 applies to all methods of external expansion, including technical mergers, consolidations, purchases of assets, subsidiary operations, joint ventures, and other combinations.

Section 7 of the Clayton Act provides that it is unlawful for a person or business to acquire stock or assets of another "where in any line of commerce or in any activity affecting commerce in any section of the country, the effect of such acquisition may be substantially to lessen competition, or to tend to create a monopoly."[15] In determining whether a merger is lawful under Section 7 of the Clayton Act, the courts must examine the elements discussed in the following paragraphs.

Line of Commerce

Determining the **line of commerce** that will be affected by a merger involves defining the relevant *product or service market*. Traditionally, the courts have done this by applying the functional interchangeability test. Under this test, the relevant line of commerce includes products or services that consumers use as substitutes. If two products are substitutes for each other, they are considered part of the same line of commerce. For example, suppose a price increase for regular coffee causes consumers to switch to decaffeinated coffee. The two products are part of the same line of commerce because they are interchangeable.

line of commerce
A market of products or services that consumers use as substitutes. If an increase in the price of one product or service leads consumers to purchase another product or service, the two products are substitutes for each other.

Section of the Country

Defining the relevant **section of the country** consists of determining the relevant *geographical market*. The courts traditionally identify this market as the geographical area that will feel the direct and immediate effects of the merger. It may be a local, state, or regional market, the entire country, or some other geographical area. For example, Anheuser-Busch and the Miller Brewing Company sell beer nationally, whereas a local brewery, such as Upper Steam, sells beer only in Michigan. If Anheuser-Busch and the Miller Brewing Company plan to merge, the relevant section of the country is the nation; if Anheuser-Bush intends to acquire a local brewery that sells beer in the West, the relevant section of the country is the western states.

section of the country
A division of the United States that is based on the relevant geographical market; the geographical area that will feel the direct and immediate effects of a merger.

Probability of a Substantial Lessening of Competition

After the relevant product or service and geographical market have been defined, the court must determine whether a merger or an acquisition is **likely to substantially lessen competition or create a monopoly**. If the court feels that a merger is likely to do either, it may prevent the merger. Section 7 tries to prevent potentially anticompetitive mergers before they occur. It deals in probabilities; an actual showing of the lessening of competition is not required.

In applying Section 7, mergers are generally classified as one of the following: *horizontal merger, vertical merger, market extension merger*, or *conglomerate merger*. Each of these is discussed in the paragraphs that follow.

probability of a substantial lessening of competition
Probability that a merger will substantially lessen competition or create a monopoly, in which case the court may prevent the merger under Section 7 of the Clayton Act.

Concept Summary Mergers: Section 7 of the Clayton Act

Element	Description
Line of commerce	The market that will be affected by a merger. It includes products or services that consumers use as substitutes for those produced or sold by the merging firms.
Section of the country	The geographical market that will be affected by a merger.
Probability of a substantial lessening of competition	If the court determines that a merger would have a probability of a substantial lessening of competition, the merger may be prohibited. The statute deals with probabilities; a showing of actual lessening of competition is not required.

Horizontal Mergers A **horizontal merger** is a merger between two or more companies that compete in the same business and geographical market. The merger of two grocery store chains that serve the same geographical market fits this definition. Such mergers are subjected to strict review under Section 7 because they clearly result in an increase in concentration in the relevant market. For example, if General Motors Corporation and Ford Motor Company tried to merge, this horizontal merger would clearly violate Section 7.

horizontal merger
A merger between two or more companies that compete in the same business and geographical market.

In the landmark case *United States v. Philadelphia National Bank*,[16] the U.S. Supreme Court adopted the *presumptive illegality test* for determining the lawfulness of horizontal mergers. This test finds horizontal mergers presumptively illegal under Section 7 if (1) the merged firm would have a 30 percent or more market share in the relevant market and (2) the merger would cause an increase in concentration of 33 percent or more in the relevant market. This presumption is rebuttable—that is, the defendants may overcome it by introducing evidence that shows that the merger does not violate Section 7.

This test is not the only criterion for evaluating the lawfulness of a merger. The court must also examine factors such as the trend toward concentration in the relevant market, the past history of the firms involved, the aggressiveness of the merged firms, the economic efficiency of the proposed merger, and consumer welfare.

vertical merger
A merger that integrates the operations of a supplier and a customer.

backward vertical merger
A vertical merger in which a customer acquires a supplier.

forward vertical merger
A vertical merger in which a supplier acquires a customer.

Vertical Mergers A **vertical merger** is a merger that integrates the operations of a supplier and a customer. For example, if Prentice Hall, Inc., a textbook publisher, acquired a paper mill, it would be a **backward vertical merger**. If a book publisher, such as Doubleday, acquired a retail bookstore chain, such as B. Dalton Bookstores, it would be a **forward vertical merger**. In examining the legality of vertical mergers, the courts usually consider such factors as the past history of the firms, the trend toward concentration in the industries involved, the barriers to entry, the economic efficiencies of the merger, and the elimination of potential competition caused by the merger.

Vertical mergers do not create an increase in market share because the merging firms serve different markets. They may, however, cause anticompetitive effects such as *foreclosing* competitors from either selling goods or services to or buying them from the merged firm. Assume that a furniture manufacturer acquires a chain of retail furniture stores. The merger is unlawful if it is likely that the merged firm will not buy furniture from other manufacturers or sell furniture to other retailers.

market extension merger
A merger between two companies in similar fields whose sales do not overlap.

Market Extension Mergers A **market extension merger** is a merger between two companies in similar fields whose sales do not overlap. The merger may expand the acquiring firm's geographical or product market. For example, a merger between two regional brewers that do not sell beer in the same geographical area is called a *geographical market extension merger*. A merger between sellers of similar products, such as a soft drink manufacturer and an orange juice producer, is called a *product market extension merger*. The legality of market extension mergers is examined under Section 7 of the Clayton Act. Market extension mergers are treated like conglomerate mergers.

conglomerate merger
A merger that does not fit into any other category; a merger between firms in totally unrelated businesses.

Conglomerate Mergers **Conglomerate mergers** are mergers that do not fit into any other category. That is, they are mergers between firms in unrelated businesses. For example, if an oil company such as Exxon merged with a clothing retailer such as Neiman-Marcus, the result would be a conglomerate merger.

The *unfair advantage theory* holds that a conglomerate merger may not give the acquiring firm an unfair advantage over its competitors in finance, marketing, or expertise. This rule is intended to prevent wealthy companies from overwhelming the competition in a given market. For example, Wal-Mart Stores, Inc., a giant discount warehouse store and one of the largest and wealthiest companies, may be prevented from acquiring Polo Ralph Lauren Corporation, a high-end manufacturer and retailer, under this theory.

Defenses to Section 7 Actions

There are two primary defenses to Section 7 actions. These defenses can be raised even if the merger would otherwise violate Section 7. The defenses are:

1. ***The failing company doctrine.*** According to this defense, a competitor may merge with a failing company if (1) there is no other reasonable alternative for the failing

company, (2) no other purchaser is available, and (3) the assets of the failing company would completely disappear from the market if the anticompetitive merger were not allowed to go through.

2. ***The small company doctrine.*** The courts have permitted two or more small companies to merge without liability under Section 7 if the merger allows them to compete more effectively with a large company.

Premerger Notification

In 1976, premerger notification rules were enacted pursuant to the **Hart-Scott-Rodino Antitrust Improvement Act**.[17] These rules require certain firms to notify the FTC and the Department of Justice of any proposed merger. This gives those agencies time to investigate and challenge any merger they deem anticompetitive. If a merger is reportable, the parties must file a notification form and wait 30 days. If within the waiting period the government sues, the suit is entitled to expedited treatment in the courts.

Hart-Scott-Rodino Antitrust Improvement Act
An act that requires certain firms to notify the FTC and the Justice Department in advance of a proposed merger. Unless the government challenges a proposed merger within 30 days, the merger may proceed.

Tying Arrangements: Section 3 of the Clayton Act

Section 3 of the Clayton Act prohibits tying arrangements involving sales and leases of goods (tangible personal property).[18] **Tying arrangements** are vertical trade restraints that involve the seller's refusal to sell a product (the *tying* item) to a customer unless the customer purchases a second product (the *tied* item). **Section 1 of the Sherman Act** forbids tying arrangements involving goods, services, intangible property, and real property.

The defendant must be shown to have had sufficient economic power in the tying product market to restrain competition in the tied product market.

A tying arrangement is lawful if there is some justifiable reason for it. For example, the protection of quality control coupled with a trade secret may save a tying arrangement.

Section 3 of the Clayton Act
A provision that prohibits tying arrangements involving sales and leases of goods.

tying arrangement
A restraint of trade in which a seller refuses to sell one product to a customer unless the customer agrees to purchase a second product from the seller.

Section 1 of the Sherman Act
A provision that prohibits tying arrangements involving goods, services, intangible property, and real property.

Consider These Examples Suppose, for example, that a manufacturer makes one patented product and one unpatented product. An illegal tie-in arrangement occurs if the manufacturer refuses to sell the patented product to a buyer unless the buyer also purchases the unpatented product. Coca-Cola Company owns the right to the formula for the syrup to make Coca-Cola, which is a trade secret. Suppose Coca-Cola requires its distributors to purchase the syrup to make Coca-Cola from it. The tying product is the Coca-Cola franchise distributorship, and the tied product is the syrup. Here, the tying arrangement is lawful because a trade secret is involved, and quality control must be preserved.

Price Discrimination: Section 2 of the Clayton Act

Businesses in the U.S. economy survive by selling their goods and services at prices that allow them to make a profit. Sellers often offer favorable terms to their preferred customers. **Price discrimination** occurs if a seller does this without just cause. The rules regarding this type of unlawful trade practices are found in **Section 2 of the Clayton Act**, which is commonly referred to as the **Robinson-Patman Act**. **Section 2(a) of the Robinson-Patman Act** contains the following basic prohibition against price discrimination in the sale of goods:

> It shall be unlawful for any person engaged in commerce, either directly or indirectly, to discriminate in price between different purchases of commodities of like grade and quality, where either or any of the purchases involved in such discrimination are in commerce, where the effect of such discrimination may be substantially to lessen

Section 2(a) of the Robinson-Patman Act
A provision that prohibits direct and indirect price discrimination by sellers of a commodity of a like grade and quality where the effect of such discrimination may be to substantially lessen competition or to tend to create a monopoly in any line of commerce.

competition or tend to create a monopoly in any line of commerce, or to injure, destroy, or prevent competition with any person who either grants or knowingly receives the benefit of such discrimination, or with customers of either of them.[19]

This section does not apply to the sale of services, real estate, intangible property, securities, leases, consignments, or gifts. Mixed sales (i.e., those involving both services and commodities) are controlled by the dominant nature of the transaction.

Direct Price Discrimination

direct price discrimination

A form of price discrimination that is readily apparent. To prove a violation of Section 2(a), the following elements must be shown: (1) The defendant sold commodities of like grade and quality (2) to two or more purchasers at different prices at approximately the same time, and (3) the plaintiff suffered injury because of the price discrimination.

To prove a violation of **Section 2(a) of the Robinson-Patman Act**, the following elements of **direct price discrimination** must be shown:

- ***Sales to two or more purchasers.*** To violate Section 2(a), price discrimination must involve sales to at least two different purchasers at approximately the same time. It is legal to make two or more sales of the same product to the same purchaser at different prices. The Robinson-Patman act requires that the discrimination occur "in commerce."
- ***Commodities of like grade and quality.*** A Section 2(a) violation must involve goods of "like grade and quality." To avoid this rule, sellers sometimes try to differentiate identical or similar products by using brand names. Nevertheless, as one court stated, "Four roses under any other name would still swill the same."[20]
- ***Injury.*** To recover damages, the plaintiff must have suffered actual injury because of the price discrimination. The injured party may be the purchaser who did not receive the favored price (*primary line injury*), that party's customers to whom the lower price could not be passed along (*secondary line injury*), and so on down the line (*tertiary line injury*).

A plaintiff who has not suffered injury because of price discrimination cannot recover. For example, assume that a wholesaler sells Michelin tires to General Motors more inexpensively than to Ford Motor Company. If Ford could have purchased comparable Michelin tires elsewhere at the lower price, it cannot recover.

Indirect Price Discrimination

indirect price discrimination

A form of price discrimination (e.g., favorable credit terms) that is less readily apparent than direct forms of price discrimination.

Because direct forms of price discrimination are readily apparent, sellers of goods have devised sophisticated ways to provide discriminatory prices to favored customers. Favorable credit terms, freight charges, and such are examples of **indirect price discrimination** that violate the Robinson-Patman Act.

Defenses to Section 2(a) Actions

The Robinson-Patman Act establishes three statutory defenses to Section 2(a) liability:

cost justification defense

A defense to a Section 2(a) action that provides that a seller's price discrimination is not unlawful if the price differential is due to "differences in the cost of manufacture, sale, or delivery" of the product.

1. ***Cost justification.*** Section 2(a) provides that a seller's price discrimination is not unlawful if the price differential is due to "differences in the cost of manufacture, sale, or delivery" of the product. This is called the **cost justification defense**. For example, quantity or volume discounts are lawful to the extent that they are supported by cost savings. Sellers may classify buyers into various broad groups and compute an average cost of selling to the group. The seller may then charge members of different groups different prices without being liable for price discrimination. The seller bears the burden of proving this defense.

   For example, if the Procter & Gamble Company can prove that bulk shipping rates make it less costly to deliver 10,000 boxes of Tide than lesser quantities, it may charge purchasers accordingly. However, Procter & Gamble may not simply lower its price per box because the buyer is a good customer.

2. ***Changing conditions.*** Price discrimination is not unlawful if it is in response to "changing conditions in the market for or the marketability of the goods." For example, the price of goods can be lowered to subsequent purchasers to reflect the deterioration of perishable goods (e.g., fish), obsolescence of seasonable goods (e.g., winter coats sold in the spring), a distress sale pursuant to a court order, or discontinuance of a business. This is called the **changing conditions defense**.
3. ***Meeting the competition.*** The **meeting the competition defense** to price discrimination is stipulated in **Section 2(b) of the Robinson-Patman Act**.[21] This defense holds that a seller may lawfully engage in price discrimination to meet a competitor's price. For example, assume that Rockport sells its "Pro Walker" shoe nationally at $100 per pair, while the Great Lakes Shoe Co. (Great Lakes), which produces and sells a comparable walking shoe, sells its product only in Michigan and Wisconsin. If Great Lakes sells its walking shoes at $75 per pair, Rockport can do the same in Michigan and Wisconsin. Rockport does not have to reduce the price of the shoe in the other 48 states. The seller can only meet, not beat, the competitor's price, however.

changing conditions defense
A price discrimination defense that claims prices were lowered in response to changing conditions in the market for or the marketability of the goods.

meeting the competition defense
A defense provided in Section 2(b) that says a seller may lawfully engage in price discrimination to meet a competitor's price.

Unfair Methods of Competition: Section 5 of the Federal Trade Commission Act

In 1914, Congress enacted the **FTC Act** and created the FTC. **Section 5 of the FTC Act** prohibits unfair methods of competition and unfair or deceptive acts or practices in or affecting commerce.[22]

Section 5, which is broader than the other antitrust laws, covers conduct that (1) violates any provision of the Sherman Act or the Clayton Act, (2) violates the spirit of those acts, (3) fills the gaps of those acts, and (4) offends public policy, or is immoral, oppressive, unscrupulous, or unethical, or causes substantial injury to competitors or consumers.

The FTC is exclusively empowered to enforce the FTC Act. It can issue interpretive rules, general statements of policy, trade regulation rules, and guidelines that define unfair or deceptive practices, and it can conduct investigations of suspected antitrust violations. It can also issue cease-and-desist orders against violators. These orders are appealable to federal court. The FTC Act provides for a private civil cause of action for injured parties. Treble damages are not available.

Section 5 of the Federal Trade Commission Act
A provision that prohibits unfair methods of competition and unfair or deceptive acts or practices in or affecting commerce.

Exemptions from Antitrust Laws

Certain industries and businesses are exempt from federal antitrust laws. The three categories of exemptions are:

1. ***Statutory exemptions.*** Certain statutes expressly exempt some forms of business and other activities from the reach of antitrust laws. **Statutory exemptions** include labor unions,[23] agricultural cooperatives,[24] export activities of American companies,[25] and insurance business that is regulated by a state.[26] Other statutes exempt railroad, utility, shipping, and securities industries from most of the reach of antitrust laws.
2. ***Implied exemptions.*** The federal courts have implied several exemptions from antitrust laws. Examples of **implied exemptions** include professional baseball (but not other professional sports) and airlines.[27] The airline exemption was granted on the ground that railroads and other forms of transportation were expressly exempt. The Supreme Court has held that professionals such as lawyers do not qualify for an

statutory exemptions
Exemptions from antitrust laws that are expressly provided in statutes enacted by Congress.

implied exemptions
Exemptions from antitrust laws that are implied by the federal courts.

implied exemption from antitrust laws.[28] The Supreme Court strictly construes implied exemptions from antitrust laws.

3. ***State action exemptions.*** The U.S. Supreme Court has held that economic regulations mandated by state law are exempt from federal antitrust laws. The **state action exemption** extends to businesses that must comply with these regulations.

state action exemptions
Exemptions from antitrust laws for regulations mandated by state law.

Consider This Example States may set the rates that public utilities (e.g., gas, electric, and cable television companies) may charge their customers. The states that set these rates and the companies that must abide by them are not liable for price-fixing in violation of federal antitrust law.

State Antitrust Laws

Most states have enacted antitrust statutes. These statutes are usually patterned after the federal antitrust statutes. They often contain the same language as well. State antitrust laws are used to attack anticompetitive activity that occurs in intrastate commerce. When federal antitrust laws are laxly applied, plaintiffs often bring lawsuits under state antitrust laws.

Art Center, Paris, France. The European Union (EU) has enacted and enforces very strong antitrust laws. The EU antitrust authorities have denied mergers of multinational companies that had been previously approved by antitrust authorities in the United States.

Terms and Concepts

Federal Antitrust Laws

Federal antitrust laws are enacted by Congress to limit anticompetitive behavior in business. Federal antitrust laws include:

1. ***Sherman Act.*** This act, enacted in 1890, makes certain restraints of trade and monopolistic acts illegal.
2. ***Clayton Act.*** This act, enacted in 1914, regulates mergers and prohibits certain exclusive dealing arrangements.
3. ***Federal Trade Commission (FTC) Act.*** This act, enacted in 1914, prohibits unfair methods of competition.
4. ***Robinson-Patman Act.*** This act, enacted in 1930, prohibits price discrimination.

Antitrust Enforcement

Each administration adopts an enforcement policy for antitrust laws. Antitrust laws are enforced more stringently at some times than at others.

Antitrust Penalties

Federal antitrust laws provide the following penalties:

1. ***Criminal sanctions.*** Criminal penalties may be assessed for violations of the Sherman Act.
2. ***Civil penalties.*** The federal government may seek civil damages, including treble damages, for violations of federal antitrust laws. Courts may issue orders for divestiture of assets, cancellation of contracts, and other remedies.
3. ***Private civil actions.*** Section 4 of the Clayton Act provides that anyone injured in his or her business or on his or her property by the defendant's violation of any federal antitrust law (except the FTC Act) may bring a civil action and recover *treble damages*, plus reasonable costs and attorneys' fees, from the defendant.
4. ***Effect of government judgment.*** A government judgment against a defendant for an antitrust violation may be used as prima facie evidence of liability in a private, civil treble damages action. A plea of *nolo contendere* or *consent decree* cannot be used as evidence in a subsequent private, civil antitrust action.

Restraints of Trade: Section 1 of the Sherman Act

Section 1 of the Sherman Act prohibits contracts, combinations, or conspiracies that cause *unreasonable restraints of trade*. It requires *concerted activity* between two or more parties. The courts apply one of the following two tests in determining the lawfulness of a restraint of trade:

1. ***Rule of reason.*** This rule requires a balancing of pro- and anticompetitive effects of the restraint. Restraints found to be unreasonable are unlawful, violating Section 1 of the Sherman Act.
2. **Per se *rule.*** This rule is applied to restraints that are inherently anticompetitive. No justification for the restraint is permitted.

Horizontal Restraint of Trade

Horizontal restraint of trade occurs when two or more competitors at the *same level of distribution* enter into a contract, combination, or conspiracy to restrain trade. Horizontal restraints include:

1. ***Price-fixing.*** In price-fixing, competitors in the same line of business agree to set the price of the goods or services they sell. Price-fixing is a *per se violation.*
2. ***Division of markets.*** In a division of markets, competitors agree that each will serve only a designated portion of a market. Also called *market sharing*. Division of markets is a *per se violation.*
3. ***Group boycott.*** In a group boycott, competitors agree not to deal with others at another level of distribution (e.g., customer or supplier). Most group boycotts are examined using the *rule of reason.*
4. ***Other horizontal agreements.*** Other horizontal agreements are examined using the *rule of reason.*

Vertical Restraint of Trade

A vertical restraint of trade occurs when two or more parties on *different levels of distribution* enter into a contract, combination, or conspiracy to restrain trade. Vertical restraints include:

1. ***Resale price maintenance.*** In resale price maintenance, a party at one level of distribution (e.g., a manufacturer) requires a party at another level of distribution (e.g., a retailer) to sell a good or service at a designated price. Also called *vertical price fixing*. Resale price maintenance is a *per se violation.*
2. ***Nonprice vertical restraints.*** Nonprice vertical restraints of trade are examined using the *rule of reason.*

Defenses to Section 1 of the Sherman Act

The following defenses may be raised against an alleged violation of Section 1 of the Sherman Act:

1. ***Unilateral refusal to deal.*** A party may unilaterally refuse to deal with another party. This does not violate Section 1 because there has been no concerted action.

2. ***Conscious parallelism.*** Conscious parallelism occurs when two or more firms act the same but without concerted action; they reached their decisions independently.
3. ***Noerr doctrine.*** Two or more parties may petition the executive, legislative, or judicial branches of government to enact laws or take other action. The Noerr doctrine does not protect petitioners or plaintiffs if their petition or lawsuit is without merit.

Monopolization: Section 2 of the Sherman Act

Section 2 of the Sherman Act prohibits the act of *monopolization* and attempts, combinations, and conspiracies to monopolize trade or commerce in a relevant market. The following elements are necessary to prove a defendant in violation of Section 2 of the Sherman Act:

1. ***Relevant market.*** The relevant market is defined as:
   a. *Relevant product or service market.* The relevant product or service market includes substitute products or services that are reasonably interchangeable with the defendant's products or services.
   b. *Relevant geographical market.* The relevant geographical market is the geographical area in which the defendant and its competitors sell the product or service.
2. ***Monopoly power.*** The defendant must possess monopoly power in the relevant market. This is defined as the power to control prices or exclude competition.
3. ***Willful act of monopolizing.*** The defendant must have engaged in a willful act of monopolization. Mere possession of a monopoly is not enough.

Defenses to Monopolization

The following defenses may be raised against an alleged violation of Section 2 of the Sherman Act:

1. ***Superior business acumen.*** A monopoly may be acquired by superior skill, foresight, or industry.
2. ***Natural monopoly.*** A monopoly may be thrust upon the defendant (e.g., only newspaper in a small town).

Mergers: Premerger Notification

The *Hart-Scott-Rodino Antitrust Improvement Act* is a federal act that requires certain firms to notify the FTC and Department of Justice in advance of a proposed merger. Unless the government challenges the proposed merger within 30 days, the merger may proceed.

Mergers: Section 7 of the Clayton Act

Section 7 of the Clayton Act prohibits acquisitions that may substantially lessen competition in any line of commerce in any section of the country. The following elements are necessary to prove a violation of Section 7 of the Clayton Act:

1. ***Line of commerce.*** The line of commerce is the market that will be affected by a merger. It includes products or services that consumers use as substitutes for those produced or sold by the merging firms.
2. ***Section of the country.*** The section of the country is the geographical market that will be affected by a merger. It includes the area that will feel the direct and immediate impact of the merger.
3. ***Probability of a substantial lessening of competition.*** If the court determines that a merger would have a probability of a substantial lessening of competition, the merger may be prohibited. The statute deals with probabilities; a showing of actual lessening of competition is not required.

Horizontal Merger

A horizontal merger is a merger between two or more firms that compete in the same business and geographical market; it is a merger between competitors at the same level of distribution.

Vertical Merger

A vertical merger is a merger between firms at different levels of distribution that integrates the operations of a supplier and a customer.

Market Extension Merger

A market extension merger is a merger of two firms in similar fields whose sales do not overlap.

1. ***Geographical market extension merger.*** A geographical market extension merger is a merger of two firms that sell the same product or service but in different geographical markets.
2. ***Product market extension merger.*** A product market extension merger is a merger of two firms that sell similar products or services in the same geographical market.

Conglomerate Merger

A conglomerate merger is a merger of firms in totally unrelated businesses. Conglomerate mergers may be challenged under the *unfair advantage theory*, which says that a merger may not give the acquiring firm an unfair advantage over its competitors in finance, marketing, or expertise.

Defenses to Section 7 Actions

The following defenses may be raised against violation of Section 7 of the Clayton Act:

1. ***Failing company doctrine.*** A competitor may merge with a failing company if (1) there is no other reasonable alternative for the failing company, (2) no other purchaser is available, and (3) the assets of the failing company would completely disappear from the market if the anticompetitive merger were not allowed to go through.
2. ***Small company doctrine.*** Two or more small companies may merge if the merger allows them to compete more effectively with a large company.

Tying Arrangements: Section 3 of the Clayton Act

1. ***Tying arrangement.*** A tying arrangement occurs when a seller refuses to sell a product (the *tying* product) to a customer unless the customer purchases a second product (the *tied* product).
2. ***Section 3 of the Clayton Act.*** This provision prohibits tying arrangements involving sales and leases of goods.
3. ***Section 1 of the Sherman Act.*** This provision prohibits tying arrangements involving goods, services, intangible property, and real property.

Price Discrimination: Section 2 of the Clayton Act

Section 2 of the Clayton Act is commonly referred to as the *Robinson-Patman Act.* It prohibits price discrimination and discriminatory fees, payments, and services. The act applies only to products, not services.

Price Discrimination

Section 2(a) of the Robinson-Patman Act prohibits a seller from discriminating in price between two or more different purchasers of commodities of *like grade and quality* where the effect may be substantially to lessen competition. *Direct* and *indirect* price discrimination are unlawful.

Defenses to Section 2(a) Actions

A seller's price discrimination is not unlawful if the price differential is due to:

1. ***Cost justification.*** This includes differences in the cost of manufacture, sale, or delivery of the product to different purchasers.
2. ***Changing conditions.*** The seller may respond to changing conditions in the market (e.g., deterioration of perishable goods).
3. ***Meeting the competition.*** *Section 2(b) of the Robinson-Patman Act* permits a seller to have a lower price in one market than in another market to meet the price competitor in the lower-priced market.

Unfair Methods of Competition: Section 5 of the FTC Act

Section 5 of the FTC Act prohibits unfair methods of competition and unfair or deceptive acts or practices. Section 5 covers conduct that (1) violates any provision of the Sherman Act or the

Clayton Act, (2) violates the spirit of those acts, (3) fills the gaps of those acts, and (4) causes substantial injury to competitors or consumers.

Exemptions from Antitrust Laws

1. ***Statutory exemptions.*** Statutes expressly exempt from federal antitrust laws: labor unions; agricultural cooperatives; export activities of American companies; insurance business regulated by states; and railroads, utility, shipping, and securities industries.
2. ***Implied exemptions.*** The courts have held that certain industries, including professional baseball and airlines, are implicitly exempt from federal antitrust laws.
3. ***State action exemptions.*** Businesses' activities that are mandated by state law are exempt from federal antitrust laws.

State Antitrust Laws

Most states have enacted state antitrust laws that attack anticompetitive activity that occurs in intrastate commerce.

Internet Exercises and Case Questions

Working the Web Internet Exercises

1. The largest antitrust case of our time, *United States v. Microsoft Corporation*, leaves a long and rich trail of documents for study. See, for example, **www.ssrn.com/update/lsn/lsn_microsoft-case.html**, which contains a lengthy list of links to articles about the famous case. List the specific sections of the antitrust laws that Microsoft was alleged to have violated.
2. Find your state's laws relating to unfair competition and restraint of trade. Are they consistent with federal law? See "Legal Information Institute: Antitrust," at **www.law.cornell.edu/topics/antitrust.html**, for an overview of antitrust law, with links to key primary and secondary sources.
3. Antitrust is an area of law deeply connected with economic theory. The intent of the law is to protect competition. So how can mergers be permitted under the Clayton Act? See Section 7 of the Clayton Act [15 U.S.C. 18].
4. Where does the United States derive its purported authority to enforce its antitrust laws extraterritorially? See **www.usdoj.gov/atr/public/guidelines/internat.htm**.

Legal Environment Cases

26.1 Price Fixing The Maricopa County Medical Society (Society) is a professional association that represents doctors of medicine, osteopathy, and podiatry in Maricopa County, Arizona. The society formed the Maricopa Foundation for Medical Care (Foundation), a nonprofit Arizona corporation. Approximately 1,750 doctors, who represent 70 percent of the practitioners in the country, belong to the foundation. The foundation acts as an insurance administrator between its member doctors and insurance companies that pay patients' medical bills.

The foundation established a maximum fee schedule for various medical services. The member doctors agreed to abide by this fee schedule when providing services to patients. The state of Arizona brought an action against the Society and the Foundation and its members, alleging price-fixing in violation of Section 1 of the Sherman Act. Who wins? *Arizona v. Maricopa County Medical Society*, 457 U.S. 332, 102 S.Ct. 2466, 1982 U.S. Lexis 5 (U.S. Sup.Ct.)

26.2 Division of Market Topco Associates, Inc., was founded in the 1940s by a group of small, local grocery store chains to act as a buying cooperative for the member stores. In this capacity, Topco procured and distributed more than 1,000 different food and related items to its members. Topco did not itself own any manufacturing or processing facilities, and the items it procured were shipped directly from the manufacturer or packer to Topco members. Topco members agreed to sell only Topco brand products within an exclusive territory. The United States sued Topco and its members, alleging a violation of Section 1 of the Sherman Act. Who wins? *United States v. Topco Associates, Inc.*, 405 U.S. 596, 92 S.Ct. 1126, 1972 U.S. Lexis 167 (U.S. Sup.Ct.)

26.3 Tying Arrangement Mercedes-Benz of North America (MBNA) was the exclusive franchiser of Mercedes-Benz dealerships in the United States. MBNA's franchise agreements required each dealer to establish a customer service department for the repair of Mercedes-Benz automobiles and for dealers to purchase Mercedes-Benz replacement parts from MBNA. At least eight independent wholesale distributors, including Metrix Warehouse, Inc., sold replacement parts for Mercedes-Benz automobiles. Because they were precluded from selling parts to Mercedes-Benz dealers, these parts distributors sold their replacement parts to independent garages that specialized in the repair of Mercedes-Benz automobiles. Evidence showed that Metrix sold replacement parts for Mercedes-Benz automobiles of equal quality and at a lower price than those sold by MBNA. Metrix sued MBNA, alleging a violation of Section 1 of the Sherman Act. Who wins? *Metrix Warehouse, Inc. v. Mercedes-Benz of North America, Inc.*, 828 F2.d 1033, 1987 U.S.App. Lexis 12341 (4th Cir.)

26.4 Resale Price Maintenance The Union Oil Company was a major oil company that operated a nationwide network of franchised service station dealers who sold Union Oil gasoline and other products throughout the United States. The franchise dealers leased their stations from Union Oil; they also signed a franchise agreement to purchase gasoline and other products on assignment from Union Oil. Both the lease and the franchise agreement were one-year contracts that Union Oil could cancel if a dealer did not adhere to the contracts. The franchise agreement provided that all dealers must adhere to the retail price of gasoline as set by Union Oil. The retail price fixed by Union Oil for gasoline during the period in question was 29.9 cents per gallon. Simpson, a franchise dealer, violated this provision in the franchise agreement and sold gasoline at 27.9 cents per gallon to meet competitive prices. Because of this, Union Oil canceled Simpson's lease and franchise agreement. Simpson sued Union Oil, alleging a violation of Section 1 of the Sherman Act. Who wins? *Simpson v. Union Oil Company*, 377 U.S. 13, 84 S.Ct. 1051, 1964 U.S. Lexis 2378 (U.S. Sup.Ct.)

26.5 Monopolization The International Business Machine Corporation (IBM) manufactured entire computer systems, including mainframes and peripherals, and provided software and support services to customers. IBM both sold and leased computers. Greyhound Computer Corporation, Inc., was a computer leasing company that bought older computers from IBM and then leased them to businesses. Thus, Greyhound was both a customer and a competitor of IBM. Prior to 1963, IBM sold its second-generation equipment at a 10 percent discount per year, up to a maximum of 75 percent. Thus, equipment on the market for several years could be purchased at a substantial discount from its original cost.

IBM's market share of this leasing market was 82.5 percent. The portion of the leasing market not controlled by IBM was dispersed among many companies, including Greyhound. IBM officials became concerned that the balance between sales and leases was turned too heavily toward sales and that the rapid increase in leasing companies occurred because of their ability to purchase second-generation computers from IBM at a substantial discount. In 1963, IBM reduced the annual discount to 5 percent per year, with a maximum of 35 percent. In 1964, the discount was changed to 12 percent after the first year, with no further discounts. Greyhound sued IBM, alleging that IBM engaged in monopolization in violation of Section 2 of the Sherman Act. Who wins? *Greyhound v. International Business Machine Corporation*, 559 F.2d 488, 1977 U.S.App. Lexis 11957 (9th Cir.)

26.6 Merger The Lipton Tea Co. was the second-largest U.S. producer of herbal teas, controlling 32 percent of the national market. Lipton announced that it would acquire Celestial Seasonings, the largest U.S. producer of herbal teas, which controlled 52 percent of the national market. R. C. Bigelow, Inc., the third-largest producer of herbal teas, with 13 percent of the national market, brought this action, alleging that the merger would violate section 7 of the Clayton Act and seeking an injunction against the merger. What type of merger was proposed? What was the relevant market? Should the merger be enjoined? *R. C. Bigelow, Inc., v. Unilever, N.V.*, 867 F.2d 102, 1989 U.S.App. Lexis 574 (2d Cir.)

26.7 Antitrust Injury The Brunswick Corporation was the second-largest manufacturer of bowling equipment in the United States. In the late 1950s, the bowling industry expanded rapidly. Brunswick's sales of lanes, automatic pinsetters, and ancillary equipment to bowling alley operators rose accordingly. Because the equipment required a major capital expenditure by bowling center operators, Brunswick extended credit for all of the purchase price except a cash down payment. It took a security interest in the equipment.

Brunswick's sales dropped in the early 1960s, when the bowling industry went into a sharp decline. In addition, many bowling center operators defaulted on their loans. By the end of 1964, Brunswick was in financial difficulty. It met with limited success when it foreclosed on its security interests and attempted to lease or sell the repossessed equipment and bowling centers. To avoid complete loss, Brunswick started running those bowling centers that would provide a positive cash flow. This made Brunswick the largest operator of bowling centers in the country, with more than five times as many bowling centers as its next-largest competitor. Because the bowling industry was so deconcentrated, however, Brunswick controlled fewer than 2 percent of the bowling centers in the country.

Pueblo Bowl-O-Mat, Inc. (Pueblo), operated three bowling centers in markets where Brunswick had repossessed bowling centers and began operating them. Pueblo sued Brunswick, alleging that Brunswick had violated Section 7 of the Clayton Act. Pueblo alleged that it had suffered injury in the form of lost profits that it would have made had Brunswick allowed the bowling centers to go bankrupt, and it requested treble damages. Is Brunswick liable? *Brunswick Corporation v. Pueblo Bowl-O-Mat, Inc.*, 429 U.S. 477, 97 S.Ct. 690, 1977 U.S. Lexis 37 (U.S. Sup.Ct.)

26.8 Price Discrimination Corn Products Refining Company manufactured corn syrup, or glucose, at two plants, one located in Chicago, Illinois, and the other in Kansas City, Missouri. Glucose was a principal ingredient of low-priced candy. Corn Products sold glucose at the same retail price to all purchasers but charged separately for freight charges. Instead of charging actual freight charges, Corn Products charged every purchaser the freight cost it would have incurred had the glucose been shipped from Chicago, even if the glucose was shipped from its Kansas City plant. This "base point pricing" system created a favored price zone for Chicago-based purchasers, which put them in a better position to compete for business. The FTC sued Corn Products, alleging that it had engaged in price discrimination in violation of Section 2(a) of the Robinson-Patman Act. Did it? *Corn Products Refining Company v. Federal Trade Commission*, 324 U.S. 726, 65 S.Ct. 961, 1945 U.S. Lexis 2749 (U.S. Sup.Ct.)

Ethics in Business

26.9 E. I. DuPont de Nemours & Co. (DuPont) is a manufacturer of chemicals, paints, finishes, fabrics, and other products. General Motors Corporation is a major manufacturer of automobiles. During the period 1917–1919, DuPont purchased 23 percent of the stock of General Motors. DuPont became a major supplier of finishes and fabrics to General Motors.

DuPont's commanding position as a General Motors supplier was not achieved until shortly after its purchase of a sizable block of General Motors stock in 1917. The company's interest in buying into General Motors was stimulated by John J. Raskob, DuPont's treasurer, and Pierre S. du Pont, DuPont's president, who acquired personal holdings of General Motors stock in

1914. General Motors had been organized six years earlier by William Durant to acquire previously independent automobile manufacturing companies—Buick, Cadillac, Oakland, and Oldsmobile. Durant later brought in Chevrolet, organized by him when he was temporarily out of power, during 1910–1915, and a bankers' group controlled General Motors. In 1915, when Durant and the bankers deadlocked on the choice of a board of directors, they resolved the deadlock through an agreement under which Pierre S. du Pont was named chairman of the General Motors board and Pierre S. du Pont, Raskob, and two nominees of Mr. du Pont were named neutral directors. By 1916, Durant settled his differences with the bankers and resumed the presidency and his controlling position in General Motors. He prevailed upon Pierre S. du Pont and Raskob to continue their interests in General Motors's affairs, which both did as members of the finance committee, working closely with Durant in matters of finances and operations and plans for future expansion.

Raskob foresaw the success of the automobile industry and the opportunity for great profit in a substantial purchase of General Motors stock. On December 19, 1917, Raskob submitted a treasurer's report to the DuPont finance committee, recommending a purchase of General Motors stock in the amount of $25 million. That report made it clear that more than just a profitable investment was contemplated. A major consideration was that an expanding General Motors would provide a substantial market needed by the burgeoning DuPont organization. Raskob's summary of reasons in support of the purchase included this statement: "Our interest in the General Motors Company will undoubtedly secure for us the entire Fabrikoid, Pyralin (celluloid) paint and varnish business of those companies, which is a substantial factor,"

General Motors was the colossus of the giant automobile industry. It accounted annually for upward of two-fifths of the total sales of automotive vehicles in the nation. Expressed in percentages, DuPont supplied 67 percent of General Motors's requirements for finishes in 1946 and 68 percent in 1947. In fabrics, DuPont supplied 52.3 percent of requirements in 1946 and 38.5 percent in 1947. Because General Motors accounted for almost one-half of the automobile industry's annual sales, its requirements for automotive finishes and fabrics must have represented approximately one-half of the relevant market for these materials.

In 1949, the United States brought an antitrust action against DuPont, alleging violation of Section 7 of the Clayton Act and seeking the divestiture of DuPont's ownership of stock in General Motors. *United States v. E. I. du Pont de Nemours & Co.*, 353 U.S. 586, 77 S.Ct. 872, 1957 U.S. Lexis 1755 (U.S. Sup.Ct)

Ethics Issues

1. What does Section 7 of the Clayton Act provide? Explain.
2. What public policy underlies Section 7?
3. Did the du Ponts act ethically in this case?
4. Did DuPont's ownership of 23 percent of the stock of General Motors constitute a vertical merger that gave DuPont illegal preferences over competitors in the sale of finishes and fabrics to General Motors in violation of Section 7 of the Clayton Act?

Endnotes

1. Antitrust Amendments Act of 1990, P.L. 101–588.
2. Antitrust Amendments Act of 1990, P.L. 101–588.
3. 15 U.S.C. Section 15.
4. *Reiter v. Sonotone Corporation,* 442 U.S. 330, 99 S.Ct. 2326, 1979 U.S. Lexis 108 (U.S. Sup.Ct.).
5. 15 U.S.C. Section 26.
6. Justice Marshall, *United States v. Topco Associates, Inc.*, 405 U.S. 596, 92 S.Ct. 1126, 1972 U.S. Lexis 167 (U.S. Sup.Ct.).
7. 15 U.S.C. Section 1.
8. 221 U.S. 1, 31 S.Ct. 502, 1911 US. Lexis 1725 (U.S. Sup.Ct.). The Court found that Rockefeller's oil trust violated the Sherman Act and ordered the trust broken up into 30 separate companies.
9. *Dr. Miles Medical Co. v. John D. Park & Sons, Co.,* 220 U.S. 373, 31 S.Ct. 376, 1911 U.S. Lexis 1685 (U.S. Sup.Ct.).
10. *Continental T.V., Inc. v. GTE Sylvania, Inc.,* 433 U.S. 36, 97 S.Ct. 2549, 1977 U.S. Lexis 134 (U.S. Sup.Ct.), reversing *United States v. Arnold Schwinn & Co.,* 388 U.S. 365, 87 S.Ct. 1856, 1967 U.S. Lexis 2965 (U.S. Sup.Ct.).
11. 250 U.S. 300, 39 S.Ct. 465, 1919 U.S. Lexis 1948 (U.S. Sup.Ct.).
12. This doctrine is the result of two U.S. Supreme Court decisions: *Eastern R.R. President's Conference v. Noerr Motor Freight, Inc.,* 365 U.S. 127, 81 S.Ct. 523, 1961 U.S. Lexis 2128 (U.S. Sup.Ct), and *United Mine Workers v. Pennington,* 318 U.S. 657, 85 S.Ct 1585, 1965 U.S. Lexis 2207 (U.S. Sup.Ct.).
13. 15 U.S.C. Section 2.
14. *William Inglis & Sons Baking Company v. ITT Continental Baking Company, Inc.*, 668 F.2d 1014, 1982 U.S.App. Lexis 21926 (9th Cir.).
15. 15 U.S.C. Section 18.
16. 374 U.S. 321, 83 S.Ct. 1715, 1963 U.S. Lexis 2413 (U.S. Sup.Ct.).
17. 15 U.S.C. Section 18(a).
18. 15 U.S.C. Section 14.
19. 15 U.S.C. Section 13(a).
20. *Hartley & Parker, Inc. v. Florida Beverage Corp.,* 307 F.2d 916, 923, 1962 U.S.App. Lexis 4196 (5th Cir).
21. 15 U.S.C. Section 13(b).
22. 15 U.S.C. Section 45.
23. Section 6 of the Clayton Act, 15 U.S.C. Section 17; the Norris-LaGuardia Act of 1932, 29 U.S.C. Sections 101–155; and the National Labor Relations Act of 1935, 29 U.S.C. Section 141 *et seq.* Labor unions that conspire or combine with nonlabor groups to accomplish a goal prohibited by federal antitrust law lose their exemption.
24. Capper-Volstrand Act of 1922, 7 U.S.C. Section 291; Cooperative Marketing Act of 1926, 15 U.S.C. Section 521.
25. Webb-Pomerene Act, 15 U.S.C. Sections 61–65.
26. McCarran-Ferguson Act of 1945, 15 U.S.C. Sections 1011–1015.
27. *Community Communications Co., Inc. v. City of Boulder,* 455 U.S. 40, 102 S.Ct. 835, 1982 U.S. Lexis 65 (U.S. Sup.Ct.).
28. *Goldfarb v. Virginia State Bar,* 421 U.S. 773, 95 S.Ct. 2004, 1975 U.S. Lexis 13 (U.S. Sup.Ct.)

27

Investor Protection and Online Securities Transactions

"Fraud is infinite in variety; sometimes it is audacious and unblushing: sometimes it pays a sort of homage to virtue, and then it is modest and retiring; it would be honesty itself, if it could only afford it."

—Lord MacNaghten
Reddaway v. Banham (1896)

Chapter Objectives

After studying this chapter, you should be able to:

1. Describe the procedure for going public and how securities are registered with the Securities and Exchange Commission.
2. Describe the requirements for qualifying for private placement, intrastate, and small offering exemptions from registration.
3. Describe insider trading that violates Section 10(b) of the Securities Exchange Act of 1934.
4. Describe the liability of tippers and tippees for insider trading.
5. Describe short-swing profits that violate Section 16(b) of the Securities Exchange Act of 1934.

Chapter Contents

- The Securities and Exchange Commission (SEC)
- Going Public: The Securities Act of 1933
- Private and Other Transactions Exempt from Registration
- Trading in Securities: The Securities Exchange Act of 1934
- Short-Swing Profits
- State Securities Laws

Prior to the 1920s and 1930s, the securities markets in this country were not regulated by the federal government. Securities were sold to investors with little, if any, disclosure. Fraud in these transactions was common.

Following the stock market crash of 1929, Congress enacted a series of statutes designed to regulate securities markets. The **Securities Act of 1933** requires disclosure by companies and others who wish to issue securities to the public. The **Securities Exchange Act of 1934** was enacted to prevent fraud in the subsequent trading of securities, including insider trading. Securities are now sold online. The SEC also regulates the sale of securities online.

Federal and state securities laws are designed to (1) require disclosure of information to investors and (2) prevent fraud. This chapter discusses federal and state securities laws and regulations that provide investor protection, as well as the sale of securities online.

Blue sky. State securities laws are often referred to as *blue-sky laws* because they help prevent investors from purchasing a piece of the blue sky.

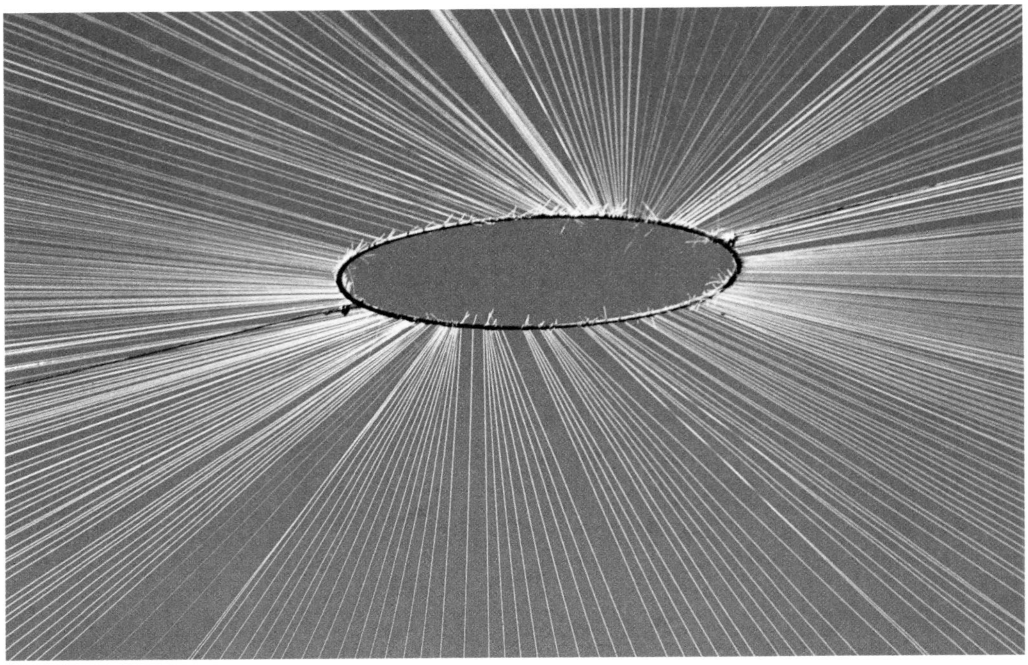

The Securities and Exchange Commission (SEC)

Securities and Exchange Commission (SEC)
A federal administrative agency that is empowered to administer federal securities laws. The SEC can adopt rules and regulations to interpret and implement federal securities laws.

The Securities Exchange Act of 1934 created the **Securities and Exchange Commission (SEC)** and empowered it to administer federal securities laws. The SEC is an administrative agency composed of five members who are appointed by the president. The major responsibilities of the SEC are:

1. Adopting rules (also called regulations) that further the purpose of the federal securities statutes. These rules have the force of law.
2. Investigating alleged securities violations and bringing enforcement actions against suspected violators. This may include a recommendation of criminal prosecution. Criminal prosecutions of violations of federal securities laws are brought by the U.S. Department of Justice.
3. Regulating the activities of securities brokers and advisors. This includes registering brokers and advisors and taking enforcement action against those who violate securities laws.

Definition of Security

A **security** must exist before securities laws apply. Securities are defined as:

1. Interests or instruments that are commonly known as securities (e.g., common stock, preferred stock, bonds, debentures, warrants).
2. Interests or instruments that are expressly mentioned in securities acts (e.g., preorganization subscription agreements; interests in oil, gas, and mineral rights; deposit receipts for foreign securities).
3. Investment contracts—that is, any contract whereby an investor invests money or other consideration in a common enterprise and expects to make a profit from the significant efforts of others. Limited partnership interests, pyramid sales schemes, and investments in farm animals accompanied by care agreements have been found to be securities under this test, which is known as the *Howey test*.[1]

In the following case, the U.S. Supreme Court held that a financial scheme constituted a security subject to federal securities laws.

security
(1) An interest or instrument that is common stock, preferred stock, a bond, a debenture, or a warrant; (2) an interest or instrument that is expressly mentioned in securities acts; and (3) an investment contract.

Case 27.1 Definition of Security

U.S. SUPREME COURT

Securities and Exchange Commission v. Edwards

540 U.S. 389, 124 S.Ct. 892, 2004 U.S. Lexis 659

Supreme Court of the United States

Background and Facts

Charles Edwards was the chairman, chief executive officer (CEO), and sole shareholder of ETS Payphones, Inc. (ETS). ETS sold payphones to the public via independent distributors. The payphones were sold to buyers in a $7,000 package deal, consisting of a payphone site lease, a 5-year leaseback by ETS, and an agreement whereby ETS would install the equipment at the site, arrange for connection and long-distance telephone service, collect coin revenues, and maintain and repair the payphones. Under the ETS contract, each payphone investor was guaranteed to receive $82 per month on his or her investment. ETS guaranteed to refund the full purchase price at the end of the lease. ETS enrolled more than 10,000 people in the payphone program, and they invested over $300 million.

In actuality, the payphones did not generate enough revenues for ETS to make the guaranteed monthly payments. After ETS defaulted on hundreds of millions of dollars of payments to investors, it filed for bankruptcy. The Securities and Exchange Commission (SEC) brought a civil action against Edwards and ETS, alleging that the defendants had failed to register the payphone sale-and-leaseback arrangement with the SEC as a security prior to selling the phones to the public and had committed securities fraud. The U.S. district court held that the payphone arrangement constituted a security and was therefore subject to federal securities laws. The U.S. Court of Appeals reversed, finding no security because the sale-and-leaseback provided for a fixed rate of return rather than capital appreciation or participation in the earnings of the enterprise. The SEC appealed to the U.S. Supreme Court.

Issue

Is the payphone sale-and-leaseback arrangement that guaranteed a fixed rate of return a security and therefore subject to federal securities laws?

In the Language of the Court

"Opportunity doesn't always knock, sometimes it rings." (ETS Payphones promotional brochure). And sometimes it hangs up. So it did for the 10,000 people who invested a total of $300 million in the payphone sale-and-leaseback arrangement touted by respondent Edwards under that slogan. Congress' purpose in enacting the securities laws was to regulate investments, in whatever form they are made and by whatever name they are called. To that end, it enacted a broad definition of "security" to encompass virtually any instrument that might be sold as an investment.

There is no reason to distinguish between promises of fixed returns and promises of variable returns. In both cases, the investing public is attracted by representations of investment income as purchasers were in this case by ETS' invitation to "watch the profits add up." Moreover, investments pitched as low risk (such as those offering a guaranteed fixed return) are particularly attractive to individuals more vulnerable to investment fraud, including older and less sophisticated investors. Under the reading respondent Edwards advances, unscrupulous marketers of investments could evade the securities laws by picking a rate of return to promise. We will not read into the securities laws a limitation not compelled by the language that would so undermine the laws' purpose. We hold that an investment scheme

(continued)

Securities and Exchange Commission v. Edwards
540 U.S. 389, 124 S.Ct. 892, 2004 U.S. Lexis 659
Supreme Court of the United States
(*continued*)

promising a fixed rate of return can be an "investment contract" and thus a "security" subject to the federal securities laws.

Decision and Remedy

The U.S. Supreme Court held that an investment arrangement that offers a fixed rate of return is a security subject to the provisions of federal securities laws. The Supreme Court reversed the decision of the Court of Appeals and remanded the case for further proceedings based on violations of securities laws and securities fraud.

Business and Ethics Questions

1. If a financial arrangement that guarantees a fixed rate of return is not found to be a security, what would be the result for society? Explain.
2. Did Edwards act ethically in this case? Is there any evidence that he acted fraudulently? Explain.
3. If Edwards had had to disclose the truth about his and ETS's investment scheme, would many people have invested? Explain.

Concept Summary *Definition of* Security

Type of Security	Definition
Common securities	Interests or instruments that are commonly known as securities, such as common stock, preferred stock, debentures, and warrants.
Statutorily defined securities	Interests and instruments that are expressly mentioned in securities acts as being securities, such as interests in oil, gas, and mineral rights.
Investment contracts	A flexible standard for defining a security. Under the Howey test, a security exists if (1) an investor invests money (2) in a common enterprise and (3) expects to make a profit from the significant efforts of others.

Going Public: The Securities Act of 1933

Securities Act of 1933
A federal statute that primarily regulates the issuance of securities by corporations, partnerships, associations, and individuals.

issuer
A business or party that sells securities to the public.

The **Securities Act of 1933** primarily regulates the issuance of securities by a corporation, a limited partnership, other businesses, or an individual.[2] **Section 5** of the Securities Act of 1933 requires securities offered to the public through the use of the mails or any other facility of interstate commerce to be registered with the SEC by means of a registration statement and an accompanying prospectus.

The business or party selling the securities to the public is called the **issuer**. The issuer may be a relatively new company (e.g., Google, Inc.) selling securities to the public through an *initial public offering (IPO)*, or it may be an established company (e.g., Microsoft Corporation) selling new securities to the public. Many issuers of securities employ **investment bankers**, which are independent securities companies, to sell their securities to the public. Issuers pay a fee to investment bankers for this service.

Registration Statement

A covered issuer must file a written **registration statement** with the SEC. The issuer's lawyer normally prepares the statement, with the help of the issuer's management, accountants, and underwriters.

registration statement
A document that an issuer of securities files with the SEC that contains required information about the issuer, the securities to be issued, and other relevant information.

A registration statement must contain descriptions of (1) securities being offered for sale; (2) the registrant's business; (3) the management of the registrant, including compensation, stock options and benefits, and material transactions with the registrant; (4) pending litigation; (5) how the proceeds from the offering will be used; (6) government regulation; (7) the degree of competition in the industry; and (8) any special risk factors. In addition, a registration statement must be accompanied by financial statements certified by certified public accountants.

Registration statements usually become effective 20 business days after they are filed, unless the SEC requires additional information to be disclosed. A new 20-day period begins each time the registration statement is amended. At the registrant's request, the SEC may "accelerate the *effective date*" (i.e., not require the registrant to wait 20 days after the last amendment is filed).

The SEC does not pass judgment on the merits of the securities offered. It decides only whether the issuer has met the disclosure requirements.

Prospectus

A **prospectus** is a written disclosure document that must be submitted to the SEC along with the registration statement. A prospectus is used as a selling tool by the issuer. It is provided to prospective investors to enable them to evaluate the financial risk of an investment.

prospectus
A written disclosure document that must be submitted to the SEC along with the registration statement and given to prospective purchasers of the securities.

A prospectus must contain the following language in capital letters and boldface (usually red) type:

> THESE SECURITIES HAVE NOT BEEN APPROVED OR DISAPPROVED BY THE SECURITIES AND EXCHANGE COMMISSION OR ANY STATE SECURITIES COMMISSION NOR HAS THE SECURITIES AND EXCHANGE COMMISSION OR ANY STATE SECURITIES COMMISSION PASSED UPON THE ACCURACY OR ADEQUACY OF THIS PROSPECTUS. ANY REPRESENTATION TO THE CONTRARY IS A CRIMINAL OFFENSE.

Internet Law & Online Commerce

Going Public Over the Internet

The SEC permits companies to issue securities over the Internet. The same federal securities laws that regulate the traditional issuance of securities also apply to the issuance of securities using the Internet. One company's Internet initial public offering (IPO) follows:

(continued)

Internet Law & Online Commerce
(continued)

The information in this prospectus is not complete and may be changed. We may not sell these securities until the registration statement filed with the Securities and Exchange Commission is effective. This prospectus is not an offer to sell these securities and is not soliciting an offer to buy these securities in any state where the offer or sale is not permitted.

SUBJECT TO COMPLETION, DATED DECEMBER 21, 2000

Peet's Coffee & Tea™

PEET'S COFFEE & TEA, INC.

3,300,000 Shares
of Common Stock

This is our initial public offering and no public market currently exists for our shares. We expect that the public offering price will be between $10.00 and $14.00 per share. This price may not reflect the market price of our shares after this offering.

THE OFFERING	PER SHARE	TOTAL
Public Offering Price	$	$
Underwriting Discount	$	$
Proceeds to Peet's	$	$
Proceeds to Selling Shareholders	$	$

Of the 3,300,000 shares being offered, we are selling 2,500,000 shares and the selling shareholders identified in this prospectus are selling 800,000 shares. We will not receive any of the proceeds from the sale of shares by the selling shareholders. We have granted the underwriters the right to purchase up to 182,623 additional shares from us and 312,377 additional shares from the selling shareholders within 30 days to cover any over- allotments. The underwriters expect to deliver shares of common stock to purchasers on , 2001.

Proposed Nasdaq National Market Symbol: PEET

OPENIPO: The method of distribution being used by the underwriters in this offering differs somewhat from that traditionally employed in firm commitment underwritten public offerings. In particular, the public offering price and allocation of shares will be determined primarily by an auction process conducted by the underwriters and other securities dealers participating in this offering. A more detailed description of this process, known as an OpenIPO, is included in "Plan of Distribution."

THIS OFFERING INVOLVES A HIGH DEGREE OF RISK. YOU SHOULD PURCHASE SHARES ONLY IF YOU CAN AFFORD A COMPLETE LOSS OF YOUR INVESTMENT. SEE "RISK FACTORS" BEGINNING ON PAGE 5.

NEITHER THE SECURITIES AND EXCHANGE COMMISSION NOR ANY STATE SECURITIES COMMISSION HAS APPROVED OR DISAPPROVED OF THESE SECURITIES OR DETERMINED IF THIS PROSPECTUS IS TRUTHFUL OR COMPLETE. ANY REPRESENTATION TO THE CONTRARY IS A CRIMINAL OFFENSE.

WR**HAMBRECHT**+**CO**

Pacific Growth Equities, Inc.

The date of this prospectus is , 2001

Limitations on Activities During the Registration Process

Section 5 of the Securities Act of 1933 limits the types of activities that an issuer, an underwriter, and a dealer may engage in during the registration process. These limitations are divided into the following three time periods:

prefiling period

A period of time that begins when an issuer first contemplates issuing securities and ends when the registration statement is filed. The issuer may not *condition* the market during this period.

waiting period

A period of time that begins when a registration statement is filed with the SEC and continues until the registration statement is declared effective. Only certain activities are permissible during the waiting period.

1. ***The prefiling period.*** The **prefiling period** begins when the issuer first contemplates issuing the securities and ends when the registration statement is filed. During this time, the issuer cannot either sell or offer to sell the securities. The issuer also cannot *condition the market* for the upcoming securities offering. This rule makes it illegal for an issuer to engage in a public relations campaign (e.g., newspaper and magazine articles and advertisements) that touts the prospects of the company and the planned securities issue. However, sending annual reports to shareholders and making public announcements of factual matters (such as the settlement of a strike) are permissible because they are considered normal corporate disclosures.
2. ***The waiting period.*** The **waiting period** begins when the registration statement is filed with the SEC and continues until the registration statement is declared effective.

   The issuer is encouraged to condition the market during this time. Thus, the issuer may (1) make oral offers to sell (including face-to-face and telephone conversations);

(2) distribute a *preliminary prospectus* (usually called a *red herring*), which contains most of the information to be contained in the final prospectus except for price; (3) distribute a *summary prospectus*, which is a summary of the important terms contained in the prospectus; and (4) publish *tombstone ads* in newspapers and other publications. Unapproved writings (which are considered illegal offers to sell) as well as actual sales are prohibited during the waiting period.

3. ***The posteffective period.*** The **posteffective period** begins when the registration statement becomes effective and runs until the issuer either sells all the offered securities or withdraws them from sale. Thus, the issuer and its underwriters and dealers may close the offers received prior to the effective date and solicit new offers and sales.

   Prior to or at the time of confirming a sale or sending a security to a purchaser, the issuer (or its representative) must deliver a *final prospectus* (also called a *statutory prospectus*) to the investor. Failure to do so is a violation of Section 5. Tombstone ads are often used during this period.

posteffective period
The period of time that begins when a registration statement becomes effective and runs until the issuer either sells all the offered securities or withdraws them from sale.

The investor may rescind his or her purchase if the issuer violates any of the prohibitions on activities during these periods. If an underwriter or a dealer violates any of these prohibitions, the SEC may issue sanctions, including the suspension of securities licenses.

Sale of Unregistered Securities

Sale of securities that should have been registered with the SEC but were not violates the Securities Act of 1933. Investors can rescind their purchase and recover damages. The U.S. government can impose criminal penalties on any person who willfully violates the Securities Act of 1933.

Regulation A Offerings

Regulation A permits issuers to sell up to $5 million of securities to the public during a 12-month period pursuant to a simplified registration process. Such offerings may have an unlimited number of purchasers who do not have to be accredited investors. For offerings exceeding $100,000, an *offering statement* must be filed with the SEC. The offering statement requires less disclosure than a registration statement and is less costly to prepare. Investors must be provided with an offering circular prior to the purchase of securities. There are no resale restrictions on the securities.

Regulation A
A regulation that permits the issuer to sell securities pursuant to a simplified registration process.

Contemporary Trend

Small Corporate Offering Registration (SCOR) Form

Small businesses often need to raise capital and must find public investors to buy company stock. In 1992, after years of investigation, the SEC amended Regulation A by adopting the **Small Corporate Offering Registration (SCOR) Form**. The SCOR form—**Form U-7**—is a question-and-answer disclosure form that small businesses can complete and file with the SEC if they plan on raising $1 million or less from the public issue of securities. An issuer must answer the questions on Form U-7, which then becomes the offering circular that must be given to prospective investors.

Form U-7 questions are so clearly and specifically drawn that they can be answered by the issuer without the help of an expensive securities lawyer. The SCOR questions require the issuer to develop a business plan that states specific company goals and how it plans to reach them. SCOR is limited to domestic businesses. A SCOR offering cannot exceed $1 million, and the offering price of the common stock or its equivalent may not be less than $5 per share. SCOR offerings are a welcomed addition for entrepreneur-owners who want to raise money through a small public offering. ■

Violations of the Securities Act of 1933

Violations of the Securities Act of 1933 may result in various penalties and remedies against the perpetrator. These penalties and remedies are discussed in the following paragraphs.

Private Actions Private parties who have been injured by violations of the Securities Act of 1933 have recourse against the violator under the following two sections:

Section 12
A provision of the Securities Act of 1933 that imposes civil liability on any person who violates the provisions of Section 5 of the act.

Section 11
A provision of the Securities Act of 1933 that imposes civil liability on persons who intentionally defraud investors by making misrepresentations or omissions of material facts in a registration statement or who are negligent for not discovering the fraud.

1. **Section 12** of the 1933 act imposes *civil liability* on any person who violates the provisions of Section 5 of the act. Violations include selling securities pursuant to an unwarranted exemption and making misrepresentations concerning the offer or sale of securities. The purchaser's remedy for a violation of Section 12 is either to rescind the purchase or to sue for damages.
2. **Section 11** of the 1933 act provides for civil liability for damages when a registration statement on its effective date misstates or omits a material fact. Liability under Section 11 is imposed on those who (1) intentionally defraud investors or (2) are negligent in not discovering the fraud. Thus, the issuer, certain corporate officers (chief executive officer, chief financial officer, chief accounting officer), directors, signers of the registration statement, underwriters, and experts (accountants who certify financial statements and lawyers who issue legal opinions that are included in a registration statement) may be liable.

due diligence defense
A defense to a Section 11 action that, if proven, makes the defendant not liable.

All defendants except the issuer may assert a **due diligence defense** against the imposition of Section 11 liability. If this defense is proven, the defendant is not liable. To establish a due diligence defense, the defendant must prove that after reasonable investigation, he or she had reasonable grounds to believe and did believe that, at the time the registration statement became effective, the statements contained therein were true and there was no omission of material facts.

SEC Actions The SEC may (1) issue a *consent order* whereby a defendant agrees not to violate securities laws in the future but does not admit to having violated securities laws in the past, (2) bring an action in federal district court to obtain an *injunction*, or (3) request the court to grant ancillary relief, such as *disgorgement of profits* by the defendant.

Section 24
A provision of the Securities Act of 1933 that imposes criminal liability on any person who willfully violates the 1933 act or the rules or regulations adopted thereunder.

Criminal Liability **Section 24** of the Securities Act of 1933 imposes *criminal liability* on any person who *willfully* violates either the act or the rules and regulations adopted thereunder.[3] A violator may be fined up to $10,000 or imprisoned up to five years, or both. Criminal actions are brought by the Department of Justice.

The following is a classic case in which the court imposed civil liability for a violation of the Securities Act of 1933.

Case 27.2
Securities Act of 1933

Escott v. BarChris Construction Corp.

283 F.Supp. 643, 1968 U.S.Dist. Lexis 3853
United States District Court, Southern District of New York

Background and Facts

In 1961, BarChris Construction Corp. (BarChris), a company primarily engaged in the construction and sale of bowling alleys, was in need of additional financing. To raise working capital, BarChris decided to issue debentures to investors. A registration statement, including a prospectus, was filed with the SEC on March 30, 1961. After two amendments, the registration statement became effective May 16, 1961. Peat, Marwick, Mitchell & Co. (Peat, Marwick) audited the financial statements of the company that were included in the registration statement and prospectus. The debentures were sold by May 24, 1961. Investors were provided a final prospectus concerning the debentures. Unbeknownst to the investors, however, the registration statement and prospectus contained the following material misrepresentations and omissions of material fact:

1. Current assets on the 1960 balance sheet were overstated by $609,689 (15 percent).

2. Contingent liabilities as of April 30, 1961, were understated by $618,853 (42 percent).
3. Sales for the quarter ending March 31, 1961, were overstated by $519,810 (32 percent).
4. Gross profits for the quarter ending March 31, 1961, were overstated by $230,755 (92 percent).
5. The backlog of orders as of March 31, 1961, was overstated by $4,490,000 (186 percent).
6. Loans to officers of BarChris of $386,615 were not disclosed.
7. Customer delinquencies and BarChris's potential liability thereto of $1,350,000 were not disclosed.
8. The use of the proceeds of the debentures to pay old debts was not disclosed.

In 1961, BarChris was failing financially, and on October 29, 1962, it filed a petition for protection to be reorganized under federal bankruptcy law. On November 1, 1962, BarChris defaulted on interest payments due to be paid on the debentures to investors. Barry Escott and other purchasers of the debentures brought this civil action against executive officers, directors, and the outside accountants of BarChris. The plaintiffs alleged that the defendants had violated Section 11 of the Securities Act of 1933 by submitting misrepresentations and omissions of material facts in the registration statement filed with the SEC.

Issue

Are the defendants liable for violating Section 11, or have they proved their due diligence defense?

In the Language of the Court

I turn now to the question of whether defendants have proved their due diligence defenses.

Russo Russo was, for all intents and purposes, the chief executive officer of BarChris. He was a member of the executive committee. He was familiar with all aspects of the business. He was thoroughly aware of BarChris's stringent financial condition in May 1961. In short, Russo knew all the relevant facts. He could not have believed that there were no untrue statements or material omissions in the prospectus. Russo has no due diligence defenses.

Vitolo and Pugliese They were the founders of the business. Vitolo was president and Pugliese was vice president. Vitolo and Pugliese each are men of limited education. It is not hard to believe that for them the prospectus was difficult reading, if indeed they read it at all. But whether it was or not is irrelevant. The liability of a director who signs a registration statement does not depend upon whether or not he read it or, if he did, whether or not he understood what he was reading. And in any case, there is nothing to show that they made any investigation of anything that they may not have known about or understood. They have not proved their due diligence defenses.

Trilling Trilling was BarChris's controller. He signed the registration statement in that capacity, although he was not a director. He was a comparatively minor figure in BarChris. He was not considered an executive officer. Trilling may well have been unaware of several of the inaccuracies in the prospectus. But he must have known of some of them. As a financial officer, he was familiar with BarChris's finances and with its books of account. Trilling did not sustain the burden of proving his due diligence defenses.

Peat, Marwick Peat, Marwick's work was in general charge of a member of the firm, Cummings, and more immediately in charge of Peat, Marwick's manager, Logan. Most of the actual work was performed by a senior accountant, Berardi, who has junior assistants, one of whom was Kennedy. Berardi was then about 30 years old. He was not yet a CPA. He had no previous experience with the bowling industry. This was his first job as a senior accountant. He could hardly have been given a more difficult assignment.

Berardi made the S-1 review in May 1961. He devoted a little over two days to it, a total of 20 1/2 hours. He did not discover any of the errors or omissions pertaining to the state of affairs in 1961, all of which were material. In conducting the S-1 review, Berardi did not examine any important financial records other than the trial balance. He asked questions, he got answers that he considered satisfactory, and he did nothing to verify them.

Accountants should not be held to a standard higher than that recognized in their profession. Berardi's review did not come up to that standard. He did not take some of the steps that Peat, Marwick's written program prescribed. He did not spend an adequate amount of time on a task of this magnitude. Most important of all, he was too easily satisfied with glib answers to his inquiries. There were enough danger signals to require some further investigation on his part. Generally accepted accounting standards required such further investigation under these circumstances. Peat, Marwick has not established its due diligence defense.

Decision and Remedy

The district court held that the defendants had failed to prove their due diligence defenses.

Business and Ethics Questions

1. Should defendants in a Section 11 lawsuit be permitted to prove a due diligence defense to the imposition of liability? Or should liability be strictly imposed?
2. Who do you think committed the fraud in this case? Did any of the other defendants act unethically?
3. Who do you think bore the burden of paying the judgment in this case?

Private and Other Transactions Exempt from Registration

Certain transactions in securities are exempt from registration. Exempt transactions are subject to the antifraud provisions of the federal securities laws. Therefore, the issuer must provide investors with adequate information—including annual reports, quarterly reports, proxy statements, financial statements, and so on—even though a registration statement is not required. The exempt transactions are discussed in the paragraphs that follow.

Nonissuer Exemption

Nonissuers, such as average investors, do not have to file a registration statement prior to reselling securities they have purchased. This is because the Securities Act of 1933 exempts from registration securities transactions not made by an issuer, an underwriter, or a dealer. For example, an investor who owns shares of IBM can resell those shares to another at any time without having to register with the SEC.

Intrastate Offerings

intrastate offering exemption
An exemption from registration that permits local businesses to raise capital from local investors to be used in the local economy without the need to register with the SEC.

The purpose of the **intrastate offerings exemption** is to permit local businesses to raise from local investors capital to be used in the local economy without the need to register with the SEC.[4] There is no limit on the dollar amount of capital that can be raised pursuant to an intrastate offering exemption. An issuer can qualify for this exemption in only one state.

Three requirements must be met to qualify for this exemption[5]:

1. The issuer must be a resident of the state for which the exemption is claimed. A corporation is a resident of the state in which it is incorporated.
2. The issuer must be doing business in that state. This requires that 80 percent of the issuer's assets be located in the state, 80 percent of its gross revenues be derived from the state, its principal office be located in the state, and 80 percent of the proceeds of the offering be used in the state.
3. The purchasers of the securities all must be residents of that state.

Private Placements

private placement exemption
An exemption from registration that permits issuers to raise capital from an unlimited number of accredited investors and no more than 35 nonaccredited investors without having to register the offering with the SEC.

An issue of securities that does not involve a public offering is exempt from the registration requirements.[6] This exemption—known as the **private placement exemption**—allows issuers to raise capital from an unlimited number of accredited investors without having to register the offering with the SEC.[7] There is no dollar limit on the amount of securities that can be sold pursuant to this exemption.

An *accredited investor* may be[8]:

1. Any natural person (including spouse) who has a net worth of at least $1 million
2. Any natural person who has had an annual income of at least $200,000 per year for the previous two years and reasonably expects to make $200,000 income in the current year
3. Any corporation, partnership, or business trust with total assets in excess of $5 million
4. Insiders of the issuers, such as executive officers and directors of corporate issuers and general partners of partnership issuers
5. Certain institutional investors, such as registered investment companies, pension plans, colleges and universities, and the like

No more than 35 *nonaccredited investors* may purchase securities pursuant to a private placement exemption. Nonaccredited investors must be sophisticated investors, however, either through their own experience and education or through representatives (such as accountants, lawyers, and business managers). General selling efforts, such as advertising to the public, are not permitted.

Small Offerings

Securities offerings that do not exceed a certain dollar amount are exempt from registration.[9] Rule 504 exempts from registration the sale of securities not exceeding $1 million during a 12-month period. The securities may be sold to an unlimited number of accredited and unaccredited investors, but general selling efforts to the public are not permitted. This is called the **small offering exemption**.

small offering exemption
An exemption from registration for the sale of securities not exceeding $1 million during a 12-month period.

Resale Restrictions

Certain *resale restrictions* are placed on securities issued pursuant to exemptions from registration. These restrictions are discussed in the following paragraphs.

Restricted Securities Securities sold pursuant to the intrastate, private placement, or small offering exemptions are called **restricted securities** because they cannot be resold for a limited period of time after their initial issue. The following restrictions apply:

restricted securities
Securities that are issued for investment purposes pursuant to the intrastate, private placement, or small offering exemption.

- Rule 147 stipulates that securities sold pursuant to an intrastate offering exemption cannot be sold to nonresidents for a period of nine months.
- Rule 144 provides that securities sold pursuant to the private placement or small offering exemption must be held for one year from the date when the securities are last sold by the issuer. After that time, investors may sell the greater of (1) one percent of the outstanding securities of the issuer or (2) the average weekly volume of trading in the securities (i.e., the four-week moving average) in any three-month period. Information about the issuer must be available to the public. Generally, all restrictions are lifted after two years.

Preventing Transfer of Restricted Securities To protect the nontransferability of restricted shares, the issuer must:

- Require the investors to sign an *affidavit* stating that they are buying the securities for investment, acknowledging that they are purchasing restricted securities, and promising not to transfer the shares in violation of the restriction.
- Place a *legend* on the stock certificate describing the restriction.
- Notify the *transfer agent* not to record a transfer of the securities that would violate the restriction.

If the issuer has taken these precautions, it will not lose its exemption from registration even if isolated transfers of stock occur in violation of the restricted period. If these precautions are not taken, the issuer may lose its exemption from registration. In that event, it has sold unregistered securities in violation of Section 5, permitting all purchasers to rescind their purchases of the securities.

Rule 144A

To establish a more liquid and efficient secondary market in unregistered securities, the SEC adopted Rule 144A. This rule permits "qualified institutional investors"—defined as institutions that own and invest at least $100 million in securities—to buy unregistered securities without being subject to the holding periods of Rule 144. This rule is designed to create an institutional market in unregistered securities as well as to permit foreign issuers to raise capital in this country from sophisticated investors without making registration process disclosures.

Exhibit 27.1
Securities Exempt from Registration

Certain *securities* are exempt from registration. Once a security is exempt, it is exempt forever. It does not matter how many times the security is transferred. Exempt securities include:

1. Securities issued by any government in the United States (e.g., municipal bonds issued by city governments)
2. Short-term notes and drafts that have a maturity date that does not exceed nine months (e.g., commercial paper issued by corporations)
3. Securities issued by nonprofit issuers, such as religious institutions, charitable institutions, and colleges and universities
4. Securities of financial institutions (e.g., banks and savings associations) that are regulated by the appropriate banking authorities
5. Securities issued by common carriers (railroads and trucking companies) that are regulated by the Interstate Commerce Commission (ICC)
6. Insurance and annuity contracts issued by insurance companies
7. Stock dividends and stock splits
8. Securities issued in a corporate reorganization where one security is exchanged for another security

Trading in Securities: The Securities Exchange Act of 1934

Securities Exchange Act of 1934
A federal statute that primarily regulates the trading in securities.

Unlike the Securities Act of 1933, which regulates the original issuance of securities, the **Securities Exchange Act of 1934** primarily regulates the subsequent trading.[10] It provides for the registration of certain companies with the SEC, the continuous filing of periodic reports by these companies to the SEC, and the regulation of securities exchanges, brokers, and dealers. It also contains provisions that assess civil and criminal liability on violators of the 1934 act and rules and regulations adopted thereunder.

Section 10(b) and Rule 10b-5

Section 10(b)
A provision of the Securities Exchange Act of 1934 that prohibits the use of manipulative and deceptive devices in the purchase or sale of securities in contravention of the rules and regulations prescribed by the SEC.

Rule 10b-5
A rule adopted by the SEC to clarify the reach of Section 10(b) against deceptive and fraudulent activities in the purchase and sale of securities.

Section 10(b) is one of the most important sections in the entire 1934 act. It prohibits the use of manipulative and deceptive devices in contravention of the rules and regulations prescribed by the SEC.

Pursuant to its rule-making authority, the SEC has adopted **Rule 10b-5**, which provides that:

> It shall be unlawful for any person, directly or indirectly, by use of any means or instrumentality of interstate commerce or of the mails, or of any facility of any national securities exchange,
> a. to employ any device, scheme, or artifice to defraud,
> b. to make any untrue statement of a material fact or to omit to state a material fact necessary in order to make the statements made, in light of the circumstances under which they were made, not misleading, or
> c. to engage in any act, practice, or course of business that operates or would operate as a fraud or deceit upon any person, in connection with the purchase or sale of any security.

Rule 10b-5 is not restricted to purchases and sales of securities of reporting companies.[11] All transfers of securities, whether made on a stock exchange, in the over-the-counter market, in a private sale, or in connection with a merger, are subject to this rule.[12] The U.S. Supreme Court has held that only conduct involving **scienter** (intentional conduct) violates Section 10(b) and Rule 10b-5. Negligent conduct is not a violation.[13]

Section 10(b) and Rule 10-b5 require reliance by the injured party on the misstatement. However, many sales and purchases of securities occur in open market transactions (e.g., over stock exchanges) where there is no direct communication between the buyer and the seller.

scienter
Intentional conduct, which is required for there to be a violation of Section 10(b) and Rule 10b-5.

Insider Trading

One of the most important purposes of Section 10(b) and Rule 10b-5 is to prevent **insider trading**. Insider trading occurs when a company employee or company advisor uses material nonpublic information to make a profit by trading in the securities of the company. This practice is illegal because it allows insiders to take advantage of the investing public.

In the *Matter of Cody, Roberts & Co.*,[14] the SEC announced that the duty of an insider who possesses material nonpublic information is to either (1) abstain from trading in the securities of the company or (2) disclose the information to the person on the other side of the transaction before the insider purchases the securities from or sells the securities to him or her.

insider trading
A situation in which an insider makes a profit by personally purchasing shares of a corporation prior to public release of favorable information or by selling shares of a corporation prior to the public disclosure of unfavorable information.

Insiders

For purposes of Section 10(b) and Rule 10b-5, *insiders* are defined as (1) officers, directors, and employees at all levels of a company; (2) lawyers, accountants, consultants, and other agents and representatives who are hired by a company on a temporary and non-employee basis to provide services or work to the company; and (3) others who owe a fiduciary duty to the company.

Consider This Example The Widget Corporation has its annual audit done by its outside CPAs, Ernest & Old, CPAs. Peter is one of the CPAs who conduct the audit. The audit discloses that the Widget Corporation's profits have doubled since last year, and Peter rightfully discloses this fact to Martha, the chief financial officer (CFO) of Widget Corporation. Both Martha and Peter are *insiders*. The earnings information is definitely *material*, and it is *nonpublic* until the corporation publicly announces its earnings in two days. Prior to the earnings information being made public, Peter and Martha buy stock in Widget Corporation at $100 per share. After the earnings information is made public, the stock of Widget Corporation increases to $150 per share. Both Peter and Martha are liable for insider trading in violation of Section 10(b) and Rule 10b-5 because they traded in the securities of Widget Corporation while in possession of inside information.

"He will lie, sir, with such volubility that you would think truth were a fool."

William Shakespeare
All's Well That Ends Well (1604)

The following two cases illustrate insider trading.

Case 27.3 Insider Trading

Securities and Exchange Commission v. Texas Gulf Sulpher Co.
401 F.2d 833 1968 U.S.App. Lexis 5797
United States Court of Appeals, Second Circuit

Background and Facts

On November 12, 1963, Texas Gulf Sulpher Co. (TGS), a mining company, drilled an exploratory hole—Kidd 55—near Timmins, Ontario. Assay reports showed that the core from this drilling proved to be remarkably high in copper, zinc, and silver. TGS kept the discovery secret, camouflaged the drill site, and diverted

(*continued*)

Securities and Exchange Commission v. Texas Gulf Sulpher Co.

401 F.2d 833 1968 U.S.App. Lexis 5797
United States Court of Appeals, Second Circuit
(*continued*)

drilling efforts to another site to allow TGS to acquire land around Kidd 55. In November, 1963, TGS stock traded at $18 per share.

Eventually, rumors of a rich mineral strike began circulating. On Saturday, April 11, 1964, the *New York Times* published an unauthorized report of TGS drilling efforts in Canada and its rich mineral strike. On Sunday, April 12, officers of TGS drafted a press release that was issued that afternoon. The press released appeared in morning newspapers of general circulation on Monday, April 13. It read, in pertinent part: "The work done to date has not been sufficient to reach definite conclusions and any statement as to size and grade of ore would be premature and possibly misleading."

The rumors persisted. On April 16, 1964, at 10:00 A.M., TGS held a press conference for the financial media. At the time of the press conference, TGS stock was trading at $37 per share. At this press conference, which lasted about 10 minutes, TGS disclosed the richness of the Timmins mineral strike and that the strike should run to at least 25 million tons in ore. Several officers, directors, and other employees of TGS who had knowledge of the mineral strike at Timmins had traded in the stock of TGS during the period November 13, 1963, to April 16, 1964. By May 15, 1964, the stock was selling at $58.

The SEC brought an action against several of these executives for insider trading in violation of Section 10(b) of the Securities Exchange Act of 1934. The SEC sought to rescind their stock purchases. The district court held against most of these executives, who then appealed.

Issue

Are the defendant executives liable for engaging in insider trading?

In the Language of the Court

The insiders here were not trading on an equal footing with the outside investors. They alone were in a position to evaluate the probability and magnitude of what seemed from the outset to be a major ore strike.

Crawford Crawford telephoned his orders to his Chicago broker about midnight on April 15 and again at 8:30 in the morning of April 16 with instructions to buy at the opening of the Midwest Stock Exchange that morning. The trial court's finding that "he sought to, and did, 'beat the news,'" is well documented by the record. Before insiders may act upon material information, such information must have been effectively disclosed in a manner sufficient to ensure its availability to the investing public. Particularly here, where a formal announcement to the entire financial news media had been promised in a prior official release known to the media, all insider activity must await dissemination of the promised official announcement.

Coates Coates was absolved by the court below because his telephone order was placed shortly before 10:20 A.M. on April 16, which was after the announcement had been made even though the news could not be considered already a matter of public information. This result seems to have been predicated upon a misinterpretation of dicta in Cody Roberts, where the SEC instructed insiders to "keep out of the market until the established procedures for public release of the information are carried out instead of hastening to execute transactions in advance of, and in frustration of, the objectives of the release." The reading of a news release, which prompted Coates into action, is merely the first step in the process of dissemination required for compliance with the regulatory objective of providing all investors with an equal opportunity to make informed investment judgments. Assuming that the contents of the official release could instantaneously be acted upon, at the minimum Coates should have waited until the news could reasonably have been expected to appear over the media of widest circulation, rather than hastening to ensure an advantage to himself and his broker son-in-law.

Decision and Remedy

The Court of Appeals held that the executives in this case had engaged in illegal insider trading.

Business and Ethics Questions

1. Should insider trading be illegal? Why or why not?
2. Did the inside executives act ethically in this case?
3. How can businesses protect against their employees engaging in insider trading? Explain.

Case 27.4 Misappropriation Theory

U.S. SUPREME COURT

United States v. O'Hagan

521 U.S. 642, 117 S.Ct. 2199, 1997 U.S. Lexis 4033
Supreme Court of the United States

Background and Facts

James O'Hagan was a partner in the law firm Dorsey & Whitney in Minneapolis, Minnesota. In July 1988, Grand Metropolitan PLC (Grand Met), a company based in London, England, hired Dorsey & Whitney to represent it in a secret tender offer for the stock of the Pillsbury Company, headquartered in Minneapolis. On August 18,

1988, O'Hagan began purchasing call options for Pillsbury stock. Each call option gave O'Hagan the right to purchase 100 shares of Pillsbury stock at a specified price. O'Hagan continued to purchase call options in August and September, and he became the largest holder of call options for Pillsbury stock. In September, O'Hagan also purchased 5,000 shares of Pillsbury common stock at $39 per share. These purchases were all made while Grand Met's proposed tender offer for Pillsbury remained secret to the public. When Grand Met publicly announced its tender offer in October 1988, Pillsbury stock increased to nearly $60 per share. O'Hagan sold his Pillsbury call options and common stock, making a profit of more than $4.3 million.

The U.S. Department of Justice charged O'Hagan with criminally violating Section 10(b) and Rule 10b-5. This was not a case of classic insider trading because O'Hagan did not trade in the stock of his law firm's client, Grand Met; therefore, the government alleged that O'Hagan was liable under the "misappropriation theory" for trading in Pillsbury stock by engaging in deceptive conduct by misappropriating the secret information about Grand Met's tender offer from his employer, Dorsey & Whitney, and from its client, Grand Met. The district court found O'Hagan guilty and sentenced him to 41 months in prison. The Eighth Circuit Court of Appeals reversed, finding that liability under Section 10(b) and Rule 10b-5 cannot be based on the misappropriation theory. The government appealed to the U.S. Supreme Court.

Issue

Can a defendant be criminally convicted of violating Section 10(b) and Rule 10b-5 based on the misappropriation theory?

In the Language of the U.S. Supreme Court

The "misappropriation theory" holds that a person commits fraud "in connection with" a securities transaction, and thereby violates Section 10(b) and Rule 10b-5, when he misappropriates confidential information for securities trading purposes, in breach of a duty owed to the source of the information. Under this theory, a fiduciary's undisclosed, self-serving use of a principal's information to purchase or sell securities, in breach of a duty of loyalty and confidentiality, defrauds the principal of the exclusive use of that information.

The classical theory targets a corporate insider's breach of duty to shareholders with whom the insider transacts; the misappropriation theory outlaws trading on the basis of nonpublic information by a corporate "outsider" in breach of a duty owed not to a trading party, but to the source of the information. The misappropriation theory comports with Section 10(b)'s language, which requires deception "in connection with the purchase or sale of any security."

Decision and Remedy

The U.S. Supreme Court held that a defendant can be criminally convicted of violating Section 10(b) and Rule 10b-5 under the misappropriation theory. The U.S. Supreme Court reversed the decision of the Court of Appeals.

Business and Ethics Questions

1. Should the misappropriation theory be recognized as a basis for criminal liability under Section 10(b) and Rule 10b-5? Do you agree with the Supreme Court's decision in this case?
2. If the Supreme Court had upheld the decision of the Court of Appeals, would ethics alone be enough to prevent persons like O'Hagan from trading on secret information?
3. Will the securities markets be more or less honest because of the Supreme Court's ruling in this case?

Tipper–Tippee Liability

A person who discloses material nonpublic information to another person is called a **tipper**. A person who receives such information is known as a **tippee**. A tippee is liable for acting on material information that he or she knew or should have known was not public. The tipper is liable for the profits made by the tippee. If the tippee tips other persons, both the tippee (who is now a tipper) and the original tipper are liable for the profits made by these remote tippees. The remote tippees are liable for their own trades if they knew or should have known that they possessed material inside information.

tipper
A person who discloses material nonpublic information to another person.

tippee
A person who receives material nonpublic information from a tipper.

Violations of the Securities Exchange Act of 1934

The civil and criminal penalties that may be assessed for violations of the Securities Exchange Act of 1934 are discussed in the following paragraphs:

- ***Private actions.*** Although Section 10(b) and Rule 10b-5 do not expressly provide for a private right of action, courts have implied such a right. Generally, a private plaintiff may seek rescission of the securities contract or recover damages (e.g., disgorgements of the illegal profits by the defendants). Private securities fraud claims

Fraud includes the pretense of knowledge when knowledge there is none.

C. J. Cardozo
Ultramares Corp. v. Touche (1931)

must be brought within two years after discovery or five years after the violation occurs, whichever is shorter.

- ***SEC actions.*** The SEC may investigate suspected violations of the Securities Exchange Act of 1934 and the rules and regulations adopted thereunder. The SEC may enter into *consent orders* with defendants, seek *injunctions* in federal district court, or seek court orders requiring defendants to *disgorge* illegally gained profits.

  In 1984, Congress enacted the **Insider Trading Sanctions Act,**[15] which permits the SEC to obtain a *civil penalty* of up to three times the illegal profits gained or losses avoided on insider trading. The fine is payable to the U.S. Treasury.

Insider Trading Sanctions Act
A federal statute that permits the SEC to obtain a civil penalty of up to three times the illegal benefits received from insider trading.

Section 32
A provision of the Securities Exchange Act of 1934 that imposes criminal liability on any person who willfully violates the 1934 act or the rules or regulations adopted thereunder.

- ***Criminal liability.*** **Section 32** of the Securities Exchange Act of 1934 makes it a criminal offense to violate willfully the provisions of the act or the rules and regulations adopted thereunder.[16] Under the Sarbanes-Oxley Act of 2002, a person who willfully violates the Securities Exchange Act of 1934 can be fined up to $5 million or imprisoned for up to 25 years, or both. A corporation or another entity may be fined up to $2.5 million.
- ***Sarbanes-Oxley Act.*** The SEC may issue an order prohibiting any person who has committed securities fraud from acting as an officer or a director of a public company.

Short-Swing Profits

Section 16(a)
A provision of the Securities Exchange Act of 1934 that defines any person who is an executive officer, a director, or a 10 percent shareholder of an equity security of a reporting company as a *statutory insider* for Section 16 purposes.

Section 16(a) of the 1934 act defines any person who is an executive officer, a director, or a 10 percent shareholder of an equity security of a reporting company as a *statutory insider* for Section 16 purposes. Statutory insiders must file reports with the SEC, disclosing their ownership and trading in the company's securities.[17] These reports must be filed with the SEC and made available on the company's Web site within two days after such a trade occurs.

Section 16(b)

Section 16(b)
A provision of the Securities Exchange Act of 1934 that requires that any profits made by a statutory insider on transactions involving *short-swing profits* belong to the corporation.

Section 16(b) requires that any profits made by a statutory insider on transactions involving *short-swing profits*—that is, trades involving equity securities occurring within six months of each other—belong to the corporation.[18] The corporation may bring a legal action to recover these profits. Involuntary transactions, such as forced redemption of securities by the corporation or an exchange of securities in a bankruptcy proceeding, are exempt. Section 16(b) is a strict liability provision. Generally, no defenses are recognized. Neither intent nor the possession of inside information need be shown.

Consider This Example Rosanne is the president of a corporation and a statutory insider who does not possess any inside information. On February 1, she purchases 1,000 shares of her employer's stock at $10 per share. On June 1, she sells the stock for $14 per share. The corporation can recover the $4,000 profit because the trades occurred within six months of each other. Rosanne would have to wait until after August 1 to sell the securities.

SEC Section 16 Rules

The SEC has adopted the following rules concerning Section 16:

- Clarify the definitions of *officer* to include only executive officers who perform policymaking functions. This would include the president, the chief executive officer, the vice presidents in charge of business units or divisions, the principal financial officer, the principal accounting officer, and the like. Officers who run day-to-day operations but are not responsible for policy decisions are not included.

- Relieve insiders of liability for transactions that occur within six months before becoming an insider. For example, if a noninsider buys shares of his or her company January 15, becomes an insider March 15, and sells the shares May 15, the January 15 purchase is not matched against the May 15 sales.
- Continue the rule that insiders are liable for transactions that occur within six months of the last transaction engaged in while an insider. For example, if an insider buys shares in his or her company April 30 and leaves the company May 15, this purchase must be matched against any sale of the company's shares that occurs on or before October 30.

Concept Summary *Section 10(b) and Section 16(b) Compared*

Element	Section 10(b) and Rule 10b-5	Section 16(b)
Covered securities	All securities.	Securities required to be registered with the SEC under the 1934 act.
Inside information	Defendant made a misrepresentation or traded on inside (or perhaps misappropriated) information.	Short-swing profits recoverable whether or not they are attributable to misappropriation or inside information.
Recovery	Belongs to the injured purchaser or seller.	Belongs to the corporation.

State Securities Laws

Most states have enacted securities laws. These laws, which are often called *blue-sky laws*, generally require the registration of certain securities and provide exemptions from registration. They also contain broad antifraud provisions. The **Uniform Securities Act** has been adopted by many states. This act is drafted to coordinate state securities laws with federal securities laws.

Ethics in Business

Sarbanes-Oxley Act Erects a Wall Between Investment Bankers and Security Analysis

Investment banking is a service provided by many securities firms, whereby they assist companies to "go public" when issuing shares to the public and otherwise selling securities. The securities firms are paid lucrative fees for providing investment banking services in assisting companies to sell their securities and finding customers to purchase these securities. These same securities firms often provide securities analysis, whereby they provide investment advice, recommending securities listed on the stock exchanges and other securities to be purchased by the public.

In the late 1990s and early 2000s, many conflicts of interest were uncovered. Investment bankers and securities analysts of the same firm shared information, and the analysts were paid or pressured by the securities firms to write glowing reports of companies that the investment bankers of the firm were earning fees from.

Congress sought to remedy this problem by enacting Section 501 of the Sarbanes-Oxley Act of 2002. Section 501 established rules for separating the investment banking and

(continued)

Ethics in Business (continued)

securities advice functions of securities firms, thus eliminating many conflicts of interest:

- Securities firms must establish structural and institutional "walls" between their investment banking and securities analysis areas. These walls must protect analysts from review, pressure, and oversight by persons employed by the investment banking area of the securities firm.
- Securities analysts must disclose in each research report or public appearance any conflicts of interest that are known or should have been known to exist at the time of publication or public appearance.

The SEC is empowered to adopt rules to enforce the provisions of Section 501.

Ethics Issues

1. Why did investment bankers of a securities firm put pressure on analysts to issue positive reports on certain companies? Was this conduct ethical?
2. Do you think Section 501 will prevent such conduct in the future? Why or why not?

Beijing, China. Foreign securities markets have developed in many countries. Each country has its own securities laws. For example, China is developing securities laws to regulate its developing securities markets.

Terms and Concepts

The Securities and Exchange Commission (SEC)

Created in 1934, the SEC is a federal administrative agency empowered to administer federal securities laws. The SEC can adopt rules and regulations to interpret and implement federal securities.

Definition of *Security*

A *security* must be found before federal securities laws apply. A *security* is defined as:

1. ***Common securities.*** These are interests or instruments that are commonly known as securities, such as common stock, preferred stock, debentures, and warrants.
2. ***Statutorily defined securities.*** These are interests and instruments that are expressly mentioned in securities acts as being securities, such as interests in oil, gas, and mineral rights.

3. ***Investment contracts.*** In investment contracts, there is a flexible standard for defining a security. Under the Howey test, a security exists if (1) an investor invests money (2) in a common enterprise and (3) expects to make a profit off the significant efforts of others.

Going Public: The Securities Act of 1933

The Securities Act of 1933 is a federal statute that primarily regulates the *issuance* of securities by corporations, partnerships, associations, and individuals.

Registration Statement

1. ***Section 5.*** Section 5 is a provision of the 1933 act that requires an issuer to register its securities with the SEC prior to selling them to the public if the securities or transaction does not qualify for an exemption from registration.
2. ***Registration statement.*** A registration statement is a document that an issuer of securities files with the SEC to register its securities. It must contain information about the issuer, the securities to be issued, and other relevant information.

Prospectus

A prospectus is a written disclosure document that is submitted to the SEC with the registration statement. It is distributed to prospective investors to enable them to evaluate the financial risk of the investment.

Limitations on Activities During the Registration Process

1. ***Prefiling period.*** The prefiling period begins when the issuer first contemplates issuing securities and ends when the registration statement is filed with the SEC. During this period, the issuer cannot (1) offer to sell securities, (2) sell securities, or (3) condition the market.
2. ***Waiting period.*** The waiting period begins when the registration statement is filed with the SEC and ends when the registration statement becomes effective. During this time, the issuer cannot (1) sell securities or (2) use unapproved writing to offer to sell the securities. The issuer may make oral offers, distribute *preliminary* and *summary prospectuses*, and publish *tombstone ads*.
3. ***Posteffective period.*** The posteffective period begins when the registration statement becomes effective and runs until the issuer either sells all of the offered securities or withdraws them from sale. The issuer may offer to sell the securities during this period. The issuer must deliver a *final prospectus* (*statutory prospectus*) to a purchaser prior to or at the time of confirming the sale or sending the security to the purchaser.

Regulation A Offerings

Regulation A is a regulation that permits an issuer to sell securities pursuant to a simplified registration process.

Small Corporate Offering Registration (SCOR) Form

Form U-7 is a question-and-answer disclosure form that permits small businesses to raise $1 million or less from the public issue of securities.

Liability Provisions of the Securities Act of 1933

1. ***Private actions.*** Private parties who have been injured by a violation of the 1933 act may sue the violator to rescind the securities contract or recover damages. The plaintiff may sue under:
   a. *Section 12.* Section 12 is a provision of the 1933 act that imposes civil liability on any person who violates the provisions of Section 5 of the act (e.g., sells unregistered securities).
   b. *Section 11.* Section 11 is a provision of the 1933 act that imposes civil liability on persons who intentionally defraud investors by making misrepresentations or omissions of material facts in the registration statement or are negligent in not discovering the fraud.
      i. *Due diligence defense.* The due diligence defense is a defense to a Section 11 action that, if proven, makes the defendant not liable. This requires the defendant to have made a reasonable investigation and had reasonable grounds to believe and did believe that the statements made in the registration statement were true.

2. ***SEC actions.*** The SEC may seek the following remedies:
   a. *Consent order.* The SEC may issue a consent order whereby a defendant agrees not to violate securities laws in the future but does not admit to having violated securities laws in the past.
   b. *Injunction.* The SEC may bring an action in federal district court to obtain an injunction.
   c. *Disgorgement of profits.* The SEC may request the court to order the defendant to disgorge illegally gained profits.
3. ***Criminal liability.*** *Section 24* of the 1933 act imposes criminal liability on any person who willfully violates either the act or the rules and regulations adopted thereunder. Criminal actions are brought by the U.S. Department of Justice.

Transactions Exempt from Registration

The following transactions are exempt from the SEC registration process:

1. ***Nonissuer exemption.*** Securities transactions *not* by an issuer, an underwriter, or a dealer are exempt from SEC registration. This covers normal purchases of securities by investors.
2. ***Intrastate offerings.*** A local business can issue securities without dollar limit without registering with the SEC if the following requirements are met:
   a. The issuer is a resident of the state (e.g., the corporation is incorporated in the state).
   b. The issuer is doing business in the state. This requires that:
      i. 80 percent of the issuer's assets are located in the state.
      ii. 80 percent of the issuer's gross revenues are derived from the state.
      iii. The issuer's principal office is located in the state.
      iv. 80 percent of the proceeds of the offering will be used in the state.
   c. The purchasers of the securities all are residents of the state.
3. ***Private placements.*** An issue of securities that does not involve a public offering is exempt from SEC registration. There is no dollar limit on the amount of securities that can be issued pursuant to this exemption. Securities can be sold to any number of *accredited investors* and to no more than 35 *nonaccredited investors.*
   a. *Accredited investors.* Accredited investors include:
      i. Any natural person (including spouse) who has a net worth of at least $1 million
      ii. Any natural person who has had an annual income of at least $200,000 per year for the previous two years and reasonably expects to make $200,000 income in the current year
      iii. Any corporation, partnership, or business trust with total assets in excess of $5 million
      iv. Insiders of the issuers, such as executive officers and directors of corporate issuers and general partners of partnership issuers
      v. Certain institutional investors, such as registered investment companies, pension plans, colleges and universities, and the like
4. ***Small offerings.*** An offering of securities that does not exceed $1 million during a 12-month period is exempt from SEC registration. The securities may be sold to any number of purchasers.

Resale Restrictions

1. ***Restricted securities.*** Securities sold pursuant to the intrastate, private placement, or small offering exemptions are called *restricted securities.*
2. ***Rule 147.*** Rule 147 is an SEC rule, which stipulates that securities sold pursuant to an *intrastate offering exemption* cannot be sold to nonresidents for a period of nine months.
3. ***Rule 144.*** Rule 144 is an SEC rule which stipulates that securities sold pursuant to the *private placement* or *small offering exemption* must be held for two years; limited sales may be made between years two and three, and then unlimited sales are permitted.
4. ***Preventing transfer of restricted securities.*** To prevent the illegal transfer of restricted securities, the issuer must take the following precautions:
   a. *Affidavit.* The issuer must require investors to sign an affidavit stating that they are buying the securities for investment and promising not to transfer the restricted securities until the restrictions no longer apply.

b. Legend. The issuer must place a legend on the stock certificate describing the restriction.

c. Transfer agent. The issuer must appoint and notify the transfer agent not to record a transfer of the securities that would violate the restriction.

5. ***Rule 144A.*** Rule 144A is an SEC rule that permits *qualified institutional investors*—defined as institutions that own and invest at least $100 million in securities—to buy unregistered securities without being subject to the holding periods of Rule 144.

Securities Exempt from Registration

The following *securities* are exempt from the SEC registration process:

1. Securities issued by any government in the United States (e.g., municipal bonds issued by city governments)
2. Short-term notes and drafts that have a maturity date that does not exceed nine months (e.g., commercial paper issued by corporations)
3. Securities issued by nonprofit issuers, such as religious institutions, charitable institutions, and colleges and universities
4. Securities of financial institutions (e.g., banks and savings associations) that are regulated by the appropriate banking authorities
5. Securities issued by common carriers (e.g., railroads and trucking companies) that are regulated by the Interstate Commerce Commission (ICC)
6. Insurance and annuity contracts issued by insurance companies
7. Stock dividends and stock splits
8. Securities issued in a corporate reorganization where one security is exchanged for another security

Trading in Securities: The Securities Exchange Act of 1934

The Securities Exchange Act of 1934 is a federal statute that primarily regulates the *trading* of securities.

Section 10(b) and Rule 10b-5

1. ***Section 10(b).*** Section 10(b) is a provision of the 1934 act that prohibits use of manipulative and deceptive devices in the purchase or sale of securities in contravention of the rules and regulations described by the SEC.
2. ***Rule 10b-5.*** Rule 10b-5 is a rule adopted by the SEC to clarify the reach of Section 10(b) against deceptive and fraudulent activities in the purchase and sale of securities.
3. ***Scienter.*** Only conduct involving *scienter* (intentional conduct) violates Section 10(b) and Rule 10b-5. Negligent conduct is not a violation.

Insider Trading

Insider trading is trading that occurs when an insider makes a profit by purchasing shares of a commodity prior to the public release of favorable information or selling shares of a corporation prior to public disclosure of unfavorable information. Insider trading violates Section 10(b) and Rule 10b-5.

Insiders

Insiders for the purposes of Section 10(b) and Rule 10b-5 include all employees of a company, independent contractors hired by the company on a temporary basis to provide services or work to the company, and others who owe a fiduciary duty to the company.

Tipper–Tippee Liability

1. ***Tipper.*** A tipper is a person who discloses material nonpublic information to another person.
2. ***Tippee.*** A tippee is a person who receives material nonpublic information from a tipper.
3. ***Tippee's liability.*** A tippee is liable for acting on material information received from a tipper if he or she knew or should have known that the information was not public. The tippee must disgorge profits made on the tip.
4. ***Tipper's liability.*** A tipper is liable for his or her own profits and the profits made by the tippee.

Liability Provisions of the Securities Exchange Act of 1934

1. ***Private actions.*** A private plaintiff has an *implied right* under Section 10(b) and Rule 10b-5 to sue to rescind a securities contract or recover damages from a defendant who has engaged in manipulative and deceptive practices that have caused the plaintiff injury.
2. ***SEC actions.*** The SEC may enter into *consent orders* with defendants, seek *injunctions* in federal district court, or seek orders requiring defendants to *disgorge* illegally gained profits.
   a. *Treble damages.* The *Insider Trading Sanctions Act of 1984* permits the SEC to obtain a civil penalty of up to three times the illegal benefits received from insider trading.
3. ***Criminal liability.*** *Section 32* of the 1934 act imposes criminal liability on any person who willfully violates the 1934 act or the rules and regulations adopted thereunder. Criminal actions are brought by the U.S. Department of Justice.

Short-Swing Profits: The Securities Exchange Act of 1934

Statutory insiders. *Section 16(a)* of the Securities Exchange Act of 1934 defines a *statutory insider* for Section 16 purposes as any person who is an executive officer, a director, or a 10 percent shareholder of any equity security of a reporting company.

1. ***Section 16(b):***
   a. *Short-swing profits.* Short-swing profits are profits made by statutory insiders on trades involving equity securities that occur within six months of each other.
   b. *Section 16(b).* Section 16(b) is a provision of the 1934 act that requires that any profits made by a statutory insider on transactions involving short-swing profits belong to the corporation.
2. ***SEC rules.*** Rules issued by the SEC clarify the persons and transactions subject to Section 16 short-swing profit rules.

State Securities Laws

Most states have enacted securities laws that regulate the issuance and trading of securities. These acts are often patterned after, and were designed to coordinate with, federal securities laws. The *Uniform Securities Act*, which is a model state securities act, has been adopted by many states.

Internet Exercises and Case Questions

Working the Web Internet Exercises

1. Using the Stanford Securities Class Action Clearinghouse site, at **securities.stanford.edu**, identify the leading sector, industry, and companies targeted in securities class action litigation.
2. Investigate the modern varieties of fraud by reading the following law review articles: "Internet Securities Fraud: Old Trick, New Medium," at **www.law.duke.edu/journals/dltr/ARTICLES/2001dltr0006.html**. "Software Disclosure and Liability Under the Securities Acts," at **www.law.duke.edu/journals/dltr/ARTICLES/2001dltr0016.html.**
3. Determine whether an athletic club membership can be a *security* by using the U.S. Securities and Exchange Commission site, at **www.sec.gov**.
4. Who qualifies as *accredited investors*? See Bloomberg Online Financial Market Info, at **bloomberg.com**.
5. What is Rule 144 stock? See The Motley Fool, at **www.fool.com**.
6. What constitutes insider trading? See MSN's Investing site, at **moneycentral.msn.com/investor/home.asp**.
7. For information on socially responsible investing, see **www.socialinvest.org**.

Legal Environment Cases

27.1 Definition of *Security* Dare To Be Great, Inc. (Dare), was a Florida corporation that was wholly owned by Glenn W. Turner Enterprises, Inc. Dare offered self-improvement courses aimed at improving self-motivation and sales ability. In return for an investment of money, the purchaser received certain tapes, records, and written materials. In addition, depending on the level of involvement, the purchaser had the opportunity to help sell the Dare courses to others and to receive part of the purchase price as a commission. There were four different levels of involvement.

The task of salespersons was to bring prospective purchasers to "Adventure Meetings." The meetings, which were conducted by Dare people and not the salespersons, were conducted in a preordained format that included great enthusiasm, cheering and charming, exuberant handshaking, standing on chairs, and shouting. The Dare people and the salespersons dressed in modern, expensive clothes, displayed large sums of cash, drove new expensive automobiles, and engaged in hard-sell tactics to induce prospects to sign their name and part with their money. In actuality, few Dare purchasers ever attained the wealth promised. The tape recordings and materials distributed by Dare were worthless. Is this sales scheme a "security" that should have been registered with the SEC? *Securities and Exchange Commission v. Glenn W. Turner Enterprises, Inc.*, 474 F.2d 476, 1973 U.S. Lexis 11903 (9th Cir.)

27.2 Definition of *Security* The Farmer's Cooperative of Arkansas and Oklahoma (Co-Op) was an agricultural cooperative that had approximately 23,000 members. To raise money to support its general business operations, the Co-Op sold promissory notes to investors that were payable upon demand. The Co-Op offered the notes to both members and nonmembers, advertised the notes as an "investment program," and offered an interest rate higher than that available on savings accounts at financial institutions. More than 1,600 people purchased the notes, worth a total of $10 million. Subsequently, the Co-Op filed for bankruptcy. A class of holders of the notes filed suit against Ernst & Young, a national firm of certified public accountants that had audited the Co-Op's financial statements, alleging that Ernst & Young had violated Section 10(b) of the Securities Exchange Act of 1934. Are the notes issued by the Co-Op "securities"? *Reeves v. Ernst & Young*, 494 U.S. 56, 110 S.Ct. 945, 1990 U.S. Lexis 1051 (U.S. Sup.Ct.)

27.3 Intrastate Offering Exemption The McDonald Investment Company was a corporation organized and incorporated in the state of Minnesota. The principal and only place of business from which the company conducted operations was located in Rush City, Minnesota. More than 80 percent of the company's assets were located in Minnesota, and more than 80 percent of its income was derived from Minnesota. On January 18, 1972, McDonald sold securities to Minnesota residents only. The proceeds from the sale were used entirely to make loans and other investments in real estate and other assets located outside the state of Minnesota. The company did not file a registration statement with the SEC. Does this offering qualify for an intrastate offering exemption from registration? *Securities and Exchange Commission v. McDonald Investment Company*, 343 F.Supp. 343, 1972 U.S.Dist. Lexis 13547 (D. Minn.)

27.4 Transaction Exemption Continental Enterprises, Inc., had 2,510,000 shares of stock issued and outstanding. Louis E. Wolfson and members of his immediate family and associates owned in excess of 40 percent of those shares. The balance was in the hands of approximately 5,000 outside shareholders. Wolfson was Continental's largest shareholder and the guiding spirit of the corporation who gave direction to and controlled the company's officers. Between August 1, 1960, and January 31, 1962, without public disclosure, Wolfson and his family and associates sold 55 percent of their stock through six brokerage houses. Wolfson and his family and associates did not file a registration statement with the SEC with respect to these sales. Do the securities sales by Wolfson and his family and associates qualify for an exemption for registration as a sale "not by an issuer, an underwriter, or a dealer"? *United States v. Wolfson*, 405 F.2d 779, 1968 U.S.App. Lexis 4342 (2d Cir.)

27.5 Insider Trading Chiarella worked as a "markup man" in the New York composing room of Pandick Press, a financial printer. Among the documents that Chiarella handled were five secret announcements of corporate takeovers. The tender offerors had hired Pandick Press to print the offers, which would later be made public when the tender offers were made to the shareholders of the target corporations. When the documents were delivered to Pandick Press, the identities of the acquiring and target corporations were concealed by black spaces or false names. The true names would not be sent to Pandick Press until the night of the final printing.

Chiarella was able to deduce the names of the target companies before the final printing. Without disclosing this knowledge, he purchased stock in the target companies and sold the shares immediately after the takeover attempts were made public. Chiarella realized a gain of $30,000 in the course of 14 months. The federal government indicted Chiarella for criminal violations of Section 10(b) of the Securities Exchange Act of 1934. Is Chiarella guilty? *Chiarella v. United States*, 1445 U.S. 222, 100 S.Ct. 1108, 1980 U.S. Lexis 88 (U.S. Sup.Ct.)

27.6 Section 10(b) Leslie Neadeau was the president of T.O.N.M. Oil & Gas Exploration Corporation (TONM). Charles Lazzaro was a registered securities broker employed by Bateman Eichler, Hill Richards, Inc. (Bateman Eichler). The stock of TONM was traded in the over-the-counter market. Lazzaro made statements to potential investors that he had "inside information" about TONM, including that (1) vast amounts of gold had been discovered in Surinam and that TONM had options on thousands of acres in the gold-producing regions of Surinam; (2) the discovery was "not publicly known, but would be subsequently announced"; and (3) when this information was made public, TONM stock, which was then selling for from $1.50 to $3.00 per share, would increase to $10.00 to $15.00 within a short period of time and might increase to $100.00 per share within a year.

The potential investors contacted Neadeau at TONM, and he confirmed that the information was not public knowledge. In reliance on Lazzaro's and Neadeau's statements, the investors purchased TONM stock. The so-called "inside information" turned out to be false, and the shares declined substantially below the purchase price. The investors sued Lazzaro, Bateman Eichler, Neadeau, and TONM, alleging violations of Section 10(b) of the Securities Exchange Act of 1934. The defendants asserted that the plaintiffs' complaint should be dismissed because they participated in the fraud. Who wins? *Bateman Eichler, Hill Richards, Inc. v. Berner*, 472 U.S. 299, 105 S.Ct. 2662, 1985 U.S. Lexis 95 (U.S. Sup.Ct.)

27.7 Insider Trading Donald C. Hoodes was the chief executive officer of the Sullair Corporation. As an officer of the corporation, he was regularly granted stock options to purchase stock of the company at a discount. On July 20, 1982, Hoodes sold 6,000 shares of Sullair common stock for $38,350. On July 31, 1982, Sullair terminated Hoodes as an officer of the corporation. On August 20, 1982, Hoodes exercised options to purchase 6,000 shares of Sullair stock that cost Hoodes $3.01 per share ($18,060) at the time they were trading at $4.50 per share ($27,000). Hoodes did not possess material nonpublic information about Sullair when he sold or purchased the securities of the company. The corporation brought suit against Hoodes to recover the profits Hoodes made on these trades. Who wins? *Sullair Corporation v. Hoodes*, 672 F.Supp. 337, 1987 U.S.Dist. Lexis 10152 (N.D. Ill.)

Ethics in Business

27.8 R. Foster Winans, a reporter for the *Wall Street Journal*, was one of the writers of the "Heard on the Street" column, a widely read and influential column in the *Journal*. This column frequently included articles that discussed the prospects of companies listed on national and regional stock exchanges and the over-the-counter market. David Carpenter worked as a news clerk at the *Journal*. The *Journal* had a conflict of interest policy that prohibited employees from using nonpublic information learned on the job for their personal benefit. Winans and Carpenter were aware of this policy.

Kenneth P. Felis and Peter Brant were stockbrokers at the brokerage house of Kidder Peabody. Winans agreed to provide Felis and Brant with information that was to appear in the "Heard" column in advance of its publication in the *Journal*. Generally, Winans would provide this information to the brokers the day before it was to appear in the *Journal*. Carpenter served as a messenger between the parties. Based on this advance information, the brokers bought and sold securities of companies discussed in the "Heard" column. During 1983 and 1984, prepublication trades of approximately 27 "Heard" columns netted profits of almost $690,000. The parties used telephones to transfer information. The *Wall Street Journal* is distributed by mail to many of its subscribers.

Eventually, Kidder Peabody noticed a correlation between the "Heard" column and trading by the brokers. After an SEC investigation, criminal charges were brought against defendants Winans, Carpenter, and Felis in U.S. district court. Brant became the government's key witness. Winans and Felis were convicted of conspiracy to commit securities, mail, and wire fraud. Carpenter was convicted of aiding and abetting the commission of securities, mail, and wire fraud. The defendants appealed their convictions. *United States v. Carpenter*, 484 U.S. 19, 108 S.Ct. 316, 1987 U.S. Lexis 4815 (U.S. Sup.Ct.)

Ethics Issues

1. What does Section 10(b) of the Securities Exchange Act of 1934 provide?
2. Can the defendants be held criminally liable for conspiring to violate, and aiding and abetting the violation of, Section 10(b) and Rule 10b-5 of securities law?
3. Did Winans act ethically in this case? Did Brant act ethically in this case? Explain.
4. What percentage of illegal insider trading and tipper–tippee trading is caught?

Endnotes

1. *Securities and Exchange Commission v. W. J. Howey Co.*, 328 U.S. 293, 66 S.Ct. 1100, 1946 U.S. Lexis 3159 (U.S. Sup.Ct.).
2. 15 U.S.C. Sections 77a–77aa.
3. 15 U.S.C. Section 77x.
4. Securities Act of 1933, Section 3(a)(11).
5. SEC Rule 147.
6. Securities Act of 1933, Section 4(2).
7. SEC Rule 506.
8. SEC Rule 501.
9. Securities Act of 1933, Section 3(b).
10. 15 U.S.C. Sections 78a–78mm.
11. Litigation instituted pursuant to Section 10(b) and Rule 10b-5 must be commenced within one year after the discovery of the violation and within three years after such violation. *Lampf, Pleva, Lipkind, Prupis & Petigrow v. Gilbertson*, 501 U.S. 350, 111 S.Ct. 2773, 1991 U.S. Lexis 3629 (U.S. Sup.Ct.).
12. The U.S. Supreme Court has held that the sale of a business is a sale of securities that is subject to Section 10(b). *See Gould v. Ruefenacht*, 471 U.S. 701, 105 S.Ct. 2308, 1985 U.S. Lexis 21 (U.S. Sup.Ct.) (where 50 percent of a business was sold), and *Landreth Timber Co. v. Landreth*, 471 U.S. 681, 105 S.Ct. 2297, 1985 U.S. Lexis 20 (U.S. Sup.Ct.) (where 100 percent of a business was sold).
13. *Ernst & Ernst v. Hochfelder*, 425 U.S. 185, 96 S.Ct. 1375, 1976 U.S. Lexis 2 (U.S. Sup.Ct.).
14. 40 SEC Section 907 (1961).
15. 15 U.S.C. Section 78 ff.
16. P.L. 98–376.
17. 15 U.S.C. Section 781.
18. 15 U.S.C. Section 78p(b).

28

Real Property and Land Use Regulation

"Property and law are born and must die together."

—Jeremy Bentham
Principles of the Civil Code, I Works 309

Chapter Objectives

After studying this chapter, you should be able to:

1. List and describe the different types of real property.
2. Describe the different types of freehold estates, concurrent ownership, and future interests in land.
3. Explain how ownership interests in real property can be transferred.
4. Explain how a landlord–tenant relationship is created.
5. Describe the various forms of land use regulation.

Chapter Contents

Private ownership of property forms the foundation of the U.S. economic system. Therefore, a comprehensive body of law has been developed to protect property rights. The law protects the right of property owners to use, sell, dispose of, control, and prevent others from trespassing on their rights.

Individuals and families own houses, farmers and ranchers own farmland and ranches, and businesses own commercial and office buildings. In addition, over half of the population rents their homes, and many businesses lease office space, stores, manufacturing facilities, and other commercial property. The parties to a **landlord–tenant relationship** have certain legal rights and duties that are governed by a mixture of real estate and contract law.

Although the United States has the most advanced private property system in the world, ownership and possession of real estate are not free from government regulation. Pursuant to constitutional authority, federal, state, and local governments have enacted myriad laws that regulate the ownership, possession, and use of real property. These laws are collectively referred to as **land use regulation**.

This chapter discusses real property, ownership of real property, transfer of real property, landlord–tenant relationships, and land use regulation.

Victorian Cottage, Mackinac Island, Michigan. The most valuable asset of many families is the home they own, such as this cottage on Mackinac Island, Michigan.

Real Property

real property
The land itself as well as buildings, trees, soil, minerals, timber, plants, and other things permanently affixed to the land.

Property is usually classified as either real or personal property. **Real property** is immovable or attached to immovable land or buildings, whereas personal property is movable. The various types of real property are discussed in the following paragraphs.

Land and Buildings

land
The most common form of real property. Land includes the land and buildings and other structures permanently attached to the land.

Land is the most common form of real property. A landowner usually purchases the *surface rights* to the land—that is, the right to occupy the land. The owner may use, enjoy, and develop the property as he or she sees fit, subject to any applicable government regulation.

Buildings constructed on land are real property. For example, houses, apartment buildings, manufacturing plants, and office buildings constructed on land are real property. Such things as radio towers and bridges are usually considered real property as well.

Subsurface Rights

The owner of land possesses **subsurface rights**, or **mineral rights**, to the earth located beneath the surface of the land. These rights can be very valuable. For example, gold, uranium, oil, or natural gas may lie beneath the surface of the land. Theoretically, mineral rights extend to the center of the earth. In reality, mines and oil wells usually extend only several miles into the earth. Subsurface rights may be sold separately from surface rights.

subsurface rights
Rights to the earth located beneath the surface of the land.

Plant Life and Vegetation

Plant life and vegetation growing on the surface of land are considered real property. Such vegetation includes both natural plant life (e.g., trees) and cultivated plant life (e.g., crops). When land is sold, any plant life growing on the land is included unless the parties agree otherwise. Plant life that is severed from the land is considered personal property.

plant life and vegetation
Real property that is growing in or on the surface of the land.

Fixtures

Certain personal property is so closely associated with real property that it becomes part of the realty. Such items are called **fixtures**. For example, kitchen cabinets, carpeting, and doorknobs are fixtures, but throw rugs and furniture are personal property.

Unless otherwise provided, if a building is sold, the fixtures are included in the sale. If the sale agreement is silent as to whether an item is a fixture, the courts make a determination on the basis of whether the item can be removed without causing substantial damage to the realty.

fixtures
Goods that are affixed to real estate so as to become part thereof.

Contemporary Trend

Air Rights

Common law provided that the owners of real property owned that property from the center of the earth to the heavens. This rule has been eroded by modern legal restrictions such as land use regulation laws, environmental protection laws, and air navigation requirements. Even today, however, the owners of land may sell or lease air space parcels above their land.

An **air space parcel** is the air space above the surface of the earth of an owner's real property. Air space parcels are valuable property rights, particularly in densely populated metropolitan areas where building property is scarce. For example, many developments have been built in air space parcels in New York City. More developments are expected to be built in air space parcels in the future. ■

Estates in Land

A person's ownership right in real property is called an **estate in land** (or **estate**). An estate is defined as the bundle of *legal rights* that the owner has to possess, use, and enjoy the property. The type of estate that an owner possesses is determined from the deed, will, lease, or other document that transferred the ownership rights to him or her.

estate
Ownership rights in real property; the bundle of legal rights that the owner has to possess, use, and enjoy the property.

freehold estate
An estate in which the owner has a present possessory interest in the real property.

A **freehold estate** is an estate in which the owner has a *present possessory interest* in the real property; that is, the owner may use and enjoy the property as he or she sees fit, subject to any applicable government regulation or private restraint. The two types of freehold estates are *estates in fee* and *life estates*.

Estate in Fee

fee simple absolute
A type of ownership of real property that grants the owner the fullest bundle of legal rights that a person can hold in real property.

A **fee simple absolute** (or **fee simple**) is the highest form of ownership of real property because it grants the owner the fullest bundle of legal rights that a person can hold in real property. It is the type of ownership most people connect with "owning" real property. A fee simple owner has the right to exclusively possess and use his or her property to the extent that the owner has not transferred any interest in the property (e.g., by lease).

If a person owns real property in fee simple, his or her ownership:

- Is infinite in duration (fee)
- Has no limitation on inheritability (simple)
- Does not end upon the happening of any event (absolute)

fee simple defeasible
A type of ownership of real property that grants the owner all the incidents of a fee simple absolute except that it may be taken away if a specified condition occurs or does not occur.

A **fee simple defeasible** (or **qualified fee**) grants the owner all the incidents of a fee simple absolute except that it may be taken away if a specified *condition* occurs or does not occur. For example, a conveyance of property to a church "as long as the land is used as a church or for church purposes" creates a qualified fee. The church has all the rights of a fee simple absolute owner except that its ownership rights are terminated if the property is no longer used for church purposes.

Life Estate

life estate
An interest in land for a person's lifetime; upon that person's death, the interest will be transferred to another party.

A **life estate** is an interest in real property that lasts for the life of a specified person, usually the grantee. For example, a conveyance of real property "to Anna for her life" creates a life estate. A life estate may also be measured by the life of a third party (e.g., "to Anna for the life of Benjamin"); this is called an *estate pour autre vie*. A life estate may be defeasible (e.g., "to John for his life but only if he continues to occupy this residence"). Upon the death of the named person, the life estate terminates, and the property reverts to the grantor or the grantor's estate or other designated person.

A life tenant is treated as the owner of the property during the duration of the life estate. He or she has the right to possess and use the property except to the extent that it would cause permanent *waste* of the property. A life tenant may sell, transfer, or mortgage his or her estate in the land. However, the mortgage cannot exceed the duration of the life estate. A life tenant is obligated to keep the property in repair and to pay property taxes.

Concurrent Ownership

co-ownership
A situation in which two or more persons own a piece of real property. Also called *concurrent ownership*.

Two or more persons may own a piece of real property. This is called **co-ownership**, or **concurrent ownership**. The following forms of co-ownership are recognized: *joint tenancy, tenancy in common, tenancy by the entirety, community property, condominiums*, and *cooperatives*.

Joint Tenancy

joint tenancy
A form of co-ownership that includes the right of survivorship.

To create a **joint tenancy**, words that clearly show a person's intent to create a joint tenancy must be used. Language such as "Marsha Leest and James Leest, as joint tenants" is usually sufficient. The most distinguished feature of a joint tenancy is the co-owners' *right of survivorship*. This means that upon the death of one of the co-owners (or **joint tenants**), the deceased person's interest in the property automatically passes to the surviving joint tenants. Any contrary provision in the deceased's will is ineffective.

Consider This Example Jones, one of four people who own a piece of property in joint tenancy, executes a will leaving all of his property to a university. Jones dies. The surviving joint tenants—not the university—acquire his interest in the piece of property. Each joint tenant has a right to sell or transfer his or her interest in the property, but such conveyance terminates the joint tenancy. The parties then become tenants in common.

Tenancy in Common

In a **tenancy in common**, the interests of a surviving *tenant in common* pass to the deceased tenant's estate and not to the co-tenants. A tenancy in common may be created by express words, such as "Ian Cespedes and Joy Park, as tenants in common." Unless otherwise agreed, a tenant in common can sell, give, devise, or otherwise transfer his or her interest in the property without the consent of the other co-owners.

tenancy in common
A form of co-ownership in which the interest of a surviving tenant in common passes to the deceased tenant's estate and not to the co-tenants.

Consider This Example Lopez, who is one of four tenants in common who own a piece of property, has a will that leaves all his property to his granddaughter. When Lopez dies, the granddaughter receives his interest in the tenancy in common, and the granddaughter becomes a tenant in common with the three other owners.

Tenancy by the Entirety

Tenancy by the entirety is a form of co-ownership of real property that can be used only by married couples. This type of tenancy must be created by express words, such as "Harold Jones and Maude Jones, husband and wife, as tenants by the entireties." A surviving spouse has the right of survivorship.

tenancy by the entirety
A form of co-ownership of real property that can be used only by married couples.

Tenancy by the entirety is distinguished from joint tenancy because neither spouse may sell or transfer his or her interest in the property without the other spouse's consent. Only about half of the states recognize tenancy by the entirety.

Community Property

Nine states—Arizona, California, Idaho, Louisiana, Nevada, New Mexico, Texas, Washington, and Wisconsin—recognize a form of co-ownership known as **community property**. This method of co-ownership applies only to married couples. It is based on the notion that a husband and wife should share equally in the fruits of the marital partnership. Under these laws, each spouse owns an equal one-half share of the *income* both spouses earned during the marriage and one-half of the *assets acquired by this income during the marriage*, regardless of who earned the income. Property that is acquired through gift or inheritance either before or during marriage remains **separate property**. Interest payments, dividends, and appreciation of separate property received or accrued during marriage is also separate property.

community property
A form of ownership in which each spouse owns an equal one-half share of the income of both spouses and the assets acquired from that income during the marriage.

When a spouse dies, the surviving spouse automatically receives one-half the community property. The other half passes to the heirs of the deceased spouse as directed by will or by state intestate statute if there is no will.

During the marriage, neither spouse can sell, transfer, or gift community property without the consent of the other spouse. Upon a divorce, each spouse has a right to one-half the community property.

The location of the real property determines whether community property law applies. For example, if a married couple who lives in a noncommunity property state purchases real property located in a community property state, community property laws apply to that property.

Property is an instrument of humanity. Humanity is not an instrument of property.

Woodrow Wilson
Speech (1912)

Consider This Example Elma is a successful brain surgeon who makes $500,000 income per year. She meets and marries Brad, a struggling actor who makes $10,000 per year. When Elma gets married, she owns $1 million of real estate and $2 million in securities, which she retains as her separate property. Brad has no separate property when he and Elma are married. After three years, Elma and Brad get a divorce. Assume that Elma has made $500,000 and Brad has made $10,000 each of the three years of their marriage, their living expenses were $110,000 per year, and they have $1.2 million of earned income saved in a bank account. During the marriage, Elma's real estate has increased in value to $1.5 million, and her securities have increased in value to $3 million. Upon divorce, Elma receives her $1.5 million in real estate and $3 million in securities as her separate property. Elma and Brad each receive $600,000 from the community property bank account.

Concept Summary *Concurrent Ownership*

Form of Ownership	Right of Survivorship	Tenant May Unilaterally Transfer His or Her Interest
Joint tenancy	Yes, deceased tenant's interest automatically passes to co-tenants.	Yes, tenant may transfer his or her interest without the consent of co-tenants. Transfer severs joint tenancy.
Tenancy in common	No, deceased tenant's interest passes to his or her estate.	Yes, tenant may transfer his or her interest without the consent of co-tenants. Transfer does not sever tenancy in common.
Tenancy by the entirety	Yes, deceased tenant's interest automatically passes to his or her spouse.	No, neither spouse may transfer his or her interest without the other spouse's consent.
Community property	Yes, when a spouse dies, the surviving spouse automatically receives one-half of the community property. The other half passes to the heirs of the deceased spouse, as directed by a valid will or by state intestate statute if there is no will.	No, neither spouse may transfer his or her interest without the other spouse's consent.

Condominium

condominium

A common form of ownership in a multiple-dwelling building where the purchaser has title to the individual unit and owns the common areas as a tenant in common with the other condominium owners.

Condominiums are a common form of ownership in multiple-dwelling buildings. Purchasers of a condominium (1) have title to their individual units and (2) own the common areas (e.g., hallways, elevators, parking areas, recreational facilities) as tenants in common with the other owners. Owners may sell or mortgage their units without the permission of the other owners. Owners are assessed monthly fees for the maintenance of common areas. In addition to dwelling units, the condominium form of ownership is offered for office buildings, boat docks, and such.

Cooperative

A **cooperative** is a form of co-ownership of a multiple-dwelling building where a corporation owns the building and the residents own shares in the corporation. Each cooperative owner leases a unit in the building from the corporation under a renewable, long-term, proprietary lease. Individual residents may not secure loans with the units they occupy. The corporation may borrow money on a blanket mortgage, and each shareholder is jointly and severally liable on the loan. Usually, cooperative owners may not sell their shares or sublease their units without the approval of the other owners.

cooperative
A form of co-ownership of a multiple-dwelling building where a corporation owns the building and the residents own shares in the corporation.

In the following case, the court had to decide how to split the proceeds from the sale of real property owned by co-owners.

Case 28.1
Joint Tenancy

Cunningham v. Hastings
556 N.E.2d 12, 1990 Ind.App. Lexis 764
Court of Appeals of Indiana

Background and Facts

On August 30, 1984, Warren R. Hastings and Joan L. Cunningham, who were unmarried, purchased a house together. Hastings paid $45,000 down payment toward the purchase price out of his own funds. The deed referred to Hastings and Cunningham as "joint tenants with the right of survivorship." Hastings and Cunningham occupied the property jointly. After their relationship ended, Hastings took sole possession of the property. Cunningham filed a complaint seeking partition of the real estate. Based on its determination that the property could not be split, the trial court ordered it to be sold. The trial court further ordered that $45,000 of the sale proceeds be paid to Hastings to reimburse him for his down payment and that the remainder of the proceeds be divided equally between Hastings and Cunningham. Cunningham appealed, alleging that Hastings should not have been given credit for the down payment.

Issue

Is Cunningham entitled to an equal share of the proceeds of the sale of the real estate?

In the Language of the Court

The parties do not dispute that the unequivocal language of the deed created a joint tenancy in the real estate. The determination of the parties' interests in the present case is simple. There are only two parties involved in the joint tenancy. Once a joint tenancy relationship is found to exist between two people in a partition action, it is axiomatic that each person owns a one-half interest. Based on this reasoning, we find that the trial court erred in allowing Hastings a $45,000 credit for the purchase price he paid. Regardless of who provided the money to purchase the land, the creation of a joint tenancy relationship entitles each party to an equal share of the proceeds of the sale upon partition. Equitable adjustments to cotenants' equal shares are allowed when the cotenants hold the property as tenants in common, not when they hold as joint tenants. The deed in the case before us unequivocally states that the parties held the property as joint tenants, not as tenants in common. The equitable adjustment of their equal shares, therefore, was improper.

Decision and Remedy

The court of appeals held that Cunningham was entitled to an equal share of the proceeds of the sale because she and Hastings owned the property as joint tenants. The court of appeals reversed the trial court's judgment and remanded the case to the trail court, with instructions to order the entire proceeds of the sale to be divided equally between Cunningham and Hastings.

Business and Ethics Questions

1. Should the law recognize so many different forms of ownership of real property? Do you think most people understand the legal consequences of taking title in the various forms?
2. Did Cunningham act ethically in demanding one-half the value of the down payment even though she had not contributed to it?
3. Could Hastings have protected the $45,000 he paid for the down payment? If so, how could he have done it?

Future Interests

A person may be given the right to possess property in the *future* rather than in the present. This right is called a **future interest**. The two forms of future interests are *reversion* and *remainder*.

future interest
The interest that a grantor retains for him- or herself or a third party.

Reversion

reversion
A right of possession that returns to the grantor after the expiration of a limited or contingent estate.

A **reversion** is a right of possession that returns to the *grantor* after the expiration of a limited or contingent estate. Reversions do not have to be expressly stated because they arise automatically by law. For example, if a grantor conveys property "to M. R. Harrington for life," the grantor has retained a reversion in the property. That is, when Harrington dies, the property reverts to the grantor or, if he or she is not living, then to his or her estate.

Remainder

remainder
A situation in which the right of possession returns to a third party upon the expiration of a limited or contingent estate.

If the right of possession returns to a *third party* upon the expiration of a limited or contingent estate, it is called a **remainder**. The person who is entitled to the future interest is called a **remainder beneficiary**. For example, a conveyance of property "to Joe for life, remainder to Meredith" is a vested remainder; the only contingency to Meredith's possessory interest is Joe's death.

Arch, St. Louis, Missouri. National Park Service, U.S. Department of the Interior. Federal, state, and local governments own substantial amounts of real property in the United States. The St. Louis Arch and surrounding areas in St. Louis, Missouri, are operated by the National Park Service.

Transfer of Ownership of Real Property

Without that sense of security which property gives, the land would still be uncultivated.

Francois Quesnay
Maximes, IV

Ownership of real property may be transferred from one person to another. Title to real property may be transferred by sale; tax sale; gift, will, or inheritance; and adverse possession. The difference methods of transfer provide different degrees of protection to the transferee.

Sale of Real Estate

sale
The passing of title from a seller to a buyer for a price. Also called a *conveyance*.

A **sale**, or **conveyance**, is the most common method for transferring ownership rights in real property. An owner may offer his or her real estate for sale either by himself or herself or by using a real estate broker. Once a buyer has been located and the parties have negotiated the terms of the sale, a **real estate sales contract** is executed by the parties. The Statute of Frauds in most states requires this contract to be in writing.

The seller delivers a deed to the buyer, and the buyer pays the purchase price at the **closing**, or **settlement**. Unless otherwise agreed, it is implied that the seller is conveying fee simple absolute title to the buyer. If either party fails to perform, the other party may sue for breach of contract and obtain monetary damages or specific performance.

Deeds

Deeds are used to convey real property by sale or gift. The seller or donor is called the **grantor**. The buyer or recipient is called the **grantee**. A deed may be used to transfer a fee simple absolute interest in real property or any lesser estate (e.g., life estate).

State laws recognize different types of deeds that provide differing degrees of protection to grantees. A **warranty deed** (i.e., a deed in which the grantor warrants that he or she has sold title to the real property) contains the greatest number of warranties and provides the most protection to grantees. A **quitclaim deed** (i.e., a deed in which the grantor transfers only whatever interest he or she has in the real property) provides the least amount of protection because only the grantor's interest is conveyed.

deed
A document that describes a person's ownership interest in a piece of real property.

grantor
The party who transfers an ownership interest in real property.

grantee
The party to whom an interest in real property is transferred.

Recording Statutes

Every state has a **recording statute** that provides that copies of deeds and other documents concerning interests in real property (e.g., mortgages, liens, easements) may be filed in a government office, where they become public records open to viewing by the public. Recording statutes are intended to prevent fraud and to establish certainty in the ownership and transfer of property. Instruments are usually filed in the **county recorder's office** of the county in which the property is located. A fee is charged to record an instrument.

recording statute
A state statute that requires a mortgage or deed of trust to be recorded in the county recorder's office of the county in which the real property is located.

Persons interested in purchasing the property or lending on the property should check these records to determine whether the grantor or borrower actually owns the property and whether any other parties (e.g., lienholders, mortgages, easement holders) have an interest in the property. The recordation of a deed is not required to pass title from the grantor to the grantee. Recording the deed gives **constructive notice** to the world of the owner's interest in the property.

A party who is concerned about his or her ownership rights in a parcel of real property can bring a **quiet title action**, which is a lawsuit, to have a court determine the extent of those rights. Public notice of the hearing must be given so that anyone claiming an interest in the property may appear and be heard. After the hearing, the judge declares who has title to the property; that is, the court "quiets title" by its decision.

quiet title action
An action brought by a party seeking an order of the court declaring who has title to disputed property. The court "quiets title" by its decision.

In the following case, the court had to decide whether a recording statute had been properly complied with.

Case 28.2
Recording Statute

The Howard Savings Bank v. Brunson
582 A.2d 1305, 1990 N.J.Super. Lexis 436
Superior Court of New Jersey

Background and Facts

In January 1986, Burl Brunson purchased a parcel of real property in Newark, New Jersey. The deed for the property was properly recorded and indexed by the county recorder on January 24, 1986. In March 1986, Brunson borrowed $50,000 from The Howard Savings Bank, secured by a mortgage that was properly recorded on May 1, 1986. The county recorder did not list the mortgage in its index for recorded documents, however. On October 6, 1987, Brunson executed and delivered a deed for the property to Jesus and Celeste Ijalba, who purchased the property from Brunson. This deed was properly recorded and indexed on November 4, 1987. On October 6, 1987, the Ijalbas borrowed money from Chrysler First Financial Services Corporation, secured by a mortgage on the property that was properly recorded and indexed on November 4, 1987. On February 9, 1988, Howard Savings Bank's mortgage from two years earlier was finally indexed by the county recorder. On May 19, 1988, Howard Savings Bank brought a foreclosure action on the property for default on its loan and claimed that its mortgage had priority over the Ijalbas' deed and Chrysler First Financial's mortgage. The defendants argued that Howard Savings Bank's mortgage did not have priority because it was not indexed, and therefore when they conducted their title search, Howard Savings Bank's mortgage did not appear in the index. The Ijalbas and Chrysler First Financial filed motions for summary judgment.

(continued)

The Howard Savings Bank v. Brunson

582 A.2d 1305, 1990 N.J.Super. Lexis 436
Superior Court of New Jersey
(continued)

Issue

Was Howard Savings Bank's mortgage on the property properly recorded so as to give notice of its existence to subsequent parties?

In the Language of the Court

The fundamental purpose of the Recording Act is to provide notice to subsequent parties in interest and the protection of purchasers and encumbrancers of real property against undisclosed titles and liens. A rule prohibiting title searchers from depending upon the alphabetical index would unduly hinder the commercial transactions in the State; lengthy title searches would cost more and would cause unreasonably long closings; potential purchasers, mortgages and lenders would hesitate to be involved in commercial transactions where they could not be confident that a reasonable search of the record would reveal prior interests or where they feared being held liable for a clerk's misindexing error; and the cost of title insurance would increase.

Obviously, one effect of finding a duty in the mortgagee to see that his instrument is properly indexed will be that the mortgagee will be required to conduct "run down" searches or to employ some other similar mechanism for ensuring that his interest is properly indexed. Yet such a practice is seen as making good business sense anyway. Furthermore, placing the burden upon the mortgagee to ensure that the requisite notice has been given is not out of step with the equitable maxim that where a loss must be borne by one of two innocent parties, equity will impose the loss on the party whose first act would have prevented the loss.

Decision and Remedy

The court held that Howard Savings Bank's mortgage was not properly recorded as to give the necessary notice to subsequent parties because it was not indexed. The court granted the defendant's motion for summary judgment.

Business and Ethics Questions

1. What are the purposes of having recording and indexing statutes?
2. Did any party act unethically in this case?
3. Howard Savings Bank and Chrysler First Financial were both innocent parties in this case. Do you think the law placed the risk of loss on the right party in this case? Explain.

Marketable Title

marketable title
Title to real property that is free from any encumbrances or other defects that are not disclosed but would affect the value of the property. Also called *good title*.

A grantor has the obligation to transfer **marketable title**, or **good title**, to the grantee. Marketable title means that the title is free from any encumbrances, defects in title, or other defects that are not disclosed but would affect the value of the property. The three most common ways of assuring marketable title are as follows:

- ***Attorney's opinion.*** An attorney examines an **abstract of title** (i.e., a chronological history of the chain of title and encumbrances affecting the property) and renders an opinion concerning the status of the title. The attorney may be sued for any losses caused by his or her negligence in rendering the opinion.
- ***Torrens system.*** The Torrens system is a method of determining title to real property in a judicial proceeding at which everyone claiming an interest in the property may appear and be heard. After the evidence is heard, the court issues a **certificate of title** to the person who is determined to be the rightful owner.
- ***Title insurance.*** The best way for a grantee to be sure that he or she has obtained marketable title is to purchase **title insurance** from an insurance company. The title insurer must reimburse the insured for any losses caused by undiscovered defects in the title. Each time a property is transferred or refinanced, a new title insurance policy must be obtained.

Adverse Possession

adverse possession
A doctrine that says a person who wrongfully possesses someone else's real property obtains title to that property if certain statutory requirements are met.

In most states, a person who wrongfully possesses someone else's real property obtains title to that property if certain statutory requirements are met. This is called **adverse possession**. Property owned by federal and state government is not subject to adverse possession.

Under this doctrine, the transfer of the property is involuntary and does not require the delivery of a deed. To obtain title under adverse possession, the wrongful possession must be:

- ***For a statutorily prescribed period of time.*** In most states, this period is between 10 and 20 years.
- ***Open, visible, and notorious.*** The adverse possessor must occupy the property so as to put the owner on notice of the possession.
- ***Actual and exclusive.*** The adverse possessor must physically occupy the premises. The planting of crops, grazing of animals, or building of a structure on the land constitutes physical occupancy.
- ***Continuous and peaceful.*** The occupancy must be continuous and uninterrupted for the required statutory period. Any break in normal occupancy terminates the adverse possession. This means that the adverse possessor may leave the property to go to work, to the store, on a vacation, and such. The adverse possessor cannot take the property by force from an owner.
- ***Hostile and adverse.*** The possessor must occupy the property without the express or implied permission of the owner. Thus, a lessee cannot claim title to property under adverse possession.

If the elements of adverse possession are met, the adverse possessor acquires clear title to the land. However, title is acquired only as to the property actually possessed and occupied during the statutory period, and not the entire tract. For example, an adverse possessor who occupies 1 acre of a 200,000-acre ranch for the statutory period of time acquires title only to the 1 acre.

In the following case, the court held that adverse possession had occurred.

Good fences make good neighbors.

Robert Frost
"Mending Wall" (1914)

Case 28.3
Adverse Possession

Witt v. Miller
845 S.W.2d 665, 1993 Mo.App. Lexis 20
Court of Appeals of Missouri

Background and Facts

Edward and Mary Shaughnessey purchased a 16-acre tract in St. Louis county in 1954. Subsequently, they subdivided 12 acres into 18 lots offered for sale and retained possession of the remaining 4-acre tract. In 1967, Charles and Elaine Witt purchased lot 12, which is adjacent to the 4-acre tract. The Witts constructed and moved into a house on their lot. In 1968, they cleared an area of land that ran the length of their property and extended 40 feet onto the 4-acre tract. The Witts constructed a pool and a deck, planted a garden, made a playground for their children, set up a dog run, and built a fence along the edge of the property line, which included the now-disputed property. Neither the Witts nor the Shaughnesseys realized that the Witts had encroached on the Shaughnesseys' property.

In February 1988, the Shaughnesseys sold the 4-acre tract to Thomas and Roseanne Miller. When a survey showed the encroachment, the Millers demanded that the Wits remove the pool and cease using the property. When the Witts refused to do so, the Millers sued to quiet title. The Witts defended, arguing that they had obtained title to the disputed property by adverse possession. The trial court held that there was no adverse possession and ruled in favor of the Millers. The Witts appealed.

Issue

Had the elements for adverse possession been met?

In the Language of the Court

We address the element of "hostile possession." Hostility does not imply animosity. There is no substantial evidence to support the finding that plaintiffs' possession was not hostile. Plaintiffs testified that they intended to possess the disputed property as their own because they believed it was part of lot 12. That intent manifests itself in plaintiffs' actions which include clearing the area, maintaining the area, planting grass and a garden, erecting a fence, installing playground equipment and a dog run, and building an above ground pool with a deck.

The evidence established plaintiffs' claim to title of the disputed property under adverse possession. The trial court's decision was not supported by substantial evidence and erroneously declared the law.

(continued)

Witt v. Miller

845 S.W.2d 665, 1993 Mo.App. Lexis 20

Court of Appeals of Missouri

(continued)

Decision and Remedy

The court of appeals held that the Witts had proven the necessary elements for adverse possession under state law. The Witts' occupation of the land was open and notorious, actual and exclusive, hostile and adverse, and continuous and peaceful, and it had been so for over the statutory period of 10 years. The court of appeals reversed the decision of the trial court and issued an order quitting title to the disputed property in the Witts' favor.

Business and Ethics Questions

1. What does the doctrine of adverse possession provide? What elements need to be proven?
2. Did the Witts act ethically in claiming title to someone else's land? Should they be allowed to benefit from their own mistake?
3. What should owners of property do to protect themselves from adverse possession claims? Explain.

Nonpossessory Interests

nonpossessory interest
A person's holding of an interest in another person's property without actually owning any part of the property.

A person may own a **nonpossessory interest** in another's real estate. Three nonpossessory interests—*easement*, *license*, and *profit*—are discussed in the following paragraphs.

Easement

easement
A given or required right to make limited use of someone else's land without owning or leasing it.

An **easement** is an interest in land that gives the holder the right to make limited use of another's property without taking anything from it. Typical easements are common driveways, party walls, and rights-of-way. Easements may be expressly created by *grant* (where an owner gives another party an easement across his or her property) or *reservation* (where an owner sells land that he or she owns but reserves an easement on the land). Easement can also be implied by (1) *implication*, where an owner subdivides a piece of property with a well, path, road, or other beneficial appurtenant that serves the entire parcel or by (2) *necessity*—for example, where "landlocked" property has an implied easement across surrounding property to enter and exit the landlocked property. Easements can also be created by *prescription*—that is, adverse possession.

There are two types of easements:

easement appurtenant
A situation created when the owner of one piece of land is given an easement over an adjacent piece of land.

- ***Easements appurtenant.*** An **easement appurtenant** is created when the owner of one piece of land is given an easement over an adjacent piece of land. The land over which the easement is granted is called the **servient estate**. The land that benefits from the easement is called the **dominant estate**. Adjacent land is defined as two estates that are in proximity to each other but do not necessarily abut each other. An easement appurtenant runs with the land. For example, if an owner sells the servient estate, the new owner acquires the benefit of the easement. If an owner sells the dominant estate, the buyer purchases the property subject to the easement.

easement in gross
An easement that authorizes a person who does not own adjacent land to use another's land.

- ***Easements in gross.*** An **easement in gross** authorizes a person who does not own adjacent land the right to use another's land. An easement in gross is a personal right because it does not depend on the easement holder owning adjacent land. Thus, there is no dominant estate. Examples of easements in gross include those granted to run power, telephone, and cable television lines across an owner's property. Commercial easements in gross run with the land.

The easement holder owes a duty to maintain and repair the easement. The owner of the estate can use the property as long as it does not interfere with the easement. For example, if a piece of property is subject to an easement for an underground pipeline, the owner of the property could graze cattle or plant crops on the land above the easement, subject to the easement holder's right to repair the pipeline.

In the following case, the court had to decide whether an easement had been created.

Case 28.4

Easement

Walker v. Ayres
1993 Del. Lexis 105
Supreme Court of Delaware

Background and Facts

Elizabeth Star Ayres and Clara Louise Quillen owned in fee simple absolute a tract of land in Sussex County known as "Bluff Point." The tract was surrounded on three sides by Rehoboth Bay and was landlocked on the fourth side by land owned by Irvin C. Walker. At one time, the two tracts had been held by a common owner. In 1878, Bluff Point was sold in fee simple absolute apart from the other holdings, thereby landlocking the parcel. A narrow dirt road, which traversed Walker's land, connected Bluff Point to a public road and was its only means of access. Ayres and Quillen sought an easement to use this road, and Walker objected. A lawsuit ensued. The trial court granted an easement. Walker appealed.

Issue

Should Ayres and Quillen's estate be granted an easement against Walker's estate?

In the Language of the Court

Based upon our review of the record, we conclude that the factual findings of the trial court are clearly sustainable. There is ample evidence in the record to support the finding that the two tracts originated from the unified holdings of one owner and that an implied easement was created by the severance which landlocked Bluff Point. The record also sufficiently supports the finding that navigable access to Bluff Point was not feasible.

Decision and Remedy

The supreme court held that an easement had been created. The supreme court affirmed the trial court's judgment granting an easement to Ayres and Quillen.

Business and Ethics Questions

1. Should easements be recognized by the law? Why or why not?
2. Did Walker act ethically in denying the easement? Did Ayres and Quillen act ethically in seeking to use Walker's property?
3. Does an easement increase or decrease the value of the servient estate? of the dominant estate?

License

A **license** grants a person the right to enter upon another's property for a specified and usually short period of time. The person granting the license is called the **licensor**; the person receiving the license is called the **licensee**. For example, a common license is a ticket to a movie theater or sporting event that grants the holder the right to enter the premises for the performance. A license does not transfer any interest in the property. A license is a personal privilege that may be revoked by the licensor at any time.

license
Permission for a person to enter upon another's property for a specified and usually short period of time.

Profit

A **profit a'pendre** (or **profit**) gives the holder the right to remove something from another's real property. Profits usually involve the right to remove gravel, minerals, grain, or timber from another's property.

profit
Permission for a person to remove something from another's real property.

Landlord–Tenant Relationship

Landlord–tenant relationships are very common in the United States because (1) over half of the population rent their homes and (2) many businesses lease office space, stores, manufacturing facilities, and other commercial property. The parties to the relationship have certain legal rights and duties that are governed by a mixture of real estate and contract law.

The tenant's interest in the property is called a **leasehold estate**, or **leasehold**. The owner who transfers the leasehold estate is called the **landlord**, or **lessor**. The party to whom the leasehold estate is transferred is called the **tenant**, or **lessee**. A landlord–tenant relationship is illustrated in Exhibit 28.1.

landlord–tenant relationship
A relationship created when the owner of a freehold estate (landlord) transfers a right to exclusively and temporarily possess the owner's property to another (tenant).

leasehold
A tenant's interest in leased property.

landlord
The owner who transfers a leasehold.

tenant
The party to whom a leasehold is transferred.

Exhibit 28.1

Landlord–Tenant Relationship

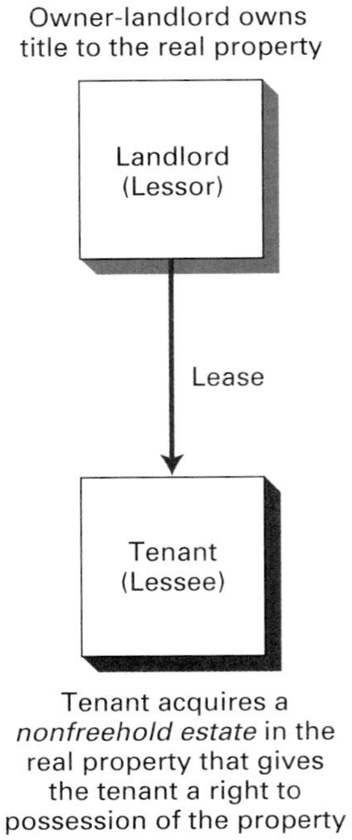

Types of Tenancy

A landlord–tenant relationship is created when the owner of a freehold estate (i.e., an estate in fee or a life estate) transfers a right to exclusively and temporarily possess the owner's property. The tenant receives a *nonfreehold estate* in the property—that is, the tenant has a right to possession of the property but not title to the property.

There are four types of *tenancies*:

tenancy for years
A tenancy created when a landlord and a tenant agree on the specific duration for a lease.

1. ***Tenancy for years.*** A **tenancy for years** is created when the landlord and the tenant agree on a specific duration for the lease. Any lease for a stated period—no matter how long or short—is called a tenancy for years. Examples of such arrangements include office space leased in a high-rise office building on a 30-year lease and a cabin leased for the summer. A tenancy for years terminates automatically, without notice, upon the expiration of the stated term.

periodic tenancy
A tenancy created when a lease specifies intervals at which payments are due but does not specify how long the lease is for.

2. ***Periodic tenancy.*** A **periodic tenancy** is created when a lease specifies intervals at which payments are due but does not specify how long the lease is for. A lease that states, "Rent is due on the first day of the month" establishes a periodic tenancy. Many such leases are created by implication. A periodic tenancy may be terminated by either party at the end of any payment interval, but adequate notice of the termination must be given. Under common law, the notice period equaled the length of the payment period. That is, a month-to-month tenancy required a one-month notice of termination.

tenancy at will
A lease that may be terminated at any time by either party.

3. ***Tenancy at will.*** A lease that may be terminated at any time by either party is a **tenancy at will**. A tenancy at will may be created expressly (e.g., "to tenant as long as landlord wishes") but is more likely to be created by implication. Most states have enacted statutes requiring minimum advance notice for the termination of a tenancy at will. The death of either party terminates a tenancy at will.

tenancy at sufferance
A tenancy created when a tenant retains possession of property after the expiration of another tenancy or a life estate without the owner's consent.

4. ***Tenancy at sufferance.*** A **tenancy at sufferance** is created when a tenant retains possession of property after the expiration of another tenancy or a life estate without the owner's consent. That is, the owner suffers the *wrongful possession* of his or her property by the holdover tenant. This is not really a true tenancy but merely the possession of property without right. Technically, a tenant at sufferance is a trespasser.

A tenant at sufferance is liable for the payment of rent during the period of sufferance. Most states require an owner to go through certain legal proceedings, called *eviction proceedings* or *unlawful detainer actions,* to evict a holdover tenant. A few states allow owners to use self-help to evict a holdover tenant if force is not used.

The Lease

The rental agreement between a landlord and a tenant is called the **lease**. Leases can generally be either oral or written, except that most Statutes of Frauds require written leases for periods of time longer than one year. The lease must contain the essential terms of the parties' agreement. The lease is often a form contract that is prepared by the landlord and presented to the tenant. This practice is particularly true of residential leases. Other leases are negotiated between the parties. For example, Bank of America's lease of a branch office would be negotiated with the owner of the building.

lease
A transfer of the right to the possession and use of real property for a set term in return for certain consideration; the rental agreement between a landlord and a tenant.

Implied Warranty of Habitability

The courts of many jurisdictions hold that an **implied warranty of habitability** applies to residential leases for their duration. This warranty provides that the leased premises must be fit, safe, and suitable for ordinary residential use. For example, unchecked rodent infestation, leaking roofs, unworkable bathroom facilities, and the like have been held to breach the implied warranty of habitability. On the other hand, a small crack in the wall or some paint peeling from a door does not breach this warranty.

implied warranty of habitability
A warranty that provides that leased premises must be fit, safe, and suitable for ordinary residential use.

If the landlord's failure to maintain or repair the leased premises affects the tenant's use of enjoyment of the premises, state statutes and judicial decisions provide various remedies. Generally, the tenant may (1) withhold from his or her rent the amount by

Soho, New York City. Many people rent apartments from landlords. The landlord and tenant owe each other certain dues.

which the defect reduced the value of the premises to him or her, (2) repair the defect and deduct the cost of repairs from the rent due for the leased premises, (3) cancel the lease if the failure to repair constitutes constructive eviction, or (4) sue for damages in the amount the landlord's failure to repair the defect reduced the value of the leasehold.

Land Use Regulation

Although the United States has the most advanced private property system in the world, the ownership and possession of real estate is not free of government regulation. Pursuant to constitutional authority, federal, state, and local governments have enacted myriad laws that regulate ownership, possession, and use of real property. These laws are collectively referred to as **land use regulation,** or **land use control**. Several forms of land use regulation are discussed in the following paragraphs.

land use regulation
The collective term for the laws that regulate the possession, ownership, and use of real property. Also called *land use control*.

Zoning

zoning ordinances
Local laws that are adopted by municipalities and local governments to regulate land use within their boundaries.

Most countries and municipalities have enacted **zoning ordinances** to regulate land use. Zoning ordinances generally (1) establish use districts within the municipality (i.e., areas are generally designated residential, commercial, or industrial); (2) restrict the height, size, and location of buildings on a building site; and (3) establish aesthetic requirements or limitations for the exterior of buildings.

A **zoning commission** usually formulates zoning ordinances, conducts public hearings, and makes recommendations to the city council, which must vote to enact an ordinance. Once a zoning ordinance is enacted, the zoning ordinance commission enforces it. If landowners believe that a zoning ordinance is illegal or that it has been applied unlawfully to them or their property, they may institute a court proceeding seeking judicial review of the ordinance or its application.

variance
An exception that permits a type of building or use in an area that would not otherwise be allowed by a zoning ordinance.

nonconforming uses
Uses and buildings that already exist in a zoned area that are permitted to continue even though they do not fit within new zoning ordinances.

An owner who wishes to use his or her property for a use different from that permitted under a current zoning ordinance may seek relief from the ordinance by obtaining a **variance**. To obtain a variance, the landowner must prove that the ordinance causes an undue hardship by preventing him or her from making a reasonable return on the land as zoned. Variances are usually difficult to obtain.

Zoning laws act prospectively; that is, uses and buildings that already exist in the zoned area are permitted to continue even though they do not fit within new zoning ordinances. Such uses are called **nonconforming uses**. For example, if a new zoning ordinance is enacted, making an area a residential zone, an existing funeral parlor is a nonconforming use.

Contemporary Trend

Rent Control

Many local communities across the country have enacted **rent control ordinances** that stipulate the amount of rent a landlord can charge for residential housing. Most of these ordinances fix the rent at a specific amount and provide for minor annual increases. Although many communities have adopted rent control ordinances, New York City has the most famous one.

Landlords, of course, oppose rent control, arguing that rent control ordinances are merely a "regulatory tax" that transfers wealth from landowners to tenants. Tenants and proponents of rent control say that it is necessary to create affordable housing, particularly in high-rent urban areas.

The U.S. Supreme Court has upheld the use of rent control. *Yee v. City of Escondido, California*, 503 U.S. 519, 112 S.Ct. 1522, 1992 U.S. Lexis 2115 (U.S. Sup.Ct.) ■

Eminent Domain

The government may use its power of **eminent domain** to acquire private property for public purposes. However, the Due Process Clause of the U.S. Constitution (and state constitutions, where applicable) requires the government to allow the owner to make a case for keeping the property. The **Just Compensation Clause** of the Fifth Amendment to the U.S. Constitution requires the government to compensate the property owner (and possibly others, such as lessees) when it exercises the power of eminent domain. Anyone who is not satisfied with the compensation offered by the government can bring an action to have the court determine the compensation to be paid. Often, the government's action is not considered a "taking," even if it causes economic losses to property owners and others.

eminent domain
A doctrine under which the government may take private property for public use, provided that just compensation is paid to the private property holder.

Just Compensation Clause
A clause of the U.S. Constitution that requires the government to compensate the property owner, and possibly others, when the government takes property under its power of eminent domain.

Consider This Example Assume that ITT has acquired a large piece of property, with the intention of erecting a commercial building at some future time. Now suppose the government wants to build a new highway that passes through the property owned by ITT. The government can use its power of eminent domain to acquire the property. There has been a "taking," so the government must pay ITT just compensation. Suppose, instead, that the government enacts a zoning law that affects ITT's property by restricting building in the area to single-family housing. Although ITT would suffer a substantial economic loss, the zoning law, nevertheless, would probably not constitute a "taking" that required the payment of compensation.

Inle Lake, Myanmar. Many countries do not have well-developed real estate laws. This house on the Inle Lake in Myanmar is built on stilts.

Terms and Concepts

Real Property

Real property is immovable. It includes land, buildings, subsurface rights, air rights, plant life, and fixtures.

Freehold Estates

A *freehold estate* is an estate in which the owner has a present possessory interest in the real property.

Estates in Fee

1. ***Fee simple absolute (or fee simple).*** Fee simple absolute is the highest form of real property ownership.
2. ***Fee simple defeasible (or qualified fee).*** A fee simple defeasible estate ends if a specified condition occurs.

Life Estates

A life estate is an interest in real property that lasts for the life of a specified person. It is called an *estate pour autre vie* if the time is measured by the life of a third person.

Concurrent Ownership

Concurrent ownership is a situation in which two or more persons jointly own real property.

1. ***Joint tenancy.*** In joint tenancy, owners may transfer their interests without the consent of co-owners. Transfer severs the joint tenancy. Under the *right of survivorship*, the interest of a deceased owner passes to his or her co-owners.
2. ***Tenancy in common.*** In tenancy in common, owners may transfer their interests without the consent of co-owners. Transfer does not sever the tenancy in common. The interest of a deceased owner passes to his or her estate.
3. ***Tenancy by the entirety.*** Tenancy by the entirety is a form of co-ownership that can be used only by married couples. Neither spouse may transfer his or her interest without the other spouse's consent. A surviving spouse has the right of survivorship.

Community Property

Community property is a form of co-ownership that applies only to married couples. Neither spouse may transfer his or her interest without the other spouse's consent. When a spouse dies, the surviving spouse automatically receives one-half the community property.

Condominium

Condominium owners have title to their individual units and own the common areas as tenants in common. Owners may transfer their interests without the consent of other owners.

Cooperative

In a cooperative, a corporation owns the building and the residents own shares of the corporation. Usually, owners may not transfer their shares without the approval of the other owners.

Future Interests

A future interest is a right to possess real property in the future rather than currently.

1. ***Reversion.*** In a reversion situation, the right to possession returns to the grantor after the expiration of a limited or contingent estate.
2. ***Remainder.*** In a remainder situation, the right to possession goes to a third person after the expiration of a limited or contingent estate. The third person is called a *remainder beneficiary*.

Sale of Real Estate

An owner may sell his or her property to another for consideration.

Deed

A deed is an instrument used to convey real property by sale or gift.

1. ***Warranty deed.*** A warranty deed provides the most protection to the grantee because the grantor makes warranties against defect in title.
2. ***Quitclaim deed.*** A quitclaim deed provides the least amount of protection to the grantee because the grantor transfers only the interest he or she has in the property.

Recording Statutes

Under recording statutes, copies of deeds and other documents concerning interests in real property (e.g., mortgages, liens) must be filed in a government office, where they become public record. This puts third parties on notice of recorded interests.

Marketable Title

A marketable title is free from any undisclosed encumbrances, defects in title, or other defects. There are several methods for assuring marketable title:

1. ***Attorney's opinion.*** An attorney may render an opinion concerning status of the title.
2. ***Torrens system.*** A court may issue a *certificate of title* to the rightful owner of the property.
3. ***Title insurance.*** A title insurer may agree to reimburse the insured for losses caused by undiscovered defects in title.

Adverse Possession

A person who occupies another's property acquires title to the property if the occupation has been:

1. For a statutory period of time (in many states, 10 to 20 years)
2. Open, visible, and notorious
3. Actual and exclusive
4. Continuous and peaceful
5. Hostile and adverse

Easements

An easement is an interest in land that gives the holder the right to make limited use of another's property without taking anything from it (e.g., driveways, party walls).

1. ***Easement appurtenant.*** An easement appurtenant gives the owner of land an easement over an adjacent piece of land.
2. ***Easement in gross.*** An easement in gross authorizes a person who does not own adjacent land the right to use another's land.

Landlord–Tenant Relationship

A landlord–tenant relationship is created when an owner of a freehold estate transfers a right to another to exclusively and temporarily possess the owner's property.

Types of Tenancy

1. ***Tenancy for years.*** A tenancy for years is a tenancy for a specified period of time.
2. ***Periodic tenancy.*** Periodic tenancy is tenancy for a period of time determined by the payment interval.
3. ***Tenancy at will.*** Tenancy at will is tenancy that may be terminated at any time by either party.
4. ***Tenancy at sufferance.*** Tenancy at sufferance is created by the wrongful possession of property.

Lease

A lease is a rental agreement between a landlord and a tenant that contains the essential terms of the parties' agreement.

Implied Warranty of Habitability

A warranty of habitability, which is implied by law in residential leases, provides that leased premises must be fit, safe, and suitable for ordinary residential use.

Zoning

Zoning ordinances are laws adopted by local governments that restrict use of property, set building standards, and establish architectural requirements.

1. ***Variance.*** A variance permits an owner to make a nonzoned use of his or her property. A variance requires permission from a zoning board.
2. ***Nonconforming use.*** A noncomforming use is a nonzoned use that is permitted (grandfathered in) when an area is rezoned.

Eminent Domain

Under the doctrine of eminent domain, the government may take private property for public use, provided that just compensation is paid to the private property holder.

1. ***Just Compensation Clause.*** This clause of the U.S. Constitution mandates that the government compensate the property owner (and possibly others, such as lessees) when it exercises the power of eminent domain.

Internet Exercises and Case Questions

Working the Web Internet Exercises

1. Some states have special laws related to land and Indian tribes. See, for example, Washington state statute RCW 64.20—Alienation of Land by Indians. Does your state have any similar laws? See "Legal Information Institute: Real Estate Transactions," at **www.law.cornell.edu/topics/real_estate.html**, for an overview of real estate law with links to key primary and secondary sources.
2. Although most real estate law is local law, there are important federal controls on certain types of transactions. See 42 U.S.C., Chapter 45—Federal Air Housing Act.
3. Is your state one that has adopted the Uniform Residential Landlord and Tenant Act? See **www.law.cornell.edu/uniform/vol7.html#lndtn**.
4. There is an ongoing and vigorous debate about government authority to regulate land use without paying compensation to the property owner. Read the law review article "Windfalls or Windmills: The Right of a Property Owner to Challenge Land Use Regulations," at **www.law.fsu.edu/journals/landuse/Vol131/ABRA.html**, for an overview of the Taking Clause of the Fifth Amendment and related issues.

Legal Environment Cases

28.1 Subsurface Rights In 1883, Isaac McIlwee owned 100 acres of land in Valley Township, Guernsey County, Ohio. In that year, he sold the property to Akron & Cambridge Coal Company (Akron & Cambridge) in fee simple but reserved in fee simple "the surface of all said lands" to himself. Over the years, the interests in the land were transferred to many different parties. As of 1981, the Mid-Ohio Coal Company owned the rights originally transferred to Akron & Cambridge, and Peter and Irene Minnich owned the rights reserved by Isaac McIlwee in 1883. The Minniches claim they posses subsurface rights to the property except for coal rights. Who wins? *Minnich v. Guernsey Savings and Loan Company*, 521 N.E.2d 489, 1987 OhioApp. Lexis 10497 (Ohio App.)

28.2 Life Estate and Remainder Baudilio Bowles died testate. His will devised to his sister, Julianita B. Vigil, "one-half of any income, rents, or profits from any real property located in Bull Creek or Colonias, New Mexico." The will contained another clause that left to his children "my interest in any real property owned by me at the time of my death, located in Bull Creek and/or Colonias, San Miguel County." The property referred to in both devises is the same property. Julianita died before the will was probated. Her heirs claim a one-half ownership interest in the real property. Bowles's children asserted that they owned all his property. Who wins? *In the matter of the Estate of Bowles*, 764 P.2d 510, 1988 N.M.App. Lexis 93 (N.M. App.)

28.3 Reversion In 1941, W. E. and Jennie Hutton conveyed land they owned to the Trustees of Schools of District Number One of the Town of Allison, Illinois (School District), by warranty deed "to be used for school purpose only; otherwise to revert to Grantor." The School District built a school on the site, commonly known as Hutton School. The Huttons conveyed the adjoining farmland and their reversionary interest in the school site to the Jacqmains, who in turn conveyed their interest to Herbert and Betty Mahrenholz in 1959. The 1.5-acre site sits in the middle of the Mahrenholz farmland. In May 1973, School District discontinued holding regular classes at Hutton School. Instead, it used the school building to warehouse and store miscellaneous school equipment, supplies, unused desks, and the like. In 1974, Mahrenholz filed suit to quiet title to the school property to themselves. Who wins? *Mahrenholz v. County Board of School Trustees of Lawrence County*, 544 N.E.2d 128, 1989 Ill.App. Lexis 1445 (Ill. App.)

28.4 Joint Tenancy Verna M. Chappell owned a piece of real property. On June 16, 1965, Chappell transferred the property to herself and her niece Bertha M. Stewart as joint tenants. When Chappell died in 1981, Chappell's gross estate was set at $28,321, which included the value of the house. Claims, debts, and charges against the estate totaled $19,451, which included a $14,040 claim by Lorna M. Rembe for services provided as conservator. The probate assets available to pay the claims and debts came to only $1,571 if the real property went to Stewart as the joint tenant. Rembe sued, alleging that the value of the real property should be used to pay off Chappell's debts and claims. Who wins? *Rembe v. Stewart*, 387 N.W.2d 313, 1986 IowaSup. Lexis 1177 (Iowa)

28.5 Tenancy by the Entirety Charles Jetter Eichman and his wife, Cora Paton Eichman, were married on August 12, 1965. In 1968, they purchased a house in Tallahassee, Florida, taking title in their joint names as husband and wife, thus creating a tenancy by the entirety. In 1971, they separated, and Cora moved to Vancouver, Canada. Charles continued to live in the marital home in Florida. In January 1975, Cora filed a petition for divorce. On March 31, 1975, Charles struck Cora on the head with a pipe, causing injuries that rendered her incapable of managing herself or her affairs and bringing to an end the divorce proceeding. A guardian was appointed for her. Charles was convicted of attempted murder and was sentenced to prison for 10 years. Cora's guardian filed an action seeking to partition the martial property located in Florida. Charles answered, alleging that an estate by the entirety is not subject to partition as long as the parties remain married. Who wins? *Eichman v. Paton*, 393 So.2d 655, 1981 Fla.App. Lexis 19454 (Fla. App.)

28.6 Easement in Gross John L. Yutterman died in 1953 and left one piece of property, located in Fort Smith, Arkansas, to his two sons and two daughters. Each child received approximately one-fourth of the property in fee simple. A 40-foot driveway divided the property. Concerning the driveway, Yutterman's will provided as follows: "Further, a specific condition of this will and of these devises is that the forty (40) foot driveway from Free Ferry Road, three hundred (300) feet Northward, shall be kept open for the common use of the devisees in this will." In 1982, one of the daughters wanted to sell her property to a third party. If the third party purchases the property, will that party have an easement to use the driveway? *Merriman v. Yutterman,* 723 S.W.2d 823, 1987 Ark. Lexis 1934 (Ark.)

28.7 Adverse Possession In 1973, Joseph and Helen Naab purchased a tract of land in a subdivision of Williamstown, West Virginia. At the time of purchase, there was both a house and a small concrete garage on the property. Evidence showed that the garage had been erected sometime prior to 1952 by one of the Naabs' predecessors in title. In 1975, Roger and Cynthia Nolan purchased a lot contiguous to that owned by the Naabs. The following year, the Nolans had their property surveyed. The survey indicated that one corner of the Naabs' garage encroached 1.22 feet onto the Nolans' property and the other corner encroached 0.91 feet over the property line. The Nolans requested that the Naabs remove the garage from their property. When the Naabs refused, a lawsuit ensued. Who wins? *Naab v. Nolan*, 327 S.E.2d 151, 1985 W.Va. Lexis 476 (W.Va.)

28.8 Implied Warranty of Habitability Sharon Love entered into a written lease agreement with Monarch Apartments for apartment 4 at 441 Winfield in Topeka, Kansas. Shortly after moving in, she experienced serious problems with termites. Her walls swelled, clouds of dirt came out, and when she checked on her children one night, she saw termites flying around the room. She complained to Monarch, which arranged for the apartment to be fumigated. When the termite problem persisted, Monarch moved Love and her children to apartment 2. Upon moving in, Love noticed that roaches crawled over the walls, ceilings, and floors of the apartment. She complained, and Monarch called an exterminator, who sprayed the apartment. When the roach problem persisted, Love vacated the premises. Did Love lawfully terminate the lease? *Love v. Monarch Apartments*, 771 P.2d 79, 1989 Kan.App. Lexis 219 (Kan. App.)

28.9 Zoning The city of Ladue was one of the finer suburban residential areas of metropolitan St. Louis. The homes in the city were considerably more expensive than those in surrounding areas and consisted of homes of traditional design such as colonial, French provincial, and English. The city set up an architectural board to approve plans for buildings that "conform to certain minimum architectural standards of appearance and conformity with surrounding structures, and that unsightly, grotesque, and unsuitable structures, detrimental to the stability of value and the welfare of surrounding property, structures, and residents, and to the general welfare and happiness of the community, be avoided." The owner of a lot in the city submitted a plan to build a house of ultramodern design. It was pyramid-shaped, with a flat top and triangular-shaped windows and doors. Although the house plans met other city zoning ordinances and building codes, the architectural board rejected the owner's petition for a building permit based on aesthetic reasons. The owner sued the city. Who wins? *State of Missouri v. Berkeley,* 458 S.W.2d 305, 1970 Mo. Lexis 902 (Mo.)

28.10 Zoning The town of Hempstead, New Hampshire, enacted a zoning ordinance "in order to retain the beauty and countrified atmosphere of the town, and to promote health, safety, morals, order, convenience, peace, prosperity, and general welfare of its inhabitants." To preserve abutting property owners' views and light, the ordinance limited the homes in the town to one-and-one-half stories. In violation of the ordinance, John M. Alexander built a shell of a second story and a new roof on his house. After the town ordered him to halt construction and denied him permission to occupy the second floor, he applied for a variance. Should the variance be granted? *Alexander v. Town of Hempstead*, 525 A.2d 276, 1987 N.H. Lexis 171 (N.H.)

Ethics in Business

28.11 On March 19, 1971, Victor and Phyllis Garber acquired a piece of real property by warranty deed. The deed was recorded on December 30, 1971. The property consisted of 80 acres enclosed by a fence that had been in place for over 50 years. The enclosed area was used to graze cattle and produce hay. Subsequently, William and Herbert Doenz acquired a piece of real property adjacent to the Garbers'. In March 1981, the Doenzes employed a surveyor to locate their land's boundaries. As a result of the survey, it was discovered that the shared fence was 20 to 30 feet inside the deed line on the Doenz property. The amount of property between the old fence and the deed line was 3.01 acres. In September 1981, the Doenzes removed the old fence and constructed a new fence along the deed line. The Garbers brought suit to quiet title. *Doenz v. Garber,* 665 P.2d 932, 1983 Wyo. Lexis 339 (Wy.)

Ethics Issues

1. Did the Doenzes act ethically in removing the fence?

2. Did the Garbers Act ethically in claiming title to property that originally belonged with the adjacent property?

3. Did the Garbers acquire title to the property between the fence and the deed through adverse possession?

29

Bankruptcy and the Bankruptcy Abuse Prevention and Consumer Protection Act of 2005

"A trifling debt makes a man your debtor, a large one makes him your enemy."

—Seneca
Epistulae Morales and Lucilium, 63–65

Chapter Objectives

After studying this chapter, you should be able to:

1. Identify and describe the major changes to federal bankruptcy law made by the Bankruptcy Abuse Prevention and Consumer Protection Act of 2005.
2. Describe a Chapter 7 liquidation bankruptcy and the means test for filing for Chapter 7 bankruptcy.
3. Describe a Chapter 13 adjustment of debts of an individual with regular income.
4. Describe how businesses are reorganized in Chapter 11 bankruptcy.
5. Describe a Chapter 12 adjustment of debts of a family farmer or fisherman with regular income.

Chapter Contents

- Bankruptcy Abuse Prevention and Consumer Protection Act of 2005
- Bankruptcy Procedure

- The Bankruptcy Estate
- Preferential and Fraudulent Transfers
- Chapter 7: Liquidation
- Chapter 13: Adjustment of Debts of an Individual with Regular Income
- Chapter 11: Reorganization
- Chapter 12: Family Farmer and Family Fisherman Bankruptcy
- Special Forms of Bankruptcy

The extension of credit from creditors to debtors in commercial and personal transactions is important to the viability of the U.S. and world economies. On occasion, however, borrowers become overextended and are unable to meet their debt obligations. The goal of bankruptcy laws is to balance the rights of debtors and creditors and provide methods for debtors to be relieved of some debt in order to obtain a "fresh start."

The founders of our country thought that the plight of debtors was so important that they included a provision in the U.S. Constitution giving Congress the authority to establish uniform federal bankruptcy laws. Congress enacted bankruptcy laws pursuant to this power. Prior to 2005, the most recent overhaul of federal bankruptcy law occurred in 1978. The 1978 law was structured to make it easier for debtors to be relieved of much of their debt by declaring bankruptcy. The 1976 act was deemed "debtor friendly" because it allowed many debtors to escape from their unsecured debts.

After a decade of lobbying by credit card companies and banks, Congress enacted the **Bankruptcy Abuse Prevention and Consumer Protection Act of 2005.** The 2005 act makes it much more difficult for debtors to escape from their debts under federal bankruptcy law. The 2005 act, which has been criticized by consumer groups for being too "creditor friendly," has been praised by many businesses, banks, and credit card issuers.

This chapter discusses federal bankruptcy law, including how the provisions of the Bankruptcy Abuse Prevention and Consumer Protection Act of 2005 have changed bankruptcy law.

Family farm, Idaho. Chapter 12 of the federal Bankruptcy Code contains special provisions for reorganizing family farmers and family fishermen.

Bankruptcy Abuse Prevention and Consumer Protection Act of 2005

Article I, section 8, clause 4 of the U.S. Constitution provides that "The Congress shall have the power . . . to establish . . . uniform laws on the subject of bankruptcies throughout the United States." Bankruptcy law is exclusively federal law; there are no state bankruptcy laws. Congress enacted the original federal Bankruptcy Act in 1878. The Bankruptcy Code is contained in Title 11 of the *United States Code* (U.S.C.).

Bankruptcy Reform Act of 1978
A federal act that substantially changed federal bankruptcy law. It made it easier for debtors to file for bankruptcy and have their unpaid debts discharged. This act was often referred to as being debtor friendly.

Federal bankruptcy law was completely revised by the **Bankruptcy Reform Act of 1978**.[1] The 1978 act substantially changed—and eased—the requirements for filing for bankruptcy. The 1978 act made it easier for debtors to rid themselves of unsecured debt, primarily by filing for Chapter 7 liquidation bankruptcy. By the year 2005, more than one million debtors per year were filing for Chapter 7 liquidation bankruptcy.

For over a decade before 2005, credit card companies, commercial banks, and other businesses lobbied Congress to pass a new bankruptcy act that would reduce the ability of some debtors to relieve themselves of unwanted debt through bankruptcy. In response, Congress enacted the **Bankruptcy Abuse Prevention and Consumer Protection Act of 2005**.[2] The 2005 act substantially amended federal bankruptcy law, making it much more difficult for debtors to escape unwanted debt through bankruptcy.

Bankruptcy Abuse Prevention and Consumer Protection Act of 2005
A federal act that substantially amended federal bankruptcy law. It makes it more difficult for debtors to file for bankruptcy and have their unpaid debts discharged.

Federal bankruptcy law, as amended, is called the **Bankruptcy Code**. The Bankruptcy Code establishes procedures for filing for bankruptcy, resolving creditors' claims, and protecting debtors' rights.

Bankruptcy Code
The name given to federal bankruptcy law, as amended.

Types of Bankruptcy

The Bankruptcy Code is divided into chapters. Chapters 1, 3, and 5 set forth definitions and general provisions that govern case administration. The provisions of these chapters generally apply to all forms of bankruptcy.

Four special chapters of the Bankruptcy Code provide different types of bankruptcy under which individual and business debtors may be granted remedy. These four types of bankruptcies, and the filing fees established by the 2005 act, are:

Chapter	Type of Bankruptcy	Filing Fee
Chapter 7	Liquidation	$200
Chapter 11	Reorganization	$1,000
Chapter 12	Adjustment of debts of a family farmer or fisherman with regular income	$200
Chapter 13	Adjustment of debts of an individual with regular income	$150

These types of bankruptcies are covered in detail in this chapter. Several special forms of bankruptcy that are also provided in the Bankruptcy Code are also covered.

"Fresh Start"

fresh start
The goal of federal bankruptcy law, which grants a debtor relief from some of his or her burdensome debts, while protecting creditors by requiring the debtor to pay more of his or her debts than would otherwise have been required prior to the 2005 act.

The primary purpose of federal bankruptcy law is to grant different forms of relief to debtors from overly burdensome debt while at the same time protecting some of the rights of creditors. The granting of bankruptcy gives debtors a **"fresh start"** by freeing them of some legal responsibility for past debts. Prior to the 2005 act, debtors were more likely to obtain an almost complete fresh start under Chapter 7 liquidation bankruptcy. With the changes made by the 2005 act, however, a debtor may sometimes obtain only a partial fresh start because he or she may have to pay more of his prepetition bankruptcy debts out of postpetition earnings than required prior to the 2005 act.

Federal bankruptcy law is designed to accomplish the following: (1) protect debtors from abusive activities by creditors in collecting debts; (2) prevent certain creditors from obtaining an unfair advantage over other creditors; (3) protect creditors from actions of a debtor that would diminish the value of the bankruptcy estate; (4) provide for the speedy, efficient, and equitable distribution of the debtor's nonexempt property to creditors; (5) require debtors to repay debts if they have the means to do so; and (6) preserve existing business relationships.

Bankruptcy Courts

Congress created a system of federal **bankruptcy courts**. These special courts are necessary because the number of bankruptcies would overwhelm the federal district courts. The bankruptcy courts are part of the federal court system, and one bankruptcy court is attached to each of the 96 U.S. district courts located across the country. The **Bankruptcy Reform Act of 2005** increased the number of bankruptcy judges to handle the increasing number and complexity of bankruptcy cases.

bankruptcy courts
Special federal courts that hear and decide bankruptcy cases.

Bankruptcy Reform Act of 2005
A federal statute that increased the number of bankruptcy judges.

Bankruptcy judges are specialists that hear bankruptcy proceedings. Pursuant to the 2005 act, bankruptcy judges are appointed by the U.S. Circuit Court of Appeals for the circuit in which the bankruptcy court district is located. Bankruptcy judges are appointed for 14-year terms. The relevant district court has jurisdiction to hear appeals from bankruptcy court. However, a Bankruptcy Appellate Panel Service, which is composed of bankruptcy judges of the relevant district, can hear and decide appeals if the parties consent.

Bankruptcy judges decide *core proceedings* regarding bankruptcy issues (e.g., allowing creditor claims, deciding preferences, confirming plans of reorganization). *Noncore* proceedings involving the debtor (e.g., personal injury lawsuits, divorce proceedings, criminal cases, other civil cases) are heard and decided by the relevant state or federal court.

United States Trustee

Federal law establishes the office of the **United States Trustee**. The U.S. Trustee is a federal government official who has the responsibility of handling and supervising many of the administrative tasks associated with a bankruptcy case.[3] The U.S. Trustee is empowered to perform many of the tasks that the bankruptcy judge had previously performed. One such task is the appointment of interim trustees to take control of a debtor's assets prior to a permanent trustee being elected by the creditors and the supervision of trustees in Chapter 7, 11, 12, and 13 cases. Each U.S. Trustee is under the general supervision of the U.S. Attorney General. The U.S. Trustee must notify the U.S. Attorney General of any action that may constitute a crime in a bankruptcy case.

United States Trustee
A federal government official who is responsible for handling and supervising many of the administrative tasks of a bankruptcy case.

Bankruptcy Procedure

The Bankruptcy Code requires that certain procedures be followed for the commencement and prosecution of a bankruptcy case. The Bankruptcy Code provides procedures and requirements for filing petitions for bankruptcy, defines the bankruptcy estate, provides certain protections to debtors during the course of bankruptcy, and establishes the rights of creditors. These issues are discussed in the following paragraphs.

Prepetition and Postpetition Counseling

The 2005 act added a new provision that requires an individual filing for bankruptcy to receive prepetition and postpetition credit and financial counseling. The debtor must receive prepetition credit counseling within 180 days prior to the debtor filing his or her petition for bankruptcy. This includes counseling on types of credit, the use of credit, and budget analysis. The counseling is to be provided by nonprofit credit counseling agencies approved by the U.S. Trustee.

In addition, the 2005 act requires that before an individual debtor receives a discharge in a Chapter 7 or Chapter 13 bankruptcy, the debtor must attend a personal financial management course approved by the U.S. Trustee. This course is designed to provide the debtor with information on responsible use of credit and personal financial planning.

The prepetition credit counseling and the postpetition financial management counseling may be provided in person, over the telephone, or on the Internet. Individuals unable to receive such services due to disability, impairment, or active military duty in a combat zone are excused from these requirements.

Filing a Bankruptcy Petition

petition
A document filed with the bankruptcy court that starts a bankruptcy proceeding.

voluntary petition
A petition filed by a debtor that states that the debtor has debts.

involuntary petition
A petition filed by creditors of a debtor that alleges that the debtor is not paying his or her debts as they become due.

A bankruptcy case is commenced when a **petition** is filed with the bankruptcy court. Two types of petitions can be filed:

1. ***Voluntary petition.*** A debtor files a **voluntary petition**. A debtor can file a voluntary petition in Chapter 7 (liquidation), Chapter 11 (reorganization), Chapter 12 (family farmer or fisherman), and Chapter 13 (adjustment of debts) bankruptcy cases. The petition has to state that the debtor has debts.
2. ***Involuntary petition.*** A creditor (or creditors) files an **involuntary petition** and places the debtor into bankruptcy. An involuntary petition can be filed in Chapter 7 (liquidation) and Chapter 11 (reorganization) cases; an involuntary petition cannot be filed in Chapter 12 (family farmer or fisherman) or Chapter 13 (adjustment of debts) cases.

   An involuntary petition must allege that the debtor is not paying his or her debts as they become due. If the debtor has 12 or more creditors, the petition must be signed by at least three of them. If there are fewer than 12 creditors, any creditor can sign the petition. The creditor or creditors who sign the petition must have valid unsecured claims of at least $12,300 in aggregate.

Form B1, a Voluntary Petition for Bankruptcy, appears as Exhibit 29.1.

Schedules

An individual debtor must submit the following schedules upon filing a voluntary petition:

1. List of secured and unsecured creditors, with addresses
2. List of all property owned
3. Statement of the financial affairs of the debtor
4. Statement of the debtor's monthly income
5. Current income and expenses

(Official Form 1) (12/03)

FORM B1 **United States Bankruptcy Court** **District of** ____________ ____________	**Voluntary Petition**
Name of Debtor (if individual, enter Last, First, Middle):	Name of Joint Debtor (Spouse) (Last, First, Middle):
All Other Names used by the Debtor in the last 6 years (include married, maiden, and trade names):	All Other Names used by the Joint Debtor in the last 6 years (include married, maiden, and trade names):
Last four digits of Soc. Sec. No./Complete EIN or other Tax I.D. No. (if more than one, state all):	Last four digits of Soc. Sec. No./Complete EIN or other Tax I.D. No. (if more than one, state all):
Street Address of Debtor (No. & Street, City, State & Zip Code):	Street Address of Joint Debtor (No. & Street, City, State & Zip Code):
County of Residence or of the Principal Place of Business:	County of Residence or of the Principal Place of Business:
Mailing Address of Debtor (if different from street address):	Mailing Address of Joint Debtor (if different from street address):
Location of Principal Assets of Business Debtor (if different from street address above):	

Information Regarding the Debtor (Check the Applicable Boxes)

Venue (Check any applicable box)

☐ Debtor has been domiciled or has had a residence, principal place of business, or principal assets in this District for 180 days immediately preceding the date of this petition or for a longer part of such 180 days than in any other District.

☐ There is a bankruptcy case concerning debtor's affiliate, general partner, or partnership pending in this District.

Type of Debtor (Check all boxes that apply)

☐ Individual(s) ☐ Railroad
☐ Corporation ☐ Stockbroker
☐ Partnership ☐ Commodity Broker
☐ Other ____________ ☐ Clearing Bank

Chapter or Section of Bankruptcy Code Under Which the Petition is Filed (Check one box)

☐ Chapter 7 ☐ Chapter 11 ☐ Chapter 13
☐ Chapter 9 ☐ Chapter 12
☐ See. 304 - Case ancillary to foreign proceeding

Nature of Debts (Check one box)

☐ Consumer/Non-Business ☐ Business

Filing Fee (Check one box)

☐ Full Filing Fee attached
☐ Filing Fee to be paid in installments (Applicable to individuals only) Must attach signed application for the court's consideration certifying that the debtor is unable to pay fee except in installments. Rule 1006(b). See Official Form No. 3.

Chapter 11 small Business (Check all boxes that apply)

☐ Debtor is a small business as defined in 11 U.S.C. & 101
☐ Debtor is and elects to be considered a small business under 11 U.S.C. & 1121(c) (Optional)

Statistical/Administrative Information (Estimates only)

☐ Debtor estimates that funds will be available for distribution to unsecured creditors.
☐ Debtor estimates that, after any exempt property is excluded and administrative expenses paid, there will be no funds available for distribution to unsecured creditors.

THIS SPACE IS FOR COURT USE ONLY

Estimated Number of Creditors	1–15	16–49	50–99	100–199	200–999	1000–over
	☐	☐	☐	☐	☐	☐

Estimated Assets							
$0 to $50,000	$50,001 to $100,000	$100,001 to $500,000	$500,001 to $1 million	$1,000,001 to $10 million	$10,000,001 to $50 million	$50,000,001 to $100 million	More than $100 million
☐	☐	☐	☐	☐	☐	☐	☐

Estimated Debts							
$0 to $50,000	$50,001 to $100,000	$100,001 to $500,000	$500,001 to $1 million	$1,000,001 to $10 million	$10,000,001 to $50 million	$50,000,001 to $100 million	More than $100 million
☐	☐	☐	☐	☐	☐	☐	☐

Exhibit 29.1

Form B1: Voluntary Petition for Bankruptcy

6. Evidence of payments received from employers within 60 days prior to the filing of the petition
7. Copy of the debtor's federal income tax return for the most recent year ending prior to the filing of the petition

All forms must be sworn under oath and signed by the debtor. In addition, an individual debtor must file a certificate stating that he or she has received the required prepetition credit counseling.

Attorney Certification

The 2005 act places a new burden on attorneys who represent debtors in bankruptcy. The 2005 act requires the attorney to certify the accuracy of the information contained in the bankruptcy petition and the schedules, under penalty of perjury. If there are any factual discrepancies, the attorney is subject to monetary fines and sanctions. Many attorneys may no longer be willing to represent debtors in bankruptcy because of this rule.

If an attorney represents a debtor in bankruptcy, the attorney will have to conduct a thorough investigation of the debtor's financial position and schedules to determine the accuracy of the information contained in the petition and schedules. The attorney may also require that accountants, appraisers, and other investigators be hired to help establish the accuracy of the information.

The new attorney certification requirement could add significantly to the cost of filing for bankruptcy. The debtor will have to pay the attorney for the additional time necessary to conduct the investigation, as well as pay for accountants, appraisers, and other professionals to help verify the accuracy of the information.

Order for Relief

order for relief
An order that occurs upon the filing of either a voluntary petition or an unchallenged involuntary petition, or an order that is granted after a trial of a challenged involuntary petition.

The filing of either a voluntary petition or an unchallenged involuntary petition constitutes an **order for relief**. If the debtor challenges an involuntary petition, a trial will be held to determine whether an order for relief should be granted. If the order is granted, the case is accepted for further bankruptcy proceedings. In the case of an involuntary petition, the debtor must file the same schedules filed by voluntary petition debtors.

Meeting of the Creditors

meeting of the creditors
A meeting of the creditors in a bankruptcy case that must occur within a reasonable time after an order for relief. The debtor must appear at this meeting.

Within a reasonable time after the court grants an order for relief (not less than 10 days or more than 30 days), the court must call a **meeting of the creditors** (also called the **first meeting of the creditors**). The bankruptcy judge cannot attend the meeting. The debtor, however, must appear and submit to questioning, under oath, by creditors. Creditors may ask questions regarding the debtor's financial affairs, disposition of property prior to bankruptcy, possible concealment of assets, and such. The debtor may have an attorney present at this meeting.

Proof of Claim and Proof of Interest

proof of claim
A document required to be filed by a creditor that states the amount of the creditor's claim against the debtor.

proof of interest
A document required to be filed by an equity security holder that states the amount of the security holder's interest against the debtor.

A creditor must file a **proof of claim** stating the amount of his or her claim against the debtor. The document for this statement is provided by the court. The proof of claim must be timely filed, which generally means within six months of the first meeting of the creditors. A secured creditor whose claim exceeds the value of the collateral may submit a proof of claim and become an unsecured claimant as to the difference. An equity security holder (e.g., a shareholder of a corporation) must file a **proof of interest**.

The proof of claim or proof of interest must be allowed by the court before a creditor or an equity security holder is permitted to participate in the bankruptcy estate. Any party of interest may object to a claim or an interest. If an objection to a claim or an interest is raised, the court will hold a hearing to determine the validity and amount of the claim or interest.

Bankruptcy Trustee

A **trustee** must be appointed in the following types of bankruptcy cases: Chapter 7 (liquidation), Chapter 12 (family farmer or family fisherman), and Chapter 13 (adjustment of debts). A trustee may be appointed in a Chapter 11 (reorganization) case upon a showing of fraud, dishonesty, incompetence, or gross mismanagement of the affairs of the debtor by current management.

trustee
A legal representative of a debtor's estate.

Trustees, who are often lawyers, accountants, or business professionals, are entitled to receive reasonable compensation for their services and reimbursement for expenses. Once appointed, a trustee becomes a legal representative of the debtor's estate. Generally, the trustee is empowered to:

- Take immediate possession of the debtor's property.
- Protect domestic-support creditors (e.g., former spouse, children of the debtor), a duty added by the 2005 act.
- Review all materials filed by the debtor.
- Separate secured and unsecured property.
- In a Chapter 7 case, file a statement as to whether the case is presumed to be an abuse under the new means test established by the 2005 act.
- Set aside exempt property.
- Investigate the debtor's financial affairs.
- Employ professionals (e.g., attorneys, accountants, appraisers) to assist in the administration of the case.
- Examine proof of claims.
- Defend, bring, and maintain lawsuits on behalf of the estate.
- Invest the property of the estate.
- Sell or otherwise dispose of property of the estate.
- Distribute the proceeds of the estate.
- Make reports to the court, creditors, debtor, and other parties of interest regarding the administration of the estate.

Automatic Stay

The filing of a voluntary or involuntary petition automatically stays (i.e., suspends) certain legal actions by creditors against the debtor or the debtor's property. This is called an **automatic stay**. The stay, which applies to collection efforts of both secured and unsecured creditors, is designed to prevent a scramble for the debtor's assets in a variety of court proceedings. The following creditor actions are stayed:

automatic stay
The suspension of certain legal actions by creditors against a debtor or a debtor's property.

1. Instituting or maintaining legal actions to collect prepetition debts
2. Enforcing judgments obtained against the debtor
3. Obtaining, perfecting, or enforcing liens against property of the debtor
4. Nonjudicial collection efforts, such as self-help activities (e.g., repossession of an automobile)

Actions to recover domestic support obligations (e.g., alimony, child support), the dissolution of a marriage, and child custody cases are not stayed in bankruptcy. An automatic stay does not preclude efforts by creditors against co-debtors and guarantors of the bankrupt debtor's debts unless the co-debtor is also in bankruptcy. Criminal actions against the debtor are not stayed. The court also has authority to issue injunctions preventing creditor activity not covered by the automatic stay provision.

relief from stay
Relief that is requested by a secured creditor that may be granted by the court if secured property is not adequately protected during a bankruptcy proceeding.

Relief from Stay A secured creditor may petition the court for **relief from stay**, which usually occurs in situations involving depreciating assets where the secured property is not adequately protected during the bankruptcy proceeding. If this situation is found, the court may grant relief from the stay. Alternatively, the court may provide adequate protection rather than grant relief from stay. In such cases, the court may (1) order cash payments equal to the amount of the depreciation, (2) grant an additional or replacement lien, or (3) grant an "indubitable equivalent" (e.g., a guarantee from a solvent party).

Discharge

discharge
An order of the court that relieves a debtor of his, her, or its legal liability to pay debts that were not paid in the bankruptcy proceeding.

In Chapter 7 (liquidation), Chapter 11 (reorganization), Chapter 12 (family farmer and family fisherman), and Chapter 13 (adjustment of debts) bankruptcies, if all the requirements are met, the court grants the debtor a **discharge** of all or some of his, her, or its debts. When discharge is granted, the debtor is relieved of responsibility to pay the discharged debts. In other words, the debtor is no longer legally liable to pay the discharged debts. Discharge is one of the primary reasons a debtor files for bankruptcy. The specifics of discharge under each type of bankruptcy are discussed in this chapter.

Exceptions to Discharge

The following debts, with the dollar limits established by the 2005 act, are not dischargeable in bankruptcy:

- Claims for income or gross receipts taxes owed to federal, state, or local governments accrued within three years prior to the filing of the petition for bankruptcy, or for such taxes for any period where the debtor made a fraudulent return or willfully attempted to evade or defeat such tax, and property taxes accrued within one year prior to the filing of the petition for bankruptcy.
- Certain fines and penalties payable to federal, state, and local government units.
- Claims based on the debtor's liability for causing willful or malicious injury to a person or property.
- Claims arising from fraud, larceny, or embezzlement by the debtor while acting in a fiduciary capacity.
- Domestic support obligations and alimony, maintenance, and child support payments resulting from a divorce decree or separation agreement.
- Unscheduled claims.
- Claims based on the consumer-debtor's purchase of luxury goods or services of more than $500 from a single creditor on or within 90 days of the order for relief. This is a rebuttable presumption that may be challenged by the debtor by proving that the expenses were incurred to support the debtor or dependants and were therefore not luxuries.
- Cash advances in excess of $750 obtained by a consumer-debtor by use of a revolving line of credit or credit cards on or within 70 days of the order for relief. This is also a rebuttable presumption.

"I will pay you some, and, as most debtors do, promise you indefinitely."
William Shakespeare
Henry IV, Pt. 11 (1597)

- Judgments and consent decrees against the debtor for liability incurred as a result of the debtor's operation of a motor vehicle, vessel, or aircraft while legally intoxicated.
- A debt that would result in a benefit to the debtor that outweighs the detrimental consequences to a spouse, former spouse, or child of the debtor.
- An amount owed to a pension, profit-sharing, or stock bonus plan, and loans owed to employee retirement plans.

Creditors who have nondischargeable claims against the debtor may participate in the distribution of the bankruptcy estate. The nondischarged balance may be pursued by the creditor against the debtor after bankruptcy.

Reaffirmation Agreement

A debtor and a creditor can enter into a **reaffirmation agreement** whereby the debtor agrees to pay the creditor for a debt that is dischargeable in bankruptcy. This might occur if the debtor wishes to repay a debt to a family member, to a bank, or to another party. A reaffirmation agreement must be entered into before discharge is granted. A reaffirmation agreement must be filed with the court. Approval by the court is required if the debtor is not represented by an attorney. If the debtor is represented by an attorney, the attorney must certify that the debtor voluntarily entered into the reaffirmation agreement and that the debtor understands the consequences of the agreement. Even if the debtor is represented by an attorney, court approval is required if the agreement will cause undue hardship on the debtor or his or her family.

reaffirmation agreement
An agreement entered into by a debtor with a creditor prior to discharge whereby the debtor agrees to pay the creditor a debt that would otherwise be discharged in bankruptcy. Certain requirements must be met for a reaffirmation agreement to be enforced.

The Bankruptcy Estate

The **bankruptcy estate** is created upon the commencement of a bankruptcy case. It includes all the debtor's legal and equitable interests in real, personal, tangible, and intangible property, wherever located, that exist when the petition is filed, and all interests of the debtor and the debtor's spouse in community property. Certain *exempt property* (which is discussed later in this section) is not part of the bankruptcy estate.

Gifts, inheritances, life insurance proceeds, and property from divorce settlements that the debtor is entitled to receive within 180 days after the petition is filed become part of the bankruptcy estate. Earnings from property of the estate—such as rents, dividends, and interest payments—are property of the estate.

Earnings from services performed by an individual debtor are not part of the bankruptcy estate in a Chapter 7 (liquidation) bankruptcy. However, the 2005 act provides that a certain amount of postpetition earnings from services performed by the debtor that are earned for up to five years after the order for relief may be required to be paid as part of the completion of Chapter 12 (family farmer or family fisherman), Chapter 11 (reorganization), and Chapter 13 (adjustment of debts) cases. These repayment plans are discussed later in this chapter.

bankruptcy estate
A debtor's property and earnings that comprise the estate of a bankruptcy proceeding.

Exempt Property

Because the Bankruptcy Code is not designed to make the debtor a pauper, certain property is exempt from the bankruptcy estate. The debtor may retain exempt property. **Exempt property** is property of the debtor that he or she can keep and that does not become part of the bankruptcy estate. The creditors cannot claim this property.

exempt property
Property that may be retained by a debtor pursuant lo federal or state law that does not become part of the bankruptcy estate.

The Bankruptcy Code establishes a list of property and assets that the debtor can claim as exempt property. The federal exemptions, with the dollar limits established by the 2005 act, are listed below.[4] Federal exemptions are adjusted every three years to reflect changes in the consumer price index.

1. Interest up to $18,450 in equity in property used as a residence and burial plots (called the "homestead exemption")
2. Interest up to $2,950 in value in one motor vehicle
3. Interest up to $475 per item in household goods and furnishings, wearing apparel, appliances, books, animals, crops, or musical instruments, up to an aggregate value of $9,850 for all items
4. Interest in jewelry up to $1,225
5. Interest in any property the debtor chooses (including cash) up to $975, plus up to $9,250 of any unused portion of the homestead exemption
6. Interest up to $1,850 in value in implements, tools, or professional books used in the debtor's trade
7. Any unmatured life insurance policy owned by the debtor
8. Professionally prescribed health aids
9. Many government benefits, regardless of value, including Social Security benefits, welfare benefits, unemployment compensation, veteran's benefits, disability benefits, and public assistance benefits
10. Certain rights to receive income, including domestic support payments (e.g., alimony, child support), certain pension benefits, profit sharing, and annuity payments
11. Interests in wrongful death benefits and life insurance proceeds to the extent necessary to support the debtor or his or her dependants
12. Personal injury awards up to $18,450
13. Retirement funds that are in a fund or an account that is exempt from taxation under the Internal Revenue Code, except that an exemption for individual retirement accounts (IRAs) shall not exceed $1 million for an individual unless the interests of justice requires this amount to be increased

"Poor bankrupt."
William Shakespeare
Romeo and Juliet (1595)

The Bankruptcy Code permits states to enact their own exemptions. States that do so may (1) give debtors the option of choosing between federal and state exemptions or (2) require debtors to follow state law. The exemptions available under state law are often more liberal than those provided by federal law.

Homestead Exemption

homestead exemption
Equity in a debtor's home that the debtor is permitted to retain.

The federal Bankruptcy Code permits homeowners to claim a **homestead exemption** in their principal residence. Many states require the debtor to file a *Declaration of Homestead* prior to bankruptcy. This document is usually filed in the county recorder's office in the county in which the real property is located. If the debtor's equity in the property (i.e., the value above the amount of mortgages and liens) exceeds the exemption limits, the trustee may sell the property to realize the excess value for the bankruptcy estate.

Consider This Example Assume that a debtor owns a principal residence worth $500,000 that is subject to a $400,000 mortgage. Therefore, the debtor owns $100,000 of equity in the property. The debtor files a petition for Chapter 7 liquidation bankruptcy. The trustee may sell the home, pay off the mortgage, pay the debtor $18,450 (applying the federal exemption), and use the remaining proceeds of $81,550 for distribution to the debtor's creditors.

Contemporary Trend

2005 Act Limits the Homestead Exemption

The Bankruptcy Code's federal homestead exemption is $18,450. Homestead exemptions under many state laws are usually higher than the federal exemption. Most states exempt between $20,000 and $100,000 of equity in a debtor's principal residence from the bankruptcy estate.

The largest exemptions are provided by Florida and Texas. Florida and Texas have no dollar amount limit on their homestead exemption, although they do limit the size of the real property that qualifies for the homestead exemption. These states have been known as "debtor's havens" for wealthy debtors who have filed for bankruptcy. Prior to the 2005 act, many wealthy debtors from other states moved their money into principal residences in Florida and Texas to benefit from these generous homestead exemptions.

The 2005 act limits abusive homestead exemptions. The 2005 act provides the following restrictions on homestead exemptions:

1. A debtor may not exempt an amount greater than $125,000 if the property was acquired by the debtor within 1,215 days (approximately three years and four months) before the filing of the petition for bankruptcy. This limit does not apply to a family farmer or to an interest transferred from a previous principal residence acquired prior to the 1,215-day period to another principal residence in the same state.
2. A debtor may not exempt an amount greater than $125,000 if the debtor has been convicted of a felony for bankruptcy fraud, securities fraud, or criminal, intentional, willful, or reckless misconduct that caused serious physical injury or death to another in the preceding five years prior to filing a petition for bankruptcy. ■

Consider These Examples Assume that a debtor owns a principal residence in Florida that he acquired 10 years ago. The equity in the property is $3 million. If the debtor files for Chapter 7 liquidation bankruptcy, the entire $3 million is shielded as exempt property. Assume, however, that the debtor owns a principal residence in Florida that has an equity value of $3 million, but that the property was acquired only 2 years prior to the debtor's filing a petition for bankruptcy. In this case, the debtor can shield only $125,000 as a homestead exemption under the 2005 act because the property was acquired within 1,215 days prior to the filing of the petition.

Preferential and Fraudulent Transfers

The Bankruptcy Code prevents debtors from making fraudulent and preferential transfers of property during certain time periods prior to bankruptcy that would unfairly benefit the debtor or some creditors at the expense of other creditors. Such payments or transfers can be voided by the court, and the recovered property or its equivalent value is placed in the bankruptcy estate for the benefit of the creditors. If a transfer is voided, a bona fide good faith purchaser must receive the value he or she paid for the property. The following paragraphs discuss preferential and fraudulent transfers that may be voided by the bankruptcy trustee.

Preferential Transfers

The Bankruptcy Code gives the bankruptcy court the power to void certain **preferential transfers** of a debtor's property made by the debtor. To be subject to voidance, the transfer of the property or the occurrence of the obligation must fall in either of two time periods: (1) to or with any party on or within 90 days of filing the petition or (2) to or with an insider between 90 days and one year of filing the petition. Insiders are defined as relatives, partners, partnerships, officers and directors of a corporation, corporations, and others who have a relationship with the debtor.

preferential transfer
A transfer of an interest in property made by a debtor (1) to or with any party on or within 90 days of filing the petition or (2) to or with an insider between 90 days and one year of filing the petition, if certain requirements are met.

To void a preferential transfer of a debtor's interest in property, the bankruptcy court must find that (1) the transfer was made to or for the benefit of a creditor, (2) the transfer was made for an *antecedent* (preexisting) debt, (3) the creditor to whom the transfer was made would receive more from the transfer than it would from a Chapter 7 liquidation of the debtor, and (4) the debtor was insolvent at the time of the transfer. Insolvency means that the debtor's debts exceed the value of the debtor's property. The Bankruptcy Code presumes that a debtor is insolvent on or within the 90 days prior to the filing of the petition; more than 90 days after the filing of the petition, the court must determine whether the debtor was insolvent.

Consider These Examples Assume that five months prior to filing a petition for bankruptcy, John purchases $30,000 of equipment on unsecured credit from a supplier. Within 90 days of filing the petition, John still owes the $30,000 to this creditor, and the payment is not due for another 120 days after the petition has been filed. Suppose that John pays this creditor $30,000 before filing the petition. In John's Chapter 7 liquidation case, however, this creditor would receive only $5,000. This payment is a voidable preferential payment because it was made within 90 days of the filing of the petition, when John was presumed to be insolvent, it paid an antecedent debt, and it gives the creditor more than it would receive in Chapter 7 liquidation.

Assume that Glen borrows $100,000 from his sister, Ida. This is an unsecured debt. On February 9, 2006, Glen is insolvent and owes $500,000 of unsecured debt, including the $100,000 he borrowed from Ida. On this day, Glen grants his sister Ida a $100,000 mortgage on his house in which he has $100,000 in equity. This converts Ida from being an unsecured creditor to being a secured creditor. Nine months later, while still owing the $400,000 to his unsecured creditors and $100,000 secured credit to Ida, Glen files a petition for bankruptcy. If Ida was an unsecured creditor, she would receive only $10,000 in a bankruptcy proceeding. The mortgage on Glen's house in favor of Ida is a preferential lien that can be voided by the bankruptcy court. This is because the mortgage was made within one year of the filing of the petition, it was made when the debtor was insolvent, it was made to an insider, it was made to pay an antecedent debt, and it gives the creditor, Ida, more than she would receive in Chapter 7 liquidation. Without this preferential mortgage, Ida would be an unsecured creditor equal to Glen's other unsecured creditors. The court will void Glen's mortgage in favor of Ida and make her an unsecured creditor again.

It is the policy of the law that the debtor be just before he be generous.

Justice Finch
Hearn 45 St. Corp. v. Jano (1940)

There are exceptions to preferential transfer avoidance rules. The following debts may be paid by the debtor without being voided as preferential payments: (1) transfers for current consideration (e.g., equipment purchased for cash), (2) credit payments made in the ordinary course of business or financial affairs of the debtor (e.g., supplies purchased on credit and paid for within the normal payment terms, such as within 30 days after purchase), (3) payments of up to $600 by a consumer-debtor to a creditor, (4) payment of up to $5,000 by a debtor for debts that are not primarily consumer debts (e.g., business debts), or (5) a transfer that was a bona fide payment of a debt for a domestic support obligation.

An otherwise preferential transfer cannot be voided if the transfer was made as a part of an alternative repayment schedule between the debtor and a creditor that was created and approved by a nonprofit budgeting and credit counseling agency.

fraudulent transfer

A transfer of a debtor's property or an obligation incurred by the debtor within two years of the petition where (1) the debtor had actual intent to hinder, delay, or defraud a creditor or (2) the debtor received less than a reasonable equivalent in value, and the debtor was insolvent or unable to pay at the time the transfer was made or the obligation was incurred.

Fraudulent Transfers

The 2005 act gives the bankruptcy court the power to void certain **fraudulent transfers** of the debtor's property and obligations incurred by the debtor within two years of the filing of the petition for bankruptcy. To void a transfer or obligation, the court must find that (1) the transfer was made or the obligation was incurred by the debtor with the actual intent to hinder, delay, or defraud a creditor or (2) the debtor received less than a reasonable equivalent in value. In addition, the debtor must have been either insolvent on the date the transfer was made or the obligation was incurred or the transfer or obligation must have been beyond the debtor's ability to pay.

Consider This Example Assume that Kathy owes her unsecured creditors $100,000. On February 9, Kathy knows that she is insolvent. Kathy owns a Mercedes-Benz automobile that is worth $55,000. On February 9, Kathy sells her Mercedes-Benz automobile to her friend Wei for $35,000. Wei is a bona fide purchaser who does not know of Kathy's financial situation. On July 1, Kathy files for Chapter 7 liquidation bankruptcy while still owing the $100,000 to her unsecured creditors. The court can void Kathy's sale of her automobile to Wei as a fraudulent transfer because it occurred within two years of the petition, Kathy received less than a reasonable equivalent in value, and Kathy was insolvent at the time of the sale. Because Wei was a bona fide purchaser, the court must repay Wei the purchase price of $35,000 to recover the automobile from her.

The 2005 act provides that transfers to or for the benefit of an insider under an employment contract and not in the ordinary course of business made within two years of the filing of the petition are voidable by the court. The 2005 act stipulates that transfers made to charitable or religious organizations by the debtor within two years of the filing of the petition are not voidable if they do not exceed 15 percent of the gross annual income of the debtor for the year in which the contribution was made and the debtor did not intend to hinder, delay, or defraud a creditor.

Fraudulent Transfer to a Trust

In recent years, many persons have established self-settled *living trusts* and have transferred their assets to these trusts. The owners and transferors usually designate themselves as trustees for the trust and make decisions regarding the investment and use of trust assets. The transferors-trustees usually name themselves as beneficiaries of the trust and therefore receive trust income and will receive the trust assets if the trust is terminated. In essence, the transferor-trustee-beneficiary has placed his or her assets in a legal entity—the living trust—but still has complete control over the trust assets. Living trusts are usually established to avoid probate upon the death of the beneficiary.

The 2005 act provides that any transfer of assets by the debtor to a living trust can be voided if (1) the transfer was made within 10 years before the debtor's filing of the petition for bankruptcy, (2) the transfer was made to a self-settled trust, (3) the debtor is the beneficiary of the trust, and (4) the debtor made the transfer with the actual intent to hinder, delay, or defraud a creditor to which the debtor was or became indebted.

Transfers made within 10 years before the date of the filing of the petition that are made in anticipation of any money judgment, settlement, civil penalty, or criminal fine incurred because of a violation of securities laws or because of fraud, deceit, or manipulation in a fiduciary capacity can be voided.

Chapter 7: Liquidation

Chapter 7 liquidation bankruptcy (also called **straight bankruptcy**) is a familiar form of bankruptcy.[5] In this type of bankruptcy proceeding, the debtor is permitted to keep a substantial portion of his or her assets (*exempt assets*), the debtor's nonexempt property is sold for cash and the cash is distributed to the creditors, and any of the debtor's unpaid debts are discharged. The debtor's future income, even if the debtor becomes rich, cannot be reached to pay the discharged debt. Thus, a debtor would be left to start life anew without the burden of his or her prepetition debts. Prior to the 2005 act, filing for Chapter 7 bankruptcy almost became part of many persons' financial planning.

Chapter 7—liquidation
A form of bankruptcy in which the debtor's nonexempt property is sold for cash, the cash is distributed to the creditors, and any unpaid debts are discharged.

The 2005 act substantially restricts the ability of many debtors to obtain a Chapter 7 liquidation bankruptcy. The 2005 act added certain median income and dollar-based means tests that must be met before a debtor is permitted to obtain a discharge of debts under Chapter 7. If these tests are not met, the 2005 act provides that the debtor's Chapter 7 proceeding may, with the debtor's consent, be dismissed or be converted to a Chapter 13 or Chapter 11 bankruptcy proceeding.

The purpose of the 2005 act's changes to Chapter 7 is to force many debtors out of Chapter 7 liquidation bankruptcy and into Chapter 13 debt adjustment bankruptcy, which requires debtors to pay some of their future income over a five-year period to pay off prepetition debts. Thus, the 2005 act reduces the number of debtors who can escape their prepetition debts entirely.

Chapter 7 Procedure

Any person, including individuals, partnerships, corporations, and other business entities, may be a debtor in a Chapter 7 proceeding. Voluntary and involuntary petitions may be filed. Most Chapter 7 filings are voluntarily filed by individuals.

Upon the filing of a Chapter 7 case, the U.S. Trustee appoints an interim trustee. A meeting of the creditors is then held, and the creditors may elect a permanent trustee at the meeting. The duty of a Chapter 7 trustee is to collect the nonexempt property of the bankruptcy estate, sell or otherwise dispose of such property, collect the money received, pay the money to the creditors and other claimants, and close the estate as quickly as possible. The trustee must act in the best interests of the parties of interest, including the debtor, secured creditors, and unsecured creditors.

The 2005 Act's Changes to Chapter 7

Prior to the 2005 act, there was a presumption in favor of granting the relief sought by the debtor under Chapter 7. Relief could be denied if the court found *substantial abuse* of Chapter 7. However, because this was rarely found, most debtors were granted relief and a fresh start free of their prepetition unsecured debts.

One of the primary purposes for the enactment of the 2005 act was to make it more difficult for individual debtors to qualify for Chapter 7 liquidation bankruptcy. To do so, the 2005 act established new *simple abuse* rules and "means testing" to determine whether a debtor should be granted relief under Chapter 7. If a debtor fails this test, a presumption of an abusive filing arises, and the Chapter 7 case can be dismissed or, with the debtor's consent, converted to a Chapter 11 or Chapter 13 case.

Thus, the goal of the 2005 act is to deny Chapter 7 discharge to debtors who have the means to pay some of their unsecured debt from postpetition earnings and steer most of these debtors into filing for Chapter 13 bankruptcy, where they have to use a portion of their postpetition earnings to pay some of their prepetition unsecured debt.

Abusive Chapter 7 Filing

abusive filing

If a Chapter 7 case is found to be an abuse of Chapter 7 liquidation bankruptcy, with the debtor's consent, the court can dismiss the case or convert the case to a Chapter 13 or Chapter 11 proceeding.

Section 707(b) of the 2005 act provides that the bankruptcy court, after notice and hearing, may dismiss a Chapter 7 liquidation case filed by an individual debtor whose debts are primarily consumer debts if the court finds that granting Chapter 7 relief to the debtor would be an **abuse** of Chapter 7. *Consumer debt* means debts incurred for personal, family, or household purposes.

Abuse is objectively determined by applying median income and means tests established by the 2005 act. Within 10 days after the first meeting of the creditors, the trustee must file a statement with the bankruptcy court about whether the debtor's Chapter 7 case is an abusive filing.

Median Income Test

The first step with regard to the means test is to determine whether the debtor's income either exceeds or is below the state's median family income for a family the same size as the debtor's family. A **state's median income** is defined as that income where half of the state's families have income above that figure and half of the state's families have incomes below that figure. For example, if a state's median income for a family of four is $65,000, then half of the state's four-member families have incomes above $65,000 and half of the state's four-member families have incomes below $65,000. Exhibit 29.2 sets forth the median income for four-person families, by state, published by the U.S. Census Bureau.

state median income
For any size family, the income where half of the state's families of this size have incomes above this figure and half of the state's families of this size have incomes below this figure.

A family's income is calculated by adding together the family's income for the six months prior to the petition, dividing by 6 to get the average monthly income for this six-month period, and then multiplying by 12 to determine the family's annual income. A debtor must include his or her spouse's income to the calculation in a two-income family.

If the debtor's family income is at or below the state's median income, there is no presumption of abuse, and the *means test* does not apply. The debtor may proceed with his or her Chapter 7 case and be granted discharge of his or her unsecured debts. Thus, it is important to note that for debtors at or below the state's median income, the 2005 act makes no changes in the ability to obtain Chapter 7 relief.

Exhibit 29.2
Median Income for Four-Person Families, by State (Estimates for 2004–2005, U.S. Census Bureau)

United States	$65,093
Alabama	55,448
Alaska	72,110
Arizona	58,206
Arkansas	48,353
California	67,814
Colorado	71,559
Connecticut	86,001
Delaware	72,680
District of Columbia	56,067
Florida	58,605
Georgia	62,294
Hawaii	71,320
Idaho	53,376
Illinois	72,368
Indiana	65,009
Iowa	64,341
Kansas	64,215
Kentucky	53,198
Louisiana	50,529
Maine	59,596
Maryland	82,363
Massachusetts	82,561
Michigan	68,602
Minnesota	76,733
Mississippi	46,570
Missouri	64,128
Montana	49,124
Nebraska	63,625
Nevada	63,005

(continued)

Exhibit 29.2
(continued)

New Hampshire	79,339
New Jersey	87,412
New Mexico	46,867
New York	69,354
North Carolina	56,712
North Dakota	57,092
Ohio	66,066
Oklahoma	50,216
Oregon	61,570
Pennsylvania	68,578
Rhode Island	71,098
South Carolina	56,433
South Dakota	59,272
Tennessee	55,401
Texas	54,554
Utah	62,032
Vermont	65,876
Virginia	71,697
Washington	69,130
West Virginia	46,169
Wisconsin	69,010
Wyoming	56,065

Means Test

For a debtor whose family income exceeds the state's median income, the 2005 act makes major changes in whether such a debtor has the ability to obtain Chapter 7 relief. If the debtor's family income is above the state's median income, a new means test applies. If a debtor's family income exceeds the state's median income, any party of interest, including the trustee and creditors, may file a motion with the court to have the debtor's Chapter 7 case dismissed.

means test
A new test added by the 2005 act that applies to debtors who have family incomes that exceed the state's median income for families of the same size.

The **means test** is a new complicated calculation that establishes, by law, a bright-line test to determine whether the debtor has the means to pay prepetition debts out of postpetition income. If it is found by this calculation that the debtor has the means to pay some of his or her prepetition debts out of postpetition income, the debtor will be denied relief under Chapter 7. The debtor's Chapter 7 proceeding will be dismissed unless the debtor approves that his or her case be converted to a Chapter 11 or Chapter 13 proceeding. The following paragraphs discuss the means test.

Calculating the Means Test Under the means test, a debtor's current monthly income is calculated by adding the debtor's last six months' income (minus certain deductions) and dividing by six. This figure is then reduced by certain monthly expenditures to get a "net amount." The 2005 act, however, does not allow the debtor to use his or her actual current expenses, but instead uses objective amounts established by Internal Revenue Service (IRS) standards. National standards establish allowances for food, clothing, personal care, and entertainment. Regional standards apply for transportation costs, and county standards apply for housing costs. Deductions are also allowed for postpetition domestic support payments, charitable contributions up to 15 percent of gross income, and school expenses up to $1,500 per child per year.

Once the net amount is calculated (average current monthly income minus allowed expenses and deductions), this net amount is multiplied by 60 (representing 60 months, or five years). Then this amount is subtracted from the state's median income for five years.

The 2005 act then places the debtor into one of the following three categories, depending on what amount results from the calculation:

1. ***Net amount less than $6,000.*** If the debtor's net amount is less than $6,000 over five years (less than $100 per month), abuse is not presumed, and the debtor is eligible for Chapter 7 relief.

   Consider This Example Assume that Sam's net amount is $80 per month, which is $4,800 over five years. Because $4,800 is less than $6,000, abuse is not presumed, and Sam is eligible for Chapter 7 relief.

2. ***Net amount between $6,000 and $9,999.*** If the debtor's net amount is between $6,000 and $9,999 for five years ($100 to $166.66 per month), the 2005 act establishes two possible outcomes: (a) If the debtor's net amount is sufficient to pay at least 25 percent of his or her unsecured debt, Chapter 7 relief is denied, or (b) if the debtor's net amount in insufficient to pay 25 percent of his or her unsecured debt, Chapter 7 relief is granted.

   Consider These Examples Assume that Amy's net amount is $7,500 over five years ($125 per month). If Amy's unsecured debt is $24,000, she can pay over 25 percent of her unsecured debt, or $6,000, from the $7,500 available. Abuse is presumed, and Amy is not eligible for Chapter 7 relief.

   However, if Amy's net amount is still $7,500 but her unsecured debt is $40,000, she cannot pay 25 percent of her debt, which is $10,000, from the $7,500 available. Abuse is not presumed, and Amy is eligible for Chapter 7 relief.

3. ***Net amount $10,000 or more.*** If the debtor's net amount is $10,000 or more over five years (equal to or greater than $166.67 per month), abuse is presumed, and the debtor is not eligible for Chapter 7 relief.

   Consider This Example Assume that Beth's net amount is $200 per month, which is $12,000 over five years. Because $12,000 is greater than $10,000, abuse is presumed, and Beth is not eligible for Chapter 7 relief.

Even if a debtor qualifies for Chapter 7 relief under the median income or means tests, the court can still deny relief if it determines that the debtor filed the Chapter 7 petition in bad faith or because of the "totality of the circumstances" of the debtor's financial situation. This determination is made on a case-by-case basis.

The trustee, a creditor, or any other party of interest can request the court to dismiss the debtor's Chapter 7 case if abuse is found. The court can convert the case to a Chapter 11 or Chapter 13 case, with the debtor's approval. In practice, although the court can dismiss the Chapter 7 case if abuse is found, in the majority of the cases, the debtor will agree to convert the case to a Chapter 13 proceeding ("adjustment of debts of an individual with regular income"). Chapter 13 requires a debtor to pay some of his or her unsecured debt for a five-year period out of his or her postpetition earnings. Chapter 13 bankruptcy is discussed later in this chapter.

Statutory Distribution of Property Under Chapter 7

If a debtor qualifies for a Chapter 7 liquidation bankruptcy, the *nonexempt property* of the bankruptcy estate must be distributed to the debtor's secured and unsecured creditors pursuant to statutory priority established by the Bankruptcy Code. The **distribution of property** to secured and unsecured debtors is discussed in the following paragraphs.

distribution of property
Nonexempt property of the bankruptcy estate must be distributed to the debtor's secured and unsecured creditors pursuant to statutory priority established by the Bankruptcy Code.

Secured Creditor Claims

The claims of secured creditors to the debtor's nonexempt property have priority over the claims of unsecured creditors. Two situations can result:

1. ***Oversecured secured creditor.*** If the value of the collateral securing the secured loan exceeds the secured interest, this makes the secured creditor an *oversecured creditor.* In this case, the property is usually sold, and the secured creditor is paid the amount of its secured interest (i.e., principal and accrued principal and interest) and reasonable fees and costs resulting from the debtor's default. The excess becomes available to satisfy the claims of the debtor's unsecured creditors. Sometimes the secured creditor is awarded the property but must remit to the trustee the difference between the market value of the property and the amount of its interest for distribution to the unsecured creditors.

   Consider This Example Assume that Edwin obtains a loan of $200,000 from City Bank to purchase a piece of investment real estate that is worth $240,000. The real estate is given as security for the loan. Several years later, when the value of the real estate is $220,000, Edwin files and qualifies for Chapter 7 relief. Edwin still owes $185,000 of the loan amount at the time of bankruptcy. In this case, City Bank will probably be awarded the real estate but must pay the bankruptcy estate $35,000 ($220,000 market value of the real estate minus $185,000 loan amount still owed).

2. ***Undersecured secured creditor.*** If the value of the collateral securing the secured loan is less than the secured interest, the secured creditor is an *undersecured creditor.* In this case, the property is usually awarded to the secured creditor. The secured creditor then becomes an unsecured creditor as to the amount still owed to it, which consists of unpaid principal and interest and reasonable fees and costs of the debtor's default.

   Consider This Example Assume that Paige obtains a loan of $200,000 from City Bank to purchase a piece of investment real estate that is worth $240,000. The real estate is given as security for the loan. Several years later, when the value of the real estate has declined to $150,000, Paige files and qualifies for Chapter 7 relief. Paige still owes $175,000 of the loan amount at the time of bankruptcy. In this case, City Bank will be awarded the real estate and becomes an unsecured creditor with a claim of $25,000 ($175,000 loan amount still owed minus $150,000 market value of the real estate).

Secured Personal Property The 2005 act added a new provision regarding secured personal property. Under the 2005 act, if personal property of an individual debtor secures a claim or is subject to an unexpired lease (e.g., an automobile lease) and is not exempt property, the debtor must either (1) surrender the personal property, (2) redeem the property by paying the secured lien in full, or (3) assume the unexpired lease.

Consider This Example Assume that Gee leases an automobile on a three-year lease. Gee files for and qualifies for Chapter 7 relief while there are still two years to go on the automobile lease, with a total amount of $12,000 to pay. Gee has three choices. First, she can surrender the personal property to the secured creditor, and the rules regarding oversecured and unsecured secured creditors will apply. Second, Gee can redeem the automobile by paying the $12,000 in full. Third, Gee can assume the unexpired lease, which will not be discharged in her Chapter 12 case, and make the payments in the future in accordance with the original lease terms.

Priority Unsecured Creditor Claims

Unsecured claims are to be satisfied out of the bankruptcy estate in order of their statutory priority, as established by the Bankruptcy Code. The statutory priority of unsecured claims, including the changes made by the 2005 act, is set forth in Exhibit 29.3. Because both individuals and businesses can be granted Chapter 7 relief, some items on this list apply primarily to individual debtors, while other items on this list apply primarily to business debtors. Each class must be paid in full before any lower class is paid anything. If a class cannot be paid in full, the claims of that class are paid pro rata (proportionately).

Small debts are like small shot; they are rattling on every side, and can scarcely be escaped without a wound; great debts are like cannon; of loud noise, but little danger.

Samuel Johnson
Letters to Joseph Simpson (1759)

Exhibit 29.3

Priority Unsecured Creditor Claims

1. Unsecured claims for domestic support obligations owed to a spouse, former spouse, or child of the debtor
2. Fees and expenses of administering the estate, including court costs, trustee fees, attorneys' fees, appraisal fees, and other costs of administration
3. In an involuntary bankruptcy, secured claims of "gap" creditors who sold goods or services on credit to the debtor in the ordinary course of the debtor's business between the date of the filing of the petition and the date of the appointment of the trustee or issuance of the order for relief (whichever occurs first)
4. Unsecured claims for wages, salary, commissions, severance pay, and sick leave pay earned by the debtor's employees within 180 days immediately preceding the filing of the petition, up to $10,000 per employee
5. Unsecured claims for contributions to employee benefit plans based on services performed within 180 days immediately preceding the filing of the petition, up to $10,000 per employee
6. Farm producers and fishermen against debtors who operate grain storage facilities or fish storage or processing facilities, respectively, up to $4,925 per claim
7. Unsecured claims for cash deposited by a consumer with the debtor prior to the filing of the petition in connection with the purchase, lease, or rental of property or the purchase of services that were not delivered or provided by the debtor, up to $2,225 per claim
8. Unsecured claims for unpaid income and gross receipts taxes owed to governments incurred during the three years preceding the bankruptcy petition, and unpaid property taxes owed to governments incurred within one year preceding the bankruptcy petition
9. Commitment by the debtor to maintain the capital of an insured depository institution such as a commercial bank or savings bank
10. Claims against the debtor for personal injuries or death caused by the debtor while he or she was intoxicated from using alcohol or drugs

Nonpriority Unsecured Creditor Claims

After the priority claims have been paid, the *nonpriority* unsecured creditors are paid. In most Chapter 7 bankruptcies, the nonpriority unsecured claims receive little, if anything, in the bankruptcy proceeding. If there is any balance remaining after the allowed claims of the creditors are satisfied, it is returned to the debtor. This, too, is an unlikely event.

Discharge

In a Chapter 7 bankruptcy, the property of the estate is sold and the proceeds are distributed to satisfy allowed claims. The remaining unpaid debts that the debtor incurred prior to the date of the order for relief are discharged. *Discharge* means that the debtor is no longer legally responsible for paying those claims. Only individual debtors may be granted discharge. The major benefit of a **Chapter 7 discharge** is that it is granted quite soon after the petition is filed. The individual debtor is not responsible for paying prepetition debts out of postpetition income, as is required in other forms of bankruptcy.

Chapter 7 discharge
The termination of the legal duty of a debtor to pay unsecured debts that remain unpaid upon the completion of a Chapter 7 proceeding.

The 2005 act stipulates that a debtor can be granted Chapter 7 relief only after eight years following Chapter 7 or Chapter 11 relief and only after six years following Chapter 12 or Chapter 13 relief. Discharge is not available to partnerships, limited liability companies, and corporations. These entities must liquidate under state law before or upon completion of the Chapter 7 proceeding.

Consider This Example Suppose that at the time that Eric is granted Chapter 7 relief, he still owes $50,000 of unsecured debt that there is no money in the bankruptcy estate to pay. This debt is composed of credit card debt, an unsecured loan from a friend, and unsecured credit from a department store. This $50,000 of unsecured credit is discharged, which means Eric is relieved of this debt and is not legally liable for its repayment. The unsecured creditors must write off this debt.

In the following case, the U.S. Supreme Court ruled that a debt was dischargeable in bankruptcy.

Case 29.1
Discharge of Debt

U.S. SUPREME COURT

Kawaauhau v. Geiger

523 U.S. 57, 118 S.Ct. 974, 1998 U.S. Lexis 1595

Supreme Court of the United States

Background and Facts

Margaret Kawaauhau sought treatment from Dr. Paul Geiger for a foot injury. Dr. Geiger examined Kawaauhau and admitted her to the hospital to attend to the risks of infection. Although Dr. Geiger knew that intravenous penicillin would have been a more effective treatment, he prescribed oral penicillin, explaining that he thought that his patient wished to minimize the cost of her treatment. Dr. Geiger then departed on a business trip, leaving Kawaauhau in the care of other physicians. When Dr. Geiger returned, he discontinued all antibiotics because he believed that the infection had subsided. Kawaauhau's condition deteriorated over the next few days, requiring the amputation of her right leg below the knee. Kawaauhau and her husband sued Dr. Geiger for medical malpractice. The jury found Dr. Geiger liable and awarded the Kawaauhaus $355,000 in damages. Dr. Geiger, who carried no malpractice insurance, filed for bankruptcy in an attempt to discharge the judgment. The bankruptcy court denied discharge, and the district court agreed. The Court of Appeals reversed and allowed discharge. The Kawaauhaus appealed to the U.S. Supreme Court.

Issue

Is a debt arising from a medical malpractice judgment that is attributable to negligent or reckless conduct dischargeable in bankruptcy?

In the Language of the Court

The Bankruptcy Code provides that a debt "for willful and malicious injury by the debtor to another" is not dischargeable. The question before us is whether a debt arising from a medical malpractice judgment, attributable to negligent or reckless conduct, falls within this statutory exception. We hold that it does not and that the debt is dischargeable. Had Congress meant to exempt debts resulting from unintentionally inflicted injuries, it might have selected an additional word or words, i.e., "reckless" or "negligent," to modify injury.

Decision and Remedy

The U.S. Supreme Court ruled that a medical malpractice judgment based on negligent or reckless conduct—and not willful conduct—is dischargeable in bankruptcy. The U.S. Supreme Court affirmed the decision of the U.S. Court of Appeals.

Business and Ethics Questions

1. What public policy is promoted by denying discharge for "willful" injurious conduct?
2. Was it ethical for Dr. Geiger not to carry malpractice insurance? Was it ethical for Dr. Geiger to file for bankruptcy to avoid paying the judgment to the Kawaauhaus?
3. Who is hurt and who is helped by this decision? Do you think this is a fair result?

Acts That Bar Discharge

> Beggars can never be bankrupt.
>
> Thomas Fuller
> *Gnomologia* (1732)

Any party of interest may file an objection to the discharge of a debt. The court will then hold a hearing. Discharge of the unsatisfied debts will be denied if the debtor:

- Made false representations about his or her financial position when he or she obtained an extension of credit.
- Transferred, concealed, removed, or destroyed property of the estate with the intent to hinder, delay, or defraud creditors within one year before the date of the filing of the petition.
- Falsified, destroyed, or concealed records of his or her financial condition.
- Failed to account for any assets.

- Failed to submit to questioning at the meeting of the creditors (unless excused).
- Failed to complete an instructional course concerning personal financial management as required by the 2005 act (unless excused).

If the discharge is obtained through fraud of the debtor, any party of interest may bring a motion to have the bankruptcy revoked. The bankruptcy court may revoke a discharge within one year after it is granted.

Contemporary Trend

Discharge of Student Loans

During college and other professional schools, many students borrow money for their tuition and living expenses. Upon graduation, when a student might have large student loans and very few assets, the student might be inclined to file for bankruptcy in an attempt to have his or her student loans discharged.

To prevent such abuse of bankruptcy law, Congress amended the Bankruptcy Code to make it more difficult for students to have their student loans discharged in bankruptcy. Student loans are defined by the Bankruptcy Code to include loans made by or guaranteed by governmental units. The 2005 act added student loans made by nongovernmental commercial institutions, such as banks, as well as funds for scholarships, benefits, or stipends granted by educational institutions.

The Bankruptcy Code now states that student loans can be discharged in bankruptcy only if the nondischarge would cause an "undue hardship" to the debtor and his or her dependants. Undue hardship is construed strictly and would be difficult for a debtor to prove unless he or she could show severe physical or mental disability or that he or she is unable to pay for the basic necessities of food or shelter for himself or herself and any dependents.

Cosigners (e.g., parents who guarantee their child's student loan) must also meet the heightened undue hardship test to discharge their obligation. ■

Chapter 13: Adjustment of Debts of an Individual with Regular Income

Chapter 13, which is called **adjustment of debts of an individual with regular income**, is a rehabilitation form of bankruptcy for individuals.[6] Chapter 13 permits qualified debtors to propose a plan to pay all or a portion of the debts that he or she owes in installments over a specified period of time, pursuant to the requirements of Chapter 13. The bankruptcy court supervises the debtor's plan for the payment.

Chapter 13—adjustment of debts of an individual with regular income
A rehabilitation form of bankruptcy that permits bankruptcy courts to supervise the debtor's plan for the payment of unpaid debts in installments over the plan period.

The debtor has several advantages under Chapter 13. These include avoiding the stigma of Chapter 7 liquidation, retaining more property than is exempt under Chapter 7, and incurring less expenses than in a Chapter 7 proceeding. The creditors have advantages, too: They may recover a greater percentage of the debts owed them than they would recover under a Chapter 7 bankruptcy.

Chapter 13 petitions are usually filed by individual debtors who do not qualify for Chapter 7 liquidation bankruptcy and by homeowners who want to protect nonexempt equity in their residence. Chapter 13 enables debtors to catch up on secured credit loans, such as home mortgages, and avoid repossession and foreclosure.

Filing the Petition

A Chapter 13 proceeding can be initiated only by the voluntary filing of a petition by an individual debtor with regular income. A creditor cannot file an involuntary petition to institute a Chapter 13 case.

Debt rolls a man over and over, binding him hand and foot, and letting him hang upon the fatal mesh until the long-legged interest devours him.

Henry Ward Beecher
Proverbs from Plymouth Pulpit (1887)

An individual with regular income means an individual whose income is sufficiently stable and regular to enable the individual to make payments under a Chapter 13 plan. Regular income may be from any source, including wages, salary, commissions, income from investments, Social Security, pension income, or public assistance. The debts of the individual debtor must be primarily consumer debt. *Consumer debt* means debts incurred by an individual for a personal, family, or household purpose.

The debtor must allege that he or she is (1) insolvent or (2) unable to pay his or her debts when they become due. The petition must state that the debtor desires to affect an extension or a composition of debts, or both. An *extension* provides for a longer period of time for the debtor to pay his or her debts. A *composition* provides for the reduction of debts. The petition must be filed in good faith.

Limitations on Who Can File for Chapter 13 Bankruptcy

The 2005 act establishes dollar limits on the secured and unsecured debt that a debtor may have in order to qualify to file for Chapter 13 bankruptcy. Only an individual with regular income alone or with his or her spouse who owe individually or with their spouse (1) noncontingent, liquidated, unsecured debts of less than $307,675 and (2) secured debts of less than $922,975 may file a petition for Chapter 13 bankruptcy. Individual debtors who exceed these dollar limits do not qualify for Chapter 13 bankruptcy. Sole proprietorships, because they are owned by individuals, may file for Chapter 13.

Chapter 13 Procedures

When (or shortly after) the petition is filed, the debtor must file a list of creditors, assets, and liabilities with the court. The court then schedules a meeting of creditors. Prior to one day before the meeting of the creditors, a Chapter 13 debtor must have filed all tax returns due for a four-year period prior to the filing of the petition for bankruptcy. The court may extend this period if the debtor can prove that the filings have not been made because of circumstances beyond the control of the debtor. The debtor must appear at the meeting of the creditors.

Creditors may submit proof of claims, which will be allowed or disallowed by the court. No creditor committees are appointed, but the court must appoint a trustee upon confirmation of the plan.

The U. S. Trustee must appoint a trustee in a Chapter 13 case. In addition to the normal duties of a trustee, in a Chapter 13 case, the trustee may appear in court and be heard concerning the confirmation of a Chapter 13 plan, and the trustee may assist the debtor in the performance of the plan.

An automatic stay goes into place after the order for relief. The stay stops creditors from commencing or continuing any civil action to collect all or part of a consumer debt from the debtor. In a Chapter 13 case, the automatic stay is also effective against the co-debtor. The court can grant a relief from the stay if the creditor's interest would be irreparably harmed by the continuation of the stay.

Property of the Estate

The property of a Chapter 13 estate consists of all nonexempt property of the debtor at the commencement of the case and nonexempt property acquired after the commencement of the case but before the case is closed. In addition, the property of the estate includes earnings and future income earned by the debtor after the commencement of the case but before the case is closed. This ensures that prepetition creditors will receive payments from the debtor's postpetition earnings and income.

The debtor remains in possession of all the property of the estate during the completion of the plan except as otherwise provided by the plan. If the debtor is self-employed, the debtor may continue to operate his or her business. In the alternative, the court may order that a trustee will operate the business if necessary.

Plan of Payment

The debtor's plan of payment must be filed no later than 90 days after the order for relief. The debtor must file information about his or her finances, including a budget of estimated income and expenses during the period of the plan. The plan may designate a class or classes of nonpriority unsecured claims. The plan may, however, treat consumer debt differently than other secured claims.

The 2005 act establishes rules as to the length of a plan under Chapter 13. The Chapter 13 plan may be either up to three years or up to five years, based on the following calculation:

- If the debtor's or debtor's and spouse's monthly income multiplied by 12 is less than the state's median income for the year for the same size family up to four members plus $525 per month for each member in excess of four members, the plan period may not exceed three years, unless the court approves a period up to five years for cause.
- If the debtor's or debtor's and spouse's monthly income multiplied by 12 is equal to or more than the state's median income for the year for the same size family up to four members plus $525 per month for each member in excess of four members, the plan period may not be longer than five years.

Modification of the Rights of Creditors

A Chapter 13 plan of payment may modify the rights of unsecured creditors and some secured creditors. Any objections they have may be voiced at the confirmation hearing held by the court. The modifications of creditors' rights permitted under a Chapter 13 plan of payment are discussed in the following paragraphs.

Secured Creditors The plan must be submitted to secured creditors for acceptance. The plan will be confirmed as to a secured creditor if that creditor has accepted the plan. If a secured creditor does not accept the plan, the court may still confirm the plan if (1) the plan permits the secured creditor to retain its lien until the payment of the underlying debt or discharge and the value of the plan's distribution to the creditor is equal to the creditor's secured interest or (2) the debtor surrenders the property securing the claim to the secured creditor. A Chapter 13 plan must provide holders of claims secured by personal property adequate protection during the plan period.

If the debtor has a purchase money security interest in a motor vehicle acquired for personal use within 910 days preceding the filing date or a purchase money security interest in other personal property that was acquired within one year preceding the filing date, the debtor must pay the secured and unsecured portions (if any) of the claim in full. If the debtor does not, the creditor can foreclose on its lien and recover the vehicle.

Consider This Example Suppose that Emmett purchased a personal automobile 700 days prior to filing a petition for Chapter 13 bankruptcy, and he borrowed $20,000 from the dealer at the time of purchase. If at the time of bankruptcy Emmett still owed $16,000 of the debt, he would have to pay this amount in full under his Chapter 13 plan, or the creditor could recover the vehicle.

Unsecured Creditors The plan will be confirmed as to an unsecured creditor if that creditor has accepted the plan. If an unsecured creditor objects to the plan, the court may still confirm the plan if (1) the plan proposes to pay an objecting unsecured creditor the amount of his or her claim or (2) the debtor agrees to commit all of his or her disposable income during the plan period to pay his or her unsecured creditors.

Disposable income is defined as current monthly income less amounts reasonably necessary to be expended for the maintenance or support of the debtor and the dependants of the debtor. Expenses include amounts necessary to pay domestic support obligations and charitable donations that do not exceed 15 percent of the debtor's gross income for the year the charitable donation is made. If a debtor earns more that the median income of the state, his or her expenses are determined by the objective IRS standards.

Consider This Example Suppose a debtor earns $3,800 per month, which is less than the median income of the state. Suppose that $3,000 is reasonably necessary to support the debtor and his or her family. If the $800 per month disposable income is committed to pay prepetition unsecured debts, the court may confirm the plan even if the debts of the unsecured creditors are substantially modified under the plan.

Confirmation of a Plan of Payment

The court can confirm a Chapter 13 plan of payment if the prior requirements are met and if the plan (1) was proposed in good faith, (2) passes the feasibility test (e.g., the debtor must be able to make the proposed payments), (3) is in the best interests of the creditors (i.e., the present value of the payments must equal or exceed the amount that the creditors would receive in a Chapter 7 liquidation proceeding), (4) the debtor has paid all domestic support obligations owed, and (5) the debtor has filed all applicable federal, state, and local tax returns.

The debtor must begin making the planned installment payments to the trustee within 30 days after the plan is filed or the order for relief, whichever is earlier. These interim payments must continue until the plan is confirmed or denied. If the plan is denied, the trustee must return the interim payments to the debtor, less any administrative costs. If the plan is confirmed, the debtor must continue making the required payments to the trustee. The trustee is responsible for remitting these payments to the creditors. The trustee is paid for administering the plan. Payments under the plan must be in equal monthly installments.

A Chapter 13 plan may be modified if the debtor's circumstances materially change. For example, if the debtor's income subsequently decreases, the court may decrease the debtor's payments under the plan. If an interested party objects to the modification, the court must hold a hearing to determine whether it should be approved.

Chapter 13 Discharge

The court will grant an order discharging the debtor from all unpaid unsecured debts covered by the plan after all the payments required under the plan are completed (which could be up to three years or up to five years). This is called a **Chapter 13 discharge**. The debtor must certify that all domestic support payments have been paid before discharge is granted. Most unpaid taxes are not discharged. Prior to the 2005 act, student loans could be discharged under Chapter 13. The 2005 act changed this and provides that student loans can be discharged only upon proving undue hardship.

Chapter 13 discharge

A discharge in a Chapter 13 case that is granted to the debtor after the debtor's plan of payment is completed (which could be up to three or up to five years).

A debtor cannot be granted Chapter 13 discharge if the debtor has received discharge under Chapter 7, 11, or 12 within the preceding four-year period or Chapter 13 relief within the prior two-year period of the order for relief in the current Chapter 13 case.

Chapter 11: Reorganization

Chapter 11 of the Bankruptcy Code provides a method for reorganizing a debtor's financial affairs under the supervision of the bankruptcy court.[7] The goal of Chapter 11 is to reorganize the debtor with a new capital structure so that it will emerge from bankruptcy as a viable concern. This option, which is referred to as **reorganization bankruptcy**, is often in the best interests of the debtor and its creditors.

Chapter 11—reorganization
A bankruptcy method that allows the reorganization of the debtor's financial affairs under the supervision of the bankruptcy court.

Reorganization Proceeding

Chapter 11 is available to individuals, partnerships, corporations, other business entities, nonincorporated associations, and railroads. It is not available to commercial banks, savings banks, credit unions, insurance companies, stockbrokers, or commodities brokers. The majority of Chapter 11 proceedings are filed by corporations that want to reorganize their capital structures by receiving discharge of a portion of their debts, obtain relief from burdensome contracts, and emerge from bankruptcy as going concerns. Much of the following discussion applies to business reorganizations.

A Chapter 11 petition may be filed voluntarily by the debtor or involuntarily by its creditors. The principles discussed earlier in this chapter regarding the filing of petitions, the first meeting of the creditors, the entry of the order for relief, automatic stay, and relief from stay also apply to Chapter 11 proceedings.

The court can dismiss a Chapter 11 case or convert the case to a Chapter 7 liquidation case upon the request of the debtor or any party of interest if the court finds that it would be in the best interests of the parties to do so.

Debtor-in-Possession

In most Chapter 11 cases, the debtor is left in place to operate the business during the reorganization proceeding. In such cases, the debtor is called a **debtor-in-possession**. The court may appoint a trustee to operate the debtor's business only upon a showing of cause, such as fraud, dishonesty, or gross mismanagement by the debtor or its management. Even if a trustee is not appointed, however, the court may appoint an examiner to investigate the debtor's financial affairs.

debtor-in-possession
A debtor who is left in place to operate the business during the reorganization proceeding.

The debtor-in-possession or trustee is empowered to operate the debtor's business during the bankruptcy proceeding. This power includes authority to enter into contracts, purchase supplies, incur debts, and so on. Some suppliers will accept only cash for their goods or services during this time, whereas others will extend credit. Credit extended by postpetition unsecured creditors in the ordinary course of business is given automatic priority as an administrative expense in bankruptcy. Further, upon notice and hearing, the court may create a secured interest by granting a postpetition unsecured creditor a lien on the debtor-in-possession's property.

Creditors' Committees

Once an order for relief is granted, the court will appoint a **creditors' committee** composed of representatives of the class of unsecured claims. The court may also appoint a committee of secured creditors and a committee of equity holders. Generally, the parties holding the seven largest creditor claims or equity interests are appointed to their requisite committees. Committee members owe a fiduciary duty to represent the interest of the class. Committees may appear at bankruptcy court hearings, participate in the negotiation of a

creditors' committee
A committee of unsecured creditors that is appointed by the court to represent the class of unsecured claims. The court can also appoint committees for secured creditors and for equity holders.

plan of reorganization, assert objections to proposed plans of reorganization, and the like. Committees can employ attorneys, accountants, appraisers, investment bankers, and other professionals.

Automatic Stay in Chapter 11

The filing of a Chapter 11 petition stays (i.e., suspends) actions by creditors to recover the debtor's property. This automatic stay suspends certain legal actions against the debtor or the debtor's property, including the ability of creditors to foreclose on assets given as collateral for their loans to the debtor. An automatic stay is extremely important to a business trying to reorganize under Chapter 11 because the debtor needs to keep its assets to stay in business.

Consider This Example UAL Corporation, the parent company of United Airlines, filed for Chapter 11 reorganization bankruptcy. At the time of filing the petition, UAL owned or leased airplanes, equipment, trucks and other vehicles, docking space at airports, warehouses, office space, and other assets. In many cases, UAL had borrowed the money to purchase or lease these assets. Most of the lenders took back a mortgage or security interest in the asset it had loaned money to UAL to purchase or lease. If UAL was not in bankruptcy and defaulted on these loans or leases, the secured creditors could use state law and foreclose on their security interests and recover these assets as collateral. UAL would be left without most of its major assets that it would need to operate its business.

When UAL filed for Chapter 11 bankruptcy, however, the automatic stay of federal bankruptcy law went into effect and prevented the secured creditors from using state law to foreclose on UAL's assets. Therefore, UAL was able to continue to operate its business while it reorganized under bankruptcy law protection. When UAL emerged from Chapter 11 bankruptcy, it still had most of its assets. The secured creditors had to be paid any arrearages that were owed by UAL to them. The secured creditors remained secured creditors during and after the bankruptcy reorganization.

Executory Contracts and Unexpired Leases

executory contract or unexpired lease

A contract or lease that has not been fully performed. With the bankruptcy court's approval, executory contracts and unexpired leases may be rejected by a debtor in bankruptcy.

Another major benefit of Chapter 11 bankruptcy is that the debtor is given the opportunity to accept or reject certain executory contracts and unexpired leases. An **executory contract or unexpired lease** is a contract or lease that has not been fully performed. For example, a contract to purchase or supply goods at a later date is an executory contract; a 20-year office lease that has 8 years left until it is completed is an unexpired lease. Other executory contracts and unexpired leases include consulting contracts, contracts to purchase or provide services, equipment leases, warehouse leases, and such.

Under the Bankruptcy Code, the debtor-in-possession (or trustee) in a Chapter 11 proceeding is given authority to assume or reject executory contracts. In general, the debtor will reject unfavorable executory contracts and assume favorable executory contracts. Court approval is necessary to reject an executory contract. The debtor is not liable for damages caused by the rejection of executory contracts and unexpired leases in bankruptcy. Note that executory contracts and unexpired leases may also be rejected in Chapter 7, Chapter 12, and Chapter 13 proceedings.

Consider This Example Suppose Import Corporation files for Chapter 11 reorganization bankruptcy. After a review of its executory contracts and unexpired leases, the corporation identifies the following unfavorable executory contracts and unexpired leases: a contract to purchase goods from a supplier that has 2 years left, a contract to deliver services to a customer that has 1 year left, a lease for office space that has 10 years left, and an equipment lease for trucks that has 3 years left. Import Corporation can reject all these contracts and leases with the court's approval. Import Corporation is not liable for any damages caused by its rejection of these executory contracts and unexpired leases.

Labor Union and Retiree Benefits Contracts

Debtors that file for Chapter 11 reorganization sometimes have collective bargaining agreements with labor unions that require the payment of agreed-upon wages and other benefits to union member-employees for some agreed-upon period in the future. Debtors also often have contracts to pay union and nonunion retired employees and their dependants medical, surgical, hospitalization, dental, and death benefits (retiree benefits). In a Chapter 11 case, union members and union retirees are represented by the responsible labor union. The court will appoint a committee to represent nonunion retirees.

The debtor and the representatives of the union members and retirees can voluntarily agree to modify the union collective bargaining agreement and retiree benefits. If such an agreement is not reached, the debtor can petition the bankruptcy court to reject the collective bargaining agreement and to modify retiree benefits. The Bankruptcy Code requires that the following multistep process be followed:

1. The debtor makes a proposal to the union or representative that sets forth its proposed modifications.
2. The debtor meets with the union or representative to discuss the proposal and confers in good faith in an attempt to reach a mutually satisfactory modification.
3. The union or representative refuses to accept the proposal without good cause.

If these steps have been taken, the court will hold a hearing. The court may order the rejection of the collective bargaining agreement or modification of retiree benefits if it finds that the "balance of equities" favors rejection or modification and that rejection or modification is necessary to the reorganization.

Plan of Reorganization

The debtor has the exclusive right to file a **plan of reorganization** with the bankruptcy court within the first 120 days after the date of the order for relief. Under the 2005 act, this period may be extended up to 18 months from the date of the order for relief. The debtor has the right to obtain creditor approval of the plan within 180 days after the date of the order. If the debtor fails to do so, any party of interest (e.g., a trustee, a creditor, an equity holder) may propose a plan up to 20 months from the date of the order. In other words, the original 180-day period cannot be extended beyond 20 months.

plan of reorganization
A plan that sets forth a proposed new capital structure for the debtor to have when it emerges from Chapter 11 reorganization bankruptcy.

The plan or reorganization should set forth the proposed new financial structure of the debtor. This includes the portion of the unsecured debt proposed to be paid by the debtor and the unsecured debt the debtor proposes to be discharged. The plan must specify the executory contracts and unexpired leases that the debtor proposes to reject that have not previously been rejected in the bankruptcy proceeding. The plan should also designate how equity holders are proposed to be treated, describe any new equity investments that are proposed to be made in the debtor, and other relevant information.

The debtor must supply the creditors and equity holders with a *disclosure statement* that contains adequate information about the proposed plan of reorganization so that they can make an informed judgment about the plan. Excerpts from a disclosure statement appear as Exhibit 29.4.

Exhibit 29.4

Excerpts from a Disclosure Statement

IN THE UNITED STATES BANKRUPTCY COURT
FOR THE NORTHERN DISTRICT OF ILLINOIS
EASTERN DIVISION

In re:	)	Chapter 11
	)	
UAL Corporation et al.,	)	
	)	Case No. 02-B-48191
Debtors.[1]	)	(Jointly Administered)
	)	Honorable Eugene R. Wedoff

DISCLOSURE STATEMENT FOR REORGANIZING DEBTORS' JOINT PLAN OF REORGANIZATION PURSUANT TO CHAPTER 11 OF THE UNITED STATES BANKRUPTCY CODE

ARTICLE 1.
SUMMARY

UAL Corporation ("UAL") is a holding company whose principal, wholly-owned subsidiary is United Air Lines, Inc. ("United"). United's operations, which consist primarily of the transportation of persons, property, and mail throughout the U.S. and abroad, accounted for most of UAL's revenues and expenses in 2004. United is one of the largest scheduled passenger airlines in the world with over 1,500 daily departures to more than 120 destinations in 26 countries and two U.S. territories. Through United's global route network, United serves virtually every major market around the world, either directly or through the Star Alliance, which is the world's largest airline network. In addition to the Star Alliance, United provides regional service into United's domestic hubs through marketing relationships with "United Express® " carriers. In 2004, United added a new low-fare brand, called Ted, designed to serve select leisure markets and to more effectively compete with low-fare carriers.

On December 9, 2002 (the "Petition Date"), UAL, United, and 26 other direct and indirect wholly-owned subsidiaries filed voluntary petitions for relief under Chapter 11 of the United States Bankruptcy Code (the "Bankruptcy Code") in the United States Bankruptcy Court for the Northern District of Illinois, Eastern Division (the "Bankruptcy Court"). The foregoing entities are sometimes referred to collectively as the "Debtors."

The Purpose of the Plan

The Debtors have concluded, after careful review of their current business operations, their prospects as ongoing business enterprises, and the estimated recoveries of Creditors in various liquidation scenarios, that the recovery of Holders of Allowed Claims will be maximized by the Debtors' continued operation as a going concern. The Debtors believe that their businesses and assets have significant value that would not be realized in a liquidation scenario, either in whole or in substantial part. According to the liquidation analysis described herein (the "Liquidation Analysis") and the other analyses prepared by the Debtors and their advisors, the value of the Debtors' Estates is considerably greater as a going concern than if they were liquidated.

Accordingly, the Debtors believe that the Plan provides the best recoveries possible for the Holders of Allowed Claims and strongly recommend that, if you are entitled to vote, you vote to accept the plan. The Debtors believe that any alternative to Confirmation of the Plan, such as liquidation or attempts by another party in interest to file a plan of reorganization, could result in significant delays, litigation, and additional costs.

confirmation
The bankruptcy court's approval of a plan of reorganization.

acceptance method
A method whereby the court confirms a plan of reorganization if the creditors accept the plan and if other requirements are met.

Confirmation of a Plan of Reorganization

There must be **confirmation** of the plan of reorganization by the bankruptcy court for the debtor to be reorganized under Chapter 11. The bankruptcy court will confirm a plan of reorganization under the **acceptance method** if (1) the plan is in the best interests of the creditors because the creditors would receive at least what they would receive in a Chapter 7 liquidation bankruptcy, (2) the plan is feasible (that is, the new reorganized company is likely to succeed), and (3) each class of creditors accepts the plan (i.e., at least one-half the number of creditors who represent at least two-thirds the dollar amount of the debt vote to accept the plan).

If a class of creditors does not accept the plan, the plan can still be confirmed by the court, using the Bankruptcy Code's **cram-down provision**. In order for the court to confirm a plan over the objection of a class of creditors, at least one class of creditors must have voted to accept the plan, the plan must be in the best interests of the creditors, the plan must be feasible, the plan must not discriminate unjustly against any creditors, and the plan must be fair and equitable.

cram-down method
A method whereby the court confirms a plan of reorganization over an objecting class of creditors if certain requirements are met.

The plan must provide for the payment in full of unpaid income, gross receipts, employment, and excise taxes incurred by the debtor within three years prior to the date of the petition and for property taxes incurred within one year prior to the date of the petition. The plan may provide that these payments be made in equal installments not to exceed five years.

Consider This Example Suppose that the BigDotCom Corporation has financial difficulties and has filed for Chapter 11 reorganization. At the time of filing for Chapter 11, the corporation has $100 million of secured credit, $100 million of unsecured credit, and common stockholders whose equity securities are now worthless. The corporation files a plan of reorganization where (1) the corporation keeps the secured assets for the business, pays the secured creditors any arrearages owed, and has the secured creditors retain their secured interests in the secured assets; (2) reduces unsecured debt by $45 million and discharges $55 million of unsecured debt; (3) eliminates the interests of the equity holders; (4) rejects specified executory contracts and unexpired leases; (5) eliminates several unprofitable product lines; (6) provides for the payment of required unpaid taxes; and (7) accepts the investment of $30 million in capital from an investment bank that wants to invest in the corporation. If this plan is approved by the court, $55 million of the corporation's unsecured debt will be discharged. The corporation will emerge from Chapter 11 as a reorganized going concern.

Individuals Filing for Chapter 11 Reorganization

Individuals may file for Chapter 11 reorganization bankruptcy. The 2005 act establishes several special rules that apply when individuals apply for Chapter 11 reorganization. The property of the estate is the same as that which would be included in the estate under a Chapter 7 or Chapter 13 proceeding, as well as all property acquired by the debtor between the time the bankruptcy was commenced and the case is closed. An individual must file a plan of reorganization. The 2005 act requires that the plan provide for the payment to creditors of a portion of the debtor's earnings from personal services earned after the commencement of the case, as necessary to complete the plan.

If an unsecured creditor objects to an individual debtor's plan, the court can cram down the plan over the objection of the creditor if (1) the plan pays the discounted value of the claim to the creditor or (2) the value of the property to be distributed under the plan is not less than the disposable income of the debtor during the five-year period from the date the first payment is due under the plan. An individual debtor's Chapter 11 plan may be modified at any time to reflect a change in the debtor's circumstances.

Once the debtor has completed the required payments under the plan, the court will grant discharge of any unpaid debts to the debtor. The court may grant discharge to a debtor who has not completed plan payments if modification of the plan is not practicable and the amount paid to the unsecured creditors has been as much as the creditor would have received in a Chapter 7 liquidation case.

Contemporary Trend

Small Business Bankruptcy

Large firms that reorganize under Chapter 11 of the Bankruptcy Code have the resources to hire lawyers, investment bankers, and other professionals to assist them in the time-consuming and expensive Chapter 11 reorganization process. Smaller firms often do not have the resources or the luxury of the time necessary to use a typical Chapter 11 proceeding.

To address this problem, the Bankruptcy Code permits a "small business," defined as one with total debts of less than $2 million, to use a simpler and fast-track form of Chapter 11 reorganization bankruptcy. Small business bankruptcy provides an efficient and cost-saving method for smaller businesses to reorganize under Chapter 11. Debtors whose primary activity is owning or operating real property, or who are members of an affiliated group with over $2 million in debt, cannot file for small business bankruptcy.

The debtor must attach its most recent financial statements and tax returns to its petition or be excused by the court from doing so. The debtor, through its senior management, must attend interviews, conferences, and a meeting of the creditors. A trustee is appointed unless the court excuses this requirement. During the bankruptcy proceeding, the debtor must file information regarding its profitability, cash flow, expenses, tax returns, and other financial information.

The Bankruptcy Code provides for a fast-track processing of a small business case. A small business debtor has 180 days after the order for relief to file its plan of reorganization. If the debtor does not file a plan, any creditor or other party of interest may submit a plan up to 300 days after the order for relief. The bankruptcy court must confirm a small business debtor's plan of reorganization within 45 days after the plan is filed, as long as the plan meets the requirements of Chapter 11. The court can extend all the time periods for cause. ■

Chapter 12: Family Farmer and Family Fisherman Bankruptcy

Beginning in 1986, family farmers were permitted to file for bankruptcy reorganization under Chapter 12 of the Bankruptcy Code. Chapter 12 was only a temporary part of the Bankruptcy Code, however, that needed to be periodically reenacted by Congress to remain law. The 2005 act made Chapter 12 a permanent part of the Bankruptcy Code and added family fishermen as debtors who could seek reorganization under its provisions. The 2005 act establishes special definitions and rules that allow family farmers and family fishermen to file for bankruptcy reorganization under **Chapter 12—adjustment of debts of a family farmer or fisherman with regular income**.[8]

Chapter 12—adjustment of debts of a family farmer or family fisherman with regular income
A form of bankruptcy reorganization permitted to be used by family farmers and family fishermen.

Family Farmer

family farmer
An individual, a corporation, or a partnership that engages in farming operations and that meets the requirements for filing for a Chapter 12 proceeding.

Chapter 12 defines a **family farmer** as:

1. An individual or an individual and spouse whose total debt does not exceed $3,273,000 and is at least 50 percent related to farming operations, and whose gross income for the preceding taxable year or each of the second and third preceding taxable years was at least 50 percent earned from farming operations; or
2. A corporation or partnership that is at least 50 percent owned by one family or one family and its relatives and such family or relatives conduct the farming operation, and more than 80 percent of the assets of the business are related to the farming operation, and the business's total debt does not exceed $3,273,000 and is at least 50 percent related to the farming operation.

Family Fisherman

Chapter 12 defines a **family fisherman** as:

family fisherman

An individual, a corporation, or a partnership that engages in commercial fishing operations and that meets the requirements for filing for a Chapter 12 proceeding.

1. An individual or an individual and spouse whose total debt does not exceed $1,500,000 and is at least 80 percent related to the commercial fishing operation and whose gross income for the preceding taxable year was at least 50 percent earned from the commercial fishing operation; or
2. A corporation or partnership that is at least 50 percent owned by one family or one family and its relatives and such family or its relatives conduct the commercial fishing operation, and more than 80 percent of the assets of the business are related to the commercial fishing operation, and the business's total debt does not exceed $1,500,000 and is at least 80 percent related to the commercial fishing operation.

Procedure and Estate

Under Chapter 12, a debtor may file a voluntary petition. Creditors cannot, however, file involuntary petitions. Upon filing for Chapter 12 bankruptcy, a trustee is appointed. The family farmer or family fisherman is a debtor-in-possession who remains in possession of the property of the estate and is permitted to operate the farming or commercial fishing operation unless cause, such as fraud, dishonesty, or gross mismanagement, is proven.

Upon the filing of the petition, an automatic stay goes into place against creditors' actions (e.g., foreclosure proceedings) against the debtor. A secured creditor can petition the court for relief from the stay if the creditor's security interest would be irreparably harmed by the stay.

In addition to the property normally included in a bankruptcy proceeding, the bankruptcy estate in a Chapter 12 case also includes (1) property that the debtor acquires after the commencement of the case and before the reorganization plan is completed, and (2) earnings from services performed by the debtor after the commencement of the case and before the reorganization plan is completed.

The debtor can convert a Chapter 12 reorganization case to a Chapter 7 liquidation case at any time.

Plan of Reorganization

The family farmer or family fisherman debtor must file a plan of reorganization within 90 days of the order for relief. Generally, the plan may provide for payments to creditors over a period no longer than three years, but the court can increase the period to up to five years based on a showing of cause. The plan of reorganization must be confirmed by the court before it becomes operable.

The plan of reorganization can modify the rights of secured creditors and unsecured creditors. The plan may treat claims for an individual debtor's consumer debt differently than other unsecured debt.

Secured Claims

Chapter 12 provides certain protections for secured creditors. A debtor's plan can be confirmed as to a secured creditor if (1) the holder of the claim has accepted the plan, (2) the debtor surrenders the property securing the claim to the secured creditor, or (3) the plan provides that the secured creditor retains the mortgage or lien securing the claim and the plan distributes property to the secured creditor that is not less than the allowed amount of the claim.

Priority Unsecured Claims

As discussed previously in this chapter, Section 507 of the Bankruptcy Code defines certain unsecured claims as priority claims and designates their priority of payment in a bankruptcy proceeding. The debtor and an unsecured creditor can voluntarily agree to the terms for the settlement of an unsecured creditor's priority claim. This can take the form of reducing the amount of the claim as well as extending the time period for the payment of the claim.

If no such agreement is reached, the plan of reorganization must (1) provide for the full payment of the claim in deferred cash payments or (2) provide for less than full payment of the claim if the plan provides that all of the debtor's projected disposable income for the plan period will be applied to make payments under the plan.

Nonpriority Unsecured Claims

The debtor and an unsecured creditor can voluntarily agree to the terms for the settlement of an unsecured creditor's nonpriority claim. If no agreement is reached, the plan can modify the claims of unsecured creditors as necessary to accomplish the reorganization. This includes reducing the amount of the claim as well as extending the period to pay the claim.

Executory Contracts

A Chapter 12 plan can provide for the assumption or rejection of executory contracts and unexpired leases. For example, suppose a family farmer is obligated under a contract to sell his harvested grain to a buyer for the next three years. The debtor can assume this contract or reject this contract, depending on what is in his best interests. If the debtor rejects the contract, the buyer cannot sue the debtor to recover damages.

Confirmation of a Chapter 12 Plan

The bankruptcy court will hold a hearing regarding the confirmation of the plan. Creditors can appear at the hearing and object to the plan. If the requirements previously discussed are met, the bankruptcy court must confirm a plan if:

1. The plan has been proposed in good faith.
2. The plan is in the best interests of each of the allowed unsecured claims because the plan pays each unsecured claim at least what such claim would have received under Chapter 7 liquidation bankruptcy.
3. The plan is feasible (that is, the debtor will be able to make the payments specified in the plan).
4. The debtor must submit all or such portion of the debtor's future earnings or other future income to the trustee as is necessary for the completion of the plan.

Cram-Down Provision

If a priority or nonpriority unsecured creditor objects to the plan, the court can cram down the plan over the objecting unsecured creditors if the plan provides any of the following: (1) The unsecured creditor is paid the discounted present value of his claim; (2) the debtor's projected disposable income received in the plan period is applied to make payments under the plan; or (3) the value of the property to be distributed under the plan is not less than the disposable income of the debtor during the plan period.

Discharge

Once the family farmer or family fisherman debtor has completed making all payments required by the plan (which is usually three years but could be up to five years), the bankruptcy court will grant the debtor discharge of all debts provided for by the plan. This is called a **Chapter 12 discharge**. For example, if the Chapter 12 plan calls for the debtor to pay 55 percent of the outstanding unsecured debt to the unsecured creditors, and this amount has been paid by the debtor during the plan period, the court will grant discharge of the unpaid 45 percent of this unsecured debt.

Chapter 12 discharge
A discharge in a Chapter 12 case that is granted to a family farmer or family fisherman debtor after the debtor's plan of payment is completed (which is usually three years but could be up to five years).

The court may grant discharge to a debtor who has not completed payments under the plan if modification of the plan is not practicable, the debtor's failure to complete the required payments is due to circumstances for which the debtor is not accountable, and the amount paid to the unsecured creditors has been as much as the creditor would have received in a Chapter 7 liquidation bankruptcy.

Ethics in Business
Bankruptcy Fraud

Most of the time, bankruptcy law is used for legitimate purposes, and the information provided by the debtor and creditors is true and complete. However, sometimes debtors or creditors abuse bankruptcy law and commit fraudulent acts in a bankruptcy proceeding.

Federal law makes it a crime for any person to devise, intend to devise, or execute a scheme or an artifice to commit fraud by filing a voluntary or involuntary petition for bankruptcy, filing a fraudulent document, or making a false or fraudulent claim in connection with a bankruptcy case [18 U.S.C. Section 157]. A person convicted of bankruptcy fraud may be fined and imprisoned for up to five years. Each case is independently examined by the court.

Section 802 of the **Sarbanes-Oxley Act**, a federal statute enacted to address business fraud, makes it a crime for anyone to knowingly alter, falsify, conceal, or make a false entry in any document with the intention to obstruct or influence the investigation of any bankruptcy case. A violation is punishable by fine or imprisonment for not more than 20 years, or both.

Ethics Issues

1. Do you think much bankruptcy fraud occurs? Give several examples.
2. Will the new provisions of the 2005 act help prevent bankruptcy fraud? Explain. ■

Special Forms of Bankruptcy

The Bankruptcy Code and other federal laws include provisions that permit special forms of bankruptcy. Some of these special forms of bankruptcy are:

- ***Railroad reorganization.*** Chapter 11 of the Bankruptcy Code provides special requirements and provisions for the reorganization of railroads.[9] The bankruptcy court is directed to consider the public interest in approving the reorganization of railroads and the abandonment of railroad lines.
- ***Municipality adjustment of debts.*** Chapter 9 of the Bankruptcy Code provides for a proceeding for adjusting the debts of a municipality.[10] Under Chapter 9, cities, towns, counties, sewage and water districts, and other local governmental units can file for bankruptcy and reorganize their debts.
- ***Stockbroker and commodity broker liquidation.*** Chapter 7 of the Bankruptcy Code provides special requirements and provisions for the liquidation bankruptcy of

stockbrokers[11] and commodity brokers.[12] This includes provisions for the treatment of customer accounts, protection of clients' property, and the processing of claims.

- ***Commercial banks, savings banks, and credit unions.*** The Bankruptcy Code does not provide for the bankruptcy of commercial banks, savings banks, or credit unions. The bankruptcy proceedings of commercial banks, savings banks, and credit unions are handled by federal governmental agencies that oversee the operation of these financial institutions.

Terms and Concepts

Bankruptcy Law

1. ***Bankruptcy Reform Act of 1978, as amended.*** This federal statute establishes the requirements and procedures for filing for bankruptcy.
2. ***Bankruptcy Abuse Prevention and Consumer Protection Act of 2005.*** This federal act substantially amends federal bankruptcy law. The 2005 act makes it more difficult for debtors to file for bankruptcy and have their unpaid debts discharged.
3. ***Bankruptcy courts.*** Bankruptcy courts have exclusive jurisdiction to hear bankruptcy cases. A bankruptcy court is attached to each federal district court. Bankruptcy judges are appointed for 14-year terms.

The "Fresh Start"

The purpose of bankruptcy is to discharge the debtor from burdensome debts.

Bankruptcy Procedure

1. ***Filing of a petition.*** The filing of a petition commences a bankruptcy case.
   a. *Voluntary petition.* A voluntary petition is filed by a debtor.
   b. *Involuntary petition.* An involuntary petition is filed by a creditor or creditors.
2. ***Order for relief.*** An order for relief designates that the bankruptcy court has accepted a case for further proceedings.
3. ***Meeting of the creditors.*** The debtor must appear at this meeting and answer questions by the creditors. Also called the *first meeting of the creditors.*
4. ***Appointments of a trustee.*** A *permanent trustee* is elected at the first meeting of the creditors.
5. ***Proof of claims.*** Each unsecured creditor must file proof of claim, stating the amount of its claim against the debtors.

Automatic Stay

The filing of a bankruptcy petition *stays* (suspends) certain legal actions against the debtor or the debtor's property.

1. ***Relief from stay.*** A secured creditor may petition the court for a relief from stay in situations involving depreciating assets and when the creditor is not adequately protected during the bankruptcy proceeding.

Property of the Bankruptcy Estate

The *bankruptcy estate* includes:

1. All the debtor's legal and equitable interests in real, personal, tangible, and intangible property at the time the petition is filed.
2. Gifts, inheritances, life insurance proceeds, and property from divorce settlements that the debtor is entitled to receive within 180 days after the petition is filed.

Exempt Property

The Bankruptcy Code permits the debtor to retain certain property that does not become part of the bankruptcy estate. Exemptions are stipulated in federal and state law.

Preferential and Fraudulent Transfers

The following transfers and preferences are voidable by the trustee:

1. ***Preferential transfer within 90 days before bankruptcy.*** In this case, transfer is for an antecedent debt and gives the creditor more than he or she would receive in bankruptcy.
2. ***Preferential transfer to an insider between 90 days and one year before bankruptcy.*** In this case, the transferee is an "insider" (e.g., relative, business associate).
3. ***Fraudulent transfer within two years before bankruptcy.*** In this case, the debtor transfers property with the actual intent to hinder, delay, or defraud creditors.

Chapter 7 Bankruptcy

In Chapter 7 bankruptcy, the debtor's nonexempt property is sold for cash, the cash is distributed to the creditors, and any unpaid debts are discharged. Also called *liquidation bankruptcy.*

Median Income and Means Tests

In order to qualify for Chapter 7 liquidation relief, the 2005 act establishes certain median income and means tests that a debtor must meet.

Priority of Distribution

Nonexempt property of the bankruptcy estate is distributed to the creditors in the following statutory priority:

1. ***Secured creditors.*** Either a secured creditor obtains the collateral or the collateral is sold and the secured creditor is paid. If the value of the collateral exceeds the secured interest, the excess becomes available to pay other creditors. If the value of the collateral is less than the secured interest, the secured creditor becomes an unsecured creditor as to the difference.
2. ***Unsecured creditors.*** Unsecured creditors are paid in the priority established by the Bankruptcy Code. Each class must be paid in full before any lower class is paid anything. If a class cannot be paid in full, the claims of that class are paid proportionately.

Chapter 7—Discharge

After the nonexempt property is distributed, the remaining unpaid claims of the debtor are *discharged*, and the debtor's legal obligation to pay these unpaid debts is terminated. Discharge is available only to individuals.

Nondischargeable Debts

The Bankruptcy Code stipulates that certain debts are not dischargeable.

Acts That Bar Discharge

A bankruptcy court may deny discharge of debts if the debtor has engaged in prohibited conduct.

Discharge of Student Loans

A student loan may be discharged after it is due only if nondischarge would cause an *undue hardship* on the debtor or his or her family.

Chapter 13—Consumer Debt Adjustment

Chapter 13 is a rehabilitation form of bankruptcy that permits bankruptcy courts to supervise the debtor's plan for the repayment of unpaid debts by installment. Called *consumer debt adjustment.*

Limitations on Who Can File Chapter 13 Bankruptcy

The 2005 act establishes limits on the dollar amount of unsecured and secured debt a debtor may have before qualifying for Chapter 13 relief.

The Plan of Payment

The debtor must file a plan of payment. The plan period cannot exceed three years unless the court approves a longer period (of up to five years). A plan may be modified if the debtor's circumstances materially change.

1. ***Trustee.*** A permanent trustee will be appointed by the court. The debtor makes payments to the trustee, who is responsible for remitting payments to the creditors.

Chapter 13 Discharge

The court will grant an order discharging the debtor from all unpaid debts covered by the plan only after all the payments required under the plan are completed.

Chapter 11—Reorganization Bankruptcy

Chapter 11 bankruptcy provides a method for reorganizing the debtor's financial affairs under the supervision of the bankruptcy court.

Reorganization Proceeding

The principles discussed for Chapter 7 regarding the filing of petitions, the first meeting of the creditors, the entry for the order for relief, and the automatic stay also apply to Chapter 11 proceedings.

Debtor-in-Possession

In most Chapter 11 cases, the debtor is left in place to operate the business during the reorganization proceeding. In such cases, the debtor is called *debtor-in-possession.*

1. ***Trustee.*** The court may appoint a trustee to operate the debtor's business only upon a showing of cause, such as fraud, dishonesty, or gross mismanagement by the debtor or its management.

Creditors' Committees

The court will appoint a committee of unsecured creditors (usually creditors holding the seven largest claims). The court may also appoint committees of secured creditors and equity holders. Committees participate in the bankruptcy proceeding and in the negotiation of a plan of reorganization.

Small Business Bankruptcy

The *Bankruptcy Reform Act of 1994* is a federal statute that provides a less-costly and faster procedure for small businesses to file, maintain, and emerge from a Chapter 11 bankruptcy proceeding.

Plan of Reorganization

This plan sets forth the debtor's proposed new capital structure. The debtor has the exclusive right to file a plan within the first 120 days after the date of the order for relief.

Disclosure Statement

The debtor must supply the creditors and equity holders with a disclosure statement that contains adequate information about the proposed plan of reorganization.

Executory Contracts

The debtor-in-possession (or trustee) may assume or reject executory contracts. A special procedure has been established for rejecting union collective bargaining agreements.

Confirmation of a Plan of Reorganization

A plan of reorganization must be confirmed by the bankruptcy court before it becomes effective. Confirmation may be by either of the following methods:

1. ***Confirmation by the acceptance method.*** This type of confirmation is established by Section 1129(a) of the Bankruptcy Code.
2. ***Confirmation by the cram-down method.*** This type or confirmation is provided for by Section 1129(b) of the Bankruptcy Code.

Chapter 11 Discharge

Upon confirmation of a plan of reorganization, the debtor is granted a discharge of all claims not included in the plan. The debtor's legal obligation to pay the discharged debts is terminated.

Chapter 12—Family Farmer and Family Fisherman Bankruptcy

Chapter 12 is a rehabilitation form of bankruptcy that provides a method for reorganizing the family farmer or family fisherman debtor's financial affairs under the supervision of the bankruptcy court.

Definition of Family Farmer and Family Fisherman

The 2005 act establishes definitions of *family farmer* and *family fisherman* based on certain debt and income associated with the farming or commercial fishing operation.

Plan of Reorganization

A plan of reorganization can only be filed by the family farmer or family fisherman debtor.

Special Forms of Bankruptcy

The Bankruptcy Code provides special chapters or sections for handling bankruptcy proceedings of railroad reorganizations, municipality adjustment of debts, and stockbroker and commodity broker liquidations.

Internet Exercises and Case Questions

Working the Web Internet Exercises

1. Check on current statistics on the number of bankruptcies filed at **www.uscourts.gov/press_releases/bankruptcyfilings82405.html** and "InterNet Bankruptcy Library—Worldwide Troubled Company Resources," at **www.bankrupt.com**.
2. What is the amount of your state's homestead exemption? More information can be found at **www.uslegalforms.com/homestead_exemption_laws.htm**.
3. The FTC has practical advice for debtors at **www.ftc.gov/bcp/conline/pubs/credit/kneedeep.htm**.
4. Why do we have bankruptcy? Theoretical underpinnings of bankruptcy are explored in "Bankruptcy's Organizing Principle," by David Gray Carlson, at **www.law.fsu.edu/journals/lawreview/backissues/263.html**.

Legal Environment Cases

29.1 Petition In March 1988, Daniel E. Beren, John M. Elliot, and Edward F. Mannino formed Walnut Street Four, a general partnership, to purchase and renovate an office building in Harrisburg, Pennsylvania. They borrowed more than $200,000 from Hamilton Bank to purchase the building and begin renovation. Disagreements among the partners arose when the renovation costs exceeded their estimates. When Beren was unable to obtain assistance from Elliot and Mannino regarding obtaining additional financing, the partnership quit paying its debts. Beren filed an involuntary petition to place the partnership into Chapter 7 bankruptcy. The other partners objected to the bankruptcy filing. At the time of the filing, the partnership owed debts of more than $380,000 and had approximately $550 in the partnership bank account. Should the petition for involuntary bankruptcy be granted? *In re Walnut Street Four,* 106 B.R. 56 1989 Bankr. Lexis 1806 (Bk.M.D. Pa.)

29.2 Bankruptcy Estate In 1983, Bill K. and Marilyn E. Hargis, husband and wife, filed a Chapter 11 bankruptcy proceeding. In 1984, more than 120 days after the bankruptcy petition was filed, Bill died. His life was insured for $700,000. His wife was the beneficiary of the policy. The bankruptcy trustee moved to recover the $700,000 as property of the bankruptcy estate. Who gets the insurance proceeds? *In re Hargis,* 887 F.2d 77, 1989 U.S.App. Lexis 16246 (5th Cir.)

29.3 Automatic Stay In 1985, James F. Kost filed a voluntary petition for relief under Chapter 11 of the Bankruptcy Code. First Interstate Bank of Greybull (First Interstate) held a first mortgage on the debtor's residence near Basin, Wyoming. Appraisals and other evidence showed that the house was worth $116,000. The debt owed to First Interstate was almost $103,000, and it was increasing at a rate of $32.46 per day. The debtor had only an 11.5 percent equity cushion in the property. Further evidence showed that the (1) Greybull/Basin area was suffering from tough economic times, (2) there were more than 90 homes available for sale in the area, (3) the real estate market in the area was declining, (4) the condition of the house was seriously deteriorating and the debtor was not financially able to make the necessary improvements, and (5) the insurance on the property had lapsed. First Interstate moved for a relief from stay so that it could foreclose on the property and sell it. Should the motion be granted? *In re Kost,* 102 B.R.829, 1989 U.S.Dist. Lexis 8316 (Bk.D. Wyo.)

29.4 Fraudulent Transfer In November 1974, Peter and Geraldine Tabala (Debtors), husband and wife, purchased a house in Clarkstown, New York. In November 1976, they purchased a Carvel ice cream business for $70,000 with a loan obtained from People's National Bank. In addition, the Carvel Corporation extended trade credit to Debtors. On October 23, 1978, Debtors conveyed their residence to their three daughters, ages 9, 19, and 20, for no consideration. Debtors continued to reside in the house and to pay maintenance expenses and real estate taxes due on the property. On the date of transfer, Debtors owed obligations in excess of $100,000. On March 28, 1980, Debtors filed a petition for Chapter 7 bankruptcy. The bankruptcy trustee moved to set aside Debtors' conveyance of their home to their daughters as a fraudulent transfer. Who wins? *In re Tabala,* 11 B.R. 405, 1981 Bankr. Lexis 3663 (Bk.S.D. N.Y.)

29.5 Preferential Payment Air Florida System, Inc. (Air Florida), an airline company, filed a voluntary petition to reorganize under Chapter 11 of the Bankruptcy Code. Within 90 days prior to the commencement of the case, Air Florida paid $13,575 to Compania Panamena de Aviacion, S.A. (COPA), in payment of an antecedent debt. This payment enabled COPA to receive more than it would have received if Air Florida were liquidated under Chapter 7. Is the payment to COPA an avoidable preferential transfer? *In re Jet Florida System, Inc. f/k/a Air Florida System, Inc.,* 105 B.R. 137, 1989 Bankr. Lexis 1629 (Bk.S.D. Fla.)

29.6 Executory Contract On October 15, 1980, The Record Company Inc. (The Record Company), entered into a purchase agreement to buy certain retail record stores from Bummbusiness, Inc. (Bummbusiness). All assets and inventory were included in the deal. The Record Company agreed to pay Bummbusiness $20,000 and to pay the $380,000 of trade debt owed by the stores. In exchange, Bummbusiness agreed not to compete with the new buyer for two years within a 15-mile radius of the stores and to use its best efforts to obtain an extension of the due dates for the trade debt. The Record Company began operating the stores but shortly thereafter filed a petition for Chapter 11 bankruptcy. At the time of the bankruptcy filing, (1) The Record Company owed Bummbusiness $10,000 and owed the trade debt of $380,000 and (2) Bummbusiness was obligated not to compete with The Record Company. Can The Record Company reject the purchase agreement? *In re The Record Company,* 8 B.R. 57, 1981 Bankr. Lexis 5157 (Bk.S.D. Ind.)

29.7 Plan of Reorganization Richard P. Friese (Debtor) filed a voluntary petition for Chapter 11 bankruptcy. In May 1989, Debtor filed a plan of reorganization that divided his creditors into three classes. The first class was administrative creditors, who were to be paid in full. The second class was unsecured creditors, who were to receive 50 percent on their claims. The IRS was the third class. It was to receive $20,000 on confirmation and the balance in future payments. No creditors voted to accept the plan. The unsecured creditors were impaired because their legal, equitable, and contractual rights were being altered. Can the bankruptcy court confirm Debtor's plan of reorganization? *In re Friese,* 103 B.R. 90, 1989 Bankr. Lexis 1309 (Bk.S.D. N.Y.)

29.8 Consumer Debt Adjustment Manuel Guadalupe (Debtor) was a tool and die machinist who was employed at Elco Industries for more than five years. He accumulated more than $19,000 in unsecured debt, including deficiencies owed after secured creditors repossessed a van (leaving a deficiency of $1,066) and a car (leaving a deficiency of $3,130). Shortly after the second automobile was repossessed, Debtor borrowed approximately $19,000 from Elco Credit Union to purchase a 1988 four-wheel-drive Chevrolet Blazer. The $472 monthly payment was to be taken directly from Debtor's earnings.

On February 28, 1989, Debtor filed a voluntary petition for Chapter 13 consumer debt adjustment. The schedule listed total secured debts of $22,132, which included the debt for the Blazer, furniture, and a camcorder. Total unsecured debt was $19,575, which included $2,160 owed to General Finance Corporation (General). Debtor's budget projected that $700 per month would be left over for funding the Chapter 13 plan after his monthly expenses were deducted from his $25,000 gross income. Secured creditors were to be paid in full; unsecured creditors would receive 10 percent of their claims. General objected to the plan. Should Debtor's Chapter 13 plan be confirmed? *In re Reyes,* 106 B.R. 155, 1989 Bankr. Lexis 1731 (Bk.N.D. Ill.)

29.9 Student Loan Donald Wayne Doyle (Debtor) obtained a guaranteed student loan to enroll in a school for training truck drivers. Due to his impending divorce, Debtor never attended the program. The first monthly installment of approximately $50 to pay the student loan became due on September 1, 1988. On September 16, 1988, Debtor filed a voluntary petition for Chapter 7 bankruptcy.

Debtor was a 29-year-old man who earned approximately $1,000 per month at an hourly wage of $7.70 as a truck driver, a job that he had held for 10 years. Debtor resided on a farm where he performed work in lieu of paying rent for his quarters. Debtor was paying monthly payments of $89 on a bank loan for his former wife's vehicle, $200 for his truck, $40 for health insurance, $28 for car insurance, $120 for gasoline and vehicular maintenance, $400 for groceries and meals, and $25 for telephone charges. In addition, a state court had ordered Debtor to pay $300 per month to support his children, ages four and five. Debtor's parents were assisting him by buying him $130 of groceries per month. Should Debtor's student loan be discharged in bankruptcy? *In re Doyle,* 106 BR. 272, 1989 Bankr. Lexis 1772 (Bk.N.D. Ala.)

29.10 Preference Rule On December 17, 1986, ZZZZ Best Co., Inc. (Debtor), borrowed $7 million from Union Bank. On July 8, 1987, Debtor filed a voluntary petition under Chapter 7 (liquidation). During the preceding 90-day period, Debtor had made two interest payments on its loan to Union Bank, totaling $100,000. The trustee of Debtor's estate filed a complaint against Union Bank to recover those interest payments as preferential transfers made within 90 days of the bankruptcy filing. Can payments on long-term debt qualify as payments within the ordinary course of business exception to the 90-day preference rule? *Union Bank v. Wolas,* 502. U.S. 151, 112 S.Ct. 527, 1991 U.S. Lexis 7174 (U.S. Sup.Ct.)

Ethics in Business

29.11 Scott Greig Keebler (Debtor) became indebted, and his debts exceeded his assets. The Internal Revenue Service (IRS) had levied his wages for nonpayment of taxes. Debtor was healthy and capable of earning a substantial income. Evidence showed that Debtor did not try his best to pay his debts, lived an affluent lifestyle, and determined not to pay his principal creditors. Debtor voluntarily quit his job and filed a voluntary petition for Chapter 7 bankruptcy. The petition stated that he was unemployed. Shortly after filing for bankruptcy, the petitioner resumed work.

Ethics Issues

1. What is the purpose of Chapter 7 bankruptcy? Explain.

2. Should Debtor's Chapter 7 case be dismissed because he filed the petition in bad faith?

Endnotes

1. 11 U.S.C. Sections 101–1330.
2. P.L. 109-8, 119 Stat. 23 (April 20, 2005).
3. 28 U.S.C. Sections 586–589b.
4. 11 U.S.C. Section 522(d).
5. 11 U.S.C. Sections 701–784.
6. 11 U.S.C. Sections 1301–1330.
7. 11 U.S.C. Sections 1101–1174.
8. 11 U.S.C. Sections 1201–1231.
9. 11 U.S.C. Sections 1161–1174.
10. 11 U.S.C. Sections 901–946.
11. 11 U.S.C. Sections 741–753.
12. 11 U.S.C. Sections 761–767.

Appendix A — The Constitution of the United States of America

We the People of the United States, in Order to form a more perfect Union, establish Justice, insure domestic Tranquility, provide for the common defense, promote the general Welfare, and secure the Blessings of Liberty to ourselves and our Posterity, do ordain and establish this Constitution for the United States of America.

Article I

Section 1. All legislative Powers herein granted shall be vested in a Congress of the United States, which shall consist of a Senate and House of Representatives.

Section 2. The House of Representatives shall be composed of Members chosen every second Year by the People of the several states, and the Electors in each State shall have the Qualifications requisite for Electors of the most numerous Branch of the State Legislature.

No Person shall be a Representative who shall not have attained to the Age of twenty five Years, and been seven Years a Citizen of the United States, and who shall not, when elected, be an Inhabitant of that State in which he shall be chosen.

Representatives and direct Taxes shall be apportioned among the several states which may be included within this Union, according to their respective Numbers, which shall be determined by adding to the whole Number of free Persons, including those bound to Service for a Term of Years, and excluding Indians not taxed, three fifths of all other Persons. The actual Enumeration shall be made within three Years after the first Meeting of the Congress of the United States, and within every subsequent Term of ten Years, in such Manner as they shall by Law direct. The number of Representatives shall not exceed one for every thirty Thousand, but each State shall have at Least one Representative; and until such enumeration shall be made, the State of New Hamp-shire shall be entitled to chuse three, Massachusetts eight, Rhode Island and Providence Plantations one, Connecticut five, New York six, New Jersey four, Pennsylvania eight, Delaware one, Maryland six, Virginia ten, North Carolina five, South Carolina five, and Georgia three.

When vacancies happen in the Representation from any State, the Executive Authority thereof shall issue Writs of Election to fill such vacancies.

The House of Representatives shall choose their Speaker and other Officers; and shall have the sole Power of Impeachment.

Section 3. The Senate of the United States shall be composed of two Senators from each State, chosen by the Legislature thereof, for six Years; and each Senator shall have one Vote.

Immediately after they shall be assembled in Consequence of the first Election, they shall be divided as equally as may be into three Classes. The Seats of the Senators of the first Class shall be vacated at the Expiration of the second Year, of the second Class at the Expiration of the fourth Year, and the third Class at the Expiration of the sixth Year, so that one third may be chosen every second Year; and if Vacancies happen by Resignation, or otherwise, during the Recess of the Legislature of any State, the Executive thereof may make temporary Appointments until the next meeting of the Legislature, which shall then fill such Vacancies.

No person shall be a Senator who shall not have attained to the Age of thirty Years, and been nine Years a Citizen of the United States, and who shall not, when elected, be an Inhabitant of that State for which he shall be chosen.

The Vice President of the United States shall be President of the Senate, but shall have no Vote, unless they be equally divided.

The Senate shall choose their other Officers, and also a President pro tempore, in the Absence of the Vice President, or when he shall exercise the Office of President of the United States.

The Senate shall have the sole power to try all Impeachments. When sitting for that Purpose, they shall be an Oath or Affirmation. When the President of the United States is tried, the Chief Justice shall preside: And no Person shall be convicted without the Concurrence of two thirds of the Members present.

Judgment in Cases of Impeachment shall not extend further than to removal from Office, and disqualification to hold and enjoy any Office of honor, Trust or Profit under the United States: but the Party convicted shall nevertheless be liable and subject to Indictment, Trial, Judgment and Punishment, according to Law.

Section 4. The Times, Places and Manner of holding Elections for Senators and Representatives, shall be prescribed in each State by the Legislature thereof: but the Congress may at any time by Law make or alter such Regulations, except as to the Places of choosing Senators.

The Congress shall assemble at least once in every Year, and such Meeting shall be on the first Monday in December, unless they shall by Law appoint a different day.

Section 5. Each House shall be the Judge of the Elections, Returns and Qualifications of its own Members, and a Majority of each shall constitute a Quorum to do Business; but a smaller Number may adjourn from day to day, and may be authorized to compel the Attendance of absent Members, in such Manner, and under such Penalties as each House may provide.

Each House may determine the Rules of its Proceedings, punish its Members for disorderly Behaviour, and, with the Concurrence of two thirds, expel a Member.

Each House shall keep a Journal of its Proceedings, and from time to time publish the same, excepting such Parts as may in their Judgment require Secrecy; and the Yeas and Nays of the Members of either House on any question shall, at the Desire of one fifth of those Present, be entered on the Journal.

Neither House, during the Session of Congress, shall, without the Consent of the other, adjourn for more than three days, nor to any other Place than that in which the two Houses shall be sitting.

Section 6. The Senators and Representatives shall receive a Compensation for their Services, to be ascertained by Law, and paid out of the Treasury of the United States. They shall in all Cases, except Treason, Felony and Breach of the Peace, be privileged from Arrest during their Attendance at the Session of their respective Houses, and in going to and returning from the same; and for any Speech or Debate in either House, they shall not be questioned in any other Place.

No Senator or Representative shall, during the Time for which he was elected, be appointed to any civil Office under the Authority of the United States, which shall have been created, or the Emoluments whereof shall have been encreased during such time; and no Person holding any Office under the United States, shall be a Member of either House during his Continuance in Office.

Section 7. All Bills for raising Revenue shall originate in the House of Representatives; but the Senate may propose or concur with Amendments as on other Bills.

Every Bill which shall have passed the House of Representatives and the Senate, shall, before it become a Law, be presented to the President of the United States; If he approve he shall sign it, but if not he shall return it, with his Objections to that House in which it shall have originated, who shall enter the Objections at large on their Journal, and proceed to reconsider it. If after such Reconsideration two thirds of that House shall agree to pass the Bill, it shall be sent, together with the Objections, to the other House, by which it shall likewise be reconsidered, and if approved by two thirds of that House, it shall become a Law. But in all such Cases the Votes of both Houses shall be determined by Yeas and Nays, and the Names of the Persons voting for and against the Bill shall be entered on the Journal of each House respectively. If any Bill shall not be returned by the President within ten Days (Sundays excepted) after it shall have been presented to him, the Same shall be a Law, in like Manner as if he had signed it, unless the Congress by their Adjournment prevent its Return, in which Case it shall not be a Law.

Every Order, Resolution, or Vote to which the Concurrence of the Senate and House of Representatives may be necessary (except on a question of Adjournment) shall be presented to the President of the United States; and before the Same shall take Effect, shall be approved by him, or being disapproved by him, shall be repassed by two thirds of the Senate and House of Representatives, according to the Rules and Limitations prescribed in the Case of a Bill.

Section 8. The Congress shall have Power to lay and collect Taxes, Duties, Imposts and Excises, to pay the Debts and provide for the common Defence and general Welfare of the United States; but all Duties, Imposts and Excises shall be uniform throughout the United States;

To borrow Money on the credit of the United States;

To regulate Commerce with foreign Nations, and among the several States, and with the Indian Tribes;

To establish an uniform Rule of Naturalization, and uniform Laws on the subject of Bankruptcies throughout the United States;

To coin Money, regulate the Value thereof, and of foreign Coin, and fix the Standard of Weights and Measures;

To provide for the Punishment of counterfeiting the Securities and current Coin of the United States;

To establish Post Offices and post Roads;

To promote the Progress of Science and useful Arts, by securing for limited Times to Authors and Inventors the exclusive Right to their respective Writings and Discoveries;

To constitute Tribunals inferior to the supreme Court;

To define and punish Piracies and Felonies committed on the high Seas, and Offenses against the Law of Nations;

To declare War, grant Letters of Marque and Reprisal, and make Rules concerning Captures on Land and Water;

To raise and support Armies, but no Appropriation of Money to that Use shall be for a longer Term than two Years;

To provide and maintain a Navy;

To make Rules for the Government and Regulation of the land and naval Forces;

To provide for calling forth the Militia to execute the Laws of the Union, suppress Insurrections and repel Invasions;

To provide for organizing, arming, and disciplining, the Militia, and for governing such Part of them as may be employed in the Service of the United States, reserving to the States respectively, the Appointment of the Officers, and the Authority of training the Militia according to the discipline prescribed by Congress;

To exercise exclusive Legislation in all Cases whatsoever, over such District (not exceeding ten Miles square) as may, by Cession of particular States, and the Acceptance of Congress, become the Seat of the Government of the United States, and to exercise like Authority over all Places purchased by the Consent of the Legislature of the State in which the Same shall be, for the Erection of Forts, Magazines, Arsenals, dock-Yards, and other needful Buildings;—And

To make all Laws which shall be necessary and proper for carrying into Execution the foregoing Powers, and all other Powers vested by this Constitution in the Government of the United States, or in any Department or Officer thereof.

Section 9. The Migration or Importation of such Persons as any of the States now existing shall think proper to admit, shall not be prohibited by the Congress prior to the Year one thousand eight hundred and eight, but a Tax or Duty may be imposed on such Importation, not exceeding ten dollars for each Person.

The Privilege of the Writ of Habeas Corpus shall not be suspended, unless when in Cases of Rebellion or Invasion the public Safety may require it.

No Bill of Attainder or ex post facto Law shall be passed.

No Capitation, or other direct, Tax shall be laid, unless in Proportion to the Census or Enumeration herein before directed to be taken.

No Tax or Duty shall be laid on Articles exported from any State.

No Preference shall be given by any Regulation of Commerce or Revenue to the Ports of one State over those of another; nor shall Vessels bound to, or from, one State, be obliged to enter, clear, or pay Duties in another.

No Money shall be drawn from the Treasury, but in Consequence of Appropriations made by Laws; and a regular Statement and Account of the Receipts and Expenditures of all public Money shall be published from time to time.

No Title of Nobility shall be granted by the United States: And no Person holding any Office of Profit or Trust under them, shall, without the Consent of the Congress, accept of any present, Emolument, Office, or Title, of any kind whatever, from any King, Prince, or foreign State.

Section 10. No State shall enter into any Treaty, Alliance, or Confederation; grant Letters of Marque and Reprisal; coin Money; emit Bills of Credit; make any Thing but gold and silver Coin a Tender in Payment of Debts; pass any Bill of Attainder, ex post facto Law, or Law impairing the Obligation of Contracts, or grant any Title of Nobility.

No State shall, without the Consent of the Congress, lay any Imposts or Duties on Imports or Exports, except what may be absolutely necessary for executing its inspection Laws: and the net Produce of all Duties and Imposts, laid by any State on Imports or Exports, shall be for the Use of the Treasury of the United States; and all such Laws shall be subject to the Revision and Control of the Congress.

No State shall, without the Consent of Congress, lay any Duty of Tonnage, keep Troops, or Ships of War in time of Peace, enter into any Agreement or Compact with another State, or with a foreign Power, or engage in War, unless actually invaded, or in such imminent Danger as will not admit of delay.

Article II

Section 1. The executive Power shall be vested in a President of the United States of America. He shall hold his Office during the Term of four Years, and, together with the Vice President, chosen for the same Term, be elected, as follows:

Each State shall appoint, in such Manner as the Legislature thereof may direct, a Number of Electors, equal to the whole Number of Senators and Representatives to which the State may be entitled in the Congress: but no Senator or Representative, or Person holding an Office of Trust or Profit under the United States, shall be appointed an Elector.

The Electors shall meet in their respective States, and vote by Ballot for two Persons, of whom one at least shall not be an Inhabitant of the same State with themselves. And they shall make a list of all the Persons voted for, and of the Number of Votes for each; which List they shall sign and certify, and transmit sealed to the Seat of the Government of the United States, directed to the President of the Senate. The President of the Senate shall, in the presence of the Senate and House of Representatives, open all the Certificates, and the Votes shall be counted. The Person having the greatest Number of Votes shall be the President, if such Number be a Majority of the whole Number of Electors appointed; and if there be more than one who have such Majority, and have an equal Number of Votes, then the House of Representatives shall immediately choose by Ballot one of them for President; and if no Person have a Majority, then from the five highest on the List the said House shall in like Manner choose the President. But in chusing the President, the Votes shall be taken by States, the Representation from each State having one Vote; A quorum for this Purpose shall consist of a Member or Members from two thirds of the States, and a Majority of all the States shall be necessary to a Choice. In every Case, after the Choice of the President, the Person having the greatest Number of Votes of the Electors shall be the Vice President. But if there should remain two or more who have equal Votes, the Senate shall choose from them by Ballot the Vice President.

The Congress may determine the Time of Choosing the Electors, and the Day on which they shall give their Votes; which Day shall be the same throughout the United States.

No Person except a natural born Citizen, or a Citizen of the United States, at the time of the Adoption of this Constitution, shall be eligible to the Office of President; neither shall any Person be eligible to that Office who shall not have attained to the Age of thirty five Years, and been fourteen Years a Resident within the United States.

In Case of the Removal of the President from Office, or of his Death, Resignation, or Inability to discharge the Powers and Duties of the said Office, the Same shall devolve on the Vice President, and the Congress may by Law provide for the Case of Removal, Death, Resignation or Inability, both of the President and Vice President, declaring what Officer shall then act as President, and such Officer shall act accordingly, until the Disability be removed, or a President shall be elected.

The President shall, at stated Times, receive for his Services, a Compensation, which shall neither be encreased nor diminished during the Period for which he shall have been elected, and he shall not receive within that Period any other Emolument from the United States, or any of them.

Before he enter on the Execution of his Office, he shall take the following Oath or Affirmation:—"I do solemnly swear (or affirm) that I will faithfully execute the Office of President of the United States, and will to the best of my

Ability, preserve, protect and defend the Constitution of the United States."

Section 2. The President shall be Commander in Chief of the Army and Navy of the United States, and of the Militia of the several States, when called into the actual Service of the United States; he may require the Opinion, in writing, of the principal Officer in each of the executive Departments, upon any Subject relating to the Duties of their respective Offices, and he shall have Power to grant Reprieves and Pardons for Offences against the United States, except in Cases of Impeachment.

He shall have Power, by and with the Advice and Consent of the Senate, to make Treaties, provided two thirds of the Senators present concur; and he shall nominate, and by and with the Advice and Consent of the Senate, shall appoint Ambassadors, other public Ministers and Consuls, Judges of the supreme Court, and all other Officers of the United States, whose Appointments are not herein otherwise provided for, and which shall be established by Law: but the Congress may by Law vest the Appointment of such inferior Officers, as they think proper, in the President alone, in the Courts of Law, or in the Heads of Departments.

The President shall have Power to fill up all Vacancies that may happen during the Recess of the Senate, by granting Commissions which shall expire at the End of their next Session.

Section 3. He shall from time to time give to the Congress Information of the State of the Union, and recommend to their Consideration such Measures as he shall judge necessary and expedient; he may, on extraordinary Occasions, convene both Houses, or either of them, and in Case of Disagreement between them, with Respect to the Time of Adjournment, he may adjourn them to such Time as he shall think proper; he shall receive Ambassadors and other public Ministers; he shall take Care that the Laws be faithfully executed, and shall Commission all the Officers of the United States.

Section 4. The President, Vice President and all civil Officers of the United States, shall be removed from Office on Impeachment for, and Conviction of, Treason, Bribery, or other high Crimes and Misdemeanors.

Article III

Section 1. The judicial Power of the United States, shall be vested in one supreme Court, and in such inferior Courts as the Congress may from time to time ordain and establish. The Judges, both of the supreme and inferior Courts, shall hold their Offices during good Behaviour, and shall, at Times, receive for their Services, a Compensation, which shall not be diminished during their Continuance in Office.

Section 2. The judicial Power shall extend to all Cases, in Law and Equity, arising under this Constitution, the Laws of the United States, and Treaties made, or which shall be made, under their Authority;—to all Cases affecting Ambassadors, other public Ministers and Consuls;—to all Cases of admiralty and maritime Jurisdiction;—to Controversies to which the United States shall be a Party;—to controversies between two or more States;—between a State and Citizens of another State;—between Citizens of different States;—between Citizens of the same State claiming Lands under Grants of different States, and between a State, or the Citizens thereof, and foreign States, Citizens or Subjects.

In all Cases affecting Ambassadors, other public Ministers and Consuls, and those in which a State shall be Party, the supreme Court shall have original Jurisdiction. In all the other Cases before mentioned, the supreme Court shall have appellate Jurisdiction, both as to Law and Fact, with such Exceptions, and under such Regulations as the Congress shall make.

The Trial of all Crimes, except in Cases of Impeachment, shall be by Jury; and such Trial shall be held in the State where the said Crimes shall have been committed; but when not committed within any State, the Trial shall be at such Place or Places as the Congress may by Law have directed.

Section 3. Treason against the United States, shall consist only in levying War against them, or in adhering to their Enemies, giving them Aid and Comfort. No Person shall be convicted of Treason unless on the Testimony of two Witnesses to the same overt Act, or on Confession in open Court.

The Congress shall have Power to declare the Punishment of Treason, but no Attainder of Treason shall work Corruption of Blood, or Forfeiture except during the Life of the Person attainted.

Article IV

Section 1. Full Faith and Credit shall be given in each State to the public Acts, Records, and judicial Proceedings of every other State. And the Congress may by general Laws prescribe the Manner in which such Arts, Records, and Proceedings shall be proved, and the Effect thereof.

Section 2. The Citizens of each State shall be entitled to all Privileges and Immunities of Citizens in the several States.

A person charged in any State with Treason, Felony, or other Crime, who shall flee from Justice, and be found in another State, shall on Demand of the executive Authority of the State from which he fled, be delivered up, to be removed to the State having Jurisdiction of the Crime.

No Person held to Service or Labour in one State, under the Laws thereof, escaping into another, shall, in Consequence of any Law or Regulation therein, be discharged from such Service or Labour, but shall be delivered up on Claim of the Party to whom such Service or Labour may be due.

Section 3. New States may be admitted by the Congress into this Union; but no new state shall be formed or erected within the Jurisdiction of any other State; nor any State be formed by the Junction of two or more States, or Parts of States, without the Consent of the Legislatures of the States concerned as well as of the Congress.

The Congress shall have Power to dispose of and make all needful Rules and Regulations respecting the Territory or other Property belonging to the United States; and nothing in this Constitution shall be so construed as to Prejudice any Claims of the United States, or of any particular State.

Section 4. The United States shall guarantee to every State in this Union a Republican Form of Government, and shall protect each of them against Invasion; and on Application of the Legislature, or of the Executive (when the Legislature cannot be convened) against domestic Violence.

Article V

The Congress, whenever two thirds of both Houses shall deem it necessary, shall propose Amendments to this Constitution, or, on the Application of the Legislatures of two thirds of the several States, shall call a Convention for proposing Amendments, which, in either Case, shall be valid to all Intents and Purposes, as Part of this Constitution, when ratified by the Legislatures of three fourths of the several States, or by Conventions in three fourths thereof, as the one or the other Mode of Ratification may be proposed by the Congress; Provided that no Amendment which may be made prior to the Year One thousand eight hundred and eight shall in any Manner affect the first and fourth Clauses in the Ninth Section of the first Article; and that no State, without its Consent, shall be deprived of its equal Suffrage in the Senate.

Article VI

All Debts contracted and Engagements entered into, before the Adoption of this Constitution, shall be as valid against the United States under this Constitution, as under the Confederation.

This Constitution, and the Laws of the United States which shall be made in Pursuance thereof; and all Treaties made, or which shall be made, under the Authority of the United States, shall be the supreme Law of the Land; and the Judges in every State shall be bound thereby, any Thing in the Constitution or Laws of any State to the Contrary notwithstanding.

The Senators and Representatives before mentioned, and the Members of the several State Legislatures, and all executive and judicial Officers, both of the United States and of the Several States, shall be bound by Oath or Affirmation, to support this Constitution; but no religious Test shall ever be required as a Qualification to any Office or public Trust under the United States.

Article VII

The Ratification of the Conventions of nine States, shall be sufficient for the Establishment of this Constitution between the States so ratifying the Same.

Amendment I [1791]

Congress shall make no law respecting an establishment of religion, or prohibiting the free exercise thereof; or abridging the freedom of speech, or the press; or the right of the people peaceably to assemble, and to petition the Government for a redress of grievances.

Amendment II [1791]

A well regulated Militia, being necessary to the security for a free State, the right of the people to keep and bear Arms, shall not be infringed.

Amendment III [1791]

No Soldier shall, in time of peace be quartered in any house, without the consent of the Owner, nor in time of war, but in a manner to be prescribed by law.

Amendment IV [1791]

The right of the people to be secure in their persons, houses, papers, and effects, against unreasonable searches and seizures, shall not be violated, and no Warrants shall issue, but upon probable cause, supported by Oath or Affirmation, and particularly describing the place to be searched, and the persons or things to be seized.

Amendment V [1791]

No person shall be held to answer for a capital, or otherwise infamous crime, unless on a presentment or indictment of a Grand Jury, except in cases arising in the land or naval forces, or in the Militia, when in actual service in time of War or public danger; nor shall any person be subject for the same offense to be twice put in jeopardy of life or limb; nor shall be compelled in any criminal case to be a witness against himself, nor be deprived of life, liberty, or property, without due process of law; nor shall private property be taken for public use, without just compensation.

Amendment VI [1791]

In all criminal prosecutions, the accused shall enjoy the right to a speedy and public trial, by an impartial jury of the State and district wherein the crime shall have been committed, which district shall have been previously ascertained by law, and to be informed of the nature and cause of the accusation; to be confronted with the Witnesses against him; to have compulsory process for obtaining witnesses in his favor, and to have the Assistance of counsel for his defence.

Amendment VII [1791]

In suits at common law, where the value in controversy shall exceed twenty dollars, the right of trial by jury shall be preserved, and no fact tried by a jury, shall be otherwise re-examined in any Court of the United States, than according to the rules of the common law.

Amendment VIII [1791]

Excessive bail shall not be required, nor excessive fines imposed, nor cruel and unusual punishments inflicted.

Amendment IX [1791]

The enumeration in the Constitution, of certain rights, shall not be construed to deny or disparage others retained by the people.

Amendment X [1791]

The powers not delegated to the United States by the Constitution, nor prohibited by it to the States, are reserved to the States respectively, or to the people.

Amendment XI [1798]

The judicial power of the United States shall not be construed to extend to any suit in law or equity, commenced or prosecuted against one of the United States by Citizens of another State, or by Citizens or Subjects of any Foreign State.

Amendment XII [1804]

The Electors shall meet in their respective states and vote by ballot for President and Vice-President, one of whom, at least, shall not be an inhabitant of the same state with themselves; they shall name in their ballots the person voted for as President, and in distinct ballots the person voted for as Vice-President, and they shall make distinct lists of all persons voted for as President, and of all persons voted for as Vice-President, and of the number of votes for each, which lists they shall sign and certify, and transmit sealed to the seat of the government of the United States, directed to the President of the Senate;—The President of the Senate shall, in the presence of the Senate and House of Representatives, open all the certificates and the votes shall then be counted;—The person having the greatest number of votes for President, shall be the President, if such number be a majority of the whole number of Electors appointed; and if no person have such majority, then from the persons having the highest numbers not exceeding three on the list of those voted for as President, the House of Representatives shall choose immediately, by ballot, the President. But in choosing the President, the votes shall be taken by states, the representation from each state having one vote; a quorum for this purpose shall consist of a member or members from two-thirds of the states, and a majority of all the states shall be necessary to a choice. And if the House of Representatives shall not choose a President whenever the right of choice shall devolve upon them, before the fourth day of March next following, then the Vice-President shall act as President, as in the case of the death or other constitutional disability of the President. The person having the greatest number of votes as Vice-President, shall be the Vice-President, if such number be a majority of the whole number of Electors appointed, and if no person have a majority, then from the two highest numbers on the list, the Senate shall choose the Vice-President; a quorum for the purpose shall consist of two-thirds of the whole number of Senators, and a majority of the whole number shall be necessary to a choice. But no person constitutionally ineligible to the office of President shall be eligible to that of the Vice-President of the United States.

Amendment XIII [1865]

Section 1. Neither slavery nor involuntary servitude, except as a punishment for crime whereof the party shall have been duly convicted, shall exist within the United States, or any place subject to their jurisdiction.
Section 2. Congress shall have power to enforce this article by appropriate legislation.

Amendment XIV [1868]

Section 1. All persons born or naturalized in the United States, and subject to the jurisdiction thereof, are citizens of the United States and of the State wherein they reside. No State shall make or enforce any law which shall abridge the privileges or immunities of citizens of the United States; nor shall any State deprive any person of life, liberty, or property, without due process of law; nor deny to any person within its jurisdiction the equal protection of the laws.
Section 2. Representatives shall be appointed among the several States according to their respective numbers, counting the whole number of persons in each State, excluding Indians not taxed. But when the right to vote at any election for the choice of electors for President and Vice President of the United States, Representatives in Congress, the Executive and Judicial officers of a State, or the members of the Legislature thereof, is denied to any of the male inhabitants of such State, being twenty-one years of age, and citizens of the United States, or in any way abridged, except for participation in rebellion, or other crime, the basis of representation therein shall be reduced in the proportion which the number of such male citizens shall bear to the whole number of male citizens twenty-one years of age in such State.
Section 3. No person shall be a Senator or Representative in Congress, or elector of President and Vice President, or hold any office, civil or military, under the United States, or under any State, who, having previously taken an oath, as a member of Congress, or as an officer of the United States, or as a member of any State legislature, or as an executive or judicial officer of any State, to support the Constitution of the United States, shall have engaged in insurrection or rebellion against the same, or given aid or comfort to the enemies thereof. But Congress may by a vote of two-thirds of each House, remove such disability.
Section 4. The validity of the public debt of the United States, authorized by law, including debts incurred for payment of pensions and bounties for services in suppressing insurrection or rebellion, shall not be questioned. But neither the United States nor any State shall assume or pay any debt or obligation incurred in aid of insurrection of rebellion against the United States, or any claim for the loss or emancipation of any slave; but all such debts, obligations and claims shall be held illegal and void.
Section 5. The Congress shall have power to enforce, by appropriate legislation, the provisions of this article.

Amendment XV [1870]

Section 1. The right of citizens of the United States to vote shall not be denied or abridged by the United States or by any State on account of race, color, or previous condition of servitude.
Section 2. The Congress shall have power to enforce this article by appropriate legislation.

Amendment XVI [1913]

The Congress shall have power to lay and collect taxes on incomes, from whatever source derived, without apportionment among the several States, and without regard to any census or enumeration.

Amendment XVII [1913]

The Senate of the United States shall be composed of two Senators from each State, elected by the people thereof, for six years; and each Senator shall have one vote. The electors in each State shall have the qualifications requisite for electors of the most numerous branch of the State legislatures.

When vacancies happen in the representation of any State in the Senate, the executive authority of each State shall issue writs of election to fill such vacancies; Provided, That the legislature of any State may empower the executive thereof to make temporary appointments until the people fill the vacancies by election as the legislature may direct.

This amendment shall not be so construed as to affect the election or term of any Senator chosen before it becomes valid as part of the Constitution.

Amendment XVIII [1919]

Section 1. After one year from the ratification of this article the manufacture, sale, or transportation of intoxicating liquors within, the importation thereof into, or the exportation thereof from the United States and all territory subject to the jurisdiction thereof for beverage purposes is hereby prohibited.
Section 2. The Congress and the several States shall have concurrent power to enforce this article by appropriate legislation.
Section 3. This article shall be inoperative unless it shall have been ratified as an amendment to the Constitution by the legislatures of the several States, as provided in the Constitution, within seven years from the date of the submission hereof to the States by the Congress.

Amendment XIX [1920]

The right of citizens of the United States to vote shall not be denied or abridged by the United States or by any State on account of sex.

Congress shall have power to enforce this article by appropriate legislation.

Amendment XX [1933]

Section 1. The terms of the President and Vice President shall end at noon on the 20th day of January, and the terms of Senators and Representatives at noon on the 3rd day of January, of the years in which such terms would have ended if this article had not been ratified; and the terms of their successors shall then begin.
Section 2. The Congress shall assemble at least once in every year, and such meeting shall begin at noon on the 3rd day of January, unless they shall by law appoint a different day.
Section 3. If, at the time fixed for the beginning of the term of the President, the President elect shall have died, the Vice President elect shall become President. If a President shall not have been chosen before the time fixed for the beginning of his term, or if the President elect shall have failed to qualify, then the Vice President elect shall act as President until a President shall have qualified; and the Congress may by law provide for the case wherein neither a President elect nor a Vice President elect shall have qualified, declaring who shall then act as President, or the manner in which one who is to act shall be selected, and such person shall act accordingly until a President or Vice President shall have qualified.
Section 4. The Congress may by law provide for the case of the death of any of the persons from whom the House of Representatives may choose a President whenever the right of choice shall have devolved upon them, and for the case of the death of any of the persons from whom the Senate may choose a Vice President whenever the right of choice shall have devolved upon them.
Section 5. Sections 1 and 2 shall take effect on the 15th day of October following the ratification of this article.
Section 6. This article shall be inoperative unless it shall have been ratified as an amendment to the Constitution by the legislatures of three-fourths of the several States within seven years from the date of its submission.

Amendment XXI [1933]

Section 1. The eighteenth article of amendment to the Constitution of the United States is hereby repealed.
Section 2. The transportation or importation into any State, Territory, or possession of the United States for delivery or use therein of intoxicating liquors, in violation of the laws thereof, is hereby prohibited.
Section 3. This article shall be inoperative unless it shall have been ratified as an amendment to the Constitution by conventions in the several States, as provided in the Constitution, within seven years from the date of the submission hereof to the States by the Congress.

Amendment XXII [1951]

Section 1. No person shall be elected to the office of the President more than twice, and no person who has held the office of President, or acted as President, for more than two years of a term to which some other person was elected President shall be elected to the office of the President more than once. But this Article shall not apply to any person holding the office of President when this article was proposed by the Congress, and shall not prevent any person who may be holding the office of President, or acting as President, during the term within which this Article becomes operative from holding the office of President, or acting as President during the remainder of such term.

Section 2. This article shall be inoperative unless it shall have been ratified as an amendment to the Constitution by the legislatures of three-fourths of the several States within seven years from the date of its submission to the States by the Congress.

Amendment XXIII [1961]

Section 1. The District constituting the seat of government of the United States shall appoint in such manner as the Congress may direct:

A number of electors of President and Vice President equal to the whole number of Senators and Representatives in Congress to which the District would be entitled if it were a State, but in no event more than the least populous State; they shall be in addition to those appointed by the States, but they shall be considered, for the purposes of the election of President and Vice President, to be electors appointed by a State; and they shall meet in the District and perform such duties as provided by the twelfth article of amendment.

Section 2. The Congress shall have power to enforce this article by appropriate legislation.

Amendment XXIV [1964]

Section 1. The right of citizens of the United States to vote in any primary or other election for President or Vice President, for electors for President or Vice President, or for Senator or Representative in Congress, shall not be denied or abridged by the United States or any State by reason of failure to pay any poll tax or other tax.

Section 2. The Congress shall have power to enforce this article by appropriate legislation.

Amendment XXV [1967]

Section 1. In case of the removal of the President from office or of his death or resignation, the Vice President shall become President.

Section 2. Whenever there is a vacancy in the office of the Vice President, the President shall nominate a Vice President who shall take office upon confirmation by a majority vote of both Houses of Congress.

Section 3. Whenever the President transmits to the President pro tempore of the Senate and the Speaker of the House of Representatives his written declaration that he is unable to discharge the powers and duties of his office, and until he transmits to them a written declaration to the contrary, such powers and duties shall be discharged by the Vice President as Acting President.

Section 4. Whenever the Vice President and a majority of either the principal officers of the executive departments or of such other body as Congress may by law provide, transmit to the President pro tempore of the Senate and the Speaker of the House of Representatives their written declaration that the President is unable to discharge the powers and duties of his office, the Vice President shall immediately assume the powers and duties of the office as Acting President.

Thereafter, when the President transmits to the President pro tempore of the Senate and the Speaker of the House of Representatives his written declaration that no inability exists, he shall resume the powers and duties of his office unless the Vice President and a majority of either the principal officers of the executive department or of such other body as Congress may by law provide, transmit within four days to the President pro tempore of the Senate and the Speaker of the House of Representatives their written declaration that the President is unable to discharge the powers and duties of his office. Thereupon Congress shall decide the issue, assembling within forty-eight hours for that purpose if not in session. If the Congress, within twenty-one days after receipt of the latter written declaration, or, if Congress is not in session, within twenty-one days after Congress is required to assemble, determines by two-thirds vote of both Houses that the President shall continue to discharge the same as Acting President; otherwise, the President shall resume the powers and duties of his office.

Amendment XXVI [1971]

Section 1. The right of citizens of the United States, who are 18 years of age or older, to vote, shall not be denied or abridged by the United States or any State on account of age.

Section 2. The Congress shall have the power to enforce this article by appropriate legislation.

Amendment XXVII [1992]

No law, varying the compensation for the services of the Senators and Representatives, shall take effect, until an election of Representatives shall have intervened.

Appendix B — Uniform Commercial Code (2000 Official Text), Article 2

Table of Sections

Article 2 Sales

Part 1. Short Title, General Construction and Subject Matter

Section

Article 2 Sales

Part 1. Short Title, General Construction and Subject Matter

§2–101. Short Title.

This Article shall be known and may be cited as Uniform Commercial Code—Sales.

§2–102. Scope; Certain Security and Other Transactions Excluded From This Article.

Unless the context otherwise requires, this Article applies to transactions in goods; it does not apply to any transaction which although in the form of an unconditional contract to sell or present sale is intended to operate only as a security transaction nor does this Article impair or repeal any statute regulating sales to consumers, farmers or other specified classes of buyers.

§2–103. Definitions and Index of Definitions.

(1) In this Article unless the context otherwise requires

(a) "Buyer" "means a person who buys or contracts to buy goods.

(b) "Good faith" in the case of a merchant means honesty in fact and the observance of reasonable commercial standards of fair dealing in the trade.

(c) "Receipt" of goods means taking physical possession of them.

(d) "Seller" means a person who sells or contracts to sell goods.

(2) Other definitions applying to this Article or to specified Parts thereof, and the sections in which they appear are:

"Acceptance"	Section 2–606.
"Banker's credit"	Section 2–325.
"Between merchants"	Section 2–104.
"Cancellation"	Section 2–106(4).
"Commercial unit"	Section 2–105.
"Confirmed credit"	Section 2–325.
"Conforming to contract"	Section 2–106.
"Contract for sale"	Section 2–106.
"Cover"	Section 2–712.
"Entrusting"	Section 2–403.
"Financing agency"	Section 2–104.
"Future goods"	Section 2–105.
"Goods"	Section 2–105.
"Identification"	Section 2–501.
"Installment contract"	Section 2–612.
"Letter of Credit"	Section 2–325.
"Lot"	Section 2–105.
"Merchant"	Section 2–104.
"Overseas"	Section 2–323.
"Person in position of seller"	Section 2–707.
"Present sale"	Section 2–106.
"Sale"	Section 2–106.
"Sale on approval"	Section 2–326.
"Sale or return"	Section 2–326.
"Termination"	Section 2–106.

(3) The following definitions in other Articles apply to this Article:

"Check"	Section 3–104.
"Consignee"	Section 7–102.
"Consignor"	Section 7–102.
"Consumer goods"	Section 9–102.
"Dishonor"	Section 3–502.
"Draft"	Section 3–104.

(4) In addition Article 1 contains general definitions and principles of construction and interpretation applicable throughout this Article.

§2–104. Definitions: "Merchant"; "Between Merchants"; "Financing Agency".

(1) "Merchant" means a person who deals in goods of the kind or otherwise by his occupation holds himself out as having knowledge

or skill peculiar to the practices or goods involved in the transaction or to whom such knowledge or skill may be attributed by his employment of an agent or broker or other intermediary who by his occupation holds himself out as having such knowledge or skill.

(2) "Financing agency" means a bank, finance company or other person who in the ordinary course of business makes advances against goods or documents of title or who by arrangement with either the seller or the buyer intervenes in ordinary course to make or collect payment due or claimed under the contract for sale, as by purchasing or paying the seller's draft or making advances against it or by merely taking it for collection whether or not the documents of title accompany the draft. "Financing agency" includes also a bank or other person who similarly intervenes between persons who are in the position of seller and buyer in respect to the goods (Section 2–707).

(3) "Between merchants" means in any transaction with respect to which both parties are chargeable with the knowledge or skill of merchants.

§2-105. Definitions: Transferability; "Goods"; "Future" Goods; "Lot"; "Commercial Unit".

(1) "Goods" means all things (including specially manufactured goods) which are movable at the time of identification to the contract for sale other than the money in which the price is to be paid, investment securities (Article 8) and things in action. "Goods" also includes the unborn young of animals and growing crops and other identified things attached to realty as described in the section on goods to be severed from realty (Section 2–107).

(2) Goods must be both existing and identified before any interest in them can pass. Goods which are not both existing and identified are "future" goods. A purported present sale of future goods or of any interest therein operates as a contract to sell.

(3) There may be a sale of a part interest in existing identified goods.

(4) An undivided share in an identified bulk of fungible goods is sufficiently identified to be sold although the quantity of the bulk is not determined. Any agreed proportion of such a bulk or any quantity thereof agreed upon by number, weight or other measure may to the extent of the seller's interest in the bulk be sold to the buyer who then becomes an owner in common.

(5) "Lot" means a parcel or a single article which is the subject matter of a separate sale or delivery, whether or not it is sufficient to perform the contract.

(6) "Commercial unit" means such a unit of goods as by commercial usage is a single whole for purposes of sale and division of which materially impairs its character or value on the market or in use. A commercial unit may be a single article (as a machine) or a set of articles (as a suite of furniture or an assortment of sizes) or a quantity (as a bale, gross, or carload) or any other unit treated in use or in the relevant market as a single whole.

§2-106. Definitions: "Contract"; "Agreement"; "Contract for Sale"; "Sale"; "Present Sale"; "Conforming" to Contract; "Termination"; "Cancellation".

(1) In this Article unless the context otherwise requires "contract" and "agreement" are limited to those relating to the present or future sale of goods. "Contract for sale" includes both a present sale of goods and a contract to sell goods at a future time. A "sale" consists in the passing of title from the seller to the buyer for a price (Section 2–401). A "present sale" means a sale which is accomplished by the making of the contract.

(2) Goods or conduct including any part of a performance are "conforming" or conform to the contract when they are in accordance with the obligations under the contract.

(3) "Termination" occurs when either party pursuant to a power created by agreement or law puts an end to the contract otherwise than for its breach. On "termination" all obligations which are still executory on both sides are discharged but any right based on prior breach or performance survives.

(4) "Cancellation" occurs when either party puts an end to the contract for breach by the other and its effect is the same as that of "termination" except that the cancelling party also retains any remedy for breach of the whole contract or any unperformed balance.

§2-107. Goods to Be Severed From Realty: Recording.

(1) A contract for the sale of minerals or the like (including oil and gas) or a structure or its materials to be removed from realty is a contract for the sale of goods within this Article if they are to be severed by the seller but until severance a purported present sale thereof which is not effective as a transfer of an interest in land is effective only as a contract to sell.

(2) A contract for the sale apart from the land of growing crops or other things attached to realty and capable of severance without material harm thereto but not described in subsection (1) or of timber to be cut is a contract for the sale of goods within this Article whether the subject matter is to be severed by the buyer or by the seller even though it forms part of the realty at the time of contracting, and the parties can by identification effect a present sale before severance.

(3) The provisions of this section are subject to any third party rights provided by the law relating to realty records, and the contract for sale may be executed and recorded as a document transferring an interest in land and shall then constitute notice to third parties of the buyer's right under the contract for sale.

Part 2. Form, Formation and Readjustment of Contract.

§2-201. Formal Requirements; Statute of Frauds.

(1) Except as otherwise provided in this section a contract for the sale of goods for the price of $500 or more is not enforceable by way of action or defense unless there is some writing sufficient to indicate that a contract for sale has been made between the parties and signed by the party against whom enforcement is sought or by his authorized agent or broker. A writing is not insufficient because it omits or incorrectly states a term agreed upon but the contract is not enforceable under this paragraph beyond the quantity of goods shown in such writing.

(2) Between merchants if within a reasonable time a writing in confirmation of the contract and sufficient against the sender is received and the party receiving it has reason to know its contents, it satisfies the requirements of subsection (1) against such party unless written notice of objection to its contents is given within 10 days after it is received.

(3) A contract which does not satisfy the requirements of subsection (1) but which is valid in other respects is enforceable

(a) if the goods are to be specially manufactured for the buyer and are not suitable for sale to others in the ordinary course of the seller's business and the seller, before notice of repudiation is received and under circumstances which reasonably indicate that the goods are for the buyer, has made either a substantial beginning of their manufacture or commitments for their procurement; or

(b) if the party against whom enforcement is sought admits in his pleading, testimony or otherwise in court that a contract for sale was made, but the contract is not enforceable under this provision beyond the quantity of goods admitted; or

(c) with respect to goods for which payment has been made and accepted or which have been received and accepted (Section 2–606).

§2-202. Final Written Expression: Parol or Extrinsic Evidence.

Terms with respect to which the confirmatory memoranda of the parties agree or which are otherwise set forth in a writing intended by the parties as a final expression of their agreement with respect to such terms as are included therein may not be contradicted by evidence of any prior agreement or of a contemporaneous oral agreement but may be explained or supplemented

(a) by course and dealing or usage of trade (Section 1–205) or by course of performance (Section 2–208); and

(b) by evidence of consistent additional terms unless the court finds the writing to have been intended also as a complete and exclusive statement of the terms of the agreement.

§2-203. Seals Inoperative.

The affixing of a seal to a writing evidencing a contract for sale or an offer to buy or sell goods does not constitute the writing a sealed instrument and the law with respect to sealed instruments does not apply to such a contract or offer.

§2-204. Formation in General.

(1) A contract for sale of goods may be made in any manner sufficient to show agreement, including conduct by both parties which recognizes the existence of such a contract.

(2) An agreement sufficient to constitute a contract for sale may be found even though the moment of its making is undetermined.

(3) Even though one or more terms are left open a contract for sale does not fail for indefiniteness if the parties have intended to make a contract and there is a reasonably certain basis for giving an appropriate remedy.

§2-205. Firm Offers.

An offer by a merchant to buy or sell goods in a signed writing which by its terms gives assurance that it will be held open is not revocable, for lack of consideration, during the time stated or if no time is stated for a reasonable time, but in no event may such period of irrevocability exceed three months; but any such term of assurance on a form supplied by the offeree must be separately signed by the offeror.

§2-206. Offer and Acceptance in Formation of Contract.

(1) Unless otherwise unambiguously indicated by the language or circumstances

(a) an offer to make a contract shall be construed as inviting acceptance in any manner and by any medium reasonable in the circumstances;

(b) an order or other offer to buy goods for prompt or current shipment shall be construed as inviting acceptance either by a prompt promise to ship or by the prompt or current shipment of conforming or non-conforming goods, but such a shipment of non-conforming goods does not constitute an acceptance if the seller reasonably notifies the buyer that the shipment is offered only as an accommodation to the buyer.

(2) Where the beginning of a requested performance is a reasonable mode of acceptance an offeror who is not notified of acceptance within a reasonable time may treat the offer as having lapsed before acceptance.

§2-207. Additional Terms in Acceptance or Confirmation.

(1) A definite and seasonable expression of acceptance or a written confirmation which is sent within a reasonable time operates as an acceptance even though it states terms additional to or different from those offered or agreed upon, unless acceptance is expressly made conditional on assent to the additional or different terms.

(2) The additional terms are to be construed as proposals for addition to the contract. Between merchants such terms become part of the contract unless:

(a) the offer expressly limits acceptance to the terms of the offer;

(b) they materially alter it; or

(c) notification of objection to them has already been given or is given within a reasonable time after notice of them is received.

(3) Conduct by both parties which recognizes the existence of a contract is sufficient to establish a contract for sale although the writings of the parties do not otherwise establish a contract. In such case the terms of the particular contract consist of those terms on which the writings of the parties agree, together with any supplementary terms incorporated under any other provisions of this Act.

§2-208. Course of Performance or Practical Construction.

(1) Where the contract for sale involves repeated occasions for performance by either party with knowledge of the nature of the performance and opportunity for objection to it by the other, any course of performance accepted or acquiesced in without objection shall be relevant to determine the meaning of the agreement.

(2) The express terms of the agreement and any such course of performance, as well as any course of dealing and usage of trade, shall be construed whenever reasonable as consistent with each other; but when such construction is unreasonable, express terms shall control course of performance and course of performance shall control both course of dealing and usage of trade (Section 1–205).

(3) Subject to the provisions of the next section on modification and waiver, such course of performance shall be relevant to show a waiver or modification of any term inconsistent with such course of performance.

§2-209. Modification, Rescission and Waiver.

(1) An agreement modifying a contract within this Article needs no consideration to be binding.

(2) A signed agreement which excludes modification or rescission except by a signed writing cannot be otherwise modified or rescinded, but except as between merchants such a requirement on a form supplied by the merchant must be separately signed by the other party.

(3) The requirements of the statute of frauds section of this Article (Section 2–201) must be satisfied if the contract as modified is within its provisions.

(4) Although an attempt at modification or rescission does not satisfy the requirements of subsection (2) or (3) it can operate as a waiver.

(5) A party who has made a waiver affecting an executory portion of the contract may retract the waiver by reasonable notification received by the other party that strict performance will be required of any term waived, unless the retraction would be unjust in view of a material change of position in reliance on the waiver.

§2-210. Delegation of Performance; Assignment of Rights.

(1) A party may perform his duty through a delegate unless otherwise agreed or unless the other party has a substantial interest in having his original promisor perform or control the acts required by the contract. No delegation of performance relieves the party delegating of any duty to perform or any liability for breach.

(2) Except as otherwise provided in Section 9–406, unless otherwise agreed all rights of either seller or buyer can be assigned except where the assignment would materially change the duty of the other party, or increase materially the burden or risk imposed on him by his contract, or impair materially his chance of obtaining return performance. A right to damages for breach of the whole contract or a right arising out of the assignor's due performance of his entire obligation can be assigned despite agreement otherwise.

(3) The creation, attachment, perfection, or enforcement of a security interest in the seller's interest under a contract is not a transfer that materially changes the duty of or increases materially the burden or risk imposed on the buyer or impairs materially the buyer's chance of obtaining return performance within the purview of subsection (2) unless, and then only to the extent that, enforcement actually results in a delegation of material performance of the seller. Even in that event, the creation, attachment, perfection, and enforcement of the security interest remain effective, but (i) the seller is liable to the buyer for damages caused by the delegation to the extent that the damages could not reasonably be prevented by the buyer, and (ii) a court having jurisdiction may grant other appropriate relief, including cancellation of the contract for sale or an injunction against enforcement of the security interest or consummation of the enforcement.

(4) Unless the circumstances indicate the contrary a prohibition of assignment of "the contract" is to be construed as barring only the delegation to the assignee of the assignor's performance.

(5) An assignment of "the contract" or of "all my rights under the contract" or an assignment in similar general terms is an assignment of rights and unless the language or the circumstances (as in an assignment for security) indicate the contrary, it is a delegation of performance of the duties of the assignor and its acceptance by the assignee constitutes a promise by him to perform those duties. This promise is enforceable by either the assignor or the other party to the original contract.

(6) The other party may treat any assignment which delegates performance as creating reasonable grounds for insecurity and may without prejudice to his rights against the assignor demand assurances from the assignee (Section 2–609).

Part 3. General Obligation and Construction of Contract

§2-301. General Obligations of Parties.

The obligation of the seller is to transfer and deliver and that of the buyer is to accept and pay in accordance with the contract.

§2-302. Unconscionable Contract or Clause.

(1) If the court as a matter of law finds the contract or any clause of the contract to have been unconscionable at the time it was made the court may refuse to enforce the contract, or it may enforce the remainder of the contract without the unconscionable clause, or it may so limit the application of any unconscionable clause as to avoid any unconscionable result.

(2) When it is claimed or appears to the court that the contract or any clause thereof may be unconscionable the parties shall be afforded a reasonable opportunity to present evidence as to its commercial setting, purpose and effect to aid the court in making the determination.

§2-303. Allocation or Division of Risks.

Where this Article allocates a risk or a burden as between the parties "unless otherwise agreed", the agreement may not only shift the allocation but may also divide the risk or burden.

§2-304. Price Payable in Money, Goods, Realty, or Otherwise.

(1) The price can be made payable in money or otherwise. If it is payable in whole or in part in goods each party is a seller of the goods which he is to transfer.

(2) Even though all or part of the price is payable in an interest in realty the transfer of the goods and the seller's obligations with reference to them are subject to this Article, but not the transfer of the interest in realty or the transferor's obligations in connection therewith.

§2-305. Open Price Term.

(1) The parties if they so intend can conclude a contract for sale even though the price is not settled. In such a case the price is a reasonable price at the time for delivery if

(a) nothing is said as to price; or

(b) the price is left to be agreed by the parties and they fail to agree; or

(c) the price is to be fixed in terms of some agreed market or other standard as set or recorded by a third person or agency and it is not so set or recorded.

(2) A price to be fixed by the seller or by the buyer means a price for him to fix in good faith.

(3) When a price left to be fixed otherwise than by agreement of the parties fails to be fixed through fault of one party the other may at his option treat the contract as cancelled or himself fix a reasonable price.

(4) Where, however, the parties intend not to be bound unless the price be fixed or agreed and it is not fixed or agreed there is no contract. In such a case the buyer must return any goods already received or if unable so to do must pay their reasonable value at the time of delivery and the seller must return any portion of the price paid on account.

§2-306. Output, Requirements and Exclusive Dealings.

(1) A term which measures the quantity by the output of the seller or the requirements of the buyer means such actual output or requirements as may occur in good faith, except that no quantity unreasonably disproportionate to any stated estimate or in the absence of a stated estimate to any normal or otherwise comparable prior output or requirements may be tendered or demanded.

(2) A lawful agreement by either the seller or the buyer for exclusive dealing in the kind of goods concerned imposes unless

otherwise agreed an obligation by the seller to use best efforts to supply the goods and by the buyer to use best efforts to promote their sale.

§2-307. Delivery in Single Lot or Several Lots.

Unless otherwise agreed all goods called for by a contract for sale must be tendered in a single delivery and payment is due only on such tender but where the circumstances give either party the right to make or demand delivery in lots the price if it can be apportioned may be demanded for each lot.

§2-308. Absence of Specified Place for Delivery.

Unless otherwise agreed

(a) the place for delivery of goods is the seller's place of business or if he has none his residence; but

(b) in a contract for sale of identified goods which to the knowledge of the parties at the time of contracting are in some other place, that place is the place for their delivery; and

(c) documents of title may be delivered through customary banking channels.

§2-309. Absence of Specific Time Provisions; Notice of Termination.

(1) The time for shipment or delivery or any other action under a contract if not provided in this Article or agreed upon shall be a reasonable time.

(2) Where the contract provides for successive performance but is indefinite in duration it is valid for a reasonable time but unless otherwise agreed may be terminated at any time by either party.

(3) Termination of a contract by one party except on the happening of an agreed event requires that reasonable notification be received by the other party and an agreement dispensing with notification is invalid if its operation would be unconscionable.

§2-310. Open Time for Payment or Running of Credit; Authority to Ship Under Reservation.

Unless otherwise agreed

(a) payment is due at the time and place at which the buyer is to receive the goods even though the place of shipment is the place of delivery; and

(b) if the seller is authorized to send the goods he may ship them under reservation, and may tender the documents of title, but the buyer may inspect the goods after their arrival before payment is due unless such inspection is inconsistent with the terms of the contract (Section 2–513); and

(c) if delivery is authorized and made by way of documents of title otherwise than by subsection (b) then payment is due at the time and place at which the buyer is to receive the documents regardless of where the goods are to be received; and

(d) where the seller is required or authorized to ship the goods on credit the credit period runs from the time of shipment but post-dating the invoice or delaying its dispatch will correspondingly delay the starting of the credit period.

§2-311. Options and Cooperation Respecting Performance.

(1) An agreement for sale which is otherwise sufficiently definite (subsection (3) of Section 2–204) to be a contract is not made invalid by the fact that it leaves particulars of performance to be specified by one of the parties. Any such specification must be made in good faith and within limits set by commercial reasonableness.

(2) Unless otherwise agreed specifications relating to assortment of the goods are at the buyer's option and except as otherwise provided in subsections (1) (c) and (3) of Section 2–319 specifications or arrangements relating to shipment are at the seller's option.

(3) Where such specification would materially affect the other party's performance but is not seasonably made or where one party's cooperation is necessary to the agreed performance of the other but is not seasonably forthcoming, the other party in addition to all other remedies

(a) is excused for any resulting delay in his own performance; and

(b) may also either proceed to perform in any reasonable manner or after the time for a material part of his own performance treat the failure to specify or to cooperate as a breach by failure to deliver or accept the goods.

§2-312. Warranty of Title and Against Infringement; Buyer's Obligation Against Infringement.

(1) Subject to subsection (2) there is in a contract for sale a warranty by the seller that

(a) the title conveyed shall be good, and its transfer rightful; and

b) the goods shall be delivered free from any security interest or other lien or encumbrance of which the buyer at the time of contracting has no knowledge.

(2) A warranty under subsection (1) will be excluded or modified only by specific language or by circumstances which give the buyer reason to know that the person selling does not claim title in himself or that he is purporting to sell only such right or title as he or a third person may have.

(3) Unless otherwise agreed a seller who is a merchant regularly dealing in goods of the kind warrants that the goods shall be delivered free of the rightful claim of any third person by way of infringement or the like but a buyer who furnishes specifications to the seller must hold the seller harmless against any such claim which arises out of compliance with the specifications.

§2-313. Express Warranties by Affirmation, Promise, Description, Sample.

(1) Express warranties by the seller are created as follows:

(a) Any affirmation of fact or promise made by the seller to the buyer which relates to the goods and becomes part of the basis of the bargain creates an express warranty that the goods shall conform to the affirmation or promise.

(b) Any description of the goods which is made part of the basis of the bargain creates an express warranty that the goods shall conform to the description.

(c) Any sample or model which is made part of the basis of the bargain creates an express warranty that the whole of the goods shall conform to the sample or model.

(2) It is not necessary to the creation of an express warranty that the seller use formal words such as "warrant" or "guarantee" or that he have a specific intention to make a warranty, but an affirmation merely of the value of the goods or a statement purporting to be merely the seller's opinion or commendation of the goods does not create a warranty.

§2-314. Implied Warranty: Merchantability; Usage of Trade.

(1) Unless excluded or modified (Section 2–316), a warranty that the goods shall be merchantable is implied in a contract for their sale if the seller is a merchant with respect to goods of that kind. Under this section the serving for value of food or drink to be consumed either on the premises or elsewhere is a sale.

(2) Goods to be merchantable must be at least such as

(a) pass without objection in the trade under the contract description; and

(b) in the case of fungible goods, are of fair average quality within the description; and

(c) are fit for the ordinary purposes for which such goods are used; and

(d) run, within the variations permitted by the agreement, of even kind, quality, and quantity within each unit and among all units involved; and

(e) are adequately contained, packaged, and labeled as the agreement may require; and

(f) conform to the promises or affirmations of fact made on the container or label if any.

(3) Unless excluded or modified (Section 2–316) other implied warranties may arise from course of dealing or usage of trade.

§2-315. Implied Warranty: Fitness for Particular Purpose.

Where the seller at the time of contracting has reason to know any particular purpose for which the goods are required and that the buyer is relying on the seller's skill or judgment to select or furnish suitable goods, there is unless excluded or modified under the next section an implied warranty that the goods shall be fit for such purpose.

§2-316. Exclusion or Modification of Warranties.

(1) Words or conduct relevant to the creation of an express warranty and words or conduct tending to negate or limit warranty shall be construed wherever reasonable as consistent with each other, but subject to the provisions of this Article on parol or extrinsic evidence (Section 2–202) negation or limitation is inoperative to the extent that such construction is unreasonable.

(2) Subject to subsection (3), to exclude or modify the implied warranty of merchantability or any part of it the language must mention merchantability and in case of a writing must be conspicuous, and to exclude or modify any implied warranty of fitness the exclusion must be by a writing and conspicuous. Language to exclude all implied warranties of fitness is sufficient if it states, for example, that "There are no warranties which extend beyond the description on the face hereof."

(3) Notwithstanding subsection (2)

(a) unless the circumstances indicate otherwise, all implied warranties are excluded by expression like "as is", "with all faults" or other language which in common understanding calls the buyer's attention to the exclusion of warranties and makes plain that there is no implied warranty; and

(b) when the buyer before entering into the contract has examined the goods or the sample or model as fully as he desired or has refused to examine the goods there is no implied warranty with regard to defects which an examination ought in the circumstances to have revealed to him; and

(c) an implied warranty can also be excluded or modified by course of dealing or course of performance or usage of trade.

(4) Remedies for breach of warranty can be limited in accordance with the provisions of this Article on liquidation or limitation of damages and on contractual modification of remedy (Sections 2–718 and 2–719).

§2-317. Cumulation and Conflict of Warranties Express or Implied.

Warranties whether express or implied shall be construed as consistent with each other and as cumulative, but if such construction is unreasonable the intention of the parties shall determine which warranty is dominant. In ascertaining that intention the following rules apply:

(a) Exact or technical specifications displace an inconsistent sample or model or general language of description.

(b) A sample from an existing bulk displaces inconsistent general language of description.

(c) Express warranties displace inconsistent implied warranties other than an implied warranty of fitness for a particular purpose.

§2-318. Third Party Beneficiaries of Warranties Express or Implied.

Note: *If this Act is introduced in the Congress of the United States this section should be omitted. (States to select one alternative.)*

Alternative A. A seller's warranty whether express or implied extends to any natural person who is in the family or household of his buyer or who is a guest in his home if it is reasonable to expect that such person may use, consume or be affected by the goods and who is injured in person by breach of the warranty. A seller may not exclude or limit the operation of this section.

Alterntive B. A seller's warranty whether express or implied extends to any natural person who may reasonably be expected to use, consume or be affected by the goods and who is injured in person by breach of the warranty. A seller may not exclude or limit the operation of this section.

Alternative C. A seller's warranty whether express or implied extends to any person who may reasonably be expected to use, consume or be affected by the goods and who is injured by breach of the warranty. A seller may not exclude or limit the operation of this section with respect to injury to the person of an individual to whom the warranty extends.

§2-319. F.O.B. and F.A.S. Terms.

(1) Unless otherwise agreed the term F.O.B. (which means "free on board") at a named place, even though used only in connection with the stated price, is a delivery term under which

(a) when the term is F.O.B. the place of shipment, the seller must at that place ship the goods in the manner provided in this Article (Section 2–504) and bear the expense and risk of putting them into the possession of the carrier; or

(b) when the term is F.O.B. the place of destination, the seller must at his own expense and risk transport the goods to that place and there tender delivery of them in the manner provided in this Article (Section 2–503);

(c) when under either (a) or (b) the term is also F.O.B. vessel, car or other vehicle, the seller must in addition at his own expense and risk load the goods on board. If the term is F.O.B. vessel the buyer must name the vessel and in an appropriate case the seller must comply with the provisions of this Article on the form of bill of lading (Section 2–323).

(2) Unless otherwise agreed the term F.A.S. vessel (which means "free alongside") at a named port, even though used only in connection with the stated price, is a delivery term under which the seller must

(a) at his own expense and risk deliver the goods alongside the vessel in the manner usual in that port or on a dock designated and provided by the buyer; and

(b) obtain and tender a receipt for the goods in exchange for which the carrier is under a duty to issue a bill of lading.

(3) Unless otherwise agreed in any case falling within subsection (1)(a) or (c) or subsection (2) the buyer must seasonably give any needed instructions for making delivery, including when the term is F.A.S. or F.O.B. the loading berth of the vessel and in an appropriate case its name and sailing date. The seller may treat the failure of needed instructions as a failure of cooperation under this Article (Section 2–311). He may also at his option move the goods in any reasonable manner preparatory to delivery or shipment.

(4) Under the term F.O.B. vessel or F.A.S. unless otherwise agreed the buyer must make payment against tender of the required documents and the seller may not tender nor the buyer demand delivery of the goods in substitution for the documents.

§2–320. C.I.F. and C. & F. Terms.

(1) The term C.I.F. means that the price includes in a lump sum the cost of the goods and the insurance and freight to the named destination. The term C. & F. or C.F. means that the price so includes cost and freight to the named destination.

(2) Unless otherwise agreed and even though used only in connection with the stated price and destination, the term C.I.F. destination or its equivalent requires the seller at his own expense and risk to

(a) put the goods into the possession of a carrier at the port for shipment and obtain a negotiable bill or bills of lading covering the entire transportation to the named destination; and

(b) load the goods and obtain a receipt from the carrier (which may be contained in the bill of lading) showing that the freight has been paid or provided for; and

(c) obtain a policy or certificate of insurance, including any war risk insurance, of a kind and on terms then current at the port of shipment in the usual amount, in the currency of the contract, shown to cover the same goods covered by the bill of lading and providing for payment of loss to the order of the buyer or for the account of whom it may concern; but the seller may add to the price the amount of the premium for any such war risk insurance; and

(d) prepare an invoice of the goods and procure any other documents required to effect shipment or to comply with the contract; and

(e) forward and tender with commercial promptness all the documents in due form and with any indorsement necessary to perfect the buyer's rights.

(3) Unless otherwise agreed the term C. & F. or its equivalent has the same effect and imposes upon the seller the same obligations and risks as a C.I.F. term except the obligation as to insurance.

(4) Under the term C.I.F. or C. & F. unless otherwise agreed the buyer must make payment against tender of the required documents and the seller may not tender nor the buyer demand delivery of the goods in substitution for the documents.

§2–321. C.I.F. or C. & F.: "Net Landed Weights"; "Payment on Arrival"; Warranty of Condition on Arrival.

Under a contract containing a term C.I.F. or C. & F.

(1) Where the price is based on or is to be adjusted according to "net landed weights", "delivered weights", "out turn" quantity or quality or the like, unless otherwise agreed the seller must reasonably estimate the price. The payment due on tender of the documents called for by the contract is the amount so estimated, but after final adjustment of the price a settlement must be made with commercial promptness.

(2) An agreement described in subsection (1) or any warranty of quality or condition of the goods on arrival places upon the seller the risk of ordinary deterioration, shrinkage and the like in transportation but has no effect on the place or time of identification to the contract for sale or delivery or on the passing of the risk of loss.

(3) Unless otherwise agreed where the contract provides for payment on or after arrival of the goods the seller must before payment allow such preliminary inspection as is feasible; but if the goods are lost delivery of the documents and payment are due when the goods should have arrived.

§2–322. Delivery "Ex-Ship".

(1) Unless otherwise agreed a term for delivery of goods "ex-ship" (which means from the carrying vessel) or in equivalent language is not restricted to a particular ship and requires delivery from a ship which has reached a place at the named port of destination where goods of the kind are usually discharged.

(2) Under such a term unless otherwise agreed

(a) the seller must discharge all liens arising out of the carriage and furnish the buyer with a direction which puts the carrier under a duty to deliver the goods; and

(b) the risk of loss does not pass to the buyer until the goods leave the ship's tackle or are otherwise properly unloaded.

§2–323. Form of Bill of Lading Required in Overseas Shipment; "Overseas".

(1) Where the contract contemplates overseas shipment and contains a term C.I.F. or C. & F. or F.O.B. vessel, the seller unless otherwise agreed must obtain a negotiable bill of lading stating that the goods have been loaded on board or, in the case of a term C.I.F. or C. & F., received for shipment.

(2) Where in a case within subsection (1) a bill of lading has been issued in a set of parts, unless otherwise agreed if the documents are not to be sent from abroad the buyer may demand tender of the full set; otherwise only one part of the bill of lading need be tendered. Even if the agreement expressly requires a full set

(a) due tender of a single part is acceptable within the provisions of this Article on cure of improper delivery (subsection (1) of Section 2–508); and
(b) even though the full set is demanded, if the documents are sent from abroad the person tendering an incomplete set may nevertheless require payment upon furnishing an indemnity which the buyer in good faith deems adequate.

(3) A shipment by water or by air or a contract contemplating such shipment is "overseas" insofar as by usage of trade or agreement it is subject to the commercial, financing or shipping practices characteristic of international deep water commerce.

§2-324. "No Arrival, No Sale" Term.

Under a term "no arrival, no sale" or terms of like meaning, unless otherwise agreed.

(a) the seller must properly ship conforming goods and if they arrive by any means he must tender them on arrival but he assumes no obligation that the goods will arrive unless he has caused the non-arrival; and
(b) where without fault of the seller the goods are in part lost or have so deteriorated as no longer to conform to the contract or arrive after the contract time, the buyer may proceed as if there had been casualty to identified goods (Section 2–613).

§2-325. "Letter of Credit" Term; "Confirmed Credit".

(1) Failure of the buyer seasonably to furnish an agreed letter of credit is a breach of the contract for sale.

(2) The delivery to seller of a proper letter of credit suspends the buyer's obligation to pay. If the letter of credit is dishonored, the seller may on seasonable notification to the buyer require payment directly from him.

(3) Unless otherwise agreed the term "letter of credit" or "banker's credit" in a contract for sale means an irrevocable credit issued by a financing agency of good repute and, where the shipment is overseas, of good international repute. The term "confirmed credit" means that the credit must also carry the direct obligation of such an agency which does business in the seller's financial market.

§2-326. Sale on Approval and Sale or Return; Rights of Creditors.

(1) Unless otherwise agreed, if delivered goods may be returned by the buyer even though they conform to the contract, the transaction is

(a) a "sale on approval" if the goods are delivered primarily for use, and
(b) a "sale or return" if the goods are delivered primarily for resale.

(2) Goods held on approval are not subject to the claims of the buyer's creditors until acceptance; goods held on sale or return are subject to such claims while in the buyer's possession.

(3) Any "or return" term of a contract for sale is to be treated as a separate contract for sale within the statute of frauds section of this Article (Section 2–201) and as contradicting the sale aspect of the contract within the provisions of this Article on parol or extrinsic evidence (Section 2–202).

§2-327. Special Incidents of Sale on Approval and Sale or Return.

(1) Under a sale on approval unless otherwise agreed

(a) although the goods are identified to the contract the risk of loss and the title do not pass to the buyer until acceptance; and
(b) use of the goods consistent with the purpose of trial is not acceptance but failure reasonably to notify the seller of election to return the goods is acceptance, and if the goods conform to the contract acceptance of any part is acceptance of the whole; and
(c) after due notification of election to return, the return is at the seller's risk and expense but a merchant buyer must follow any reasonable instructions.

(2) Under a sale or return unless otherwise agreed

(a) the option to return extends to the whole or any commercial unit of the goods while in substantially their original condition, but must be exercised reasonably; and
(b) the return is at the buyer's risk and expense.

§2-328. Sale by Auction.

(1) In a sale by auction if goods are put up in lots each lot is the subject of a separate sale.

(2) A sale by auction is complete when the auctioneer so announces by the fall of the hammer or in other customary manner. Where a bid is made while the hammer is falling in acceptance of a prior bid the auctioneer may in his discretion reopen the bidding or declare the goods sold under the bid on which the hammer was falling.

(3) Such a sale is with reserve unless the goods are in explicit terms put up without reserve. In an auction with reserve the auctioneer may withdraw the goods at any time until he announces completion of the sale. In an auction without reserve, after the auctioneer calls for bids on an article or lot, that article or lot cannot be withdrawn unless no bid is made within a reasonable time. In either case a bidder may retract his bid until the auctioneer's announcement of completion of the sale, but a bidder's retraction does not revive any previous bid.

(4) If the auctioneer knowingly receives a bid on the seller's behalf or the seller makes or procures such a bid, and notice has not been given that liberty for such bidding is reserved, the buyer may at his option avoid the sale or take the goods at the price of the last good faith bid prior to the completion of the sale. This subsection shall not apply to any bid at a forced sale.

Part 4. Title, Creditors and Good Faith Purchasers

§2-401. Passing of Title; Reservation for Security; Limited Application of This Section.

Each provision of this Article with regard to the rights, obligations and remedies of the seller, the buyer, purchasers or other third parties applies irrespective of title to the goods except where the provision refers to such title. Insofar as situations are not covered by the other provisions of this Article and matters concerning title become material the following rules apply:

(1) Title to goods cannot pass under a contract for sale prior to their identification to the contract (Section 2–501), and unless otherwise explicitly agreed the buyer acquires by their identification a special property as limited by this Act. Any retention or reservation by the seller of the title (property) in goods shipped or delivered to the buyer is limited in effect to a reservation of a security interest. Subject to these provisions and to the provisions of the Article on

Secured Transactions (Article 9), title to goods passes from the seller to the buyer in any manner and on any conditions explicitly agreed on by the parties.

(2) Unless otherwise explicitly agreed title passes to the buyer at the time and place at which the seller completes his performance with reference to the physical delivery of the goods, despite any reservation of a security interest and even though a document of title is to be delivered at a different time or place; and in particular and despite any reservation of a security interest by the bill of lading

(a) if the contract requires or authorizes the seller to send the goods to the buyer but does not require him to deliver them at destination, title passes to the buyer at the time and place of shipment; but

(b) if the contract requires delivery at destination, title passes on tender there.

(3) Unless otherwise explicitly agreed where delivery is to be made without moving the goods.

(a) if the seller is to deliver a document of title, title passes at the time when and the place where he delivers such documents; or

(b) if the goods are at the time of contracting already identified and no documents are to be delivered, title passes at the time and place of contracting.

(4) A rejection or other refusal by the buyer to receive or retain the goods, whether or not justified, or a justified revocation of acceptance revests title to the goods in the seller. Such revesting occurs by operation of law and is not a "sale".

§2-402. Rights of Seller's Creditors Against Sold Goods.

(1) Except as provided in subsections (2) and (3), rights of unsecured creditors of the seller with respect to goods which have been identified to a contract for sale are subject to the buyer's rights to recover the goods under this Article (Sections 2–502 and 2–716).

(2) A creditor of the seller may treat a sale or an identification of goods to a contract for sale as void if as against him a retention of possession by the seller is fraudulent under any rule of law of the state where the goods are situated, except that retention of possession in good faith and current course of trade by a merchant-seller for a commercially reasonable time after a sale or identification is not fraudulent.

(3) Nothing in this Article shall be deemed to impair the rights of creditors of the seller

(a) under the provisions of the Article on Secured Transactions (Article 9); or

(b) where identification to the contract or delivery is made not in current course of trade but in satisfaction of or as security for a pre-existing claim for money, security or the like and is made under circumstances which under any rule of law of the state where the goods are situated would apart from this Article constitute the transaction a fraudulent transfer or voidable preference.

§2-403. Power to Transfer; Good Faith Purchase of Goods; "Entrusting".

(1) A purchaser of goods acquires all title which his transferor had or had power to transfer except that a purchaser of a limited interest acquires rights only to the extent of the interest purchased. A person with voidable title has power to transfer a good title to a good faith purchaser for value. When goods have been delivered under a transaction of purchase the purchaser has such power even though

(a) the transferor was deceived as to the identity of the purchaser, or

(b) the delivery was in exchange for a check which is later dishonored, or

(c) it was agreed that the transaction was to be a "cash sale", or

(d) the delivery was procured through fraud punishable as larcenous under the criminal law.

(2) Any entrusting of possession of goods to a merchant who deals in goods of that kind gives him power to transfer all rights of the entruster to a buyer in ordinary course of business.

(3) "Entrusting" includes any delivery and any acquiescence in retention of possession regardless of any condition expressed between the parties to the delivery or acquiescence and regardless of whether the procurement of the entrusting or the possessor's disposition of the goods have been such as to be larcenous under the criminal law.

(4) The rights of other purchasers of goods and of lien creditors are governed by the Articles on Secured Transactions (Article 9). [Bulk Transfers/Sales (Article 6)* and Documents of Title (Article 7)].

Part 5. Performance

§2-501. Insurable Interest in Goods; Manner of Identification of Goods.

(1) The buyer obtains a special property and an insurable interest in goods by identification of existing goods as goods to which the contract refers even though the goods so identified are non-conforming and he has an option to return or reject them. Such identification can be made at any time and in any manner explicitly agreed to by the parties. In the absence of explicit agreement identification occurs.

(a) when the contract is made if it is for the sale of goods already existing and identified;

(b) if the contract is for the sale of future goods other than those described in paragraph (c), when goods are shipped, marked or otherwise designated by the seller as goods to which the contract refers;

(c) when the crops are planted or otherwise become growing crops or the young are conceived if the contract is for the sale of unborn young to be born within twelve months after contracting or for the sale of crops to be harvested within twelve months or the next normal harvest season after contracting, whichever is longer.

(2) The seller retains an insurable interest in goods so long as title to or any security interest in the goods remains in him and where the identification is by the seller alone he may until default or insolvency or notification to the buyer that the identification is final substitute other goods for those identified.

(3) Nothing in this section impairs any insurable interest recognized under any other statute or rule of law.

§2-502. Buyer's Right to Goods on Seller's Insolvency.

(1) Subject to subsections (2) and (3) and even though the goods have not been shipped a buyer who has paid a part or all of the price of goods in which he has a special property under the provisions of the immediately preceding section may on making and keeping good a tender of any unpaid portion of their price recover them from the seller if:

(a) in the case of goods bought for personal, family, or household purposes, the seller repudiates or fails to deliver as required by the contract; or

(b) in all cases, the seller becomes insolvent within ten days after receipt of the first installment on their price.

(2) The buyer's right to recover the goods under subsection (1)(a) vests upon acquisition of a special property, even if the seller had not then repudiated or failed to deliver.

(3) If the identification creating his special property has been made by the buyer he acquires the right to recover the goods only if they conform to the contract for sale.

§2-503. Manner of Seller's Tender of Delivery.

(1) Tender of delivery requires that the seller put and hold conforming goods at the buyer's disposition and give the buyer any notification reasonably necessary to enable him to take delivery. The manner, time and place for tender are determined by the agreement and this Article, and in particular

(a) tender must be at a reasonable hour, and if it is of goods they must be kept available for the period reasonably necessary to enable the buyer to take possession; but

(b) unless otherwise agreed the buyer must furnish facilities reasonably suited to the receipt of the goods.

(2) Where the case is within the next section respecting shipment tender requires that the seller comply with its provisions.

(3) Where the seller is required to deliver at a particular destination tender requires that he comply with subsection (1) and also in any appropriate case tender documents as described in subsections (4) and (5) of this section.

(4) Where goods are in the possession of a bailee and are to be delivered without being moved

(a) tender requires that the seller either tender a negotiable document of title covering such goods or procure acknowledgment by the bailee of the buyer's right to possession of the goods; but

(b) tender to the buyer of a non-negotiable document of title or of a written direction to the bailee to deliver is sufficient tender unless the buyer seasonably objects, and receipt by the bailee of notification of the buyer's rights fixes those rights as against the bailee and all third persons; but risk of loss of the goods and of any failure by the bailee to honor the non-negotiable document of title or to obey the direction remains on the seller until the buyer has had a reasonable time to present the document or direction, and a refusal by the bailee to honor the document or to obey the direction defeats the tender.

(5) Where the contract requires the seller to deliver documents

(a) he must tender all such documents in correct form, except as provided in this Article with respect to bills of lading in a set (subsection (2) of Section 2–323); and

(b) tender through customary banking channels is sufficient and dishonor of a draft accompanying the documents constitutes non-acceptance or rejection.

§2-504. Shipment by Seller.

Where the seller is required or authorized to send the goods to the buyer and the contract does not require him to deliver them at a particular destination, then unless otherwise agreed he must

(a) put the goods in the possession of such a carrier and make such a contract for their transportation as may be reasonable having regard to the nature of the goods and other circumstances of the case; and

(b) obtain and promptly deliver or tender in due form any document necessary to enable the buyer to obtain possession of the goods or otherwise required by the agreement or by usage of trade; and

(c) promptly notify the buyer of the shipment.

Failure to notify the buyer under paragraph (c) or to make a proper contract under paragraph (a) is a ground for rejection only if material delay or loss ensues.

§2-505. Seller's Shipment Under Reservation.

(1) Where the seller has identified goods to the contract by or before shipment:

(a) his procurement of a negotiable bill of lading to his own order or otherwise reserves in him a security interest in the goods. His procurement of the bill to the order of a financing agency or of the buyer indicates in addition only the seller's expectation of transferring that interest to the person named.

(b) a non-negotiable bill of lading to himself or his nominee reserves possession of the goods as security but except in a case of conditional delivery (subsection (2) of Section 2–507) a non-negotiable bill of lading naming the buyer as consignee reserves no security interest even though the seller retains possession of the bill of lading.

(2) When shipment by the seller with reservation of a security interest is in violation of the contract for sale it constitutes an improper contract for transportation within the preceding section but impairs neither the rights given to the buyer by shipment and identification of the goods to the contract nor the seller's powers as a holder of a negotiable document.

§2-506. Rights of Financing Agency.

(1) A financing agency by paying or purchasing for value a draft which relates to a shipment of goods acquires to the extent of the payment or purchase and in addition to its own rights under the draft and any document of title securing it any rights of the shipper in the goods including the right to stop delivery and the shipper's right to have the draft honored by the buyer.

(2) The right to reimbursement of a financing agency which has in good faith honored or purchased the draft under commitment to or authority from the buyer is not impaired by subsequent discovery of defects with reference to any relevant document which was apparently regular on its face.

§2-507. Effect of Seller's Tender; Delivery on Condition.

(1) Tender of delivery is a condition to the buyer's duty to accept the goods and, unless otherwise agreed, to his duty to pay for them. Tender entitles the seller to acceptance of the goods and to payment according to the contract.

(2) Where payment is due and demanded on the delivery to the buyer of goods or documents of title, his right as against the seller to retain or dispose of them is conditional upon his making the payment due.

§2-508. Cure by Seller of Improper Tender or Delivery; Replacement.

(1) Where any tender or delivery by the seller is rejected because non-conforming and the time for performance has not yet expired, the seller may seasonably notify the buyer of his intention to

cure and may then within the contract time make a conforming delivery.

(2) Where the buyer rejects a non-conforming tender which the seller had reasonable grounds to believe would be acceptable with or without money allowance the seller may if he reasonably notifies the buyer have a further reasonable time to substitute a conforming tender.

§2-509. Risk of Loss in the Absence of Breach.

(1) Where the contract requires or authorizes the seller to ship the goods by carrier

(a) if it does not require him to deliver them at a particular destination, the risk of loss passes to the buyer when the goods are duly delivered to the carrier even though the shipment is under reservation (Section 2–505); but

(b) if it does require him to deliver them at a particular destination and the goods are there duly tendered while in the possession of the carrier, the risk of loss passes to the buyer when the goods are there duly so tendered as to enable the buyer to take delivery.

(2) Where the goods are held by a bailee to be delivered without being moved, the risk of loss passes to the buyer

(a) on his receipt of a negotiable document of title covering the goods; or

(b) on acknowledgment by the bailee of the buyer's right to possession of the goods; or

(c) after his receipt of a non-negotiable document of title or other written direction to deliver, as provided in subsection (4)(b) of Section 2–503.

(3) In any case not within subsection (1) or (2), the risk of loss passes to the buyer on his receipt of the goods if the seller is a merchant; otherwise the risk passes to the buyer on tender of delivery.

(4) The provisions of this section are subject to contrary agreement of the parties and to the provisions of this Article on sale on approval (Section 2–327) and on effect of breach on risk of loss (Section 2–510).

§2-510. Effect of Breach on Risk of Loss.

(1) Where a tender or delivery of goods so fails to conform to the contract as to give a right of rejection the risk of their loss remains on the seller until cure or acceptance.

(2) Where the buyer rightfully revokes acceptance he may to the extent of any deficiency in his effective insurance coverage treat the risk of loss as having rested on the seller from the beginning.

(3) Where the buyer as to conforming goods already identified to the contract for sale repudiates or is otherwise in breach before risk of their loss has passed to him, the seller may to the extent of any deficiency in his effective insurance coverage treat the risk of loss as resting on the buyer for a commercially reasonable time.

§2-511. Tender of Payment by Buyer; Payment by Check.

(1) Unless otherwise agreed tender of payment is a condition to the seller's duty to tender and complete any delivery.

(2) Tender of payment is sufficient when made by any means or in any manner current in the ordinary course of business unless the seller demands payment in legal tender and gives any extension of time reasonably necessary to procure it.

(3) Subject to the provisions of this Act on the effect of an instrument on an obligation (Section 3–310), payment by check is conditional and is defeated as between the parties by dishonor of the check on due presentment.

§2-512. Payment by Buyer Before Inspection.

(1) Where the contract requires payment before inspection nonconformity of the goods does not excuse the buyer from so making payment unless

(a) the non-conformity appears without inspection; or

(b) despite tender of the required documents the circumstances would justify injunction against honor under this Act (Section 5–109(b)).

(2) Payment pursuant to subsection (1) does not constitute an acceptance of goods or impair the buyer's right to inspect or any of his remedies.

§2-513. Buyer's Right to Inspection of Goods.

(1) Unless otherwise agreed and subject to subsection (3), where goods are tendered or delivered or identified to the contract for sale, the buyer has a right before payment or acceptance to inspect them at any reasonable place and time and in any reasonable manner. When the seller is required or authorized to send the goods to the buyer, the inspection may be after their arrival.

(2) Expenses of inspection must be borne by the buyer but may be recovered from the seller if the goods do not conform and are rejected.

(3) Unless otherwise agreed and subject to the provisions of this Article on C.I.F. contracts (subsection (3) of Section 2–321), the buyer is not entitled to inspect the goods before payment of the price when the contract provides

(a) for delivery "C.O.D." or on other like terms; or

(b) for payment against documents of title, except where such payment is due only after the goods are to become available for inspection.

(4) A place or method of inspection fixed by the parties is presumed to be exclusive but unless otherwise expressly agreed it does not postpone identification or shift the place for delivery or for passing the risk of loss. If compliance becomes impossible, inspection shall be as provided in this section unless the place or method fixed was clearly intended as an indispensable condition failure of which avoids the contract.

§2-514. When Documents Deliverable on Acceptance; When on Payment.

Unless otherwise agreed documents against which a draft is drawn are to be delivered to the drawee on acceptance of the draft if it is payable more than three days after presentment; otherwise, only on payment.

§2-515. Preserving Evidence of Goods in Dispute.

In furtherance of the adjustment of any claim or dispute

(a) either party on reasonable notification to the other and for the purpose of ascertaining the facts and preserving evidence has the right to inspect, test and sample the goods including such of them as may be in the possession or control of the other; and

(b) the parties may agree to a third party inspection or survey to determine the conformity or condition of the goods and may agree that the findings shall be binding upon them in any subsequent litigation or adjustment.

Part 6. Breach, Repudiation and Excuse

§2-601. Buyer's Rights on Improper Delivery.

Subject to the provisions of this Article on breach in installment contracts (Section 2–612) and unless otherwise agreed under the sections on contractual limitations of remedy (Sections 2–718 and 2–719), if the goods or the tender of delivery fail in any respect to conform to the contract, the buyer may

(a) reject the whole; or
(b) accept the whole; or
(c) accept any commercial unit or units and reject the rest.

§2-602. Manner and Effect of Rightful Rejection.

(1) Rejection of goods must be within a reasonable time after their delivery or tender. It is ineffective unless the buyer seasonably notifies the seller.

(2) Subject to the provisions of the two following sections on rejected goods (Sections 2–603 and 2–604),

(a) after rejection any exercise of ownership by the buyer with respect to any commercial unit is wrongful as against the seller; and
(b) if the buyer has before rejection taken physical possession of goods in which he does not have a security interest under the provisions of this Article (subsection (3) of Section 2–711), he is under a duty after rejection to hold them with reasonable care at the seller's disposition for a time sufficient to permit the seller to remove them; but
(c) the buyer has no further obligations with regard to goods rightfully rejected.

(3) The seller's rights with respect to goods wrongfully rejected are governed by the provisions of this Article on Seller's remedies in general (Section 2–703).

§2-603. Merchant Buyer's Duties as to Rightfully Rejected Goods.

(1) Subject to any security interest in the buyer (subsection (3) of Section 2–711), when the seller has no agent or place of business at the market of rejection a merchant buyer is under a duty after rejection of goods in his possession or control to follow any reasonable instructions received from the seller with respect to the goods and in the absence of such instructions to make reasonable efforts to sell them for the seller's account if they are perishable or threaten to decline in value speedily. Instructions are not reasonable if on demand indemnity for expenses is not forthcoming.

(2) When the buyer sells goods under subsection (1), he is entitled to reimbursement from the seller or out of the proceeds for reasonable expenses of caring for and selling them, and if the expenses include no selling commission then to such commission as is usual in the trade or if there is none to a reasonable sum not exceeding ten percent on the gross proceeds.

(3) In complying with this section the buyer is held only to good faith and good faith conduct hereunder is neither acceptance nor conversion nor the basis of an action for damages.

§2-604. Buyer's Options as to Salvage of Rightfully Rejected Goods.

Subject to the provisions of the immediately preceding section on perishables if the seller gives no instructions within a reasonable time after notification of rejection the buyer may store the rejected goods for the seller's account or reship them to him or resell them for the seller's account with reimbursement as provided in the preceding section. Such action is not acceptance or conversion.

§2-605. Waiver of Buyer's Objections by Failure to Particularize.

(1) The buyer's failure to state in connection with rejection a particular defect which is ascertainable by reasonable inspection precludes him from relying on the unstated defect to justify rejection or to establish breach

(a) where the seller could have cured it if stated reasonably; or
(b) between merchants when the seller has after rejection made a request in writing for a full and final written statement of all defects on which the buyer proposes to rely.

(2) Payment against documents made without reservation of rights precludes recovery of the payment for defects apparent on the face of the documents.

§2-606. What Constitutes Acceptance of Goods.

(1) Acceptance of goods occurs when the buyer

(a) after a reasonable opportunity to inspect the goods signifies to the seller that the goods are conforming or that he will take or retain them in spite of their non-conformity; or
(b) fails to make an effective rejection (subsection (1) of Section 2–602), but such acceptance does not occur until the buyer has had a reasonable opportunity to inspect them; or
(c) does any act inconsistent with the seller's ownership; but if such act is wrongful as against the seller it is an acceptance only if ratified by him.

(2) Acceptance of a part of any commercial unit is acceptance of that entire unit.

§2-607. Effect of Acceptance; Notice of Breach; Burden of Establishing Breach After Acceptance; Notice of Claim or Litigation to Person Answerable Over.

(1) The buyer must pay at the contract rate for any goods accepted.

(2) Acceptance of goods by the buyer precludes rejection of the goods accepted and if made with knowledge of a non-conformity cannot be revoked because of it unless the acceptance was on the reasonable assumption that the non-conformity would be reasonably cured but acceptance does not of itself impair any other remedy provided by this Article for non-conformity.

(3) Where a tender has been accepted

(a) the buyer must within a reasonable time after he discovers or should have discovered any breach notify the seller of breach or be barred from any remedy; and
(b) if the claim is one for infringement or the like (subsection (3) of Section 2–312) and the buyer is sued as a result of such a breach he must so notify the seller within a reasonable time after he receives notice of the litigation or be barred from any remedy over for liability established by the litigation.

(4) The burden is on the buyer to establish any breach with respect to the goods accepted.

(5) Where the buyer is sued for breach of a warranty or other obligation for which his seller is answerable over

(a) he may give his seller written notice of the litigation. If the notice states that the seller may come in and defend and that if the seller does not do so he will be bound in any action against him by his buyer by any determination of fact common to the two litigations, then unless the seller after reasonable receipt of the notice does come in and defend he is so bound.

(b) if the claim is one for infringement or the like (subsection (3) of Section 2–312) the original seller may demand in writing that his buyer turn over to him control of the litigation including settlement or else be barred from any remedy over and if he also agrees to bear all expense and to satisfy any adverse judgment, then unless the buyer after reasonable receipt of the demand does turn over control the buyer is so barred.

(6) The provisions of subsection (3), (4) and (5) apply to any obligation of a buyer to hold the seller harmless against infringement or the like (subsection (3) of Section 2–312).

§2-608. Revocation of Acceptance in Whole or in Part.

(1) The buyer may revoke his acceptance of a lot or commercial unit whose non-conformity substantially impairs its value to him if he has accepted it

(a) on the reasonable assumption that its non-conformity would be cured and it has not been reasonably cured; or

(b) without discovery of such non-conformity if his acceptance was reasonably induced either by the difficulty of discovery before acceptance or by the seller's assurances.

(2) Revocation of acceptance must occur within a reasonable time after the buyer discovers or should have discovered the ground for it and before any substantial change in condition of the goods which is not caused by their own defects. It is not effective until the buyer notifies the seller of it.

(3) A buyer who so revokes has the same rights and duties with regard to the goods involved as if he had rejected them.

§2-609. Right to Adequate Assurance of Performance.

(1) A contract for sale imposes an obligation on each party that the other's expectation of receiving due performance will not be impaired. When reasonable grounds for insecurity arise with respect to the performance of either party the other may in writing demand adequate assurance of due performance and until he receives such assurance may if commercially reasonable suspend any performance for which he has not already received the agreed return.

(2) Between merchants the reasonableness of grounds for insecurity and the adequacy of any assurance offered shall be determined according to commercial standards.

(3) Acceptance of any improper delivery or payment does not prejudice the aggrieved party's right to demand adequate assurance of future performance.

(4) After receipt of a justified demand failure to provide within a reasonable time not exceeding thirty days such assurance of due performance as is adequate under the circumstances of the particular case is a repudiation of the contract.

§2-610. Anticipatory Repudiation.

When either party repudiates the contract with respect to a performance not yet due the loss of which will substantially impair the value of the contract to the other, the aggrieved party may

(a) for a commercially reasonable time await performance by the repudiating party; or

(b) resort to any remedy for breach (Section 2–703 or Section 2–711), even though he has notified the repudiating party that he would await the latter's performance and has urged retraction; and

(c) in either case suspend his own performance or proceed in accordance with the provisions of this Article on the seller's right to identify goods to the contract notwithstanding breach or to salvage unfinished goods (Section 2–704).

§2-611. Retraction of Anticipatory Repudiation.

(1) Until the repudiating party's next performance is due he can retract his repudiation unless the aggrieved party has since the repudiation cancelled or materially changed his position or otherwise indicated that he considers the repudiation final.

(2) Retraction may be by any method which clearly indicates to the aggrieved party that the repudiating party intends to perform, but must include any assurance justifiably demanded under the provisions of this Article (Section 2–609).

(3) Retraction reinstates the repudiating party's rights under the contract with due excuse and allowance to the aggrieved party for any delay occasioned by the repudiation.

§2-612. "Installment Contract"; Breach.

(1) An "installment contract" is one which requires or authorizes the delivery of goods in separate lots to be separately accepted, even though the contract contains a clause "each delivery is a separate contract" or its equivalent.

(2) The buyer may reject any installment which is non-conforming if the non-conformity substantially impairs the value of that installment and cannot be cured or if the non-conformity is a defect in the required documents; but if the non-conformity does not fall within subsection (3) and the seller gives adequate assurance of its cure the buyer must accept that installment.

(3) Whenever non-conformity or default with respect to one or more installments substantially impairs the value of the whole contract there is a breach of the whole. But the aggrieved party reinstates the contract if he accepts a non-conforming installment without reasonably notifying of cancellation or if he brings an action with respect only to past installments or demands performance as to future installments.

§2-613. Casualty to Identified Goods.

Where the contract requires for its performance goods identified when the contract is made, and the goods suffer casualty without fault of either party before the risk of loss passes to the buyer, or in a proper case under a "no arrival, no sale" term (Section 2–324) then

(a) if the loss is total the contract is avoided; and

(b) if the loss is partial or the goods have so deteriorated as no longer to conform to the contract the buyer may nevertheless demand inspection and at his option either treat the contract as avoided or accept the goods with due allowance from the contract price for the deterioration or the deficiency in quantity but without further right against the seller.

§2-614. Substituted Performance.

(1) Where without fault of either party the agreed berthing, loading, or unloading facilities fail or an agreed type of carrier becomes unavailable or the agreed manner of delivery otherwise becomes commercially impracticable but a commercially reasonable

substitute is available, such substitute performance must be tendered and accepted.

(2) If the agreed means or manner of payment fails because of domestic or foreign governmental regulation, the seller may withhold or stop delivery unless the buyer provides a means or manner of payment which is commercially a substantial equivalent. If delivery has already been taken, payment by the means or in the manner provided by the regulation discharges the buyers obligation unless the regulation is discriminatory, oppressive or predatory.

§2-615. Excuse by Failure of Presupposed Conditions.

Except so far as a seller may have assumed a greater obligation and subject to the preceding section on substituted performance:

(a) Delay in delivery or non-delivery in whole or in part by a seller who complies with paragraphs (b) and (c) is not a breach of his duty under a contract for sale if performance as agreed has been made impracticable by the occurrence of a contingency the non-occurrence of which was a basic assumption on which the contract was made or by compliance in good faith with any applicable foreign or domestic governmental regulation or order whether or not it later proves to be invalid.

(b) Where the causes mentioned in paragraph (a) affect only a part of the seller's capacity to perform, he must allocate production and deliveries among his customers but may at his option include regular customers not then under contract as well as his own requirements for further manufacture. He may so allocate in any manner which is fair and reasonable.

(c) The seller must notify the buyer reasonably that there will be delay or non-delivery and, when allocation is required under paragraph (b), of the estimated quota thus made available for the buyer.

§2-616. Procedure on Notice Claiming Excuse.

(1) Where the buyer receives notification of a material or indefinite delay or an allocation justified under the preceding section he may by written notification to the seller as to any delivery concerned, and where the prospective deficiency substantially impairs the value of the whole contract under the provisions of this Article relating to breach of installment contracts (Section 2–612), then also as to the whole,

(a) terminate and thereby discharge any unexecuted portion of the contract; or

(b) modify the contract by agreeing to take his available quota in substitution.

(2) If after receipt of such notification from the seller the buyer fails so to modify the contract within a reasonable time not exceeding thirty days the contract lapses with respect to any deliveries affected.

(3) The provisions of this section may not be negated by agreement except in so far as the seller has assumed a greater obligation under the preceding section.

Part 7. Remedies

§2-701. Remedies for Breach of Collateral Contracts Not Impaired.

Remedies for breach of any obligation or promise collateral or ancillary to a contract for sale or not impaired by the provisions of this Article.

§2-702. Seller's Remedies on Discovery of Buyer's Insolvency.

(1) Where the seller discovers the buyer to be insolvent he may refuse delivery except for cash including payment for all goods therefore delivered under the contract, and stop delivery under this Article (Section 2–705).

(2) Where the seller discovers that the buyer has received goods on credit while insolvent he may reclaim the goods upon demand made within ten days after the receipt, but if misrepresentation of solvency has been made to the particular seller in writing within three months before delivery the ten day limitation does not apply. Except as provided in this subsection the seller may not base a right to reclaim goods on the buyer's fraudulent or innocent misrepresentation of solvency or of intent to pay.

(3) The seller's right to reclaim under subsection (2) is subject to the rights of a buyer in ordinary course or other good faith purchaser under this Article (Section 2–403). Successful reclamation of goods excludes all other remedies with respect to them.

§2-703. Seller's Remedies in General.

Where the buyer wrongfully rejects or revokes acceptance of goods or fails to make a payment due on or before delivery or repudiates with respect to a part or the whole, then with respect to any goods directly affected and, if the breach is of the whole contract (Section 2–612), then also with respect to the whole undelivered balance, the aggrieved seller may

(a) withhold delivery of such goods;

(b) stop delivery by any bailee as hereafter provided (Section 2–705);

(c) proceed under the next section respecting goods still unidentified to the contract;

(d) resell and recover damages as hereafter provided (Section 2–706);

(e) recover damages for non-acceptance (Section 2–708) or in a proper case the price (Section 2–709);

(f) cancel.

§2-704. Seller's Right to Identify Goods to the Contract Notwithstanding Breach or to Salvage Unfinished Goods.

(1) An aggrieved seller under the preceding section may

(a) identify to the contract conforming goods not already identified if at the time he learned of the breach they are in his possession or control;

(b) treat as the subject of resale goods which have demonstrably been intended for the particular contract even though those goods are unfinished.

(2) Where the goods are unfinished an aggrieved seller may in the exercise of reasonable commercial judgment for the purposes of avoiding loss and of effective realization either complete the manufacture and wholly identify the goods to the contract or cease manufacture and resell for scrap or salvage value or proceed in any other reasonable manner.

§2-705. Seller's Stoppage of Delivery in Transit or Otherwise.

(1) The seller may stop delivery of goods in the possession of a carrier or other bailee when he discovers the buyer to be insolvent (Section 2–702) and may stop delivery of carload, truckload, planeload or larger shipments of express or freight when the buyer repudiates or fails to make a payment due before delivery or if for any other reason the seller has a right to withhold or reclaim the goods.

(2) As against such buyer the seller may stop delivery until
(a) receipt of the goods by the buyer; or
(b) acknowledgment to the buyer by any bailee of the goods except a carrier that the bailee holds the goods for the buyer; or
(c) such acknowledgment to the buyer by a carrier by reshipment or as warehouseman; or
(d) negotiation to the buyer of any negotiable document of title covering the goods.

(3) (a) To stop delivery the seller must so notify as to enable the bailee by reasonable diligence to prevent delivery of the goods.
(b) After such notification the bailee must hold and deliver the goods according to the directions of the seller but the seller is liable to the bailee for any ensuing charges or damages.
(c) If a negotiable document of title has been issued for goods the bailee is not obliged to obey a notification to stop until surrender of the document.
(d) A carrier who has issued a non-negotiable bill of lading is not obliged to obey a notification to stop received from a person other than the consignor.

§2-706. Seller's Resale Including Contract for Resale.

(1) Under the conditions stated in Section 2–703 on seller's remedies, the seller may resell the goods concerned or the undelivered balance thereof. Where the resale is made in good faith and in a commercially reasonable manner the seller may recover the difference between the resale price and the contract price together with any incidental damages allowed under the provisions of this Article (Section 2–710), but less expenses saved in consequence of the buyer's breach.

(2) Except as otherwise provided in subsection (3) or unless otherwise agreed resale may be at public or private sale including sale by way of one or more contracts to sell or of identification to an existing contract of the seller. Sale may be as a unit or in parcels and at any time and place and on any terms but every aspect of the sale including the method, manner, time, place and terms must be commercially reasonable. The resale must be reasonably identified as referring to the broken contract, but it is not necessary that the goods be in existence or that any or all of them have been identified to the contract before the breach.

(3) Where the resale is at private sale the seller must give the buyer reasonable notification of his intention to resell.

(4) Where the resale is at public sale
(a) only identified goods can be sold except where there is a recognized market for a public sale of futures in goods of the kind; and
(b) it must be made at a usual place or market for public sale if one is reasonably available and except in the case of goods which are perishable or threaten to decline in value speedily the seller must give the buyer reasonable notice of the time and place of the resale; and
(c) if the goods are not to be within the view of those attending the sale the notification of sale must state the place where the goods are located and provide for their reasonable inspection by prospective bidders; and
(d) the seller may buy.

(5) A purchaser who buys in good faith at a resale takes the goods free of any rights of the original buyer even though the seller fails to comply with one or more of the requirements of this section.

(6) The seller is not accountable to the buyer for any profit made on any resale. A person in the position of a seller (Section 2–707) or a buyer who has rightfully rejected or justifiably revoked acceptance must account for any excess over the amount of his security interest, as hereinafter defined (subsection (3) of Section 2–711).

§2-707. "Person in the Position of a Seller".

(1) A "person in the position of a seller" includes as against a principal an agent who has paid or become responsible for the price of goods on behalf of his principal or anyone who otherwise holds a security interest or other right in goods similar to that of a seller.

(2) A person in the position of a seller may as provided in this Article withhold or stop delivery (Section 2–705) and resell (Section 2–706) and recover incidental damages (Section 2–710).

§2-708. Seller's Damages for Non-Acceptance or Repudiation.

(1) Subject to subsection (2) and to the provisions of this Article with respect to proof of market price (Section 2–723), the measure of damages for non-acceptance or repudiation by the buyer is the difference between the market price at the time and place for tender and the unpaid contract price together with any incidental damages provided in this Article (Section 2–710), but less expenses saved in consequence of the buyer's breach.

(2) If the measure of damages provided in subsection (1) is inadequate to put the seller in as good a position as performance would have done then the measure of damages is the profit (including reasonable overhead) which the seller would have made from full performance by the buyer, together with any incidental damages provided in this Article (Section 2–710), due allowance for costs reasonably incurred and due credit for payments or proceeds of resale.

§2-709. Action for the Price.

(1) When the buyer fails to pay the price as it becomes due the seller may recover, together with any incidental damages under the next section, the price
(a) of goods accepted or of conforming goods lost or damaged within a commercially reasonable time after risk of their loss has passed to the buyer; and
(b) of goods identified to the contract if the seller is unable after reasonable effort to resell them at a reasonable price or the circumstances reasonably indicate that such effort will be unavailing.

(2) Where the seller sues for the price he must hold for the buyer any goods which have been identified to the contract and are still in his control except that if resale becomes possible he may resell them at any time prior to the collection of the judgment. The net proceeds of any such resale must be credited to the buyer and payment of the judgment entitles him to any goods not resold.

(3) After the buyer has wrongfully rejected or revoked acceptance of the goods or has failed to make a payment due or has repudiated (Section 2–610), a seller who is held not entitled to the price under this section shall nevertheless be awarded damages for non-acceptance under the preceding section.

§2-710. Seller's Incidental Damages.

Incidental damages to an aggrieved seller include any commercially reasonable charges, expenses or commissions incurred in stopping delivery, in the transportation, care and custody of goods after the buyer's breach, in connection with return or resale of the goods or otherwise resulting from the breach.

§2-711. Buyer's Remedies in General; Buyer's Security Interest in Rejected Goods.

(1) Where the seller fails to make delivery or repudiates or the buyer rightfully rejects or justifiably revokes acceptance then with respect to any goods involved, and with respect to the whole if the breach goes to the whole contract (Section 2–612), the buyer may cancel and whether or not he has done so may in addition to recovering so much of the price as has been paid

(a) "cover" and have damages under the next section as to all the goods affected whether or not they have been identified to the contract; or

(b) recover damages for non-delivery as provided in this Article (Section 2–713).

(2) Where the seller fails to deliver or repudiates the buyer may also

(a) if the goods have been identified recover them as provided in this Article (Section 2–502); or

(b) in a proper case obtain specific performance or replevy the goods as provided in this Article (Section 2–716).

(3) On rightful rejection of justifiable revocation of acceptance a buyer has a security interest in goods in his possession or control for any payments made on their price and any expenses reasonably incurred in their inspection, receipt, transportation, care and custody and may hold such goods and resell them in like manner as an aggrieved seller (Section 2–706).

§2-712. "Cover"; Buyer's Procurement of Substitute Goods.

(1) After a breach within the preceding section the buyer may "cover" by making in good faith and without unreasonable delay any reasonable purchase of or contract to purchase goods in substitution for those due from the seller.

(2) The buyer may recover from the seller as damages the difference between the cost of cover and the contract price together with any incidental or consequential damages as hereinafter defined (Section 2–715), but less expenses saved in consequence of the seller's breach.

(3) Failure of the buyer to effect cover within this section does not bar him from any other remedy.

§2-713. Buyer's Damages for Non-Delivery or Repudiation.

(1) Subject to the provisions of this Article with respect to proof of market price (Section 2–723), the measure of damages for nondelivery or repudiation by the seller is the difference between the market price at the time when the buyer learned of the breach and the contract price together with any incidental and consequential damages provided in this Article (Section 2–715), but less expenses saved in consequence of the seller's breach.

(2) Market price is to be determined as of the place for tender or, in cases of rejection after arrival or revocation of acceptance, as of the place of arrival.

§2-714. Buyer's Damages for Breach in Regard to Accepted Goods.

(1) Where the buyer has accepted goods and given notification (subsection (3) of Section 2–607) he may recover as damages for any non-conformity of tender the loss resulting in the ordinary course of events from the seller's breach as determined in any manner which is reasonable.

(2) The measure of damages for breach of warranty is the difference at the time and place of acceptance between the value of the goods accepted and the value they would have had if they had been as warranted, unless special circumstances show proximate damages of a different amount.

(3) In a proper case any incidental and consequential damages under the next section may also be recovered.

§2-715. Buyer's Incidental and Consequential Damages.

(1) Incidental damages resulting from the seller's breach include expenses reasonably incurred in inspection, receipt, transportation and care and custody of goods rightfully rejected, any commercially reasonable charges, expenses or commissions in connection with effecting cover and any other reasonable expense incident to the delay or other breach.

(2) Consequential damages resulting from the seller's breach include

(a) any loss resulting from general or particular requirements and needs of which the seller at the time of contracting had reason to know and which could not reasonably be prevented by cover or otherwise; and

(b) injury to person or property proximately resulting from any breach of warranty.

§2-716. Buyer's Right to Specific Performance or Replevin.

(1) Specific performance may be decreed where the goods are unique or in other proper circumstances.

(2) The decree for specific performance may include such terms and conditions as to payment of the price, damages, or other relief as the court may deem just.

(3) The buyer has a right of replevin for goods identified to the contract if after reasonable effort he is unable to effect cover for such goods or the circumstances reasonably indicate that such effort will be unvailing or if the goods have been shipped under reservation and satisfaction of the security interest in them has been made or tendered. In the case of goods bought for personal, family, or household purposes, the buyer's right of replevin vests upon acquisition of a special property, even if the seller had not then repudiated or failed to deliver.

§2-717. Deduction of Damages From the Price.

The buyer on notifying the seller of his intention to do so may deduct all or any part of the damages resulting from any breach of the contract from any part of the price still due under the same contract.

§2-718. Liquidation or Limitation of Damages; Deposits.

(1) Damages for breach by either party may be liquidated in the agreement but only at an amount which is reasonable in the light of the anticipated or actual harm caused by the breach, the difficulties of proof of loss, and the inconvenience of nonfeasibility of otherwise obtaining an adequate remedy. A team fixing unreasonably large liquidated damages is void as a penalty.

(2) Where the seller justifiably withholds delivery of goods because of the buyer's breach, the buyer is entitled to restitution of any amount by which the sum of his payments exceeds

(a) the amount to which the seller is entitled by virtue of terms liquidating the seller's damages in accordance with subsection (1), or

(b) in the absence of such terms, twenty percent of the value of the total performance for which the buyer is obligated under the contract or $500, whichever is smaller.

(3) The buyer's right to restitution under subsection (2) is subject to offset to the extent that the seller establishes

(a) a right to recover damages under the provisions of this Article other than subsection (1), and

(b) the amount or value of any benefits received by the buyer directly or indirectly by reason of the contract.

(4) Where a seller has received payment in goods their reasonable value or the proceeds of their resale shall be treated as payments for the purposes of subsection (2); but if the seller has notice of the buyer's breach before reselling goods received in part performance, his resale is subject to the conditions laid down in this Article on resale by an aggrieved seller (Section 2–706).

§2-719. Contractual Modification or Limitation of Remedy.

(1) Subject to the provisions of subsections (2) and (3) of this section and of the preceding section on liquidation and limitation of damages,

(a) the agreement may provide for remedies in addition to or in substitution for those provided in this Article and may limit or alter the measure of damages recoverable under this Article, as by limiting the buyer's remedies to return of the goods and repayment of the price or to repair and replacement of non-conforming goods or parts; and

(b) resort to a remedy as provided is optional unless the remedy is expressly agreed to be exclusive, in which case it is the sole remedy.

(2) Where circumstances cause an exclusive or limited remedy to fail of its essential purpose, remedy may be had as provided in this Act.

(3) Consequential damages may be limited or excluded unless the limitation or exclusion is unconscionable. Limitation of consequential damages for injury to the person in the case of consumer goods is prima facie unconscionable but limitation of damages where the loss is commercial is not.

§2-720. Effect of "Cancellation" or "Rescission" on Claims for Antecedent Breach.

Unless the contrary intention clearly appears, expressions of "cancellation" or "rescission" of the contract or the like shall not be construed as a renunciation or discharge of any claim in damages for an antecedent breach.

§2-721. Remedies for Fraud.

Remedies for material misrepresentation or fraud include all remedies available under this Article for non-fraudulent breach. Neither rescission or a claim for rescission of the contract for sale nor rejection or return of the goods shall bar or be deemed inconsistent with a claim for damages or other remedy.

§2-722. Who Can Sue Third Parties for Injury to Goods.

Where a third party so deals with goods which have been identified to a contract for sale as to cause actionable injury to a party to that contract

(a) a right of action against the third party is in either party to the contract for sale who has title to or a security interest or a special property or an insurable interest in the goods; and if the goods have been destroyed or converted a right of action is also in the party who either bore the risk of loss under the contract for sale or has since the injury assumed that risk as against the other,

(b) if at the time of the injury the party plaintiff did not bear the risk of loss as against the other party to the contract for sale and there is no arrangement between them for disposition of the recovery, his suit or settlement is, subject to his own interest, as a fiduciary for the other party to the contract;

(c) either party may with the consent of the other sue for the benefit of whom it may concern.

§2-723. Proof of Market Price: Time and Place.

(1) If an action based on anticipatory repudiation comes to trial before the time for performance with respect to some or all of the goods, any damages based on market price (Section 2–708 or Section 2–713) shall be determined according to the price of such goods prevailing at the time when the aggrieved party learned of the repudiation.

(2) If evidence of a price prevailing at the times or places described in this Article is not readily available the price prevailing within any reasonable time before or after the time described or at any other place which in commercial judgment or under usage of trade would serve as a reasonable substitute for the one described may be used, making any proper allowance for the cost of transporting the goods to or from such other place.

(3) Evidence of a relevant price prevailing at a time or place other than the one described in this Article offered by one party is not admissible unless and until he has given the other party such notice as the court finds sufficient to prevent unfair surprise.

§2-724. Admissibility of Market Quotations.

Whenever the prevailing price or value of any goods regularly bought and sold in any established commodity market is in issue, reports in official publications or trade journals or in newspapers or periodicals of general circulation published as the reports of such market shall be admissible in evidence. The circumstances of the preparation of such a report may be shown to affect its weight but not its admissibility.

§2-725. Statute of Limitations in Contracts for Sale.

(1) An action for breach of any contract for sale must be commenced within four years after the cause of action has accrued. By the original agreement the parties may reduce the period of limitation to not less than one year but may not extend it.

(2) A cause of action accrues when the breach occurs, regardless of the aggrieved party's lack of knowledge of the breach. A breach of warranty occurs when tender of delivery is made, except that where a warranty explicitly extends to future performance of the goods and discovery of the breach must await the time of such performance the cause of action accrues when the breach is or should have been discovered.

(3) Where an action commenced within the time limited by subsection (1) is so terminated as to leave available a remedy by another action for the same breach such other action may be commenced after the expiration of the time limited and within six months after the termination of the first action unless the termination resulted from voluntary discontinuance or from dismissal for failure or neglect to prosecute.

(4) This section does not alter the law on tolling of the statute of limitations nor does it apply to causes of action which have accrued before this Act becomes effective.

Appendix C—Sarbanes-Oxley Act of 2002 (Excerpts)

Title I—Public Company Accounting Oversight Board

Sec. 101 Establishment; Administrative Provisions.

(a) Establishment of Board.—There is established the Public Company Accounting Oversight Board, to oversee the audit of public companies that are subject to the securities laws, and related matters, in order to protect the interests of investors and further the public interest in the preparation of informative, accurate, and independent audit reports for companies the securities of which are sold to, and held by and for, public investors. The Board shall be a body corporate, operate as a nonprofit corporation, and have succession until dissolved by an Act of Congress.

Sec. 102 Registration with the Board.

(a) Mandatory Registration.—It shall be unlawful for any person that is not a registered public accounting firm to prepare or issue, or to participate in the preparation or issuance of, any audit report with respect to any issuer.

(b) Application for Registration.—

(1) Form of application.—A public accounting firm shall use such form as the Board may prescribe, by rule, to apply for registration under this section.

Sec. 104 Inspections of Registered Public Accounting Firms.

(a) In General.—The Board shall conduct a continuing program of inspections to assess the degree of compliance of each registered public accounting firm and associated persons of that firm with this Act, the rules of the Board, the rules of the Commission, or professional standards, in connection with its performance of audits, issuance of audit reports, and related matters involving issuers.

(b) Inspection Frequency.—

(1) In general.—Subject to paragraph (2), inspections required by this section shall be conducted—

(A) annually with respect to each registered public accounting firm that regularly provides audit reports for more than 100 issuers; and

(B) not less frequently than once every 3 years with respect to each registered public accounting firm that regularly provides audit reports for 100 or fewer issuers.

Sec. 105 Investigations and Disciplinary Proceedings.

(a) In General.—The Board shall establish, by rule, subject to the requirements of this section, fair procedures for the investigation and disciplining of registered public accounting firms and associated persons of such firms.

(b) Disciplinary Procedures.—

(4) Sanctions.—If the Board finds, based on all of the facts and circumstances, that a registered public accounting firm or associated person thereof has engaged in any act or practice, or omitted to act, in violation of this Act, the rules of the Board, the provisions of the securities laws relating to the preparation and issuance of audit reports and the obligations and liabilities of accountants with respect thereto, including the rules of the Commission issued under this Act, or professional standards, the Board may impose such disciplinary or remedial sanctions as it determines appropriate, subject to applicable limitations under paragraph (5), including—

(A) temporary suspension or permanent revocation of registration under this title;

(B) temporary or permanent suspension or bar of a person from further association with any registered public accounting firm;

(C) temporary or permanent limitation on the activities, functions, or operations of such firm or person (other than in connection with required additional professional education or training);

(D) a civil money penalty for each such violation, in an amount equal to—

(i) not more than $100,000 for a natural person or $2,000,000 for any other person; and

(ii) in any case to which paragraph (5) applies, not more than $750,000 for a natural person or $15,000,000 for any other person;

(E) censure;

(F) required additional professional education or training; or

(G) any other appropriate sanction provided for in the rules of the Board.

(5) Intentional or other knowing conduct.—The sanctions and penalties described in subparagraphs (A) through (C) and (D)(ii) of paragraph (4) shall only apply to—

(A) intentional or knowing conduct, including reckless conduct, that results in violation of the applicable statutory, regulatory, or professional standard; or

(B) repeated instances of negligent conduct, each resulting in a violation of the applicable statutory, regulatory, or professional standard.

Title II—Auditor Independence

Sec. 201 Services Outside the Scope of Practice of Auditors.

(a) Prohibited Activities.—Section 10A of the Securities Exchange Act of 1934 (15 U.S.C. 78j–l) is amended by adding at the end of the following:

"(g) Prohibited Activities.—Except as provided in subsection (h), it shall be unlawful for a registered public accounting firm (and any associated person of that firm, to the extent determined appropriate by the Commission) that performs for any issuer any audit required by this title or the rules of the Commission under this title or, beginning 180 days after the date of commencement of the operations of the Public Company Accounting Oversight Board established under section 101 of the Sarbanes-Oxley Act of 2002 (in this section referred to as the 'Board'), the rules of the Board, to provide to that issuer, contemporaneously with the audit, any non-audit service, including—

"(1) bookkeeping or other services related to the accounting records or financial statements of the audit client;
"(2) financial information systems design and implementation;
"(3) appraisal or valuation services, fairness opinions, or contribution-in-kind reports;
"(4) actuarial services;
"(5) internal audit outsourcing services;
"(6) management functions or human resources;
"(7) broker or dealer, investment adviser, or investment banking services;
"(8) legal services and expert services unrelated to the audit; and
"(9) any other service that the Board determines, by regulation, is impermissible.

"(h) Preapproval Required for Non-Audit Services.—A registered public accounting firm may engage in any non-audit service, including tax services, that is not described in any of paragraphs (1) through (9) of subsection (g) for an audit client, only if the activity is approved in advance by the audit committee of the issuer, in accordance with subsection (i)."

Sec. 206 Conflicts of Interest.

Section 10A of the Securities Exchange Act of 1934 (15 U.S.C. 78j–l), as amended by this Act, is amended by adding at the end the following:

"(l) Conflicts of Interest.—It shall be unlawful for a registered public accounting firm to perform for an issuer any audit service required by this title, if a chief executive officer, controller, chief financial officer, chief accounting officer, or any person serving in an equivalent position for the issuer, was employed by that registered independent public accounting firm and participated in any capacity in the audit of that issuer during the 1-year period preceding the date of the initiation of the audit."

Title III—Corporate Responsibility

Sec. 301 Public Company Audit Committees.

Section 10A of the Securities Exchange Act of 1934 (15 U.S.C. 78f) is amended by adding at the end the following:

"(m) Standards Relating to Audit Committees.—

"(2) Responsibilities relating to registered public accounting firms.—The audit committee of each issuer, in its capacity as a committee of the board of directors, shall be directly responsible for the appointment, compensation, and oversight of the work of any registered public accounting firm employed by that issuer (including resolution of disagreements between management and the auditor regarding financial reporting) for the purpose of preparing or issuing an audit report or related work, and each such registered public accounting firm shall report directly to the audit committee.

"(3) Independence.—

"(A) In general.—Each member of the audit committee of the issuer shall be a member of the board of directors of the issuer, and shall otherwise be independent.

"(B) Criteria.—In order to be considered to be independent for purposes of this paragraph, a member of an audit committee of an issuer may not, other than in his or her capacity as a member of the audit committee, the board of directors, or any other board committee—

"(i) accept any consulting, advisory, or other compensatory fee from the issuer; or
"(ii) be an affiliated person of the issuer or any subsidiary thereof.

Sec. 302 Corporate Responsibility for Financial Reports.

(a) Regulations Required.—The Commission shall, by rule, require, for each company filing periodic reports under section 13(a) or 15(d) of the Securities Exchange Act of 1934 (15 U.S.C. 78m, 78o(d)), that the principal executive officer or officers and the principal financial officer or officers, or persons performing similar functions, certify in each annual or quarterly report filed or submitted under either such section of such Act that—

(1) the signing officer has reviewed the report;
(2) based on the officer's knowledge, the report does not contain any untrue statement of a material fact or omit to state a material fact necessary in order to make the statements made, in light of the circumstances under which such statements were made, not misleading;
(3) based on such officer's knowledge, the financial statements, and other financial information included in the report fairly present in all material respects the financial condition and results of operations of the issuer as of, and for, the periods presented in the report;
(4) the signing officers—
    (A) are responsible for establishing and maintaining internal controls;
    (B) have designed such internal controls to ensure that material information relating to the issuer and its consolidated subsidiaries is made known to such officers by others within those entities, particularly during the period in which the periodic reports are being prepared;
    (C) have evaluated the effectiveness of the issuer's internal controls as of a date within 90 days prior to the report; and
    (D) have presented in the report their conclusions about the effectiveness of their internal controls based on their evaluation as of that date;
(5) the signing officers have disclosed to the issuer's auditors and the audit committee of the board of directors (or persons fulfilling the equivalent function)—
    (A) all significant deficiencies in the design or operation of internal controls which could adversely affect the issuer's ability to record, process, summarize, and report financial data and have identified for the issuer's auditors any material weaknesses in internal controls; and
    (B) any fraud, whether or not material, that involves management or other employees who have a significant role in the issuer's internal controls; and
(6) the signing officers have indicated in the report whether or not there were significant changes in

internal controls or in other factors that could significantly affect internal controls subsequent to the date of their evaluation, including any corrective actions with regard to significant deficiencies and material weaknesses.

Sec. 303 Improper Influence on Conduct of Audits.

(a) Rules to Prohibit.—It shall be unlawful, in contravention of such rules or regulations as the Commission shall prescribe as necessary and appropriate in the public interest or for the protection of investors, for any officer or director of an issuer, or any other person acting under the direction thereof, to take any action to fraudulently influence, coerce, manipulate, or mislead any independent public or certified accountant engaged in the performance of an audit of the financial statements of that issuer for the purpose of rendering such financial statements materially misleading.

Title IV—Enhanced Financial Disclosures

Sec. 401 Disclosures in Periodic Reports.

(a) Disclosures Required.—Section 13 of the Securities Exchange Act of 1934 (15 U.S.C. 78m) is amended by adding at the end the following:

"(i) Accuracy of Financial Reports.—Each financial report that contains financial statements, and that is required to be prepared in accordance with (or reconciled to) generally accepted accounting principles under this title and filed with the Commission shall reflect all material correcting adjustments that have been identified by a registered public accounting firm in accordance with generally accepted accounting principles and the rules and regulations of the Commission.

"(j) Off-Balance Sheet Transactions.—Not later than 180 days after the date of enactment of the Sarbanes-Oxley Act of 2002, the Commission shall issue final rules providing that each annual and quarterly financial report required to be filed with the Commission shall disclose all material off-balance sheet transactions, arrangements, obligations (including contingent obligations), and other relationships of the issuer with unconsolidated entities or other persons, that may have a material current or future effect on financial condition, changes in financial condition, results of operations, liquidity, capital expenditures, capital resources, or significant components of revenues or expenses."

(b) Commission Rules on Pro Forma Figures.—Not later than 180 days after the date of enactment of the Sarbanes-Oxley Act of 2002, the Commission shall issue final rules providing that pro forma financial information included in any periodic or other report filed with the Commission pursuant to the securities laws, or in any public disclosure or press or other release, shall be presented in a manner that—

(1) does not contain an untrue statement of a material fact or omit to state a material fact necessary in order to make the pro forma financial information, in light of the circumstances under which it is presented, not misleading; and

(2) reconciles it with the financial condition and results of operations of the issuer under generally accepted accounting principles.

Sec. 402 Enhanced Conflict of Interest Provisions.

(a) Prohibition on Personal Loans to Executives.—Section 13 of the Securities Exchange Act of 1934 (15 U.S.C. 78m), as amended by this Act, is amended by adding at the end the following:

(k) Prohibition on Personal Loans to Executives.—

(1) In general.—It shall be unlawful for any issuer (as defined in section 2 of the Sarbanes-Oxley Act of 2002), directly or indirectly, including through any subsidiary, to extend or maintain credit, to arrange for the extension of credit, or to renew an extension of credit, in the form of a personal loan to or for any director or executive officer (or equivalent thereof) of that issuer. An extension of credit maintained by the issuer on the date of enactment of this subsection shall not be subject to the provisions of this subsection, provided that there is no material modification to any term of any such extension of credit or any renewal of any such extension of credit on or after that date of enactment.

Sec. 406 Code of Ethics for Senior Financial Officers.

(a) Code of Ethics Disclosure.—The Commission shall issue rules to require each issuer, together with periodic reports required pursuant to section 13(a) or 15(d) of the Securities Exchange Act of 1934, to disclose whether or not, and if not, the reason therefor, such issuer has adopted a code of ethics for senior financial officers, applicable to its principal financial officer and comptroller or principal accounting officer, or persons performing similar functions.

(b) Changes in Codes of Ethics.—The Commission shall revise its regulations concerning matters requiring prompt disclosure on Form 8-K (or any successor thereto) to require the immediate disclosure by means of the filing of such form, dissemination by the Internet or by other electronic means, by any issuer of any change in or waiver of the code of ethics for senior financial officers.

(c) Definition.—In this section, the term "code of ethics" means such standards as are reasonably necessary to promote—

(1) honest and ethical conduct, including the ethical handling of actual or apparent conflicts of interest between personal and professional relationships;

(2) full, fair, accurate, timely, and understandable disclosure in the periodic reports required to be filed by the issuer; and

(3) compliance with applicable governmental rules and regulations.

Title V—Analyst Conflicts of Interest

Sec. 501 Treatment of Securities Analysts by Registered Securities Associations and National Securities Exchanges.

(a) Rules Regarding Securities Analysts.—The Securities Exchange Act of 1934 (15 U.S.C. 78a et seq.) is amended by inserting after section 15C the following new section:

"Sec. 15D. Securities Analysts and Research Reports

"(a) Analyst Protections.—The Commission, or upon the authorization and direction of the Commission, a registered securities association or national securities exchange, shall have adopted, not later than 1 year after the date of enactment of this section, rules reasonably designed to address conflicts of interest that can arise when securities analysts recommend equity securities in research reports and public appearances, in order to improve the objectivity of research and provide investors with more useful and reliable information, including rules designed—

"(1) to foster greater public confidence in securities research, and to protect the objectivity and independence of securities analysts, by—

"(A) restricting the prepublication clearance or approval of research reports by persons employed by the broker or dealer who are engaged in investment banking activities, or persons not directly responsible for investment research, other than legal or compliance staff;

"(B) limiting the supervision and compensatory evaluation of securities analysts to officials employed by the broker or dealer who are not engaged in investment banking activities; and

"(C) requiring that a broker or dealer and persons employed by a broker or dealer who are involved with investment banking activities may not, directly or indirectly, retaliate against or threaten to retaliate against any securities analyst employed by that broker or dealer or its affiliates as a result of an adverse, negative, or otherwise unfavorable research report that may adversely affect the present or prospective investment banking relationship of the broker or dealer with the issuer that is the subject of the research report, except that such rules may not limit the authority of a broker or dealer to discipline a securities analyst for causes other than such research report in accordance with the policies and procedures of the firm;

"(2) to define periods during which brokers or dealers who have participated, or are to participate, in a public offering of securities as underwriters or dealers should not publish or otherwise distribute research reports relating to such securities or to the issuer of such securities;

"(3) to establish structural and institutional safeguards within registered brokers or dealers to assure that securities analysts are separated by appropriate informational partitions within the firm from the review, pressure, or oversight of those whose involvement in investment banking activities might potentially bias their judgment or supervision; and

"(4) to address such other issues as the Commission, or such association or exchange, determines appropriate.

"(b) Disclosure.—The Commission, or upon the authorization and direction of the Commission, a registered securities association or national securities exchange, shall have adopted, not later than 1 year after the date of enactment of this section, rules reasonably designed to require each securities analyst to disclose in public appearances, and each registered broker or dealer to disclose in each research report, as applicable, conflicts of interest that are known or should have been known by the securities analyst or the broker or dealer, to exist at the time of the appearance or the date of distribution of the report, including—

"(1) the extent to which the securities analyst has debt or equity investments in the issuer that is the subject of the appearance or research report;

"(2) whether any compensation has been received by the registered broker or dealer, or any affiliate thereof, including the securities analyst, from the issuer that is the subject of the appearance or research report, subject to such exemptions as the Commission may determine appropriate and necessary to prevent disclosure by virtue of this paragraph of material nonpublic information regarding specific potential future investment banking transactions of such issuer, as is appropriate in the public interest and consistent with the protection of investors;

"(3) whether an issuer, the securities of which are recommended in the appearance or research report, currently is, or during the 1-year period preceding the date of the appearance or date of distribution of the report has been, a client of the registered broker or dealer, and if so, stating the types of services provided to the issuer;

"(4) whether the securities analyst received compensation with respect to a research report, based upon (among any other factors) the investment banking revenues (either generally or specifically earned from the issuer being analyzed) of the registered broker or dealer; and

"(5) such other disclosures of conflicts of interest that are material to investors, research analysts, or the broker or dealer as the Commission, or such association or exchange, determines appropriate.

"(c) Definitions.—In this section—

"(1) the term 'securities analyst' means any associated person of a registered broker or dealer that is principally responsible for, and any associated person who reports directly or indirectly to a securities analyst in connection with, the preparation of the substance of a research report, whether or not any such person has the job title of 'securities analyst'; and

"(2) the term 'research report' means a written or electronic communication that includes an analysis of equity securities of individual companies or industries, and that provides information reasonably sufficient upon which to base an investment decision."

(b) Enforcement.—Section 21B(a) of the Securities Exchange Act of 1934 (15 U.S.C. 78u–2(a)) is amended by inserting "15D," before "15B".

(c) Commission Authority.—The Commission may promulgate and amend its regulations, or direct a registered securities association or national securities exchange to promulgate and amend its rules, to carry out section 15D of the Securities Exchange Act of 1934, as added by this section, as is necessary for the protection of investors and in the public interest.

Title VI—Commission Resources and Authority

Sec. 602 Appearance and Practice Before the Commission.

The Securities Exchange Act of 1934 (15 U.S.C. 78a et seq.) is amended by inserting after section 4B the following:

"Sec 4C. Appearance and Practice Before the Commission

"(a) Authority to Censure.—The Commission may censure any person, or deny, temporarily or permanently, to any person the privilege of appearing or practicing before the Commission in any way, if that person is found by the Commission, after notice and opportunity for hearing in the matter—

"(1) not to possess the requisite qualifications to represent others;
"(2) to be lacking in character or integrity, or to have engaged in unethical or improper professional conduct; or
"(3) to have willfully violated or willfully aided and abetted the violation of, any provision of the securities laws or the rules and regulations issued thereunder."

Title VII—Studies and Reports

Sec. 705 Study of Investment Banks.

(a) GAO Study.—The Comptroller General of the United States shall conduct a study on whether investment banks and financial advisers assisted public companies in manipulating their earnings and obfuscating their true financial condition. The study should address the rule of investment banks and financial advisers—

(1) in the collapse of the Enron Corporation, including with respect to the design and implementation of derivatives transactions, transactions involving special purpose vehicles, and other financial arrangements that may have had the effect of altering the company's reported financial statements in ways that obscured the true financial picture of the company;
(2) in the failure of Global Crossing, including with respect to transactions involving swaps of fiberoptic cable capacity, in the designing transactions that may have had the effect of altering the company's reported financial statements in ways that obscured the true financial picture of the company; and
(3) generally, in creating and marketing transactions which may have been designed solely to enable companies to manipulate revenue streams, obtain loans, or move liabilities off balance sheets without altering the economic and business risks faced by the companies or any other mechanism to obscure a company's financial picture.

Title VIII—Corporate and Criminal Fraud Accountability

Sec. 801 Short Title.

This title may be cited as the "Corporate and Criminal Fraud Accountability Act of 2002".

Sec. 802 Criminal Penalties for Altering Documents.

(a) In General.— Chapter 73 of title 18, United States Code, is amended by adding at the end the following:

§1519. Destruction, alteration, or falsification of records in Federal investigations and bankruptcy

"Whoever knowingly alters, destroys, mutilates, conceals, covers up, falsifies, or makes a false entry in any record, document, or tangible object with the intent to impede, obstruct, or influence the investigation or proper administration of any matter within the jurisdiction of any department or agency of the United States or any case filed under Title 11, or in relation to or contemplation of any such matter or case, shall be fined under this title, imprisoned not more than 20 years, or both.

§1520. Destruction of corporate audit records

"(a) (1) Any accountant who conducts an audit of an issuer of securities to which section 10A(a) of the Securities Exchange Act of 1934 (15 U.S.C. 78j–1(a)) applies, shall maintain all audit or review workpapers for a period of 5 years from the end of the fiscal period in which the audit or review was concluded."

Sec. 807 Criminal Penalties for Defrauding Shareholders of Publicly Traded Companies.

(a) In General.— Chapter 63 of title 18, United States Code, is amended by adding at the end the following:

§1348. Securities fraud

"Whoever knowingly executes, or attempts to execute, a scheme or artifice—

"(1) to defraud any person in connection with any security of an issuer with a class of securities registered under section 12 of the Securities Exchange Act of 1934 (15 U.S.C. 78l) or that is required to file reports under section 15(d) of the Securities Exchange Act of 1934 (15 U.S.C. 78o(d)); or
"(2) to obtain, by means of false or fraudulent pretenses, representations, or promises, any money or property in connection with the purchase or sale of any security of an issuer with a class of securities registered under section 12 of the Securities Exchange Act of 1934 (15 U.S.C. 78l) or that is required to file reports under section 15(d) of the Securities Exchange Act of 1934 (15 U.S.C. 78o(d));

shall be fined under this title, or imprisoned not more than 25 years, or both."

Title IX—White-Collar Crime Penalty Enhancements

Sec. 901 Short Title.

This title may be cited as the "White-Collar Crime Penalty Enhancement Act of 2002".

Sec. 906 Corporate Responsibility for Financial Reports.

(a) In General.— Chapter 63 of title 18, United States Code, is amended by inserting after section 1349, as created by this Act, the following:

§1350. Failure of corporate officers to certify financial reports

"(a) Certification of Periodic Financial Reports.—Each periodic report containing financial statements filed by an issuer with the Securities Exchange Commission pursuant to section 13(a) or 15(d) of the Securities Exchange Act of 1934 (15 U.S.C. 78m(a) or 78o(d)) shall be accompanied by a written statement by the chief executive officer and chief financial officer (or equivalent thereof) of the issuer.

"(b) Content.—The statement required under subsection (a) shall certify that the periodic report containing the financial statements fully complies with the requirements of section 13(a) or 15(d) of the Securities Exchange Act of 1934 (15 U.S.C. 78m or 78o(d)) and that information contained in the periodic report fairly presents, in all material respects, the financial condition and results of operations of the issuer.

"(c) Criminal Penalties.—Whoever—

"(1) certifies any statement as set forth in subsections (a) and (b) of this section knowing that the periodic report accompanying the statement does not comport with all the requirements set forth in this section shall be fined not more than $1,000,000 or imprisoned not more than 10 years, or both; or

"(2) willfully certifies any statement as set forth in subsections (a) and (b) of this section knowing that the periodic report accompanying the statement does not comport with all the requirements set forth in this section shall be fined not more than $5,000,000, or imprisoned not more than 20 years, or both."

(b) Clerical Amendment.—The table of sections at the beginning of Chapter 63 of title 18, United States Code, is amended by adding at the end the following:

"1350. Failure of corporate officers to certify financial reports."

Title X—Corporate Tax Returns

Sec. 1001 Sense of the Senate Regarding the Signing of Corporate Tax Returns by Chief Executive Officers.

It is the sense of the Senate that the Federal income tax return of a corporation should be signed by the chief executive officer of such corporation.

Title XI—Corporate Fraud Accountability

Sec. 1101 Short Title.

This title may be cited as the "Corporate Fraud Accountability Act of 2002".

Sec. 1102 Tampering with a Record or Otherwise Impeding an Official Proceeding.

Section 1512 of title 18, United States Code, is amended—

(1) by redesignating subsections (c) through (i) as subsections (d) through (j), respectively; and

(2) by inserting after subsection (b) the following new subsection:

"(c) Whoever corruptly—

"(1) alters, destroys, mutilates, or conceals a record, document, or other object, or attempts to do so, with the intent to impair the object's integrity or availability for use in an official proceeding; or

"(2) otherwise obstructs, influences, or impedes any official proceeding, or attempts to do so,

shall be fined under this title or imprisoned not more than 20 years, or both."

Sec. 1105 Authority of the Commission to Prohibit Persons from Serving as Officers or Directors.

"(a) Securities Exchange Act of 1934.—Section 21C of the Securities Exchange Act of 1934 (15 U.S.C. 78u–3) is amended by adding at the end the following:

"(f) Authority of the Commission to Prohibit Persons from Serving as Officers or Directors.—In any cease-and-desist proceeding under subsection (a), the Commission may issue an order to prohibit, conditionally or unconditionally, and permanently or for such period of time as it shall determine, any person who has violated section 10(b) or the rules or regulations thereunder, from acting as an officer or director of any issuer that has a class of securities registered pursuant to section 12, or that is required to file reports pursuant to section 15(d), if the conduct of that person demonstrates unfitness to serve as an officer or director of any such issuer."

"(b) Securities Act of 1933.—Section 8A of the Securities Act of 1933 (15 U.S.C. 77h–l) is amended by adding at the end of the following:

"(f) Authority of the Commission to Prohibit Persons from Serving as Officers or Directors.—In any cease-and-desist proceeding under subsection (a), the Commission may issue an order to prohibit, conditionally or unconditionally, and permanently or for such period of time as it shall determine, any person who has violated section 17(a)(1) or the rules or regulations thereunder, from acting as an officer or director of any issuer that has a class of securities registered pursuant to section 12 of the Securities Exchange Act of 1934, or that is required to file reports pursuant to section 15(d) of that Act, if the conduct of that person demonstrates unfitness to serve as an officer or director of any such issuer."

Glossary

abandoned property Property that an owner has discarded with the intent to relinquish his or her rights in it and mislaid or lost property that the owner has given up any further attempts to locate.

abatement If the property the testator leaves is not sufficient to satisfy all the beneficiaries named in a will and there are both general and residuary bequests, the residuary bequest is abated first (i.e., paid last).

absolute priority rule A rule that says a reorganization plan is fair and equitable to an impaired class of unsecured creditors or equity holders if no class below it receives anything in the plan.

acceptance A manifestation of assent by the offeree to the terms of the offer in a manner invited or required by the offer as measured by the objective theory of contracts. [Section 50 of the Restatement (Second) of Contracts]. Occurs when a buyer or lessee takes any of the following actions after a reasonable opportunity to inspect the goods: (1) signifies to the seller or lessor in words or by conduct that the goods are conforming or that the buyer or lessee will take or retain the goods despite their nonconformity or (2) fails to effectively reject the goods within a reasonable time after their delivery or tender by the seller or lessor. Acceptance also occurs if a buyer acts inconsistently with the seller's ownership rights in the goods.

acceptance method The bankruptcy court must approve a plan of reorganization if (1) the plan is in the best interests of each class of claims and interests, (2) the plan is feasible, (3) at least one class of claims votes to accept the plan, and (4) each class of claims and interests is nonimpaired.

accession Occurs when the value of personal property increases because it is added to or improved by natural or manufactured means.

accommodation A shipment that is offered to the buyer as a replacement for the original shipment when the original shipment cannot be filled.

accommodation party A party who signs an instrument and lends his or her name (and credit) to another party to the instrument.

accord An agreement whereby the parties agree to accept something different in satisfaction of the original contract.

accord and satisfaction The settlement of a contract dispute.

accountant malpractice Occurs when the accountant breaches the duty of reasonable care, knowledge, skill, and judgment that he or she owes to a client when providing auditing and other accounting services to the client.

act of monopolizing A required act for there to be a violation of Section 2 of the Sherman Act. Possession of monopoly power without such act does not violate Section 2.

act of state doctrine States that judges of one country cannot question the validity of an act committed by another country within that other country's borders. It is based on the principle that a country has absolute authority over what transpires within its own territory.

action for an accounting A formal judicial proceeding in which the court is authorized to (1) review the partnership and the partners' transactions and (2) award each partner his or her share of the partnership assets.

actus reus "Guilty act"—the actual performance of the criminal act.

ademption A principle that says if a testator leaves a specific devise of property to a beneficiary, but the property is no longer in the estate when the testator dies, the beneficiary receives nothing.

adequate assurance of performance A party to a sales or lease contract may demand an adequate assurance of performance from the other party if there is an indication that the contract will be breached by that party.

adjudged insane A person who has been adjudged insane by a proper court or administrative agency. A contract entered into by such a person is void.

administrative agencies Agencies that the legislative and executive branches of federal and state governments establish.

administrative dissolution Involuntary dissolution of a corporation that is ordered by the secretary of state if the corporation has failed to comply with certain procedures required by law.

administrative law judge (ALJ) A judge, presiding over administrative proceedings, who decides questions of law and fact concerning the case.

Administrative Procedure Act (APA) An act that establishes certain administrative procedures that federal administrative agencies must follow in conducting their affairs.

administrative subpoena An order that directs the subject of the subpoena to disclose the requested information.

adverse action A denial or revocation of credit or a change in the credit terms offered.

adverse possession When a person who wrongfully possesses someone else's real property obtains title to that property if certain statutory requirements are met.

advertisement A general advertisement is an invitation to make an offer. A specific advertisement is an offer.

affirmative action Policy that provides that certain job preferences will be given to minority or other protected class applicants when an employer makes an employment decision.

AFL-CIO The 1955 combination of the AFL and the CIO.

after-acquired property Property that the debtor acquires after the security agreement is executed.

agency The principal-agent relationship: the fiduciary relationship "which results from the manifestation of consent by one person to another that the other shall act in his behalf and subject to his control, and consent by the other so to act."

agency by ratification An agency that occurs when (1) a person misrepresents him- or herself as another's agent when in fact he or she is not and (2) the purported principal ratifies the unauthorized act.

agency law The large body of common law that governs agency; a mixture of contract law and tort law.

agency shop An establishment where an employee does not have to join the union, but must pay a fee equal to the union dues.

agent A person who has been authorized to sign a negotiable instrument on behalf of another person. The party who agrees to act on behalf of another.

agreement The manifestation by two or more persons of the substance of a contract.

agreement of conversion Document that states the terms for converting an existing business to an LLC.

aiding and abetting the commission of a crime Rendering support, assistance, or encouragement to the commission of a crime; harboring a criminal after he or she has committed a crime.

air pollution Pollution caused by factories, homes, vehicles, and the like that affects the air.

alien corporation A corporation that is incorporated in another country.

alien LLC An LLC that is organized in another country.

allonge A separate piece of paper attached to the instrument on which the indorsement is written.

altered check A check that has been altered without authorization that modifies the legal obligation of a party.

alternative dispute resolution (ADR) Methods of resolving disputes other than litigation.

Americans with Disabilities Act (ADA) of 1990. Imposes obligations on employers and providers of public transportation, telecommunications, and public accommodations to accommodate individuals with disabilities.

annual financial statement A statement provided to the shareholders that contains a balance sheet, an income statement, and a statement of changes in shareholder equity.

annual shareholders' meeting Meeting of the shareholders of a corporation that must be held annually by the corporation to elect directors and to vote on other matters.

answer The defendant's written response to the plaintiff's complaint that is filed with the court and served on the plaintiff.

anti-assignment clause A clause that prohibits the assignment of rights under the contract.

anticipatory breach A breach that occurs when one contracting party informs the other that he or she will not perform his or her contractual duties when due.

anticipatory repudiation The repudiation of a sales or lease contract by one of the parties prior to the date set for performance.

antideficiency statute A statute that prohibits deficiency judgments regarding certain types of mortgages, such as those on residential property.

anti-delegation clause A clause that prohibits the delegation of duties under the contract.

antidilution statutes State laws that allow persons and companies to register trademarks and service marks.

antitrust laws A series of laws enacted to limit anticompetitive behavior in almost all industries, businesses, and professions operating in the United States.

apparent agency Agency that arises when a principal creates the appearance of an agency that in actuality does not exist. Agency that arises when a franchisor creates the appearance that a franchisee is its agent when in fact an actual agency does not exist.

appeal The act of asking an appellate court to overturn a decision after the trial court's final judgment has been entered.

appellant The appealing party in an appeal. Also known as petitioner.

appellate body A panel of seven judges selected from WTO member nations that hears and decides appeals from decisions by the dispute settlement body.

appellee The responding party in an appeal. Also known as respondent.

appropriate bargaining unit The group that a union seeks to represent.

approval clause A clause that permits the assignment of the contract only upon receipt of an obligor's approval.

arbitration A form of ADR in which the parties choose an impartial third party to hear and decide the dispute. A nonjudicial method of dispute resolution whereby a neutral third party decides the case.

arbitration clause A clause in contracts that requires disputes arising out of the contract to be submitted to arbitration. A clause contained in many international contracts that stipulates that any dispute between the parties concerning the performance of the contract will be submitted to an arbitrator or arbitration panel for resolution.

arraignment A hearing during which the accused is brought before a court and is (1) informed of the charges against him or her and (2) asked to enter a plea.

arrest warrant A document for a person's detainment based upon a showing of probable cause that the person committed the crime.

arson Willfully or maliciously burning another's building.

Article 2A (Leases) Article of the UCC that governs lease of goods.

Article 4 of the UCC Establishes the rules and principles that regulate bank deposit and collection procedures.

Article 7 of the UCC An article of the Uniform Commercial Code that provides a detailed statutory scheme for the creation, perfection, and foreclosure on common carriers' and warehouse operators' liens. Article of the Uniform Commercial Code that governs documents of title.

Article 8 of the UCC The article of the UCC that governs transfer of securities.

Article 9 of the UCC An article of the Uniform Commercial Code that governs secured transactions in personal property.

articles of incorporation The basic governing documents of the corporation. These documents must be filed with the secretary of state of the state of incorporation.

articles of organization The formal documents that must be filed at the secretary of state's office of the state of organization of an LLC to form the LLC.

articles of termination Document that is filed with the secretary of state that terminates the LLC as of the date of filing or upon a later effective date specified in the document.

assault The threat of immediate harm or offensive contact or any action that arouses reasonable apprehension of imminent harm. Actual physical contact is unnecessary.

assent Assent to enter into a contract may be manifested in any manner sufficient to show agreement, including express words or conduct of the parties.

assignee The party to whom the right has been transferred. The transferee in an assignment situation. The party to whom rights have been transferred.

assignment The transfer of contractual rights by the obligee to another party. The transfer of rights under a contract. A transfer by a tenant of his or her rights under a lease to another.

assignment and delegation Transfer of both rights and duties under the contract.

assignor The party who transfers the rights. The transferor in an assignment situation. The obligee who transfers the right.

assumption of duties When a delegation of duties contains the term assumption, I assume the duties, or other similar language; the delegatee is legally liable to the obligee for nonperformance.

assumption of the risk A defense a defendant can use against a plaintiff who knowingly and voluntarily enters into or participates in a risky activity that results in injury. A defense in which the defendant must prove that (1) the plaintiff knew and appreciated the risk and (2) the plaintiff voluntarily assumed the risk

Attachment The creditor has an enforceable security interest against the debtor and can satisfy the debt out of the designated collateral.

attempt to commit a crime When a crime is attempted but not completed.

attestation The action of a will being witnessed by two or three objective and competent people.

attorney-client privilege A rule that says a client can tell his or her lawyer anything about the case without fear that the attorney will be called as a witness against the client.

attribution procedure A procedure using codes, algorithms, identifying words or numbers, encryption, callback, or other acknowledgment to verify an authentication of a record.

at-will employees Employees who do not have employment contracts.

at-will LLC An LLC that has no specified term of duration.

auction with reserve Unless expressly stated otherwise, an auction is an auction with reserve; that is, the seller retains the right to refuse the highest bid and withdraw the goods from sale.

auction without reserve An auction in which the seller expressly gives up his or her right to withdraw the goods from sale and must accept the highest bid.

audit The verification of a company's books and records pursuant to federal securities laws, state laws, and stock exchange rules that must be performed by an independent CPA.

authenticate Signing the contract or executing an electronic symbol, sound, or message attached to, included in, or linked with the record.

authorized shares The number of shares provided for in the articles of incorporation.

automatic stay The result of the filing of a voluntary or involuntary petition; the suspension of certain actions by creditors against the debtor or the debtor's property.

backward vertical merger A vertical merger in which the customer acquires the supplier.

bailee A holder of goods who is not a seller or a buyer (e.g., a warehouse or common carrier). A holder of goods who is not a seller or a buyer (e.g., a warehouse).

bailee's rights Depending on the type of bailment, bailees may have the right to (1) exclusive possession of the bailed property, (2) use of the bailed property, and (3) compensation for work done or services provided.

bailment A transaction where an owner transfers his or her personal property to another to be held, stored, delivered, or for some other purpose. Title to the property does not transfer.

bailment at will A bailment without a fixed term; can be terminated at any time by either party.

bailment for a fixed term A bailment that terminates at the end of the term or sooner by mutual consent of the parties.

bailment for the sole benefit of the bailee A gratuitous bailment that benefits only the bailee. The bailee owes a duty of utmost care to protect the bailed property.

bailment for the sole benefit of the bailor A gratuitous bailment that benefits only the bailor. The bailee owes only a duty of slight care to protect the bailed property.

bailor The owner of property in a bailment.

bait and switch A type of deceptive advertising that occurs when a seller advertises the availability of a low-cost discounted item but then pressures the buyer into purchasing more expensive merchandise.

bank check A certified check, a cashier's check, or a traveler's check, the payment for which the bank is solely or primarily liable.

Bankruptcy Code The name given to the Bankruptcy Reform Act of 1978, as amended.

bankruptcy estate An estate created upon the commencement of a Chapter 7 proceeding that includes all the debtor's legal and equitable interests in real, personal, tangible, and intangible property, wherever located, that exist when the petition is filed, minus exempt property.

bargained-for exchange Exchange that parties engage in that leads to an enforceable contract.

battery Unauthorized and harmful or offensive physical contact with another person. Direct physical contact is not necessary.

bearer paper Bearer paper is negotiated by delivery; indorsement is not necessary.

beneficiary A person or organization designated in the will that receives all or a portion of the testator's property at the time of the testator's death. The person who is to receive the life insurance proceeds when the insured dies. Person for whose benefit a trust is created.

bequest A gift of personal property by will. Also known as a legacy.

bilateral contract A contract entered into by way of exchange of promises of the parties; "a promise for a promise."

bill of lading A document of title that is issued by a carrier when goods are received for transportation.

blank indorsement An indorsement that does not specify a particular indorsee. It creates bearer paper.

board of directors A panel of decision makers, the members of which are elected by the shareholders.

bona fide occupational qualification (BFOQ) Employment discrimination based on a protected class (other than race or color) is lawful if it is job related and a business necessity. This exception is narrowly interpreted by the courts.

bond A long-term debt security that is secured by some form of collateral.

breach Failure of a party to perform an obligation in a sales or lease contract.

breach of contract If a contracting party fails to perform an absolute duty owed under a contract.

breach of the duty of care A failure to exercise care or to act as a reasonable person would act.

bribery When one person gives another person money, property, favors, or anything else of value for a favor in return. Often referred to as a payoff or "kickback."

building A structure constructed on land.

building codes State and local statutes that impose specific standards on property owners to maintain and repair leased premises.

burglary Taking personal property from another's home, office, commercial, or other type of building.

business brief Laws cannot be written in advance to anticipate every dispute that could arise in the future. Therefore, general principles are developed to be applied by courts and juries to individual disputes. This flexibility in the law leads to some uncertainty in predicting results of lawsuits.

business judgment rule A rule that protects the decisions of the board of directors, who act on an informed basis, in good faith, and in the honest belief that the action taken was in the best interests of the corporation and its shareholders. A rule that says directors and officers are not liable to the corporation or its shareholders for honest mistakes of judgement.

buyer in the ordinary course of business A person who in good faith and without knowledge of another's ownership or security interest in goods buys the goods in the ordinary course of business from a person in the business of selling goods of that kind [UCC 1–201(9)].

bylaws A detailed set of rules adopted by the board of directors after the corporation is incorporated that contains provisions for managing the business and the affairs of the corporation.

cancellation The termination of a contract by a contracting party upon the material breach of the contract by the other party. A buyer or lessee may cancel a sales or lease contract if the seller or lessor fails to deliver conforming goods or repudiates the contract or if the buyer or lessee rightfully rejects the goods or justifiably revokes acceptance of the goods.

case brief A summary of each of the following items of a case: 1. Case name and citation 2. Key facts 3. Issue presented 4. Holding of the court 5. Court's reasoning.

cashier's check A check issued by a bank where the customer has paid the bank the amount of the check and a fee. The bank guarantees the payment of the check.

causation A person who commits a negligent act is not liable unless his or her act was the cause of the plaintiff's injuries. The two types of causation that must be proven are (1) causation in fact (actual cause) and (2) proximate cause (legal cause).

causation in fact or actual cause The actual cause of negligence. A person who commits a negligent act is not liable unless causation in fact can be proven.

caveat emptor "Let the buyer beware," the traditional guideline of sales transactions.

certificate of amendment A document that keeps the certificate of limited partnership current.

certificate of authority Formal document that must be issued by the secretary of state of a state before a foreign LLC may conduct business in that state.

certificate of deposit (CD) A two-party negotiable instrument that is a special form of note created when a depositor deposits money at a financial institution in exchange for the institution's promise to pay back the amount of the deposit plus an agreed-upon rate of interest upon the expiration of a set time period agreed upon by the parties.

certificate of interest Document that evidences a member's ownership interest in an LLC.

certificate of limited partnership A document that two or more persons must execute and sign that makes the limited partnership legal and binding.

certificate of partnership A document that a partnership must file with the appropriate state government agency in some states to acknowledge that the partnership exists.

certificate of registration A document permitting a foreign limited partnership to transact business in a foreign state.

certified check A type of check where a bank agrees in advance (certifies) to accept the check when it is presented for payment.

certified public accountant (CPA) An accountant who has met certain educational requirements, has passed the CPA examination, and has had a certain number of years of audit experience.

chain of distribution All manufacturers, distributors, wholesalers, retailers, lessors, and subcomponent manufacturers involved in a transaction.

chain-style franchise The franchisor licenses the franchisee to make and sell its products or distribute services to the public from a retail outlet serving an exclusive territory.

changing conditions defense A price discrimination defense that claims prices were lowered in response to changing conditions in the market for or the marketability of the goods.

Chapter 7 liquidation bankruptcy The most familiar form of bankruptcy; the debtor's nonexempt property is sold for cash, the cash is distributed to the creditors, and any unpaid debts are discharged.

Chapter 11 A bankruptcy method that allows reorganization of the debtor's financial affairs under the supervision of the Bankruptcy Court.

Chapter 13 A rehabilitation form of bankruptcy that permits the courts to supervise the debtor's plan for the payment of unpaid debts by installments.

charging order A document that the court issues against the debtor-partner's partnership interest in order to satisfy a debt.

check An order by the drawer to the drawee bank to pay a specified sum of money from the drawer's checking account to the named payee (or holder). A distinct form of draft drawn on a financial institution and payable on demand.

choice of forum clause Clause in an international contract that designates which nation's court has jurisdiction to hear a case arising out of the contract. Also known as a forum-selection clause.

choice of law clause Clause in an international contract that designates which nation's laws will be applied in deciding a dispute.

closely held corporation A corporation owned by one or a few shareholders.

closing The finalization of a real estate sales transaction that passes title to the property from the seller to the buyer.

codicil A separate document that must be executed to amend a will. It must be executed with the same formalities as a will.

C.O.D. shipment A type of shipment contract where the buyer agrees to pay the shipper cash upon the delivery of the goods.

collateral Security against repayment of the note that lenders sometimes require; can be a car, a house, or other property. The property that is subject to the security interest.

collateral contract A promise where one person agrees to answer for the debts or duties of another person.

collecting bank The depository bank and other banks in the collection process (other than the payor bank).

collective bargaining The act of negotiating contract terms between an employer and the members of a union.

collective bargaining agreement The resulting contract from a collective bargaining procedure.

collision insurance Insurance that a car owner purchases to insure his or her car against risk of loss or damage.

coming and going rule A rule that says a principal is generally not liable for injuries caused by its agents and employees while they are on their way to or from work.

Commerce Clause A clause of the U.S. Constitution that grants Congress the power "to regulate commerce with foreign nations, and among the several states, and with Indian tribes."

commercial impracticability Nonperformance that is excused if an extreme or unexpected development or expense makes it impractical for the promisor to perform.

commercial speech Speech used by businesses, such as advertising. It is subject to time, place, and manner restrictions.

common carrier A firm that offers transportation services to the general public.

common law Developed by judges who issued their opinions when deciding a case. The principles announced in these cases became precedent for later judges deciding similar cases.

common law of contracts Contract law developed primarily by state courts.

common stock A type of equity security that represents the residual value of the corporation.

common stock certificate A document that represents the common shareholder's investment in the corporation.

common stockholder A person who owns common stock.

comparative negligence A doctrine under which damages are apportioned according to fault. A doctrine that applies to strict liability actions that says a plaintiff who is contributorily negligent for his or her injuries is responsible for a proportional share of the damages.

compensatory damages An award of money intended to compensate a nonbreaching party for the loss of the bargain; they place the nonbreaching party in the same position as if the contract had been fully performed by restoring the "benefit of the bargain." Damages that are generally equal to the difference between the value of the goods as warranted and the actual value of the goods accepted at the time and place of acceptance.

competent party's duty of restitution If a minor has transferred money, property, or other valuables to the competent party before disaffirming the contract, that party must place the minor back into status quo.

complaint The document the plaintiff files with the court and serves on the defendant to initiate a lawsuit.

complete performance Occurs when a party to a contract renders performance exactly as required by the contract; discharges that party's obligations under the contract.

comprehensive insurance A form of property insurance that insures an automobile from loss or damage from causes other than collision.

conciliation A form of mediation in which the parties choose an interested third party to act as the mediator.

concurrent condition A condition that exists when the parties to a contract must render performance simultaneously; each party's absolute duty to perform is conditioned on the other party's absolute duty to perform.

concurrent jurisdiction Jurisdiction shared by two or more courts.

condition A qualification of a promise that becomes a covenant if it is met. There are three types of conditions: conditions precedent, conditions subsequent, and concurrent conditions.

condition precedent based on satisfaction Clause in a contract that reserves the right to a party to pay for the items or services contracted for only if they meet his or her satisfaction.

condition subsequent A condition, if it occurs or doesn't occur, that automatically excuses the performance of an existing contractual duty to perform.

condominium A common form of ownership in a multiple-dwelling building where the purchaser has title to the individual unit and owns the common areas as a tenant in common with the other condominium owners.

confirmation The bankruptcy court's approval of a plan of reorganization.

confusion Occurs if two or more persons commingle fungible goods; title is then acquired by confusion.

conglomerate merger A merger that does not fit into any other category; a merger between firms in totally unrelated businesses.

consequential damages Foreseeable damages that arise from circumstances outside the contract. To be liable for these damages, the breaching party must know or have reason to know that the breach will cause special damages to the other party.

consideration Something of legal value given in exchange for a promise.

consignee The person to whom the bailed goods are to be delivered.

consignment An arrangement where a seller (the consignor) delivers goods to a buyer (the consignee) for sale.

consignor The person shipping the goods. The bailor.

Consolidated Omnibus Budget Reconciliation Act (COBRA) Federal law that permits employees and their beneficiaries to continue their group health insurance after an employee's employment has ended.

consolidation The act of a court to combine two or more separate lawsuits into one lawsuit. Occurs when two or more corporations combine to form an entirely new corporation.

conspicuous A requirement that warranty disclaimers be noticeable to the average person.

Constitution of the United States of America The supreme law of the United States.

constructive trust An equitable trust that is imposed by law to avoid fraud, unjust enrichment, and injustice.

consumer expectation test A test to determine merchantability based on what the average consumer would expect to find in food products.

Consumer Leasing Act (CLA) An amendment to the TILA that extends the TILA's coverage to lease terms in consumer leases.

Consumer Product Safety Act (CPSA) A federal statute that regulates potentially dangerous consumer products and created the Consumer Product Safety Commission.

Consumer Product Safety Commission (CPSC) An independent federal regulatory agency empowered to (1) adopt rules and regulations to interpret and enforce the Consumer Product Safety Act, (2) conduct research on safety, and (3) collect data regarding injuries.

consumer protection laws Federal and state statutes and regulations that promote product safety and prohibit abusive, unfair, and deceptive business practices.

contracts contrary to public policy Contracts that have a negative impact on society or that interfere with the public's safety and welfare.

contributory negligence A doctrine that says a plaintiff who is partially at fault for his or her own injury cannot recover against the negligent defendant. A defense that says a person who is injured by a defective product but has been negligent and has contributed to his or her own injuries cannot recover from the defendant.

controlling shareholder A shareholder that owns a sufficient number of shares to control the corporation effectively.

convenant of good faith and fair dealing Under this implied covenant, the parties to a contract not only are held to the express terms of the contract but are also required to act in "good faith" and deal fairly in all respects in obtaining the objective of the contract.

Convention Treaty that is sponsored by an international organization.

conversion of personal property A tort that deprives a true owner of the use and enjoyment of his or her personal property by taking over such property and exercising ownership rights over it.

cooling-off period Requires a union to give an employer at least 60 days' notice before a strike can commence.

cooperative A form of co-ownership of a multiple-dwelling building where a corporation owns the building and the residents own shares in the corporation.

co-ownership When two or more persons own a piece of real property. Also called concurrent ownership.

copyright infringement When a party copies a substantial and material part of the plaintiff's copyrighted work without permission. A copyright holder may recover damages and other remedies against the infringer.

Copyright Revision Act of 1976 Federal statute that (1) establishes the requirements for obtaining a copyright and (2) protects copyrighted works from infringement.

corporate citizenship A theory of responsibility that says a business has a responsibility to do good.

corporate seal A design containing the name of the corporation and the date of incorporation that is imprinted by the corporate secretary using a metal stamp on certain legal documents.

corporation A fictitious legal entity that is created according to statutory requirements.

corporations codes State statutes that regulate the formation, operation, and dissolution of corporations.

cost justification defense A defense in Section 2(a) action that provides that a seller's price discrimination is not unlawful if the price differential is due to "differences in the cost of manufacture, sale, or delivery" of the product.

counteroffer A response by an offeree that contains terms and conditions different from or in addition to those of the offer. A counteroffer terminates an offer.

Court of Appeals for the Federal Circuit A court of appeals in Washington, DC, that has special appellate jurisdiction to review the decisions of the Claims Court, the Patent and Trademark Office, and the Court of International Trade.

Court of Chancery Court that granted relief based on fairness. Also called equity court.

covenant An unconditional promise to perform.

covenant of good faith and fair dealing Under this implied covenant, the parties to a contract not only are held to the express terms of the contract but also are required to act in "good faith" and deal fairly in all respects in obtaining the objective of the contract.

covenant of quiet enjoyment A covenant that says a landlord may not interfere with the tenant's quiet and peaceful possession, use, and enjoyment of the leased premises.

cover Right of a buyer or lessee to purchase or lease substitute goods if a seller or lessor fails to make delivery of the goods or repudiates the contract or if the buyer or lessee rightfully rejects the goods or justifiably revokes their acceptance. The licensee's right to engage in a commercially reasonable substitute transaction after the licensor has breached the contract.

cram down method A method of confirmation of a plan of reorganization where the court forces an impaired class to participate in the plan of reorganization.

crashworthiness doctrine A doctrine that says automobile manufacturers are under a duty to design automobiles so they take into account the possibility of harm from a person's body striking something inside the automobile in the case of a car accident.

credit report Information about a person's credit history that can be secured from a credit bureau.

creditor The lender in a credit transaction.

creditor beneficiary Original creditor who becomes a beneficiary under the debtor's new contract with another party.

creditor beneficiary contract A contract that arises in the following situation: (1) a debtor borrows money, (2) the debtor signs an agreement to pay back the money plus interest, (3) the debtor sells the item to a third party before the loan is paid off, and (4) the third party promises the debtor that he or she will pay the remainder of the loan to the creditor.

creditor–debtor relationship Created when a customer deposits money into the bank; the customer is the creditor and the bank is the debtor.

creditors' committee The creditors holding the seven largest unsecured claims are usually appointed to the creditors' committee. Representatives of the committee appear at Bankruptcy Court hearings, participate in the negotiation of a plan of reorganization, assert objections to proposed plans and so on.

crime A crime is a violation of a statute for which the government imposes a punishment.

criminal conspiracy When two or more persons enter into an agreement to commit a crime and an overt act is taken to further the crime.

criminal fraud Obtaining title to property through deception or trickery. Also known as false pretenses or deceit.

critical legal thinking The process of specifying the issue presented by a case, identifying the key facts in the case and applicable law, and then applying the law to the facts to come to a conclusion that answers the issue presented.

cross-complaint Filed by the defendant against the plaintiff to seek damages or some other remedy.

crossover worker A person who does not honor a strike who either (1) chooses not to strike or (2) returns to work after joining the strikers for a time.

crown jewel A valuable asset of the target corporation's that the tender offeror particularly wants to acquire in the tender offer.

cruel and unusual punishment A clause of the Eighth Amendment that protects criminal defendants from torture or other abusive punishment.

cumulative voting A shareholder can accumulate all of his or her votes and vote them all for one candidate or split them among several candidates.

cure An opportunity to repair or replace defective or nonconforming goods.

custom The second source of international law, created through consistent, recurring practices between two or more nations over a period of time that have become recognized as binding.

damages A buyer or lessee may recover damages from a seller or lessor who fails to deliver the goods or repudiates the contract; damages are measured as the difference between the contract price (or original rent) and the market price (or rent) at the time the buyer or lessee learned of the breach.

damages for accepted nonconforming goods A buyer or lessee may accept nonconforming goods and recover the damages caused by the breach from the seller or lessor or deduct the damages from any part of the purchase price or rent still due under the contract.

danger invites rescue doctrine Doctrine that provides that a rescuer who is injured while going to someone's rescue can sue the person who caused the dangerous situation.

debenture A long-term unsecured debt instrument that is based on the corporation's general credit standing.

debt collector An agent who collects debts for other parties.

debt securities Securities that establish a debtor-creditor relationship in which the corporation borrows money from the investor to whom the debt security is issued.

debtor The borrower in a credit transaction.

debtor-in-possession A debtor who is left in place to operate the business during the reorganization proceeding.

declaration of duties If the delegatee has not assumed the duties under a contract, the delegatee is not legally liable to the obligee for nonperformance.

decree of judicial dissolution A decree of dissolution that is granted to a partner whenever it is not reasonably practical to carry on the business in conformity with the limited partnership agreement.

deed A writing that describes a person's ownership interest in a piece of real property.

deed of trust An instrument that gives the creditor a security interest in the debtor's property that is pledged as collateral.

defamation of character False statement(s) made by one person about another. In court, the plaintiff must prove that (1) the defendant made an untrue statement of fact about the plaintiff and (2) the statement was intentionally or accidentally published to a third party.

default Failure to make scheduled payments when due, bankruptcy of the debtor, breach of the warranty of ownership as to the collateral, and other events defined by the parties to constitute default.

defect Something wrong, inadequate, or improper in manufacture, design, packaging, warning, or safety measures of a product.

defect in design A defect that occurs when a product is improperly designed.

defect in manufacture A defect that occurs when the manufacturer fails to (1) properly assemble a product, (2) properly test a product, or (3) adequately check the quality of the product.

defect in packaging A defect that occurs when a product has been placed in packaging that is insufficiently tamperproof.

defective formation Occurs when (1) a certificate of limited partnership is not properly filed, (2) there are defects in a certificate that is filed, or (3) some other statutory requirement for the creation of a limited partnership is not met.

deferred posting rule A rule that allows banks to fix an afternoon hour of 2:00 P.M. or later as a cutoff hour for the purpose of processing items.

deficiency judgment Judgment of a court that permits a secured lender to recover other property or income from a defaulting debtor if the collateral is insufficient to repay the unpaid loan. A judgment that allows a secured creditor to successfully bring a separate legal action to recover a deficiency from the debtor entitles the secured creditor to recover the amount of the judgment from the debtor's other property.

delegatee The party to whom the duty has been transferred.

delegation doctrine A doctrine that says when an administrative agency is created, it is delegated certain powers; the agency can only use those legislative, judicial, and executive powers that are delegated to it.

delegation of duties A transfer of contractual duties by the obligor to another party for performance.

delegator The obligor who transferred his or her duty.

demand instrument An instrument payable on demand.

demand note A note payable on demand.

deponent Party who gives his or her deposition.

deposition Oral testimony given by a party or witness prior to trial. The testimony is given under oath and is transcribed.

depository bank The bank where the payee or holder has an account.

derivative lawsuit A lawsuit a shareholder brings against an offending party on behalf of the corporation when the corporation fails to bring the lawsuit.

destination contract A sales contract that requires the seller to deliver conforming goods to a specific destination. The seller bears the risk of loss during transportation. A contract that requires the seller to deliver the goods either to the buyer's place of business or to another destination specified in the sales contract.

devise A gift of real estate by will.

direct lawsuit A lawsuit that a shareholder can bring against the corporation to enforce his or her personal rights as a shareholder.

disability insurance Insurance that provides a monthly income to an insured who is disabled and cannot work.

disaffirmance The act of a minor to rescind a contract under the infancy doctrine. Disaffirmance may be done orally, in writing, or by the minor's conduct.

discharge Actions or events that relieve certain parties from liability on negotiable instruments. There are three methods of discharge: (1) payment of the instrument; (2) cancellation; and (3) impairment of the right of recourse. The termination of the legal duty of a debtor to pay debts that remain unpaid upon the completion of a bankruptcy proceeding. Creditors' claims that are not included in a Chapter 11 reorganization are discharged. A discharge is granted to a debtor in a Chapter 13 consumer debt adjustment bankruptcy only after all the payments under the plan are completed by the debtor.

discharge in bankruptcy A real defense against the enforcement of a negotiable instrument; bankruptcy law is intended to relieve debtors of burdensome debts, including negotiable instruments.

disclosure statement A statement that must contain adequate information about the proposed plan of reorganization that is supplied to the creditors and equity holders.

discovery A legal process during which both parties engage in various activities to discover facts of the case from the other party and witnesses prior to trial.

dishonored Occurs when an instrument has been presented for payment and payment has been refused.

disparate impact discrimination Occurs when an employer discriminates against an entire protected class. An example would be where a facially neutral employment practice or rule causes an adverse impact on a protected class.

disparate treatment discrimination Occurs when an employer discriminates against a specific individual because of his or her race, color, national origin, sex, or religion.

disposition of collateral If a secured creditor repossesses collateral upon a debtor's default, he or she may sell, lease, or otherwise dispose of it in a commercially reasonable manner.

disposition of goods A seller or lessor who is in possession of goods at the time the buyer or lessee breaches or repudiates the contract may in good faith resell, release, or otherwise dispose of the goods in a commercially reasonable manner and recover damages, including incidental damages, from the buyer or lessee.

dispute settlement body A board comprised of one representative from each WTO member nation that reviews panel reports.

dissension When an individual director opposes the action taken by the majority of the board of directors.

dissenting shareholder appraisal rights Shareholders who object to a proposed merger, share exchange, or sale or lease of all or substantially all of the property of a corporation have a right to have their shares valued by the court and receive cash payment of this value from the corporation.

dissolution "The change in the relation of the partners caused by any partner ceasing to be associated in the carrying on of the business" [UPA § 29].

distinctive A brand name that is unique and fabricated.

distribution of assets Upon the winding-up of a dissolved partnership, the assets of the partnership are distributed in the following order [UPA § 40(b)]: (1) Creditors (except partners who are creditors), (2) Creditor-partners, (3) Capital contributions, (4) Profits.

distribution of property Nonexempt property of the bankruptcy estate must be distributed to the debtor's secured and unsecured creditors pursuant to the statutory priority established by the Bankruptcy Code.

distributional interest A member's ownership interest in an LLC that entitles the member to receive distributions of money and property from the LLC. The ownership interest that a member has in an LLC.

distributorship franchise The franchisor manufactures a product and licenses a retail franchisee to distribute the product to the public.

diversity of citizenship A case between (1) citizens of different states, (2) a citizen of a state and a citizen or subject of a foreign country, and (3) a citizen of a state and a foreign country where a foreign country is the plaintiff.

dividend Distribution of profits of the corporation to shareholders.

division of markets When competitors agree that each will serve only a designated portion of the market.

doctrine of sovereign immunity States that countries are granted immunity from suits in courts of other countries.

doctrine of strict liability in tort A tort doctrine that makes manufacturers, distributors, wholesalers, retailers, and others in the chain of distribution of a defective product liable for the damages caused by the defect irrespective of fault.

document of title An actual piece of paper, such as warehouse receipt or bill of lading, that is required in some transactions of pick up and delivery. A negotiable instrument developed to represent the interests of the different parties in a transaction that uses storage or transportation between the parties.

domain name A unique name that identifies an individual's or company's Web site.

domestic corporation A corporation in the state in which it was formed.

domestic limited partnership A limited partnership in the state in which it was formed.

domestic LLC An LLC in the state in which it is organized.

donee A person who receives a gift.

donee beneficiary The third party on whom the benefit is to be conferred.

donee beneficiary contract A contract entered into with the intent to confer a benefit or gift on an intended third party.

donor A person who gives a gift.

double jeopardy clause A clause of the Fifth Amendment that protects persons from being tried twice for the same crime.

draft A three-party instrument that is an unconditional written order by one party that orders the second party to pay money to a third party.

Dram Shop Act Statute that makes taverns and bartenders liable for injuries caused to or by patrons who are served too much alcohol.

drawee of a check The bank where the drawer has his or her account.

drawee of a draft The party who must pay the money stated in the draft. Also called the acceptor of a draft.

drawer of a check The checking account holder and writer of the check.

drawer of a draft The party who writes the order for a draft.

dual-purpose mission An errand or other act that a principal requests of an agent while the agent is on his or her own personal business.

due diligence defense A defense to a Section 11 action that, if proven, makes the defendant not liable.

Due Process Clause A clause that provides that no person shall be deprived of "life, liberty, or property" without due process of the law.

duress Occurs where one party threatens to do a wrongful act unless the other party enters into a contract.

duty not to willfully or wantonly injure The duty an owner owes a trespasser to prevent intentional injury or harm to the trespasser when the trespasser is on his or her premises.

duty of accountability A duty that an agent owes to maintain an accurate accounting of all transactions undertaken on the principal's behalf.

duty of care The obligation we all owe each other not to cause any unreasonable harm or risk of harm. The obligation partners owe to use the same level of care and skill that a reasonable person in the same position would use in the same circumstances. A breach of the duty of care is negligence. A duty owed by a member of a member-managed LLC and a manager of a manager-managed LLC to not engage in (1) a known violation of law, (2) intentional conduct, (3) reckless conduct, or (4) grossly negligent conduct that injures the LLC. A duty that corporate directors and officers have to use care and diligence when acting on behalf of the corporation.

duty of loyalty A duty owed by a member of a member-managed LLC and a manager of a manager-managed LLC to be honest in his or her dealings with the LLC and to not act adversely to the interests of the LLC. A duty that a partner owes not to act adversely to the interests of the partnership. A duty that directors and officers have not to act adversely to the interests of the corporation and to subordinate their personal interests to those of the corporation and its shareholders.

duty of notification An agent's duty to notify the principal of information he or she learns from a third party or other source that is important to the principal.

duty of obedience A duty that partners must adhere to the provisions of the partnership agreement and the decisions of the partnership. A duty that directors and officers of a corporation have to act within the authority conferred upon them by the state corporation statute, the articles of incorporation, the corporate bylaws, and the resolutions adopted by the board of directors.

duty of ordinary care The duty an owner owes an invitee or a licensee to prevent injury or harm when the invitee or licensee steps on the owner's premises. Collecting banks are required to exercise ordinary care in presenting and sending checks for collection.

duty of performance An agent's duty to a principal that includes (1) performing the lawful duties expressed in the contract and (2) meeting the standards of reasonable care, skill, and diligence implicit in all contracts.

duty of reasonable care The duty that a reasonable bailee in like circumstances would owe to protect the bailed property.

duty of slight care A duty not to be grossly negligent in caring for something in one's responsibility.

duty of strict liability A duty that common carriers owe that says if the goods are lost, damaged, destroyed, or stolen, the common carrier is liable even if it was not at fault for the loss.

duty of utmost care A duty of care that goes beyond ordinary care that says common carriers and innkeepers have a responsibility to provide security to their passengers or guests.

duty to compensate A duty that a principal owes to pay an agreed-upon amount to the agent either upon the completion of the agency or at some other mutually agreeable time.

duty to cooperate A duty that a principal owes to cooperate with and assist the agent in the performance of the agent's duties and the accomplishment of the agency.

duty to indemnify A duty that a principal owes to protect the agent for losses the agent suffered during the agency because of the principal's misconduct.

duty to inform A duty a partner owes to inform his or her co-partners of all information he or she possesses that is relevant to the affairs of the partnership.

duty to reimburse A duty that a principal owes to repay money to the agent if the agent spent his or her own money during the agency on the principal's behalf.

easement A right to use someone else's land without owning or leasing it. A given or required right to make limited use of someone else's land without owning or leasing it.

easement appurtenant A situation created when the owner of one piece of land is given an easement over an adjacent piece of land.

easement in gross An easement that authorizes a person who does not own adjacent land to use another's land.

e-commerce The sale of goods and services by computer over the Internet.

economic duress Occurs when one party to a contract refuses to perform his or her contractual duties unless the other party pays an increased price, enters into a second contract with the threatening party, or undertakes a similar action.

electronic mail (e-mail) Electronic written communication between individuals using computers connected to the Internet.

elements of a bailment The following three elements are necessary to create a bailment: (1) personal property, (2) delivery of possession, and (3) a bailment agreement.

emancipation When a minor voluntarily leaves home and lives apart from his or her parents.

embezzlement The fraudulent conversion of property by a person to whom that property was entrusted.

eminent domain Power of the government to acquire private property for public purposes. The taking of private property by the government for public use, provided just compensation is paid to the private property holder.

Employee Retirement Income Security Act (ERISA) A federal act designed to prevent fraud and other abuses associated with private pension funds.

employer-employee relationship A relationship that results when an employer hires an employee to perform some form of physical service.

employer lockout Act of the employer to prevent employees from entering the work premises when the employer reasonably anticipates a strike.

employment relationships (1) Employer–employee, (2) principal–agent, and (3) principal–independent contractor.

endorsement An addition to an insurance policy that modifies it.

engagement A formal entrance into a contract between a client and an accountant.

entity theory A theory that holds that partnerships are separate legal entities that can hold title to personal and real property, transact business in the partnership name, sue in the partnership name, and the like.

entrepreneur A person who forms and operates a new business either by him- or herself or with others.

entrustment rule: buyer in the ordinary course of business A person who in good faith and without knowledge that the sale violates the ownership or security interests of a third party buys the goods in the ordinary course of business from a person in the business of selling goods of that kind. A buyer in the ordinary course of business takes the goods free of any third-party security interest in the goods.

enumerated powers Certain powers delegated to the federal government by the states.

Environmental Protection Agency (EPA) An administrative agency created by Congress in 1970 to coordinate the implementation and enforcement of the federal environmental protection laws.

Equal Access to Justice Act An act that was enacted to protect persons from harassment by federal administrative agencies.

Equal Credit Opportunity Act (ECOA) A federal statute that prohibits discrimination in the extension of credit based on sex, marital status, race, color, national origin, religion, age, or receipt of income from public assistance programs.

equal dignity rule A rule that says that agents' contracts to sell property covered by the Statute of Frauds must be in writing to be enforceable.

Equal Employment Opportunity Commission (EEOC) The federal administrative agency responsible for enforcing most federal antidiscrimination laws.

equal opportunity in employment The right of all employees and job applicants (1) to be treated without discrimination and (2) to be able to sue employers if they are discriminated against.

Equal Pay Act of 1963 Protects both sexes from pay discrimination based on sex; extends to jobs that require equal skill, equal effort, equal responsibility, and similar working conditions.

Equal Protection Clause A clause that provides that a state cannot "deny to any person within its jurisdiction the equal protection of the laws."

equity A doctrine that permits judges to make decisions based on fairness, equality, moral rights, and natural law.

equity securities Representation of ownership rights to the corporation. Also called stocks.

Establishment Clause A clause to the First Amendment that prohibits the government from either establishing a state religion or promoting one religion over another.

estate Ownership rights in real property; the bundle of legal rights that the owner has to possess, use, and enjoy the property.

estate pour autre vie A life estate measured in the life of a third party.

ethical fundamentalism When a person looks to an outside source for ethical rules or commands.

ethical relativism A moral theory that holds that individuals must decide what is ethical based on their own feelings as to what is right or wrong.

ethics A set of moral principles or values that governs the conduct of an individual or a group.

European Court of Justice The Judicial branch of the European Union, located in Luxembourg. It has jurisdiction to enforce European Union law.

European Union (Common Market) Comprises many countries of Western Europe; created to promote peace and security plus economic, social, and cultural development.

exclusionary rule A rule that says evidence obtained from an unreasonable search and seizure can generally be prohibited from introduction at a trial or administrative proceeding against the person searched.

exclusive agency contract A contract a principal and agent enter into that says the principal cannot employ any agent other than the exclusive agent.

exclusive jurisdiction Jurisdiction held by only one court.

exclusive license A license that grants the licensee exclusive rights to use informational rights for a specified duration.

exculpatory clause A contractual provision that relieves one (or both) of the parties to the contract from tort liability for ordinary negligence.

executed contract A contract that has been fully performed on both sides; a completed contract.

executive branch The part of the government that consists of the President and Vice President.

executive order An order issued by a member of the executive branch of the government.

executive powers Powers that administrative agencies are granted, such as the investigation and prosecution of possible violations of statutes, administrative rules, and administrative orders.

executory contract A contract that has not been fully performed. With court approval, executory contracts may be rejected by a debtor in bankruptcy.

exempt property Property that may be retained by the debtor pursuant to federal or state law; debtor's property that does not become part of the bankruptcy estate.

express agency An agency that occurs when a principal and an agent expressly agree to enter into an agency agreement with each other.

express authorization A stipulation in the offer that says the acceptance must be by a specified means of communication.

express contract An agreement that is expressed in written or oral words.

express partnership General partnership created by words, either verbal or written.

express powers Powers given to a corporation by (1) the U.S. Constitution, (2) state constitutions, (3) federal statutes, (4) state statutes, (5) articles of incorporation, (6) bylaws, and (7) resolutions of the board of directors.

express trust A trust created voluntarily by the settlor.

express warranty Any affirmation of fact or promise by the licensor about the quality of its software or information. A warranty that is created when a seller or lessor makes an affirmation that the goods he or she is selling or leasing meet certain standards of quality, description, performance, or condition.

extortion Threat to expose something about another person unless that other person gives money or property. Often referred to as "blackmail."

extradition Sending a person back to a country for criminal prosecution.

extreme duress Extreme duress, but not ordinary duress, is a real defense against enforcement of a negotiable instrument.

failure to provide adequate instructions A defect that occurs when a manufacturer does not provide detailed directions for safe assembly and use of a product.

failure to warn A defect that occurs when a manufacturer does not place a warning on the packaging of products that could cause injury if the danger is unknown.

Fair Credit and Charge Card Disclosure Act of 1988 An amendment to the TILA that requires disclosure of certain credit terms on credit- and charge-card solicitations and applications.

Fair Credit Reporting Act (FCRA) An amendment to the TILA that protects customers who are subjects of a credit report by setting out guidelines for credit bureaus.

Fair Debt Collection Practices Act (FDCPA) An act enacted in 1977 that protects consumer-debtors from abusive, deceptive, and unfair practices used by debt collectors.

Fair Labor Standards Act (FLSA) A federal act enacted in 1938 to protect workers; prohibits child labor and establishes minimum wage and overtime pay requirements.

Fair Packaging and Labeling Act A federal statute that requires the labels on consumer goods to identify the product; the manufacturer, processor, or packager of the product and its address; the net quantity of the contents of the package; and the quantity of each serving.

fair price rule A rule that says any increase in price paid for shares tendered must be offered to all shareholders, even those who have previously tendered their shares.

fair use doctrine A doctrine that permits certain limited use of a copyright by someone other than the copyright holder without the permission of the copyright holder.

false imprisonment The intentional confinement or restraint of another person without authority or justification and without that person's consent.

federal administrative agencies Administrative agencies that are part of the executive or legislative branch of government.

Federal Insurance Contributions Act (FICA) A federal act that says employees and employers must make contributions into the Social Security fund.

Federal Patent Statute of 1952 Federal statute that establishes the requirements for obtaining a patent and protects patented inventions from infringement.

federal question A case arising under the U.S. Constitution, treaties, or federal statutes and regulations.

Federal Reserve System A system of 12 regional Federal Reserve banks that assist banks in the collection of checks.

Federal Trade Commission (FTC) Federal government agency empowered to enforce federal franchising rules. Federal administrative agency empowered to enforce the Federal Trade Commission Act and other federal consumer protection statutes.

Federal Unemployment Tax Act (FUTA) A federal act that requires employers to pay unemployment taxes; unemployment compensation is paid to workers who are temporarily unemployed.

federalism The U.S. form of government; the federal government and the 50 state governments share powers.

fee simple absolute A type of ownership of real property that grants the owner the fullest bundle of legal rights that a person can hold in real property.

fee simple defeasible A type of ownership of real property that grants the owner all the incidents of a fee simple absolute except that it may be taken away if a specified condition occurs or does not occur.

felony The most serious type of crime; inherently evil crime. Most crimes against the person and some business-related crimes are felonies.

fictitious payee rule A rule that says that a drawer or maker is liable on a forged or unauthorized indorsement of a fictitious payee.

fiduciary duty Duty of loyalty, honesty, integrity, trust, and confidence owed by directors and officers to their corporate employers. The duty the directors of a corporation owe to act carefully and honestly when acting on behalf of the corporation.

final order rule A rule that says the decision of an administrative agency must be final before judicial review can be sought.

final prospectus A final version of the prospectus that must be delivered by the issuer to the investor prior to or at the time of confirming a sale or sending a security to a purchaser.

final settlement Occurs when the payor bank (1) pays the check in cash, (2) settles for the check without having a right to revoke the settlement, or (3) fails to dishonor the check within certain statutory time periods.

finance lease A three-party transaction consisting of the lessor, the lessee, and the supplier.

financing statement A document filed by a secured creditor with the appropriate government office that constructively notifies the world of his or her security interest in personal property.

fixed amount A requirement of a negotiable instrument that ensures that the value of the instrument can be determined with certainty.

fixed amount of money A negotiable instrument must contain a promise or order to pay a fixed amount of money.

fixtures Goods that are affixed to real estate so as to become part thereof.

fixtures Personal property that is permanently affixed to the real property, such as built-in cabinets in a house.

floating lien A security interest in property that was not in the possession of the debtor when the security agreement was executed; includes after-acquired property, future advances, and sale proceeds.

Food and Drug Administration (FDA) Federal administrative agency that administers and enforces the federal Food, Drug, and Cosmetic Act (FDCA) and other federal consumer protection laws.

Food, Drug, and Cosmetic Act (FDCA) A federal statute enacted in 1938 that provides the basis for the regulation of much of the testing, manufacture, distribution, and sale of foods, drugs, cosmetics, and medicinal products.

Foreclosure Legal procedure by which a secured creditor causes the judicial sale of the secured real estate to pay a defaulted loan.

Foreign Commerce Clause Clause of the U.S. Constitution that vests Congress with the power "to regulate commerce with foreign nations."

foreign corporation A corporation in any state or jurisdiction other than the one in which it was formed.

foreign limited partnership A limited partnership in all other states than the one in which it was formed.

foreign LLC An LLC in any state other than the one in which it is organized.

Foreign Sovereign Immunities Act Exclusively governs suits against foreign nations that are brought in federal or state courts in the United States; codifies the principle of qualified or restricted immunity.

foreign substance test A test to determine merchantability based on foreign objects that are found in food.

foreseeability standard A rule that an accountant is liable for negligence to third parties who are foreseeable users of the client's financial statements. Provides the broadest standard for holding accountants liable to third parties for negligence.

forged indorsement The forged signature of a payee or holder on a negotiable instrument.

forged instrument A check with a forged drawer's signature on it.

forgery Fraudulently making or altering a written document that affects the legal liability of another person. A real defense against the enforcement of a negotiable instrument; the unauthorized signature of a maker, drawer, or indorser.

formal contract A contract that requires a special form or method of creation.

forum-selection clause Contract provision that designates a certain court to hear any dispute concerning nonperformance of the contract.

forward vertical merger A vertical merger in which the supplier acquires the customer.

four legals Four notices or actions that prevent the payment of a check if they are received by the payor bank before it has finished its process of posting the check for payment.

Fourteenth Amendment Amendment that was added to the U.S. Constitution in 1868. It contains the Due Process, Equal Protection, and Privileges and Immunities clauses.

franchise Established when one party licenses another party to use the franchisor's trade name, trademarks, commercial symbols, patents, copyrights, and other property in the distribution and selling of goods and services.

franchise agreement An agreement that the franchisor and the franchisee enter into that sets forth the terms and conditions of the franchise.

fraud by concealment Occurs when one party takes specific action to conceal a material fact from another party.

fraud in the inception Occurs if a person is deceived as to the nature of his or her act and does not know what he or she is signing. A real defense against the enforcement of a negotiable instrument; a person has been deceived into signing a negotiable instrument thinking that it is something else.

fraud in the inducement Occurs when the party knows what he or she is signing, but has been fraudulently induced to enter into the contract. A personal defense against the enforcement of a negotiable instrument; a wrongdoer makes a false statement to another person to lead that person to enter into a contract with the wrongdoer.

fraudulent transfer Occurs when (1) a debtor transfers property to a third person within one year before the filing of a petition in bankruptcy and (2) the transfer was made by the debtor with an intent to hinder, delay, or defraud creditors.

Free Exercise Clause A clause to the First Amendment that prohibits the government from interfering with the free exercise of religion in the United States.

Freedom of Information Act An act that was enacted to give the public access to documents in the possession of federal administrative agencies. There are many exceptions to disclosure.

freedom of speech The right to engage in oral, written, and symbolic speech protected by the First Amendment.

freehold estate An estate where the owner has a present possessory interest in the real property.

fresh start The goal of federal bankruptcy law: To discharge the debtor from burdensome debts and allow him or her to begin again.

frolic and detour When an agent does something during the course of his employment to further his own interests rather than the principal's.

frustration of purpose A doctrine which excuses the performance of contractual obligations if (1) the object or benefit of a contract is made worthless to a promisor, (2) both parties knew what the purpose was, and (3) the act that frustrated the purpose was unforeseeable.

FTC franchise rule A rule set out by the FTC that requires franchisors to make full presale disclosures to prospective franchisees.

future advances Personal property of the debtor that is designated as collateral for future loans from a line of credit.

future goods Goods not yet in existence (ungrown crops, unborn stock animals).

future interest The interest that the grantor retains for him- or herself or a third party.

gambling statutes Statutes that make certain forms of gambling illegal.

gap-filling rule A rule that says an open term can be "read into" a contract.

general duty A duty that an employer has to provide a work environment "free from recognized hazards that are causing or are likely to cause death or serious physical harm to his employees."

general gift Gift that does not identify the specific property from which the gift is to be made.

general partners Partners in a limited partnership who invest capital, manage the business, and are personally liable for partnership debts.

general partnership An association of two or more persons to carry on as co-owners of a business for profit [UPA § 6(1)].

general principles of law The third source of international law, consisting of principles of law recognized by civilized nations. These are principles of law that are common to the national law of the parties to the dispute.

general-jurisdiction trial court A court that hears cases of a general nature that are not within the jurisdiction of limited jurisdiction trial courts. Testimony and evidence at trial are recorded and stored for future reference.

generally accepted accounting principles (GAAPs) Standards for the preparation and presentation of financial statements.

generally accepted auditing standards (GAASs) Standards for the methods and procedures that must be used to conduct audits.

generally known dangers A defense that acknowledges that certain products are inherently dangerous and are known to the general population to be so.

general-purpose clause A clause often included in the articles of incorporation that authorizes the corporation to engage in any activity permitted corporations by law.

generic name A term for a mark that has become a common term for a product line or type of service and therefore has lost its trademark protection.

genuineness of assent The requirement that a party's assent to a contract be genuine.

gift A transfer of property from one person to another without exchange of money. A voluntary transfer of title to property without payment of consideration by the donee. To be a valid gift, three elements must be shown: (1) donative intent, (2) delivery, and (3) acceptance.

gift causa mortis A gift that is made in contemplation of death.

gift inter vivos A gift made during a person's lifetime that is an irrevocable present transfer of ownership.

gift promise An unenforceable promise because it lacks consideration.

good faith Honesty in fact in the conduct or transaction concerned. The good faith test is subjective.

good faith purchaser for value A person to whom good title can be transferred from a person with voidable title. The real owner cannot reclaim goods from a good faith purchaser for value.

good faith subsequent lessee A person to whom a lease interest can be transferred from a person with voidable title. The real owner cannot reclaim the goods from the subsequent lessee until the lease expires.

Good Samaritan law Statute that relieves medical professionals from liability for ordinary negligence when they stop and render aid to victims in emergency situations.

good title Title that is free from any encumbrances or other defects that are not disclosed but would affect the value of the property.

goods Tangible things that are movable at the time of their identification to the contract.

government contractor defense A defense that says a contractor who was provided specifications by the government is not liable for any defect in the product that occurs as a result of those specifications.

Government in the Sunshine Act An act that was enacted to open certain federal administrative agency meetings to the public.

grace period A period of time after the actual expiration date of a payment but during which the insured can still pay an overdue premium without penalty.

grantee The party to whom an interest in real property is transferred.

grantor The party who transfers an ownership interest in real property.

greenmail The purchase by a target corporation of its stock from an actual or perceived tender offeror at a premium.

group boycott When two or more competitors at one level of distribution agree not to deal with others at another level of distribution.

group insurance plan An insurance plan that is sold to all the members of a single group, often all the employees of one employer.

guaranteeing collection A form of accommodation where the accommodation party guarantees collection of a negotiable instrument; the accommodation party is secondarily liable on the instrument.

guaranteeing payment A form of accommodation where the accommodation party guarantees payment of a negotiable instrument; the accommodation party is primarily liable on the instrument.

guarantor The person who agrees to pay the debt if the primary debtor does not. The third person who agrees to be liable in a guaranty arrangement.

guaranty arrangement An arrangement where a third party promises to be secondarily liable for the payment of another's debt.

guaranty contract The contract between the guarantor and the original creditor.

guest statute Statute that provides that if a driver of a vehicle voluntarily and without compensation gives a ride to another person, the driver is not liable to the passenger for injuries caused by the driver's ordinary negligence.

hardship discharge A discharge granted if (1) the debtor fails to complete the payments due to unforeseeable circumstances, (2) the unsecured creditors have been paid as much as they would have been paid in a Chapter 7 liquidation proceeding, and (3) it is not practical to modify the plan.

Hart-Scott-Rodino Antitrust Improvement Act Requires certain firms to notify the FTC and the Justice Department in advance of a proposed merger. Unless the government challenges the proposed merger within 30 days, the merger may proceed.

hazardous waste Solid waste that may cause or significantly contribute to an increase in mortality or serious illness or pose a hazard to human health or the environment if improperly managed.

health insurance Purchased to help cover the costs of medical treatment, surgery, or hospital care.

holder What the transferee becomes if a negotiable instrument has been transferred by negotiation. A person who is in possession of a negotiable instrument that is drawn, issued, or indorsed to him or his order, or to bearer, or in blank.

holder in due course (HDC) A holder who takes a negotiable instrument for value, in good faith, and without notice that it is defective or is overdue.

holographic will Will that is entirely handwritten and signed by the testator.

homeowners policy A comprehensive insurance policy that includes coverage for the risks covered by a fire insurance policy as well as personal liability insurance.

honor Payment of a drawer's properly drawn check by the drawee bank.

horizontal merger A merger between two or more companies that compete in the same business and geographical market.

horizontal restraint of trade A restraint of trade that occurs when two or more competitors at the same level of distribution enter into a contract, combination, or conspiracy to restrain trade.

hung jury A jury that cannot come to a unanimous decision about the defendant's guilt. The government may choose to retry the case.

identification of goods Distinguishing the goods named in the contract from the seller's or lessor's other goods.

illegal consideration A promise to refrain from doing an illegal act. Such a promise will not support a contract.

illusory promise A contract into which both parties enter, but one or both of the parties can choose not to perform their contractual obligations. Thus the contract lacks consideration.

Immigration Reform and Control Act of 1986 (IRCA) A federal statute that makes it unlawful for employers to hire illegal immigrants.

immoral contract A contract whose objective is the commission of an act that is considered immoral by society.

immunity from prosecution The government agrees not to use any evidence given by a person granted immunity against that person.

impairment of right of recourse Certain parties (holders, indorsers, accommodation parties) are discharged from liability on an instrument if the holder (1) releases an obligor from liability or (2) surrenders collateral without the consent of the parties who would benefit by it.

implied agency An agency that occurs when a principal and an agent do not expressly create an agency, but it is inferred from the conduct of the parties.

implied authorization Mode of acceptance that is implied from what is customary in similar transactions, usage of trade, or prior dealings between the parties.

implied exemptions Exemptions from antitrust laws that are implied by the Federal courts.

implied partnership General partnership implied from the conduct of the parties.

implied powers Powers beyond express powers that allow a corporation to accomplish its corporate purpose.

implied term A term in a contract that can reasonably be supplied by the courts.

implied trust A trust that is implied by law or from the conduct of the parties.

implied warranties The law implies certain warranties on transferors of negotiable instruments. There are two types of implied warranties: transfer and presentment.

implied warranty of authority An agent who enters into a contract on behalf of another party impliedly warrants that he or she has the authority to do so.

implied warranty of fitness for a particular purpose An implied warranty that information is fit for the licensee's purpose that applies if the licensor (1) knows of any particular purpose for which the computer information is required and (2) knows that the licensee is relying on the licensor's skill or judgment to select or furnish suitable information.

implied warranty of fitness for human consumption A warranty that applies to food or drink consumed on or off the premises of restaurants, grocery stores, fast-food outlets, and vending machines.

implied warranty of habitability A warranty that provides that the leased premises must be fit, safe, and suitable for ordinary residential use.

implied warranty of informational content An implied warranty that there is no inaccuracy in the informational content caused by the merchant-licensor's failure to perform with reasonable care.

implied warranty of merchantability Unless properly disclosed, a warranty that is implied that sold or leased goods are fit for the ordinary purpose for which they are sold or leased, and other assurances.

implied warranty of merchantability of the computer program An implied warranty that the copies of the computer program are within the parameters permitted by the licensing agreement, that the computer program has been adequately packaged and labeled, and that the program conforms to any promises or affirmations of fact on the container or label.

implied-in-fact condition A condition that can be implied from the circumstances surrounding a contract and the parties' conduct.

implied-in-fact contract A contract where agreement between parties has been inferred because of their conduct.

impossibility of performance Nonperformance that is excused if the contract becomes impossible to perform; must be objective impossibility, not subjective.

imposter A person who impersonates a payee and induces a maker or drawer to issue an instrument in the payee's name and to give it to the imposter.

imposter rule A rule that says if an imposter forges the indorsement of the named payee, the drawer or maker is liable on the instrument and bears the loss.

imputed knowledge Information that is learned by the agent that is attributed to the principal.

in pari delicto When both parties are equally at fault in an illegal contract.

in personam jurisdiction Jurisdiction over the parties to a lawsuit.

in rem jurisdiction Jurisdiction to hear a case because of jurisdiction over the property of the lawsuit.

in transit A state in which goods are in the possession of a bailee or carrier and not in the hands of the buyer, seller, lessee, or lessor.

inaccessibility exception A rule that permits employees and union officials to engage in union solicitation on company property if the employees are beyond reach of reasonable union efforts to communicate with them.

incidental beneficiary A party who is unintentionally benefited by other people's contracts.

incidental damages When goods are resold or released, incidental damages are reasonable expenses incurred in stopping delivery, transportation charges, storage charges, sales commissions, and so on.

incontestability clause A clause that prevents insurers from contesting statements made by insureds in applications for insurance after the passage of a stipulated number of years.

incorporation by reference When integration is made by express reference in one document that refers to and incorporates another document within it.

incorporator The person or persons, partnerships, or corporations that are responsible for incorporation of a corporation.

indemnification Right of a partner to be reimbursed for expenditures incurred on behalf of the partnership.

indenture agreement A contract between the corporation and the holder that contains the terms of a debt security.

independent contractor A person who contracts with another to do something for him who is not controlled by the other nor subject to the other's right to control with respect to his physical conduct in the performance of the undertaking [Restatement (Second) of Agency].

indictment The charge of having committed a crime (usually a felony), based on the judgment of a grand jury.

indirect price discrimination A form of price discrimination (e.g., favorable credit terms) that is less readily apparent than direct forms of price discrimination.

indorsee The party to whom a check is indorsed. The person to whom a negotiable instrument is indorsed.

indorsement The signature (and other directions) written by or on behalf of the holder somewhere on the instrument.

indorsement for deposit or collection An indorsement that makes the indorsee the indorser's collecting agent (e.g., "for deposit only").

indorsement of a check Occurs when a payee indorses a check to another party by signing the back of the check.

indorser The person who indorses a negotiable instrument. The payee who indorses a check to another party.

indorsers' liability Unqualified indorsers are secondarily liable on negotiable instruments they indorse; qualified indorsers disclaim liability and are not secondarily liable on instruments they indorse.

infancy doctrine A doctrine that allows minors to disaffirm (cancel) most contracts they have entered into with adults.

inferior performance Occurs when a party fails to perform express or implied contractual obligations that impair or destroy the essence of the contract.

informal contract A contract that is not formal. Valid informal contracts are fully enforceable and may be sued upon if breached.

information The charge of having committed a crime (usually a misdemeanor), based on the judgment of a judge (magistrate).

injunction A court order that prohibits a person from doing a certain act.

injury The plaintiff must suffer personal injury or damage to his or her property to recover monetary damages for the defendant's negligence.

innkeepers' statutes State statutes that limit an innkeeper's common law liability. An innkeeper can avoid liability for loss caused to a guest's property if (1) a safe is provided in which the guest's valuable property may be kept and (2) the guest is notified of this fact.

innocent misrepresentation Occurs when a person makes a statement of fact that he or she honestly and reasonably believes to be true, even though it is not. Occurs when an agent makes an untrue statement that he or she honestly and reasonably believes to be true.

INS Form 1–9 A form that must be filled out by all U.S. employers for each employee; states that the employer has inspected the employee's legal qualifications to work.

insane, but not adjudged insane A person who is insane but has not been adjudged insane by a court or administrative agency. A contract entered into by such person is generally voidable. Some states hold that such a contract is void.

Insecticide, Fungicide, and Rodenticide Act A federal statute that requires pesticides, herbicides, fungicides, and rodenticides to be registered with the EPA; the EPA may deny, suspend, or cancel registration.

inside director A member of the board of directors who is also an officer of the corporation.

insider trading When an insider makes a profit by personally purchasing shares of the corporation prior to public release of favorable information or by selling shares of the corporation prior to the public disclosure of unfavorable information.

Insider Trading Sanctions Act of 1984 A federal statute that permits the SEC to obtain a civil penalty of up to three times the illegal benefits received from insider trading.

installment contract A contract that requires or authorizes the goods to be delivered and accepted in separate lots.

instrument Term that means negotiable instrument.

insurable interest A person who purchases insurance must have a personal interest in the insured item or person.

insurance A means for persons and businesses to protect themselves against the risk of loss.

insured The party who pays a premium to a particular insurance company for insurance coverage.

insurer The insurance company that underwrites the insurance coverage.

intangible property Rights that cannot be reduced to physical form such as stock certificates, certificates of deposit, bonds, and copyrights.

integration The combination of several writings to form a single contract.

intellectual property rights Intellectual property rights, such as patents, copyrights, trademarks, trade secrets, trade names, and domain names are very valuable business assets. Federal and state laws protect intellectual property rights from misappropriation and infringement.

intended beneficiary A third party who is not in privity of contract but who has rights under the contract and can enforce the contract against the obligor.

intentional infliction of emotional distress A tort that says a person whose extreme and outrageous conduct intentionally or recklessly causes severe emotional distress to another person is liable for that emotional distress. Also known as the tort of outrage.

intentional interference with contractual relations A tort that arises when a third party induces a contracting party to breach the contract with another party.

intentional misrepresentation Intentionally defrauding another person out of money, property, or something else of value. When a seller or lessor fraudulently misrepresents the quality of a product and a buyer is injured thereby. Occurs when one person consciously decides to induce another person to rely and act on a misrepresentation. Also called fraud. Occurs when an agent makes an untrue statement that he or she knows is not true.

intentional tort A category of torts that requires that the defendant possessed the intent to do the act that caused the plaintiff's injuries. Occurs when a person has intentionally committed a wrong against (1) another person or his or her character, or (2) another person's property.

inter vivos trust A trust that is created while the settlor is alive.

intermediary bank A bank in the collection process that is not the depository or payor bank.

intermediate appellate court An intermediate court that hears appeals from trial courts.

intermediate scrutiny test Test that is applied to classifications based on protected classes other than race (e.g., sex or age).

International Court of Justice The judicial branch of the United Nations that is located in The Hague, the Netherlands. Also called the World Court.

International law Law that governs affairs between nations and that regulates transactions between individuals and businesses of different countries.

Internet A collection of millions of computers that provide a network of electronic connections between computers.

interpretive rules Rules issued by administrative agencies that interpret existing statutory language.

interrogatories Written questions submitted by one party to another party. The questions must be answered in writing within a stipulated time.

interstate commerce Commerce that moves between states or that affects commerce between states.

intervention The act of others to join as parties to an existing lawsuit.

intoxicated person A person who is under contractual incapacity because of ingestion of alcohol or drugs to the point of incompetence.

intrastate offering exemption An exemption from registration that permits local businesses to raise capital from local investors to be used in the local economy without the need to register with the SEC.

invasion of the right to privacy A tort that constitutes the violation of a person's right to live his or her life without being subjected to unwarranted and undesired publicity.

involuntary petition A petition filed by creditors of the debtor; alleges that the debtor is not paying his or her debts as they become due.

issued shares Shares that have been sold by the corporation.

joint and several liability Partners are jointly and severally liable for tort liability of the partnership. This means that the plaintiff can sue one or more of the partners separately. If successful, the plaintiff can recover the entire amount of the judgment from any or all of the defendant-partners.

joint liability Partners are jointly liable for contracts and debts of the partnership. This means that a plaintiff must name the partnership and all of the partners as defendants in a lawsuit.

joint tenancy A form of co-ownership that includes the right of survivorship.

joint will A will that is executed by two or more testators.

judgment on the underlying debt A right granted to a secured creditor to relinquish his or her security interest in the collateral and sue a defaulting debtor to recover the amount of the underlying debt.

judicial branch The part of the government that consists of the Supreme Court and other federal courts.

judicial decision A decision about an individual lawsuit issued by federal and state courts.

judicial decisions and teachings The fourth source of international law, consisting of judicial decisions and writings of the most qualified legal scholars of the various nations involved in the dispute.

judicial decree of dissolution Order of the court that dissolves a partnership. An application or petition must be filed by a partner or an assignee of a partnership interest with the appropriate state court; the court will issue a judicial decree of dissolution if warranted by the circumstances.

judicial dissolution Occurs when a corporation is dissolved by a court proceeding instituted by the state.

jurisdiction The authority of a court to hear a case.

jurisprudence The philosophy or science of law.

Just Compensation Clause Clause in the U.S. Constitution that mandates that the government must compensate owners and lessees for property taken under the power of eminent domain.

Kantian or duty ethics A moral theory that says that people owe moral duties that are based on universal rules, such as the categorical imperative "do unto others as you would have them do unto you."

land The most common form of real property; includes the land and buildings and other structures permanently attached to the land.

land pollution Pollution of the land that is generally caused by hazardous waste being disposed of in an improper manner.

land sales contract Arrangement where the owner of real property agrees to sell the property to a purchaser, who agrees to pay the purchase price to the owner-seller over an agreed-upon period of time.

land use control The collective term for the laws that regulate the possession, ownership, and use of real property.

landlord The owner who transfers the leasehold.

landlord–tenant relationship A relationship created when the owner of a freehold estate (landlord) transfers a right to exclusively and temporarily possess the owner's property to another (tenant).

Lanham Trademark Act (as amended) Federal statute that (1) establishes the requirements for obtaining a federal mark and (2) protects marks from infringement.

lapse of time An offer terminates when a stated time period expires. If no time is stated, an offer terminates after a reasonable time.

larceny Taking another's personal property other than from his or her person or building.

law That which must be obeyed and followed by citizens subject to sanctions or legal consequences; a body of rules of action or conduct prescribed by controlling authority, and having binding legal force.

law court A court that developed and administered a uniform set of laws decreed by the kings and queens after William the Conqueror; legal procedure was emphasized over merits at this time.

lease The transfer of the right to use real property for a specified period of time. A transfer of the right to the possession and use of the named goods for a set term in return for certain consideration. A transfer of the right to the possession and use of the real property for a set term in return for certain consideration; the rental agreement between a landlord and a tenant.

leasehold A tenant's interest in the property.

legal entity An LLC is a separate legal entity—an artificial person—that can own property, sue and be sued, enter into and enforce contracts, and such.

legal insanity A state of contractual incapacity as determined by law.

legally enforceable contract If one party fails to perform as promised, the other party can use the court system to enforce the contract and recover damages or other remedy.

legislative branch The part of the government that consists of Congress (the Senate and the House of Representatives).

lessee The person who acquires the right to possession and use of goods under a lease.

lessor The person who transfers the right of possession and use of goods under the lease.

liability insurance Automobile insurance that covers damages that the insured causes to third parties.

libel A false statement that appears in a letter, newspaper, magazine, book, photograph, movie, video, and so on.

license A contract that transfers limited rights in intellectual property and informational rights. Grants a person the right to enter upon another's property for a specified and usually short period of time.

licensee The party who is granted limited rights in or access to intellectual property or informational rights owned by the licensor.

licensing agreement Detailed and comprehensive written agreement between the licensor and licensee that sets forth the express terms of their agreement.

licensing statute Statute that requires a person or business to obtain a license from the government prior to engaging in a specified occupation or activity.

licensor The owner of intellectual property or informational rights who transfers rights in the property or information to the licensee.

licensor's damages If a licensee breaches a contract, the licensor may sue and recover monetary damages from the licensee caused by the breach.

life estate An interest in the land for a person's lifetime; upon that person's death, the interest will be transferred to another party.

life insurance A form of insurance where the insurer is obligated to pay a specific sum of money upon the death of the insured.

limited liability Members are liable for the LLC's debts, obligations, and liabilities only to the extent of their capital contributions. Liability that shareholders have only to the extent of their capital contribution. Shareholders are generally not personally liable for debts and obligations of the corporation.

limited liability company (LLC) An unincorporated business entity that combines the most favorable attributes of general partnerships, limited partnerships, and corporations.

limited liability company codes State statutes that regulate the formation, operation, and dissolution of LLCs.

limited liability partnership (LLP) A type of partnership that has no general partner. All partners have limited liability. A special form of partnership where all partners are limited partners and there are no general partners.

limited partners Partners in a limited partnership who invest capital but do not participate in management and are not personally liable for partnership debts beyond their capital contributions.

limited partnership A special form of partnership that has both limited and general partners.

limited partnership agreement A document that sets forth the rights and duties of the general and limited partners; the terms and conditions regarding the operation, termination, and dissolution of the partnership; and so on.

limited-jurisdiction trial court A court that hears matters of a specialized or limited nature.

line of commerce Includes products or services that consumers use as substitutes. If an increase in the price of one product or service leads consumers to purchase another product or service, the two products are substitutes for each other.

lineal descendants Children, grandchildren, great-grandchildren, and so on of the testator.

liquidated damages Damages to which parties to a contract agree in advance if the contract is breached. Damages that are specified in the contract rather than determined by the court. Damages that will be paid upon a breach of contract and that are established in advance

litigation The process of bringing, maintaining, and defending a lawsuit.

long-arm statute A statute that extends a state's jurisdiction to nonresidents who were not served a summons within the state.

lost property When a property owner leaves property somewhere because of negligence, carelessness, or inadvertence.

mail fraud The use of mail to defraud another person.

mailbox rule A rule that states that an acceptance is effective when it is dispatched, even if it is lost in transmission.

main purpose or leading object exception If the main purpose of a transaction and an oral collateral contract is to provide pecuniary benefit to the guarantor, the collateral contract does not have to be in writing to be enforced.

maker of a CD The bank (borrower).

maker of a note The party who makes the promise to pay (borrower).

management Unless otherwise agreed, each partner has a right to participate in the management of the partnership and has an equal vote on partnership matters.

manager-managed LLC An LLC that has designated in its articles of organization that it is a manager-managed LLC.

marine insurance Insurance that owners of vessels purchase to insure against loss or damage to the vessel and its cargo caused by perils at sea.

Marine Protection, Research, and Sanctuaries Act A federal statute enacted in 1972 that extends environmental protection to the oceans.

mark The collective name for trademarks, service marks, certification marks, and collective marks that all can be trademarked.

market extension merger A merger between two companies in similar fields whose sales do not overlap.

material alteration A partial defense against enforcement of a negotiable instrument by an HDC. An HDC can enforce an altered instrument in the original amount for which the drawer wrote the check.

material breach A breach that occurs when a party renders inferior performance of his or her contractual duties.

maximizing profits A theory of social responsibility that says a corporation owes a duty to take actions that maximize profits for shareholders.

mediation A form of ADR in which the parties choose a neutral third party to act as the mediator of the dispute.

Medicinal Device Amendment to the FDCA An amendment enacted in 1976 that gives the FDA authority to regulate medicinal devices and equipment.

meeting of the creditors A meeting of the creditors in a bankruptcy case that must occur not less than 10 days nor more than 30 days after the court grants an order for relief.

meeting the competition defense A defense provided in Section 2(b) that says a seller may lawfully engage in price discrimination to meet a competitor's price.

member An owner of an LLC.

member-managed LLC An LLC that has not designated that it is a manager-managed LLC in its articles of organization.

mens rea "Evil intent"—the possession of the requisite state of mind to commit a prohibited act.

merchant A person who (1) deals in the goods of the kind involved in the transaction or (2) by his or her occupation holds himself or herself out as having knowledge or skill particular to the goods involved in the transaction.

merger Occurs when one corporation is absorbed into another corporation and ceases to exist.

merger clause A clause in a contract that stipulates that it is a complete integration and the exclusive expression of the parties' agreement. Parol evidence may not be introduced to explain, alter, contradict, or add to the terms of the contract.

midnight deadline The midnight of the next banking day following the banking day on which the bank received the "on them" check for collection.

minor A person who has not reached the age of majority.

minor breach A breach that occurs when a party renders substantial performance of his or her contractual duties.

minor's duty of restoration As a general rule, a minor is obligated only to return the goods or property he or she has received from the adult in the condition it is in at the time of disaffirmance.

mirror image rule States that for an acceptance to exist, the offeree must accept the terms as stated in the offer.

misdemeanor A less serious crime; not inherently evil but prohibited by society. Many crimes against property are misdemeanors.

mislaid property When an owner voluntarily places property somewhere and then inadvertently forgets it.

misrepresentation An assertion that is made that is not in accord with the facts.

misuse A defense that relieves a seller of product liability if the user abnormally misused the product. Products must be designed to protect against foreseeable misuse.

mitigation A nonbreaching party is under a legal duty to avoid or reduce damages caused by a breach of contract.

mixed sale A sale that involves the provision of a service and a good in the same transaction.

mobile sources Sources of air pollution such as automobiles, trucks, buses, motorcycles, and airplanes.

Model Business Corporation Act (MBCA) A model act drafted in 1950 that was intended to provide a uniform law for regulation of corporations.

monetary damages An award of money.

money A "medium of exchange authorized or adopted by a domestic or foreign government." [UCC 1–201(24)]

monopoly power The power to control prices or exclude competition measured by the market share the defendant possesses in the relevant market.

moral minimum A theory of social responsibility that says a corporation's duty is to make a profit while avoiding harm to others.

mortgage A collateral arrangement where a property owner borrows money from a creditor who uses a deed as collateral for repayment of the loan.

mortgage An interest in real property given to a lender as security for the repayment of a loan.

mortgagee The creditor in a mortgage transaction.

mortgagor The owner-debtor in a mortgage transaction.

motion for judgment on the pleadings Motion that alleges that if all the facts presented in the pleadings are taken as true, the party making the motion would win the lawsuit when the proper law is applied to these asserted facts.

motion for summary judgment Motion that asserts that there are no factual disputes to be decided by the jury; if so, the judge can apply the proper law to the undisputed facts and decide the case without a jury. These motions are supported by affidavits, documents, and deposition testimony.

motivation test A test to determine the liability of the principal; if the agent's motivation in committing the intentional tort is to promote the principal's business, then the principal is liable for any injury caused by the tort.

mutual benefit bailment A bailment for the mutual benefit of the bailor and bailee. The bailee owes a duty of ordinary care to protect the bailed property.

mutual mistake of fact A mistake made by both parties concerning a material fact that is important to the subject matter of the contract.

mutual mistake of value A mistake that occurs if both parties know the object of the contract, but are mistaken as to its value.

mutual wills Occur where two or more testators execute separate wills that leave their property to each other on the condition that the survivor leave the remaining property on his or her death as agreed by the testators.

national courts The courts of individual nations.

National Labor Relations Board (NLRB) A federal administrative agency that oversees union elections, prevents employers and unions from engaging in illegal and unfair labor practices, and enforces and interprets certain federal labor laws.

necessaries of life A minor must pay the reasonable value of food, clothing, shelter, medical care, and other items considered necessary to the maintenance of life.

negligence A tort related to defective products where the defendant has breached a duty of due care and caused harm to the plaintiff. Failure of a corporate director or officer to exercise the duty of care while conducting the corporation's business.

negligence per se Tort where the violation of a statue or ordinance constitutes the breach of the duty of care.

negligent infliction of emotional distress A tort that permits a person to recover for emotional distress caused by the defendant's negligent conduct.

negotiable instrument Commercial paper that must meet these requirements: (1) be in writing, (2) be signed by the maker or drawer, (3) be an unconditional promise or order to pay, (4) state a fixed amount of money, (5) not require any undertaking in addition to the payment of money, (6) be payable on demand or at a definite time, and (7) be payable to order or to bearer. A special form of contract that satisfies the requirement established by Article 3 of the UCC. Also called commercial paper.

negotiation Transfer of a negotiable instrument by a person other than the issuer to a person who thereby becomes a holder.

New York standard fire insurance form A standard fire insurance policy that protects the homeowner from loss caused by fire, lightning, smoke, and water damage.

no evidence of forgery, alteration, or irregularity requirement A holder cannot become an HDC to an instrument that is apparently forged or altered or is so otherwise irregular or incomplete as to call into question its authenticity.

Noise Control Act A federal statute enacted in 1972 that authorizes the EPA to establish noise standards for products sold in the United States.

noise pollution Unwanted sound from planes, manufacturing plants, motor vehicles, construction equipment, stereos, and the like.

nominal damages Damages awarded when the nonbreaching party sues the breaching party even though no financial loss has resulted from the breach; usually consists of $1 or some other small amount.

nonattainment areas Regions that do not meet air quality standards.

nonconforming uses Uses and buildings that already exist in the zoned area that are permitted to continue even though they do not fit within new zoning ordinances.

noncupative will Oral will that is made before a witness during the testator's last illness.

nonfreehold estate An estate in which the tenant has a right to possession of the property but not title to the property.

nonnegotiable contract Fails to meet the requirements of a negotiable instrument and, therefore, is not subject to the provisions of UCC Article 3.

nonpossessory interest When a person holds an interest in another person's property without actually owning any part of the property.

nonprice vertical restraints Restraints of trade that are unlawful under Section 1 of the Sherman Act if their anticompetitive effects outweigh their procompetitive effects.

nonprofit corporation A corporation that is formed to operate charitable institutions, colleges, universities, and other not-for-profit entities.

nonrestrictive indorsement An indorsement that has no instructions or conditions attached to the payment of the funds.

note An instrument that evidences the borrower's debt to the lender. A debt security with a maturity of five years or less.

notice of dishonor The formal act of letting the party with secondary liability to pay a negotiable instrument know that the instrument has been dishonored.

novation An agreement that substitutes a new party for one of the original contracting parties and relieves the exiting party of liability on the contract.

Nuclear Regulatory Commission (NRC) Federal agency that licenses the construction and opening of commercial nuclear power plants.

Nuclear Waste Policy Act of 1982 A federal statute that says the federal government must select and develop a permanent site for the disposal of nuclear waste.

objective theory of contracts A theory that says that the intent to contract is judged by the reasonable person standard and not by the subjective intent of the parties.

obligation An action a party to a sales or lease contract is required by law to carry out.

obscene speech Speech that (1) appeals to the prurient interest, (2) depicts sexual conduct in a patently offensive way, and (3) lacks serious literary, artistic, political, or scientific value.

Occupational Safety and Health Act A federal act enacted in 1970 that promotes safety in the workplace.

offensive speech Speech that is offensive to many members of society. It is subject to time, place, and manner restrictions.

offer The manifestation of willingness to enter into a bargain, so made as to justify another person in understanding that his assent to that bargain is invited and will conclude it. [Section 24 of Restatement (Second) of Contracts]

offeree The party to whom an offer to enter into a contract is made. The party to whom an offer has been made.

offeror The party who makes an offer to enter into a contract. The party who makes an offer.

officers Employees of the corporation who are appointed by the board of directors to manage the day-to-day operations of the corporation.

on them item A check presented for payment by the payee or holder where the depository bank and the payor bank are not the same bank.

on us item A check that is presented for payment where the depository bank is also the payor bank. That is, the drawer and payee or holder have accounts at the same bank.

one year rule An executory contract that cannot be performed by its own terms within one year of its formation must be in writing.

one-year "on sale" doctrine A doctrine that says a patent may not be granted if the invention was used by the public for more than one year prior to the filing of the patent application.

operating agreement An agreement entered into among members that governs the affairs and business of the LLC and the relations among members, managers, and the LLC.

order Decision issued by an administrative law judge.

order for relief The filing of either a voluntary petition, an unchallenged involuntary petition, or a grant of an order after a trial of a challenged involuntary petition.

order paper Order paper is negotiated by (1) delivery and (2) indorsement.

order to pay A drawer's unconditional order to a drawee to pay a payee.

ordinances Laws enacted by local government bodies such as cities and municipalities, countries, school districts, and water districts.

ordinary bailments (1) Bailments for the sole benefit of the bailor, (2) bailments for the sole benefit of the bailee, and (3) bailments for the mutual benefit of the bailor and bailee.

organizational meeting A meeting that must be held by the initial directors of the corporation after the articles of incorporation are filed.

original tenor The original amount for which the drawer wrote the check.

outside director A member of the board of directors who is not an officer of the corporation.

outstanding shares Shares of stock that are in shareholder hands.

overdraft The amount of money a drawer owes a bank after it has paid a check despite insufficient funds in the drawer's account.

pac-man tender offer Occurs when a corporation that is the target of a tender offer makes a reverse tender offer for the stock of the tender offeror.

palming off Unfair competition that occurs when a company tries to pass one of its products as that of a rival.

panel A panel of three WTO judges that hears trade disputes between member nations and issues a "panel report."

parol evidence Any oral or written words outside the four corners of the written contract.

parol evidence rule A rule that says if a written contract is a complete and final statement of the parties' agreement, any prior or contemporaneous oral or written statements that alter, contradict, or are in addition to the terms of the written contract are inadmissible in court regarding a dispute over the contract. There are several exceptions to this rule.

part performance An equitable doctrine that allows the court to order an oral contract for the sale of land or transfer of another interest in real property to be specifically performed if it has been partially performed and performance is necessary to avoid injustice.

partner's interest A partner's share of profits and surplus of the partnership.

partnership agreement A written partnership agreement that the partners sign. Also called articles of partnership.

partnership at will A partnership with no fixed duration.

partnership capital Money and property contributed by partners for the permanent use of the partnership.

partnership for a term A partnership with a fixed duration.

partnership property Property that is originally brought into the partnership on account of the partnership and property that is subsequently acquired by purchase or otherwise on account of the partnership or with partnership funds.

past consideration A prior act or performance. Past consideration (e.g., prior acts) will not support a new contract. New consideration must be given.

patent infringement Unauthorized use of another's patent. A patent holder may recover damages and other remedies against a patent infringer.

payable on demand or at a definite time requirement A negotiable instrument must be payable either on demand or at a definite time.

payee of a CD The depositor (lender).

payee of a check The party to whom the check is written.

payee of a draft The party who receives the money from a draft.

payee of a note The party to whom the promise to pay is made (lender).

payor bank The bank where the drawer has a checking account and on which the check is drawn.

penal codes A collection of criminal statutes.

per capita A distribution of the estate that makes each grandchild and great-grandchild of the deceased inherit equally with the children of the deceased.

per se rule A rule that is applicable to those restraints of trade considered inherently anticompetitive. Once this determination is made, the court will not permit any defenses or justifications to save it.

per stirpes A distribution of the estate that makes grandchildren and great-grandchildren of the deceased inherit by representation of their parent.

perfect tender rule A rule that says if the goods or tender of a delivery fail in any respect to conform to the contract, the buyer may opt either (1) to reject the whole shipment, (2) to accept the whole shipment, or (3) to reject part and accept part of the shipment.

perfection by possession of the collateral If a secured creditor has physical possession of the collateral, no financing statement has to be filed; the creditor's possession is sufficient to put other potential creditors on notice of his or her secured interest in the property.

perfection of a security interest Establishes the right of a secured creditor against other creditors who claim an interest in the collateral.

periodic tenancy A tenancy created when a lease specifies intervals at which payments are due but does not specify how long the lease is for.

permanency requirement A requirement of negotiable instruments that says they must be in a permanent state, such as written on ordinary paper.

permanent trustee A legal representative of the bankruptcy debtor's estate, usually an accountant or lawyer; elected at the first meeting of the creditors.

personal articles floater An addition to the homeowners policy that covers specific valuable items.

personal defense A defense that can be raised against enforcement of a negotiable instrument by an ordinary holder but not against an HDC.

personal property Property that consists of tangible property such as automobiles, furniture, and jewelry; intangible property such as securities, patents, and copyrights; and instruments, chattel paper, documents of title, and accounts.

personal satisfaction test Subjective test that applies to contracts involving personal taste and comfort.

petition A document filed with the bankruptcy court that sets the bankruptcy proceedings into motion.

petition for certiorari A petition asking the Supreme Court to hear one's case.

petitioner The party appealing the decision of an administrative agency.

physical or mental examination A court may order another party to submit to a physical or mental examination prior to trial.

picketing The action of strikers walking in front of the employer's premises carrying signs announcing their strike.

piercing the corporate veil A doctrine that says if a shareholder dominates a corporation and uses it for improper purposes, a court of equity can disregard the corporate entity and hold the shareholder personally liable for the corporation's debts and obligations.

plaintiff The party who files the complaint.

plan of reorganization A plan that sets forth a proposed new capital structure for the debtor to have when it emerges from reorganization bankruptcy. The debtor has the exclusive right to file the first plan of reorganization; any party of interest may file a plan thereafter.

plant life and vegetation Real property that is growing in or on the surface of the land.

plea bargain When the accused admits to a lesser crime than charged. In return, the government agrees to impose a lesser sentence than might have been obtained had the case gone to trial.

pleadings The paperwork that is filed with the court to initiate and respond to a lawsuit.

point sources Sources of water pollution such as paper mills, manufacturing plants, electric utility plants, and sewage plants.

police power The power of states to regulate private and business activity within their borders.

policy The insurance contract.

portability requirement A requirement of negotiable instruments that says they must be able to be easily transported between areas.

possession A lease grants the tenant exclusive possession of the leased premises for the term of the lease or until the tenant defaults on the obligations under the lease.

possessory lien Lien obtained by a bailee on bailed property for the compensation owed by the bailor to the bailee.

Postal Reorganization Act An act that makes the mailing of unsolicited merchandise an unfair trade practice.

posteffective period The period of time that begins when the registration statement becomes effective and runs until the issuer either sells all of the offered securities or withdraws them from sale.

potential competition theory A theory that reasons that the real or implied threat of increased competition keeps businesses more competitive. A merger that would eliminate this perception can be enjoined under Section 7.

potential reciprocity theory A theory that says if Company A, which supplies materials to Company B, mergers with Company C (which in turn gets its supplies from Company B), the newly merged company can coerce Company B into dealing exclusively with it.

power of attorney An express agency agreement that is often used to give an agent the power to sign legal documents on behalf of the principal.

precedent A rule of law established in a court decision. Lower courts must follow the precedent established by higher courts.

preemption doctrine The concept that federal law takes precedence over state or local law.

preemptive rights Rights that give existing shareholders the option of subscribing to new shares being issued in proportion to their current ownership interest.

preexisting duty A promise lacks consideration if a person promises to perform an act or do something he or she is already under an obligation to do.

preferential lien Occurs when (1) a debtor gives an unsecured creditor a secured interest in property within 90 days before the filing of a petition in bankruptcy, (2) the transfer is made for a preexisting debt, and (3) the creditor would receive more because of this lien than it would as an unsecured creditor.

preferential transfer Occurs when (1) a debtor transfers property to a creditor within 90 days before the filing of a petition in bankruptcy, (2) the transfer is made for a preexisting debt, and (3) the creditor would receive more from the transfer than it would from Chapter 7 liquidation.

preferential transfer to an insider A transfer of property by an insolvent debtor to an "insider" within one year before the filing of a petition in bankruptcy.

preferred stock A type of equity security that is given certain preferences and rights over common stock.

preferred stock certificate A document that represents a shareholder's investment in preferred stock in the corporation.

preferred stockholder A person who owns preferred stock.

prefiling period A period of time that begins when the issuer first contemplates issuing the securities and ends when the registration statement is filed. The issuer may not condition the market during this period.

Pregnancy Discrimination Act Amendment to Title VII that forbids employment discrimination because of "pregnancy, childbirth, or related medical conditions."

premises liability The liability of landlords and tenants to persons injured on their premises.

premium The money paid to the insurance company.

presentment A demand for acceptance or payment of an instrument made upon the maker, acceptor, drawee, or other payor by or on behalf of the holder.

presentment across the counter When a depository physically presents the check for payment at the payor bank instead of depositing an "on them" check for collection.

presentment warranties Any person who presents a draft or check for payment or acceptance makes the following three warranties to a drawee or acceptor who pays or accepts the instrument in good faith: (1) The presenter has good title to the instrument or is authorized to obtain payment or acceptance of the person who has good title, (2) the instrument has not been materially altered, and (3) the presenter has no knowledge that the signature of the maker or drawer is unauthorized.

pretrial hearing A hearing before the trial in order to facilitate the settlement of a case. Also called a settlement conference.

pretrial motion A motion a party can make to try to dispose of all or part of a lawsuit prior to trial.

price-fixing Occurs where competitors in the same line of business agree to set the price of the goods or services they sell: raising, depressing, fixing, pegging, or stabilizing the price of a commodity or service.

primary liability Absolute liability to pay a negotiable instrument, subject to certain real defenses.

principal A person who authorizes an agent to sign a negotiable instrument on his or her behalf. The party who employs another person to act on his or her behalf.

principal–agent relationship An employer hires an employee and gives that employee authority to act and enter into contracts on his or her behalf.

priority The order in which conflicting claims of creditors in the same collateral are solved.

Privacy Act An act stipulating that federal administrative agencies can maintain only information about an individual that is relevant and necessary to accomplish a legitimate agency purpose.

private corporation A corporation formed to conduct privately owned business.

private nuisance A nuisance that affects or disturbs one or a few people.

private placement exemption An exemption from registration that permits issuers to raise capital from an unlimited number of accredited investors and no more than 35 nonaccredited investors without having to register the offering with the SEC.

Private Securities Litigation Reform Act of 1995 Provides a safe harbor from liability for companies that make forward-looking statements that are accompanied by meaningful cautionary statements of risk factors.

Privileges and Immunities Clause A clause that prohibits states from enacting laws that unduly discriminate in favor of their residents.

privity of contract The state of two specified parties being in a contract.

pro rata rule A rule that says shares must be purchased on a pro rata basis if too many shares are tendered.

probability of a substantial lessening of competition If there is a probability that a merger will substantially lessen competition or create a monopoly, the court may prevent the merger under Section 7 of the Clayton Act.

probate court A specialized state court that supervises the administration and settlement of an estate.

procedural due process Due process that requires the respondent to be given (1) proper and timely notice of the allegations or charges against him or her and (2) an opportunity to present evidence on the matter.

procedural due process Requires that the government must give a person proper notice and hearing of the legal action before that person is deprived of his or her life, liberty, or property.

process of certification The accepting bank writes or stamps the word certified on the ordinary check of an account holder and sets aside funds from that account to pay the check.

processing plant franchise The franchisor provides a secret formula or process to the franchisee, and the franchisee manufactures the product and distributes it to retail dealers.

production of documents Request by one party to another party to produce all documents relevant to the case prior to the trial.

products liability The liability of manufacturers, sellers, and others for the injuries caused by defective products.

professional corporation A corporation formed by lawyers, doctors, or other professionals.

professional malpractice The liability of a professional who breaches his or her duty of ordinary care.

profit Grants a person the right to remove something from another's real property.

profit corporation A corporation created to conduct a business for profit that can distribute profits to shareholders in the form of dividends.

promise to pay A maker's (borrower's) unconditional and affirmative undertaking to repay a debt to a payee (lender).

promissory estoppel An equitable doctrine that prevents the withdrawal of a promise by a promisor if it will adversely affect a promisee who has adjusted his or her position in justifiable reliance on the promise. An equitable doctrine that permits enforcement of oral contracts that should have been in writing. It is applied to avoid injustice.

promissory note A two-party negotiable instrument that is an unconditional written promise by one party to pay money to another party.

promoter A person or persons who organize and start the corporation, negotiate and enter into contracts in advance of its formation, find the initial investors to finance the corporation, and so forth.

promoters' contracts A collective term for such things as leases, sales contracts, contracts to purchase property, and employment contracts entered into by promoters on behalf of the proposed corporation prior to its actual incorporation.

proof of claim A document required to be filed by unsecured creditors that states the amount of their claim against the debtor.

proper dispatch An acceptance must be properly addressed, packaged, and posted to fall within the mailbox rule.

prospectus A written disclosure document that must be submitted to the SEC along with the registration statement and given to prospective purchasers of the securities.

provisional credit Occurs when a collecting bank gives credit to a check in the collection process prior to its final settlement. Provisional credits may be reversed if the check does not "clear."

proximate cause or legal cause A point along a chain of events caused by a negligent party after which this party is no longer legally responsible for the consequences of his or her actions.

proxy The written document that a shareholder signs authorizing another person to vote his or her shares at the shareholders' meetings in the event of the shareholder's absence.

proxy card Written document signed by a shareholder that authorizes another person to vote the shareholder's shares.

proxy contest When opposing factions of shareholders and managers solicit proxies from other shareholders, the side that receives the greatest number of votes wins the proxy contest.

proxy statement A document that fully describes (1) the matter for which the proxy is being solicited, (2) who is soliciting the proxy, and (3) any other pertinent information.

public corporation A corporation formed to meet a specific governmental or political purpose.

public nuisance A nuisance that affects or disturbs the public in general.

public policy exception An exception to the employment-at-will doctrine that states an employee cannot be discharged if such discharge violates the public policy of the jurisdiction.

publicly held corporation A corporation that has many shareholders and whose securities are often traded on national stock exchanges.

punitive damages Damages that are awarded to punish the defendant, to deter the defendant from similar conduct in the future, and to set an example for others.

purchase money security interest An interest a creditor automatically obtains when it extends credit to a consumer to purchase consumer goods.

purchasing property The most common method of acquiring title to personal property.

qualified individual with a disability A person who (1) has a physical or mental impairment that substantially limits one or more of his or her major life activities, (2) has a record of such impairment, or (3) is regarded as having such impairment.

quasi contract An equitable doctrine that permits the recovery of compensation even though no enforceable contract exists between the parties.

quasi in rem jurisdiction Jurisdiction allowed a plaintiff who obtains a judgment in one state to try to collect the judgment by attaching property of the defendant located in another state.

quasi- or implied-in-law contract An equitable doctrine whereby a court may award monetary damages to a plaintiff for providing work or services to a defendant even though no actual contract existed. The doctrine is intended to prevent unjust enrichment and unjust detriment.

quiet title action An action brought by a party seeking an order of the court declaring who has title to disputed property. The court "quiets title" by its decision.

quorum The required number of shares that must be represented in person or by proxy to hold a shareholders' meeting. The RMBCA establishes a majority of outstanding shares as a quorum. The number of directors necessary to hold a board of directors' meeting or transact business of the board.

Racketeer Influenced and Corrupt Organizations Act (RICO) A federal statute that provides for both criminal and civil penalties.

radiation pollution Emissions from radioactive wastes that can cause injury and death to humans and other life and can cause severe damage to the environment.

ratification The act of a minor after the minor has reached the age of majority by which he or she accepts a contract entered into when he or she was a minor. When a principal accepts an agent's unauthorized contract. The acceptance by a corporation of an unauthorized act of a corporate officer or agent.

rational basis test Test that is applied to classifications not involving a suspect or protected class.

Rawls's social contract A moral theory that says each person is presumed to have entered into a social contract with all others in society to obey moral rules that are necessary for people to live in peace and harmony.

real defense A defense that can be raised against both holders and HDCs.

real property The land itself as well as buildings, trees, soil, minerals, timber, plants, crops, and other things permanently affixed to the land.

reasonable person test Objective test that applies to commercial contracts and contracts involving mechanical fitness.

receiving stolen property A person (1) knowingly receives stolen property and (2) intends to deprive the rightful owner of that property.

reclamation The right of a seller or lessor to demand the return of goods from the buyer or lessee under specified situations.

record date A date specified in the corporate bylaws that determines whether a shareholder may vote at a shareholders' meeting. A date that determines whether a shareholder receives payment of a declared dividend.

recording statute A state statute that requires the mortgage or deed of trust to be recorded in the county recorder's office of the county in which the real property is located.

recovery of damages A seller or lessor may recover damages measured as the difference between the contract price (or rent) and the market price (or rent) at the time and place the goods were to be delivered, plus incidental damages, from a buyer or lessee who repudiates the contract or wrongfully rejects tendered goods.

recovery of goods from an insolvent seller or lessor A buyer or lessee who has wholly or partially paid for goods before they are received may recover the goods from a seller or lessor who becomes insolvent within 10 days after receiving the first payment; the buyer or lessee must tender the remaining purchase price or rent due under the contract.

recovery of lost profits If the recovery of damages would be inadequate to put the seller or lessor in as good a position as if the contract had been fully performed by the buyer or lessee, the seller or lessor may recover lost profits, plus an allowance of overhead and incidental damages, from the buyer or lessee.

recovery of the purchase price or rent A seller or lessor may recover the contracted-for purchase price or rent from the buyer or lessee if the buyer or lessee (1) fails to pay for accepted goods, (2) breaches the contract and the seller or lessor cannot dispose of the goods, or if (3) the goods are damaged or lost after the risk of loss passes to the buyer or lessee.

red light doctrine A doctrine that says a holder cannot qualify as an HDC if he or she has notice of an unauthorized signature or an alteration of the instrument or any adverse claim against or defense to its payment.

redeemable preferred stock Stock that permits the corporation to buy back the preferred stock at some future date.

reformation An equitable doctrine that permits the court to rewrite a contract to express the parties' true intentions.

registered agent A person or corporation that is empowered to accept service of process on behalf of the corporation.

registration statement Document that an issuer of securities files with the SEC that contains required information about the issuer, the securities to be issued, and other relevant information.

regular meeting A meeting held by the board of directors at the time and place established in the bylaws.

regulatory statute A licensing statute enacted to protect the public.

rejection Express words or conduct by the offeree that rejects an offer. Rejection terminates the offer.

rejection of nonconforming goods If the goods or the seller's or lessor's tender of delivery fails to conform to the contract, the buyer or lessee may (1) reject the whole, (2) accept the whole, or (3) accept any commercial unit and reject the rest.

relevant geographical market A relevant market that is defined as the area in which the defendant and its competitors sell the product or service.

relevant product or service market A relevant market that includes substitute products or services that are reasonably interchangeable with the defendant's products or services.

relief from stay May be granted in situations involving depreciating assets where the secured property is not adequately protected during the bankruptcy proceedings; asked for by a secured creditor.

religious discrimination Discrimination against a person solely because of his or her religion or religious practices.

remainder If the right of possession returns to a third party upon the expiration of a limited or contingent estate.

replacement cost insurance Insurance that pays the cost to replace the damaged or destroyed property up to the policy limits.

replacement workers Workers who are hired to take the place of striking workers. They can be hired on either a temporary or permanent basis.

replevin An action by a buyer or lessor to recover scarce goods wrongfully withheld by a seller or lessor.

reply Filed by the original plaintiff to answer the defendant's cross-complaint.

repossession A right granted to a secured creditor to take possession of the collateral upon default by the debtor.

res ipsa loquitur Tort where the presumption of negligence arises because (1) the defendant was in exclusive control of the situation and (2) the plaintiff would not have suffered injury but for someone's negligence. The burden switches to the defendant(s) to prove they were not negligent.

resale price maintenance A per se violation of Section 1 of the Sherman Act; occurs when a party at one level of distribution enters into an agreement with a party at another level to adhere to a price schedule that either sets or stabilizes prices.

rescission An action to rescind (undo) the contract. Rescission is available if there has been a material breach of contract, fraud, duress, undue influence, or mistake.

residence contents broad form Insurance that renters purchase to cover loss or damage to their possessions.

residuary gift Gift of the estate left after the debts, taxes, and specific and general gifts have been paid.

Resource Conservation and Recovery Act (RCRA) A federal statute that authorizes the EPA to regulate facilities that generate, treat, store, transport, and dispose of hazardous wastes.

respondeat superior A rule that says an employer is liable for the tortious conduct of its employees or agents while they are acting within the scope of its authority.

Restatement of the Law of Contracts A compilation of model contract law principles drafted by legal scholars. The Restatement is not law.

restitution Returning of goods or property received from the other party to rescind a contract; if the actual goods or property is not available, a cash equivalent must be made.

restricted securities Securities that were issued for investment purposes pursuant to the intrastate, private placement, or small offering exemption.

restrictive covenant A private agreement between landowners that restricts the use of their land.

restrictive indorsement An indorsement that contains some sort of instruction from the indorser.

resulting trust A trust that is created by the conduct of the parties.

retained earnings Profits retained by the corporation and not paid out as dividends.

retention of collateral If a secured creditor repossesses collateral upon a debtor's default, he or she may propose to retain the collateral in satisfaction of the debtor's obligation.

revenue-raising statute A licensing statute with the primary purpose of raising revenue for the government.

reverse discrimination Discrimination against a group that is usually thought of as a majority.

reversion A right of possession that returns to the grantor after the expiration of a limited or contingent estate.

Revised Model Business Corporation Act (RMBCA) A revision of the MBCA in 1984 that arranged the provisions of the act more logically, revised the language to be more consistent, and made substantial changes in the provisions.

Revised Uniform Limited Partnership Act (RULPA) A 1976 revision of the ULPA that provides a more modern, comprehensive law for the formation, operation, and dissolution of limited partnerships.

revocation Withdrawal of an offer by the offeror terminates the offer. Reversal of acceptance. Termination of a will.

reward To collect a reward, the offeree must (1) have knowledge of the reward offer prior to completing the requested act and (2) perform the requested act.

right of inspection A right that shareholders have to inspect the books and records of the corporation.

right of redemption A right that says the mortgagor has the right to redeem real property after default and before foreclosure. Requires the mortgagor to pay the full amount of the debt incurred by the mortgagee because of the mortgagor's default.

A right granted to a defaulting debtor or other secured creditor to recover the collateral from a secured creditor before he or she contracts to dispose of it or exercises his or her right to retain the collateral. Requires the redeeming party to pay the full amount of the debt and expenses caused by the debtor's default.

right to cure A licensor has the right to cure a contract under certain conditions.

River and Harbor Act A federal statute enacted in 1886 that established a permit system for the discharge of refuse, wastes, and sewage into U.S. navigable waterways.

robbery Taking personal property from another person by use of fear or force.

Rule 10b-5 A rule adopted by the SEC to clarify the reach of Section 10(b) against deceptive and fraudulent activities in the purchase and sale of securities.

rule of reason A rule that holds that only unreasonable restraints of trade violate Section 1 of the Sherman Act. The court must examine the pro- and anticompetitive effects of the challenged restraint.

rules and regulations Adopted by administrative agencies to interpret the statutes that they are authorized to enforce.

Sabbath law A law that prohibits or limits the carrying on of certain secular activities on Sundays.

Safe Drinking Water Act A federal statute enacted in 1974 and amended in 1986 that authorizes the EPA to establish national primary drinking water standards.

sale The passing of title from a seller to a buyer for a price. Also called a conveyance.

sale on approval A type of sale in which there is no actual sale unless and until the buyer accepts the goods.

sale or return contract A contract that says that the seller delivers goods to a buyer with the understanding that the buyer may return them if they are not used or resold within a stated or reasonable period of time.

sale proceeds The resulting assets from the sale, exchange, or disposal of collateral subject to a security agreement.

satisfaction The performance of an accord.

scienter Means international conduct. Scienter is required for there to be a violation of Section 10(b) and Rule 10b-5.

search warrant A warrant issued by a court that authorizes the police to search a designated place for specified contraband, articles, items, or documents. The search warrant must be based on probable cause.

secondary boycott picketing A type of picketing where unions try to bring pressure against an employer by picketing his or her suppliers or customers.

secondary liability Liability on a negotiable instrument that is imposed on a party only when the party primarily liable on the instrument defaults and fails to pay the instrument when due.

secondary meaning When an ordinary term has become a brand name.

Section 1 of the Sherman Act Prohibits contracts, combinations, and conspiracies in restraint of trade.

Section 10(b) A provision of the Securities Exchange Act of 1934 that prohibits the use of manipulative and deceptive devices in the purchase or sale of securities in contravention of the rules and regulations prescribed by the SEC.

Section 11 A provision of the Securities Act of 1933 that imposes civil liability on persons who intentionally defraud investors by making misrepresentations or omissions of material facts in the registration statement or who are negligent for not discovering the fraud.

Section 11(a) A section of the Securities Act of 1933 that imposes civil liability on accountants and others for (1) making misstatements or omissions of material facts in a registration statement or (2) failing to find such misstatements or omissions.

Section 12 A provision of the Securities Act of 1933 that imposes civil liability on any person who violates the provisions of Section 5 of the act.

Section 14(a) Provision of the Securities Exchange Act of 1934 that gives the SEC the authority to regulate the solicitation of proxies.

Section 14(e) A provision of the Williams Act that prohibits fraudulent, deceptive, and manipulative practices in connection with a tender offer.

Section 16(a) A section of the Securities Exchange Act of 1934 that defines any person who is an executive officer, a director, or a 10 percent shareholder of an equity security of a reporting company as a statutory insider for Section 16 purposes.

Section 2 of the Sherman Act Prohibits the act of monopolization and attempts or conspiracies to monopolize trade.

Section 2(a) of the Robinson-Patman Act Prohibits direct and indirect price discrimination by sellers of a commodity of a like grade and quality where the effect of such discrimination may be to substantially lessen competition or to tend to create a monopoly in any line of commerce.

Section 3 of the Clayton Act Prohibits tying arrangements involving sales and leases of goods.

Section 5 of the FTC Act Prohibits unfair and deceptive practices.

Section 7 of the NLRA A law that gives employees the right to join together and form a union.

Section 8(a) of the NLRA A law that makes it an unfair labor practice for an employer to interfere with, coerce, or restrain employees from exercising their statutory right to form and join unions.

Section 8(b) of the NLRA A law that prohibits unions from engaging in unfair labor practices that interfere with a union election.

Section 16(b) A section of the Securities Exchange Act of 1934 that requires that any profits made by a statutory insider on transactions involving short-swing profits belong to the corporation.

Section 18(a) A section of the Securities Exchange Act of 1934 that imposes civil liability on any person who makes false or misleading statements in any application, report, or document filed with the SEC.

Section 24 A section of the Securities Act of 1933 that makes it a criminal offense for any person to (1) willfully make any untrue statement of material fact in a registration statement filed with the SEC, (2) omit any material fact necessary to ensure that the statements made in the registration statement are not misleading, or (3) willfully violate any other provision of the Securities Act of 1933 or rule or regulation adopted thereunder.

Section 32 A provision of the Securities Exchange Act of 1934 that imposes criminal liability on any person who willfully violates the 1934 act or the rules or regulations adopted thereunder.

Section 32(a) A section of the Securities Exchange Act of 1934 that makes it a criminal offense for any person willfully and knowingly to make or cause to be made any false or misleading statement in any application, report, or other document required to be filed with the SEC pursuant to the Securities Exchange Act of 1934 or any rule or regulation adopted thereunder.

Section 552 of the Restatement (Second) of Torts A rule that an accountant is liable only for negligence to third parties who are members of a limited class of intended users of the client's financial statements. Provides a broader standard for holding accountants liable to third parties for negligence than the Ultramares doctrine.

section of the country A division of the country that is based on the relevant geographical market; the geographical area that will feel the direct and immediate effects of the merger.

secured credit Credit that requires security (collateral) that secures payment of the loan.

secured transaction A transaction that is created when a creditor makes a loan to a debtor in exchange for the debtor's pledge of personal property as security.

Securities Act of 1933 A federal statute that primarily regulates the issuance of securities by corporations, partnerships, associations, and individuals.

Securities and Exchange Commission (SEC) Federal administrative agency that is empowered to administer federal securities laws. The SEC can adopt rules and regulations to interpret and implement federal securities laws.

Securities Exchange Act of 1934 A federal statute that primarily regulates the trading in securities.

security An interest or instrument that is common stock, preferred stock, a bond, a debenture, or a warrant, (2) an interest or instrument that is expressly mentioned in securities acts, and (3) an investment contract.

security agreement The agreement between the debtor and the secured party that creates or provides for a security interest.

self-dealing If the directors or officers engage in purchasing, selling, or leasing of property with the corporation, the contract must be fair to the corporation; otherwise, it is voidable by the corporation. The contract or transaction is enforceable if it has been fully disclosed and approved.

Self-Employment Contributions Act A federal act that says self-employed persons must pay Social Security taxes equal to the combined employer-employee amount.

self-incrimination The Fifth Amendment states that no person shall be compelled in any criminal case to be a witness against him- or herself.

service mark A mark that distinguishes the services of the holder from those of its competitors.

service of process A summons is served on the defendant to obtain personal jurisdiction over him or her.

settlement of the estate The process of a deceased's property being collected, debts and taxes being paid, and the remainder of the estate being distributed.

settlor or trustor Person who creates a trust.

sex discrimination Discrimination against a person solely because of his or her gender.

sexual harassment Lewd remarks, touching, intimidation, posting pinups, and other verbal or physical conduct of a sexual nature that occur on the job.

share exchange When one corporation acquires all the shares of another corporation and both corporations retain their separate legal existence.

shareholder voting agreements Agreement between two or more shareholders agreeing on how they will vote their shares.

shipment contract A contract that requires the seller to ship the goods to the buyer via a common carrier. The buyer bears the risk of loss during transportation. A sales contract that requires the seller to send the goods to the buyer, but not a specifically named destination.

short-form merger A merger between a parent corporation and a subsidiary corporation that does not require the vote of the shareholders of either corporation or the board of directors of the subsidiary corporation.

sight draft A draft payable on sight. Also called a demand draft.

signature Any name, word, or mark used in lieu of a written signature; any symbol that is (1) handwritten, typed, printed, stamped, or made in almost any other manner and (2) executed or adopted by a party to authenticate a writing.

signature liability A person cannot be held contractually liable on a negotiable instrument unless his or her signature appears on the instrument. Also called contract liability.

signature requirement A negotiable instrument must be signed by the drawer or maker. Any symbol executed or adopted by a party with a present intent to authenticate a writing qualifies as his or her signature.

signer A person signing an instrument who acts in the capacity of (1) a maker of notes and certificates of deposit, (2) a drawer of drafts and checks, (3) a drawee who certifies or accepts checks and drafts, (4) an indorser who indorses an instrument, (5) an agent who signs on behalf of others, or (6) an accommodation party.

slander Oral defamation of character.

small claims court A court that hears civil cases involving small dollar amounts.

small offering exemption For the sale of securities not exceeding $1 million during a 12-month period.

social host liability Rule that provides that social hosts are liable for injuries caused by guests who become intoxicated at a social function. States vary as to whether they have this rule in effect.

Social Security Federal system that provides limited retirement and death benefits to covered employees and their dependents.

sole proprietorship A form of business where the owner is actually the business; the business is not a separate legal entity.

sources of international law Those things that international tribunals rely on in settling international disputes.

special bailees Includes common carriers, warehouse companies, and innkeepers.

special federal courts Federal courts that hear matters of specialized or limited jurisdiction.

special indorsement An indorsement that contains the signature of the indorser and specifies the person (indorsee) to whom the indorser intends the instrument to be payable. Creates order paper.

special meeting A meeting convened by the board of directors to discuss new shares, merger proposals, hostile takeover attempts, and so forth.

special shareholders' meetings Meetings of shareholders that may be called to consider and vote on important or emergency issues, such as a proposed merger or amending the articles of incorporation.

specific duty An OSHA standard that addresses a safety problem of a specific duty nature (e.g., requirement for a safety guard on a particular type of equipment).

specific gift Gift of a specifically named piece of property.

specific performance A remedy that orders the breaching party to perform the acts promised in the contract; usually awarded in cases where the subject matter is unique, such as in contracts involving land, heirlooms, and paintings. Judgment of the court ordering a licensor to specifically perform the license by making the contracted-for unique information available to the licensee. A decree of the court that orders a seller or lessor to perform his or her obligations under the contract; usually occurs when the goods in question are unique, such as art or antiques.

stakeholder interest A theory of social responsibility that says a corporation must consider the effects its actions have on persons other than its stockholders.

stale check A check that has been outstanding for more than six months.

standing to sue The plaintiff must have some stake in the outcome of the lawsuit.

stare decisis Latin: "to stand by the decision." Adherence to precedent.

state action exemptions Business activities that are mandated by state law are exempt from federal antitrust laws.

state administrative agencies Administrative agencies that states create to enforce and interpret state law.

state antitakeover statutes Statutes enacted by state legislatures that protect corporations incorporated in or doing business in the state from hostile takeovers.

state supreme court The highest court in a state court system; it hears appeals from intermediate state courts and certain trial courts.

statement of disassociation A document filed with the secretary of state that gives constructive notice that a member has disassociated from an LLC.

statement of policy A statement issued by administrative agencies announcing a proposed course of action that an agency intends to follow in the future.

stationary sources Sources of air pollution such as industrial plants, oil refineries, and public utilities.

statute Written law enacted by the legislative branch of the federal and state governments that establishes certain courses of conduct that must be adhered to by covered parties.

Statute of Frauds State statute that requires certain types of contracts to be in writing.

statute of limitations Statute that establishes the time period during which a lawsuit must be brought; if the lawsuit is not brought within this period, the injured party loses the right to sue.

statute of repose A statute that limits the seller's liability to a certain number of years from the date when the product was first sold.

Statute of Wills A state statute that establishes the requirements for making a valid will.

statutory exemptions Exemptions from antitrust laws that are expressly provided in statutes enacted by Congress.

stock dividend Additional shares of stock paid as a dividend.

stop-payment order An order by a drawer of a check to the payor bank not to pay or certify a check.

stopping delivery of goods in transit A seller or lessor may stop delivery of goods in transit if he or she learns of the buyer's or lessee's insolvency or if the buyer or lessee repudiates the contract, fails to make payment when due, or gives the seller or lessor some other right to withhold the goods.

straight voting Each shareholder votes the number of shares he or she owns on candidates for each of the positions open.

strict liability Liability without fault.

strict liability standard Common law duty that says innkeepers are liable for lost, damaged, or stolen goods of guests even if they were not at fault for the loss.

strict or absolute liability Standard for imposing criminal liability without a finding of mens rea (intent).

strict scrutiny test Test that is applied to classifications based on race.

strike A cessation of work by union members in order to obtain economic benefits or correct an unfair labor practice.

subject matter jurisdiction Jurisdiction over the subject matter of a lawsuit.

sublease When a tenant transfers only some of his or her rights under the lease.

sublessee The new tenant in a sublease situation.

sublessor The original tenant in a sublease situation.

subrogation If an insurance company pays a claim to an insured for liability or property damage caused by a third party, the insurer succeeds to the right of the insured to recover from the third party.

substantial performance Performance by a contracting party that deviates only slightly from complete performance.

substantive due process Due process that requires that the statute or rule that the respondent is charged with violating be clearly stated.

substantive due process Requires that government statutes, ordinances, regulations, or other laws be clear on their face and not overly broad in scope.

substantive rules Government regulation that has the force of law and must be adhered to by covered persons and businesses.

subsurface rights Rights to the earth located beneath the surface of the land.

summons A court order directing the defendant to appear in court and answer the complaint.

superseding event A defendant is not liable for injuries caused by a superseding or intervening event for which he or she is not responsible.

supervening event An alteration or modification of a product by a party in the chain of distribution that absolves all prior sellers from strict liability.

supervening illegality The enactment of a statute, regulation, or court decision that makes the object of an offer illegal. This action terminates the offer.

supramajority voting requirement A requirement that a greater than majority of shares constitutes a quorum of the vote of the shareholders.

Supremacy Clause A clause of the U.S. Constitution that establishes that the federal Constitution, treaties, federal laws, and federal regulations are the supreme law of the land.

Surety The third person who agrees to be liable in a surety arrangement.

surety arrangement An arrangement where a third party promises to be primarily liable with the borrower for the payment of the borrower's debt.

taking for value requirement A holder must give value for the negotiable instrument to qualify as an HDC.

taking in good faith requirement A holder must take the instrument in good faith to qualify as an HDC.

taking possession A method of acquiring ownership of unowned personal property.

taking without notice of defect requirement A person cannot qualify as an HDC if he or she has notice that the instrument is defective in certain ways.

tangible property All real property and physically defined personal property such as buildings, goods, animals, and minerals.

target corporation The corporation that is proposed to be acquired in a tender offer situation.

Tax Reform Act (1976) An act that imposes criminal liability on accountants and others who prepare federal tax returns if they (1) willfully understate a client's tax liability, (2) negligently understate the tax liability, or (3) wrongfully indorse a client's tax refund check.

tax sale A method of transferring property ownership that involves a lien on property for unpaid property taxes. If the lien remains unpaid after a certain amount of time, a tax sale is held to satisfy the lien.

tenancy at sufferance A tenancy created when a tenant retains possession of property after the expiration of another tenancy or a life estate without the owner's consent.

tenancy at will A lease that may be terminated at any time by either party.

tenancy by the entirety A form of co-ownership of real property that can be used only by married couples.

tenancy for years A tenancy created when the landlord and the tenant agree on a specific duration for the lease.

tenancy in common A form of co-ownership where the interest of a surviving tenant in common passes to the deceased tenant's estate and not to the co-tenants.

tenant The party to whom the leasehold is transferred.

tender of delivery The obligation of the seller to transfer and deliver goods to the buyer in accordance with the sales contract.

tender of performance Tender is an unconditional and absolute offer by a contracting party to perform his or her obligations under the contract. Occurs when a party who has the ability and willingness to perform offers to complete the performance of his or her duties under the contract.

tender offer An offer that an acquirer makes directly to a target corporation's shareholders in an effort to acquire the target corporation.

tender offeror The party that makes a tender offer.

term LLC An LLC that has a specified term of duration.

termination The ending of a corporation that occurs only after the winding-up of the corporation's affairs, the liquidation of its assets, and the distribution of the proceeds to the claimants.

termination by acts of the parties An agency may be terminated by the following acts of the parties: (1) mutual agreement, (2) lapse of time, (3) purpose achieved, and (4) occurrence of a specified event.

termination by operation of law An agency is terminated by operation of law, including: (1) death of the principal or agent, (2) insanity of the principal or agent, (3) bankruptcy of the principal, (4) impossibility of performance, (5) changed circumstances, and (6) war between the principal's and agent's countries.

termination statement A document filed by the secured party that ends a secured interest because the debt has been paid.

testamentary trust A trust created by will: The trust comes into existence when the settlor dies.

testator The person who makes a will.

thermal pollution Heated water or material discharged into waterways that upsets the ecological balance and decreases the oxygen content.

through bill of lading A bill of lading that provides that connecting carriers may be used to transport the goods to their destination.

time draft A draft payable at a designated future date.

time instrument An instrument payable (1) at a fixed date, (2) on or before a stated date, (3) at a fixed period after sight, or (4) at a time readily ascertainable when the promise or order is issued. An instrument that specifies a definite date for payment of the instrument.

time note A note payable at a specific time.

tippee The person who receives material nonpublic information from a tipper.

tipper A person who discloses material nonpublic information to another person.

title Legal, tangible evidence of ownership of goods.

Title I of the Landrum-Griffin Act Referred to as labor's "bill of rights" that gives each union member equal rights and privileges to nominate candidates for union office, vote in elections, and participate in membership meetings.

title insurance Insurance that owners of real property purchase to insure that they have clear title to the property.

Title VII of the Civil Rights Act of 1964 (Fair Employment Practices Act) Intended to eliminate job discrimination based on five protected classes: race, color, religion, sex, or national origin.

tort A wrong. There are three categories: (1) intentional torts, (2) unintentional torts (negligence), and (3) strict liability.

tort of misappropriation of the right to publicity An attempt by another person to appropriate a living person's name or identity for commercial purposes.

toxic air pollutants Air pollutants that cause serious illness or death to humans.

toxic substances Chemicals used for agricultural, industrial, and mining uses that cause injury to humans, birds, animals, fish, and vegetation.

Toxic Substances Control Act A federal statute enacted in 1976 that requires manufacturers and processors to test new chemicals to determine their effect on human health and the environment before the EPA will allow them to be marketed.

trade acceptance A sight draft that arises when credit is extended (by a seller to a buyer) with the sale of goods. The seller is both the drawer and the payee, and the buyer is the drawee.

trade secret A product formula, pattern, design, compilation of data, customer list, or other business secret. Ideas that make a franchise successful but that do not qualify for trademark, patent, or copyright protection.

trademark A distinctive mark, symbol, name, word, motto, or device that identifies the goods of a particular business.

trademark infringement Unauthorized use of another's mark. The holder may recover damages and other remedies from the infringer.

transfer Any passage of an instrument other than its issuance and presentment for payment.

transfer warranties Any of the following five implied warranties: (1) The transferor has good title to the instrument or is authorized to obtain payment or acceptance on behalf of one who does have good title; (2) all signatures are genuine or authorized; (3) the instrument has not been materially altered; (4) no defenses of any party are good against the transferor; and (5) the transferor has no knowledge of any insolvency proceeding against the maker, or acceptor, or the drawer of an unaccepted instrument.

traveler's check A form of check sold by banks and other issuers. They are issued without a named payee. The purchaser fills in the payee's name when he or she uses the check to purchase goods or services.

Treaty Clause Clause of the U.S. Constitution that states the president "shall have the power . . . to make treaties, provided two-thirds of the senators present concur."

treasury shares Shares of stock repurchased by the company itself.

treaties The first source of international law, consisting of agreements or contracts between two or more nations that are formally signed by an authorized representative and ratified by the supreme power of each nation.

trespass to land A tort that interferes with an owner's right to exclusive possession of land.

trespass to personal property A tort that occurs whenever one person injures another person's personal property or interferes with that person's enjoyment of his or her personal property.

trial briefs Documents submitted by the parties' attorneys to the judge that contain legal support for their side of the case.

trier of fact The jury in a jury trial; the judge where there is not a jury trial.

trust A legal arrangement established when one person transfers title to property to another person to be held and used for the benefit of a third person.

trust corpus The property held in trust.

trustee Person who holds legal title to the trust corpus and manages the trust for the benefit of the beneficiary or beneficiaries.

tying arrangement A restraint of trade where a seller refuses to sell one product to a customer unless the customer agrees to purchase a second product from the seller.

UCC Statute of Frauds A rule that requires all contracts for the sale of goods costing $500 or more and lease contracts involving payments of $1,000 or more to be in writing.

UCC statute of limitations A rule that provides that an action for breach of any written or oral sales or lease contract must commence within four years after the cause of action accrues. The parties may agree to reduce the limitations period to one year.

ultra vires act An act by a corporation that is beyond its express or implied powers.

ultramares doctrine A rule that an accountant is liable only for negligence to third parties who are in privity of contract or a privity-like relationship with the accountant. Provides the narrowest standard for holding accountants liable to third parties for negligence.

unauthorized signature A signature made by a purported agent without authority from the purported principal.

unconditional Promises to pay and orders to pay must be unconditional in order for them to be negotiable.

unconditional promise or order to pay requirement A negotiable instrument must contain either an unconditional promise to pay (note or CD) or an unconditional order to pay (draft or check).

unconscionable disclaimer A disclaimer that is so oppressive or manifestly unfair that it will not be enforced by the court.

undue influence Occurs where one person takes advantage of another person's mental, emotional, or physical weakness and unduly persuades that person to enter into a contract; the persuasion by the wrongdoer must overcome the free will of the innocent party.

unenforceable contract A contract where the essential elements to create a valid contract are met, but there is some legal defense to the enforcement of the contract.

unfair advantage theory A theory that holds that a merger may not give the acquiring firm an unfair advantage over its competitors in finance, marketing, or expertise.

unfair competition Competition that violates the law.

Uniform Commercial Code Comprehensive statutory scheme that includes laws that cover aspects of commercial transactions.

Uniform Computer Information Transactions Act (UCITA) A model act that provides uniform and comprehensive rules for contracts involving computer information transactions and software and information licenses.

Uniform Franchise Offering Circular (UFOC) A uniform disclosure document that requires the franchisor to make specific presale disclosures to prospective franchisees.

Uniform Gift to Minors Act and Revised Uniform Gift to Minors Act Acts that establish procedures for adults to make gifts of money and securities to minors.

The Uniform Limited Liability Company Act (ULLCA) A model act that provides comprehensive and uniform laws for the formation, operation, and dissolution of LLCs.

Uniform Partnership Act (UPA) Model act that codifies partnership law. Most states have adopted the UPA in whole or in part.

Uniform Probate Code (UPC) A model law promulgated to establish uniform rules for the creation of wills, the administration of estates, and the resolution of conflicts in settling estates.

Uniform Securities Act An act that has been adopted by many states; it was drafted to coordinate state securities laws with federal securities laws.

Uniform Simultaneous Death Act An act that provides that if people who would inherit property from each other die simultaneously, each person's property is distributed as though he or she survived.

unilateral contract A contract in which the offeror's offer can be accepted only by the performance of an act by the offeree; a "promise for an act."

unilateral mistake When only one party is mistaken about a material fact regarding the subject matter of the contract.

unilateral refusal to deal A unilateral choice by one party not to deal with another party. This does not violate Section 1 of the

Sherman Act because there is not concerted action.

uninsured motorist coverage Automobile insurance that provides coverage to the driver and passengers who are injured by an uninsured motorist or hit-and-run driver.

unintentional tort or negligence A doctrine that says a person is liable for harm that is the foreseeable consequence of his or her actions.

union shop An establishment where an employee must join the union within a certain number of days after being hired.

United Nations An international organization created by multilateral treaty in 1945 to promote social and economic cooperation among nations and to protect human rights.

U.S. Constitution The fundamental law of the United States of America. It was ratified by the states in 1788.

U.S. courts of appeals The federal court system's intermediate appellate courts.

U.S. district courts The federal court system's trial courts of general jurisdiction.

U.S. Supreme Court The Supreme Court was created by Article III of the U.S. Constitution. The Supreme Court is the highest court in the land. It is located in Washington, DC.

unprotected speech Speech that is not protected by the First Amendment and may be forbidden by the government.

unqualified indorsement An indorsement whereby the indorser promises to pay the holder or any subsequent indorser the amount of the instrument if the maker, drawer, or acceptor defaults on it.

unqualified indorser An indorser who signs an unqualified indorsement to an instrument.

unreasonable search and seizure Any search and seizure by the government that violates the Fourth Amendment.

unsecured credit Credit that does not require any security (collateral) to protect the payment of the debt.

usurping a corporate opportunity A director or officer steals a corporate opportunity for him- or herself.

usury law A law that sets an upper limit on the interest rate that can be charged on certain types of loans.

utilitarianism A moral theory that dictates that people must choose the action or follow the rule that provides the greatest good to society.

valid contract A contract that meets all of the essential elements to establish a contract; a contract that is enforceable by at least one of the parties.

variance An exception that permits a type of building or use in an area that would not otherwise be allowed by a zoning ordinance.

venue A concept that requires lawsuits to be heard by the court with jurisdiction that is nearest the location in which the incident occurred or where the parties reside.

vertical merger A merger that integrates the operations of a supplier and a customer.

vertical restraint of trade A restraint of trade that occurs when two or more parties on different levels of distribution enter into a contract, combination, or conspiracy to restrain trade.

violation A crime that is neither a felony nor a misdemeanor that is usually punishable by a fine.

voidable contract A contract where one or both parties have the option to avoid their contractual obligations. If a contract is avoided, both parties are released from their contractual obligations.

voidable title Title that a purchase has if the goods were obtained by (1) fraud, (2) a check that is later dishonored, or (3) impersonating another person.

voidable transfer An unusual payment or transfer of property by the debtor on the eve of bankruptcy that would unfairly benefit the debtor or some creditors at the expense of other creditors. Such transfer may be avoided by the bankruptcy court.

void contract A contract that has no legal effect; a nullity.

void title A thief acquires no title to the goods he or she steals.

voluntary dissolution A corporation that has begun business or issued shares can be dissolved upon recommendation of the board of directors and a majority vote of the shares entitled to vote.

voluntary petition A petition filed by the debtor; states that the debtor has debts.

voting trust The shareholders transfer their stock certificates to a trustee who is empowered to vote the shares.

waiting period A period of time that begins when the registration statement is filed with the SEC and continues until the registration statement is declared effective. Only certain activities are permissible during the waiting period.

warehouse company A bailee engaged in the business of storing property for compensation. Owes a duty of reasonable care to protect the bailed property.

warehouse receipt A written document issued by a person who is engaged in the business of storing goods for hire.

warranties of quality Seller's or lessor's assurance to buyer or lessee that the goods meet certain standards of quality. Warranties may be expressed or implied.

warranty A buyer's or lessee's assurance that the goods meet certain standards. A representation of the insured that is expressly incorporated in the insurance contract.

warranty against infringements A seller or lessor who is a merchant who regularly deals in goods of the kind sold or leased automatically warrants that the goods are delivered free of any third-party patent, trademark, or copyright claim.

warranty against interference The lessor warrants that no person holds a claim or interest in the goods that arose from an act or omission of the lessor that will interfere with the lessee's enjoyment of his or her leasehold interest.

warranty disclaimer Statements that negate express and implied warranties.

warranty of fitness for a particular purpose A warranty that arises where a seller or lessor warrants that the goods will meet the buyer's or lessee's expressed needs.

warranty of good title Sellers warrant that they have valid title to the goods they are selling and that the transfer of title is rightful.

warranty of no security interests Sellers of goods warrant that the goods they sell are delivered free from any third-party security interests, liens, or encumbrances that are unknown to the buyer.

waste Occurs when a tenant causes substantial and permanent damage to the leased premises that decreases the value of the property and the landlord's reversionary interest in it.

water pollution Pollution of lakes, rivers, oceans, and other bodies of water.

wetlands Areas that are inundated or saturated by surface water or ground water that support vegetation typically adapted for life in such conditions.

white-collar crimes Crimes usually involving cunning and deceit rather than physical force.

will A declaration of how a person wants his or her property distributed upon death.

will or inheritance A way to acquire title to property that is a result of another's death. If a person dies with a will, his or her property is distributed to the beneficiaries as designated in the will. If a person dies without a will, his or her property is distributed to the heirs as stipulated in the state's intestate statute.

Williams Act An amendment to the Securities Exchange Act of 1934 made in 1968 that specifically regulates all tender offers.

winding-up Process of liquidating the partnership's assets and distributing the proceeds to satisfy claims against the partnership. The process of preserving and selling the assets of the LLC and distributing the money and property to creditors and members.

winding-up and liquidation The process by which a dissolved corporation's assets are collected, liquidated, and distributed to creditors, shareholders, and other claimants.

wire fraud The use of telephone or telegraph to defraud another person.

withholding delivery The act of the seller or lessor purposefully refusing to deliver goods to the buyer or lessee upon breach of the sales or lease contract by the buyer or lessee or the insolvency of the buyer or lessee.

work product immunity A state statute that says an accountant's work papers cannot be used in a court action in that state; federal courts do not recognize this statute.

workers' compensation acts Acts that compensate workers and their families if workers are injured in connection with their jobs.

work-related test A test to determine the liability of a principal; if an agent commits an intentional tort within a work-related time or space, the principal is liable for any injury caused by the agent's intentional tort.

World Trade Organization (WTO) An international organization of more than 130 member nations created to promote and enforce trade agreements among member nations.

World Wide Web An electronic connection of millions of computers that support a standard set of rules for the exchange of information.

writ of certiorari An official notice that the Supreme Court will review one's case.

written order A stop-payment order that is good for six months after the date it is written.

wrongful disassociation Occurs when a member withdraws from (1) a term LLC prior to the expiration of the term or (2) an at-will LLC when the operating agreement eliminates a member's power to withdraw.

wrongful discharge The discharge of an employee in violation of a statute, an employment contract, or public policy, or tortiously. As a result, the employee can recover damages and other remedies.

wrongful dishonor Occurs when there are sufficient funds in a drawer's account to pay a properly payable check, but the bank does not do so.

wrongful dissolution When a partner withdraws from a partnership without having the right to do so at that time.

wrongful eviction A violation of the covenant of quiet enjoyment. Also called unlawful eviction.

wrongful termination The termination of an agency contract in violation of the terms of the agency contract. The nonbreaching party may recover damages from the breaching party. Termination of a franchise without just cause.

zoning commission A local administrative body that formulates zoning ordinances, conducts public hearings, and makes recommendations to the city council.

zoning ordinances Local laws that are adopted by municipalities and local governments to regulate land use within their boundaries. Zoning ordinances are adopted and enforced to protect the health, safety, morals, and general welfare of the community.

Case Index

*Cases cited or discussed are in roman type. Principal cases are in **bold type.***

R

S

T

U

V

W

Y

Z

Subject Index

D

E

J

K

L

M

Q

T

U

Cases